ENCYCLOPEDIA OF
HISTORICAL TREATIES
AND ALLIANCES

ENCYCLOPEDIA OF
HISTORICAL TREATIES AND ALLIANCES

FROM ANCIENT TIMES TO WORLD WAR I

Charles L. Phillips and Alan Axelrod

Facts On File, Inc.

Encyclopedia of Historical Treaties and Alliances

Facts On File, Inc.
11 Penn Plaza
New York NY 10001

Library of Congress Cataloging-in-Publication Data

Phillips, Charles L., 1948–
    Encyclopedia of historical treaties and alliances / by Charles L. Phillips and Alan Axelrod.
        p. cm.
    Includes bibliographical references and index.
    ISBN 0-8160-3090-0 (alk. paper)
    I. Treaties History—Encyclopedias. I. Axelrod, Alan, 1952– II. Title.

KZ1160 .P48 2001   00-044269
341.3'7'09—dc21

Facts On File books are available at special discounts when purchased in bulk quantities for businesses, associations, institutions, or sales promotions. Please call our Special Sales Department in New York at (212) 967-8800 or (800) 322-8755.

You can find Facts On File on the World Wide Web at http://www.factsonfile.com

Text design by Erika K. Arroyo
Cover design by Cathy Rincon

Printed in the United States of America

VB FOF 10 9 8 7 6 5 4 3 2 1

This book is printed on acid-free paper.

CONTENTS

~✑

VOLUME 2

ALPHABETICAL LIST OF TREATIES

INTRODUCTION

Those who enjoy contemplating, reading about, and studying the past are accustomed to thinking of history in terms of people and events. Scholars, writers, and historians understand that these people and events are reconstructions rather than realities and that such reconstructions are based most often on documents of one kind or another. Certainly, few historical documents are of greater moment than treaties, the instruments through which tribes, states, and nations have sought to define themselves and their relations to others. Quite literally as old as recorded time, treaties are signposts of historically significant events and windows on historical eras, yet for casual readers and students of history alike they usually figure as little more than passing references or footnotes to what they see as the main story. Historians have focused discussion on astonishingly few of these documents, and it is difficult to find historical treatments of treaties themselves. Those works that do deal with treaties in any depth usually focus on agreements currently in effect, while books concerned with historical treaties seem content to treat them simply as documents, reprinting them with only the most cursory of introductory and interpretive information.

Our approach here is to look at treaties as seminal documents that help to illuminate their times and to explicate their historical significance through an understanding of the circumstances in which they were created and an assessment of their impact. By placing each document fully in context, we have sought to remove the abstraction with which diplomatic texts are often viewed, and by focusing on the treaties themselves, we have attempted to trace more concretely than others typically do the growth and development of modern diplomacy and international relations. Neither a survey of world agreements currently in effect nor a sourcebook of historical documents, this book is intended as a reference on the great treaties in world history and a history of treaty making that provides detailed information on critical agreements and alliances not easily found in either narrative works on specific periods or in history reference books.

The arrangement of the book is historical and analytical, rather than alphabetical, as in most encyclopedias. We have divided the work into historical eras and geopolitical areas, reflecting the development of world diplomacy from its beginnings in antiquity to its state at the end of the second millennium. Each of these divisions includes an introductory essay setting the treaties that follow in an overall historical and diplomatic context. Rather than treating the documents within each era strictly chronologically, however, we have divided them into analytical categories by type of treaty—mutual defense treaties and military alliances, for example, are all grouped together, as are peace treaties and truces, trade agreements and commercial treaties, multinational conventions and agreements, and weapons treaties. Treaties whose main import is none of these, we have grouped under a miscellaneous category called "Diplomatic Treaties." Also included in the encyclopedia are agreements and understandings—charters, declarations, annexations—that are not treaties in the strictest sense but which function in their historical context as diplomatic documents. These are most frequently grouped under the categories of "Annexations and Territorial Agreements" (though that category, too, includes true treaties) and "Declarations and Proclamations." Within each category the arrangement of the documents is chronological.

This scheme is a result of our historical intent and our determination to focus on the treaties themselves as discrete events. Dividing the book into eras allows us to follow in general the development of diplomacy; grouping treaties into categories helps us show the impact of one treaty and one set of negotiations on other treaties and negotiations years, sometimes decades, apart; and employing geopolitical areas lets us more fully develop the historical context in which the treaties came into existence. For similar reasons there is some overlap in the historical eras and geopolitical areas—for example, between the "Age of Reason," which deals with the diplomacy of the developing nation states in Europe, and "A New World," which covers the treaty making of expanding empires in the Western Hemisphere both among themselves and with the Native American tribes and nations.

While some of the events in both periods happened simultaneously and were closely related, they also led in different directions. The Seven Year's War may have been a worldwide event, but in Europe it enhanced the power and prestige of some nations at the expense of others and helped to create the Great Powers and their entangling alliances. In America at the same time, the war was not even called by its European name but instead became known as the French and Indian War. It sparked the development of a sense of common purpose among British colonies and led ultimately to the American Revolution and a different kind of treatment of and treaty making with the aboriginal inhabitants. During the "Epoch of Napoleon," Europe was trying to come to terms with the rise of one of history's great personalities, while Americans were in contrast building a nation and fending off the continuing colonial ambitions of Europe's imperial powers. Thus, the Louisiana Purchase was negotiated by Napoleon for strategic reasons related to his European conflicts, but its greater significance lay in the tremendous impact it had on the development of the continental United States, an impact that had little to do with European diplomacy of any stripe. Instead, it was related to other events and treaties covered in "Western Diplomacy and Continental Expansion." On the other hand, once the United States had expanded across the continent, Americans began to compete with the Great Powers of Europe for colonial possessions throughout the world, and the American treaty making with and annexation of Hawaii, for example, is covered with other such colonial agreements by other nations under "The New Imperialism."

Within this general historical and analytical framework, we have included each treaty as a separate entry. For each entry we provide a summary of the treaty for quick reference so that at a glance the reader can glean the essential information about the document. We have followed these summaries with a concise history of the events leading up to the creation of the document. We then discuss the terms of the treaty, quoting liberally from the document itself and, when warranted, reproducing the entire treaty—to illustrate the treaty's major provisions, to provide historical texts that are sometimes hard to come by, to give a feel for the language or historical period, and sometimes as a text emblematic of those in its era or category. Finally, we discuss the significance of the treaty, its relation to the era and its diplomacy, and its consequences for the future. In the discussions of a treaty's historical context, its terms, and its consequences, we have provided cross-references to other treaties or agreements related to its development through the use of SMALL CAPITAL LETTERS.

In many cases, historical treaties are known by different names, such as the Veterans' Treaty, which is officially titled the Treaty with the Indians Living in the Country of the Oneidas, and is sometimes referred to that way. Some treaties are now commonly referred to by one title but in the past have been called something else, such as the Adams-Onís Treaty, once called variously the Transconti-nental Treaty and the Purchase of Florida. Frequently, a number of treaties have the same title, such as the several known individually as the Treaty of Paris. And especially with more recent treaties, the official title can be a bureaucratic monstrosity such as the Convention on the Prohi-bition of the Use, Stockpiling, Production and Transfer of Anti-Personnel Mines and on Their Destruction, more popularly called the Land Mine Ban Treaty. We have treated each case individually, usually opting for the more popular title but in any case seeking to avoid confusion. The Veteran's Treaty and the Land-Mine Ban Treaty, for example, appear under those titles, with the alternate, more official appellation following in parenthesis. The Adams-Onís Treaty appears under that title alone, since the earlier names have fallen out of general use. Treaties with the same name are distinguished in some way, either followed by an alternate name in parentheses for some, such as the Treaty of Constantinople (Unkiar Skelessi), which was concluded on July 8, 1833, to distinguish it from the September 29, 1913, Treaty of Constantinople, or simply followed by the year in which it was concluded, such as the Treaty of Paris (1763), Treaty of Paris (1783), Treaty of Paris (1856), etc. Alternate names for treaties still in use are included in the index, and we have also provided an alphabetical listing of all the treaties in the encyclopedia, with their dates and page numbers, as well as a chronological list of treaties by year.

In all of this—the organizational scheme, the treatment of the individual treaties, and the use of more popular and historically telling titles—we have made it our goal to make this work easy to use by its likely readers. The same goal governed our selection of the treaties. Not all historical treaties are included here, for to do so would swell the work beyond convenience, but most of the major agreements are. Some treaties, especially in the initial chapters, which lay the groundwork for modern diplomacy, are included both as treaties significant in themselves but more important as samples of the kinds of agreements typical of their periods. Others are included among major treaties of an era, not because they are especially significant in and of themselves, as was the North Atlantic Treaty, which established NATO during the era we call "Cold War, Peaceful Coexistence," but because they so perfectly capture the temper of the times, such as the Hot Line Memorandum during that same period. Others, especially in the "Epilogue: A New World Order," are included to indicate trends in treaty making or strains in diplomacy in addition to their unquestioned historical importance. We decided to treat the agreements since the end of the cold war as emblematic rather than comprehensive for a number of reasons: we are in a transition period in international relations during which precisely what will prove historically significant is unknowable; current treaties are readily available elsewhere, especially through the internet sites of universities and governmental agencies; most major contemporary treaties are multilateral, involving hundreds of countries, and so immensely detailed that to quote even portions of them would take many more volumes than we were willing to inflict on the public; and treaties now in force are also in flux, being constantly amended and renegotiated, which, once again, dims the value of considering them as completed historical documents.

Indeed, instead of a constantly updated work on current affairs, we have tried to produce a historical work of enduring value that will actually be read and used by those interested in the subject or wishing to learn about it, rather than one simply referred to on occasion to retrieve the text of a forgotten treaty or picked up to produce a quick term paper on contemporary diplomacy and then placed back on the shelf. We have attempted to use treaties as historians typically use events and historical personalities: as jumping-off points, opportunities to describe the events and the milieus in which they occurred, handy guides to the past, much more fascinating in context and never to be considered in isolation from other events and action. Looking to the past to understand treaties in the fullness of time, we have hoped to recapture something of the pregnancy of significance with which they were once imbued and through which they helped to engender the present.

—Charles Phillips and Alan Axelrod

Part One
THE ANCIENT WORLD

INTRODUCTION

Although many of the current precepts and principles of international law, foreign policy, diplomacy, and treaty making stem most immediately from Europe's early medieval period, Europe of course did not develop in a vacuum. Those in the ancient world made and broke treaties, too, and some of this diplomacy—Roman legal terms and methods, for example—would have lasting impact on that of later ages.

Indeed, diplomacy precedes recorded history, although we cannot read unwritten treaties, and terms trusted to memory could hardly be elaborate. One suspects that except as traditions, the earliest treaties were difficult to abide by or to enforce. The first "international" law no doubt sprang from intertribal relations. Though war—as we have come to understand the term—was then uncommon, raids and feuds were not. Certainly, defensive alliances existed. Heralds traveled from tribe to tribe carrying some emblem, such as a message stick, of their sacred, probably inviolable, credentials. And envoys—many of them perhaps women, valued for their sanctity and sexual wiles—were received with great ceremony in the treating for peace. In the Middle East, with the birth of cities around the fourth millennium B.C.E. and the invention of written language around the third, treaties could be made that outlasted the memory of a few lifetimes, and a few of them withstood the winds and sands of Sumer to intrigue modern scholars.

Still, our knowledge of any treaties made by early peoples is quite limited by the scarcity of evidence. There exists a trace of Egyptian diplomacy in the 14th century B.C.E., where diplomatic correspondence of a sort took place between the pharaoh's court and a Hittite king, but these cuneiform tablets were in Akkadian, the language of Babylon, and not in the ancient Egyptian or Hittite tongues. And no treaties of any kind have been found in West Africa before the ninth century B.C.E. China's Sung dynasty treated with Khitan in 1004 B.C.E., when the latter invaded the Middle Kingdom and a few battles led to victory by neither side. This exchange of sworn documents between the two empires pledged each to a peaceful coexistence that adumbrated modern international treaties. Certainly by the eighth century B.C.E., China boasted leagues and missions and an organized diplomatic corps. India, too, was practicing a cosmopolitan diplomacy by the fourth century, which argues for earlier treaty making.

The best documented of the early diplomacy, though, remains that of the eastern Mediterranean, where Babylonian (Akkadian) had begun to serve as the world's first diplomatic language at least as early as 3000 B.C.E.. There—in the region that gave us the first wheeled vehicles, the first system of writing, the first codes of law, the first city-states—records dating from the third millennium indicate treaties between the constantly warring city-states of Mesopotamia, such as Lagash and Umma. There, too, scholars later found the oldest treaties for which full texts survived, dating from about 1280 B.C.E., between Egypt's Ramses II and a number of Hittite leaders, as well as much evidence of Assyrian diplomacy in the seventh century B.C.E.. From this region also comes the Bible, which—along with other evidence—documents the diplomatic relations of Hebrew tribes amongst themselves and with others.

Despite the tracks of this earlier diplomacy, the traceable origins of modern treaty making lie in ancient Greece. Classical Greek civilization developed many of the elements used in treaty making today, including archives, a diplomatic vocabulary, and tenets of conduct and laws for the interaction of sovereign bodies that resemble the principles of modern international relations. Truces, treaties, alliances, neutralities, conferences, and commercial conventions were common to the Greeks. To serve as inviolable messengers between warring city-states, the Greeks employed heralds, protected by the messenger god Hermes, Zeus's own herald, who not coincidentally was associated with a shifty craftiness, even knavery and theft, as well as with uncanny persuasiveness and remarkable eloquence. Greek envoys, skilled in oratory, went on diplomatic missions, while a different class of consular agents called *proxeni* resided in foreign cities and specialized in commercial negotiations. The Greeks favored heralds as contacts during wartime because they were protected by the gods. These heralds, who traveled alone, made safe passage for the envoys who followed them and who traveled in groups in order to keep check on each of the other envoys' loyalty. It was a wise precaution since an important secondary function of the envoys as well as for the *proxeni* was the gathering of information, i.e., spying. The Greeks required their envoys not only to be silver tongued but also to be at least 50 years old and politically prominent. Unlike these men, the *proxeni* were citizens of the cities in which they resided rather than of the city-states that employed them. At first, *proxeni* only negotiated for one city-state while living in another, but their consularships eventually became far-flung. By 550 B.C.E., notes the Greek historian Herodotus, there were *proxeni* in Egypt.

References to Greek diplomacy lace both the *Iliad* and the *Odyssey*, but outside Greek literature the first direct evidence of treaty making centers around the Olympic Games of 776 B.C.E.. A hundred years later, the once religious amphictyonic leagues, which had developed extraterritorial rights and full-time secretariats, were serving interstate diplomatic functions. By 500 B.C.E. Sparta had been aggressively forming alliances for more than half a century and had created the Peloponnesian League. Mediation among Greek city-states had become commonplace by the time Sparta's great rival, Athens, in the next century cobbled together the Delian League against the Persian threat to its seaborne power. The fourth century witnessed eight congresses in 25 years between the Greeks and the Persians, at which even the smallest states could speak up.

Like much else Greek, this interstate system of multilateral negotiations became a Roman inheritance. As Rome expanded, it not only conquered, it negotiated. To some of the lands it vanquished, Rome offered by treaty limited self-government, even as it negotiated compacts with other sovereign states under Greek international law. Like the Greeks, Rome's missions included envoys and attachés granted immunity in their persons, property, and official correspondence. Rome sent its envoys abroad with written instructions. The *nuntius*, or messenger, went to towns, but for more complicated missions the Romans employed a *legatio*, an embassy of a dozen ambassadors called *legati*. Organized under a president, the *legati* were, like Greek envoys, leading citizens and skilled orators. They were received with great ceremony, and in the early days of the Republic, they worked at the behest of the Senate, which conducted foreign policy. Later a department of foreign affairs grew up, and still later the emperor had the final say in matters multinational.

The Romans were serious about their laws and their archives. They put their archives in the hands of trained professionals, who developed new methods of deciphering and authenticating ancient documents. Some Roman archivists specialized in precedents and procedures based on archival holdings. As these became more formal, they tended to preoccupy Roman diplomacy. While Roman archival work served as an example to diplomats in later ages, the city's major historical influence on treaty making was legal. The Romans applied civil law to treaties, stressing the sanctity of contracts for international compacts as well as for private agreements. Clearly related to the archival focus—since the authenticity and preservation of written contracts is essential to their ability to continue functioning as binding agreements—Roman legalism more importantly meant that contract law became the basis for treaties. Documents such as the TREATY OF BRUNDISIUM were both territorial agreements, dividing up the empire, and contracts for civil marriages.

At the same time, the Romans had rules for relations with foreigners that were different from the civil law covering citizens. Later these laws for foreign relations merged with the Greek concept of natural law, which, like everything else, the Romans felt the urge to codify. Theses—ideal codes based on reason applying to all peoples in the world and supported by a belief in the sanctity of treaties—were the elements necessary for the birth of international law. Absorbed by the Catholic Church (and thus preserved even after the collapse of the Western Roman Empire), Roman concepts underlay the international law that came to govern foreign relations in medieval Europe.

TREATIES

INSCRIPTION FIXING BOUNDARIES BETWEEN LAGASH AND UMMA

TREATY AT A GLANCE

Completed
Circa 3100 B.C.E.

Signatories
Lagash and Umma

Overview
This is one of the earliest known treaties. It fixed the boundary between the Sumerian cities of Lagash and Umma, two of a number of warring city-states located in ancient Mesopotamia.

Amid a swirl of qualifications and second guesses, archaeologists and scholars place the birth of a recognizable civilization—that is, of a population located in urban centers using a written language—to Mesopotamia at the turn of the fourth to the third millennium. A Sumerian empire, consisting of a number of city-states, such as Uruk and Kish, came into being, and, though constantly threatened by clashes between separatist forces, produced dynasties that could be recorded in great lists of kings. Although scholars sometimes debate the exact form "war" might have actually taken among these city-states, wars of some kind characterized the history of Mesopotamia. The Middle Eastern story began to take on a shape we might recognize today as historical with the coming of the Akkad dynasty around 2520 B.C.E. The Akkads, founders of the Babylonian Empire, left behind reports about the city-state of Lagash and its capital at Girsu, reports that covered its troubled relations with its nearby rival, Umma. For many generations before the coming of Sargon of Akkad, Lagash and Umma fought over the fertile fields located in a region called Gu'edena. Among the corpus of inscriptions and clay tablets relating the story of nine rulers, their institutions, and their wars, scholars have found an inscription indicating that several generations earlier a "king of Kish" named Mesilim served as an arbiter between the two cities. Whether Kish had simply intervened in the clash and Mesilim served as an overlord in dictat-ing the peace or he was invited to do so is less clear than the fact that he set the course of the boundary between the two cities. Drawing the line between Lagash and Umma, Mesilim's "treaty" had caused a dike reinforcing the boundary to be built.

How long the cities adhered to the terms of the treaty is unknown, but certainly by 2600 B.C.E. the rulers of Umma were regularly crossing the old border. According to the Stele of Vultures, by the middle of the 24th century B.C.E., Lagash's King Ennatum vanquished the Umman king and forced him to take an elaborate oath, invoking no less than six divinities, that he would stick to his side of the dike. Still, the battles over the border raged on under Ennatum's successors, especially Entemena. The warfare sometimes favored Lagash, sometimes Umma, as rival infantries took the field and war chariots strapped to wild asses clashed. When Urukagina came to the Lagashan throne, he was defeated by Umma's Lugalzagesi, who inflicted great damage on the city and destroyed many of its sacred sites. Lugalzagesi was in turn overthrown by Sargon, who established Akkad rule.

Though the best documented, Umma was not Lagash's only rival. Lagash fought other Sumerian cities, such as Kish and Mari, these sometimes separately and sometimes in combination with Umma, in a pattern of changing, short-lived alliances for which, perhaps, the boundary with Umma, as Lagash's closest enemy, served as a pretext.

TREATY OF BRUNDISIUM

TREATY AT A GLANCE

Completed
40 B.C.E. at Brundisium (present-day Brindisi, Italy)

Signatories
Gaius Julius Caesar (Octavian) and Mark Antony

Overview
Following the final fall of the Republic and the murder of Julius Caesar, a period of political chaos engulfed Rome out of which rose the Second Triumvirate, a coalition of shared power among Lepidus, Octavian, and Mark Antony. By the Treaty of Brundisium, Antony and Octavian attempted to bring order to the empire by dividing up its lands and arranging a state marriage between Antony and Octavian's sister. The effort failed, the triumvirate collapsed, and Octavian defeated both Lepidus and Antony to become the first Roman emperor, Augustus Caesar.

Historical Background

Following the Punic Wars, the Roman Republic began to lose its authority as Rome itself expanded toward a worldwide empire. By the time Julius Caesar, a Roman general, began his rise to power, the former peasant militiamen of the Republic had become professional soldiers who owed their allegiance not to the Roman state, much less to the Senate, but to the individual generals upon whom their fortunes literally depended. Inevitably, Rome's legions became a political tool. For a generation, Rome's fate was decided by powerful generals as its politics became quite fluid, filled with intrigue, and expensive.

From this volatile combination, three men emerged within a few years to claim leadership of the state: a renowned and revered old general named Gnaeus Pompey; a wealthy landowner, speculator, and moneylender named Marcus Crassus; and Julius Caesar himself, the scion of an obscure patrician family, but also a skilled writer, spellbinding orator, astute politician, and accomplished general. The three men formed a coalition, an informal compact called later the First Triumvirate.

After Crassus was killed in a foreign war in Parthia, Pompey colluded with a powerful oligarchy in the Senate to trump up charges of treason against Caesar, who had been appointed governor of Gaul. Ordered to return alone to Rome to face the charges, Caesar came instead with his extensive and loyal army,

and Pompey fled to Egypt, where he was put to death by the nominally independent country's teenaged king, Ptolemy XIII. Caesar, arriving in Egypt in pursuit of Pompey, quickly replaced Ptolemy with Ptolemy's sister, Cleopatra. Cleopatra and Caesar became lovers; she was pregnant with Caesar's child when he returned to Rome to a hero's welcome and a humbled but secretly seething Senate. Declared dictator, he announced his intentions to assume the position for life, which lead the Senate oligarchy to plot his assassination. On the Ides of March in 44 B.C.E. some 60 senators surrounded Caesar in the Forum as he presided over the assembly and stabbed him 23 times.

News of Caesar's death reached his 18-year-old grandnephew and protégé, Gaius Octavius, in Apollonia, a Greek city on the Adriatic coast, where he was completing his education. Octavius rushed back to Italy to find he had been named in the dictator's will as his adopted son and heir. Urged on by his stepfather and others, Octavian decided to take up what was bound to be a perilous inheritance, and he proceeded on to Rome, where he would discover there were others vying for the position his dead "father" had created: Caesar's chief lieutenant, the swaggering and handsome Marcus Antonius, called Mark Antony by English historians; Caesar's second in command, Marcus Aemilius Lepidus, who succeeded the great Roman as chief priest in the state religion; and two powerful senators, Marcus Junius Brutus and Gaius Cassius Longinus, who had led the assassination conspiracy.

Antony, who had assumed he would be Caesar's heir, had taken possession of his papers and assets and refused to hand over any of Caesar's funds. Upon his arrival in Rome, Octavian paid from his own pocket the late dictator's bequests that Antony had refused to pay and underwrote the public games instituted by Caesar to ingratiate himself with the Roman populace. In the process, Octavian managed to win a considerable number of Caesar's former troops to his cause. Brutus and Cassius left Rome, more or less ignoring the new pretender to power, and took command of the eastern half of the empire. The Senate, encouraged by Cicero, broke with Antony and swung its support to the young man who was now calling himself Gaius Julius Caesar. Cicero had assumed Octavian (as historians by tradition continue to refer to him before the point he assumed the title "Augustus") would be easier for the Senate to manipulate than either Antony or Lepidus, and eventually he would pay for that mistake with his life.

After several months of battling for supremacy, the three men agreed to a division of power in a coalition called the Second Triumvirate. Formed in part to seek retribution against Caesar's assassins, this triumvirate, unlike the first, became official when the Senate in 43 B.C.E. granted to the triumvirs five years of autocratic power in order to reconstitute the fractured state. Antony and Octavian hunted down the two leading tyrannicides in Macedonia, where both Brutus and Cassius chose suicide on the battlefield rather than capture at Philippi. The triumvirs then turned on Rome itself, drawing up a list of proscribed enemies and executing some 200 senators and some 2,000 nobles. Among the senators, at Antony's insistence, was Cicero, whose head and hands were nailed to the Rostra in the Forum, one nail—in brute mockery of the great orator's eloquence—driven through his tongue. Finally, the triumvirs had Julius Caesar officially recognized as a god of the Roman state, which enhanced Octavian's prestige. To Antony, the coalition's senior partner, went the Eastern Empire and Gaul.

Upon his return to Italy, Octavian found himself embroiled in the Perusine War against Antony's brother over the settlement of Octavian's veterans. Pompey's son, Sextus Pompeius, also was causing trouble, having seized Sicily and Rome's sea routes. To appease Sextus and win time to finish the Perusine conflict, Octavian married one of his relatives, but this did not stop Sextus from making overtures to Antony once the war was concluded. Meanwhile, Antony had formed a strong political bond with Egypt's wealthy queen and Caesar's former lover Cleopatra, and soon that bond had become a romantic one as well. Octavian was no doubt relieved when Antony rejected Sextus's blandishments. In 40 B.C.E., Octavian and Antony reached a fresh understanding in the Treaty of Brundisium.

Terms

Under the new agreement, Octavian was to have the whole of the western empire, including Gaul and excepting Africa, which went to Lepidus. Italy itself was declared neutral ground, although in fact it was controlled by Octavian. Antony kept the eastern half of the empire, but having spent—much to the dismay of Rome—the previous winter with Cleopatra, he now agreed under the treaty to a marriage with Octavian's sister, Octavia. The treaty delighted the peoples of the empire, east and west, since it seemed to promise an end to generations of social strife and occasional civil war. And just as Antony was closely linking his future to Octavian by marrying into his family, Octavian sought to strengthen his ties to the Senate aristocracy, many of whom supported either Antony or Sextus, by a new marriage of his own to Livia Drusilla.

Consequences

The goodwill established by the treaty did not last, and in the long run, provisions of the treaty themselves became sources of discord. Reconciliation with Sextus proved abortive, and Lepidus, unhappy with his portion of power, rebelled. Antony's true love lay in Egypt, not in Italy, and when he returned to Cleopatra, the insult was not only to his new wife but to her brother as well. In 37 B.C.E., with Antony's reluctant help, Octavian destroyed Sextus. In 36 B.C.E., when Lepidus attacked, Octavian defeated him and placed him under guard for the rest of his life. In 32 B.C.E. Octavian renounced the triumvirate outright, and Antony responded by divorcing Octavia. Urged on by Octavian, the Senate the next year declared war on Antony. Octavian himself accompanied the Roman ships that defeated Antony and Cleopatra at the Battle of Actium in 31 B.C.E.. Like Brutus and Cassius before them, the pair chose suicide over capture by the now clearly ruthless Octavian.

Octavian went on to reign as Caesar Augustus, the first Roman emperor. The Republic had died, replaced by the rule of a single strong man. Under such rule would grow a Roman Empire whose glory became the touchstone of civilization thereafter, but such rule also created the problem of succession, which the Roman Empire never solved. Instead, the habit of political assassination, having brought Augustus to power, would plague his empire throughout its history.

Part Two
MEDIEVAL ROOTS

INTRODUCTION

Modern treaty making and the international law underlying it have their roots in three developments of the Western world. First, as the Middle Ages waned, Europe's feudal community disintegrated into a society made up of separate nation-states. Then that society, for various reasons, including technological advances, spread across the globe. And third, as it spread, an emerging world society witnessed the concentration of sovereignty in the hands of a rapidly declining number of great powers.

The modern use of some Roman terms and a few legal techniques stretching back to Byzantine diplomacy lingers on principally because of the influence of the church on international relations, fading though it is. However, such continuity as exists in the international law underlying the contemporary making of treaties dates from the early Middle Ages. As Rome fell apart in the fifth century C.E., diplomacy suffered. Whereas monarchs of various ilks negotiated directly with nearby rulers, sometimes employing envoys if the negotiations took place at a distance, the pope continued to use *legati*—men of some standing, skilled at oration, who served as ambassadors—as had the Romans.

Both types of diplomacy continued over the next three centuries, but the major diplomatic developments took place in the East. There, after Western Rome fell, the Byzantine Empire—Eastern Rome— flourished for a thousand years. The very word *byzantine* today connotes something about its diplomacy as well as its rule: subtle, twisting, treacherously complex. Byzantium had a department of foreign affairs and a bureau to deal with foreign envoys, both marked by spectacular if hollow ceremoniousness aimed at humiliating and intimidating outsiders and hinting at a grandeur and power the empire scarcely possessed.

Perhaps fittingly, the first professional diplomats were Byzantines. Given elaborate instructions, enjoined at all costs to be polite, they were expected to entertain as lavishly as money permitted, promote sales of Byzantine wares, and push trade where they could. From at least the 12th century onward, they were also expected to spy on their hosts. As Byzantium grew ever more laden by elaborate ceremony and its strength waned, this intelligence allowed the emperors to play states off against each other, which began the tradition of using skillful, subtle, even treacherous diplomacy to make up for a lack of true power. As it often would in centuries to come, such diplomacy signaled not just decadence but impending collapse.

As the Byzantine Empire tumbled into various feudal kingdoms in the 11th century, the papal West rekindled its diplomacy. Although the church was probably at its weakest in Constantinople and during the 13th century when it came under attack from the Holy Roman Emperors, popes nevertheless practiced an active diplomacy. Their emissaries outranked secular envoys at every court; they made the sanctity of legates—inherited from the Romans—a matter of canon law; they sometimes served as arbiters in secular disputes; and their legates tried to impose whenever possible the "Peace of God" and the "Truce of God." Beginning around 1400, church lawyers set down rules for papal envoys. Kings and emperors often applied these rules to their own emissaries, adopting canonical dictates about their status, privilege, and conduct. Modern international conferences also meet and conduct their business by many of the rules first set down for medieval church councils.

In the Middle Ages, courts and kings, councils and popes sent or received emissaries, but they did not always know what properly to call them, or at least they weren't consistent in the titles they used. For a period, *nuncius* might mean any envoy, though more strictly the term was supposed to apply only to a messenger. In general, it depended on the importance of the matters under negotiation. For very important matters, such as major conferences and significant peaces, the pope would send a legate. Other times he settled for a *nuncius* (nuncio). Already in the 10th century, some secular rulers were using nuncios as agents; by the 12th, they did so commonly. The nuncio—always male—represented his prince or his pope, spoke for him, conveyed his will, acted in his name, and carried letters of credence to prove it. Usually he could not commit his principal to an agreement without checking first, however, thus he mostly negotiated draft agreements. Such men served the purpose for short-range diplomacy, treating between nearby kingdoms, where meetings could be set up fairly easily and traveling back and forth to get agreement and approval did not consume an inordinate amount of time.

As feudal bonds loosened, Crusades were undertaken, and trade began to spread, though something more supple became required for effective negotiation. In the 12th century, the church looked back into Roman civil law and came up with the concept of a procurator with *plenta potens*, or "full powers," and then applied the idea to diplomacy. These plenipotentiaries could both negotiate and conclude treaties, but their principals did not let them attend ceremonies—that remained the privilege of nuncii. In practice, rulers often vested both offices in one man.

The word *ambassador* finally appeared on the scene at the end of the 12th century. Taken from the Latin *ambactiare*, meaning "to go on a mission," it was first used in Italy, then spread to France, and by the time Geoffrey Chaucer was writing *Troilus and Crieseyde*, the English were using it. Loosely used to describe an envoy, the title did not always mean its holder was the agent of some sovereign, though by the 15th century, most kings and princes called their emissaries ambassadors. Popes stuck to legates and nuncios. Ambassadors, like the nuncios, carried credentials—which a procurator had no need to carry—but an ambassador could not commit his prince to a treaty unless he was expressly granted authority to do so as a plenipotentiary.

The Crusades, in addition to opening up trade, brought back to Europe a renewed interest in the East. Venice in particular, a city whose trade relations with Constantinople stretched back to Byzantine days, had borrowed much from Byzantium's diplomatic style. The Venetians gave their ambassadors written instructions, which was unheard of in the West, and they kept an archive with registered and cataloged treaties. As trade relations in the West became extensive, Venice's diplomacy became byzantine not only in its elaborateness and extension, but in its very soul, as the Venetians began using envoys to spy on their host countries. Venice even "debriefed" its ambassadors upon their return, requiring them to file a *relazione*, or final report, at first by oral presentation, by the 15th century in writing.

Other Italian city-states copied Venice's diplomatic system, and later so did France and Spain. By the 16th century, resident embassies had become commonplace throughout Europe. There were so many ambassadors swarming about the capitals of Europe, representing so many sovereigns, that disputes arose of who took precedence in this diplomatic corps. Much of today's diplomatic protocol was fashioned in the 1500s. By the 17th century, the focus of diplomacy had begun to shift from sovereign to state, from representing the king's interests to representing the nation's, and in 1626 Cardinal Richelieu set up in France the first truly modern ministry.

As the various ambassadors went about the work of aggrandizing their principal, nation, or king—at the expense of the next nation or prince—the premises of international law they had inherited from the Middle Ages were simple enough. First, in the absence of an agreed-upon state of truce or peace, war was not only assumed but considered the fundamental state of international relations, even among independent Christian communities. Next, unless foreigners had some kind of individual dispensation, a safe conduct award, treaty protection, or diplomatic immunity, rulers felt free to treat them at their absolute discretion. Finally, the high seas were open, a no-man's land where anyone might do as he pleased. From these basics Europe would develop a more complex diplomacy—as its society and its politics grew more complex—and fashion the increasingly intricate treaties of a modern world in the making.

TREATIES

TREATY BETWEEN CHARLEMAGNE AND MICHAEL I RANGABE

TREATY AT A GLANCE

Completed
811

Signatories
Charlemagne and Michael I Rangabe

Overview
Years after being anointed the first Holy Roman Emperor by Pope Leo III, European colossus Charlemagne finally secured recognition of his title from the new Byzantine emperor Michael I Rangabe, who agreed to a split in sovereignty over the old Roman Empire into East and West, marking the secular incarnation of the long-standing religious schism between the Catholic and Orthodox Churches.

Historical Background

When the Frankish king Pepin founded the Carolingian dynasty in 751, the Christian Church was in the midst of a schism between Rome and Constantinople over the Byzantine Empire's ban on the use of holy icons in worship. Pepin, anointed by Pope Boniface, answered Rome's call to restore lands taken from the church by the Lombards. The only trouble was that these lands, which became the Papal States (sometimes called the Republic of Saint Peter), had belonged to the Byzantine Church and were considered part of the empire by Constantinople. For Pepin's service the new Roman pope Stephan reenacted his coronation and bestowed on the Frank and his heirs the title of Patrician of Rome. Thus, when Pepin's son Charles came to the throne at the age of 26 in 768, his fortunes were already cast with Rome. Under Charles's reign the Franks grew more powerful still, and soon his clerics were calling him in Latin Carolus Magnus—"Charles the Great," or in French Charlemagne.

Charlemagne's tremendous success rested on two skills. One was his ability to compel loyalty at all levels of Frankish society. Expanding on the practice of vassalage begun by his forebears, the mayors of the palace, who exchanged grants of land for the fealty of soldiers and others sworn to serve them, Charlemagne made personal vassals of all those in authority—counts, dukes, and churchmen as well as ranking officials—and encouraged them to develop their own networks of vassals in turn. Charlemagne's second talent was for war. Rarely did a year pass that he and his knights and foot soldiers failed to embark on some campaign, penetrating the Pyrenees to the southwest, marching across upper Germany to the North Sea and across Saxony to the Baltic in the north, conquering Bavaria and bursting onto the central basin of the Danube to the east. When the Lombards again assaulted the Papal States, he promptly defeated them, this time annexing the land himself and taking the title king of the Lombards. Late in his life, Charlemagne settled his capital at Aachen in today's western Germany. Thus had he laid the grounds for both the feudal society of medieval Europe and the Holy Roman Empire.

Although Charlemagne was clearly the colossus of the West, Byzantium still dominated eastern Europe. Hoping to dissuade the Franks from absorbing the remaining Byzantine holdings in southern Italy and Sicily, Byzantine emissaries approached Charlemagne in 781 with a proposal of marriage between the 11-year-old Byzantine emperor, Constantine VI, and the Frankish king's eight-year-old daughter, Rotrud. The proposal did not account for Constantine's widowed mother, Irene, who ruled the empire as regent. Marriage alliances were central to medieval diplomacy, and Charlemagne welcomed the opportunity to link his royal house with an empire that still enjoyed enormous prestige, if not the power it once had. The children were duly betrothed, and Rotrud began learning Greek and Byzantine customs.

The arrangement collapsed under Irene's vaulting ambitions, however. She sent an army to invade Benveneto, an independent duchy south of Rome, and Charlemagne came to its aid. She then sponsored an ecumenical council at Nicea, without inviting Charlemagne or any of his bishops, which rescinded the 60-year-old ban on icons, thus removing the most divisive issue between Byzantium and Rome. In 791, after a falling-out with her son, Irene engineered his overthrow and had him blinded to prevent his return to power. Then she assumed the title not of empress but of emperor of the Byzantines.

In Rome an outraged Pope Leo III announced that he considered the throne vacant because no male occupied it and had Charlemagne declared Emperor of the Romans, a title that had traditionally been Constantinople's to bestow. Charlemagne spent the remainder of his life working to secure Byzantine recognition and heal the rift between the Eastern and Western Roman Empires. Years of much negotiation and some fighting followed, during which time Irene was deposed and her son Nicephorus was killed fighting the Bulgarians. Meanwhile, a new emperor, the son-in-law of Nicepherous, Michael I Rangabe, was about to assume the throne. With Byzantium menaced by the Bulgarians and others, Michael agreed, upon his accession in 811, to Byzantine's long-withheld recognition of Charlemagne's imperial title.

Terms

After some excruciatingly painful moments, during which one scribe warned Michael that "barbarians" and "those who have arisen from among foreign peoples" were not "eligible for imperial dignity," the Byzantine ruler ratified a treaty that accepted the notion of coequal emperors, presiding side by side, over the East and West in the Roman Empire. In return Charlemagne agreed to the cession of several cities on the Adriatic and of Venice to Byzantium.

Consequences

The treaty was of little help to Michael I Rangabe. Not only had he recognized a barbarian as his co-emperor, he also supported the proponents of the use of icons and soon found himself faced by a revolt of the Iconoclasts, who sought to replace him with a son of the former emperor Constantine V. The revolt in turn left an opening for the Bulgarian kahn, Krum, to capture the Byzantine city of Develtus and carry off all its inhabitants into captivity. After putting down the revolt, Michael was able to turn his full attention to the Bulgarians. Though he won a number of victories, in 813 the desertion of one of his generals, Leo, cost the Byzantines Adrianople. Later that year Leo deposed Michael to become Leo V. From Michael's brief rule, Byzantines bearing his family name would go on to triumphs never dreamed of in these years, and the next four centuries would be remembered as Byzantium's Golden Age.

The treaty had, however, established a Roman Emperor in the West, and these European emperors would come to Byzantium's rescue in the Crusades and ultimately grow to overshadow the Eastern emperors. Indeed, long after Byzantium had fallen into the trashbin of history, men holding the title of Holy Roman Emperor would make their imprint on the development and fate of Europe and the world.

TREATY BETWEEN RICHARD THE LIONHEARTED AND SALADIN

TREATY AT A GLANCE

Completed
Autumn 1192 at Jerusalem

Signatories
Crusaders under Richard and Muslims under Saladin

Overview
Called on a Third Crusade to retake Jerusalem from its Muslim captors, Richard the Lionhearted ended by signing a compromise peace with the Muslim general Saladin, whom he had come to admire.

Historical Background

In 1188 the Kurdish general Salah a-Din Yusuf ibn Ayyub, head of an Islamic army determined to retake land lost to Christian Crusaders, engineered through a string of victories the fall of Jerusalem. A distraught Pope Gregory VIII, with a great bull that linked the disaster in Palestine to the sins of Christians everywhere, summoned the Third Crusade, promising the remission of all sins to anyone who accepted the call in a repentant frame of mind. Ships sailed from Brittany, France, Flanders, England, Germany, Denmark with small squadrons of local volunteers, knights and barons, professional archers and spearmen—all headed to fight the infidel who had become infamous in Christian Europe over the last decade under the name "Saladin."

For those forces from earlier Crusades already in the region who, supplemented by a trickle of early-arriving galleys from Norman Sicily, were now besieging the city of Acre in Tripoli—and in turn being besieged by Saladin's warriors—the news came that reinforcement was imminent. The 67-year-old emperor of Germany, Frederick Barbarossa, it was said, was marching eastward. Rumor had it, too, that Philip II and Richard the Lionhearted, the feuding kings of France and England, had patched up their differences and were on the high seas with a huge, combined army. Richard in particular was known as a fierce warrior, one who led his knights into battle personally and wielded his great sword with skill and abandon.

For once the Christians had enough money. For three, nearly four generations, prominent European families had been supporting the Crusades, and their coffers had been depleted, or so they said. In any case, recognizing the strains their kingdoms had begun to feel by the last decade of the 10th century, monarchs, with the pope backing them, had begun to look for new ways of coming up with the funds to subsidize Crusaders. Philip and Richard both levied taxes, immense taxes, to pay for this latest outing, amounting to some 10 percent of all the movable property belonging to those choosing not to go on crusade. The Saladin tithe, folks called it, and the funds went to supplement other levies and contributions.

Frederick Barbarossa discovered he would have to fight his way across the Byzantine Empire territories, because the Byzantines—who had started the Crusade craze in the first place by calling on the Western pope for help when Constantinople was threatened by infidel hordes—had, assuming Saladin invincible, allied themselves with the Muslims. Barbarossa crossed Anatolia, slaughtering thousands of Seljuks as he went, and fought his way into Christian-held territory. When he tried to swim an especially wide river, he drowned, probably after suffering a heart attack, and his leaderless German hordes fell apart. As they staggered into Antioch, one pleased Arab described them as "looking like disinterred corpses." The Christians clearly would have to wait for the French and English fleet to break out of the double siege still going on, with the Christian army surrounding Acre, and Saladin surrounding them.

The two kings landed in the summer of 1191. On the way, Richard had stopped to take Cyprus from Isaac Comnenus, a Greek rebelling against Byzantium who had recently installed himself as the new king. Then he sold the island to the Knights Templar, after exacting a 50 percent tax from the liberated Cypriots. Now he and Philip began to squabble over who got to be king of the no-doubt-soon-to-be-restored Jerusalem. The Crusaders stayed unified enough to crush Acre, which surrendered in July, and force Saladin to withdraw, but Philip, disgruntled with Richard's dominance in the Crusade, took the first opportunity to head back to France. Once there, he attacked with some success Richard's territories on the Continent.

Left in sole command, Richard marched on to Jaffa, the gateway to the best route to Jerusalem. Saladin's Turkish cavalry skirmished with Richard all along the way, and when the latter reached Arsuf, Saladin, waiting in ambush with his entire host, attacked. At Arsuf, Saladin learned just how good a general he was up against. Richard, a careful but skilled tactician, absorbed the ambush, letting Saladin commit his main forces to the battle, and when the Muslim rearguard charged too soon, the Lionhearted struck. Afterward, Saladin could get no Muslin army to face Richard again, so he withdrew into the hills of Judea, destroying the countryside as he went, poisoning wells, damming springs, and in general creating an artificial wilderness in an already arid land.

Richard understood what Saladin was doing, and the Englishman was astute enough at logistics to realize as well that even if he took Jerusalem, the Christians would never be able to hold onto it. During the course of their fighting and maneuvering, Saladin had been extremely courteous to the foreign king, and Richard in turn, had come to appreciate both Saladin's manner and his skill. Something like an understanding grew between them, if not a friendship, and both began to seek some road short of bloodshed out of the impasse they had created. At one point, Richard even suggested to the astonished Saladin that Richard's sister might marry Saladin's brother, who would then rule all Palestine, Christian and Muslim together. Saladin rejected the idea but continued to work with Richard until, sometime in the autumn of 1192, they agreed to a treaty.

Terms

Under the truce, the Christian Franks were left in their coastal cities of the Holy Land, and the True Cross, housed in Jerusalem, was returned to them. In addition, Christians were allowed free passage to the city, which nevertheless stayed in Muslim hands.

Consequences

Five months into the peace, Saladin died of a fever. Revered by enemy and foe alike, his story and personality became celebrated in songs and plays, and a century later Dante Alighieri gave Saladin an honored spot in Hell in his *Divine Comedy*. Richard returned to England after some travail—which included being held for ransom by Philip II—to find that his brother John, ruling in his absence, had managed to botch the job, upset much of the kingdom, and pave the way, after Richard's death, for the signing of the MAGNA CARTA.

Most of the Christian powers knew that the treaty of 1192 was the best they could hope for, but it was not what they had wanted. The Crusaders had set out to save their souls by recapturing the city where Christ had suffered for them, and the peace seemed too much of a compromise. In 1197 Barbarossa's son, Henry VI, tried again. Although he had learned enough from his father's mistakes to travel to the Holy Land by sea, he nevertheless died suddenly en route, like his father, and the Germans, once again leaderless, managed to recapture only Beirut. A Fourth Crusade, preached throughout Europe in 1197, wound up sacking Byzantium rather than fighting Muslims.

MAGNA CARTA

TREATY AT A GLANCE

Completed
June 15, 1215, at Runnymede, England

Signatories
King John and the barons of England

Overview
Resentments, already strong among the English barons, against the royal house of Anjou burst into rebellion when the long-absent King John, defeated in his French wars, returned permanently to his island realm. The resulting treaty, the Magna Carta, brought the civil war temporarily to an end but established forever the "rights of an Englishman" to be protected from arbitrary rule not supported by the consent of the governed.

Historical Background

England had been conquered in the 11th century by William, duke of Normandy, who replaced its Anglo-Saxon landholding nobility with his Norman vassals. These lords, having received their lands by direct royal grant, were beholden only to the monarch. As a result, the feudal system took a clearer shape in England than it did in France.

By the middle of the 12th century, feudal relations had grown more muddled. Henry Plantagenet, count of Anjou, added the English throne to his existing French possessions, and to administer his vast holdings—stretching from the Scottish border to the Pyrenees—he governed through local officials, to whom he sent written instructions. Henry was himself constantly on the move with an itinerant court that migrated from province to province, and the administration of England was only one of his many preoccupations. His heirs Richard the Lionhearted, and Richard's brother and successor John, followed Henry's lead. Richard, distracted by his crusading, was in England for only a year of his 11-year reign; John, apart from a three-week visit for his coronation in 1199, spent the first four years of his rule fighting over French properties with Philip II.

From Henry's day, English vassals had resented the expansion of the Angevin kings' administration. These sovereigns always seemed to be demanding money and interfering in local and private affairs, but at least they were not around much to irritate the vassals personally.

That changed, however, when John lost his French provinces to Philip in 1214. Deprived of his favorite haunts on the Continent, he was forced to take up nearly permanent residence in his English domain, as were many of his vassals, who had held lands widely spread in France.

Few of these vassals held much affection for their king. Lacking the resources of his Capetian enemy, he had exhausted his English coffers by exporting huge quantities of silver to pay for his French expedition, and many of the lords and barons he had summoned to feudal service failed to show up and campaign or to send any of the knights they owed him. Furthermore, during his long absence the kingdom had been left in the hands of administrators, many of them not English, who were accountable only to him. Under John succession dues, payable by a baron on accession to his title, rose from 100 to as high as 10,000 marks. Fines from the king's justices for even the most minor of misdemeanors shot up. In his time John stooped to blackmail and extortion, for example, forcing one northern baron to pay for the king's silence about the baron's sexual liaison with another man's wife. On another occasion, he extracted a fee simply to allow a lady to leave court and "lie one night" with her husband.

The result was a sharp increase in the already existing friction between the king and the powerful magnates of the land. During the winter following his return from France, he attempted to collect payments in lieu of service from those who had refused to campaign. The barons rebelled, demanding that the

Angevin regime's despotic innovations be tossed aside and England be returned to the customs of Anglo-Saxon days. John played for time, taking Crusader vows to put himself and his property under the protection of the church, then sending hastily to Aquitaine and Flanders for mercenaries to smash the rebellion. Before the French legions could arrive, however, the English nobles repudiated their oaths of fealty and took up arms. They failed to capture the important town of Northampton, but they took both Bedford and London, the latter never much of a Plantagenet stronghold.

Under pressure from his more moderate advisers, John asked for a truce. In June 1215, the two sides conducted detailed negotiations at the meadow of Runnymede, about 20 miles up the Thames River from London.

Terms

The Magna Carta, or "Great Charter," as the document they produced became known, consisted of 63 clauses of specific promises extracted from King John to redress the lords' complaints in return for their renewed loyalty. Certain clauses were simply restatements of time-honored customs that John and his ancestor kings had come to ignore. Some paragraphs took the time to name royal agents hated by the barons, who thus announced that the careers of these lickspittles were at an end. The barons made sure to reward London's merchant community for its support of their rebellion by attempting to standardize currency and weights and measures.

The force of the more important provisions were not so mundane, however. Instead, they sought to assert the rule of law over the arbitrary power of the king. One central paragraph outlawed extraordinary payments to the king without the "common counsel" of the realm. Perhaps the severest limitation of royal power came from John's agreement to nominate 25 barons as a tribunal to hear complaints about breaches of the charter, which created a body with the right to restrain a king by force if necessary.

This central document in both English and American history reads as follows.

PREAMBLE

John, by the grace of God, king of England, lord of Ireland, duke of Normandy and Aquitaine, and count of Anjou, to the archbishop, bishops, abbots, earls, barons, justiciaries, foresters, sheriffs, stewards, servants, and to all his bailiffs and liege subjects, greetings. Know that, having regard to God and for the salvation of our soul, and those of all our ancestors and heirs, and unto the honor of God and the advancement of his holy Church and for the rectifying of our realm, we have granted as underwritten by advice of our venerable fathers, Stephen, archbishop of Canterbury, primate of all England and cardinal of the holy Roman Church, Henry, archbishop of Dublin, William of London, Peter of Winchester, Jocelyn of Bath and Glastonbury, Hugh of Lincoln, Walter of Worcester, William of Coventry, Benedict of Rochester, bishops; of Master Pandulf, subdeacon and member of the household of our lord the Pope, of brother Aymeric (master of the Knights of the Temple in England), and of the illustrious men William Marshal, earl of Pembroke, William, earl of Salisbury, William, earl of Warenne, William, earl of Arundel, Alan of Galloway (constable of Scotland), Waren Fitz Gerold, Peter Fitz Herbert, Hubert De Burgh (seneschal of Poitou), Hugh de Neville, Matthew Fitz Herbert, Thomas Basset, Alan Basset, Philip d'Aubigny, Robert of Roppesley, John Marshal, John Fitz Hugh, and others, our liegemen.

1. In the first place we have granted to God, and by this our present charter confirmed for us and our heirs forever that the English Church shall be free, and shall have her rights entire, and her liberties inviolate; and we will that it be thus observed; which is apparent from this that the freedom of elections, which is reckoned most important and very essential to the English Church, we, of our pure and unconstrained will, did grant, and did by our charter confirm and did obtain the ratification of the same from our lord, Pope Innocent III, before the quarrel arose between us and our barons: and this we will observe, and our will is that it be observed in good faith by our heirs forever. We have also granted to all freemen of our kingdom, for us and our heirs forever, all the underwritten liberties, to be had and held by them and their heirs, of us and our heirs forever.

2. If any of our earls or barons, or others holding of us in chief by military service shall have died, and at the time of his death his heir shall be full of age and owe "relief", he shall have his inheritance by the old relief, to wit, the heir or heirs of an earl, for the whole baroncy of an earl by £100; the heir or heirs of a baron, £100 for a whole barony; the heir or heirs of a knight, 100s, at most, and whoever owes less let him give less, according to the ancient custom of fees.

3. If, however, the heir of any one of the aforesaid has been under age and in wardship, let him have his inheritance without relief and without fine when he comes of age.

4. The guardian of the land of an heir who is thus under age, shall take from the land of the heir nothing but reasonable produce, reasonable customs, and reasonable services, and that without destruction or waste of men or goods; and if we have committed the wardship of the lands of any such minor to the sheriff, or to any other who is responsible to us for its issues, and he has made destruction or waster of what he holds in wardship, we will take of him amends, and the land shall be committed to two lawful and discreet men of that fee, who shall be responsible for the issues to us or to him to whom we shall assign them; and if we have given or sold the wardship of any such land to anyone and he has therein made destruction or waste, he shall lose that wardship, and it shall be transferred to two lawful and discreet men of that fief, who shall be responsible to us in like manner as aforesaid.

5. The guardian, moreover, so long as he has the wardship of the land, shall keep up the houses, parks, fishponds, tanks,

mills, and other things pertaining to the land, out of the issues of the same land; and he shall restore to the heir, when he has come to full age, all his land, stocked with ploughs and wainage, according as the season of husbandry shall require, and the issues of the land can reasonable bear.

6. Heirs shall be married without disparagement, yet so that before the marriage takes place the nearest in blood to that heir shall have notice.

7. A widow, after the death of her husband, shall forthwith and without difficulty have her marriage portion and inheritance; nor shall she give anything for her dower, or for her marriage portion, or for the inheritance which her husband and she held on the day of the death of that husband; and she may remain in the house of her husband for forty days after his death, within which time her dower shall be assigned to her.

8. No widow shall be compelled to marry, so long as she prefers to live without a husband; provided always that she gives security not to marry without our consent, if she holds of us, or without the consent of the lord of whom she holds, if she holds of another.

9. Neither we nor our bailiffs will seize any land or rent for any debt, as long as the chattels of the debtor are sufficient to repay the debt; nor shall the sureties of the debtor be distrained so long as the principal debtor is able to satisfy the debt; and if the principal debtor shall fail to pay the debt, having nothing wherewith to pay it, then the sureties shall answer for the debt; and let them have the lands and rents of the debtor, if they desire them, until they are indemnified for the debt which they have paid for him, unless the principal debtor can show proof that he is discharged thereof as against the said sureties.

10. If one who has borrowed from the Jews any sum, great or small, die before that loan be repaid, the debt shall not bear interest while the heir is under age, of whomsoever he may hold; and if the debt fall into our hands, we will not take anything except the principal sum contained in the bond.

11. And if anyone die indebted to the Jews, his wife shall have her dower and pay nothing of that debt; and if any children of the deceased are left under age, necessaries shall be provided for them in keeping with the holding of the deceased; and out of the residue the debt shall be paid, reserving, however, service due to feudal lords; in like manner let it be done touching debts due to others than Jews.

12. No scutage not aid shall be imposed on our kingdom, unless by common counsel of our kingdom, except for ransoming our person, for making our eldest son a knight, and for once marrying our eldest daughter; and for these there shall not be levied more than a reasonable aid. In like manner it shall be done concerning aids from the city of London.

13. And the city of London shall have all its ancient liberties and free customs, as well by land as by water; furthermore, we decree and grant that all other cities, boroughs, towns, and ports shall have all their liberties and free customs.

14. And for obtaining the common counsel of the kingdom anent the assessing of an aid (except in the three cases aforesaid) or of a scutage, we will cause to be summoned the archbishops, bishops, abbots, earls, and greater barons, severally by our letters; and we will moreover cause to be summoned generally, through our sheriffs and bailiffs, and others who hold of us in chief, for a fixed date, namely, after the expiry of at least forty days, and at a fixed place; and in all letters of such summons we will specify the reason of the summons. And when the summons has thus been made, the business shall proceed on the day appointed, according to the counsel of such as are present, although not all who were summoned have come.

15. We will not for the future grant to anyone license to take an aid from his own free tenants, except to ransom his person, to make his eldest son a knight, and once to marry his eldest daughter; and on each of these occasions there shall be levied only a reasonable aid.

16. No one shall be distrained for performance of greater service for a knight's fee, or for any other free tenement, than is due therefrom.

17. Common pleas shall not follow our court, but shall be held in some fixed place.

18. Inquests of novel disseisin, of mort d'ancestor, and of darrein presentment shall not be held elsewhere than in their own county courts, and that in manner following; We, or, if we should be out of the realm, our chief justiciar, will send two justiciaries through every county four times a year, who shall alone with four knights of the county chosen by the county, hold the said assizes in the county court, on the day and in the place of meeting of that court.

19. And if any of the said assizes cannot be taken on the day of the county court, let there remain of the knights and freeholders, who were present at the county court on that day, as many as may be required for the efficient making of judgments, according as the business be more or less.

20. A freeman shall not be amerced for a slight offense, except in accordance with the degree of the offense; and for a grave offense he shall be amerced in accordance with the gravity of the offense, yet saving always his "contentment"; and a merchant in the same way, saving his "merchandise"; and a villein shall be amerced in the same way, saving his "wainage" if they have fallen into our mercy: and none of the aforesaid amercements shall be imposed except by the oath of honest men of the neighborhood.

21. Earls and barons shall not be amerced except through their peers, and only in accordance with the degree of the offense.

22. A clerk shall not be amerced in respect of his lay holding except after the manner of the others aforesaid; further, he shall not be amerced in accordance with the extent of his ecclesiastical benefice.

23. No village or individual shall be compelled to make bridges at river banks, except those who from of old were legally bound to do so.

24. No sheriff, constable, coroners, or others of our bailiffs, shall hold pleas of our Crown.

25. All counties, hundred, wapentakes, and trithings (except our demesne manors) shall remain at the old rents, and without any additional payment.

26. If anyone holding of us a lay fief shall die, and our sheriff or bailiff shall exhibit our letters patent of summons for a debt which the deceased owed us, it shall be lawful for our sheriff or bailiff to attach and enroll the chattels of the deceased, found upon the lay fief, to the value of that debt, at the sight of law worthy men, provided always that nothing whatever be thence removed until the debt which is evident shall be fully paid to us; and the residue shall be left to the executors to ful-

fill the will of the deceased; and if there be nothing due from him to us, all the chattels shall go to the deceased, saving to his wife and children their reasonable shares.

27. If any freeman shall die intestate, his chattels shall be distributed by the hands of his nearest kinsfolk and friends, under supervision of the Church, saving to every one the debts which the deceased owed to him.

28. No constable or other bailiff of ours shall take corn or other provisions from anyone without immediately tendering money therefor, unless he can have postponement thereof by permission of the seller.

29. No constable shall compel any knight to give money in lieu of castle-guard, when he is willing to perform it in his own person, or (if he himself cannot do it from any reasonable cause) then by another responsible man. Further, if we have led or sent him upon military service, he shall be relieved from guard in proportion to the time during which he has been on service because of us.

30. No sheriff or bailiff of ours, or other person, shall take the horses or carts of any freeman for transport duty, against the will of the said freeman.

31. Neither we nor our bailiffs shall take, for our castles or for any other work of ours, wood which is not ours, against the will of the owner of that wood.

32. We will not retain beyond one year and one day, the lands those who have been convicted of felony, and the lands shall thereafter be handed over to the lords of the fiefs.

33. All kydells for the future shall be removed altogether from Thames and Medway, and throughout all England, except upon the seashore.

34. The writ which is called praecipe shall not for the future be issued to anyone, regarding any tenement whereby a freeman may lose his court.

35. Let there be one measure of wine throughout our whole realm; and one measure of ale; and one measure of corn, to wit, "the London quarter"; and one width of cloth (whether dyed, or russet, or "halberget"), to wit, two ells within the selvedges; of weights also let it be as of measures.

36. Nothing in future shall be given or taken for awrit of inquisition of life or limbs, but freely it shall be granted, and never denied.

37. If anyone holds of us by fee-farm, either by socage or by burage, or of any other land by knight's service, we will not (by reason of that fee-farm, socage, or burage), have the wardship of the heir, or of such land of his as if of the fief of that other; nor shall we have wardship of that fee-farm, socage, or burage, unless such fee-farm owes knight's service. We will not by reason of any small serjeancy which anyone may hold of us by the service of rendering to us knives, arrows, or the like, have wardship of his heir or of the land which he holds of another lord by knight's service.

38. No bailiff for the future shall, upon his own unsupported complaint, put anyone to his "law", without credible witnesses brought for this purpose.

39. No freemen shall be taken or imprisoned or disseised or exiled or in any way destroyed, nor will we go upon him nor send upon him, except by the lawful judgment of his peers or by the law of the land.

40. To no one will we sell, to no one will we refuse or delay, right or justice.

41. All merchants shall have safe and secure exit from England, and entry to England, with the right to tarry there and to move about as well by land as by water, for buying and selling by the ancient and right customs, quit from all evil tolls, except (in time of war) such merchants as are of the land at war with us. And if such are found in our land at the beginning of the war, they shall be detained, without injury to their bodies or goods, until information be received by us, or by our chief justiciar, how the merchants of our land found in the land at war with us are treated; and if our men are safe there, the others shall be safe in our land.

42. It shall be lawful in future for anyone (excepting always those imprisoned or outlawed in accordance with the law of the kingdom, and natives of any country at war with us, and merchants, who shall be treated as if above provided) to leave our kingdom and to return, safe and secure by land and water, except for a short period in time of war, on grounds of public policy— reserving always the allegiance due to us.

43. If anyone holding of some escheat (such as the honor of Wallingford, Nottingham, Boulogne, Lancaster, or of other escheats which are in our hands and are baronies) shall die, his heir shall give no other relief, and perform no other service to us than he would have done to the baron if that barony had been in the baron's hand; and we shall hold it in the same manner in which the baron held it.

44. Men who dwell without the forest need not henceforth come before our justiciaries of the forest upon a general summons, unless they are in plea, or sureties of one or more, who are attached for the forest.

45. We will appoint as justices, constables, sheriffs, or bailiffs only such as know the law of the realm and mean to observe it well.

46. All barons who have founded abbeys, concerning which they hold charters from the kings of England, or of which they have long continued possession, shall have the wardship of them, when vacant, as they ought to have.

47. All forests that have been made such in our time shall forthwith be disafforsted; and a similar course shall be followed with regard to river banks that have been placed "in defense" by us in our time.

48. All evil customs connected with forests and warrens, foresters and warreners, sheriffs and their officers, river banks and their wardens, shall immediately by inquired into in each county by twelve sworn knights of the same county chosen by the honest men of the same county, and shall, within forty days of the said inquest, be utterly abolished, so as never to be restored, provided always that we previously have intimation thereof, or our justiciar, if we should not be in England.

49. We will immediately restore all hostages and charters delivered to us by Englishmen, as sureties of the peace of faithful service.

50. We will entirely remove from their bailiwicks, the relations of Gerard of Athee (so that in future they shall have no bailiwick in England); namely, Engelard of Cigogne, Peter, Guy, and Andrew of Chanceaux, Guy of Cigogne, Geoffrey of Martigny with his brothers, Philip Mark with his brothers and his nephew Geoffrey, and the whole brood of the same.

51. As soon as peace is restored, we will banish from the kingdom all foreign born knights, crossbowmen, serjeants, and mercenary soldiers who have come with horses and arms to the kingdom's hurt.

52. If anyone has been dispossessed or removed by us, without the legal judgment of his peers, from his lands, castles, franchises, or from his right, we will immediately restore them to him; and if a dispute arise over this, then let it be decided by the five and twenty barons of whom mention is made below in the clause for securing the peace. Moreover, for all those possessions, from which anyone has, without the lawful judgment of his peers, been disseised or removed, by our father, King Henry, or by our brother, King Richard, and which we retain in our hand (or which as possessed by others, to whom we are bound to warrant them) we shall have respite until the usual term of crusaders; excepting those things about which a plea has been raised, or an inquest made by our order, before our taking of the cross; but as soon as we return from the expedition, we will immediately grant full justice therein.

53. We shall have, moreover, the same respite and in the same manner in rendering justice concerning the disafforestation or retention of those forests which Henry our father and Richard our brother afforested, and concerning the wardship of lands which are of the fief of another (namely, such wardships as we have hitherto had by reason of a fief which anyone held of us by knight's service), and concerning abbeys founded on other fiefs than our own, in which the lord of the fee claims to have right; and when we have returned, or if we desist from our expedition, we will immediately grant full justice to all who complain of such things.

54. No one shall be arrested or imprisoned upon the appeal of a woman, for the death of any other than her husband.

55. All fines made with us unjustly and against the law of the land, and all amercements, imposed unjustly and against the law of the land, shall be entirely remitted, or else it shall be done concerning them according to the decision of the five and twenty barons whom mention is made below in the clause for securing the peace, or according to the judgment of the majority of the same, along with the aforesaid Stephen, archbishop of Canterbury, if he can be present, and such others as he may wish to bring with him for this purpose, and if he cannot be present the business shall nevertheless proceed without him, provided always that if any one or more of the aforesaid five and twenty barons are in a similar suit, they shall be removed as far as concerns this particular judgment, others being substituted in their places after having been selected by the rest of the same five and twenty for this purpose only, and after having been sworn.

56. If we have disseised or removed Welshmen from lands or liberties, or other things, without the legal judgment of their peers in England or in Wales, they shall be immediately restored to them; and if a dispute arise over this, then let it be decided in the marches by the judgment of their peers; for the tenements in England according to the law of England, for tenements in Wales according to the law of Wales, and for tenements in the marches according to the law of the marches. Welshmen shall do the same to us and ours.

57. Further, for all those possessions from which any Welshman has, without the lawful judgment of his peers, been disseised or removed by King Henry our father, or King Richard our brother, and which we retain in our hand (or which are possessed by others, and which we ought to warrant), we will have respite until the usual term of crusaders; excepting those things about which a plea has been raised or an inquest made by our order before we took the cross; but as soon as we return (or if perchance we desist from our expedition), we will immediately grant full justice in accordance with the laws of the Welsh and in relation to the foresaid regions.

58. We will immediately give up the son of Llywelyn and all the hostages of Wales, and the charters delivered to us as security for the peace.

59. We will do towards Alexander, king of Scots, concerning the return of his sisters and his hostages, and concerning his franchises, and his right, in the same manner as we shall do towards our other barons of England, unless it ought to be otherwise according to the charters which we hold from William his father, formerly king of Scots; and this shall be according to the judgment of his peers in our court.

60. Moreover, all these aforesaid customs and liberties, the observances of which we have granted in our kingdom as far as pertains to us towards our men, shall be observed by all of our kingdom, as well clergy as laymen, as far as pertains to them towards their men.

61. Since, moreover, for God and the amendment of our kingdom and for the better allaying of the quarrel that has arisen between us and our barons, we have granted all these concessions, desirous that they should enjoy them in complete and firm endurance forever, we give and grant to them the underwritten security, namely, that the barons choose five and twenty barons of the kingdom, whomsoever they will, who shall be bound with all their might, to observe and hold, and cause to be observed, the peace and liberties we have granted and confirmed to them by this our present Charter, so that if we, or our justiciar, or our bailiffs or any one of our officers, shall in anything be at fault towards anyone, or shall have broken any one of the articles of this peace or of this security, and the offense be notified to four barons of the foresaid five and twenty, the said four barons shall repair to us (or our justiciar, if we are out of the realm) and, laying the transgression before us, petition to have that transgression redressed without delay. And if we shall not have corrected the transgression (or, in the event of our being out of the realm, if our justiciar shall not have corrected it) within forty days, reckoning from the time it has been intimated to us (or to our justiciar, if we should be out of the realm), the four barons aforesaid shall refer that matter to the rest of the five and twenty barons, and those five and twenty barons shall, together with the community of the whole realm, distrain and distress us in all possible ways, namely, by seizing our castles, lands, possessions, and in any other way they can, until redress has been obtained as they deem fit, saving harmless our own person, and the persons of our queen and children; and when redress has been obtained, they shall resume their old relations towards us. And let whoever in the country desires it, swear to obey the orders of the said five and twenty barons for the execution of all the aforesaid matters, and along with them, to molest us to the utmost of his power; and we publicly and freely grant leave to everyone who wishes to swear, and we shall never forbid anyone to swear. All those, moreover, in the land who of themselves and of their own accord are unwilling to swear to the twenty five to help them in constraining and molesting us, we shall by our command compel the same to swear to the effect foresaid. And if any one of the five and twenty barons shall have died or departed from the land, or be incapacitated in any other manner which would prevent the foresaid provisions being carried out, those of the said twenty five barons

who are left shall choose another in his place according to their own judgment, and he shall be sworn in the same way as the others. Further, in all matters, the execution of which is entrusted to these twenty five barons, if perchance these twenty five are present and disagree about anything, or if some of them, after being summoned, are unwilling or unable to be present, that which the majority of those present ordain or command shall be held as fixed and established, exactly as if the whole twenty five had concurred in this; and the said twenty five shall swear that they will faithfully observe all that is aforesaid, and cause it to be observed with all their might. And we shall procure nothing from anyone, directly or indirectly, whereby any part of these concessions and liberties might be revoked or diminished; and if any such things has been procured, let it be void and null, and we shall never use it personally or by another.

62. And all the will, hatreds, and bitterness that have arisen between us and our men, clergy and lay, from the date of the quarrel, we have completely remitted and pardoned to everyone. Moreover, all trespasses occasioned by the said quarrel, from Easter in the sixteenth year of our reign till the restoration of peace, we have fully remitted to all, both clergy and laymen, and completely forgiven, as far as pertains to us. And on this head, we have caused to be made for them letters testimonial patent of the lord Stephen, archbishop of Canterbury, of the lord Henry, archbishop of Dublin, of the bishops aforesaid, and of Master Pandulf as touching this security and the concessions aforesaid.

63. Wherefore we will and firmly order that the English Church be free, and that the men in our kingdom have and hold all the aforesaid liberties, rights, and concessions, well and peaceably, freely and quietly, fully and wholly, for themselves and their heirs, of us and our heirs, in all respects and in all places forever, as is aforesaid. An oath, moreover, has been taken, as well on our part as on the art of the barons, that all these conditions aforesaid shall be kept in good faith and without evil intent. Given under our hand—the above named and many others being witnesses—in the meadow which is called Runnymede, between Windsor and Staines, on the fifteenth day of June, in the seventeenth year of our reign.

The Magna Carta was no abstract attempt to define the law. Objective inquiries and the taking down of evidence were already well established, although ancient customs such as trial by ordeal or judicial dueling were by no means dead. Instead, by creating an advisory body, a parliament, comprising in theory all who held land directly from the king; by devoting so many of the clauses to making royal justice more prompt, effective, and available; and by, in effect, taking control of the royal purse strings, the English barons had forced John to concede that neither he nor any future king of England held an entitlement to proceed against free men on the sovereign's whim.

Consequences

In time the Magna Carta would come to be viewed as a milestone in the march away from autocracy and toward government by the direct consent of those governed. More immediately, though, the Great Charter failed to stop England from collapsing into chaos. Ambitious barons, still hoping to overthrow their now even weaker king, renewed the conflict with the assistance of French troops sent by Philip II. Although the French temporarily occupied London, the barons failed to make much headway against King John's mercenaries.

As the French invasion bogged down, John, already ill with dysentery, died shortly after falling into the tidewaters of the Wellstream River, which he was attempting to cross as a shortcut in rejoining troops from whom he had become separated during a rebel siege in Cambridge. English loyalists backed John's quickly crowned nine-year-old son, Henry III, and they won a decisive victory in March 1217. After a fleet carrying reinforcements was destroyed by the English in August, Philip's son, the future Louis VIII, headed back to France under a face-saving truce, and the Magna Carta was reissued, this time without the committee of 25 barons. Since the renewal of the Magna Carta agreement confirmed that Henry would not reverse the gains of the civil war, the rebel party melted away.

The gulf between the king and magnates, however, would continue to widen. In 1225, for example, another reissue of the Great Charter in return for a general grant of money temporarily reassured the barons. The conflict had become endemic, though, which showed in the subsequent separate development of France and England, once ruled as one land. In France autocratic power was secure, and the kingdom came to be ruled by an absolute monarch through a large body of royal administrators whose actions were little hindered by the need to consult with local assemblies. In England the king was held in check by his own subjects, and a tradition of opposition, growing out of the Magna Carta, resurfaced regularly throughout the century, a tradition that ultimately led to a permanent parliament and a "constitutional" monarchy.

TREATY OF BRÉTIGNY

TREATY AT A GLANCE

Completed
May 8, 1360, at Brétigny (present-day Brétigny-sur-Orge), France

Signatories
England and France

Overview
After Edward, the Black Prince, captured and held for ransom the French king John II during the Hundred Years' War, a peace was signed at Brétigny that lasted for nearly a decade before hostilities broke out again between an England whose lands had been much expanded on the Continent and a France that had used the time to revitalize its armies and alliances.

Historical Background

Disputes between England's King Edward III, duke of Aquitaine and count of Ponthieu, and Philip VI of France concerning English territories Edward claimed in France were a decisive factor among many interrelated and complex reasons for the 1337 outbreak of the Hundred Years' War (which actually went on for some 150 years). At the famous Battle of Poitiers in 1356, Edward of Woodstock, Edward III's soldier-son, who was known as the Black Prince, took the new French king, John II, Philip's son and heir, prisoner and returned with him to London. Having captured the king and humiliated the illustrious French knights, the English had good reason to believe that they could conclude the war on their terms. In John's absence, his son Charles, the dauphin, managed to inspire the French with new determination. Backed by the pope, the dauphin's army forced the English to raise a siege they had invested at Rheims, after which Edward's army abandoned hope of marching on Paris.

The French, too, however, had reason to negotiate a truce. Decades of war and devastation and the constant demands for taxes had led to unrest and resentment among the French. After the capture of their king, angry subjects castigated the upper classes, and in the countryside a bloody rebellion known as the Jacquerie (after the common nickname for a peasant, "Jacques Good-man") set the poor, inflamed with generations of stored-up wrath, to raiding castles and massacring the inhabitants. In 1358 an alliance of French nobles and neighboring princes, who abandoned for the moment their traditional rivalries, responded with a savagery matching that of the peasants, laying waste to the land all around.

By 1360 everybody needed some space in which to breathe. When representatives of both sides met for negotiations at Brétigny, a small settlement south of Paris, the French, thanks to Charles, were able to bargain from a position of some strength.

Terms

The treaty appeared to make massive concessions to the English, considerably extending the English domains in France, giving Edward III full sovereignty over more than a third of John II's nation. In exchange Edward was expected to renounce his claim to the French throne and give up any thought of sovereignty outside those rather vast areas delineated by the treaty.

The agreement was partially ratified at Calais the coming autumn, but certain key clauses—regarding each king's renunciation over the other's newly agreed-to territories—were separated into another document, which never received the seal of either king. Nevertheless, as the new decade opened, both sides seemed to feel their honor and ambitions had been satisfied.

Consequences

John was released from captivity in London that year, when the French sent the agreed-to £500,000 and sent three of his sons as hostages back to England.

When one of those sons broke parole, John—ever chivalrous—voluntarily returned to London and to jail, where he died in 1364. Importantly, France enjoyed nine years of peace, affording the peasantry some relief and giving the French time to reorganize their armies, put their finances in order, and cement new alliances. Working hard at precisely that was the dauphin, now ruling as Charles V, who initiated an energetic diplomatic campaign to win new friends and political alliances and gradually unraveled those Edward had put together.

Hostilities would begin again in 1369. Both kings would have to die and their sons replace them, and a saint named Joan of Arc appear, before the war would at last come to an end in the next century. No peace treaty would be signed until well afterward, in 1492, and even as late as 1815 English kings continued to call themselves kings of France on official documents.

Part Three

THE BIRTH OF MODERN DIPLOMACY

INTRODUCTION

In many ways, the PEACE OF WESTPHALIA on October 24, 1648, signals the true beginning of modern diplomacy. In it we can see the coming into being of the secular state and a system of international relations based on the existence of sovereign powers that are interrelated by competition for territorial expansion and by alliances that serve their mutual interests. At Westphalia the Reformation came to an end, and with it, the religious conflicts stretching back to the decline of the moral authority of the Catholic Church in the late Middle Ages. The pope, naturally, tried to condemn the treaty, but Catholic powers in the emerging Europe ratified it anyway. The signatories enshrined this treaty rather than, say, the latest papal bull, as the fundamental territorial settlement in Europe, a settlement that lasted for all intents and purposes down to the time of the CONGRESS OF VIENNA in 1815.

The Emerging Secular State

The treaty's "subject" is the Thirty Years' War. Although fought by many nations, most of the destruction took place within the Holy Roman Empire, a loose concoction of nearly 1,000 semi-independent, small states, in theory controlled from Vienna by the emperor, Ferdinand II, a Hapsburg. The House of Hapsburg then ruled nearly half of modern-day Europe, including Spain and portions of Italy and the Low Countries, i.e., the Netherlands. Ferdinand's bailiwick among the family holdings covered today's Germany, the former Czechoslovakia, and Austria and included part of Hungary, Poland, and what until recently was called Yugoslavia. His lands stretched north and south from the Baltic to the Adriatic Seas, east and west from the Carpathian Mountains to the Rhine River.

The spark that set off the conflagration was religion. Christianity, since medieval times a source of unity in western Europe, had been transfigured by the 16th century's Protestant Reformation into a casus belli between emerging nations. Some within the Holy Roman Empire itself, many Scandinavians, even more English and Scots, and most of the Swiss had converted to Lutheranism or Calvinism or some other Protestant sect, while the Italians, the Spanish, and majority of those in the empire—along with the Hapsburg rulers—remained loyal to the pope in Rome. The new schism cut the old diplomatic ties, and traditional allies such as Spain and England those days were at odds over theology. Since religious affinities did not follow territorial boundaries, all the major states found themselves dealing with religious minorities whose first loyalties were to creed, not king.

The Holy Roman Empire had from the beginning been based on a delicate balance between individual principalities and their would-be rulers in Vienna. In 1618, when Ferdinand attempted to reassert his imperial authority over apostate Bohemia by debarring Protestants from public office and shutting down their two major churches, the precarious balance was not so much upset as destroyed. In Prague, the Bohemian capital, an anti-imperial revolt broke out, and—like dominos—not only the German states but neighboring European powers fell into the fighting. At first the alliances were mostly based on religious affiliation, Protestant England, Sweden, Denmark, and the Dutch Republic falling in with Bohemia; Catholic Spain, Poland, and the papal state marching along the imperial front. But the intentions of individual belligerents varied, and sometimes changed moment to moment as events unfurled, between the holy and the profane, the aggressive and defensive, self-assertion and self-preservation. First among the more secular issues was the longing of many German princes and dukes and the rising nation-states butting up against the Holy Roman Empire to counteract and contain the multinational power and the imperial ambitions of the Hapsburg clan.

The long struggle fell roughly into two phases. In the first, local issues dominated, the most heartfelt being religious. After 1635, however, politics, naked and raw, took over, and the goal of the warmongers was nothing less than altering the balance of power in Hapsburg-dominated Europe. By the beginning of the second phase, the war had taken on a momentum all its own. On a continent divided into two camps, diplomacy had become nigh unto impossible—no neutral parties existed to mediate disputes, fighting was the only way to resolve issues, no one had the edge to win the fighting, so the war dragged on and on and on. None of this was helped by the fact that early nation-states collected few taxes and had no base to support standing armies, so rulers hired mercenaries. These soldiers of fortune had begun to appear toward the end of the Middle Ages, when the ancient obligations of feudal vassals to fight for their lords was waning under the impact of the Crusades, which gave the mercenaries combat experience. The profession had grown, and by the 17th century, mercenaries were indispensable to the conduct of war in Europe.

Rulers farmed out the task of recruiting and leading the hireling armies to privately paid generals—ambitious adventurers and unscrupulous entrepreneurs, they were men like Count Peter Ernst von Mansfield. The bastard son of a minor Catholic prince, Mansfield began his military career in the Hapsburg army. His illegitimate birth blocked his rise through the ranks, so early on he switched allegiance to the Protestants, leading in the course of the first eight years the troops of Savoy, France, England, and the Netherlands. Some of those hired by Mansfield and his ilk might once have had religious feelings, but most were no better than their bosses. Many were conscripted, kidnapped more or less, while some joined up to escape the gallows or the harsh poverty the war was fast bringing in its wake. Conditions were filthy, pay uncertain, and death—more by disease than in battle—omnipotent. Mutiny and desertion were, necessarily, savagely punished. Since wages came through regimental commanders, the soldiers' loyalty lay with them rather than a cause or a king, even when—as routinely happened—the officers skimmed the take from the rulers who hired them.

Often the cash dried up entirely. Princes ran out of money, or lost heart, or disliked the job their hirelings were doing. When the duke of Savoy, for example, cut off Mansfield's men, Mansfield complained that "neither they nor their horses can live on air" and turned them loose on the citizens. Mercenary armies frequently extracted such payment from the common folk, sometimes as taxes, sometimes in free board and lodging, often as simple booty, looting being one of the attractions of a soldier's life. They traveled about, these armies, with a train of servants, wives, children, prostitutes, freebooters, and traders, wreaking havoc and visiting vicious depredations on villagers, who, often driven to extremes, sometimes struck back. Both villager and mercenary mutilated as well as murdered, and civilians and soldiers alike were drawn into a spiral of violence that was proving nearly impossible to stop. The destruction was so great that even the highborn belligerents had been drained of all desires except a longing for peace.

By then Germany's population as a whole had fallen by 20 percent, higher in the areas of heaviest fighting. There, up to three-quarters of the people had disappeared from the land as a result of disease, the war, and a mass migration to the cities, where walls and payoffs kept most armies at bay. In Württemberg, a southern duchy much visited by the war, the 450,000 inhabitants living there in 1620 had dwindled to 100,000 by 1639. Germany was not the only country devastated by the three decades of conflict. In Sweden, for example, wholesale conscription had stripped the land of its adult males.

By the 1640s all Europe was in the mood for peace. Achieving it turned out to be harder than hoped, involving something new and cumbersome—an international conference of nation-states. The meetings dragged on for four years and were held simultaneously in two cities. The French and their Roman Catholic allies met with the Hapsburg emperor at Münster in northwest Germany; the Swedes and their Protestant delegates met him 30 miles away at Osnabrück. In the end, all the delegates stuck to the task at hand and produced on October 24, 1648, the Peace of Westphalia.

Starting as an internal dispute within the Holy Roman Empire, the Thirty Years' War had swelled to involve most of the nations in Europe. The common folk saw it not so much in terms of battles won or territories gained or theologies defined and protected, but as a long orgy of violence, a glimpse of Hell created by men on Earth. The rulers who began and backed the war imagined it had been a means of establishing the status quo in Europe, a status quo that would last for almost a century. Historians came to view the war more broadly as the failure of the Austrian Hapsburgs to sustain the Counter-Reformation. Under the banner of this Counter-Reformation, said these historians, the Hapsburgs had marched all the way to the Baltic to establish their hegemony over the Holy Roman Empire. But in the end, they were thwarted by the jealousy of Catholic Bavaria and, more important, by the powerful and effective military intervention after 1635 of Lutheran Sweden under its warrior-king Gustavus

Adolphus. He in turn was supported by money from a Catholic France then dominated by Cardinal Richelieu. Thus was the Thirty Years' War—and Europe—secularized, as considerations of power and diplomatic advantage superseded religion when first Sweden, then France, decided to crush Hapsburg Germany.

As a result of the war, the Calvinist, or "Reform" Church, now gained status equal to that of Lutheranism, and by and large various territorial rulers in the Holy Roman Empire could establish public worship as they saw fit. Not only did Westphalia make official Germany's religious disunity, it confirmed as well its political fragmentation by allowing member states to conclude treaties with foreign powers. It would be two centuries before the diverse German states could be welded into a power sufficiently unified to truly threaten again the Continent's stability.

Left in peace for the time being to rebuild their lives and livelihoods, the war-weary German people did so with surprising speed. By 1700 much of Germany had returned to its prewar housing and population levels, as the Thirty Years' War became both a memory and a byword for calamity. Some of the emerging nations in Europe fared better than others. Protestant Sweden gained a commanding post on Germany's Baltic coast, though it was now in no position economically or militarily to exploit the gain. On the other hand, Catholic France got 10 imperial towns in Alsace and three strategic fortresses at Metz, Toul, and Verdun, all of which laid the basis for the emerging French ascendancy in Europe.

With the Peace of Westphalia, the threat of Hapsburg domination had subsided, and it was the turn of others, notably France, to kindle territorial longings. Meanwhile, the Roman Catholic Church role of universal mediator in international disputes, long in decline, had been forever diminished, and henceforth it would be the new rulers of nations doing the treaty making and deploying the diplomats.

The New Absolutes

Throughout Europe, in the wake of the Hapsburg decline, the 17th century would witness the growth of governments concentrated in the hands of rulers with nearly despotic powers. This centralizing of the affairs of state found a theoretical expression and theological justification in the belief that sovereignty was vested exclusively by "divine right" in a nation-state's ruler, who was under no obligation to share his authority with anyone, certainly no political body. Though subject to no agency of state, this new monarch was portrayed in the political thought of the period as a champion of individual rights and liberties. Diplomatic

theorists such as Cardinal Jean Richelieu argued that the absolute power of the king, exercised from a central seat of government, was an advance over the old warring influences of regional nobles and magistrates so obvious in Hapsburg lands. Concentrated rule meant greater efficiency and control. When these new absolute monarchs began to achieve some economic as well as military success, the system seemed justified.

Such absolutism reached its apotheosis in France, where the nation's young king, Louis XIV, became for all Europe the very emblem of the absolute monarch. Coming to the throne at the age of 14 during the year the peace was concluded at Westphalia, Louis was under the tutelage of his powerful guardian and adviser, Cardinal Jules Mazarin. Not until Mazarin's death in 1661 would Louis take the kind of personal command over every aspect of his nation's political life that became the keystone to his view of kingship. He lived a long life, till 1715, and his reign established the House of Bourbon as a rival to the Hapsburgs, while he himself embodied an entire era of political development. Right away, in 1662, Louis had adopted the Sun as his personal symbol, and even then he had already decided to build a palace that would be a fitting setting for his conception of royal majesty. The court of the "Sun King" created at Versailles became the French seat of government for more than a century, and in its halls and gardens, a tableau of absolute power was played out day by day as if on a plush, extended stage.

Actually setting the stage for Louis XIV's ascendancy in Europe, however, were events stretching back to the end of the Thirty Years' War. One of the major reasons that the negotiations at Münster had been so protracted was the obstinacy of the Spanish branch of the Hapsburg family. Its rule had been crumbling since the early 1600s, but the Spanish royal house was dealt a decisive blow by the French at Rocroi in 1643. Staving off the inevitable, the Iberian Hapsburgs used the relatively brief (five-year) period of civil unrest that followed Louis's ascension to prolong its weak hold on the throne until 1659, when Mazarin used some astute diplomacy to isolate them entirely. Forming a League of the Rhine, a bloc of French client states in northwestern Germany, and a second alliance with the new English lord protector, Oliver Cromwell, Mazarin trapped the Spanish in the southern Netherlands, and they were defeated by the English at the Battle of the Dunes in Dunkirk in 1658. Cut off from the rest of Europe and desiccated militarily, Spain concluded the TREATY OF THE PYRENEES in 1659. France got important towns in the Netherlands, which resulted in an extended northeast frontier that considerably diminished any Hapsburg military threat and provided the basis for Louis XIV's future wars of expansion. The peace, then, humbled the Spanish Hapsburgs and brought Spain's history as a great power virtually to an end, while establishing the Pyrenees as the "natural" border between the two nations.

With the death of Cardinal Mazarin, Louis began his long personal rule. During his life, the French monarchy achieved its greatest internal cohesion and international power. His wars were a push toward, and a consolidation of, what he perceived as France's natural borders, especially in the northeast. There lay the possessions still of the Spanish and Austrian Hapsburgs, and Louis—after marriage to a Spanish princess—laid claim to them, all of them. He backed up this spurious assertion of his right to the whole of the Spanish Netherlands with a brilliant diplomatic and military isolation of both the Netherlands and the Dutch Republic. Though his armies won impressive victories, he fell short of complete dominance when England grew alarmed about the growing French power. The Triple Alliance of England, the United Netherlands, and Sweden marked the start of an Anglo-Dutch collaboration aimed at using the Spanish Netherlands as a buffer against French aggression. The Alliance and Louis fought the so-called War of Devolution, which ended in 1668.

Next, in the Dutch War of 1672, Louis struck directly at the Dutch. Diplomacy—and a secret bribe to the Stuart king, Charles II—kept the English from coming to the aid of the United Netherlands, but the war proved unpopular in England and the Dutch got help from the Austrian Hapsburgs and Frederick the Great's grandfather, the elector of Brandenburg. The large French armies were finally stopped by a young William of Orange, who cut Holland's dikes and held out behind his watery defenses. Unable to defeat the Dutch in what became a naval conflict, Louis grabbed some land from the decrepit Spanish king and let the matter go. The 1678 PEACE OF NIJMEGEN, ending the Dutch war, left a still successfully imperial France that in the 1680s would reach the high-water mark of its territorial expansion before the coming of Napoleon.

From the end of that decade forward, however, Louis would find it increasingly difficult to maintain French preeminence on the Continent. A series of military defeats would combine with economic difficulties internally—not unconnected with the costly wars of expansion—to increase social dissent and set the stage for an inexorable weakening of the old regime during the course of the coming century. When the Austrian Hapsburgs found themselves threatened by Turkey on the Danube, and England and Brandenburg fell victim to the lure of French bribes, Louis was tempted to overreach. Subtle, even tortured, interpretations of international treaties in his favor led Louis to declare a number of border towns, notably Strasbourg, to belong completely to France, which along with his seizure of Luxembourg and brutal attacks on Protestant minorities excited his enemies to form the League of Augsburg, which in turned paved the way for the Grand Alliance of 1689.

The Protestant Prince of Orange was the heart and soul of that alliance. He unseated the Catholic ruler of England, James II, and took the English throne in 1688, a move watched with benevolent neutrality by the Holy Roman Emperor, with impotent silence by the pope, and with much joy by the English Protestant majority. Closing off a century of revolution in England, the reign of William and Mary married the resources of two great sea powers, creating a mighty navy and commercial marine in support of an industrially expanding mercantile nation whose aim was clearly set against French hegemony. Thus, the allies proved inexhaustible in the War of the League of Augsburg, and by the 1697 TREATY OF RYSWICK, Louis was forced to renounce most of his military conquests. It was not an auspicious beginning for the century, which would witness a long diplomatic and armed duel between the English and the French over who would reign supreme in Europe and, indeed, in the world.

TREATIES

PEACE OF WESTPHALIA

TREATY AT A GLANCE

Completed
October 24, 1648, at Münster, Westphalia (in present-day Germany)

Signatories
Holy Roman Empire (and allies) and France (and allies)

Overview
The Peace of Westphalia was the culmination of a four-year peace process ending the last of the series of European wars known collectively as the Thirty Years' War. The Peace of Westphalia created an enduring compromise between Protestants and Roman Catholics by ending the Holy Roman Empire as a significant political entity, replacing it with a recognition of the virtual sovereignty of the German states. The treaty established France as the major European power, and it made Sweden the dominant Baltic nation.

Historical Background

The long, debilitating conflict known as the Thirty Years' War was the last major European war of religion and the first struggle for secular power that engulfed virtually all of Europe, although it was fought mainly on German soil. It began as a religious struggle between rival leagues of Catholic and Protestant states within the Holy Roman Empire in 1618. The religious issues were essentially solved by the Peace of Prague in 1635 between the Lutheran states and the Hapsburgs, so the closing phase of the conflict, from 1635 to 1648, was primarily a struggle over secular power.

The series of wars began on May 23, 1618, with the so-called Defenestration of Prague, when a group of Protestant Bohemian nobles hurled two royal Catholic governors of their country out of the windows of the Hradcany Palace in protest of the absolutist and Catholic policies of their king, Ferdinand of Hapsburg, who would shortly be elected Holy Roman Emperor Ferdinand II. The Bohemian War was a holy war, with both sides convinced that defeat meant nothing less than annihilation. Thus motivated, the combatants scrambled for allies, quickly widening the conflict. The Bohemians appealed to Gabor Bethlen, Protestant prince of Transylvania, who, in turn, was encouraged to join the fray by his overlord, the Ottoman sultan of Turkey. The Ottomans saw this as a chance to wrest the crown of Hungary from the Hapsburgs. The Bohemians also elected Frederick V of the Palatinate as their new king, hoping thereby to secure the support of Frederick's father-in-law, James I of England, and Frederick's uncle, Maurice of Nassau, who was virtual ruler of the United Provinces of the Netherlands. For his part, Ferdinand called on Poland for alliance and on his cousins Maximilian, duke of Bavaria and leader of the Catholic League of German princes, and Philip III, the Hapsburg king of Spain.

The first decisive battle in this early phase of the conflict came on November 8, 1620, when Maximilian's general, Count von Tilly, defeated Bohemian forces at White Mountain near Prague. The newly crowned Frederick summarily lost his crown (thereby earning the epithet of "the Winter King"), though he continued to wage war, using mercenary leaders (principally Ernst, count von Mansfeld) as well as troops sent by the English and Dutch. Nevertheless, in 1623 the Palatinate was overrun by Spanish and Bavarian troops, and Frederick's electoral vote was transferred to Maximilian of Bavaria.

In the meantime, in 1621 the Dutch and Spanish had renewed a war that had begun years earlier as the Revolt of the Netherlands. Spanish and Dutch hostilities ranged to the Caribbean, the South Atlantic, and the Indian Ocean. The Dutch captured the Gold Coast, parts of Angola, and half of Brazil from the Portuguese. The Dutch then lost both Angola and Brazil back to Portugal, after Portugal had reasserted its independence from Spain in 1640.

On the European continent, it was Dutch funds and Spanish professional soldiers who helped drive the war. Spanish troops fought in Germany, Italy, and

France, while the Dutch provided much-needed finance to their Protestant allies. In April 1626 Hapsburg loyalist Albrect von Wallenstein, whose career would later become the subject of a famous play by German Romantic poet Friedrich Schiller, won a major victory against the mercenary Count von Mansfield, and in July Dutch-backed Denmark suffered a major defeat that prompted Emperor Ferdinand boldly to issue the Edict of Restitution on March 29, 1629, restoring to the Catholic Church all property taken by the Protestants since 1552. The vacuum left by Denmark's May 1629 withdrawal from the war, however, was soon filled by another Scandinavian power, Sweden, under Gustavus II Adolphus, who landed in Pomerania to begin a series of successful campaigns against the imperial armies, although he himself was killed in the process.

While these events were being played out, Louis XIII of Catholic France, traditional rival of the House of Hapsburg for dominance in Europe, grew increasingly concerned over the Hapsburg victories. At this point, the conflict ceased to be a religious struggle and had become a war for secular power. To be sure, France had been convulsed by civil war against its own Protestant subjects, the Huguenots, but once this group had been suppressed, France leaped into the Thirty Years' War against Spain in northern Italy. Following the death of Gustavus Adolphus and a major Swedish defeat at Nordlingen in September 1634, France formally declared war on Spain in 1635, allying itself with the United Provinces, Sweden, and some German Protestant princes.

With the complex of alliances in place, peace would not be easy to achieve, for no single treaty between any two states could end the war. Moreover, with religious allegiance replaced by political ends, even more combatants joined the fray. In 1640 both Catalonia and Portugal rebelled against Spain—although all three nations were Catholic. In 1643 the Protestant King Christian of Denmark sought to check the growing power of Protestant Sweden by reigniting the traditional rivalry for the control of the Sound (Øresund), the northwestern entrance to the Baltic. The Danes lost, relinquishing control over the Sound.

Wearily, diplomats started the tortuous peace process. Beginning in 1643, the combatants met in peace congresses in the Westphalian cities of Münster and Osnabrück. However, no side would consent to a truce during the negotiations; therefore, positions continually shifted according to the ongoing fortunes of war. The most comprehensive treaty, the Peace of Westphalia, was five years in the making, and the important TREATY OF THE PYRENEES, between France and Spain, was not forthcoming until 1659. Warfare between Sweden and Poland and between Sweden and Denmark was not finally quelled until 1660.

Terms

The Peace of Westphalia was a compromise. The Holy Roman Emperor accepted French claims to Upper Alsace. Sweden obtained the bishoprics of Bremen and Verden and divided Pomerania with Brandenburg, whose prince-elector also secured Magdeburg. Bavaria retained the Upper Palatinate and the Palatinate electorate, and Swiss independence was recognized. The German princes were granted virtual sovereignty, obtaining the right to make alliances and choose their religion for themselves and their subjects, thereby effectively bringing to an end the real power of the Holy Roman Empire. This most momentous historical event was conveyed not in some sweeping "declaration of independence" but primarily in a single unpretentious article—article LXIV—tucked among 128 very particular and exacting provisions.

Peace Treaty between the Holy Roman Emperor and the King of France and Their Respective Allies

In the name of the most holy and individual Trinity: Be it known to all, and every one whom it may concern, or to whom in any manner it may belong, That for many Years past, Discords and Civil Divisions being stir'd up in the *Roman* Empire, which increas'd to such a degree, that not only all *Germany*, but also the neighbouring Kingdoms, and *France* particularly, have been involv'd in the Disorders of a long and cruel War: And in the first place, between the most Serene and most Puissant Prince and Lord, *Ferdinand* the Second, of famous Memory, elected *Roman* Emperor, always August, King of *Germany*, *Hungary*, *Bohemia*, *Dalmatia*, *Croatia*, *Slavonia*, Arch-Duke of *Austria*, Duke of *Burgundy*, *Brabant*, *Styria*, *Carinthia*, *Carniola*, Marquiss of *Moravia*, Duke of *Luxemburgh*, the Higher and Lower *Silesia*, of *Wirtemburg* and *Teck*, Prince of *Suabia*, Count of *Hapsburg*, *Tirol*, *Kyburg* and *Goritia*, Marquiss of the Sacred *Roman* Empire, Lord of *Burgovia*, of the Higher and Lower *Lusace*, of the Marquisate of *Slavonia*, of Port *Naon* and *Salines*, with his Allies and Adherents on one side; and the most Serene, and the most Puissant Prince, *Lewis* the Thirteenth, most Christian King of *France* and *Navarre*, with his Allies and Adherents on the other side. And after their Decease, between the most Serene and Puissant Prince and Lord, *Ferdinand* the Third, elected *Roman* Emperor, always August, King of *Germany*, *Hungary*, *Bohemia*, *Dalmatia*, *Croatia*, *Slavonia*, Arch-Duke of *Austria*, Duke of *Burgundy*, *Brabant*, *Styria*, *Carinthia*, *Carniola*, Marquiss of *Moravia*, Duke of *Luxemburg*, of the Higher and Lower *Silesia*, of *Wirtemburg* and *Teck*, Prince of *Suabia*, Count of *Hapsburg*, *Tirol*, *Kyburg* and *Goritia*, Marquiss of the Sacred *Roman* Empire, *Burgovia*, the Higher and Lower *Lusace*, Lord of the Marquisate of *Slavonia*, of Port *Naon* and *Salines*, with his Allies and Adherents on the one side; and the most Serene and most Puissant Prince and Lord, *Lewis* the Fourteenth, most Christian King of *France* and *Navarre*, with his Allies and Adherents on the other side: from whence ensu'd great Effusion of Christian Blood, and the Desolation of several Provinces. It has at last happen'd, by the effect of Divine Goodness, seconded by the Endeavours of the most Serene Republick of *Venice*, who in this sad time, when all *Christendom* is imbroil'd, has not ceas'd to contribute its Counsels for the publick Welfare and Tranquillity; so that on the side, and the other, they have form'd Thoughts of an universal Peace. And for this purpose, by a mutual Agreement and Covenant of both Partys, in the year of our Lord 1641. the 25th of *December*, N.S. or the 15th O.S. it was resolv'd at *Hamburgh*, to hold an Assembly of Plenipotentiary Ambassadors, who should render themselves at *Munster* and *Osnabrug* in *Westphalia* the 11th of *July*, N.S. or the 1st of the said month O.S. in the year 1643. The Plenipotentiary Ambassadors on the one side, and the other, duly establish'd, appearing at the prefixt time, and on the behalf of his Imperial Majesty, the most illustrious and most excellent Lord, *Maximilian* Count of *Trautmansdorf* and *Weinsberg*, Baron of *Gleichenberg*, *Neustadt*, *Negan*, *Burgau*, and *Torzenbach*, Lord of *Teinitz*, Knight of the Golden Fleece, Privy Counsellor and Chamberlain to his Imperial Sacred Majesty, and Steward of his Houshold; the Lord *John Lewis*, Count of *Nassau*, *Catzenellebogen*, *Vianden*, and *Dietz*, Lord of *Bilstein*, Privy Counsellor to the Emperor, and Knight of the Golden Fleece; Monsieur *Isaac Volmamarus*, Doctor of Law, Counsellor, and President in the Chamber of the most Serene Lord Arch-Duke *Ferdinand Charles*. And on the behalf of the most Christian King, the most eminent Prince and Lord, *Henry* of *Orleans*, Duke of *Longueville*, and *Estouteville*, Prince and Sovereign Count of *Neuschaftel*, Count of *Dunois* and *Tancerville*, Hereditary Constable of *Normandy*, Governor and Lieutenant-General of the same Province, Captain of the *Cent Hommes d'Arms*, and Knight of the King's Orders, &c. as also the most illustrious and most excellent Lords, *Claude de Mesmes*, Count *d'Avaux*, Commander of the said King's Orders, one of the Superintendents of the Finances, and Minister of the Kingdom of *France &c.* and *Abel Servien*, Count *la Roche* of *Aubiers*, also one of the Ministers of the Kingdom of *France*. And by the Mediation and Interposition of the most illustrious and most excellent Ambassador and Senator of *Venice*, *Aloysius Contarini* Knight, who for the space of five Years, or thereabouts, with great Diligence, and a Spirit intirely impartial, has been inclin'd to be a Mediator in these Affairs. After having implor'd the Divine Assistance, and receiv'd a reciprocal Communication of Letters, Commissions, and full Powers, the Copys of which are inserted at the end of this Treaty, in the presence and with the consent of the Electors of the Sacred *Roman* Empire, the other Princes and States, to the Glory of God, and the Benefit of the Christian World, the following Articles have been agreed on and consented to, and the same run thus.

I

That there shall be a Christian and Universal Peace, and a perpetual, true, and sincere Amity, between his Sacred Imperial Majesty, and his most Christian Majesty; as also, between all and each of the Allies, and Adherents of his said Imperial Majesty, the House of *Austria*, and its Heirs, and Successors; but chiefly between the Electors, Princes, and States of the Empire on the one side; and all and each of the Allies of his said Christian Majesty, and all their Heirs and Successors, chiefly between the most Serene Queen and Kingdom of *Swedeland*, the Electors respectively, the Princes and States of the Empire, on the other part. That this Peace and Amity be observ'd and cultivated with such a Sincerity and Zeal, that each Party shall endeavour to procure the Benefit, Honour and Advantage of the other; that thus on all sides they may see this Peace and Friendship in the *Roman* Empire, and the Kingdom of *France* flourish, by entertaining a good and faithful Neighbourhood.

II

That there shall be on the one side and the other a perpetual Oblivion, Amnesty, or Pardon of all that has been committed since the beginning of these Troubles, in what place, or what manner soever the Hostilitys have been practis'd, in such a manner, that no body, under any pretext whatsoever, shall practice any Acts of Hostility, entertain any Enmity, or cause any Trouble to each other; neither as to Persons, Effects and Securitys, neither of themselves or by others, neither privately nor openly, neither directly nor indirectly, neither under the colour of Right, nor by the way of Deed, either within or without the extent of the Empire, notwithstanding all Covenants made before to the contrary: That they shall not act, or permit to be acted, any wrong or injury to any whatsoever; but that all that has pass'd on the one side, and the other, as well before as during the War, in Words, Writings, and Outrageous Actions, in Violences, Hostilitys, Damages and Expences, without any respect to Persons or Things, shall be entirely abolish'd in such a manner that all that might be demanded of, or pretended to, by each other on that behalf, shall be bury'd in eternal Oblivion.

III

And that a reciprocal Amity between the Emperor, and the Most Christian King, the Electors, Princes and States of the Empire, may be maintain'd so much the more firm and sincere (to say nothing at present of the Article of Security, which will be mention'd hereafter) the one shall never assist the present or future Enemys of the other under any Title or Pretence whatsoever, either with Arms, Money, Soldiers, or any sort of Ammunition; nor no one, who is a Member of this Pacification, shall suffer any Enemys Troops to retire thro' or sojourn in his Country.

IV

That the Circle of *Burgundy* shall be and continue a Member of the Empire, after the Disputes between *France* and *Spain* (comprehended in this Treaty) shall be terminated. That nevertheless, neither the Emperor, nor any of the States of the Empire, shall meddle with the Wars which are now on foot between them. That if for the future any Dispute arises between these two Kingdoms, the abovesaid reciprocal Obligation of not aiding each others Enemys, shall always continue firm between the Empire and the Kingdom of France, but yet so as that it shall be free for the States to succour; without the bounds of the Empire, such or such Kingdoms, but still according to the Constitutions of the Empire.

V

That the Controversy touching *Lorain* shall be refer'd to Arbitrators nominated by both sides, or it shall be terminated by a Treaty between *France* and *Spain*, or by some other friendly means; and it shall be free as well for the Emperor, as Electors, Princes and States of the Empire, to aid and advance this Agreement by an amicable Interposition, and other Offices of Pacification, without using the force of Arms.

VI

According to this foundation of reciprocal Amity, and a general Amnesty, all and every one of the Electors of the sacred *Roman* Empire, the Princes and States (therein comprehending the Nobility, which depend immediately on the Empire) their Vassals, Subjects, Citizens, Inhabitants (to whom on the account of the *Bohemian* or *German* Troubles or Alliances, contracted here and there, might have been done by the one Party or the other, any Prejudice or Damage in any manner, or under what pretence soever, as well in their Lordships, their fiefs, Underfiefs, Allodations, as in their Dignitys, Immunitys, Rights and Privileges) shall be fully re-establish'd on the one side and the other, in the Ecclesiastick or Laick State, which they enjoy'd, or could lawfully enjoy, notwithstanding any Alterations, which have been made in the mean time to the contrary.

VII

If the Possessors of Estates, which are to be restor'd, think they have lawful Exceptions, yet it shall not hinder the Restitution; which done, their Reasons and Exceptions may be examin'd before competent Judges, who are to determine the same.

VIII

And tho by the precedent general Rule it may be easily judg'd who those are, and how far the Restitution extends; nevertheless, it has been thought fit to make a particular mention of the following Cases of Importance, but yet so that those which are not in express Terms nam'd, are not to be taken as if they were excluded or forgot.

IX

Since the Arrest the Emperor has formerly caus'd to be made in the Provincial Assembly, against the moveable Effects of the Prince Elector of *Treves*, which were transported into the Dutchy of *Luxemburg*, tho releas'd and abolish'd, yet at the instance of some has been renew'd; to which has been added a Sequestration, which the said Assembly has made of the Jurisdiction of *Burch*, belonging to the Archbishoprick, and of the Moiety of the Lordship of St. *John*, belonging to *John Reinbard* of *Soeteren*, which is contrary to the Concordat's drawn up at Ausburg in the year 1548 by the publick interposition of the Empire, between the Elector of Treves, and the Dutchy of *Burgundy*: It has been agreed, that the abovesaid Arrest and Sequestration shall be taken away with all speed from the Assembly of *Luxemburg*, that the said Jurisdiction, Lordship, and Electoral and Patrimonial Effects, with the sequestred Revenues, shall be releas'd and restor'd to the Elector; and if by accident some things should be Imbezel'd, they shall be fully restor'd to him; the Petitioners being refer'd, for the obtaining a determination of their Rights, to the Judge of the Prince Elector, who is competent in the Empire.

X

As for what concerns the Castles of *Ehrenbreitstein* and *Homestein*, the Emperor shall withdraw, or cause the Garisons to be withdrawn in the time and manner limited hereafter in the Article of Execution, and shall restore those Castles to the Elector of *Treves*, and to his Metropolitan Chapter, to be in the Protection of the Empire, and the Electorate; for which end the Captain, and the new Garison which shall be put therein by the Elector, shall also take the Oaths of Fidelity to him and his Chapter.

XI

The Congress of *Munster* and *Osnabrug* having brought the *Palatinate* Cause to that pass, that the Dispute which has lasted for so long time, has been at length terminated; the Terms are these.

XII

In the first place, as to what concerns the House of *Bavaria*, the Electoral Dignity which the Electors *Palatine* have hitherto had, with all their Regales, Offices, Precedencys, Arms and Rights, whatever they be, belonging to this Dignity, without excepting any, as also all the *Upper Palatinate* and the County of *Cham*, shall remain, as for the time past, so also for the future, with all their Appurtenances, Regales and Rights, in the possession of the Lord *Maximilian*, Count *Palatine* of the *Rhine*, Duke of *Bavaria*, and of his children, and all the *Willielmine* Line, whilst there shall be any Male Children in being.

XIII

Reciprocally the Elector of *Bavaria* renounces entirely for himself and his Heirs and Successors the Debt of Thirteen Millions, as also all his Pretensions in *Upper Austria*; and shall deliver to his Imperial Majesty immediately after the Publication of the Peace, all Acts and Arrests obtain'd for that end, in order to be made void and null.

XIV

As for what regards the House of *Palatine*, the Emperor and the Empire, for the benefit of the publick Tranquillity, consent, that by virtue of this present Agreement, there be establish'd an eighth Electorate; which the Lord *Charles Lewis*, Count *Palatine* of the *Rhine*, shall enjoy for the future, and his Heirs, and the Descendants of the *Rudolphine* Line, pursuant to the Order of Succession, set forth in the Golden Bull; and that by this Investiture, neither the Lord *Charles Lewis*, nor his Successors shall have any Right to that which has been given with the Electoral Dignity to the Elector of *Bavaria*, and all the Branch of *William*.

XV

Secondly, that all the *Lower Palatinate*, with all and every the Ecclesiastical and Secular Lands, Rights and Appurtenances, which the Electors and Princes *Palatine* enjoy'd before the Troubles of *Bohemia*, shall be fully restor'd to him; as also all the Documents, Registers and Papers belonging thereto; annulling all that hath been done to the contrary. And the Emperor engages, that neither the Catholick King, nor any other who possess any thing thereof, shall any ways oppose this Restitution.

XVI

Forasmuch-as that certain Jurisdictions of the *Bergstraet*, belonging antiently to the Elector of *Mayence*, were in the year 1463 mortgag'd to the House *Palatine* for a certain Sum of Money: upon condition of perpetual Redemption, it has been agreed that the same Jurisdictions shall be Restor'd to the present Elector of *Mayence*, and his Successors in the Archbishoprick of *Mayence*, provided the Mortgage be paid in ready Mony, within the time limited by the Peace to be concluded; and that he satisfies the other Conditions, which he is bound to by the Tenor of the Mortgage-Deeds.

XVII

It shall also be free for the Elector of *Treves*, as well in the Quality of Bishop of *Spires* as Bishop of *Worms*, to sue before competent Judges for the Rights he pretends to certain Ecclesiastical Lands, situated in the Territorys of the *Lower Palatinate*, if so be those Princes make not a friendly Agreement among themselves.

XVIII

That if it should happen that the Male Branch of *William* should be intirely extinct, and the *Palatine* Branch still subsist, not only the *Upper Palatinate*, but also the Electoral Dignity of the Dukes of *Bavaria*, shall revert to the said surviving *Palatine*, who in the mean time enjoys the Investiture: but then the eighth Electorate shall be intirely suppress'd. Yet in such case, nevertheless, of the return of the *Upper Palatinate* to the surviving *Palatines*, the Heirs of any *Allodian* Lands of the *Bavarian* Electors shall remain in Possession of the Rights and Benefices, which may lawfully appertain to them.

XIX

That the Family-Contracts made between the Electoral House of *Heidelberg* and that of *Nieuburg*, touching the Succession to the Electorate, confirm'd by former Emperors; as also all the Rights of the *Rudolphine* Branch, forasmuch as they are not contrary to this Disposition, shall be conserv'd and maintain'd entire.

XX

Moreover, if any *Fiefs* in Juliers shall be found open by lawful Process, the Question shall be decided in favour of the House Palatine.

XXI

Further, to ease the Lord *Charles Lewis*, in some measure, of the trouble of providing his Brothers with Appenages, his Imperial Majesty will give order that forty thousand Rixdollars shall be paid to the said Brothers, in the four ensuing Years; the first commencing with the Year 1649. The Payment to be made of ten thousand Rixdollars yearly, with five per Cent Interest.

XXII

Further, that all the *Palatinate* House, with all and each of them, who are, or have in any manner adher'd to it; and above all, the Ministers who have serv'd in this Assembly, or have formerly serv'd this House; as also all those who are banish'd out of the *Palatinate*, shall enjoy the general Amnesty here above promis'd, with the same Rights as those who are comprehended therein, or of whom a more particular and ampler mention has been made in the Article of Grievance.

XXIII

Reciprocally the Lord *Charles Lewis* and his Brothers shall render Obedience, and be faithful to his Imperial Majesty, like the other Electors and Princes of the Empire; and shall renounce their Pretensions to the *Upper Palatinate*, as well for themselves as their Heirs, whilst any Male, and lawful Heir of the Branch of *William* shall continue alive.

XXIV

And upon the mention which has been made, to give a Dowry and a Pension to the Mother Dowager of the said Prince, and to his Sisters; his Sacred Imperial Majesty (according to the Affection he has for the *Palatinate* House) has promis'd to the said Dowager, for her Maintenance and Subsistence, to pay once for all twenty thousand Rixdollars; and to each of the Sisters of the said Lord *Charles Lewis*, when they shall marry, ten thousand

Rixdollars, the said Prince *Charles Lewis* being bound to disburse the Overplus.

XXV

That the said Lord *Charles Lewis* shall give no trouble to the Counts of *Leiningen* and of *Daxburg*, nor to their Successors in the *Lower Palatinate*; but he shall let them peaceably enjoy the Rights obtain'd many Ages ago, and confirm'd by the Emperors.

XXVI

That he shall inviolably leave the Free Nobility of the Empire, which are in *Franconia*, *Swabia*, and all along the *Rhine*, and the Districts thereof, in the state they are at present.

XXVII

That the Fiefs confer'd by the Emperor on the Baron *Gerrard* of *Waldenburg*, call'd *Schenck-heeren*, on *Nicholas George Reygersberg*, Chancellor of *Mayence*, and on *Henry Brombser*, Baron of *Rudeheim*; *Item*, on the Elector of *Bavaria*, on Baron *John Adolph Wolff*, call'd *Meternicht*, shall remain firm and stable: That nevertheless these Vassals shall be bound to take an Oath of Fidelity to the Lord *Charles Lewis*, and to his Successors, as their direct Lords, and to demand of him the renewing of their Fiefs.

XXVIII

That those of the Confession of *Augsburg*, and particularly the Inhabitants of *Oppenheim*, shall be put in possession again of their Churches, and Ecclesiastical Estates, as they were in the Year 1624. as also that all others of the said Confession of *Augsburg*, who shall demand it, shall have the free Exercise of their Religion, as well in publick Churches at the appointed Hours, as in private in their own Houses, or in others chosen for this purpose by their Ministers, or by those of their Neighbours, preaching the Word of God.

XXIX

That the Paragraphs, Prince *Lewis Philip*, &c. Prince *Frederick*, &c. and Prince *Leopold Lewis*, &c. be understood as here inserted, after the same manner they are contain'd in the Instrument, or Treaty of the Empire with *Swedeland*.

XXX

That the Dispute depending between the Bishops of *Bamberg* and *Wirtzberg* on the one, and the Marquiss of *Brandenburg*, *Culmbach*, and *Onalzbach*, on the other side, touching the Castle, Town, Jurisdiction, and Monastery of *Kitzingen* in *Franconia*, on the Main, shall be amicably compos'd; or, in a judicial manner, within two years time, upon pain of the Person's losing his Pretensions, that shall delay it: and that, in the mean time, the Fort of *Wirtzberg* shall be surrender'd to the said Lords Marquisses, in the same state it was taken, according as it has been agreed and stipulated.

XXXI

That the Agreement made, touching the Entertainment of the Lord *Christian William*, Marquiss of *Brandenburg*, shall be kept as if recited in this place, as it is put down in the fourteenth Article of the Treaty between the Empire and *Swedeland*.

XXXII

The Most Christian King shall restore to the Duke of *Wirtemberg*, after the manner hereafter related, where we shall mention the withdrawing of Garisons, the Towns and Forts of *Hohenwiel*, *Schorendorff*, *Turbingen*, and all other places, without reserve, where he keeps Garisons in the Dutchy of *Wirtemberg*. As for the rest, the Paragraph, THE HOUSE OF WIRTEMBERG, &c. shall be understood as inserted in this Place, after the same manner it's contain'd in the Treaty of the Empire, and of *Swedeland*.

XXXIII

That the Princes of *Wirtemberg*, of the Branches of *Montbeillard*, shall be re-establish'd in all their Domains in *Alsace*, and wheresoever they be situated, but particularly in the three Fiefs of *Burgundy*, *Clerval*, and *Passavant*: and both Partys shall re-establish them in the State, Rights and Prerogatives they enjoy'd before the Beginning of these Wars.

XXXIV

That *Frederick*, Marquiss of *Baden*, and of *Hachberg*, and his Sons and Heirs, with all those who have serv'd them in any manner whatsoever, and who serve them still, of what degree they may be, shall enjoy the Amnesty above-mention'd, in the second and third Article, with all its Clauses and Benefices; and by virtue thereof, they shall be fully re-establish'd in the State Ecclesiastical or Secular, in the same manner as the Lord *George Frederick* Marquiss of *Baden* and of *Hachberg*, possess'd, before the beginning of the Troubles of *Bohemia*, whatever concern'd the lower Marquisate of *Baden*, call'd vulgarly *Baden Durlach*, as also what concern'd the Marquisate of *Hachberg*, and the Lordships of *Rottelen*, *Badenweiller*, and *Sausenberg*, notwithstanding, and annulling all the Changes made to the contrary. After which shall be restor'd to Marquiss *Frederick*, the Jurisdictions of *Stein* and *Renchingen*, without being charg'd with Debts, which the Marquiss William has contracted during that time, by Reason of the Revenues, Interests and Charges, put down in the Transaction pass'd at *Etlingen* in the Year 1629. and transfer'd to the said William Marquiss of *Baden*, with all the Rights, Documents, Writings, and other things appertaining; so that all the Plea concerning the Charges and Revenues, as well receiv'd as to receive, with their Damages and Interests, to reckon from the time of the first Possession, shall be intirely taken away and abolish'd.

XXXV

That the Annual Pension of the Lower Marquisate, payable to the Upper Marquisate, according to former Custom, shall by virtue of the present Treaty be intirely taken away and annihilated; and that for the future nothing shall be pretended or demanded on that account, either for the time past or to come.

XXXVI

That for the future, the Precedency and Session, in the States and Circle of *Swabia*, or other General or Particular Assemblys of the Empire, and any others whatsoever, shall be alternative in the two Branches of *Baden*; *viz.* in that of the Upper, and that of the Lower Marquisate of Baden: but nevertheless this Precedency shall remain in the Marquiss *Frederick* during his Life. It has been agreed, touching the Barony of *Hohengerolt Zegk* that if Madam, the Princess of *Baden*, verifies the Rights of her Pretension upon the said Barony by authentick Documents, Restitution shall be made her, according to the Rights and Contents of the said Documents, as soon as Sentence shall be pronounc'd. That the Cognizance of this Cause shall be terminated within two Years after the Publication of the Peace: And lastly, no Actions, Transaction, or Exceptions, either general or particular, nor Clauses comprehended in this Treaty of Peace, and whereby

they would derogate from the Vigour of this Article, shall be at any time alledg'd by any of the Partys against this special Agreement. The Paragraphs, the Duke of *Croy*, &c. As for the Controversy of *Naussau-Siegen*, &c. To the Counts of *Naussau*, *Sarrepont*, &c. The House of *Hanau*, &c. *John Albert* Count of *Solms*, &c. as also, Shall be re-establish'd the House of *Solms*, *Hohensolms*, &c. The Counts of *Isemburg*, &c. The *Rhinegraves*, &c. The Widow of Count *Ernest* of *Sainen*, &c. The Castle and the County of *Flackenstein*, &c. Let also the House of *Waldeck* be re-establish'd, &c. *Joachim Ernest* Count of *Ottingen*, &c. Item, The House of *Hohenlo*, &c. *Frederick Lewis*, &c. The Widow and Heirs of the Count of *Brandenstein*, &c. The Baron *Paul Kevenhuller*, &c. shall be understood to be inserted in this place word by word, as they are put down in the Instruor Treaty between the Empire and *Swedeland*.

XXXVII

That the Contracts, Exchanges, Transactions, Obligations, Treatys, made by Constraint or Threats, and extorted illegally from States or Subjects (as in particular, those of *Spiers* complain, and those of *Weisenburg* on the *Rhine*, those of *Landau*, *Reitlingen*, *Hailbron*, and others) shall be so annull'd and abolish'd, that no more Enquiry shall be made after them.

XXXVIII

That if Debtors have by force got some Bonds from their Creditors, the same shall be restor'd, but not with prejudice to their Rights.

XXXIX

That the Debts either by Purchase, Sale, Revenues, or by what other name they may be call'd, if they have been violently extorted by one of the Partys in War, and if the Debtors alledge and offer to prove there has been a real Payment, they shall be no more prosecuted, before these Exceptions be first adjusted. That the Debtors shall be oblig'd to produce their Exceptions within the term of two years after the Publication of the Peace, upon pain of being afterwards condemn'd to perpetual Silence.

XL

That Processes which have been hitherto enter'd on this Account, together with the Transactions and Promises made for the Restitution of Debts, shall be look'd upon as void; and yet the Sums of Money, which during the War have been exacted *bona fide*, and with a good intent, by way of Contributions, to prevent greater Evils by the Contributors, are not comprehended herein.

XLI

That Sentences pronounc'd during the War about Matters purely Secular, if the Defect in the Proceedings be not fully manifest, or cannot be immediately demonstrated, shall not be esteem'd wholly void; but that the Effect shall be suspended until the Acts of Justice (if one of the Partys demand the space of six months after the Publication of the Peace, for the reviewing of his Process) be review'd and weigh'd in a proper Court, and according to the ordinary or extraordinary Forms us'd in the Empire: to the end that the former Judgments may be confirm'd, amended, or quite eras'd, in case of Nullity.

XLII

In the like manner, if any Royal, or particular Fiefs, have not been renew'd since the Year 1618. nor Homage paid to whom it belongs; the same shall bring no prejudice, and the Investiture shall be renew'd the day the Peace shall be concluded.

XLIII

Finally, That all and each of the Officers, as well Military Men as Counsellors and Gownmen, and Ecclesiasticks of what degree they may be, who have serv'd the one or other Party among the Allies, or among their Adherents, let it be in the Gown, or with the Sword, from the highest to the lowest, without any distinction or exception, with their Wives, Children, Heirs, Successors, Servants, as well concerning their Lives as Estates, shall be restor'd by all Partys in the State of Life, Honour, Renown, Liberty of Conscience, Rights and Privileges, which they enjoy'd before the abovesaid Disorders; that no prejudice shall be done to their Effects and Persons, that no Action or accusation shall be enter'd against them; and that further, no Punishment be inflicted on them, or they to bear any damage under what pretence soever: And all this shall have its full effect in respect to those who are not Subjects or Vassals of his Imperial Majesty, or of the House of *Austria*.

XLIV

But for those who are Subjects and Hereditary Vassals of the Emperor, and of the House of *Austria*, they shall really have the benefit of the Amnesty, as for their Persons, Life, Reputation, Honours: and they may return with Safety to their former Country; but they shall be oblig'd to conform, and submit themselves to the Laws of the Realms, or particular Provinces they shall belong to.

XLV

As to their Estates that have been lost by Confiscation or otherways, before they took the part of the Crown of *France*, or of *Swedeland*, notwithstanding the Plenipotentiarys of *Swedeland* have made long instances, they may be also restor'd. Nevertheless his Imperial Majesty being to receive Law from none, and the Imperialists sticking close thereto, it has not been thought convenient by the States of the Empire, that for such a Subject the War should be continu'd: And that thus those who have lost their Effects as aforesaid, cannot recover them to the prejudice of their last Masters and Possessors. But the Estates, which have been taken away by reason of Arms taken for *France* or *Swedeland*, against the Emperor and the House of *Austria*, they shall be restor'd in the State they are found, and that without any Compensation for Profit or Damage.

XLVI

As for the rest, Law and Justice shall be administer'd in *Bohemia*, and in all the other Hereditary Provinces of the Emperor, without any respect; as to the Catholicks, so also to the Subjects, Creditors, Heirs, or private Persons, who shall be of the Confession of *Augsburg*, if they have any Pretensions, and enter or prosecute any Actions to obtain Justice.

XLVII

But from this general Restitution shall be exempted things which cannot be restor'd, as Things movable and moving, Fruits gather'd, Things alienated by the Authority of the Chiefs of the Party, Things destroy'd, ruin'd, and converted to other uses for the publick Security, as publick and particular Buildings, whether sacred or profane, publick or private Gages, which have been, by surprize of the Enemys, pillag'd, confiscated, lawfully sold, or voluntarily bestow'd.

XLVIII

And as to the Affair of the Succession of Juliers, those concern'd, if a course be not taken about it, may one day cause great Troubles in the Empire about it; it has been agreed, That the Peace being concluded it shall be terminated without any Delay, either by ordinary means before his Imperial Majesty, or by a friendly Composition, or some other lawful ways.

XLIX

And since for the greater Tranquillity of the Empire, in its general Assemblys of Peace, a certain Agreement has been made between the Emperor, Princes and States of the Empire, which has been inserted in the Instrument and Treaty of Peace, concluded with the Plenipotentiarys of the Queen and Crown of *Swedeland*, touching the Differences about Ecclesiastical Lands, and the Liberty of the Exercise of Religion; it has been found expedient to confirm,and ratify it by this present Treaty, in the same manner as the abovesaid Agreement has been made with the said Crown of *Swedeland*; also with those call'd the *Reformed*, in the same manner, as if the words of the abovesaid Instrument were reported here verbatim.

L

Touching the Affair of *Hesse Cassel*, it has been agreed as follows: In the first place, The House of *Hesse Cassel*, and all its Princes, chiefly Madam *Emelie Elizabeth* Landgravine of Hesse, and her Son Monsieur *William* and his Heirs, his Ministers, Officers, Vassals, Subjects, Soldiers, and others who follow his Service in any manner soever, without any Exception, notwithstanding Contracts to the contrary, Processes, Proscriptions, Declarations, Sentences, Executions and Transactions; as also notwithstanding any Actions and Pretensions for Damages and Injuries as well from Neutrals, as from those who were in Arms, annull'd by the General Amnesty here before establish'd, and to take place from the beginning of the War in *Bohemia*, with a full Restitution (except the Vassals, and Hereditary Subjects of his Imperial Majesty, and the House of Austria, as is laid down in the Paragraph, *Tandemomnes*, &c.) shall partake of all the Advantages redounding from this Peace, with the same Rights other States enjoy, as is set forth in the Article which commences, *Unanimi*, &c.

LI

In the second place, the House of *Hesse Cassel*, and its Successors, shall retain, and for this purpose shall demand at any time, and when it shall be expir'd, the Investiture of his Imperial Majesty, and shall take the Oath of Fidelity for the Abby of *Hitsfield*, with all its Dependencys, as well Secular as Ecclesiastical, situated within or without his Territorys (as the Deanery of *Gellingen*) saving nevertheless the Rights possess'd by the House of *Saxony*, time out of mind.

LII

In the third place, the Right of a direct Signiory over the Jurisdictions and Bayliwick of *Schaumburg*, *Buckenburg*, *Saxenhagen*, and *Stattenhagen*, given heretofore and adjudged to the Bishoprick of *Mindau*, shall for the future belong unto Monsieur *William*, the present Landgrave of *Hesse*, and his Successors in full Possession, and for ever, so as that the said Bishop, and no other shall be capable of molesting him; saving nevertheless the Agreement made between *Christian Lewis*, Duke of *Brunswick* and *Lunenburg*, and the Landgravine of *Hesse*, and *Philip* Count of *Lippe*, as also the Agreement made between the said Land-gravine, and the said Count.

LIII

It has been further agreed, That for the Restitution of Places poss-sess'd during this War, and for the Indemnity of *Madam*, the Landgravine of *Hesse*, who is the Guardian, the Sum of Six Hundred Thousand Rixdollars shall be given to her and her Son, or his Successors Princes of *Hesse*, to be had from the Archbishopricks of *Mayence* and *Cologne*, from the Bishopricks of *Paderborn* and *Munster*, and the Abby of *Fulden*; which Sum shall be paid at *Cassel* in the term of eight Months, to reckon from the Day of the Ratification of the Peace, at the peril and charge of the Solvent: and no Exception shall be used to evade this promis'd Payment, on any Pretence; much less shall any Seizure be made of the Sum agreed on.

LIV

And to the end that *Madam*, the Landgravine, may be so much the more assur'd of the Payment, she shall retain on the Conditions following, *Nuys*, *Cuesfeldt*, and *Newhaus*, and shall keep Garisons in those Places which shall depend on her alone; but with this Limitation, That besides the Officers and other necessary Persons in the Garisons, those of the three above-nam'd Places shall not exceed the number of Twelve Hundred Foot, and a Hundred Horse; leaving to *Madam*, the Landgravine, the Disposition of the number of Horse and Foot she shall be pleas'd to put in each of these Places, and whom she will constitute Governor.

LV

The Garisons shall be maintain'd according to the Order, which has been hitherto usually practis'd, for the Maintenance of the *Hessian* Soldiers and Officers; and the things necessary for the keeping of the Forts shall be furnish'd by the Arch-bishopricks and Bishopricks, in which the said Fortresses are situated, without any Diminution of the Sum above-mention'd. It shall be allow'd the Garisons, to exact the Money of those who shall retard Payment too long, or who shall be refractory, but not any more than what is due. The Rights of Superiority and Jurisdiction, as well Ecclesiastical as Secular, and the Revenues of the said Castles and Towns, shall remain in the Arch-bishop of *Cologne*.

LVI

As soon as after the Ratification of Peace, Three Hundred Thousand Rixdollars shall be paid to *Madam*, the Landgravine, she shall give up *Nuys*, and shall only retain *Cuesfeldt* and *Newhaus*; but yet so as that the Garison of *Nuys* shall not be thrown into the other two Places, nor nothing demanded on that account; and the Garisons of *Cuesfeldt* shall not exceed the Number of Six Hundred Foot and Fifty Horse. That if within the term of nine Months, the whole Sum be not paid to *Madam* the Landgravine, not only *Cuesfeldt* and *Newhaus* shall remain in her Hands till the full Payment, but also for the remainder, she shall be paid Interest at Five per Cent. and the Treasurers and Collectors of the Bayliwicks appertaining to the abovesaid Arch-bishopricks, Bishopricks and Abby, bordering on the Principality of *Hesse*, shall oblige themselves by Oath to *Madam* the Landgravine, that out of the annual Revenues, they shall yearly pay the Interest of the remaining Sum notwithstanding the Prohibitions of their Masters. If the Treasurers and Collectors delay the Payment, or alienate the Revenues, *Madam* the Landgravine shall have liberty to constrain them to pay, by all

sorts of means, always saving the Right of the Lord Proprietor of the Territory.

LVII

But as soon as *Madam* the Landgravine has receiv'd the full Sum, with all the Interest, she shall surrender the said Places which she retain'd for her Security; the Payments shall cease, and the Treasurers and Collectors, of which mention has been made, shall be freed, from their Oath: As for the Bayliwicks, the Revenues of which shall be assign'd for the Payment of the Sum, that shall be adjusted before the Ratification of the Peace; and that Convention shall be of no less Force than this present Treaty of Peace.

LVIII

Besides the Places of Surety, which shall be left, as aforesaid, to *Madam* the Landgravine, which she shall restore after the Payment, she shall restore, after the Ratification of the Peace, all the Provinces and Bishopricks, as also all their Citys, Bayliwicks, Boroughs, Fortresses, Forts; and in one word, all immoveable Goods, and all Rights seiz'd by her during this War. So, nevertheless, that as well in the three Places she shall retain as Cautionary, as the others to be restor'd, the said Lady Landgravine not only shall cause to be convey'd away all the Provisions and Ammunitions of War she has put therein (for as to those she has not sent thither, and what was found there at the taking of them, and are there still, they shall continue;) but also the Fortifications and Ramparts, rais'd during the Possession of the Places, shall be destroy'd and demolish'd as much as possible, without exposing the Towns, Borroughs, Castles and Fortresses, to Invasions and Robberys.

LIX

And tho *Madam* the Landgravine has only demanded Restitution and Reparation of the Arch-bishopricks of *Mayence*, *Cologne*, *Paderborn*, *Munster*, and the Abby of *Fulden*; and has not insisted that any besides should contribute any thing for this Purpose: nevertheless the Assembly have thought fit, according to the Equity and Circumstances of Affairs, that without prejudice to the Contents of the preceding Paragraph, which begins, *Conventum praterea est*, &c. IT HAS BEEN FURTHER AGREED, the other States also on this and the other side the *Rhine*, and who since the first of *March* of this present Year, have paid Contributions to the *Hessians*, shall bear their Proportion *pro Rata* of their preceding Contributions, to make up the said Sum with the Arch-bishopricks, Bishopricks and Abby above-named, and forward the Payments of the Garisons of the Cautionary Towns. If any has suffer'd Damage by the delay of others, who are to pay their share, the Officers or Soldiers of his Imperial Majesty, of the most Christian King, and of the Landgravine of *Hesse*, shall not hinder the forcing of those who have been tardy; and the *Hessian* Soldiers shall not pretend to except any from this Constraint, to the prejudice of this Declaration, but those who have duly paid their Proportion, shall thereby be freed from all Charges.

LX

As to the Differences arisen between the Houses of *Hesse Cassel*, and of *Darmstadt*, touching the Succession of *Marburg*; since they have been adjusted at *Cassel*, the 14th of *April*, the preceding Year, by the mutual Consent of the Interested Partys, it has been thought good, that that Transaction, with all its

Clauses, as concluded and sign'd at *Cassel* by both Partys, should be intimated to this Assembly; and that by virtue of this present Treaty, it shall be of the same force, as if inserted word by word: and the same shall never be infring'd by the Partys, nor any other whatsoever, under any pretence, either by Contract, Oath, or otherways, but ought to be most exactly kept by all, tho perhaps some of the Partys concern'd may refuse to confirm it.

LXI

As also the Transaction between the Deceas'd monsieur *William*, Landgrave of *Hesse*, and Messieurs *Christian* and *Wolrad*, Counts of *Waldeck*, made the 11th of *April*, 1635. and ratify'd to Monsieur *George*, Landgrave of *Hesse*, the 14th of *April* 1648. shall no less obtain a full and perpetual force by virtue of this Pacification, and shall no less bind all the Princes of *Hesse*, and all the Counts of *Waldeck*.

LXII

That the Birth-right introduc'd in the House of *Hesse Cassel*, and in that of *Darmstadt*, and confirm'd by His Imperial Majesty, shall continue and be kept firm and inviolable.

LXIII

And as His Imperial Majesty, upon Complaints made in the name of the City of *Basle*, and of all *Switzerland*, in the presence of their Plenipotentiarys deputed to the present Assembly, touching some Procedures and Executions proceeding from the Imperial Chamber against the said City, and the other united *Cantons* of the *Swiss* Country, and their Citizens and Subjects having demanded the Advice of the States of the Empire and their Council; these have, by a Decree of the 14th of May of the last Year, declared the said City of *Basle*, and the other *Swiss-Cantons*, to be as it were in possession of their full Liberty and Exemption of the Empire; so that they are no ways subject to the Judicatures, or Judgments of the Empire, and it was thought convenient to insert the same in this Treaty of Peace, and confirm it, and thereby to make void and annul all such Procedures and Arrests given on this Account in what form soever.

LXIV

And to prevent for the future any Differences arising in the Politick State, all and every one of the Electors, Princes and States of the *Roman* Empire, are so establish'd and confirm'd in their antient Rights, Prerogatives, Libertys, Privileges, free exercise of Territorial Right, as well Ecclesiastick, as Politick Lordships, Regales, by virtue of this present Transaction: that they never can or ought to be molested therein by any whomsoever upon any manner of pretence.

LXV

They shall enjoy without contradiction, the Right of Suffrage in all Deliberations touching the Affairs of the Empire; but above all, when the Business in hand shall be the making or interpreting of Laws, the declaring of Wars, imposing of Taxes, levying or quartering of Soldiers, erecting new Fortifications in the Territorys of the States, or reinforcing the old Garisons; as also when a Peace of Alliance is to be concluded, and treated about, or the like, none of these, or the like things shall be acted for the future, without the Suffrage and Consent of the Free Assembly of all the States of the Empire: Above all, it shall be free perpetually to each of the States of the Empire, to make Alliances with Strangers for their Preservation and Safety; provided, nevertheless, such Alliances be not against the Emperor, and the Empire, nor against the Publick Peace, and this Treaty, and without prejudice to the Oath by which every one is bound to the Emperor and the Empire.

LXVI

That the Diets of the Empire shall be held within six Months after the Ratification of the Peace; and after that time as often as the Publick Utility, or Necessity requires. That in the first Diet the Defects of precedent Assemblys be chiefly remedy'd; and that then also be treated and settled by common Consent of the States, the Form and Election of the Kings of the *Romans*, by a Form, and certain Imperial Resolution; the Manner and Order which is to be observ'd for declaring one or more States, to be within the Territorys of the Empire, besides the Manner otherways describ'd in the Constitutions of the Empire; that they consider also of re-establishing the Circles, the renewing the Matricular-Book, the re-establishing suppress'd States, the moderating and lessening the Collects of the Empire, Reformation of Justice and Policy, the taxing of Fees in the Chamber of Justice, the Due and requisite instructing of ordinary Deputys for the Advantage of the Publick, the true Office of Directors in the Colleges of the Empire, and such other Business as could not be here expedited.

LXVII

That as well as general as particular Diets, the free Towns, and other States of the Empire, shall have decisive Votes; they shall, without molestation, keep their Regales, Customs, annual Revenues, Libertys, Privileges to confiscate, to raise Taxes, and other Rights, lawfully obtain'd from the Emperor and Empire, or enjoy'd long before these Commotions, with a full Jurisdiction within the inclosure of their Walls, and their Territorys: making void at the same time, annulling and for the future prohibiting all Things, which by Reprisals, Arrests, stopping of Passages, and other prejudicial Acts, either during the War, under what pretext soever they have been done and attempted hitherto by private Authority, or may hereafter without any preceding formality of Right be enterpris'd. As for the rest, all laudable Customs of the sacred *Roman* Empire, the fundamental Constitutions and Laws, shall for the future be strictly observ'd, all the Confusions which time of War have, or could introduce, being remov'd and laid aside.

LXVIII

As for the finding out of equitable and expedient means, whereby the Prosecution of Actions against Debtors, ruin'd by the Calamitys of the War, or charg'd with too great Interests, and whereby these Matters may be terminated with moderation, to obviate greater inconveniences which might arise, and to provide for the publick Tranquillity; His Imperial Majesty shall take care to hearken as well to the Advices of his Privy Council, as of the Imperial Chamber, and the States which are to be assembled, to the end that certain firm and invariable Constitutions may be made about this Matter And in the mean time the alledg'd Reasons and Circumstances of the Partys shall be well weigh'd in Cases brought before the Sovereign Courts of the Empire, or Subordinate ones of States and no body shall be oppress'd by immoderate Executions; and ail this without prejudice to the Constitution of *Holstein*.

LXIX

And since it much concerns the Publick, that upon the Conclusion of the Peace, Commerce be re-establish'd, for that end it has been agreed, that the Tolls, Customs, as also the Abuses of the Bull of *Brabant*, and the Reprisals and Arrests, which proceeded from thence, together with foreign Certifications, Exactions, Detensions; *Item*, The immoderate Expences and Charges of Posts, and other Obstacles to Commerce and Navigation introduc'd to its Prejudice, contrary to the Publick Benefit here and there, in the Empire on occasion of the War, and of late by a private Authority against its Rights and Privileges, without the Emperor's and Princes of the Empire's consent, shall be fully remov'd; and the antient Security, Jurisdiction and Custom, such as have been long before these Wars in use, shall be re-establish'd and inviolably maintain'd in the Provinces, Ports and Rivers.

LXX

The Rights and Privileges of Territorys, water'd by Rivers or otherways, as Customs granted by the Emperor, with the Consent of the Electors, and among others, to the Count of *Oldenburg* on the *Viserg*, and introduc'd by a long Usage, shall remain in their Vigour and Execution. There shall be a full Liberty of Commerce, a secure Passage by Sea and Land: and after this manner all and every one of the Vassals, Subjects, Inhabitants and Servants of the Allys, on the one side and the other, shall have full power to go and come, to trade and return back, by Virtue of this present Article, after the same manner as was allowed before the Troubles of Germany; the Magistrates, on the one side and on the other, shall be oblig'd to protect and defend them against all sorts of Oppressions, equally with their own Subjects, without prejudice to the other Articles of this Convention, and the particular laws and Rights of each place. And that the said Peace and Amity between the Emperor and the Most Christian King, may be the more corroborated, and the publick Safety provided for, it has been agreed with the Consent, Advice and Will of the Electors, Princes and States of the Empire, for the Benefit of Peace:

LXXI

First, That the chief Dominion, Right of Sovereignty, and all other Rights upon the Bishopricks of *Metz*, *Toul*, and *Verdun*, and on the Citys of that Name and their Dioceses, particularly on *Mayenvick*, in the same manner they formerly belong'd to the Emperor, shall for the future appertain to the Crown of *France*, and shall be irrevocably incorporated therewith for ever, saving the Right of the Metropolitan, which belongs to the Archbishop of *Treves*.

LXXII

That Monsieur *Francis*, Duke of *Lorain*, shall be restor'd to the possession of the Bishoprick of *Verdun*, as being the lawful Bishop thereof; and shall be left in the peaceable Administration of this Bishoprick and its Abbys (saving the Right of the King and of particular Persons) and shall enjoy his Patrimonial Estates, and his other Rights, wherever they may be situated (and as far as they do not contradict the present Resignation) his Privileges, Revenues and Incomes; having previously taken the Oath of Fidelity to the King, and provided he undertakes nothing against the Good of the State and the Service of his Majesty.

LXXIII

In the second place, the Emperor and Empire resign and transfer to the most Christian King, and his Successors, the Right of direct Lordship and Sovereignty, and all that has belong'd, or might hitherto belong to him, or the sacred *Roman* Empire, upon *Pignerol*.

LXXIV

In the third place the Emperor, as well in his own behalf, as the behalf of the whole most Serene House of *Austria*, as also of the Empire, resigns all Rights, Propertys, Domains, Possessions and Jurisdictions, which have hitherto belong'd either to him, or the Empire, and the Family of *Austria*, over the City of Brisac, the Landgraveship of *Upper* and *Lower Alsatia*, *Suntgau*, and the Provincial Lordship of ten Imperial Citys situated in *Alsatia*, viz. *Haguenau*, *Calmer*, *Sclestadt*, *Weisemburg*, *Landau*, *Oberenheim*, *Rosheim*, *Munster* in the Valley of *St. Gregory*, *Keyerberg*, *Turingham*, and of all the villages, or other Rights which depend on the said Mayoralty; all and every of them are made over to the most Christian King, and the Kingdom of *France*; in the same manner as the City of *Brisac*, with the Villages of *Hochstet*, *Niederrimsing*, *Hartem* and *Acharren* appertaining to the Commonalty of *Brisac*, with all the antient Territory and Dependence; without any prejudice, nevertheless, to the Priviliges and Libertys granted the said Town formerly by the House of *Austria*.

LXXV

Item, The said Landgraveship of the one, and the other *Alsatia*, and *Suntgau*, as also the Provincial Mayoralty on the ten Citys nominated, and their Dependencys.

LXXVI

Item, All the Vassals, Subjects, People, Towns, Boroughs, Castles, Houses, Fortresses, Woods, Coppices, Gold or Silver Mines, Minerals, Rivers, Brooks, Pastures; and in a word, all the Rights, Regales and Appurtenances, without any reserve, shall belong to the most Christian King, and shall be for ever incorporated with the Kingdom *France*, with all manner of Jurisdiction and Sovereignty, without any contradiction from the Emperor, the Empire, House of *Austria*, or any other: so that no Emperor, or any Prince of the House of *Austria*, shall, or ever ought to usurp, nor so much as pretend any Right and Power over the said Countrys, as well on this, as the other side the *Rhine*.

LXXVII

The most Christian King shall, nevertheless, be oblig'd to preserve in all and every one of these Countrys the Catholick Religion, as maintain'd under the Princes of *Austria*, and to abolish all Innovations crept in during the War.

LXXVIII

Fourthly, By the Consent of the Emperor and the whole Empire, the most Christian King and his Successors shall have perpetual Right to keep a Garison in the Castle of *Philipsburg*, but limited to such a number of Soldiers, as may not be capable to give any Umbrage, or just Suspicion to the Neighbourhood; which Garison shall be maintain'd at the Expences of the Crown of *France*. The Passage also shall be open for the King into the Empire by Water, when, and as often as he shall send Soldiers, Convoys, and bring necessary things thither.

LXXIX

Nevertheless the King shall pretend to nothing more than the Protection and safe Passage of his Garison into the Castle of *Philipsburg*: but the Property of the Place, all Jurisdiction, Possession, all its Profits, Revenues, Purchases, Rights, Regales,

Servitude, People, Subjects, Vassals, and every thing that of old in the Bishoprick of *Spire*, and the Churches incorporated therein, had appertain'd to the Chapter of *Spire*, or might have appertain'd thereto; shall appertain, and be intirely and inviolably preserv'd to the same Chapter, saving the Right of Protection which the King takes upon him.

LXXX

The Emperor, Empire, and Monsieur the Arch Duke of *Insprug*, *Ferdinand Charles*, respectively discharge the Communitys, Magistrates, Officers and Subjects of each of the said Lordships and Places, from the Bonds and Oaths which they were hitherto bound by, and ty'd to the House of *Austria*; and discharge and assign them over to the Subjection, Obedience and Fidelity they are to give to the King and Kingdom of *France*; and consequently confirm the Crown of *France* in a full and just Power over all the said Places, renouncing from the present, and for ever, the Rights and Pretensions they had thereunto: Which Cession the Emperor, the said Arch-Duke and his Brother (by reason the said Renunciation concerns them particularly) shall confirm by particular Letters for themselves and their Descendants; and shall so order it also, that the Catholick King of *Spain* shall make the same Renunciation in due and authentick form, which shall be done in the name of the whole Empire, the same Day this present Treaty shall be sign'd.

LXXXI

For the greater Validity of the said Cessions and Alienations, the Emperor and Empire, by virtue of this present Treaty, abolish all and every one of the Decrees, Constitutions, Statutes and Customs of their Predecessors, Emperors of the sacred *Roman* Empire, tho they have been confirm'd by Oath, or shall be confirm'd for the future; particularly this Article of the Imperial Capitulation, by which all or any Alienation of the Appurtenances and Rights of the Empire is prohibited: and by the same means they exclude for ever all Exceptions hereunto, on what Right and Titles soever they may be grounded.

LXXXII

Further it has been agreed, That besides the Ratification promis'd hereafter in the next Diet by the Emperor and the States of the Empire, they shall ratify anew the Alienations of the said Lordships and Rights: insomuch, that if it shou'd be agreed in the Imperial Capitulation, or if there shou'd be a Proposal made for the future, in the Diet, to recover the Lands and Rights of the Empire, the abovenam'd things shall not be comprehended therein, as having been legally transfer'd to another's Dominion, with the common Consent of the States, for the benefit of the publick Tranquillity; for which reason it has been found expedient the said Seigniorys shou'd be ras'd out of the Matricular-Book of the Empire.

LXXXIII

Immediately after the Restitution of *Benfield*, the Fortifications of that Place shall be ras'd, and of the Fort *Rhinau*, which is hard by, as also of *Tabern* in *Alsatia*, of the Castle of *Hohember* and of *Newburg* on the *Rhine*: and there shall be in none of those Places any Soldiers or Garison.

LXXXIV

The Magistrates and the Inhabitants of the said City of Tabern shall keep an exact Neutrality, and the King's Troops shall freely pass thro' there as often as desir'd. No Forts shall be erected on the Banks of this side the Rhine, from Basle to Philipsburg; nor shall any Endeavours be made to divert the Course of the River, neither on the one side or the other.

LXXXV

As for what concerns the Debts wherewith the Chamber of *Ensisheim* is charg'd, the Arch-Duke *Ferdinand Charles* shall undertake with that part of the Province, which the most Christian King shall restore him, to pay one third without distinction, whether they be Bonds, or Mortgages; provided they are in authentick form, and that they have a particular Mortgage, either on the Provinces to be restor'd, or on them which are to be transfer'd; or if there be none, provided they be found on the Books of Accounts, agreeing with those of Receipts of the Chamber of *Ensisheim*, until the Expiration of the year 1632, and have been inserted amonst the Debts of the publick Chamber, and the said Chamber having been oblig'd to pay the Interests: the Arch-Duke making this Payment, shall keep the King exempt from the same.

LXXXVI

And as for those Debts which the Colleges of the States have been charg'd with by the Princes of the House of *Austria*, pursuant to particular Agreements made in their Provincial Assemblys, or such as the said States have contracted in the name of the Publick, and to which they are liable; a just distribution of the same shall be made between those who are to transfer their Allegiance to the King of *France*, and them that continue under the Obedience of the House of *Austria*, that so either Party may know what proportion of the said Debt he is to pay.

LXXXVII

The most Christian King shall restore to the House of *Austria*, and particularly to the Arch-Duke *Ferdinand Charles*, eldest Son to Arch-Duke *Leopold*, four Forest-Towns, viz. *Rheinselden*, *Seckingen*, *Laussenberg* and *Waltshutum*, with all their Territorys and Bayliwicks, Houses, Villages, Mills, Woods, Forests, Vassals, Subjects, and all Appurtenances on this, or the other side the *Rhine*.

LXXXVIII

Item, The County of *Hawenstein*, the *Black Forest*, the *Upper* and *Lower Brisgaw*, and the Towns situate therein, appertaining of Antient Right to the House of *Austria*, viz. *Neuburg*, *Friburg*, *Edingen*, *Kenzingen*, *Waldkirch*, *Willingen*, *Bruenlingen*, with all their Territorys; as also, the Monasterys, Abbys, Prelacys, Deaconrys, Knight-Fees, Commanderships, with all their Bayliwicks, Baronys, Castles, Fortresses, Countys, Barons, Nobles, Vassals, Men, Subjects, Rivers, Brooks, Forests, Woods, and all the Regales, Rights, Jurisdictions, Fiefs and Patronages, and all other things belonging to the Sovereign Right of Territory, and to the Patrimony of the House of *Austria*, in all that Country.

LXXXIX

All *Ortnaw*, with the Imperial Citys of *Ossenburg*, *Gengenbach*, *Cellaham* and *Harmospach*, forasmuch as the said Lordships depend on that of *Ortnaw*, so that no King of *France* can or ought ever to ; pretend to or usurp any Right or Power over the said Countrys situated on this and the other side the *Rhine*: nevertheless, in such a manner, that by this present Restitution, the Princes of *Austria* shall acquire no new Right; that for the future, the Commerce and Transportation shall be free to the Inhabitants on both sides of the *Rhine*, and the adjacent Provinces. Above all, the Navigation of the *Rhine* be free, and none of the partys shall be permitted to hinder Boats going up or coming down, detain, stop, or molest them under any pretence whatsoever, except the Inspection and Search which is usually done to Merchandizes: And it shall not be permitted to impose upon the *Rhine* new and unwonted Tolls, Customs, Taxes, Imposts, and other like Exactions; but the one and the other Party shall contented with the Tributes, Dutys and Tolls that were paid before these Wars, under the Government of the Princes of *Austria*.

XC

That all the Vassals, Subjects, Citizens and Inhabitants, as well on this as the other side the *Rhine*, who were subject to the House of *Austria*, or who depended immediately on the Empire, or who acknowledg'd for Superiors the other Orders of the Empire, notwithstanding all Confiscations, Transferrings, Donations made by any Captains or Generals of the *Swedish* Troops, or Confederates, since the taking of the Province, and ratify'd by the most Christian King, or decreed by his own particular Motion; immediately after the Publication of Peace, shall be restor'd to the possession of their Goods, immovable and stable, also to their Farms, Castles, Villages, Lands, and Possessions, without any exception upon the account of Expences and Compensation of Charges, which the modern Possessors may alledge, and without Restitution of Movables or Fruits gather'd in.

XCI

As to Confiscations of Things, which consist in Weight, Number and Measure, Exactions, Concussions and Extortions made during the War; the reclaiming of them is fully annull'd and taken away on the one side and the other, in order to avoid Processes and litigious Strifes.

XCII

That the most Christian King shall be bound to leave not only the Bishops of *Strasburg* and *Basle*, with the City of *Strasburg*, but also the other States or Orders, Abbots of *Murbach* and *Luederen*, who are in the one and the other *Alsatia*, immediately depending upon the *Roman* Empire; the Abess of *Andlavien*, the Monastery of *St. Bennet* in the Valley of *St. George*, the Palatines of *Luzelstain*, the Counts and Barons of *Hanaw*, *Fleckenstein*, *Oberstein*, and all the nobility of *Lower Alsatia*; *Item*, the said ten Imperial Citys, which depend on the Mayory of *Haganoc*, in the Liberty and Possession they have enjoy'd hitherto, to arise as immediately dependent upon the *Roman* Empire; so that he cannot pretend any Royal Superiority over them, but shall rest contented with the Rights which appertain'd to the House of *Austria*, and which by this present Treaty of Pacification, are yielded to the Crown of *France*. In such a manner, nevertheless, that by the present Declaration, nothing is intended that shall derogate from the Sovereign Dominion already hereabove agreed to.

XCIII

Likewise the most Christian King, in compensation of the things made over to him, shall pay the said Archduke *Ferdinand Charles* three millions of *French* Livres, in the next following Years 1649 1650, 1651, on St. *John Baptist's* Day, paying yearly one third of the said Sum at *Basle* in good Money to the Deputys of the said Archduke.

XCIV

Besides the said Sum, the most Christian King shall be oblig'd to take upon him two Thirds of the Debts of the Chamber of *Ensisheim* without distinction, whether by Bill or Mortgage, provided they be in due and authentic Form, and have a special Mortgage either on the Provinces to be transfer'd, or on them to be restor'd; or if there be none, provided they be found on the Books of Accounts agreeing with those of the Receits of the Chamber of *Ensisheim*, until the end of the Year 1632, the said Sums having been inserted among the Debts of the Community, and the Chamber having been oblig'd to pay the Interests: And the King making this Payment, the Archduke shall be exempted for such a proportion. And that the same may be equitably executed, Commissarys shall be deputed on the one side and the other, immediately after the signing of this present Treaty, who before the Payment of the first Sum, shall agree between them what Debts every one has to pay.

XCV

The most Christian King shall restore to the said Archduke *bona fide*, and without delay, all Papers, Documents of what nature so-ever, belonging to the Lands which are to be surrender'd to him, even as many as shall be found in the Chancery of the Government and Chamber of *Ensisheim*, or of *Brisac*, or in the Records of Officers, Towns, and Castles possess'd by his Arms.

XCVI

If those Documents be publick, and concern in common and jointly the Lands yielded to the King, the Archduke shall receive authentick Copys of them, at what time and as often as he shall demand them.

XCVII

Item, For fear the Differences arisen between the Dukes of *Savoy* and *Mantua* touching *Montserrat*, and terminated by the Emperor *Ferdinand* and *Lewis* XIII. Fathers to their Majestys, shou'd revive some time or other to the damage or Christianity; it has been agreed, That the Treaty of *Cheras* of the 6th of *April* 1631. with the Execution thereof which ensu'd in the *Montserrat*, shall continue firm for ever, with all its Articles: *Pignerol*, and its Appurtenances, being nevertheless excepted, concerning which there has been a decision between his most Christian Majesty and the Duke of *Savoy*, and which the King of *France* and his Kingdom have purchas'd by particular Treatys, that shall remain firm and stable, as to what concerns the transferring or resigning of that Place and its Appurtenances. But if the said particular Treatys contain any thing which may trouble the Peace of the Empire, and excite new Commotions in *Italy*, after the present War, which is now on foot in that Province, shall be at an end, they shall be look'd upon as void and of no effect; the said Cession continuing nevertheless unviolable, as also the other Conditions agreed to, as well in favour of the Duke of *Savoy* as the most Christian King: For which reason their Imperial and most Christian Majestys promise reciprocally, that in all other things relating to the said Treaty of *Cheras*, and its Execution, and particularly to *Albe*, *Trin*, their Territorys, and the other places, they never shall contravene them either directly or indirectly, by the way of Right or in Fact; and that they neither shall succour nor countenance the Offender, but rather by their common Authority shall endeavour that none violate them under any pretence whatsoever; considering that the most

Christian King has declar'd, That he was highly oblig'd to advance the Execution of the said Treaty, and even to maintain it by Arms; that above all things the said Lord, the Duke of *Savoy*, notwithstanding the Clauses abovemention'd, shall be always maintain'd in the peaceable possession of *Trin* and *Albe*, and other places, which have been allow'd and assign'd him by the said Treaty, and by the Investiture which ensu'd thereon of the Dutchy of *Montserrat*.

XCVIII

And to the end that all Differences be extirpated and rooted out between these same Dukes, his most Christian Majesty shall pay to the said Lord, the Duke of *Mantua*, four hundred ninety four thousand Crowns, which the late King of blessed Memory, *Lewis* XIII. had promis'd to pay to him on thu Duke of *Savoy's* Discount; who by this means shall together with his Heirs and Successors be discharg'd from this Obligation, and secur'd from all Demands which might be made upon him of the said Sum, by the Duke of *Mantua*, or his Successors; so that for the future neither the Duke of *Savoy*, nor his Heirs and Successors, shall receive any Vexation or Trouble from the Duke of *Mantua*, his Heirs and Successors, upon this subject, or under this pretence.

XCIX

Who hereafter, with the Authority and Consent of their Imperial and most Christian Majestys, by virtue of this solemn Treaty of Peace, shall have no Action for this account against the Duke of *Savoy*, or his Heirs and Successors.

C

His Imperial Majesty, at the modest Request of the Duke of *Savoy*, shall together with the Investiture of the antient Fiefs and States, which the late *Ferdinand* II. of blessed memory granted to the Duke of *Savoy*, *Victor Amadeus*, also grant him the Investiture of the Places, Lordships, States, and all other Rights of *Montserrat*, with their Appurtenances, which have been surrender'd to him by virtue of the abovesaid Treaty of *Cheras*, and the Execution thereof which ensu'd; as also, of the Fiefs of *New Monsort*, of *Sine*, *Monchery*, and *Castelles*, with their Appurtenances, according to the Treaty of Acquisition made by the said Duke *Victor Amadeus*, the 13th of *October* 1634. and conformable to the Concessions or Permissions, and Approbation of his Imperial Majesty; with a Confirmation also of all the Privileges which have been hitherto granted to the Dukes of *Savoy*, when and as often as the Duke of *Savoy* shall request and demand it.

CI

Item, It has been agreed, That the Duke of *Savoy*, his Heirs and Successors, shall no ways be troubled or call'd to an account by his Imperial Majesty, upon account of the Right of Sovereignty they have over the Fiefs of *Rocheveran*, *Olme*, and *Casoles*, and their Appurtenances, which do not in the least depend on the *Roman* Empire, and that all Donations and Investitures of the said Fiefs being revok'd and annul'd, the Duke shall be maintain'd in his Possession as rightful Lord; and if need be, reinstated: for the same reason his Vassal the *Count de Verrue* shall be re-instated in the same Fiefs of *Olme* and *Casoles*, and in the Possession of the fourth part of *Rocheveran*, and in all his Revenues.

CII

Item, It is Agreed, That his Imperial Majesty shall restore to the Counts *Clement* and *John* Sons of *Count Charles Cacheran*, and to his Grandsons by his Son *Octavian*, the whole Fief of *la Roche d'Arazy*, with its Appurtenances and Dependencys, without any Obstacle whatever.

CIII

The Emperor shall likewise declare, That within the Investiture of the Dutchy of *Mantua* are comprehended the Castles of *Reygioli* and *Luzzare*, with their Territorys and Dependencys, the Possession whereof the Duke of *Guastalla* shall be oblig'd to render to the Duke of *Mantua*, reserving to himself nevertheless, the Right of Six Thousand Crowns annual Pension, which he pretends to, for which he may sue the Duke before his Imperial Majesty.

CIV

As soon as the Treaty of Peace shall be sign'd and seal'd by the Plenipotentiarys and Ambassadors, all Hostilitys shall cease, and all Partys shall study immediately to put in execution what has been agreed to; and that the same may be the better and quicker accomplish'd, the Peace shall be solemnly publish'd the day after the signing thereof in the usual form at the Cross of the Citys of *Munster* and of *Osnabrug*. That when it shall be known that the signing has been made in these two Places, divers Couriers shall presently be sent to the Generals of the Armys, to acquaint them that the Peace is concluded, and take care that the Generals chuse a Day, on which shall be made on all sides a Cessation of Arms and Hostilitys for the publishing of the Peace in the Army; and that command be given to all and each of the chief Officers Military and Civil, and to the Governors of Fortresses, to abstain for the future from all Acts of Hostility: and if it happen that any thing be attempted, or actually innovated after the said Publication, the same shall be forthwith repair'd and restor'd to its former State.

CV

The Plenipotentiarys on all sides shall agree among themselves, between the Conclusion and the Ratification of the Peace, upon the Ways, Time, and Securitys which are to be taken for the Restitution of Places, and for the Disbanding of Troops; of that both Partys may be assur'd, that all things agreed to shall be sincerely accomplish'd.

CVI

The Emperor above all things shall publish an Edict thro'out the Empire, and strictly enjoin all, who by these Articles of Pacification are oblig'd to restore or do any thing else, to obey it promptly and without tergi-versation, between the signing and the ratifying of this present Treaty; commanding as well the Directors as Governors of the Militia of the Circles, to hasten and finish the Restitution to be made to every one, in conformity to those Conventions, when the same are demanded. This Clause is to be inserted also in the Edicts, That whereas the Directors of the Circles, or the Governors of the Militia of the Circles, in matters that concern themselves, are esteem'd less capable of executing this Affair in this or the like case and likewise if the Directors and Governors of the Militia of the Circles refuse this Commission, the Directors of the neighbouring Circle, or the Governors of the Militia of the Circles shall exercise the Function, and officiate in the execution of these Restitutions in the other Circles, at the instance of the Partys concern'd.

CVII

If any of those who are to have something restor'd to them, suppose that the Emperor's Commissarys are necessary to be present at the Execution of some Restitution (which is left to their Choice) they shall have them. In which case, that the effect of the things agreed on may be the less hinder'd, it shall be permitted as well to those who restore, as to those to whom Restitution is to be made, to nominate two or three Commissarys immediately after the signing of the Peace, of whom his Imperial Majesty shall chuse two, one of each Religion, and one of each Party, whom he shall injoin to accomplish without delay all that which ought to be done by virtue of this present Treaty. If the Restorers have neglected to nominate Commissioners, his Imperial Majesty shall chuse one or two as he shall think fit (observing, nevertheless, in all cases the difference of Religion, that an equal number be put on each side) from among those whom the Party, to which somewhat is to be restor'd, shall have nominated, to whom he shall commit the Commission of executing it, notwithstanding all Exceptions made to the contrary; and for those who pretend to Restitutions, they are to intimate to the Restorers the Tenour of these Articles immediately after the Conclusion of the Peace.

CVIII

Finally, That all and every one either States, Commonaltys, or private Men, either Ecclesiastical or Secular, who by virtue of this Transaction and its general Articles, or by the express and special Disposition of any of them, are oblig'd to restore, transfer, give, do, or execute any thing, shall be bound forthwith after the Publication of the Emperor's Edicts, and after Notification given, to restore, transfer, give, do, or execute the same, without any Delay or Exception, or evading Clause either general or particular, contain'd in the precedent Amnesty, and without any Exception and Fraud as to what they are oblig'd unto.

CIX

That none, either Officer or Soldier in Garisons, or any other whatsoever, shall oppose the Execution of the Directors and Governors of the Militia of the Circles or Commissarys, but they shall rather promote the Execution; and the said Executors shall be permitted to use Force against such as shall endeavour to obstruct the Execution in what manner soever.

CX

Moreover, all Prisoners on the one side and the other, without any distinction of the Gown or the Sword, shall be releas'd after the manner it has been covenanted, or shall be agreed between the Generals of the Armys, with his Imperial Majesty's Approbation.

CXI

The Restitution being made pursuant to the Articles of Amnesty and Grievances, the Prisoners being releas'd, all the Soldiery of the Garisons, as well the Emperor's and his Allys, as the most Christian King's, and of the Landgrave of Hesse, and their Allys and Adherents, or by whom they may have been put in, shall be drawn out at the same time, without any Damage, Exception, or Delay, of the Citys of the Empire, and all other Places which are to be restor'd.

CXII

That the very Places, Citys, Towns, Boroughs, Villages, Castles, Fortresses and Forts which have been possess'd and retain'd, as well in the Kingdom of Bohemia, and other Countrys of the Empire and Hereditary Dominions of the House of Austria, as in the other Circles of the Empire, by one or the other Army, or have been surrender'd by Composition; shall be restor'd without delay to their former and lawful Possessors and Lords, whether they be mediately or immediately States of the Empire, Ecclesiastical or Secular, comprehending therein also the free Nobility of the Empire: and they shall be left at their own free disposal, either according to Right and Custom, or according to the Force this present Treaty ought to have, notwithstanding all Donations, Infeoffments, Concessions (except they have been made by the free-will of some State) Bonds for redeeming of Prisoners, or to prevent Burnings and Pillages, or such other like Titles acquir'd to the prejudice of the former and lawful Masters and Possessors. Let also all Contracts and Bargains, and all Exceptions contrary to the said Restitution cease, all which are to be esteem'd void; saving nevertheless such things as have been otherwise agreed on in the precedent Articles touching the Satisfaction to made to his most Christian Majesty, as also some Concessions and equivalent Compensations granted to the Electors and Princes of the Empire. That neither the Mention of the Catholick King, nor Quality of the Duke of *Lorain* given to Duke *Charles* in the Treaty between the Emperor and *Swedeland*, and much less the Title of Landgrave of *Alsace*, given to the Emperor, shall be any prejudice to the most Christian King. That also which has been agreed touching the Satisfaction to be made to the *Swedish* Troops, shall have no effect in respect to his Majesty.

CXIII

And that this Restitution of possess'd Places, as well by his Imperial Majesty as the most Christian King, and the Allys and Adherents of the one and the other Party, shall be reciprocally and *bona fide* executed.

CXIV

That the Records, Writings and Documents, and other Moveables, be also restor'd; as likewise the Cannon found at the taking of the Places, and which are still in being. But they shall be allow'd to carry off with them, and cause to be carry'd off, such as have been brought thither from other parts after the taking of the Places, or have been taken in Battels, with all the Carriages of War, and what belongs thereunto.

CXV

That the Inhabitants of each Place shall be oblig'd, when the Soldiers and Garisons draw out, to furnish them without Money the necessary Waggons, Horses, Boats and Provisions, to carry off all things to the appointed Places in the Empire; which Waggons, Horses and Boats, the Governors of the Garisons and the Captains of the withdrawing Soldiers shall restore without any Fraud or Deceit. The Inhabitants of the States shall free and relieve each other of this trouble of carrying the things from one Territory to the other, until they arrive at the appointed Place in the Empire; and the Governors or other Officers shall not be allow'd to bring with him or them the lent Waggons, Horses and Boats, nor any other thing they are accommodated with, out of the limits they belong unto, much less out of those of the Empire.

CXVI

That the Places which have been restor'd, as, well Maritime as Frontiers, or in the heart of the Country shall from henceforth and for ever be exempted from all Garisons, introduc'd during the Wars, and left (without prejudice in other things to every one's Right) at the full liberty and disposal of their Masters.

CXVII

That it shall not for the future, or at present, prove to the damage and prejudice of any Town, that has been taken and kept by the one or other Party; but that all and every one of them, with their Citizens and Inhabitants, shall enjoy as well the general Benefit of the Amnesty, as the rest of this Pacification. And for the Remainder of their Rights and Privileges, Ecclesiastical and Secular, which they enjoy'd before these Troubles, they shall be maintain'd therein; save, nevertheless the Rights of Sovereignty, and what depends thereon, for the Lords to whom they belong.

CXVIII

Finally, that the Troops and Armys of all those who are making War in the Empire, shall be disbanded and discharg'd; only each Party shall send to and keep up as many Men in his own Dominion, as he shall judge necessary for his Security.

CXIX

The Ambassadors and Plenipotentiarys of the Emperor, of the King, and the States of the Empire, promise respectively and the one to the other, to cause the Emperor, the most Christian King, the Electors of the Sacred *Roman* Empire, the Princes and States, to agree and ratify the Peace which has been concluded in this manner, and by general Consent; and so infallibly to order it, that the solemn Acts of Ratification be presented at *Munster,* and mutually and in good form exchang'd in the term of eight weeks, to reckon from the day of signing.

CXX

For the greater Firmness of all and every one of these Articles, this present Transaction shall serve for a perpetual Law and establish'd Sanction of the Empire, to be inserted like other fundamental Laws and Constitutions of the Empire in the Acts of the next Diet of the Empire, and the Imperial Capitulation; binding no less the absent than the present, the Ecclesiasticks than Seculars, whether they be States of the Empire or not: insomuch as that it shall be a prescrib'd Rule, perpetually to be follow'd, as well by the Imperial Counsellors and Officers, as those of other Lords, and all Judges and Officers of Courts of Justice.

CXXI

That it never shall be alledg'd, allow'd, or admitted, that any Canonical or Civil Law, any general or particular Decrees of Councils, any Privileges, any Indulgences, any Edicts, any Commissions, Inhibitions, Mandates, Decrees, Rescripts, Suspensions of Law, Judgments pronounc'd at any time, Adjudications, Capitulations of the Emperor, and other Rules and Exceptions of Religious Orders, past or future Protestations, Contradictions, Appeals, Investitures, Transactions, Oaths, Renunciations, Contracts, and much less the Edict of 1629. or the Transaction of *Prague,* with its Appendixes, or the Concordates with the Popes, or the Interims of the Year 1548. or any other politick Statutes, or Ecclesiastical Decrees, Dispensations, Absolutions, or any other Exceptions, under what pretence or colour they can be invented; shall take place against this Convention, or any of its Clauses and Articles neither shall any inhibitory or other Processes or Commissions be ever allow'd to the Plaintiff or Defendant.

CXXII

That he who by his Assistance or Counsel shall contravene this Transaction or Publick Peace, or shall oppose its Execution and the abovesaid Restitution, or who shall have endeavour'd, after the Restitution has been lawfully made, and without exceeding the manner agreed on before, without a lawful Cognizance of the Cause, and without the ordinary Course of Justice, to molest those that have been restor'd, whether Ecclesiasticks or Laymen; he shall incur the Punishment of being an Infringer of the publick Peace, and Sentence given against him according to the Constitutions of the Empire, so that the Restitution and Reparation may have its full effect.

CXXIII

That nevertheless the concluded Peace shall remain in force, and all Partys in this Transaction shall be oblig'd to defend and protect all and every Article of this Peace against any one, without distinction of Religion; and if it happens any point shall be violated, the Offended shall before all things exhort the Offender not to come to any Hostility, submitting the Cause to a friendly Composition, or the ordinary Proceedings of Justice.

CXXIV

Nevertheless, if for the space of three years the Difference cannot be terminated by any of those means, all and every one of those concern'd in this Transaction shall be oblig'd to join the injur'd Party, and assist him with Counsel and Force to repel the Injury, being first advertis'd by the injur'd that gentle Means and Justice prevail'd nothing; but without prejudice, nevertheless, to every one's Jurisdiction, and the Administration of Justice conformable to the Laws of each Prince and State: and it shall not be permitted to any State of the Empire to pursue his Right by Force and Arms; but if any difference has happen'd or happens for the future, every one shall try the means of ordinary Justice, and the Contravener shall be regarded as an Infringer of the Peace. That which has been determin'd by Sentence of the Judge, shall be put in execution, without distinction of Condition, as the Laws of the Empire enjoin touching the Execution of Arrests and Sentences.

CXXV

And that the publick Peace may be so much the better preserv'd intire, the Circles shall be renew'd; and as soon as any Beginnings of Troubles are perceiv'd, that which has been concluded in the Constitutions, of the Empire, touching the Execution and Preservation of the Public Peace, shall be observ'd.

CXXVI

And as often as any would march Troops thro' the other Territorys, this Passage shall be done at the charge of him whom the Troops belong to, and that without burdening or doing any harm or damage to those whole Countrys they march thro'. In a word, all that the Imperial Constitutions determine and ordain touching the Preservation of the publick Peace, shall be strictly observ'd.

CXXVII

In this present Treaty of Peace are comprehended such, who before the Exchange of the Ratification or in six months after, shall be nominated by general Consent, by the one or the other Party; mean time by a common Agreement, the Republick of *Venice* is therein compriz'd as Mediatrix of this Treaty. It shall also be of no prejudice to the Dukes of Savoy and Modena, or to what they shall act, or are now acting in Italy by Arms for the most Christian King.

CXXVIII

In Testimony of all and each of these things, and for their greater Validity, the Ambassadors of their Imperial and most Christian Majestys, and the Deputys, in the name of all the Electors, Princes, and States of the Empire, sent particularly for this end (by virtue of what has been concluded the 13th of *October*, in the Year hereafter mention'd, and has been deliver'd to the Ambassador of *France* the very day of signing under the Seal of the Chancellor of *Mentz*) *viz*. For the Elector of *Mayence*, Monsieur *Nicolas George de Reigersberg*, Knight and Chancellor; for the Elector of *Bavaria*, Monsieur *John Adolph Krebs*, Privy Counsellor; for the Elector of *Brandenburg*, Monsieur *John Count* of *Sain* and *Witgenstein*, Lord of *Homburg* and *Vallendar*, Privy Counsellor.

In the Name of the House of *Austria*, M. *George Verie*, Count of *Wolkenstein*, Counsellor of the Emperor's Court; *M. Corneille Gobelius*, Counsellor of the Bishop of *Bamberg*; *M. Sebastian William Meel*, Privy Counsellor to the Bishop of *Wirtzburg*; M. *John Earnest,* Counsellor of the Duke of *Bavaria's* Court; *M. Wolff Conrad* of *Thumbshirn*, and *Augustus Carpzovius*, both Counsellors of the Court of *Saxe-Altenburg* and *Coburg*; *M. John Fromhold*, Privy Counsellor of the House of *Brandenburg-Culmbac*, and *Onolzbac*; *M. Henry Laugenbeck*, J.C. to the House of *Brunswick-Lunenburg*; *James Limpodius*, J.C. Counsellor of State to the Branch of *Calemburg*, and Vice-Chancellor of *Lunenburg*. In the Name of the Counts of the Bench of Wetteraw, M. *Matthews Wesembecius*, J. D. and Counsellor.

In the Name of the one and the other Bench, M. *Marc Ottoh* of *Strasburg*, M. *John James Wolff* of *Ratisbon*, M. *David Gloxinius* of *Lubeck*, and *M. Lewis Christopher Kres* of *Kressenstein*, all Syndick Senators, Counsellors and Advocates of the Republick of *Noremberg*; who with their proper Hands and Seals have sign'd and seal'd this present Treaty of Peace, and which said Deputys of the several Orders have engag'd to procure the Ratifications of their Superiors in the prefix'd time, and in the manner it has been covenanted, leaving the liberty to the other Plenipotentiarys of States to sign it, if they think it convenient, and send for the Ratifications of their Superiors: And that on condition that by the Subscription of the abovesaid Ambassadors and Deputys, all and every one of the other States who shall abstain from signing and ratifying the present Treaty, shall be no less oblig'd to maintain and observe what is contain'd in this present Treaty of Pacification, than if they had subscrib'd and ratify'd it; and no Protestation or Contradiction of the Council of Direction in the *Roman* Empire shall be valid, or receiv'd in respect to the Subscription and said Deputys have made.

Done, pass'd and concluded at *Munster* in *Westphalia*, the 24th Day of *October*, 1648.

Consequences

In addition to ending the hegemony of the Holy Roman Empire, the Peace of Westphalia made Sweden the dominant power in the Baltic and elevated France over Spain as the dominant power in western Europe.

The cost of the war was staggering and was borne not by princes but by their people. In Brandenburg, Mecklenburg, Pomerania, the Palatinate, Württemberg, and parts of Bavaria, it is estimated that more than half of the civilian population perished. In the language of the treaty, "Discords and Civil Divisions being stir'd up in the Roman Empire . . . increas'd to such a degree, that not only all Germany, but also the neighboring Kingdoms, and France particularly, have been involv'd in the Disorders of a long and cruel War."

TREATY OF THE PYRENEES

TREATY AT A GLANCE

Completed
November 7, 1659, at Isle of the Pheasants, in the estuary
of the Bidassoa River, the Pyrenees

Signatories
France and Spain

Overview
The major phase of the Thirty Years' War was concluded by the
PEACE OF WESTPHALIA in 1648; however, largely because of the
obstinacy of the Spanish Hapsburgs, war between Spain and
France continued for another decade, even though the Spanish
position had been badly weakened by the long war. It was not until
the Spanish were entirely isolated militarily and diplomatically
that the Treaty of the Pyrenees was concluded.

Historical Background

Beginning in 1618, the Thirty Years' War grew to engulf
all of Europe. All of the major combatants, except for
France and Spain, made peace in 1648. Despite the
fact that the Spanish Hapsburgs had been in decline
throughout the 17th century, and although the French
had dealt them a stunning defeat at the Battle of Rocroi
in 1643, King Philip IV exploited the civil war in
France—the Fronde, during 1648–53—to prolong the
struggle in hopes of achieving some diplomatic gains
and preventing France from achieving dominance in
western Europe. Despite the Wars of the Fronde, Louis
XIV's minister, Cardinal Jules Mazarin, maneuvered
diplomatically to isolate Spain's position in the southern Netherlands by creating the League of the Rhine,
effectively a bloc of French client-states in northwestern Germany, and by forging an alliance with England's
lord protector, Oliver Cromwell.

As a result of the latter, Spanish forces were
soundly defeated at Dunkirk in the Battle of the Dunes
on June 14, 1658. This blow motivated the negotiations that ultimately resulted in the Treaty of the Pyrenees.

Terms

The treaty brought to France several key towns in the
southern Netherlands, considerably extending France's
northeastern frontier, thereby reducing the Hapsburg
military threat there and laying the foundation for the
young Louis XIV's future wars of expansion. France
also gained Roussillon and parts of the Cerdagne, so
that the Pyrenees became the enduring "natural" border between France and Spain.

XLII

And as concerning the Countrys and Places taken by
the Arms of *France*, during this War towards *Spain*; as
it had been formerly agreed by the Negotiation begun
in Madrid, in the Year 1656. upon which this present
Treaty is grounded, that the *Pyrenean* Mountain, which
antiently had divided the Gauls from Spain, should
also make henceforth the division of both the said
Kingdoms: It hath been concluded and agreed, that
the Lord the Most Christian King shall remain in possession, and shall effectually enjoy the whole County
and Viquery of *Roussillon*, and the County and Viquery
of *Conflans*, the Countrys, Towns, Places, Castles, Boroughs, Villages and Places, which make up the said
Counties and Viqueries of *Roussillon* and *Conflans*:
And to the Lord the Catholick King, shall remain the
County and Viquery of *Cerdana*, and the whole Principality of *Catalonia*, with the Viquerys, Places, Towns,
Castles, Boroughs, Hamlets, Places and Countrys, that
make up the said County of *Cerdana*, and the Principality of *Catalonia*, Provided, that if there be found any
Place of the County and Viquery of *Conflans* only, and
not of *Roussillon*, that be in the said *Pyrenean* Mountains towards *Spain*, it shall likewise remain to his
Catholick Majesty: As likewise, if any Place be found

of the said County and Viquery of *Cerdana* only, and not of *Catalonia*, that be in the said *Pyrenean* Mountains, towards *France*, it shall remain to his Most Christian Majesty. And that the said Division might be concluded, Commissioners shall be presently appointed on both sides, who shall together, bona fide, declare which are the *Pyrenean* Mountains, which according to the tenor of this Article, ought hereafter to divide both Kingdoms, and shall mark the limits they ought to have: And the said Commissioners shall meet upon the place at the furthest a Month after the subscribing of the present Treaty, and within the space of another Month after, shall conclude the matter, and declare, with common consent, the Premises. Provided, that if then they cannot agree among themselves concerning it, they shall presently send the Grounds of their Opinions to the two Plenipotentiarys of both the Lords and Kings; who taking notice of the Difficultys and Differences happen'd thereupon, shall conclude the Business betwixt them, so that it shall not be suffer'd that Arms be taken up again about the same.

Although its historical implications were great, the Treaty of the Pyrenees was in large part a catalog of Spanish cessions to France rather than a manifesto or statement of principles. It was therefore a lengthy and rather dry document, although its very nature as a catalog was in itself instructive, for it was no mean feat to catalog towns, provinces, and other entities at the fringes of countries that were still making the transition from collections of feudal holdings to modern nationhood.

XL

Sixthly, His Catholick Majesty, for certain Considerations hereafter particularly express'd in another Article of the present Treaty, doth promise and oblige himself to put into the hands of his most Christian Majesty the Town and Place of *Avennes*, situate between the *Sambre* and the *Maze*, with the Appurtenances, Dependences, Annexes and Dominions thereof, with all the Artillery and warlike Ammunitions that are now therein, to remain to his said Most Christian Majesty seiz'd of the said Place of *Avennes*, and effectually to enjoy the same, and the said Appurtenances, Dependences, Annexes and Dominions, after the same manner, and with the same right of Possession, Sovereignty and other things, which his Catholick Majesty doth now enjoy there. And because it hath been reported, that within the said Place of *Avennes*, and the Appurtenances, Dependences, Annexes and Dominions thereof, the ordinary Jurisdiction, the Rents and other Profits do belong to the Prince of *Chimay*, it hath been declar'd and agreed between the said Lords and Kings, that whatsoever is contain'd within the Walls and Fortifications of the said Prince shall have no kind of Right, Rent or Jurisdiction, within the said Walls, and Fortifications; it being only reserv'd to him to keep whatsoever in time past did belong to him out of the

said Place, in the Villages, Countrys and Forests of the said Dependence of *Avennes*, in the same manner as he hath hitherto possess'd the same: provided also, as hath been said before, that the Sovereignty and the high Dominion of the said Villages, Countrys and Forests of the said Dependence of *Avennes*, shall belong and remain to his Most Christian Majesty; the said Lord the Catholick King having taken upon himself to indemnify the said Prince of *Chimay* for the Interest he may have in what is taken from him by the present Treaty within the Precincts of the said Place, as aforesaid.

XLI

The said Places of *Arras*, *Hesdin*, *Bapaume*, *Bethune*, and the Towns of *Lillers*, *Lens*, County of *St. Pol*, *Teroane*, *Pas*, and their Bayliwicks; as also all the other Bayliwicks and Chatellanys of *Artois* (except only as aforesaid the Towns and Bayliwicks of *Ayre* and *St. Omer*, their Appurtenances, Dependences, Annexes and Dominions) as also Renty, in case it be not found to be any of the Dependences of *Ayre* or of *St. Omer*; together with the places of *Greveling*, and the Forts *Philip*, the *Sluice* and *Hannuin*, *Bourburg* and *St. Venent*, in *Flanders*; the Places of *Landrecy* and *Quesnoy*, in the *Heyneult*; as also those of *Avennes*, *Merienburg* and *Philippeville*, which are to be put into the hands of the most Christian King, as aforesaid: And likewise the Places of *Thionville*, *Montmedy*, and *Demvilliers*, the Town and Provostship of *Ivoy*, *Chavency*, *Chateau* and the Provostship thereof, and *Marville* in *Luxembourg*, their Bayliwicks, Chatellanys, Governments, Provostships, Territorys, Dominions, Lordships, Appurtenances, Dependences and Annexes shall remain, by the present Treaty of Peace, unto the said Lord the most Christian King, and to his Successors and Assigns, irrevocably and for ever; and with the same rights of Sovereignty, Propriety, Regality, Patronage, Wardianship, Jurisdiction, Nomination, Prerogatives and Preeminences upon the Bishopricks, Cathedral Churches, and other Abbys, Priorys, Dignitys, Parsonages, or any other Benefices whatsoever, being within the limits of the said Countrys, Places and Bayliwicks so yielded, of whatsoever Abbys the said Priorys may hold and depend, and all other Rights formerly belonging to the said Lord the Catholick King, tho not particularly related here. And his most Christian Majesty shall never hereafter be troubled nor molested by any way whatsoever, either of Right or of Fact, by the said Lord the Catholick King, his Successors, or any Prince of his House, or any other whatsoever, under any pretence or occasion that may happen in the said Sovereignty, Propriety, Jurisdiction, Prerogative, Possession and Enjoyment of all the said Countrys, Towns, Places, Castles, Lands, Lordships, Provostships, Dominions, Chatellanys and Bayliwicks, and of all the Places and other things depending of them. And for that effect, the said Lord the Catholick King, for himself and for his Heirs, Successors and Assigns, doth renounce unto, quit, yield and transfer, as his Plenipotentiary in his

Name by the present irrevocable Treaty of Peace, hath renounced to, quitted, yielded and for ever transfer'd, in the behalf and to the benefit of the said Lord the most Christian King, his Heirs, Successors and Assigns, all the Rights, Actions, Pretensions, Regalities, Patronage, Wardianship, Jurisdiction, Nomination, Prerogatives and Preeminences upon the said Bishopricks, Cathedral Churches, and other Abbys, Priorys, Dignitys, Parsonages, and any other Benefices whatsoever within the Precincts of the said Countrys, Places and Bayliwicks so yielded, of what Abbys soever the said Priorys do hold or depend: And generally, without retaining or reserving any thing, all other Rights which the said Lord the Catholick King, or his Heirs and Successors have and pretend, or may have and pretend for what cause and occasion soever, upon the said Countrys, Places, Castles, Forts, Lands, Lordships, Dominions, Chatellanys and Bayliwicks, and upon all the Places depending of them as aforesaid: Which, together with all the Men, Vassals, Subjects, Boroughs, Villages, Hamlets, Forests, Lands, and other things whatsoever depending of them, without keeping or reserving anything, the said Lord the Catholick King, both for himself and for his Successors, doth consent to be from this time forth and for ever united and incorporated to the Crown of *France*; all Laws, Customs, Statutes and Constitutions made to the contrary, even such as may have been confirmed by Oath, in any wise notwithstanding. To which, and to all Clauses derogatory to former derogatory Clauses, it is expressly derogated by the present Treaty, for the effect of the said Renunciations and Cessions; which shall be valid and shall take place, the particular Expression or Specification not derogating to the general, nor the general to the particular, and excluding for ever all Exceptions, upon what right, title, cause or pretence soever they may be grounded. And the said Lord the Catholick King doth declare, consent, will and understand, that the Men, Vassals and Subjects of the said Countrys, Towns and Lands yielded to the Crown of *France* as aforesaid, be and remain quitted and absolv'd from henceforth and for ever of the faith, homage, service and oath of Fidelity, they, all, or any of them may have done to him, or to his Predecessors the Catholick Kings; and withal of all obedience, subjection and vassalage which they for that cause might owe unto him: The said Lord the Catholick King, willing that the said faith and homage, and oath of Fidelity become and remain void and of none effect, as if they had never been taken.

Consequences

If the Peace of Westphalia ended the hegemony of the Holy Roman Empire, also checking the Austrian Hapsburgs' efforts to consolidate their position in Germany by means of the Holy Roman Empire, the Treaty of the Pyrenees brought the Spanish Hapsburgs to their knees, ending Spain's long-held position as one of the greatest of European powers.

PEACE OF NIJMEGEN

TREATIES AT A GLANCE

Completed
August 10 and September 17, 1678, and February 3, 1679,
at Nijmegen (Nimeguen), East Netherlands

Signatories
France, Holland, Spain, and the Holy Roman Empire

Overview
The Peace of Nijmegen ended Louis XIV's second major war of
conquest, and successfully for him, bringing Alsace and a
chunk of the Spanish Netherlands under his control and setting
the stage for further glory and gain.

Historical Background

For at least a decade, since the regent Cardinal Jules Mazarin had died and left Louis XIV to pursue his dreams of glory, the Sun King had longed for the Belgian Netherlands, which he saw as the "natural boundary" for France in Europe. His plottings had come a cropper back in 1668, when the new Triple Alliance of England, Sweden, and Holland had prevented Louis from grabbing the Low Countries in his War of Devolution. Since then he had been working to split the Alliance and isolate Holland. He secretly bribed the Swedes to quit the league, and he put England's King Charles II on a pension. Charles, wrangling with a Parliament just then unhappy it had ever restored the Stuarts to the throne after Oliver Cromwell lopped off the first Charles's head, needed the money to shore up his authority so he could rule single-handed and absolute like all the best kings of the time, like King Louis, in fact.

With Charles in his pocket and Sweden shunted to the sidelines, Louis attacked Holland in 1672. The English dutifully declared war as well, then attempted to blockade and invade the Netherlands. As Dutch admiral M. A. De Ruyter held the French and English fleets at bay, young William of Orange opened Holland's dikes, flooded the region, rallied the Dutch army behind the "Water Line," and staved off the invasion. Back home Charles floated a Declaration of Indulgences so unpopular that in 1673 Parliament passed the Test Act, cutting off his funds for the war, forcing him not only to treat with the Dutch and pull England out of the

war but again to ally the British with France's growing number of enemies. These now included a coalition of Holland with Spain, the Hapsburgs, and German Lorraine. This "Grand Alliance" drove the French out of the Dutch Republic by the end of 1673.

Between 1674 and 1678, though, with Sweden as his only effective ally, Louis turned this second war of conquest around. He advanced steadily into the Southern, or Spanish, Netherlands and along the Rhine, defeating badly the poorly coordinated Alliance forces with easy regularity. He won major victories in Alsace and Lorraine in 1675, and in 1676 he crushed both the Spanish army and the combined Dutch and Spanish navy in and off Sicily (where De Ruyter was mortally wounded).

Despite his strong military position—French had by now pretty much overrun Holland—Louis was facing financial ruin at home and feared the English would make good their threat and reenter the war alongside the Alliance. Thus, in 1678 he decided to make peace.

Terms

The treaties of Nijmegen helped put Alsace on the road to becoming a French province, forced the Alliance's elector of Brandenburg to give his conquests in Pomerania to Sweden, and generously aggrandized France in the Spanish Netherlands, but they left the Dutch Republic intact.

The Treaty of Peace between France and Holland Concluded at Nimeguen [Nimegen], August 10, 1678

I

There shall be a good, firm and inviolable peace betwixt his most Christian Majesty and the states, &c.

II

If any prizes shall be taken on either side, four weeks after the publication of the peace, in the Baltick, or north sea, from New-foundland to the channel's mouth; within the space of six weeks after the said publication, from the channel to Cape St. Vincent; ten weeks after it in the Mediterranean, and as far as the Equinoctial; and eight months after it beyond the line, they shall be restored, with recompence for damages.

III

There shall be perpetual friendship between the said king and states, and their subjects, and no resenting of damages, or offences, during the war.

IV

They shall procure one another's good, and not consent to any treaties to the damage of each other.

V

Estates seized and confiscated on account of the war to be restored.

VI

The count d'Auvergne to be restored to the marquisate of Bergen-opzome, with all its rights, the same being confiscated by the states for his being in the French service.

VII

Each side to hold all it is now possessed of within or without Europe.

VIII

But his most Christian Majesty to restore Maestricht, with all its dependencies.

IX

The states shall maintain the Catholic religion, and the professors of it, in Maestricht, according to the capitulation of 1632.

X

The king may carry away from Maestricht all the artillery, ammunition and provisions, and the garrison their effects; but without exacting any thing from the inhabitants, or doing any hurt.

XI

Prisoners of war on both sides shall be discharged without ransom.

XII

Contributions demand by the governor of Maestricht shall be payable till the ratification of this treaty.

XIII

The states shall not directly or indirectly assist the enemies of France, or its allies; and shall be guarantees for all engagements Spain shall enter into with his most Christian Majesty.

XIV

If through inadvertancy, or otherwise, there be any want in the observance of this treaty, it shall be repaired, without any breach of friendship.

XV

If any breach should happen between France and Holland, the subjects on both sides shall have six months to withdraw themselves and their effects.

XVI

As for what concerns the Prince of Orange, all that is contained in a writing made particularly relating to his interests, shall be observed as if inserted word for word in this treaty.

XVII

The King of Great Britain shall be comprehended in this treaty. . . .

XVIII and XIX

[Contain the Princes and States admitted to this treaty.]

XX

The King of Great Britain, and such others as shall think fit, may be guarantees of this treaty.

XXI

The ratifications shall be exchanged within six weeks.

A SEPARATE ARTICLE CONCERNING THE PRINCE OF ORANGE

The principality of Orange shall immediately after the ratification of this treaty, be restored to the Prince of Orange, with all other lands belonging to him in France, and other countries under his Majesty's subjection.

The Treaty of Commerce Betwixt France and Holland Concluded at Nimeguen, August 10, 1678

I

The subjects on both sides shall enjoy the same liberty, as before the war.

II

All hostilities shall cease, and neither side to take commissions as privateers, or letters of reprisal from any Princes, or States, at enmity with the other.

III

This is the same with the second article in the treaty of peace.

IV

All former letters of mart and reprisal are declared void.

V

The subjects on neither side, nor their goods, shall be liable to arrests and seisures, for debts owing by the king and states.

VI

The subjects on both sides shall live in friendship, and enjoy all liberty in commerce and navigation.

VII

The subjects on both sides shall pay no other duties in one another's dominions than the natives do.

VIII

Ships of war belonging to either party shall have free access into ports, harbours, &c. of the other.

IX

Ships of war on either side may conduct the prizes they take from their enemies, where they think good, without being tied to any duties, or be liable to be stopped, or to give any account of the value of the said prizes. But neither side shall give refuge in their ports to such as shall have taken any prizes from the other.

X

The subjects of each party shall, in the dominions of the other, be exempted from the law of Aubain, by which the goods of foreigners dying, escheat to the crown; but their said goods shall pass to their heirs either by will, deed, or even if they die intestate, without any letters of naturalization; but they shall be treated as natural born subjects, and not liable to such taxes as are laid upon strangers.

XI

Ships driven into ports shall not be compelled to unlade, or pay any duties.

XII

Neither ships, men, nor goods, shall be seized on any pretence whatsoever. . . .

XXX

His Majesty and the States may at any time cause to be built or freighted, as many ships of war, or trade as they shall think fit, in one another's countries, and buy such quantities of ammunition, honestly and at reasonable prices; but neither shall grant the like permission to one another's enemies, if they be the aggressors.

XXXI

Ships driven by storm, or otherwise, on the coasts of either ally, shall be saved, with all the goods, for the proprietors; and those punished who shall commit any inhumanities in such cafes.

XXXII

Neither side shall receive any pirates, or exiles, but shall cause them to be pursued, punished and driven out.

XXXIII

The subjects on both sides, may make use of such lawyers, notaries, &c. as they shall think fit, who shall be appointed to them by the judges, and may keep books of trade in what language they please.

XXXIV

Both parties may settle consuls in one anothers estates, who shall enjoy all the privileges belonging to their function.

XXXV

Neither side shall suffer any vessel, in the service of another, to make prize, within their ports, &c. upon one another's subjects; and if any such thing should happen, either party shall procure reparation.

XXXVI

If through inadvertency any thing should be wanting in the observance of this treaty, it shall not cause a breach, but reparation shall be made for the contravention.

XXXVII

If any breach shall happen between France and Holland, nine months shall be allowed the subjects of each party to retire and withdraw their effects.

XXXVIII

This treaty shall be in force twenty-five years from the day of signing, and the ratifications shall be exchanged within six weeks.

SEPARATE ARTICLE

The equality to be observed in relation to the subject of each nation as to duties, &c. according to the seventh article of this treaty, shall not derogate from the imposition of fifty sols per ton, imposed in France upon the ships of strangers, but the subjects of the States shall pay the same as well as other strangers; but it shall be only once in each voyage; and the said ships, if laden with salt, shall pay but half the said fifty sols. The States may lay the like imposition on strangers' ships, but must not exceed.

The Treaty of Peace between France and Spain Concluded at Nimeguen, September 17, 1678.

I

It is agreed, that there be a firm and lasting peace, and perpetual alliance, between the most Christian and Catholic Kings, their heirs, subjects, &c.

II

The cessation of all hostilities signed the 19th of August shall continue; and if any thing contrary shall happen, reparation shall be made.

III

All that has been done during this war, shall be buried in perpetual oblivion.

IV

The most Christian King shall restore to his Catholic Majesty the fortress of Charleroy, the towns of Binch, Ath, Oudenarde, and Countray, with all their dependencies, excepting the verge of Menin, and the town of Conde.

V

The most Christian King promises also to restore the town and duchy of Limberg, with its dependencies, the country beyond the Maese, the town and citadel of Ghent, fort Rodenhers, the land of Waes, the town of Lewe, and that of St. Guislan, the fortifications whereof shall be raised; also the town of Puicerda in Catalonia, with all their dependencies.

VI

The places above-mentioned shall remain to his Catholic Majesty, with all their rights, prerogative, &c.

VII

The most Christian and Catholic Kings shall restore to one another whatsoever may have been taken till the proclaiming of the peace.

VIII

The restitution of the above mentioned places shall be made without any delay, in the same condition they now are without making any demands, for fortification, or otherwise.

IX

All judgments given, and other proceedings at law, in the said places under his most Christian Majesty, shall remain valid.

X

The eastern and western sluices of Newport, and the fort of Vierbout, at the end of the western sluice, with other parts belonging to the fortifications of Newport, shall remain in the hands of his Catholic Majesty.

XI

The most Christian King shall remain possessed of and enjoy the county of Burgundy, commonly called Franche Compte, with all its towns and dependencies, comprehending the city of Bezanzon, as also the towns of Valenciennes, Bouchain and Conde; also Cambray and Cambresis, Aire, St. Omer, Ypres, Warvick, Warneton, Poperinghen, Bailleul, Cassel, Bavay and Maubeuge, with their dependencies.

XII

The said county of Burgundy, and all other places named, with their dependencies, shall for ever remain to the most Christian King, his heirs and successors, with all their rights, sovereignties, &c,

XIII

His Catholic Majesty obliges himself to procure from the Bishop and Chapter of Liege, with the consent of the Emperor and Empire, they shall yield up to the most Christian King the town of Dinant, within a year after the peace shall be concluded with the Emperor; and in case he cannot prevail to have it so yielded up, does promise to deliver to his most Christian Majesty, in lieu of it, the town of Charlemont

XIV

To prevent all difficulties arising about lands lying within each other's bounds, it is agreed, that all the lands, &c. comprehended within the provost-ships belonging to his most Christian Majesty, beyond the Sambre, shall be exchanged for others lying more conveniently for his Catholic Majesty.

XV

Commissioners shall be appointed on both sides for adjusting the said exchange; as also for ascertaining all mortgages on the places restored.

XVI

If the difficulties about the exchange cannot be adjusted, neither side shall impose new duties upon goods, unless they be transported into another dominion to be there spent, or sent farther off.

XVII

The said Kings may carry away all their artillery and ammunition from the places they restore.

XVIII

Contributions on both sides shall continue till the 16th of October next, and the arrears then due shall be paid within three months.

XIX

The most Christian King shall receive all duties in the places he restores to the Catholic King till the day of the restitution.

XX

All papers, &c. relating to the places restored, shall be delivered up.

XXI

All the subjects on both sides shall be restored to the estates, dignities, &c. they possessed before the war, which have been seized on account of the said war; but they shall claim none of the profits during the war.

XXII

Nor any debts, effects, or moveables confiscated before the proclaiming of peace.

XXIII

The restoring of the said subjects on both sides shall be performed according to the 21st and 22d articles, notwithstanding the many grants, confiscations, &c. all which shall be void. The said persons may freely return to their homes; or, in case they shall rather chuse to stay elsewhere, they may appoint any unsuspected persons to receive their revenues, &c.

XXIV

Such as have benefices legally conferred on them on both sides, shall enjoy them for their lives, without prejudice to the rights of the patrons.

XXV

All prelates, &c. named to their benefices, by the said Kings, before or since the war, shall enjoy the same, provided the persons be capable and qualified as was requisite before the war.

XXVI

No part of the Pyrenean treaty is hereby made void, excepting what relates to Portugal; nor the treaty of Aix-la-Chapelle any farther than is here specified.

XXVII

His Catholic Majesty promises neither directly nor indirectly to assist his own allies against France or its allies.

XXVIII

His Britannick Majesty, as mediator, shall be included in this treaty. . . .

XXI

All Princes that please may be guarantees of this treaty.

XXXII

This treaty shall be registered in the parliaments of France, and in the Chamber of Accounts in Paris; as also in the great council, and other councils, and Chambers of account of his Catholic Majesty, &c.

The Treaty of Peace between the Emperor and King of France Concluded at Nimeguen, February 3, 1679

I

There shall be an universal and sincere peace and true friendship between their Imperial and most Christian Majesties and their allies, &c.

II

The treaty of Munster shall be the foundation of this treaty.

III

Philipsburg having been taken by the Emperor during the war, Friburg by France, it is agreed.

IV

That his most Christian Majesty shall renounce all pretensions to that peace.

V

That the Emperor for ever quit to the most Christian King the town of Friburg, with all its dependencies, rights, &c. the town still retaining its privileges, and the Bishop of Constance his rights.

VI

His most Christian Majesty shall at all times have free passage through the territories of the Empire from Brisack to Friburg.

VII

The provisions for Friburg shall not be liable to any new or ancient duties, the same from Brisgaw; other merchandise to pay no more than are paid by the Emperor's subjects.

VIII

Commissioners to be appointed in a-year to consider what lawful debts are to be paid by the town of Friburg.

IX

All papers, records, &c. found at Friburg when taken, to be restored, unless they jointly concern the said town of Friburg, and then to be kept in such place as shall be agreed on, that authentic copies may be had upon occasion.

X

All persons shall have liberty in a year to depart Friburg, and to carry away their goods, or to sell either moveables, or immoveables.

XI

The said town of Friburg may be restored, in case their Majesties can agree on an equivalent.

XII

The Duke of Lorain shall be restored to those states, places and goods, his uncle possessed in the year 1670.

XIII

The town of Nancy, with it's district, shall remain for ever incorporated in the Crown of France, and the Duke of Lorain does renounce all right to it.

XIV

For the better communication between the said town of Nancy and the dominions of France, ways half a league broad shall be marked out by commissioners on both sides of St. Didier to Nancy, from Nancy to Alsatia, from Nancy to Besanzon in Burgundy, and from Nancy to Metz.

XV

All villages, houses, lands, &c. with their dependencies, situate within the said ways, shall belong to his most Christian Majesty; but so that whatsoever is beyond them shall remain to the Duke.

XVI

The city and provostship of Longwick, with its dependencies, shall for ever remain to the most Christian King, for which the King shall give the Duke provostship.

XVII

In consideration for the city of Nancy, the King conveys to the Duke the town, suburbs and district of Toul forever.

XVIII

In case the district of Toul shall be found of less value than that of Nancy, the same shall be otherwise made good to the Duke.

XIX

The right of presenting the Bishop of Toul shall belong to the Duke.

XX

Those who are possessed of benefices by the King shall not be disturbed by the Duke.

XXI

All proceedings at law under the King shall stand good.

XXII

The deeds and writing that were at Nancy and Bar shall be restored to the Duke.

XXIII

The Bishop of Strasburg, his brother and nephew, Princes of Furstemburg, shall be restored to all their rights, honours, revenues, &c. the first of them to his liberty, and all proceedings against him be buried in oblivion.

XXIV

All subjects on both sides shall be restored to the honours, dignities, estates, &c. which they enjoyed, before the war or falling to them during the same; but nothing to be demanded of the profits during the war.

XXV

The agreement made between the Emperor and Sweden, shall be looked upon as if inserted in this treaty.

XXVI

The Emperor and most Christian King shall use their utmost endeavours to conclude a peace, and to that end first a cessation of arms between the said most Christian King and the King of Sweden on the one part, and the King of Denmark the Elector of Brandenburg, the Bishop of Munster, and the Princes of Lunenburg, on the other. But if their good offices should want effect, the Emperor and Empire shall give no assistance nor winter quarters to the said enemies of France and Sweden; and the most Christian King shall be still allowed to keep garrisons in Chastelet, Huy, Verviers, Aix-la-Chapelle, Dueren, Linnick, Nuys and Zons, which places he shall restore when the war is ended.

XXVII

Places shall be restored bona fide within a month after the ratification of the peace, excepting those in the foregoing article.

XXVIII

The difference about the castle and duchy of Bouillon between the Bishop of Liege and the Dukes of Bouillon, shall be amicably adjusted.

XXIX

All acts of hostility shall cease immediately after signing this treaty of peace; and if any thing be done otherwise within fourteen days, it shall be repaired.

XXX

Contributions shall continue to be paid on both sides till the ratifications; the arrears be paid within four months after, and security given for the same; so that no force shall be used for recovering of them.

XXXI

All things stipulated in the treaty of Munster, concerning the Montserrat, shall remain in full force.

XXXII

The King of Great Britain shall be included in this treaty as mediator.

XXXIII

Those to be also comprehended, who shall be named in six months by both parties.

XXXIV

All Princes and States may be guarantees for the performance of this treaty.

XXXV

The ratifications shall be exchanged within eight weeks after signing.

XXXVI

No protestation or contradiction from the directory of the Empire, against the subscription of this treaty, shall be received or esteemed valid.

Consequences

Confirmed at Nijmegen as Europe's new strongman, Louis would continue his agenda of conquest until he established a French ascendancy on the Continent. Eventually, however, he would overextend his rule, provoke the formation of another "Grand Alliance," and nearly bankrupt the French state, thus laying the groundwork for the French Revolution of the coming century.

TREATY OF RYSWICK

TREATY AT A GLANCE

Completed
September 20, 1697, at Ryswick Castle, Holland

Signatories
France and the Grand Alliance (Great Britain, Holland [the United Provinces], Hapsburg Austria [the Holy Roman Empire], Spain, France, Sweden, and various German states

Overview
The Treaty of Ryswick stalled the successful expansion of Louis XIV after the War of the Grand Alliance and launched Great Britain, then under the new monarchs William (of Orange) and Mary, on a century of worldwide competition with the French.

Historical Background

French monarch Louis the XIV's aggressions in the Dutch War of 1672–78 had led England, Holland (the United Provinces), and the Austrian Hapsburgs to form a defensive alliance, called the League of Augsburg, and later—after 1689—the Grand Alliance. This time around, Louis hoped for a brief, unimpeded war in Germany, but those hopes were dashed when England's Glorious Revolution toppled King James II and brought William of Orange to the British throne—and into the lists against French expansion.

Louis supported an attempted restoration of the Stuarts to the English throne to distract William II, but when former king James landed his force in Ireland, the Dutch and English forces handed him a sound drubbing at the Battle of the Boyne. Louis then used his navy, the finest at the time in Europe, to try to cripple the Grand Alliance on the high seas, and his warships did indeed score a major victory at the 1690 Battle of Beachy Head. Two years later, however, the Anglo-Dutch fleet struck back at the Battle of La Hogue and so wrecked Louis's ships that his navy was thereafter all but useless to him.

Confined to fighting on the Continent, Louis was now at a distinct disadvantage since the Alliance had swelled to include Savoy, Sweden, Spain, the Holy Roman Empire, Bavaria, Saxony, and the German Palatine. The Sun King had already been fighting them by the time he lost his navy, sometimes collectively, sometimes one at a time. Back in 1690, in a brilliant double envelopment at the Battle of Fleurus, the French cavalry had surrounded and dispatched some 14,000 English, German, and Spanish troops, killing 6,000 and taking 8,000 prisoner. In those days he had seemed invincible, and despite his losses at sea, he continued to build his reputation at Namur, a key city in the Low Countries, which he attacked and where he gained a bloody victory. Other victories, some of them virtual massacres, strained the Alliance, and Saxony withdrew in 1694 and signed a separate peace in 1696.

After the death of his undefeated star general, Marshal Luxembourg, in 1695, Louis was defeated when he again attacked Namur, at which point he had had enough. He entered into secret peace negotiations with King William III, and the war finally came to an end with a peace conference conducted between September 20 and October 30, 1697, at Ryswick Castle in Holland.

Terms

In the Treaty (or more accurately, treaties) of Ryswick, Louis recognized William's right to the British Crown; the Dutch received important trade concessions; and France and some in the Grand Alliance gave up their conquests of the past two decades.

The Treaty of Peace between William III, King of Great Britain, and Lewis [Louis] XIV, the King of France

I

THAT there be an universal and perpetual Peace and a true and sincere Friendship, between the most Serene and Mighty Prince

William III King of *Great Britain*, and the most Serene and Mighty Prince *Lewis XIV* the most Christian King, their Heirs and Successors, and between the Kingdoms, States and Subjects of both; and that the same be so sincerely and inviolably observed and kept, that the one shall promote the Interest, Honour and Advantage of the other; and that on both sides a faithful Neighbourhood, and true Observation of Peace and Friendship, may daily flourish and encrease.

II

That all Enmitys, Hostilitys, Discords and Wars, between the said King of *Great Britain* and the most Christian King, and their Subjects, cease and be abolish'd; so that on both sides they forbear and abstain hereafter from all Plundering, Depredation, Harm-doing, Injurys and Infestation whatsoever, as well by Land as by Sea, and on fresh waters every where; and especially throughout all the Kingdoms, Territorys, Dominions and Places belonging to each other, of what Condition soever they be.

III

That all Offences, Injurys, Damages, which the said King of *Great Britain* and his Subjects, or the said most Christian King and his Subjects have suffer'd from each other during this War, shall be forgotten, so that neither on account of them, or for any other cause or pretence, neither Party, or the Subjects of either, shall hereafter do, cause or suffer to be done any Hostility, Enmity, Molestation or Hindrance to the other, by himself or others, secretly or openly, directly or indirectly, by colour by Right or way of Fact.

IV

And since the most Christian King was never more desirous of any thing than that the Peace be firm and inviolable, the said King promises and agrees for himself and his Successors, that he will on no account whatsoever disturb the said King of *Great Britain*, in the free possession of the Kingdoms, Countrys, Lands or Dominions which he now enjoys; and therefore engages his Honour, upon the Faith and Word of a King, that he will not give or afford any Assistance, directly or indirectly, to any Enemy or Enemys of the said King of *Great Britain*; and that he will in no manner whatsoever favour the Conspiracys or Plots which any Rebels, or ill-dispos'd Persons, may in any Place excite or contrive against the said King: and for that end promises and engages, That he will not assist with Arms, Ammunition, Ships, Provisions or Mony, or in any other way, by Sea or Land, any Person or Persons who shall hereafter, under any pretence whatsoever, disturb or molest the said King of *Great Britain*, in the free and full Possession of his Kingdoms, Countrys, Lands and Dominions. The King and Successors, Kings of *Great Britain*, That he will inviolably do and perform the same towards the said most Christian King, his Kingdoms, Countrys, Lands, and Dominions.

V

That there be a free use of Navigation and Commerce between the Subjects of both the said Kings, as was formerly in the time of Peace and before the Declaration of the late War, so that every one of them may freely come into the Kingdoms, Marts, Ports and Rivers of either of the said Kings with their Merchandizes, and may there continue and Trade without and Molestation; and shall use and enjoy all Libertys, Immunitys and Privileges granted by solemn Treatys and ancient Customs.

VI

That the ordinary Administration of justice shall be restor'd and set open throughout the Kingdoms and Dominions of both Kings; so that it shall be free for all the Subjects of either to claim and obtain their Rights, Pretentions and Actions, according to the Laws, Constitutions and Statutes of each Kingdom.

VII

The most Christian King shall restore to the said King of *Great Britain*, all Countrys, Islands, Forts and Colonys wheresoever situated, which the *English* did possess before the Declaration of this present War; and in like manner the King of *Great Britain* shall restore to the most Christian King all Countrys, Islands, Forts and Colonys, wheresoever situated, which the *French* did possess before the said Declaration of War. And this Restitution shall be made on both sides, within the space of six Months, or sooner, if it can be done. And to that end immediately after the Ratification of this Treaty, each of the said Kings shall deliver, or cause to be deliver'd to the other, or to Commissioners authoriz'd in his Name for that purpose, all Acts of Concession, Instruments, and necessary Orders, duly made and in proper Form, so that they may have their Effect.

VIII

Commissioners shall be appointed on both sides, to examine and determine the Rights and Pretentions which either of the said Kings hath to the Places situated in *Hudson's Bay*: But the Possession of those Places which were taken by the *French* during the Peace that preceded this present War, and were retaken by the *English* during this War, shall be left to the French by virtue of the foregoing Article. The Capitulation made by the *English* on the fifth of *September*, 1696. shall be observ'd, according to its Form and Tenor; Merchandizes therein mention'd shall be restor'd; the Governor of the Fort taken there shall be set at liberty, if it be not already done; the Differences arisen concerning the Execution of the said Capitulation, and the value of the Goods there lost, shall be adjudged and determin'd by the said Commissioners, who immediately after the Ratification of the present Treaty shall be invested with sufficient Authority for settling the Limits and Confines of the Lands to be restor'd on either side by virtue of the foregoing Article, and likewise for exchanging of Lands, as may conduce to the mutual Interest and Advantage of both Kings.

And to this end the Commissioners, so appointed, shall within the space of Three Months from the time of the Ratification of the present Treaty, meet in the City of *London*; and within Six Months, to be reckon'd from their First Meeting, shall determine all Differences and Disputes which may arise concerning this matter: After which, the Articles the said Commissioners shall agree to, shall be ratify'd by both Kings, and shall have the same Force and Vigour, as if they were inserted Word for Word in the present Treaty.

IX

All Letters, as well of Reprisal as of Marque and Counter-Marque, which hitherto have for any cause been granted on either side, shall be, and remain null and void; Nor shall any the like Letters be hereafter granted by either of the said Kings against the subjects of the other, unless it be first made manifest, that Right hath been deny'd; and it shall not be taken for a denial of Right, unless the Petition of the Person, who desires Letters of Reprisal to be granted to him, be first shewn to the Minister residing there on the part of the King, against whose Subjects those Letters are desired; That within the space of Four Months or sooner, he may inquire into the contrary, or procure that Satisfaction be made with all speed from the Party offending, to the Complainant. But if the King against whose Subjects Reprisals are demanded, have no Minister residing there, Letters of Reprisal shall not be granted till after the space of Four Months, to be reckon'd from the day on which his Petition was made and presented to the King against whose Subjects Reprisals are desir'd, or to his Privy-Council.

X

For cutting off all matter of Dispute and Contention, which may arise concerning the Restitution of Ships, Merchandises, and other movable Goods, which either Party may complain to be taken and detain'd from the other, in Countrys, and on Coasts far distant, after the Peace is concluded, and before it be notify'd there; All ships, Merchandises, and other movable Goods, which shall be taken by either side, after the Signing and Publication of the present Treaty, within the space of Twelve Days in the *British* and *North Seas*, as far as the Cape St. *Vincent*; within the space of Ten Weeks beyond the said Cape, and on this side of the *Equinoctial Line* or *Equator*, as well in the Ocean and *Mediterranean* Sea as elsewhere; Lastly within the space of Six Months beyond the said Line throughout the whole World, shall belong and remain unto the Possessors, without any exception or further distinction of Time or Place, or any Consideration to be had of Restitution or Compensation.

XI

But if it happens thro' Inadvertency or Imprudence, or any other Cause whatever, that any Subject of either of the said Two Kings shall do or commit any thing by Land or Sea, or on Fresh Water, any where, contrary to the present Treaty, or that any particular Article thereof is not fulfill'd; this Peace and good correspondence between the said Two Kings shall not on that account be interrupted or infringed but shall remain in its former Force, Strength and Vigour, and the said Subject only shall answer for his own Fact, and undergo the Punishment to be inflicted, according to the Custom and Law of Nations.

XII

But if (which God forbid) the Differences now composed between the said Kings should at any time be renew'd, break out into open War, the Ships, Merchandises and all kind of movable Goods of either Party, which shall be found to be and remain in the Ports and Dominions of the adverse Party, shall not be confiscated or brought under any Inconveniency, but the whole space of Six Months shall be allow'd to the Subjects of both of the said Kings, that they may carry away and transport the foresaid Goods, and any thing else that is theirs, whither they shall think fit, without any molestation.

XIII

For what concerns the Principality of *Orange*, and other Lands and Dominions belonging to the said King of *Great Britain*; the separate Article of the Treaty of *Nimeguen*, concluded between the most Christian King and the States General of the United Provinces the 10th day of *August* 1678, shall according to its Form and Tenor, have full effect; and all things that have been innovated and alter'd, shall be restor'd as they were before. All Decrees, Edicts, and other Acts of what kind soever they be without exception, which are in any manner contrary to the said Treaty, or were made after the conclusion thereof, shall be held to be null and void, without any revival or consequence for the future: And all things shall be restor'd to the said King in the same state, and in the same manner, as he held and enjoy'd them before he was dispossess'd thereof in the time of the War, which was ended by the said Treaty of *Nimeguen*, or which he ought to have held and enjoy'd according to the said Treaty. And that an end may be put to all Trouble, Differences, Processes and Questions, which may arise concerning the same, both the said Kings will name Commissioners, who with full and summary Power may compose and settle all these matters. And forasmuch as by the Authority of the most Christian King, King of *Great Britain* was hindered from enjoying the Revenues, Rights and Profits, as well as his Principality of *Orange* as of other his Dominions, which after the conclusion of the Treaty of *Nimeguen*, until the Declaration of the present War, were under the Power of the said most Christian King, the said most Christian King will restore, and cause to be restor'd in reality with effect, and with the interest due, all those Revenues, Rights and Profits, according to the Declarations and Verifications that shall be made before the said Commissioners.

XIV

The Treaty of Peace concluded between the most Christian King, and the late Elector of *Brandenburg* at *St. Germains en Laye*, the 29th of June 1679. shall be restor'd in all its Articles, and remain in its former Vigour between his sacred most Christian Majesty and his Electoral Highness of *Brandenburg*.

XV

Whereas 'twill greatly conduce to the publick Tranquillity that the Treaty be observ'd, which concluded between his Sacred most Christian Majesty and his Royal Highness of *Savoy*, on the Ninth of *August*, 1696. 'tis agreed that the said Treaty shall be confirm'd by this Article.

XVI

Under this present Treaty of Peace shall be comprehended those who shall be nam'd by either Party, with common consent, before the exchange of Ratifications, or within six Months after. But in the mean time, the most Serene and Mighty Prince WILLIAM King of *Great Britain*, and the most Serene and Mighty Prince LEWIS the most Christian King, gratefully acknowledging the sincere Offices and indefatigable Endeavours, which have been employ'd by the most Serene and Mighty Prince *Charles* K. of *Sweden*, by the interposition of his Mediation, in bringing this happy Work of the Peace, with the Divine Assistance, to the desir'd Conclusion: and to show the like Affection to him, 'tis by consent of all Parties stipulated and agreed, That his said Sacred Royal Majesty of *Sweden* shall with all his Kingdoms, Countrys, Provinces and Rights, be included in this Treaty, and comprehended in the best manner in the present Pacification.

XVII

Lastly, the solemn Ratifications of this present Agreement and Alliance made in due form, shall be deliver'd on both sides, and mutually and duly exchang'd at the Royal Palace of *Reswick*, in the Province of *Holland*, within the space of Three Weeks, to be reckon'd from the Day of the Subscription, or sooner if it may be.

In Testimony of all and every the things before-mention'd, and for their greater Force, and to give them all the Vigour and full Authority they ought to have, the underwritten Ambassadors Extraordinary and Plenipotentiarys, together with the Illustrious and most Excellent the Extraordinary Ambassador Mediator, have sign'd and seal'd the present Instrument of Peace. Done, &c.

SEPARATE ARTICLE

Besides all that is concluded and stipulated by the Treaty of Peace sign'd this present day, the 20th of *September*, it is moreover agreed by the present Separate Article, which shall have the same Force and Effect as if it was inserted word for word in the said Treaty, that the most Christian King shall covenant and agree, and by the present Article he does covenant and agree, That it shall be *free* for the Emperor and the Empire, until the first day of *November* next, to accept the Conditions of Peace lately proposed by the the most Christian King, according to the Declaration made on the first day of this present Month, unless in the mean time it shall be otherwise agreed between his Imperial Majesty and the Empire, and his most Christian Majesty. And in case his Imperial Majesty does not within the time prefix'd accept those Conditions, or that it be no otherwise agreed between his Imperial Majesty and the Empire, and his most Christian Majesty; the said Treaty shall have its full effect, and be duly put in execution, according to its Form and Tenor: and it shall not be lawful for the King of *Great Britain*, directly or indirectly, on any Account or Cause whatsoever, to act contrary to the said Treaty.

Treaty of Peace between Lewis [Louis] XIV, King of France, and the United Provinces; Concluded at Reswick [Ryswick], September the 20th, 1697

In the Name of God and the most Holy Trinity, be it known to all present and to come, that during the course of the bloodiest War, *Europe* hath been afflicted with for a long time, it hath pleas'd the Divine Providence to prepare Christendom to put an end to its Miserys, by forming an ardent Desire of Peace in the Heart of the most High, most Excellent, and most Potent Prince *Lewis* XIV. by the Grace of God, most Christian King of *France* and *Navarre*; his most Christian Majesty having nothing more in view than to render the same by the justness of the Terms solid and perpetual; and the Lords the States General of the United Provinces of the *Low-Countrys*, being desirous seriously to concur, and as much as in them lies to restore the publick Tranquillity, and to re-enter into the ancient Friendship and Affection of his most Christian Majesty, have in the first place consented to acknowledge for this end the Mediation of the most High, most Potent, and most Excellent Prince, *Charles* XI of Glorious Memory, by the Grace of God, King of *Sweden*, of the *Goths* and *Vandals*: But the precipitate Death of that Prince, having thwarted the hope all *Europe* had justly entertain'd in respect to the happy effect of his Counsel and good Offices, his most Christian Majesty and the said Lords the States General persisting in their Resolution forthwith to put a stop to the Effusion of so much Christian Blood, have judg'd they could do no better than to continue to own in the same Quality, the most Potent Prince *Charles* XII, King of *Sweden*, his Son and Successor; who on his part hath also continu'd

the same Endeavours for promoting the Peace between his most Christian Majesty and the said Lords the States General, in the Conferences held for this end in the Castle of *Reswick*, in the Province of *Holland*, between the Ambassadors Extraordinary and Plenipotentiarys nam'd on both sides, viz., on the part of his most Christian Majesty, the Sieur *Nicholas Augustus de Harlay*, Knight, Lord of *Bonncuil*, Count of *Celi*, Counsellor in ordinary to his Majesty in his Council of State, the Sieur *Lewis Verjus*, Kt. Count de *Crecy*, Counsellor in ordinary to the King in his Council of State, Marquiss of *Treon*, Baron of *Convay*, Lord of *Boulay*, the two Churches of *Fort Isle* and *Menillet*, and other Places; and the Sieur *Francis de Callieres*, Kt. Lord of *Callieres*, *Rochechelly* and *Gigny*: and on the part of the Lords the States General, the Sieurs *Anthony Heinfius*, Counsellor and Pensioner of the States of *Holland* and *Westfriezland*, Keeper of the Great Seal, and Superintendent of the Fiefs of the same Province; *Everhard de Weede*, Lord of *Weede*, *Dykvelt*, *Rotelles*, and other Places, Lord Foncier of the Town of *Qudwater*, Dean and Principal of the Imperial Chapter of *St. Mary* in *Utrecht*, *Dyck-Grave* of the *Rhine* in the Province of *Utrecht*, President of the States of the said Province; and *William de Haren*, Grietman of *Bilt*, Deputy from the Nobility to the States of *Friezland*, and Curator of the University of *Franeker*, Deputy in their Assembly on the part of the States of *Holland*, *Utrecht* and *Friezland*: who having implor'd the Divine Assistance, and communicated their full Powers respectively to one another, and having duly exchang'd them by the Intervention and Mediation of the Baron *de Lillienroot*, Ambassador Extraordinary and Plenipotentiary of the King of *Sweden*, who hath perform'd the Office of Mediator with great Prudence, Capacity, and all manner of Candor and Equity; they have, to the Glory of God and the Good of *Christendom*, agreed upon Articles, the Tenour whereof here follows.

I

There shall be for the future between his most Christian Majesty and his Successors, Kings of *France* and *Navarre*, and his Kingdoms on the one part, and the Lords the States General of the United Provinces on the other, a good, firm, faithful and inviolable Peace: and from hence forward all Acts of Hostility, be they of what nature they will, shall cease and be laid aside, between the said King and the said Lords the States General, as well by Sea and on other Waters, as by Land, in all their Kingdoms, Countrys, Provinces and Seignorys; and for all their Subjects and Inhabitants, let them be of what quality and condition they will, without exception of Places or Persons.

II

There shall be a General Amnesty and Oblivion of all that hath been done on either part upon the account of the last War; whether for those, who being born Subjects of *France*, and oblig'd to serve the most Christian King, upon the account of the Imployments and Estates which they posses'd within the boundarys of *France*, have enter'd into and continu'd in the Service of the Lords the States General of the United Provinces, or for those who being born Subjects of the said States General of the United Provinces, or engag'd to serve them by reason of the Imployments and Estates which they possess'd within the Dominions of the United Provinces, enter'd into or continu'd in the Service of his most Christian Majesty: And the said Persons of what Quality and Condition soever they be, without any exception, may and shall re-enter upon, and be effectually allow'd to be restor'd to the Possession and peaceable Enjoyment of all their Estates, Honours, Dignitys, Privileges, Franchises, Rights, Exemptions, Constitutions and Libertys, without their being examin'd, disturbed or incommoded, in general or particular, be the Cause or Pretence what it will upon the account of any thing that has happen'd since the beginning of the said War. And in consequence of this Treaty, and after the same shall be ratify'd, as well by his most Christian Majesty, as by the said Lords the States General, it shall be free for all and every of them in particular, without any Letters of Abolition or Pardon, personally to return into their Houses, and the Enjoyment of their Lands and all other Goods, and to dispose of them as they please.

III

And if any Prizes are taken on either side in the *Baltick Sea*, or that of the *North* from *Terneuse* to the end of the *British* Channel, in the space of four Weeks, or from the end of the Channel to Cape St. *Vincent* in six Weeks time, and beyond that in the *Mediterranean*, and as far as the Line in the space of ten Weeks, and beyond the Line and all the World over in eight Months time, to reckon from the Day of the Publishing of this Peace at *Paris* and the *Hague*: the said Prizes and the Damages done on either side beyond the time limited, shall be accounted for, and all that which shall be taken shall be restor'd, with Reparation of all Damages that may have been sustain'd.

IV

Moreover there shall be between the said King and the said Lords the States General, and their Subjects and Inhabitants reciprocally, a sincere, firm and perpetual Friendship and good Correspondence as well by Sea as by Land, in all and every Place and Places as well within as without *Europe*, without resenting any Offences and Damages that may have been sustain'd as well heretofore as upon the account of the said Wars.

V

And his Majesty and the Lords the States General, by virtue of this Friendship and Correspondence, shall procure and sincerely promote the Good and Prosperity of one another, by yielding all Support, Aid, Counsel and real Assistance, upon all Occasions, and at all Times, to each other; and shall not for the future consent to any Treatys or Negotiations that may be injurious to either side; but shall break them, and mutually inform one another of them, with care and sincerity, as soon as they shall come to the knowledge of them.

VI

Those whose Estates have been seiz'd and confiscated upon the account of the said War, their Heirs, or Assigns, be they of what Quality or Religion soever they will, shall enjoy their Estates, and take possession of them by their own private Authority, and in virtue of this Treaty, without having any need to have recourse to Law, notwithstanding all Incorporations with the Exchequer, Engagements, Donations, Preparatory or Definitive Sentences given for Default or Contempt, in the absence of the Partys, and unheard; Treatys, Agreements, and Transactions, any Renunciations that may have been made of the said Transactions, to exclude the Party from the said Estates, which ought to belong to them; and all and every the Estates, and Rights, which are to be restor'd in conformity to this Treaty, or ought to be restor'd reciprocally to the first Owners, their Heirs or Assigns,

may be sold by the said Proprietors, without being hindred for the want of the consent of any particular Person; and afterwards, the Proprietors of Rents, which on behalf of the Fife shall be constituted in lieu of the sold Estates, as also the rents and Suits being at the Charge of the Fife respectively, may dispose of the Propriety of the same by Sale or otherwise, as they do their other Goods or Estates.

VII

And as the Marquisate of *Bergenopzoom*, with all the Rights and Revenues depending thereon, and generally all the Lands and Goods belonging to the Count *d'Auvérgne* Colonel-General of the Light-Horse of *France*, and which are within the Dominion of the said Lords the States General of the *United Provinces*, have been seized and confiscated upon account of the War, to which this present Treaty ought to put a happy end; it's agreed, That the said Count *d'Auvérgne* shall be restor'd to the Possession of the said Marquisate of *Bergenopzoom*, with its Appurtenances and Dependences; as also to his Rights, Actions, Privileges, Usages and Prerogatives, which he enjoy'd when the Declaration of the War was made.

VIII

All the Countrys, Towns, Places, Lands, Forts, Islands and Seigniorys, as well within as without *Europe*, which may have been taken and seiz'd since the beginning of this War, shall be restor'd on either side, in the same condition as the Fortifications were in when taken, and as to other Buildings in the state they are now, without damaging or destroying any of them, and also without pretending to any Reparation of Damage for what had been demolish'd of them; and particularly the Fort and Settlement of *Pontichery* shall be restor'd on the said Terms to the *French East-India* Company; and as to the Artillery carry'd thither by the *Dutch East-India Company*, as also the Ammunition, Provisions, Slaves and all other Effects, it shall be free for them to dispose of them as they please, as they may in like manner of the Lands, Rights and Privileges they have acquir'd as well of the Prince as of the Inhabitants of the Country.

IX

All Prisoners of War shall be releas'd on both sides, without any Distinction or Reserve, and without paying any Ransom.

X

The raising of Contributions shall cease on both sides, upon the day of the Exchange of the Ratifications of this present Treaty; and any Arrears of the said Contributions, which have been demanded and agreed to, shall not be exacted, but all Pretensions which may depend upon this account, under what title or pretence soever they may be, shall be entirely abolish'd both on the one side and the other: So also Contributions on either side, in respect to the Dominions of the most Christian and Catholick Kings, shall cease upon the exchange of the said Ratifications of this Treaty.

XI

That this Treaty may be made as firm as possible, and so continue, his Majesty and the States General have moreover agreed, and being satisfy'd with the same, they shall, as they do, make as well a general as a particular Renunciation of all manner of Pretensions, as well for, the time past as for the present, be they what they will, that one Party might pretend to upon the other, that so they may for the future cut off all occasions that may arise, and prevent new Differences.

XII

The ordinary course of justice shall be free and open on both sides, and the Subjects both of the one and the other Dominion may pursue their Rights, Suits and Pretensions, according to the Laws and Statutes of each Country; and then without any Distinction, obtain all the Satisfaction that is justly due to them: And if any Letters of Reprisals have been granted on either side, whether before or after the Declaration of the last War, they shall be revok'd and annull'd, saving to the Partys to whom the same have been granted, the Liberty to have right done them by the ordinary Proceedings at Law.

XIII

If thro' Inadvertency or otherwise, any Infraction or other Inconvenience should happen in this Treaty, on the part of his said Majesty, or the said Lords the States General and their Successors; this Peace and Alliance shall for all that continue in its full force, without coming upon that account to any Breach of the Friendship and good Correspondence between them: but the said Contraventions shall immediately be repair'd; and if they happen thro' the fault of some private Men, they only shall be punish'd and chastis'd for them.

XIV

And that the Commerce and Friendship between the said King and the said States General of the *United Provinces* of the *Low-Countrys*, may be the better secur'd for the future, it's concluded and agreed on, That in case hereafter any Interruption of Friendship or Rupture should happen between the Crown of *France* and the States General (which God forbid) the Subjects both of the one and the other Dominion shall always have nine Months time allow'd them to withdraw with their Effects, and to carry them whithersoever they please: This they shall be allow'd to do, as also to sell or transport their Goods and Movables with all Freedom, without giving them any trouble, or pretending, during the said nine Months, to the seizing of their Effects, much less to confine their Persons.

XV

The Treaty of Peace between the most Christian King and the late Elector of *Brandenburg* made at St. *Germain en Laye*, the 29th of June, 1679, shall be re-establish'd between his most Christian Majesty and his Electoral Highness of Brandenburg that now is, in all its Points and Articles.

XVI

As it concerns the publick Tranquillity, that the Peace concluded between his most Christian Majesty and his Royal Highness the Duke of *Savoy*, on the 9th of *August*, 1696. should be exactly observ'd; it's agreed, That the same is confirm'd by this Treaty.

XVII

And as his Majesty and the Lords the States General acknowledg the powerful Offices of the King of *Sweden*, who by his good Counsels and Persuasions hath contributed to the promotion of the publick Safety and Tranquillity; it's agreed by both Partys, That his said *Swedish* Majesty, together with his Kingdoms, shall by name be comprehended in this present Treaty, in the best Form that can be.

XVIII

In this present Treaty of Peace and Alliance, all those who shall be nam'd before the Exchange of the Ratifications, and within six Months after they shall be exchanged, shall be comprehended in this Treaty of Peace and Alliance.

XIX

In like manner, on the part of the States General, the King of *Great Britain*, the King of *Spain*, and all their Allys, who within the space of six Months, to reckon from the exchange of the Ratifications, shall declare their Acceptance of the Peace; as also the thirteen laudable Cantons of *Switzerland*, with their Allys and Confederates, and particularly in the best manner and form that can be, the Republicks and Evangelick Cantons of *Zurich*, *Bern*, *Glaris*, *Basil*, *Schashausen* and *Appenzel*, with all their Allys and Confederates; namely the Republick of *Geneva* and its Dependences, the Town and Country of *Neuschattel*, the Towns of *St. Gall*, *Milhausen* and *Bienne*; also the *Grisons*, and their Dependences, the Citys of *Bremen* and *Embden*; and finally, all Kings, Princes and States, Towns and particular Persons, the Lords the States General do agree, upon their Request made to them shall be comprehended therein.

XX

The said King and the said Lords the States General do consent that the King of *Sweden* as Mediator, and all other Princes and Potentates, who have a mind to come into the same Engagement, may give to his Majesty and the said Lords the States General their Promises and Obligations of Guaranty, for the Execution of every thing that is contain'd in this present Treaty.

XXI

The present Treaty shall be ratify'd and approv'd by the King and Lords the States General, and the Ratifications produc'd within the space of three Weeks or sooner, if it can be done, to reckon from the day of signing.

XXII

And for the greater Confirmation of this Treaty of Peace, and all the Points and Articles contain'd therein, this same Treaty shall be publish'd, verify'd and registred in the Court of Parliament of *Paris*, and in all other Parliments of the Kingdom of *France*, and Chamber of Accounts in *Paris*; as also the said Treaty shall in like manner be publish'd, verify'd and register'd by the said Lords the States General, in the Courts and other Places where such Publications, Verifications and Registrings were wont to be made.

In witness whereof, we his Majesty's Ambassadors, and those of the Lords the States General, by virtue of our respective Powers, have in their Names sign'd these Presents with our own Hands, and set to our Seals. Done at *Reswick* in *Holland*, September the 20th, 1697.

Sign'&
(L.S.) N. LILLIENROOT.
(L.S.) A. IFTEYNSIUS.
(L.S.) E. DF WEEDE.
(L.S.) W. V. HAREN.
(L.S.) N. A. DE HARLAY BONNEUIL.
(L.S.) VERJUS DE CRECY.
(L.S.) DE CALLIERES.

SEPARATE ARTICLE

Besides what has been agreed and concluded on by the Treaty of Peace, between the Ambassadors Extraordinary and Plenipotentiarys of the most Christian King, and those of the Lords the States General of the *United Provinces*, on the 20th of *September*, 1697. it has been farther agreed by this separate Article, which shall have the same force and virtue as if it were inserted word for word in the said Treaty; that his most Christian Majesty will allow, as he does by this present Article, the Emperor and Empire till the first of *November* next, to accept of the Terms of Peace propos'd last by his most Christian Majesty, pursuant to his Declaration of the first of this instant *September*, unless his Imperial Majesty and the Empire may otherways agree with his most Christian Majesty; and in case that the Emperor and Empire shall not accept of the said Terms, or do not otherwise agree with his said most Christian Majesty, the said Treaty of Peace shall have its full power and whole effect, and be executed according to its Tenor and Form so as that the said Lords the States shall neither directly nor indirectly contravene the same under any pretence whatsoever.

In witness whereof, we his Majesty's Ambassadors, and those of the States General, by virtue of our respective Powers, have in their Names, sign'd this separate Article with our own Hands, and set to our Seals. *Reswick* in *Holland*, September 20, 1697.

Sign'd:
(L.S.) A. HFYNSIUS.
(L.S.) E. DE WEEDE.
(L.S.) W. V. HAREN.
(L.S.) N. A. DE HARLAY BONNEUIL.
(L.S.) VERJUS DE CRECY.
(L.S.) DE CALLIERFS.

Treaty of Peace Between Lewis [Louis] XIV, King of France, and Charles II. King of Spain, Concluded at Reswick, September 20, 1697

In the name of God and of the most Holy Trinity, to all present and to come. Be it known that during the Course of the most bloody War wherewith Europe hath been afflicted for a long time, it pleas'd the Divine Providence to prepare Matters to put an end to the Evils of Christendom, by preserving an ardent Desire of Peace in the Hearts of the most high, most excellent, and most potent Prince *Lewis* XIV. By the Grace of God most Christian King of *France* and *Navarre*, and of the most high, most excellent and most potent Prince *Charles* II. Catholick King of the *Spains*: who being equally desirous to concur in good earnest, and as much as in them lies, towards the re-establishing of the publick Tranquillity, and having nothing more in view than to render the same solid and perpetual, by the Equitableness of the Terms; their Majestys have in the first place unanimously agreed to acknowledge for this purpose the Mediation of the most high, most excellent, and most potent Prince of glorious Memory *Charles* XI, by the Grace of God King of *Sweden*, of the *Goths* and *Vandals*: But his unexpected Death having cross'd the hopes, which all Europe had justly conceiv'd of the happy Effects of his Counsels and good Offices; their said Majestys persisting in a Resolution to put a stop as soon as possible to the Effusion of so much Christian Blood, have bethought themselves, that they could do no better than in the same quality to continue to acknowledge the most high, most excellent, and most potent Prince *Charles* XII, King of *Sweden* his Son and Successors, who on his part hath also continu'd the same Endeavours for promoting a Peace between their most Christian and Catholick Majestys, in the Conferences held for this and in the Castle of *Reswick* in the province of *Holland*, between the Ambassadors Extraordinary and Plenipotentiarys nam'd on both sides, viz. for the most Christian King the Sieur *Nickalas Augustus de Harlay*, Knight, Lord of *Bonneuil*, Count of *Cely*, Counsellor in Ordinary to his Majesty in his Council of State; the Sieur *Lewis Verjus*, Knight, Count of *Crecy*, Counsellor in Ordinary to the King in his Counsel of State, Marquiss of *Treon*, Baron of *Couvay*, Lord of *Boulay*, of the two Churches of *Fort Isle* and *Meuillet*, and other Places; the Sieur *Francis de Callieres*, Knight, Lord of *Callieres de la Rochechelly*, and of *Gigny*: and on the part of his Catholick Majesty, *Don Francisco Bernardo de Quires*, Knight of the Order of St. *James*, Counseling to the King in his Royal and Supreme Council of *Castile*; *Don Lewis Alexander de Stockart* Count of *Tremont*, Baron of *Gaesbeke*, Counsellor in the Supreme Council of State for the *Netherlands* at *Madrid* and of that of State and Privy Council in the Low-Countrys: Why after having implor'd the Divine Assistance, and respectively communicated their full Powers to one another, and having duly exchang'd the same by the means and intervention of *Nicholas* Baron *de Lillienroot*, Ambassador Extraordinary and Plenipotentiary from his Majesty the King of *Sweden*, who hath discharg'd the Function of Mediator with so much Prudence, Capacity and Equitableness, they have, to the Glory of God and the Good of *Christendom* agreed on the Articles here following:

I

It is concluded and agreed, that for the future there shall be a good, firm and durable Peace, Confederacy, and perpetual Alliance between the most Christian and Catholick Kings, their Children born and to be born, their Heirs and Successors, their Kingdoms, Territorys, Countrys and Subjects; that they shall love one another as good Brothers, promoting with all their Might the Good, Honour and Reputation of each other, and avoiding in good earnest, and as much as possibly they can, every thing that may occasion a prejudice to either side.

II

In consequence of this Peace and good Union, all Acts of Hostility shall cease between the said Kings, their Subjects and Vassals, as well by Sea and other Waters as by Land, and generally in all Places where War hath been wag'd by their Majesty's Arms, as well between whole Armys as the Garisons of Places: And if they shall contravene the same, by taking one or more Places, whether by Attack, Surprize or Intelligence; and also if they make any Prisoners, or commit other Acts of Hostility by chance or otherwise, Reparation shall be made for such contravention on both sides with all Sincerity, without any delay or difficulty; Restitution being made without any diminution of that which has been seiz'd, and those that have been made Prisoners shall be deliver'd up without any Ransom or Charge.

III

All Causes of Enmity and Misunderstanding shall be forgot and for ever abolished; There shall be a perpetual Oblivion and Amnesty on both sides of every thing transacted during this War, or upon the account of it; without seeking for the future, under any pretence whatever, either directly or indirectly, any amends by way of Law-Suit or otherwise, let the Pretence be what it will; and neither shall their said Majestys, their Subjects, Servants and Adherents show any Resentment, nor pretend to any Reparation for the same.

IV

Gironne, Reses and *Velver* shall be restor'd and put into the possession of his Catholick Majesty, in the State they were taken, together with the Artillery found therein at the same time; and in general all the other Towns, Places, Forts and Chastellanys whatsoever, which during this War have been possess'd by the Arms of his most Christian Majesty in the Principality of *Catalonia*, or elsewhere in *Spain*, together with their Appurtenances, Dependences and things annext to them, shall be restor'd in the Condition they are at present, without retaining, reserving, weakening or damnifying any thing appertaining to them. The City of *Barcelona*, the Fort and Fortifications depending thereon, together with all the Artillery, shall also be restor'd into the hands, and put under the Dominion and Sovereignty of the Catholick King, in the same Condition all was found at the time they were taken, with all the Appurtenances, Dependences and other matters annext thereunto.

V

The City and Fortress of *Luxemburg*, in the Condition 'tis at this day, without demolishing, changing, diminishing, weakening or worsting any of the Works, Forts and Fortifications of the same, with the Artillery found therein at the time it was taken; together with the Province and Dutchy of *Luxemburg*, and the County of *Chiny* in all their Circumstances, and every thing comprehended therein, with their Appurtenances, Dependences and things annext, shall be given up, put into the hands, and under the Power, Sovereignty, Dominion and Possession of the Catholick King, in good earnest, to be enjoy'd by the said Catholick King, in the same manner as it was or might have been at and before the Treaty of *Nimeguen*, without withholding or reserving any thing, save what has been yielded to his said most Christian Majesty by the aforesaid Treaty of Peace.

VI

The Fortress of *Charleroy* shall in like manner be put into the hands, and under the Power and Dominion of his Catholick Majesty, with its Dependences, in the Condition 'tis now, without breaking, demolishing, weakening or otherwise damnifying any thing therein; as also the Artillery that was in it at the time it was taken.

VII

The City of *Mons*, the Capital of the Province of *Hainault*, shall also be put into the Possession, and under the Dominion and Sovereignty of his Catholick Majesty, together with its Works and Fortifications, in the State they are at present, without breaking, demolishing, weakening or worsting any thing belonging thereunto; together with the Artillery found therein at the time it was taken; also the Bayliwick, Provostship, Appurtenances and Dependences of the same Town, in all the parts thereof, in the same manner as the Catholick King did, or

might enjoy the same at and before the said Treaty: As also the Town of *Aeth*, in the Condition it was found when last taken, without breaking, demolishing, weakening, or damnifying any thing therein with the Artillery found there at the same time; also the Bayliwick, Chastellany, Appurtenances, Dependences and Annexes of the said Town, as they were yielded up by the Treaty of *Nimeguen*, except the Places hereafter nam'd, *viz.* the Burg of St. *Anthony Vaux, Guarrain, Romecroix, Bethome, Constantine*, the Fief of *Paradis*; the said last Places being within the Boundarys of the County of *Tourney*: and the said Fief of *Paradis*; together with the Villages of *Kans, Kavines, Meles, Mourcourt, Kain, le Mont de St. Audeberg*, call'd *de la Trinity, Fontenay, Maulray, Hernies, Calvralle* and *Wier*, with their Parishes, Appurtenances and Dependences, without any reserve, shall remain in the possession of the most Christian King; the Province of *Hainault*, continuing however under the Dominion of his Catholick Majesty, yet without prejudice to what has been yielded to his most Christian Majesty by the preceding Treatys.

VIII

The Town of *Courtray* shall be put into the hands, and under the Dominion and Sovereignty of the Catholick King, in the condition 'tis now, together with the Artillery found therein when it was last taken; as also the Chastellany of the said Town, Appurtenances, Dependences, and other things annext thereto, conformable to the Treaty of *Nimeguen*.

IX

The said most Christian King shall also restore to his Catholick Majesty, all the Towns, Places, Forts, Castles and Ports, which his Armys have or might have posses'd to the day of the Peace, and even after it, in what place of the World soever they are; as his said Catholick Majesty shall in like manner restore to his most Christian Majesty, all the Places, Forts, Castles and Ports, which his Armies might have seiz'd during this War, even to the day of the proclaiming of the Peace, be they where they will.

X

All the Places, Towns, Boroughs and Villages, which the most Christian King has seiz'd, and made Reunions of, since the Treaty of *Nimeguen*, in the Provinces of *Luxemburg, Namur, Brabant, Flanders, Hainault*, and other Provinces of the *Netherlands* (according to the List of the said Reunions produc'd on the behalf of his Catholick Majesty, in the Acts of this Negotiation, a Copy whereof shall be annex'd to this present Treaty) shall wholly and always remain in the possession of his Catholick Majesty, except the eighty two Towns, Boroughs, Places and Villages contain'd in the excepted List, produc'd also on the part of his most Christian Majesty, and to which he makes Pretension on the account of being Dependences upon the Towns of *Charlemont, Maubeuge*, and other Places yielded to his most Christian Majesty by the Treatys of *Aix-la-Chapelle* and *Nimeguen*: In respect to which eighty two Villages only, a List whereof shall in like manner be annex'd to this present Treaty, it's mutually agreed, that presently after the signing of the present Treaty, Commissioners shall be nam'd on both sides, as well to regulate to which of the two Kings the said eighty two Towns, Boroughs, Places or Villages, or any of them ought to belong, as to agree to make Exchanges for the Places and Villages within the Confines of the Countrys under the Dominion both of the one and the other: And in case the said Commissioners cannot agree, their most Christian and Catholick Majestys shall put the same to the final determination of the States General of the *United Provinces*, whom the said Lords the Kings have mutually consented to be Arbitrators; yet without being a Bar to the Plenipotentiarys of the most Christian and Catholick Kings agreeing otherwise amicably about them between themselves, and even before the Ratification of this Treaty, if it be possible; provided all Difficultys as well in reference to the said Reunion, as to the Limits and Dependences, shall on either side be intirely silenc'd and determin'd: In consequences whereof all Suits, Sentences, Separations, Incorporations, Commissions, Decrees, Confiscations, Reunions, Declarations, Regulations, Edicts, and in general all Acts whatsoever, denounc'd in the name on the behalf of his most Christian Majesty, upon the account of the said Reunions, whether by the Parliament or Chamber set up at *Metz*, or by any other Tribunals of justice, Intendant, Commissions, Delegations against his Catholick Majesty and his Subjects, shall cease, and be revok'd and annull'd for ever, as if they had never been; and moreover the Generality of the said Provinces shall belong to his Catholick Majesty, except all those Towns and Places, together with their Appurtenances and Dependences, that have been yielded to his most Christian Majesty by the preceding Treatys.

XI

All the said Places, Towns, Boroughs and Villages, Circumstan-Oces, Dependences and Annexes, quitted and yielded by his most Christian Majesty, without any reserve, shall be put again into the possession of his Catholick Majesty, to be enjoy'd by him, together with all the Privileges, Advantages, Profits and Revenues depending thereupon, with the same extent, and the same Rights of Property, Dominion and Sovereignty, as he enjoy'd them before the last War, and at and before the Treatys of *Aix-la-Chapelle* and *Nimeguen*, and all in the same manner as he might or ought to have enjoy'd the same.

XII

The Restitution of the said Places shall be perform'd on the part of the most Christian King, really and sincerely, without any delay or difficulty, under any Cause or Pretence, in respect to him or them who shall be deputed by the said Catholick King, immediately after the Ratification of this Treaty, without demolishing, weakening, diminishing, or any way damaging the said Towns, and without pretending to or demanding the Reimbursement of any Charges, on the account of Fortifications, publick Edifices, and Buildings erected in the said Places; nor the payment of that which might be due to Soldiers and military Persons, that are found there at the time of the Restitution.

XIII

The most Christian King shall withdraw out of all the said Places, which he restores to the Catholick King, and all the Artillery which his said Majesty had caus'd to be brought into the said Places since they have been taken as also all the Pouder, Ball, Provision, and Ammunition found there, at the time they are put into the hands of his said Catholick Majesty; and those Persons whom the most Christian King shall depute for this end, may for the space of two months make use of the Waggons and Boats of the Country: The Passage, as well by Water as by Land, shall be free for them to carry the said Ammunition into the most neigh-

bouring Places belonging to his most Christian Majesty: The Governors, Commanders, Officers and Magistrates of the Places and Countrys thus restor'd, shall facilitate, as much as in them lies, the removal away and carriage of the said Ammunition and Artillery: The Officers, Soldiers and military Men, who do evacuate the said Places, may also from thence withdraw and carry away the Movables appertaining to them, but yet so as that they are not allow'd to exact any thing from the Inhabitants of the said Places, or of the open Country, nor to damnify the Houses, or to take away any thing belonging to the Inhabitants.

XIV

The Prisoners, of what Quality or Condition soever they be, shall on both sides be set at liberty, and without any ransom, as soon as the Ratifications are exchang'd, they paying their Debts, and whatever they lawfully ow'd there. And if any Persons have been put on board the Gallys of their said Majestys, by reason and because of the Misfortune of the said Wars only, be it for what cause or occasion soever, they shall forthwith be set at liberty without any delay or difficulty, be the cause or the occasion what it will, and without demanding upon that account any thing for their Ransom or Maintenance.

XV

The Subjects of either side, be they who they will, may, having regard to the Usages, Laws and Customs of the respective Countrys, by virtue of this Peace and strict Friendship, go, come, tarry, traffick and return to and from each other's Countrys, as good Traders, as they please, as well as by Sea as by Land, and other Waters, to trade and deal together; and shall be supported and protected in each other's Countrys as good Subjects, paying the just Customs requir'd in all the usual Places and others, which shall be laid by the said Kings or their Successors.

XVI

All the Papers, Letters and Documents appertaining to the Countrys, Lands and Signiorys, which are yielded and restor'd to the said Kings by the present Treaty of Peace, shall be produc'd and deliver'd up sincerely on each side, within three months after the Ratifications of this Treaty shall be exchang'd, in what Places soever the said Papers and Documents may be found, even those which might have been taken away out of the Citadel of *Ghent*, and the Chamber of Accounts at *Lisle*.

XVII

Contributions settled or demanded on either side, Reprisals, Demands of Forage, Corn, Wood, Cattle, Utensils, and other forts of Impositions on the Countrys of either of the two Sovereigns, shall cease presently after the Ratification of this Treaty; and all the Arrears or Parts thereof that may be due shall be demanded on neither side, under any Title or pretence whatsoever.

XVIII

All the Subjects on either side, as well Ecclesiastical as Secular Bodys, Communitys, Universitys and Colleges, are restor'd as well to the enjoyment of their Honours, Dignitys and Benefices, of which they were possess'd before the War, as to all and every their Rights, Movables and Immovables, Rents of Redemption, whereof the Principal is in being, and passable Rents, seiz'd and enjoy'd since the said times, as well upon the account of the War, as for having follow'd the contrary Party; together with their Rights, Actions and Successions to the Survivors, even since the War began: yet without demanding or pretending to satisfaction for the Produce and Income receiv'd or due during the War, since the seizing of the said immovable Goods, Revenues and Benefices, to the day of the publication of this Treaty.

XIX

In like manner they cannot demand nor pretend to any Debts, Effects and Movables, which have been confiscated before the said day; so as that neither the Creditors of such Debts, the Depositors of such Effects and their Heirs, or any pretending thereunto, shall not sue for, nor pretend to recover the same: Which Re-establishments, in the form aforesaid, shall be in favour of those who have follow'd the contrary Party; insomuch that by the means of this Treaty they are to return into the favour of their Prince and Sovereign, as also into the possession of their Goods and Estates, as they are found to exist at the concluding and signing of this Treaty.

XX

And the restoring of the said Subjects both on the one and the other side, shall be done pursuant to the 21st and 22d Articles of the Treaty of Nimeguen, notwithstanding all or any of the Donations, Concessions, Declarations, Confiscations, Commissions, preparatory and definitive Sentences, given for contumacy in the absence of Partys, and the same unheard: Which Sentences and judgments thereupon shall be void and of none effect, as if never given and pronounc'd; with full and entire liberty for the said Partys to return into the Countrys, out of which they had withdrawn before, personally to enjoy their Goods and Movables, Rents and Revenues, or to fix their Abode of the said Countrys, wheresoever they please, and at their own Choice and Election without using any Constraint upon them on that account. And in case they shall rather chuse to dwell elsewhere, they may depute or entrust such unsuspected Persons, as they shall think fit, to manage and enjoy their said Goods, Rents and Revenues; but this shall not extend to Benefices that require Residence, which ought to be personally serv'd.

XXI

The 24th and 25th Articles of the said Treaty of *Nimeguen* concerning Benefices shall be executed; and consequently those who have had Benefices confer'd upon them by either of the two Kings, who in the time of the Collation possess'd the Towns and Countrys where the said Benefices were situated, shall be maintain'd in the possession and enjoyment of the said Benefices.

XXII

The Subjects on both sides shall have liberty and full power to sell, exchange, alienate, and otherwise to dispose, as well by Deed as last Will and Testament, of their Goods, and movable and immovable Effects, which they have or shall have in the Dominions of the other Sovereign; and any one may buy them, Subjects or Foreigners, so as that there is no need of any Grant, Leave, or other Act whatsoever, for this Sale or Buying, but only this Treaty.

XXIII

As there are Rents laid upon the Generality of some Provinces, part of which are possess'd by his most Christian Majesty, and the other by the Catholick King; it's concluded and agreed, that each shall pay his Quota, and Commissioners shall be nam'd to regulate the Proportion each King ought to pay.

XXIV

Rents lawfully fix'd or due upon the Domains by the preceding Treatys, and the payment whereof shall appear in the Accounts given to the Chambers of Accounts by the Receivers of their most Christian and Catholick Majestys, before the said Cessions, shall be paid by their said Majestys to the Creditors of the said Rents be they under whole Dominion they will, whether *Frenchmen*, *Spaniards*, or any other Nation, without any distinction.

XXV

And as a good and firm Peace is made by this Treaty as well by Sea as by Land, between the said Kings in all their Kingdoms, Countrys, Territorys, Provinces and Signiorys; and that all Hostilitys ought to cease for the future: It's stipulated, that if any Prizes are taken on either side in the *Baltick*, or in the *North Sea*, from *Terncuse* in *Norway* to the end of the *British* Channel, in the space of four Weeks; from the end of the said Channel as far as *Cape St. Vincent*, in the space of six Weeks; and from thence in the *Mediterranean*, and as far as the *Line*, in the space of six Months; beyond the Line, and all the other parts of the World, in the space of eight Months, to reckon from the day of proclaiming this present Treaty: the said Prizes which shall be taken on either side, after the said Terms, shall be restor'd with satisfaction made for the Damages sustain'd by such Capture.

XXVI

In case of a Rupture, which God forbid, there shall be six Months time given to the Subjects on either side, to withdraw and carry off their Effects and Persons whither they please; and they shall be allow'd to do it with all freedom, and without any let or hindrance; and none are suffer'd to seize the said Effects, much less are their Persons to be detain'd.

XXVII

The Troops on either side shall withdraw presently after the ratifying of this Treaty, into the Countrys and Territorys of their own Sovereigns, and into such Parts and Places as are reciprocally to remain and belong to their Majestys, pursuant to this Treaty, without tarrying, under any pretence whatsoever, in the Dominions of the other Sovereign, nor in like manner in the Places which hereafter ought to remain and belong to him: And as soon as the Treaty is signed there shall be a Cessation of Arms and Hostilitys in all Places under the Dominions of the said Kings, as well by Sea and other Waters as by Land.

XXVIII

It hath also been agreed, that the receiving of Dutys and Customs, which the most Christian King is in possession of, in all the Countrys which he surrenders to the day of the actual Restitution of the Places upon which the said Countrys are dependent; and that that which shall be in Arrear after the said Restitution, shall be faithfully paid to them who have farm'd the same; as also that at the same time the Proprietors of Woods, confiscated within the Dependences of those Places which ought to be restor'd to his Catholick Majesty, shall re-enter upon possession of their Goods, and of all the Wood which they shall find on the Spot: it being always understood, that the selling or cutting of all Wood shall cease on either side, on the day of the signing of the present Treaty.

XXIX

The Treaty of *Nimeguen*, and the preceding ones, shall be put in execution according to their form and tenor, except in the Points and Articles from which they have before derogated, or wherein, in the last place some alteration is made in the present Treaty.

XXX

All Law-Proceedings and Judgments pronounc'd between private Persons by the judges or other Officers of his most Christian Majesty, who have been fixed as well in the Towns and Places which he hath enjoyed by virtue of the Treaty of *Aix-la-Chapelle*, and which since have been yielded to his Catholick Majesty, as in those that belong to the most Christian King, by virtue of the Treaty of *Nimeguen*, or which he has been in possession of since the said Treaty; and in like manner the Decrees of the Parliament of Tourney, made in respect to Differences and Law-Suits, prosecuted by the Inhabitants of the said Towns and their Dependences, during the time that they have been subject to his most Christian Majesty, shall take place and have their full effect, as if the said King continu'd Lord and Possessor of the said Towns and Countrys; and the said Judgments and Decrees shall not be revok'd, question'd and annul'd, nor the execution of them retarded or hindred. However, it shall be lawful for Persons to have a rehearing of the Cause, according to the Order and Disposition of the Laws and Ordinances; the Judgments nevertheless remaining in their full force and virtue, without any prejudice to that which is stipulated in this respect in the 21st Article of the said Treaty of *Nimeguen*.

XXXI

The Town and Castle of *Dinaut* shall be restor'd by the most Christian King to the Bishop and Prince of *Liege*, in the state it was when possessed by the King's Arms.

XXXII

His most Christian Majesty having express'd his Desire that the Isle of *Ponza* in the *Mediterranean* be restor'd to the Duke of *Parma*, his Catholic Majesty, in consideration of the Offices of his most Christian Majesty, has been pleas'd to declare, that he will withdraw the Soldiers he may have there, and put that Island into the Power and Possession of the Duke of *Parma*, as soon as this Treaty shall be ratify'd.

XXXIII

As it conduces to the publick Tranquillity, that the Peace concluded at *Turin* on the 29th of *August*, 1696. between the most Christian King and his Royal Highness of *Savoy*, should also be exactly observ'd, it hath been thought convenient to confirm it by, and to comprehend it in the present Treaty, in all its Points or Articles, such as are contain'd in the Copy sign'd and seal'd by the Plenipotentiarys of *Savoy*, and which shall be annext to this present Treaty: for the maintenance of which Treaty, and this now in hand, their Majestys give their Guaranty to his Royal Highness.

XXXIV

Their said Majestys acknowledging the good Offices and Endeavours which the most Serene King of *Sweden* hath contin-ually imploy'd for the restoring of Peace; they have agreed, that his *Swedish* Majesty shall by name be comprehended in this present Treaty, in the best form and manner that can be.

XXXV

All those who shall be nam'd on either part by common Consent, before the Exchange of the Ratifications, shall be comprehended in this Peace, Alliance and Friendship, within the space of six months after they shall be exchanged.

XXXVI

The said most Christian and Catholick Kings consent, that his *Swedish* Majesty in quality of Mediator, and all other Kings, Princes and States, who are willing to enter into the like Engagements, may give their Promises and Obligations of Guaranty to their Majestys, for the Execution of all that is contain'd in this present Treaty.

XXXVII

And for the greater confirmation of this Treaty of Peace, and all the Points and Articles contain'd therein, the present Treaty shall be publish'd, verify'd and registered as well in the Grand Council and other Councils and Chambers of Accounts belonging to the said Catholick King in the *Low-Countrys*, as in the other Councils of the Crowns of *Castile* and *Arragon*, all pursuant and according to the form contain'd in the Treaty of *Nimeguen*, in the Year 1678; as in like manner the said Treaty shall be publish'd, verify'd and register'd in the Court of the Parliament of *Paris*, and in all other Parliaments of the Kingdom of *France*, and in the Chamber of Accounts in the said city of *Paris*: of which Publications and Registerings, Extracts shall be taken and deliver'd on both sides within the space of three Months after the publication of this Treaty.

XXXVIII

The Points and Articles abovemention'd, together with the Contents of each of them, have been treated of, agreed to, passed and stipulated between the said Ambassadors Extraordinary and Plenipotentiarys of the said Catholick and most Christian Kings, in their Majestys Name; which Plenipotentiarys, by virtue of the Powers they receiv'd, have promis'd, and do promise, under the penalty of all and every the respective Estates, in Possession or Reversion, of the Kings, their Masters, that they shall be inviolably observ'd and fulfill'd, to have them sincerely and unfeignedly ratify'd, without any Addition made thereunto; and to produce the Ratifications in authentick Form; wherein this whole Treaty shall be inserted word for word, within six Weeks, to commence from the Day of the Date of this Treaty, and sooner, if possible. Besides, the said Plenipotentiarys have, and do promise in the said Names, that when the said Letters of Ratification are produc'd, the said most Christian King shall as soon as may be, in the presence of such Person or Persons as the Catholick King deputes solemnly swear upon the Cross, Evangelists, Canons of the Mass, and his Honour, to observe and fully, really, and in all sincerity to observe and fulfil all the Articles contain'd in this present Treaty; and the same shall also be done as soon as possible, by the said Lord the Catholick King, in the presence of such Person or Persons as the most Christian King shall depute. In witness of all which the said Plenipotentiarys have subscrib'd their Names to this present Treaty, and put to their Seals. *Done at* Reswick *in* Holland, Sept. *the 20th*, 1697. Thus sign'd in the Original:

(L.S.) LILLIENROOT.
(L.S.) DON FRANCISCO BERNARDO DE QUIROS.
(L.S.) THE COUNT DE TIREMONT.
(L.S.) HARLAY BONNEUIL.
(L.S.) VERJUS DE CRECY.
(L.S.) FRANCIS DE CALLIERES.

SEPARATE ARTICLE OF THE TREATY OF PEACE
BETWEEN LEWIS [LOUIS] XIV, KING OF FRANCE,
AND CHARLES II, KING OF SPAIN,
CONCLUDED AT RESWICK,
SEPTEMBER THE 20TH, 1697

Over and above what has been concluded and agreed on by the Treaty of Peace between the Ambassadors extraordinary and Plenipotentiarys of the most Christian King, and those of the Catholick King, this 20th day of *September* 1697. It's further agreed by this present Separate Article, which shall have the same virtue and force as if it were inserted word for word in the said Treaty, that his most Christian Majesty shall allow, as by this present Article he does allow, the Emperor and the Empire to the first of *November* next, to accept of the terms of Peace propos'd last by his most Christian Majesty, pursuant to a Declaration made on the first Day of this instant *September*, if his Imperial Majesty and the Empire cannot agree any other way with his most Christian Majesty: And in case they do not within the said time accept of the said Conditions, or do not agree some other way with his most Christian Majesty, this Treaty of Peace shall have its full and entire force, and be executed according to its Tenour and Form, without being any way contraven'd by the said Catholick King, directly or indirectly, under any pretence whatsoever. In witness whereof we the Ambassadors of his most Christian and Catholick Majestys, by virtue of our respective Powers, have in their Names sign'd this separate Article with our own Hands, and put our Seals thereto, at the Castle of Reswick, in the Province of Holland, September 20, 1697.

(L.S.) DON FRANCISCO BERNARDO DE QUIROS.
(L.S.) COUNT DE TIREMONT.
(L.S.) N. LILLIENROOT.
(L.S.) OF HARLAY BONNEUIL.
(L.S.) DE CALLIERES.

Consequences

At Ryswick the glory days of Louis's reign came to a close. French fortunes would soon reach their nadir at the turn of the new century during the War of the Spanish Succession and the Seven Years' War, as a result of which the French lost their entire New World empire and began the long tumble into a national economic disaster that, ultimately, led to revolution and the overthrow of Louis's ancien régime.

Part Four
THE AGE OF REASON

INTRODUCTION

Since the beginning of the Renaissance, the sovereigns of Europe's emerging nation-states had characteristically attempted to enlarge upon their authority and assume new rights, especially in the administration of justice and finance. Not all of them became the kind of absolute monarch that Louis XIV became in France, but then not all of them had the way paved for them by such brilliant and devious diplomats as Cardinals Richelieu and Mazarin. If Frederick the Great's absolutism was limited by the fractured nature of the Holy Roman Empire, or Charles I by the growing power of Parliament, the kind of power and freedom of action practiced by the "Sun King" in France was their ideal, something to emulate.

Absolute monarchy had evolved out of conflicts within and challenges outside the state, notably war. Once in authority, the national kings with their fashionably professional armies continued to fight, and the constant pressure of their recurrent warfare reinforced their hold on power. The expanded powers of the absolute monarchs, especially their increasing control of the purse strings of the state, allowed them a broad range of patronage. They introduced to the courts of Europe some original thinkers; the age soon witnessed the rise of many others. This new intellectual cadre was an outgrowth of the philosophical chaos first spawned by the attack of radical theologians and cynical political theorists on the Catholic Church's waning medieval order. Fresh, innovative philosophers, political pamphleteers, and scientists—Montesquieu, Berkeley, Locke, Hume, Kepler, Descartes, Bacon, Newton, Voltaire, Rousseau, Kant, to name but a few—were fomenting an intellectual turmoil called the Enlightenment in the wake of the tumultuous rise of the modern nation-state.

Kings such as Louis the XIV and Sweden's Gustavus II Adolphus had imagined themselves God's Lieutenant or First Servant of the State in response to a generation of courtiers and political theoreticians, men like Cardinal Richelieu and Niccolò Machiavelli, who had found the traditional constitutions of medieval society wanting yet whose classical education and religious upbringing had schooled them to look for strong rulers within a hierarchy. The more unsettling Enlightenment thinkers, however, did not necessarily support the idea of an absolute monarchy within a strong secular state; to the contrary, some of them raised expectations, especially among the merchant class, that undercut such hierarchical obsessions.

This only reinforced the ruling classes' now well-established attraction to strong monarchs as protectors of ancient privileges and as bulwarks against social change. For 150 years, Europe's upper classes remained disposed toward the ethos of absolutism, and kings fought continuous wars to expand their "divine rights" and their nations' power at the expense of other ruling houses and other nations. The diplomacy of the age often reflected these tensions, offering broad religious, moral, and proprietorial assertions to settle what were, in effect, the disputes of a few families grown recently powerful.

The New Equilibrium

When the War of the Spanish Succession broke out at the turn of the new century in 1701, the ancien régime of Louis XIV was already suffering a decline. Louis in many ways had taught Europe what a nation could be, and now he was to pay for that lesson. Under the TREATY OF RYSWICK, near the end of the century past, Louis had been forced, following his war with the League of Augsburg, to renounce most of his great military conquests. With the TREATY OF UTRECHT in 1713, French fortunes would reach not quite their nadir—since heroic military efforts and clever diplomacy allowed Louis to recoup some losses—but nevertheless, French expansion under the old regime came to a definite standstill.

It had all started with the growing decrepitude of the Spanish Empire. The Austrian Hapsburgs had been harrying the ailing, incompetent, and, most important, heirless Spanish king, Charles II, with claims to some of his Iberian holdings that had already been recognized under earlier agreements. Before he could straighten out the mess with the Hapsburgs, the old king died and left a deathbed will ceding the whole of the empire to the duke of Anjou, the grandson of Louis XIV. The Sun King tried to appease the Hapsburgs with offers of land and other concessions recognizing many of their previous claims, but they were having none of it.

Then there were the English and the Dutch, rising commercial powers, who feared that the French might establish hegemony in Spanish America and the Spanish—that is, the southern—Netherlands. These conditions led to the second Grand Alliance against the French. The duke of Marlborough was brilliant on the battlefield, smashing French-allied Bavaria at Blenheim, and the French suffered gravely at Ramillies and Oudenarde. Then the fall of the bellicose Whig government in Britain and extraordinary French efforts at the Battle of Malpaquet, indicating a stiffening resistance, led to the opening of negotiations in 1711.

Not only did Utrecht signal the eclipse of the Sun King, it also marked the virtual vanishing of the Spanish from any real role in the affairs of the evolving European state system. Even though a Bourbon—Philip V—did indeed succeed to the Spanish throne, it was agreed that it would remain permanently separated from the French, and it did. Austria got the Spanish lands in Italy and the southern Netherlands, although the Dutch insisted they be allowed to throw up a line of fortresses there to serve as a barrier against the Hapsburgs. The real winners at Utrecht, however, were the English. They got Hudson Bay, Nova Scotia, and Newfoundland—enough to put them in a good position when it came time to eliminate the French entirely from the North American continent come the Seven Years' War. From Spain, England took Gibraltar and Minorca, the better to protect her expanding Mediterranean trade, and, not insignificantly, the exclusive right to traffic slaves in Spain's American possessions, which soon became a general trading privilege for all the New World. In short, Utrecht not only promoted British commercial interests but more than that confirmed her commercial supremacy. In a broader sense, the Peace of Utrecht established an equilibrium in Europe that would last virtually unchallenged until 1740.

Rising Stars

When Frederick II came to the throne of Prussia in 1740, the realm he inherited had been a kingdom for only two generations. A hundred years before, Germany had been a patchwork of several hundred supposedly independent principalities, fragmented states that had achieved their autonomy by challenging the authority of the House of Hapsburg's unwieldy Holy Roman Empire during the horrors of the Thirty Years' War. Frederick's great-grandfather, Frederick Wilhelm, was a Hohenzollern prince and elector of Brandenburg who ruled over a number of scattered territories in the north of the old Empire. Sometimes by war, sometimes by diplomacy, more often by astute marriages, the House of Hohenzollern had brought together distant and disparate holdings. Berlin, the old heartland of the electorate, lay some 400 miles from the Baltic province of East Prussia, from which it was cut off by a good-sized slab of Poland, while far to the west lay small counties like Cleves, Mark, and Ravensburg, the last of these closer to Amsterdam than Berlin. Yet Frederick Wilhelm, the Great Elector, by sheer will, somehow began to weld these scattered lands into a state ruled by a centralized government.

For this kingdom, Frederick Wilhelm's son was granted a crown by the Hapsburg emperor and began calling himself Frederick I, king *in* Prussia. (He could not style himself king *of* Prussia, since East Prussia was ruled by Poland; nor could he claim to be king of Brandenburg, since that would give him the right to grant titles of nobility within the Holy Roman Empire, an enterprise profitable enough that the Hapsburgs wanted it for themselves.)

In 1713, Frederick Wilhelm I succeeded his father, Frederick I, and immediately abandoned the French manners and excessive ostentation of the first king in Prussia's court. He lived frugally, fostered what would become the famed Prussian military style, and continued the work of his grandfather and namesake: strengthening the state and expanding and improving his army. When he produced an heir, he tried to regulate his life just as he was regulating his army and his country, and when young Frederick II showed a liking for such unmanly pastimes as card games, flute playing, and novel reading in addition to his military drills, his father subjected the boy to a series of public humiliations. An aborted plot to escape to England and beg for asylum led to the court-martial and beheading of the young friend who helped Frederick come up with the plan, and Frederick himself was tossed in jail. He gave up and formally submitted to his father, who left Frederick at his death a well-structured if puritanical military state and an army mustering 80,000 troops, equal to that of an Austria 10 times the size of Prussia. Despite his father, the 28-year-old Frederick who acceded to his throne was an admirer of Voltaire and determined to create a Prussia embracing the best principles of the Enlightenment. On the other hand, thanks to his father, Frederick was ready for military challenge when it came.

This time it was the Hapsburgs who were at the root of the new instability in the European system. Emperor Charles VI, like the Spanish king 40 years before, was about to die without an heir, at least without a male heir. His plan had been to leave the rule of Austria, Hungary, Bohemia, and the southern Netherlands to his daughter Maria Theresa. Although her sex barred her from ruling in Germany as Holy Roman Emperor in her own right, she could share the crown with her husband if he were elected emperor. To these ends Charles secured a "Pragmatic Sanction" guaranteeing Maria Theresa the succession to all the Hapsburg domains signed by the major European states, including Prussia. When she came to the throne the same year as Frederick, however, he seized the Austrian province of Silesia with relative ease for, as he said, the "reason of state." Since Bavaria, Spain, and France also wanted to plunder what they now perceived as an Austria grown weak, Frederick's action sparked a general conflict called the War of the Austrian Succession.

Maria Theresa, herself a mere 23 upon her accession, had, like Frederick, abandoned her beloved youthful pursuits—riding, dancing, and playing music—to immerse herself in the affairs of state. Unschooled in politics, she was stubborn and deeply religious, both of which helped her in the long run, not only to secure her hereditary lands, but also to reign over them effectively for four decades. Yet just now she was new to the job and unsure of herself, and she soon came to terms with Frederick by ceding him Silesia. That did not stop the others, who continued to fight on in Bohemia and in the Austrian Netherlands. There the French achieved some noteworthy successes, but Maria Theresa did not give up.

Meanwhile, Austria's ally, Britain, which was winning the war at sea and threatening France's rich West Indian colonies, figured it was time to bring hostilities to a close. The British warned Maria Theresa they would cut the subsidies to her and her army unless she would agree to negotiate. While the 1748 treaty of AIX-LA-CHAPELLE saw no changes in territory, really, outside Prussia's taking possession of Silesia, it did signal the emergence of Brandenburg-Prussia under Frederick "the Great" as a major player among the European nations, one of the two German keys—the other being Austria—to a new balance of power on the Continent.

A Spark in the Wilderness

Britain became the maintainer of that new balance in the 1750s. The British saw it as essential that they preserve Prussia and use her as a counterweight to French power on the Continent, especially since France was now a threat to the Austrian Netherlands. In large measure this had to do with the struggle for empire going on between the French and the British, particularly in colonial North America. England's colonies were mostly gathered into compact settlements along the Atlantic seaboard, while the French, much fewer in number, had nevertheless been spreading down from Canada into the vast American interior and effectively expanding the French fur trade with the American Indians. A France fully occupied in Europe was a France that could ill afford the expense and attention required to secure its hold on the Ohio and Mississippi Valleys, instead relying on the thin string of far-flung and weakly garrisoned forts and trading posts it had been establishing.

After the War of the Austrian Succession, Frederick the Great turned conservative, concentrating on holding Silesia. Meanwhile, Maria Theresa, determined to win it back, turned to yet another woman who had come to occupy a European throne. Empress Elizabeth, daughter of Peter the Great, had—with the support of the Imperial Guard—seized power in Russia in 1741. Now she and Maria Theresa entered into secret agreements that contemplated the near-dismemberment of Prussia. Thus it was that Britain rushed to Frederick's side, supplying Prussia now with the vital British subsidies that had once sustained Austria.

Meanwhile, in 1754 an undeclared war had begun smoldering along the French and British frontiers in North America. Since the conflict between France's European and colonial interests was weakening her hand, she undertook a famous "reversal of alliances" in the so-called Diplomatic Revolution of 1756, in which the French agreed to support their old enemy, the House of Hapsburg, in its bid to reclaim Silesia in return for the cession to France of the long-coveted southern Netherlands. Thus, France, Austria, and Russia were linked against England and Prussia, and the stage was set for a major European conflict with ramifications in America and India.

This virtual world war waited only for a spark. In America, an unknown young militia major named George Washington, sent into the Ohio wilderness to warn off the French, bungled the job and massacred a French diplomatic mission he thought was a war party, murdering in the process a French nobleman. As a scandalized Europe prepared for a general war, Frederick of Prussia—aware via the British of the secret Austro-Russian plans to chop up his kingdom—struck first through Saxony. On August 26, 1756, began the Seven Years' War.

Initially successful, Frederick was soon desperate. Although the French had been defeated in Germany, they increased their subsidies to Austria, which enabled Austria and the Russians to inflict an almost complete defeat on Frederick. Near exhaustion, he continued to struggle on, however, and in 1761 Elizabeth, who had been chiefly responsible for maintaining the alliance, died in January 1762.

Her German-born nephew Karl Peter Ulrich became Czar Peter III. An admirer of Frederick, the czar began peace negotiations. The 1763 treaty of HUBERTS-BURG returned Austria and Prussia to the status quo antebellum, with Prussia retaining Silesia. France was not so lucky. That same year the TREATY OF PARIS, resulting from protracted negotiations between both nations, saw France's withdrawal from much of her empire, as determined by her severe losses at sea. While both agreed to refrain in the future from helping their respective German allies, France surrendered all her North American holdings and was decisively checked in her ambitions in the East toward India. The defeat virtually created the "second" English empire, launching the new "Great Britain" as the world's great sea power.

The French, in a way, later got their revenge. Their withdrawal from the North American interior led to squabbling between Great Britain and her North American colonists, who wanted to expand rapidly into the Ohio Valley when the mother country wanted them to stay where they were and take care of the business of enriching London. The revolt of the 13 American colonies afforded France the opportunity to strike back at her rival. The French concluded an alliance with the United States in 1778 and launched an undeclared war on England. In 1779 France was joined in this effort by Spain. French military support, French loans, and the French Navy helped the American revolutionaries hand Britain a decisive defeat, and she recognized American independence in the 1783 TREATY OF PARIS. But revenge often destroys its host; ultimately, these efforts on behalf of the Americans fueled the fiscal crisis that sparked the French Revolution.

Balancing Act

Upon reflection, both Maria Theresa and Frederick the Great were dissatisfied with the outcome of the Seven Years' War—the former had failed to reclaim Silesia; the latter to take Saxony. For her part, Russia, making advances against Turkey, was now worried about Austria on her flank. These worries and dissatisfaction, added to the abrupt decline of French prestige in eastern Europe, helped place Poland squarely on the agenda of the three powers. In particular, Russia's interest had become keen. The new czar, who proved something of a weakling, had back in 1744 married a German-born princess named Sophia Augusta Fredericka, from the small and obscure state of Anhalt-Zerbst, who was restyled Grand Duchess Catherine Alekseyevna. To history, she would become known as Catherine the Great, the third of this triad of remarkable enlightenment rulers to face off in Europe at mid-century.

Catherine had one of her lovers, Stanislaus Ponia-towski, elected to the Polish throne in 1764 and thus had Poland become a virtual protectorate of Russia. Nevertheless, Catherine was ready enough to placate Austria and Prussia if need be, and Frederick, anxious to avoid being drawn into some Austro-Russian conflict, saw Poland as a vehicle for working out their differences and, in the process, just maybe gaining something for himself in compensation for Russia's and Austria's potential gains in Turkey. The FIRST PARTITION OF POLAND came on July 25, 1772, when the Polish "republic" lost nearly a third of its territory. Prussia got West Prussia and Ermeland, thus uniting East Prussia with electorial Brandenburg; Austria wound up with Galicia; and Russia took the rest, making what remained of Poland an official dependency.

In the early 1790s, the Poles struck back. A national resurgence had already begun to question Catherine's authority when in May the Polish Diet adopted a new constitution favoring a strong monarchy and colluding with Austria and Prussia to make sure they opposed the election of another of Catherine's pawns to their new throne. By then, however, the Turkish war was coming to an end, the two German powers were embroiled in the French Revolution, and Catherine took the opportunity to invade and defeat Poland in a matter of some six weeks. A shrewd diplomat, she was careful not to unite the Germans against Russia, by arranging for the SECOND PARTITION OF POLAND in 1793. When Prussia got Danzig, Thorn, and Posen, and Russia got four times the Polish territory it previously controlled but Austria was left out in the cold, the humiliation would run deep, ultimately contributing to the tension between Austria and Prussia during the Napoleonic Wars.

Incredibly, if hopelessly, the Poles rallied yet again under Tadeusz Kościuszko, who—with surprising effectiveness—held out in Warsaw till November of 1794. This time Catherine needed Austrian help in plans she had for Turkey, so in the THIRD PARTITION OF POLAND, Austria enlarged Galicia and secured Kraków. Prussia got Warsaw. Poland disappeared.

The extinction of Poland signified the triumph of the principle of the "balance" of power in a Europe based on absolutist states enjoying immense freedom to maneuver diplomatically without regard to custom, religion, or public opinion. While the German powers, urged on by the famous Russian autocrat, chopped up Poland, they yet allowed by neglect the French Revolution to burst through its national boundaries and sweep over the Continent. No longer would warfare and diplomacy be linked simply with the "reason of state" but increasingly with the interests of ethnic nations and social classes—and that would signal sooner or later the end of the old regimes of the Enlightenment's "Age of Reason."

TREATIES

Peace Treaties and Truces

TREATY OF UTRECHT

TREATY AT A GLANCE

Completed
April 12 and July 13, 1713, at Utrecht, the Netherlands

Signatories
Great Britain, France, and Spain (Portugal, Savoy, Sweden, Tuscany, Parma, Venice, Genoa, and Danzig also subscribed to the treaty)

Overview
The Treaty of Utrecht ended the War of the Spanish Succession as well as its North American phase, Queen Anne's War. Not only did the treaty bring about a basic equilibrium in Europe until about 1740, it established the foundation of the English hegemony in North America, giving to Great Britain the Hudson Bay region, Nova Scotia, and Newfoundland. By the Anglo-Spanish agreement that is part of the Treaty of Utrecht (signed July 13, 1713), Spain ceded Gibraltar and Minorca to Great Britain and the *asientio* (privilege) of exclusively introducing African slaves into its American possessions, a right that was subsequently extended to general trading privileges. The Utrecht documents and an additional agreement, the TREATY OF RASTADT (March 16, 1714), marked the end of French aggrandizement under the ancien régime and the dramatic diminution of Spain as a power among the European states.

Historical Background

When Spain's Hapsburg king Charles II (1661–1700) chose a Bourbon as his successor, Louis XIV laid claim to the Spanish throne, and England, fearing a powerful French-Spanish union, formed an anti-French alliance with Holland and Austria. For a dozen years from 1701, England and its allies battled France, Italy, Germany, Spain, and the Spanish Netherlands in the War of the Spanish Succession, until a peace accord was reached in 1713, the Treaty of Utrecht. The forces of the Holy Roman Empire fought on into 1714, after the Treaty of Utrecht, until coming to terms under the Treaty of Rastadt. Simultaneously, in North America, Britain and France contested from 1702 to 1713 for control of the continent in what was called Queen Anne's War.

In both Europe and North America, the war was extraordinarily costly. While England's duke of Marl-borough fought a series of brilliant campaigns—particularly at Donauworth and Blenheim in 1704 and at Ramillies in 1706—the Allies suffered serious defeats in 1707, only to best the French again the following year, in fighting always costly for the victor. In America, English forces took Port Royal, the major French stronghold in Acadia (Nova Scotia and New Brunswick). Despite this, French colonials allied with Indians continually harried, terrorized, and ravaged the settlements of New England.

When Charles III of Barcelona became Holy Roman Emperor Charles VI in 1711, Britain, victorious but reeling under the heavy price of its triumphs, feared an alliance between Austria and Spain. Accordingly, Queen Anne recalled Marlborough (and her armies in consequence suffered a defeat at the Battle of Denain in 1712) and commenced peace talks with France.

Terms

That both nations were weary of the long war was evident in the language of the Treaty of Utrecht, which spoke of "healing . . . the Miserys of the Wasted World" by making an end to "the War which was unhappily kindled, and has been obstinately carry'd on above ten years, being both cruel and destructive, by reason of the frequency of Battles, and the Effusion of Christian Blood." What the nations seemed to learn was that dynastic privileges and nationalist rights were inferior to establishing and maintaining a balance of power, which the framers of the Utrecht treaty expressed as "faithful Friendship":

> All Offenses, Injurys, and Damages, which the aforesaid Queen of Great Britain, and her subjects, or the aforesaid most Christian King, and his Subjects, have suffered the one from the other, during the War, shall be buried in Oblivion; so that neither on account, or under pretence thereof, or of any other thing, shall either hereafter, of the Subjects of either, do or give, cause or suffer to be done or given to the other, any Hostility, Enmity, Molestation, or Hindrance, by themselves, or by others, secretly or openly, directly or indirectly, under color of Right, or by any way of fact.

More specifically, the treaty acknowledged that "the most destructive Flame of War . . . arose chiefly from hence, that the Security and Libertys of Europe could by no means bear the Union of the Kingdoms of France and Spain under one and the same King" and made its principal thrust clear: "that this Evil"—the union of France and Spain under one crown—"should in all times to come be obviated, by means of Renunciations drawn in the most effectual Form, and executed in the most solemn Manner."

Treaty of Utrecht

Whereas the most destructive Flame of War which is to be extinguished by this Peace, arose chiefly from hence, that the Security and Libertys of Europe could by no means bear the Union of the Kingdoms of France and Spain under one and the same King: And whereas it has at length been brought to pass by the Assistance of the Divine Power, upon the most earnest Instances of her Sacred Royal Majesty of Great Britain, and with the Consent both of the most Christian and of the Catholick King, that this Evil should in all times to come be obviated, by means of Renunciations drawn in the most effectual Form, and executed in the most solemn Manner, the Tenor whereof is as follows.

LETTERS PATENT BY THE KING, WHICH ADMIT THE
RENUNCIATION OF THE KING OF SPAIN
TO THE CROWN OF FRANCE, AND
THOSE OF MONSIEUR THE DUKE OF BERRY
AND OF MONSIEUR THE DUKE OF ORLÉANS,
TO THE CROWN OF SPAIN.

LEWIS, by the Grace of God, King of France and Navarre: To all People present and to come, Greeting. During the various Revolutions of a War, wherein we have fought only to maintain the Justice of the Rights of the King, our most dear and most beloved Grandson to the Monarchy of Spain, we have never ceased to desire Peace. The greatest Successes did not at all dazzle us, and the contrary Events, which the Hand of God made use of to try us rather than to destroy us, did not give birth to that Desire in us, but found it there. But the Time marked out by Divine Providence for the Repose of Europe was not yet come; the distant Fear of seeing one Day our Crown and that of Spain upon the Head of one and the same Prince, did always make an equal Impression on the Powers which were united against us; and this Fear, which had been the principal Cause of the War, seemed also to lay an insuperable Obstacle in the way to Peace. At last, after many fruitless Negotiations, God being moved with the Sufferings and Groans of so many People, was pleased to open a surer way to come at so difficult a Peace. But the same Alarms still subsisting, the first and principal Condition, which was proposed to us by our most dear and most beloved Sister the Queen of Great Britain, as the essential and necessary Foundation of Treating, was, That the King of Spain, our said Brother and Grandson, keeping the Monarchy of Spain and of the Indies, should renounce for himself and his Descendants for ever, the Rights which his Birth might at any time give him and them to our Crown; that on the other hand, our most dear and most beloved Grandson the Duke of Berry, and our most dear and most beloved Nephew the Duke of Orleans, should likewise renounce for themselves, and for their Descendants, Male and Female for ever, their Rights to the Monarchy of Spain and the Indies. Our said Sister caused it to be represented to us, that without a formal and positive Assurance upon this Point, which alone could be the Bond of Peace, Europe would never be at rest; all the Powers which share the same being equally persuaded, That it was for their general Interest, and for their common Security, to continue a War, whereof no one could foresee the End, rather than to be exposed to behold the same Prince become one day Master of two Monarchys, so powerful as those of France and Spain. But as this Princess (whose indefatigable Zeal for re-establishing the general Tranquillity we cannot sufficiently praise) was sensible of all the Reluctancy we had to consent that one of our Children, so worthy to inherit the Succession of our Forefathers, should necessarily be excluded from it, if the Misfortunes wherewith it has pleased God to afflict us in our Family, should moreover take from us, in the Person of the Dauphin, our most dear and most beloved great Grandson, the only Remainder of those Princes which our Kingdom has so justly lamented with us; she entered into our Pain, and after having jointly sought out gentler means of securing the Peace, we agreed with our said Sister to propose the King of Spain other Dominions, inferior indeed to those which he possesses, yet the Value thereof would so much the more increase under his Reign, in as much as in that case he would preserve his Rights, and annex to our Crown a part of the said Dominions, if he came one time or other to succeed us. We employed therefore the strongest Reasons to persuade him to accept this Alternative. We gave him to understand, that the Duty of his Birth was the first which he ought to consult; that he owed himself to his House, and to his Country, before he was obliged to Spain; that if he were wanting to his first Engagements, he would perhaps one day in vain regret his having abandoned those Rights, which he would be no more able to maintain. We added to these Reasons the personal motives of Friendship and of tender Love, which we thought likely to move him; the Pleasure we should have in seeing him from time to time near us, and in passing some part of our days with him, which we might promise ourselves from the Neighborhood of the Dominions that were offered him; the Satisfaction of instructing him ourselves concerning the State of our Affairs, and of relying upon him for the future; so that, if God should preserve to us the Dauphin, we could give our Kingdom, in the Person of the King our Brother and Grandson, a Regent instructed in the Art of Government; and that, if this Child so precious to us and to our Subjects, were also taken from us, we shou'd at least have the Consolation of leaving to our People a virtuous King, fit to govern them, and who would likewise annex to our Crown very considerable Dominions. Our Instances, reiterated with all the force, and with all the tender affection necessary to persuade a Son who so justly deserves those Efforts which we made for preserving him to France, produced nothing but reiterated Refusals on his part, ever to abandon such brave and faithful Subjects, whose Zeal for him had been distinguished in those Conjunctures, when his Throne seemed to be the most shaken. So that persisting with an invincible Firmness in his first Resolution, asserting likewise, that it was more glorious and more advantageous for our House, and for our Kingdom, than that which we pressed him to take, he declared in the Meeting of the States of the Kingdom of Spain, assembled at Madrid for that purpose, that for obtaining a general Peace, and securing the Tranquillity of Europe by a Ballance of Power, he of his own proper Motion, of his own free Will, and without any Constraint, renounced for himself, for his Heirs and Successors for ever and ever, all Pretensions, Rights and Titles, which he, or any of his Descendants, have.at present, or may have at any time to come whatsoever, to the Succession of our Crown: That he held for excluded therefrom himself, his Children, Heirs, and Descendants for ever: That he consented for himself and for them, that now, as well as then, his Right, and that of his Descendants, should pass over and be transferred to him among the Princes, whom the Law of Succession, and the Order of Birth calls, or shall call to inherit our Crown, in default of our said Brother and Grandson the King of Spain, and of his Descendants, as it is more amply specified in the Act of Renunciation, approved by the States of his Kingdom; and consequently he declared, that he desisted particularly from the Right which hath been added to that of his Birth, by our Letters Patent of the Month of December 1700, whereby we declared, that it was our Will, that the King of Spain and his Descendants should always preserve the Rights of their Birth and Original, in the same manner as if they resided actually in our Kingdom; and from the Registry which was made of our said Letters Patent, both in our Court of Parliament, and in our Chamber of Accounts at Paris, we are sensible as King and as Father, how much it were to be desired that the general Peace could have been concluded without a Renunciation, which makes so great a Change in our Royal House, and in the antient Order of succeeding to our Crown: but we are yet more sensible how much it is our Duty to secure speedily to our Subjects a Peace which

is so necessary for them. We shall never forget the Efforts which they made for us, during the long continuance of a War, which we could not have supported, if their Zeal had not been much more extensive than their Power. The Welfare of a People so faithful, is to us a supreme Law, which ought to be preferred to any other Consideration. It is to this Law that We this day sacrifice the Right of a Grandson, who is so dear to us; and by the Price which the general Peace will cost our tender Love, we shall at least have the Comfort of shewing our Subjects, that even at the Expence of our Blood, they will always keep the first place in our Heart.

For these Causes, and other important Considerations us thereunto moving, after having seen in our Council the said Act of Renunciation of the King of Spain our said Brother and Grandson, of the fifth of November last, as also the Acts of Renunciations, which our said Grandson the Duke of Berry, and our said Nephew the Duke of Orleans, made reciprocally of their Rights to the Crown of Spain, as well for themselves as for their Descendants Male and Female, in consequence of the Renunciation of our said Brother and Grandson the King of Spain, the whole hereunto annexed, with a Copy collated of the said Letters Patent of the Month of December 1700, under the Counter-Seal of our Chancery; of our special Grace, full Power, and Royal Authority, we have declared, decreed and ordained, and by these Presents signed with our Hand, we do declare, decree and ordain, we will, and it is our Pleasure, That the said Act of Renunciation of our said Brother and Grandson the King of Spain, and those of our said Grandson the Duke of Berry, and of our said Nephew the Duke of Orleans, which we have admitted, and do admit, be registered in all our Courts of Parliament, and Chambers of our Accounts in our Kingdom, and other Places where it shall be necessary, in order to their being executed according to their Form and Tenor. And consequently, we will and intend, that our said Letters Patent of the Month of December 1700, be and remain null, and as if they had never been made; that they be brought back to us, and that in the Margin of the Resisters of our said Court of Parliament, and of our said Chamber of Accounts, where the Enrolment of the said Letters Patent is, the Extract of these Presents be placed and inserted, the better to signify our Intention as to the Revocation, and Nullity of the said Letters. We will that in conformity to the said Act of Renunciation of our said Brother and Grandson the King of Spain, he be from henceforth looked upon and considered as excluded from our Succession; that his Heirs, Successors, and Descendants be likewise excluded for ever, and looked upon as incapable of enjoying the same. We understand that in failure of them, all Rights to our said Crown, and succession to our Dominions, which might at any time whatsoever belong and appertain to them, be and remain transferred to our most dear, and most beloved Grandson the Duke of Berry, and to his Children and Descendants, being Males born in lawful Marriage; and successively in failure of them, to those of the Princes of our Royal House, and their Descendants, who in Right of their Birth, or by the Order established since the Foundation of our Monarchy, ought to succeed to our Crown. And so we command our beloved and trusty Counsellors, the Members of our Court of Parliament at Paris, that they do cause these Presents, together with the Acts of Renunciation made by our said Brother and Grandson the King of Spain, by our said Grandson the Duke of Berry, and by our said Nephew the Duke of Orleans, to be read, publish'd and registered, and the Contents thereof to be kept, peaceably, and perpetually; ceasing, and causing to cease all Molestations and Hindrances, notwithstanding any Laws, Statutes, Usages, Customs, Decrees, Regulations, and other matters contrary thereunto: whereto, and to the Derogations of the Derogations therein contained, we have derogated, and do derogate by these Presents, for this purpose only and without being brought into Precedent. For such is our Pleasure.

And to the end that this may be a matter firm and lasting for ever, we have caused our Seal to be affixed to these Presents. Given at Versailles, in the Month of March in the Year of our Lord 1713, and of our Reign the 70th. Sign'd Lewis, and underneath, by the King, Phelypeaux. Vise, Phelypeaux. And sealed with the Great Seal on green Wax, with strings of red and green Silk.

Read and published, the Court being assembled, and registered among the Rolls of the Court, the King's Attorney General being heard and moving for the same, to the end that they may be executed according to their Form and Tenor, in pursuance of, and in conformity to, the Acts of this Day. At Paris, in Parliament the 15th of March, 1713.

Sign'd
DONGOIS

For his part, King Philip V of Spain reciprocally renounced any claim to the French throne for himself or his heirs. By the July 13, 1713, agreement, Spain pledged "free Use of Navigation and Commerce" between itself and England, ceded Minorca and Gibraltar, and, through the Pacto de el Assiento de Negros, granted Great Britain an exclusive right to introduce African slaves into her American possessions.

Consequences

The Treaty of Utrecht set the terms for European politics and international relations for a generation. Its provision on African slavery became the basis for Britain's general slave-trading privileges in Spanish America, and this in turn resulted in the gradual erosion of the Spanish hegemony in North America. In the long term effectively removing Spain from the centuries-long imperial struggles in the Western Hemisphere, the treaty cleared the field for the battle to continue ever more directly between France and England, although each new escalation of the New World fight inevitably involved jockeying for position on the Continent, as well.

There would be other wars in which Spain played a role, of course, and which spilled over into the Americas—the European struggle for the Austrian succession, for example, which the American colonists knew as the War of Jenkins' Ear and King George's War successively, but each flash of fire in the wilderness would hone the contention more finely to one primarily between France and England. The French, like Spain before them, were economically inhibited from supporting their colonies in the vast American interior the way the English could maintain their snug settlements along the Atlantic seaboard, so instead they allied themselves more closely with the native populations and, like Spain before them, intermarried with and converted the Indians. The British colonials were more wont simply to take their lands. Thus, when what historians would later call the "Great War for Empire" finally broke out in Europe at mid-century after several smaller conflicts, the British colonials in America, hardly seeing Spain's participation as of any consequence at all, described what the Europeans would call the Seven Years' War more accurately from their point of view as simply the "French and Indian War."

TREATY OF RASTADT (AND BADEN)

TREATY AT A GLANCE

Completed
March 6, 1714, and September 7, 1714, at Rastadt
(present-day Rastatt, Germany)

Signatories
Holy Roman Empire and France

Overview
When the rest of Europe reached a settlement to the War of the Spanish Succession in the 1713 TREATY OF UTRECHT, Holy Roman Emperor Charles VI fought on alone against France for more than a year before reaching a separate peace, which—like Utrecht—became part of the foundation of Europe's international relations.

Historical Background

The long, 12-year War of the Spanish Succession over Louis XIV's claim to the Spanish throne came to a close for most of the belligerents—England, Holland, and Austria on the one side, France and Spain on the other—in an international peace settlement called the Treaty of Utrecht that set the stage for European politics and international relations for at least a generation. But Charles VI, emperor of the Holy Roman Empire and a Hapsburg, was not happy with allowing a French Bourbon to sit on a Spanish throne he believed by right belonged to his house. He continued to fight the French "Sun King" for another year or so. Not until March and September 1714 did Charles come to an official settlement with the French in the Treaties of Rastadt and Baden, and not even then—though he at least admitted the war was over—did he fully accept the accord the rest of Europe had come to during the previous spring and summer.

Terms

Charles made the Rastadt peace in his own name and half a year later at Baden he signed on behalf of the various states of the Holy Roman Empire. In these treaties, he renounced his own claims to the Spanish throne, but he did not actually make peace with Spain itself, and he continued stubbornly to insist that the Bourbon Philip V was not actually the king of Spain. In return, France recognized the Hapsburg emperor as the ruler of some former Spanish possessions: Milan, Tuscany,

Naples, the southern Netherlands, and Sardinia. For ceding Strasbourg and Alsace to France and permitting the electors of Bavaria and Cologne—Louis XIV's allies in the war—to recover their possessions currently under his control, Charles recovered Breisach, Kehl, and Freiburg east of the Rhine. All of these conditions harked back to treaties concluded in the century past before the issue of a Spanish succession once again clouded relations between the two powers: the PEACE OF WESTPHALIA, the PEACE OF NIJMEGEN, and the TREATY OF RYSWICK.

The Treaty of Rastadt was an important document in the long decline of the Hapsburgs and of the French ascendancy. It involved, however, not only the dynastic and political concerns of His Imperial Majesty, Charles VI, and His Most Christian Majesty, Louis XIV but also the lives of their dependencies and subjects, who had suffered through more than a decade of war. In its attempt to rectify some of the damage done to the people of France and the Holy Roman Empire as well as to establish the status quo antebellum, the treaty provided something of a snapshot of the times.

Treaty of Peace between the Holy Roman Emperor and the King of France

In the name of the Most Holy and Indivisible Trinity, let it be known to all and everyone whom it concerns or whom it may in any manner concern, that Europe, having been agitated for several years by long and bloody Wars, enveloping her principal

States and Kingdoms, it has pleased God, who holds in his hand the hearts of all Kings, to being the hearts of these Sovereigns to a full recognition, and to prepare the way toward an end to the war first begun between the Most Serene and Powerful Prince and Lord, his Highness, Leopold, elected Holy Roman Emperor, most August, King of Germany, Hungary, Bohemia, etc., of renowned memory, and, since his death, between the Most Serene and Powerful Prince and Lord, his Highness Joseph, his Son, most August, King of Germany, etc., of renowned memory, and after his death, between the most Serene and Powerful Prince and Lord, his Highness, Charles VI, most August, King of Germany, *Castille, Aragon,* Leon, the Two Sicilies, *Jerusalem, Hongrie, Boheme, Dalmatie, Croacie, Esclavonie, Navarre, Granade, Tolede, Valence, Gallice, Majorque, Seville, Sardaigne, Cordue, Corse, Murcie, Algarbes, Alger, Gibraltar, Isles de Canarie, les Indes,* the islands and mainland of l'Ocean, Archduke of Austria, Duke of *Bourgone, Brabant, Milan, Stirie, Carinthie, Carniole,* Limburg, Luxemburg, *Gueldres, Witemburg,* High and Low Silesia, *Calabre;* Prince of *Suabe, Catalogne, Asturie;* Marquis of the Holy Roman Empire, or Burgaw, *Moravie,* High and Low Lusace, Count of Hapsburg, Flanders, *Tyrol, Frioul, Kybourg, Gorice, Artois, Namur, Roussillon,* and of *Cerdaigne,* Lord of the *Esclavone Marche* of *Port Mahon,* and of *Salins, Biscaye, Molline, Tripoli,* and *Malines,* etc., and the Holy Roman Empire; and the Most Serene and Powerful Prince and Lord, His Majesty, Louis XIV, Most Catholic King of France and Navarre. His Imperial Majesty and His Most Christian Majesty, wishing nothing more ardently than, by the restoration of a firm and immutable Peace, to bring about an end to the desolation of so many Provinces and the spilling of so much Christian Blood, they have agreed that, in order to accomplish this more promptly, Conferences held at Rastadt between the Commanders-in-Chief of the two Armies, to whom they have granted their full powers. They have also established their Extraordinary and Plenipotentiary Ambassadors to this end, that is, for the Emperor, the Most High Prince and Lord Eugéne de Savoie, etc., and for the Most Christian King, the Most High and Excellent Lord, Louis Hector, Duke de Villars, Peer and Marshal of France, etc.; These, having implored Divine assistance and having exchanged their full powers, of which copies are inserted word for word at the end of this Treaty, have agreed, for the Holy Name of God and for the good of the Christian Republic, upon reciprocal conditions of Peace and Friendship, which follow.

I

There shall be a universal, Christian Peace and Perpetual Friendship, true and sincere, between His Imperial Majesty and His Most Christian Majesty and their Heirs, Successors, and all Kingdoms and Provinces. One shall not for any reason undertake any action toward the destruction or harm of the other and shall not lend aid under any name whatever, to those who would wish to undertake or do damage in any manner. His Imperial Majesty and the Empire, and His Most Christian Majesty shall not aid or protect rebel subjects or anyone disobeying one or the other, but on the contrary, they shall seriously preserve all that concerns the service, honor and benefit of any sort, past and future.

II

On each side there shall be a perpetual Pardon and Amnesty for all that has been done since the beginning of the war, in all man-ners and in all places that the Hostilities took place. Thus, for none of these things, under no pretext, shall one or the other do, or permit to be done, directly or indirectly, within or outside of the boundaries of the Empire and inherited Lands of His Imperial Majesty and of the Kingdom of France, any wrong notwithstanding any pacts concluded heretofore. All wrongs, committed by either side in words, acts of hostility and destruction, and expense incurred, without taking into account persons or property, are completely annulled, so that all demands and claims in these matters shall be forgotten.

III

The Treaties of Westphalia, Nimeguen, Ryswick are considered to be the basis of this Treaty; consequently, after the exchange of Ratifications, the said Treaties shall be totally carried out in regard both to the Spiritual and Temporal and shall be inviolably observed in the future, according to what shall expressly be stipulated in the Treaty, restoring all in the Empire and its possessions as prescribed by the Treaty of Ryswick concerning changes made during this war, or before, as well as what has not been carried out, if it is actually found that some article has not been executed, or that the execution of it has in the meantime been changed.

IV

In conformance with the above mentioned Treaty of Ryswick, his Most Christian Majesty shall restore to the Emperor the city and the fortress of Old Brisack in its entirety and in the condition it now is in, with the storage-houses, arsenals, fortifications, ramparts, walls, towers and other public and private edifices and all the dependencies situated on the right high bank of the Rhine, leaving to the Most Christian King those on the left, namely the fort called Mortier, all according to the clauses and conditions in article 20 of the Treaty concluded at Ryswick in October, 1697, by the deceased Emperor Leopold and the Most Christian King.

V

His Most Christian Majesty equally restores to His Imperial Majesty and to the Most Serene House of Austria the city and fortresses of Fribourg, as well as the fort Saint Pierre, the fort called the *Star* (l'Étoile) and all other forts constructed or repaired, there or elsewhere in the Black Forest, or in the remainder of *Brisgaw,* all as it is now, with nothing demolished or marred, and with it, the villages of *Lehem, Merzhaufen,* and *Kirchzarren,* and with all their Laws and archives and all their written documents as they were when His Most Christian Majesty recently took possession of them, whether they are still in these lands or have been taken elsewhere, save and excepting the Diocesan Law and other laws and revenues of the Bishopric of Constance.

VI

The fort of Kehl built by His Most Christian Majesty on the right bank of the Rhine at the end of the Pont de Strasbourg shall likewise be restored to the Emperor in its entirety, with nothing demolished, and with all its rights and dependencies.

As for the for of La Pile, and others built on islands in the Rhine below Strasbourg, they shall be completely razed at the expense of the Most Christian King in such manner that they shall not be able to be rebuilt afterwards by one party or the other; these cessions, demolitions of the strongholds and fortifications mentioned above shall be completed in the terms of the following articles, that is to say, beginning at the day of the exchange of Ratifications of this solemn and total Treaty of Peace between His Imperial Majesty, the Empire, and His Most Christian Majesty. Navigation and other uses of the River shall remain free and open to the subjects of the two Parties and to all those wishing to pass by, sail, or transport merchandise, without permitting either one side or the other to undertake to divert the course of the said River in such a way as to render its flow and navigation or other uses more difficult. Nor, especially, can they demand new tolls or taxes or increase old ones, or oblige vessels to land on one bank rather than the other, to lay open their cargo or to receive any, but shall be at the choice of each individual.

VII

The said places, fortresses, and castles of Brisack, Fribourg, and Kehl shall be restored to His Imperial Majesty with all jurisdictions and dependencies, with all artillery and munitions that were there when His Most Christian Majesty occupied them during this War, as written in the inventories that have been made; these supplies shall be delivered with no reserve or exception, in good faith and with no delay, prevention, or any pretext, to those who shall be chosen to this end after exchange of Ratifications of the total and solemn Treaty of Peace between His Imperial Majesty, the Empire, and His Most Christian Majesty by His Imperial Majesty alone, or in case of differences of places, by Him and by the Empire. These dependencies, having made known their full powers to the Intendants, Governors, or French Officers of those places that are to be restored, the said towns, citadels, forts and strongholds, with all their privileges, benefits, revenues and emoluments and all other things whatsoever included, shall return to the jurisdiction and total possession, power and sovereignty of His Imperial Majesty, the Empire, and the House of Austria as they formerly belonged to them and have since been held by His Christian Majesty holding or reserving any right or pretention to the abovesaid places or their jurisdiction.

In addition, nothing shall be demanded for the expenses used on the fortifications and public and private buildings. The entire restoration cannot be postponed for any reason, whatever it may be, in the terms prescribed below. Therefore, all French garrisons shall be totally evacuated without molesting or annoying the citizens and inhabitants, causing them any loss or harm, nor especially the other subjects of His Imperial Majesty or the Empire, on pretext of debt or pretense of any nature.

Nor shall it be permitted for the French Troops to remain any longer than the time stipulated in the terms below in the places that are to be restored, or any others that shall not belong to His Most Christian Majesty; they shall not establish winter quarters nor have any period of stay, but they are obliged to withdraw without halting into the lands of the said Majesty.

VIII

His Most Christian Majesty promises equally to have razed at his expense the fortifications built opposite Huningue on the right bank and on the island of the Rhine, as well as the bridge constructed over the Rhine at this place, giving up the foundations and building to the Family of Baden. Likewise, the fort of Sellingue, the forts in the isles between the fort of Sellingue and the Fort Louis, and as for the land of the destroyed fort, it shall be given up, along with its buildings to the Family of Baden. He promises to destroy that part of the bridge leading from said fort of Sellingue to the Fort Louis., and the fort built on the right bank of the Rhine opposite said Fort Louis without it ever being possible for them to be restored by either of the Parties. It is well understood that the Fort Louis and the Island shall remain in the power of the Most Christian King. His said Majesty promises to have razed at his expense all forts, entrenchments, ways and bridges specified in the Treaty of Ryswick. either along the Rhine, on the Rhine, or anywhere else in the Empire and its possessions it shall not be permitted to rebuild them.

IX

The Most Christian King promises equally to gave the castle of Bitsch, with all its possessions evacuated, as well as the castle of Hombourg, having beforehand razed the fortification making it impossible for them to be rebuilt, but in such a manner, nevertheless, that the said castle and town adjoining them shall not be damaged but shall remain completely whole.

X

Thirty days after the exchange of Ratifications of the total and solemn Peace Treaty made between His Imperial Majesty, the Empire, and His Most Christian Majesty, and even earlier, if such is possible, the areas and fortified places, this named above and those that are to be restored according to this Treaty and that of Ryswick, the words of which shall be held as included in this Treaty and executed as if they had been inserted word for word, shall be placed in the hands of those authorized to that end by the Emperor, the States of the Empire, or by other particular Princes who are to possess them by virtue of the Treaty of Ryswick. It is not permitted to demolish the fortifications or the buildings, public and private, nor to impair the state in which they all are now, nor to demand anything for the expenses incurred in the said places or on account of them. Also, the archives and documents, belonging either to HIs Imperial Majesty or to the Empire on one hand, or to the places to be restored by His Most Christian Majesty on the other, must be returned.

XI

As the intention of the Most Christian King is to fulfill as promptly as possible the terms of this Treaty, His Majesty promises that the places he promised to have razed, at his expense, shall be razed. The most important, in the period of two months after the exchange of Ratification of the total and solemn Peace Treaty to be made by His Imperial Majesty, the Empire, and His Most Christian Majesty, and the less important, in the period of one month after the Ratifications.

XII

And since His Most Christian Majesty truly and in good faith wishes to reestablish a sincere union with the Emperor and the Empire, he promises and binds himself to restore, when treating with the Electors, Princes and States of the General Congress with the emperor and the Empire, to them and to the subjects and vassals of the said Empire as well, clerical or secular, and to all in general named in the Treaty of Ryswick, even though they are not all expressly named here, the lands, fortifications, and possessions that He has come to own in the course of the present War, either by arms, confiscation, or by any other means whatsoever. Likewise, He promises to execute fully and promptly all the clauses and conditions of the Treaty of Ryswick that He has not expressly been excused from fulfilling by this Treaty, if there be one that has not been executed since the conclusion of the Peace of Ryswick.

XIII

His Imperial Majesty, wishing equally to show his desire to contribute to the satisfaction of His Most Christian Majesty and to maintain with him in the future a sincere friendship and perfect understanding, and in virtue of the Peace of Ryswick reestablished by this Treaty, consents that the town of Landau, with all its dependencies, consisting of the villages of Nussdorff, Danheim, Queicheim, with their districts as His Most Christian Majesty held before the War, shall remain, fortified, in his power, His Imperial Majesty being obliged to make great effort to obtain the consent of the Empire for this at the preparation and conclusion of the solemn Treaty of Peace between His Imperial Majesty, the Empire, and His Most Christian Majesty

XIV

The House of Brunswick-Hanover having been elevated by the Emperor, with the consent of the Empire, to the rank of Elector, His Most Christian Majesty shall recognize, in virtue of the Treaty, the dignity of the Electoral Rank of the said House.

XV

Concerning the House of Bavaria, His Imperial Majesty and the Empire, for reasons of public tranquility, agree that, in virtue of the total and solemn Treaty to be concluded by the Emperor, and the Empire, His Lordship, Joseph-Clement, Archbishop of Cologne and his Lordship, Maximilian Emanuel of Bavaria shall be completely restored to all their lands, titles, revenues and goods, electoral rights, privileges and others, and in all their claims and dues, as They held before this War and which belonged to the Archbishop of Cologne and other churches named below, or to the House of Bavaria, directly or indirectly.

As soon as the meetings begin, they shall be able to send to the Congress of the Treaty to be called by His Imperial Majesty, the Empire, and His Most Christian Majesty, representatives with full power, though without title, to negotiate for them and to look after their interests, with no obstacle. Also, in good faith, all furniture, precious stones and jewelry and other effects of whatever nature shall be restored to them, as well as the munitions and the artillery specified in the authenticated inventories that are to be brought out from various places; that is, all those that may have been removed on orders from the Emperor or by his glorious predecessors, beginning at the occupation of Bavaria, of the palaces, castles, towns, fortresses and other places, which belonged to them and shall belong to them again with the exception of the artillery belonging to neighboring cities and states, which have been returned to them; likewise, all archives and papers shall be restored.

And his Lordship the Archbishop of Cologne shall be restored his Archbishopric of Cologne, his Bishoprics of Hildesheim, Ratisbonne, Liege, and the Prepositure of Berchtolsgaden, without any basis for legal action any pretention or claim, being allowed to alter its total restoration; excepting, however, the rights of those who might have such claims and who shall be allowed, after the reestablishment of the two Electors, to pursue them according to the ways of Justice established in the Empire, as it was before the present War; excepting also

the privileges of the Chapters (of Canons) states of the Archbishopric of Cologne and of other churches previously established, according to their Unions, treaties, and constitutions.

And as for the city of Bonn, in time of peace there shall not be any garrison at all, but its protection shall be confined to the burgers of the city; as for the *Garde du Corps*, and the Palace Guard, they shall be restricted to simple companies of these guards; this shall be agreed to by the Emperor and the Empire. Let it be well understood, however, that in time of war or threat of war, His Imperial Majesty and the Empire can place there as many troops as the war demands, all in conformity with the laws and constitution of the Empire. It is understood also that on condition of the total restitution, the said Lords of the House of Bavaria shall renounce forever and shall be considered to have forfeited their claims, satisfactions, reimbursements, whatsoever that they might have wished to make against the Emperor, the Empire and the House of Austria on account of the present War, without compromising, nevertheless the former rights and pretentions they may have had before this war. They shall be permitted to pursue these, as before, by the ways of justice established in the Empire. However, this total restitution shall not give them any new right against anyone. All those who would want to formulate new pretentions on account of this War, against the House of Bavaria and the abovesaid Archbishopric, Bishoprics and Provostships, shall renounce and be considered to have forfeited all claims, satisfactions or reimbursement.

In virtue of the total restitution of the abovesaid Lords, Joseph-Clement, Archbishop of Cologne and Maximilian of Bavaria shall give obedience and shall keep faithful to His Imperial Majesty, as well as to the other Electors and Princes of the Empire and shall ask and duly receive from His Imperial Majesty the renewal of Investiture for their Electorates, Principalities, fiefs, title and rights in the manner and in the time prescribed by the laws of the Empire; and also all that has been done on one side or the other during this War shall be forgotten for perpetuity.

XVI

The Ministers and officers, ecclesiastic or military, political or civil, of whatever condition they may be, having served on one side or the other, the subjects and vassals of His Imperial Majesty, the Empire and the House of Austria or the domestics of any sort of the House of Bavaria and of the Lord Archbishop of Cologne, shall equally be restored to the possessions of all their goods, charges, honors and dignities as before the War, and they shall enjoy a total pardon for all that has passed, on condition that this same amnesty be completely reciprocal for those of the subjects, vassals, ministers or domestics who may in the course of this War have adhered to the side of His Imperial Majesty, and the Empire, and they, on this account, shall not be molested or disturbed in any manner whatsoever.

XVII

As for the time at which the total restitution as specified in the two preceding articles is to be made, it shall, in the total and solemn Peace Treaty to be made between the Emperor, the Empire and the Most Christian King be set at thirty days after the ratification of the said Treaty, as it has been agreed upon for the evacuation of the places that His Most Christian Majesty promises to restore to His Imperial Majesty and to the Empire.

This shall be carried out in such a manner that the one and the other, as well as the restitution to the Emperor of the states and lands now possessed by the House of Bavaria in the Low Countries shall be done at the same time.

XVIII

If, after the total restitution, the House of Bavaria finds it convenient to effect some exchanges of its lands for others, His Most Christian Majesty shall not oppose it.

XIX

His Most Christian Majesty having returned or having had returned to the Estates-General of the United Provinces, in favor of the House of Austria, all that His Said Majesty or His Allies still possessed of the Low Countries, together called Spanish, as the late King Charles II of Spain possessed them or should have possessed them according to the Treaty of Ryswick. His Most Christian Majesty consents that the Emperor shall take possession of said Spanish Low Countries himself, and his heirs and successors, now and for always, totally and in peace, according to the order of succession established by the House of Austria, excepting, the agreements that the Emperor will enter into with said Estates-General of the United Provinces concerning their border and the restoration of the said places. It is well understood that the King of Prussia shall retain all that he now possesses and occupies of the upper region of Gueldres, that is, the town of Gueldres, the prefecture, the bailiwick and the lower bailiwick of Gueldres, with all that belongs to and is dependent upon it as especially the cities, bailiwicks and manors of Sthralen, Wachtendonck, Midelaar, Walbeck, Aertsen, Asserden and de Weel, as well as Racy and Klein Kevelaar, with all their dependencies and possessions. In addition, to the said King of Prussia shall be given the village of Krickenbeck with all that depends upon and belongs to it and the country of Kessel, equally, with all its possessions and dependencies and all that is contained in the said village and district, with no exception, if not for Erkelens with its possessions and dependencies, which in all shall belong to the said king and to his Heirs and successors, the Princes of Prussia, with all the rights, prerogatives, revenues and advantages of whatever name, in the same manner that the House of Austria and particularly the Late King of Spain possessed them, as always with the charges and mortgages, the conservation of the Roman Catholic Religion and the privileges of the states.

XX

And since, besides the provinces, cities, fortified places, and fortresses possessed by the late King of Spain Charles II on the day of his death, the Most Christian King has, as much for himself as for the Princes his Heirs and Successors, born and not yet born, ceded to the Estates General in favor of the House of Austria all the rights he has had or could have ever on the town of Menin, with all its fortifications and its acreage, on the town and citadel of Tournay, with all Tournesis, without reserving any of his rights thereon, nor on any of their dependencies, possessions, annexes, territories and enclosures. His Majesty consents that the Estates General shall give up to the Emperor the said towns, places, territories, dependencies, possessions, annexes and enclosures, as soon as they shall have convened with His Imperial Majesty, for him to enjoy, as well as his Heirs and Successors, totally, peacefully, and forever, as well as the Spanish Low Countries, which belonged to the late King of Spain

Charles II on the day of his death; be it understood nevertheless that the said restitution of the Spanish Low Countries, towns, places and fortresses ceded by the Most Christian King shall not be made by the said Estates-General until after the Ratification of the Treaties of peace between His Imperial Majesty, the Empire, and His Most Christian Majesty; be it understood also that Saint Armand with its dependencies and Mortagne without dependencies, shall remain in the power of His Most Christian Majesty on condition nevertheless that it shall not be permitted to make at Mortagne any fortification or dam of any nature whatsoever.

XXI

Likewise, the Most Christian King confirms the cession in favor of the Emperor and of the House of Austria, which His Imperial Majesty has already made in favor of that House to the Estates-General of the United Provinces, for himself as well as for the Princes, His Heirs and Successors, born or not yet born, of all his rights to Furnes and Furnambacht, including the eight parishes and the fort of la Knocque, as well as on the towns of Loo and Dixmude with their dependencies, the town of Ypres with its castleward, Russelaer included, with the other dependencies, which shall henceforth be Poperingue, Varneton, Commines and Warwick, these last three, inasmuch as they are situated on the side of the Lys near Ypres, and with this, all that is dependent upon the Places specified above. His Most Christian Majesty reserves no claim whatsoever on these rights thus ceded to the Emperor, His Heirs and Successors, of any of the said towns, strongholds, fortifications and lands, nor any of their possessions, dependencies, annexes or enclosures. He further consents that the Estates-General may yield them to the House of Austria to enjoy them irrevocably and forever, as soon as they have agreed with Him upon the border and the Ratifications of the Peace Treaties between the Emperor, the Empire and His Most Christian Majesty have been exchanged.

XXII

Navigation on the Lys, from the mouth of the Danube on upwards shall be free and no payment or tariff shall be established.

XXIII

There shall be on either side a reciprocal pardon for all wrongs, hurts, and offenses committed in word and deed or in any manner whatsoever, during the course of this War, by the subjects of the Spanish Low Countries and of the places and lands ceded, or restituted, and no investigation of any sort shall be introduced.

XXIV

By means of this Peace, the subjects of His Most Christian Majesty and those of the said Spanish Low Countries and of places ceded by His Most Christian Majesty shall, while keeping the laws and customs of the country, be able to come, go, live, transport, return, bargain and negotiate together, as good merchants, and even to sell, exchange, give away or otherwise dispose of their goods and personal effects, furnishings and structures, which they have or shall have on either side; and each one shall be able to buy these, be he subject or not, without the need for any permission on either side, other than this Treaty.

The subjects of the places and lands reciprocally ceded or restituted shall be permitted, as are subjects of the said Spanish

Low Countries, to leave the said places and Spanish Low Countries to go and live where they wish, during the period of a year, with the power to sell to whomever they please, or to dispose otherwise of their effects, goods, furnishings and structures, before and after their having left, and without being impeded directly or indirectly.

XXV

These same subjects on either side, ecclesiastic, secular, corps, communities, universities and colleges shall be returned to the possession of their honors, dignities, and benefits that they had earned before the war, as well as in the possession of each and every one of their rights, goods, furnishings and structures, and incomes, seized or occupied during the present War, all of their rights, legal actions and successions coming to them even after the War had begun, and never having to furnish anything of the fruits and incomes received or having expired in the course of the War, up until the date of publication of the present Treaty. These re-establishments shall take place reciprocally, all donations, concessions, declarations, confiscations, sentences given of default in which the parties had not appeared, all shall be null and void. A total liberty shall be given these people to return to the lands from which they had withdrawn because of the War, so that now they may enjoy their goods and their incomes in person or through procurers, according to the laws and customs of the countries and states. In these restorations are included also those who, in the last War followed the side of one of the two contracting Powers. However, the arrests and judgements given in the parlements, councils and other high courts or in lower ones, and which are not expressly excluded by this Treaty, shall all be carried out and shall have their full effect; and those who, in virtue of the said seizures and judgements are now in possession of lands and manors and other goods, shall be maintained without wrong, nevertheless to the parties believing themselves to have been wronged by the said judgements, and wanting to petition by the ordinary channels and before competent judges.

XXVI

Concerning the incomes assumed on the totality of several provinces of the Low Countries, one part of which may be owned by His Most Christian Majesty, His Imperial Majesty, or others, it has been agreed that each one shall pay his part, and commissioners shall be named to regulate the portions to be paid by each side.

XXVII

Whereas, in the lands, towns, and fortifications of the Catholic Low Countries, which the Most Christian King has ceded to the Emperor, several privileges have been granted by His Most Christian Majesty to capable persons, the said privileges thus accorded shall be left to those presently holding them; and everything that concerns the Catholic, Apostolic and Roman Church shall be maintained in such a state as it was before the War in regard to the magistrates, who can only be Roman Catholics, as in the past, as well as to the bishops, chapters, monasteries, the possession of the Order of Malta, and all the clergy in general, who all shall be restored to and maintained in their churches, their liberty, franchises, immunities, rights, prerogatives and honors, as they have been under the preceding Roman Catholic Sovereign. Each and every one of the said clergy provided with any ecclesiastic possession, command,

conanate, provostship, or other privilege shall keep it without being dispossessed of it, shall enjoy the benefits and gains coming from it, and shall be able to administer and look after it as before. Likewise, the pensioners shall benefit as in the past from the pensions assigned to their benefits, whether they be created in the courts of Rome or by commissions assigned before the present War, without their being impeded for any cause or pretext whatever,

XXVIII

The communities and inhabitants of all the places, cities and lands ceded by His Most Christian Majesty in the Catholic Low Countries by this Treaty, shall be preserved and maintained with the full enjoyment of all their privileges, prerogatives, customs, exemptions, rights and concessions, popular and individual, hereditary offices and charges, with the same honor, wages, benefits and exemptions as those they enjoyed under His Most Christian Majesty; this applies only to the communities and inhabitants of the places, towns and lands that His Majesty held since the conclusion of the Treaty of Ryswick and not to the towns, places and lands owned by the late King of Spain, Charles II at the time of his death. These communities and inhabitants shall keep the benefits of the privileges, prerogatives, customs, rights, individual and popular concessions, charges and hereditary offices as they held at the death of the said late King of Spain.

XXIX

Likewise, the ecclesiastic privileges, direct and indirect, conferred during the present War by one of the parties, in places or lands then subject to them, to capable persons, according to the rule of their appointment and legitimate status set down on this subject, or according to canon dispositions set down by the Pope, the said ecclesiastic benefits shall be left to the present possessors; no one henceforth shall disturb or impede them in the legitimate holding and administration of these, nor in the collecting of their fruits, and they shall not themselves be called for any reason past or present before justice, or disturbed or molest on this account in any way; on condition, nevertheless, that they fulfill their duties toward those to whom they are bound by virtue of the said privileges.

XXX

His Imperial Majesty and His Most Christian Majesty shall not, for any reason, henceforth disturb the peace that has been established by this Treaty, take up arms, and begin, on whatever pretext, any hostile act against each other; on the contrary, they shall work sincerely and in good faith, as true friends, to strengthen more and more that mutual friendship and perfect understanding so necessary for the well-being of Christianity. And because the Most Christian King, sincerely reconciled with His Imperial Majesty, wishes henceforth to cause him no disturbance or ill, His Most Christian Majesty promises and binds to allow His Imperial Majesty to enjoy in peace and tranquility all the lands and places he now possesses and which have heretofore been held by the Kings of the House of Austria in Italy, that is to say, the Kingdom of Naples as His Imperial Majesty now possesses it, the Duchy of Milan, as His Imperial Majesty possesses that equally, the Island and Kingdom of Sardinia, as well as the ports and settlements on the coasts of Tuscany, which the said Imperial Majesty now owns and which have been owned heretofore by the Kings of Spain and the House of Austria, together with all the rights attached to the abovesaid states of Italy, which His Imperial Majesty possesses, as the Kings of Spain have, from Philip I to the recently deceased King. The said Most Christian Majesty give his royal word never to disturb the Empire or the House of Austria in this possession, either directly or indirectly, under any pretext or in any manner whatsoever, nor to oppose its possession, which His Imperial Majesty and the House of Austria now have or may have in the future, either by negotiation, treaty or any other legitimate and peaceful means, in such manner that, however, the Neutrality of Italy shall not be troubled. The Emperor promises and binds himself not to trouble said Neutrality or the peace of Italy, and, consequently, not to employ arms for any cause or occurrence whatsoever, but on the contrary, to follow and observe punctually the promises His Imperial Majesty has made in the Treaty of Neutrality concluded at Utrecht, March 14, 1713, which article shall be considered as repeated herein and shall be exactly observed by His Imperial Majesty, provided that it be observed similarly by the other side, and that He not be attacked there. To the same end, His said Imperial Majesty binds Himself to permit every Prince of Italy to enjoy in peace the states he now possesses, with no wrong done to the rights and claims of anyone.

XXXI

In order to have the Princes and states of Italy taste the fruits of the peace between the Emperor and His Most Christian Majesty, not only shall a perfect neutrality be kept there, but true and prompt justice shall be rendered by His Imperial Majesty to the Princes and Vassals of the Empire in the matter of the other places and lands in Italy that have never been held by the Kings of Spain or the House of Austria, and upon which the said Princes may have legitimate claims, such as the Duke of Guastulle, Pico de la Mirandole and the Prince of Castiglioni, without interrupting the Peace and Neutrality of Italy nor giving cause to arrive at a new war.

XXXII

Aside from the abovesaid pretentions, the Marshal, Duke de Villars being charged with several others on which he shall have to insist in the name of His Most Christian Majesty, such as those of Her Ladyship, the widowed Duchess de Elbeuf, because the inheritance and matrimonial agreements of the late Duchess de Mantone, her daughter; that of Her Ladyship the Princess de Ursins, the Princess Piombin, and finally the Duke de Saint Pierre concerning the principality of Sabionette, and on the other side, Prince Eugéne de Savoie also charged with several claims on which he shall have to insist in the name of His Imperial Majesty, that is, several claims of His Lordship the Duke de Lorraine, excluding those comprised in the Treaty of Ryswick and those in the preceding articles concerning the said Treaty; that of the Duke of Modene as well as that of the House of Aremberg, of the House of Ligne, and finally on the repayment of debts left by the French troops in the Duchy of Milan, which would all take too long a time if they were settled in this Treaty, it has been decided to postpone the discussion to the meetings to be established for that total, solemn Peace Treaty between His Imperial Majesty, the Empire, and His Most Christian Majesty, in which it shall be permitted to represent their rights and to produce their titles and reasons, which being well examined, His Imperial Majesty and His Most Christian Majesty promise to

attend only to justice; none of this, moreover, shall change or delay the execution of the Peace.

XXXIII

Since the present arrangements have not left to His Imperial Majesty time to consult the Electors, Princes and States of the Empire on the conditions of the Peace, nor leaving to the latter time to consent in the customary manner in the name of all the Empire to the conditions of this Treaty, which involves them, His Imperial Majesty promises that said Electors, Princes and States shall at once send in the name of the Empire, their full powers or else a Deputation of their own Body, equally bearing full powers, chosen to work on the solemn treaty to be made between the Emperor, the Empire, and His Most Christian Majesty. His Imperial Majesty gives his word that the said Deputation, or those charged with the full powers shall give their consent in the name of all the Empire to the points agreed upon by His Imperial Majesty and His Most Christian Majesty in the present Treaty, which He promises and binds Himself to fulfill.

XXIV

As it is stated in the Article above that the Electors, Princes, and States of the Empire shall send in the name of the Empire's a Deputation of their Body, or else their full powers for the meeting on the total and solemn Treaty of Peace to be made between His Imperial Majesty, the Empire, and His Most Christian Majesty in the place to be chosen and designated to that end, the Emperor and the Most Christian King agree on fixing the location in a neutral country outside of the Empire and the Kingdom of France, and for that reason they have given thought to the Territory of Switzerland, in which, by His Imperial Majesty or by His Most Christian Majesty, three towns shall be named from which one is to be chosen in the following manner: His Imperial Majesty naming and proposing three towns, His Most Christian Majesty shall choose the one that shall serve for the meeting, or, if His Most Christian Majesty proposes three towns, His Imperial Majesty shall have the choice of the one of the three He prefers. These propositions and choices shall take place at the time when the Treaty is signed, so that there shall be no delay nor time lost in concluding the total and solemn Peace between His Imperial Majesty, the Empire, and His Most Christian Majesty. Their Plenipotentiary Ministers shall be able to convene the 15th day of April next, or the first of May at the latest, in the place chosen for holding the meetings. During these same, the Electors, Princes and States of the Empire having claims and reasons, aside from what falls to them by the stipulated execution of the Treaty of Ryswick, to make themselves heard in particular in the total Peace Treaty to be made, shall be allowed to produce them, and His Most Christian Majesty promises to be attentive to the demands of justice; nevertheless, in order that the end of the said meetings not be delayed, it is agreed by both Parties to end it with the conclusion of the total Peace Treaty, in two months or three at the latest, beginning with the day of the opening of the meetings.

XXXV

At the moment when this Treaty is signed, all hostilities and violence on the part of the Emperor and the Empire as well as on the part of the Most Christian King shall cease, and from the day of exchange of Ratifications, His Most Christian Majesty shall no longer demand from the Empire contributions for provisions for His troops, nor shall His Imperial Majesty and the Empire ask it from the States of His Most Christian Majesty; all other demands made on account of the present War, by His Imperial Majesty, the Empire, and His Most Christian Majesty shall cease.

Political prisoners as well as prisoners of war on either side shall be returned without ransom, and fifteen days after the Ratification of this Treaty, each Prince shall withdraw his troops from the Low Countries into his own lands. His Imperial Majesty pledges Himself to withdraw His troops in the same time, and to have those of the States of the Empire withdraw, from the lands of the Archbishop of Cologne and those of Bavaria, which lands and states, moreover, shall be restored in the manner and terms specified by Articles XV, XVI, XVII, and XVIII of the present Treaty.

XXXVI

The Commerce forbidden, during the War, between the subjects of His Imperial Majesty, the Empire, and His Most Christian Majesty shall be restored immediately after the Ratification of the Treaty, with the same liberty it had before the War, and each and everyone, particularly the citizens and inhabitants of the Hanseatic Cities, shall enjoy every sort of protection on land and sea, in conformance with Article 52 of the Peace of Ryswick.

XXXVII

This Treaty shall be ratified by the Emperor and by the Most Christian King, and the exchange of the Ratifications shall be made in the Palace of Rastadt in the period of one month after the signing, or earlier, if such is possible.

In testimony whereof the above said Extraordinary and Plenipotentiary Ambassadors of His Imperial Majesty and of His Most Christian Majesty have signed the present Treaty with their own hand and have placed the seals of their arms. Done this the sixth day of March, 1714, at the Palace of Rastadt.

LE M. DUC DE VILLARS
EUGÈNE DE SAVOIE

Consequences

Because Charles refused to recognize the Bourbon king sitting on the throne of Spain, a state of war continued technically to exist between the Empire and Spain until 1720, although nobody paid that detail much mind. The settlement of the Treaty of Rastadt, like the final settlement at Utrecht the year before, became part of the foundation of European diplomacy and influenced international relations on the Continent for a generation or more.

TREATY OF AIX-LA-CHAPELLE

TREATY AT A GLANCE

Completed
October 18, 1748, at Aix-la-Chapelle, France
(present-day Aachen, Germany)

Signatories
Great Britain, Hapsburg Empire (Austria, Hungary, Bohemia, etc.),
Sardinia, the United Provinces of the Low Countries (Netherlands),
and Prussia, France, Spain, Modena, and Genoa

Overview
The TREATY OF UTRECHT, concluded in 1713, ended the War of the
Spanish Succession and was intended to bring about a permanent
peace in Europe through a stable balance of power there. In fact,
relative peace and stability endured until 1740. In that year, the
Holy Roman Emperor, Charles VI of Austria, died without a male
heir. By virtue of the Pragmatic Sanction (1713), Charles's daughter Maria Theresa had been guaranteed possession of the Hapsburg
lands, but nevertheless, Frederick II (the Great) of Prussia seized
the Austrian province of Silesia, touching off the War of the Austrian Succession (1740–48). The Treaty of Aix-la-Chapelle, which
concluded the war, brought little territorial change to Europe,
except for the Prussian possession of Silesia; however, it did mark
the emergence of Prussia as a major military power in Europe.

Historical Background

Following the death of her father, Holy Roman
Emperor Charles VI, in 1740, Maria Theresa found
herself assailed by several claimants challenging the
Pragmatic Sanction of 1713, which guaranteed her
possession of Austria and the other Hapsburg domains.
Some European powers were poised to carve up the
loose empire, and Frederick II of Prussia actually
invaded one province, Silesia, in 1740, starting the
First Silesian War. France, Spain, Bavaria, and Saxony
rallied to Frederick's cause. Great Britain, which had
come to blows with Spain over colonial and trade
issues in North and Central America, igniting the War
of Jenkins's Ear in 1739, sided with Maria Theresa.

For eight years, from 1740 to 1748, central Europe
was engulfed in war, which extended to North America (as King George's War) and colonial India (as the
Carnatic Wars). Thus, the War of the Austrian Succession might be considered a world war and was a
drawn-out prelude to the Seven Years' War of 1756–63
(called in America the French and Indian War), the
first truly global conflict.

After Maria Theresa's forces lost their first large-
scale encounter with Frederick in 1741 and Prague fell
to the French and Bavarians that same year, the
empress ceded Silesia to Prussia in 1742, hoping
thereby to secure Frederick's neutrality as she moved
to retake Prague and to invade Bavaria. Her victories in
Prague and Bavaria persuaded Saxony to re-ally itself
with her, and Sardinia worked against the forces of
Spain and Naples. Thus bolstered, Maria Theresa's
forces were able to push the French army toward the
Rhine, where it was met in battle by British forces
under the direction of George II, who scored a decisive
victory at Dettingen, Bavaria, on June 27, 1743. Following this the French retreated west across the Rhine
and turned their attention to Austria's territories in the
Netherlands. In the meantime, Frederick II reentered
the conflict in 1744, prosecuting what has been called
the Second Silesian War.

The French, defeated in Bavaria, achieved brilliant
success in the Austrian Netherlands, defeating a combined British, Dutch, and Hanoverian army under the
duke of Cumberland at Fontenoy on May 11, 1745.

The town of Tournai surrendered to the French, who also took Brussels. While these military actions were taking place, Bavaria's claimant to the Austrian throne died, prompting Bavaria to make a separate peace with Maria Theresa, securing the return of lands Austria had taken and pledging its support of Maria Theresa's husband, Francis I, as Holy Roman Emperor. With Prussian forces now isolated in Silesia, Maria Theresa moved against Frederick II, who, however, struck pre-emptively at Hohenfriedberg on June 4, 1745, routing her army. Frederick defeated two more of Maria Theresa's armies advancing against Berlin (at Hennersdorf on November 24, 1745, and at Kesseldorf, near Dresden, on December 14, 1745), prompting the empress to sign the Treaty of Dresden, affirming Prussia's control of Silesia in return for Frederick's support of her husband's accession to the Holy Roman throne.

Although the original cause of the war—the question of the Austrian succession—had been resolved, bitter, ruinous, and non-decisive combat continued in India and especially in North America, where the War of Jenkins's Ear had dissolved into King George's War, fought mainly by the British against colonial Spain and France. As in the earlier Queen Anne's War (1702–13), the American phase of the War of the Spanish Succession-combat in North America was largely a campaign of wilderness guerrilla action heavily involving France's Indian allies, who harried and terrorized English settlers.

The War of the Austrian Succession and its associated conflicts in America and India were ended less on account of the powers involved having achieved their political and military objectives than from a general state of exhaustion on all sides.

Terms

The Treaty of Aix-la-Chapelle was far less eloquent than the TREATY OF UTRECHT, which ended the War of the Spanish Succession with vivid evocations of the devastation of war and almost poetic aspirations to universal amity. In contrast, the language of Aix-la-Chapelle was straightforward and dispassionate, yet it also recognized the necessity of a European community of interest superior to destructive nationalist ambitions: "Europe sees the day, which Divine Providence had pointed out for the reestablishment of its repose. A general peace succeeds to the long and bloody war . . ."

There shall be a Christian, universal and perpetual peace, as well by sea as land, and a sincere and lasting friendship between the eight powers above-mentioned, and between their heirs and successors, kingdoms, states, provinces, countries, subjects and vassals, of what rank and condition soever they may be, without exception of places or persons. So that the high contracting powers may have the greatest attention to maintain between them and their said states and subjects, this reciprocal friendship and correspondence, not permitting any sort of hostilities to be committed, on one side or the other, on any cause, or under any pretence whatsoever; and avoiding everything that may, for the future, disturb the union happily reestablished between them; and, on the contrary, endeavouring to procure, on all occasions, whatever may contribute to their mutual glory, interest and advantage, without giving any assistance or protection, directly or indirectly, to those who would injure or prejudice any of the contracting parties.

Aside from the cession of Silesia to Prussia, the Treaty of Aix-la-Chapelle was an example of a document restoring the status quo antebellum, reestablishing conditions as they were prior to war. The construction and language of Aix-la-Chapelle were strikingly modern, taking special pains to reiterate and reaffirm existing treaties and agreements:

The treaties of Westphalia of 1648; those of Madrid, between the crowns of England and Spain, of 1667, and 1670; the treaties of peace of Nimegen of 1678, and 1679; of Ryswick of 1697; of Utrecht of 1713; of Baden of 1714; the treaty of the Triple Alliance of the Hague of 1717; that of the Quadruple Alliance of London of 1718; and the treaty of peace of Vienna of 1738, serve as a basis and foundation to the general peace, and to the present treaty; and, for this purpose, they are renewed and confirmed in the best form, and as if they were herein inserted, word for word; so that they shall be punctually observed for the future in all their tenour, and religiously executed on the one side and the other; such points however, as have been derogated from in the present treaty, excepted.

The treaty also carefully spelled out the disposition of prisoners of war, the removal of occupation forces (within six weeks), and the dismantling of fortifications.

Consequences

The Treaty of Aix-la-Chapelle was a "modern"-sounding legal and diplomatic document that (in contrast to the Treaty of Utrecht) makes scant mention of aspiration toward universal or lasting peace. It was the product of exhaustion rather than genuine resolution, a mere truce, really. Although it restored the status quo in America too, giving Louisburg back to France, its very focus on that fort caught the attention of both countries and made them aware of the increasing strength, and thus increasing importance, of Britain's American subjects. That awareness itself would spark the even more destructive Seven Years' War to come.

TREATY OF HUBERTSBURG

TREATY AT A GLANCE

Completed
February 15, 1763, at Château de Hubertsburg, Prussia

Signatories
Prussia and Austria (encompassing Hungary and Bohemia)

Overview
With the TREATY OF PARIS (1763), the Treaty of Hubertsburg concluded the Seven Years' War. Whereas the Treaty of Paris, among Britain, France, and Spain (plus Portugal), reshaped the world by delivering much of the North American continent into British hands, the Treaty of Hubertsburg, between Prussia and Austria, restored the status quo antebellum but most significantly confirmed Prussia's retention of Silesia, the disputed area that had largely provoked the present conflict as well as the earlier War of the Austrian Succession (1740–48).

Historical Background

The Treaty of Hubertsburg, along with Treaty of Paris (1763), concluded what many historians consider the first true world war in the modern period. Frederick II the Great of Prussia enjoyed initial success in what he conceived as a brief, decisive, and preemptive war against Maria Theresa's Austria, but the conflict soon escalated into the Seven Years' War and went badly for the Prussian monarch. Russia and Sweden were both allied with Maria Theresa against Prussia.

At the lowest ebb of Frederick's fortunes, however, Russia's empress Elizabeth died and was succeeded by Czar Peter III, an ardent admirer of Prussia's "benevolent despot." He promptly withdrew from the war and initiated peace negotiations. Sweden, always under Russian sway, also withdrew from the conflict. That left Maria Theresa to fight Frederick on her own; she chose the better part of valor and opted for a peace, which Frederick was quite willing to accept.

Terms

Somewhat in contrast to the other great document of the Seven Years' War, the Treaty of Paris (1763), the Treaty of Hubertsburg took on a personal tone, framing the conflict in terms of a dispute between monarchs rather than nations:

I

Henceforth, there shall be an inviolable and perpetual peace together with a sincere unity and perfect friendship between, on the one hand, Her Apostolic Majesty, Empress and Queen of Hungary and Bohemia and, on the other His Majesty, the King of Prussia, their heirs and successors and all their states and subjects so that, in the future, the two High Contracting Parties shall not commit or allow to be committed any act of hostility whether secretly or in public, direct or indirect, nor shall they under any conceivable pretext undertake anything that might be detrimental to the other. Rather shall they concentrate on maintaining mutual friendship and agreement between themselves and their states and subjects, shunning anything that might in the future alter the unity so fortunately restored and shall endeavor at all times to further their mutual glory, interest and advantage.

Also, while it had long been conventional to include a treaty article forestalling any subsequent actions of vengeance by consigning to "oblivion" wrongs and injuries committed on any and all sides, Hubertsburg again assumed a deliberate, direct, plain, and even personal tone:

II

Both sides shall grant a general amnesty and totally wipe from their memory all hostilities, losses, damages and injuries whatever their nature, committed or sustained on either side during the recent disturbances. Hostilities shall nevermore be alluded to nor shall any compensation be claimed under any pretext or in any name. No subject on either side shall ever be troubled but shall enjoy this amnesty and all its effects to the full, despite the decrees sent out and published; all orders for confiscation shall be withdrawn and goods confiscated or sequestrated shall be returned to their owners, from whom they were taken during the recent disturbances.

As in essence a status quo antebellum document, the Treaty of Hubertsburg provided insight into such highly consequential human details attending the cessation of hostilities as the settlement of debts and the disposition of prisoners of war:

VI

Levies and deliveries of any kind together with all requests for recruits, settlers, wagons, horses etc. and all forced contributions in general, will cease the day the present Treaty is signed; all that may be exacted, seized or collected after that date shall be handed back in good faith and without delay.

Both sides shall waive all arrears of levies and taxes; bills of exchange or other promises in writing given concerning these things, shall be declared null and void and shall be handed back free of charge to those who issued them. Also, hostages taken or given in connection with these same things, shall be freed without ransom and all the above shall be effected immediately following the exchange of ratifications of the present Treaty.

VII

Both sides shall hand over their prisoners of war in good faith, without ransom and regardless of their number or military rank, though not until after having paid the debts they contracted while in captivity. Both sides shall renounce to what may have been supplied or advanced to these prisoners for their maintenance and keep and the same shall be done with the sick or wounded immediately after their recovery. For this purpose, each side shall appoint generals and commissaries who, immediately after the exchange of the ratifications, shall proceed to exchange all prisoners of war in certain places yet to be determined.

All that is stipulated in this article shall also apply to the states of the Empire, in accordance with the general stipulation mentioned in Article XIX. However, as His Majesty, the King of Prussia and the States of the Empire have themselves contributed towards the maintenance and keep of their respective prisoners of war, and that certain individuals may have made advances for this purpose, the High Contracting Parties do not intend by the above stipulations to derogate from the claims these individuals may have concerning this matter.

Article 20 provided that the two "High Contracting Parties have agreed to include their friends and allies in the present peace Treaty and they reserve their right to name them in a separate act that shall have the same binding force as though it were inserted word for word in this treaty, and it shall also be ratified by the two High Contracting Parties."

The "separate act" was signed on March 12 and 20 in order to avoid postponing implementation of "this stipulation." Included by virtue of the separate act were Maria Theresa's allies, the kings of Sweden and Poland (who was also the elector of Saxony), "and all the Princes and States of the Empire who are her friends or allies"; and Frederick's allies, the king of England, the duke of Brunswick-Lunebourg, and the landgrave of Hesse-Cassel. Most significant was the sense of urgency that motivated both Article 20 and the separate act that followed it within a month.

There were also two secret articles, which provided a window on the workings of diplomacy among Europe's family of monarchs:

SECRET ARTICLES

I

His Majesty the King of Prussia, Elector of Brandenburg, wishing to give Her Apostolic Majesty, Empress and Queen of Hungary and Bohemia, a proof of his friendship as well as of the pleasure he derives from entering into anything that pleases this Princess, promises to vote for His Royal Highness, Archduke Joseph in the coming election of the Holy Roman Emperor.

II

His Majesty the Emperor and Her Majesty the Empress and Queen having decided, in a convention with His Most Serene Highness of Modene, the marriage of one of the younger Archdukes to the Princess of Modene, granddaughter of the above-mentioned Duke and, having determined to speak to the Emperor and the Empire that the succession to the states of Modene go to whichever Archduke marries the said Princess; His Majesty, the King of Prussia, most gladly, inasfar as it depends on him, shall enter into anything that may please Their Imperial Majesties, pledges his word now and forever to vote for this should the need arise; Their Majesties in turn, assure His Prussian Majesty of their gratitude and of their sincere desire of giving him proof of their friendship whenever they have the opportunity of so doing.

Consequences

In signing the treaty, clearly both sides were highly motivated to end the war quickly. Frederick recognized that his resources were exhausted, while Maria Theresa understood that further prosecution of the war without Russia and Sweden was hopeless. The settlement between them was direct and personal, and out of such bonds was the fabric of European diplomacy created.

Annexations and Territorial Agreements

FIRST PARTITION OF POLAND

TREATY AT A GLANCE

Completed
(1) July 25, 1772, at St. Petersburg, Russia; (2) September 18, 1773,
at Warsaw, Poland; (3) March 15–18, 1775, at Warsaw;
(4) February 9, 1776, at Warsaw; (5) August 22, 1776, at Warsaw

Signatories
(1) Russia and Prussia; Russia and Austria; Prussia and Austria;
(2) Poland and Russia; Poland and Prussia; Poland and Austria;
(3) Poland and Russia; Poland and Prussia; Poland and Austria;
(4) Poland and Austria; (5) Poland and Prussia

Overview
The first of three partitions of Poland (see SECOND PARTITION OF
POLAND and THIRD PARTITION OF POLAND) that divided the Polish
kingdom among its three powerful neighbors, Russia, Austria, and
Prussia, was initiated in 1772 (the other two came in 1793 and
1795). The First Partition gave Russia part of northeast Poland,
while the balance of power in eastern Europe was maintained by
Austria's annexation of Galicia and Prussia's annexation of Polish
Pomerania and Ermeland. This was accomplished by a complex of
treaties and "separate instruments" drawn up between 1772 and
1776.

Historical Background

The TREATY OF PARIS (1763) and the TREATY OF HUBERTS-
BURG (1763), ending the Seven Years' War, left Austria
and Prussia dissatisfied, because Austria had failed in
its bid to regain Silesia from Prussia, while Prussia had
failed to acquire Saxony. In the meantime, Russia was
making advances against its traditional rival Ottoman
Turkey and was concerned to forestall aggression from
Austria. In 1764 Catherine II the Great of Russia engineered the election of a puppet monarch in Poland,
Stanislaus Poniatowski, thereby making the nation a
virtual Russian satellite. She proposed to use Poland
as a means of placating both Prussia and Austria in
order to maintain a balance of power that would protect her as she carried out her campaign against
Turkey. Therefore, the three powers carved the Polish
prize. To Austria, Poland yielded Galicia; to Prussia,
the territories of West Prussia and Ermeland; and to
Russia went almost one-third of the remaining terri-

tory, while what was left of Poland became a Russian
dependency.

Terms

The treaty document of July 25, 1772, began by asserting Russia's role as protector of Poland and protector of
the general peace:

In the name of the Very Sainted Trinity.
　　The spirit of faction, turmoils and civil war that has
been agitating the Kingdom of Poland for so many
years, and the anarchy which every day gathers there
new forces to the point of annihilating all the authority of a regular government, causing justified fears of a
forthcoming total decomposition of the State, and of
disturbing the interests of all her neighbors, impairing
the good harmony existing among them, and kindling
a general war, now, due to these disturbances, difficulties resulted between Her Imperial Majesty of all the
Russias and the Ottoman Porte; at the same time, the

neighboring powers of the Republic have ancient and legitimate claims and rights which they have never been able to maintain and which they risk to lose forever, unless they take measures to assert them and reinstall tranquility and order in the interior of this Republic and secure for her a political existence more in harmony to the interests of her neighbors.

The First Partition of Poland was not a single unified treaty but a complex of 15 separate treaties and "separate instruments," spanning 1772 to 1776 and variously involving Russia, Prussia, Austria, and—almost incidentally—Poland. For example, in the first of the treaties, Catherine II unilaterally divides Poland between Russia and Prussia:

I

Her Majesty the Empress of all the Russias, for herself and for her descendants, heirs and successors, shall take into her possession within the time and terms provided by the article that follows, the rest of Polish Livonia as well as the part of the Palatinate of Polotsk which is beyond the Dzwina river, and likewise the Palatinate of Witebsk; thus, the Dzwina river will form the natural border between the two states up to the special frontier of the Witebsk Palatinate with that of Polotsk, following this border up to the point where the borders of the three Palatinates, that is, of Polotsk, Witebsk and of Minsk have joined; from said point the boundary will be extended in a straight line up to the source of the river Druc, towards the place called Ordwa and from there down this river to where it joins the Dnieper; thus all the Palatinate of Mscislaw both this side and beyond the Dnieper, and the two extremities of the Minsk Palatinate underneath and above that of Mscislaw beyond the new border and the Dnieper, will belong to the Empire of all the Russias; and from the mouth of the Druc river the Dnieper will be the border between the two states preserving, however, to the city of Kiiow and to its district the border which they now have on the other side of this river.

III

Her Imperial Majesty of all the Russias, for herself and her descendants, heirs and successors, guarantees formally to His Majesty the King of Prussia the countries and districts of Poland, which by virtue of a mutual accord, His said Majesty shall take into possession; which consist of all of Pomerania, the city of Danzig with its territory excluded, as well as in the districts of Greater-Poland beyond the Notec (Netze), along this river from the frontier of the *Nouvelle-Marche* to the Vistula near Fordon and Solitz; so that the Netze shall form the border of the States of His Prussian Majesty, and that this river will belong entirely to Him; and also, inasmuch as His said Majesty shall not make further claims on the several other districts of Poland bordering Silesia and Prussia which His Majesty could rightfully claim, and by waiving at the same time all his aspirations to the city of Danzig and its territory, shall, in compensation,

take the rest of Polish Prussia, notably the Palatinate of Malborg or Marienburg, the city of Elbing included, with the Bishopric of Warmie and the Palatinate of Chelmno (Culm), excepting only the city of Thorn which shall be preserved with all its territory under the domination of the Republic of Poland.

Moreover, the motive of balancing this gift to Prussia against Russia's war with the Ottomans was made explicit by Article 4:

IV

As Her Imperial Majesty of all the Russias, who has been waging war for more than three years, a special war against the Ottoman Empire just because of Poland, has communicated with full confidence to His Majesty the King of Prussia the definitive conditions under which she would consent to make peace with the Porte and that by means of this new plan Her said Majesty would neither insist upon the conquest nor even upon the independence of Walachia and Moldavia, and hence would no longer insist on the first conditions which were directly contrary to the immediate interest of the States of His Prussian Majesty. His Majesty the King of Prussia, conforming to his sentiments of sincere friendship for Her Imperial Majesty of all the Russians, promises to continue his sincere endeavors towards a desirable success of the negotiations of the Congress, consequently towards the good offices to which She has committed herself on behalf of the two belligerent parties.

An additional treaty document similarly disposed of Austria's portion of Poland, and further treaties defined the relation between Austria and Prussia with regard to the Polish partition. It was not until the fourth document, concluded on September 18, 1773, that Poland itself was included in the agreement. After imposing and defining the surrender of Polish territories to Russia in Article 2, Article 6 presented a solemn guarantee:

VI

Her Imperial Majesty of all the Russias formally and explicitly guaranties, in the strongest manner, to His Majesty the King of Poland and his successors, and to the Republic of Poland, all the present possessions, according to the extension and in the state in which they remain after the Treaties concluded between the most serene Republic of Poland and their Majesties the Empress-Queen of Hungary and Bohemia and the King of Prussia. Likewise, His Majesty the King and the Republic of Poland guarantee to Her Imperial Majesty of all the Russias and her successors the present possessions in Europe, according to the extent and in the state they exist after the conclusion of the same Treaties. And the two High Contracting Parties declare that it is as a result of this new state of affairs that article II of their Treaty of 1768 should be extended and executed.

The next two treaties in this First Partition complex were between Prussia and Poland and Austria and Poland, with Poland consenting to the cession of territories to these nations. Finally, the various "separate instruments" that followed the basic treaties defined the government of what remained of Poland and the commercial relations among Poland, Russia, Prussia, and Austria.

Consequences

The partition served only to humiliate the Poles, who acted to strengthen their central government, adopting a new constitution on May 3, 1791, which abolished the elective monarchy that had been engineered by Russia and replaced it with a hereditary kingship meant to place the crown beyond such foreign manipulation. Simultaneously, it introduced liberal reforms abolishing feudal legal and social practices. In response to the resurgence of Poland, Russia intervened militarily and concluded a Second Partition with Prussia in 1793.

SECOND PARTITION OF POLAND

TREATY AT A GLANCE

Completed
January 23, 1793, and December 23, 1794/ January 23, 1795,
at St. Petersburg, Russia

Signatories
Russia and Prussia

Overview
The second of three partitions of Poland, including a FIRST PARTI-
TION OF POLAND and a THIRD PARTITION OF POLAND, this treaty gave
Russia most of eastern Poland and gave Prussia Gdansk and the
region known as Great Poland.

Historical Background

As noted, the Seven Years' War left Austria and Prussia
disgruntled because Austria had failed to take back
Silesia from Prussia and Prussia had failed to gain Saxony. For its part, Russia was making advances against
Ottoman Turkey and sought a means of forestalling
aggression from Austria. In 1764 Catherine II the Great
of Russia had installed a puppet monarch in Poland;
with the First Partition, she used what had become a
satellite nation as a means of placating both Prussia
and Austria in order to maintain a balance of power to
protect her as she carried out her campaign against
Turkey.

Humiliated by these high-handed encroachments
into their sovereignty, the Poles reformed and strengthened their government, adopting a new constitution on
May 3, 1791, which replaced the elective monarchy
with hereditary kingship and abolished the trappings of
what had been a hopelessly outmoded feudal state. Now
fearful that Poland would indeed revive as a nation and
fight to recover its lands, Russia invaded and concluded
the Second Partition (1793) with Prussia, which
Poland, where a revolt had broken out in response to
the Russian repression, was not invited to sign.

Terms

In contrast to the lengthy and complex First Partition
treaty, made up of 15 separate documents, the Second
Partition was simple and direct. As the signatories had
justified the First Partition on the grounds of putting
an end to the "spirit of faction, turmoils and civil war

. . . agitating the Kingdom of Poland," the language of
the Second Partition was even more sweeping. It
defined the partition as a kind of diplomatic duty in a
world turned upside down by revolution:

In the Name of the Most Holy and Indivisible Trinity.

The troubles which shake Europe in the wake of
the deadly Revolution that has occurred in France
present the aspect of an imminent and universal danger in the growth and extension of which they appear
liable, if the Powers whose interest it is to maintain
order, the only solid foundation for the general safety
and peace, do not hasten to make provision by the
most rigorous and effective of means. Her Majesty the
Empress of all the Russias and His Majesty the King of
Prussia, forthwith upon the successful renewal of the
treaties of friendship and alliance which have existed
between them, have hastened to bring their entire
attention to bear upon a matter of such importance,
and having communicated with mutual confidence
Their ideas and Their thoughts on this matter, They
have found all the more cause for concern, for They
have seen definite indications that this same spirit of
dangerous rebellion and innovation which at present
reigns in France is on the verge of breaking out in the
Kingdom of Poland, which immediately borders Their
respective possessions. This state of affairs has naturally caused Their Imperial and Royal Majesties to
realize the necessity for increasing Their precautions
and efforts towards protecting Their subjects from the
effects of an evil and often contagious example, and at
the same time to contrive in such a manner that these
efforts might procure both the present and future
safety, and compensation for the exorbitant expense
which they must inevitably necessitate. In order that
in this sense they might determine and assure their

respective interests, as well as those of His Majesty the Holy Roman Emperor, King of Hungary and of Bohemia, their mutual Ally who shares their principles and unites with them in the same goal; Their said Majesties have deemed it advisable to fix and conclude between them an explicit and formal agreement, and at the same time one that will be secret. And to this end They have chosen, named and authorized that is to say: Her Majesty the Empress of all the Russias Count Jean d'Ostermann, Her Vice Chancellor, present Privy Counselor, Senator etc., etc.; Count Alexandre de Besborodko, present Privy Counselor, *Premier-maître* of the Court etc., and Count Arcadi de Morcoff, Privy Counselor, member of the Council of Foreign Affairs etc.; and His Majesty the King of Prussia, Count Henri Leopold de Goltz, Colonel of the cavalry in his armies and Envoy Extraordinary and Minister Plenipotentiary to the Court of Her Majesty the Empress of all the Russias; which Plenipotentiaries, after having made known and exchanged their full powers, entered into agreement on the following articles.

The balance of the treaty defined the partition and asserted conditions intended to maintain a balance of power between Russia and Prussia and with Austria:

Her Majesty the Empress of all the Russias pledges that as long as shall last the troubles now caused by the insurrection in France and her invasion of Germany, and in the hereditary States of her Allies, His Majesty the Holy Roman Emperor and His Majesty the King of Prussia, to maintain her land and sea forces in this state of fearsome armament in which they are now held ready, so that they may be at hand both to defend her own States against any possible attack and to lend aid and assistance to her Allies according to the cases stipulated by the Treaties, as well as to repress and contain, at the first requisition that shall be made, any rebellion or other trouble which might arise in either Poland or in some province belonging to the said High Allies which lies contiguous to this State.

ARTICLE II

For compensation of the expenses which such armament will entail and for reasons of safety and general peace revealed here above, Her Majesty the Empress of all the Russias, for Herself and her Descendants, Heirs and Successors, shall take possession, at the time and in the manner stipulated by the following article, of the lands and provinces situated and included in the line marked on the map, which line begins with the settlement of Druya, which is located at the *Cape of Simigalle* and on the left bank of the *Dvina*; from there it extends to *Naroca* and *Doubrava* progressing along the border of the *Palatinate* of *Vilna* to the settlement of *Stolpezc*, continuing to Nisviecz, then to *Pinsk* and from there running through Kuniew between *Vischgrodeck* and *Novogrebla* near the border of *Galicia*, which it follows up until the river *Dniester*. It ends finally, still following the course of this river, at *Jagor-*

lic, the present day frontier of Russia on that particular side, so that all the lands, cities and districts designated here above will belong forever to the Empire of Russia and are guaranteed to her from this time forth by His Majesty the King of Prussia in the most formal and most binding manner.

ARTICLE III

Her Imperial Majesty of all the Russias shall occupy by the body of her troops the places and districts which by virtue of the preceding article She proposes to join to her States and She fixes for this taking of possession the period from next 25 March to 10 April old style of the current year, pledging herself to state nothing until that time regarding her views and her plans.

ARTICLE IV

His Majesty the King of Prussia pledges on his side to continue to make common cause with His Majesty the Holy Roman Emperor in the war which Their Majesties are now waging against the French rebels and to make neither a separate peace nor a separate truce until They have accomplished the goal that They announced in Their joint declarations, and have forced these disturbers of the peace to renounce their hostile enterprises abroad and their criminal attempts within the Kingdom of France.

ARTICLE V

As compensation for the expenses that this war has entailed and will entail in the future, as well as for the other considerations which are shared by His Majesty the King of Prussia and Her Majesty the Empress of all the Russias, His Prussian Majesty will take possession of the lands, cities and districts located and included in the line drawn on the map from *Czenstochowe* through *Rawa* to *Soldau*, also adding the city of Dantzig together with its territory; so that these lands, provinces and cities will belong forever to the Prussian Monarchy and are henceforth guaranteed to this Monarchy by Her Majesty the Empress of all the Russias in the most formal and most binding of manners.

ARTICLE VI

The taking of possession of the localities and districts indicated here above will be carried out in the name of His Prussian Majesty in the same fashion and at the same time as that of the Lands transmitted to Her Majesty the Empress of all the Russias by virtue of Article II of the present agreement.

ARTICLE VII

And by virtue of a series of bonds of friendship and Treaties which unite Her Majesty the Empress of all the Russias with His Majesty the King of Prussia to Their mutual ally His Majesty the Holy Roman Emperor, as well as in consideration of the assent which this latter has seen fit to give to the present agreement and for the part that he has taken in the events which have warranted his action, Their said Imperial and Royal Majesties pledge to contrive and advance his interests to the same extent as Their own;

They undertake by virtue of the present article between Themselves, as well as between His Majesty the Holy Roman Emperor not to fail to employ, when such time will arrive, and when They will be required to do so, any of Their good services, nor any other effective means which will be in Their power, in order to assist Him to obtain the exchange which he desires to make of his hereditary States of the Low Countries for Bavaria, and adding such advantages as shall be compatible with the general agreement.

ARTICLE VIII

In consequence of the present stipulation the two High contracting Parties will, immediately upon final drafting of the present Act, hasten to communicate in secret to His Majesty the Holy Roman Emperor and will invite him to accede formally to it, and likewise to give his guarantee to all the stipulations which have here been declared, as well as to the real results which will follow, Her Majesty the Empress of all the Russias and His Majesty the King of Prussia pledge by virtue of the present article to His Majesty the Holy Roman Emperor a perfectly reciprocal guarantee relative to the above mentioned exchange of the Low Countries for Bavaria, as soon as it shall be brought into effect.

ARTICLE IX

If in hatred for the present agreement and of its results one of the two High Contracting Powers finds itself attacked by no matter what third Power, the other will join forces with her and will assist her with all his might and means until the ceasing of all hostilities has been achieved.

ARTICLE X

As it will be necessary to arrive at a definite arrangement with the Republic of Poland regarding their respective acquisitions, Her Majesty the Empress of all the Russias and His Majesty the King of Prussia pledge reciprocally to give to Their Ambassadors or respective Ministers accredited to the Court of Warsaw, as well as to Their generals commanding Their troops in Poland, the most precise instructions so that they may move together in common accord and in perfect harmony between themselves in order to support this negotiation with the action that will be most appropriate in assuring success.

ARTICLE XI

The present convention will be ratified in six weeks or earlier, if this will be possible.

In witness whereof we the Plenipotentiaries of Her Imperial Majesty of all the Russias and His Prussian Majesty have signed etc.

Done at St. Petersburg the 12/23 January 1793.

(L.S.) COMTE JEAN D'OSTERMANN.
(L.S.) COMTE DE GOLTZ.
(L.S.) ALEXANDRE COMTE BESBORODKO.
(L.S.) ARCADI DE MORCOFF.

His said Imperial Majesty and Royal Apostolic having nothing closer to his heart than to give at every occasion to Her Imperial Majesty of all the Russias, his Ally, all the proofs of friendship which are in his power; He has enabled in consequence of his most ample powers Count Louis de Cobenzl etc. to proceed in his name to this accession. The latter therefore declares, that His Imperial Majesty and Royal Apostolic adheres by virtue of the present Act to the above mentioned Agreement insofar as it concerns the direct interests of the two Imperial Courts, the exchange of Bavaria for the Low Countries and the acquisitions made in virtue of this Agreement by the Imperial Court of Russia, to which Court only until the court of Berlin has in turn acceded to the arrangement agreed upon between the two Imperial Courts relative to the new Partition of Poland, His Majesty the Emperor formally and solemnly guarantees the above mentioned acquisitions.

In witness whereof We Plenipotentiary of His Majesty the Holy Roman Emperor and Royal Apostolic have in virtue of our full powers signed the present Act of accession, have had set to it the seal of our arms, and have exchanged it for the Act of acceptance made in the name of Her Imperial Majesty of all the Russias.
Done at St. Petersburg December 23, 1794
January 3, 1795

(L.S.) COBENZL

Consequences

This second land grab prompted Tadeusz Kościuszko to lead a national revolt in 1794, which was soon crushed by Russia and Prussia, which, along with Austria, imposed on the beleaguered nation a Third Partition in 1795.

THIRD PARTITION OF POLAND

TREATY AT A GLANCE

Completed
October 24, 1795, at St. Petersburg, Russia

Signatories
Russia, Prussia, and Austria

Overview
The third of three partitions of Poland—including a FIRST PARTITION OF POLAND and a SECOND PARTITION OF POLAND—this treaty accomplished the final dismemberment of Poland, dividing among Russia, Prussia, and Austria what remained after the Second Partition.

Historical Background

The conclusion of the Seven Years' War left Austria and Prussia dissatisfied because Austria had failed to regain Silesia from Prussia, while Prussia had failed to acquire Saxony. Russia, having turned its attention to acquiring territory from Ottoman Turkey, wanted to forestall aggression from Austria. Having installed a puppet monarch in Poland in 1764, Catherine II the Great of Russia instigated the First Partition, by which she gave Prussia and Austria portions of Poland in order to placate them, maintaining a balance of power to protect her as she carried out her campaign against Turkey. Humiliated by these encroachments, the Poles reformed and strengthened their government, adopting a new constitution on May 3, 1791, which replaced the elective monarchy with hereditary kingship and abolished the trappings of what had been a hopelessly outmoded feudal state. In response, Russia invaded Poland and with Prussia concluded the Second Partition (1793), seizing even more territory.

This prompted the Polish patriot Tadeusz Kościuszko to lead a national revolt in 1794, which ultimately failed as a result of combined Russian and Prussian intervention. Following the defeat of Kościuszko, Russia and Prussia invited Europe's third great power, Austria, to participate in this third attempt to settle the Polish "problem" as it had in the first—a bid to make this agreement a more legitimate and, therefore, lasting "international" arrangement. The three drew up the Third Partition (1795), by which they absorbed all that was left of Poland.

Terms

The treaty of the First Partition was a lengthy and complex diplomatic agreement of 15 separate documents. The treaty of the Second Partition, in contrast, was simple and direct. The Third Partition was even briefer and, in fact, the product of haste. Whereas most treaties present the conclusions of negotiations, the Third Partition in large part was a promise that conclusions would be reached in the future. Also in contrast to the documents of the First and Second Partitions, the Third Partition made no attempt to rationalize the Polish dismemberment as either a means of restoring order to Poland or avoiding a general revolution in eastern Europe. Instead, the treaty was framed as the product of a desire "to find a more perfect and final accord concerning the stipulations contained" in the Second Partition and to "fix more precisely the limits that are to separate the respective States of three Powers adjoining Poland after the total partition of that state."

The Third Partition of Poland was, in effect, the reductio ad absurdum of the politics of late 18th-century maneuver, the politics of creating and maintaining a balance of power at the cost of some client state. The brief document is reproduced here in its entirety.

In the Name of the Most Holy and Indivisible Trinity.
    Her Majesty, the Empress of all the Russias, and His Majesty, the King of Prussia, desiring to find a more perfect and final

accord concerning the stipulations contained in the Declaration issued here at St. Petersburg on December 23, 1794 (January 3, 1795), by the two Imperial Courts and recently transmitted to the Court of Berlin, and desiring to fix more precisely the limits that are to separate the respective States of three Powers adjoining Poland after the total partition of that state, have thus chosen and named to this end their Plenipotentiaries, that is to say: for Her Majesty, the Empress, Count Jean d'Ostermann, Vice Chancellor, Private Advisor, Senator, and Knight of the Orders of St. Andre, etc.; His Lordship, Count Alexandre de Besborodko, Grand Master of the Court, Privy-Councillor, Director-General of the Guard, and Knight of the Orders of St. Andre, etc.; and His Lordship Arcadi de Morcoff, Privy-Councillor, Member of the Council on Foreign Affairs, etc.; and for His Majesty, the King of Prussia, His Lordship, Count Frederick Bogislaw Emanuel de Tauentzien, His special Envoy and Minister Plenipotentiary to the Court of Russia, Chamberlain, Colonel of the Infantry and Aide-de-Camp, Knight of the Order of Merit and of the Order of St. John of Jerusalem, who all having convened, together with the Plenipotentiary of His Majesty, the Holy Roman Emperor, His Lordship, Count Louis de Cobenzl, Grand Cross of the Royal Order of St. Stephen of Hungary, His Chamberlain, Private Councillor, Special Plenipotentiary Ambassador to Her Imperial Majesty of all the Russias, and having thus made known and having exchanged their full powers, all found to be in good order, have agreed upon the following articles:

ARTICLE I

The Declaration referred to in the Preamble of this Act is taken, as if it had been inserted word for word, to be the immutable base of the present accord in all that concerns the acquisitions of Her Majesty, the Empress of all the Russias. Therefore, Her Imperial Majesty shall keep possession of all the lands, cities, districts and other domains that are thereby designated, and His Prussian Majesty guarantees to Her the perpetual use and possession of these.

ARTICLE II

His Majesty, the Holy Roman Emperor, because of his friendship toward His Prussian Majesty, yields in His favor that extremity of land extending in a straight line from Swydry on the Vistula to the confluence of the Bug and the Narew, in such a manner that all this district shall be contained in the portion ceded, according to the terms of that same Declaration, to His Prussian Majesty, and of which His Imperial Majesty grants him equally the perpetual use and possession.

ARTICLE III

The demarcation of the future boundaries between the States of Austria and Prussia in the Province of Cracow (Cracovie) remaining undecided, and the two contracting parties, moved by the mutual desire to see it settled in a manner suitable for the securing of a distinct border, fitting and proper and sheltered from all invasions, it has been agreed that it shall be determined and fixed in a conciliatory manner by demarcating commissioners, who shall be sent to the area by both parties, and to whom Her Imperial Majesty of all the Russias shall join one on her behalf to serve as conciliator and arbitrator in the case of differences of opinion between the commissioners of the interested parties; and the latter, because of their confidence in the impartiality of Her Imperial Majesty, and in her equal friendship toward them, promise and contract themselves to abide entirely by Her opinions and her decisions in this matter. In addition, it is agreed that all work on this demarcation shall be completed within the period of three months from the date of the signing of this Treaty. In the meantime, all the territory marked out on the map of Zanoni by a line drawn from the point where the river Sola flows into the Vistula, between Grozow and Gromiec, then passing diagonally by Krzeszowice and continuing, skirting and leaving to the right the cities of Skala and Michnow, and ending at Czarnowice on the Pilice, from whence it follows the course of that river, shall remain occupied by the troops of His Prussian Majesty until the work of the Demarcation in question be completed and confirmed according to the order established above.

ARTICLE IV

His Majesty, the Holy Roman Emperor and His Majesty, the King of Prussia solemnly guarantee to each other in advance the territories that shall be awarded to them respectively after the findings of the joint Commission and the arbitration of Her Imperial Majesty of all the Russias, and these same territories shall be guaranteed in a like manner by Her said Majesty.

ARTICLE V

But the city of Cracow, as well as other lands ceded according to this Treaty and the above-mentioned Declaration of December 23, 1794 (January 3, 1795) to His Majesty, the Holy Roman Emperor, and where there would still be troops of His Prussian Majesty, shall be evacuated in the space of six weeks after the signing of this Treaty and returned to those charged by His Majesty, the Holy Roman Emperor to receive and take possession of them.

ARTICLE VI

In a like manner shall the evacuation and relinquishing of the lands and cities now occupied by the troops of Her Majesty, the Empress of all the Russias, and ceded by this agreement to His Prussian Majesty be carried out.

ARTICLE VII

If, in hostility to this Treaty of Partition and its consequences, one of the three high contracting Powers finds Herself attacked by whatever power it may be, the two others shall join Her and assist Her with all their strength and their means, until the total cessation of that attack.

ARTICLE VIII

This Treaty shall be ratified in the manner customary to the two contracting Courts, and the ratifications shall be exchanged in the space of six weeks or less, if such be possible.

In testimony whereof, We, the respective Plenipotentiaries have signed and affixed our seals.

At Saint Petersburg on this Thirteenth (Twenty-fourth) day of October, 1795.

(L. S.) COUNT JEAN D'OSTERMANN
(L.S.) COUNT ALEXANDER DE BESBORODKO
(L. S.) ARCADI MORCOFF
(L. S.) COUNT FREDERICK BOGISLAS
EMANUEL DE TAUENTZIEN

Consequences

The partitions of Poland were not simply examples of more powerful nations victimizing a less powerful one—although they were that. More important, the partitions marked the ascendancy of true nation-states over what was, in effect, an outmoded feudal country. Although Poland was ostensibly a republic, it was really an oligarchy conducted by a group of nobles. It was therefore internally weak and unable to withstand the onslaught of more modern states.

The partitions were also an example of a new kind of European diplomacy that would dominate the 19th and 20th centuries to come. It was a diplomacy of grand strategies and the creation of an elusive balance of power. Much as the two world wars of the 20th century would do, the Seven Years' War—perhaps the globe's first "world war"—prompted the great European powers to search for a new way of asserting their dominance. Engineering the balance of power by preying upon dependent nations was the solution enacted by the partitions of Poland.

The restoration of the Polish state would not be accomplished until the end of World War I.

Part Five

A NEW WORLD

INTRODUCTION

North America was born in the European struggle for empire, its ideological creation shaped especially by the conflict between England and France. During the early 17th century, both countries began establishing themselves on the continent, and by the mid-1600s both were in a position to challenge the New World monopoly that Spain had built during a century of exploration and conquest. Though both the French and English fought sporadic backwoods battles with Spain, they soon became much more concerned about their respective relations with the various Indian "nations" they encountered than about the fragmented outposts of the Spanish Empire.

The Spanish thought of North America as the "Northern Mystery," essentially a missionary outpost of their empire centered in Mexico. The French saw the same region as the great "sea of the West," a vast potential reserve of fur—a land fit, perhaps, for the establishment of trading posts but not to occupy and colonize with French families and French farms. The British, inching their way onto the continent in earnest during the early 17th century, were the first to define the vast American interior geographically as a destination and to treat traveling to that destination in itself as an ideological and economic enterprise. It was not the Spanish, nor the French, but the British colonials who first went "westering," that is, who first moved westward, not merely to explore, conquer, and exploit, but also to people a new world.

The diplomacy of this New World was certainly entangled with that of the old, and treaties dealing with the internecine struggles in Europe often had major repercussions upon the European empires in the Western Hemisphere. How these empires were established and settled also had an impact on European diplomacy, and in the case of the Seven Years' War, the conflict itself was ignited in the interior wilderness of North America. Finally, it was the economic and social structures of the individual European countries themselves that determined the nature of their enterprises outside national borders and dictated the subject and style of the treaty making with those they encountered in their imperial adventures.

Savage Land

After John Cabot, a Genovese sailor hired by England's Henry VII, made landfall in June 1497 along the southern shore of Newfoundland and laid claim to North America for the Crown, England ignored the continent for nearly 80 years. Not until the Elizabethan period, when the British Isles wholeheartedly entered the competition with Spain for overseas empire, did English sea dogs take up exploring again. Sir Francis Drake sailed the *Golden Hind* up the California coast in 1578; Sir Humphrey Gilbert tried to establish a colony in Newfoundland in 1583; after Sir Walter Raleigh's colony at Roanoke foundered in 1587, Jamestown was established in 1607.

The colonization of America by the English, however, would quickly take on a different cast than that by either the Spanish or the French. As had the Dutch before them, the English would form land and trading companies to provide the men and money that made settlement in North America possible. They recruited settlers, transported them across the Atlantic, and subsidized the colonies they established. Corporations such as the London Company, the Plymouth Company, and the old Dutch West Indies Company invested substantial sums trying to establish colonies that would produce minerals, furs, and other commodities to sell in the world market. In addition, the companies acquired from the Indians large tracts of lands that they used as manors in hopes of receiving rental income. Over time, the English companies—again, like the Dutch before them—failed to produce large returns for their investors from trade, not least because the French were so well positioned in the Indian trade. Speculation in land, on the other hand, proved more promising. It became commonplace for first the Dutch, then the English, government to charter companies, grant them huge tracts of land and administrative powers, and send them off to settle land in the New World.

Thus, while the more adventuresome French, much fewer in number, remained primarily traders and spread westward down the St. Lawrence and into the expanses of the interior, the English immigrants established compact little settlements all along the Atlantic coast on company lands. As these English seaboard colonies were established and grew in the 18th century, investments in land farther inland to the west promised a rapid turnover of capital and at least the hope of renewed profit. New land companies sprang into existence, some of them purely local affairs, others corporations that took investments both from the colonists and from English capitalists. American colonials, men like Conrad Weisner, Christopher Gist, and George Croghan, hirelings of the investment companies and historical prototypes of western "frontiersmen," explored the North American interior from the compact seacoast settlements. Driven by land speculation and, increasingly, the fur trade, they would traipse the Ohio Valley as far west as the Mississippi. The aggressive search for new fields of investment by such companies was a contributing factor in the growing friction between English colonies and the French-allied Indian tribes, who resisted encroachments on the fur trade and who resented having the land they used bought and sold by others.

The British also differed in many ways from the French and—ultimately—from the Spanish, too, in their attitudes toward the American Indians. Shortly before the English began migrating to America, the Crown had decided to add Ireland to its kingdom and encouraged private colonization of the isle. Just as the Moorish conflicts had colored Spanish attitudes toward the New World in the 15th century, the subjugation of Ireland in the mid-16th century became a training exercise for Elizabethan colonizers in demonizing those they intended to conquer in the Americas.

Indeed, the same cultivated gentlemen who invaded Ireland in the 1560s and '70s—Sir Humphrey Gilbert, Baron De La Warr, Sir Francis Drake, Walter Raleigh—spearheaded the colonization of the New World in the 1610s and '20s, and they carried with them their habits of thought and action and applied them to the indigenous peoples of the New World.

The Elizabethan aristocrats professed to believe that at least the Irish could be, with effort, civilized. If they could be so improved, the Irish then must not be inherently savage. In other words, their character was a question not of nature, of race, so much as one of culture, that is to say, of class. In Virginia the English colonial upper class continued the Irish colonial tradition of viewing the "savages" as ignorant heathens, primitives capable through force—and dispossession of their savage wilderness—of improvement. But in New England, those settling the land were not dominated by Elizabethan adventurer-aristocrats but by social radicals on intense religious crusades. During their "errand into the wilderness" to build a gleaming and godly "city upon a hill," American Indian savagery became radicalized for them. Although the Puritans, like all Europeans in the New World, paid lip service to conversion, there was never really much room for Indians among the elect. More commonly to the Puritan, the Indian was a demon, fit generally—as Increase Mather put it—for "utter extirpation."

From the beginning, English settlers in America fought the Indians with a ferocity to match the early Spanish conquistadores. What Columbus did to the Arawak, what Cortez did to the Aztec, what Pizarro did to the Inca, the British colonials in Massachusetts and Virginia did to the Pequot and Powhatan. Throughout the 17th century the English colonists conducted a series of brutal wars of conquest and dispossession that much reduced the American Indian tribes east of the Allegheny and Appalachian Mountains. The Iroquois, who were superb politicians and who had succeeded in establishing their confederation as a clearinghouse for the Indian trade, were among the few tribes that managed to hold their own, even to thrive, with the British. The success of these wars—and the growing arrogance with which the colonies usurped Indian lands in their wake—led to a boom in real estate speculation. This boom in turn led land speculators in London and in the several seaboard colonies to form new and rival companies, companies that began to lay fanciful claim to western lands beyond the Appalachians.

At length, it mattered little to the American Indians whether the English invaders saw them as wild men or devils, as children of culture or nature, as a problem of class or race—in any case, the British worked to destroy Indian society. This double vision—the urge both to civilize and to eradicate the Indians—served to blind colonial America to some of the horror of its enterprise in the New World. It would become a major legacy of the British Empire that lay at the heart of the history of American diplomacy for centuries to come. For at bottom, because the English had come to settle, they were wont to displace the Indians from their tribal lands, either by legal chicanery or, if necessary, by forced eviction. The French, on the other hand, interested in commerce and conversion, more often moved into the native wigwams, married the sachems' daughters, and introduced the tribes to Mother

Church. Thus, the French had little reason to enter into elaborate treaty relations except as a check on other foreign encroachments, while the British dealt with the Indians both as enemies to be vanquished and nations whose territories were subject to favorable treaty negotiation.

The Rabble

The British were different from the French (and the Spanish) in a third—and significant—way that had a major impact on their colonial empire and the history of North American diplomacy. England, in advance of the rest of Europe, was undergoing its industrial revolution. A complex development, closely associated with a revolution in agricultural productivity, the industrial revolution shook people loose from traditional ways of life wherever it occurred. Under its impact, artisans became factory workers, and millions of rural farmers became urban wage earners. Most of those moving from countryside to city, from agriculture to industry, remained in their homelands, but in the early stages of industrialization, the movement of people—like the growth of investment capital—was greater than the market could bear. Over time, England—and Europe to follow—would reach a kind of equilibrium, absorbing its own workers in its own wage market. During this transition period, however, many new workers, having abandoned the mill or farm, could not find a place in domestic cities. They migrated overseas. England's early industrialization meant two things important for our purposes—the English colonies had the finest industrial goods for trade with the Indians, and these colonies were filled with tens of thousands of English-speaking people, as compared to the few thousand French and Spanish in America.

The Elizabethan colonizers certainly did not understand that they were going through a great economic change destined to make them dominant in the New World. It was clear to them, however, that in America, they would need servants and laborers since the Indians were not easily domesticated; besides, the latter so far outnumbered the Europeans that it was not politic to enslave many of them. It just so happened that they could find such servitors in contemporary England. Part of a vast underclass of miserably poor whites who came to the English colonies from British cities glad to be rid of them, these indentured servants were to be the outcasts of a changing society. So many tens of thousands of these "surplus inhabitants" were shipped to America in the 18th century that when the traffic was cut off by the American Revolution, a crisis struck the English justice system. With prisons over-flowing, ships filled with the indigent and the criminal lay off London and became festering death traps until the British came up with transshipment to Australia. Long before then, however, the American elite had found another way to bring workers to their plantations. In fact it was in 1619, just 12 years after the founding of Jamestown, that a certain Dutch ship appeared in Chesapeake Bay carrying what the Virginians saw as an exotic new cargo—African slaves. At first the colonial aristocracy much preferred the indentured servants to the slaves. They spoke the same language, however badly. Since they had something to work for—freedom from debt and servitude, nominally within seven years—they did not have to be "broken," as the blacks did. Plus, the notion of a lifetime of slavery and its potential profits was not yet fully realized: a planter had to pay for a slave as well as his or her upkeep; the indentured servant did not represent an initial cash outlay. And servant supply was no problem: there were always more poor back home. There was only one major problem with indentured servitude that the Virginia elite belatedly discovered—what to do with the indentured when their service was up, especially since more than half the colonists who came to the shores of North America during colonial times came as servants. Colonial officialdom hit upon a happy expedient: monopolize the good land in the east and force the landless whites west into the wilderness, where they would run up against the savages and become a buffer for the seaboard rich against Indian troubles. The poor would be kept at a distance and depend on the seaboard establishment for the goods and guns needed to survive.

Not that the seaboard rich exactly wanted to protect the poor. Indeed, they soon were worried about the very freedoms they had offered them. Since every free white man was required by law to carry a gun to defend his colony, and the industrial revolution, among other things, produced firearms in abundance, before long much of the "rabble" was armed. Military historians have pointed out how many innovations in gun making occurred in the British Isles, especially in Scotland, and the surprising numbers in which those guns made their way to the backwoods of English America. Probably the first mass of poor people to be fully armed, they hardly surprisingly came quickly to believe that power emanated from the barrel of a gun.

The landed elite—especially after Bacon's Rebellion in 1676 revealed the revolutionary potential of the indigent and indentured masses—not only grew to mistrust the poor but were afraid even to organize them for military service. After the rebellion, the aristocrats turned wholesale to enforced bondage, and they began offering their former white servants a number of new benefits. In 1705 the Virginia Assembly passed a law giving every freed indentured male 10 bushels of corn, 30 shillings, and a gun. Every freed woman got 15 bushels and 40 shillings. And all newly freed servants got 50 acres of land west of the Tidewater.

Thus was the American West born, as a politically expedient solution to Virginia's turbulent class struggles. "Shiftless" whites would be sent into the wilderness to hack out a subsistence living and fight the "savages" who inhabited the place, while back East black slaves would toil endlessly to wrest profits from sprawling tobacco, rice, indigo, and cotton plantations. Obscuring common class interests, race became the social construction under which America would be settled and civilized, dominating diplomatic relations with the Indians and requiring ever more cheap land, first west of the Tidewater, then up the hollows of the mountains, and finally beyond the Appalachians themselves.

This is why Virginia—almost inevitably—eventually wanted the Ohio Valley for itself and was in effect willing to go to war with the world to get it. This is also why, henceforth when the British dealt with the Indians, their treaty making was not merely a matter of negotiating the cessation of hostilities or the cession of land, but of moderating relations between Indians, whom the Crown needed as allies, and settlers, whose volatility it sought to control.

French and Indian War

Not only European politics, then, but the internal development of colonial lands during the 18th century pushed the three-way struggle for New World empires to center more and more on the French and English in North America. If the English made considerable gains in the competition of the fur trade, it was because, much to France's chagrin, they could supply more cheaply the textiles and hardware the Indians, grown quickly dependent on European technology, demanded in exchange for fur. Still, the wide-roaming French trappers, mostly hard-boiled coureurs de bois—literally, "runners of the woods," who were as casual with their lives as any old English sea dog and as accomplished in woodcraft as the Indians—hunted beside the Indians, went on raids with them, sometimes confessed to the same priests as they did, and were often married into their families. When push came to shove, blood relatives simply made better comrades-in-arms than mere trading partners. It was no accident that the majority of the native Americans opted to ally themselves with the easygoing French Canadians rather than with the rigid and land-hungry British colonials.

The French used their special relationship with the American Indians each time the conflict between the two imperialist powers heated up, leading their indigenous friends in raids on the outlying English settlements in New England and New York. And each time, the English protected themselves by an uneasy alliance with the Iroquois, who controlled the Mohawk Valley and the St. Lawrence River, the two major approaches to the interior of the subcontinent. By mid-century three times already the situation in Europe had led to wars that inflamed the American frontier, their origins evident in the names given them by the British colonials: King William's War (called the War of the Grand Alliance in Europe, 1689–97); Queen Anne's War (War of the Spanish Succession, 1702–13); and King George's War (War of the Austrian Succession, 1744–48). With the signing of each new soon-to-be-violated peace treaty, sovereignty shifted back and forth between the two powers over various of their holdings in North America, and nobody in Europe or America expected the most recent of them, the 1748 TREATY OF AIX-LA-CHAPELLE, to hold much longer.

The French continued to consolidate their hold on the far West, only now more often with soldiers than with trappers and divines. Even as the French spread into the Far West, though, the English were encroaching on Ohio. Much as the Spanish had sent missionaries and explorers into the Southwest to build a string of missions and presidios in response to French settlement along their northern borders, the French marched into the Ohio Valley with the intention of building a string of forts to protect the land in which both their king and their Indian allies had an interest.

It was the British land companies that first raised the cry of "invasion"—against the French. None of the land companies was more aggressive than the Ohio Company of Virginia. The company had been organized by a Tidewater aristocrat named Thomas Lee late in King George's War (1747) when he realized that backwoods land too hazardous for new settlement during the hostilities would be a real estate gold mine if peace came. The company had the backing of powerful men. The Quaker John Hanbury, a London merchant whose business interests stretched from Hudson Bay to the Baltic Sea, was a partner. The London Board of Trade's imperialist president, George Dunk, Lord Halifax, supported the company's plans, hoping that by granting Lee's request for half a million acres on the Ohio River, he could diminish France's influence over the Indians of the West. The grant, which came in March 1749, called for settlement by 100 families within seven years. The charter angered the French because they claimed the area as their own. It infuriated the Ohio Indians, who regarded the Allegheny-Appalachian mountain range as their barrier against further European encroachment.

Thus did the heedless greed of a few headstrong men—Lee, Hanbury, Halifax—light a fire in the wilderness that spread to become a conflagration throughout the world. The French, provoked by the Ohio Company's new charter, sent an army of 2,200 men, complete with artillery—the largest European force thus far mustered in North America—under Ange Duquesne de Menneville, marquis Duquesne, who had become governor of New France on July 1, 1752, to secure the region and protect the thin lifeline extending from Montreal to New Orleans. In response Lord Halifax, in August 1753, pushed the British cabinet toward a declaration of war based on misunderstandings and wishful thinking about the Iroquois. He used as his pretext for war the 1713 TREATY OF UTRECHT, which had stipulated that the Iroquois were British subjects. Since, so argued the British, the Iroquois had launched trade wars—actually, more a series of raids on other tribes—from 1701 to 1726, the Ohio country belonged to them by right of "conquest," although the Iroquois, not being Europeans, never in fact occupied or controlled the area, as the word "conquest" implies. Still, said the British, the Ohio was the Confederacy's, the people of the Five Nations were British subjects, and accordingly, Halifax asserted British rights to these Iroquois lands.

Such claims grew from the cross-purposes, misunderstandings, and attitudes of mind by which the fur-trading French, the fur-trapping Indians, and the land-hungry British were unwittingly dragging the world itself closer to war. Many of the Ohio Indian peoples, for example, doubted the wisdom of dealing with the English at all, reasoning that because the French so apparently had the upper hand, perhaps they would be better allies than enemies. From the Iroquois point of view, neither the French nor the British belonged in Ohio. (Neither perhaps did the Iroquois, but that was a different matter.) The Iroquois League had a long-standing, and perfectly logical, policy of playing the Europeans against each other, taking sides—usually with the British—only when it was advantageous to the Iroquois. For over a century, it had made the Iroquois a force to be reckoned with in North America. Because France was pressing its claims in Ohio more forcefully just now, traditional Iroquois diplomacy would have called for seeking closer alliance with the English in the hopes that the position of both the European sides in Ohio would be weakened.

Halifax argued before the cabinet, that the French, by trading throughout the Ohio Valley—and despite the fact they had been doing so for a century—had actually invaded Virginia. In this climate, as the cabinet debated a declaration of war in London, Governor Robert Dinwiddie of Virginia received authorization from the Crown to evict the French from territory the English now claimed to be under his jurisdiction. Dinwiddie commissioned a 21-year-old Virginia militia officer named George Washington to carry an ultima-

tum to the French in the wilds of the Ohio Valley. When Washington first marched into the area in 1753, France and England had been fighting each other steadily for a hundred years, but the young colonial soldier, in effect a hireling of the Ohio Company, was probably only dimly aware that the world was teetering on the brink of war.

In the dusky dark of December 11, 1753, his beleaguered band of wilderness diplomats, some on gaunt horses, others afoot, straggled up to Fort LeBoeuf near Lake Erie and announced their presence to the garrison of forlorn and despairing troops. At a sad little outpost in the middle of nowhere, the mighty French and British Empires once again came face to face and squared off for yet another trial by arms. The commander of the French "invasion" force at the fort was Captain Jacques Le Gardeur, sieur de Sainte-Pierre. He had seen a lifetime of action at frontier posts in Acadia and Wisconsin and on campaigns in the Lake of the Woods region and down the Mississippi to the backwoods of Alabama. Hospitable and urbane, he responded to Washington with the utmost care, but at length he said no, the French had not the least intention of withdrawing from the Ohio country.

Washington returned to Virginia, where he was promoted to lieutenant colonel and sent back into the Ohio country, this time to teach the French interlopers a lesson. This he did in May 1754 by ambushing what he thought was a French war party but which turned out to be instead a French diplomatic mission bringing to him the same message he had the year before brought the French: stay out of Ohio. In the course of the ambush, one of Washington's Indian allies murdered and scalped the French commander, a young aristocrat named Joseph Coulon de Villiers de Jumonville. When news of the doings in Ohio reached Europe, the French declared the unprovoked ambush barbaric and contrary to every principle of international relations and called Washington an assassin.

Thus, as Horace Walpole would later observe, "the volley fired by a young Virginian in the backwoods of America set the world on fire." Washington's appearance in the Ohio Valley sparked a conflict that would spread from the American wilderness over vast stretches of Europe and across the high seas to the edge of the Near East. The issue that had touched off the war was control of the upper Ohio, and its outcome would be the opening of the American West to English-speaking settlers.

The conflict in America was, however, merely one theater of the much larger European war, and the American struggle was originally directed by armchair from London. By the time it was over, France, Austria, Sweden, a number of small German states, and Spain took up arms against England and Frederick the

Great's Prussia. In Europe the fighting came to be known as the Great War for the Empire. The English called it the Seven Years' War. The American colonists dubbed this first truly worldwide conflict the French and Indian War.

In America's French and Indian War, the Indians often bore the brunt of the fighting and almost always did most of the dying. After them, however, the greatest number of casualties would be suffered by the white settlers along what would become known as the western frontier. Indeed, much of the passionate and mutual hatred that sprang up between Native Indian and American pioneer, so central to future diplomatic relations between the United States and American Indians, had its roots in the French and Indian War, where the French used the Indians as instruments of deliberate terror and the British used their "beastly" backwoodsmen as a sacrificial advance guard. As a measure of the importance of Indian allies, the British won battles only when the Indians abandoned the French when the British managed to muster Indian allies themselves, or when Indians were involved on neither side. While the shortsighted English either failed to use Indian allies effectively or openly spurned them, the French exploited them, though they professed to find doing so distasteful.

On the other hand, Indian leaders were quite aware that whichever side ultimately prevailed, it prevailed against them; it was their land for which the French and the English fought. But the Indians could hardly ignore the struggle in their midst. The Iroquois for the most part, with the exception of the pro-English Mohawk, sought to remain neutral. Most of the other tribes sided in varying degrees with the French, hoping to eke out some advantage thereby or hoping merely to survive.

In 1762, Spain came late into the Seven Years' War on the side of France and was quickly neutralized by British sea power. On February 15, 1762, Martinique fell to the English, followed by St. Lucia and Grenada. On August 12, 1762, Havana yielded to a two-month siege, and Manila fell on October 5. On November 3, France concluded the secret Treaty of San Ildefonso with Spain, in which it ceded to that country all of its territory west of the Mississippi and the Île d'Orleans in Louisiana. By the TREATY OF PARIS, concluded on February 10, 1763, France ceded all of Louisiana to Spain and the rest of its North American holdings to Great Britain. The king of France had abandoned his Indian allies—and the New World—entirely.

The British, after seven bitter and often inept years of combat, had not only at last forced the surrender of New France, they were free to turn the full force of their rapacity against the Indians. As far as Great Britain was concerned, the French and Indian War had established its control of the upper Ohio and made it the dominant power on the North American continent. For the colonials, victory meant the opening of the trans-Appalachian West. Hard on the heels of the Treaty of Paris came colonial petitions to King George to settle in Illinois and what is today West Virginia. The colony of Virginia calmly asserted claims to a territory encompassing present-day West Virginia, Kentucky, Ohio, Indiana, Illinois, Michigan, Wisconsin, and parts of Minnesota.

In September 1763 the land speculation firm called the Mississippi Company, led by the ubiquitous George Washington, received a royal grant of 2 1/2 million acres between the Ohio and Wisconsin Rivers for settlement by Virginia soldiers who fought in the war. Trading and land companies had helped precipitate the French and Indian War.

Now that France was out of the picture and colonial America's official border was with Spain along the Mississippi, all the land between the Appalachian Mountains and that border appeared to land speculators "unimproved" land ripe for "opening." Despite promises to the Indians made in the heat of battle, despite the guarantees of earlier treaties, despite disapproval from the British Crown, despite the continued threat of determined and ferocious Indian attacks, would-be pioneers poured into the newly opened West.

Backwoods Revolution

The pattern of European promise and betrayal on the frontier had been established, and the French and Indian War would become, from the point of view of the Indians themselves, merely the first in a series of wars waged by the various Algonquian tribes of the Old Northwest, first against England and later against the United States. From their great victory over General Braddock on the meadowlands of Fort Duquesne in 1755, through the vicious and cruel border skirmishes of Pontiac's Rebellion and the American Revolution, to their final defeat by "Mad" Anthony Wayne at Fallen Timbers in 1794, the Algonquians' objective would be to force the English-speaking aliens to withdraw. The great worldwide conflagrations in which France lost Canada and Louisiana and in which England was to lose its 13 seaboard colonies were minor concerns to the Algonquians in their 40-year struggle to liberate themselves and their lands from the British immigrants' belief that there now existed an American West that belonged to them.

The Algonquians in particular felt betrayed by the French, who had deserted them, and felt threatened by the English, who seemed simply to ignore the treaty-established boundary of the Allegheny-Appalachian mountain range. On April 27, 1763, an Ottawa chief called a grand council of the tribes in the vicinity of Detroit and urged them to join his band in an attack upon the nearby fort—one of many coordinated attacks by the tribes of the Old Northwest in a great, year-long Indian uprising that came to be called (after the Ottawa chief) Pontiac's Rebellion. If the border skirmishes of the French and Indian War had been harsh, the frenzy of Pontiac's Rebellion was horrifying. This time settlers, not Indians, suffered the greatest number of casualties. The victims were generally those who had violated the treaty bans against invading Indian territory. The exuberantly brutal Indians inflicted incredible tortures and mutilations on the captured, and practiced ritual cannibalism on the fallen. The savagery, however, was not confined to one side of the conflict. The British commander in chief, Lord Amherst, responded to news of the Indian uprising with orders to extirpate the belligerents, taking no prisoners but putting "to death all that fall into your hands." A brutal vigilantism sprung up among white settlers as well in response to the Indian attacks, and mobs stabbed, hacked, and mutilated even peaceful Indians long after Pontiac had sued for peace.

King George used Pontiac's Rebellion as an excuse for reasserting his control over the American colonies. By the royal PROCLAMATION OF 1763, he declared the hostilities over and limited white settlement by and large to the territory east of the Appalachians. But the Indians gained no lasting benefit from the hard-fought struggle. If anything, the failure of Indian alliances to hold during the uprising encouraged the Americans. Furthermore, the king's decree, which the colonials took as a challenge, seemed to push the Americans further along the path to a rebellion of their own. Royal troops ostensibly sent to enforce the new frontier line declared by the king wound up billeted in seacoast cities policing the colonials. The new taxes, enacted in part to support such troop strength, enraged the merchant class.

The colonies got their first taste of victory against the mother country in the successfully protested passage of the Stamp Act in 1765. For a decade resentments between Crown and colony seethed. During those 10 years, the Americans moved steadily closer to a break with Great Britain as they came to reach the irreversible conclusion that Parliament had no right to tax or otherwise interfere with the daily activities of the colonies. The growing hostilities reached the boiling point on April 19, 1775, when 700 British troops—on the march since the night before toward a colonial arsenal at Concord—faced off along the way at Lexington against a small and confused ragtag force of Massachusetts militia calling themselves Minutemen. Someone fired a shot, the British broke ranks and returned fire, and within minutes eight of the militia lay dead on the village green. The American Revolution had begun.

The French, delighted to further embarrass the country with which it had been at war over colonial possessions for the last two centuries, had secretly offered the Americans aid from the start, but with Burgoyne's surrender at Saratoga, the French came out of the closet. To make sure the English and the Patriots reached no reconciliation, the French struck an alliance with America in 1778. France's ally, Spain, made no deal with the rebels but provided help nevertheless in the South and West. The Russians formed the League of Armed Neutrality, which the French backed, and the Dutch—also enemies of the English at the time—tolerated the anti-British French-American alliance. The British Empire, which had claimed to rule the Seven Seas for decades was in effect at war with the whole world.

If her enemies did not mount full-fledged sea battles against her, their privateers raided merchant ships, exasperated her navy, and drove up her insurance rates. Any British army in America was likely to have its retreat cut off, if only temporarily, and that is precisely what happened when George Washington, with the help of the French navy, trapped His Majesty's troops at Yorktown. Peace feelers that formally had gotten nowhere suddenly led to earnest negotiation. Suspicious of their French ally—who wanted to reward Spain at American expense—the Patriots made a separate peace under the 1783 TREATY OF PARIS, a diplomatic triumph that granted the United States independence and set its boundaries. A great empire was humbled, and a new nation was born.

A major legacy of the Revolution to diplomatic history was the sudden appearance of a new contestant, the United States, in the centuries-old European conflict over North American colonies—now the unsettled lands west of the 1763 Proclamation Line, where the United States had the advantage of proximity as opposed to imperial might. The Revolution saw the collapse of the Iroquois Confederacy, since most of its tribes had sided with the British, and the loss of their vast holdings to the new Americans. Treaty relations with the Iroquois, which included the settling of the tribes on reserved and much-diminished territories, served as a model for later diplomacy with the Indians farther west.

Though the infant nation was in effect a competitor for empire in the American West, its approach to the conquest and settlement of those lands differed from those of the three principal European imperialist nations, Spain, France, and England. Land had always been a key to the English-speaking settlements, and now the individual states found themselves having to negotiate their various and conflicting claims to the American West. The new federal government served not only as a mediator for these claims but ultimately as the repository of such territories, which the states—reluctantly, in some cases—ceded to that government. New laws, such as the NORTHWEST ORDINANCE, specified how territories and states were to be formed from western lands "gained" by the United States as a result of the Revolution. New political leaders spawned by the Revolution, such as Thomas Jefferson, found, at least in theory, new uses for western land. Even those who explored the West for the United States often did so with purposes that in some respects differed from those of the Europeans before them.

Having discovered a way to incorporate conquered land directly into the body politic, which in effect is what the Northwest Ordinance allowed for, Americans were poised at the end of the 18th century for a massive expansion that would eventually bring them a continental empire. Already, as settlers crossed the mountains and made their way toward the Mississippi, expansion was causing troubles with the European imperialists and with New Englanders, who worried about the extension of slavery and the waning of their region's influence. All of these would be much exasperated by the purchase of half the continent from France a few years later, but in 1800, having vanquished Britain, the Iroquois Confederacy, and the Algonquians of the Northwest, the United States was already a New World empire.

TREATIES

Mutual Defense Treaties, Military Alliances, and Nonaggression Pacts

MAYFLOWER COMPACT

```
TREATY AT A GLANCE

Completed
November 11, 1620, in Provincetown Harbor, Cape Cod
(in present-day Massachusetts)

Signatories
The male passengers, "Pilgrim" and "Stranger" alike,
aboard the Mayflower

Overview
A pact between the zealous members of the Pilgrim sect and other
passengers immigrating to America to form a civil body politic tol-
erant of all aboard the English ship Mayflower, the compact be-
came the basis for the foundation of Plymouth Colony and the
launching of Puritan settlement in New England.
```

Historical Background

In 1620 rough seas off the coast of Nantucket evidently forced Captain Christopher Jones of the *Mayflower* to alter his course from the mouth of the Hudson River toward Cape Cod, where he deposited his passengers—including some 50 members of a religious sect who would soon come to be called Pilgrims—outside the jurisdiction of Virginia, much to the chagrin of those aboard who were not Pilgrims. The two groups settled their differences by signing a brief statement of self-government drafted by the Pilgrims, which became known as the Mayflower Compact, the first written constitution in North America.

Some later claimed the Pilgrims had bribed the good captain to alter his course. The Pilgrims had arranged the nine-month journey with the permission of the Virginia Company and the backing of London merchants, who charged the Plymouth Company, as the Pilgrims' corporation was known, a handsome interest on the funds they advanced the group. The Pilgrims were a sect of the Separatists, themselves a splinter group of the Puritans. The Puritans rejected the wordy ceremoniousness of the Church of England as too "popish" and hoped to cleanse the church of all traces of Roman Catholicism. Those Puritans who thought the Anglican Church too corrupt to be purified wanted complete autonomy for their congregations, and the Pilgrims were so extreme in their Separatist views that the English authorities banned them outright. Pilgrims who did not go underground fled the country, and a small band hailing from Scrooby, Nottinghamshire, settled in Leyden, Holland. There, though their theology was acceptable, their culture was alien, and the group at length opted for a second course: a fresh start in America.

They struck their deal with the London merchants, hoping to establish the Kingdom of God in the English colonies, but they took with them on the voyage a number of men at least nominally faithful to the Church of England, whom they called Strangers and who had very different goals from the otherworldly religious cult: to get rich, to own a bit of land, to live the good life on the earth just as it was. Needless to say, the trip did not go smoothly. With Pilgrims numbering only some 50 of the 102 passengers on board when Captain Jones, for whatever reason, altered course, some sort of arrangement was necessary to stave off a true mutiny.

Terms

Signing the Mayflower Compact, in which the signatories vowed to create a "Civil Body Politic" and abide by laws created for the good of the colony as a whole, were some of the most headstrong and determined men in American history: Pilgrims such as William Brewster, John Carver, Edward Winslow, and William Bradford; Strangers such as the ship's cooper, John Alden, and army captain Miles Standish.

Agreement between the Settlers at New Plymouth: 1620

IN THE NAME OF GOD, AMEN. We, whose names are underwritten, the Loyal Subjects of our dread Sovereign Lord King James, by the Grace of God, of Great Britain, France, and Ireland, King, Defender of the Faith, &c. Having undertaken for the Glory of God, and Advancement of the Christian Faith, and the Honour of our King and Country, a Voyage to plant the first Colony in the northern Parts of Virginia; Do by these Presents, solemnly and mutually, in the Presence of God and one another, covenant and combine ourselves together into a civil Body Politick, for our better Ordering and Preservation, and Furtherance of the Ends aforesaid: And by Virtue hereof do enact, constitute, and frame, such just and equal Laws, Ordinances, Acts, Constitutions, and Officers, from time to time, as shall be thought most meet and convenient for the general Good of the Colony; unto which we promise all due Submission and Obedience.

IN WITNESS whereof we have hereunto subscribed our names at Cape-Cod the eleventh of November, in the Reign of our Sovereign Lord King James, of England, France, and Ireland, the eighteenth, and of Scotland the fifty-fourth, Anno Domini; 1620.

MR. JOHN CARVER	MR. WILLIAM BRADFORD
MR EDWARD WINSLOW	MR. WILLIAM BREWSTER
ISAAC ALLERTON	MYLES STANDISH
JOHN ALDEN	JOHN TURNER
FRANCIS EATON	JAMES CHILTON
JOHN CRAXTON	JOHN BILLINGTON
JOSES FLETCHER	JOHN GOODMAN
MR. SAMUEL FULLER ,	MR. CHRISTOPHER MARTIN
MR. WILLIAM MULLINS	MR. WILLIAM WHITE
MR. RICHARD WARREN	JOHN HOWLAND
MR. STEVEN HOPKINS	DIGERY PRIEST
THOMAS WILLIAMS	GILBERT WINSLOW
EDMUND MARGESSON	PETER BROWN
RICHARD BRITTERIDGE	GEORGE SOULE
EDWARD TILLY	JOHN TILLY,
FRANCIS COOKE	THOMAS ROGERS
THOMAS TINKER	JOHN RIDGDALE
EDWARD FULLER	RICHARD CLARK
RICHARD GARDINER	MR. JOHN ALLERTON,
THOMAS ENGLISH	EDWARD DOTEN
	EDWARD LIESTER

Consequences

Pilgrim and stranger alike came ashore at the site of present-day Provincetown at the worst possible time of year. Winter was settling in, and nearly half the colonists died before a supply ship arrived in the spring of 1621. The Pilgrims viewed as a blessing from God the appearance of Squanto and Samoset, local Indians who had learned English from earlier explorers and who helped the Pilgrims plant crops and build homes. In the fall of 1621, the Pilgrims and their Indian friends gathered to celebrate the harvest, an event that is commemorated yearly in the American holiday of Thanksgiving. There is irony enough in such commemoration, since the friendship between Puritan and Indian did not last, and the Puritan's theological tendency to see the American Indians as "devils" to be exterminated rather than "savages" to be converted would give Indians throughout North America cause to rue the help provided by Squanto and Samoset.

After the colony's original governor died during the first harsh winter in the New World, the settlers selected William Bradford as his replacement. A wise and equitable citizen ruler, Bradford was also an able chronicler. His *History of Plimmoth Plantation* recounts the separatists' life in Holland and in the New World and was the first instance in which the English settlers were called Pilgrims. Among the struggles Bradford examined in his book was one between the Pilgrims and the "Particulars." These individuals had paid their own way to the New World and did not believe they were responsible for contributing to the payments due the Virginia Company. In addition, the Particulars wanted no part in the colony's work to raise funds to bring over more Pilgrims. To end the quarrel between the two factions and to relieve the colony of its mounting debts, a group of prosperous colonists agreed to assume the debts to the Virginia Company in exchange for greater access to land and control of the fur trade with the Indians. These men, whom Bradford called the Undertakers, agreed to pay the Virginia Company £200 a year for nine years.

As the years passed, more and more Pilgrims and Particulars flocked to the fledgling colony. Towns were created throughout the region of Plymouth. Each town had at least one church congregation, independent of all others and in strong control of the religious and secular lives of the townspeople. Only those individuals who freely professed their conversion were admitted to the congregation. The Pilgrims, unlike those who would soon be neighboring Puritans in the Massachusetts Bay Colony, did not forbid the unconverted from participating in the colony's affairs. With the Mayflower Compact as a foundation, the Pilgrims were able to develop the broad enfranchisement necessary for managing a colony that boasted any number of Particulars and Strangers, a toleration—always setting aside the Indians—that would become the hallmark of American civil life.

The Mayflower Compact would also foster a penchant for written constitutions among New England's colonies. In 1629 five English ships bursting with Puritan émigrés sailed into Massachusetts Bay, the first of many more that would bring to Britain's newest colony the 20-odd settlers who participated in what has come to be called the Great Puritan Migration. Mostly Anglican Puritans, these early arrivals were inspired by the New World success of their more radical fellow countrymen who had established Plymouth a decade earlier. The first Puritans founded Naumkeg, later called Salem, and by the time John Winthrop arrived the next year, carrying a royal charter for the new joint-stock venture called the Massachusetts Bay Company, 11 more ships had deposited a thousand more Puritan immigrants.

To Boston, which Winthrop founded and named after England's great Puritan city, they came in the thousands every year for 12 years, chased out of their mother country by a king who grew ever more intolerant of their disputatiousness, their rigid morality, their grim industriousness, and their seditious religious ideology. No doubt about it: they were an argumentative lot, constantly fighting among themselves—usually over church matters, sometimes over land. Squabble by squabble, it seemed, they settled New England. If, ecclesiastically, the Puritans were as intolerant as the king they had fled, politically they were dangerous radicals, as the brethren they had left behind in England proved in 1649, when Puritan champion Oliver Cromwell overthrew King Charles I and chopped off his head.

The coming of the English Commonwealth would spell the end of the Great Puritan Migration. Though English Puritans continued to settle in New England for a year or two in search of a better fortune than the tumultuous economy of the Glorious Revolution could offer them, by the time Connecticut, New Haven, Plymouth, and the Massachusetts Bay Colony formed the New England Confederation in 1643 in order to settle border disputes (and promote land acquisition from the Indians, mostly through a series of military conquests), the absolute dominance of the Puritans had begun to decline. New England and American politics and foreign relations would continue to be affected, however, by the strange mixture of moral authoritarianism and political democracy that make up the Pilgrim legacy.

TAUNTON AGREEMENT

TREATY AT A GLANCE

Completed
April 10, 1671, at Taunton, Plymouth Colony
(in present-day Massachusetts)

Signatories
Plymouth Colony and the Wampanoag Indians of Massachusetts

Overview
This brief document—just over 200 words—is typical of the legal instruments by which European colonists in America sought to dominate their American Indian neighbors, both to neutralize them as military threats and to exploit them as "clients" or even "subjects" in order to legitimate questionable claims to territory and sovereignty. The humiliating terms Plymouth Colony imposed on the Wampanoag chief Metacom, called King Philip by the English, through the Taunton Agreement led directly to King Philip's War (1675–76), proportionate to population the costliest war in American history.

Historical Background

Massasoit, chief of the Wampanoag and longtime friend of the Plymouth colonists, died in 1661 at the age of 81. His son Wamsutta, whom the English called Alexander, succeeded him and continued the tradition of friendship. However, under Wamsutta, the Wampanoag divided their loyalty between two English colonies, Rhode Island and Plymouth, which competed for the purchase of Indian lands and which both sought to establish a protectorate over the Wampanoag in order to put backbone into their weak and tenuous charters. Plymouth officials sought to intimidate Alexander by forcibly taking him to Duxbury to pressure him into selling land to Plymouth in preference to Rhode Island. During his captivity, Alexander fell ill and, though released, died on the journey home.

Alexander's 24-year-old brother, Metacom or Metacomet, whom the English called Philip, succeeded Wamsutta as chief and broadcast the opinion that the colonists had poisoned Alexander. From this point on, friction between Plymouth Colony and King Philip steadily increased. A skilled diplomat, forceful speaker, and charismatic leader, King Philip patiently forged alliances with neighboring tribes. Plymouth authorities, fearful of his activities and seeking to intimidate him as they had Alexander,

summoned King Philip to Plymouth Town on August 6, 1664, to answer charges of plotting against the colony. He denied the accusations but signed a document pledging to seek permission from the colony before selling any land.

Peaceful if uneasy relations prevailed between the Indians and the English until 1665, when a land dispute between colonists and the Narragansett Indians brought the region to the brink of war. Seizing a chance to exploit the rift between the English and a rival tribe, King Philip warned New York colonial authorities that the Narragansett were plotting war against them. The Narragansett chief, Ninigret, responded by accusing Philip of hostile designs, and in 1667 Philip was again summoned to Plymouth. This time he was defiant. Declaring the Plymouth governor "but a subject," Philip insisted he would treat only with his "brother," King Charles of England. When Charles came to see him, Philip said, he would be ready.

For four more years, the mutual animosity intensified. Early in 1671, Philip, outraged when a new Plymouth settlement, Swansea, encroached on his land, staged an armed display for the benefit of the town's citizens. On April 10, 1671, he was summoned to Taunton to sign an agreement acknowledging and apologizing for such "plotting."

Terms

The document, given below in its entirety, bound the Wampanoag to surrender their arms and compelled King Philip to acknowledge submission to the British Crown and to Plymouth Colony.

Whereas my Father, my Brother, and my self, have formally submitted ourselves and our People unto the Kings Majesty of England, and to the Colony of New Plimouth, by solemn Covenant under our Hand; but I having of late through my Indiscretion, and the Naughtiness of my Heart, violated and broken this my Covenant with my Friends, by taking up Arms, with evil intent against them, and that groundlessly; I being now deeply sensible of my Unfaithfulness and Folly, so desire at this Time solemnly to renew my Covenant with my ancient Friends, my Fathers Friends above mentioned, and do desire that this may testify to the World against me if ever I shall again fail in my Faithfulness towards them (that I have now, and at all Times found so kind to me) or any other of the English Colonies; and as a real Pledge of my true Intentions for the Future to be Faithful and Friendly, I do freely engage to resign up unto the Government of New Plimouth, all my English Arms, to be kept by them for their Security, so long as they shall see Reason. For true Performance of the Premises, I have hereunto set my Hand, together with the Rest of my Council.

In Presence of	The Mark of P. *Philip*
William Davis.	The Mark of V. *Tavoser*
William Hudson.	The Mark of *Capt. Wisposke*
Thomas Brattle.	The Mark of *T. Woonkaponchant*
	The Mark of *Nimrod*

Consequences

After signing the document, Philip attempted to incite a dispute between Plymouth and Massachusetts by pointing out that his retroactive pledge to Plymouth undermined the validity of land titles Massachusetts had earlier secured from the Wampanoag. Canny though this strategy was, it backfired, serving to unite the two colonies against Philip. Toward the end of September, the chief was once more hauled into a Plymouth court, where he was tried for breaking the Taunton Agreement. Fined £100, he was now forbidden to wage war against other Indians without authority from the colonial government.

Philip, outraged and offended, bided his time, sealing an alliance against the English with the Nipmuck Indians as well as with his tribe's former rivals, the Narragansett. Early in 1675, King Philip probably murdered John Sassamon, an Indian employed by the colonists to spy on him. Summoned to answer charges of murder, Philip made no secret of his contempt for his accusers, who were compelled at length to release him for lack of evidence.

On June 11, 1675, shortly after his release, the Wampanoag armed near Swansea and Plymouth Town. Cattle were killed and houses looted in the outlying settlements, from which colonists began to retreat. Although it would not be declared officially by the "United Colonies" (Massachusetts, Plymouth, Rhode Island, Connecticut, New Hampshire, and Maine) until September 9, 1675, King Philip's War had begun. Before it ended—with Philip's defeat and death on August 12, 1676—it would devastate half the towns of New England, virtually bankrupt the fledgling colonies, and kill one in 16 men of military age as well as many older men, women, and children. At least three thousand Indians perished in the war—mostly Wampanoag, Narragansett, and Nipmuck—and many who did not die were deported to the West Indies as slaves. In proportion to population, King Philip's War must be counted as the costliest in American history.

Peace Treaties and Truces

TREATY OF PARIS (1763)

TREATY AT A GLANCE

Completed
February 10, 1763, at Paris

Signatories
Great Britain, France, Spain, and Portugal

Overview
Together with the TREATY OF HUBERTSBURG, the Treaty of Paris brought to a formal conclusion what many historians call the first world war: the Seven Years' War, which in its North American phase was called the French and Indian War. Signed by the principal combatants, Britain, France, and Spain (in addition to Portugal), the treaty not only brought an interval of peace to Europe, it reshaped the colonial world. France lost to Britain all of its North American possessions, except Louisiana, which it had earlier ceded to Spain; French troops were excluded from Bengal, thereby ending the French imperial drive in India and laying the foundation for British domination of the subcontinent; in Africa, France yielded Senegal to the British. France retained a few colonies: Saint Pierre and Miquelon (in the Gulf of Saint Lawrence); Saint Lucia, St-Domingue (Haiti), Guadeloupe, and Martinique (in the West Indies); and Pondichery and Chandernagor (in India). Spain recovered Cuba and the Philippines, which it had lost in the course of the war, but ceded Florida to Britain.

Historical Background

The Seven Years' War, which spanned 1756 to 1763, pitted Britain and Prussia against Austria, France, Russia, Saxony, Sweden, and, after 1762, Spain (which jointly ruled Portugal). The war may be viewed, in part, as a continuation of the issues that had ignited the War of the Austrian Succession (1740–48): the contest between Prussia and Austria for possession of Silesia and for political dominance in central Europe, and the struggle between Britain and France for military and naval supremacy and for colonial dominance.

The most intense prelude to the war came in North America, where British and French interests had begun sporadic fighting in 1754. In Europe hostilities commenced on August 29, 1756, when Frederick II the Great of Prussia, seeking to preempt an attack from Maria Theresa of Austria and Elizabeth of Russia, launched a surprise offensive through the electorate of Saxony, a minor Austrian ally. Frederick's strategy was to check Austria and Russia with a quick war, but despite minor victories, Frederick was unable to achieve swift victory and soon found himself embroiled in a desperate struggle that was involving nation after nation. Sweden aligned itself against Prussia, and Frederick's advance into Bohemia led to a Prussian defeat at Kolin in June 1757. Russian forces marched into East Prussia in August, and Austrian troops overran Berlin, occupying it for several days in October. Frederick came back with massive victories at Rossbach on November 5 and at Leuthen the next month, thereby saving his kingdom from conquest. Moreover, these victories bought him the time he needed to orchestrate the major campaigns of the next four years.

The nations aligned against Prussia failed to coordinate their forces adequately. Great Britain provided some finance and maintained an army in northwestern Germany to defend Hanover (a British royal possession) from French attack. Although Frederick won the day at Zorndorf in 1758 and again at Leignitz and Torgau in 1760, the victories were costly, draining his resources and causing a steady decline in his military fortunes. When he met the Russians at Kunersdorf on August 12, 1759, his forces were soundly defeated, and by the end of 1761, the Austrians had moved into Saxony and Silesia, and Russians held Prussian Pomerania.

Although Frederick's position appeared hopeless, he was rescued by the death of the Russian empress Elizabeth in January 1762, for she was succeeded by Peter III, who was a great admirer of Frederick. Peter summarily withdrew from the war, leaving Austria to face Prussia alone. This prompted an Austrian treaty with Prussia, the TREATY OF HUBERTSBURG, on February 15, 1763, which affirmed Prussian sovereignty over Silesia.

During all of this, Britain and France fought the bulk of their war on the soil of their contested colonial possessions, especially those in North America and India. In May 1756, about two years after the outbreak of hostilities on the Virginia frontier, Britain declared war on France. Both sides called upon colonial militias and Indian allies to do much of the fighting, but the British, who had treated the native peoples poorly, had far fewer Indian allies than the French. Moreover, the British regular army officers who had been sent to take charge of the war regarded colonial troops with contempt. Both of these factors contributed to early English defeats at the hands of the brilliant French commander Montcalm. The British fort at Oswego on Lake Ontario fell in 1756, and in 1757 Fort William Henry at the south end of Lake George was taken.

With British colonial fortunes at their nadir, William Pitt (the Elder) became Britain's new prime minister and instituted new policies of increased aid to the American colonies, which included a reformed attitude toward the Indians, as well as colonial troops. At the same time, France was finding it increasingly difficult to support its colonies. The tide of the French and Indian War began to turn in favor of the English in 1758, and 1759 brought victory after victory, culminating in the fall of Quebec to the British September 12–13, 1759. In 1760 Lord Amherst completed the conquest of Canada by taking Montreal, and by the end of the year, the French hegemony in North America had come to an end.

This did not mean an immediate end to the war, however. Except for a handful of "traditional" military engagements, the French and Indian War was largely a guerrilla war, fought more by settlers against Indians (allied with French or British interests) than by one army against another. Combat continued between the British and the Cherokee Indians in the south until 1761 and between settlers and Indians throughout the Ohio country. In 1762 the Spanish entered the fray against Britain but were rapidly defeated, principally because of British sea power. The exhausted combatants entered into negotiations that produced the Treaty of Paris early in 1763.

Terms

As historians have frequently pointed out, the Seven Years' War and the French and Indian War grew directly out of earlier conflicts: the War of the League of Augsburg (in North America, King William's War), the War of the Spanish Succession (in North America, Queen Anne's War), and the War of the Austrian Succession (in North America, King George's War). The framers of the Treaty of Paris clearly recognized this as well, and Article 2 of the document sweepingly subsumed the treaties resolving these conflicts:

II

The Treaties of Westphalia of 1648; those of Madrid between the crowns of Great-Britain and Spain of 1667, and 1670; the treaties of peace of Nimeguen of 1678, and 1679; of Ryswick of 1697; those of peace and of commerce of Utrecht of 1713; that of Baden of 1714; the treaty of the triple alliance of the Hague of 1717; that of the quadruple alliance of London of 1718; the treaty of peace of Vienna of I 738; the definitive treaty of Aix-la-Chapelle of 1748; and that of Madrid, between the crowns of Great-Britain and Spain, of 1750; as well as the treaties between the crowns of Spain and Portugal, of the 13th of February, 1668; of the 6th of February, 1715; and of the 12th of February, 1761; and that of the 11th of April, 1713, between France and Portugal, with the guaranties of Great-Britain; serve as a basis and foundation to the peace, and to the present treaty: and for this purpose, they are all renewed and confirmed in the best form, as well as all the general, which subsisted between the high contracting parties before the war, as if they were inserted here word for word, so that they are to be exactly observed, for the future, in their whole tenor, and religiously executed on all sides, in all their points, which shall not be derogated from by the present treaty, notwithstanding all that may have been stipulated to the contrary by any of the high contracting parties: and all the said parties declare, that they will not suffer any privilege, favor, or indulgence to subsist, contrary to the treaties above confirmed, except what shall have been agreed and stipulated by the present treaty.

Similarly sweeping is the language through which North America east of the Mississippi is apportioned to

Great Britain. The contrast between Article 7 of the Treaty of Paris, carving up "virgin land," and, say, the language of the 17th-century TREATY OF THE PYRENEES, apportioning quasi-feudal holdings between France and Spain, is dramatic. In place of the earlier document's many complex, cataloglike recitations of place names and detailing of ancient rights and holdings, the Treaty of Paris provides a single paragraph:

VII

In order to re-establish peace on solid and durable foundations, and to remove for ever all subject of dispute with regard to the limits of the British and French territories on the continent of America; it is agreed, that, for the future, the confines between the dominions of his Britannick Majesty, and those of his most Christian Majesty, in that part of the world, shall be fixed irrevocably by a line drawn along the middle of the River Mississippi, from its source, to the River Iberville, and from thence, by a line drawn along the middle of this River, and the Lakes Maurepas and Pontchatrain, to the sea; and for this purpose, the most Christian King cedes in full right, and guaranties to his Britannick Majesty, the River and Port of the Mobile, and every thing which he possesses, or ought to possess, on the left side of the River Mississippi, except the town of New Orleans, and the island in which it is situated, which shall remain to France; provided that the navigation of the River Mississippi, shall be equally free, as well to the subjects of Great Britain, as to those of France, in its whole breadth and length, from its source to the sea, and expressly that part, which is between the said island of New Orleans, and the right bank of that River, as well as the passage both in and out of its mouth: It is further stipulated, that the vessels belonging to the subjects of either nation, shall not be stopped, visited, or subjected to the payment of any duty whatsoever. The stipulations, inserted in the IVth article, in favor of the inhabitants of Canada, shall also take place, with regard to the inhabitants of the countries ceded by this article.

While other articles detailed the cessions of Great Britain to France and Spain, it was the starkly simple Article 7 that constituted the heart of the treaty, making it a document that quite literally altered the face of the world.

Consequences

Few treaties have been so decisive and far reaching. By this single document, Britain acquired all of North America east of the Mississippi River, including Canada and Florida. Yet this proved less a boon to Great Britain than it did to her colonists. With the French and Spanish removed from the frontiers, the Indians were left without foreign support for their resistance to British expansion. As colonists migrated inland, connections with the mother country grew increasingly tenuous, and for their part, even coastal colonials no longer felt as dependent on Britain for defense. Thus, the Treaty of Paris provided some of the conditions under which an increasing number of colonists began to think of independence. The treaty may therefore be read as an opening chord in the prelude to the American Revolution.

DELAWARE INDIAN TREATY

> ## TREATY AT A GLANCE
>
> *Completed*
> September 17, 1778, Fort Pitt (present-day Pittsburgh, Pennsylvania)
>
> *Signatories*
> United States and the Delaware Indians
>
> *Overview*
> The treaty was an attempt to neutralize the threat of the Delaware (Lenni Lenape) tribe, which was largely allied with the British during the American Revolution.

Historical Background

American Indians were involved, in varying degrees, in all conflicts fought on the North American continent. During the French and Indian War and the wars preceding it, British and French interests each had their Indian allies and auxiliaries (the French more than the British). During the American Revolution, most Indian tribes and groups who did not succeed in remaining neutral sided with the British against the Americans. They reasoned that a British victory would result in enforcement of the PROCLAMATION OF 1763, which prohibited white settlement west of the Allegheny Mountains, and generally stem the tide of invasion into their lands. More realistically, most Indian tribes were aware that an American victory would ensure invasion, whereas a British victory might at least forestall it.

For the most part, the Delaware Indians had cooperated with the British in the frontier regions of the Cherry Valley, the Mohawk Valley, and the Wyoming Valley of New York and Pennsylvania, terrorizing settlers during 1778. The treaty concluded at Fort Pitt on September 17 not only sought to end this but to strike up an alliance with the Delaware.

Terms

Characteristically, the language of the treaty was modeled on that of European examples, except for the reference to "wise men of the United States," a phrase the framers of the treaty doubtless thought would be highly comprehensible to the Indians.

ARTICLE I
THAT all offenses or acts of hostilities by one, or either of the contracting parties against the other, be mutu-

ally forgiven, and buried in the depth of oblivion, never more to be had in remembrance.

ARTICLE II
That a perpetual peace and friendship shall from henceforth take place, and subsist between the contracting parties aforesaid, through all succeeding generations: and if either of the parties are engaged in a just and necessary war with any other nation or nations, that then each shall assist the other in due proportion to their abilities, till their enemies are brought to reasonable terms of accommodation: and that if either of them shall discover any hostile designs forming against the other, they shall give the earliest notice thereof, that timeous measures may be taken to prevent their ill effect.

ARTICLE III
And whereas the United States are engaged in a just and necessary war, in defence and support of life, liberty and independence, against the King of England and his adherents, and as said King is yet possessed of several posts and forts on the lakes and other places, the reduction of which is of great importance to the peace and security of the contracting parties, and as the most practicable way for the troops of the United States to some of the posts and forts is by passing through the country of the Delaware nation, the aforesaid deputies, on behalf of themselves and their nation, do hereby stipulate and agree to give a free passage through their country to the troops aforesaid, and the same to conduct by the nearest and best ways to the posts, forts or towns of the enemies of the United States, affording to said troops such supplies of corn, meat, horses, or whatever may be in their power for the accommodation of such troops, on the commanding officer's, &c. paying, or engaging to pay, the full value of whatever they can supply them with. And the said deputies, on the behalf of their nation, engage to

join the troops of the United States aforesaid, with such a number of their best and most expert warriors as they can spare, consistent with their own safety, and act in concert with them; and for the better security of the old men, women and children of the aforesaid nation, whilst their warriors are engaged against the common enemy, it is agreed on the part of the United States, that a fort of sufficient strength and capacity be built at the expense of the said States, with such assistance as it may be in the power of the said Delaware Nation to give, in the most convenient place, and advantageous situation, as shall be agreed on by the commanding officer of the troops aforesaid, with the advice and concurrence of the deputies of the aforesaid Delaware Nation, which fort shall be garrisoned by such a number of the troops of the United States, as the commanding officer can spare for the present, and hereafter by such numbers, as the wise men of the United States in council, shall think most conducive to the common good.

More than most of the many later treaties between Indians and whites, the Delaware document attempted to establish the basis of an ongoing relationship between the interests of the American settlers and the Native Americans. Article 4 provided for the establishment of a system of criminal justice in cases involving whites and Indians, and Article 5 established a basis of trade:

ARTICLE IV

For the better security of the peace and friendship now entered into by the contracting parties, against all infractions of the same by the citizens of either party, to the prejudice of the other, neither party shall proceed to the infliction of punishments on the citizens of the other, otherwise than by securing the offender or offenders by imprisonment, or any other competent means, till a fair and impartial trial can be had by judges or juries of both parties, as near as can be to the laws, customs and usages of the contracting parties and natural justice: The mode of such trials to be hereafter fixed by the wise men of the United States in Congress assembled, with the assistance of such deputies of the Delaware nation, as may be appointed to act in concert with them in adjusting this matter to their mutual liking. And it is further agreed between the parties aforesaid, that neither shall entertain or give countenance to the enemies of the other, or protect in their respective states, criminal fugitives or slaves, but the same to apprehend, and secure and deliver to the State or States, to which such enemies, criminals, servants or slaves respectively belong.

ARTICLE V

Whereas the confederation entered into by the Delaware nation and the United States, renders the first dependent on the latter for all the articles of clothing, utensils and implements of war, and it is judged not only reasonable, but indispensably necessary, that the aforesaid Nation be supplied with such articles from time to time, as far as the United States may have it in their power, by a well-regulated trade, under the conduct of an intelligent, candid agent, with an adequate salary, one more influenced by the love of his country, and a constant attention to the duties of his department by promoting the common interest, than the sinister purposes of converting and binding all the duties of his office to his private emolument: Convinced of the necessity of such measures, the Commissioners of the United States, at the earnest solicitation of the deputies aforesaid, have engaged in behalf of the United States, that such a trade shall be afforded said nation, conducted of such principals of mutual interest as the wisdom of the United States in Congress assembled shall think most conducive to adopt for their mutual convenience.

Article VI directly addressed the Delawares' concerns about invasion, seeking to meet British propaganda head-on:

ARTICLE VI

Whereas the enemies of the United States have endeavored, by every article in their power, to possess the Indians in general with an opinion, that it is the design of the States aforesaid, to extirpate the Indians and take possession of their country: to obviate such false suggestion, the United States do engage to guarantee to the aforesaid nation of Delawares, and their heirs, all their territorial rights in the fullest and most ample manner, as it hath been bounded by former treaties, as long as they the said Delaware nation shall abide by, and hold fast the chain of friendship now entered into. And it is further agreed on between the contracting parties should it for the future be found conducive for the mutual interest of both parties to invite any other tribes who have been friends to the interest of the United States, to join the present confederation, and to form a state whereof the Delaware nation shall be the head, and have a representation in Congress: Provided, nothing contained in this article to be considered as conclusive until it meets with the approbation of Congress. And it is also the intent and meaning of this article, that no protection or countenance shall be afforded to any who are at present our enemies, by which they might escape the punishment they deserve.

Consequences

As white-Indian treaties go, the Fort Pitt treaty was evenhanded and admirably clear. Unfortunately, it was also largely ineffective. The government of the United States was no more effective than the colonial administration of Great Britain in regulating and restraining the expansion of settlement into Indian lands. As for the Delaware, many Delaware groups continued to cooperate with the British throughout the balance of the Revolution, and those led by Joseph Brant

(Thayendanegea) in the Ohio Valley during 1781 were devastatingly effective.

The continued hostility was not so much a result of the Delaware having violated the 1778 treaty as it was an instance of the flaw that would prove fatal in most white-Indian treaties: tribal organization was characteristically loose to the point that Euro-Americans would regard as anarchy. So-called chiefs were seldom sovereigns in the European or American sense, embodying the collective will of the people or the nation. Chiefs usually led factions, not tribes, and, at that, they did not so much lead as they convinced and persuaded through force of personality. This meant that, although a particular chief or set of chiefs might assent to a treaty, many members of the tribe might not regard themselves bound by it. British and American officials alike persistently refused to acknowledge the fact that Indian tribes were not nations and their chiefs were not sovereigns.

TREATY OF PARIS (1783)

TREATY AT A GLANCE

Completed
September 3, 1783, at Paris

Signatories
Great Britain and the United States

Overview
From an American point of view, the Treaty of Paris (1783) marks the successful conclusion of the War of Independence. From the British point of view, it betokens the nation's first major colonial loss. The treaty did end the American Revolution, and it was the instrument by which Great Britain recognized the independence of the United States. It also specified the boundaries of the United States in order "that all disputes which might arise in future . . . may be prevented," and it gave the United States fishing rights off Newfoundland. Related documents also stipulated that navigation of the Mississippi River would be free not only to the United States and Britain but to France, Spain, and Holland as well and restored Florida to Spain and Senegal to France.

Historical Background

The American Revolution gave birth to the United States, transforming a colony into a nation. It was the product of the colonists' desire for political and economic independence from a mother country that had grown unresponsive to their needs and repressive of their aspirations and ambitions. It was also the product of the so-called Age of Reason, a period in which a number of eloquent philosophers proposed that the natural and just state of humankind was liberty, which, in the words Thomas Jefferson used in the DECLARATION OF INDEPENDENCE, was an "unalienable right," along with "life" and "the pursuit of happiness." Thus, the American Revolution was an act of pragmatism, spiritual desire, and philosophical inclination.

As early as 1759, small-scale disputes broke out between Britain and the colonies over vetoes of measures enacted by colonial assemblies and other acts. When King George issued the PROCLAMATION OF 1763, prohibiting settlement west of the Appalachian divide, anti-British sentiment greatly increased. Next came taxation of the colonists for the first time in their history. This was distasteful enough, but in the absence of colonial representation in Parliament, it struck many as nothing less than tyranny. Although many of the taxes were rescinded during the 1760s, relations between the colonies and the mother country continued to deteriorate.

Finally, in 1773 Parliament passed the Tea Act, by which British tea exporters were allowed to sell directly to American retailers, cutting out American wholesale merchants. The tea thus imported into the colonies was taxed at a modest rate. The reaction was the famous Boston Tea Party, in which colonists, disguised as Indians, threw 340 tea chests off ships and into Boston Harbor. In retaliation, Parliament passed the so-called Intolerable Acts, which closed the port of Boston, interfered with town and provincial government, removed royal officials and functionaries from colonial jurisdiction, and provided for the quartering of troops in Boston. The other colonies rallied to defend Massachusetts, forming the Continental Congress in September 1774 to denounce the acts. The British responded by sending more troops to Boston, and at Lexington and Concord, the colonial militia and the British regulars clashed on April 19, 1775. The Revolution had begun, although a formal Declaration of Independence was not signed until July 4, 1776.

The odds against the colonists seemed enormous. Britain had substantial resources, a very good army, and a superb navy. Moreover, the population of America was by no means unanimous in its support of the rebellion. Nevertheless, George Washington, chosen as supreme commander of the Patriot forces, was able to raise large armies, and American diplomats, most notably Benjamin Franklin, John Adams, and John Jay, were able to secure aid from sympathetic foreign powers, particularly the French.

The Continental Army and the various colonial militias won few of the war's formal, fixed battles, but even when they lost, they exacted a heavy toll on the British, who were hard pressed for reinforcements. And if the militia was not always at its best in a full-dress battle, it was efficient in fighting the Revolution's internal enemies, including British-allied Indians and Loyalist colonials. Washington's genius lay in his ability to exploit whatever advantages he possessed while holding his army together through military adversity and through such hardships as critical shortages of food, clothing, and equipment and often bitter winter weather.

While the hard-pressed Patriots enjoyed often-inspired leadership and the ability to move quickly and deftly, the British government was increasingly divided over the question of American independence. The war was prosecuted by the conscientious but obstinate George III and his dull-witted prime minister Lord North. Britain's generals were cut from the same cloth as its political leaders and characteristically failed to tailor their campaigns to the conditions of wilderness America.

Under these conditions, the war dragged on, as neither side won decisive victories and as negotiations repeatedly failed. The deadlock began to break in October 1781 at Yorktown, Virginia, where Patriot forces, aided by a French fleet under the Comte de Grasse, defeated General Cornwallis, who surrendered his nearly 8,000 troops on October 19, 1781. Fighting continued until 1783, but after Yorktown, British leaders lost any remaining enthusiasm for subduing the rebellious colonies. To be sure, British armies continued to occupy key American cities and frontier outposts, but the American negotiators at the Paris peace conference, John Jay, Benjamin Franklin, and John Adams, showed great genius in exploiting the rivalry between France and England. After protracted negotiation, the Americans were able to obtain British recognition of their independence in return for an understanding that the new United States would not fall into the French orbit.

Terms

The central document of the Treaty of Paris was remarkably concise and plainspoken.

Treaty of Paris
Paris, September 3, 1783
Peace Treaty between Great Britain and
the United States of America

In the name of the Most Holy and Undivided Trinity.

It having pleased the Divine Providence to dispose the hearts of the most serene and most potent Prince George the Third, by the Grace of God King of Great Britain, France, and Ireland, Defender of the Faith, Duke of Brunswick and Luneburg, Arch-Treasurer and Prince Elector of the Holy Roman Empire, Szca., and of the United States of America, to forget all past misunderstandings and differences that have unhappily interrupted the good correspondence and friendship which they mutually wish to restore; and to establish such a beneficial and satisfactory intercourse between the two countries, upon the ground of reciprocal advantages and mutual convenience, as may promote and secure to both perpetual peace and harmony: And having for this desirable end already laid the foundation of peace and reconciliation, by the provisional articles, signed at Paris, on the 30th of Nov'r, 1782, by the commissioners empowered on each part, which articles were agreed to be inserted in and to constitute the treaty of peace proposed to be concluded between the Crown of Great Britain and the said United States, but which treaty was not to be concluded until terms of peace should be agreed upon between Great Britain and France, and His Britannic Majesty should be ready to conclude such treaty accordingly; and the treaty between Great Britain and France having since been concluded, His Britannic Majesty and the United States of America, in order to carry into full effect the provisional articles above mentioned, according to the tenor thereof, have constituted and appointed, that is to say, His Britannic Majesty on his part, David Hartley, esqr., member of the Parliament of Great Britain; and the said United States on their part, John Adams, esqr., late a commissioner of the United States of America at the Court of Versailles, late Delegate in Congress from the State of Massachusetts, and chief justice of the said State, and Minister Plenipotentiary of the said United States to their High Mightinesses the States General of the United Netherlands; Benjamin Franklin, esq're, late Delegate in Congress from the State of Pennsylvania, president of the convention of the said State, and Minister Plenipotentiary from the United States of America at the Court of Versailles; John Jay, esq're, late president of Congress, and chief justice of the State of New York, and Minister Plenipotentiary from the said United States at the Court of Madrid, to be the Plenipotentiaries for the concluding and signing the present definitive treaty; who, after having reciprocally communicated their respective full powers, have agreed upon and confirmed the following articles:

ARTICLE I

His Britannic Majesty acknowledges the said United States, viz. New Hampshire, Massachusetts Bay, Rhode Island, and Providence Plantations, Connecticut, New York, New Jersey, Pennsylvania, Delaware, Maryland, Virginia, North Carolina, South Carolina, and Georgia, to be free, sovereign and independent States; that he treats with them as such, and for himself, his heirs and successors, relinquishes all claims to the Government, propriety and territorial rights of the same, and every part thereof.

ARTICLE II

And that all disputes which might arise in future, on the subject of the boundaries of the said United States may be prevented, it is hereby agreed and declared, that the following are, and shall be their boundaries, viz: From the northwest angle of Nova Scotia, viz. that angle which is formed by a line drawn due north from the source of Saint Croix River to the Highlands; along the said Highlands which divide those rivers that empty themselves into the river St. Lawrence, from those which fall into the Atlantic Ocean, to the northwesternmost head of Connecticut River; thence down along the middle of that river, to the forty-fifth degree of north latitude; from thence, by a line due west on said latitude, until it strikes the river Iroquois or Cataraquy; thence along the middle of said river into Lake Ontario, through the middle of said lake until it strikes the communication by water between that lake and Lake Erie; thence along the middle of said communication into Lake Erie, through the middle of said lake until it arrives at the water communication between that lake and Lake Huron; thence along the middle of said water communication into the Lake Huron; thence through the middle of said lake to the water communication between that lake and Lake Superior; thence through Lake Superior northward of the Isles Royal and Phelipeaux, to the Long Lake; thence through the middle of said Long Lake, and the water communication between it and the Lake of the Woods, to the said Lake of the Woods; thence through the said lake to the most northwestern point thereof, and from thence on a due west course to the river Mississippi; thence by a line to be drawn along the middle of the said river Mississippi until shall intersect the northernmost part of the thirty-first degree of north latitude. South, by a line to be drawn due east from the determination of the line last mentioned, in the latitude of thirty-one degrees north of the Equator, to the middle of the river Apalachicola or Catahouche; thence along the middle thereof to its junction with the Flint River; thence strait to the head of St. Mary's River; and thence down along the middle of St. Mary's River to the Atlantic Ocean. East, by a line to be drawn along the middle of the river St. Croix, from its mouth in the Bay of Fundy to its source, and from its source directly north to the aforesaid Highlands, which divide the rivers that fall into the Atlantic Ocean from those which fall into the river St. Lawrence; comprehending all islands within twenty leagues of any part of the shores of the United States, and lying between lines to be drawn due east from the points where the aforesaid boundaries between Nova Scotia on the one part, and East Florida on the other, shall respectively touch the Bay of Fundy and the Atlantic Ocean; excepting such islands as now are, or heretofore have been, within the limits of the said province of Nova Scotia.

ARTICLE III

It is agreed that the people of the United States shall continue to enjoy unmolested the right to take fish of every kind on the Grand Bank, and on all the other banks of Newfoundland; also in the Gulph of Saint Lawrence, and at all other places in the sea where the inhabitants of both countries used at any time heretofore to fish. And also that the inhabitants of the United States shall have liberty to take fish of every kind on such part of the coast of Newfoundland as British fishermen shall use (but not to

dry or cure the same on that island) and also on the coasts, bays and creeks of all other of His Britannic Majesty's dominions in America; and that the American fishermen shall have liberty to dry and cure fish in any of the unsettled bays, harbors and creeks of Nova Scotia, Magdalen Islands, and Labrador, so long as the same shall remain unsettled; but so soon as the same or either of them shall be settled, it shall not be lawful for the said fishermen to dry or cure fish at such settlements, without a previous agreement for that purpose with the inhabitants, proprietors or possessors of the ground.

ARTICLE IV

It is agreed that creditors on either side shall meet with no lawful impediment to the recovery of the full value in sterling money, of all bona fide debts heretofore contracted.

ARTICLE V

It is agreed that the Congress shall earnestly recommend it to the legislatures of the respective States, to provide for the restitution of all estates, rights and properties which have been confiscated, belonging to real British subjects, and also of the estates, rights and properties of persons resident in districts in the possession of His Majesty's arms, and who have not borne arms against the said United States. And that persons of any other description shall have free liberty to go to any part or parts of any of the thirteen United States, and therein to remain twelve months, unmolested in their endeavors to obtain the restitution of such of their estates, rights and properties as may have been confiscated; and that Congress shall also earnestly recommend to the several States a reconsideration and revision of all acts or laws regarding the premises, so as to render the said laws or acts perfectly consistent, not only with justice and equity, but with that spirit of conciliation which, on the return of the blessings of peace, should universally prevail. And that Congress shall also earnestly recommend to the several States, that the estates, rights and properties of such last mentioned persons, shall be restored to them, they refunding to any persons who may be now in possession, the *bona fide* price (where any has been given) which such persons may have paid on purchasing any of the said lands, rights or properties, since the confiscation. And it is agreed, that all persons who have any interest in confiscated lands, either by debts, marriage settlements or otherwise, shall meet with no lawful impediment in the prosecution of their just rights.

ARTICLE VI

That there shall be no future confiscations made, nor any prosecutions commenc'd against any person or persons for, or by reason of the part which he or they may have taken in the present war; and that no person shall, on that account, suffer any future loss or damage, either in his person, liberty or property; and that those who may be in confinement on such charges, at the time of the ratification of the treaty in America, shall be immediately set at liberty, and the prosecutions so commenced be discontinued.

ARTICLE VII

There shall be a firm and perpetual peace between His Britannic Majesty and the said States, and between the subjects of the one and the citizens of the other, wherefore all hostilities, both by sea and land, shall from henceforth cease: All prisoners on both sides shall be set at liberty, and His Britannic Majesty shall, with all convenient speed, and without causing any destruction, or carrying away any negroes or other property of the American inhabitants, withdraw all his armies, garrisons and fleets from the said United States, and from every post, place and harbor within the same; leaving in all fortifications the American artillery that may be therein: And shall also order and cause all archives, records, deeds and papers, belonging to any of the said States, or their citizens, which, in the course of the war, may have fallen into the hands of his officers, to be forthwith restored and deliver'd to the proper States and persons to whom they belong.

ARTICLE VIII

The navigation of the river Mississippi, from its source to the ocean, shall for ever remain free and open to the subjects of Great Britain, and the citizens of the United States.

ARTICLE IX

In case it should so happen that any place or territory belonging to Great Britain or to the United States, should have been conquer'd by the arms of either from the other, before the arrival of the said provisional articles in America, it is agreed, that the same shall be restored without difficulty, and without requiring any compensation.

ARTICLE X

The solemn ratification of the present treaty, expedited in good and due form, shall be exchanged between the contracting parties, in the space of six months, or sooner if possible, to be computed from the day of the signature of the present treaty. In witness whereof, we the undersigned, their Ministers Plenipotentiary, have in their name and in virtue of our full powers, signed with our hands the present definitive treaty, and caused the seals of our arms to be affix'd thereto.

Done at Paris, this third day of September, in the year of our Lord one thousand seven hundred and eighty-three.

[SEAL.]	D. HARTLEY.
[SEAL.]	JOHN ADAMS
[SEAL.]	B. FRANKLIN
[SEAL.]	JOHN JAY

Consequences

The treaty not only brought the Revolutionary War to an end, recognized American independence, defined the boundaries of the United States, and ensured American fishing rights in Newfoundland, it also gave birth to a new nation in the world and, in doing so, to a wholly new idea of nationhood. It would take the British a while to come to terms with what they had done, which was to shut down one empire—called by many historians the First British Empire, concentrated on the seacoasts of America—and establish a second empire stretching across whole continents all over the globe, in Canada, Australia, India, and Africa.

Despite the language of the treaty, following the LOUISIANA PURCHASE of 1803 and subsequent expansion into the interior of the subcontinent by the United States, disputes did arise between the two nations over the precise boundaries of U.S. sovereignty in the American West. The Americans would have to fight a second war, the War of 1812, before the British would leave them to themselves in North America below Canada. And the American Revolution would inspire an age of revolutions, beginning in France before the century was out and spreading in the 19th century to the Latin American holdings of those other venerable New World imperialist powers Portugal and Spain.

SECOND TREATY OF FORT STANWIX
(TREATY WITH THE SIX NATIONS)

TREATY AT A GLANCE

Completed
October 22, 1784 at Fort Stanwix (present-day Rome), New York

Signatories
United States and the Mohawk, Onondaga, Oneida, Cayuga,
Seneca, and Tuscarora Indians

Overview
This was the treaty by which the American revolutionaries ended
the hostilities between themselves and the Six Nations of the Iroquois Confederacy and the hostilities among the Six Nations tribes
that grew out of the Revolution and its conflicting alliances. In
effect, the treaty marked the end of the centuries-old confederacy
and the reduction of the Iroquois tribes to what would later be
called dependent nations.

Historical Background

Insofar as the American Revolution was fought for the
West, it was a war for the future. As such, in the West,
it was more a war against the Indians than a revolt
against the British. For it was Indian land that the new
Americans were laying claim to in the West, and it was
the Iroquois League and the powerful Algonquian
tribes of the upper Ohio that stood in the way of those
claims, the last bastion against white settlement of the
Old Northwest and the frontier regions of today's
American South. For these Indian tribes, the Revolution was but another stage in their resistance to foreign
conquest, and they fought by and large not to aid the
Loyalists or the rebels but to keep European settlers
behind the Alleghenies and the Appalachians.

When British authorities began to recognize that
the western boundary they had drawn for the American settlers in the PROCLAMATION OF 1763 was unrealis-
tic given the colonies' land-hungry settlers and
ambitious fur traders, they tried to alleviate some of
the pressure being brought by the colonials through
negotiating land cessions from the Iroquois. The great
British Indian agent Sir William Johnson, connected by
marriage to the Six Nations, met with 3,400 Iroquois
near present-day Rome, New York, to sign the First
Treaty of Fort Stanwix in 1768. In return for £10,000
worth of gifts and goods, the Iroquois allowed Johnson

to open up vast tracts of land in what are now western
Pennsylvania, Kentucky, West Virginia, and New York
to white exploration and settlement. The only trouble
was that much of the land, especially to the south, did
not belong to the Iroquois except in their own minds,
which even the British recognized. They negotiated
two new agreements with the Cherokee, setting the
boundaries of what is now West Virginia, but there was
not much they could do with the Algonquian tribes of
the Ohio, like the Shawnee, who considered much of
the region their own hunting grounds and were loath
to let them go.

Although the American rebellion came to the frontier relatively late, it proved especially virulent there.
As usual, frontiersmen and Indians suffered in a series
of raids and counterraids. As earlier in the century,
when the European empires had enlisted the aid of
those they considered savages in a contest for possession of the continent, now both the British and Americans courted Indian allies. Most Indians sided with the
British, both because they believed—quite correctly—
that the British Empire was the more powerful force
and because they saw a British victory as the better
hope for containing white settlement. The British
argued—not only persuasively but also accurately—
that colonial victory would mean a steady push westward that would drive the Indians before it. Defeat of
the revolutionaries, however, would result in enforce-

ment of the royal Proclamation of 1763. Clearly, in wooing Indian support, the British had learned something from the French and Indian War.

Fortunately for the American Patriots, however, the British had not learned enough. British-allied Indians ran rampant on the frontier, especially in upstate New York, in the back counties of Pennsylvania, and in the fledgling settlement of Kentucky. Some historians have claimed that had the British treated the Indians with more trust and respect, equipped them better, and used them more, their alliance might well have won the war. The British as always saw the Indians as expendable savages, though, and racial solidarity sometimes outweighed political expedience. On the western frontiers of the South, in western Virginia and the Carolinas, as well as west of the Proclamation line, in Tennessee and Kentucky, Cherokee raided isolated and far-flung backwoods settlements. In 1776 John Stuart, the British superintendent of Indian affairs in the region, was so appalled by the ferocity of the Indian attacks that he actually warned Tennessee settlers—rebels—of impending raids.

On the western frontiers of Pennsylvania and New York, the British-Indian alliance threatened to wipe out the trans-Allegheny pioneer settlements. The combined force of Tory colonel John Butler's Rangers and Mohawks under Chief Joseph Brant (known to the Indians as Thayendanega) raked the Mohawk and Wyoming Valleys during 1778 and 1779, until George Washington, in command of the Revolutionary Army, was able to divert troops from the principal action in the East in order to relieve the West. A force of 25 hundred under the rebel general John Sullivan combined with a smaller force of 15 hundred under General James Clinton and pushed into Iroquois country, burning to the ground some 40 Iroquois towns and destroying the Indians' harvest. And that, Sullivan and Clinton assumed, was that. They were wrong. The truly brutal warfare only intensified the Indians' will to fight, and the Mohawk Valley remained subject to combined Indian-Tory raids until the autumn of 1781.

More than simply a few battles were lost by the Iroquois in the Revolutionary War, for in the heat of the fighting, the centuries-old Iroquois Confederacy had torn itself apart. Part mutual defense league, part trade association, the confederacy was based on one primary rule: no member of any of the confederated tribes would ever take up arms against a member of another tribe. Through all the temptations afforded by the coming of the Europeans, none had done so before the Revolutionary Battle of Oriskany. There the Oneida and the Tuscarora sided with the colonials while the other tribes—the Mohawk, Onondaga, Cayuga, and Seneca—fought with the British, and the Iroquois League vanished into the fog of war.

Terms

When the American Revolution ended, the newly emancipated citizens of the United States still had Indian enemies to come to terms with, especially in the Ohio Valley and the rest of the Northwest, where the Algonquian-speaking tribes were still engaged in their long resistance. But the once-mighty Iroquois the new Americans treated as an already vanquished foe, and the Second Treaty of Fort Stanwix, ending the war with the confederacy, was short and brutal. Discouraged from further resistance, the Iroquois reluctantly agreed to redraw their eastern borders, established in 1768, and were persuaded to yield both a small section of western New York and vast acreage of rich land in western Pennsylvania, making up one-fourth the area of today's state.

Articles concluded at Fort Stanwix, or the twenty-second day of October, one thousand seven hundred and eighty-four, between Oliver Wolcott, Richard Butler, and Arthur Lee, Commissioners Plenipotentiary from the United States, in Congress assembled, on the one Part, and the Sachems and Warriors of the Six Nations, on the other. The United States of America give peace to the Senecas, Mohawks, Onondagas and Cayugas, and receive them into their protection upon the following conditions:

ARTICLE I
Six hostages shall be immediately delivered to the commissioners by the said nations, to remain in possession of the United States, till all the prisoners, white and black, which were taken by the said Senecas, Mohawks, Onondagas and Cayugas, or by any of them, in the late war, from among the people of the United States, shall be delivered up.

ARTICLE II
The Oneida and Tuscarora nations shall be secured in the possession of the lands on which they are settled.

ARTICLE III
A line shall be drawn, beginning at the mouth of a creek about four miles east of Niagara, called Oyonwayea, or Johnston's Landing-Place, upon the lake named by the Indians Oswego, and by us Ontario; from thence southerly in a direction always four miles east of the carrying-path, between Lake Erie and Ontario, to the mouth of Tehoseroron or Buffaloe Creek on Lake Erie; thence south to the north boundary of the state of Pennsylvania; thence west to the end of the said north boundary; thence south along the west boundary of the said state, to the river Ohio; the said line from the mouth of the Oyonwayea to the Ohio, shall be the western boundary of the lands of the Six Nations, so that the Six Nations shall and do yield to the United States, all claims to the country west of the said boundary, and then they shall be secured in the peaceful possession of the lands they inhabit east and north of the same, reserving only six miles square round the fort of Oswego, to the United States, for the support of the same.

ARTICLE IV

The Commissioners of the United States, in consideration of the present circumstances of the Six Nations, and in execution of the humane and liberal views of the United States upon the signing of the above articles, will order goods to be delivered to the said Six Nations for their use and comfort.

OLIVER WOLCOTT
RICHARD BUTLER
ARTHUR LEE

MOHAWKS:
ONOGWENDAHONJI, HIS X MARK
TOUIGHNATOGON, HIS X MARK

ONONDAGAS:
OHEADARIGHTON, HIS X MARK
KENDARINDGON, HIS X MARK

SENEKAS:
TAYAGONENDAGIGHTI, HIS X MARK
TEHONWAEAGHRIGAGIJ HIS X MARK

ONEIDAS:
OTYADONENGHTI, HIS X MARK
DAGAHEARI, HIS X MARK

CAYUGA:
ORAGHGOANENDAGEN, HIS X MARK

TUSCARORAS:
ONONGHSAWENGHTI, HIS X MARK
THARONDAWAGON, HIS X MARK

SENEKA ABEAL:
KAYENTHOGHKE, HIS X MARK

WITNESSES:
SAM. JO. ATLEE
WM. MACLAY

FRAS. JOHNSTON
JAMES DEAN
SAML. MONTGOMERY
DERICK LANE, CAPTAIN

PENNSYLVANIA COMMISSIONERS:
JOHN MERCER, LIEUTENANT
AARON HILL
ALEXANDER CAMPBELL
SAML. KIRKLAND, MISSIONARY
WILLIAM PENNINGTON, LIEUTENANT
MAHLON ELORD, ENSIGN
HUGH PEEBLES.

Consequences

Having acknowledged defeat in the Second Treaty of Fort Stanwix, the Iroquois League effectively came to an end. The relinquishment of claims to additional territory west of the Ohio would continue the long dispute between the Algonquians, especially the Shawnee, and the former British colonials over who owned that land. Following the British Crown's self-serving lead, the United States chose to assert the old but quite spurious claim of the Iroquois to the region, which of course they had now ceded to the new nation in such treaties as the TREATY OF FORT HARMAR and the TREATY OF CANANDAIGUA, WHICH led to continued misunderstanding and much bloodshed for decades to come.

VETERANS' TREATY
(TREATY WITH THE INDIANS
LIVING IN THE COUNTRY OF THE ONEIDAS)

TREATY AT A GLANCE

Completed
December 2, 1794

Signatories
The United States and the Oneida and Tuscarora Nations

Overview
Ten years after the American Revolution, the United States agreed by treaty to compensate the Oneida and Tuscarora Indians for the losses they suffered during the war as allies of the rebellious colonists.

Historical Background

The least populous of the tribes of the Iroquois League, the Oneida during the 17th century occupied only one palisaded town of 60 to 100 longhouses before the town was destroyed by a French-backed Canadian expedition in 1696. Afterward the tribe split into the Oneida (or Upper Castles) and the Canawaroghere. In the early 1700s the Oneida were joined by Tuscarora from North Carolina, who thus became the sixth of the Six Nations now making up the former five-nation Iroquois Confederacy.

These two closely related tribes, then, supported the American cause during the Revolutionary War, which created a schism in the league since all the others—the Mohawk, Onondaga, Cayuga, and Seneca—backed the British. The Oneida were hit hard by the Iroquois Loyalists under Mohawk chief Joseph Brant early in the war, and they retired behind American lines. They fought a bloody battle against their former confederates at Oriskany Creek, but mostly they served the Americans as scouts. Returning to their homes near today's Rome and Utica, New York, after the war, they took in remnants of the Mohegan tribe (called the Stockbridge Indians).

Terms

Ten years after the war, in the flush of victory over the Algonquin of the Old Northwest and post-Revolution-ary explosion in land sales, the United States signed the Veterans' Treaty, or the Treaty with the Indians Living in the Country of the Oneidas, under which the new federal government planned to compensate the Oneida for their losses during the war.

A Treaty between the United States and the Oneida, Tuscarora and Stockbridge Indians, Dwelling in the Country of the Oneidas.

WHEREAS, in the late war between Great-Britain and the United States of America, a body of the Oneida and Tuscarora and the Stockbridge Indians, adhered faithfully to the United States, and assisted them with their warriors; and in consequence of this adherence and assistance, the Oneidas and Tuscaroras, at an unfortunate period of the war, were driven from their homes, and their houses were burnt and their property destroyed: And as the United States in the time of their distress, acknowledged their obligations to these faithful friends, and promised to reward them: and the United States being now in a condition to fulfil the promises then made: the following articles are stipulated by the respective parties for that purpose; to be in force when ratified by the President and Senate.

ARTICLE I
The United States will pay the sum of five thousand dollars, to be distributed among individuals of the Oneida and Tuscarora nations, as a compensation for their individual losses and serv-

ices during the late war between Great-Britain and the United States. The only man of the Kaughnawaugas now remaining in the Oneida country, as well as some few very meritorious persons of the Stockbridge Indians, will be considered in the distribution.

ARTICLE II

For the general accommodation of these Indian nations, residing in the country of the Oneidas, the United States will cause to be erected a complete grist-mill and saw-mill, in a situation to serve the present principal settlements of these nations. Or if such one convenient situation cannot be found, then the United States will cause to be erected two such grist-mills and saw-mills, in places where it is now known the proposed accommodation may be effected. Of this the United States will judge.

ARTICLE III

The United States will provide, during three years after the mills shall be completed, for the expense of employing one or two suitable persons to manage the mills, to keep them in repair, to instruct some young men of the three nations in the arts of the miller and sawyer, and to provide teams and utensils for carrying on the work of the mills.

ARTICLE IV

The United States will pay one thousand dollars, to be applied in building a convenient church at Oneida, in the place of the one which was there burnt by the enemy, in the late war.

ARTICLE V

In consideration of the above stipulations to be performed on the part of the United States, the Oneida, Tuscarora and Stockbridge Indians afore-mentioned, now acknowledge themselves satisfied, and relinquish all other claims of compensation and rewards for their losses and services in the late war. Excepting only the unsatisfied claims of such men of the said nations as bore commissions under the United States, for any arrears which may be due to them as officers.

In witness whereof, the chiefs of those nations, residing in the country of the Oneidas, and Timothy Pickering, agent for the United States have hereto set their hands and seals, at Oneida, the second day of December, in the year one thousand seven hundred and ninety four.

TIMOTHY PICKERING
WOLF TRIBE:
ODOTSAIHTE, HIS X MARK,
KONNOQUENYAU, HIS X MARK,
HEAD SACHEMS OF THE ONEIDAS.
JOHN SKENENDO, ELDEST WAR CHIEF, HIS X MARK,
BEAR TRIBE:
LODOWIK KOHSANWETAU, HIS X MARK,
CORNELIUS KAUHIKTOTON, HIS X MARK,

THOS. OSAUHATAUGAUNLOT, HIS X MARK
WAR CHIEFS.
TURTLE TRIBE:
SHONOHLEYO, WAR CHIEF, HIS X MARK,
PETERKONNAUTERLOOK, SACHEM, HIS X MARK.
DANIEL TEOUNESLEES, SON OF SKEN ENDO.
WAR CHIEF, HIS X MARK

TUSCARORAS:
THAULONDAUWAUGON, SACHEM, HIS X MARK,
KANATJOGH, OR NICHOLAS CUSIEK, WAR CHIEF,
HIS X MARK,

Witnesses to the signing and sealing of the agent of the United States, and of the chiefs of the Oneida and Tuscarora nations:

S. KIRKLAND,
JAMES DEAN, INTERPRETER.

Witnesses to the signing and sealing of the four chiefs of the Stockbridge Indians, whose names are below:

SAML. KIRKLAND,
JOHN SERGEANT.

STOCKBRIDGE INDIANS:
HENDRICK AUPAUMUT,
JOSEPH QUONNEY,
JOHN KONKAPOT,
JACOB KONKAPOT,

Consequences

In the years following the treaty, the Oneida fought amongst themselves over Quaker missions to the tribe, their traditional religion, and the sale of Oneida lands, ultimately breaking into factions. Some settled in Canada along the Thames River; others emigrated to Green Bay, Wisconsin; and a few families remained in Oneida County, New York, on a reservation, or at nearby Onondaga. In the late 20th century, descendants, concentrated in Canada, Wisconsin, and central New York, were estimated at 3,000. Visited with new riches courtesy of a major gambling casino at Turning Stone in central New York, the Oneida—amid much controversy—have begun buying up major tracts of land that traditionally belonged to the tribe in Oneida County and along the New York Thruway.

TREATY OF FORT GREENVILLE

TREATY AT A GLANCE

Completed
August 3, 1795, at Fort Greenville, Northwest Territory

Signatories
United States and the Wyandot, Delaware, Shawnee, Ottawa, Chippewa, Potawatomi, Miami, Kickapoo, Piankeshaw, and Kaskaskia Indian tribes, in addition to two Indian groups known as the Eel River and Weeas

Overview
Despite the TREATY OF PARIS, which ended the American Revolution in 1783, British interests as well as the Indian tribes that had fought on the side of the British during the Revolution realized that the new United States had, in actuality, very little control over what was called at the time the Northwest: the trading frontier of the Ohio River Valley and the upper Midwest. When the United States attempted to assert its authority over this territory, many of the Indians, aided and abetted by British traders, waged war against settlers and the army. After suffering two disastrous defeats, the United States scored a decisive victory, which was followed by the Treaty of Fort Greenville, securing white occupation of lands northwest of the Ohio River, establishing a "permanent" boundary to white settlement west of the present state of Ohio, and instituting a program of compensation for territory lost by the Indians. With the Indian threat neutralized, the British in the region acknowledged U.S. authority as well.

Historical Background

The Treaty of Easton had established the Allegheny Mountains as the limit of white settlement in October 1758, and the PROCLAMATION OF 1763 reaffirmed the intention of the Easton treaty, generally setting the Appalachians as the limit to westward expansion. Neither of these agreements proved enforceable, and if anything, the Proclamation of 1763 galvanized colonial resistance to the "restrictive" and "repressive" policies of King George III, paving the way for the American Revolution.

Following this War of Independence, it was the policy of the United States to regard those Indians who had allied themselves with the British as a conquered people. This did not mean that the government simply seized Indian territory. Although it did not recognize civil rights for the Indians, the government did attempt to regulate white settlement in Indian lands and offered to buy territory (cheaply, to be sure) rather than appropriate it. In some places and with some Indian peoples, this policy was moderately successful, but the Shawnee and a number of other "western" tribes resisted negotiation and declined all government offers. While the British may have lost the Revolution, the Shawnee and allied tribes had, if anything, soundly defeated the Americans west of the Ohio, and they were therefore inclined to concede nothing.

In January 1786 U.S. negotiators met with some three hundred Shawnees and informed their leader, Tame Hawk, that the Ohio country was henceforth United States territory. When Tame Hawk countered that the land had been and would remain Shawnee, the negotiators threatened war, whereupon Tame Hawk agreed to relinquish the entire Miami Valley. As was often, indeed usually, the case with negotiations, agreements, and treaties between the government and Native Americans, the authority of any individual or group of individuals to speak for a tribe or other specific group of Indians was by no means clear. In the case of the Miami cession, many Shawnee and Miami bands immediately repudiated Tame Hawk's agreement, and led by the Shawnee Blue Jacket and the Miami Little Turtle, these bands intensified raiding throughout the region. The conflict quickly escalated to full-scale frontier warfare and was called Little Turtle's War.

George Rogers Clark, the somewhat superannuated and bibulous hero of the Revolution, led a large militia force against Shawnee, Ottawa, and Miami in the fall of 1786, but his untrained, ill-equipped, and uncommitted troops soon deserted and disbanded. The campaign was not so much lost as it fell apart. In the meantime, another militia force, under Colonel Benjamin Logan, attacked Shawnee villages on the Miami River, inciting even wider Indian participation in the war against the settlers. The frontier was convulsed with sporadic violence for the next four years, until General Josiah Harmar led 1,133 poorly trained militiamen and 330 army regulars into the Miami and Maumee region near present-day Cincinnati. On October 19, 1790, Little Turtle easily routed Harmar's advance guard, and on October 21 he ambushed the army's rear guard, resulting in a rout.

One year later, on October 4, 1791, General Arthur St. Clair, governor of the newly created Northwest Territory, began what he called a "punitive expedition" against the Shawnee and allied tribes. Inexperienced in frontier warfare, St. Clair encamped on a vulnerable plateau above the upper Wabash River. On November 4, 1791, Little Turtle and Blue Jacket attacked the camp from three directions, killing 623 officers and men (along with 24 civilian teamsters) and wounding 271 soldiers. In proportion to the number of troops engaged, about 1,400, it stands as the worst defeat the U.S. Army has ever suffered.

Following the defeat of St. Clair, President Washington put federal forces under General "Mad" Anthony Wayne, an experienced commander well versed in the ways of wilderness warfare. After carefully mustering and patiently preparing his troops, Wayne scored a massively decisive victory at the Battle of Fallen Timbers August 17–20, 1794, bringing an end to Little Turtle's War and inducing the combatant tribes to sign the Treaty of Fort Greenville.

Terms

The two most important provisions of the treaty were the establishment of peace and "friendly intercourse" between the United States and the Indian tribes, and the demarcation of boundaries between white and Indian settlements:

ARTICLE III

The general boundary line between the lands of the United States, and the lands of the said Indian tribes, shall begin at the mouth of Cayahoga river, and run thence up the same to the portage between that and the Tuscarawas branch of the Muskingum; thence down that branch to the crossing place above Fort Lawrence; thence westerly to a fork of that branch of the great Miami river running into the Ohio, at or near which fork stood Loromie's store, and where commences the portage between the Miami of the Ohio, and St. Mary's river, which is a branch of the Miami, which runs into Lake Erie; thence a westerly course to Fort Recovery, which stands on a branch of the Wabash; then south-westerly in a direct line to the Ohio, so as to intersect that river opposite the mouth of Kentucky or Cuttawa river. And in consideration of the peace now established; of the goods formerly received from the United States; of those now to be delivered, and of the yearly delivery of goods now stipulated to be made hereafter, and to indemnify the United States for the injuries and expenses they have sustained during the war; the said Indian tribes do hereby cede and relinquish forever, all their claims to the lands lying eastwardly and southwardly of the general boundary line now described; and these lands, or any part of them, shall never hereafter be made a cause or pretence, on the part of the said tribes or any of them, of war or injury to the United States, or any of the people thereof.

And for the same considerations, and as an evidence of the returning friendship of the said Indian tribes, of their confidence in the United States, and desire to provide for their accommodation, and for that convenient intercourse, which will be beneficial to both parties, the said Indian tribes do also cede to the United States the following pieces of land; to wit.

(1) One piece of land six miles square at or near Loromie's store before mentioned.

(2) One piece two miles square at the head of the navigable water or landing on the St. Mary's river, near Girty's town.

(3) One piece six miles square at the head of the navigable water of the Au-Glaize river.

(4) One piece six miles square at the confluence of the Au-Glaize and Miami rivers, where Fort Defiance now stands.

(5) One piece six miles square at or near the confluence of the rivers St. Mary's and St. Joseph's, where Fort Wayne now stands, or near it.

(6) One piece two miles square on the Wabash river at the end of the portage from the Miami of the lake, and about eight miles westward from Fort Wayne.

(7) One piece six miles square at the Ouatanon or old Weea towns on the Wabash river.

(8) One piece twelve miles square at the British fort on the Miami of the lake at the foot of the rapids.

(9) One piece six miles square at the mouth of the said river where it empties into the Lake.

(10) One piece six miles square upon Sandusky lake, where a fort formerly stood.

(11) One piece two miles square at the lower rapids of Sandusky river.

(12) The post of Detroit and all the land to the north, the west and the south of it, of which the Indian title has been extinguished by gifts or grants to the French or English governments; and so much more land to be annexed to the district of Detroit as shall be comprehended between the river Rosine on the south, lake St. Clair on the north, and a line, the general course whereof shall be six miles distant from the west end of lake Erie, and Detroit river.

(13) The post of Michillimackinac, and all the land on the island, on which that post stands, and the main land adjacent, of which the Indian title has been extinguished by gifts or grants to the French or English governments; and a piece of land on the main to the north of the island, to measure six miles on lake Huron, or the straight between lakes Huron and Michigan, and to extend three miles back from the water of the lake or straight, and also the island De Bois Blanc, being an extra and voluntary gift of the Chippewa nation.

(14) One piece of land six miles square at the mouth of Chikago river emptying into the south-west end of lake Michigan, where a fort formerly stood.

(15) One piece twelve miles square at or near the mouth of the Illinois river, emptying into the Mississippi.

(16) One piece six miles square at the old Piorias fort and village, near the south end of the Illinois lake on said Illinois river: And whenever the United States shall think proper to survey and mark the boundaries of the lands hereby ceded to them, they shall give timely notice thereof to the said tribes of Indians, that they may appoint some of their wise chiefs to attend and see that the lines are run according to the terms of this treaty.

And the said Indian tribes will allow to the people of the United States a free passage by land and by water, as one and the other shall be found convenient, through their country, along the chain of posts herein before mentioned; that is to say, from the commencement of the portage aforesaid at or near Loromie's store, thence along said portage to the St. Mary's, and down the same to Fort Wayne, and then down the

Miami to lake Erie: again from the commencement of the portage at or near Loromie's store along the portage from thence to the river Au-Glaize, and down the same to its junction with the Miami at Fort Defiance: again from the commencement of the portage aforesaid, to Sandusky river, and down the same to Sandusky bay and lake Erie, and from Sandusky to the post which shall be taken at or near the foot of the rapids of the Miami of the lake: and from thence to Detroit. Again from the mouth of Chikago, to the commencement of the portage, between that river and the Illinois, and down the Illinois river to the Mississippi, also from Fort Wayne along the portage aforesaid which leads to the Wabash, and then down the Wabash to the Ohio. And the said Indian tribes will also allow to the people of the United States the free use of the harbors and mouths of rivers along the lakes adjoining the Indian lands, for sheltering vessels and boats, and liberty to land their cargoes where necessary for their safety.

The Treaty of Greenville, like many government-Indian treaties before and after it, provided for a program of compensation for Indian lands ceded: a lump sum of $20,000 in goods and an annual payment of $9,500 in goods. A vitally important side effect of the treaty was that by effectively neutralizing Indian resistance in the area, it compelled British interests in the area—chiefly traders—to acknowledge and abide by U.S. authority. In effect, then, the Treaty of Greenville enforced in fact the territorial gains and sovereignty in the Northwest that the United States had gained in theory as a result of the Revolutionary War.

Consequences

To a surprising degree, the treaty did succeed in bringing peace to the region, not the "perpetual peace" promised, but almost 15 years of relative quiet, which was more stability than the Northwest had known since mid-century. The attempt to define boundaries of Indian and white settlement, however, was as futile as it was elaborate, and the boundaries established by the Treaty of Greenville were doomed to almost instant violation.

Annexations and Territorial Agreements

TREATY OF FORT HARMAR
(TREATY WITH THE SIX NATIONS)

TREATY AT A GLANCE

Completed
January 1, 1789, at Fort Harmar (in present-day Marietta, Ohio)

Signatories
United States and the Six Nations

Overview
The Iroquois, five years after being forced to sign the SECOND TREATY OF FORT STANWIX ending their involvement in the American Revolution and signaling the end of the Iroquois League itself, met once again with U.S. treaty makers to reaffirm the terms of the peace treaty and to clarify their relations with the new federal government.

Historical Background

During the United States War of Independence a schism developed among the Six Nations of the Iroquois League. The Oneida and the Tuscarora sided with the rebelling colonials, while the rest of the confederacy backed the British. Led by Chief Joseph Brant and his Mohawk Loyalists, the Onondaga, Cayuga, and Seneca tribes raided out of Niagara and decimated a number of American settlements on the isolated Indian frontier. In 1779 U.S. Major General John Sullivan mounted a retaliatory expedition of some 4,000 American troops, who burned to the ground Iroquois fields, orchards, and granaries, ultimately defeating the Loyalist Indians near present-day Elmira, New York. When the Iroquois accepted the terms dictated to them in the SECOND TREATY OF FORT STAN-WIX, they were in effect admitting that their age-old confederacy had come to and end.

The Six Nations were unhappy with the treaty, which had not made a clear enough distinction between the lands the tribes were ceding to the United States and those still belonging to the tribes though currently unoccupied by them. For the Americans, too, some of its provisions remained problematic. The Iroquois Confederacy, with the backing of the British, had long claimed hegemony over vast transmontane lands in the Ohio Valley and beyond by the spurious "right of conquest." The trouble was, the Algonquian tribes, still putting up a fierce resistance to American encroachments into the trans-Allegheny regions, believed those lands belonged to them.

It was important for the new federal government to reiterate the old British claim to Iroquois "conquest" lands by proxy in order to deal with both the hostile Algonquian tribes and its own rapacious settler-squatters. Thus, five years after the Fort Stanwix peace, the United States met again with the Iroquois to reaffirm the terms of that peace, only now placing emphasis on the land ceded by the league.

Terms

The Treaty of Fort Harmar, which reiterated the Second Treaty of Fort Stanwix, focused on the land cession portions of the earlier treaty, more fully describing the boundary lines of the Six Nations and carefully pointing out the land "reserved" for the Indians. Both here, and in the separate article specifically describing criminal jurisdiction between the Indians and the United States, we can see the initial steps toward formulating a general Indian policy for the new nation, a policy that, in all its future twists and turns, aimed always at annexing Indian land and reducing individual Indians to virtual wards of the state.

137

Articles of a treaty made at Fort Harmar, the ninth day of January, in the year of our Lord one thousand seven hundred and eighty-nine, between Arthur St. Clair, esquire, Governor of the territory of the United States of America, northwest of the river Ohio, and Commissioner plenipotentiary of the said United States, for removing all causes of controversy, regulating trade, arid settling boundaries, between the Indian nations in the northerly department and the said United States, of the one part, and the sachems and warriors of the Six Nations, of the other part:

ARTICLE 1

WHEREAS the United States, in congress assembled, did, by their commissioners, Oliver Wolcott, Richard Butler, and Arthur Lee, esquires, duly appointed for that purpose, at a treaty held with the said Six Nations, viz: with the Mohawks, Oneidas, Onondagas, Tuscaroras, Cayugas, and Senekas, at fort Stanwix, on the twenty-second day of October, one thousand seven hundred and eighty-four, give peace to the said nations, and receive them into their friendship and protection: And whereas the said nations have now agreed to and with the said Arthur St. Clair, to renew and confirm all the engagements and stipulations entered into at the before mentioned treaty at fort Stanwix: and whereas it was then and there agreed, between the United States of America and the said Six Nations, that a boundary line should be fixed between the lands of the said Six Nations and the territory of the said United States, which boundary line is as follows, viz: Beginning at the mouth of a creek, about four miles east of Niagara, called Ononwayea, or Johnston's Landing Place, upon the lake named by the Indians Oswego, and by us Ontario; from thence southerly, in a direction always four miles east of the carrying place, between lake Erie and lake Ontario, to the mouth of Tehoseroton, or Buffalo creek, upon lake Erie; thence south, to the northern boundary of the state of Pennsylvania; thence west, to the end of the said north boundary; thence south, along the west boundary of the said state to the river Ohio. The said line, from the mouth of Ononwayea to the Ohio, shall be the western boundary of the lands of the Six Nations, so that the Six Nations shall and do yield to the United States, all claim to the country west of the said boundary; and then they shall be secured in the possession of the lands they inhabit east, north, and south of the same, reserving only six miles square, round the fort of Oswego, for the support of the same. The said Six Nations, except the Mohawks none of whom have attended at this time, for and in consideration of the peace then granted to them, the presents they then received, as well as in consideration of a quantity of goods, to the value of three thousand dollars, now delivered to them by the said Arthur St. Clair, the receipt whereof they do hereby acknowledge, do hereby renew and confirm the said boundary line in the words beforementioned, to the end that it may be and remain as a division line between the lands of the said Six Nations and the territory of the United States, forever. And the undersigned Indians, as well in their own names as in the name of their respective tribes and nations, their heirs and descendants, for the considerations beforementioned, do release, quit claim, relinquish, and cede, to the United States of America, all the lands west of the said boundary or division line, and between the said line and the strait, from the mouth of Ononwayea and Buffalo Creek, for them, the said United States of America, to have and to hold the same, in true and absolute propriety, forever.

ARTICLE 2

The United States of America confirm to the Six Nations all the lands which they inhabit, lying east and north of the beforementioned boundary line, and relinquish and quit claim to the same and every part thereof, excepting only six miles square round the fort of Oswego, which six miles square round said fort is again reserved to the United States by these presents.

ARTICLE 3

The Oneida and Tuscarora nations, are also again secured and confirmed in the possession of their respective lands.

ARTICLE 4

The United States of America renew and confirm the peace and friendship entered into with the Six Nations, (except the Mohawks) at the treaty beforementioned, held at fort Stanwix, declaring the same to be perpetual. And if the Mohawks shall, within six months, declare their assent to the same, they shall be considered as included.

Done at Harmar, on the Muskingum, the day and year first above written.

In witness whereof, the parties have hereunto, interchangeably, set their hands and seals.

AR. ST. CLAIR,
CAGEAGA, or DOGS ROUND THE FIRE,
SAWEDOWA, or THE BLAST,
KIONDUSHOWA, or SWIMMING FISH,
ONEAHYE, or LANCING FEATHER
SOHAEAS, or FALLING MOUNTAIN,
OTACHSAKA, or BROKEN TOMAHAWK, HIS X MARK,
TEKAHIAS, or LONG TREE, HIS X MARK,
ONEENSETEE, or LOADED MAN, HIS X MARK,
KIAHTULAHO, or SNAKE AQUEIA, OR BANDY LEGS
KIANDOGEWA, or BIG TREE, HIS X MARK,
OWENEWA, or THROWN IN THE WATER HIS X MARK
GYANTWAIA, or CORN PLANTER, HIS X MARK,
GYASOTA, or BIG CROSS, HIS X MARK,
KANNASSEE, or NEW ARROW,
ACHIOUT, or HALF TOWN,
ANACHOUT, or THE WASP, HIS X MARK,
CHISHEKOA, or WOOD BUG, HIS X MARK,
SESSEWA, or BIG BALE OF A KETTLE,
SCIAHOWA, or COUNCIL KEEPER,
TEWANIAS, or BROKEN TWIG
SONACHSHOWA, or FULL MOON
CACHUNWASLE, or TWENTY CANOES
HICKONQUASH, or TEARING ASUNDER,

In presence of:

JOS. HARMAR, LIEUTENANT-COLONEL COMMANDING FIRST REGIMENT AND BRIGADIER-GENERAL BY BREVET,
RICHARD BUTLER,
JNO. GIBSON,

WILL. M'CURDY, CAPTAIN,
ED. DENNY, ENSIGN FIRST U. S. REGIMENT,
A. HARTSHORN, ENSIGN,
ROBT. THOMPSON, ENSIGN, FIRST U. S. REGIMENT,
FRAN. BELLE, ENSIGN,
JOSEPH NICHOLAS.

SEPARATE ARTICLE

Should a robbery or murder be committed by an Indian or Indians of the Six Nations, upon the citizens or subjects of the United States, or by the citizens or subjects of the United States, or any of them, upon any of the Indians of the said nations, the parties accused of the same shall be tried, and if found guilty, be punished according to the laws of the state, or of the territory of the United States, as the case may be, where the same was committed. And should any horses be stolen, either by the Indians of the said nations, from the citizens or subjects of the United States, or any of them, or by any of the said citizens or subjects from any of the said Indians, they may be reclaimed into whose possession soever they may have come; and, upon due proof, shall be restored, any sale in open market notwithstanding; and the persons convicted shall be punished with the utmost severity the laws will admit. And the said nations engage to deliver the persons that may be accused, of their nations, of either of the beforementioned crimes, at the nearest post of the United States, if the crime was committed within the territory of the United States; or to the civil authority of the state, ire it shall have happened within any of the United States.

AR. ST. CLAIR.

Consequences

Clearly the Indians hit hardest by the Revolution, the Iroquois afterward found their confederation torn asunder and their lands thoroughly occupied. They were, in fact, largely a conquered people and had little choice but to accept confinement to relatively small areas of central New York and northern Pennsylvania. The term "reservation" is not used here, and reservations would not become a dominant factor in U.S.-Indian relations until President Ulysses S. Grant's Peace Policy was formulated after the American Civil War. Nevertheless, the first Indian reservation in North America, Edge Pillock, in New Jersey, had been established in 1758 and become home to about 100 Unami, and the concept was clearly in the minds of those American diplomats dealing with the Iroquois tribes in the wake the Revolution.

Five years after the Treaty of Fort Harmar, the Americans would finally succeed in crushing the 40-year resistance of Algonquian tribes in the Old Northwest (roughly the triangle between the Ohio, the Mississippi and the Great Lakes) to European encroachments on their vast hunting grounds. Now the United States no longer needed the diplomatic fiction of Iroquois hegemony over the transmontane Ohio lands that the Americans had inherited from the British. Policy makers met once again with the Iroquois to draw up a new TREATY OF CANANDAIGUA, which would indeed describe the much-diminished lands being set aside for Iroquois habitation as reservations.

TREATY OF CANANDAIGUA
(TREATY WITH THE SIX NATIONS)

TREATY AT A GLANCE

Completed
November 11, 1794. at Konandaigua
(present-day Canandaigua, New York)

Signatories
United States and the Six Nations

Overview
Ten years after the American Revolution, U.S. treaty makers met with the Six Nations to pledge mutual recognition of lands relinquished by and reserved for the Indians at the end of the war and since.

Historical Background

The American Revolution played out its social implications on the western frontier. In the 10 years following the conflict, an explosive expansion, exceeding in pace and extent the experience of any previous generation, brought new settlements to a backcountry only recently taken from the American Indians. Western New York, where the Iroquois had been devastated by American raids in 1779 and abandoned by their British allies in 1783, was the vanguard of the developing nation.

The Iroquois found their confederation torn asunder as a consequence of the Revolution, and many of their extensive lands were taken away by treaty. To their former hunting grounds came men like William Cooper, father of future novelist James Fenimore Cooper, who took advantage of the Revolutionary upheavals in land titles to grab vast tracts formerly claimed by Indians, Loyalists, and Tories, for speculation and development. Establishing frontier communities on the spots occupied by Indian villages, land speculators such as Cooper and the thousands of settlers they brought in their wake steadily obliterated the marks made by their Indian predecessors.

Since the Revolution, the Americans had engaged in a sporadic war with the numerous Algonquian-speaking tribes of the Old Northwest, which encompassed the lands bordered by the Allegheny and Appalachian Mountains on the east, the Mississippi River on the west, and stretching from the Great Lakes in the north to the bottom tip of the Ohio River in the south. The Iroquois League had long exercised a kind of diplomatic hegemony over much of this region, especially the meadows of the Great Lakes and the Ohio Valley. It was an hegemony originally based on their role as middlemen in the fur trade, which was then often called the Indian trade, between the British seacoast settlements and the fur-trapping Algonquian tribes in the Old Northwest.

In fact, when the Iroquois launched a series of trade wars in the early 18th century against their major Indian rivals in the fur traffic—principally the Huron, but also a host of smaller tribes—the British used the Iroquois success to make of the confederacy a useful diplomatic tool. Arguing that by long-recognized European tradition, there existed a presumption of ownership over territories won by "right of conquest," the British encouraged Iroquois claims to vast stretches of the American interior because, by treaty and proclamation, the Iroquois were loyal subjects and wards of the British Crown, and thus, their lands, so to speak, were Crown lands.

Just as the British employed this diplomatic fiction to good effect against the French, the Iroquois wielded it to sustain their intermediary status with other Indian tribes, including not only the Algonquian but also the Caddo- and Muskogee-speaking tribes of the American South. Over time, the Iroquois came to serve as the diplomatic emissaries of the American Indians, and confederacy diplomats were brought into negotiations with the European settlers to speak for such tribes as the Shawnee—always to the benefit of the Iroquois. The Indians in general seemed to recognize this function as particular to the Iroquois, and such Iroquois diplomacy would outlast the confederacy itself. After the War of 1812, Iroquois diplomats were still operating among some Sioux-speaking tribes west of the Mississippi, and even later a few Iroquois emissaries were found roaming the Pacific Northwest.

Because of their diplomatic standing with the Algonquians and because of the title, however spurious, they had long been considered to hold in the Ohio, the Iroquois were treated less harshly after the Revolution by the Americans than other tribes might have been who sided with the British. As long as the Shawnee and other Algonquians held out in the Ohio, the Americans needed the Iroquois—even those, unlike the Oneida and the Tuscarora, who had been "disloyal"—especially the Seneca, the "keepers of the Western gate," whose lands around present-day Buffalo, New York, overlapped those of the Great Lakes Algonquian tribes.

In 1794, however, the hostile peoples of the Northwest had been defeated by "Mad" Anthony Wayne at the Battle of Fallen Timbers. With the Algonquian's 40-year resistance to encroachment by English-speaking settlers at an end, the Iroquois had become entirely superfluous to American needs in the Ohio. Congress turned its attention toward the disposition of the region that had come into American possession as a result of the Algonquian wars. The following year the United States forced the defeated tribes to sign, many of them reluctantly, the TREATY OF GREENVILLE. Now, the United States owned the Northwest, and later that year Congress passed the Land Ordinance of 1795, and three years later the NORTHWEST ORDINANCE to map out the legal guidelines of its future settlement.

Meanwhile, it was in this context of settling up in the Ohio in the wake of "Mad" Anthony Wayne's great 1794 victory, that U.S. treaty makers had met in 1794 with the thoroughly demoralized Iroquois before treating fully with the Algonquian or launching legislative expansion plans. The United States wished further to reduce Iroquois holdings and make sure the tribal members themselves understood precisely which of their former lands remained available to them as reservations and under what circumstances they would receive support from the federal government whose wards they had become.

Terms

Reiterating some of the conditions and promises contained in the SECOND TREATY OF FORT STANWIX and the TREATY OF FORT HARMAR, in the Treaty of Canandaigua the Iroquois and the United States each pledged not to disturb the other in lands that had been relinquished or reserved and more carefully than before defined the territory of the Seneca Nation.

A Treaty between the United States of America, and the Tribes of Indians Called the Six Nations

The President of the United States having determined to hold a conference with the Six Nations of Indians, for the purpose of removing from their minds all causes of complaint, and establishing a firm and permanent friendship with them; and Timothy Pickering being appointed sole agent for that purpose; and the agent having met and conferred with the Sachems, Chiefs and Warriors of the Six Nations, in a general council: Now, in order to accomplish the good design of this conference, the parties have agreed on the following articles; which, when ratified by the President, with the advice and consent of the Senate of the United States, shall be binding on them and the Six Nations.

ARTICLE I

Peace and friendship are hereby firmly established, and shall be perpetual, between the United States and the Six Nations.

ARTICLE II

The United States acknowledge the lands reserved to the Oneida, Onondaga and Cayuga Nations, in their respective treaties with the state of New-York, and called their reservations, to be their property; and the United States will never claim the same nor disturb them or either of the Six Nations, nor their Indian friends residing thereon and united with them in the free use and enjoyment thereof: but the said reservations shall remain theirs, until they choose to sell the same to the people of the United States, who have the right to purchase.

ARTICLE III

The land of the Seneka nation is bounded as follows: Beginning on Lake Ontario, at the north-west corner of the land they sold to Oliver Phelps, the line runs westerly along the lake, as far as O-yong-wong-yeh Creek, at Johnson's Landing-place, about four miles eastward from the fort of Niagara; then southerly up that creek to its main fork, then straight to the main fork of Stedman's creek, which empties into the river Niagara, above fort Schlosser, and then onward, from that fork, continuing the same straight course, to that river; (this line, from the mouth of O-yong-wong-yeh Creek to the river Niagara, above fort Schlosser, being the eastern boundary of a strip of land, extending from the same line to Niagara river, which the Seneka nation ceded to the King of Great-Britain, at a treaty held about thirty years ago, with Sir William Johnson;) then the line runs along the river Niagara to Lake Erie; then along Lake Erie to the north-east corner of a triangular piece of land which the United States conveyed to the state of Pennsylvania, as by the President's patent, dated the third day of March, 1792; then due south to the northern boundary of that state; then due east to the south-west corner of the land sold by the Seneka nation to Oliver Phelps; and then north and northerly, along Phelps's line, to the place of beginning on Lake Ontario. Now, the United States acknowledge all the land within the aforementioned boundaries, to be the property of the Seneka nation; and the United States will never claim the same, nor disturb the Seneka nation, nor any of the Six Nations, or of their Indian friends residing thereon and united with them, in the free use and enjoyment thereof: but it shall remain theirs, until they choose to sell tie same to the people of the United States, who have the right to purchase.

ARTICLE IV

The United States having thus described and acknowledged what lands belong to the Oneidas, Onondagas, Cayugas and Senekas, and engaged never to claim the same, nor to disturb them, or any of the Six Nations, or their Indian friends residing thereon and united with them, in the free use and- enjoyment thereof: Now, the Six Nations, and each of them, hereby engage that they will never claim any other lands within the boundaries of the United States; nor ever disturb the people of the United States in the free use and enjoyment thereof.

ARTICLE V

The Seneka nation, all others of the Six Nations concurring, cede to the United States the right of making a wagon road from Fort Schlosser to Lake Erie, as far south as Buffaloe Creek; and the people of the United States shall have the free and undisturbed use of this road, for the purposes of travelling and transportation. And the Six Nations, and each of them, will forever allow to the people of the United States, a free passage through their lands, and the free use of the harbors and rivers adjoining and within their respective tracts of land, for the passing and securing of vessels and boats, and liberty to land their cargoes where necessary for their safety.

ARTICLE VI

In consideration of the peace and friendship hereby established, and of the engagements entered into by the Six Nations; and because the United States desire, with humanity and kindness, to contribute to their comfortable support; and to render the peace and friendship hereby established, strong and perpetual; the United States now deliver to the Six Nations, and the Indians of the other nations residing among and united with them, a quantity of goods of the value of ten thousand dollars. And for the same considerations, and with a view to promote the future welfare of the Six Nations, and of their Indian friends aforesaid, the United States will add the sum of three thousand dollars to the one thousand five hundred dollars, heretofore allowed them by an article ratified by the President, on the twenty-third day of April, 1792;(1) making in the whole, four thousand five hundred dollars; which shall be expended yearly forever, in purchasing clothing, domestic animals, implements of husbandry and other utensils suited to their circumstances, and in compensating useful artificers, who shall reside with or near them, and be employed for their benefit. The immediate application of the whole annual allowance now stipulated, to be made by the superintendent appointed by the President for the affairs of the Six Nations, and their Indian friends aforesaid.

ARTICLE VII

Lest the firm peace and friendship now established should be interrupted by the misconduct of individuals, the United States and Six Nations agree, that for injuries done by individuals on either side, no private revenge or retaliation shall take place; but, instead thereof, complaint shall be made by the party injured to the other: BY the Six Nations or any of them, to the President of the United States, or the Superintendent by him appointed: and by the Superintendent, or other person appointed by the President, to the principal chiefs of the Six Nations, or of the nation to which the offender belongs: and

such prudent measures shall then be pursued as shall be necessary to preserve our peace and friendship unbroken; until the legislature (or great council) of the United States shall make other equitable provision for the purpose.

NOTE. It is clearly understood by the parties to this treaty, that the annuity stipulated in the sixth article, is to be applied to the benefit of such of the Six Nations and of their Indian friends united with them as aforesaid, as do or shall reside within the boundaries of the United States: For the United States do not interfere with nations, tribes or families, of Indians elsewhere resident.

In witness whereof, the said Timothy Pickering, and the sachems and war chiefs of the said Six Nations, have hereto set their hands and seals.

Done at Konondaigua, in the State of New York, the eleventh day of November in the year one thousand seven hundred and ninety four.

TIMOTHY PICKERING,
ONOYEAHNEE, HIS X MARK,
KONNEATORTEEOOH, HIS X MARK, OR HANDSOME LAKE,
TOKENHYONHAU, HIS X MARK, ALIAS CAPTAIN KEY
ONESHAUEE, HIS X MARK
HENDRICK AUPAURNUT,
DAVID NEESOONHUK HIS X MARK,
KANATSOYH, ALIAS NICHOLAS KUSIK,
SOHHONTEOQUENT, HIS X MARK
OODUHTSAIT, HIS X MARK,
KONOOHQUNG, HIS X MARK
TOSSONGGAULOLUS, HIS X MARK,
JOHN SKENENDOA, HIS X MARK
ONEATORLEEOOH, HIS X MARK,
KUSSANWATAU, HIS X MARK,
EYOOTENYOOTANOOK, HIS X MARK,
KOHNYEAUGONG, HIS X MARK, ALIAS JAKE STROUD
SHAGUIESA, HIS X MARK
TEEROOS, HIS X MARK, ALIAS CAPTAIN PRANTUP,
SOOSHAOOWAU, HIS X MARK,
HENRY YOUNG BRANT, HIS X MARK
SONHYOOWAUNA, HIS X MARK, OR BIG SKY
ONSAHHAH, HIS X MARK
EOTOSHAHENH, HIS X MARK,
KAUKONDANALYA, HIS X MARK,
NONDIYAUKA, HIS X MARK,
KOSSISHTOWAU, HIS X MARK
OOJAUGENTA, HIS X MARK, OR FISH CARRIER
TOHEONGGO, HIS X MARK,
OOTAGUASSO, HIS X MARK,
JOONONDAUWAONCH, HIS X MARK,
KIYANHAONH, HIS X MARK,
OOTAUJEAUGENH, HIS X MARK, OR BROKEN AXE
TAUHOONDOS, HIS X MARK, OR OPEN THE WAY,
TWAUKEWASHA, HIS X MARK,
SEQUIDONGQUEE, HIS X MARK, ALIAS LITTLE BEARD,
KODJEOTE, HIS X MARK OR HALF TOWN,
KENJAUARLGUS, HIS X MARK, OR STINKING FISH,
SOONOHQUAUKAU, HIS X MARK,
TWENNIYANA, HIS X MARK,

JISHKAAGA, HIS X MARK, OR GREEN GRASSHOPPER,
ALIAS LITTLE BILLY
TUGGEHSHOTTA, HIS X MARK,
TEHONGYAGAUNA, HIS X MARK,
TEHONGYOOWNSH, HIS X MARK,
E;ONNEYOOWESOT, HIS X MARK
TIOOHQUOTTAKAUNA, HIS X MARK, OR WOODS ON
FIRE
TAOUNDAUDEESH, HIS X MARK
HONAYAWNS, HIS X MARK, ALIAS FARMER'S BROTHER,
SOGGOCYAWAUTHAU, HIS X MARK ALIAS RED JACKET
KONYOOTIAYOO, HIS X MARK
SANHTAKAONGYEES, HIS X MARK, OR TWO SKIES OF A
LENGTH,
OUNNASHATTAKAU, HIS X MARK,
KAUNGYANEHQUEE, HIS X MARK,
SOOAYOOWAU, HIS X MARK,
KANJEAGAONH, HIS X MARK, OR HEAP OF DOGS
SOONOOHSHOOWAU, HIS X MARK
THAOOWAUNIAS, HIS X MARK,
SOONONGJOOWAU, HIS X MARK,
KIANTU HAUKA, HIS X MARK, ALIAS CORNPLANTER,
IIAUNEHSHONGGOO, HIS X MARK,

WITNESSES:

ISRAEL CHAPIN   WILLIAM SHEPARD, JR.
JAMES SMEDLEY.   JOHN WICKHAM
AUGUSTUS PORTER   JAMES K. GARNSEV
WILLIAM EWING   ISRAEL CHAPIN, JR.
HORATIO JONES   JOSEPH SMITH
JASPER PARISH, INTERPRETERS   HENRY ABEELE

Consequences

Once upon a time occupying fortress-like settlements, the Iroquois had abandoned these over the centuries to avoid European-borne diseases and to create villages that better serviced the fur trade. Now those villages had also vanished in the 1780s and '90s. After the Treaty of Canandaigua, of the Six Nations, only the Onondaga, Seneca, and Tuscarora remained in New York, settling on their reservations. The Mohawk and Cayuga withdrew to Canada. A generation later, most of the Oneida departed for Wisconsin. Outside the reservations, all that remained of the Iroquois in the Mohawk Valley and in today's central New York were the occasional Indian peddlers who visited Cooperstown and other Yankee villages to sell venison, fish, brooms, medicines, bark or willow baskets, and deerskin moccasins—or worse yet, to beg for gifts of food.

Although in the late 20th century, some of the Six Nations enjoyed a renaissance of sorts, based upon income from new gambling casinos, only in the fiction of William Cooper's son would they find again anything like the glory of the Iroquois League during its heyday. Ironically enough, when the Seneca and the Oneida, flush with the proceeds of the gaming tables, came under attack for buying up vast parcels of former tribal lands in western and central New York (and thus removing them from local property tax rolls), it was to the Treaties of Fort Stanwix, Fort Harmar, and Canadaigua that they turned to press legal claims against bitterly angry Americans trying to block tribal expansion and resentful of the "special" treatment by the federal government such treaties afforded the Indians.

DIPLOMATIC TREATIES

JAY'S TREATY WITH GREAT BRITAIN

TREATY AT A GLANCE

Completed
November 19, 1794, at London

Signatories
United States and Great Britain

Overview
After the American Revolution, friction between the new republic and Great Britain resumed, in particular over Britain's continuing occupation of outposts in the Old Northwest. Chief Justice Jay was sent to England to negotiate a treaty that would preserve U.S. sovereignty while averting a new war with England.

Historical Background

The TREATY OF PARIS, which ended the American Revolution in 1783, called for the British evacuation of posts on the western frontier. This the British government refused to do. Even worse, many Americans believed that the British in the West were purposely inducing the Indians to attack local settlers. Boundaries between British North America and United States territory were also disputed. On their part, the British claimed that Americans had refused to pay prerevolutionary debts owed British creditors and to compensate Loyalists for property confiscated during the Revolution. The Anglo-American crisis reached a critical stage when Britain began regularly seizing American ships and "impressing" American sailors into British service in its war against revolutionary France.

News of the seizures and impressments prompted in Congress a demand for strong anti-British measures. But arch-Federalist Alexander Hamilton, George Washington's secretary of the treasury and increasingly the "power behind the throne" of the administration, felt sure that Britain would respond by declaring war on the United States, if Congress did not push the United States to declare war first. The country's blood was up, and war hysteria was sweeping the land. Volunteer defense committees appeared suddenly and everywhere mobs attacked British seamen and tarred and feathered pro-British Americans, mean-

ing staunch Federalists. To stave off the rush to battle, Hamilton persuaded Washington to send a special mission to London and seems to have imagined heading it himself.

Instead, Washington assigned the task to John Jay, who was something of Hamilton's alter ego. Jay had abundant experience as a diplomat, all of it bad. As envoy to Spain during the Revolution, he had flubbed the chance to gain either alliance with the rebellion or recognition of American independence. As secretary of foreign affairs under the Articles of Confederation, he had conducted nigh to disastrous negotiation with Don Diego de Gardoqui, sent by Spain in 1785 to the United States to wring from Congress formal recognition of its exclusive control over the Mississippi. Jay's defenders argued it was not so much that he was unskilled in diplomacy as that in both cases, the opposing side held most, if not all, the cards. This time at least, with England bogged down in the European quagmire created by Napoleon, Jay was certainly in a strong position to play the Great Game.

Thomas Jefferson, George Washington's increasingly alienated secretary of state, had all along been advocating that the United States make it clear to the English they could not count on continued American neutrality in the Napoleonic Wars unless they made concessions in the West and stopped treating New England's merchant fleet so high-handedly. When Jefferson, frustrated by Hamilton's growing influence over the president, resigned, the Virginian who replaced him, Edmund Randolph, took up the same refrain. He instructed Jay to consult with Russia, Sweden, and Denmark about an armed neutrality to pressure Great Britain into stopping its seizures of neutral ships and its impressing of anyone who spoke the king's English.

As it turned out, Denmark and Sweden, which shared the American view of neutral rights at sea, took the first step, inviting the United States to form with them a neutral alliance shortly after Jay left for Europe. Randolph urged Washington to accept, arguing it would strengthen Jay's hand immensely, but Hamilton persuaded the president to decline on the spurious grounds it would jeopardize Jay's mission by unnecessarily antagonizing the British. Hamilton went further than merely convincing a Washington whose ear he always had. To put the best light on his actions would be to say that Hamilton, eager to create a friendly climate of opinion in England for Jay's negotiations, informed George Hammond, British minister to the United States, of George Washington's decision to reject the assistance of other neutrals. Jay's strong hand was weakened immeasurably since Lord Grenville, British foreign secretary, with Hamilton's insider's information to guide him, felt sanguine in conceding almost nothing. Little wonder that Jay's Treaty became the low-water mark of foreign affairs during the administration of George Washington.

Terms

The treaty reads in part as follows:

ARTICLE 1

There shall be a firm, inviolable, and universal peace, and a true and sincere friendship between His Britannic Majesty, His Heirs, and Successors, and the United States of America; and between their respective countries, territories, cities, towns, and people of every degree, without exception of persons or places.

ARTICLE II

His Majesty will withdraw all his troops and garrisons from all posts and places within the boundary lines assigned by the treaty of peace to the United States. This evacuation shall take place on or before June 1, 1796, and all the proper measures shall in the interval be taken by concert between the government of the United States and His Majesty's governor-general in America for settling the previous arrangements which may be necessary respecting the delivery of the said posts. The United States, in the meantime, at their discretion, extending their settlements to any part within the said boundary line, except within the precincts or jurisdiction of any of the said posts. All settlers and traders within the precincts or jurisdiction of the said posts shall continue to enjoy, unmolested, all their property of every kind, and shall be protected therein. They shall be at full liberty to remain there, or to remove with all or any part of their effects; and it shall also be free to them to sell their lands, houses, or effects, or to retain the property thereof, at their discretion.

Such of them as shall continue to reside within the said boundary lines shall not be compelled to become citizens of the United States, or to take any oath of allegiance to the government thereof; but they shall be at full liberty so to do if they think proper~ and they shall make and declare their election within one year after the evacuation aforesaid. And all persons who shall continue there after the expiration of the said year, without having declared their intention of remaining subjects of His Britannic Majesty, shall be considered as having elected to become citizens of the United States.

ARTICLE III

It is agreed that it shall at all times be free to His Majesty's subjects, and to the citizens of the United States, and also to the Indians dwelling on either side of the said boundary line, freely to pass and repass by land or inland navigation into the respective territories and countries of the two parties, on the continent of America (the country within the limits of the Hudson's Bay Company only excepted) and to navigate all the lakes, rivers, and waters thereof, and freely to carry on trade and Commerce with each other.

But it is understood that this article does not extend to the admission of vessels of the United States into the seaports, harbors, bays, or creeks of His Majesty's said territories; nor into such parts of the rivers in His Majesty's said territories as are between the mouth thereof and the highest port of entry from the sea, except in small vessels trading bona fide between Montreal and Quebec, under such regulations as shall be established to prevent the possibility of any frauds in this respect. Nor to the admission of British vessels from the sea into the rivers of the United States beyond the highest ports of entry for foreign vessels from the sea.

The River Mississippi shall, however, according to the treaty of peace, be entirely open to both parties; and it is further agreed that all the ports and places on its eastern side, to whichsoever of the parties belonging, may freely be resorted to and used by both parties in as ample a manner as any of the Atlantic ports or places of the United States, or any of the ports or places of His Majesty in Great Britain.

All goods and merchandise whose importation into His Majesty's said territories in America shall not be entirely prohibited may freely, for the purposes of commerce, be carried into the same, in the manner aforesaid, by the citizens of the United States; and such goods and merchandise shall be subject to no higher or other duties than would to payable by His Majesty's subjects on the importation of the same from Europe into the said territories. And, in like manner, all goods and merchandise whose importation into the United States shall not be wholly prohibited may freely, for the purposes of commerce, be carried into the same, in the manner aforesaid, by His Majesty's subjects, and such goods and merchandise shall be subject to no higher or other duties than would be payable by the citizens of the United States on the importation of the same in American vessels into the Atlantic ports of the said states. And all goods not prohibited to be exported from the said territories respectively may, in like manner, be carried out of the same by the two parties respectively, paying duty as aforesaid. . . .

ARTICLE IV

Whereas it is uncertain whether the River Mississippi extends so far to the northward as to be intersected by a line to be drawn due west from the Lake of the Woods, in the manner mentioned in the treaty of peace . . . it is agreed that measures shall be taken . . . for making a joint survey of the said river from one degree of latitude below the Falls of St. Anthony to the principal source or sources of the said river, and also of the parts adjacent thereto; and that if, on the result of such survey, it should appear that the said river would not be intersected by such a line as is above mentioned, the two parties will thereupon proceed by amicable negotiation to regulate the boundary line in that quarter as well as all other points to be adjusted between the said parties. . . .

ARTICLE V.

Whereas doubts have arisen what river was truly intended under the name of the River St. Croix, mentioned in the said treaty of peace, and forming a part of the boundary therein described; that question shall he referred to the final decision of commissioners to be appointed. . . .

ARTICLE VI

Whereas it is alleged by diverse British merchants and others, His Majesty's subjects that debts, to a considerable amount, which were bona fide contracted before the peace, still remain owing to them by citizens or inhabitants of the United States, and that by the operation of various lawful impediments since the peace, not only the full recovery of the said debts has been delayed but also the value and security thereof have been, in several instances, impaired and lessened, so that by the ordinary course of judicial proceedings the British creditors cannot now obtain, and actually have and receive full and adequate compensation for the losses and damages which they have thereby sustained: It is agreed that in all such cases where full compensation for such losses and damages cannot, for whatever reason, be actually obtained, had, and received by the said creditors in the ordinary course of justice, the United States will make full and complete compensation for the same to the said creditors. But it is distinctly understood that this provision is to extend to such losses only as have been occasioned by the lawful impediments aforesaid, and is not to extend to losses occasioned by such insolvency of the debtors or other causes as would equally have operated to produce such loss, if the said impediments had not existed; nor to such losses or damages as have been occasioned by the manifest delay or negligence or willful omission of the claimant. . . .

ARTICLE VII

Whereas complaints have been made by diverse merchants and others, citizens of the United States, that during the course of the war in which His Majesty is now engaged they have sustained considerable losses and damage, by reason of irregular or illegal captures or condemnations of their vessels and other property, under color of authority or commissions from His Majesty, and that from various circumstances belonging to the said cases adequate compensation for the losses and damages so sustained cannot now be actually obtained, had, and received by the ordinary course of judicial proceedings; it is agreed that in all such cases where adequate compensation cannot, for whatever reason, be now actually obtained, had, and received by the said merchants and others, in the ordinary course of justice, full and complete compensation for the same will be made by the British government to the said complainants. But it is distinctly

understood that this provision is not to extend to such losses or damages as have been occasioned by the manifest delay or negligence or willful omission of the claimant. . . .

And whereas certain merchants and others, His Majesty's subjects, complain that in the course of the war they have sustained loss and damage by reason of the capture of their vessels and merchandise, taken within the limits and jurisdiction of the States and brought into the ports of the same, or taken by vessels originally armed in ports of the said States: It is agreed that in all such cases where restitution shall not have been made . . . the complaints of the parties shall be and hereby are referred to the commissioners . . . who are hereby authorized and required to proceed in the like manner relative to these as to the other cases committed to them; and the United States undertake to pay to the complainants or claimants in specie, without deduction, the amount of such sums as shall be awarded to them respectively by the said commissioners, and at the times and places which in such awards shall be specified; and on condition of such releases or assignments to be given by the claimants as in the said awards may be directed. And it is further agreed that not only the now-existing cases of both descriptions but also all such as shall exist at the time of exchanging the ratifications of this treaty shall be considered as being within the provisions, intent, and meaning of this article. . . .

ARTICLE IX

It is agreed that British subjects who now hold lands in the territories of the United States, and American citizens who now hold lands in the dominions of His Majesty, shall continue to hold them according to the nature and tenure of their respective estates and titles therein; and may grant, sell, or devise the same to whom they please, in like manner as if they were natives; and that neither they nor their heirs or assigns shall, so far as may respect the said lands and the legal remedies incident thereto, be regarded as aliens.

ARTICLE X

Neither the debts due from individuals of the one nation to individuals of the other, nor shares nor monies which they may have in the public funds, or in the public or private banks, shall ever in any event of war or national differences be sequestered or confiscated, it being unjust and impolitic that debts and engagements contracted and made by individuals, having confidence in each other and in their respective governments, should ever be destroyed or impaired by national authority on account of national differences and discontents.

ARTICLE XI

It is agreed between His Majesty and the United States of America that there shall be a reciprocal and entirely perfect liberty of navigation and commerce between their respective people, in the manner, under the limitations, and on the conditions specified in the following articles:

ARTICLE XII

His Majesty consents that it shall and may be lawful, during the time hereinafter limited, for the citizens of the United States to carry to any of His Majesty's islands and ports in the West Indies from the United States, in their own vessels, not being above the burden of seventy tons, any goods or merchandises, being of the growth, manufacture, or produce of the said States, which it is or may be lawful to carry to the said islands or ports from the said States in British vessels; and that the said American vessels shall be subject there to no other or higher tonnage duties or charges than shall be payable by British vessels in the ports of the United States; and that the cargoes of the said American vessels shall be subject there to no other or higher duties or charges than shall be payable on the like articles if imported there from the said States in British vessels.

And His Majesty also consents that it shall be lawful for the said American citizens to purchase, load, and carry away in their said vessels to the United States, from the said islands and ports. all such articles, being of the growth. manufacture, or produce of the said islands, as may now by law be carried from thence to the said States in British vessels, and subject only to the same duties and charges on exportation to which British vessels and their cargoes are or shall be subject in similar circumstances. . . .

ARTICLE XIII

His Majesty consents that the vessels belonging to the citizens of the United States of America shall be admitted and hospitably received in all the seaports and harbors of the British territories in the East Indies. And that the citizens of the said United States may freely carry on a trade between the said territories and the said United States in all articles of which the importation or exportation respectively to or from the said territories shall not be entirely prohibited; provided only that it shall not be lawful for them, in any time of war between the British government and any other power or state whatever, to export from the said territories, without the special permission of the British government there, any military stores, or naval stores, or rice.

The citizens of the United States shall pay for their vessels, when admitted into the said ports, no other tonnage duty than shall be payable on British vessels when admitted into the ports of the United States. And they shall pay no other or higher duties or charges on the importation or exportation of the cargoes of the said vessels than shall be payable on the same articles when imported or exported in British vessels. But it is expressly agreed that the vessels of the United States shall not carry any of the articles exported by them from the said British territories to any port or place except to some port or place in America, where the same shall be unladen, and such regulations shall be adopted by both parties as shall from time to time be found necessary to enforce the due and faithful observance of this stipulation.

It is also understood that the permission granted by this article is not to extend to allow the vessels of the United States to carry on any part of the coasting trade of the said British territories; but vessels going with their original cargoes, or part thereof, from one port of discharge to another are not to be considered as carrying on the coasting trade. Neither is this article to be construed to allow the citizens of the said States to settle or reside within the said territories, or to go into the interior parts thereof, without the permission of the British government established there.

And if any transgression should be attempted against the regulations of the British government in this respect, the observance of the same shall and may be enforced against the citizens of America in the same manner as against British subjects or others transgressing the same rule. And the citizens of the United States, whenever they arrive in any port or harbor in the said territories, or if they should be permitted, in manner aforesaid, to go to any other place therein, shall always be subject to the laws, government, and jurisdiction of what nature established in such harbor, port, or place, according as the same may be. The citizens of the United States may also touch for refreshment at the island of St. Helena, but subject in all respects to such regulations as the British government may from time to time establish there.

ARTICLE XIV

There shall be between all the dominions of His Majesty in Europe and the territories of the United States a reciprocal and perfect liberty of commerce and navigation. . . .

ARTICLE XV

It is agreed that no other or higher duties shall be paid by the ships or merchandise of the one party in the ports of the other than such as are paid by the like vessels or merchandise of all other nations. . . .

ARTICLE XVI

It shall be free for the two contracting parties, respectively, to appoint consuls for the protection of trade, to reside in the dominions and territories aforesaid; and the said consuls shall enjoy those liberties and rights which belong to them by reason of their function. . . .

ARTICLE XVII

It is agreed that in all cases where vessels shall be captured or detained on just suspicion of having on board enemy's property, or of carrying to the enemy any of the articles which are contraband of war, the said vessel shall be brought to the nearest or most convenient port; and if any property of an enemy should be found on board such vessel, that part only which belongs to the enemy shall be made prize, and the vessel shall be at liberty to proceed with the remainder without any impediment. . . .

ARTICLE XVIII

And whereas the difficulty of agreeing on the precise cases in which alone provisions and other articles not generally contraband may be regarded as such, renders it expedient to provide against the inconveniences and misunderstandings which might thence arise; it is further agreed that whenever any such articles so becoming contraband, according to the existing laws of nations, shall for that reason be seized, the same shall not be confiscated, but the owners thereof shall be speedily and completely indemnified. . . .

And whereas it frequently happens that vessels sail for a port or place belonging to an enemy without knowing that the same is either besieged, blockaded, or invested, it is agreed that every vessel so circumstanced may be turned away from such port or place; but she shall not be detained, nor her cargo, if not contraband, be confiscated, unless after notice she shall again attempt to enter, but she shall be permitted to go to any other port or place she may think proper; nor shall any vessel or goods of either party that may have entered into such port or place before the same was besieged, blockaded, or invested by the other. and be found therein after the reduction or surrender of such place, be liable to confiscation but shall be restored to the owners or proprietors there.

ARTICLE XIX

And that more abundant care may be taken for the security of the respective subjects and citizens of the contracting parties, and to prevent their suffering injuries by the men of war or privateers either party, all commanders of ships of and privateers, and all others the said subjects and citizens, shall forbear doing any damage to those of the other party, or committing any outrage against them, and if act to the contrary, they shall be punished, and shall also be bound in their persons and estates to make satisfaction and reparation for all damages. . . .

ARTICLE XX

It is further agreed that both said contracting parties shall not only refuse to receive any pirates into any of it ports, havens, or towns, or permit any their inhabitants to receive, protect, harbor, conceal, or assist them in any manner, will bring to condign punishment all such inhabitants as shall be guilty of such offenses.

And all their ships, with the goods or merchandises taken by them and brought to the port of either of the said parties, shall be seized as far as they can be discovered and shall be restored to the owners, or their factors or agents, duly deputed and authorized in writing by them (proper evidence being first given in the Court of Admiralty for proving the property), even in case such effects should have passed into their hands by sale, if it be proved that the buyers knew or had good reason to believe suspect that they had been piratically taken.

ARTICLE XXI

It is likewise agreed that the subjects and citizens of the two nations shall not do any acts of hostility or violence against each other, nor accept commissions or instructions so to act from any foreign prince or state, enemies to the other party; nor shall the enemies of one of the parties permitted to invite, or endeavor to enlist their military service, any of the subjects citizens of the other party; and the laws all such offenses and aggressions be punctually executed. And if any subject or citizen of the said parties respectively shall accept any foreign commission or letters of marque for arming any vessel to act as a privateer against the other party, and be taken by the other party, it is hereby declared to be lawful for the said party to treat and punish the said subject or citizen having such commission or letters of marque as a pirate.

ARTICLE XXII

It is expressly stipulated, that neither of the said contracting parties will order or authorize any acts of reprisal against the other, on complaints of injuries or damages, until the said party shall first have presented to the other a statement thereof, verified by competent proof and evidence, and demanded justice and satisfaction, and the same shall either have been refused or unreasonably delayed. . . .

ARTICLE XXVI

If at any time a rupture should take place (which God forbid) between His Majesty and the United States, the merchants and others of each of the two nations, residing in the dominions of the other, shall have the privilege of remaining and continuing their trade, so long as they behave peaceably and commit no offense against the laws; and in case their conduct should render them suspected, and the respective governments should think proper to order them to remove, the term of twelve months from the publication of the order shall he allowed them for that purpose, to remove with their families, effects, and property; but this favor shall not he extended to those who shall act contrary to the established laws. . . .

ARTICLE XXVII

It is further agreed that His Majesty and the United States, on mutual requisitions, by them respectively, or by their respective ministers or officers authorized to make the same, will deliver up to justice all persons who, being charged with murder or forgery, committed within the jurisdiction of either, shall seek an asylum within any of the countries of the other, provided that this shall only be done on such evidence of criminality as, according to those who make the laws of the place where the fugitive or person so charged shall be found, would justify his apprehension and commitment for trial, if the offense had there been committed. The expense of such apprehension and delivery shall be borne and defrayed by those who make the requisition and receive the fugitive.

ARTICLE XXVIII

It is agreed that the first ten articles of this treaty shall be permanent, and that the subsequent articles, except the 12th, shall be limited in their duration to twelve years.

Consequences

Jay's Treaty did avert war, and it ensured Anglo-American trade, thereby providing badly needed customs revenues to the new government. Moreover, the treaty secured the British evacuation of the frontier forts and obtained a limited right of American ships to trade in the British West Indies. On other points, the treaty temporized, referring the question of debt repayment and the settlement of boundary disputes to joint commissions.

Jay's Treaty, however, was not popular with the American public, who considered it so pro-British as to be treasonous. It did not stop the British from arming hostile Indians out West; it did not keep English sea captains from shanghaiing American sailors. The treaty exacerbated the growing split of the body politic into "factions," i.e., parties, of Democratic-Republicans and Federalists. In some places, Jay was burned in effigy, and the Democratic-Republicans generally denounced the document as a Federalist sellout to Britain. Nevertheless, the usually Federalist-leaning president George Washington pressed for ratification, and the Senate complied by June 1795, albeit with deletion of a provision limiting American trade in the West Indies.

The issues surrounding the treaty's more serious shortcomings—its failure to address the British encouragement of their Indian allies on the western frontiers, to provide for the compensation claims of Loyalists, or to prevent impressment of American sailors or the seizure of U.S. ships on the high seas—would ultimately lead to the War of 1812.

PROCLAMATIONS AND DECLARATIONS
PROCLAMATION OF 1763

TREATY AT A GLANCE

Completed
October 7, 1763, London

Signatory
Unilateral declaration of King George III

Overview
At the close of the French and Indian War, King George issued the Proclamation of 1763, setting the boundary beyond which English colonials could not settle. This only encouraged American pioneers to flout royal authority and paved the way for revolution.

Historical Background

The British Crown emerged from the long, arduous, and dirty French and Indian War acutely aware of the insecurity of its western borders, caused in large measure by the volatility of pioneer-Indian relations. Pontiac's Rebellion, an Indian uprising that followed fast on the heels of the Seven Years' War, had only underscored this volatility. By the Treaty of Easton, concluded in October 1758, the English colonies had agreed to prohibit white settlement west of the Allegheny Mountains.

English victories in the later years of the French and Indian War, however, combined with the completion of the Forbes Road (built to transport General Forbes's army to the site of Fort Duquesne, modern-day Pittsburgh), prompted settlers to violate the treaty almost immediately. King George used Pontiac's Rebellion, which occurred in the new transmontane American West, as an excuse to reassert his control over the expansionist ambitions of the American colonies by treating with the Indians to limit further encroachments on their lands. On October 7, 1763, he issued a royal proclamation that set the boundary beyond which British colonials could not settle.

Terms

The Proclamation of 1763 reasserted the Easton treaty, this time backing it with the authority of the Crown.

Henceforth, except for a settlement in the upper Ohio, British subjects were forbidden west of the Appalachians.

The new proclamation line was not a "border" in the usual European sense of a demarcation between two established nations nor exactly a "frontier" in the Old World sense of a fortified line of defense separating hostile sovereign powers. For political reasons, the king defined the border as the line behind which he would allow "civilization" (the word itself had just come into common usage) to flourish and beyond which "savagery" would be contained. The Native Americans, the "savages," he in effect claimed as his private wards, who had the use of his land as a hunting ground as long as his "Royal Will and Pleasure" decreed. Colonials could not trespass on that land without his blessing. All of this, in time, gave the word "frontier" a new meaning as the advancing edge of white settlement and the march of "civilization" into the wilderness.

Proclamation of 1763
from the Royal Proclamation on
North America, 7 October 1763

Whereas we have taken into our royal consideration the extensive and valuable acquisitions in America secured to our Crown by the late definitive treaty of peace concluded at Paris on the

---

10th day of February last; and being desirous that all our loving subjects, as well of our kingdom as of our colonies in America, may avail themselves, with all convenient speed, of the great benefits and advantages which must accrue therefrom to their commerce, manufactures, and navigation; we have thought fit, with the advice of our Privy Council, to issue this our Royal Proclamation, hereby to publish and declare to all our loving subjects that we have, with the advice of our said Privy Council, granted our letters patent under our Great Seal of Great Britain, to erect within the countries and islands ceded and confirmed to us by said treaty, four distinct and separate governments, styled and called by the names of Quebec, East Florida, West Florida, and Grenada, and limited and bounded as follows, viz.:

First, the Government of Quebec, bounded on the Labrador coast by the river St. John, and from thence by a line drawn from the head of that river, through the lake St. John, to the south end of the lake Nipissim; from whence the said line, crossing the river St. Lawrence and the lake Champlain in 45 degrees of north latitude, passes along the high lands which divide the rivers that empty themselves into the said river St. Lawrence from those which fall into the sea; . . .

Secondly, the Government of East Florida, bounded to the westward by the Gulf of Mexico and the Apalachicola River; to the northward, by a line drawn from that part of the said river where the Chatahoochee and Flint Rivers meet, to the source of the St. Mary's river, and by the course of the said river to the Atlantic Ocean; . . .

Thirdly, the Government of West Florida, bounded to the ...westward, by the Lake Pontchartrain, the lake Maurepas, and the river Mississippi; to the northward, by a line drawn due east from that part of the river Mississippi which lies in 31 degrees north latitude, to the river Apalachicola or Chatahoochee; and to the eastward, by the said river. . . .

We have also, with the advice of our Privy Council aforesaid, annexed to our Province of Georgia all the lands lying between the rivers Altamaha and St. Mary's. . . .

*   *   *

And whereas it is just and reasonable, and essential to our interest and the security of our colonies, that the several nations or tribes of Indians with whom we are connected, and who live under our protection, should not be molested or disturbed in the possession of such parts of our dominions and territories as, not having been ceded to or purchased by us, are reserved to them, or any of them, as their hunting-grounds; we do therefore, with the advice of our Privy Council, declare it to be our royal will and pleasure, that no Governor or commander in chief, in any of our colonies of Quebec, East Florida, or West Florida, do presume, upon any pretence whatever, to grant warrants of survey, or pass any patents for lands beyond the bounds of their respective governments, as described in their commissions; as also that no Governor or commander in chief of our other colonies or plantations in America do presume for the present, and until our further pleasure be known, to grant warrants of survey or pass patents for any lands beyond the heads or sources of any of the rivers which fall into the Atlantic Ocean from the west or northwest; or upon any lands whatever, which, not hav-

ing been ceded to or purchased by us, as aforesaid, are reserved to the said Indians, or any of them.

And we do further declare it to be our royal will and pleasure, for the present as aforesaid, to reserve under our sovereignty, protection, and dominion, for the use of the said Indians, all the land and territories not included within the limits of our said three new governments, or within the limits of the territory granted to the Hudson's Bay Company; as also all the land and territories lying to the westward of the sources of the rivers which fall into the sea from the west and northwest as aforesaid; and we do hereby strictly forbid, on pain of our displeasure, all our loving subjects from making any purchases or settlements whatever, or taking possession of any of the lands above reserved, without our special leave and license for that purpose first obtained.

And we do further strictly enjoin and require all persons whatever, who have either willfully or inadvertently seated themselves upon any lands within the countries above described, or upon any other lands which, not having been ceded to or purchased by us, are still reserved to the said Indians as aforesaid, forthwith to remove themselves from such settlements.

And whereas great frauds and abuses have been committed in the purchasing lands of the Indians, to the great prejudice of our interests, and to the great dissatisfaction of the said Indians; in order, therefore, to prevent such irregularities for the future, and to the end that the Indians may be convinced of our justice and determined resolution to remove all reasonable cause of discontent, we do, with the advice of our Privy Council, strictly enjoin and require, that no private person do presume to make any purchase from the said Indians of any lands reserved to the said Indians within those parts of our colonies where we have thought proper to allow settlement; but that if at any time any of the said Indians should be inclined to dispose of the said lands, the same shall be purchased only for us, in our name, at some public meeting or assembly of the said Indians, to be held for that purpose by the Governor or commander in chief of our colony respectively within which they shall lie: and in case they shall lie within the limits of any proprietary government, they shall be purchased only for the use and in the name of such proprietaries, conformable to such directions and instructions as we or they shall think proper to give for that purpose. And we do, by the advice of our Privy Council, declare and enjoin, that the trade with the said Indians shall be free and open to all our subjects whatever, provided that every person who may incline to trade with the said Indians do take out a license for carrying on such trade, from the Governor or commander in chief of any of our colonies respectively where such person shall reside, and also give security to observe such regulations as we shall at any time think fit, by ourselves or commissaries to be appointed for this purpose, to direct and appoint for the benefit of the said trade. And we do hereby authorize, enjoin, and require the Governors and commanders in chief of all our colonies respectively, as well those under our immediate government as those under the government and direction of proprietaries, to grant such licenses without fee or reward, taking especial care to insert therein a condition that such license shall be void, and the security forfeited, in case the person to whom the same is granted shall refuse or neglect to observe such regulations as we shall think proper to prescribe as aforesaid.

And we do further expressly enjoin and require all officers whatever, as well military as those employed in the management and direction of Indian affairs within the territories reserved as aforesaid, for the use of the said Indians, to seize and apprehend all persons whatever who, standing charged with treasons, misprisions of treason, murders, or other felonies or misdemeanors, shall fly from justice and take refuge in the said territory, and to send them under a proper guard to the colony where the crime was committed of which they shall stand accused, in order to take their trial for the same.

Given at our Court at St. James's, the 7th day of October 1763, in the third year of our reign.

Consequences

The proclamation did much to conciliate the hostile Indians during Pontiac's Rebellion, but like the earlier Easton agreement, it was soon honored more in the breach than in the observance and would in the long run prove impossible to enforce. Indeed, to many frontier settlers, it seemed a dare that had to be accepted, almost an invitation to cross into proscribed territory.

The proclamation's boundary line, says historian Francis Jennings, was the historical reality behind the great American myth of the frontier. There would be many such boundaries declared in the future, and each would be breached by white settlers just as they defiantly crossed this one, although the movement was not inexorably westward, but sometimes to the west, sometimes south, sometimes north—wherever Indian lands were officially demarcated.

For now, having established a frontier, King George argued that an army of occupation was necessary to colonial security and sent more troops to patrol the forts built along the border he had marked off between the colonials and the Indians. But the army of occupation did not stay in the backwoods for long. Once the Crown was certain that French influence was truly vanquished and that the Indians were pacified for the moment by treaty, the army marched from the western forts to the coastal towns, where it could more effectively impose the king's "Will and Pleasure" on the colonists themselves.

At the same time, the settlers who crossed the proclamation line were subject to raids from resentful Indians. When, now and again, such raiding became prevalent along the frontier, settlers looked to royal colonial officials for aid. Since the settlers were in violation of the law, however, they had placed themselves beyond the king's protection. Hence, assistance from the Crown's armed forces was not always forthcoming, which steadily widened the gulf not only between Tidewater civilization and the frontier settlements, but more importantly between the colonies themselves and the mother country. The proclamation line also encouraged American pioneers to flout royal authority. In 1774, when the border erupted, the British could not hold the line. Sent initially to patrol the frontier, troops removed to the east and were billeted in American homes, which only caused more resentment. Taxes passed to pay for increased troop strengths in America was one of the factors that eventually led to open rebellion.

Not only did such colonial policies help spark the American Revolution, they also shaped the frontier pattern of American expansion ever afterward. Settlers moved onto Indian lands without the sanction of—and often against the wishes of—official government policy, then demanded the protection of the government against Indian reprisals, establishing a western legacy of both dependence upon centralized authority and resentment of it.

DECLARATION OF INDEPENDENCE

TREATY AT A GLANCE

Completed
July 4, 1776, at Philadelphia, Pennsylvania

Signatories
Members of the Continental Congress

Overview
On July 4, 1776, the Continental Congress of the English settlements along the North American Atlantic seacoast, then in rebellion against Great Britain, passed *The Unanimous Declaration of the Thirteen United States of America*, a document, popularly known as the Declaration of Independence, that set out, briefly and with supreme eloquence, the fundamental premises of American nationhood.

Historical Background

Three days before the Continental Congress passed the Declaration of Independence, Richard Henry Lee, one of Virginia's delegates to the Congress, rose in the swelling heat of the Philadelphia meetinghouse where the outlaw legislature had gathered during the rebellion they had fomented against Great Britain. Lee proposed a resolution declaring that "these United Colonies are, and of a right ought to be, free and independent States." Lee's draft proposal called for the newly declared nation to form foreign alliances and to prepare a plan for confederation.

Congress passed Lee's proposal but, in what would become a time-honored legislative tradition, sent the draft to committee for debate and amendment. The assembly appointed Massachusetts delegate John Adams, internationally known philosopher Benjamin Franklin, New York conservative Robert Livingston, and Connecticut Yankee Roger Sherman but fell to wrangling over a fifth member, which southern delegates argued should be one of their own to achieve balance. At Adams's suggestion, Congress named compromise candidate Thomas Jefferson, a Virginian who had a reputation as a fine writer.

To Jefferson fell the task of drafting the committee's report, a resolution whose language would be acceptable to all delegates. Jefferson, whose wife was sick and who longed to be home working on his own state's new constitution, then being drafted in the Virginia House of Burgesses, set to work quickly, producing a powerful and incisive summary of Whig political thought that was much influenced by English philosopher John Locke, among others. "We hold these truths to be self evident," he wrote, "that all men are created equal, that they are endowed by their Creator with certain unalienable Rights." Following Locke, Jefferson declared that chief among these rights were "Life, Liberty and Property." Jefferson later crossed out "property" and inserted the phrase "the pursuit of Happiness." He wrote on, "to secure these rights, Governments are instituted among Men, deriving their just powers from the consent of the governed."

The promise held in these phrases became the cornerstone of American democracy, but at the time it was the more concrete declarations that concerned the committee and the delegates. For years the colonials had based their resistance against England on the belief that they were fighting not the divinely chosen English king, whose loyal subjects they remained, but his ministers and his parliament. Not until the Crown had waged war against the colonies for 14 months and George III had finally declared the colonies in open rebellion and put them officially outside his protection did the Americans turn against the king. Radical English expatriate Thomas Paine had crystallized American sentiment in a tract entitled *Common Sense*, published at the beginning of 1776, and Thomas Jefferson set about to document specifically why the former colonies felt that the "royal brute" who occupied the English throne deserved their hatred instead of their allegiance.

Jefferson produced a catalog of George III's tyrannies, among them the slave trade, contending that the king had "waged a cruel war against humane nature" by assaulting a "distant people" and carrying them into slavery in "another hemisphere." This was too much for Jefferson's fellow slaveholders in the South, especially in South Carolina, the largest slaveholding state, where slaves far outnumbered white settlers, and certain Yankee traders who had made fortunes from what Jefferson called the "execrable commerce." Together, representatives of these southern and Yankee interests deleted the section when it came before Congress.

Terms

The document as amended and passed by the Continental Congress reads*:

When in the course of human events, it becomes necessary for one people to dissolve the political bands which have connected them with another, and to assume among the powers of the earth, the separate and equal station to which the laws of nature and of nature's God entitle them, a decent respect to the opinions of mankind requires that they should declare the causes which impel them to the separation.

We hold these truths to be self-evident:

That all men are created equal; that they are endowed by their Creator with certain unalienable rights; that among these are life, liberty, and the pursuit of happiness; that, to secure these rights, governments are instituted among men, deriving their just powers from the consent of the governed; that whenever any form of government becomes destructive of these ends, it is the right of the people to alter or to abolish it, and to institute new government, laying its foundation on such principles, and organizing its powers in such form, as to them shall seem most likely to effect their safety and happiness. Prudence, indeed, will dictate that governments long established should not be changed for light and transient causes; and accordingly all experience hath shown that mankind are more disposed to suffer, while evils are sufferable than to right themselves by abolishing the forms to which they are accustomed. But when a long train of abuses and usurpations, pursuing invariably the same object, evinces a design to reduce them under absolute despotism, it is their right, it is their duty, to throw off such government, and to provide new guards for their future security. Such has been the patient sufferance of these colonies; and such is now the necessity which constrains them to alter their former systems of government. The history of the present King of Great Britain is a history of repeated injuries and usurpations, all having in direct object the establishment of an absolute tyranny over these states.

To prove this, let facts be submitted to a candid world.

He has refused his assent to laws, the most wholesome and necessary for the public good.

* Capitalization and punctuation of the original document have been amended.

He has forbidden his governors to pass laws of immediate and pressing importance, unless suspended in their operation till his assent should be obtained; and, when so suspended, he has utterly neglected to attend to them.

He has refused to pass other laws for the accommodation of large districts of people, unless those people would relinquish the right of representation in the legislature, a right inestimable to them, and formidable to tyrants only.

He has called together legislative bodies at places unusual uncomfortable, and distant from the depository of their public records, for the sole purpose of fatiguing them into compliance with his measures.

He has dissolved representative houses repeatedly, for opposing, with manly firmness, his invasions on the rights of the people.

He has refused for a long time, after such dissolutions, to cause others to be elected; whereby the legislative powers, incapable of annihilation, have returned to the people at large for their exercise; the state remaining, in the mean time, exposed to all the dangers of invasions from without and convulsions within.

He has endeavored to prevent the population of these states; for that purpose obstructing the laws for naturalization of foreigners; refusing to pass others to encourage their migration hither, and raising the conditions of new appropriations of lands.

He has obstructed the administration of justice, by refusing his assent to laws for establishing judiciary powers.

He has made judges dependent on his will alone, for the tenure of their offices, and the amount and payment of their salaries.

He has erected a multitude of new offices, and sent hither swarms of officers to harass our people and eat out their substance.

He has kept among us, in times of peace, standing armies, without the consent of our legislatures.

He has affected to render the military independent of, and superior to, the civil power.

He has combined with others to subject us to a jurisdiction foreign to our Constitution and unacknowledged by our laws, giving his assent to their acts of pretended legislation:

For quartering large bodies of armed troops among us;

For protecting them, by a mock trial, from punishment for any murders which they should commit on the inhabitants of these states;

For cutting off our trade with all parts of the world;

For imposing taxes on us without our consent;

For depriving us, in many cases, of the benefits of trial by jury;

For transporting us beyond seas, to be tried for pretended offenses;

For abolishing the free system of English laws in a neighboring province, establishing therein an arbitrary government, and enlarging its boundaries, so as to render it at once an example and fit instrument for introducing the same absolute rule into these colonies;

For taking away our charters, abolishing our most valuable laws, and altering fundamentally the forms of our governments;

For suspending our own legislatures, and declaring themselves invested with power to legislate for us in all cases whatsoever.

He has abdicated government here, by declaring us out of his protection and waging war against us.

He has plundered our seas, ravaged our coasts, burned our towns, and destroyed the lives of our people.

He is at this time transporting large armies of foreign mercenaries to complete the works of death, desolation, and tyranny already begun with circumstances of cruelty and perfidy scarcely paralleled in the most barbarous ages, and totally unworthy the head of a civilized nation.

He has constrained our fellow-citizens, taken captive on the high seas, to bear arms against their country, to become the executioners of their friends and brethren, or to fall themselves by their hands.

He has excited domestic insurrection among us, and has endeavored to bring on the inhabitants of our frontiers the merciless Indian savages, whose known rule of warfare is an undistinguished destruction of all ages, sexes, and conditions.

In every stage of these oppressions we have petitioned for redress in the most humble terms; our repeated petitions have been answered only by repeated injury. A prince, whose character is thus marked by every act which may define a tyrant, is unfit to be the ruler of a free people.

Nor have we been wanting in our attentions to our British brethren. We have warned them, from time to time, of attempts by their legislature to extend an unwarrantable jurisdiction over us. We have reminded them of the circumstances of our emigration and settlement here. We have appealed to their native justice and magnanimity; and we have conjured them, by the ties of our common kindred, to disavow these usurpations which would inevitably interrupt our connections and correspondence. They too, have been deaf to the voice of justice and of consanguinity. We must, therefore, acquiesce in the necessity which denounces our separation, and hold them as we hold the rest of mankind, enemies in war, in peace friends.

We, therefore, the representatives of the United States of America, in General Congress assembled, appealing to the Supreme Judge of the world for the rectitude of our intentions, do, in the name and by the authority of the good people of these colonies solemnly publish and declare, That these United Colonies are, and of right ought to be, FREE AND INDEPENDENT STATES; that they are absolved from all allegiance to the British crown and that all political connection between them and the state of Great Britain is, and ought to be, totally dissolved; and that, as free and independent states, they have full power to levy war, conclude peace, contract alliances, establish commerce, and do all other acts and things which independent states may of right do. And for the support of this declaration, with a firm reliance on the protection of Divine Providence, we mutually pledge to each other our lives, our fortunes, and our sacred honor.

[SIGNED BY] JOHN HANCOCK [PRESIDENT]

[NEW HAMPSHIRE]
JOSIAH BARTLETT
WM. WHIPPLE
MATTHEW THORNTON

[MASSACHUSETTS BAY]
SAML. ADAMS
JOHN ADAMS
ROBT. TREAT PAINE
ELBRIDGE GERRY

[RHODE ISLAND]
STEP. HOPKINS
WILLIAM ELLERY

[CONNECTICUT]
ROGER SHERMAN
SAM'EL HUNTINGTON
WM. WILLIAMS
OLIVER WOLCOTT

[NEW YORK]
WM. FLOYD
PHIL. LIVINGSTON
FRANS. LEWIS
LEWIS MORRIS

[NEW JERSEY]
RICHD. STOCKTON
JNO. WITHERSPOON
FRAS. HOPKINSON
JOHN HART
ABRA. CLARK

[PENNSYLVANIA]
ROBT. MORRIS
BENJAMIN RUSH
BENJA. FRANKLIN
JOHN MORTON
GEO. CLYMER
JAS. SMITH
GEO. TAYLOR
JAMES WILSON
GEO. ROSS

[DELAWARE]
CAESAR RODNEY
GEO. READ
THO. M'KEAN

[MARYLAND]
SAMUEL CHASE
WM. PACA
THOS. STONE
CHARLES CARROLL OF
CARROLLTON

[VIRGINIA]
GEORGE WYTHE
RICHARD HENRY LEE
TH. JEFFERSON
BENJA. HARRISON
THS. NELSON, JR.
FRANCIS LIGHTFOOT LEE
CARTER BRAXTON

[NORTH CAROLINA]
WM. HOOPER
JOSEPH HEWES
JOHN PENN

[SOUTH CAROLINA]
EDWARD RUTLEDGE
THOS. HAYWARD, JUNR.
THOMAS LYNCH, JUNR.
ARTHUR MIDDLETON.

[GEORGIA]
BUTTON GWINNETT
LYMAN HALL
GEO. WALTON

Consequences

The Declaration proved a much-needed rallying cry for the Revolution, one of which both Jefferson and Adams were always proud and for which Jefferson, much to Adams's chagrin, became famous. Moreover, it became a document for the ages, one of the seminal historical statements in the history of humankind, and one that formed the backdrop for nearly every assertion of human rights and dignity thereafter. More immediately, in making the banishment of the word "slavery" from the declaration the price of their endorsement, the southerners overlooked the word "equality" and the central role it played in the declaration. By adopting an instrument of independence that promised the equality of all men, the new American nation ultimately doomed the "peculiar institution" of slavery, although at what would prove to be the immense cost of a bloody civil war decades later that would almost destroy the country and its promise.

NORTHWEST ORDINANCE

TREATY AT A GLANCE

Enacted
July 13, 1787, New York City

Signatories
Passed by the U.S. Congress

Overview
One of the more important pieces of legislation passed by Congress under the Articles of Confederation, the Northwest Ordinance specified how territories and states were to be formed from the land gained by the United States—the Old Northwest—as a result of the American Revolution.

Historical Background

In America in the late 18th century it happened that there was a parson from Ipswich, Massachusetts, one Manasseh Cutler, who, like a Chaucerian cleric, had a healthier appetite for the finer things in life than for the spiritual. Purchasing lands in a new country, he declared, appeared to be the only thing he could do to secure a living for himself and his family. He was tapped by the newly formed Ohio Company to act as what may have been the new nation's first lobbyist. His task was to cajole Congress into allowing the company to buy land at the minimum price of one dollar per acre as mandated by the Ordinance of 1785, but to pay that dollar in grossly depreciated Continental currency, in effect securing a price of eight or nine cents an acre. President George Washington himself approved this plan. It would, after all, enable his loyal Revolutionary Army officers to buy land with the devalued currency.

The land ordinance also specified that no speculative grants of land were to be made before at least seven ranges had been surveyed, and some congressmen rightly objected that the Ohio Company's petition should be put off until this was done. To their naysaying, Cutler replied with a threat to buy lands from individual states but then added honey to his vinegar: he offered the recalcitrant legislators an opportunity to invest in another land corporation, the Scioto Company, in which the Confederation's secretary of the treasury, William Duer, and Arthur St. Clair, the president of the Continental Congress, were already principal investors.

That was not all Cutler obtained from Congress. In order to lure settlers to the new lands, he helped to persuade the legislators to formulate an ordinance that would guarantee stable government for the West. The result was the famed Northwest Ordinance. Passed at the height of the Indian resistance to trans-Appalachian expansion, it was an effort both to appease discontented frontiersmen and to impose some order on them, and it was one of the most important pieces of legislation passed under the Articles of Confederation.

Terms

The law called for the land of what was then considered the Northwest to be divided into three to five territories. Congress would appoint a governor, a secretary, and three judges to administer each territory. When the adult population of a territory reached 5,000, elections would be held to form a legislature and to select a nonvoting representative to Congress. A territory could write a constitution and apply for statehood when the adult male population reached 60,000. In other words, the ordinance established goals for, and thus encouraged, western expansion. Such expansion was still de facto an invasion of Indian land, but the occupation of that land now had a de jure political purpose: statehood.

An Ordinance for the Government of the Territory of the United States Northwest of the River Ohio

Be it ordained by the United States in Congress assembled, That the said territory, for the purposes of temporary government, be one district, subject, however, to be divided into two districts, as future circumstances may, in the opinion of Congress, make it expedient.

Be it ordained by the authority aforesaid, That the estates, both of resident and nonresident proprietors in the said territory, dying intestate, shall descent to, and be distributed among their children, and the descendants of a deceased child, in equal parts; the descendants of a deceased child or grandchild to take the share of their deceased parent in equal parts among them: And where there shall be no children or descendants, then in equal parts to the next of kin in equal degree; and among collaterals, the children of a deceased brother or sister of the intestate shall have, in equal parts among them, their deceased parents' share; and there shall in no case be a distinction between kindred of the whole and half blood; saving, in all cases, to the widow of the intestate her third part of the real estate for life, and one third part of the personal estate; and this law relative to descents and dower, shall remain in full force until altered by the legislature of the district. And until the governor and judges shall adopt laws as hereinafter mentioned, estates in the said territory may be devised or bequeathed by wills in writing, signed and sealed by him or her in whom the estate may be (being of full age), and attested by three witnesses; and real estates may be conveyed by lease and release, or bargain and sale, signed, sealed and delivered by the person being of full age, in whom the estate may be, and attested by two witnesses, provided such wills be duly proved, and such conveyances be acknowledged, or the execution thereof duly proved, and be recorded within one year after proper magistrates, courts, and registers shall be appointed for that purpose; and personal property may be transferred by delivery; saving, however to the French and Canadian inhabitants, and other settlers of the Kaskaskies, St. Vincents and the neighboring villages who have heretofore professed themselves citizens of Virginia, their laws and customs now in force among them, relative to the descent and conveyance, of property.

Be it ordained by the authority aforesaid, That there shall be appointed from time to time by Congress, a governor, whose commission shall continue in force for the term of three years, unless sooner revoked by Congress; he shall reside in the district, and have a freehold estate therein in 1,000 acres of land, while in the exercise of his office.

There shall be appointed from time to time by Congress, a secretary, whose commission shall continue in force for four years unless sooner revoked; he shall reside in the district, and have a freehold estate therein in 500 acres of land, while in the exercise of his office. It shall be his duty to keep and preserve the acts and laws passed by the legislature, and the public records of the district, and the proceedings of the governor in his executive department, and transmit authentic copies of such acts and proceedings, every six months, to the Secretary of Congress: There shall also be appointed a court to consist of three judges, any two of whom to form a court, who shall have a common law jurisdiction, and reside in the district, and have each therein a freehold estate in 500 acres of land while in the exercise of their offices; and their commissions shall continue in force during good behavior.

The governor and judges, or a majority of them, shall adopt and publish in the district such laws of the original States, criminal and civil, as may be necessary and best suited to the circumstances of the district, and report them to Congress from time to time: which laws shall be in force in the district until the organization of the General Assembly therein, unless disapproved of by Congress; but afterwards the Legislature shall have authority to alter them as they shall think fit.

The governor, for the time being, shall be commander in chief of the militia, appoint and commission all officers in the same below the rank of general officers; all general officers shall be appointed and commissioned by Congress.

Previous to the organization of the general assembly, the governor shall appoint such magistrates and other civil officers in each county or township, as he shall find necessary for the preservation of the peace and good order in the same: After the general assembly shall be organized, the powers and duties of the magistrates and other civil officers shall be regulated and defined by the said assembly; but all magistrates and other civil officers not herein otherwise directed, shall during the continuance of this temporary government, be appointed by the governor.

For the prevention of crimes and injuries, the laws to be adopted or made shall have force in all parts of the district, and for the execution of process, criminal and civil, the governor shall make proper divisions thereof; and he shall proceed from time to time as circumstances may require, to lay out the parts of the district in which the Indian titles shall have been extinguished, into counties and townships, subject, however, to such alterations as may thereafter be made by the legislature.

So soon as there shall be five thousand free male inhabitants of full age in the district, upon giving proof thereof to the governor, they shall receive authority, with time and place, to elect a representative from their counties or townships to represent them in the general assembly: Provided, That, for every five hundred free male inhabitants, there shall be one representative, and so on progressively with the number of free male inhabitants shall the right of representation increase, until the number of representatives shall amount to twenty five; after which, the number and proportion of representatives shall be regulated by the legislature: Provided, That no person be eligible or qualified to act as a representative unless he shall have been a citizen of one of the United States three years, and be a resident in the district, or unless he shall have resided in the district three years; and, in either case, shall likewise hold in his own right, in fee simple, two hundred acres of land within the same; Provided, also, That a freehold in fifty acres of land in the district, having been a citizen of one of the states, and being resident in the district, or the like freehold and two years residence in the district, shall be necessary to qualify a man as an elector of a representative.

The representatives thus elected, shall serve for the term of two years; and, in case of the death of a representative, or removal from office, the governor shall issue a writ to the county or township for which he was a member, to elect another in his stead, to serve for the residue of the term.

The general assembly or legislature shall consist of the governor, legislative council, and a house of representatives. The Legislative Council shall consist of five members, to continue in office five years, unless sooner removed by Congress; any three of whom to be a quorum: and the members of the Council shall be nominated and appointed in the following manner, to wit: As soon as representatives shall be elected, the Governor shall appoint a time and place for them to meet together; and, when met, they shall nominate ten persons, residents in the district, and each possessed of a freehold in five hundred acres of land, and return their names to Congress; five of whom Congress shall appoint and commission to serve as aforesaid; and, whenever a vacancy shall happen in the council, by death or removal from office, the house of representatives shall nominate two persons, qualified as aforesaid, for each vacancy, and return their names to Congress; one of whom congress shall appoint and commission for the residue of the term. And every five years, four months at least before the expiration of the time of service of the members of council, the said house shall nominate ten persons, qualified as aforesaid, and return their names to Congress; five of whom Congress shall appoint and commission to serve as members of the council five years, unless sooner removed. And the governor, legislative council, and house of representatives, shall have authority to make laws in all cases, for the good government of the district, not repugnant to the principles and articles in this ordinance established and declared. And all bills, having passed by a majority in the house, and by a majority in the council, shall be referred to the governor for his assent; but no bill, or legislative act whatever, shall be of any force without his assent. The governor shall have power to convene, prorogue, and dissolve the general assembly, when, in his opinion, it shall be expedient.

The governor, judges, legislative council, secretary, and such other officers as Congress shall appoint in the district, shall take an oath or affirmation of fidelity and of office; the governor before the president of congress, and all other officers before the Governor. As soon as a legislature shall be formed in the district, the council and house assembled in one room, shall have authority, by joint ballot, to elect a delegate to Congress, who shall have a seat in Congress, with a right of debating but not voting during this temporary government.

And, for extending the fundamental principles of civil and religious liberty, which form the basis whereon these republics, their laws and constitutions are erected; to fix and establish those principles as the basis of all laws, constitutions, and governments, which forever hereafter shall be formed in the said territory: to provide also for the establishment of States, and permanent government therein, and for their admission to a share in the federal councils on an equal footing with the original States, at as early periods as may be consistent with the general interest:

It is hereby ordained and declared by the authority aforesaid, That the following articles shall be considered as articles of compact between the original States and the people and States in the said territory and forever remain unalterable, unless by common consent, to wit:

ARTICLE 1

No person, demeaning himself in a peaceable and orderly manner, shall ever be molested on account of his mode of worship or religious sentiments, in the said territory.

ARTICLE 2

The inhabitants of the said territory shall always be entitled to the benefits of the writ of habeas corpus, and of the trial by jury; of a proportionate representation of the people in the legislature; and of judicial proceedings according to the course of the common law. All persons shall be bailable, unless for capital offenses, where the proof shall be evident or the presumption great. All fines shall be moderate; and no cruel or unusual punishments shall be inflicted. No man shall be deprived of his liberty or property, but by the judgment of his peers or the law of the land; and, should the public exigencies make it necessary, for the common preservation, to take any person's property, or to demand his particular services, full compensation shall be made for the same. And, in the just preservation of rights and property, it is understood and declared, that no law ought ever to be made, or have force in the said territory, that shall, in any manner whatever, interfere with or affect private contracts or engagements, bona fide, and without fraud, previously formed.

ARTICLE 3

Religion, morality, and knowledge, being necessary to good government and the happiness of mankind, schools and the means of education shall forever be encouraged. The utmost good faith shall always be observed towards the Indians; their lands and property shall never be taken from them without their consent; and, in their property, rights, and liberty, they shall never be invaded or disturbed, unless in just and lawful wars authorized by Congress; but laws founded in justice and humanity, shall from time to time be made for preventing wrongs being done to them, and for preserving peace and friendship with them.

ARTICLE 4

The said territory, and the States which may be formed therein, shall forever remain a part of this Confederacy of the United States of America, subject to the Articles of Confederation, and to such alterations therein as shall be constitutionally made; and to all the acts and ordinances of the United States in Congress assembled, conformable thereto. The inhabitants and settlers in the said territory shall be subject to pay a part of the federal debts contracted or to be contracted, and a proportional part of the expenses of government, to be apportioned on them by Congress according to the same common rule and measure by which apportionments thereof shall be made on the other States; and the taxes for paying their proportion shall be laid and levied by the authority and direction of the legislatures of the district or districts, or new States, as in the original States, within the time agreed upon by the United States in Congress assembled. The legislatures of those districts or new States, shall never interfere with the primary disposal of the soil by the United States in Congress assembled, nor with any regulations Congress may find necessary for securing the title in such soil to the bona fide purchasers. No tax shall be imposed on lands the property of the United States; and, in no case, shall nonresident proprietors be taxed higher than residents. The navigable waters leading into the Mississippi and St. Lawrence, and the carrying places between the same, shall be common highways and forever free, as well to the inhabitants of the said territory as to the citizens of the United States, and those of any other States that may be admitted into the confederacy, without any tax, impost, or duty therefor.

ARTICLE 5

There shall be formed in the said territory, not less than three nor more than five States; and the boundaries of the States, as soon as Virginia shall alter her act of cession, and consent to the same, shall become fixed and established as follows, to wit: The western State in the said territory, shall be bounded by the Mississippi, the Ohio, and Wabash Rivers; a direct line drawn from the Wabash and Post Vincents, due North, to the territorial line between the United States and Canada; and, by the said territorial line, to the Lake of the Woods and Mississippi. The middle State shall be bounded by the said direct line, the Wabash from Post Vincents to the Ohio, by the Ohio, by a direct line, drawn due north from the mouth of the Great Miami, to the said territorial line, and by the said territorial line. The eastern State shall be bounded by the last mentioned direct line, the Ohio, Pennsylvania, and the said territorial line: Provided, however, and it is further understood and declared, that the boundaries of these three States shall be subject so far to be altered, that, if Congress shall hereafter find it expedient, they shall have authority to form one or two States in that part of the said territory which lies north of an east and west line drawn through the southerly bend or extreme of Lake Michigan. And, whenever any of the said States shall have sixty thousand free inhabitants therein, such State shall be admitted, by its delegates, into the Congress of the United States, on an equal footing with the original States in all respects whatever, and shall be at liberty to form a permanent constitution and State government: Provided, the constitution and government so to be formed, shall be republican, and in conformity to the principles contained in these articles; and, so far as it can be consistent with the general interest of the confederacy, such admission shall be allowed at an earlier period, and when there may be a less number of free inhabitants in the State than sixty thousand.

ARTICLE 6

There shall be neither slavery nor involuntary servitude in the said territory, otherwise than in the punishment of crimes whereof the party shall have been duly convicted: Provided, always, That any person escaping into the same, from whom labor or service is lawfully claimed in any one of the original States, such fugitive may be lawfully reclaimed and conveyed to the person claiming his or her labor or service as aforesaid.

Be it ordained by the authority aforesaid, That the resolutions of the 23rd of April, 1784, relative to the subject of this ordinance, be, and the same are hereby repealed and declared null and void.

While the ordinance placed certain restrictions on the constitutions of new states and banned slavery from the newly occupied region (a ban that would have future political consequences), it also called for religious freedom, trial by jury, and state government–supported education, all of which would ensure that any new territory politically and institutionally closely resembled the states. This in turn allowed the law to offer pioneers—once they had settled in sufficient numbers to create a state—a voice in Congress equal to that of the original 13 colonies.

Consequences

It was precisely in this piece of legislation that the new country displayed the genius of its revolution-spawned republicanism. The Northwest Ordinance was, in fact, a document for the political handling of colonized land. The "mother country" east of the Appalachians, understanding the psychology of colonial peoples, declared that it would treat its western lands not as colonies but, in the long run, as full partners in a single nation. Alone among the expansive imperial powers of the 18th and 19th centuries, the United States established an orderly method, at least on paper, for creating a coherent polity from conquered land. The ordinance served as a model for the transition from territory to statehood in both the trans-Appalachian West and the trans-Mississippi West as the U.S. population expanded westward.

Thus, a Congress in need of money, and an Ohio Company willing to provide it in return for 1 1/2 million acres at greatly depreciated prices, came to create the structure by which new territories, the United States's own colonies, would be transformed into states and become equal partners in the body politic. As the original states, which in centuries past had laid claims to the land stretching west from their current borders, were forced to relinquish those claims under the new land policies, they either ceded the western lands to the federal government or sold them to the big land companies. American companies like Phelps & Gorham, Scottish-owned Pilteney and Associates, the Dutch-controlled Holland Land Company, and the Ohio and Yazoo Companies created a pattern of speculation and colonization of the West later adopted and expanded upon by the land grant railroads.

After passage of the Northwest Ordinance, land speculation ran rampant as the companies invested millions of dollars in wildernesses far from any kind of transportation and unlikely to be turned into farms any time soon. Eventually the companies, and various individuals, who had borrowed heavily to finance their investments could no longer carry their landholdings, at which point would come the inevitable crash, as land companies were forced to liquidate their holdings and collapse into bankruptcy. The boom-and-bust cycles in part established by land speculation, in part fed by them, would come to dominate the American economy, especially the economy of the American West.

Part Six

EPOCH OF NAPOLEON

INTRODUCTION

For some 20 years the history of Europe at the end of the 18th and beginning of the 19th centuries was intertwined and inseparable from the fortunes of a single man, Napoleon Bonaparte. From his relatively obscure origins in Corsica, Bonaparte's military prowess and political acumen would sweep him to personal dominance over most of the Continent. At its height, Napoleon's empire stretched from Spain to the Russian border. Napoleon directly ruled France, Catalonia, the Netherlands, the Dalmatian coast, and northern Italy, while members of his family reigned over Spain, modern-day Germany and Poland, and the rest of Italy. For some of these countries, French occupation brought a centralized rule and liberal institutions that provided them for the first time with a true sense of national identity. Even after his downfall in 1815, the empire's legal codes and administrative systems would continue to operate for decades or longer in the once-occupied territories. Certainly, the history of diplomacy during the first decades of the new century centered on doings of the man who made himself Emperor Napoleon I.

Europe was not the world, nor was Bonaparte's rise the only dramatic change during the half-century he walked the earth. In Great Britain an industrial revolution had been gathering the force that would make Britain the world's first capitalist society, one whose steam-driven commercial success became both the envy of and the model for other nations. In the long run, this industrialization would have a more profound effect on Europe than all of Napoleon's armies.

As the economies and influence of Britain, France, and a few European powers expanded, other nations were in decline. Weakened by imported opium and British sea power, the once-mighty China had fallen to its knees and was soon to become a vassal of Western traders. The aging and ailing Spanish Empire tottered on the brink of dissolution even before Napoleon's meddling doomed its future at the hands of Latin American revolutionaries. The native populations of North America and the black kingdoms of Africa were being crushed, the former by English-speaking Americans spreading west from their seaboard settlements across the Appalachians toward the Mississippi, the latter by British and Dutch settlers flowing inland east and north from the Cape of Good Hope.

These were the beginnings of movements whose impacts were yet to come (and whose development will be covered in other parts of this work) during the years when Napoleon was changing the history of France and of the world. Eventually, a Europe much rattled by revolution would meet at Vienna to try to put the Old World back together, only to discover that Europe as conceived by the conservative representatives of the traditional regimes had vanished. Ultimately, in the wake of the great French Revolution and the rise to power of one of the preeminent personalties of the 19th century, Napoleon Bonaparte, the old regimes of continental Europe thoroughly, if quietly, would modernize their governments and internationalize their diplomacy.

Fall of the Ancien Régime

Napoleon did not spring from the earth *ab ovo*, but like all men was a creature of his place and time, and his rise would have been impossible without the massive social upheaval of the French Revolution. A decade before the close of the 18th century, France was the most powerful nation on the continent of Europe, perhaps (depending on whether you were talking to an Englishman or not) in the world. It was certainly the most populous occidental country. But France's political system was more creaky than was apparent before French revolutionaries began openly to excoriate the ancien régime in front of revolution-minded assemblies and mobs. An absolute monarchy stitched together in the previous century by the crafty and capable Cardinal Richelieu to center around Louis XIV at his new palace in Versailles, the kingdom was only as strong as the man at the top, a fact that became clear when the Sun King's successors, the lazy Louis XV and the dithering Louis XVI, enfeebled royal authority.

The cost of Louis XIV's absolute power had been the corruption of French society. The entire economic and legal system was not simply corrupt but fecklessly inefficient, and the state's finances often tottered on ruin. Already a source of deep resentment for the country's growing bourgeoisie, the system was stretched intolerably by the foreign adventures and imperial wars typical of the 18th century's rival European ruling houses: the War of the Grand Alliance in Europe, the War of the Spanish Succession, the War of the Austrian Succession, the Seven Year's War. The latest of these, playing itself out 3,000 miles from Paris across the Atlantic Ocean, was the American Revolution. There the French had helped British colonials achieve independence against the nation's archrival, Britain, only to provoke a fiscal crisis at home. Along with new war debts also came the liberal ideas of the Enlightenment for which the former colonists had been fighting, placing both new financial and new intellectual burdens on the French. When the French middle class and many of the country's forward-thinking aristocrats realized that the government against which the North Americans had fought was much less oppressive than their own, the political costs of the adventure became clear. By the 1780s, the French state was close to a bankruptcy both economic and moral.

The result was the French Revolution, and foreign reaction to the French Revolution (and to the consequent rise of Napoleon), which was everywhere severe, would affect the international relations of Europe for a generation. An Assembly of Notables called by the hapless Louis XVI to work out France's growing financial problems became a National Assembly controlled by the French middle class but always operating under pressure from the Paris mob and the radical revolutionary debating clubs that sprang up in the city. With the American Revolution as an example, the Assembly produced a Declaration of the Rights of Man, created a National Convention to write a constitution, and then imprisoned Louis XVI in Paris when he and his unpopular queen, Austrian-born Marie Antoinette, were caught trying to flee the country.

When the Revolution inspired an uprising in the Austrian Netherlands, Leopold II, emperor of Austria, already upset by the antiecclesiastical bent of the Assembly in Paris and by the ill treatment of his sister, Marie Antoinette, began plotting an armed response.

Together, Leopold and the king of Prussia, Frederick Wilhelm II, issued a joint declaration calling on other European monarchs to help them restore Louis to the French throne. In response, the left-wing Gironde took control of the Revolution and launched a preemptive war on Austria. The ill-trained revolutionary troops fared poorly and merely provoked the invasion of France that summer by Austria's ally, Prussia.

Under the strain of war, the delicate French economy collapsed, and the dangerous, widespread discontent fostered by food shortages and rising prices led the Assembly to declare a national emergency. This in turn led to the rise of the Jacobin Club—so named for its original meeting place, the former monastery of the Dominicans of Saint James—led by an impeccably dressed, incorruptible but austere and rigid lawyer from Arras named Maximilien Robespierre. Under Robbespierre, the Revolution went blood-simple. Aristocrats and enemies of the state were prosecuted and guillotined, including one named Citizen Capet, otherwise known as Louis XVI, king of France.

The king's execution on January 21, 1793, sparked royalist insurrections, notably in the Vendée, and set off a wave of outraged protest from the governments of Europe. In response the National Convention in quick succession declared war on Britain, Holland, and Spain. Other provincial cities joined the Vendée insurrection as discontent boiled over into civil war. The crisis put France on a war footing, which led to the infamous Reign of Terror at home. A Revolutionary Tribunal, set up to sniff out traitors, now saw treason in what a few months before would have passed for simple political opposition. By April full power had flowed into the hands of the newly created Committee of Public Safety.

In Jacobin hands the Committee proved an extremely effective machine for winning wars. The Jacobins increased conscription to levies unheard of before, raising by August a force of some 650,000 men, many of them true believers, who far outnumbered those in the ranks of the small professional armies then invading France. Given the needed training, the necessary tools, and the right leader—all of which they were soon to receive—they would make a mighty force indeed. Even now, their mass was pushing the foreigners and the émigré aristocrats back beyond French borders. The Mediterranean port town of Toulon, for example, had been handed over to the encroaching British by royalist traitors to the Revolution, but republican troops recaptured the site in December 1793. Leaders back in Paris, reading over official dispatches, noted that the republican success was being attributed in large degree to an unknown Corsican artillery officer and strong Jacobin supporter by the name of Napoleon Bonaparte.

From Hero of the Revolution to Emperor of Europe

Destined to become perhaps the most brilliant figure in military history, Napoleon Bonaparte was not so much a product of the French Revolution as its chief beneficiary. Born on August 5, 1769, in Ajaccio, Corsica, a politically turbulent island recently acquired by the French Crown from the Republic of Genoa, and given a more or less typical military upbringing, Napoleon had ambitions to establish a solid dynasty within France and to create a French-dominated empire in Europe. If he was never the reincarnation of a typical 14th-century condottiere some biographers later made him out to be, Napoleon from the beginning shared few if any of the traditions, and adopted almost none of the prejudices, of his new country, remaining Corsican by temperament as well as birth. Through education and his own reading, he was a man of the 18th century, of its belief both in enlightenment and in absolutism. He spent the twilight years of the ancien régime on leisurely garrison duty reading the works of military theorist J. P. du Teil and Enlightenment philosophers Voltaire and Rousseau, steeping himself in both strategy and tactics of war and the liberal ideas sweeping France.

While Napoleon believed political change was imperative, as a career officer he seemed leery of radical social reform, and he always moved steadily to consolidate his personal power. Joining the Jacobins early in his career in Grenoble, he made fiery speeches declaiming against nobles, monks, and bishops and in 1791 put down a revolt against French revolutionary rule in his native Corsica. Thereafter, he rose by personal connection and opportune action. He came to the attention of the Paris revolutionaries through Maximilien Robespierre's brother Justin via a pamphlet he wrote as a young artillery officer, which argued fervently for united action by all republicans rallied around the Jacobins. When the French artillery commander at the port of Toulon was wounded during an attack in August 1793, Napoleon stepped in to save the town from British occupation. Augustin Robespierre, who was political governor of Toulon, wrote to his brother Maximilien, by then the leading figure behind the current Reign of Terror, praising the "transcendent merit" of the young republican officer.

With such powerful backing, Napoleon quickly worked his way up the ranks of the Revolutionary Army, while the Revolutionary Tribunal quickly worked its way through French society. The first to fall victim to the guillotine were French aristocrats and captured or returned émigrés; they were followed by a number of republican generals who had committed the new crime of suffering defeat in battle; then Marie

Antoinette faced the same fate as her late husband, Louis Capet, after she was convicted of treason in a infamously unfair trial. The Girondist deputies were guillotined shortly after Marie Antoinette. When Robespierre redefined even those who backed his rise to power as counterrevolutionaries, the less radical Jacobins trundled to the scaffold, followed the next week by some of Robespierre's closet former associates.

Robespierre still saw traitors everywhere, and he and his Montagnard faction of the Jacobins no longer truly controlled the tiger they were riding. After Robespierre demanded yet another purge of its deputies to eradicate even more enemies of the republic, the Convention, its members clearly conscious they were voting to save their own necks, ordered the arrest and execution of Citizen Robespierre. Now, for the first time since the beheading of the king, the Paris guillotine fell idle. The Great Terror had burned itself out, and as a protégé of the Robespierres, Napoleon was arrested in Nice and imprisoned on charges of conspiracy and treason, although the charges were soon dropped due to lack of evidence. He was not, however, restored to his command. Under the new assembly, whose members feared his intense ambitions and worried about his former relations with the Montagnards, his prospects looked bleak indeed. For months he tramped about the city from office to office, but his efforts brought no new command. At one point he considered offering his services as a mercenary to the sultan of Turkey.

Then, in October 1795, his luck changed. Under threat from enraged mobs in Paris, the National Convention entrusted Vicomte Paul de Barras with almost dictatorial powers to defend the government. Unwilling to rely on the loyalty of the commander of the Army of the Interior, Barras, who had heard of Bonaparte's service at Toulon, appointed him second in command. Thus it was Napoleon who, rapidly assembling some artillery, coolly dispersed the insurrectionists with a "whiff of grapeshot," leaving several hundred people dead and wounded, thereby saving the Convention, the republic, and his own career. The massacre confirmed the new Directory as the supreme authority in the land, and the Directory, whose five members included Barras, rewarded Napoleon with full command of the Army of the Interior.

Now a hero of the Revolution, his future was ensured. As head of the Army of the Interior, Bonaparte was aware of every political development in France, and he became a trusted military adviser to the Directory. Meanwhile, he had taken up with Barras's former mistress, an attractive Creole named Josephine Tascher de La Pagerie. She was the widow of Alexandre de Beauharnais, a republican general guillotined during the Reign of Terror, mother of two children, and the source of many rumored affairs. The two were to be married in March 1796, and the approving Barras gave Napoleon command of the Revolution's war in Italy.

Napoleon worked the appointment for all it was worth, and by April 1797 he had swept the Austrians from northern Italy and marched to within 75 miles of Vienna. On his own initiative, he negotiated the TREATY OF CAMPO FORMIO in open disregard for regular diplomatic channels and of any legal authority. The Directory did not much like it, but Napoleon Bonaparte had gotten the Holy Roman Empire to surrender a good deal of its Italian territory to a new French-dominated government he called the Cisalpine Republic and to let go of its holdings in the Rhineland and the Netherlands, as well.

Besides, the Directory itself, never truly popular, subject throughout its short, four-year tenure to unrest from both the left and the right, needed Napoleon as much as he needed the Directory. Only the Directory's military efforts were truly crowned with success, partly because France now had the most efficient system of conscription in Europe. In return, the army's help became indispensable to the Directory's survival, which introduced the generals to politics and made the coup d'état thenceforth a part of French political life.

Napoleon's next military assignment was in Egypt, but he was soon recalled. Chronically unstable, the Directory suffered reverses in two French elections, and an attempted military coup by Directory members failed to purge the government of newly elected royalists; renewed repressions by the Directory only made the situation worse. When British prime minister William Pitt organized and financed a fresh anti-French alliance, the Second Coalition, which included Naples, Austria, Russia, and the Ottoman Empire, many doubted the Directory's ability to wage war successfully against it, and some of the Directory's members were convinced that only military dictatorship could prevent a restoration of the monarchy. The Directors ordered the return of Napoleon to "save" the Revolution.

Napoleon was delighted. The British had destroyed his fleet in Egypt, and his army was left sick and stranded in the shadow of the pyramids. He was on his way to Paris to seek new orders even before he had received the Directory's recall, and once there, he took advantage of the changed circumstances to seize power. By the time he arrived on October 14, 1799, French victories in Switzerland and Holland had stayed the danger of invasion, and the most recent counterrevolutionary risings at home had fizzled, so the republic no longer needed saving, but in collusion with members of the Directory, Napoleon plotted a coup. On 18 Brumaire (November 9), he struck. As planned, the five-man Directory was replaced by three

consuls, including—as yet another reward for services rendered to the Revolution—General Bonaparte. When the Jacobins in the Assembly refused to accept the abrogation of the constitution, Bonaparte's troops drove them from their chambers. A few hours later, a handful of more tractable deputies murmured assent to the changes and gave a semblance of legality to the coup, but the bayonets remained, and the message was clear: not just the Directory but the Revolution was dead, and First Consul Napoleon Bonaparte was master of France.

The mood of the nation favored the First Consul, and there was remarkably little opposition. Racked by years of revolutionary terror and lawlessness, still faced with a formidable royalist faction, the people—whose yearning for stability was almost tangible—were willing to hand over authority to one strong man. Buttressed by a new and highly authoritarian constitution that a plebiscite of his weary fellow citizens backed almost unanimously, Napoleon radically restructured the French national debt, setting the French economy on a sound footing. He encouraged the development of industry and the improvement of the educational system, and he initiated an ambitious program of construction inspired by the classical examples of imperial Rome. He created the Code Napoleon, which codified civil law by amalgamating the old customs of northern France with the Roman law of the south. Also included was a new criminal code to be enforced by judges. These changes were sweeping, and over the years the code would be extended to regulate and transform every aspect of French life and then, as it came to cover Napoleon's conquests, the life of much of Europe. One provision in particular, insisting on the equal division of property between sons, did more than the Revolution to destroy the power of France's—then the Empire's—landed gentry. Equally significant, the First Consul concluded a concordant with Pope Pius VII reestablishing Roman Catholicism as the state religion.

Needing peace at home and abroad to give time for his reforms to take effect, Napoleon moved decisively in May 1800 to bring an end to the War of the Second Coalition. When Napoleon crushed the Austrians in June, William Pitt resigned as British prime minister, and the incoming government—its members emotionally fatigued by almost a decade of fruitless fighting—signed the TREATY OF AMIENS on March 27, 1802. With Great Britain still deeply suspicious and France full of expansionist ambition, the peace was destined to be not much more than a brief truce. It did nevertheless provide Napoleon nearly 15 months to complete his civic and clerical reforms and to reshape his army. A grateful France made Napoleon First Consul for life on August 2, 1802.

From that time forward, international relations within Europe would be at the whim of Napoleon. He needed his empire building to shore up his rule in France; the stronger he grew at home, the larger an empire this soldier of fortune par excellence sought to conquer. To the chagrin of the British, much of France's newfound energy seemed devoted to ship-building, and not just to constructing ships of the line, but also flat-bottomed barges that could only, they decided, be intended for an invasion of their island.

Worse still, in 1803 Napoleon set about once again to reshaping the face of Europe. In Holland he occupied the Batavian Republic and in Switzerland the Helvetic Republic. He annexed Savoy-Piedmont, then took the first step toward abolishing the Holy Roman Empire by means of the Imperial Recess of 1803, which consolidated free cities and minor states dominated by the Holy Roman Empire. He also attempted to recover the Caribbean island of Haiti, which had rebelled against French colonial domination. To help fund these adventures and to ensure, at the very least, America's neutrality in what was surely the coming war with Britain, Napoleon sold Louisiana—ceded to France by its ally, Spain in 1800—to the United States at a cut-rate price in the LOUISIANA PURCHASE. This deal extracted vague promises of friendship in an exchange that fell far short of what Bonaparte wanted: the Americans to fight England again.

Britain was even more irritated by Napoleon's determination to turn Europe into a huge market reserved exclusively for French goods. Not only did France control the entire continental coastline from Genoa to Antwerp, it was also charging extortionate customs duties that much affronted the commercially minded island sea power. Thus, Napoleon's renewed aggression in Europe, coupled with his refusal to grant trade concessions to Britain, led the English (on the slim pretext that he was not living up to the Treaty of Amiens) to reignite war in May 1803.

As Napoleon prepared an army of 170,000 troops to invade England, an assassination scheme, financed by the British, was discovered. Alarmed by the plot, the French Senate, nudged along by Napoleon, petitioned the First Consul to establish a hereditary dynasty. Once more Bonaparte eagerly seized opportunity, and on December 2, 1804, as Pope Pius VII looked on, he crowned himself emperor.

The Return of Talleyrand

Almost as important, in terms of foreign affairs, as the rise of Napoleon was the return to grace of Charles-Maurice de Talleyrand-Périgord. As a French statesman and diplomat, Talleyrand would become noted for his capacity for survival, holding high office not only during the French Revolution and the subsequent Napoleonic Empire but also at the restoration of the Bourbon monarchy and under King Louis-Philippe. From an impoverished but ancient aristocratic family, left clubfooted by a childhood accident, Talleyrand had under the ancien régime become a typical court cleric before rising to fame as the veritable "Bishop of the Revolution" when he engineered the adoption of the Civil Constitution of the Clergy that proved so pernicious to the success of the Revolution.

The first bishop to take the revolutionary loyalty oath, for which he was excommunicated by the pope, Talleyrand was recognized for his skills as a clever negotiator and was posted as a minister to London in 1791, where he helped keep England neutral until the massacre of royalist prisoners alienated whatever sympathy the British had for revolutionary France. Denounced at home by the National Convention after the overthrow of the monarchy, Talleyrand was also attached in England by counterrevolutionary émigrés who demanded his expulsion. When the British complied with these demands in January 1794, Talleyrand—hardly able to return to a France in the throes of the Terror—embarked for the United States.

After the fall of Robespierre, Talleyrand petitioned the National Convention to remove his name from the list of émigrés since, he pointed out, he had left France on an official passport. His request granted, Talleyrand returned to Paris in September 1796. There, with the help of his political connections on the Directory, he regained his standing as a diplomat and was named French foreign minister in the summer of 1797. It was Talleyrand who confirmed Napoleon's conclusion of the Treaty of Campo Formio. It was Talleyrand who, with Napoleon, would execute France's grand strategy in the coming years of guaranteeing French security by creating a ring of satellite republics around the nation's borders in Italy and the Netherlands and, also, in Switzerland. It was Talleyrand who seconded Napoleon's proposal to strike at Britain by occupying Egypt and threatening its lucrative trade route to India. It would be Talleyrand who exercised his diplomatic skills to divide the victorious allies at the Congress of Vienna following the defeat and exile of the emperor.

Rise and Fall of the Empire

Abrogating the republic for which he had for so long and so ostentatiously fought, Napoleon quickly created a royal court populated by former republicans and royalists alike. Not content merely to create a dynasty for France, he sketched out a new European aristocracy, eventually installing members of his family on the thrones of newly created kingdoms of Naples, Holland, Westphalia, and Spain. In 1809 he divorced Josephine because she had failed to bear a male heir. On April 2, 1810, he married Marie-Louise, daughter of the Austrian emperor, and a son (whom Napoleon immediately crowned the king of Rome) was born to the couple within a year.

From the moment he became emperor, Napoleon was almost constantly at war. Great Britain proved his most dogged opponent, but Prussia and Austria also joined in the series of coalitions stretched together to stop Napoleon's march across Europe. Backed by an entirely new kind of army—ideologically conscripted rather than professionally recruited—he was a master strategist, particularly skilled at the rapid deployment of masses of troops and mobile field artillery. Until 1812, with some important exceptions, he was usually successful. One of those exceptions came in October of 1805, when British admiral Horatio Nelson annihilated the French navy at the Battle of Trafalgar off the coast of Spain. Preoccupied with Austria and Russia, Napoleon was certainly not aware that the battle, which cost Nelson his life, was one of the turning points in history. In the short term, it meant he had to call off his elaborate plans to invade England; in the long run, Nelson's victory ensured that the British navy would rule the seas for more than a century.

Forcing the Russians to capitulate and sign the TREATY OF PRESSBURG after his single greatest military victory, at Austerlitz in December, Napoleon abolished the Holy Roman Empire and organized in its stead the Confederation of the Rhine, a French protectorate of German states. In an attempt to ease hostilities with England, Napoleon offered to return Hanover to British control, which provoked a war with Prussia in September, though Napoleon easily defeated this Fourth Coalition. Once again he forced major concessions from Prussia and its ally, Czar Alexander I, in the TREATIES OF TILSIT, creating the French-controlled Grand Duchy of Warsaw, gaining Russian recognition of other European entities spawned by Napoleon, and removing from Prussia all lands between the Rhine and Elbe Rivers.

The emperor now enjoyed unparalled sway over Europe, but he was not satisfied. Unable to defeat England by military means, he instituted in 1806 the Continental System, a blockade of British trade intended to destroy England's economy. Britain calmly responded with the Orders in Council, which called for its own naval blockade of Napoleonic Europe. The Continental System and the British response created tremendous unrest throughout Europe, and Portugal immediately announced that it would not participate. Napoleon launched the Peninsular War to compel Portugal's obedience, which provoked unrest in Spain and

led to the abdication of King Charles IV and his son Ferdinand VII. When Napoleon replaced them with his brother, Joseph Napoleon, a popular revolt broke out in Spain and in Spanish holdings around the world. With Napoleon embroiled on the Iberian Peninsula, Austria formed the Fifth Coalition, won a few early victories, then lost decisively. Napoleon's marriage to Marie-Louise followed the 1809 armistice with Austria and the TREATY OF SCHÖNBRUNN.

By 1809, then, Napoleonic France had directly annexed the Low Countries and western Germany and set up satellite kingdoms in eastern Germany and Italy, in Spain, and in Poland. Despite the enmity his empire was stirring up, Napoleon hoped that his union with one of Europe's oldest royal families, in addition to providing an heir, would guarantee him Austrian friendship and bring peace to Europe. Instead, English-backed guerrillas continued to threaten his grasp on Spain and Portugal, and now Russia—nervous about the substantial French forces in Poland— also refused to participate in the Continental System.

These irritations would provoke Napoleon, after 1810, to clearly overreach himself. Following an enormous effort requiring every country in Europe, including a reluctant Prussia, to contribute a contingent, the emperor managed to assemble some 650,000 troops along the Russian frontier, where he planned one of his lightning campaigns that would destroy the Russian forces in six weeks and allow him to impose a humiliating peace. The invasion failed miserably in the cold Russian winter, though, and by December 1812 the Prussians had deserted the Grand Army and turned against the French; the Austrians had likewise withdrawn and were growing increasingly restive; and even stalwart Italy was turning its back on Napoleon.

They would all hail the formation of yet another anti-French Coalition—the Sixth—consisting of Prussia, Russia, Britain, and Sweden. This time the forces arrayed against France would no longer be armies of mercenaries but those of nations fighting for their freedom. Even though, in Paris, the emperor built a new army, with which he defeated Coalition forces in 1813 and brought about a brief armistice, the French themselves had lost their enthusiasm for a European empire. Napoleon's ideal of conquest was no longer that of the French nation. In August, Austria joined the Sixth Coalition, Napoleon's own father-in-law having mobilized against him. Napoleon promptly defeated Austrian troops at Dresden, but, badly outnumbered, the French were in turn trounced at the Battle of the Nations at Leipzig October 16–19, 1813. Napoleon retreated across the Rhine but refused to surrender any conquered territory.

The next year, when coalition armies invaded France itself, the emperor prevailed against each attempt to penetrate to Paris until repeated mauling of his dwindling forces prompted a mutiny of his marshals and the fall of the capital on March 31, 1814. A few days later, on April 4, Napoleon abdicated in favor of his son. The allies rejected this "solution," and Napoleon abdicated unconditionally on April 6. He was exiled to the British-controlled island of Elba. In a matter of days, the empire had vanished. In Napoleon's place the victors had enthroned the Bourbon Louis XVIII, whose brother had lost his head to the Revolution some 21 years before. On May 30, the new king signed the FIRST PEACE OF PARIS, which Talleyrand negotiated to retain those "natural" frontiers of France in place since 1792. A great congress was summoned at Vienna to set in order a post-Napoleonic Europe, but within weeks, thanks to Talleyrand's diplomacy, the allies' wartime unity had begun to evaporate, and the diplomats were engaged in bitter squabbles.

They had at least managed to agree to the creation of a moderately powerful state in the Netherlands as a buffer against a resurgent plan, when the congress was interrupted by news that Napoleon had escaped from exile and was on his way to Paris. He had landed, with a few hundred followers, at Cannes on March 1, 1815, well aware that the new King Louis was unpopular, that the peasants feared a restoration of the aristocracy would cost them all they had gained in the Revolution, and that the middle class hated a reactionary regime threatening to its own class hegemony. Troops sent by the king to arrest Napoleon instead joined him, and yet again a Bourbon monarch fled Paris. Napoleon occupied the city, which joyfully acclaimed the return of its emperor, on March 20, while the CONGRESS OF VIENNA spurned Napoleon's claim that his intentions were peaceful and labeled him an outlaw.

Seeking to forestall combined attack by Russian and Austrian armies, Napoleon decided to strike first in order to divide and destroy Prussian and Anglo-Dutch armies in Belgium. Indeed, Napoleon prevailed against the Austrians at Ligny on June 16 and against the British at Quatre-Bras on the same day, but he was defeated at Waterloo by the duke of Wellington reinforced by troops under Gebhard von Blücher on June 18, 1815. The duke of Wellington claimed that his victory at Waterloo was not assured, but even had Napoleon won, the world was determinedly arrayed against him and would have quickly crushed his restoration. Now he was on the run, a mere fugitive, reaching the port of Rochefort in early July hoping to find a ship to take him to America. The British, always his biggest nemesis, were still strictly enforcing their blockade, and Napoleon simply had no way out.

Napoleon returned to Paris, abdicated for the second time on June 22, and surrendered to the captain of the *Bellerophon*, a British warship, cheekily seeking asylum in England. The British demurred, and he was exiled again, this time to the desolate South Atlantic island of Saint Helena. There he composed his memoirs and grew increasingly ill. Some authorities believe that he succumbed, like his father, to cancer of the stomach (on May 5, 1821). Others have theorized that he died of gradual arsenic poisoning, which may have been the result of a deliberate assassination effort or only due to overmedication with the arsenic-based drugs popular at the time.

Diplomatic Fallout, Historical Impact

The Congress of Vienna, shocked enough by Napoleon's escape to leave off its bickering, picked up where it had left off in March. Both a diplomatic conference and a glittering social occasion, the delegates discussed the fate of their world amid a gala of balls and receptions where old Europe celebrated its survival. Austria's foreign minister, Prince Klemens Metternich, whose shadow stretched long over the future of Europe, dominated the proceedings as diplomats from Britain, Russia, and Prussia worked to restore a balance of power that would ensure that their old order would continue to thrive indefinitely.

Much of their attention focused on the undoing of Napoleon's reforms in Europe, but—terrified by both the Revolution and the attendant nationalism that gave rise to France's empire—they hoped to do more than merely restore the balance of power. They wanted to come up with a settlement designed to prevent any such events from recurring. Thus, all the powers, including the constitutionally governed Britain, placed great emphasis on principles of legitimacy for monarchies. Some of Napoleon's innovations, long envied and often imitated, the congress itself was not willing to forego. Having striven to copy his efficient and centralized administration, they retained the improved bureaucratic and fiscal systems he had imposed on his conquests, and where these conflicted with the old feudal aristocracy, they often set aside old and once-cherished privileges, quietly, carefully modernizing their governments. Napoleon's Civil Code they left intact also, underpinning the legal systems not just of France but also of Holland, Belgium, Italy—wherever had trod the troops of the Grand Army.

Napoleon's rise had created many changes beyond remedy to the European peacemakers, indeed beyond remedy by the art of diplomacy altogether. Not only did his conquests cement the spread of revolutionary legislation to much of western Europe and destroy the old order inherited from the 18th century in major sections of the Continent, but also in such areas as Belgium, western Germany, and northern Italy, it consolidated what before had been scattered territories; this welter of states was never truly restored. Such developments, added to an intense resentment toward Napoleonic hegemony, did indeed spark a growing nationalism in these areas and in Spain and Poland. Even Prussia and Russia, less seduced by the siren call of revolution, had been forced to introduce political reforms to strengthen their states and resist Napoleon's war machine.

Napoleon's impact was felt outside Europe as well, most spectacularly in Latin America. When Bonaparte placed his brother on the Spanish throne, he dealt Spanish-speaking republicans in Central and South America a winning hand. All Creole society united in its opposition to the despised Joseph, and—at first shouting "Long Live King Ferdinand!"—mobs drove French emissaries out of capitals across the lower half of the Western Hemisphere. Then Spanish officialdom itself, increasingly viewed as the puppet of a French usurper, came under attack. For a year, Spanish viceroys clung to power, but in 1810 Latin America's Creole population as a whole, acting in remarkable unanimity, arose in a huge spasm of republican anger and deposed their already powerless rulers. The rebellions struck every Latin country in the New World but Peru and culminated in the first Mexican Revolution in 1811. Years later Spain and Portugal would make a feeble stab at reclaiming some of their lost colonial empires, but by then the United States, backed by Great Britain, was determined to stop them, setting the stage for U.S. president James Monroe to issue the seminal MONROE DOCTRINE.

Most significantly perhaps, Great Britain, protected by the English Channel from Napoleon's preeminent army, was also transformed by the long series of conflicts. Fifteen years of continuous war against the French emperor (and 10 years of war against the French Revolution before that), although proving arduous for those at the front on land or sea, was nevertheless a godsend for British industrialists. Honed by Napoleon's constant pressure, the Royal Navy came to rule the waves, not only protecting the island kingdom from invasion, but also keeping the ocean lanes open for British exports. The navy enforced the Orders in Council, which not only blockaded France and her allies but also permitted neutrals to trade with the enemy only if they paid duty on their cargoes. While this ultimately provoked the War of 1812 with the United States, it also gave Britain's fledgling industries the security they needed to expand.

Britain's military victories in the Napoleonic Wars also expanded its own empire. French possessions in the Carribbean and Mediterranean soon joined its growing—and captive—imperial market. When Holland fell to France, the British seized Dutch territories in Africa and Asia. The expanded colonial demands for British goods helped offset the decline in trade with a continental Europe squeezed by economic sanctions, but more lastingly, it stoked the fires of Britain's industrial revolution and gave rise to one of the greatest colonial empires the world had ever seen.

Even the protection afforded by the British navy and the expanding industrial economy that ultimately helped to wear Napoleon down, could not prevent the French revolutionary example from spurring a new wave of democratic agitation in British society. Thus, Britain showed up in Vienna as anxious to conserve some of the old order as the Europeans coming under Metternich's sway. The Treaty of Vienna they produced disappointed the growing number of nationalists, who had hoped for an officially united Germany and Italy, and it certainly daunted democrats and liberals, but—thanks in no small measure to Talleyrand—it was not truly reactionary nor as punitive toward France as it might have been. After Vienna, conservatism dominated the diplomatic and political agenda of Europe through the mid-1820s at least, with major governments, even in Britain, employing police agents to ferret out revolutionary agitators. The balance of power worked out at the congress would preserve the peace in Europe for more than half a century, but in the long run the conservative political order it worked to reestablish was doomed by the boost given to national movements in the Napoleonic era.

TREATIES

Peace Treaties and Truces

TREATY OF CAMPO FORMIO

TREATY AT A GLANCE

Completed
October 17, 1797, at Campo Formio, Italy

Signatories
France and Austria

Overview
The Treaty of Campo Formio ended the first phase of the French Revolutionary Wars following Napoleon Bonaparte's triumphal Italian campaigns. Austria ceded the Austrian Netherlands (present-day Belgium) and the Ionian Islands to France and recognized the French-sponsored Cisalpine Republic in Italy. Austria received Venice and its territories.

Historical Background

Napoleon Bonaparte's series of victories in the French Revolutionary Wars, which ended with the 1802 TREATY OF AMIENS, began with astounding successes in northern Italy and brought about the collapse of the First Coalition of European powers formed against the new republic. In 1792 France's new National Assembly, pressed by the moderate republican Girondists, had declared war on Austria's Emperor Francis II for signing the Declaration of Pillnitz, which called for the restoration of France's ancien régime. The duke of Brunswick, Charles William Ferdinand, led the Austrians and their allied Prussian troops across the Rhine, threatening to destroy Paris if the revolutionaries harmed the royal family, who considered themselves more or less prisoners in their own country. The French resented the demands, and that resentment led them to abolish the monarchy, if not yet the monarch.

In the first year of the wars, revolutionary France defeated the invaders at Valmy and then pressed on to attack the Austrian Netherlands. There, too, the French army was victorious, defeating the Austrians at Jemappes and afterward overrunning today's Belgium. The successful French offensive pushed the Prussians back across the Rhine, in November 1792 a French army conquered Savoy and Nice, and flush with these early victories, the French began bold talk of exporting their revolution. The French Constitutional Convention offered aid to seekers of liberty everywhere, it opened the Scheldt estuary to French commerce, and in 1793 it guillotined the erstwhile king, who the French had taken to calling "Citizen Capet."

Alarmed by all this, the powers of Europe—Britain, Holland, Spain, Austria, Prussia, and Russia—were provoked into forming the First Coalition against France. The allies enjoyed early victories at Neerwinden, Mainz, and Kaiserslautern, and they evicted the much demoralized French from the Austrian Netherlands. The French quickly regrouped, however, introducing mass mobilization to form a huge army made up of a new kind of trooper, the citizen-soldier, and took the offensive. Once again they drove the Prussians back, and in 1794 a Russia distracted by unrest in Poland withdrew from the coalition. French success in Holland forced the Dutch to a peace, and the revolutionaries renamed their conquest the Batavian Republic. In 1795 Prussia and Spain followed Holland to the negotiating table.

That year, too, the new five-man governing Directory, which had replaced the old Convention, planted the young Bonaparte atop the Revolution's army in Italy. Jailed the year before as Jacobin heads rolled in the streets of Paris, a newly sprung Napoleon had not only saved the government from a Paris mob but also married up in the world to Josephine de Beauharnais.

Now the once obscure Corsican artilleryman cum hero-general was confronting the troops of the Holy Roman Empire, whose Hapsburg monarch ruled northern Italy and the Netherlands and claimed allegiance from all the German states in between.

Rallying the troops under his new command, Napoleon took the offensive on April 12, 1796. In succession he defeated and separated the Austrian and the Sardinian armies, then marched on Turin. When the Sardinian king, Victor Amadeus III, asked for an armistice and then sued for peace, Nice and Savoy, occupied by the French since 1792, were annexed to the republic. Bonaparte fought on against the Austrians, occupying Milan before he was held up at Mantua. While his army besieged the great fortress, he signed armistices with the duke of Parma, the duke of Modena, and ultimately with Pope Pius VI. He took an interest in the political organization of Italy, setting up a republican regime in Lombardy. In October 1796 he merged Modena and Reggio nell'Emilia with the Papal States of Bologna and Ferrara to create the Cisalpine Republic. He even sent an expeditionary force to recover Corsica after the British had evacuated.

Meanwhile, four times Austrian armies had swept down from the Alps to relieve Mantua, and four times Bonaparte had routed them. With the last Austrian defeat at Rivoli in January 1797, Mantua itself capitulated and Napoleon wasted no time in marching on Vienna. He had hied his army within about 60 miles of the Austrian capital before the House of Hapsburg sued for an armistice. With Austria standing alone against Napoleon in Italy, Francis II felt he had no choice but to come to terms with France, which he did in a preliminary peace signed on April 18, 1797, at Leoben.

Back in Paris, royalist gains in the latest election occupied Napoleon's attention, as he urged the Directory on to a coup in July, which failed. Bonaparte then dispatched one of his generals and several officers to mount another. This one, the coup d'état of 18 Fructidor (September 4, 1797) proved successful. Having eliminated the royalists' friends from the government and legislative councils, the young general saw his prestige rise again. Hailed as the savior of the Directory, he turned to conclude—to the dismay of the Directory itself—the Treaty of Campo Formio as he thought best.

Terms

Essentially, in exchange for Dalmatia and Venetia, Francis II recognized all of the conquests of the French Republic, including the long-cherished French dream of establishing hegemony over Italy. In addition, the treaty provided for a congress to be convened at Rastadt to determine the future of Germany:

XX

A Convention shall take place at Rastadt, composed of Plenipotentiaries of the Germanic Empire and those of the Republic of France to institute Peace between the two powers. This Convention shall take place a month following the signature of the present Treaty or sooner, if possible.

However, Austria stacked the deck by promising in secret articles to the Treaty of Campo Formio just which limited parts of the left bank of the Rhine France might receive.

17th of October Secret Articles and Additional Agreements of the Campo Formio Treaty of 26 Vendémiaire An. 6.

I

His Majesty, the Emperor, King of Hungary and Bohemia agrees to extending the frontiers of the Republic of France to the boundary line set in writing as follows and pledges to employ his good offices following peace with the German Empire to secure for the Republic of France this boundary line. That is to say:

The left bank of the Rhine River from the Suisse frontier below Bale to the junction of the Nette River below Andernach, including the bridgehead of Manheim on the left bank of the Rhine River and the city and fortress of Mayance, both banks of the Nette River from the mouth to the source near Bruch, from there a boundary line passing through Senscherode and Borley to Kerpen and from that city to Udelhofen, Blandenheim, Marmagen, Jactenizt, Cale, Gemund, including all the districts and suburbs of these communities, then the two banks of the Olff River to its mouth in the Roer River, the two banks of the Roer River, including Heimbach, Nideggen, Duren and Juliers with its districts and suburbs and all the river villages and suburbs to Limnich, from there a boundary line crossing Roffems and Thalens, Dalen, Hilas, Papdermod Laterforst, Radenberg, Haversloo, if these are situated on the line drawn, Anderheide, Halderkirchen, Wambach, Herrigen, and Grobray, with the city of Venloo and its district. Should the good offices of His Majesty, the Emperor, King of Hungary and Bohemia not be able to convince the Germanic Empire to consent to these terms, His Majesty, the Emperor formally pledges himself to allocate to the Army of the Empire only that share which shall be normally used in the forts, thereby not encroaching on the amity which has been established between His said Majesty and the Republic of France.

II

His Majesty, the Emperor, King of Hungary and Bohemia shall also use his good offices when pacification takes place with the Germanic Empire:

(1) To secure free navigation rights for the Republic of France and the Emperor's States situated on the right bank of the river from Huningue to the entrance of the Republic of Batavia's territory.

(2) To see that the owner of the German section situated opposite the mouth of the Moselle River shall never, under any pretext be allowed to obstruct free navigation, entry and exit of ships, boats or others at the mouth of the River.

(3) To assure for the Republic of France free navigation of the Meuse River and see that all tolls and other claims which might be established from Venloo to its entry into the territory of Batavia be stopped.

III

To the Republic of France, His Imperial and Royal Majesty renounces for himself and his successors all sovereignty and propriety of the County of Falkenstein and its annexes.

IV

The countries which His Majesty, the Emperor, King of Hungary and Bohemia shall possess by virtue of Article VI. of the official Treaty signed today and which shall also serve as compensation for and replace countries renounced in Article III. and VII. of said Treaty as well as Article III. as stated above.

These renunciations will be validated only when His Imperial and Royal Majesty's troops will occupy the countries he acquires as effected by said articles.

V

The Republic of France shall use its good offices to see that His Majesty, the Emperor obtains the Archbishopric of Salzburg and the section of Bavaria situated between the Archbishopric of Salzburg, the Inn and Salza Rivers and the Tyrol River, including the city of Wasserbourg on the right bank of the Inn River with a district of 3,000 meters.

VI

His Imperial and Royal Majesty shall cede to the Republic of France, when Peace is declared in the Empire, full sovereignty and propriety of Frickthal and all territories which belong to the Austrian realm on the left bank of the Rhine River between Zurich and Bale providing that His Majesty obtains upon a peace declaration an equal compensation in Germany, approved and declared convenient thereof.

The Republic of France will then unite these countries to the Republic of Helvetia providing convenient and mutual arrangements, showing no prejudices to His Majesty, the Emperor and King and his Empire.

VII

It is agreed between the two contracting powers, upon cessation of hostilities in the German Empire, that should the Republic of France gain territorial acquisitions in Germany, His Majesty, the Emperor, King of Hungary and Bohemia shall also obtain reciprocal and equal lands. The same understanding shall apply in reverse should His Imperial and Royal Majesty acquire any territories, thus allowing the Republic of France to gain equal and proportionate territories.

VIII

To Prince de Nassau Dietz, formerly Stadthouder of Holland, a territorial indemnity shall be given; however this indemnity shall not be allocated in the neighborhood of any Austrian possession or in the Republic of Batavia.

IX

Since the Republic of France has no difficulty restituting to the King of Prussia his possessions on the left bank of the Rhine River: there shall, therefore, be no question of securing new acquisitions for the King of Prussia although the two contracting Powers mutually guarantee each other such acquisitions.

X

If the King of Prussia consents to ceding to the Republic of France and to the Republic of Batavia small portions of its territory which are situated on the left bank of the Meuse River, and also the gore of Sevenaer and other possessions near the Issel River, His Majesty, the Emperor, King of Hungary and Bohemia shall use his good offices to assist in these matters and have these territories taken over by the German Empire.

Should the present article not be executed, the preceding one shall stand as is and be executed in full.

XI

His Majesty, the Emperor, does not object to the Republic of France's disposition of his landed Imperial Majesty's estates in feudal tenure in the Republic of Liguria.

His Majesty the Emperor shall bring his good offices together with those of the Republic of France in ar effort to influence the Germanic Empire to renounce its sovereign rights in Italy and especially in countries which are part of the Cisalpine and Liguria Republics and also countries situated between the Toscane River and the States of Parma, the Liguria Republic and Lacquoise and the former Modena which landed estates in feudal tenure shall make up the Cisalpine Republic.

XII

When peace is declared in the Germanic Empire, His Majesty, the Emperor, King of Hungary and Bohemia and the Republic of France shall unite their good offices in an effort to obtain for the different Princes and the States of the Empire adequate and proper compensations. The aforementioned who may have suffered loss of territories and certain rights under the present Treaty of Peace and its stipulations or when said concluded Treaty is drawn up with the Germanic Empire and in particular with the Electors of Mayence, Treves, and Cologne, the Palatin Elector de Baviere the Duc de Wurtemberg and Teck, the Margrave de Bode, the Duc de Deux-Pont, the Landgraves of Hesse-Cassel and Darmstadt, the Princes de Nassau Sarbruck, de Salm Kyrbourg, Loewenstein-Wertheim and de Wiedrunkel, and the Count de la Leyen, shall receive these compensations as regulated in common accord with the Republic of France.

XIII

His Majesty, the Emperor's troops shall evacuate the city and fortress of Mayance, Ehrenbreitstein, Philippsbourg, Manheim, Konigstein, Ulm, and Ingolstadt and all the territories belonging to the Germanic Empire, including its hereditary States within twenty days following the exchange of ratifications of the present Treaty.

XIV

The present secret articles shall stand in full force and validity as if they were inserted word for word in the original Treaty of Peace signed of this day.

They shall be ratified at the same time by the two contracting parties and the acts of ratification in due form shall be exchanged at Rastadt.

Done and signed at Camp-Formio the 17th of October, 1797 (27 vendemiaire an 6.) of the Republic of France one and indivisible.

BONAPARTE;
MARQUIS DE GALLO;
LOUIS, COMTE DE COBENZL;
MAJOR-GENERAL COMTE DE MEERVEILDT;
BARON DE DEGELMANN.

Articles 3 through 5 of the main part of the treaty defined the Austrian cessions and concessions directly to France:

III

His Majesty, the Emperor, King of Hungary and Bohemia, renounces in favor of the Republic of France, for himself and his successors, all claims, rights and titles to the Belgian provinces, known as the Austrian Netherlands. The Republic of France shall possess these territories for perpetuity, have full sovereignty and ownership including all territorial benefits resulting thereby.

IV

All pre-war mortgage debts on the aforemen-tioned territories whose contracts shall be attested to be official and legal shall be honored by the Republic of France. The Plenipotentiaries of His Majesty, the Emperor, King of Hungary and Bohemia shall submit these as soon as possible to the Plenipotentiaries of the Republic of France. This to be done before final ratifications have started in order that the two contracting powers may at the time they convene be properly informed of all necessary, pertinent and additional data relating to the article in question.

V

His Majesty, the Emperor, King of Hungary and Bohemia agrees to the Republic of France having full sovereignty and possession of the Venetian Isles of the Levant; that is to say Corfu, Zente, Cephalona, Saint-Maura, Cerigo, as well as other independent Isles, such as Butrint, Larta, Vonitsa and in general all the Venetian sites in Albania situated lower than the Gulf of Lodrino.

By Articles 7 and 8, Austria acknowledged the Cisalpine Republic:

VII

His Majesty, the Emperor, King of Hungary and Bohemia renounces in perpetuity for himself and his successors and executors, in favor of the Cisalpine Republic, all rights and titles emanating from these rights which His said Majesty could hold on these territories and possessed before the war and which now comprise the Cisalpine Republic. The Cisalpine Republic shall own these in full sovereignty and propriety, with all territorial benefits thereof.

VIII

His Majesty, the Emperor, King of Hungary and Bohemia, recognizes the Cisalpine Republic as an independent and autonomous power.

This Republic's territory will include the former section of Austrian Lombardy, Bergamo, Brescia, the city and fortress of Mantu, Mantuan, Peschiera, part of the former Venetian Isles, west and south of the border designated in Article VI. for the Italian frontier States of His Majesty, the Emperor; Modena, the principalities of Massa and Carrara and the three legations of Bologna, Ferrara and Romana.

Article 6 confirmed Austria in the possession of Venetia and Dalmatia:

VI

The Republic of France agrees to His Majesty, the Emperor and King retaining possession in full sovereignty and ownership of the countries listed as follows; that is to say, Istria, Dalmatia, the Adriatique Venetian Iles, the mouth of the Cattaro, the city of Venice and all countries situated in boundaries within the hereditary States of His Majesty, the Emperor and King, the Adriatique Sea and a border line starting from the Tyrol River, following the Falls situated in front of the Gardola, then crossing the Lake of Garda to Cise; from there, a military border to San-Giacomo, giving both parties equal advantages; this border to be decided upon by officers assigned to the engineer corps of their respective regiments and nominated by each contracting Parties before the exchange of ratifications of the present Treaty. The lines of demarcation shall then pass through the Adige River at San-Giacomo, follow the left bank of this river to the mouth of the Blanc Canal, including the section of Porto-Legnago, which is to be found on the right bank of the Adige River and which shall include a district encompassing three thousand meters. The border will then continue on, skirting the right bank of the Blanc Canal, the left bank of the Tartarus River, the left bank of the Canal of Polesina, up to the mouth of the Po River, following the left bank of the river to the sea.

Consequences

With the Treaty of Campo Formio, Bonaparte began reshaping the map of Europe, a habit that would continue throughout his career. The Directory, disturbed by Napoleon's extralegal assumption of authority, let it be known that it was displeased because the treaty had ceded Venice to the Austrians but did not secure the left bank of the Rhine for France. On the other hand, not only had Napoleon reorganized parts of Europe, he had, like a good radical republican, spread the Revolution to northern Italy, encouraging Jacobin propaganda in Venetia. Returning to Paris with a victory in hand after five years of war on the Continent, Bonaparte's popularity, despite the naysaying of the politicians, reached new heights. The glory was his, and a new figure was strutting across the stage of world history. Moreover, his consolidation of the northern Italian republics led many Italian patriots to hope for the future formation of a single and indivisible "Italian Republic" modeled on the French. As would often be the case, out of Bonaparte's conquests was born a new nationalism.

TREATY OF AMIENS

TREATY AT A GLANCE

Completed
March 27, 1802, at Amiens, France

Signatories
Great Britain and the French Republic, Spain, and
the Batavian Republic (Holland)

Overview
The Treaty of Amiens marked the end of the French Revolutionary
Wars and may be seen as the overture to the Napoleonic Wars of
1803–15. By this treaty, France was confirmed in its recent Continental acquisitions (except for southern Italy), and Great Britain
surrendered most of its recent naval conquests.

Historical Background

The French Revolutionary Wars were fought between
France and the other European powers in the wake of
the French Revolution, from 1792 to 1802. After the
brief hiatus created by the Treaty of Amiens, the wars
continued as the Napoleonic Wars. The French Revolutionary Wars ranged from the Caribbean to the
Indian Ocean but were concentrated primarily in Holland (the Low Countries), the Rhineland, and Lombardy.

The French Revolution charged the traditional
antagonisms between France and its neighbors, particularly Austria, with ideological significance and
urgency. Every conflict became a de facto confrontation between what the revolutionaries defined as
democracy versus the old aristocratic order. The
French republicans, fearing Austrian support of an
armed assembly of displaced French nobles at
Coblentz, declared war on Austria and Prussia in April
1792. At first the war went disastrously for France, and
the Prussian army advanced closer and closer to Paris
until it was stopped at the Battle of Valmy (September
20, 1792). The Prussians retired, and the French next
defeated the Austrians at Jemappes (November 6,
1792), then overran the Austrian Netherlands (Belgium). In response, Britain, Holland, Sardinia, and
Spain aligned themselves as the First Coalition against
France. In 1793 the Coalition repelled a French invasion of Holland at the Battle of Neerwinden (March
18), then attacked France on every frontier, seeking to
exploit the internal dissent that swept France.

Radical republican factions seized power through
the Reign of Terror in order to suppress civil war, and
the republic quickly built the world's first national con-
script army. By 1794 this massive force was making
rapid advances throughout Europe. The Battle of Fleurus (June 26, 1794) resulted in French conquest of the
Low Countries. In 1795 Prussia declared its neutrality,
and Holland and Spain became, for all practical purposes, satellites of France. In October 1797 Austria
made peace with France by the TREATY OF CAMPO
FORMIO after suffering defeat in the extraordinary Italian campaign (1796–97) conducted by Napoleon
Bonaparte.

The events culminating in Campo Formio isolated
Great Britain, which had acted as the chief source of
funds for the anti-French alliances. The nation was
vulnerable to invasion, but the French fleet proved no
match for the Royal Navy, which defeated it at the
Glorious First of June (1794) and then dealt a decisive
blow to the Spanish fleet off Cape St. Vincent (February 14, 1797) and to the Dutch fleet at Camperdown
(October 11, 1797). Turning from its plans against
England, the French Directory approved Napoleon's
1798 proposal to conquer Egypt. Despite a brilliant
land campaign, Napoleon's gains were largely nullified
by Admiral Horatio Nelson's victory over the French
fleet in the Battle of the Nile (August 1, 1798) and by
the Turks' successful defense of Acre.

In the meantime, while Napoleon was fighting in
Egypt, a Second Coalition, consisting of Britain, Aus-
tria, Russia, and Turkey, was formed against France.
This, too, failed, and the French Republic was again

175

victorious. On September 25, 1799, Russian armies were turned back at Zurich, leaving the Austrians exposed and forcing them to retire from the Rhine. A planned Anglo-Russian landing in Holland had to be aborted. Next, Napoleon returned from Egypt to defeat the Austrians at the spectacular Battle of Marengo (June 14, 1800). This, coupled with another French victory at Hohenlinden (December 3, 1800), prompted the Austrians to make peace at Luneville on February 9, 1801. Britain, now isolated, struck out at the Danish fleet at Copenhagen (April 2, 1801) and also destroyed Napoleon's Egyptian army at Alexandria (August 1801). However, aware of its exposure, Britain sued for peace at Amiens.

Terms

Although the Treaty of Amiens served as an entr'acte between the French Revolutionary Wars and the Napoleonic Wars, it was framed in the usual language of permanence. The body of the treaty, Articles 3 through 11 stipulated the disposition of prizes won and lost during the wars. In sum, France retained all that it had taken on the Continent, except for southern Italy, while Great Britain surrendered most of what it had won by sea.

I

There shall be peace, friendship; and good understanding between his Majesty the King of the United Kingdom of Great Britain and Ireland, his heirs and successors, on the one part; and the French Republic, his Majesty the King of Spain, his heirs and successors and the Batavian Republic, on the other part. The contracting parties shall give the greatest attention to maintain between themselves and their states a perfect harmony, and without allowing, on either side, any kind of hostilities, by sea or by land, to be committed for any cause, or under any pretence whatsoever.

They shall carefully avoid everything which might hereafter affect the union happily re-established, and they shall not afford any assistance or protection, directly or indirectly, to those who should cause prejudice to any of them.

II

All the prisoners on either side, as well by land as by sea, and the hostages carried away or given during the war, and to this day, shall be restored, without ransom, in six weeks at latest, to be computed from the day of the exchange of the ratifications of the present treaty, and on paying the debts which they have contracted during their captivity. Each contracting party shall respectively discharge the advances which have been made by any of the contracting parties for the subsistence and maintenance of the prisoners in the countries where they have been detained. For this purpose, a commission shall be appointed by agreement, which shall be specially charged to ascertain and regulate the compensation which may be due to either of the contracting powers. The time and place where the said commissioners shall take into account the expenses occasioned not only by the prisoners of the respective nations, but also by the foreign troops, who, before they were made prisoners, were in the pay, or at the disposal of any of the contracting parties.

III

His Britannic Majesty restores to the French Republic and her allies, namely, his Catholic Majesty and the Batavian republic, all the possessions and colonies which belonged to them respectively, and which had been occupied or conquered by the British forces in the course of the war, with the exception of the island of Trinidad, and the Dutch possessions in the island of Ceylon.

IV

His Catholic Majesty cedes and guarantees, in full right and sovereignty to his Britannic Majesty, the island of Trinidad.

V

The Batavian republic cedes and guarantees, in full right and sovereignty to his Britannic Majesty, all the possessions and establishments in the island of Ceylon, which belonged, before the war, to the republic of the United Provinces, or to their East India Company.

VI

The Cape of Good Hope remains in full sovereignty to the Batavian republic, as it was before the war.

The ships of every description belonging to the other contracting parties, shall have the right to put in there, and to purchase such supplies as they may stand in need of as heretofore, without paying any other duties than those to which the ships of the Batavian republic are subjected.

VII

The territories and possessions of her Most Faithful Majesty are maintained in their integrity, such as they were previous to the commencement of the war.

Nevertheless, the limits of French and Portuguese Guiana shall be determined by the river Arawari, which falls into the ocean below North Cape, near the Isle Neuve, and the Island of Penitence, about a degree and one third of north latitude. These limits shall follow the course of the river Arawari, from that of its mouth which is at the greatest distance from the North Cape to its source, and thence in a direct line from its source to the river Branco, towards the west. The northern bank of the river Arawari, from its mouth to its source, and the lands which are situated to the north of the line of the limits above fixed, shall consequently belong in full sovereignty to the French republic. The southern bank of the said river from its source, and all the lands to the southward of the said line of demarcation, shall belong to her Most Faithful Majesty. The navigation of the river Arawari shall be common to both nations.

The arrangements which have taken place between the courts of Madrid and of Lisbon, for the settlement of their frontiers in Europe, shall, however, be executed conformably to the treaty of Badajos.

VIII

The territories, possessions, and rights of the Ottoman Porte are hereby maintained in their integrity, such as they were previous to the war.

IX

The republic of the Seven Islands is hereby acknowledged.

X

The islands of Malta, Gozo, and Comino shall be restored to the Order of St. John of Jerusalem, and shall be held by it upon the same conditions on which the Order held them previous to the war, and under the following stipulations:

(1) The Knights of the Order, whose *langues* shall continue to subsist after the exchange of the ratifications of the present treaty, are invited to return to Malta, as soon as that exchange shall have taken place. They shall there form a general Chapter, and shall proceed to the election of a Grand Master, to be chosen from amongst the natives of those nations which preserve *langues*, if no such election have been already made since the exchange of the ratification of the preliminary articles of peace. It is understood that an election which shall have been made subsequent to that period, shall alone be considered as valid, to the exclusion of every other which shall have taken place at any time previous to the said period.

(2) The governments of Great Britain and the French republic, being desirous of placing the Order of St. John, and the island of Malta, in a state of entire independence on each of those powers, do agree, that there shall be henceforth no English nor French *langues*; and that no individual belonging to either of the said powers shall be admissible into the Order.

(3) A Maltese *langue* shall be established, to be supported out of the land revenues and commercial duties of the island. There shall be dignities, with appointments, and an auberge appropriated to this langue; no proofs of nobility shall be necessary for the admission of Knights of the said *langue*; they shall be competent to hold every office, and to enjoy every privilege in the like manner as the Knights of the other langues. The municipal, revenue, civil, judicial, and other offices under the government of the island, shall be filled, at least in the proportion of one half, by native inhabitants of Malta, Gozo, and Comino.

(4) The forces of his Britannic Majesty shall evacuate the island and its dependencies, within three months after the exchange of the ratifications, or sooner if it can be done: at that period the island shall be delivered up to the Order in the state in which it now is, provided that the Grand Master, or commissioners fully empowered according to the statutes of the Order, be upon the island to receive possession; and that the force to be furnished by his Sicilian Majesty, as hereafter stipulated, shall be arrived there.

(5) The garrison of the island shall, at all times, consist at least one half of native Maltese; and the Order shall have the liberty of recruiting for the remainder of the garrison from the natives of those countries only that shall continue to possess *langues*. The native Maltese troops shall be officered by Maltese: the supreme command of the garrison, as well as the appointment of the officers, shall be invested in the Grand Master of the Order; and he shall not be at liberty to divest himself of it, even for a time, except in favor of a Knight of the Order, and in consequence of the opinion of the council of the Order.

(6) The independence of the islands of Malta, Gozo, and Comino, as well as the present arrangement, shall be under the protection and guarantee of Great Britain, France, Austria, Russia, Spain, and Prussia.

(7) The perpetual neutrality of the Order, and of the island of Malta and its dependencies, is hereby declared.

(8) The ports of Malta shall be open to the commerce and navigation of all nations, who shall pay equal and moderate duties. These duties shall be applied to the support of the Maltese *langue*, in the manner specified in paragraph 3, to that of the civil and military establishments of the island, and to that of a Lazaretto, open to all flags.

(9) The Barbary States are excepted from the provisions of the two preceding paragraphs, until, by means of an arrangement to be made by the contracting parties, the system of hostility which subsists between the said Barbary States, the Order of St. John, and the powers possessing *langues*, or taking part in the formation of them, shall be terminated.

(10) The Order shall be governed, both in spiritual and temporal matters, by the same statutes that were in force at the time when the Knights quitted the island, so far as the same shall not be derogated from by the present treaty.

(11) The stipulations contained in paragraphs 3, 5, 7, 8, and 10, shall be converted into laws and perpetual statutes of the Order, in the customary manner. And the Grand Master, (or if he should not be in the island at the time of its restitution to the Order, his representative,) as well as his successors, shall be bound to make oath to observe them punctually.

(12) His Sicilian Majesty shall be invited to furnish two thousand men, natives of his dominions, to serve as a garrison for the several fortresses upon the island. This force shall remain there for one year, from the period of the restitution of the island to the Knights; after the expiration of which term, if the Order of St. John shall not, in the opinion of the guarantying powers, have raised a sufficient force to garrison the island and its dependencies, in the manner proposed in paragraph 5, the Neapolitan troops shall remain, until they shall be relieved by another force, judged to be sufficient by the said powers.

(13) The several powers specified in paragraph 6, *vide'licet*, Great Britain, France, Austria, Russia, Spain, and Prussia, shall be invited to accede to the present arrangement.

XI

The French forces shall evacuate the kingdom of Naples and the Roman territory: the English forces shall in like manner evacuate Porto Ferrajo, and generally all the ports and islands which they may occupy in the Mediterranean, or in the Adriatic.

Consequences

By the Treaty of Amiens, a general peace was reestablished in Europe, but Napoleon Bonaparte's success in the French Revolutionary Wars had allowed him to maneuver politically at home into a position of near dictatorial powers, and Bonaparte's notion of international peace bore little resemblance to that of, say, Great Britain. Already First Consul of the French Republic, Bonaparte's prestige was such that his friends—with a few hints from Napoleon—proposed to offer him a "token of national gratitude." A referendum was mounted to answer the simple question "Shall Napoleon Bonaparte be consul for life?" The vote was overwhelmingly yes, and Napoleon assumed the reins of state with the right to name his own successor.

If the Treaty of Amiens marked for the British the absolute limit beyond which they were never prepared to go, for Napoleon it marked the starting point of a new French ascendancy in the world. Future wars were inevitable.

TREATY OF PRESSBURG

TREATY AT A GLANCE

Completed
December 26, 1805, at Pressburg
(present-day Bratislava, Czech Republic)

Signatories
France and Austria

Overview
The Treaty of Pressburg was the fruit of Napoleon's signal victory over the Austrians and Russians at the Battle of Austerlitz (December 2, 1805). By this treaty, Austria conveyed to Napoleon Venice and Dalmatia (recognizing Napoleon as king of Italy), as well as surrendering territories to Bavaria, Württemberg, and Baden.

Historical Background

The French Revolutionary Wars (see the introduction to this chapter, TREATY OF CAMPO FORMIO, and TREATY OF AMIENS) evolved, like the Revolution itself, into a prosecution of Napoleon Bonaparte's personal ambitions. Emerging from those wars as First Consul for Life, Napoleon was determined to recover St-Domingue, which had rebelled and renamed itself Haiti; to occupy Louisiana, which had been ceded to France by Spain in 1800; and perhaps to reconquer Egypt. In any case, it was clear he intended to extend French influence in both the Mediterranean and the Indian Ocean, and he was advancing France beyond what the rest of Europe considered its natural frontiers: incorporating the Piedmont into his revolutionary republic, imposing a democratic and French-friendly government on the Swiss Confederation, and compensating dispossessed German princes for their former Rhine territories with shares in the ecclesiastical states he had secularized.

The English were upset by all this, by France's peacetime expansions, and especially by the First Consul's attempt to reserve half of Europe as a market for French goods without lowering customs duties. In the midst of a maritime commercial explosion of its own, Great Britain could barely tolerate the fact that one state, one man, should command the coast of the Continent from Genoa to Antwerp, and over Malta the English dug in their heels. The British had taken Malta when the French occupation collapsed during the last stage of the Revolutionary Wars. By the Treaty of Amiens, they were supposed to give it back to the

Knights Hospitallers, from whom Napoleon had seized it. Using some excuse—that the French had not yet evacuated certain Neapolitan ports—the British refused to leave the island.

As French-British relations grew strained over England's defiance of the precarious peace terms, the British used the brouhaha as the pretext for declaring a new war in 1803. Bonaparte raised a large army, but he could not hold back the British as they seized French colonial possessions one after the other. Although for now he had only Great Britain to fight, Napoleon realized he could only hope for victory by landing his Grand Army on the British Isles, while they in turn knew that they could only ultimately defeat the French by forming another continental coalition against him. Bonaparte concentrated his troops at Boulogne and gathered nearly 2,000 ships between Brest and Antwerp, but his problem remained the same as it had always been: to cross the Channel, he needed control of the seas, and the French fleet was still far inferior to the British navy. Even when he induced Spain to declare war against Britain in December 1804, the combined fleets were no match for anything more than a squadron of English ships. Napoleon decided that if he massed the French-Spanish armada in the Antilles, he could lure a British squadron into these waters and defeat it, which in turn would give him rough parity with Britain at sea.

Meanwhile, Napoleon, now acclaimed emperor of France, annexed Genoa and crowned himself king of Italy, an act that gave the British all they needed to succeed in organizing a new anti-French coalition, the

Third Coalition, also consisting of Austria, Russia, Sweden, and Naples. Abandoning his plans for the moment to invade England, the emperor sent his Grand Army against the Austrians at Ulm, winning an overwhelming victory there in October 1805. That same month, his scheme for defeating Britain at sea came a cropper. France's Mediterranean squadron, under Admiral Pierre de Villeneuve, had earlier in the summer arrived in the Antilles to find no Spanish fleet awaiting. Alone, pursued by England's great admiral Horatio Nelson, and not daring to attack him, Villeneuve turned sail toward Europe and took refuge off the Spanish coast at Cadiz in July 1805. The English threw up a blockade, and there Villeneuve remained until October, when, goaded by accusations of cowardice from his emperor, he decided to run the blockade with the help of a Spanish squadron. Off Cape Trafalgar on October 21, 1805, Lord Nelson attacked the Franco-Spanish fleet and utterly destroyed it, losing his own life in the battle. A decisive victory, Trafalgar put paid to any danger of invasion and gave Great Britain rule of the high seas.

Less concerned with the long-term implications than he might otherwise have been, Napoleon remained occupied with the war he was fighting inland. In mid-November he occupied Vienna, then routed the Russians and Austrians at the Battle of Austerlitz on December 2, 1805, eliminating the Austrians from the coalition and evicting them from Italy under the ensuing Treaty of Pressburg.

Terms

Following the French emperor's most celebrated victory so far, the Treaty of Pressburg forced Austria to renounce all influence in Italy and cede not only Venetia and Dalmatia to Napoleon but also vast territories in Germany to his protégés Bavaria, Württemberg, and Baden. It allowed the French to dethrone the Bourbons in Naples and bestow that kingdom on Napoleon's brother Joseph. Furthermore, it created a French-controlled federation that embraced all western Germany. The principal articles of the treaty enumerated Austria's cessions to Napoleon:

IV

The Emperor of Germany and of Austria renounces not only for himself but also for his heirs and successors, to the part of the states of the Republic of Venice, ceded to him by the Treaties of Campo Formio and Luneville, which shall be united forever with the Kingdom of Italy.

V

H. M. the Emperor of Germany and of Austria recognizes H. M. the Emperor of the French as King of Italy.

It is agreed, however, in conformity to the declaration made by H. M. the Emperor of the French, at the time he took the Crown of Italy, that as soon as the powers named in that declaration shall have fulfilled the conditions found expressed therein, the Crowns of France and Italy shall be separated forever, and can no longer, in any case, be united over the same head. H. M. the Emperor of Germany and Austria engages himself to recognize, at the time of separation, the successor whom H. M. the Emperor of the French shall have chosen as King of Italy.

VI

The present Treaty is declared common to Their Most Serene Highnesses, the Electors of Bavaria, of Wurtemberg and of Baden, and to the Batavian Republic, all allies in the present war of H. M. the Emperor of the French, King of Italy.

VII

The Electors of Bavaria and of Wurtemberg having taken the title of King, without however, ceasing to belong to the German confederation, H. M. the Emperor of Germany and of Austria recognizes them in title and rank.

VIII

H. M. the Emperor of Germany and Austria renounces, for himself, his respective heirs and successors as well as for the Princes of His House, their heirs and successors, the principalities, seigniorages, domains and territories hereinafter designated:

Cedes and abandons, to His Majesty the King of Bavaria, the Margraviate of Burgau and its dependencies; the Principality of Eichstadt; the part of the territory of Passau belonging to His Royal Highness, the Elector of Salzburg, situated between Bohemia, Austria, the Danube and the Inn, the County of Tyrol, including the Principalities of Brixen and of Trent; the seven seigniorages of the Voralberg with their enclaves; the County of Hohenems; the County of Konigsegg-Rothenfels; the seigniorages of Tetnang and Argen, and the city and territory of Lindau;

To His Majesty, the King of Wurtemberg the five cities known as the cities of the Danube, to wit: Ehingen, Munderkingen, Reidlingen, Mengen and Sulgau, with their dependencies; the upper and lower County of Hohenberg, the Landgraviate of Nellenburg and the Prefecture of Altorff, with their dependencies (the city of Constance excepted), the part of Brisgau, forming an enclave in the Wurtemberg possessions and located to the East of a line drawn from Schlegelberg to Molbach; and the cities and territories of Willingen and Brentingen:

To His Highness, the Elector of Baden the Brisgau (to the exception of the enclave and of the separated portions, designated hereinabove) the Ortenau, and their dependencies; the city of Constance and the Commandery of Meinau.

The aforementioned principalities, seigniorages, domains and territories shall be owned respectively by

Their Majesties the Kings of Bavaria and of Wurtemberg and by His Most Serene Highness the Elector of Baden, either in suzerainty or in full ownership and sovereignty, in the same manner, with the same rights and prerogatives as H. M. the Emperor of Germany and of Austria possessed them, or the Princes of the House, and not otherwise. . .

XV

H. M. the Emperor of Germany and of Austria, as much for himself, his heirs and successors as for the Princes of His House, their heirs and successors, renounces all rights, either of sovereignty or suzerainty, all pretensions whatsoever, present or future, over all the states, without exception, of Their Majesties, the Kings of Bavaria and of Wurtemberg and of His Most Serene Highness the Elector of Baden and, generally, over all the states, domains and territories included in the circles [boundaries] of Bavaria, Franconia and Swabia, as well as any title or claim over the said domains and territories; and reciprocally, all pretensions, present or future, of the said states, to the charge of the House of Austria or its Princes, are and shall remain extinguished [abolished] forever; however, the renunciations, contained in the present article, in no manner concern the properties which are, by Article XI, or shall be, by virtue of Art. XII above, granted to their Royal Highnesses, the Archdukes designated in the said articles.

It was characteristic of Napoleon's style as a ruler and statesman that the treaty bore his personal signature in addition to that of his minister Talleyrand. Hitherto, monarchs had not customarily signed the treaty instruments, leaving that entirely to their plenipotentiaries.

> We have approved and approve the above Treaty, in each and all of the articles contained therein; declare that it is accepted, ratified and confirmed and promise that it shall be observed without violation. In faith of which, We have given these presents, signed by Our hand, countersigned and sealed with Our Imperial seal.
>
> At the Palace of Schönbrunn, 6 Nivôse an 14 [27 December, 1805]
>
> Signed:
> NAPOLEON

Consequences

The Treaty of Amiens separated the French Revolutionary Wars from the Napoleonic Wars; the Treaty of Pressburg was the first major treaty of the latter wars and had far-reaching effects. Not only did Napoleon achieve recognition as king of Italy and establish a veritable French imperium in central Europe; as a direct result of Pressburg, the Holy Roman Empire was dissolved (on August 6, 1806), most of the smaller German states disappeared, and the larger ones were grouped together as the Confederation of the Rhine, with Napoleon as Protector. Finally, Austerlitz and the Treaty of Pressburg heralded the ultimate collapse of the Third Coalition against Napoleon.

The treaty could hardly offset Trafalgar, though. Pressburg would have a long-term impact on European history mostly because, like other treaty settlements by Napoleon, it lit the fire of union in German hearths, but the implications of Trafalgar were both more immediate and even more wide ranging. It was one of those battles that changed the world, making possible the ascendancy of the British Empire in the 19th century and giving Britain a freedom of movement on the seas that would not be effectively challenged for another hundred years.

TREATY OF TILSIT

TREATY AT A GLANCE

Completed
July 7 and 9, 1807, at Tilsit, East Prussia (present-day Sovetsk, Russia)

Signatories
France and Russia (July 7); France and Prussia (July 9)

Overview
The Treaty of Tilsit ended the War of the Third Coalition, in which Russia, Prussia, and Austria were allied against Napoleonic France, giving Napoleon I almost total control over Europe.

Historical Background

While Napoleon's defeat of Austria at the Battle of Austerlitz and the resulting TREATY OF PRESSBURG heralded the collapse of the Third Coalition, the fighting continued for a while beyond the Hapsburg's withdrawal from the allied cause. Just a month before, in September 1806, Prussia had joined the Coalition, only now to be promptly defeated at Jena and Auerstadt. Russia acquitted herself better in the inconclusive fighting at Eylau in February 1807, briefly checking the French advance on the Russian frontier. Come summer, however, the French emperor was ready to push on, crushing Russian resistance. Napoleon's defeat of the Russians at the very hard-fought Battle of Friedland (June 14, 1807) brought the War of the Third Coalition to an end.

While the Russian czar, Alexander I, might well have continued the struggle, he was weary of his alliance with the British and chose instead to negotiate with Napoleon. The talks between the two autocrats commenced on June 25 on a raft in the Neman River near the East Prussian town of Tilsit. Subsequently, King Frederick Wilhelm III of Prussia also took part in the discussions.

Terms

The negotiations resulted in two documents collectively known as the Treaty of Tilsit. The documents signed on July 7 brought peace between France and Russia. Czar Alexander I recognized Napoleon's European conquests and—by secret articles within the treaty—agreed to mediate between France and Britain and to ally Russia with the French if mediation failed.

The terms Napoleon planned to propose to Britain were harsh. The British nation would abandon its colonial conquests since 1803 and would rescind the Orders in Council, which prohibited neutral trade with France and its allies.

By the document of July 9, Frederick William III ceded most of Prussia's territory west of the Elbe River to the French-controlled Kingdom of Westphalia. Prussia's Polish provinces were ceded to the newly created Duchy of Warsaw. Moreover, Prussia agreed to reduce the size of its army and to allow for the garrisoning of French troops within its borders. Finally, Prussia joined the Continental System, Napoleon's latest scheme against the stubborn English, a grand, worldwide economic embargo of trade with Great Britain.

Articles 4–9 of the July 7 document of the Treaty of Tilsit redefined Russia's western frontiers, taking territory from Prussia and giving it to Russia:

IV

His Majesty, the Emperor Napoleon, out of regard for His Majesty, the Emperor of all the Russias, and wishing to give proof of his sincere desire to unite the two nations in lasting friendship and trusting bonds, agrees to restitute to His Majesty, the King of Prussia—ally of His Majesty, the Emperor of all the Russias, all the conquered countries, cities and territories named as follows, that is to say: The section of the Duchy of Magdebourg situated to the right of the Elbe River, Priegnitz, the Uckermark River, *la moyenne et la Nouvelle Marche de Brandebourg*, with the exception of *Cotbuser Kreis*, or Circle of Cotbus in Basse-Lusace, which shall belong to His Majesty, the King of Saxony; the Duchy of Pomerania; high, low and new Silesia with the County of Glatz; the section of the Netze River district, situated north of the causeway going from Driesen to Schneidemuhl to the Vistula River via

Waldau, following the borders of the Circle of Brombert, the navigation right on the river of Netze and the Bromberg Canal, from Driesen to the Vistula River, reciprocally and free of all tolls: the Pomerelie River, the Isle of Nogat and the Vistula River, to the west of Old Prussia and north of the Circle of Culm, the Ermeland River, and finally the Kingdom of Prussia as it was the 1st of January 1772, with the strongholds of Spandau, Stettin, Custrin, Glogau, Breslau, Schweidnitz, Neisse, Brieg, Kosel and Glatz, and generally all the strongholds, citadels, castles and forts of the above mentioned countries in the State where said strongholds, citadels, castles and forts are to be found now, and also the town and citadel of Graudenz.

V

The provinces which were part of the Kingdom of Poland as of the first of January I 772, and which have passed on since then at various periods to Prussia shall, with the exception of countries named in the preceding article and those specified in Article IX of this Treaty, be possessed in full sovereignty by His Majesty, the King of Saxony. These possessions shall be given the name of Duchy of Varsovie and be governed by constitutions which shall assure the people privileges and liberties in conformance to their neighbors tranquility and welfare.

VI

The city of Danzig surrounded with a two kilometer radius shall be given its independence under the protection of His Majesty, the King of Prussia and His Majesty, the King of Saxony and shall be governed by the laws which were in effect at the time she ceased to govern herself.

VII

In order to communicate between the Kingdom of Saxony and the Duchy of Varsovie, the King of Saxony shall have free use of military roads crossing the possessions of His Majesty, the King of Prussia. The particular road, number of troops permitted to travel it, and bivouac areas shall be determined at a special meeting to take place between their Majesties under the mediators of France.

VIII

Neither His Majesty, the King of Prussia nor His Majesty, the King of Saxony or the city of Danzig shall have the authority to establish tolls and taxes of any kind or prohibit the navigation of the Vistula River.

IX

In order to establish natural borders between Russia and the Duchy of Varsovie the following territory surrounding the actual Russian frontiers shall be united for perpetuity to the Russian Empire: from the Bug River to the mouth of the Lossosna River; a border line starting at the mouth of the Thalweg-Bobra River, the Thalweg-Narew River to Suratz, from the Lisa River to its source near the village of Mien, from the tributary of the Nurzeck, taking its source from the same vil-

lage, from the Nurzeck River to its mouth above Nurr, and finally from the Thalweg of the Bug River ascending from it to the actual Russian frontiers.

Article 10, however, explicitly protected the private property of individuals, the general realignment of territories notwithstanding:

X

No individual, of whatever class or station in life domiciled or owning properties in territories specified in the preceding article shall be affected in anyway by the exchange be it in his rights, rank and status or his properties, pensions and revenues or any other benefits coming to him; nor shall he be pursued in anyway, be it politically or militarily for any part he played in the present hostilities being terminated by this Treaty. Said specifications shall apply to individuals domiciled in the Old Kingdom of Poland which shall be restituted to His Majesty, the King of Prussia and be known as the Duchy of Varsovie.

The July 9 document imposed most of the territorial cessions and other concessions on Prussia:

III

His Majesty, the King of Prussia recognizes His Majesty, the King of Naples, Joseph Napoleon and His Majesty, the King of Holland, Louis Napoleon.

IV

His Majesty, the King of Prussia in like manner recognizes the Confederation of the Rhine River, the actual State possessed by each Sovereign which partake in it, the titles given to some among them, either by the Confederations act or by Treaties of subsequent accession. Said Majesty promises to recognize, upon notification given to him by His Majesty, the Emperor Napoleon, the Sovereign who shall in the near future become members of the Confederation on a par in rank which shall be given to them by the Charter admitting them to the Confederation.

V

The present Treaty of Peace and Friendship is declared in effect for Their Majesties, the King of Naples and the King of Holland, and all confederate sovereigns of the Rhine River, allies of His Majesty, the Emperor Napoleon.

VI

His Majesty, the King of Prussia also recognizes His Highness, Prince Jerome Napoleon as King of Westphalia.

VII

His Majesty, the King of Prussia cedes in full propriety and sovereignty to the Kings, Princes or Grand Dukes who shall be designated by His Majesty, the Emperor of the French, King of Italy, all the Duchies, Marquisates, Principalities, Counties, Seigniories, and generally all the territories or part thereof as well as the domains and properties which His said Majesty, the King of Prussia possessed officially or otherwise, between the Rhine River and the Elbe River at the beginning of the present war.

VIII

The Kingdom of Westphalia shall be composed of possessions ceded by His Majesty, the King of Prussia to the left of the Elbe River and other States now in the possession of His Majesty, the Emperor Napoleon.

IX

His Majesty the King of Prussia shall recognize the arrangements made by His Majesty, Emperor Napoleon, as stated in the two preceding articles, in the same manner as if these were effected and incorporated in the present Treaty.

X

His Majesty the King of Prussia renounces for himself, his inheritors and successors, all actual or eventual rights which he might have or might claim,

1) on all territories, without exception, situated between the Rhine River and the Elbe River other than those designated in Article VII.

2) on those possessions belonging to His Majesty, the King of Saxony and the House of Anhalt, which are situated on the right of the Elbe River. Likewise, all actual or eventual rights and claims of States situated between the Elbe River and the Rhine River on territories in the possession of His Majesty, the King of Prussia, as they shall be recognized in the present Treaty, are and shall be obliterated for perpetuity.

XI

All pacts, agreements, treaties of alliance, manifest or secret, which might have been concluded between Prussia and any of the countries situated to the left of the Elbe River, and which would not have been broken during the present war, shall become obsolete and shall be considered null and void.

XII

His Majesty, the King of Prussia cedes in all propriety and sovereignty the *cotbuser kreis* or Circle of Cotbus in Basse-Lusace to His Majesty, the King of Saxony.

XIII

His Majesty, the King of Prussia renounces for perpetuity possession of all the provinces which had belonged to the Kingdom of Poland and after the 1st of January 1772 passed at various periods under Prussian rule, with the exception of Ermeland and countries situated west of Old Prussia, east of Pomerania, north of the Circle of Culm, following a line going from the Vistula River at Schneidemuhl through Waldau following the confines of the Circle of Bromberg and the seawall going from Schneidemuhl to Driesen which shall with the city of and citadel of Grandenz

and villages of Neudorff, Parschken and Swierkorzy, continue to be possessed in all propriety and sovereignty by His Majesty, the King of Prussia.

XIV

His Majesty, the King of Prussia also renounces for perpetuity possession of the city of Danzig.

On a raft anchored in the middle of the Neman River, the emperor of France and the czar of all the Russias had forced Prussia to give up half her territory and, in effect, divided up the control of Europe, Napoleon taking the west and Alexander the east.

As the negotiations drew to a close, Alexander promised vaguely to make an attack on British possessions in India.

Consequences

The British, after Tilsit, once again found themselves dangerously isolated. Nevertheless, they moved quickly and used their superb navy to seize the Danish and Portuguese fleets before Napoleon could secure them. The two powers blockaded one another's ports. To be sure, the Continental System created economic hardship in Britain, but in no way approaching the degree Napoleon had hoped for. Smuggling was common, and Britannia, courtesy of Trafalgar, continued to rule the waves and to trade actively and openly with its colonies. Moreover, the Continental System caused drastic shortages of goods throughout Europe and greatly inflated prices on many commodities, creating much discontent, especially in the Netherlands and northern Germany.

With the Continental System faltering, Napoleon invaded Spain in order, ultimately, to gain a foothold in Spanish America, which would give him a badly needed economic advantage. The Spanish people, however, staged widespread resistance to the occupation, giving England an opportunity to land troops on the Iberian Peninsula. This breached Napoleon's blockade and prompted Austria to enter the fray against Napoleon. The armies clashed at the Battle of Wagram, which resulted in total defeat for the Austrians, who agreed to the humiliating TREATY OF SCHÖNBRUNN (October 14, 1809). Despite Wagram, Napoleon had reached the high-water mark of his power as resistance to the Continental System grew, culminating in Russia's break with it, which prompted Napoleon's invasion of Russia in June 1812, abruptly abrogating the Treaty of Tilsit.

TREATY OF SCHÖNBRUNN (TREATY OF VIENNA)

TREATY AT A GLANCE

Completed
October 14, 1809, at Schönbrunn, Vienna
(with a Military Convention done on October 27)

Signatories
France and Austria

Overview
After England landed troops on the Iberian peninsula against Napoleon, Austria engaged the French at the Battle of Wagram (July 5–6, 1809), suffering a crushing defeat. The result was the Treaty of Schönbrunn, imposing harsh penalties on Austria, reaffirming Napoleon's dominance in Europe, but also marking the zenith of that dominance.

Historical Background

Following the humiliating concessions made by Prussia and the less humiliating accord with Russia, both made in the TREATY OF TILSIT (July 7–9, 1807), Napoleon moved in November and December 1807 against Portugal. His Continental System—aimed at killing the world's trade with archenemy England—was failing, and he realized that for the blockade to work, he needed to enforce it vigorously throughout Europe. That meant seizing a Portugal that had made clear from the beginning its opposition to Napoleon's trade restrictions. Spain's Charles IV allowed French troops passage across the Iberian peninsula, and they soon occupied Lisbon. The presence of Napoleon's legions in northern Spain, however, did not sit well with Charles's subjects, and they rebelled, forcing him to abdicate in favor of his son, Ferdinand VII.

Napoleon saw in the abdication a chance to rid Europe and himself of the last Bourbon rulers, and he preemptorily summoned the Spanish royal family to Bayonne in April 1808. There he removed both Charles and Ferdinand from the throne and interned them in the château of French foreign minister Charles-Maurice de Talleyrand-Périgord. In their stead he named his brother Joseph Bonaparte, king of Naples, as the new ruler of Spain.

Spaniards were no happier with a Bonaparte on the throne than they were with a Bonaparte army roaming the countryside. When Napoleon brutally suppressed an uprising in Madrid, the insurrection spread across the whole of the peninsula. Encouraged at the sight of an Iberia up in arms, the British decided to use the area as a bridgehead on the Continent and sent a small force under the energetic Arthur Wellesley (subsequently the duke of Wellington) to support the rebellion. The French, after setbacks at Bailen and Vimeiro, surrendered Lisbon.

Napoleon met with his reluctant ally, Alexander of Russia, at the Congress of Erfurt in September and October 1808 to extract promises of help in a situation that might well become desperate. Despite the august company of princes assembled by Napoleon, the czar made no clear commitments. So damaged was Napoleon's prestige by the sensational blows he had received during what could only be considered a national uprising in Spain and Portugal that even Talleyrand—always a harbinger of informed French opinion—had grown dismayed by his emperor's policies and was already negotiating with Alexander behind Bonaparte's back.

With little choice, Napoleon personally led an expedition onto the peninsula during November 1808 through January 1809. Taking most of his Grand Army with him, he nearly defeated the British, who narrowly escaped at Coruna in early 1809. Thus was Napoleon on the brink of putting down the entire revolt when Austria, seeing him preoccupied in Spain, attempted to regain her autonomy. The Hapsburgs attacked Bavaria in hopes of rousing all Germany against a common foe, but they only succeeded in catching Napoleon's undivided attention. Turning east, he soon entered Vienna.

Not only, however, did the Austrians hold him off both in Tyrol and north of the Danube, they also forced him to backtrack at Essling-Aspern in May 1809. It was a hint of weakness that gave new heart to the British, who launched an abortive expedition to the Netherlands as small revolts sprang up all across Europe. The French emperor recrossed the Danube and once again soundly defeated the Hapsburgs on July 6 at the Battle of Wagram, however.

Terms

The Treaty of Schönbrunn relieved Austria of its Illyrian provinces and basically rounded out the Continental System, although too late to save it from failure as a blockade. Article 3 of the treaty enumerated the cessions Austria was forced to make to France and French interests:

III

His Majesty, the Emperor of Austria, King of Hungary and Bohemia, for himself as well as for his heirs and successors, Princes of His House, their heirs and respective successors, give up the principalities, seigniorial domains and territories designated below, as well as any title whatsoever that might derive from their possession and from the properties, whether they belong to the State or are possessed by virtue of a particular title, that these lands include.

I) He cedes and abandons to His Majesty the Emperor of the French to become part of the Confederation of the Rhine and to be at the disposal of the Sovereigns of the Confederation:

The lands of Salzburg and Berchtesgaden, the part of Upper Austria, located above a line which begins at the Danube near the village of Strass, and including Weissenkirch, Wildersdorff, Michelbach, Gruit Mukenhoffen, Helst, Jeding; from there the road as far as Schwanstadt, the city of Schwanstadt on the Aller and continuing by ascending the course of this river and the lake of the same name up to the point where this lake touches upon the frontier of the lands of Salzburg;

His Majesty, the Emperor of Austria shall in ownership only of the woods belonging to the Salzkammergut, which are part of the territory of Mondace, and the right to export the cuttings, without having any right of sovereignty which He may exercise on this territory;

2) He equally cedes to His Majesty, the Emperor of the French, King of Italy, the county of Gorizia, the territory of Montfalcone, the government and the city of Trieste, Carniola with its enclaves on the gulf of Trieste; the circle of Villach in Carinthia and all the lands situated to the right of the Save, beginning at the point where this river leaves Carniola, and following it up to the frontier of Bosnia, that is to say: part of provincial Croatia, six districts of military Croatia, Fiume and the Hungarian coast-line, Austrian Istria or the district of Castua, the islands subordinate to the lands which have been ceded, and all lands under no matter what name situated on the right bank of the Save, the Thalweg of this river serving as the border between the two States.

Lastly, the manorial domain of Rhazums, enclaved in the land of Grisons.

3) He cedes and abandons to His Majesty the King of Saxony the enclaves belonging to Bohemia and included in the territory of the Kingdom of Saxony, that is to say; the parishes and villages of Guntersdorff, Taubentranke, Gerlachsheim, Lenkersdorff, Schirgiswalde, Winkel etc.

4) He cedes and abandons to His Majesty, the King of Saxony to be reunited to the Duchy of Warsaw, all of western or New Galicia, one district around Cracow on the right bank of the Vistula which shall be specified here below, and the circle of Zamosc in eastern Galicia.

The district around Cracow on the right bank of the Vistula, before Podgorze, shall be equidistant from Podgorze to Wieliczka, the boundary line shall pass by Wieliecka and shall bear upon Scavina to the west and to the east of the river which flows into the Vistula at Brzdegy.

Wieliczka and all the territory of the salt mines shall belong in common to the Emperor of Austria and to the King of Saxony; justice shall be rendered here in the name of the municipal authority. There shall be troops only for the police, and each of the two nations will maintain an equal number of them. The Austrian salts at Wieliczka may be transported on the Vistula across the Duchy of Warsaw, without being subject to any toll. Grains coming from Austrian Galicia may be exported by way of the Vistula.

Between His Majesty the Emperor of Austria and His Majesty the King of Saxony a boundary may be fixed, such as the Sacu, from the point where it touches the circle of Zamosc up to its junction with the Vistula.

5) He cedes and abandons to His Majesty, the Emperor of Russia, in the most eastern part of former Galicia, a territory containing four hundred thousand souls, in which the city of Brody may not be included. This territory shall be settled amiably between the commissioners of the two Empires.

Article 12 of the October 14 document called for the creation of a "military convention . . . in order to regulate the respective terms of the evacuation of the different provinces restored to His Majesty the Emperor of Austria." The convention also regulated the "evacuation of that part of Croatia that has been ceded to His Majesty, the Emperor of the French . . ." The convention, signed on October 27, illustrated the gritty mechanics of postwar cleanup.

Military Convention Concluded in Consequence of Article 12 of the Treaty of Vienna between France and Austria; Signed at Schönbrunn on the 27th of October, 1809

ARTICLE I

The first evacuation, that of Moravia, must take place within fifteen days after the exchange of ratifications; this province shall be completely evacuated by the fourth day of November.

ARTICLE II

The circle of Brunn shall be evacuated on the twelfth day of November and the return shall be effected by an officer, to be named by the Commander in Chief of the third body, to the Austrian officer who shall have been designated to receive it.

ARTICLE III

The circle of Znaim shall be evacuated on the second day of November and the return shall be effected by an officer named by the Commander in Chief of the fourth body, to the Austrian officer who shall have been designated to receive it.

ARTICLE IV

The military equipment which his now in the localities of Brunn and Znaim shall be maintained and returned.

ARTICLE V

During the month which follows the evacuation of these two circles, troops stationed in the city of Brunn may not exceed one battalion and one detachment of one hundred horses, and for the city of Znaim they may not exceed one battalion; which is approximately the garrison of these two localities in peace time.

ARTICLE VI

The second evacuation, that of Hungary, the city of Vienna and its surrounding territory, and of the part of Galicia which Austria shall retain, must take place one month after ratification. On the twentieth day of November the French and allied troops shall leave the places, billets, and stations that they still occupy on Hungarian soil and will proceed to occupy the first boundary line established by Article VIII here below.

ARTICLE VII

If the conditions of the Treaty relative to the payment of the stipulated sums, whether in liquid monies or in bills of exchange, are fulfilled, the keys of the city of Vienna shall be returned by the present governor to the officer who shall be designated by His Majesty the Emperor of Austria. The police in this city shall continue to be made up of the civilian guard.

ARTICLE VIII

By the twentieth day of November the city of Vienna and its surrounding territory, that is to say the part of the circle of *Unter-Wiener-Wald* to the east of the first boundary line, shall be entirely evacuated by the French troops.

This line will pass by Tuln;
From Tuln to Stassdorf
    to Baumgarten
    to Siegarokirchen
    to Rappolden
    to Krakeng
    to Henirichberg
    to Wirtshaus de Preissbaum
    to the chateau of Breitenfurt
    to Striegau by Hochleitn and Forstenerhaus
    to Siltindorf by Fulzfrazenberg
    to Rhorberg to Siegenfeld
    to Baden to the *charité* of Neustadt near the gate
        and in front of Gunzeldorf
        and from there to Ebenfurth.

It is understood that the city of Baden shall be occupied by no billets, but only by a police guard from each army and of equal numbers, because of the baths which the wounded and sick from the two armies shall be able to use alike.

ARTICLE IX

The circle of Untersmain-Hartsberg, which is part of Lower Austria, will not be evacuated until the twentieth day of December. Until this time, the foreguard of the French army shall occupy a line which shall follow the great road of Znaim, from Stokerau up to the frontier of Moravia.

It is understood that up until the twentieth day of December no Austrian troops shall be established in that part of aforementioned circle which is not occupied by French troops.

On the Znaim road shall be allowed complete liberty of communication, transport and passage, except for troops and artillery.

ARTICLE X

On the same day, the twentieth of November, all of the section of Galicia to be retained by Austria, shall be entirely evacuated.

The circles in this part which are occupied by Polish troops, if there are such, shall be returned by an officer to be named by the Commander of the Polish army, and those occupied by the Russians will be returned by an officer to be named by the Commander of the Russian army.

To assure the execution of this article, the present convention shall be sent to the Russian and Polish armies by superior officers in the French and Austrian armies.

ARTICLE XI

The third evacuation, that of Lower Austria, shall take place two months after the exchange of ratifications, and the districts which this province contains shall be evacuated on the 20 of December.

During this evacuation, as for all the others, the stations evacuated by the French troops shall not be reoccupied by Austrian troops until twenty-four hours after the departure of the former, and during fifteen days following the evacuation of Lower Austria, no large body of troops should be stationed near Saint Pölten.

ARTICLE XII

The fourth and last evacuation, that of the remainder of provinces and districts not ceded by the Treaty, shall take place within two months and one half after ratifications, and the said provinces and districts will be entirely evacuated by the 4 of January, 1810.

ARTICLE XIII

The Commander of the Russian army and the Commander of the Austrian army shall each name commissioners for the execution of the present convention: these commissioners shall agree provisionally upon a territory in eastern Galicia, on the Russian border, of which the population equals four hundred thousand souls, and which must be ceded by Austria to Russia, until the courts of Russia and Austria have agreed upon its final boundaries.

ARTICLE XIV

The coast and the part of Croatia ceded to the Emperor of the French, King of Italy shall be occupied in the following manner:

On the 14 of November the city of Fiume and the Hungarian coast shall be put in the hands of the French troops.

The taking possession of the whole coast as far as Dalmatia, and of the entire part of Croatia ceded to the Emperor of the French, King of Italy up to the Thalweg of the Save, shall follow immediately and in such a manner that the Austrian troops will leave on locality, no station, no port, until they have been relieved by French troops, who in order to reach these various points shall follow the steps or ordinary movements of the Austrian troops.

In such a way that in consequence of the principle established by Article XI here above, the Austrian troops which shall have been relieved at Fiume as well as at the stations along the Hungarian coast, cannot arrive in following their movement by successive steps until the 27 of November at Karlstadt; the French troops shall not occupy this place until the 28 of November.

ARTICLE XV

After occupation by the French troops of all the lands up to the Save, passage shall be left free on the various roads and even in the localities occupied by the French troops; lodgings and all necessary assistance shall be furnished the Austrian troops withdrawing by daily steps to arrive beyond the Save.

Free passage through the islands dependent upon the coast, and delivered over to the French troops in order to enter the ports of this coast, and the aforementioned ports beyond the Save, shall also be allowed on all the roads and in all the localities occupied by French troops, for the transport of all military effects, baggage and all property whether belonging to the Austrian government or private individuals, until the 4 of January 1810, final date set for the evacuations.

ARTICLE XVI

During the evacuation of the coast, the French troops shall take possession of the islands dependent upon the said coast and which are in the power of Austrian troops where these latter are garrisoned.

For the execution of the present article the commissioners named by His Majesty, the Emperor of the French, King of Italy, and the Emperor of Austria, shall determine, according to circumstances, the manner and the time of the final evacuation, plus the occupation of the various islands dependent upon the aforementioned coast.

ARTICLE XVII

All the stores, artillery and marine supplies, as well as all properties whatsoever belonging either to His Majesty the Emperor of Austria or to private individuals, which were not able to be evacuated nor sold within the terms of the evacuation period, will be under the guard and surveillance of the Austrian commissioners.

ARTICLE XVIII

The French hospitals which shall not have been able to be completely evacuated in the time interval established by the Treaty and by the present convention relative to the successive evacuations, shall remain under the surveillance of a French commander and administrator.

In each hospital shall be left a sergeant and six men for the internal police.

ARTICLE XIX

All stores of food staples, artillery and any other object which could not have been evacuated or sold at the time of the restoration of the city of Vienna, shall remain under the guard of French commissioners, as French property.

The same shall hold for all stores of salt, wood, tobacco and others that Austria does not purchase.

Done at Vienna on the 26 of October, 1809.

Signed:
COUNT DUMAS
The General of the Division.
THE BARON DE STRAUCH
Field Marshal Lieutenant.
MAYER DE HELDENFELD
Lieutenant General.

Ratified by we, Plenipotentiary of His Majesty, the Emperor of the French, King of Italy, Alexander Prince de Neuchâtel and Major General Wagram;

And by we Plenipotentiary of His Majesty the Emperor of Austria, Count de Wrena, Grand Chamberlain.

Signed:
ALEXANDER.
COUNT R. DE WRENA.

Consequences

Following Austria's defeat, Bonaparte turned his attention back to Spain and Portugal. Despite some defeats there, by 1810 he was at the zenith of his power and considered himself the heir to Charlemagne. Although the Treaty of Schönbrunn indeed marked a great French triumph, it also signified the high-water mark of French dominion in Europe. With the failure of the Continental System, France's principal means of control had become fear, and that was quickly destined to bring about rebellion and revolt against France throughout Europe and, ultimately, the Emperor Napoleon's downfall.

FIRST PEACE OF PARIS

TREATY AT A GLANCE

Completed
May 30, 1814, at Paris

Signatories
Great Britain and France (treaties containing the same stipulations verbatim were concluded simultaneously between France and Austria, France and Prussia, and France and Russia)

Overview
The First Peace of Paris followed the abdication of Napoleon and his exile to Elba. With the "legitimate" Bourbon dynasty restored, the anti-French allies treated their enemy liberally, restoring France's borders to their 1792 extent and allowing her to retain most of her colonies.

Historical Background

With Napoleon's dynastic marriage to Austria's Marie-Louise following the TREATY OF SCHÖNBRUNN, the political map of Europe—complicated beyond measure before 1796—was much simplified. France's new frontiers coincided neither with the geographical features nor the ethnic realities of Europe as a whole, but by reducing the number of states, amalgamating populations, constantly redrawing borderlines, and prorogating Revolutionary civics, Napoleon had prepared the ground for eventual German and Italian unity and fostered new national feelings that would in turn give rise to the first resistance against French domination.

From 1809 onward, Spanish guerrillas, sometimes backed by British ships and British troops, were harassing the French. While Napoleon was preoccupied in Austria, in fact, the British under Arthur Wellesley—later ennobled by a grateful government in London as the duke of Wellington—returned to drive the French from Portugal and invade Spain, winning an important victory at Talvera on July 28, 1809. Napoleon sent reinforcements to lance what he described as his "Spanish ulcer" and enforce the Continental System in the only way he could after losing his fleet at Trafalgar.

Freshly spilled blood did restore French ascendancy for the moment, but in 1811 Wellington's forces began their inexorable recovery of Portugal's frontier fortress. Although the Spanish field armies had been smashed and scattered by Napoleon's marshals the year before, guerrillas continued the struggle and, with new

British aid, proved effective. Without the British, the guerrillas would hardly have survived; without the guerrillas, the outnumbered British would have been swept away by the more experienced French. Together, supplied by the Royal Navy, Wellington's regulars and the Spanish irregulars were devastating, although at an appalling cost to Spain's civil population.

In 1812 the national Cortes, convened at Cadiz by the insurrectionaries, promulgated a constitution inspired by both the French Revolution and by British institutions. This in turn would spark revolutions throughout the old Spanish Empire's holdings in the New World. For now, it cheered the allies on to Salamanca and Madrid, where they evicted the French from southern Spain altogether.

Just as Napoleon felt able to return his full attention to Spain, his founding of a dynasty with Marie-Louise completed, France's relations with Russia worsened. Ever since the Congress of Erfurt in the fall of 1808, the czar had shown himself increasingly less willing to deal with Napoleon as a trusted ally or to enforce his Continental System of trade restrictions against the British. By the summer of 1812, Napoleon had massed his troops in Poland to intimidate Alexander into staying the course, but in June 1812, after attempts to heal the rift had failed, the czar made peace with Great Britain, and Napoleon's Grand Army invaded Russia.

The Russians retreated, adopting a "scorched-earth" defense that kept the French army from the approaches to Moscow until the beginning of

September. At Borodino the Russian commander, Mikhail Kutuzov, engaged Napoleon in a savage, bloody, indecisive battle that did not prevent the French from entering Moscow a week later, after the Russians had abandoned the city. A huge fire broke out that same day, although no one knows whether it was deliberately set by the Russians or occurred accidently at the hands of French looters. In any case, it destroyed the greater part of the town, and afterward Alexander refused to treat with Napoleon. Stranded in the heart of Russia with winter coming on, Napoleon withdrew. Early snows made the retreat disastrous. By December, although he managed to preserve himself and the core of his Grand Army, much of his forces were destroyed or deserted him.

The catastrophe cheered all Europe. Though Wellington had earlier failed to take Burgos, in 1813 he routed the French at Vitoria and pursued them back into their home country. Napoleon's Prussian allies, smelling weakness in the Russian and Spanish setbacks, formed a new coalition with Russia, Sweden, and Austria to wage a "War of Liberation." Having pursued Napoleon's army into France itself, Wellington laid siege to Bayonne and Bordeaux, where his efforts merged with the general allied effort. This brought the so-called Peninsular War, which had brutalized Spain and detonated Latin American revolutions, to a close.

Meanwhile, at the "Battle of Nations" in Leipzig on October 16–19, 1813, Coalition powers defeated the Grand Army. Napoleon rejected the allies' offer of a peace that stipulated France's pre-1792 frontiers on the Rhine and along the Alps as its "natural" borders, and stubbornly held his ground. But in March 1814, Paris was captured by the allies, and Napoleon relinquished the battle, abdicating as emperor and accepting, under the Peace of Paris, exile from Europe to the island of Elba.

Terms

The liberality of the First Peace of Paris demonstrated that the allied nations did not see themselves as fighting France so much as Napoleon. With the emperor's unconditional abdication and his exile to Elba, the victorious powers were willing to restore France to its 1792 borders and to allow it to retain most of its colonial possessions. Nevertheless, most of Napoleon's continental conquests were erased by virtue of the treaty:

II

The Kingdom of France retains its limits entire, as they existed on the 1st of January, 1792. It shall further receive the increase of Territory comprised within the line established by the following Article:

III

On the side of Belgium, Germany, and Italy, the ancient Frontiers shall be re-established as they existed the 1st of January, 1792, extending from the North Sea, between Dunkirk and Nieuport, to the Mediterranean between Cagnes and Nice, with the following modifications:

(1) In the Department of Jemappes, the Cantons of Dour, Merbesle-Chateau, Beaumont, and Chimay, shall belong to France; where the line of demarcation comes in contact with the Canton of Dour, it shall pass between that Canton and those of Boussu and Paturage, and likewise further on it shall pass between the Canton of Merbesle-Chateau and those of Binch and Thuin.

(2) In the Department of Sambre and Meuse, the Cantons of Walcourt, Florennes, Beauraing, and Gedinne, shall belong to France; where the demarcation reaches that Department, it shall follow the line which separates the said Cantons from the Department of Jemappes, and from the remaining Cantons of the Department of Sambre and Meuse.

(3) In the Department of the Moselle, the new demarcation, at the point where it diverges from the old line of Frontier, shall be formed by a line to be drawn from Perle to Fremersdorff, and by the limit which separates the Canton of Tholey from the remaining Cantons of the said Department of the Moselle.

(4) In the Department of La Sarre, the Cantons of Saarbruck and Arneval shall continue to belong to France, as likewise the portion of the Canton of Lebach which is situated to the south of a line drawn along the confines of the Villages of Herchenbach, Ueberhofen, Hilsbach, and Hall (leaving these different places out of the French Frontier) to the point where, in the neighborhood of Querselle (which place belongs to France), the line which separates the Cantons of Arneval and Ottweiler reaches that which separates the Cantons of Arvenal and Lebach. The Frontier on this side shall be formed by the line above described, and afterwards by that which separates the Canton of Arneval from that of Bliescastel.

(5) The Fortress of Landau having, before the year 1792, formed an insulated point in Germany, France retains beyond her Frontiers a portion of the Departments of Mount Tonnerre and of the Lower Rhine, for the purpose of uniting the said Fortress and its radius to the rest of the Kingdom. The new demarcation from the point in the neighborhood of Obersteinbach (which place is left out of the limits of France) where the Boundary between the Department of the Moselle, and that of Mount Tonnerre, reaches the Department of the Lower Rhine, shall follow the line which separates the Cantons of Wissenbourg and Bergzabern (on the side of France) from the Cantons of Permasens, Dahn, and Annweiler (on the side of Germany), as far as the point near the Village of Vollmersheim, where that line touches the ancient radius of the Fortress of Landau. From this radius,

which remains as it was in 1792, the new Frontier shall follow the arm of the River de la Queich, which on leaving the said radius at Queichheim (that place remaining to France) flows near the Villages of Merlenheim, Knittelsheim, and Belheim (these places also belonging to France) to the Rhine, which from thence shall continue to form the boundary of France and Germany.

The main stream (Thalweg) of the Rhine shall constitute the Frontier; provided, however, that the changes which may hereafter take place in the course of that river shall not affect the property of the Islands. The right of possession in these Islands shall be re-established as it existed at the Signature of the Treaty of Luneville.

(6) In the Department of the Doubs, the Frontier shall be so regulated as to commence above the Ranconniere near Locle, and follow the Crest of the Jura between the Cerneux-Pequignot and the Village of Fontenelles, as far as the peak of that Mountain, situated about 7,000 or 8,000 feet to the North-West of the Village of La Brevine, where it shall again fall in with the ancient Boundary of France.

(7) In the Department of the Leman, the Frontiers between the French Territory, the Pays de Vaud, and the different portions of the Territory of the Republic of Geneva (which is to form part of Switzerland) remain as they were before the incorporation of Geneva with France. But the Cantons of Frangy and of St. Julien, (with the exception of the districts situated to the North of a line drawn from the point where the River of La Laire enters the Territory of Geneva near Chancy, following the confines of Sesequin, Laconex, and Seseneuve, which shall remain out of the limits of France), the Canton of Reignier, (with the exception of the portion to the East of a line which follows the confines of the Muraz, Bussy, Pers, and Cornier, which shall be out of the French limits), and the Canton of La Roche (with the exception of the places called La Roche, and Armanoy with their districts) shall remain to France. The Frontier shall follow the limits of these different Cantons, and the line which separates the Districts continuing to belong to France, from those which she does not retain.

(8) In the Department of Mont-Blanc, France acquires the Sub-Prefecture of Chambery, with the exception of the Cantons of L'Hôpital, St. Pierre d'Albigny, la Rocette, and Montmelian, and the Sub-Prefecture of Annecy, with the exception of the portion of the Canton of Faverges, situated to the East of a line passing between Ourechaise and Marlens on the side of France, and Marthod and Ugine on the opposite side, and which afterwards follows the crest of the mountains as far as the Frontier of the Canton of Thones; this line, together with the limit of the Cantons before mentioned, shall on this side form the new Frontier.

On the side of the Pyrenees, the Frontiers between the 2 Kingdoms of France and Spain remain such as they were the 1st of January, 1792, and a Joint Commission shall be named on the part of the 2 Crowns for the purpose of finally determining the line.

France on her part renounces all rights of Sovereignty, *Suzeraineté*, and of possession, over all the Countries, Districts, Towns, and places situated beyond the Frontier above described, the Principality of Monaco being replaced on the same footing on which it stood before the 1st of January, 1792 .

The Allied Powers assure to France the possession of the Principality of Avignon, of the Comté of Venaissin, of the Comté of Montbeliard, together with the several insulated Territories which formerly belonged to Germany, comprehended within the Frontier above described, whether they have been incorporated with France before or after the 1st of January, 1792 .

The Powers reserve to themselves, reciprocally, the complete right to fortify any point in their respective States which they may judge necessary for their security.

To prevent all injury to private property, and protect, according to the most liberal principles, the property of Individuals domiciliated on the Frontiers, there shall be named, by each of the States bordering on France, Commissioners who shall proceed, conjointly with French Commissioners, to the delineation of the respective Boundaries.

As soon as the Commissioners shall have performed their task, maps shall be drawn, signed by the respective Commissioners, and posts shall be placed to point out the reciprocal boundaries.

Even more generously, all war indemnities were forgiven:

XVIII

The Allied Powers, desiring to offer His Most Christian Majesty a new proof of their anxiety to arrest, as far as in them lies, the bad consequences of the disastrous epoch fortunately terminated by the present Peace, renounce all the sums which their Governments claim from France, whether on account of contracts, supplies, or any other advances whatsoever to the French Government, during the different Wars which have taken place since 1792 .

His Most Christian Majesty, on his part, renounces every claim which he might bring forward against the Allied Powers on the same grounds. In execution of this Article, the High Contracting Parties engage reciprocally to deliver up all titles, obligations, and documents which relate to the Debts they may have mutually cancelled.

The First Peace of Paris provided for the CONGRESS OF VIENNA:

XXXII

All the Powers engaged on either side in the present War, shall, within the space of 2 months, send Plenipotentiaries to Vienna, for the purpose of regulating, in General Congress; the arrangements which are to complete the provisions of the present Treaty.

Consequences

The process of completing the "provisions of the present Treaty" would involve nothing less than an attempt to engineer a new balance of power in Europe in the wake of all Napoleon had done to upset it. But even as Louis XVIII ascended to the restored Bourbon throne and the Congress of Vienna met to decide in detail the fate of Europe, Napoleon, having arrived on Elba after a hazardous journey during which he barely escaped assassination, kept a close watch on the Continent. He knew the diplomats thought the island too close to home and wanted to remove him to some distant island in the South Atlantic, and he heard the criticism to which the Bourbon Restoration was soon exposed. He accused Austria of preventing Marie-Louise and his son from joining him in exile, although in truth she had taken a new lover and had no plans to give up her life. As a final insult, the French government refused to pay Napoleon's allowance, and he feared he was in danger of being reduced to penury.

All of these drove Bonaparte to action. On March 1, 1815, he returned like a thunderbolt to France for one last hurrah in the long saga of what had become in many respects his personal war with Europe.

SECOND PEACE OF PARIS

TREATY AT A GLANCE

Completed
November 20, 1815, at Paris

Signatories
Great Britain, Austria, and Prussia and France

Overview
The FIRST PEACE OF PARIS (May 30, 1814), which was concluded after the initial defeat and abdication of Napoleon I, treated France with considerable liberality, forgiving war indemnities and restoring it to its 1792 frontiers. The Second Peace of Paris, which followed the defeat of Napoleon after he returned from exile on Elba, was much harsher, assessing an indemnity, reducing France to its 1790 boundaries, and providing for the allied garrisoning of the French frontiers.

Historical Background

While in exile on Elba, Napoleon—brooding over his fate and unhappy with his treatment—became intensely aware of France's dissatisfaction over the restoration of the Bourbon dynasty. He boldly returned to France in 1815. Landing at Cannes on March 1 with a detachment of his guard, he was greeted by many, not as a fallen emperor, but as the embodiment of the spirit of the revolution and the returning savior of the nation's glory. As he crossed the Alps, the republican peasantry rallied round him, and near Grenoble he won over the soldiers sent to arrest him. King Louis XVIII fled in terror, and Napoleon marched into Paris on March 20, commencing the period known as the Hundred Days. Napoleon knew that his exhausted nation and greatly reduced army were in no condition to take on all of Europe. Accordingly, he proclaimed peaceful intentions, but the allies, meeting at the CONGRESS OF VIENNA, declared him an outlaw and summarily prepared for renewed war.

To rally the French masses to his cause, he probably should have allied himself once more with the Jacobins, but he was afraid to do so and alienate the bourgeoisie whose support he needed more and whose predominance he himself had always ensured. The bourgeoisie feared above everything a revival of the socialist experiments France had suffered at the hands of Jacobin radicals in 1793 and 1794. So all Napoleon had to offer was a political regime not unlike that of Louis XVIII, except with himself at the top. Enthusiasm ebbed, and his latest adventure seemed a dead end.

In these circumstances, Napoleon, as always, chose action. Rather than adopt a defensive posture, Napoleon determined that his only chance was to separate the Prussian and Anglo-Dutch armies in order to defeat them in detail in what is now Belgium. He took the field and won several victories before he was defeated by the duke of Wellington and Gebhard von Blücher at perhaps the most famous battle in history, Waterloo, on June 18, 1815.

Returning to Paris, Napoleon abdicated for the second time on June 23. He took flight to Aix, where he surrendered to the captain of the British warship *Bellerophon*, and was exiled to the island of Saint Helena. Following this the anti-French allies empowered Great Britain to represent their collective interests in a Second Peace of Paris.

Terms

This document adopted a very different tone from the conciliatory First Peace of Paris. Although the Second Peace was far more punitive against France, it even more sharply separated the deeds of Napoleon from those of the French nation:

> *In the Name of the Most Holy and Undivided Trinity.*
> The Allied Powers having by their united efforts, and by the success of their arms, preserved France and

Europe from the convulsions with which they were menaced by the late enterprise of Napoleon Bonaparte, and by the revolutionary system reproduced in France, to promote its success; participating at present with His Most Christian Majesty in the desire to consolidate, by maintaining inviolate the Royal authority, and by restoring the operation of the Constitutional Charter, the order of things which had been happily re-established in France, as also in the object of restoring between France and her neighbors those relations of reciprocal confidence and goodwill which the fatal effects of the Revolution and of the system of conquest had for so long a time disturbed; persuaded, at the same time, that this last object can only be obtained by an arrangement framed to secure to the Allies proper indemnities for the past and solid guarantees for the future, they have, in concert with His Majesty the King of France, taken into consideration the means of giving effect to this arrangement; and being satisfied that the indemnity due to the Allied Powers cannot be either entirely territorial or entirely pecuniary, without prejudice to France in the one or other of her essential interests, and that it would be more fit to combine both the modes, in order to avoid the inconvenience which would result, were either resorted to separately, their Imperial and Royal Majesties have adopted this basis for their present transactions; and agreeing alike as to the necessity of retaining for a fixed time in the frontier provinces of France a certain number of allied troops, they have determined to combine their different arrangements, founded upon these bases, in a definitive treaty. For this purpose, and to this effect, His Majesty the King of the United Kingdom of Great Britain and Ireland, for himself and his allies on the one part, and His Majesty the King of France and Navarre on the other part, have named their plenipotentiaries to discuss, settle and sign the said definitive treaty; namely, His Majesty the King of the United Kingdom of Great Britain and Ireland, the Right Honorable Robert Stewart, Viscount Castlereagh, Knight of the Most Noble Order of the Garter, His said Majesty's Principal Secretary of State for Foreign Affairs, etc., and the Most Illustrious and Most Noble Lord Arthur, Duke, Marquess, and Earl of Wellington, Marquess of Douro, Viscount Wellington, of Talavera and of Wellington, and Baron Douro of Wellesley, a member of His said Majesty's Most Honorable Privy Council, a Field Marshal of his Armies, Colonel of the Royal Regiment of Horse Guards, Knight of the Most Noble Order of the Garter, etc.

And His Majesty the King of France and of Navarre, the Sieur Armand Emanuel du Plessis Richelieu, Duke of Richelieu, Peer of France, First Gentleman of the Chamber of His Most Christian Majesty, his Minister and Secretary of State for Foreign Affairs, and President of the Council of his Ministers, etc.,

Who having exchanged their full powers, found to be in good and due form, have signed the following articles. . . .

Especially noteworthy was the fact that Napoleon was singled out as a menace and that he was referred to not as Napoleon I, emperor of France, but as Napoleon Bonaparte, a mere individual without legitimate claim to rule.

Following the preamble, Article 1 established the new frontiers of France, contracted from their 1792 extent essentially to the borders as they existed in 1790, prior to the conquests of the Wars of the Revolution. Article 4 assessed an indemnity against France of 700,000,000 francs. Article 5 provided for garrisoning of frontier outposts—in effect, for France's own good:

V

The state of uneasiness and of fermentation, which after so many violent convulsions, and particularly after the last catastrophe, France must still experience, not withstanding the paternal intentions of her King, and the advantages secured to every class of his subjects by the Constitutional Charter, requiring, for the security of the neighboring States, certain measures of precaution and of temporary guarantee, it has been judged indispensable to occupy, during a fixed time, by a corps of Allied troops certain military positions along the frontiers of France, under the express reserve, that such occupation shall in no way prejudice the sovereignty of His Most Christian Majesty, nor the state of possession, such as it is recognized and confirmed by the present treaty. The number of these troops shall not exceed 150,000 men. The Commander-in-Chief of this army shall be nominated by the Allied Powers. This army shall occupy the fortresses of Condé, Valenciennes, Bouchain, Cambray, Le Quesnoy, Maubeuge, Landrecies, Avesnes, Rocroy, Givet with Charlemont, Mezières, Sedan, Montmedy, Thionville, Longwy, Bitsch, and the Tête-de-Pont of Fort Louis. As the maintenance of the army destined for this service is to be provided by France, a special convention shall regulate everything which may relate to that object.

This convention, which shall have the same force and effect as if it were inserted word for word in the present treaty, shall also regulate the relations of the army of occupation with the civil and military authorities of the country. The utmost extent of the duration of this military occupation is fixed at five years. It may terminate before that period if, at the end of three years, the Allied Sovereigns, after having, in concert with His Majesty the King of France, maturely examined their reciprocal situation and interests, and the progress which shall have been made in France in the re-establishment of order and tranquillity, shall agree to acknowledge that the motives which led them to that measure have ceased to exist. But whatever may be the result of this deliberation, all the fortresses and positions occupied by the Allied troops, shall, at the expiration of five years, be evacuated without further delay, and given up to His Most Christian Majesty, or to his heirs and successors.

An "Additional Convention" subjoined to the treaty detailed the composition of the 150,000-man army that would occupy a military line in France. Within the "Additional Convention," Article 1 specified that the army would be made up of troops from all the allied nations, and Article 2 spelled out the French responsibility for maintaining and provisioning the force:

II

This army shall be maintained by the French Government in the manner following:-

The lodging, the fuel and lighting, the provisions and forage, are to be furnished in kind.

It is agreed that the total amount of daily rations shall never exceed 200,000 for men and 50,000 for horses, and that they shall be issued according to the tariff annexed to the present convention.

With respect to the pay, the equipment, the clothing, and other incidental matters, the French Government will provide for such expense by the payment of a sum of 50,000,000 francs per annum, payable in specie from month to month, from the 1st of December of the year 1815, into the hands of the Allied commissioners.

But the Allied Powers, in order to concur as much as possible in everything which can satisfy His Majesty the King of France, and relieve his subjects, consent that only 30,000,000 francs on account of pay shall be paid in the first year, on condition of the difference being made up in the subsequent years of the occupation.

An "Additional Article" dealt with deserters from the proposed allied garrison:

ADDITIONAL ARTICLE
PARIS, NOVEMBER 20, 1815
[DESERTERS]

The High Contracting Parties having agreed, by Art. V of the treaty of this day, to occupy for a certain period with an Allied army military positions in France; and being desirous of anticipating all that might hazard the order and discipline which it is so important to maintain in that army, it is determined upon by the present additional article, that every deserter who, from either of the corps of the said army, should go over to the French side, shall immediately be arrested by the French authorities, and delivered up to the nearest commander of the Allied troops, in like manner as all deserters from the French troops who might come over towards the Allied army shall be immediately delivered up to the nearest French commandant.

The tenor of this article is to apply equally to such deserters from either side, who may have forsaken their colors previously to the signature of the treaty; the same to be without delay restored and delivered up to the respective corps to which they may belong.

The present additional article shall have the same force and validity as if it were inserted, word for word, in the military convention of this day.

In faith whereof the respective plenipotentiaries have signed it, and have affixed thereunto the seal of their arms.

Done at Paris, the 20th November, in the year of our Lord, 1815.

[Seals and signatures]

An "Annexed Convention" spelled out the terms by which France was obligated to make the indemnity payment over a five-year period.

Consequences

Napoleon died in exile on Saint Helena on May 5, 1821. His fall had set loose a torrent of hostile books designed to sully his reputation, but his death made him a legendary figure who would be celebrated as a romantic hero and the embodiment of modern individuality. For some he remained recent history's most monstrous tyrant, at least until the rise of another strongman, Adolf Hitler, made Napoleon's strides across the human stage seem almost benign by comparison.

Multinational Conventions and Agreements

CONGRESS OF VIENNA

TREATY AT A GLANCE

Completed
June 9, 1815, at Vienna

Signatories
Great Britain, Austria, France, Portugal, Prussia, Russia, Spain, and Sweden

Overview
The general treaty of June 9, 1815, resulted from a congress held from September 1814 through June 1815. The business of the congress was, pursuant to the FIRST PEACE OF PARIS, to reestablish a balance of power in Europe and, to the extent possible, restore pre-Napoleonic dynasties.

Historical Background

With Napoleon presumably in permanent exile on the island of Elba, the powers of Europe convened in Vienna, where after 25 years of almost constant war stretching back to the French Revolution, the old order was ready to reassert its control over Europe and establish a stable, conservative international settlement. Austria's Francis I (formerly Holy Roman Emperor Francis II) hosted the unprecedented congress, attended by Alexander I of Russia, Frederick William III of Prussia, and many lesser rulers and monarchs. Of even greater significance was the galaxy of diplomats present, including Viscount Castlereagh, representing Great Britain; Prince Karl August von Hardenberg, Prussia; Count Karl Robert Nesselrode, Russia; Prince Klemens von Metternich, Austria; and the highly flexible Charles-Maurice de Talleyrand-Périgord, foreign minister under Napoleon and now in service to the restored Bourbon government.

In the course of the congress, Napoleon made his dramatic return from Elba, landing at Cannes on March 1. The powers gathered in Vienna paid no heed to Napoleon's protestations of peaceful intentions but instead outlawed the returned exile and prepared for war. As massive Russian and Austrian forces assembled, Napoleon decided to act decisively to separate and defeat the Prussian and Anglo-Dutch armies in what is now Belgium. He did win several initial victories before he met defeat at the hands of the duke of Wellington and Gebhard von Blücher at Waterloo on June 18, 1815.

Terms

In the meantime, Talleyrand had emerged as Europe's premiere diplomat and power broker. He played brilliantly upon the differences among the four dominant powers at Vienna and broke a deadlock over the demands of Russia for all of Poland, and of Prussia for all of Saxony. Talleyrand supported Castlereagh and Metternich to force Russia and Prussia to reduce their claims. The final result: Prussia was given two-fifths of Saxony, and Russia received most of the Grand Duchy of Warsaw.

As to the west, the aim of the dominant powers was to erect barriers against future French aggression. Belgium was given to the Netherlands; the Rhineland and Westphalia to Prussia; Nice and Savoy to Sardinia; and Lombardy and Venetia went to Austria. A new but loose German Confederation was established, chiefly to facilitate defense. Switzerland was neutralized under an international guarantee that endures to this day. Denmark ceded Norway to Sweden in exchange for Lauenburg. In Spain, Portugal, and Italy, the pre-Napoleonic dynasties were restored.

The lengthy document of June 9 was in large part a detailed redivision of Europe. Typical was Article 23:

ARTICLE XXIII

His Majesty the King of Prussia having in consequence of the last war, reassumed the possession of the provinces and territories which had been ceded by the Peace of Tilsit it is acknowledged and declared by the present Article that His Majesty, his heirs and successors, shall possess anew, as formerly, in full property and Sovereignty, the following countries, that is to say:

Those of his ancient provinces of Poland specified in Article II;

The City of Dantzig and its territory, as the latter was determined by the Treaty of Tilsit;

The Circle of Cottbus;

The Old March;

The part of the Circle of Magdeburg situated on the left bank of the Elbe, together with the Circle of the Saale;

The Principality of Halberstadt, with the Lordships of Derenburg, and of Hassenrode;

The Town and Territory of Quedlinburg (save and except the rights of Her Royal Highness the Princess Sophia Albertine of Sweden, Abbess of Quedlinburg, conformable to the arrangements made in 1803);

The Prussian part of the County of Mansfeld;

The Prussian part of the County of Hohenstein;

The Eichsfeld;

The Town of Nordhausen with its territory;

The Town of Mühlhausen with its territory;

The Prussian part of the district of Trefourt with Dorla;

The Town and Territory of Erfurth, with the exception of Klein-Brembach and Berlstedt, inclosed in the Principality of Weimar, ceded to the Grand Duke of Saxe-Weimar by Article XXXIX;

The Bailiwick of Wandersleben, belonging to the County of Unter-gleichen;

The Principality of Paderborn, with the Prussian part of the Bailiwicks of Schwallenberg, Oldenburg, and Stoppelberg, and the jurisdictions (*Gerichte*) of Hagendorn and Odenhausen, situated in the territory of Lippe;

The County of Mark, with the part of Lipstadt belonging to it;

The County of Werden;

The County of Essen;

The part of the Duchy of Cleves on the right bank of the Rhine, with the town and fortress of Wesel; the part of the Duchy, situated on the left bank, specified in Article XXV;

The secularized Chapter of Elten;

The Principality of Munster, that is to say, the Prussian part of the former Bishopric of Munster, with the exception of that part which has been ceded to His Britannic Majesty, King of Hanover, in virtue of Article XXVII;

The secularized Provostship of Cappenburg;

The County of Tecklenburg;

The County of Lingen, with the exception of that part ceded to the kingdom of Hanover by Article XXVII;

The Principality of Minden;

The County of Ravensburg;

The secularized Chapter of Herford;

The Principality of Neufchatel, with the County of Valengin, such as their Frontiers are regulated by the Treaty of Paris, and by Article LXXVI of this General Treaty.

The same disposition extends to the rights of Sovereignty and *suzeraineté* over the County of Wernigerode, to that of high protection over the County of Hohen-Limbourg, and to all the other rights or pretensions whatsoever which His Prussian Majesty possessed and exercised, before the Peace of Tilsit, and which he has not renounced by other Treaties, Acts, or Conventions.

The German Confederation was established by Articles 53–64, which provide a virtual constitution for the body:

ARTICLE LIII

The Sovereign Princes and Free Towns of Germany, under which denomination, for the present purpose, are comprehended their Majesties the Emperor of Austria, the Kings of Prussia, of Denmark, and of the Netherlands; that is to say:—

The Emperor of Austria and the King of Prussia, for all their possessions which anciently belonged to the German Empire;

The King of Denmark, for the Duchy of Holstein;

And the King of the Netherlands, for the Grand Duchy of Luxembourg; establish among themselves a perpetual Confederation, which shall be called 'The Germanic Confederation.'

ARTICLE LIV

The object of this Confederation is the maintenance of the external and internal safety of Germany, and of the Independence and Inviolability of the Confederated States.

ARTICLE LV

The Members of the Confederation, as such, are equal with regard to their rights; and they all equally engage to maintain the Act which constitutes their union.

ARTICLE LVI

The affairs of the Confederation shall be confided to a Federative Diet, in which all the Members shall vote by their Plenipotentiaries, either individually or collectively, in the following manner, without prejudice to their rank:—

1. Austria	1 Vote
2. Prussia	1 Vote
3. Bavaria	1 Vote
4. Saxony	1 Vote
5. Hanover	1 Vote
6. Wurtemberg	1 Vote
7. Baden	1 Vote
8. Electoral Hessell	1 Vote
9. Grand Duchy of Hesse	1 Vote
10. Denmark, for Holstein	1 Vote

11. The Netherlands, for Luxembourg	1 Vote
12. Grand-Ducal and Ducal House of Saxony	1 Vote
13. Brunswick and Nassau	1 Vote
14. Mecklenburg-Schwerin and Strelitz	1 Vote
15. Holstein-Oldenburg, Anhalt and Schwartzburg	1 Vote
16. Hohenzollern, Liechtenstein, Reuss, Schaumburg-Lippe, Lippe and Waldeck	1 Vote
17. The Free Towns of Lubeck, Frankfort, Bremen and Hamburgh	1 Vote

Total 17 Votes.

ARTICLE LVII

Austria shall preside at the Federative Diet. Each State of the Confederation has the right of making propositions, and the presiding State shall bring them under deliberation within a definite time.

ARTICLE LVIII

Whenever fundamental laws are to be enacted, changes made in the fundamental laws of the Confederation, measures adopted relative to the Federative Act itself, and organic institutions or other arrangements made for the common interest, the Diet shall form itself into a General Assembly, and, in that case, the distribution of votes shall be as follows, calculated according to the respective extent of the individual States:—

Austria shall have	4 Votes
Prussia	4 Votes
Saxony	4 Votes
Bavaria	4 Votes
Hanover	4 Votes
Wurtemberg	4 Votes
Baden	3 Votes
Electoral Hesse	3 Votes
Grand Duchy of Hesse	3 Votes
Holstein	3 Votes
Luxembourg	3 Votes
Brunswick	2 Votes
Mecklenburg-Schwerin	2 Votes
Nassau	2 Votes
Saxe-Weimar	1 Vote
Saxe-Gotha	1 Vote
Saxe-Coburg	1 Vote
Saxe-Meiningen	1 Vote
Saxe-Hildburghausen	1 Vote
Mecklenburg-Strelitz	1 Vote
Holstein-Oldenburg	1 Vote
Anhalt-Dessau	1 Vote
Anhalt-Bernburg	1 Vote
Anhalt-Kothen	1 Vote
Schwartzburg-Sondershausen	1 Vote
Schwartzburg-Rudolstadt	1 Vote
Hohenzollern-Heckingen	1 Vote
Liechtenstein	1 Vote
Hohenzollern-Sigmaringen	1 Vote
Waldeck	1 Vote
Reuss (Elder Branch)	1 Vote

Reuss (Younger Branch)	1 Vote
Schaumburg-Lippe	1 Vote
Lippe	1 Vote
The Free Town of Lubeck	1 Vote
The Free Town of Frankfort	1 Vote
The Free Town of Bremen	1 Vote
The Free Town of Hamburgh	1 Vote

Total 69 Votes.

The Diet in deliberating on the organic laws of the Confederation shall consider whether any collective votes ought to be granted to the ancient Mediatised State of the Empire.

ARTICLE LIX

The question, whether a subject is to be discussed by the General Assembly, conformably to the principles above established, shall be decided in the Ordinary Assembly by a majority of votes. The same Assembly shall prepare the drafts of resolutions which are to be proposed to the General Assembly, and shall furnish the latter with all the necessary information, either for adopting or rejecting them.

The plurality of votes shall regulate the decisions, both in the Ordinary and General Assemblies, with this difference, however, that in the Ordinary Assembly, an absolute majority shall be deemed sufficient, while, in the other, two-thirds of the votes shall be necessary to form the majority.

When the votes are even in the Ordinary Assembly, the President shall have the casting vote; but when the Assembly is to deliberate on the acceptance or change of any of the fundamental laws, upon organic institutions, upon individual rights, or upon affairs of religion, the plurality of votes shall not be deemed sufficient, either in the Ordinary or in the General Assembly.

The Diet is permanent: it may, however, when the subjects submitted to its deliberation are disposed of, adjourn for a fixed period, which shall not exceed four months.

All ulterior arrangements relative to the postponement or the dispatch of urgent business which may arise during the recess shall be reserved for the Diet, which will consider them when engaged in preparing the organic laws.

ARTICLE LX

With respect to the order in which the members of the Confederation shall vote, it is agreed, that while the Diet shall be occupied in framing organic laws, there shall be no fixed regulation; and whatever may be the order observed on such an occasion, it shall neither prejudice any of the members, nor establish a precedent for the future. After framing the organic laws, the Diet will deliberate upon the manner of arranging this matter by a permanent regulation, for which purpose it will depart as little as possible from those which have been observed in the ancient Diet, and more particularly according to the Reces of the Deputation of the Empire in 1803. The order to be adopted shall in no way affect the rank and precedence of the members of the Confederation except in as far as they concern the Diet.

ARTICLE LXI

The Diet shall assemble at Frankfort on the Maine. Its first meeting is fixed for the 1st of September, 1815.

ARTICLE LXII

The first object to be considered by the Diet after its opening shall be the framing of the fundamental laws of the Confederation, and of its organic institutions, with respect to its exterior, military, and interior relations.

ARTICLE LXIII

The States of the Confederation engage to defend not only the whole of Germany, but each individual State of the Union, in case it should be attacked, and they mutually guarantee to each other such of their possessions as are comprised in this Union.

When war shall be declared by the Confederation, no member can open a separate negotiation with the enemy, nor make peace, nor conclude an armistice, without the consent of the other members.

The Confederated States engage, in the same manner, not to make war against each other, on any pretext, nor to pursue their differences by force of arms, but to submit them to the Diet, which will attempt a mediation by means of a Commission. If this should not succeed, and a juridical sentence becomes necessary, recourse shall be had to a well organized Austregal Court (*Austrägalinstanz*), to the decision of which the contending parties are to submit without appeal.

ARTICLE LXIV.

The Articles comprised under the title of *Particular Arrangements*, in the Act of the Germanic Confederation, as annexed to the present General Treaty, both in original and in a French translation, shall have the same force and validity as if they were textually inserted herein.

Annexed to the June 9 document was a series of 17 treaties, declarations, and protocols de-signed to enact the provisions of the Congress of Vienna. An "Epitome of the Seventeen Documents" outlined the relationship between the treaties among various powers and particular articles in the Congress treaty of June 9. The "Epitome" gives some idea of the extent and complexity of the issues the Congress of Vienna managed to resolve:

Epitome of the Seventeen Documents Annexed to the Congress Treaty of Vienna

ANNEX I

Treaty between Austria and Russia respecting Poland. Signed at Vienna April 21 / May 3, 1815.

Articles 1, 2, 3. 4, 5 were embodied in the principal Treaty as, respectively, 5, 3, 4, 6, and 1. They had reference to the new Austro-Russian frontiers, &c. Article 6 enabled inhabitants to leave the country on its transfer. Articles 7, 8, 9 were embodied in the principal Treaty as Articles 11, 12, and 13, general amnesty and sequestrations. Articles 10 to 23, property of proprietors having estates on both sides of boundary line. Articles 24 to 29, navigation of rivers in Poland, tariffs, &c. (see Article 14 of principal Treaty). Articles 30 and 40 related to loans and debts, surrender of documents, evacuation of territories, &c.

ANNEX II

Treaty between Russia and Prussia relating to Poland, signed at Vienna April 21 / May 3, 1815 .

Articles 1, 2, 3, 4, 5, 6, 7 are embodied in substance in the principal Treaty as Articles 2, 6, 11, 12, 13 respectively. The remaining provisions of the Treaty are very similar to those of the Austro-Russian Treaty (see Annex I).

ANNEX III

Additional Treaty between Austria, Prussia, and Russia relative to Cracow. Signed at Vienna April 21 / May 3, 1815.

Articles 1, 2, 3, 6, embodied in principal Treaty as Articles 6, 7, 8, 9. This Treaty constituted Cracow a free, neutral, and independent town under the protection of Austria, Prussia, and Russia, with consequent conditions and privileges. [By a treaty between the same Powers dated November 6, 1846, the above additional Treaty was abrogated, the independence of Cracow was put an end to, and the territory incorporated with Austrian dominions. The British and French Governments protested against this infraction of the Treaty of Vienna. The constitution of Cracow, which was appended to this Annex, disappeared with the Treaty which created it.]

ANNEX IV

Treaty between Prussia and Saxony (also between Austria and Saxony and between Russia and Saxony) on the subject of territorial reconstruction. Signed at Vienna May 18, 1815.

Articles 2, 4, 13, 16, 21, were incorporated in the principal Treaty as Articles 15, 16, 20, 21, and 22. They related to territorial changes, religious property, amnesty, emigration, &c.

Article 17 concerned the navigation of the Elbe. Article 19, supply of salt from Prussia duty free. Article 22, recognition by Saxony of sovereign rights of Austria, Prussia, and Russia in portions of Poland, &c. [Great Britain acceded to this Treaty.]

ANNEX V

Declaration of King of Saxony on Rights of House of Schonburg, Vienna, May 18, 1815. Act of Acceptation by the five Powers, May 29, 1815.

ANNEX VI

Treaty (territorial), Prussia and Hanover. Vienna, May 29, 1815.

Articles 1, 2, 4, 5, 6 embodied in the principal Treaty as Articles 27, 28, 29, 30, 31. Reciprocal cessions. Prussia, Hanover, Brunswick, Oldenburg, navigation of the Ems, debts, &c.

ANNEX VII

Convention (territorial), Prussia and Saxe-Weimar. Vienna, June 1, 1815.

Article 3 was embodied in the principal Treaty as Article 39.

ANNEX VIII

Convention (territorial), Prussia and Nassau. Vienna, May 31, 1815.

This convention contains a stipulation (Article 5) relating to the fortress of Ehrenbreititein, enabling Prussia to erect military works within a certain radius of the fortress 'even in those communes which may remain under the Sovereignty of the House of Nassau.'

ANNEX IX

Act concerning the Federative Constitution of Germany. Vienna, June 8, 1815.

Articles 1 to 11, first paragraph, are embodied in the principal Treaty as Articles 53 to 63. This Act established a Confederation of the Sovereign Princes and Free Towns of Germany (17 in number), including Denmark for the Duchy of Holstein and the Netherlands for the Grand Duchy of Luxembourg, forming together the Germanic Confederation for the maintenance of the safety of Germany and the independence of the confederated States. Austria was also a member of this Confederation. A Federative Diet was formed to sit at Frankfort, each of the I 7 members having one vote, and a General Assembly in which the number of votes to each member was apportioned according to the respective extent of the individual States. The Act further contained stipulations on various matters bearing on the regulation of affairs.

ANNEX X

Treaty, Great Britain, &c. and Netherlands. Vienna, May 31, 1815.

Union of the Netherlands and Belgium,33 cessions of territory, Luxembourg, boundaries, &c. Articles I to 8 were embodied in the principal Treaty as Articles 65 to 73. Appended to the Treaty is an Act of the Netherlands Government of July 21, 1814, accepting the sovereignty of the Belgian Provinces.

ANNEX XIA

Declaration (8 Powers) respecting Helvetic Confederacy. Vienna, March 20, 1815.

Articles 1 to 8 are, with certain omissions, embodied in the principal Treaty as Articles 74, 75, 76, 77, 79, 81, 82, 83. They deal with the integrity of the Cantons, the addition of 3 new Cantons, and stipulations for regrouping of territory, military roads and other internal arrangements.

ANNEX XIB

Act of Acceptance by Switzerland of the above Declaration. Zurich, May 27, 1815.

ANNEX XII

Protocol (8 Powers). Vienna, March 29, 1815.

Cessions by Sardinia to Geneva. Passage of troops. Protection of Catholic religion in ceded territory, &c.

ANNEX XIII

Treaty, Austria and Sardinia (also Great Britain, Russia, Prussia, and France). Vienna, May 20, 1815.

Articles 1 to 8 embodied in principal Treaty as Articles 85 to 92. Boundaries of Sardinia, union of Genoa, fortifications, cessions to Geneva, neutrality of Chablais and Faucigny, passage of troops, &c. Appended to this Annex are the conditions respecting the government of Genoa, Geneva, &c.

ANNEX XIV

Conditions attaching to union of Genoa with Sardinia.

ANNEX XV.

Declaration (8 Powers). Vienna, February 8, 1815.

Proposed universal abolition of the Slave Trade; to be a subject for separate negotiations between the Powers.

ANNEX XVI

Regulations. Vienna, March 1815.

Embodied in the principal Treaty as Articles 108 to 116. Navigation of rivers. General arrangements, uniformity of system, &c. The Rhine, Neckar, Maine, Moselle, Meuse, Scheltd.

ANNEX XVII

Regulations. Vienna, March 19, 1815.

Concerning the Rank and Precedence of Diplomatic Agents.

The above epitome gives roughly the purport of the 17 annexes to the Vienna Congress Treaty of June 9, 1815.

Consequences

The Congress of Vienna created a European settlement that endured for some 40 years, establishing a relatively stable balance of power. Yet it was shortsighted to the extent that it ignored nationalist yearnings, leaving the nations of Europe open to internal revolt, which culminated in the revolutions of 1848.

Part Seven
WILDERNESS DIPLOMACY AND CONTINENTAL EXPANSION

INTRODUCTION

In the 19th century, the trans-Mississippi region of today's United States was transformed by the country's expansionist initiatives into the "American" West, which resembled (in relation to the nation east of the great river) something very much like the colonies of the European imperialist powers. A mass migration changed what had been for the most part an Indian and Hispanic land of small villages and tribal communities into a colonial dependency dominated by a growing capitalist economy and peopled by a workforce of millions of Anglo-Americans, African-Americans, and European, Mexican, and Chinese immigrants. The migration took place under the political imprint of the American nation, which rearranged the social and physical landscape of the West.

Although gains in territory at the expense of Mexico, France, Great Britain, and independent Indian tribes were perhaps the most obvious attribute of American expansion into the trans-Mississippi region, it also involved the growth of federal power, the imposition of a national political definition on the region, and the gradual creation of a bureaucratic state to administer the newly designated American lands. In all, the "winning of the West" was a tale not of steady military triumphs and absolute diplomatic successes, but of migrations in fits and starts, of Native American resistance and political intrigues, and of enterprises launched and abandoned, which only in the retelling became an account of progressive victory and national glory. The diplomacy of this period, too, was not a matter merely of making treaties between long-established sovereign powers to end a war or settle a dispute but also of passing federal laws, negotiating land deals, and declaring foreign policy doctrines, all of which were in many ways dictated by a new nation's internal politics.

Thomas Jefferson and Early Expansion

The ideas, politics, and institutions that governed the expansion of the United States into the trans-Mississippi West were born and developed east of the river in periods prior to 1800. The very concept of a peculiar region considered uniquely "western," for example, had a political pedigree stretching back to colonial times. In fact, the American West itself was a political and cultural construction before it was ever a landed reality. As such, the American West had been invented by Virginia planters who feared it was too dangerous to allow the indentured servants they had previously preferred to slaves to remain in their seaboard colony. Colonial politics, then, shaped the "frontier" pattern of western settlement in which settlers moved onto Indian lands without the sanction, and often against the wishes of, official government policy, then demanded the protection of the government against Indian reprisals. This established a western legacy of both dependence upon centralized authority and resentment of it.

Not colonial, however, but post-Revolutionary politics provided the legal means by which national expansion would be accomplished. After the Revolution, Americans poured into the trans-Appalachian West. Some were Revolutionary soldiers who were granted lands in the Ohio region for their service in the rebellion; others were representatives of eastern land companies seeking quick profits from speculative booms in western real estate; still others poor commoners after cheap land or a new living as "long hunters" and trappers. The mostly Algonquian tribes of the Old Northwest, the triangle of land bounded by the Ohio and Mississippi Rivers and the Great Lakes, fought a 40-year resistance against such encroachments, from Pontiac's Rebellion just after the French and Indian War until their defeat by "Mad" Anthony Wayne at the Battle of Fallen Timbers in 1794.

During this period, at the height of the Indian resistance, the new U.S. Congress, urged on by the Ohio Company, would pass the NORTHWEST ORDINANCE in 1787. An effort to appease discontented frontiersmen and to impose some order on them, it was one of the most important pieces of legislation passed under the Articles of Confederation. The Northwest Ordinance specified how territories and states were to be formed from land "gained" by the United States as a result of the Revolution. Here the new country displayed the genius of its Revolution-spawned republicanism, for the Northwest Ordinance was in fact a document for the political handling of colonized land. The "mother country" east of the Appalachians, understanding the psychology of colonial peoples, declared that it would treat what it was careful not to call its western colonies not as colonies at all, but in the long run as full partners in a single nation. Alone among the expansive imperial powers of the 18th and 19th centuries, the United States established an orderly method, at least on paper, for creating a coherent polity from conquered land. The ordinance was to serve as a model for the transition from territory to statehood in the trans-Mississippi West as the U.S. population expanded westward.

The United States's first venture west of the Mississippi came in 1803 with President Thomas Jefferson's purchase of France's vast holdings in North America. The LOUISIANA PURCHASE and its aftermath was an early, if nearly accidental, form of imperialism that served as a long prelude to the more vigorous and self-conscious imperial expansion that began in the 1840s. That the federal government, for exigent geopolitical reasons, purchased the land far in advance of its settlement by U.S. citizens would be one of the attributes distinguishing trans-Mississippi expansion from early expansion into the trans-Appalachian West, which in many ways was more associated with nation building than with imperial adventures.

If national expansion's frontier ideology was a legacy of colonial times, if its legal machinery was the child of post–Revolutionary War land speculation, then its agent in the trans-Mississippi West was the federal government. The federal government taking these first, tentative steps west of the great river, however, was not the highly centralized state of a powerful young nation hungry for empire but the decentralized republican government of a weak and disorganized new country, one in many ways struggling to survive in a world filled with strong empires, each with a stake still in North America. Indeed, it was more the weakness of the United States's government, its fears and worries, than its strength that led it westward.

At the end of the 18th century, Britain, Spain, and France continued to push their New World interests even as they fought among themselves. The United States, despite its all-but-official refusal to enter into European alliances, remained nevertheless caught up in the centuries-old struggle for empire. England, deeply involved in the fur trade with the American Indians, encouraged Indian resistance movements in the Old Northwest and continued to do so even after Anthony Wayne's victory at Fallen Timbers in 1794 and the subsequent TREATY OF FORT GREENVILLE "secured" the region for the United States. A source of anxiety for the westerners moving into the Ohio Valley, Kentucky, and Tennessee, Indian troubles were not a concern for New Englanders, who engaged in a lively trade with the British. This in turn led Spain, fearful that the United States would throw its small but strategic weight behind the British, to threaten to cut off trade along the Mississippi. It also conspired with Kentuckians and Tennesseans to leave the union they had only recently joined (Kentucky became the first "western" state in 1792, Tennessee the second in 1796).

American envoy to Spain Thomas Pinckney negotiated a treaty in 1795 to keep the Mississippi open, which alleviated the danger of secession by Kentucky and Tennessee. But Americans occupying the Ohio and Mississippi River valleys continued to worry both about English perfidy with the Indians and Spanish possession of New Orleans. For all the voraciousness they would eventually show toward trans-Mississippi lands, Americans at the time were not much interested in the region and were infinitely more concerned with the American West of the day, which included the states of Kentucky and Tennessee as well as the territories of present-day Ohio, Indiana, Illinois, Michigan, Alabama, and Mississippi.

In 1800 Thomas Jefferson was elected president. That same year Spain gave Louisiana back to France by secret treaty, and Napoleon Bonaparte made plans to make it the footstool of a New World empire just as soon as he had reclaimed St-Domingue (present-day Haiti), which France had lost to a recent slave rebellion. About the time the United States became aware of the transfer, Spain, which still retained formal possession of Louisiana, closed the port of New Orleans to American trade. The two events—Spain's transfer of Louisiana to France and its revoking the U.S. right of deposit in New Orleans—shocked and angered western settlers and worried Jefferson, who feared he might be forced to change his basic foreign policy and ally the United States with Great Britain if this was a foretaste of Napoleon's future policy.

Jefferson sent envoys to Paris to negotiate a treaty with France, and Napoleon, bogged down in his adventure in Haiti, offered the United States one of the greatest real estate deals in history. In the Louisiana Purchase, Jefferson's Democratic-Republican administration bought an empire, although no one knew exactly, or agreed upon, its true extent. Federalist-dominated New England, not at all happy with the purchase, argued that the region was useless because it was too vast to be governed and was therefore a threat to republican government. The Yankees worried that if the nation survived an expansion into these western lands, the West and the South would combine to dominate government at the expense of New England. Jefferson and the Republicans responded that the Louisiana Purchase ensured that plenty of land would be available to future generations, especially to the yeoman farmers they considered the true backbone of the republic. The political and philosophical argument surrounding the Louisiana Purchase produced two additional characteristics of national expansion into the trans-Mississippi West. On the one hand, each official step westward threatened to break apart the political balance between North and South upon which national unity had been based, and on the other, each official step was justified by the Jeffersonian claim that the country was establishing an "empire of liberty" that would ensure the future prosperity and progress of the nation as a whole.

Even as Jefferson was planning—and the Congress was (sometimes secretly) funding—such endeavors as the Lewis and Clark Expedition into Louisiana and Zebulon Pike's exploration of today's Southwest (which most historians agree was a spy mission into Spanish territory), some Federalists were conspiring with Jefferson's ambitious Democratic-Republican vice president, Aaron Burr, to detach New England and New York from the Union. When Burr lost his bid to become governor of New York (and thus any such plan went awry), he blamed Alexander Hamilton and killed him in a duel. Fleeing into the trans-Appalachian lands to escape arrest, Burr was drawn to another plot, one that included approaches both to Spain and Britain as well as to disgruntled French-speaking residents of Louisiana to establish an independent empire in the West. While the Burr Conspiracy was something of a comic opera, it did reveal the dangers of a weak and faction-ridden federal government when it came to administering a western empire, although a relatively weak central government was precisely the kind of government presumed by Jefferson's "empire of liberty."

A plot that threatened to make the point far more seriously than Burr's skullduggery, however, was brewing in the region around the same time. Beginning about 1805, the great Shawnee sachem Tecumseh began building, with British encouragement, a pan-tribal Indian alliance that he hoped would result in an Indian confederacy, an American Indian state, stretching from the Great Lakes to the Gulf of Mexico. The young republic's vulnerability was further underscored when Great Britain and Napoleonic France went to war. Although the United States declared itself neutral, both of the belligerents ignored its neutrality and disrupted at will American trade on the high seas. Even more odious to Americans, the British navy arrogantly impressed U.S. sailors into service on its own ships. By 1811 a full-scale Indian uprising led by Tecumseh and his Indian-mystic brother, called the Prophet, was again under way in the Ohio and Mississippi River valleys, and westerners were calling for another war with England.

The War of 1812

Jefferson had been drawn into the Louisiana Purchase because he hoped to avoid becoming embroiled in European disputes, but in many ways, his action only hurried such entanglement. The purchase increased internal and sectional conflicts, highlighted the federal government's weakness, and made the country more a target of international concern and manipulation, as became clear when Great Britain and Napoleon each basically forbade Americans from trading with the other.

Americans fought the War of 1812 against Great Britain officially to protect U.S. sovereignty, the nation's right to remain neutral and engage in foreign trade at sea in the face of the British Orders in Council. Under these the British navy enforced a worldwide blockade against Napoleonic France, forced neutral merchant ships to pay a duty on cargo bound for France, confiscated American ships with abandon, and impressed American sailors into service on as regular basis. But New England—the section of the country most involved in the international trafficking—did not support the war, resisted raising troops (and sometimes refused to do so), and toward the end of the conflict, held a convention that resolved to secede from the Union unless the United States withdrew from the war.

In contrast, the Republican "War Hawks," who took control of Congress in 1812 and pushed the new administration of James Madison into battle, were led by a westerner, Kentuckian Henry Clay, and were for the most part westerners or the product of recent "Indian frontiers" in the western regions of states North and South. Although they took up the cry in support of shanghaiied American sailors, they were more concerned with the budding of a hostile, pan-Indian state stuck smack in the middle of the subcontinent and the tribes of this confederacy being secretly armed by British agents and fur traders, who were operating out of forts they were supposed to have abandoned under the terms of the 1783 TREATY OF PARIS, ending the American Revolution. Extreme nationalists, the War Hawks frequently talked of taking Canada from the British, which antiwar Virginian John Randolph claimed was the bellicose young West's true goal.

In general the war went badly for the United States. The Americans failed to achieve any of their official aims and actually lost ground diplomatically in the 1814 peace talks at Ghent. At best, they managed to settle for what the TREATY OF GHENT claimed was a return to the "status quo antebellum." Still, Tecumseh was killed at the Battle of the Thames, his Indian confederacy was destroyed, and British influence over the tribes was greatly diminished. This, along with Tennessee-lawyer-turned-American-general Andrew Jackson's defeat of the Creek at Horseshoe Bend and his famous victory in New Orleans, helped to explain the feeling, especially in the West, that the United States had essentially won the war. Certainly, the war created a much stronger sense of an American nation and bound the trans-Appalachian West, formerly a seething cauldron of sedition, firmly to the republic.

In the war's wake, a country that had for the most part hugged the Atlantic seaboard and sought its prosperity in foreign trade began spilling into Trans-Appalachia. In the next six years, five "western" states—Louisiana (1812), Indiana (1816), Mississippi (1817), Illinois (1818), and Alabama (1819)—entered the Union. In Congress, westerner Henry Clay launched an economic program he called the American System. A combination of government-sponsored internal improvements and government protection of infant industry, the program presaged the central role the federal government would later play in the economy of the trans-Mississippi West. At the same time, the rise of the American West as a self-conscious section raised serious questions about the nation's traditional political balance.

The war had also given the country its first true military hero since George Washington: Andrew Jackson. Not a Virginia aristocrat like Washington but a westerner cut from the same cloth as the common folk pouring into the new states, Jackson had a career that would eventually lead to the White House, and his rise was not unrelated to a major postwar issue: the "Indian question." By banishing any vestige of British support for the Indians of the region, the War of 1812 deprived Tecumseh's followers of their last European ally against the Americans, who now began a heated debate about what to do with those tribes still resident in the United States. Since the Louisiana Purchase, many high-ranking state and federal officials had been considering moving them west of the Mississippi, and indeed the bulk of the purchase was viewed in those days by settler and politician alike as "Indian Territory" and not

yet an extension of the American West just waiting for future expansion. Perhaps because of that, the postwar migration of white settlers seemed to stop for the most part at the great river.

Indeed, the decades following the War of 1812 were not characterized so much by expansion as by consolidation, not by imperial adventures but by nation building. For European imperialists, the distinction between mother country and colony remained clear, but in the United States the colonies became, by law, the mother country. The war had created the circumstances under which the United States was willing to make the trans-Appalachian lands into an American West, a regional partner in a single nation. Expanding that nation beyond the Mississippi—even into U.S. territory—would create serious political problems, as became clear when Missouri tried to join the nation in 1819.

When the nation did begin to expand in earnest into the "unorganized" region beyond the Mississippi, the mold for that expansion had already been cut. Like earlier expansions, it would be characterized by a frontier ideology; the treatment of Indians as savages; the promotion of agrarian values; the justification that Americans were creating a unique empire of liberty; the dispossession of many of those inhabiting the region; the introduction of social, legal, and political models established in the East; the attempt to incorporate conquered lands into the American polity; subsequent sectional clashes that threatened the Union; and a federal government that served as the general agent of expansion and the major promoter and protector of the region's economy.

Expansion and International Policy

If English-speaking settlers had been moving into the trans-Appalachian regions of North American since before the French and Indian War, not until after the War of 1812 could they do so with impunity; if the American Revolution founded the political republic called the United States, the War of 1812 secured the nation to house it. In times past, Europe's battles over empire had served to hold the westward expansion of English-speaking settlers somewhat in check.

Now events in Europe created a situation that, if anything, proved favorable to the birth of new states between the mountains and the Mississippi. In February 1815, Napoleon Bonaparte escaped from his forced exile on the Corsican isle of Elba and picked up where he had left off in his war with England. Four months later, he met absolute defeat at the hands of a British force commanded by the duke of Wellington, and two centuries of on-again, off-again worldwide conflict came to a close with the SECOND PEACE OF PARIS. The Americans had been drawn into the major European conflagrations six times, four times as British colonials, twice allied with France against England. Garnering immense international prestige with Wellington's victory at the Battle of Waterloo, England went on to establish the Pax Britannica, an extended period of relative peace and stability among the European Great Powers, basically guaranteed by the might of the English navy. With the long three-way European struggle for empire in the New World at an end, the United States—sans any urge or need to take sides—flourished. In one of the great ironies of history, the hated British navy's mastery of the seas enabled the Americans in the coming years first to undergo a period of undisturbed and intense internal development and, ultimately, to embark upon an era of territorial expansion unmatched outside the rise of the great Mediterranean and Asian empires of the ancient past.

Significantly, the Pax Britannica meant that Native Americans were, for the first time in centuries, deprived of European allies. For just as the English-speaking newcomers had been caught up in six international conflicts, so too had the Indians. They may not have known it, since they made their various alliances for local reasons, throwing in with those close at hand who seemed most powerful, taking up arms against those who at the time were most flagrantly stealing their land. It hardly mattered, however, that the Indians did not fight to maintain some faraway European balance of power. The practical results of their alliances meant that most of them most of the time took sides against the American settlers, colonial or Patriot, and when the European conflicts came to a halt, these settlers—not England, France, or Spain—were in control of the vast American interior, of trans-Appalachia and the Louisiana Purchase lands. In short, the Indians, like France, lost the centuries-long struggle to control the American West. Under the Pax Britannica the American frontier—in the European sense of a fortified border region between hostile sovereign powers—disappeared. It was an America free at last from "the broils of Europe" that allowed the United States in the decades following the War of 1812 to concentrate on the consolidation of the political and territorial gains it had made in the early part of the century in order to build a nation. And it was a nation that had no tolerance for Indians.

It was not only France and the Native American tribes that suffered under the coming of the Pax Britannica, nor only the United States that flourished. The new world order also saw the final collapse of the old Spanish Empire and the birth of an independent Latin America. Importantly for an expanding United States, those new lands included what had once been called the Northern Mystery. For 300 years the land north of modern-day Mexico had "belonged" to Spain. California, New Mexico, Arizona, and Texas—the Mexican borderlands that would become the American Southwest—had been a fragment of the world's then-oldest Western empire. In the late 18th century, Spain had made various efforts to revitalize its northern provinces, setting up a buffer between itself and the United States in hopes of vitiating the "foreign" threat to its North American frontier. Spain's real problems with its empire, however, had proved to be internal rather than external. In 1808 Napoleon's invasion of Iberia led to a destabilization of the mother country that ultimately cost Spain nearly all its holdings in the New World.

It had been the liberals in the Cortes, Spain's traditionally weak parliament, who led the resistance against the French, and it was these same liberals who promulgated reforms during the political chaos created by Napoleon's invasion. They established a representative government under the liberal Spanish Constitution of 1812. Provincial legislatures and town councils cropped up everywhere in both the mother country and the empire. After Napoleon's defeat and exile to Elba, the Spanish monarchy launched a restoration, dissolving the representative bodies or suspending their privileges, which in turn led to a revolt within Spain by the liberals and their supporters in the military.

In the long run, though republican government was restored, an empire was lost, for, meanwhile, the republican movement that began in Spain took firm root in the colonies of the Western Hemisphere. Having a taste of independence, the Latin Americans did not sit still for the restoration of Spain's "legitimate" monarchy and the reconstruction of the old colonial empire. Over the next decade the world witnessed the great Central and South American liberations, led by such men as San Martín, Bolívar, and O'Higgins. In Mexico, the upheavals were fed not only by the liberals' desire for representative government but also by mestizo discontent with social conditions. The mixture created a cycle of revolt and repression that lasted until Mexico's war for independence became the climax of the New World revolutions.

When Spain—with the ardent support of Europe's Great Powers, whose "Holy Alliance" was dedicated to the suppression of revolution wherever it occurred—sought to destroy these fledgling republics, the United States decided to make itself heard in world politics. Eschewing England's offer to issue a joint proclamation, President James Monroe and Secretary of State John Quincy Adams in 1823 came up with a doctrine that formally recognized the new republics and specifically warned against the intervention of any European power, England included, in the affairs of the Western Hemisphere.

In truth, no American president then had the power to back up the MONROE DOCTRINE, but it formed the backdrop for the rise to power of the one man who seemed to embody the boldness and the bellicosity of the expanding North American nation: Andrew Jackson. Jackson's seizure of Spanish Pensacola on May 26, 1818, not only embarrassed President Monroe, it also demonstrated that Spain could not defend Florida. His reckless conduct added little to his reputation among the country's leaders in Washington, and one faction in Congress even sought to censure the general for his execution of two British subjects he found working with the Spanish. The effort failed as Jackson's popularity soared, however, and his conduct both during and after the War of 1812, especially with the Indians, made American settlement possible from the Tennessee River to the Gulf of Mexico. The man who would soon become president himself had, it seemed to many Americans, almost single-handed redirected the course of the country's expansionist ambitions from Canada toward the Southwest and Texas.

More popular in the West than ever, Old Hickory (as his troops had begun calling Jackson during the 1812 war) was elected the first American president from the region in 1828 by the "common men," who had begun to participate in large numbers in national elections. Once in office, Jackson completed the conquest of the trans-Appalachian West by removing the Indian tribes east of the Mississippi, under the INDIAN REMOVAL ACT, to the "surplus" lands of the Louisiana Purchase, in the process opening up the old Southwest of Alabama, Mississippi, and Louisiana to the slave-based seacoast economy of the plantation South. Under Jackson's administration the American economy would boom as he moved these Indians to make room for big plantations, all in the name of small homesteaders and common folk. Much as a generation later in the trans-Mississippi West, the buffalo (and the hunting cultures that depended on it) would be destroyed to make way for cattle (and the ranching culture that came with it), in the trans-Appalachian West, Jackson would replace the Indians with black slaves, the woods with cotton fields.

The Indians might protest, and they did, but squatters and land speculators waited for neither the state nor the federal government to resolve the disputed claims they raised; they instead overran Indian lands and, whenever they could, swindled Indians out of their property. Georgia, Alabama, and Mississippi had all passed legislation abolishing tribal government and placing Indians under state jurisdiction by the time Congress, at Jackson's urging, passed the Indian Removal Act in 1830, calling for new treaties under which the "Civilized Tribes"—the Choctaw, Chikasaw, Cherokee, Creek, and Seminole, living in Georgia, Alabama, Mississippi, and Florida—would migrate to Indian Territory in present-day Oklahoma. When the Cherokee took their case to the Supreme Court in 1832, the Court ruled that the state laws and the persecution of Indians was unconstitutional, but Jackson simply refused to enforce the decision. Some of the tribes mounted an armed resistance, but in the end all were forced out of their traditional homes.

As part of this general trend during Jackson's terms in office to turn the Southwest into a slave-based, cotton economy, Texas, long a hotbed of filibustering, would declare itself independent of a Mexico that had only recently declared itself independent of Spain. Though Jackson's personal friend, and perhaps initially his agent in Texas, Sam Houston would become the Lone Star Republic's first president, domestic pressure would keep both Jackson and his hand-picked successor, Martin Van Buren, from annexing the republic as the newest and largest U.S. territory. Not until after the election of 1844 would a lame-duck president, John Tyler, sneak the annexation through Congress, and by then the new president and the country were eyeing prizes even bigger than Texas.

Expansion and Domestic Politics

Until 1844 the federal government played a mostly reactive role in continental expansion. This was true, despite the fact that American filibusters, settlers, missionaries, and merchants actively undercut attempts by both Mexican and British authorities to maintain their sovereignty over major stretches of the North America, the former in present-day Texas, the Southwest, and California, the latter in what is now Washington and Oregon. Like Texas, the Oregon region had not been included in the Louisiana Purchase, although under a series of agreements beginning in 1818, the United States and Great Britain had established a joint occupation of the Far Northwest. Despite these diplomatic successes and the sympathy elected officials felt for pioneers headed to the area, the federal government—foundering on sectional issues and incapable of forging a national consensus on expansion—in the long run proved both unwilling and unable to acquire the Oregon territory, just as it could not manage to annex Texas after its Anglo revolution.

During the decade that Congress first debated, then ignored, then debated again Texas annexation, American settlers—many of them Christian evangelists attracted by the possibility of Indian converts and whose missionary zeal had been fired by the Second Great Awakening sweeping through much of the

Northeast—began to settle in Oregon country. The continuing overland migration to Oregon supported American claims in the region, and it was no accident that it came at a time, the mid-1840s, when the country was witnessing a resurgence of republican imperialism, justified by an expanded rationale fed by new religious convictions and taking as its point of departure old Jeffersonian arguments about the West representing an empire of liberty.

Responding to what was clearly a reluctance on the part of many, perhaps most, Americans at the time to push the nation beyond its existing borders, the new expansionists claimed that an empire west of the Mississippi not only represented a triumph for liberty, it was also ordained. Not merely Texas and Oregon, but Canada, Mexico, Cuba, and in fact all the lands of North America belonged to the United States because of the moral superiority of its dominant Anglo-Saxon race. Not until after the presidential election of 1844 would the term *manifest destiny* pop up in the writings of New York journalist John O'Sullivan during the final debate over Texas annexation. This was yet clearly the idea toward which the powerful coterie of expansionists, led by Senator Robert Walker, within the administration of John Tyler were working toward when they made national expansion the central issue of the election of 1844.

Concentrating first on Texas, the expansionists tried to persuade the southerners that an independent Texas would inevitably come under British influence, abolish slavery, become a mecca for runaway slaves, and totally undermine the southern way of life. To those northerners adamantly opposed to any annexation that would allow another slave state into the Union, the expansion lobby advanced another, diametrically opposed argument, one that played on northern racism. As both free blacks and slaves moved south, they would drain the border states of their race and undermine slavery there as an institution; sooner or later, all Africans, lured by tropical climates and "kindred" races south of the new border, would pass on through Texas and settle in Latin America, emptying the United States of black people. If most northerners did not buy the notion that Texas would serve as a "safety valve" to protect the United States from racial turmoil, enough northern Democrats were entranced by the idea—containing slavery by expanding it—that the expansionists succeeded in turning the annexation of Texas from a sectional issue into a partisan one in time for the election.

Their triumph came as a total surprise to the two leading candidates. In fact, Henry Clay and Martin Van Buren, each of whom fully expected to receive the presidential nomination from his respective party, found the unsettled Texas question a source of embarrass-ment precisely because it had become so wrapped up in the slavery controversy. After apparently consulting in private, they tried to remove the issue from the campaign entirely by making separate but quite similar statements opposing annexation of Texas without prior consent from Mexico. The statement did not hurt Clay's bid for the nomination. There was never any question whom the Whig convention in Baltimore would declare as the party's hopeful, and the Whigs adopted a platform on which Clay could run that avoided taking any stand whatsoever on Texas, or indeed on most of the other major national issues of the day. Van Buren was not so lucky. As a result of his tepid response to expansion, the Democrats, also meeting in Baltimore, deadlocked over his nomination and eventually picked American history's first dark horse candidate, James Polk, a Tennessee-born protégé of Andrew Jackson and a strong expansionist.

During the general election, the Democrats, to avoid the accusation of sectional favoritism, constructed a platform that cleverly combined a demand for annexing Texas with a demand for the acquisition of Oregon. The latter demand grew from the attempt the expansionist lobby had been making to link the Texas safety valve theory with commercial arguments for expansion. Most Americans were still enthralled by Andrew Jackson's gloss on Thomas Jefferson's ideal republic: a country primarily of farmers that also offered ample commercial opportunity to the common man. North and South, they agreed that the United States needed foreign markets to absorb the large agricultural surpluses American farmers, North and South, could produce. Without them, they believed, the economy would shrivel, as it had after the Panic of 1837. Given the depression that followed, politicians, including Polk, saw the struggle for markets in apocalyptic terms. They proclaimed that America could dominate world markets by controlling raw materials, even as they fretted incessantly about other countries, especially England, developing other sources of supply or choking off the markets American merchants needed. Hence, they argued, England wanted Texas as an alternate source of raw cotton in order to ruin the American South.

The same argument, however spurious, could be applied to California and New Mexico. These Mexican territories were important sources of raw materials for America's ongoing market revolution. New Mexico of course had the long-established Santa Fe trade, but California also exported hides to New England, where immigrant Irish factory workers manufactured boots and shoes. Through California's strategic harbors came the sperm oil of whales that lubricated the American economy as a crucial fuel, and the U.S. whaling industry plied the Pacific from the California ports they needed for repair and supply. Polk of course was aware of this. Like the expansionists whose standard-bearer he was about to become, he wanted to promote American trade with the Pacific rim. When he came to outline the objectives of his administration for his secretary of the navy, George Bancroft, the acquisition of California would be second only to the settlement of the Oregon question (Texas having by then been annexed).

By combining the expansionists' desires of the South and West, the Democrats had not only once again managed to dangle territory out West as a solution to the economic problems and class conflicts obscured by tense racial issues, they had also found a winning formula for the election. Polk won by a small plurality, 38,000 popular votes, and by a margin of 170 to 105 in the Electoral College. Thus, he came into office a dark horse candidate elected by a slim margin, determined to follow an aggressive imperial policy that enjoyed only weak support from the American people. While voters may narrowly have approved the idea of adding Texas and Oregon to the United States, few wanted a war with either Britain or Mexico in order to do so. Almost certainly, any hint of U.S. military action to acquire New Mexico and California would have reversed the results of the election.

In any case, both of the northern provinces of Mexico were already drifting toward some kind of political and economic accommodation with the United States. Perhaps a truly inspired leader could have risen above the sectional pressures of the moment, made the bare majority who had voted for expansion into a true consensus, and pulled off the kind of diplomatic coup Thomas Jefferson had with the Louisiana Purchase. Polk—dedicated to the platform that got him elected when no one thought he could be, and thus committed to geographic expansion regardless of cost—was not that leader. Instead, America found itself launched on what would generally come to be considered by most historians one of the more shameful episodes in its history, a series of events that in their perfidy rivaled the country's treatment of the Indians.

Polk partly achieved his expansionist ends even before his inauguration. Texas was annexed in the last days of the Tyler administration via a joint resolution by Congress, hotly and bitterly debated and barely passed. Immediately after Congress passed the resolution, Irish workers in New York and Boston, and Lowell, Massachusetts, who were adamantly opposed to the spread of slavery and of black labor, and who made up the bulk of the common soldiers in the small American army, demonstrated against annexation. Mexico instantly severed diplomatic relations with the United States. A Texas convention accepted the offer made by Congress in the summer of 1845.

In the four months before Texas voters ratified the resolution in October, Polk did everything he could to ensure that war with Mexico would follow fast on the heels of Texas's joining the Union in February 1846. As war loomed with Mexico, Polk moved to resolve the Oregon issue with Britain. America wanted to set the boundary between Canada and the United States at the 54th parallel, Britain at the 44th. Having run for office on his willingness to fight Britain for the higher boundary, Polk maintained in public a belligerent tone, but behind the scenes he compromised and accepted a division of Oregon along the 49th parallel. The English, for their own reasons, did not wish to push the issue to war, and Polk could not afford to fight both them and Mexico.

Afterward, Polk called for war against Mexico on the slimmest of pretenses: that Mexicans had fired on an expeditionary force he sent to police the border. Congress gave him what he asked for, passing a declaration of war by overwhelming majorities in both the House and the Senate, which appropriated $10 million to the war effort and authorized Polk to recruit an army of 50,000 volunteers.

The country was probably not as united as the vote, stampeded through Congress, indicated. Whigs, who felt they had no choice but to support military measures, were far less enthusiastic than Democrats. Young Abraham Lincoln, after his election in 1846 to Congress, would introduce his famous "spot resolutions," which demanded the administration show him the exact spot where the American blood had been shed as the president claimed to justify the war. Irish workers, once again, staged a demonstration in New York and called the war a plot by slave owners. Soon, they were joined by the New England Workingmen's Association. Some newspapers, like Horace Greeley's *New York Tribune*, loudly opposed the war from the start. Whig opposition grew throughout the war, and ultimately, the war's unpopularity would snowball after it became clear that Polk had deliberately provoked a fight and that despite his protestations, the Mexican War was a war of conquest. Abolitionists and antislavery Whigs, calling themselves Conscience Whigs, accused Polk of launching a war of aggression to enhance the "Slave Power" South. In 1847 the Massachusetts legislature resolved that the war was "unconstitutionally commenced by order of the President" and that it was waged for the "dismemberment of Mexico."

Most historians now agree that national expansion was less the outcome of a widely shared belief in manifest destiny and more the result of a compromised achievement of expansionists who, for a few years, persuaded Americans that expansion was the means to solve problems that, if left unchecked, would destroy the republic. The government, and James Polk, acted more from fear of Europe and anxiety over sectional wrangling than from confidence of purpose. Certainly, once Mexico was defeated, Americans had second thoughts, and Polk found that sectional splits prevented him from gaining all the territory he wanted. It was a furious president who accepted the TREATY OF GUADALUPE HIDALGO, negotiated by Nicholas Trist, whom he considered an unauthorized agent, under the direction of General Winfield Scott, whom he considered a political rival. But accept it he did, because he was convinced that the antiwar sentiment rampant in the United States allowed him no room to reject it.

For $15 million and the assumption of claims from U.S. citizens against Mexico, the federal government acquired all of modern California, Nevada, and Utah, most of New Mexico and Arizona, and a good deal of Colorado. It was perhaps the greatest land grab in all human history, except for Ivan the Terrible's subjugation of Siberia in 1581, and still it was not enough. Five years later, the government would buy the rest of the present-day continental United States from Mexico in the $10-million Gadsden Purchase, the core of the GADSDEN TREATY. The empire failed to match the dreams of the expansionists, who wanted Canada, Mexico, Central America, and the Caribbean, but it was certainly enough land to fuel to a white-hot intensity the unsettled question of whether the West should be slave or free. As Ralph Waldo Emerson remarked, the nation might have swallowed the territory, but inevitably the territory would consume the nation.

TREATIES

Peace Treaties and Truces

TREATY OF FORT JACKSON

TREATY AT A GLANCE

Completed
August 9, 1814, Fort Jackson, Florida

Signatories
United States and the Creek Nation

Overview
The Creek War was fought toward the end of the War of 1812 between the Red Stick faction of the Creek Nation and the United States. The Treaty of Fort Jackson, which followed Andrew Jackson's victory at the Battle of Horseshoe Bend (March 27, 1814), ended the war and extorted some 23 million acres of land not only from the hostile Red Stick Creek, but also from the White Sticks, who had sided with the United States.

Historical Background

In the Battle of the Thames (October 5, 1813), American forces effectively crushed a confederacy of American Indians led by Shawnee war chief Tecumseh and his British allies in the Old Northwest. The American victory dramatically and decisively reversed the course of the War of 1812, but it by no means ended the white-Indian hostilities associated with the war. In Georgia, Tennessee, and the Mississippi Territory, the Creek were engaged in an intratribal war between those who advocated cooperation with the whites and those bent on driving the whites out of their land. The latter faction, known as the Upper Creek, or Red Sticks, fought against the Americans in the War of 1812, while the tribe's peace faction—the Lower Creek, or White Sticks—cooperated with the Americans. The Red Sticks were in part equipped by the Spanish in Pensacola, Florida. The worst catastrophe for settlers in Creek country came on August 30, 1813, when Red Sticks under William Weatherford (Red Eagle) attacked Fort Mims on the lower Alabama River, resulting in the deaths of some 400 whites. The Tennessee legislature authorized $300,000, a staggering sum for that time and place, to outfit a large army under Andrew Jackson, who quickly and terribly swept through Red Stick country. In March 1814, with his militiamen augmented by 600 regulars from the U.S.

Thirty-ninth Infantry, Jackson attacked Horseshoe Bend, a peninsula on the Tallapoosa River. After a day-long battle on March 27, 1814, some 750 of a force of 900 Red Stick warriors lay dead. Following this victory, Jackson concluded a preliminary treaty, the provisions of which were subsequently formalized in the Treaty of Fort Jackson.

Terms

Although the preamble of the treaty is filled with high-sounding self-justification, the document is perhaps more honest than most agreements made between the United States and Native Americans in that it is almost entirely one-sided. Its chief provision is the cession of a vast tract of Creek land, amounting to some 23 million acres. The treaty makes no distinction between the Red Sticks, against whom the Creek War had been fought, and the White Sticks, who had sided with the forces of the United States. The territorial cession represented land belonging to the entire Creek Nation, Red Stick and White Stick alike.

Only two concessions are made to the Creek: a guarantee of the "integrity of [Creek] territory eastwardly and northwardly of the said line to be run and described as mentioned in the first article," and a pledge to assist the Creek ("reduced to extreme want, and not at present having the means of subsistence") by providing "gratuitously the necessaries of life."

The treaty is brief enough to be reproduced in its entirety.

Treaty of Fort Jackson

FORT JACKSON, AUGUST 9, 1814
*Made on behalf of the President of the
United States of America, and the Chiefs, Deputies,
and Warriors of the Creek Nation*

WHEREAS an unprovoked, inhuman, and sanguinary war, waged by the hostile Creeks against the United States, hath been repelled, prosecuted and determined, successfully, on the part of the said States, in conformity with principles of national justice and honorable warfare—And whereas consideration is due to the rectitude of proceeding dictated by instructions relating to the re-establishment of peace: Be it remembered, that prior to the conquest of that part of the Creek nation hostile to the United States, numberless aggressions had been committed against the peace, the property, and the lives of citizens of the United States, and those of the Creek nation in amity with her, at the mouth of Duck river, Fort Mimms, and elsewhere, contrary to national faith, and the regard due to an article of the treaty concluded at New-York, in the year seventeen hundred ninety, between the two nations: That the United States, previously to the perpetration of such outrages, did, in order to ensure future amity and concord between the Creek nation and the said states, in conformity with the stipulations of former treaties, fulfil, with punctuality and good faith, her engagements to the said nation: that more than two-thirds of the whole number of chiefs and warriors of the Creek nation, disregarding the genuine spirit of existing treaties, suffered themselves to be instigated to violations of their national honor, and the respect due to a part of their own nation faithful to the United States and the principles of humanity, by impostures [impostors,] denominating themselves Prophets, and by the duplicity and misrepresentation of foreign emissaries, whose governments are at war, open or understood, with the United States. Wherefore,

I

The United States demand an equivalent for all expenses incurred in prosecuting the war to its termination, by a cession of all the territory belonging to the Creek nation within the territories of the United States, lying west, south, and south-eastwardly, of a line to be run and described by persons duly authorized and appointed by the President of the United States—Beginning at a point on the eastern bank of the Coosa river, where the south boundary line of the Cherokee nation crosses the same; running from thence down the said Coosa river with its eastern bank according to its various meanders to a point one mile above the mouth of Cedar creek, at Fort Williams, thence east two miles, thence south two miles, thence west to the eastern bank of the said Coosa river, thence down the eastern bank thereof according to its various meanders to a point opposite the upper end of the great falls, (called by the natives Woetumka,) thence east from a true meridian line to a point due north of the mouth of Ofucshee, thence south by a like meridian line to the mouth of Ofucshee on the south side of the Tallapoosa river, thence up the same, according to its various meanders, to a point where a direct course will cross the same at the distance of ten miles from the mouth thereof, thence a direct line to the mouth of Summochico creek, which empties into the Chatahouchie river on the east side thereof below the Eufaulau town, thence east from a true meridian line to a point which shall intersect the line now dividing the lands claimed by the said Creek nation from those claimed and owned by the state of Georgia: Provided, nevertheless, that where any possession of any chief or warrior of the Creek nation, who shall have been friendly to the United States during the war, and taken an active part therein, shall be within the territory ceded by these articles to the United States, every such person shall be entitled to a reservation of land within the said territory of one mile square, to include his improvements as near the center thereof as may be, which shall inure to the said chief or warrior; and his descendants, so long as he or they shall continue to occupy the same, who shall be protected by and subject to the laws of the United States; but upon the voluntary abandonment thereof, by such possessor or his descendants, the right of occupancy or possession of said lands shall devolve to the United States, and be identified with the right of property ceded hereby.

II

The United States will guarantee to the Creek nation, the integrity of all their territory eastwardly and northwardly of the said line to be run and described as mentioned in the first article.

III

The United States demand, that the Creek nation abandon all communication, and cease to hold any intercourse with any British or Spanish post, garrison, or town; and that they shall not admit among them, any agent or trader, who shall not derive authority to hold commercial, or other intercourse with them, by license from the President or authorized agent of the United States.

IV

The United States demand an acknowledgment of the right to establish military posts and trading houses, and to open roads within the territory, guaranteed to the Creek nation by the second article, and a right to the free navigation of all its waters.

V

The United States demand, that a surrender be immediately made, of all the persons and property, taken from the citizens of the United States, the friendly part of the Creek nation, the Cherokee, Chickasaw, and Choctaw nations, to the respective owners; and the United States will cause to be immediately restored to the formerly hostile Creeks, all the property taken from them since their submission, either by the United States, or by any Indian nation in amity with the United States, together with all the prisoners taken from them during the war.

VI

The United States demand the capture and surrender of all the prophets and instigators of the war, whether foreigners or natives, who have not submitted to the arms of the United States, and become parties to these articles of capitulation, if ever they shall be found within the territory guaranteed to the Creek nation by the second article.

VII

The Creek nation being reduced to extreme want, and not at present having the means of subsistence, the United States, from motives of humanity, will continue to furnish gratuitously the necessaries of life, until the crops of corn can be considered competent to yield the nation a supply, and will establish trading houses in the nation, at the discretion of the President of the United States, and at such places as he shall direct, to enable the nation, by industry and economy, to procure clothing.

VIII

A permanent peace shall ensue from the date of these presents forever, between the Creek nation and the United States, and between the Creek nation and the Cherokee, Chickasaw, and Choctaw nations.

IX

If in running east from the mouth of Summochico creek, it shall so happen that the settlement of the Kennards, fall within the lines of the territory hereby ceded, then, and in that case, the line shall be run east on a true meridian to Kitchofoonee creek, thence down the middle of said creek to its junction with Flint River, immediately below the Oakmulgee town, thence up the middle of Flint river to a point due east of that at which the above line struck the Kitchofoonee creek, thence east to the old line herein before mentioned, to wit: the line dividing the lands claimed by the Creek nation, from those claimed and owned by the state of Georgia.

The parties to these presents, after due consideration for themselves and their constituents, agree to, ratify and confirm the preceding articles, and constitute them the basis of a permanent peace between the two nations; and they do hereby solemnly bind themselves, and all the parties concerned and interested, to a faithful performance of every stipulation contained therein. In testimony whereof, they have hereunto interchangeably set their hands and affixed their seals, the day and date above written.

TUSTUNNUCCEE THLUCCO, Speaker for the
Upper Creeks
MICCO AUPOCCAU, of Toukaubatche
TUSTUNNUCCEE HOPPOIEE, Speaker of the
Lower Creeks
MICCO ACHULEE, of Cowetau
WILLIAM M'INTOSH, Major of Cowetau
TUSREE ENEAH, of Cussetau
FAUE EMAUTLA, of Cussetau
TOUKAUBATCHEE TUSTUNNUCCEE, of Hitchetee
NOBLE KINNARD, of Hitchetee
HOPOIEE HUTKEE, of Souwagoolo

HOPOIEE HUTKEE, for HOPOIEE YOHOLO,
of Souwogoolo
FOLAPPO HAUJO, of Eufaulau, on Chattohochee
PACHEE HAUJO, of A palachoocla
TIMPOEECHEE BERNARD, Captain of Uchees
IJCHEE MICCO
YOHOLO MICCO, of Rialijee
SO-COS-XEE EMAUTLA, of Kialijee
CHOOC-CHAU HAUJO, of Woccocoi
ESHOLOCTEE, of Nauchee
YOHOLO MICCO, of Tallapoosa Eufaulau
STIN-THEL-LIS HAUJO, of Abecoochee
OCPUSREE YOHOLO, of Tou-ta-cau-gee
JOHN O'XELLY, of Coosa
ENEAH THLUCCO, of Immookfau
ESPOKOKOKE HAUJO, of Wewoka
ENEAH THLUCCO ElOPOLEE, of Talesee
EFAU HAUJO, of Puccan Tallahassee
TALESEE FIXICO, of Ocheobofau
NOMATLEE EMAUTLA, or CAPTAIN ISAACS of
Cousaudee
TUSKECEE EMAUTLA, or JOHN CARB of Tuskegee
ALEXANDER CRAYSON, of Hillabee
LOWEE, of Ocmulgee
NOCOOSEE EMAUTLA, of Chuskee Tallafau
WILLIAM M'INTOSH, for HOPOLEE HAUJO,
of Oose-oo-chee
WILLIAM M'INTOSH, for CHEHAHAW TUSTUNNUC-
CEE, of Chehahaw
WILLIAM M'INTOSH, for SPOKEKEE
TUSTUNNUCCEE, of O-tel-k-who-yon-nee

Done at Fort Jackson, in presence of CHARLES CASSEDY, Acting Secretary. BENJ. HAWKINS, Agent for Indian Affairs. RETURN J. MEIGS, A. C. NATION. ROBERT BUTLER, Adjutant General United States' Army. J. C. WARREN, Assistant Agent for Indian Affairs. GEORGE MAYFIELD, ALEXANDER CORNELS, GEORGE LOWRETT, Public Interpreters.

[To the Indian names are subjoined a mark and seal.]

Consequences

The guarantee of territorial integrity was soon violated by the state of Georgia and by the federal government's INDIAN REMOVAL ACT of 1830. The delivery of the promised provisions was subject to the vagaries of an inadequate and corrupt Indian agency system.

TREATY OF GHENT

TREATY AT A GLANCE

Completed
December 24, 1814, at Ghent, Belgium

Signatories
United States and Great Britain

Overview
With exaggeration called "the second War of Independence," the War of 1812 was largely instigated by expansionist interests in the United States and was fought over territorial boundaries. A costly war for both sides, it was concluded by the Treaty of Ghent, which officially restored the status quo antebellum.

Historical Background

For generations American schoolchildren had been taught that the War of 1812 was fought over a noble principle: the British, at war with Napoleon and badly in need of sailors for the Royal Navy, frequently intercepted and boarded neutral vessels, including ships of the United States, and summarily "impressed" into the service of Britain men arbitrarily deemed to be British subjects. Chiefly for this reason, it has often been said, the United States declared war on Great Britain on June 18, 1812. The fact is, however, that Great Britain had agreed, two days earlier, on June 16, to cease interfering with commerce on the high seas, effective June 23. Significantly, the Treaty of Ghent makes no mention of the impressment issue, precisely because it had ceased to be an issue, in any official sense, even before the war began.

The real source of the conflict was the American hunger for land, the most attractive parcel of which was Spanish Florida, which in 1812 extended as far west as the Mississippi River. Since Spain was allied with Great Britain against Napoleon, war with Britain would also mean war with Spain, and victory over Britain in such a war would mean the acquisition of Florida, which would be joined to the vast territories acquired by the LOUISIANA PURCHASE. There were other issues that interested western expansionists, as well. To the degree that former British impressment practices had disrupted trade, the U.S. coastal as well as interior economies suffered, and the West was particularly hard hit by a depression. Many westerners also believed, with varying degrees of justification, that British interests in Canada were arming Indians south of the bor-

der in an effort to drive out American settlers and eliminate trade competition. Finally, the borders between Canada and the United States were chronically in dispute. Using all of these causes, Henry Clay of Kentucky led the so-called War Hawks in an ultimately successful campaign to push President James Madison into a declaration of war.

It was, however, one thing to entertain bellicose sentiments and quite another to make good on them. Ill-manned, ill-equipped, ill-led, and poorly organized, the armed forces of the United States were hardly in a position to conduct an effective war against a major European power, especially one that had been on a war footing for most of the decade. The early campaigns were disastrous for the United States, which faced not only British troops but their Indian auxiliaries, including those led by the brilliant Tecumseh. Throughout 1812 the frontier suffered great devastation, but in 1813 Commander Oliver Hazard Perry scored a miraculous victory against the British fleet on Lake Erie, and William Henry Harrison defeated the British and Tecumseh's forces at the Battle of the Thames. However, the following year, with Napoleon in full retreat, the British were able to commit more troops to the war in America and struck a cruel blow by invading and burning the United States capital at Washington, D.C., sending President Madison and the War Hawk Congress into full flight. Later that year, U.S. forces recovered by successfully defending Baltimore from capture and pushing back invaders from Canada largely as a result of a naval victory on Lake Champlain. Exhausted and desirous of avoiding a protracted war, the British agreed to negotiate terms.

Terms

Negotiators from neither side approached the conference table feeling the flush of victory. In fact, the war's most decisive land battle came after the Ghent agreement had been concluded but before word of it had reached the combatant armies. General Andrew Jackson routed British forces at the Battle of New Orleans, lending an air of American triumph to a war that had no victor in any official sense.

The Treaty of Ghent proclaimed a "firm and universal peace between His Britannic Majesty and the United States," but it was actually more of an armistice than a settled treaty. It recognized that the chief cause of the dispute was territorial, but it left the determination of the precise boundary between the United States and Canada and the resolution of disputed claims to various islands and bodies of water located in the borderlands to a commission that was to consist of representatives of the United States and Great Britain. The commission would address the boundary issues in all their complexity:

ARTICLE IV

Whereas it was stipulated by the second article in the treaty of peace of one thousand seven hundred and eighty-three, between His Britannic Majesty and the United States of America, that the boundary of the United States should comprehend all islands within twenty leagues of any part of the shores of the United States, and lying between lines to be drawn due east from the points where the aforesaid boundaries, between Nova Scotia on the one part, and East Florida on the other, shall respectively touch the Bay of Fundy and the Atlantic Ocean, excepting such islands as now are, or heretofore have been, within the limits of Nova Scotia; and whereas the several islands in the Bay of Passamaquoddy, which is part of the Bay of Fundy, and the Islands of Grand Menan, in the said Bay of Fundy, are claimed by the United States as being comprehended within their aforesaid boundaries, which said islands are claimed as belonging to His Britannic Majesty, as having been, at the time of and previous to the aforesaid treaty of one thousand seven hundred and eighty-three, within the limits of the Province of Nova Scotia; In order, therefore, finally to decide upon these claims, it is agreed that they shall be referred to two Commissioners to be appointed in the following manner, viz: One Commissioner shall be appointed by His Britannic Majesty, and one by the President of the United States, by and with the advice and consent of the Senate thereof; and the said two Commissioners so appointed shall be sworn impartially to examine and decide upon the said claims according to such evidence as shall be laid before them on the part of His Britannic Majesty and of the United States respectively. The said Commissioners shall meet at St. Andrews, in the Province of New Brunswick, and shall have power to adjourn to such other place or places as they shall think fit. The said Commissioners shall, by a declaration or report under their hands and seals, decide to which of the two contracting parties the several islands of the aforesaid do respectively belong, in conformity with the true intent of the said treaty of peace of one thousand seven hundred and eighty-three. And if the said Commissioners shall agree in their decision, both parties shall consider such decision as final and conclusive. It is further agreed that, in event of the two Commissioners differing upon all or any of the matters so referred to them, or in the event of both or either of the said Commissioners refusing, or declining, or wilfully omitting to act as such, they shall make, jointly or separately, a report or reports, as well to the Government of His Britannic Majesty as to that of the United States, stating in detail the points on which they differ, and the grounds upon which their respective opinions have been formed, or the grounds upon which they, or either of them, have so refused, declined, or omitted to act. And His Britannic Majesty and the Government of the United States hereby agree to refer the report or reports of the said Commissioners to some friendly sovereign or State, to be then named for that purpose, and who shall be requested to decide on the differences which may be stated in the said report or reports, or upon the report of one Commissioner, together with the grounds upon which the other Commissioner shall have refused, declined or omitted to act, as the case may be. And if the Commissioner so refusing, declining or omitting to act, shall also wilfully omit to state the grounds upon which he has so done, in such manner that the said statement may be referred to such friendly sovereign or State, together with the report of such other Commissioner, then such sovereign or State shall decide *ex parte* upon the said report alone. And His Britannic Majesty and the Government of the United States engage to consider the decision of such friendly sovereign or State to be final and conclusive on all the matters so referred.

A modest, relatively brief, and dry document, the Treaty of Ghent did touch on two additional profound issues: the disposition of the Indians and the traffic in slaves. The former is discussed in Article 9:

ARTICLE IX

The United States of America engages to put an end, immediately after the ratification of the present treaty, to hostilities with all the tribes or nations of Indians with whom they may be at war at the time of such ratification; and forthwith to restore to such tribes or nations, respectively, all the possessions, rights and privileges which they may have enjoyed or been entitled to in one thousand eight hundred and eleven, previous to such hostilities: Provided always that such tribes or nations shall agree to desist from all hostilities against the United States of America, their citizens and subjects, upon the ratification of the present treaty being notified to such tribes or nations, and shall so desist accordingly. And His Britannic Majesty engages, on his part, to put an end immediately after the ratification of the present treaty, to hostilities with all the tribes or nations of Indians with whom he may be at war at the time of such ratification, and forthwith to restore to such tribes or nations respectively all the possessions, rights and privileges which they may have enjoyed or been entitled to in one thousand eight hundred and eleven, previous to such hostilities: Provided always that such tribes or nations shall agree to desist from all hostilities against His Britannic Majesty, and his subjects, upon the ratification of the present treaty being notified of such tribes or nations, and shall so desist accordingly.

More timid, but still significant, was the brief Article 10, concerning slavery:

ARTICLE X

Whereas the traffic in slaves is irreconcilable with the principles of humanity and justice, and whereas both His Majesty and the United States are desirous of continuing their efforts to promote its entire abolition, it is hereby agreed that both the contracting parties shall use their best endeavors to accomplish so desirable an object.

Consequences

The commission created by the treaty ultimately failed to resolve many of the most important disputed claims, especially the U.S.-Canadian boundary from the source of the Saint Croix River to the Saint Lawrence. The commissioners, appointed subsequently, met for the last time on April 13, 1822, then in desperation agreed in 1827 to leave the decision in the hands of a neutral third party, the king of the Netherlands, who delivered his award on January 10, 1831. It was rejected by both sides, and the boundary (as well as other disputed claims) was left in dispute for more than a decade afterward.

Americans had heard about the Treaty of Ghent at around the same time the news reached them of Andrew Jackson's crushing blow against the British in the Battle of New Orleans. The stunning British defeat, which came after the war ended, provided at least the feel of victory, even though none of the avowed American war aims—defending American commerce, vindicating republican independence—had truly been achieved. Indeed, on the frontier, westerners might be excused for believing that America had lost, since the treaty forbade all military activity there until the United States had concluded subsequent treaties with the "Indian allies of the English." That left the Indians free to roam the territory at will, while the local American authorities, at least in theory, were hamstrung by international agreement. The Indians knew it, launching their most destructive raids of the war during the six months it took to bring them to terms.

Still, they were brought to terms, chiefly because the withdrawal of the British from U.S. territory meant the collapse of various alliances with western Indian tribes, most notably the Sioux, who agreed by treaty to recognize the sovereignty of the United States over Missouri Territory. Because of the war, the United States secured a stronger claim to the Far Northwest, while in the South the war with the Red Stick Creek pushed American settlement, under the TREATY OF FORT JACKSON, to the Spanish border.

Indeed, Jackson's victories at Horseshoe Bend and New Orleans provided the West with its greatest hero since Daniel Boone, and westerners were not about to give that up for doubts about whether the Treaty of Ghent represented anything other than a cessation of the hostilities they had forced on a reluctant East. It was one of the many ways in which the War of 1812 helped to bind the West solidly to the rest of the country. The war also finished the Federalists as an effective political party. In short, though the Treaty of Ghent returned the two nations to the status quo ante—literally, "the way things were [before the war]"—this official result is misleading. In a broad sense the war, bumbling and disastrous as much of it had been, fostered a new patriotism and forged a sense of national identity and national purpose that would lead to imperial expansion westward.

TREATY OF FORT ARMSTRONG

TREATY AT A GLANCE

Completed
September 21, 1832, at Rock Island, Illinois

Signatories
United States and the Sac and Fox Indian tribes

Overview
The Black Hawk War of 1832 was the last major Indian-white conflict east of the Mississippi River. It was led by the charismatic Sac chief Black Hawk and was ended by the Treaty of Fort Armstrong, which secured additional cessions from the tribes.

Historical Background

In 1804 representatives of the Sac and Fox, two closely connected tribes, agreed to cede to the U.S. government all of the tribal lands in Illinois. Although, as a consequence of the treaty, the Indians were required to remove to Iowa on the west bank of the Mississippi River, they were permitted to remain in Illinois until the lands they had ceded were actually sold. Before all of the Indians had moved, however, the Sac leader Black Hawk (1767–1838) repudiated the 1804 treaty. He resisted white settlement by fighting on the side of the British during the War of 1812, and then, when the Indians were finally ordered into Iowa in 1828, he worked to forge an anti-American alliance with the Winnebago, Potawatomi, and Kickapoo. In this he failed, but during 1829, 1830, and 1831, he returned with his band east across the Mississippi for spring planting, terrorizing local whites.

When Black Hawk's so-called British Band returned in 1832, a military force was organized to repulse them. For 15 weeks, Black Hawk was pursued into Wisconsin and then westward toward the Mississippi. He unsuccessfully sought aid from other tribes, and on August 3, 1832, the remnants of the British Band were attacked as they attempted to flee west across the river. Black Hawk escaped, was refused succor by other tribes, and soon surrendered. He was imprisoned briefly, then permitted to settle in a Sac village on the Des Moines River. While he was in prison, General Winfield Scott, in charge of the American expedition, concluded the treaty on September 1921 at Fort Armstrong with the surviving Sac and Fox who had failed to escape.

Terms

The Treaty of Fort Armstrong began with a preamble which, without mentioning Black Hawk by name, referred to "certain lawless and desperate leaders" who violated treaties and began an "unprovoked" war:

> WHEREAS, under certain lawless and desperate leaders, a formidable band, constituting a large portion of the Sac and Fox nation, left their country in April last, and, in violation of treaties, commenced an unprovoked war upon unsuspecting and defenseless citizens of the United States, sparing neither age nor sex; and whereas, the United States, at a great expense of treasure, have subdued the said hostile band, killing or capturing all its principal Chiefs and Warriors—the said States, partly as indemnity for the expense incurred, and partly to secure the future safety and tranquillity of the invaded frontier, demand of the said tribes, to the use of the United States, a cession of a tract of the Sac and Fox country, bordering on said frontier, more than proportional to the numbers of the hostile band who have been so conquered and subdued.

By Article 1 of the Fort Armstrong agreement, the Sac and Fox ceded a vast portion of the Mississippi Valley, agreeing to live within the confines of a reservation set aside for them. In return, the United States agreed to pay a modest annuity:

> ARTICLE I
> Accordingly, the confederated tribes of Sacs and Foxes hereby cede to the United States forever, all the lands to which the said tribes have title, or claim, (with the exception of the reservation hereinafter made,) included within the following bounds, to wit: Beginning on the Mississippi river, at the point where the Sac and Fox northern boundary line, as established by

the second article of the treaty of Prairie du Chien, of the fifteenth of July, one thousand eight hundred and thirty, strikes said river; thence, up said boundary line to a point fifty miles from the Mississippi, measured on said line; thence, in a right line to the nearest point on the Red Cedar of the Ioway, forty miles from the Mississippi river; thence, in a right line to a point in the northern boundary line of the State of Missouri, fifty miles, measured on said boundary, from the Mississippi river; thence, by the last mentioned boundary to the Mississippi river, and by the western shore of said river to the place of beginning. And the said confederated tribes of Sacs and Foxes hereby stipulate and agree to remove from the lands herein ceded to the United States, on or before the first day of June next; and, in order to prevent any future misunderstanding, it is expressly understood, that no band or party of the Sac or Fox tribes shall reside, plant, fish, or hunt on any portion of the ceded country after the period just mentioned.

ARTICLE II

Out of the cession made in the preceding article, the United States agree to a reservation for the use of the said confederated tribes, of a tract of land containing four hundred square miles, to be laid off under the directions of the President of the United States, from the boundary line crossing the Ioway river, in such manner that nearly an equal portion of the reservation may be on both sides of said river, and extending downwards, so as to include Ke-o-kuck's principal village on its right bank, which village is about twelve miles from the Mississippi river.

ARTICLE III

In consideration of the great extent of the foregoing cession, the United States stipulate and agree to pay to the said confederated tribes, annually, for thirty successive years, the first payment to be made in September of the next year, the sum of twenty thousand dollars in specie.

Article 5 further agreed to discharge tribal debts to Indian traders:

ARTICLE V

The United States, at the earnest request of the said confederated tribes, further agree to pay to Farnham and Davenport, Indian traders at Rock Island, the sum of forty thousand dollars without interest, which sum will be in full satisfaction of the claims of the said traders against the said tribes, and by the latter was, on the tenth day of July, one thousand eight hundred and thirty-one, acknowledged to be justly due, for articles of necessity, furnished in the course of the seven pre-ceding years, in an instrument of writing of said date, duly signed by the Chiefs and Headmen of said tribes, and certified by the late Felix St. Vrain, United States' agent, and Antoine Le Claire, United States' Interpreter, both for the said tribes.

The only mention of Black Hawk came in Article 7, which acknowledged that most Sac and Fox prisoners of war had been released, save for Black Hawk and other leaders of the war, who "shall be held as hostages for the future good conduct of the late hostile bands, during the pleasure of the President of the United States."

An interesting fillip to this treaty was Article 11, which provided for a "suitable present" to be given to the tribes "on their pointing out to any United States agent . . . the position or positions of one or more mines, supposed by the said tribes to be of a metal more valuable than lead or iron."

Consequences

Despite what the Treaty of Fort Armstrong claimed, Black Hawk had repudiated the 1804 agreements on the grounds that those who had made the cession of Illinois lands did not fairly represent the Sac and Fox tribes. To his thinking, then, the war he had just lost was not "unprovoked," since those earlier agreements were invalid. This points up a common flaw of white-Indian treaties in North America. Oftentimes, such treaties were concluded by compliant individuals who did not necessarily represent the majority will of the tribe. The problem was compounded by the fact that tribal chiefs were not analogous to European sovereigns or the United States chief executive. They did not rule their tribes so much as they led by force of personality and persuasion. Often, a given chief held sway over a particular tribal faction only. Keokuk, whose name appears first on the Treaty of Fort Armstrong, was an Indian eager to cooperate with the government. Because of this, U.S. officials readily decided that he—and other similarly tractable individuals—had the authority to conclude a treaty on behalf of the tribe.

Black Hawk's defeat and humiliation dispirited resistance from the so-called Civilized Tribes of the Southeast, whom President Andrew Jackson was at that moment seeking to move west of the Mississippi by various treaties and agreements attendant to the INDIAN REMOVAL ACT.

TREATY OF GUADALUPE HIDALGO

TREATY AT A GLANCE

Completed
February 2, 1848, at Guadalupe Hidalgo, Mexico

Signatories
United States and Mexico

Overview
The principal U.S. motive for declaring war against Mexico in 1846 was western expansion at Mexico's expense. For its part, Mexico wished to restrain expansion and punish what it deemed U.S. "insolence." Expansionism was sufficient to whip up war fever in the United States, but officials found more immediate justification for war in Mexico's failure to make restitution for losses suffered by U.S. citizens during various internal uprisings, in Mexico's generally "barbarous" policies with regard to foreign nationals, and in the Mexican government's rebuff of a U.S. mission to negotiate the purchase of California. The United States enjoyed great success in the Mexican War, and by the Treaty of Guadalupe Hidalgo, the nation realized great territorial gains in the Southwest in return for $15 million and the assumption of U.S. citizens' claims against Mexico.

Historical Background

The Mexican state of Texas was colonized mainly by Americans beginning in the 1820s. Having won its independence in 1835–36, Texas sought annexation to the United States. The U.S. government demurred, however, since annexation would not only lead inevitably to war with Mexico but would upset the tenuous balance of slave versus free states, giving the southern bloc undue influence. However, by the late 1840s, both France and England were courting an independent Texas as a potential military ally and trading partner. Citing this, outgoing president John Tyler urged Congress to adopt an annexation resolution, which Tyler signed just three days before the expiration of his term. On June 16, 1845, the Congress of the Republic of Texas accepted, and Tyler's successor, President James K. Polk, admitted Texas to the Union on December 29.

Just as the Texas question was being settled, it became apparent that England and France had also set their sights on California, which was held tenuously by Mexico. Stirred to action, President Polk offered Mexico $40 million for California, but Mexican president Herrera rebuffed Polk's minister, John Slidell, whereupon Polk sanctioned a covert separatist movement in the territory. In the meantime, John Charles Frémont, exploring potential transcontinental railroad routes for the U.S. Bureau of Topographical Engineers, took matters into his own hands, leading the so-called Bear Flag Rebellion, a relatively minor uprising that nevertheless succeeded in gaining California's independence from Mexico.

While the Bear Flag Rebellion was under way in California, Texas became the focus of a boundary dispute with Mexico. When it was part of Mexico, Texas had been bounded on the south by the Nueces River. Independent Texas claimed the Rio Grande as its southern boundary, a claim the United States enforced when the republic entered the Union. Throughout 1845 the United States and Mexico built up troop strength on either side of the Nueces. After Slidell's mission was rebuffed in January 1846, President Polk ordered General Zachary Taylor to advance to the north bank of the Rio Grande. A clash was inevitable, and the United States declared war on May 13, 1846.

Although the war was unpopular in New England, where many saw it as an unjust imperialist adventure, elsewhere volunteers were so numerous that recruiters had to turn many of them away. Nevertheless, the American army was ill trained and ill equipped. The Mexican forces, more numerous and often splendidly uniformed, were even less prepared for battle than the Americans. Their leadership was also markedly inferior, and the Americans, usually outnumbered, progressed from one decisive triumph to another. Soon General Taylor's armies were thrusting deep into Mexico.

In July 1846 Antonio López de Santa Anna, exiled to Cuba after a rebellion had ended his dictatorship of Mexico, proposed aiding the United States in reaching a successful conclusion to the war in return for a payment (to him personally) of $30 million and safe conduct to Mexico. Although the Americans balked at the money, they did allow Santa Anna to return to Mexico, where he immediately set about putting together an army to crush Taylor. By January 1847 Santa Anna had gathered 18,000 men, hurling some 15,000 of them against Taylor's 4,800-man force at Buena Vista. Remarkably, Taylor prevailed, forcing Santa Anna to withdraw on February 23.

At this point and chiefly for political reasons, President Polk replaced Taylor with General Winfield Scott, a hero of the War of 1812, who prosecuted the war with far greater vigor than Taylor had. Scott completed the invasion of Mexico with lightning speed, pushing Santa Anna all the way to Mexico City, which fell on September 17, when Santa Anna surrendered.

Terms

Peace talks, which had begun on August 27, even before the invasion of Mexico City, and which had been broken off by the Mexicans on September 7, resumed on November 22. It fell to a reluctant and somewhat junior State Department official, Nicholas P. Trist, to hammer out a treaty. General Scott persuaded a dubious President Polk that the political situation in Mexico was too unstable to permit the convention of a more august U.S. negotiating team. Scott reasoned that it was critical to conclude a treaty while there was still a semblance of a recognized Mexican government with which to treat.

Considering the magnitude of the American victory, the terms of the Treaty of Guadalupe Hidalgo were generous. The United States gained New Mexico (which also included parts of the present states of Utah, Nevada, Arizona, and Colorado) and California as well as Mexican renunciation of its claims to Texas above the Rio Grande. In return, the United States agreed to pay $15 million and to assume all claims of U.S. citizens against Mexico, which amounted to an additional $3,250,000, as subsequently determined by

a specially appointed commission. In addition, restitution was made for customs duties Mexico had been unable to collect because of the war.

Despite the customary pledges of "peace and friendship, which shall confer reciprocal benefits upon the citizens of both" nations, the framers of Guadalupe Hidalgo approached their task with considerable realism. The boundary line was meticulously specified, and the treaty provided for special survey maps to be commissioned. The treaty writers specified that the line was to be "religiously respected by each of the two republics, and no change shall ever be made therein, except by the express and free consent of both nations, lawfully given by the General Government of each, in conformity with its own constitution." The treaty also anticipated the possibility of renewed hostilities and set forth rules of "humane" warfare:

ARTICLE XXII

If (which is not to be expected, and which God forbid) war should unhappily break out between the two republics, they do now, with a view to such calamity, solemnly pledge themselves to each other and to the world to observe the following rules; absolutely where the nature of the subject permits, and as closely as possible in all cases where such absolute observance shall be impossible:

(1) The merchants of either republic then residing in the other shall be allowed to remain twelve months, (for those dwelling in the interior,) and six months, (for those dwelling at the seaports,) to collect their debts and settle their affairs; during which periods they shall enjoy the same protection, and be on the same footing, in all respects, as the citizens or subjects of the most friendly nations; and, at the expiration thereof, or at any time before, they shall have full liberty to depart, carrying off all their effects without molestation or hindrance, conforming therein to the same laws which the citizens or subjects of the most friendly nations are required to conform to. Upon the entrance of the armies of either nation into the territories of the other, women and children, ecclesiastics, scholars of every faculty, cultivators of the earth, merchants, artisans, manufacturers, and fishermen, unarmed and inhabiting unfortified towns, villages, or places, and in general all persons whose occupations are for the common subsistence and benefit of mankind, shall be allowed to continue their respective employments, unmolested in their persons. Nor shall their houses or goods be burnt or otherwise destroyed, nor their cattle taken, nor their fields wasted, by the armed force into whose power, by the events of war, they may happen to fall; but if the necessity arise to take anything from them for the use of such armed force, the same shall be paid for at an equitable price. All churches, hospitals, schools, colleges, libraries, and other establishments for charitable and beneficent purposes, shall be respected, and all persons connected with the same, protected in

the discharge of their duties, and the pursuit of their vocations.

(2) In order that the fate of prisoners of war may be alleviated, all such practices as those of sending them into distant, inclement, or unwholesome districts, or crowding them into close and noxious places, shall be studiously avoided. They shall not be confined in dungeons, prison-ships, or prisons; nor be put in irons, or bound, or otherwise restrained in the use of their limbs. The officers shall enjoy liberty on their paroles, within convenient districts, and have comfortable quarters; and the common soldier shall be disposed in cantonments, open and extensive enough for air and exercise, and lodged in barracks as roomy and good as are provided by the party in whose power they are for its own troops. But if any officer shall break his parole by leaving the district so assigned him, or any other prisoner shall escape from the limits of his cantonment, after they shall have been designated to him, such individual, officer, or other prisoner, shall forfeit so much of the benefit of this article as provides for his liberty on parole or in cantonment. And if any officer so breaking his parole, or any common soldier so escaping from the limits assigned him, shall afterwards be found in arms, previously to his being regularly exchanged, the person so offending shall be dealt with according to the established laws of war. The officers shall be daily furnished, by the party in whose power they are, with as many rations, and of the same articles, as are allowed, either in kind or by commutation, to officers of equal rank in its own army; and all others shall be daily furnished with such ration as is allowed to a common soldier in its own service; the value of all which supplies shall, at the close of the war, or at periods to be agreed upon between the respective commanders, be paid by the other party, on a mutual adjustment of accounts for the subsistence of prisoners; and such accounts shall not be mingled with or set off against any others, nor the balance due on them be withheld, as a compensation or reprisal for any cause whatever, real or pretended. Each party shall be allowed to keep a commissary of prisoners, appointed by itself, with every cantonment of prisoners, in possession of the other; which commissary shall see the prisoners as often as he pleases; shall be allowed to receive, exempt from all duties or taxes, and to distribute, whatever comforts may be sent to them by their friends; and shall be free to transmit his reports in open letters to the party by whom he is employed.

And it is declared that neither the pretence that war dissolves all treaties, nor any other whatever, shall be considered as annulling or suspending the solemn covenant contained in this article. On the contrary, the state of war is precisely that for which it is provided; and, during which, its stipulations are to be as sacredly observed as the most acknowledged obligations under the law of nature or nations.

The Mexican-American borderlands had been traditionally plagued by Indian hostility, and the framers of Guadalupe Hidalgo attempted to provide for the restriction of Indian incursion from the acquired territories into the newly reconfigured Mexico:

ARTICLE XI

Considering that a great part of the territories, which, by the present treaty, are to be comprehended for the future within the limits of the United States, is now occupied by savage tribes, who will hereafter be under the exclusive control of the Government of the United States, and whose incursions within the territory of Mexico would be prejudicial in the extreme, it is solemnly agreed that all such incursions shall be forcibly restrained by the Government of the United States whensoever this may be necessary; and that when they cannot be prevented, they shall be punished by the said government, and satisfaction for the same shall be exacted—all in the same way, and with equal diligence and energy, as if the same incursions were meditated or committed within its own territory, against its own citizens.

It shall not be lawful, under any pretext whatever, for any inhabitant of the United States to purchase or acquire any Mexican, or any foreigner residing in Mexico, who may have been captured by Indians inhabiting the territory of either of the two republics; nor to purchase or acquire horses, mules, cattle, or property of any kind, stolen within Mexican territory by such Indians.

And in the event of any person or persons, captured within Mexican territory by Indians, being carried into the territory of the United States, the Government of the latter engages and binds itself, in the most solemn manner, so soon as it shall know of such captives being within its territory, and shall be able so to do, through the faithful exercise of its influence and power, to rescue them and return them to their country, or deliver them to the agent or representative of the Mexican Government. The Mexican authorities will, as far as practicable, give to the Government of the United States notice of such captures; and its agents shall pay the expenses incurred in the maintenance and transmission of the rescued captives; who, in the mean time, shall be treated with the utmost hospitality by the American authorities at the place where they may be. But if the Government of the United States, before receiving such notice from Mexico, should obtain intelligence, through any other channel, of the existence of Mexican captives within its territory, it will proceed forthwith to effect their release and delivery to the Mexican agent, as above stipulated.

For the purpose of giving to these stipulations the fullest possible efficacy, thereby affording the security and redress demanded by their true spirit and intent, the Government of the United States will now and hereafter pass, without unnecessary delay, and always vigilantly enforce, such laws as the nature of the subject may require. And, finally, the sacredness of this obligation shall never be lost sight of by the said Government, when providing for the removal of the Indians from any portion of the said territories, or for its being settled by citizens of the United States; but, on the contrary, special care shall then be taken not to place its Indian occupants under the necessity of seeking new homes, by committing those invasions which the United States have solemnly obliged themselves to restrain.

Consequences

The treaty's proposals for humane warfare anticipated later international conventions and accords, especially those concluded as a result of the First International Peace Conference, often called the HAGUE CONVENTION, in 1899 and in subsequent such conferences. More immediately, many in the United States thought the terms of the treaty were too generous, and some called for nothing less than "All Mexico!" (which became a familiar slogan). President Polk had his own second thoughts, but Scott and Trist convinced him that having obtained Mexican surrender on terms proposed by the duly appointed U.S. negotiator, it would not be proper to abrogate them. Vast as the territorial acquisitions were, Jefferson Davis, secretary of war in 1853, engineered additional acquisitions by means of the GADSDEN TREATY of December 30, 1853. By then American officials had realized that the task of policing the Hidalgo cessions as set out in the treaty represented a military project of enormous, even hopeless scope, and Article 11 was abrogated by the Gadsden Treaty, which, in exchange for $10 million, bought the remaining tracts that make up the present-day continental United States.

Annexations and Territorial Agreements

THE LOUISIANA PURCHASE

TREATY AT A GLANCE

Completed (Ratified)
October 20, 1803

Signatories
United States and France

Overview
Hailed as the greatest real estate deal in history, the Louisiana Purchase doubled the size of the United States and put it squarely on the road to a continental empire. At the same time, it deepened the sectional disputes among the states, and such divisions ultimately led to civil war.

Historical Background

The vast stretch of Louisiana, settled by the French, now in the hands of the Spanish, had long been the focus of intrigue abroad. When the American West—the territory between the Appalachians and the Mississippi—began filling fast in the late 18th century, not only Thomas Jefferson but other U.S. policy makers looked toward the "Far West," and Louisiana became the focus of increasing pressure at home. There was talk in high circles of taking Louisiana by force. Doubtless that would have happened at some point, but then Napoleon Bonaparte made his presence felt on the already well-trod stage of western American empire. In a secret treaty concluded on October 1, 1800, Spain ceded Louisiana to France in exchange for certain territories in Tuscany and a promise that France would maintain the territory as a buffer between the United States and Mexico.

The same year that Spain gave Louisiana back to France by secret treaty, Thomas Jefferson became president of the United States of America. Napoleon had plans for Louisiana, as he had plans for most of the world, but he could hardly move to make the territory the focus of a New World empire while he was embroiled in a slave rebellion in Haiti and a series of conflicts on the European continent. In fact, he was so overextended already that he immediately disappointed Spain by abandoning the war that would have

given her the Tuscan territory he promised. A dispute developed between the two, and Spain continued to administer Louisiana.

Just about the time the United States became aware of the secret transfer, a suspicious and ailing Spain closed the port of New Orleans to American trade. The transfer of Louisiana and the closing of New Orleans raised the ire of many westerners and made the new president quite anxious. Jefferson feared, among other things, that he might be forced by his political enemies to change his basic foreign policy and ally the United States with Great Britain. Although Jefferson, like many Americans, believed that only Britain, with its mighty navy, could stand up to Napoleon, he had from Revolutionary War days been a strident Anglophobe and an ardent Francophile. As America's former minister to France, he had fully supported the French Revolution, which ultimately led to Napoleon's rise to power. Like many westerners, Jefferson was convinced that British fur traders continued to agitate the Indians in the West, including Ohio, which was just then preparing for statehood, and he despised British condescension toward its former colony, so shabbily treating the British minister in social settings that he nearly provoked formal protests.

Yet Jefferson also knew that a West controlled by Napoleon's France was a far greater threat than that same territory administered by a feeble Spain. Surely, he and many others reasoned, the apparently departing Iberians would not have acted to close New Orleans without Napoleon's backing. Thus the very presence of France as a neighbor might mean both a blockage of westward expansion indefinitely and a threat to a substantial portion of the nation's trade. For the time being, France was still an ally of the United States, and—despite Spain's suspension of the right of deposit—Napoleon at least posed no overt and immediate threat to the security of the new nation. But war loomed between France and Britain, and in any such war Britain would likely seize the Louisiana territory. In either case—whether France took control of New Orleans or whether Britain grabbed the port in battle— the United States would be choked off at the Mississippi. Many westerners, and some in Congress, were now openly calling for the territory to be taken by force of arms. Jefferson realized he might soon find his weak new republic obliged to choose sides and dragged into a general European conflict.

Jefferson sent New York's Robert Livingston to Paris to negotiate a treaty. Not long afterward, he dispatched James Monroe, a fellow Virginian, with instructions to offer to buy the city of New Orleans and Florida (west of the Perdido River) from France for no more than $9 million. Meanwhile, Napoleon's army, which had been fighting in the West Indies, was dying there—not from English bullets but from yellow fever and guerrilla warfare with the formerly enslaved islanders. Fearful of being bogged down in a pestiferous corner of the world, Napoleon decided to retreat from the Americas, at least for the time being. He still feared British usurpation of the Louisiana territory, and he also needed money to finance his European wars.

The perfect expedient was to sell the territory—all of it—to the United States. On April 11, 1803, even before Monroe had arrived in Paris to negotiate for the purchase of New Orleans, Napoleon's prime minister, the duke of Talleyrand, asked Livingston (whose title was U.S. minister to France) how much Jefferson would offer for the whole of Louisiana. Negotiations proceeded after Monroe arrived and were concluded in a treaty signed on May 2, 1803. Basically, Napoleon's misadventure in Haiti led him to offer the United States one of the greatest real estate deals in history: 900,000 square miles of trans-Mississippi territory for 60 million francs, or about $15 million.

Terms

The Louisiana Purchase came in three parts: a treaty of cession and two conventions, one for the payment of 60 million francs ($11,250,000), the other for claims American citizens had made against France for 20 million francs ($3,750,000).

Treaty between the United States of America and the French Republic

The President of the United States of America and the First Consul of the French Republic in the name of the French People desiring to remove all Source of misunderstanding relative to objects of discussion mentioned in the Second and fifth articles o f the Convention of the 8th Vendémiaire an 9/30 September 1800 relative to the rights claimed by the United States in virtue of the Treaty concluded at Madrid the 27 of October 1795, between His Catholic Majesty & the Said United States, & willing to Strengthen the union and friendship which at the time of the Said Convention was happily reestablished between the two nations have respectively named their Plenipotentiaries to wit The President of the United States, by and with the advice and consent o f the Senate of the Said States; Robert R. Livingston Minister Plenipotentiary of the United States and James Monroe Minister Plenipotentiary and Envoy extraordinary of the Said States near the Government of the French Republic; And the First Consul in th e name of the French people, Citizen Francis Barbé Marbois Minister of the public treasury who after having respectively exchanged their full powers have agreed to the following Articles.

ARTICLE I

Whereas by the Article the third of the Treaty concluded at St Ildefonso the 9th Vendémiaire an 9/1st October 1800 between the First Consul of the French Republic and his Catholic Majesty it was agreed as follows.

"His Catholic Majesty promises and engages on his part to cede to the French Republic six months after the full and entire execution of the conditions and Stipulations herein relative to his Royal Highness the Duke of Parma, the Colony or Province of Louisiana with the Same extent that it now has in the hand of Spain, & that it had when France possessed it; and Such as it Should be after the Treaties subsequently entered into between Spain and other States."

And whereas in pursuance of the Treaty and particularly of the third article the French Republic has an incontestible title to the domain and to the possession of the said Territory-The First Consul of the French Republic desiring to give to the United States a strong proof of his friendship doth hereby cede to the United States in the name of the French Republic for ever and in full Sovereignty the said territory with all its rights and appurtenances as fully and in the Same manner as they have bee n acquired by the French Republic in virtue of the above mentioned Treaty concluded with his Catholic Majesty.

ARTICLE II

In the cession made by the preceeding article are included the adjacent Islands belonging to Louisiana all public lots and Squares, vacant lands and all public buildings, fortifications, barracks and other edifices which are not private property.-The

Archives, papers & documents relative to the domain and Sovereignty of Louisiana and its dependencies will be left in the possession of the Commissaries of the United States, and copies will be afterwards given in due form to the Magistrates and Municipal officers of such of the said papers and documents as may be necessary to them.

ARTICLE III

The inhabitants of the ceded territory shall be incorporated in the Union of the United States and admitted as soon as possible according to the principles of the federal Constitution to the enjoyment of all these rights, advantages and immunities of citizens of the United States, and in the mean time they shall be maintained and protected in the free enjoyment of their liberty, property and the Religion which they profess.

ARTICLE IV

There Shall be Sent by the Government of France a Commissary to Louisiana to the end that he do every act necessary as well to receive from the Officers of his Catholic Majesty the Said country and its dependencies in the name of the French Republic if it has not been already done as to transmit it in the name of the French Republic to the Commissary or agent of the United States.

ARTICLE V

Immediately after the ratification of the present Treaty by the President of the United States and in case that of the first Consul's shall have been previously obtained, the commissary of the French Republic shall remit all military posts of New Orleans and other parts of the ceded territory to the Commissary or Commissaries named by the President to take possession—the troops whether of France or Spain who may be there shall cease to occupy any military post from the time of taking possession and shall be embarked as soon as possible in the course of three months after the ratification of this treaty.

ARTICLE VI

The United States promise to execute Such treaties and articles as may have been agreed between Spain and the tribes and nations of Indians until by mutual consent of the United States and the said tribes or nations other Suitable articles Shall have been agreed upon.

ARTICLE VII

As it is reciprocally advantageous to the commerce of France and the United States to encourage the communication of both nations for a limited time in the country ceded by the present treaty until general arrangements relative to commerce of both nations may be agreed on; it has been agreed between the contracting parties that the French Ships coming directly from France or any of her colonies loaded only with the produce and manufactures of France or her Said Colonies; and the Ships of Spain coming directly from Spain or any of her colonies loaded only with the produce or manufactures of Spain or her Colonies shall be admitted during the Space of twelve years in the Port of New-Orleans and in all other legal ports-of-entry within the ceded territory in the Same manner as the Ships of the United States coming directly from France or Spain or any of their Colonies without being Subject to any other or greater duty on merchandize or other or greater tonnage than that paid by the citizens of the United. States.

During that Space of time above mentioned no other nation Shall have a right to the Same privileges in the Ports of the ceded territory—the twelve years Shall commence three months after the exchange of ratifications if it Shall take place in France or three months after it Shall have been notified at Paris to the French Government if it Shall take place in the United States; It is however well understood that the object of the above article is to favour the manufactures, Commerce, freight and navigation of France and of Spain So far as relates to the importations that the French and Spanish Shall make into the Said Ports of the United States without in any Sort affecting the regulations that the United States may make concerning the exportation of t he produce and merchandize of the United States, or any right they may have to make Such regulations.

ARTICLE VIII

In future and for ever after the expiration of the twelve years, the Ships of France shall be treated upon the footing of the most favoured nations in the ports above mentioned.

ARTICLE IX

The particular Convention Signed this day by the respective Ministers, having for its object to provide for the payment of debts due to the Citizens of the United States by the French Republic prior to the 30th Sept. 1800 (8th Vendémiaire an 9) is approved and to have its execution in the Same manner as if it had been inserted in this present treaty, and it Shall be ratified in the same form and in the Same time So that the one Shall not be ratified distinct from the other.

Another particular Convention Signed at the Same date as the present treaty relative to a definitive rule between the contracting parties is in the like manner approved and will be ratified in the Same form, and in the Same time and jointly.

ARTICLE X

The present treaty Shall be ratified in good and due form and the ratifications Shall be exchanged in the Space of Six months after the date of the Signature by the Ministers Plenipotentiary or Sooner if possible.

In faith whereof the respective Plenipotentiaries have Signed these articles in the French and English languages; declaring nevertheless that the present Treaty was originally agreed to in the French language; and have thereunto affixed their Seals.

Done at Paris the tenth day of Floreal in the eleventh year of the French Republic; and the 30th of April 1803.

ROBT R LIVINGSTON [SEAL]
JAS. MONROE [SEAL]
BARBÉ MARBOIS [SEAL]

Convention between the United States of America and the French Republic

The President of the United States of America and the First Consul of the French Republic in the name of the French people, in consequence of the treaty of cession of Louisiana which has been Signed this day; wishing to regulate definitively every thing which has relation to the Said cession have authorized to this effect the Plenipotentiaries, that is to say the President of the United States has, by and with the advice and consent of the Senate of the Said States, nominated for their Plenipotentiaries, Robert R. Livingston, Minister Plenipotentiary of the United States, and James Monroe, Minister Plenipotentiary and Envoy-Extraordinary of the Said United States, near the Government of the French Republic; and the First Consul of the French Republic, in the name of the French people, has named as Plenipotentiary of the Said Republic the citizen Francis Barbé Marbois: who, in virtue of their full powers, which have been exchanged this day, have agreed to the followings articles:

ARTICLE 1

The Government of the United States engages to pay to the French government in the manner Specified in the following article the sum of Sixty millions of francs independent of the Sum which Shall be fixed by another Convention for the payment of the debts due by France to citizens of the United States.

ARTICLE 2

For the payment of the Sum of Sixty millions of francs mentioned in the preceeding article the United States shall create a Stock of eleven millions, two hundred and fifty thousand Dollars bearing an interest of Six per cent: per annum payable half yearly in London Amsterdam or Paris amounting by the half year to three hundred and thirty Seven thousand five hundred Dollars, according to the proportions which Shall be determined by the french Government to be paid at either place: The principal of the Said Stock to be reimbursed at the treasury of the United States in annual payments of not less than three millions of Dollars each; of which the first payment Shall commence fifteen years after the date of the exchange of ratifications:—this Stock Shall be transferred to the government of France or to Such person or persons as Shall be authorized to receive it in three months at most after the exchange of ratifications of this treaty and after Louisiana Shall be taken possession of the name of the Government of the United States.

It is further agreed that if the french Government Should be desirous of disposing of the Said Stock to receive the capital in Europe at Shorter terms that its measures for that purpose Shall be taken So as to favour in the greatest degree possible the credit of the United States, and to raise to the highest price the Said Stock.

ARTICLE 3

It is agreed that the Dollar of the United States Specified in the present Convention shall be fixed at five francs 3333/100000 or five livres eight Sous tournois.

The present Convention Shall be ratified in good and due form, and the ratifications Shall be exchanged the Space of Six months to date from this day or Sooner if possible.

In faith of which the respective Plenipotentiaries have Signed the above articles both in the french and english languages, declaring nevertheless that the present treaty has been originally agreed on and written in the french language; to which they have hereunto affixed their Seals.

Done at Paris the tenth of Floreal eleventh year of the French Republic/ 30th April 1803 ./

ROBT R LIVINGSTON [SEAL]

JAS. MONROE [SEAL]
BARBÉ MARBOIS [SEAL]

Convention between the United States of America and the French Republic

The President of the United States of America and the First Consul of the French Republic in the name of the French People having by a Treaty of this date terminated all difficulties relative to Louisiana, and established on a Solid foundation the friendship which unites the two nations and being desirous in complyance with the Second and fifth Articles of the Convention of the 8th Vendé miaire ninth year of the French Republic (30th September 1800) to Secure the payment of the Sums due by France to the citizens of the United States have respectively nominated as Plenipotentiaries that is to Say The President of the United States of America by and with the advise and consent of their Senate Robert R. Livingston Minister Plenipotentiary and James Monroe Minister Plenipotentiary and Envoy Extraordinary of the Said States near the Government of the French Republic: and the First Consul in the name of the French People the Citizen Francis Barbé Marbois Minister of the public treasury; who after having exchanged their full powers have agreed to the following articles.

ARTICLE 1

The debts due by France to citizens of the United States contracted before the 8th Vendé miaire ninth year of the French Republic/30th September 1800/ Shall be paid according to the following regulations with interest at Six per Cent; to commence from the period when the accounts and vouchers were presented to the French Government.

ARTICLE 2

The debts provided for by the preceeding Article are those whose result is comprised in the conjectural note annexed to the present Convention and which, with the interest cannot exceed the Sum of twenty millions of Francs. The claims comprised in the Said note which fall within the exceptions of the following articles, Shall not be admitted to the benefit of this provision.

ARTICLE 3

The principal and interests of the Said debts Shall be discharged by the United States, by orders drawn by their Minister Plenipotentiary on their treasury, these orders Shall be payable Sixty days after the exchange of ratifications of the Treaty and the Conventions Signed this day, and after possession Shall be given of Louisiana by the Commissaries of France to those of the United States.

ARTICLE 4

It is expressly agreed that the preceding articles Shall comprehend no debts but Such as are due to citizens of the United States who have been and are yet creditors of France for Supplies for embargoes and prizes made at Sea, in which the appeal has been properly lodged within the time mentioned in the Said Convention 8th Vendé miaire ninth year, /30th Sept 1800/

ARTICLE 5

The preceding Articles Shall apply only, First: to captures of which the council of prizes Shall have ordered restitution, it being well understood that the claimant cannot have recourse to the United States otherwise than he might have had to the Government of the French republic, and only in case of insufficiency of the captors—2d the debts mentioned in the Said fifth Article of the Convention contracted before the 8th Vendé miaire an 9/30th September 1800 the payment of which has been heretofore claimed of the actual Government of France and for which the creditors have a right to the protection of the United States;— the Said 5th Article does not comprehend prizes whose condemnation has been or Shall be confirmed: it is the express intention of the contracting parties not to extend the benefit of the present Convention to reclamations of American citizens who Shall have established houses of Commerce in France, England or other countries than the United States in partnership with foreigner s, and who by that reason and the nature of their commerce ought to be regarded as domiciliated in the places where Such house exist.—All agreements and bargains concerning merchandize, which Shall not be the property of American citizens, are equally excepted from the benefit of the said Conventions, Saving however to Such persons their claims in like manner as if this Treaty had not been made.

ARTICLE 6

And that the different questions which may arise under the preceding article may be fairly investigated, the Ministers Plenipotentiary of the United States Shall name three persons, who Shall act from the present and provisionally, and who shall have full power to examine, without removing the documents, all the accounts of the different claims already liquidated by the Bureaus established for this purpose by the French Republic, and to ascertain whether they belong to the classes designated by the present Convention and the principles established in it or if they are not in one of its exceptions and on their Certificate, declaring that the debt is due to an American Citizen or his representative and that it existed before the 8th Vendé miaire 9th year/30 September 1800 the debtor shall be entitled to an order on the Treasury of the United States in the manner prescribed by the 3d Article.

ARTICLE 7

The Same agents Shall likewise have power, without removing the documents, to examine the claims which are prepared for verification, and to certify those which ought to be admitted by uniting the necessary qualifications, and not being comprised in the exceptions contained in the present Convention.

ARTICLE 8

The Same agents Shall likewise examine the claims which are not prepared for liquidation, and certify in writing those which in their judgement ought to be admitted to liquidation.

ARTICLE 9

In proportion as the debts mentioned in these articles Shall be admitted they Shall be discharged with interest at Six per Cent: by the Treasury of the United States.

ARTICLE 10

And that no debt shall not have the qualifications above mentioned and that no unjust or exorbitant demand may be admitted, the Commercial agent of the United States at Paris or such other agent as the Minister Plenipotentiary or the United States Shall think proper to nominate shall assist at the operations of the Bureaus and cooperate in the examinations of the claims; and if this agent Shall be of the opinion that any debt is not completely proved, or if he shall judge that it is not comprised in t he principles of the fifth article above mentioned, and if notwithstanding his opinion the Bureaus established by the french Government should think that it ought to be liquidated, he shall transmit his observations to the board established by the United States, who, without removing documents, shall make a complete examination of the debt and vouchers which Support it, and report the result to the Minister of the United States.—The Minister of the United States Shall transmit his observations in all Such cases to the Minister of the treasury of the French Republic, on whose report the French Government Shall decide definitively in every case.

The rejection of any claim Shall have no other effect than to exempt the United States from the payment of it, the French Government reserving to itself, the right to decide definitively on Such claim So far as it concerns itself.

ARTICLE 11

Every necessary decision Shall be made in the course of a year to commence from the exchange of ratifications, and no reclamation Shall be admitted afterwards.

ARTICLE 12

In case of claims for debts contracted by the Government of France with citizens of the United States Since the 8th Vendé miaire 9th year/30 September 1800 not being comprised in this Convention may be pursued, and the payment demanded in the Same manner as if it had not been made.

ARTICLE 13

The present convention Shall be ratified in good and due form and the ratifications Shall be exchanged in Six months from the date of the Signature of the Ministers Plenipotentiary, or Sooner if possible.

In faith of which, the respective Ministers Plenipotentiary have signed the above Articles both in the french and english languages, declaring nevertheless that the present treaty has been originally agreed on and written in the french language, to which they have hereunto affixed their Seals.

Done at Paris, the tenth of Floreal, eleventh year of the French Republic. 30th April 1803.

ROBT R LIVINGSTON [SEAL]
JAS. MONROE [SEAL]
BARBÉ MARBOIS

Consequences

To the Spanish, the Louisiana Purchase must have seemed like yet more Napoleonic treachery. When Napoleon had failed to win Tuscany for Spain, he abrogated one major provision of the secret Treaty of Ildefonso. Now he reneged on the other major provision, to make Louisiana a buffer against U.S. expansion. To the president of the United States, though, the purchase was a windfall that matched his wildest imaginings. Significantly, in January 1803—a full three months before the deal was struck with Napoleon—Jefferson had requested congressional funding for a cross-continental survey of the Louisiana territory and beyond. In others words, the president of the United States had been planning an expedition to the Pacific across what was at the time foreign soil.

In truth, of course, Jefferson had long been musing on the Far West. As early as 1783, while serving in Congress, he asked George Rogers Clark, the Indian-fighting Revolutionary War hero, if he would be interested in an expedition up the Missouri River. To be sponsored privately, the expedition was meant to head off British attempts to secure a foothold in the Far West. When Clark turned him down, Jefferson continued to search for western explorers. While minister to France, he encouraged John Ledyard to undertake a one-man journey across Siberia, followed by a trek across North America beginning on the Pacific coast. Suspicious Russians deported the would-be explorer, thus scuttling Ledyard's plans but not Jefferson's hopes for a western expedition.

Not until Jefferson became president did he have at last the authority to launch his long-desired expedition. The final catalyst seems to have been British fur trader Alexander Mackenzie's publication in 1802 of the account of his continental crossing in Canada from 1792 to 1793. In his book, Mackenzie urged England to develop a transcontinental trade route, which aroused Jefferson's fears of British preemption in the Far West. The newly elected Jefferson selected as his personal secretary Meriwether Lewis because of the young man's knowledge of the "Western country," and by the summer of 1803, the expedition planned and the necessary supplies obtained, Lewis was on his way over the Appalachians to Pittsburgh.

Contrary to popular notions, then, the Louisiana Purchase came after, not before, the planning of the Lewis and Clark expedition. Indeed, Jefferson may have sent James Monroe to Paris to buy New Orleans thinking that a presence at the mouth of the Mississippi would imply a further claim to the territory between that river and the Northwest coast, which Lewis was going to explore. In any event, Jefferson's Democratic-Republican administration was able to buy rather than merely stake a claim to an empire, although no one knew exactly, or agreed upon, its true extent. The purchase and the transfer did, however, create more favorable conditions for the expedition and made it more urgent as an assertion of American sovereignty.

Jefferson may have gotten a bargain in the Louisiana Purchase, but it was one that would give any self-respecting real-estate attorney fits, for while the Gulf of Mexico was fixed as the southern boundary of the purchase and the Mississippi as the eastern boundary, there was no clear understanding as to whether the purchase included West Florida and Texas. Moreover, the purchase posed constitutional problems, since the Constitution made no provision for the purchase of foreign territory. In addition, the acquisition of Louisiana had enormous implications for the nation's development. It represented a major increase in the constitutionally implied powers of the president and set the stage for future westward expansion. While in effect negating the claims of Native Americans who inhabited the territory, the purchase established the colonial hold of the United States over the region's 50,000 French Creoles.

And it further disrupted the domestic tranquility of the republic itself. Until recently, the writers of textbooks and Jefferson's often fawning biographers have frequently praised without question the Louisiana Purchase as a diplomatic masterpiece that doubled the size of the country. That at least is not the way it appeared to Alexander Hamilton and the Federalist Party he headed. Indeed, Federalist-dominated New England and the Federalists in New York were not at all happy with the purchase. They remained convinced that America should have grabbed the territory by force, and they had no faith at all in Napoleon's promise to honor the purchase. When a French author described the deal as a "pledge of friendship" between America and France, they were quick to condemn Jefferson for betraying the country's traditional neutrality and pointed to the language indicating that, as far as trade went, France had achieved "favored nation" status. They argued as well that the region was useless because it was too vast to be governed. It was a threat, they said, to republican government. They worried that if the nation survived an expansion into these western lands, the West and the South would combine to dominate government at their expense. Jefferson and the Republicans responded that the purchase was its own solution. It ensured plenty of land would be available to future generations, especially to the yeoman farmers and the common folk whom they felt made up the true heart of American public.

Despite many doubts, the Senate ratified the treaty on October 20, 1803, and the United States took formal possession of the territory on December 20.

In the long run, both sides in the argument over the significance of the purchase proved to be right. Out of the Louisiana Territory there would eventually emerge the states of Louisiana, Arkansas, Iowa, Missouri, Nebraska, North Dakota, South Dakota,

Oklahoma, and parts of Kansas, Minnesota, Colorado, Montana, and Wyoming. While the costs were cheap at three cents an acre, and common folk did flock to the new lands in great numbers, there was a steep price to be paid in blood and treasure and civility. Each step westward threatened to break apart the political balance between North and South upon which national unity had been based. Indian removal and the "cultural genocide" of Native America was hastened by the purchase. And, as the question of whether or not to allow slavery in these new lands grew ever more prominent, major political efforts, such as the Missouri Compromise of 1820 and the Compromise of 1850, became necessary just to hold the country together. In many ways, the Louisiana Purchase can be understood as one of the long-term causes of the American Civil War.

ADAMS-ONÍS TREATY

TREATY AT A GLANCE

Completed
February 22, 1819, at Washington, D.C.

Signatories
United States and Spain

Overview
Agreement by which the United States acquired Florida and established the first claim of the United States to lands extending to the West Coast, the Adams-Onís Treaty proved pivotal to the creation of the Monroe Doctrine and to the annexation of Texas.

Historical Background

The War of 1812 left in place one traditional frontier, the border between the Americans and Spain, the first of Europe's imperial powers to exploit the New World. Enfeebled, corrupted, and much impoverished by the centuries of warfare, Spain still supported, sometimes with British connivance, its Indian proxies in what was then considered part of the Spanish American Southwest: Florida and the gulf regions of Georgia, Alabama, and Mississippi.

Andrew Jackson, the Hero of New Orleans, Old Hickory himself, was determined to change all that. In the spring of 1815, when Andrew Jackson arrived home from the war, his world had changed utterly. Transformed from a country squire into a national hero, he was the most famous American of his day, he was out of debt, and he was ready to claim his place in U.S. history. Already his admirers were speaking of a more glamorous future in which he might lead the country. During the Creek conflict, Jackson had for the first time begun systematically to save his correspondence. After the 1812 war, he agreed to have an aide write a biography of his life. He attended postwar banquets held around the country in his honor. With his wife, Rachel, he traveled to Washington, D.C., stopping along the way to be feted and saluted for his accomplishments. Soon he would commission the first of many portraits of himself in uniform, his Napoleonic spit curls, de reguer for military men of the period, much in evidence. He was one of only two major generals in the U.S. Army to be retained after the war, and if he enjoyed the rest and peace of being back home with his family and his standing as the toast of

the nation, the calm was short-lived. By 1817 Jackson was again at war with the Indians, and by the spring of 1818, he had pushed his way into Spanish Florida.

The trouble stretched back to Horseshoe Bend. After Jackson's victory there, the fortunes of the Creek merged with those of the closely related Seminole. Red Stick remnants, loath to live under the draconian peace imposed by Jackson under the TREATY OF FORT JACKSON, drifted south to join the renegades in Spanish Florida. As the War of 1812 drew to a close, the British built a fort in the panhandle at Prospect Bluff, 15 miles up the Apalachicola River. When the British withdrew from the fort during the summer of 1815, they left it to the Seminole and a band of fugitive slaves. The Americans claimed that Negro Fort, as it soon became known, posed a threat to navigation on the Apalachicola, the Flint, and the Chattahoochee, all important water routes into Florida, Georgia, and Alabama. More important, southern slaveholders were outraged and alarmed that the Seminole were sheltering their escaped "property."

Major General Jackson, claiming that he was responding to the pleas of the states and territories involved, dispatched troops in the spring of 1816 to attack the Indians and recapture as many fugitive slaves as possible. When they exploded Negro Fort, killing about 300 blacks, including men, women, and children, and 30 Seminole, the outraged Indians went to war. In this, the First Seminole War had begun. Jackson's orders were vague, and he intended to make the most of them, interpreting his mission as nothing less than the conquest of the entire Florida peninsula. During the course of his conquest, Jackson captured Lieutenant Robert Armbrister of the British Royal

Marines and Alexander Arbuthnot, an elderly Scottish trader. Jackson, frustrated with the elusiveness and effectiveness of his Indian foes, who were accomplished at guerrilla-style war, now charged both Armbrister and Arbuthnot with aiding the Indians and being in league with the Spanish. Following a summary trial, he hanged the two of them. Then, on May 26, 1818, with rash arrogance, Jackson seized Spanish Pensacola.

When news of his actions reached home, his popularity among the common folk, especially in the West, soared, but his reckless conduct in Florida added nothing to his reputation among the country's leaders in Washington. One faction in Congress even sought to censure Jackson for executing the two Britons and grabbing Pensacola, but the effort failed. Jackson, touchy as ever about his reputation, never forgave those involved. More important, Jackson's highhanded conduct was potentially embarrassing to President James Monroe because the unauthorized invasion of Spanish territory threatened to scuttle treaty negotiations under way between Secretary of State John Quincy Adams and foreign minister Luis de Onís over Spain's claims to the gulf and Florida lands. Adams made the best of a bad situation. Refusing to apologize for Jackson's behavior, he threw the onus on the Spanish for utterly failing to preserve order in Florida. It worked, for, if nothing else, Jackson's conquest demonstrated to Spain that it could not effectively defend Florida.

Terms

With Spain's hold over the peninsula already tenuous, Onís arranged for the transfer of the Floridas (East and West) to the United States. In exchange, the federal government would assume payment of $5 million worth of claims that Americans held against Spain. The Adams-Onís Treaty also established the border between Spanish America and the Louisiana Territory, drawing the line along the Sabine, Red, and Arkansas Rivers to the Rocky Mountains, and from there west to the Pacific along the 42nd parallel. The United States gave up its rather spurious claim to Texas, Spain her equally spurious claim to the Pacific Northwest.

Treaty of Amity, Settlement, and Limits between the United States of America and His Catholic Majesty

The United States of America and His Catholic Majesty, desiring to consolidate, on a permanent basis, the friendship and good correspondence which happily prevails between the two parties, have determined to settle and terminate all their differences and pretensions, by a treaty, which shall designate, with precision, the limits of their respective bordering territories in North America.

With this intention the President of the United States has furnished with their full powers John Quincy Adams, Secretary of State of the said United States; and His Catholic Majesty has appointed the Most Excellent Lord Don Luis De Onís, Gonzales, Lopez y Vara, Lord of the Town of Rayaces, Perpetual Regidor of the Corporation of the city of Salamanca, Knight Grand Cross of the Royal American Order of Isabella the Catholic, decorated with the Lys of La Vendée, Knight Pensioner of the Royal and Distinguished Spanish Order of Charles the Third, Member of the Supreme Assembly of the said Royal Order; of the Council of His Catholic Majesty; his Secretary, with Exercise of Decrees, and His Envoy Extraordinary and Minister Plenipotentiary near the United States of America.

And the said Plenipotentiaries, after having exchanged their powers, have agreed upon and concluded the following articles:

ARTICLE I

There shall be a firm and inviolable peace and sincere friendship between the United States and their citizens and His Catholic Majesty, his successors and subjects, without exception of persons or places.

ARTICLE II

His Catholic Majesty cedes to the United States, in full property and sovereignty, all the territories which belong to him, situated to the eastward of the Mississippi, known by the name of East and West Florida. The adjacent islands dependent on said provinces, all public lots and squares, vacant lands, public edifices, fortifications, barracks, and other buildings, which are not private property, archives and documents, which relate directly to the property and sovereignty of said provinces, are included in this article. The said archives and documents shall be left in possession of the commissaries or officers of the United States, duly authorized to receive them.

ARTICLE III

The boundary-line between the two countries, west of the Mississippi, shall begin on the Gulph of Mexico, at the mouth of the river Sabine, in the sea, continuing north, along the western bank of that river, to the 32d degree of latitude; thence, by a line due north, to the degree of latitude where it strikes the Rio Roxo of Nachitoches, or Red River; then following the course of the Rio Roxo westward, to the degree of longitude 100 west from London and 23 from Washington; then, crossing the said Red River, and running thence, by a line due north, to the river Arkansas; thence, following the course of the southern bank of the Arkansas, to its source, in latitude 42 north; and thence, by that parallel of latitude, to the South Sea. The whole being as laid down in Melish's map of the United States, published at Philadelphia, improved to the first of January, 1818. But if the source of the Arkansas River shall be found to fall north or south of latitude 42, then the line shall run from the said source due south or north, as the case may be, till it meets the said parallel of latitude 42, and thence, along the said parallel, to the South Sea: All the islands in the Sabine, and the said Red and Arkansas

Rivers, throughout the course thus described. to belong to the United States; but the use of the waters, and the navigation of the Sabine to the sea, and of the said rivers Roxo and Arkansas, throughout the extent of the said boundary, on their respective banks, shall be common to the respective inhabitants of both nations.

The two high contracting parties agree to cede and renounce all their rights, claims, and pretensions to the territories described by the said line, that is to say: The United States hereby cede to His Catholic Majesty, and renounce forever, all their rights, claims, and pretensions, to the territories lying west and south of the above-described line; and, in like manner, His Catholic Majesty cedes to the said United States all his rights, claims, and pretensions to any territories east and north of the said line, and for himself, his heirs, and successors, renounces all claim to the said territories forever.

ARTICLE IV

To fix this line with more precision, and to place the landmarks which shall designate exactly the limits of both nations, each of the contracting parties shall appoint a Commissioner and a surveyor, who shall meet before the termination of one year from the date of the ratification of this treaty at Nachitoches, on the Red River, and proceed to run and mark the said line, from the mouth of the Sabine to the Red River, and from the Red River to the river Arkansas, and to ascertain the latitude of the source of the said river Arkansas, in conformity to what is above agreed upon and stipulated and the line of latitude 42, to the South Sea: they shall make out plans, and keep journals of their proceedings, and the result agreed upon by them shall be considered as part of this treaty, and shall have the same force as if it were inserted therein. The two Governments will amicably agree respecting the necessary articles to be furnished to those persons, and also as to their respective escorts, should such be deemed necessary.

ARTICLE V

The inhabitants of the ceded territories shall be secured in the free exercise of their religion, without any restriction; and all those who may desire to remove to the Spanish dominions shall be permitted to sell or export their effects, at any time whatever, without being subject, in either case, to duties.

ARTICLE VI

The inhabitants of the territories which His Catholic Majesty cedes to the United States, by this treaty, shall be incorporated in the Union of the United States as soon as may be consistent with the principles of the Federal Constitution, and admitted to the enjoyment of all the privileges, rights, and immunities of the citizens of the United States.

ARTICLE VII

The officers and troops of His Catholic Majesty, in the territories hereby ceded by him to the United States, shall be withdrawn, and possession of the places occupied by them shall be given within six months after the exchange of the ratifications of this treaty, or sooner if possible, by the officers of His Catholic Majesty to the commissioners or officers of the United States duly appointed to receive them; and the United States shall furnish the transports and escort necessary to convey the Spanish officers and troops and their baggage to the Havana.

ARTICLE VIII

All the grants of land made before the 24th of January, 1818, by His Catholic Majesty, or by his lawful authorities, in the said territories ceded by His Majesty to the United States, shall be ratified and confirmed to the persons in possession of the lands, to the same extent that the same grants would be valid if the territories had remained under the dominion of His Catholic Majesty. But the owners in possession of such lands, who, by reason of the recent circumstances of the Spanish nation, and the revolutions in Europe, have been prevented from fulfilling all the conditions of their grants, shall complete them within the terms limited in the same, respectively, from the date of this treaty; in default of which the said grants shall be null and void. All grants made since the said 24th of January, 1818, when the first proposal, on the part of His Catholic Majesty, for the cession of the Floridas was made, are hereby declared and agreed to be null and void.

ARTICLE IX

The two high contracting parties, animated with the most earnest desire of conciliation, and with the object of putting an end to all the differences which have existed between them, and of confirming the good understanding which they wish to be forever maintained between them, reciprocally renounce all claims for damages or injuries which they, themselves, as well as their respective citizens and subjects, may have suffered until the time of signing this treaty.

The renunciation of the United States will extend to all the injuries mentioned in the convention of the 11th of August, 1802.

2. [sic] To all claims on account of prizes made by French privateers, and condemned by French Consuls, within the territory and jurisdiction of Spain.

3. To all claims of indemnities on account of the suspension of the right of deposit at New Orleans in 1802.(2)

4. To all claims of citizens of the United States upon the Government of Spain, arising from the unlawful seizures at sea, and in the ports and territories of Spain, or the Spanish colonies.

5. To all claims of citizens of the United States upon the Spanish Government, statements of which, soliciting the interposition of the Government of the United States have been presented to the Department of State, or to the Minister of the United States in Spain, the date of the convention of 1802 and until the signature of this treaty.

The renunciation of His Catholic Majesty extends,

1. To all the injuries mentioned in the convention of the 11th of August, 1802.

2. To the sums which His Catholic Majesty advanced for the return of Captain Pike from the Provincias Internas

3. To all injuries caused by the expedition of Miranda, that was fitted out and equipped at New York.

4. To all claims of Spanish subjects upon the Government of the United States arising from unlawful seizures at sea, or within the ports and territorial Jurisdiction of the United States.

Finally, to all the claims of subjects of His Catholic Majesty upon the Government of the United States in which the interposition of his Catholic Majesty's Government has been solicited, before the date of this treaty and since the date of the convention of 1802, or which may have been made to the department of foreign affairs of His Majesty, or to his Minister of the United States

And the high contracting parties, respectively, renounce all claim to indemnities for any of the recent events or transactions of their respective commanders and officers in the Floridas.

The United States will cause satisfaction to be made for the injuries, if any, which, by process of law, shall be established to have been suffered by the Spanish officers, and individual Spanish inhabitants, by the late operations of the American Army in Florida.

ARTICLE X

The convention entered into between the two Governments, on the 11th of August, 1802, the ratifications of which were exchanged the 21st December, 1818, is annulled.

ARTICLE XI

The United States, exonerating Spain from all demands in future, on account of the claims of their citizens to which the renunciations herein contained extend, and considering them entirely cancelled, undertake to make satisfaction for the same, to an amount not exceeding five millions of dollars. To ascertain the full amount and validity of those claims, a commission, to consist of three Commissioners, citizens of the United States, shall be appointed by the President, by and with the advice and consent of the Senate, which commission shall meet at the city of Washington, and, within the space of three years from the time of their first meeting, shall receive, examine, and decide upon the amount and validity of all the claims included within the descriptions above mentioned. The said Commissioners shall take an oath or affirmation, to be entered on the record of their proceedings, for the faithful and diligent discharge of their duties; and, in case of the death, sickness, or necessary absence of any such Commissioner, his place may be supplied by the appointment, as aforesaid, or by the President of the United States, during the recess of the Senate, of another Commissioner in his stead.

The said Commissioners shall be authorized to hear and examine, on oath, every question relative to the said claims, and to receive all suitable authentic testimony concerning the same. And the Spanish Government shall furnish all such documents and elucidations as may be in their possession, for the adjustment of the said claims, according to the principles of justice, the laws of nations, and the stipulations of the treaty between the two parties of 27th October, 1795; the said documents to be specified. when demanded, at the instance of the said Commissioners.

The payment of such claims as may be admitted and adjusted by the said Commissioners, or the major part of them, to an amount not exceeding five millions of dollars, shall be made by the United States, either immediately at their Treasury, or by the creation of stock, bearing an interest of six per cent. per annum, payable from the proceeds of sales of public lands within the territories hereby ceded to the United States, or in such other manner as the Congress of the United States may prescribe by law.

The records of the proceedings of the said Commissioners, together with the vouchers and documents produced before them, relative to the claims to be adjusted and decided upon by them, shall, after the close of their transactions, be deposited in the Department of State of the United States; and copies of them, or any part of them, shall be furnished to the Spanish Government, if required' at the demand of the Spanish Minister in the United States.

ARTICLE XII

The treaty of limits and navigation, of 1795, remains confirmed in all and each one of its articles excepting the 2, 3, 4, 21, and the second clause of the 22d article, which, having been altered by this treaty, or having received their entire execution, are no longer valid.

With respect to the 15th article of the same treaty of friendship, limits, and navigation of 1795, in which it is stipulated that the flag shall cover the property, the two high contracting parties agree that this shall be so understood with respect to those powers who recognize this principle; but if either of the two contracting parties shall be at war with a third party, and the other neutral, the flag of the neutral shall cover the property of enemies whose government acknowledge this principle, and not of others.

ARTICLE XIII

Both contracting parties, wishing to favor their mutual commerce, by affording in their ports every necessary assistance to their respective merchant-vessels, have agreed that the sailors who shall desert from their vessels in the ports of the other, shall be arrested and delivered up, at the instance of the consul, who shall prove, nevertheless, that the deserters belonged to the vessels that claimed them, exhibiting the document that is customary in their nation: that is to say, the American Consul in a Spanish port shall exhibit the document known lay the name of articles, and the Spanish Consul in American ports the roll of the vessel; and if the name of the deserter or deserters are claimed shall appear in the one or the other, they shall be arrested, held in custody, and delivered to the vessel to which they shall belong.

ARTICLE XIV

The United States hereby certify that they have not received any compensation from France for the injuries they suffered from her privateers, Consuls, and tribunals on the coasts and in the ports of Spain, for the satisfaction of which provision is made by this treaty; and they will present an authentic statement of the prizes made, and of their true value, that Spain may avail herself of the same in such manner as she may deem just and proper.

ARTICLE XV

The United States, to give to His Catholic Majesty a proof of their desire to cement the relations of amity subsisting between the two nations, and to favor the commerce of the subjects of His Catholic Majesty, agree that Spanish vessels, coming laden only with productions of Spanish growth or manufactures, directly from the ports of Spain, or of her colonies, shall be admitted, for the term of twelve years, to the ports of Pensacola and St. Augustine, in the Floridas, without paying other or higher duties on their cargoes, or of tonnage, than will be paid by the vessels of the United States. During the said term no other nation shall enjoy the same privileges within the ceded territories. The twelve years shall commence three months after the exchange of the ratifications of this treaty.

ARTICLE XVI

The present treaty shall be ratified in due form, by the contracting parties, and the ratifications shall be exchanged in six months from this time, or sooner if possible.

In witness whereof we, the underwritten Plenipotentiaries of the United States of America and of His Catholic Majesty, have signed, by virtue of our powers, the present treaty of amity, settlement, and limits, and have thereunto affixed our seals, respectively.

Done at Washington this twenty-second day of February, one thousand eight hundred and nineteen.

JOHN QUINCY ADAMS. [L. S.]

LUIS DE ONÍS. [L. S.]

Consequences

With the cession, Jackson left Florida, and the First Seminole War came to an end. Some of the surviving Seminole remained in the inland portion of northern Florida, while others moved to central Florida, near present-day Orlando. The Red Stick Creek, including their half-Scot, half-Creek leader, Peter McQueen, occupied the area around Tampa Bay, far from Alabama and Georgia. McQueen, aging and exhausted, died a few years later—no one knows exactly when. Meanwhile, Congress delayed approval of the treaty until 1821. Andrew Jackson, ambitious as ever, delighted to preside over the formal ouster of Spain, and hoping to vindicate his reputation in the wake of the attempted censure, resigned his army commission and accepted appointment from President Monroe as the first governor of the Florida Territory.

It seemed to many that Jackson had almost single-handed made American settlement possible from the Tennessee River to the Gulf of Mexico and redirected the course of the country's expansionist ambitions from Canada toward the Southwest and Texas. The Adams-Onís Treaty itself proved critically important to those ambitions. By resolving the long-term dispute with Spain, it finalized the LOUISIANA PURCHASE. As a result, Adams and President James Monroe were in a position in December 1823 to declare the Western Hemisphere off limits to further European colonization in a statement of policy later known as the MONROE DOCTRINE. Through the provisions of the treaty, the United States had access to the first transcontinental river route to the Columbia River area. By giving up U.S. claims to Texas, the treaty fueled the agitation for the "reannexation" of that region, which proslavery expansionists claimed had been wrongly thrown away by the treaty. And the western boundary established by the treaty acknowledged California and today's Southwest to be Mexican territory, which set the stage for the U.S. conquest of those lands during the 1846–48 war with Mexico.

INDIAN REMOVAL ACT

TREATY AT A GLANCE

Completed
May 28, 1830, at Washington, D.C.

Signatories
United States Congress and President Andrew Jackson

Overview
The Indian Removal Act was a law authorizing the president of the United States to conclude several treaties with those Native American tribes still residing east of the Mississippi for their removal to putatively comparable land in "Indian Territory" west of the river, which ultimately would become the state of Oklahoma. The act, and the treaties which followed, became the occasion for massive deportation of tribes such as the Cherokee, the Creek, the Choctaw, and the Seminole, a cruel "final solution" to an "Indian problem" that had been the subject of debate for decades.

Historical Background

The Cherokee, who lived primarily in northwestern Georgia and northeastern Alabama (as well as the southeastern corner of Tennessee and the southwestern corner of North Carolina), had declared themselves a sovereign nation in 1827 and adopted a constitution similar to that of the United States. When the Georgia state legislature decreed in response on December 20, 1828, that all Indian residents would come under state jurisdiction within six months, Andrew Jackson was just about to assume office as president of the United States. By then gold had been discovered on Cherokee tribal lands. Thousands of whites invaded Cherokee territory and staked claims, destroying Indian property, seizing Indian livestock, beating up Indians who protested, selling alcohol to weaken resistance and judgment, forcing Indians to sign leases, killing the game Cherokee needed for food. The new president ordered in federal troops to remove the whites, but he also commanded the Cherokee to stop mining their gold. Immediately, Jackson began to hammer out his Indian policy.

To be fair to Jackson, every U.S. president before him, not merely Jefferson, had contemplated transferring the Indians beyond the limits of white settlement, even beyond the United States proper. George Washington imagined a western "Chinese wall" to separate whites and Indians. In order to pacify Indians after the War of 1812, James Madison considered exchanging areas in the trans-Mississippi West for Indian lands in the trans-Appalachian region. And James Monroe followed the advice of his secretary of war, John C. Calhoun, in adopting a policy of Indian removal in 1825.

Jackson's immediate predecessor, John Quincy Adams, responded to an impending constitutional crisis by laying the groundwork for the removal legislation enacted during Jackson's administration. Not just Georgia but all the southern states debated legislation aimed at circumventing federal protection of Indian lands and rights. Not only did southerners covet fertile and mineral-rich Indian land, they were alarmed by the flight of fugitive slaves into Indian territory. The Seminole and others repeatedly refused to return the fugitives, and the federal government was unwilling to compel them to do so. President Adams repeatedly turned down requests from the southern states for the summary removal of the Indians, and he even threatened to call in the army to protect tribesmen against the depredations of the states. Facing a showdown between states' rights and federal authority, Adams reluctantly agreed to a plan for removing the eastern tribes to the trans-Mississippi.

But it was Jackson who signed the legislation, Jackson—and his Indian agents and treaty commissioners—who shamelessly manipulated the law and interfered with internal Indian affairs well beyond the point of fraud in order to compel them to give up their land and head out west, and it was Andrew Jackson whose name would rightly be forever linked to the government policy of Indian "removal." Jackson's personal attitude toward the Indians has, in modern times, become more controversial than it was during his own day. His experience with Native Americans had been in large measure that they were hostile nations allied to the country's European enemies. He also understood—again from personal experience—that Americans were going to expand onto Indian lands regardless of laws passed in Washington, and thus he held little hope for a permanent peace with the tribes. He justified removal as the better alternative to assimilation, which he did not think possible, or extermination, which he believed likely otherwise.

From the moment he took office, Jackson collaborated and conspired behind the scenes against the current laws of the United States with his old friends in Georgia, Alabama, and Mississippi, but with the American public, he was more circumspect. Efforts to "civilize" the Indians had failed, he explained. White settlers had been purchasing their lands in ever greater numbers, which in turn had driven the Indians ever deeper into the wilderness, where they continued their "wandering state." Although it was true, he admitted, that a few had taken up farming, established political institutions, and created a civil society, even these "nations" with their "foreign" governments simply could not be tolerated within sovereign state boundaries and would have to submit to the proper authorities. Besides, such nations could not survive long within white society, anyway. Like earlier tribes, they would disappear.

Saddened by the injustice of it all, Jackson said, he nevertheless felt compelled in the interest of "humanity and national honor" to avoid this "great calamity" and "preserve this much injured race" by setting aside a district west of the United States's borders and removing the Indians there, where they could form their own governments and live in peace "as long as the grass grows, or water runs."[1] The flinty Jackson, orphaned scion of Scotch-Irish immigrants, worked hard to counteract sentiment for the Indians themselves. Though it may be a hard thing to ask them to "leave the graves of their fathers," that is precisely what "our ancestors did" and "our children are doing now," Jackson argued. What good had weeping done for the Indians of the past? It had certainly never stopped "progress."[2]

To Congress in his 1829 message, Jackson, whose style had always been imperial, made his position and his conclusion clear: "I informed the Indians inhabiting parts of Georgia and Alabama that their attempt to establish an independent government would not be countenanced by the Executive of the United States, and advised them to emigrate beyond the Mississippi or submit to the laws of those States." As Jackson saw it, he had done his duty to his "red children, and if any failure of my good intentions arises, it will be attributable to their want of duty to themselves, not to me." It would, in other words, be their fault, not his.

The Indians, understandably enough, clearly saw chicanery behind the metaphysics. Cherokee leader John Ross—who like Jackson was the son of a Scotch-Irish immigrant, but who was born of a Cherokee mother—responded that "the perpetrator of a wrong" had decided not to forgive "his victims." Many in Congress, too, questioned Jackson's motives and doubted the good sense of removal.

A troubled national legislature passed by a narrow margin the Indian Removal Act of 1830.

Terms

Congress did what it could to salvage its own conscience. It authorized removal not by fiat and force, but by land exchanges. It provided for funds and protection in helping the Indians move, implying that only if they failed to do so were they at the mercy of the states:

An Act to Provide for an Exchange of Lands with the Indians Residing in Any of the States or Territories, and for Removal West of the River Mississippi

Be it enacted . . . , That it shall and may be lawful for the President of the United States to cause so much of any territory belonging to the United States, west of the Mississippi, not included in any state or organized territory, and to which the Indian title has been extinguished, as he may judge necessary, to be divided into a suitable number of districts, for the reception of such tribes or nations of Indians as may choose to exchange the lands where they now reside, and remove there; and to cause each of such districts to be so described by natural or artificial marks, as to be easily distinguished from every other.

Sec. 2. And be it further enacted, That it shall and may be lawful for the President to exchange any or all of such districts, so to be laid off and described, with any tribe or nation of Indians now residing within the limits of any of the states or territories, and with which the United States have existing treaties, for the whole or any part or portion of the territory claimed and occupied by such tribe or nation, within the bounds of any one or more of the states or territories, where the land claimed and occupied by the Indians, is owned by the United States, or the United States are bound to the state within which it lies to extinguish the Indians' claim thereto.

Sec. 3. And be it further enacted, That in the making of any such exchange or exchanges, it shall and may be lawful for the President solemnly to assure the tribe or nation with which the exchange is made, that the United States will forever secure and guaranty to them, and their heirs or successors, the country so exchanged with them; and if they prefer it, that the United States will cause a patent or grant to be made and executed to them for the same: Provided always, That such land shall revert to the United States, if the Indians become extinct, or abandon the same.

Sec. 4. *And be it further enacted,* That if, upon any of the lands now occupied by the Indians, and to be exchanged for, there should be such improvements as add value to the land claimed by any individual or individuals of such tribes or nations, it shall and may be lawful for the President to cause such value to be ascertained by appraisement or otherwise, and to cause such ascertained value to be paid to the person or persons rightfully claiming such improvements. And upon the payment of such valuation, the improvements so valued and paid for, shall pass to the United States, and possession shall not afterwards be permitted to any of the same tribe.

Sec. 5. *And be it further enacted,* That upon the making of any such exchange as is contemplated by this act, it shall and may be lawful for the President to cause such aid and assistance to be furnished to the emigrants as may be necessary and proper to enable them to remove to, and settle in, the country for which they may have exchanged; and also, to give them such aid and assistance as may be necessary for their support and subsistence for the first year after their removal.

Sec. 6. *And be it further enacted,* That it shall and may be lawful for the President to cause such tribe or nation to be protected, at their new residence, against all interruption or disturbance from any other tribe or nation in the country to which they may remove, as contemplated by this act, that he is now authorized to have over them at their present places of residence: Provided, That nothing in this act contained shall be construed as authorizing or directing the violation of any exiting treaty between the United States and any of the Indian tribes.

Sec. 7. *And be it further enacted,* That it shall and may be lawful for the President to have the same superintendence and care over any tribe or nation in the country to which they may remove, as contemplated by this act, that he is now authorized to have over them at their present places of residence: Provided, That nothing in this act contained shall be construed as authorizing or directing the violation of any existing treaty between the United States and any of the Indian tribes.

Sec. 8. *And be it further enacted,* That for the purpose of giving effect to the provisions of this act, the sum of five hundred thousand dollars is hereby appropriated, to be paid out of any money in the treasury, not otherwise appropriated.

Consequences

In practice, Jackson's government, both officially and unofficially, was ruthless and devious in its use of the law. Jackson removed the troops from Cherokee Territory, and the Georgian prospectors and squatters rushed in, beginning once more the process of tribal disintegration from food shortages, whiskey, white attack, and Indian-on-Indian violence. Alabama and Mississippi followed Georgia in passing state legislation that abolished tribal government and placed Indians under state jurisdiction. Jackson, backed now by federal law, moved to uproot some 70,000 Indians from their homes and drive them west of the Mississippi River.

CHOCTAW AND CHICKASAW

In September, after passage of the removal act, Jackson's federal commissioners met with the Choctaw at Dancing Rabbit Creek to negotiate a treaty for buying their land and moving them out west. The Choctaw rejected the offer, and many of them left, assuming the meeting was over. But the commissioners knew better than to take "no" for an answer; they offered the 50 remaining delegates secret bribes of money and land, and the treaty was signed. Choctaw land east of the Mississippi, some 10 1/2 million acres, went to the U.S. government in return for financial help in leaving, compensation for lost property, and a federal guarantee they would never again be required to move. For the 20,000 Choctaw in Mississippi, most of whom hated the treaty, the pressure to move became intense. In the fall of 1831, some began the long journey west. Others soon followed. On through the summer they came, and a major cholera epidemic struck western Mississippi.

The Chickasaw signed removal treaties in 1832 and 1834 providing for the federal government to sell on their behalf the lands vacated and hold the proceeds in trust for Chickasaw use.

THE CREEK

The Creek decided to tough it out. They had been fighting for their land since the arrival of Columbus, against Spaniards, English, French, and Americans, and they simply refused to budge. By 1836 both the federal and the state governments had lost patience with them and used as a pretext recent Creek attacks on squatting whites to declare that the Indian nation, by making war, had abrogated its rights under the TREATY OF WASHINGTON (1826).

Now the army forced the Creek to move. The military gathered the Creek up in batches of a couple thousand. Those the soldiers decided were rebels or rebel sympathizers they manacled and chained together. The army hired private contractors to march the Indians west. The contractors provided the Creek neither with food, nor shelter, nor clothing, nor blankets, nor medical attention. By midwinter some 15,000 stretched from border to border across Arkansas.

Observers there said they could tell where the Creeks were marching by the howling of the wolf packs that stalked them and by the circling of buzzards who fed on the fallen.

Eight hundred Creek thought they had escaped by promising to help the army fight Seminole in Florida. The government guaranteed the safety of their families back in Alabama. While the warriors were gone, land-hungry whites attacked their families, robbed them, raped the women, and drove them off the land. The army rounded the remnants up and sent them to a stockaded camp in Mobile Bay for their own protection. When the braves returned from the brutal Second Seminole War, the government reunited them with their family members who had not died of starvation or disease in Mobile and shipped them all west. On the way, in New Orleans they were ravaged by an outbreak of yellow fever. Six hundred Creek were crowded onto the aged and rotting steamboat *Monmouth* when it sank in the Mississippi above the city, drowning over half the Indians aboard.

SEMINOLE

The Seminole, as usual, decided to fight. Like other tribes, they were persecuted and subjected to unremitting pressure to accept removal. As if depredations suffered at the hands of the whites were not enough, a devastating drought in 1831 worked great hardship on the tribe. Faced with annihilation, Seminole leaders signed a provisional removal treaty on May 9, 1832, which stipulated that removal was conditional on tribal approval of the site selected for resettlement. A party of seven Seminole headed west to inspect the site. The report of those who had seen the proposed site of resettlement did nothing to make the Seminole anxious to give up their familiar lands.

Secretary of War Cass decreed that all tribes removed to Indian Territory be lumped into a single political unit, an expedient that would help the government to deal with them, but an idea most tribes found abhorrent. Certainly, the Seminole did not want to merge their identity even with the closely-related Creek, much less any other tribe. For them, it was not entirely an ethnic issue. The Creek had been compelled to compensate Georgia planters for fugitive slaves they had harbored. The Seminole feared that the Creek would in turn, appropriate their slaves.

As for the blacks, they recognized that their treatment by the Seminole was far more generous than they would experience at the hands of whites or Creek. The Seminole did not practice plantation slavery. Slaves often lived in their own villages, their children frequently became free, there was much intermarriage, and several Seminole villages were mixed Indian-black. In general, the blacks enjoyed considerable influence

among the Seminole, and they reinforced the Indians' resolve not to be removed.

The Second Seminole War began in 1835, when—after announcing that any Seminole leader planning to move west would have to be killed—Seminole Chief Osceola had the major proponent of removal, Charley Ematha, assassinated in broad daylight outside the Seminole agency. Despite everything Henry Clay—a critic of Indian removal as well as an implacable political foe of Jackson—tried to do to stop it, Congress appropriated funds for the war. Whig colleague Daniel Webster summed up the partisan fatigue in dealing with Jackson by invoking the unity across party lines summoned by frontier metaphysics, a kind of unity, based on executive fait accompli, that would become a marked feature of American colonial actions.

For seven long years, a series of white commanders successively tried and successively failed to win the war: Edmund Gaines, Duncan Clinch, Winfield Scott, Robert Call, Thomas Jesup, Zachary Taylor, Alexander McComb, Walker Armistead, and William Worth, essentially in that order. General Jesup did succeed in capturing Osceola on October 21, 1837, but not through military skill. He requested a conference at Osceola's camp, over which the chief raised a white flag of truce. Despite the flag, Jesup had the chief seized and consigned him to a prison cell at Fort Moultrie, South Carolina. Although he was treated reasonably well in prison, he fell ill and died on January 30, 1838.

Others continued to lead the resistance after Osceola's death, but between 1835 and 1842, some three thousand Seminole submitted to removal and were shipped to Indian Territory. The cost to the Americans was high: for every two Seminoles who were sent West, one soldier died, 1,500 American troops in all. The war cost the federal government $20 million, and it ended in 1842 not through any victory on either side but because the government simply stopped trying to flush out the remaining Seminole who had hidden themselves deep in the Everglades.

Thirteen years after the Second Seminole War petered out, a party of surveyors working in the Great Cypress Swamp stole or vandalized some crops belonging to followers of Seminole Chief Billy Bowlegs. The Indians approached the whites, demanding compensation or, failing that, an apology. Neither was given, and from 1855 to 1858, a pattern of Indian raiding was again established, as settlers, traders, and trappers fell under sporadic attack. The regular army and militiamen were called in, but, as in the Second Seminole War, their efforts were largely ineffective against Indian guerrillas whose knowledge of the dense swamp lands made them virtually undetectable.

This third Seminole conflict was brought to an end when Seminoles who had earlier moved to Indian

Territory were brought back to Florida to negotiate on behalf of the whites. Accepting a cash settlement, Billy Bowlegs and his followers at last emigrated to Indian Territory. A significant number of Seminoles, however, have never left the Florida Everglades and remain there today.

CHEROKEE

Shortly after Congress passed the Indian Removal Act and Jackson recalled federal troops from Cherokee land, Georgia passed a law making it a crime for a white person to remain in Indian territory without taking an oath to the state of Georgia. The white missionaries in Cherokee territory declared openly their sympathies for the Indians and their belief that the Cherokee had the right to remain in Georgia. Georgia sent in the militia.

The Cherokee appealed to the U.S. Supreme Court and won. In *Worcester v. Georgia*, Chief Justice John Marshall, for the majority, declared that the Georgia law under which Samuel Worcester (a federal postmaster who refused to leave Cherokee territory when Georgia ordered the whites out) had been jailed violated U.S. treaties with the Cherokee, and those treaties, under the American Constitution, were binding on the states. Georgia's Indian laws were unconstitutional. Furthermore, President Jackson's efforts in support of the Georgia laws were illegal. The matter was a question of states' rights, and just as South Carolina had no right to nullify tariffs, Georgia had no right to legislate the Cherokee out of existence.

By the laws of the United States of America, its chief executive was legally required to enforce the terms of the Cherokee treaties. The president refused to enforce the Court's decision. Georgia ignored John Marshall's order. Instead, the state put Cherokee land on sale and moved the militia back in to crush any resistance.

As whites took Cherokee property, burned their homes, closed their schools, mistreated their women, and sold liquor in their churches, the Cherokee followed a policy of strict nonviolence. Two factions emerged among their numbers. A minority Treaty Party, led by Major Ridge, favored compliance with removal. A majority National Party, led by John Ross, opposed removal. Unlike most nationalist Indian groups, however, Ross's party did not advocate a desperate armed conflict against inevitably superior white forces. If resistance to removal should fail, they wanted at least to be in position to secure the most favorable terms possible for the sale of the ceded lands, so that they might be able to purchase land somewhere beyond the territorial limits and jurisdiction of the United States.

The Jackson administration severed the Gordian knot of conflicting Cherokee factions by deciding to deal solely with members of the Treaty faction, arbitrarily investing in them the authority to represent the Cherokee nation, even though they represented a mere 1,000 of the 17,000 Cherokee living in the South. A treaty was concluded on December 29, 1835, calling for the completion of removal by 1838, and following Senate ratification of the agreement, Jackson effectively abolished the National Party by forbidding it to hold meetings to discuss the treaty or alternative courses of action. Furthermore, Jackson warned John Ross that the United States would recognize no Cherokee government prior to removal west of the Mississippi and that any attempt to resist removal would be met by force of arms.

Despite Jackson's threats, the National Party worked during the period 1835–1838—albeit to no avail—to expose the fraud that had been perpetrated. During this period, too, the state of Georgia and various individuals did their best to cheat the Cherokee out of their removal funds. By the 1838 deadline, only 2,000 Cherokee had emigrated. Martin Van Buren, who had succeeded Jackson as president, approached the task of removal with some vigor. Except for a handful who successfully managed to hide in the mountains of Tennessee, the Cherokee of the South were penned into the camps during the long, hot summer. In the fall and winter of 1838–39, they were marched off to Indian Territory along what came to be called the Trail of Tears. Fifteen thousand followed the 1,200-mile route, always cold, always short of food, always sick at heart, often just sick. Four thousand died along the way.

Callous in conception, often brutal in its execution, Indian removal suited the longstanding commitment to national expansion Jackson and his political party shared with most southerners and westerners. That it tended to enrich the southern planter class of which Jackson was a member probably seemed only natural to him, an inevitable consequence of progress, and that it spread the institution of slavery, every bit as callous and brutal as removal, would hardly have given Jackson pause—it was the way of life he knew, the economic system that had allowed a pauper like himself to become rich and powerful. More immediately, of all President Jackson's policies, Indian removal probably gave him the least trouble politically, since his opponents were concentrated in the Northeast and the policy's harshest critics were a small group of humanitarians, most all of them already affiliated with anti-Jackson parties. When Jackson came to retire, he clearly considered the near-completion of Indian removal to be the major achievement of his presidency.

1. Howard Zinn, *A People's History of the United States* (New York: HarperCollins, 1980), 132.
2. Alan Axelrod, *Chronicle of the Indian Wars: From Colonial Times to Wounded Knee* (New York: Prentice Hall General Reference, 1993), 137–47.

GADSDEN TREATY

TREATY AT A GLANCE

Completed
December 30, 1853, at Mexico City

Signatories
United States and Mexico

Overview
Through the Gadsden Purchase, framed within the Gadsden Treaty, Mexico ceded to the United States a 29,670-square-mile rectangle of territory in the Mesilla Valley, south of the Gila River. This was in addition to the vast territory ceded by the TREATY OF GUADALUPE HIDALGO, which ended the Mexican War in 1848, and marks the present boundary between Mexico and the United States.

Historical Background

During the late 1840s and early 1850s, the United States launched a series of westward expeditions with the purpose of determining the most practical route for the long-contemplated transcontinental railroad, which would link the nation's two coasts. The definition of "practical" depended largely on the various regional commitments of the planners involved, and all regions, from north to south, had their advocates.

Jefferson Davis, destined in the next decade to become president of the Confederacy but at the time secretary of war under President Franklin Pierce, was anxious to run the highly strategic transcontinental railroad through the South. Accordingly, he supported the adoption of an extreme southerly route. Unfortunately, it soon became apparent that a significant portion of this right-of-way ran through territory that had not been explicitly acquired from Mexico by virtue of the Treaty of Guadalupe Hidalgo, and a dispute over the boundary ensued. Davis persuaded President Pierce to commission James Gadsden, minister to Mexico, to negotiate purchase of the additional required territory.

Terms

Gadsden undertook his mission on May 19, 1853, originally offering $15 million for the acquisition of almost 30,000 square miles of territory in the Mesilla valley, south of the Gila River. By the time the treaty, which authorized the purchase, was concluded on December 30, 1853, the purchase price had been reduced to $10 million, of which $7 million was to be paid immediately and the remainder withheld until the survey was completed and approved:

ARTICLE 1
The Mexican Republic agrees to designate the following as her true limits with the United States for the future: Retaining the same dividing line between the two Californias. as already defined and established, according to the 5th article of the treaty of Guadalupe Hidalgo, the limits between the two republics shall be as follows: Beginning in the Gulf of Mexico, three leagues from land, opposite the mouth of the Rio Grande, as provided in the fifth article of the treaty of Guadalupe Hidalgo; thence, as defined in the said article, up the middle of that river to the point where the parallel of 31° 47' north latitude crosses the same; thence due west one hundred miles; thence south to the parallel of 31° 20' north latitude: thence along the said parallel of 31° 20' to the 111th meridian of longitude west of Greenwich; thence in a straight line to a point on the Colorado River twenty English miles below the junction of the Gila and Colorado Rivers; thence up the middle of the said river Colorado until it intersects the present line between the United States and Mexico.

For the performance of this portion of the treaty, each of the two Governments shall nominate one commissioner, to the end that, by common consent, the two thus nominated, having met in the city of Paso del Norte, three months after the exchange of the ratifications of this treaty, may proceed to survey and

243

mark out upon the land the dividing line stipulated by this article, where it shall not have already been surveyed and established by the mixed commission, according to the treaty of Guadalupe, keeping a journal and making proper plans of their operations. For this purpose, if they should judge it is necessary, the contracting parties shall be at liberty each to unite to its respective commissioner scientific or other assistants, such as astronomers and surveyors, whose concurrence shall not be considered necessary for the settlement and ratification of a true line of division between the two republics; that line shall be alone established upon which the commissioners may fix, their consent in this particular being considered decisive and an integral part of this treaty, without necessity of ulterior ratification or approval, and without room for interpretation of any kind by either of the parties contracting.

The dividing line thus established shall, in all time, be faithfully respected by the two Governments, without any variation therein, unless of the express and free consent of the two, given in conformity to the principles of the law of nations, and in accordance with the constitution of each country, respectively.

In consequence, the stipulation in the 5th article of the treaty of Guadalupe upon the boundary line therein described is no longer of any force, wherein it may conflict with that here established, the said line being considered annulled and abolished wherever it may not coincide with the present, and in the same manner remaining in full force where in accordance with the same.

While the purchase, which established the present Mexican-American boundary, is the key aspect of the Gadsden Treaty, another important provision is the abrogation of Article 11 of the Treaty of Guadalupe Hidalgo, by which the United States had pledged to prevent Indians from leaving its newly acquired territory in order to settle in (and presumably raid) territory still held by Mexico. Fulfilling this treaty condition would have entailed an extensive, expensive, and ultimately hopeless military enterprise. Although Indians were not considered citizens of the United States, the forcible restraint of anyone, citizen or not, from leaving the United States would also have been a constitutionally questionable and morally repugnant task.

Consequences

The only tangible result of the various expansionist schemes in the 1850s, the Gadsden Purchase rounded out the continental frontiers of the United States. The transcontinental railroad, however, did not follow Davis's hoped-for route. The Civil War intervened, and Davis became president of the Confederate States of America, while the railroad took a more northerly route after the war.

Proclamations and Declarations

MONROE DOCTRINE

TREATY AT A GLANCE

Completed
December 2, 1823, at Washington, D.C.

Signatories
Unilateral declaration by the United States

Overview
An outgrowth of English and American fears that continental powers would attempt to restore Spain's colonies in the Western Hemisphere after the fall of Napoleon, the Monroe Doctrine was a declaration of U.S. foreign policy, in James Monroe's annual message to Congress, that recognized newly independent republics in Latin America and outlawed foreign intervention in their affairs, which became a cornerstone of future U.S. diplomacy.

Historical Background

By the second decade of the 19th century an aggressive and expansive nationalism had become one of the more dominant themes in American foreign policy. In an earlier era, both George Washington and John Adams had taken pains to keep their infant and fragile republic free of the "broils of Europe." Neutrality and isolation were perhaps wise for so young a country, suffering internally from regional wranglings, although even in those wranglings Europe had its influence. The Federalists, strong in New England, were attracted to financial, trade, and foreign policies that favored Britain, whose commerce was essential to the region's developing industrial economy. Republicans, strongest in the South, leaned toward those that favored France, with whose recent revolution the party leaders, especially Thomas Jefferson, felt a close affinity. Jefferson's LOUISIANA PURCHASE in 1803 from France and the westward movement it fostered would swing the balance toward the Republicans, who, following the War of 1812, occupied the White House and controlled the Congress for half a century.

Regardless of the TREATY OF GHENT, which ended the 1812 conflict without the hoped-for territorial gains in Canada or Florida, General Andrew Jackson's victories during the war gave the nation a new faith in its own strength and fed a growing expansionist hunger. Jackson himself would seize Spanish Florida in 1818 when he was supposedly on a mission to subdue the Seminole, and the ADAMS-ONÍS TREATY would make the seizure official in 1819.

Meanwhile, Central and Latin American countries had begun a series of rebellions against a Spain weakened by the Napoleonic Wars. Following Napoleon's final defeat by the British, Spain, with the help of Portugal and of others in the so-called Holy Alliance, declared their opposition to revolution of any kind and their intention of reconstructing the old empire in America. Britain, now the world's dominant sea power, was just as determined to prevent such a development, and the British approached U.S. president James Monroe with the suggestion that the two countries issue a joint proclamation barring the rest of Europe from American affairs.

Secretary of State John Quincy Adams was mindful of the expansionist ambitions of some of his countrymen, and he was cognizant of the likelihood of conflict with Britain itself at some point in the Pacific Northwest. He was also aware that Britain was right, that other European powers, should they succeed in crushing the newly born republics, would continue their colonization of America. Indeed, the British, other Europeans, even the Russians might well establish new empires at the very borders of the United States. While Monroe was amenable to the British suggestion of a joint warning—and so for that matter were his two venerable advisers, former presidents Thomas Jefferson and James Madison—Adams was vehemently opposed. He would not have the United States, he said, appear to be a mere "cock-boat in the wake of a British man-of-war." Adams was successful in insisting upon unilateral action, and Monroe issued the "proclamation," disguised as two widely separated passages in an annual message to Congress in December 1823, which in time would become known as the Monroe Doctrine.

Terms

Under the Monroe Doctrine, the United States formally recognized the new republics that had sprung up among the ruins of the Spanish Empire and took a firm stand against European intervention in the Western Hemisphere:

> At the proposal of the Russian Imperial Government, made through the minister of the Emperor residing here, a full power and instructions have been transmitted to the minister of the United States at St. Petersburg to arrange by amicable negotiations the respective rights and interests of the two nations on the northwest coast of this continent. A similar proposal had been made by His Imperial Majesty to the Government of Great Britain, which has likewise been acceded to. The Government of the United States has been desirous by this friendly proceeding of manifesting the great value which they have invariably attached to the friendship of the Emperor and their solicitude to cultivate the best understanding with his Government. In the discussions to which this interest has given rise and in the arrangements by which they may terminate the occasion has been judged proper for asserting, as a principle in which the rights and interests of the United States are involved, that the American continents, by the free and independent condition which they have assumed and maintain, are henceforth not to be considered as subjects for future colonization by any European powers. . . .

> It was stated at the commencement of the last session that a great effort was then making in Spain and Portugal to improve the condition of the people of those countries, and that it appeared to be conducted with extraordinary moderation. It need scarcely be remarked that the result has been so far very different from what was then anticipated. Of events in that quarter of the globe, with which we have so much intercourse and from which we derive our origin, we have always been anxious and interested spectators. The citizens of the United States cherish sentiments the most friendly in favor of the liberty and happiness of their fellow-men on that side of the Atlantic. In the wars of the European powers in matters relating to

themselves we have never taken any part, nor does it comport with our policy so to do. It is only when our rights are invaded or seriously menaced that we resent injuries or make preparation for our defense. With the movements in this hemisphere we are of necessity more immediately connected, and by causes which must be obvious to all enlightened and impartial observers. The political system of the allied powers is essentially different in this respect from that of America. This difference proceeds from that which exists in their respective Governments; and to the defense of our own, which has been achieved by the loss of so much blood and treasure, and matured by the wisdom of their most enlightened citizens, and under which we have enjoyed unexampled felicity, this whole nation is devoted. We owe it, therefore, to candor and to the amicable relations existing between the United States and those powers to declare that we should consider any attempt on their part to extend their system to any portion of this hemisphere as dangerous to our peace and safety. With the existing colonies or dependencies of any European power we have not interfered and shall not interfere. But with the Governments who have declared their independence we have, on great consideration and on just principles, acknowledged, we could not view any interposition for the purpose of oppressing them, or controlling in any other manner their destiny, by any European power in any other light than as the manifestation of an unfriendly disposition toward the United States. In the war between those new Governments and Spain we declared our neutrality at the time of their recognition, and to this we have adhered, and shall continue to adhere, provided no changed shall occur which, in the judgment of the competent authorities of this Government, shall make a corresponding change on the part of the United States indispensable to their security.

> The late events in Spain and Portugal show that Europe is still unsettled. Of this important fact no stronger proof can be adduced than that the allied powers should have thought it proper, on any principle satisfactory to themselves, to have interposed by force in the internal concerns of Spain. To what extent such interposition may be carried, on the same principle, is a question in which all independent powers whose governments differ from theirs are interested, even those most remote, and surely none more so than the United States. Our policy in regard to Europe, which was adopted at an early stage of the wars which have so long agitated that quarter of the globe, nevertheless remains the same, which is, not to interfere in the internal concerns of any of its powers; to consider the government de facto as the legitimate government for us; to cultivate friendly relations with it, and to preserve those relations by a frank, firm, and manly policy, meeting in all instances the just claims of every power, submitting to injuries from none. But in regard to these continents circumstances are eminently and conspicuously different. It is impossible that the allied

powers should extend their political system to any portion of either continent without endangering our peace and happiness; nor can anyone believe that our southern brethren, if left to themselves, would adopt it of their own accord. It is equally impossible, therefore, that we should behold such interposition in any form with indifference. If we look to the comparative strength and resources of Spain and those new Governments, and their distance from each other, it must be obvious that she can never subdue them. It is still the true policy of the United States to leave the parties to themselves, in the hope that other powers will pursue the same course. . . .

Consequences

The Monroe Doctrine was first declaimed during that upsurge of flamboyant nationalism characteristic of the years following the Treaty of Ghent, a period historians have designated the Era of Good Feelings. Some ironies seem unavoidable; for example, the "era" could hardly have been possible except for the Pax Britannica, a stretch of relative stability in European history born in the defeat of Napoleon and maintained by the ascent of the British navy to its unassailable mastery of the seas. The simple truth was that for all Adams's bluster about not being a "cock-boat," the United States lacked the power to enforce Monroe's bold new principles. For decades, Latin American independence was protected precisely by British man-of-wars, not by presidential pronouncements. The second obvious irony is that not least among the new republics proclaiming their independence of Spain had been Mexico, a country soon to suffer at the hands of the United States something of the same fate the Monroe Doctrine imagined for new republics at the hands of Europe.

In one respect, as Monroe's speech itself makes clear, the doctrine did not represent a truly new direction for American foreign policy. Despite its somewhat bellicose message and the implication that the United States would not remain neutral if it came to keeping Europe out of Latin America with, say, British help, in large measure the doctrine was a reinforcement of the deep strain of "isolationism" from European affairs already long evident in the country's diplomatic history. That isolation would be necessary for the nation's continued expansion across the continent and especially for the elimination of the Native American "threat" within its own borders. For the first time in the North American subcontinent's history, the Indians were themselves isolated from European allies, who in the past had helped them resist the encroachment of white Americans onto their lands.

There was also an implied threat to peoples other than the Europeans in the thinking behind the proclamation, since the United States would decide for itself who was free and independent. In the long run, this would develop into the belief that the U.S. government knew what was best for the entire hemisphere, that it was basically free to meddle in the internal affairs of its neighbors, if always in the name of freedom. Central and Latin American republics, however much they might have welcomed the immediate recognition of their independence, would one day come to rue the hegemony the Monroe Doctrine claimed for the "colossus of the North" in their half of the world. Mexico was only the first to feel the steely hand stretched forth in the velvet glove of friendship, and the Mexicans developed a saying that would chill the blood of many a Latin American diplomat: "Poor Mexico: so far from God, so close to the United States."

Isolationism remained the basic tenet of American foreign policy, with significant lapses, until World War II. But even as the United States became an imperial power in its own right in the late 19th and early 20th centuries, even after it assumed the mantle of world power after the Great War, even when it became one of two superpowers in the post–World War II cold war, the Monroe Doctrine continued to play a significant role in its diplomacy as the basis for the nation's claim that it should be free from intervention by powers outside the Americas and free to protect its vital interests at any cost within them. Hence, it was no surprise to hear President John F. Kennedy invoke the Monroe Doctrine during the Cuban Missile Crisis as he prepared his country for nuclear armageddon against Russia, if necessary, to protect American rights in the Western Hemisphere, rights first proclaimed to the world in 1823.

Part Eight

THE AMERICAN CIVIL WAR

INTRODUCTION

The treaty making of the American Civil War was not the result of diplomacy between two sovereign powers, for sovereignty of person over slave and of nation over section lay at the heart of the issues over which the war was being fought. At several points during the conflict, peace feelers, usually from a beleaguered South but also from a beleaguered U.S. president, were undertaken, always to founder on the question of sovereignty. Formulated in just such terms, these attempts at peace meant that the South was continuing to mask its dedication to the "peculiar institution" of slavery with high-toned rhetoric about states' rights, the combination that had led to the war in the first place. Even after the South, nearing physical and economic exhaustion, was nominally ready to give up Negro bondage, the question of sovereignty remained a sticking point. Indeed, it would be under the banner of sovereignty—so-called white sovereignty—that a defeated South continued to try to deny emancipated slaves full participation in the American nation secured by the Civil War. Thus, while the end of the fighting was not a matter of treaties but of truces and amnesties granted by a sovereign nation to several states in rebellion, the peace itself consisted of amendments and legislation passed by Congress and, ultimately, of national presidential elections a decade later.

None of this should obscure the fact that despite what the participants said at the time or what Southern apologists have said since, the Civil War was fought to resolve the question of slavery. It was only over the question of slavery that the South unequivocally asserted the sovereign rights of the individual states, all other matters—tariffs and sectional influence in Congress, for example—having proved pliable to debate and compromise and legislative remedy. If money was the root of all evil, slavery was the evil root of sectional conflict in the United States, a root that predated the formation of the Union and lay at the bottom of the growing rift in that Union since it was formed. Ultimately, the South did not so much rebel against the Union as it resisted the threat of a revolution in its social and economic institutions posed by continuing the Union. Unable to remain both a slaveholding society and be part of the United States, the South chose disunion. The peace after the war was not simply about reunion, which would have been easily enough accomplished, but about instituting the social revolution for which the war had been fought and over which both sides continued to struggle after the fighting ceased.

The background for understanding the treaty making of the Civil War, then, is not the war itself. Indeed, the war is better seen as presaging the coming "total" warfare of the 20th century, where industrial might and weaponry were more decisive than the bravery or brilliance of the combatants. Instead, that understanding lies with the history and development of slavery as the "peculiar institution" underlying Southern society and the flashpoint of regional conflict, for if the war presaged the future of battlefield fighting, the peace sought to undo the American past.

The Peculiar Institution

It was in 1619, merely 12 years after the founding of Jamestown, that Dutch traders imported black slaves for sale to the Virginia tobacco farmers, the first step in the establishment of a "peculiar institution" that would survive for more than two centuries, make a mockery of the American Revolution's promise of equality, blight millions of lives, fuel sectional rivalries into bitter hatred, and lead the new nation to the brink of destruction. For the wealthy planters who bought them, black slaves represented nothing more than a new source of cheap labor, one that—unlike indentured servants, who worked (at least in theory) for only seven years to repay their passage—would be perpetually under the planters' control. In the early colonial period, few could afford the prohibitive costs of purchasing African slaves, so indentured servitude remained the predominant method by which planters exploited the labor force. Toward the end of the 17th century, the prices of slaves began to fall, and as living conditions improved in the colonies, planters who bought slaves could expect to get a full lifetime of work from their chattel. Even at twice the price of indentured servants, African slaves had become a bargain.

In South Carolina, especially, slavery fast grew essential to the colony's economy. By the 1730s, rice plantations covered the tidal and inland swamps of the Low Country. Indigo thrived in the drier regions of the colony, where rice would not grow. Within a few years of the founding of South Carolina's great rice plantations, black slaves outnumbered the white population. Planters forced slaves to work under abysmal conditions in swamplands infested by mosquitoes, and black men and women died in alarming numbers from malaria and a wide range of infectious diseases. Many others fell disabled from exhaustion and poor diet, together with diseases. The planters simply imported more Africans, finding it cheaper to buy new slaves than to sustain the ones they owned. South Carolina strictly enforced the slave codes and allowed masters to treat their chattel as they saw fit, without restriction. Often plantation owners lived in Charleston, leaving the operation of their plantations and the supervision of their slaves to overseers, many of whom—more concerned about the commissions they received on good harvests than with their management of black labor—became widely infamous for their mistreatment of slaves.

Southerners were not the only Americans to engage in slavery as a means of economic improvement. The New England shipping industry relied on the importation of slaves as a part of its "triangular" trade. The trade took many different forms, but in one version traders shipped molasses refined in the West Indies to New England for use in the distillation of rum. They then shipped rum to Africa in trade for slaves, whom they transported to the West Indies. New England slave traders then hawked the Africans on the auction blocks in Charleston, New York, and other busy port cities along the eastern seaboard.

In the South, however, American slavery flourished both as an economic system—allowing a few planters to grow rich from the forced labor of the Africans who cultivated their tobacco, rice, indigo, and later cotton—and as a system for strict racial control. The casual bigotry of the early European settlers became a virulent racism in the service of the South's regionalist ideology. Planters and traders kept questions of morality and human decency in abeyance dur-

ing the 17th and 18th centuries, when the economic benefits of slavery were evident for both the South and the North and the balance of sectional interests could serve as a basis for compromise. But westward expansion of the new nation threatened that balance even as slavery developed into the South's own peculiar institution, the bleak rockbed of its cherished way of life, and grew increasingly irrelevant economically to the rapidly industrializing North.

The tensions inherent in the diverging economies of the two regions were underscored by slavery, and the institution from the beginning proved politically volatile. By the time of the American Revolution, the interests of the North and South were different enough that slavery was an issue in the drafting of the DECLARATION OF INDEPENDENCE, and it would remain an issue in the subsequent drafting of both the NORTHWEST ORDINANCE and the Constitution. Jefferson had wanted to include a mention of the slave trade in the Declaration and blame the foul practice on George III, but other southerners in the Continental Congress objected to any mention of slavery at all, and they prevailed. The Northwest Ordinance, probably the most important piece of legislation passed under the Articles of Confederation because it determined how the United States would handle new lands, prompted the debate over whether slavery should be allowed to spread with the nation. A compromise was reached, barring slavery from the western lands "won" during the war but allowing slavery to flourish below the old Northwest. The question of whether slaves were property or people was raised during the debates of the Constitutional Convention, where southerners wanted them considered property except when it came to representation in Congress, when they wanted them counted as people. Again a compromise was reached, each slave considered as three-fourths a human at census time but otherwise treated like any other chattel.

Slavery of course was not the only point of contention between North and South. The issues were complicated, often involving the balance of power between the two regions in Congress. They wrangled over trade policies and foreign affairs. Mercantile New England's Federalists frequently sought to shore up commerce with Britain, while the agricultural South's Democratic-Republicans felt a special affinity for revolutionary France. But slavery was a spark. Any new territory that allowed slaveholding, it was assumed, would align itself with the South. Since slavery seemed antithetical to the founding principles of the Republic, it was an easier issue on which to take the high ground than, say, economic self-interest or political influence in Congress. As black bondage became embedded in the South's self-image and the power of the Democratic-Republican Party grew, slavery became increasingly the one issue over which neither side was willing to compromise. By the time of the LOUISIANA PURCHASE, the pattern was already in place if not yet obvious: new lands or policies would threaten to upset the regional balance in Congress, the extension of slavery would become the flashpoint for a political crisis, a new compromise would be reached not quite satisfying to either side, and the nation would edge closer to outright civil conflict.

The Long Debate

New England was the section threatening to secede from the Union when Thomas Jefferson bought the vast interior territory of Louisiana from Napoleon Bonaparte—a threat that, made once too often toward the end of the War of 1812, effectively ended the already waning political life of the Federalist Party. In 1819, 22 United States senators were from northern states, and 22 from southern states.

This balance, carefully preserved with the admission of each new state since the revolution, was about to be upset as Missouri petitioned Congress for statehood as a slaveholding state. When Missouri submitted its application, Representative James Talmadge of New York introduced an amendment calling for a ban on the "further introduction of slavery" and for the emancipation of all slaves born in the new state of Missouri once they reached the age of 25. The House of Representatives passed Talmadge's amendment, but the Senate, where the North-South split was even, saw the matter differently. The senators rejected the amendment and adjourned without reaching a decision on Missouri statehood.

When Congress reconvened, the debate on Missouri's application resumed in earnest. Northern senators claimed that Congress had the right to ban slavery in new states. Southern senators countered that new states, like the original 13, had the right to determine whether or not to allow slavery within their borders. After protracted and agonizing debate, a two-part compromise was finally reached in March 1820, called variously the Compromise of 1820 or the Missouri Compromise. First, Missouri would be allowed to join the Union as a slave state, but at the same time, Maine, which had been part of Massachusetts, would be admitted as a free state.

No one was completely satisfied by the compromise, but it did help to preserve the Union for some 30 years. Northerners were dissatisfied because the compromise failed to ban slavery from the Louisiana territories. Southerners were distressed that the law set a precedent for future congressional action regarding slavery. The Missouri Compromise opened the eyes of many political leaders to the real volatility of the issue

of slavery and to see the debate as a prologue to a disaster yet to come. Jefferson said the sectional debate over slavery, like a fire bell in the night, filled him with terror. John Quincy Adams called the compromise the title page to a great tragic volume.

While the law would remain in force until the Kansas-Nebraska Act of 1854, the positions on slavery began to grow more radical. It seemed that slavery was vanishing through the civilized world except in the American South, where it grew stronger. Napoleon had outlawed it in his empire, and soon the British would too. Among the Europeans, only backward Russia still relied on human bondage when the American Civil War broke out, and even the czar would free the serfs before the Americans freed their slaves.

During the 1830s, a secret network of individuals committed to helping escaped slaves find their way north to freedom became more thoroughly organized and acquired the name by which it would be known until the Civil War: the Underground Railroad. The network had actually existed since the days of the revolution, as evidenced by some comments George Washington made on the aid Quakers gave to runaway slaves. By the early 19th century, most of the individuals working in the loosely knit network were free blacks living in the North. Harriet Tubman, herself an escaped slave, was among the most active Underground Railroad workers. She is reported to have made 19 trips into the South, risking her own freedom to help some 300 slaves flee northward. White abolitionists, growing in number, also participated in the railroad's activities. The Underground Railroad was most helpful to slaves living in the Upper South. Those in Louisiana, southern Georgia, Alabama, and Mississippi had little hope of reaching the southernmost "terminal" of the railroad, but even slaves in the Upper South had extreme difficulty reaching the safety of the railroad's embrace.

Still, by the time the antislavery newspaper *The Liberator* appeared in 1831, the abolitionist crusade was in full swing in the North. Alarmed by the willingness of northern citizens to help the slaves, the southerners raved about being deprived of their property. They blamed abolitionist agitation for such slave revolts in the South as the one led by Nat Turner in 1831. Northern states responded by enacting "personal liberty" laws prohibiting state officials from helping southerners recapture their runaway slaves. By 1842, when the Supreme Court declared in *Prigg v. Pennsylvania* that the states were not required to enforce the Fugitive Slave Act, the southerners had grown rabid in their denunciations of the North's attempts to destroy what they called their "way of life."

Early in the 1830s, southerners thought they had found a solution this northern "attack": nullification.

When Andrew Jackson became president in March 1829, the nation was embroiled in these arguments over slavery and slavery-related issues, such as protective tariffs and the price of western lands. Northern states feared that low prices set on western lands would not only bankrupt the treasury but would attract southerners sympathetic to slavery to the trans-Mississippi. They also advocated tariffs to protect their industries, while southerners opposed them since they hurt the trade of their major cash crop, cotton. In 1832 Congress passed a new tariff that southerners, already outraged at the abolitionist fever spreading rapidly through the North, thought not merely excessive but a deliberate attempt at destroying their economy. Radicals in the South Carolina legislature combined their hatred of abolition with their resentment of the new tariff and resolved that the state would not yield. On November 24, 1832, a special convention called by the state legislature passed the Ordinance of Nullification, which prohibited the collection of duties after February 1, 1833. In addition, the legislature called for raising and arming a military force.

The state was determined to put the authority of the central government to a severe test, but South Carolinians did not realize how determined President Jackson was to compel their compliance with federal law. They reasoned that Jackson, himself a slaveholder and cotton ginner, had backed the state of Georgia when it refused to acquiesce to the Supreme Court's decision in *Worcester v. Georgia*, which held that the state had no jurisdiction over the actions of American Indians on their own land. But Jackson's action in that instance of "nullification" had been motivated by his desire to compel the Cherokee to remove to Indian Territory under the INDIAN REMOVAL ACT. The matter of South Carolina's attempting to nullify a law of Congress was different, and Jackson prepared to take military measures against the state, issuing a Proclamation to the People of South Carolina, in which he declared that "disunion by armed force is treason," even as he pleaded with Congress to reconsider the tariff. The South Carolina radicals backed down 10 days before nullification was scheduled to begin. When a compromise tariff was passed by Congress in March 1833, the state legislature repealed the Nullification Ordinance altogether. While the ultimate crisis was averted, sectional tensions continued to mount. Radicals in South Carolina and elsewhere in the South came to believe that only secession from the Union would protect their way of life.

Leading South Carolina's fight during the Nullification Crisis was native son John C. Calhoun. He was actually Andrew Jackson's vice president and a member of the new Democratic Party, which Jackson had led out of Thomas Jefferson's old Republican Party, taking most of the South and the West with him. Calhoun, who resigned the vice presidency, would become the major spokesman for states' rights and one of a remarkable triumvirate of senators that dominated the two decades before the Civil War. Another was Daniel Webster, who represented the once-Federalist New England and had become the Whig Party's foremost spokesman for the Union at any cost. Between these two there was Henry Clay, a Whig but also a slaveholding Kentuckian who would become known as the Great Compromiser. All three wanted to be president, but tainted by the social struggles of the time, none of them ever achieved his goal.

All three, however, had a major impact on the debate over the admission of California as a state, where Congress—threatened by the mounting regional tensions over whether new territories should be admitted with or without slavery—hammered out a new political compromise, the Compromise of 1850. The discovery of gold in California in 1848 brought to a boil the long-simmering sectional differences over slavery. More than 80,000 people from the eastern states and territories flooded into California in 1849 alone, making the establishment of a territorial government an urgent necessity. The question of whether territories and new states would be slave-holding or free had been settled—so most people thought—by the Missouri Compromise of 1820, which prohibited slavery in all parts of the Louisiana Purchase north of the latitude of 36° 30'.

Then, in 1846 David Wilmot, a congressman from Pennsylvania, introduced an amendment to a bill appropriating $2 million to facilitate negotiations with Mexico for "territorial adjustments" as a way of bringing an end to the Mexican War. His amendment, the Wilmot Proviso, as it came to be called, would have prohibited slavery in any land acquired by the United States as a result of the war. In opposition to the proviso, John C. Calhoun, now South Carolina's senator, proposed four resolutions, during February 19 and 20, 1847, that articulated the South's position with regard to slavery. Calhoun proposed that the territories were the common and joint property of the states; that Congress, as agent for the states, had no right to make laws discriminating between the states and depriving any state of its full and equal right in any territory acquired by the United States; that the enactment of any national law pertaining to slavery would be a violation of the Constitution and states' rights; that the people had the right to form their state governments as they chose, the Constitution imposing no conditions for the admission of a state except that its government should be republican. Calhoun warned that failure to maintain a balance between the interests of the South and those of the North would result in political revolution, anarchy, civil war, and widespread disaster, threatening that, if "trampled" upon, the South would resist.

During the next three years, various compromises on the issue of slavery in new territories and states were proposed, including an extension of the line drawn by the Missouri Compromise across the full breadth of the continent, but the atmosphere in Congress and in the country itself had changed much since 1820. Most northerners were no longer willing to allow slavery to extend into any territory, no matter whether it lay above or below the compromise line.

Faced with a widening gulf of irreconcilable positions, Senator Lewis Cass of Michigan proposed that territories should be organized without mention of slavery, a solution which had a venerable American pedigree. Then, Cass said, when the territory wrote its own constitution in preparation for admission to statehood, the citizens of the territory would decide for themselves whether to be free or slave. Called popular sovereignty, the concept held great appeal for President Zachary Taylor, who was faced with the decision of what to do about California. He proposed that popular sovereignty be allowed to run its course and that California should be admitted directly as a state. The controversy over whether slavery would be allowed in California would be avoided, since no territorial government would be set up and since the state of California would determine the issue for itself.

Southern states were horrified by Taylor's proposal. They reasoned that since not only California but also New Mexico would doubtless organize themselves as free states, the balance of slave versus free states as represented in the Senate would be destroyed. Some compensation was required, and the aging Henry Clay, who had been among the framers of the Missouri Compromise, worked with Daniel Webster to devise a plan that would satisfy the South. California would be admitted to the Union as a free state. Other territories in the Southwest would be organized without mention of slavery. The slave trade in the District of Columbia would be abolished, but the federal government would pass a stronger fugitive slave law to prevent slaves from being declared free. The final leg of the complicated compromise called for the federal government's assumption of debts slaveholding Texas had incurred before it was annexed by the United States.

The Compromise of 1850 was subjected to excruciatingly protracted negotiations and debate. It pleased no one absolutely, but it offered North and South sufficient concessions to preserve the Union for another tense decade, as extremists on both sides slid inexorably toward civil war. Ardent abolitionists saw the new Fugitive Slave Law as caving in to southern pressures. With the admission of California as a free state, and the likely admission of New Mexico and Utah as free states in the future, Southern states' rights fanatics saw looming the certain end of any power they had in Congress. The rumblings of disunion could be clearly heard behind the public facade of the compromise.

One of those who would contribute to those rumblings was a homemaker in Brunswick, Maine, named Harriet Beecher Stowe, who two years later published a novel entitled *Uncle Tom's Cabin, or Life among the Lowly*, which more than any other piece of writing, whether political treatise or newspaper editorial, promoted popular support for abolition. Stowe reported later that she had been moved to write the book after the passage of the Fugitive Slave Act, a bill included in the Compromise of 1850. Telling the story of Tom, Eliza, and Eva, slaves under the control of the evil New England slave overseer Simon Legree, the novel became an immediate commercial success, selling 10,000 copies in one week and 300,000 nationally within a year. Translated into dozens of languages, it sold 2 million copies worldwide during its first year. The book was adapted for the New York stage, where it was performed 18 times a week. The publication of an anti-slavery book by a woman had another important result, in that it created a legitimate place for women in the abolition movement.

Southerners were naturally outraged by *Uncle Tom's Cabin* and its immediate popularity. They claimed that Stowe had no knowledge of slavery as it existed in the South and that she had exaggerated the mistreatment of slaves. Northerners, on the other hand, discounted southern criticism as biased, and thousands of people who had been undecided over the issue flocked to the abolition movement. When Abraham Lincoln later met Mrs. Stowe, he reportedly called her "the little lady who wrote the book that made this big war."

Due to the work of people like Stowe, the abolition crusade was hitting its crest just as Congress in 1854 passed the Kansas-Nebraska Act, throwing the decision of whether to allow slavery into territories seeking statehood back to the respective territories. The move caused border warfare to erupt in Kansas and brought yet closer the likelihood of armed conflict between the states. If Congress thought it had averted disaster in 1850 by shuffling once more to delay the national showdown over slavery, the Kansas-Nebraska Act revealed what a last-ditch effort the Compromise of 1850 had been. When the territories of Nebraska and Kansas applied for statehood in 1854, Congress collectively threw up its hands, officially repealed the Missouri Compromise, which the Compromise of 1850 had already more or less gutted, and passed the Kansas-Nebraska Act, which left the question of slavery up to the popular sovereignty of the two want-to-be states.

The act spawned a new antislavery Republican Party and led U.S. Senator David P. Atchison of

Missouri, who had already broken with his hoary and respected fellow senator Thomas H. Benton over slavery, to swear he would let the new territories sink in hell before allowing them to be organized as Free-Soil states. Abolitionists in the North organized the Emigrant Aid Society and financed free settlers in Kansas. New England authors such as William Cullen Bryant and John Greenleaf Whittier mounted one of history's great propaganda campaigns, quickly aided by newspaperman Horace Greeley and correspondents sent by eastern papers to report on the Kansas-Missouri border "situation."

In response, fearing and hating those they called "Yankee slave-stealers" and egged on by Atchison, thousands of pro-slavery Missourians, mainly from the tobacco- and hemp-growing western counties, flooded into Kansas to vote illegally and then return home to their farms. Overwhelming the Kansas settlers, the majority of whom were probably Free-Soilers, they elected a territorial legislature that immediately legalized slavery and won official recognition from the federal government. Free-Soilers poured in from Iowa to settle the land, formed their own legislature, set their capital up at Lawrence, and petitioned Congress for admission as a free state. Open warfare broke out along the Kansas-Missouri border. Atchison resigned his seat in the Senate to lead the fight on the ground, organized a posse of Missourians, and, in the guise of answering a U.S. marshal's summons, raided Lawrence. Called afterward "border ruffians" by Greeley, the posse set fire to a hotel and a few houses, chopped up a printing press, arrested several free state leaders, and killed three others in the process.

A monomaniacal abolitionist named John Brown retaliated by murdering five pro-slavery settlers along the Pottawatomie Creek, then mutilating their bodies. Ideologically motivated assassination had begun. By the time the federal government could join with the governments of Missouri and Kansas to bring the guerrilla fighting in "Bleeding Kansas" more or less to an end in 1858, 200 people were dead, and $2 million worth of property had gone up in smoke.

Meanwhile, a year earlier, at the height of the bloodletting, the U.S. Supreme Court had decided to enter the controversy over slavery by addressing the question of Congress's power over the peculiar institution in the territories, the question at issue in the Dred Scott case. A St. Louis slave, Dred Scott had been trying to win his freedom through the courts. Scott had belonged to John Emerson, an army surgeon who was stationed first in Illinois, then in the Wisconsin Territory, and finally in Missouri. Scott accompanied Emerson to each new station until the surgeon's death in 1846. Scott then sued Emerson's widow for his freedom, claiming that he was a citizen of Missouri and free by virtue of his travels with Emerson in Illinois, where slavery was banned by the Northwest Ordinance, and in the Wisconsin Territory, where it was banned by the Missouri Compromise.

When the state court decided against him, he and his lawyers appealed to the Supreme Court. Sentiment among the justices was almost evenly split. Antislavery justices John McLean of Ohio and Benjamin R. Curtis of Massachusetts believed that Scott should be freed because of the Missouri Compromise. Southern justices hoped that the Court's ruling would, quite to the contrary, nullify the compromise itself. Chief Justice Roger B. Taney ruled first that neither free blacks nor slaves were citizens, so they could not sue in the federal courts. The justice also ruled that the Illinois law banning slavery had no force over Scott and his owners after he returned to Missouri, where slavery was allowed. In addition, the Court ruled that the Wisconsin Territory laws had no force either, because the Missouri Compromise, which outlawed slavery there, was unconstitutional. The Court based its ruling on the Fifth Amendment, which prohibits the government from depriving an individual of property without due process of law. The justices saw any law that deprived an individual of property solely because the owner had taken his property into a different territory as a violation of the Fifth Amendment.

Politically, the Dred Scott decision had an immediate impact. Republicans, struggling to get their new political party on sound footing, viewed the ruling as an attempt by southern justices to destroy them. Northern and western Democrats saw the ruling as an attack on the policy of popular sovereignty. Northern abolitionists saw the ruling as an attempt by the Supreme Court, a majority of whose justices were from the South, to extend slavery by legal fiat. To the utter amazement and outrage of the abolitionists, the Court had invoked the Bill of Rights in a ruling that denied freedom to a black man. For Southern slave owners, the decision implied that slavery was safe—and according to their reading, should be protected—everywhere in the nation. In short, the Dred Scott decision changed the terms of the national debate on slavery and made the Civil War inevitable. From an argument over how the West should be settled, it had become a battle over the nature of property itself.

Those new terms to the argument were obvious the following year, 1858, in the great Lincoln-Douglas debates. The two men were running for the Senate in perhaps the most important contest so far for the Republican Party, formed in 1854 on the ruins of a Whig Party that had lost favor among northern and western voters who could never forgive the passage of the Kansas-Nebraska Act. During the debate over the act, Congress had acquiesced to Democratic senator

Stephen Douglas's proposal to repeal that part of the Missouri Compromise that banned slavery north of the 36° 30' line. Instead of such an arbitrary boundary, Douglas suggested, popular sovereignty should be allowed to run its course in the new territories to be established in the West.

The move discredited the Whigs, and in their place the ranks of the new Republicans, who had been gathering in a series of political meetings in the upper Midwest, swelled. Early members of the party included former Free-Soilers, conscience Whigs, and anti-Nebraska Democrats, all of whom were united in their opposition to the expansion of slavery. Before long the party spread from the states of the old Northwest Territory to New England. In the congressional elections of 1854, the new party won more than a hundred seats in the House of Representatives. By the time of the next presidential election, the party was ready with a candidate, John C. Frémont, and a slogan, "Free soil, free speech, and Frémont." Although Frémont lost the election to Democrat James Buchanan, the party made a good showing, carrying 11 of 16 northern states.

In the 1858 Senate elections, Stephen A. Douglas was up for reelection, and the Republicans were ready with a candidate named Abraham Lincoln. A former member of the Illinois state legislature and former United States congressman, Lincoln challenged Douglas to a series of debates that captured the attention of the national press. The strategies of both men were to exaggerate the differences between them. Douglas tried to portray Lincoln as a radical abolitionist; Lincoln, to portray Douglas as favoring slavery. In reality, the candidates were more similar than not. Both favored banning slavery in the territories, but neither thought it possible to abolish slavery by political action. Douglas ultimately won the election, in part because of his stance, known as the Freeport Doctrine, on the Dred Scott decision. In explaining his position on the Supreme Court ruling, Douglas maintained that a territory could exclude slavery before it became a state by declining to enact laws that were required for slavery to exist.

Although the Republicans lost the Senate seat for Illinois, elsewhere they made great gains, and Lincoln's performance in the debates garnered him renown in the country and respect in his new party. The North swung heavily to the Republican Party, further discomfiting the South, where radicals were soon declaiming that if a Republican were elected president in 1860, they would secede from the Union. That Republican, of course, would be Abraham Lincoln, and secession, followed by war, would indeed come.

Meanwhile, just how deeply divided the country had grown was made abundantly clear by John Brown's raid on Harpers Ferry, Virginia (now West Virginia), on October 16, 1859. To Brown it seemed that the federal government itself had fallen captive to the hated slavers of the South, and he had been planning his attack since 1857, after moving to Boston from Kansas, where he was a wanted man for the massacre he and his sons perpetrated on pro-slave families living along Pottawatomie Creek. In Boston, Brown became associated with a number of noted abolitionists, including Samuel Howe, Thomas Wentworth Higgens, Theodore Parker, Franklin Sanborn, George L. Stearns, and Gerrit Smith, who raised funds for Brown, bought guns, and supplied his family with a house. With the escaped slave and prominent member of the Massachusetts Anti-Slavery Society Frederick Douglass as an adviser, Brown developed his plans to take the federal arsenal at Harpers Ferry and use the guns and ammunition to arm slaves for a rebellion he expected to follow once the blacks held in bondage realized that Douglass was with him. Leading 21 followers, Brown seized the armory, cut telegraph wires, and spread some of his fighters throughout the area to raid plantations.

There followed, however, no spontaneous slave revolt and no appearance by Frederick Douglass. Instead, on the morning of October 17, federal troops commanded by Colonel Robert E. Lee retook the arsenal, killed 10 of Brown's men, and took Brown prisoner. The state of Virginia charged Brown with treason, conspiracy, and murder. During his trial and after his conviction and execution by hanging, abolitionists made of him a martyr. On the day of Brown's hanging, December 2, 1859, Ralph Waldo Emerson and William Lloyd Garrison memorialized him at a huge gathering of abolitionists in Boston.

While northern abolitionists took up his martyrdom as the new standard of their cause, southerners reacted to the raid with exaggerated alarm. For northerner and southerner alike, Brown's bloody raid—a harbinger of the horrific conflict shortly to come—only served to strengthen the acrimonious forces already trying to tear the country apart. Discussion of compromise grew less and less common amid the acrid talk that turned readily to violence. A collision course had long been set, and fewer people than ever held any hope that the course might change. In the end, the split was so bitter that it took no overt action like Brown's to spark a civil war. All it took, instead, was the simple choice of a Republican president by a majority of the voters in a perfectly legal and politically legitimate national election.

The Course of the War

At 4:30 A.M. on April 12, 1861, a hotheaded South Carolina rebel fired on Fort Sumter, beginning four years of bloodshed and bitterness called the Civil War.

Although the population and industrial might of the North outweighed the technology and numbers of men the South could muster, the cream of the U.S. Army officer corps felt allegiance to the Southern states. Thus, Confederate forces were, in the main, more ably commanded than those of the North, especially early in the war. The Confederates stunned Union loyalists with victories at Bull Run (or Manassas, July 21, 1861), the so-called Seven Days (during the Peninsular Campaign of Union commander George B. McClellan), the Second Battle of Bull Run (Second Manassas, August 29–30, 1862), Fredericksburg (December 13, 1862), and Chancellorsville (May 2–4, 1863).

It was not until Antietam (Sharpsburg), on September 17, 1862, that the Union was able to claim something approaching a victory—sufficiently credible to enable Lincoln to issue, from what he felt was a position of strength, the preliminary EMANCIPATION PROCLAMATION, which brought the slavery issue to the fore of the conflict. For the Union, the Civil War now took on an added moral dimension, officially becoming more than a struggle to save the Union: it was now a crusade to abolish slavery. After General Robert E. Lee invaded Pennsylvania, the Union forces under General George G. Meade turned back the Confederate army at Gettysburg (July 1–3, 1863), also at great cost. Gettysburg is usually cited as the turning point of the war in favor of the Union. Not only was an invading army repulsed and Northern morale lifted, the Southern defeat discouraged both England and France from supporting the Confederate cause.

Still, the war ground on. Union general Ulysses S. Grant scored important triumphs in the war's western theater, at Shiloh (April 6–7, 1862), Vicksburg (under siege from October 1862 to July 4, 1863), and Chattanooga (November 23–25, 1863). Union control of the lower Mississippi began with the victory of Admiral David Farragut, who captured New Orleans in April 1862. Black troops were recruited into the Union Army but were used mainly for guard duty, domestic work, and hard labor. They saw action first in the western campaign, where they suffered defeat at Fort Pillow in 1863 and were massacred afterward by angry Confederates, a trend that continued throughout the war. Late in the war, a desperate Confederacy considered manumitting slaves in exchange for service in the rebel army, but loud protests from Southern politicians killed the notion aborning.

In 1864, after a series of mediocre commanding generals, Lincoln finally appointed Grant as the Union's general-in-chief. Slowly, inexorably, he forced Lee's army back toward the Confederate capital of Richmond, Virginia, fighting the bitter Wilderness Campaign through May and June 1864. Grant's chief lieutenant, General William Tecumseh Sherman, advanced, in the meantime, through Tennessee and Georgia to Atlanta, which he captured, occupied, and finally burned (September–November 1864) before continuing on his infamously destructive March to the sea. Sherman, a brilliant strategist, introduced a concept that would become a terrifying hallmark of modern warfare. He called it "total war," by which he meant taking the battle not just to the opposing army but to the civilian populations as well, reducing their will and their means to support the fight.

Yet the will of the South was not easy to break, and the bloody conflict refused to end. Occasional and unofficial peace offers were floated by both sides, but they all came to grief over the bedrock contentions by Lincoln that the states in rebellion were still part of the Union and by Jefferson Davis that they were, in themselves, sovereign—providing no common ground for talks. Finally, General Philip Sheridan defeated Confederate general George E. Pickett at Five Forts (April 1, 1865), and Grant took heavily fortified Petersburg after a long campaign that stretched from June 1864 to April 2, 1865, when Grant at last took Richmond. A week later, at Appomattox Court House, General Robert E. Lee surrendered his Army of Northern Virginia to General Grant, effectively ending the Civil War.

Most of the Northern boys who fought in the Civil War joined up in order to preserve the Union, and Southern leaders and soldiers always protested that they were not fighting simply to preserve slavery, which was even to them an embarrassing cause, but to save their cherished way of life. During the war itself, even Abraham Lincoln held onto the notion for as long as he could that his only goal was to reunite those in rebellion with their former brethren in one nation. But the Radical Republicans who controlled the Congress were neither so blasé nor so forgiving as Lincoln. They knew the war was about slavery, and they meant to conquer the South and abolish it.

They constantly pushed Lincoln in the first two years of the war to abolish slavery by proclamation, and he constantly resisted them until, facing a midterm election in which Democrats who sought an immediate peace might well make inroads into Congress, he realized his position was no longer politically tenable. Only then did Lincoln issue his famous Emancipation Proclamation. Similarly, it was not until he was facing a tough reelection battle himself in 1864 that he could bring himself to proclaim an amnesty for those who would give up fighting on terms much less harsh than the congressional radicals were urging. Despite what the radicals saw as his timidity and the Confederates of course saw as his tyranny, Lincoln did manage to redefine the nature of the American experiment in government with, among other things, his now quite famous Gettysburg Address, with its seminal claim that the

United States was a "government of the people, by the people, for the people."

Reconstruction

Clearly, Lincoln had in mind a milder reconstruction for the rebellious Southern states than the congressional members of his party, but that hardly kept defeated Southerners from hating the man who had led the Union to victory. John Wilkes Booth's assassination of Abraham Lincoln at Ford's Theatre in Washington, D.C., on the night of April 14, 1865, was meant as an act of vengeance on behalf of Booth's humiliated South.

Perhaps it is historically fitting that the first assassination of an American president would be the bitter fruit of so ugly a conflict, but certainly Lincoln's death made matters worse for the country. With Lincoln gone, the Radical Republicans in Congress were certain to take over the process of Reconstruction and push much faster for enfranchisement of the slaves recently freed by the Thirteenth Amendment. Booth's murder deprived the country of a great man, and it condemned the South to a very hard, slow road of postwar recovery in which Southerners continued to resist social change imposed by congressional fiat, and Republicans saw in that resistance only evidence of further sedition.

Andrew Johnson, who became president of the United States upon Lincoln's assassination, also became at the same time a victim of the passions and mistrust that would characterize the postwar period as much as they had characterized the war itself, hardly a surprise given that the Civil War was as destructive an episode as any in American history ever would be. Johnson attempted to carry out the conciliatory program of Reconstruction he believed, based on Lincoln's second inaugural speech, that Lincoln had favored at the time of his death. But Johnson, a cantankerous and prickly individual, was no Abe Lincoln. Radical Republicans were suspicious of the new president (a former governor of Tennessee), eager to avenge Lincoln's death at the hands of "another" Southerner like Johnson, and impatient with foot-dragging on social issues by those but recently in open rebellion. The Radical-controlled Congress rejected Johnson's moderate stance on Reconstruction. Supported by the American public and swayed by social reformers, Congress overrode Johnson's veto of civil rights legislation twice and then proposed the Fourteenth Amendment, which extended full citizenship to blacks and prohibited states from enacting laws abridging that citizenship.

During the 1866 congressional elections, Johnson campaigned against those congressmen who had supported the amendment, but to no avail. The Republicans won large majorities in both houses and quickly passed a series of hard-nosed Reconstruction measures, which Johnson vetoed and which Congress overrode.

As a result, there arose a classic example of the periodic struggles over the separation of powers to which the American republic is prone when ideological conflicts are conducted as moral crusades. Johnson's stubbornness in his dealings with Congress had made him many enemies, and that legislative body was determined to get rid of him—or at least to curb the powers of the presidency, which had been greatly magnified by the Civil War itself. First, Congress passed laws that gave it more authority over the army, over amending the Constitution, and over presidential appointment, including cabinet members.

The Radicals did not stop at these measures. They next passed the Tenure of Office Act of 1867, which required the consent of the Senate before removing a Senate-approved appointee from office. When Johnson, in flagrant violation of the new law, dismissed Secretary of War Edwin M. Stanton in February 1868, the House of Representatives invoked the powers granted it by the Constitution to impeach the president. In 11 articles of impeachment, Congress held that Johnson had violated the law. The articles were upheld by the House of Representatives but fell short of passage in the Senate on May 16, 1868, by a single vote. Johnson was left to serve out his term.

Congress enjoyed and exercised such power immediately after of the Civil War because Americans wanted to believed the four years of carnage had been about something. For the clear majority it was, at least in retrospect, about slavery, and they were consequently impatient with backsliding on black enfranchisement. The Radical Republicans, for all their opportunism and vindictiveness, had put their fingers on the moral pulse of America, which is why they were returned to office again and again in numbers sufficient to control Congress. But even in the name of a good cause, trumped-up impeachment was a bad policy. Had the Radicals been successful, they would have set a disastrous precedent, paving the way for the future settlement of disagreements between the president and the Congress through impeachment. As it was, the bitterness of political struggle between Congress and Johnson mirrored the bitterness of the war between North and South, and that bitterness would continue to mark American policy throughout the Reconstruction years.

In response to the Radical Reconstructionist revolutionary social agenda on race, a "white supremacy" movement developed in the South, at first clandestine and then more and more public, which fostered the disenfranchisement of black voters and the legally enforced segregation of the two races under a series of

"Jim Crow" laws. These white "redeemers" intimidated those blacks who did try to vote or to take advantage of Reconstruction by terrorizing them with nighttime raids and lynchings, they rewrote state constitutions to exclude government action of almost any ilk, and they created the "Solid South" as a block of Southern states that could be relied upon to support the Democratic Party.

The battle between the Redeemer South and the Reconstruction North came to a climax in the close and confusing results of the Hayes-Tilden presidential election of 1876, which—because of the Reconstruction rules governing the electoral votes of former Confederate states—produced no Electoral College majority for either candidate, despite the fact that Samuel Tilden won the popular vote. The election was thrown into the House of Representatives. As months passed with no resolution on who was actually the new president of the United States, the threat of disunion once more raised its head. At length, the Republicans bargained away the remaining political leverage they held over the Democratic Solid South under Reconstruction, agreeing to cease their attempts to create legal equality between the races in exchange for seeing their man, Rutherford B. Hayes, assume the presidency. Quite quickly, black Southerners became politically and economically second-class citizens, exploited frequently more harshly than they had been even under slavery, as once again the nation learned to compromise on the issue of race and equality.

TREATIES

Peace Treaties and Truces

AMERICAN CIVIL WAR TRUCE DOCUMENTS

TREATY AT A GLANCE

Completed
April 7–9, 1865, at Appomattox Court House, Virginia

Signatories
United States and Confederate States of America

Overview
The American Civil War did not end with General Robert E. Lee's celebrated surrender at Appomattox Court House on April 9, 1865 (indeed, the last Confederate units, in the West, surrendered on May 26), but the defeat of Lee's Army of Northern Virginia and the truce that followed have always been regarded as the symbolic end to the conflict.

Historical Background

The seeds of civil war had been sown when the framers of the nation's constitution failed to deal definitively with the issue of slavery. For economic, political, and moral reasons, slavery eroded national unity from the beginning, ineluctably dividing the slaveholding, slave-dependent Southern states from the "free" states of the North. A series of compromises staved off armed conflict through the first half of the 19th century, but on December 20, 1860, South Carolina became the first of the Southern states to secede from the Union. Mississippi, Florida, Alabama, Georgia, Louisiana, and Texas followed early in 1861, and at 4:30 A.M. on April 12, 1861, South Carolinians commenced firing on Fort Sumter. These were the opening shots of a four-year conflict, which would cost at least a half-million battle deaths and would shatter many more lives.

Although the population and industrial might of the North far outweighed the technology and numbers of men the South could muster, the best of the U.S. Army officer corps felt allegiance to their native South, and the Confederate forces were for the most part more skillfully commanded than those of the North. It was not until the Battle of Antietam (Sharpsburg), on September 17, 1862, that the Union military effort achieved, by its victory, sufficient credibility to enable Lincoln to issue, from what he felt was a position of strength, the preliminary EMANCIPATION PROCLAMATION,

the first step toward the liberation of the slaves. By officially bringing the slavery issue to the forefront of the conflict, the Emancipation Proclamation invested the Civil War with an added moral dimension. Not only was it a struggle to save the Union, it was now a crusade to abolish slavery.

If Antietam was the first marginal Union victory, the Battle of Gettysburg (July 1–3, 1863) was the turning point of the war in favor of the Union. Not only was Robert E. Lee's army driven from Northern soil, but the Southern defeat ended Confederate hopes for aid from England and France. The war nevertheless continued through the spring of 1865, with the Southern states suffering economic hardship and their forces and material dwindling. Union general Philip Sheridan defeated Confederate general George F. Pickett at Five Forts on April 1, 1865, and Grant took heavily fortified Petersburg, Virginia, after a campaign that stretched from June 1864 to April 2, 1865. On that day General Grant took Richmond, the Confederate capital through most of the war. A week later at Appomattox Court House, Lee surrendered his Army of Northern Virginia to General Grant.

Terms

Like most of the principal commanders on both sides, Grant and Lee knew and respected one another, having served together during the U.S.–Mexican War of 1846–48. The great armistice began with a note from Grant to Lee:

Headquarters Armies of the United States,
General R. E. Lee, Commanding C.S. Army:
April 7, 1865—5 p.m.
General:

The result of the last week must convince you of the hopelessness of further resistance on the part of the Army of Northern Virginia in this struggle. I feel that it is so, and regard it as my duty to shift from myself the responsibility of any further effusion of blood by asking of you the surrender of that portion of the C. S. Army known as the Army of Northern Virginia.

Very respectfully, your obedient servant,
U. S. GRANT,
Lieutenant-General,
Commanding Armies of the
United States.

Lee replied:

April 7, 1865.
Lieut. Gen. U. S. Grant,
Commanding Armies of the United States:
General:

I have received your note of this date. Though not entertaining the opinion you express of the hopelessness of further resistance on the part of the Army of Northern Virginia, I reciprocate your desire to avoid useless effusion of blood, and therefore, before considering your proposition, ask the terms you will offer on condition of its surrender.

R. E. LEE,
General.

The correspondence continued:

Headquarters Armies of the United States,
General R. E. Lee,
Commanding C.S. Army:
April 9, 1865.
General:

Your note of yesterday is received. As I have no authority to treat on the subject of peace the meeting proposed for 10 a.m. to-day could lead to no good. I will state, however, general, that I am equally anxious for peace with yourself, and the whole North entertain the same feeling. The terms upon which peace can be had are well understood. By the South laying down their arms they will hasten that most desirable event, save thousands of human lives, and hundreds of millions of property not yet destroyed. Sincerely hoping that all our difficulties may be settled without the loss of another life, I subscribe myself,

Very respectfully, your obedient servant,
U. S. GRANT,
Lieutenant-General, U.S. Army.

Lieut. Gen. U. S. Grant,
Commanding U.S. Armies:
April 9, 1865.
General:

I received your note of this morning on the picket-line, whither I had come to meet you and ascertain definitely what terms were embraced in your proposal of yesterday with reference to the surrender of this army. I now request an interview in accordance with the offer contained in your letter of yesterday for that purpose.

Very respectfully, your obedient servant,
R. E. LEE, *General.*

Lieut. Gen. U.S. Grant,
Commanding U.S. Armies:
April 9, 1865.
General:

I ask a suspension of hostilities pending terms of the surrender of this army, in the my former communication to-day.

Very respectfully,
R. E. LEE, *General.*

Headquarters Army of Northern Virginia,
Lieut. Gen. U. S. Grant,
Commanding U.S. Armies:
April 9, 1865.
General:

I sent a communication to you to-day from the picket-line, whither I had gone in hopes of meeting you in pursuance of the request contained in my letter of yesterday. [Union] Major-General [George] Meade informs me that it would probably expedite matters to send a duplicate through some other part of your lines. I therefore request an interview, at such time and place as you may designate, to discuss the terms of the surrender of this army in accordance with your offer to have such an interview, contained in your letter of yesterday.

Very respectfully, your obedient servant,
R. E. LEE, *General.*

Headquarters Armies of the United States,
April 9, 1865.
General R. E. Lee,
Commanding C.S. Army:

Your note of this date is but this moment (11.50 a. m.) received. In consequence of my having passed from the Richmond and Lynchburg road to the Farmville and Lynchburg road I am at this writing about four miles west of Walker's Church, and will push forward to the front for the purpose of meeting you. Notice sent to me on this road where you wish the interview to take place will meet me.

Very respectfully, your obedient servant,
U. S. GRANT,
Lieutenant-General.

Headquarters Armies of the United States,
Appomattox Court-House, Va., April 9, 1865.
General R. E. Lee,
Commanding C.S. Army:
General:

In accordance with the substance of my letter to you of the 8th instant, I propose to receive the surrender of the Army of Northern Virginia on the following terms, to wit: Rolls of all the officers and men to be made in duplicate—one copy to be given to an officer to be designated by me, the other to be retained by such officer or officers as you may designate; the officers to give their individual paroles not to take up arms against the Government of the United States until properly exchanged, and each company or regimental commander sign a like parole for the men of their commands. The arms, artillery, and public property to be parked and stacked, and turned over to the officers appointed by me to receive them. This will not embrace the side-arms of the officers, nor their private horses or baggage. This done, each officer and man will be allowed to return to their homes, not to be disturbed by United States authority so long as they observe their paroles and the laws in force where they may reside.

Very respectfully,
U. S. GRANT,
Lieutenant-General.

Headquarters Army of Northern Virginia,
Lieut. Gen. U. S. Grant,
Commanding Armies of the United States:
April 9, 1865.
General:

I have received your letter of this date containing the terms of surrender of the Army of Northern Virginia as proposed by you. As they are substantially the same as those expressed in your letter of the 8th instant, they are accepted. I will proceed to designate the proper officers to carry the stipulations into effect.

Very respectfully, your obedient servant,
R. E. LEE, *General.*

Consequences

The two men met at the nearby home of Wilmer McLean (whose former house at Manassas had been hit by a Yankee shell during the war's first major battle, Bull Run) to sign the peace. The formal ceremony of surrender three days later was conducted with suitable dignity. When Stonewall Jackson's old brigade stepped forward to stack arms and surrender flags, the Union bugler blew a call to shift from order arms to carry arms. Thus the Union troops gave their Southern brethren the U.S. Army's salute of honor.

Diplomatic Treaties

TREATY OF WASHINGTON

TREATY AT A GLANCE

Completed
May 8, 1871, at Washington, D.C.

Signatories
United States and Great Britain

Overview
The Treaty of Washington settled the so-called Alabama Claims, compensating damages suffered by American merchant shipping during the Civil War as a result of attack by Confederate cruisers (notably the *Alabama*), which had been constructed in British shipyards contrary to the nation's declared neutrality.

Historical Background

British government sympathies during the American Civil War were largely with the Confederacy, especially since the Southern states supplied much of the cotton that kept British cloth mills humming. However, the Confederacy's commitment to slavery was anathema to British policy and conscience, so the nation declared itself officially neutral in the conflict, and arms and munitions suppliers as well as shipbuilders were prohibited by act of Parliament from supplying either the Union or the Confederacy.

In practice, the British neutrality laws were often honored more in the breach than in the observance, and the Confederacy purchased a fortune in arms and vessels from British suppliers. Following the conclusion of the Civil War, a period of bitter dispute ensued between the United States and Great Britain over the latter's responsibility for damages incurred by U.S. shipping at the hands of Confederate naval personnel and raiders sailing in British-built vessels. The most infamous of the British-built Confederate warships was the C.S.S. *Alabama*, which slipped out of Liverpool in the summer of 1862. Under the command of Raphael Semmes, it captured almost seventy U.S. merchant ships. Postwar U.S. claims against Great Britain were collectively called the Alabama Claims.

The treaty was negotiated by U.S. president Ulysses S. Grant's secretary of state, Hamilton Fish, the only official member of that administration Grant did not fire for corruption or incompetence in office. Able, honest, and dignified, Fish sought to put an end to the nettlesome and strident demands of American chauvinists who were talking of acquiring Canada as compensation for the damage done by the *Alabama* and other commerce-raiders built in Britain.

Terms

The 1871 Treaty of Washington did not settle the Alabama Claims, but instead embodied an agreement between the two nations to submit the issue of claims to international arbitration:

ARTICLE I

Whereas differences have arisen between the Government of the United States and the Government of Her Britannic Majesty, and still exist, growing out of the acts committed by the several vessels which have given rise to the claims generically known as the "Alabama Claims": And whereas Her Britannic Majesty has authorized her High Commissioners and Plenipotentiaries to express, in a friendly spirit, the regret felt by Her Majesty's Government for the escape, under whatever circumstances, of the Alabama and other vessels from British ports, and for the depredations committed by those vessels:

Now, in order to remove and adjust all complaints and claims on the part of the United States, and to provide for the speedy settlement of such claims which are not admitted by Her Britannic Majesty's

Government, the high contracting parties agree that all the said claims, growing out of acts committed by the aforesaid vessels, and generically known as the "Alabama Claims," shall be referred to a tribunal of arbitration to be composed of five Arbitrators, to be appointed in the following manner, that is to say: One shall be named by the President of the United States; one shall be named by Her Britannic Majesty; His Majesty the King of Italy shall be requested to name one; the President of the Swiss Confederation shall be requested to name one; and His Majesty the Emperor of Brazil shall be requested to name one.

In case of the death, absence, or incapacity to serve of any or either of the said Arbitrators, or, in the event of either of the said Arbitrators omitting or declining or ceasing to act as such, the President of the United States, or Her Britannic Majesty, or His Majesty the King of Italy, or the President of the Swiss Confederation, or His Majesty the Emperor of Brazil, as the case may be, may forthwith name another person to act as Arbitrator in the place and stead of the Arbitrator originally named by such head of a State.

And in the event of the refusal or omission for two months after receipt of the request from either of the high contracting parties of His Majesty the King of Italy, or the President of the Swiss Confederation, or His Majesty the Emperor of Brazil, to name an Arbitrator either to fill the original appointment or in the place of one who may have died, be absent, or incapacitated, or who may omit, decline, or from any cause cease to act as such Arbitrator, His Majesty the King of Sweden and Norway shall be requested to name one or more persons, as the case may be, to act as such Arbitrator or Arbitrators.

The treaty thus established the principle of international arbitration to resolve peacefully disputes between nations. And the treaty outlined the principles that should govern neutral nations in time of war:

ARTICLE VI

In deciding the matters submitted to the Arbitrators, they shall be governed by the following three rules, which are agreed upon by the high contracting parties as rules to be taken as applicable to the case, and by such principles of international law not inconsistent therewith as the Arbitrators shall determine to have been applicable to the case.

Rules

A neutral Government is bound—

First, to use due diligence to prevent the fitting out, arming, or equipping, within its jurisdiction, of any vessel which it has reasonable ground to believe is intended to cruise or to carry on war against a Power with which it is at peace; and also to use like diligence to prevent the departure from its jurisdiction of any vessel intended to cruise or carry on war as above, such vessel having been specially adapted, in whole or in part, within such jurisdiction, to warlike use.

Secondly, not to permit or suffer either belligerent to make use of its ports or waters as the base of naval operations against the other, or for the purpose of the renewal or augmentation of military supplies or arms, or the recruitment of men.

Thirdly, to exercise due diligence in its own ports and waters, and, as to all persons within its jurisdiction, to prevent any violation of the foregoing obligations and duties.

Her Britannic Majesty has commanded her High Commissioners and Plenipotentiaries to declare that Her Majesty's Government cannot assent to the foregoing rules as a statement of principles of international law which were in force at the time when the claim mentioned in Article I arose, but that Her Majesty's Government, in order to evince its desire of strengthening the friendly relations between the two countries and of making satisfactory provision for the future, agrees that in deciding the questions between the two countries arising out of those claims, the Arbitrators should assume that Her Majesty's Government had undertaken to act upon the principles set forth in these rules.

And the high contracting parties agree to observe these rules as between themselves in future, and to bring them to the knowledge of other maritime Powers, and to invite them to accede to them.

Acting in accordance with these principles, a panel of American, British, Brazilian, Swiss, and Italian arbitrators met in 1872 in Geneva. The panel awarded the United States the sum of $15.5 million.

The Geneva Award under Articles I to XI of the Convention of 1871 Made by the Tribunal of Arbitration Constituted by Virtue of the First Article of the Treaty Concluded at Washington the 8th of May 1871, between the United States and Great Britain

The United States of America and Her Britannic Majesty having agreed by Article I. of the treaty concluded and signed at Washington the 8th of May 1871, to refer all the claims "generically know as the Alabama claims" to a tribunal of arbitration to be compose of five arbitrators named:

One by the President of the United States,

One by Her Britannic Majesty,

One by His Majesty the King of Italy,

One by the President of the Swiss Confederation,

One by his Majesty the Emperor of Brazil;

And the President of the United States, Her Britannic Majesty His Majesty the King of Italy, the President of the Swiss Confederation, and His Majesty the Emperor of Brazil having respectively named their arbitrators, to wit:

The President of the United States, Charles Francis Adams, esquire;

Her Britannic Majesty, Sir Alexander James Edmund Cockburn, baronet a member of Her Majesty's privy council, lord chief justice of England;

His Majesty the King of Italy, His Excellency Count Frederick Sclopis of Salerno, a knight of the order of the Annunciata, minister of state, senator of the Kingdom of Italy;

The President of the Swiss Confederation, M. James Stampfli;

His Majesty the Emperor of Brazil, His Excellency Marcos Antonio d' Araujo, Viscount d' Itajuba, a grandee of the Empire of Brazil, member of the council of H. M. the Emperor of Brazil, and his envoy extraordinary and minister plenipotentiary in France.

And the five arbitrators above named having assembled at Geneva (In Switzerland) in one of the chambers of the Hotel de Ville on the 15th of December, 1871, in conformity with the terms of the second article of the treaty of Washington of the 8th of May of that year, and having proceeded to the inspection and verification of their respective powers, which were found duly authenticated, the tribunal of arbitration was declared duly organized.

The agents named by each of the high contracting parties, by virtue of the same article II, to wit:

For the United States of America, John C. Bancroft Davis, esquire;

And for Her Britannic Majesty, Charles Stuart Aubrey, Lord Tenterden, a peer of the United Kingdom, companion of the Most Honorable Order of the Bath, assistant under secretary of state for foreign affairs;

Whose powers were found likewise duly authenticated, then delivered to each of the arbitrators the printed case prepared by each of the two parties, accompanied by the documents, the official correspondence, and other evidence on which each relied, in conformity with the terms of the third article of the said treaty.

In virtue of the decision made by the tribunal at its first session, the counter case and additional documents, correspondence, and evidence referred to in article four of the said treaty were delivered by the respective agents of the two parties to the secretary of the tribunal on the 15th of April, 1872, at the chamber of conference at the Hotel de Ville of Geneva.

The tribunal, in accordance with the vote of adjournment passed at their second session, held on the 16th of December, 1871, reassembled at Geneva on the 15th of June 1872; and the agent of each of the parties duly delivered to each of the arbitrators, and to the agent of the other party, the printed argument referred to in article V of the said treaty.

The tribunal having since fully taken into their consideration the treaty, and also the cases, counter cases, documents, evidence, and arguments, and likewise all other communications made to them by the two parties during the progress of their sittings and having impartially and carefully examined the same,

Has arrived at the decision embodied in the present award:

Whereas, having regard to the VIth and VIIth articles of the said treaty, the arbitrators are bound under the terms of the said VIth article, "in deciding the matters submitted to them, to be governed by the three rules therein specified and by such principles of international law, not inconsistent therewith, as the arbitrators shall determine to have been applicable to the case;"

And whereas the "due diligence" referred to in the first and third of the said rules ought to be exercised by neutral Governments in fact proportion to the risks to which either of the belligerents may be exposed, from a failure to fulfill the obligations of neutrality on their part;

And whereas the circumstances out of which the facts constituting the subject matter of the present controversy arose were of a nature to call for the exercise on the part of Her Britannic Majesty's Government of all possible solicitude for the observance of the rights and the duties involved in the proclamation of neutrality issued by her Majesty on the 13th day of May 1861;

And whereas the effects of a violation of neutrality committed by means of the construction, equipment and armament of a vessel are not done away with by any commission which the Government of the belligerent power, benefitted by the violation of neutrality, may afterwards have granted to that vessel; and the ultimate step, by which the offense is completed cannot be admissible as a ground for the absolution of the offender, nor can the consummation of his fraud become the means of establishing his innocence;

And whereas the privilege of extraterritoriality accorded to vessels of war has been admitted into the law of Nations, not as an absolute right, but solely as a proceeding founded on the principle of courtesy and mutual deference between different nations, and therefore can never be appealed to for the protection of acts done in violation of neutrality;

And whereas the absence of a previous notice cannot be regarded as a failure in any consideration required by the law of nations in those cases in which a vessel carries with it its own condemnation;

And whereas in order to impart to any supplies of coal a character inconsistent with the second rule prohibiting the use of neutral ports or waters as a base of naval operations for a belligerent it is necessary that the said supplies should be connected with special circumstances of time, of persons, or of place, which may combine to give them such character;

And whereas with respect to the vessel called the Alabama, it clearly results from all the facts relative to the construction of the ship at first designated by the number "290" in the port of Liverpool and its equipments and armament in the vicinity of Terceira through the agency of the vessels called the "Agrippina" and the "Bahama," dispatched from Great Britain to that end, that the British Government failed to use due diligence in the performance of its neutral obligations; and especially that it omitted, notwithstanding the warnings and official representations made by the diplomatic agents of the United States during the construction of the said number "290," to take in due time any effective measures of prevention, and that those orders which it did give at last, for the detention of the vessel, were issued so late that their execution was not practicable;

And whereas after the escape of that vessel, the measures taken for its pursuit and its arrest were so imperfect as to lead to no result, and therefore cannot be considered sufficient to release Great Britain from the responsibility already incurred;

And whereas, in spite of the violations of the neutrality of Great Britain committed by the "290," this same vessel, later known as the confederate cruiser Alabama, was on several occasions freely admitted into the ports of colonies of Great Britain, instead of being proceeded against as it ought to have been in any and every port within British jurisdiction in which it might have been found;

And whereas the Government of Her Britannic Majesty cannot justify itself for a failure in due diligence on the plea of insufficiency of the legal means of action which it possessed:

For the arbitrators for the reasons above assigned and the fifth for the reasons separately signed by him,

Are of opinion—

That Great Britain has in this case failed by omission, to fulfil the duties prescribed in the first and the third of the rules, established by the VIth article of the treaty of Washington.

And whereas, with respect to the vessel called the "Florida" it results from all the facts relative to the construction of the "Oreto" in the port of Liverpool, and to its issue therefrom, which facts failed to induce the authorities in Great Britain to resort to measures adequate to prevent the violation of the neutrality of that nation, notwithstanding the warnings and repeated representations of the agents of the United States, that Her Majesty's Government has failed to use due diligence to fulfill the duties of neutrality;

And whereas it likewise results from all the facts relative to the stay of the "Oreto" at Nassau, to her issue from that port, to her enlistment of men, to her supplies, and to her armament, with the cooperation of the British vessel "Prince Alfred" at Green Cay, that there was negligence on the part of the British colonial authorities;

And whereas, notwithstanding the violation with Great Britain committed by the Oreto, this same vessel later known as the confederate cruiser Florida, was nevertheless on several occasions freely admitted into the ports of British colonies;

And whereas the judicial acquittal of the "Oreto" at Nassau cannot relieve Great Britain from the responsibility incurred by her under the principles of international law; nor can the fact of the entry of the Florida into the confederate port of Mobile, and of its stay there during four months extinguish the responsibility previously to that time incurred by Great Britain;

For these reasons,

The tribunal by a majority of four voices to one is of opinion—

That Great Britain has in this case failed by omission to fulfil the duties prescribed in the first, in the second, and in the third of the rules established by article VI. of the treaty of Washington.

And whereas, with respect to the vessel called the "Shenandoah," it results from all the facts relative to the departure from London of the merchant vessel "The Sea King" and to the transformation of that ship into a confederate cruiser under the name of the Shenandoah near the Island of Madeira, that the Government of Her Britannic Majesty is not chargeable with any failure, down to that date, in the use of all diligence to fulfill the duties of neutrality;

But whereas its results from all the facts connected with the stay of the Shenandoah at Melbourne, and especially with the augmentation which the British Government itself admits to have been clandestinely effected of her force, by the enlistment of men within that port, that there was negligence on the part of the authorities of that place:

For these reasons,

The tribunal is unanimously of opinion—

That Great Britain has not failed by any act or omission, "to fulfil any of the duties prescribed by the three rules of article VI in the treaty of Washington or by the principles of law not inconsistent therewith," in respect to the vessel called the Shenandoah, during the period of time anterior to her entry into the port of Melbourne;

And by a majority of three to two voices, the tribunal decided that Great Britain has failed, by omission to fulfil the duties prescribed by the second and third of rules aforesaid, in the case of this same vessel, from and after her entry into Hobson's Bay, and is therefore responsible for all acts committed by that vessel after her departure from Melbourne on the 18 day of February 1865.

And so far as relates to the vessels called—The Tuscaloosa, (tender to the Alabama), The Clarence, The Tacony and The Archer, (tenders to the Florida),

The tribunal is unanimously of opinion—

That such tenders or auxiliary vessels, being properly regarded as accessories, must necessarily follow the lot of their principals, and be submitted to the same decision which applies to them respectively.

And so far as relates to the vessel called "Retribution,"

The tribunal by a majority of three to two voices is of opinion—

That Great Britain has not failed by any act or omission to fulfill any of the duties prescribed by the three rules of article VI in the treaty of Washington, or by the principles of international law not inconsistent therewith.

And so far as relates to the vessels called—The Georgia, The Sumter, The Nashville, The Tallahassee, and The Chickamauga, respectively.

The tribunal is unanimously of opinion—

That Great Britain has not failed, by any act or omission to fulfill any of the duties prescribed by the three rules of article VI. in the treaty of Washington or by the principles of international law not inconsistent therewith.

And so far as relates to the vessels called—The Sallie, The Jefferson Davis, The Music, The Boston and the V. H. Joy, respectively,

The tribunal is unanimously of opinion—

That they ought to be excluded from consideration for want of evidence.

And whereas, so far as relates to the particulars of the indemnity claimed by the United States, the cost of pursuit of the confederate cruisers, are not, in the judgment of the tribunal, properly distinguishable from the general expenses of the war carried on by the United States.

The tribunal is therefore of opinion, by a majority of three to two voices—

That there is no ground for awarding to the United States any sum by way of indemnity under this head.

And whereas prospective earnings cannot properly be made the subject of compensation, inasmuch as they depend in their nature upon future and uncertain contingencies:

The tribunal is unanimously of opinion—

That there is no good ground for awarding to the United States any sum by way of indemnity under this head.

And whereas in order to arrive at an equitable compensation for the damages which have been sustained, it is necessary to set aside all double claims for the same losses, and all claims for "gross freights" so far as they exceed "net freights";

And whereas it is just and reasonable to allow interest at a reasonable rate;

And whereas, in accordance with the spirit and letter of the treaty of Washington, it is preferable to adopt the form of adjudication of a sum in gross, rather than refer the subject of compensation for a further discussion and deliberation to a board of assessors, as provided by article X of the said treaty;

The tribunal, making use of the authority conferred upon it by article VII of the said/treaty, by a majority of four voices to one awards to the United States a sum of $15,500,000 in gold as the indemnity to be paid by Great Britain to the United States, for the Satisfaction of all the claims referred to the consideration of the tribunal, conformably to the provisions contained in article VII of the aforesaid treaty.

And, in accordance with the terms of article XI of the said treaty the tribunal declares that "all the claims referred to in the treaty as submitted to the tribunal are hereby fully, perfectly, and finally settled."

Further it declares, that "each and every one of the said claims whether the same may or may not have been presented to the notice of, or made, preferred, or laid before the tribunal, shall henceforth be considered and treated as finally settled, barred, and inadmissible."

In testimony whereof this present decision an award has been made in duplicate and signed by the arbitrators who have given their assent thereto, the whole being in exact conformity with the provisions of article VII of the said treaty of Washington.

Made and concluded at the Hotel de Ville of Geneva, in Switzerland, the 14th day of the month of September, in the year of our Lord, One thousand eight hundred and seventy-two.

CHAS. FRANCIS ADAMS.
FREDERICK SCLOPIS.
STAMPELI.
VICOMTE D'ITAJUBA.

The treaty also included less important articles governing U.S. fishing rights in Canadian waters and navigation of the St. Lawrence River.

Consequences

The principal significance of the Treaty of Washington was that it laid the foundation for international law governing disputes between nations. In addition to the $15.5 million awarded to the Americans by the special Geneva tribunal, $2 million went to British subjects for damages suffered during the war. One dispute, over the channel between Vancouver Island and the state of Washington, was judged by the German emperor, and in a declaration issued May 8, 1871, Kaiser Wilhelm I judged in favor of the United States. By expressing "regret" in the treaty itself about the *Alabama* and submitting to arbitration, the British stilled agitation in the United States for more draconian measures and thus fed a growing Anglo-American rapport, but by accepting the results of the arbitration gracefully, both parties lent credence to the treaty and its techniques, thus furthering the possibilities for international peace.

Proclamations and Declarations

EMANCIPATION PROCLAMATION

> **TREATY AT A GLANCE**
>
> *Completed (Ratified)*
> January 1, 1863, at Washington, D.C.
>
> *Signatory*
> Unilateral declaration by the president of the United States
>
> *Overview*
> On September 23, 1862, President Abraham Lincoln issued the Emancipation Proclamation, which was to take effect officially on January 1, 1863. However radical it appeared at the time, the proclamation in retrospect appears to be something of a dry, legalistic, perhaps even timid, little document. It nevertheless changed the course of the Civil War and of American history.

Historical Background

Slavery is such a manifest evil that today some find it difficult to sympathize with Abraham Lincoln's caution and delay in issuing the Emancipation Proclamation during the American Civil War. Lincoln's letter to *New York Tribune* editor Horace Greeley, written on August 22, 1862, just before the president was ready to announce the proclamation, still sometimes troubles his admirers: "If I could save the Union," Lincoln wrote in part, "without freeing any slave, I would do it; and if I could save it by freeing all the slaves, I would do it; and if I could save it by freeing some and leaving others alone, I would also do that."

That Lincoln personally hated slavery is beyond doubt, but as president he was bound to abide by the Constitution, which protected slavery in slave states. He was also fearful that emancipation would alienate Northern Democrats and send the four slaveholding border states into the embrace of the Confederacy. Lincoln therefore began cautiously. If he dared not simply free the slaves, he could seize them as enemy property—as contraband of war—and refuse to return them to their owners. In August 1861 Congress made the contraband policy official, passing an act that conferred contraband status on all slaves who had been used in support of the Confederate war effort. In March of the next year, Congress passed legislation forbidding army officers from returning any fugitive slaves. With these two acts, the Union moved closer to emancipation.

It was a series of Union defeats during the first half of 1862 that at last moved Lincoln's hand. Emancipation, which many Northerners had come to see as a moral imperative, now appeared to be a military necessity, as well. The South had to be deprived of as much of its labor force as possible. In July 1862 Congress passed a new and stronger confiscation act, which freed slaves who had belonged to owners engaged in rebellion, and a militia act, authorizing the president to use freed slaves in the army as laborers or even soldiers.

Lincoln was now on the verge of declaring emancipation outright and was held back only by Secretary of State William H. Seward, who convinced the president that the Emancipation Proclamation would ring hollow in the absence of a Union military victory. When the Union declared victory in the bloody and inconclusive Battle of Antietam, fought on September 17, 1862, Lincoln felt free to move ahead.

Terms

Immediately, Lincoln issued his "preliminary" proclamation, warning that the slaves living in states still in rebellion on January 1, 1863, would be declared "forever free." When the deadline passed, Lincoln issued the "final" proclamation, which explicitly committed the armed forces of the United States to liberate the slaves.

The Emancipation Proclamation

WHEREAS, on the twenty-second day of September in the year of our Lord one thousand eight hundred and sixty-two, a proclamation was issued by the President of the United States, containing, among other things, the following, to wit:

That on the first day of January, in the year of our Lord one thousand eight hundred and sixty-three, all persons held as slaves within any State, or designated part of a State, the people whereof shall then be in rebellion against the United States, shall be then, thenceforward, and forever free: and the Executive Government of the United States, including the military and naval authority thereof, will recognize and maintain the freedom of such persons, and will do no act or acts to repress such persons, or any of them, in any efforts they may make for their actual freedom.

That the Executive will, on the first day of January aforesaid, by proclamation, designate the States and parts of States, if any, in which the people thereof respectively shall then be in rebellion against the United States; and the fact that any State, or the people thereof, shall on that day be in good faith represented in the Congress of the United States by members chosen thereto at elections wherein a majority of the qualified voters of such State shall have participated, shall in the absence of strong countervailing testimony be deemed conclusive evidence that such State and the people thereof are not then on rebellion against the United States.

Now, therefore, I, Abraham Lincoln, President of the United States, by virtue of the power in me vested as Commander-in-Chief of the Army and Navy of the United States, in time of actual armed rebellion against the authority and government of the United States, and as a fit and necessary war measure for suppressing said rebellion, do, on this the first day of January, in the year of our Lord one thousand eight hundred and sixty-three, and in accordance with my purpose so to do, publicly proclaimed for the full period of 100 days from the first day mentioned above, order and designate as the States and parts of States wherein the people thereof, respectively, are this day in rebellion against the United States, the following, to wit:

Arkansas, Texas, Louisiana (except the parishes of St. Bernard, Plaquemines, Jefferson, St. John, St. Charles, St. James, Ascension, Assumption, Terre Bonne, Lafourche, St. Mary, St. Martin, and Orleans, including the city of New Orleans), Mississippi, Alabama, Florida, Georgia, South Carolina, North Carolina, and Virginia (except the forty-eight counties designated as West Virginia, and also the counties of Berkeley, Accomac, Northampton, Elizabeth City, York, Princess Anne, and Norfolk, including the cities of Norfolk and Portsmouth), and which excepted parts are for the present left precisely as if this proclamation were not issued.

And by virtue of the power and for the purpose aforesaid, I do order and declare that all persons held as slaves within said designated States and parts of States are, and henceforth shall be, free; and that the Executive Government of the United States, including the military and naval authorities thereof, shall recognize and maintain the freedom of said persons.

And I hereby enjoin upon the people so declared to be free to abstain from all violence, unless in necessary self-defense; and I recommend to them that, in all cases where allowed, they labor faithfully for reasonable wages.

And I further declare and make known that such persons of suitable condition will be received into the armed service of the United States to garrison forts, positions, stations, and other places, and to man vessels of all sorts in said service.

And upon this act, sincerely believed to be an act of justice, warranted by the Constitution upon military necessity, I invoke the considerate judgment of mankind and the gracious favor of Almighty God.

In witness whereof, I have hereunto set my hand and caused the seal of the United States to be affixed.

[SEAL.]

Done at the city of Washington, the first day of January, in the year of our Lord one thousand eight hundred and sixty-three, and of the independence of the United States the eighty-seventh.

By the President:

ABRAHAM LINCOLN
WILLIAM H. SEWARD, Secretary of State

Consequences

Sweeping as the Emancipation Proclamation was in the context of the times, it nevertheless did not apply to slaves in the border states or to those in areas of the Confederacy presently under the control of the Union army, for these areas were not "in rebellion" against the United States.

When the war was over, all the carnage needed to be "about" something, and the proclamation ensured that for most people it would be about slavery. And because the war was officially about slavery, the limitations of the Emancipation Proclamation itself would be overcome by the Thirteenth Amendment (see CIVIL WAR AND RECONSTRUCTION AMENDMENTS TO THE CONSTITUTION OF THE UNITED STATES), which was passed by the Senate on April 8, 1864, and (after a struggle) by the House on January 31, 1865. By December 18, 1865, three-quarters of the states reunified by war's end ratified the measure, which outlawed slavery throughout the nation forever.

PROCLAMATION OF AMNESTY AND PARDON FOR THE CONFEDERATE STATES

```
┌─────────────────────────────────────────────┐
│              TREATY AT A GLANCE               │
│                                               │
│                  Proclaimed                   │
│         May 29, 1865, at Washington, D.C.     │
│                                               │
│                                               │
│                  Signatory                    │
│   Unilateral declaration by the president of  │
│              the United States                │
│                                               │
│                                               │
│                   Overview                    │
│   After the end of the Civil War, President   │
│   Andrew Johnson issued a broad amnesty and   │
│   pardon for citizens of the former           │
│   Confederacy.                                │
└─────────────────────────────────────────────┘
```

Historical Background

During the Civil War, on December 8, 1863, President Abraham Lincoln issued an amnesty proclamation in an effort to set up loyal governments in Southern states that were then under Union control, which included Louisiana, Tennessee, and Arkansas. Lincoln appointed provisional governors and authorized each of them to call a convention to create a new state government as soon as 10 percent of the voters in the 1860 presidential election had signed oaths of loyalty to the Union. Although governments were duly formed, Congress refused to recognize them. Instead, in 1864 Congress passed the Wade-Davis Reconstruction Bill, which would have delayed readmission of the Southern states until 50 percent of a state's 1860 voters had signed loyalty oaths. Lincoln responded with a pocket veto.

President Lincoln fell to the bullet of John Wilkes Booth before the matter was resolved, and his vice president, Andrew Johnson, adopted a modified form of the Wade-Davis plan.

Terms

With a few exceptions enumerated in his proclamation of May 29, 1865, Johnson issued an amnesty to anyone who would take an oath to be loyal to the Union in the future. Enough ex-Confederates signed the loyalty oath to permit the rapid creation of new state governments, and Johnson's amnesty required only that the new states ratify the Thirteenth Amendment, freeing the slaves (see CIVIL WAR AND RECONSTRUCTION AMENDMENTS TO THE CONSTITUTION OF THE UNITED STATES), abolish slavery in their own constitutions, repudiate debts

incurred while in rebellion, and declare secession null and void. By the end of 1865, all of the secessionist states but Texas had completely complied.

Johnson's proclamation follows. Of particular interest is the 13th exception to those covered by the amnesty: the wealthy.

Whereas, the President of the United States, on the 8th day of December, A.D. 1863, and on the 26th day of March, A.D. 1864, did, with the object to suppress the existing rebellion, to induce all persons to return to their loyalty, and to restore the authority of the United States, issue proclamations offering amnesty and pardon to certain persons who had, directly or by implication, participated in the said rebellion; and

Whereas, many persons who had so engaged in said rebellion have, since the issuance of said proclamations, failed or neglected to take the benefits offered thereby; and

Whereas, many persons who have been justly deprived of all claim to amnesty and pardon thereunder by reason of their participation, directly or by implication, in said rebellion and continued hostility to the government of the United States since the date of said proclamations, now desire to apply for and obtain amnesty and pardon.

To the end, therefore, that the authority of the government of the United States may be restored and that peace, order, and freedom may be established, I, Andrew Johnson, President of the United States, do proclaim and declare that I hereby grant to all persons who have, directly or indirectly, participated in the existing rebellion, except as hereinafter excepted, amnesty and pardon, with restoration of all rights of property, except as to slaves and except in cases where legal proceedings under the laws of the United States providing for the confiscation of property of persons engaged in rebellion have been instituted; but upon the condition, nevertheless, that every such person shall take and subscribe the following oath (or affirmation) and thenceforward keep, and maintain said oath inviolate, and which oath shall be registered for permanent preservation and shall be of the tenor and effect following, to wit:

I,   , do solemnly swear (or affirm), in presence of Almighty God, that I will henceforth faithfully support, protect, and defend the Constitution of the United States and the Union of the States thereunder, and that I will in like manner abide by and faithfully support all laws and proclamations which have been made during the existing rebellion with reference to the emancipation of slaves. So help me God.

The following classes of persons are excepted from the benefits of this proclamation:

First, all who are or shall have been pretended civil or diplomatic officers or otherwise domestic or foreign agents of the pretended Confederate government.

Second, all who left judicial stations under the United States to aid the rebellion.

Third, all who shall have been military or naval officers of said pretended Confederate government above the rank of colonel in the army or lieutenant in the navy.

Fourth, all who left seats in the Congress of the United States to aid the rebellion.

Fifth, all who resigned or tendered resignations of their commissions in the Army or Navy of the United States to evade duty in resisting the rebellion.

Sixth, all who have engaged in any way in treating otherwise than lawfully as prisoners of war persons found in the United States service as officers, soldiers, seamen, or in other capacities.

Seventh, all persons who have been or are absentees from the United States for the purpose of aiding the rebellion.

Eighth, all military and naval officers in the Rebel service who were educated by the government in the Military Academy at West Point or the United States Naval Academy.

Ninth, all persons who held the pretended offices of governors of states in insurrection against the United States.

Tenth, all persons who left their homes within the jurisdiction and protection of the United States and passed beyond the Federal military lines into the pretended Confederate States for the purpose of aiding the rebellion.

Eleventh, all persons who have been engaged in the destruction of the commerce of the United States upon the high seas and all persons who have made raids into the United States from Canada or been engaged in destroying the commerce of the United States upon the lakes and rivers that separate the British Provinces from the United States.

Twelfth, all persons who, at the time when they seek to obtain the benefits hereof by taking the oath herein prescribed, are in military, naval, or civil confinement or custody, or under bonds of the civil, military, or naval authorities, or agents of the United States as prisoners of war, or persons detained for offenses of any kind, either before or after conviction.

Thirteenth, all persons who have voluntarily participated in said rebellion and the estimated value of whose taxable property is over $20,000.

Fourteenth, all persons who have taken the oath of amnesty as prescribed in the President's proclamation of December 8, A.D. 1863, or an oath of allegiance to the government of the United States since the date of said proclamation and who have not thenceforward kept and maintained the same inviolate.

Provided, that special application may be made to the President for pardon by any person belonging to the excepted classes, and such clemency will be liberally extended as may be consistent with the facts of the case and the peace and dignity of the United States.

The secretary of state will establish rules and regulations for administering and recording the said amnesty oath, so as to insure its benefit to the people and guard the government against fraud.

Consequences

Johnson's amnesty was hardly an end to the problems of Reconstruction. Congress, protesting that the conditions of presidential Reconstruction returned power to the same people who had tried so bloodily to destroy the Union and noting, too, that Johnson's program failed to protect the rights of freedmen (emancipated slaves), passed the Freedmen's Bureau Act and the Civil Rights Act in 1866. Johnson vetoed these acts, insisting that the Southern states were immediately entitled to representation in Congress. Congress refused to recognize the legitimacy of the new governments of the Southern states and overrode Johnson's vetoes.

Additionally, Congress introduced the Fourteenth Amendment to the Constitution, which declared blacks to be citizens, prohibited states from discriminating against any class of citizens, and barred former Confederate leaders from federal or state office until such time as Congress removed the disqualification. When the new Southern state governments refused to ratify this amendment, Congress passed a series of Reconstruction Acts in 1867 that effectively put the South under military occupation. The new regime was called Radical Reconstruction and made the federal government responsible for the protection of the ex-slaves.

Congress agreed to recognize new state governments only after they had guaranteed equal civil and political rights regardless of race and had ratified the Fourteenth Amendment. Confederate leaders were barred from voting in the process that created the new state governments. President Johnson attempted to foil Congress by declining to enforce the laws, thereby bringing about a situation that ultimately resulted in his impeachment. He narrowly escaped removal from office. As to the nation, it suffered through two decades of punitive Reconstruction, which resulted in more, rather than less, racial bitterness and repression.

PROCLAMATION OF PROVISIONAL GOVERNMENT FOR NORTH CAROLINA

TREATY AT A GLANCE

Proclaimed
May 29, 1865, at Washington, D.C.

Signatory
Unilaterally declared by the president of the United States

Overview
This proclamation is one of the documents that concluded the Civil War. It is typical of the documents creating provisional governments for the states of the former Confederacy during Reconstruction.

Historical Background

The assassination of President Abraham Lincoln on the eve of the war's end threw Radical Republicans into a storm of doubt. They feared that Vice President Andrew Johnson—now president—would accede to Democratic demands for a liberal, essentially status quo Reconstruction policy. In this context of mutual suspicion, Johnson began proclaiming provisional governments in defeated Southern states to reestablish public order, meet the peace terms so far imposed by the United States (ratifying the Thirteenth Amendment to the Constitution, which freed the slaves, abolishing slavery in their state constitutions, repudiating debts incurred during the rebellion, and declaring their secession null and void), and bring their states back into the Union as soon as practicable. The proclamation for North Carolina was first and typical.

Terms

Johnson's and the Radical Congress's views notwithstanding, the provisional state governments Johnson proclaimed were fashioned in accordance with Lincoln's moderate Reconstruction policies.

Whereas, the 4th Section of the 4th Article of the Constitution of the United States declares that the United States shall guarantee to every state in the Union a republican form of govern-

ment and shall protect each of them against invasion and domestic violence; and

Whereas, the President of the United States is by the Constitution made commander in chief of the Army and Navy, as well as chief civil executive officer of the United States, and is bound by solemn oath faithfully to execute the office of President of the United States and to take care that the laws be faithfully executed; and

Whereas, the rebellion, which has been waged by a portion of the people of the United States against the properly constituted authorities of the government thereof in the most violent and revolting form, but whose organized and armed forces have now been almost entirely overcome, has in its revolutionary progress deprived the people of the state of North Carolina of all civil government; and

Whereas, it becomes necessary and proper to carry out and enforce the obligations of the United States to the people of North Carolina in securing them in the enjoyment of a republican form of government:

Now, therefore, in obedience to the high and solemn duties imposed upon me by the Constitution of the United States and for the purpose of enabling the loyal people of said state to organize a state government whereby justice may be established, domestic tranquillity insured, and loyal citizens protected in all their rights of life, liberty, and property, I, Andrew Johnson, President of the United States and commander in chief of the Army and Navy of the United States, do hereby appoint William W. Holden provisional governor of the state of North Carolina, whose duty it shall be, at the earliest practicable period, to prescribe such rules and regulations as may be necessary and proper for convening a convention composed of delegates to be chosen by that portion of the people of said state who are loyal to the United States, and no others, for the purpose of altering or amending the constitution thereof, and with authority to exercise within the limits of said state all the powers necessary and proper to enable such loyal people of the state of North Carolina to restore said state to its constitutional relations to the Federal government and to present such a republican form of state government as will entitle the state to the guarantee of the United States therefor and its people to protection by the United States against invasion, insurrection, and domestic violence:

Provided, that in any election that may be hereafter held for choosing delegates to any state convention as aforesaid no person shall be qualified as an elector or shall be eligible as a member of such convention unless he shall have previously taken and subscribed the oath of amnesty as set forth in the President's proclamation of May 29, A.D. 1865, and is a voter qualified as prescribed by the constitution and laws of the state of North Carolina in force immediately before the 20th day of May, A.D. 1861, the date of the so-called ordinance of secession; and the said convention, when convened, or the legislature that may be thereafter assembled, will prescribe the qualification of electors and the eligibility of persons to hold office under the constitution and laws of the state—a power the people of the several states composing the Federal Union have rightfully exercised from the origin of the government to the present time.

And I do hereby direct:

First, that the military commander of the department and all officers and persons in the military and naval service aid and assist the said provisional governor in carrying into effect this proclamation; and they are enjoined to abstain from in any way hindering, impeding, or discouraging the loyal people from the organization of a state government as herein authorized.

Second, that the secretary of state proceed to put in force all laws of the United States the administration whereof belongs to the State Department applicable to the geographical limits aforesaid.

Third, that the secretary of the treasury proceed to nominate for appointment assessors of taxes and collectors of customs and internal revenue, and such other officers of the Treasury Department as are authorized by law, and put in execution the revenue laws of the United States within the geographical limits aforesaid. In making appointments the preference shall be given to qualified loyal persons residing within the districts where their respective duties are to be performed; but if suitable residents of the districts shall not be found, then persons residing in other states or districts shall be appointed.

Fourth, that the postmaster general proceed to establish post offices and post routes and put into execution the postal laws of the United States within the said state, giving to loyal residents the preference of appointment; but if suitable residents are not found, then to appoint agents, etc., from other states.

Fifth, that the district judge for the judicial district in which North Carolina is included proceed to hold courts within said state in accordance with the provisions of the act of Congress. The attorney general will instruct the proper officers to libel and bring to judgment, confiscation, and sale property subject to confiscation and enforce the administration of justice within said state in all matters within the cognizance and jurisdiction of the Federal courts.

Sixth, that the secretary of the navy take possession of all public property belonging to the Navy Department within said geographical limits and put in operation all acts of Congress in relation to naval affairs having application to the said state.

Seventh, that the secretary of the interior put in force the laws relating to the Interior Department applicable to the geographical limits aforesaid.

Consequences

How close Johnson's plans might ultimately have been to Lincoln's own we do not know. Certainly, the fears of Congressional leaders concerning the new president were well grounded. Johnson was a Southerner who believed in white supremacy and in the concept of state's rights. He believed that Congress had no power to interfere in the internal affairs of a state. Accordingly, he would ultimately oppose Radical Republican legislation to protect the rights of ex-slaves in the South (see CIVIL WAR AND RECONSTRUCTION AMENDMENTS TO THE CONSTITUTION OF THE UNITED STATES) and would try—without success—to stop Congress from replacing the Southern state governments he had authorized with new ones. The intense friction with Congress would eventually lead to impeachment proceedings against Johnson.

PROCLAMATIONS ENDING THE CIVIL WAR

TREATY AT A GLANCE

Proclaimed
April 2 and August 20, 1866, at Washington, D.C.

Signatory
Unilateral declaration by the president of the United States

Overview
General Robert E. Lee surrendered his Army of Northern Virginia at Appomattox Court House on April 9, 1865, and the last Confederate units, in the West, surrendered on May 26, 1865. Since the United States did not want to recognize the former Confederate States as having constituted a legitimate nation, no treaty ended the war. Instead, the president issued two proclamations.

Historical Background

The proclamation of April 2, 1866, applied to those states "in rebellion" that had ratified the Thirteenth Amendment to the Constitution (which freed the slaves) that had abolished slavery in their state constitutions, that had repudiated debts incurred during the rebellion, and that had declared the secession null and void. The proclamation encompassed Georgia, South Carolina, Virginia, North Carolina, Tennessee, Alabama, Louisiana, Arkansas, Mississippi, and Florida. Only Texas at first refused to comply with the proclamation terms, but it ultimately did and was encompassed in a second proclamation of August 20, 1866.

Terms

The proclamations read as follows.

By the President of the United States of America
A Proclamation

Whereas by proclamations of the Fifteenth and 19th of April, 1861, the President of the United States, in virtue of the power vested in him by the Constitution and the laws, declared that the laws of the United States were opposed and the execution thereof obstructed in the States of South Carolina, Georgia, Alabama, Florida, Mississippi, Louisiana, and Texas by combinations too powerful to be suppressed by the ordinary course of judicial proceedings or by the powers vested in the marshals by law; and

Whereas by another proclamation, made on the 16th day of August, in the same year, in pursuance of an act of Congress approved July 13, 1861, the inhabitants of the States of Georgia, South Carolina, Virginia, North Carolina, Tennessee, Alabama, Louisiana, Texas, Arkansas, Mississippi, and Florida (except the inhabitants of that part of the State of Virginia lying west of the Allegheny Mountains and of such other parts of that State and the other States before named as might maintain a loyal adhesion to the Union and the Constitution or might be from time to time occupied and controlled by forces of the United States engaged in the dispersion of insurgents) were declared to be in a state of insurrection against the United States; and

Whereas by another proclamation, of the 1st day of July, 1862, issued in pursuance of an act of Congress approved June 7, in the same year, the insurrection was declared to be still existing in the States aforesaid, with the exception of certain specified counties in the State of Virginia; and

Whereas by another proclamation, made on the 2d day of April, 1863, in pursuance of the act of Congress of July 13, 1861, the exceptions named in the proclamation of August 16, 1861, were revoked and the inhabitants of the States of Georgia, South Carolina, North Carolina, Tennessee, Alabama, Louisiana, Texas, Arkansas, Mississippi, Florida, and Virginia (except the forty-eight counties of Virginia designated as West Virginia and the ports of New Orleans, Key West, Port Royal, and Beaufort, in North Carolina) were declared to be still in a state of insurrection against the United States; and

Whereas the House of Representatives, on the 22d day of July, 1861, adopted a resolution in the words following, namely:

Resolved by the House of Representatives of the Congress of the United States, That the present deplorable civil war has been forced upon the country by the disunionists of the Southern States now in revolt against the constitutional Government and in arms around the capital; that in this national emergency Congress, banishing all feelings of mere passion or resentment, will recollect only its duty to the whole country; that this war is not waged upon our part in any spirit of oppression, nor for any purpose of conquest or subjugation, nor purpose of overthrowing or interfering with the rights or established institutions of those States, but to defend and maintain the supremacy of the Constitution and to preserve the Union, with all the dignity, equality, and rights of the several States unimpaired; and that as soon as these objects are accomplished the war ought to cease.

And whereas the Senate of the United States, on the 25th day of July, 1861, adopted a resolution in the words following, to wit:

Resolved, That the present deplorable civil war has been forced upon the country by the disunionists of the Southern States now in revolt against the constitutional Government and in arms around the capital; that in this national emergency Congress, banishing all feeling of mere passion or resentment, will recollect only its duty to the whole country; that this war is not prosecuted upon our part in any spirit of oppression, nor for any purpose of conquest or subjugation, nor purpose of overthrowing or interfering with the rights or established institutions of those States, but to defend and maintain the supremacy of the Constitution and all laws made in pursuance thereof and to preserve the Union, with all the dignity, equality, and rights of the several States unimpaired; that as soon as these objects are accomplished the war ought to cease.

And whereas these resolutions, though not joint or concurrent in form, are substantially identical, and as such may be regarded as having expressed the sense of Congress upon the subject to which they relate; and

Whereas by my proclamation of the 13th day of June last the insurrection in the State of Tennessee was declared to have been suppressed, the authority of the United States therein to be undisputed, and such United States officers as had been duly commissioned to be in the undisturbed exercise of their official functions; and

Whereas there now exists no organized armed resistance of misguided citizens or others to the authority of the United States in the States of Georgia, South Carolina, Virginia, North Carolina, Tennessee, Alabama, Louisiana, Arkansas, Mississippi, and Florida, and the laws can be sustained and enforced therein by the proper civil authority, State or Federal, and the people of said States are well and loyally disposed and have conformed or will conform in their legislation to the condition of affairs growing out of the amendment to the Constitution of the United States prohibiting slavery within the limits and jurisdiction of the United States; and

Whereas in view of the before-recited premises, it is the manifest determination of the American people that no State of its own will has the right or the power to go out of, or separate itself from, or be separated from, the American Union, and that therefore each State ought to remain and constitute an integral part of the United States; and

Whereas the people of the several before-mentioned States have, in the manner aforesaid, given satisfactory evidence that they acquiesce in this sovereign and important resolution of national unity; and

Whereas it is believed to be a fundamental principle of government that people who have revolted and who have been overcome and subdued must either be dealt with so as to induce them voluntarily to become friends or else they must be held by absolute military power or devastated so as to prevent them from ever again doing harm as enemies, which last-named policy is abhorrent to humanity and to freedom; and

Whereas the Constitution of the United States provides for constituent communities only as States, and not as Territories. dependencies, provinces, or protectorates; and

Whereas such constituent States must necessarily be, and by the Constitution and laws of the United States are, made equals and placed upon a like footing as to political rights, immunities, dignity, and power with the several States with which they are united; and

Whereas the observance of political equality, as a principle of right and justice, is well calculated to encourage the people of the aforesaid States to be and become more and more constant and persevering in their renewed allegiance; and

Whereas standing armies, military occupation, martial law, military tribunals, and the Suspension of the privilege of the writ of *habeas corpus* are in time of peace dangerous to public liberty, incompatible with the individual rights of the citizen, contrary to the genius and spirit of our free institutions, and exhaustive of the national resources, and ought not, therefore, to be sanctioned or allowed except in cases of actual necessity for repelling invasion or suppressing insurrection or rebellion; and

Whereas the policy of the Government of the United States from the beginning of the insurrection to its overthrow and final suppression has been in conformity with the principles herein set forth and enumerated:

Now, therefore, I, Andrew Johnson, President of the United States, do hereby proclaim and declare that the insurrection which heretofore existed in the States of Georgia, South Carolina, Virginia, North Carolina, Tennessee, Alabama, Louisiana, Arkansas, Mississippi, and Florida is at an end and is henceforth to be so regarded.

In testimony whereof I have hereunto set my hand and caused the seal of the United States to be affixed.

[SEAL]

Done at the city of Washington, this 2d day of April, A.D. 1866, and of the Independence of the United States of America the ninetieth.

By the President:
ANDREW JOHNSON.
WILLIAM H. SEWARD, Secretary of State.

By the President of the United States of America A Proclamation

Whereas by proclamations of the Fifteenth and 19th of April, 1861, the President of the United States, in virtue of the power vested in him by the Constitution and the laws, declared that the laws of the United States were opposed and the execution thereof obstructed in the States of South Carolina, Georgia, Alabama, Florida, Mississippi, Louisiana, and Texas by combinations too powerful to be suppressed by the ordinary course of judicial proceedings or by the powers vested in the marshals by law; and

Whereas by another proclamation, made on the 16th day of August, in the same year, in pursuance of an act of Congress approved July 13, 1861, the inhabitants of the States of Georgia, South Carolina, Virginia, North Carolina, Tennessee, Alabama, Louisiana, Texas, Arkansas, Mississippi, and Florida (except the inhabitants of that part of the State of Virginia lying west of the Alleghany Mountains, and except also the inhabitants of such other parts of that State and the other States before named as might maintain a loyal adhesion to the Union and the Constitution or might be from time to time occupied and controlled by forces of the United States engaged in the dispersion of insurgents) were declared to be in a state of insurrection against the United States; and

Whereas by another proclamation, of the 1st day of July, 1862, issued in pursuance of an act of Congress approved June 7, in the same year, the insurrection was declared to be still existing in the States aforesaid, with the exception of certain specified counties in the State of Virginia; and

Whereas by another proclamation, made on the 2d day of April, 1863, in pursuance of the act of Congress of July 13, 1861, the exceptions named in the proclamation of August 16, 1861, were revoked and the inhabitants of the States of Georgia, South Carolina, North Carolina, Tennessee, Alabama, Louisiana, Texas, Arkansas, Mississippi, Florida, and Virginia (except the forty-eight counties of Virginia designated as West Virginia and the ports of New Orleans, Key West, Port Royal, and Beaufort, in North Carolina) were declared to be still in a state of insurrection against the United States; and

Whereas by another proclamation, of the 15th day of September, 1863, made in pursuance of the act of Congress approved March 3, 1863, the rebellion was declared to be still existing and the privilege of the writ of habeas corpus was in certain specified cases suspended throughout the United States, said suspension to continue throughout the duration of the rebellion or until said proclamation should, by a subsequent one to be issued by the President of the United States, be modified or revoked; and

Whereas the House of Representatives, on the 22d day of July, 1861, adopted a resolution in the words following, namely:

Resolved by the House of Representatives of the Congress of the United States, That the present deplorable civil war has been forced upon the country by the disunionists of the Southern States now in revolt against the constitutional Government and in arms around the capital; that in this national emergency Congress, banishing all feelings of mere passion or resentment, will recollect only its duty to the whole country; that this war is not waged upon our part in any spirit of oppression, nor for any purpose of conquest or subjugation, nor purpose of overthrowing or interfering with the rights or established institutions of those States, but to defend and maintain the supremacy of the Constitution and to preserve the Union, with all the dignity, equality, and rights of the several States unimpaired; and that as soon as these objects are accomplished the war ought to cease.

And whereas the Senate of the United States, on the 25th day of July, 1861, adopted a resolution in the words following, to wit:

Resolved, That the present deplorable civil war has been forced upon the country by the disunionists of the Southern States now in revolt against the constitutional Government and in arms around the capital; that in this national emergency Congress, banishing all feeling of mere passion or resentment, will recollect only its duty to the whole country; that this war is not prosecuted upon our part in any spirit of oppression, nor for any purpose of conquest or subjugation, nor purpose of overthrowing or interfering with the rights or established institutions of those States, but to defend and maintain the supremacy of the Constitution and all laws made in pursuance thereof and to preserve the Union, with all the dignity, equality, and rights of the several States unimpaired; that as soon as these objects are accomplished the war ought to cease.

And whereas these resolutions, though not joint or concurrent in form, are substantially identical, and as such have hitherto been and yet are regarded as having expressed the sense of Congress upon the subject to which they relate; and

Whereas the President of the United States, by proclamation of the 13th of June, 1865, declared that the insurrection in the State of Tennessee had been suppressed, and that the authority of the United States therein was undisputed, and that such United States officers as had been duly commissioned were in the undisturbed exercise of their official functions; and

Whereas the President of the United States, by further proclamation, issued on the 2d day of April, 1866, did promulgate and declare that there no longer existed any armed resistance of misguided citizens or others to the authority of the United States in any or in all the States before mentioned, excepting only the State of Texas, and did further promulgate and declare that the laws could be sustained and enforced in the several States before mentioned, except Texas, by the proper civil authorities, State or Federal, and that the people of the said States, except Texas, are well and loyally disposed and have conformed or will conform in their legislation to the condition of affairs growing out of the amendment to the Constitution of the United States prohibiting slavery within the limits and jurisdiction of the United States;

And did further declare in the same proclamation that it is the manifest determination of the American people that no State, of its own will, has a right or power to go out of, or separate itself from, or be separated from, the American Union; and that, therefore, each State ought to remain and constitute an integral part of the United States;

And did further declare in the same last-mentioned proclamation that the several aforementioned States, excepting Texas, had in the manner aforesaid given satisfactory evidence that they acquiesce in this sovereign and important resolution of national unity; and

Whereas the President of the United States in the same proclamation did further declare that it is believed to be a fundamental principle of government that the people who have revolted and who have been overcome and subdued must either be dealt with so as to induce them voluntarily to become friends or else they must be held by absolute military power or devastated so as to prevent them from ever again doing harm as enemies, which last-named policy is abhorrent to humanity and to freedom; and

Whereas the President did in the same proclamation further declare that the Constitution of the United States provides for constituent communities only as States, and not as Territories, dependencies, provinces, or protectorates;

And further, that such constituent States must necessarily be, and by the Constitution and laws of the United States are, made equals and placed upon a like footing as to political rights, immunities, dignity, and power with the several States with which they are united;

And did further declare that the observance of political equality, as a principle of right and justice, is well calculated to encourage the people of the before-named States, except Texas, to be and to become more and more constant and persevering in their renewed allegiance; and

Whereas the President did further declare that standing armies, military occupation, martial law, military tribunals, and the suspension of the writ of *habeas corpus* are in time of peace dangerous to public liberty, incompatible with the individual rights of the citizen, contrary to the genius and spirit of our free institutions, and exhaustive of the national resources, and ought not, therefore, to be sanctioned or allowed except in cases of actual necessity for repelling invasion or suppressing insurrection or rebellion;

And the President did further, in the same proclamation, declare that the policy of the Government of the United States from the beginning of the insurrection to its overthrow and final suppression had been conducted in conformity with the principles in the last-named proclamation recited; and

Whereas the President, in the said proclamation of the 2d of April, 1866, upon the grounds therein stated and hereinbefore recited, did then and thereby proclaim and declare that the insurrection which heretofore existed in the several States before named, except in Texas, was at an end and was henceforth to be so regarded; and

Whereas subsequently to the said 2d day of April, 1866, the insurrection in the State of Texas has been completely and everywhere suppressed and ended and the authority of the United States has been successfully and completely established in the said State of Texas and now remains therein unresisted and undisputed, and such of the proper United States officers as have been duly commissioned within the limits of the said State are now in the undisturbed exercise of their official functions; and

Whereas the laws can now be sustained and enforced in the said State of Texas by the proper civil authority, State or Federal, and the people of the said State of Texas, like the people of the other States before named, are well and loyally disposed and have conformed or will conform in their legislation to the condition of affairs growing out of the amendment of the Constitution of the United States prohibiting slavery within the limits and jurisdiction of the United States; and

Whereas all the reasons and conclusions set forth in regard to the several States therein specially named now apply equally and in all respects to the State of Texas, as well as to the other States which had been involved in insurrection; and

Whereas adequate provision has been made by military orders to enforce the execution of the acts of Congress, aid the civil authorities, and secure obedience to the Constitution and laws of the United States within the State of Texas if a resort to military force for such purpose should at any time become necessary:

Now, therefore, I, Andrew Johnson, President of the United States, do hereby proclaim and declare that the insurrection which heretofore existed in the State of Texas is at an end and is to be henceforth so regarded in that State as in the other States before named in which the said insurrection was proclaimed to be at an end by the aforesaid proclamation of the 2d day of April, 1866;

And I do further proclaim that the said insurrection is at an end and that peace, order, tranquillity, and civil authority now exist in and throughout the whole of the United States of America.

In testimony whereof I have hereunto set my hand and caused the seal of the United States to be affixed.

[SEAL.]

Done at the city of Washington, this 20th day of August, A.D. 1866, and of the Independence of the United States of America the ninety-first.

By the President:
ANDREW JOHNSON.
WILLIAM H. SEWARD, Secretary of State.

Consequences

Unfortunately, the two momentous proclamations would prove inadequate to heal the wounds of war and readily reunite the nation. To so daunting a task, the wise and infinitely charitable judgment and strong leadership of Abraham Lincoln might well have been equal, but his assassination on April 14, 1865, brought the irascible and unpopular Vice President Andrew Johnson into the White House. The process of Reconstruction, begun with the proclamations, became a vindictive and opportunistic struggle (see CIVIL WAR AND RECONSTRUCTION AMENDMENTS TO THE CONSTITUTION OF THE UNITED STATES) that greatly prolonged the sufferings of the South and contributed to racial resentments and outright hatred that have yet to be fully resolved in the United States.

CIVIL WAR AND RECONSTRUCTION AMENDMENTS TO THE CONSTITUTION OF THE UNITED STATES

```
TREATY AT A GLANCE

Ratified
December 1865, July 1868, and March 1870


Signatories
Three-fourths of the states of the United States,
including all those formerly in rebellion


Overview
In 1865, 1866, and 1870, the U.S. Congress, determined to carry
through its plan for "Reconstruction" of the Confederacy follow-
ing the Civil War—a plan bitterly opposed by the defeated South—
passed the Thirteenth, Fourteenth, and Fifteenth Amendments to
the Constitution. In time these articles would play a revolutionary
role in American society far beyond their immediate effects of
extending the franchise to former African-American slaves and set-
ting the conditions under which former Confederates could be
rehabilitated and hold office.
```

Historical Background

Five days after General Robert E. Lee surrendered at Appomattox Court House, President Abraham Lincoln was assassinated while attending a performance of *Our American Cousin* at Ford's Theatre in Washington, D.C. With his death, Andrew Johnson came to office determined to treat the recently defeated Confederacy as mildly as Lincoln had apparently intended, given the reconciliatory tone of his second inaugural address.

The Radical Republicans who controlled Congress, however, were wary of the new president, a Democrat (the Democratic Party had been considered a vehicle of sedition throughout the war) and a Southerner himself. When Johnson proposed readmitting the rebel states to full partnership in the Union as soon as they had ratified the Thirteenth Amendment abolishing slavery and had elected congressional representatives, Congress balked. Three-fourths of those states reunified at war's end had ratified the amendment by December 18, 1865, but members of Congress refused to seat the predictably all-white slates of newly elected Southern senators and representatives.

Instead, the House and Senate formed a joint Committee on Reconstruction and named Senator William P. Fessenden of Maine to head it. While the committee conducted public hearings, many of which focused on the mistreatment of blacks in the South, Congress passed a bill to extend the Freedman's Bureau and passed the Civil Rights Act, which stated that blacks were citizens of the United States and that no state could restrict their rights to testify in court or to own property. Johnson vetoed both measures, but Congress overrode the vetoes. April 9, 1866, the date on which Congress overrode the veto of the Civil Rights Act, marked a shift in the direction of Reconstruction. Congress had wrested control of the process from the president.

Two months after the Civil Rights Bill became law, Congress passed and submitted to the states the Fourteenth Amendment, whose five sections redefined American citizenship as including every man born or naturalized in the United States. In July 1868, when the Fourteenth Amendment was ratified by the necessary three-fourths of the states, Congress was ready to go beyond both it and the Thirteenth Amendment in abolishing slavery and protecting freedmen. That same month, Congress submitted to the states the Fifteenth Amendment, which prohibited the states from denying the vote to any man on the basis of "race, color, or previous condition of servitude."

Terms

The Thirteenth Amendment, originally passed by the Senate on April 8, 1864, ran into trouble in the House and was not cleared for submission to the various states until January 31, 1865. Caught up in the squabble between Congress and the executive branch over Reconstruction, the amendment ratified at the end of that year was nevertheless elegant:

ARTICLE XIII

Sec. 1. Neither slavery nor involuntary servitude, except as a punishment for crime whereof the part shall have been duly convicted, shall exist within the United States, or any place subject to their jurisdiction.

Sec. 2. Congress shall have power to enforce this article by appropriate legislation.

The Fourteenth Amendment not only extended the definition of American citizenship, it also barred states from passing laws abridging the rights of those citizens and punished those states that prohibited eligible voters under its definitions from voting by proportionally decreasing those states' representation in Congress. The last two sections dealt exclusively with those who participated in the recent rebellion, prohibiting, among other things, former Confederates from holding state or federal offices unless pardoned by Congress:

ARTICLE XIV

Sec. 1. All persons born or naturalized in the United States and subject to the jurisdiction thereof, are citizens of the United States and of the State wherein they reside. No State shall make or enforce any law which shall abridge the privileges or immunities of citizens of the United States; nor shall any state deprive any person of life, liberty, or property without due process of law; nor deny to any person within its jurisdiction the equal protection of the laws.

Sec. 2. Representatives shall be appointed among the several states according to their respective numbers, counting the whole number of persons in each State, excluding Indians not taxed. But when the right to vote at any election for the choice of electors for President and Vice-President of the United States, Representatives in Congress, the executive and judicial officers of a State, or the members of the legislature thereof, is denied any of the male inhabitants of such State, being twenty-one years of age, and citizens of the United States, or in any way abridged, except for participation in rebellion, or other crime, the basis of representation therein shall be reduced in the proportion which the number of such male citizens shall bear to the whole number of male citizens twenty-one years of age in such State.

Sec. 3. No person shall be a Senator or Representative in Congress or elector of President and Vice-President, or hold any office, civil or military, under the United States, or under any State, who, having previously taken an oath, as a member of Congress, or as an officer of the United States, or as a member of any State legislature, or as an executive or judicial officer of any State; to support the Constitution of the United States, shall have engaged in insurrection or rebellion against the same, or given aid or comfort to the enemies thereof. But Congress may by a vote of two-thirds of each house, remove such disability.

Sec. 4. The validity of the public debt of the United States, authorized by law, including debts incurred for payment of persons and bounties for services in suppressing insurrection or rebellion, shall not be questioned. But neither the United States nor any State shall assume or pay any debt or obligation incurred in aid of insurrection or rebellion against the United States, or any claim for loss of emancipation of any slave; but all such debts, obligations and claims shall be held illegal and void.

Sec. 5. The Congress shall have power to enforce, by appropriate legislation, the provisions of this article.

After passage of the Fourteenth Amendment, the only Southern state to ratify it was Tennessee. Angered by the South's recalcitrance, Congress then passed a series of Reconstruction Acts. The first, enacted on March 2, 1867, put all the South except Tennessee under military government, with a major general in charge of each state. The only way a state could shed military rule was by ratifying a new state constitution that included provisions for black enfranchisement and for the disenfranchisement of ex-Confederates. Congressional approval of the new constitution and the state's ratification of the Fourteenth Amendment were required before a state would be readmitted.

Because the first Reconstruction Act was vague as to how the new state constitutions were to be drafted, Congress passed a second act that empowered the military to register voters in the Southern states and to supervise the election of delegates to constitutional conventions. Once the constitutions were drafted, a majority of registered voters had to approve them. White Southerners figured out a way to defeat the new constitutions: they simply refrained from voting. Congress then decided that approval by a majority of those actually voting was all that was required for ratification, and between June 1868, with the admission of Arkansas, and July 1870, with the admission of Georgia, all the Southern states were brought reluctantly back into the Union.

The Fifteenth Amendment, then, was aimed at preventing the newly "reconstructed" states from now taking back all that had been gained for former black slaves. Of the three amendments, this is perhaps the one that would in the future affect the broadest number of Americans:

ARTICLE XV

Sec. 1. The right of citizens of the United States to vote shall not be denied or abridged by the United States or by any State on account of race, color, or previous condition of servitude.

Sec. 2. The Congress shall have power to enforce this article by appropriate legislation.

Ratification of the Fifteenth Amendment was secured in March 1870.

Consequences

By the time the Fifteenth Amendment was passed, many white Southerners, reacting to what they considered oppression by an American government bent on social revolution, had organized secret societies, such as the Ku Klux Klan, the Knights of the White Camellia, and the Pale Faces, to intimidate blacks and keep them away from the polls to which they now had rights. Within a few years, these secret societies gave way to public movements, such as the Mississippi Plan. As part of this movement, whites no longer hid behind masks, nor did they confine their terrorist activities to nighttime. Instead, they openly paraded about and captured and killed many militant, and some not-so-militant, blacks. Calling themselves "redeemers," they intended to take back their states from those Northerners they saw as exploiting their defeat, whom they called carpetbaggers, and to get free of the meddlesome federal government's policy of Reconstruction.

The redeemers rewrote their state constitutions, creating laissez-faire tracts suspicious and distrustful of any legislative body. They also framed new laws aimed just as surely at disenfranchising blacks as Reconstruction legislation had aimed at protecting them. Such pieces of legislation were called Jim Crow laws, taking their nickname from the antebellum minstrel show that had given the Confederacy its national anthem, "Dixie." As more and more formerly moderate Southerners joined the ranks of militant racists, the redeemer movement gave birth to the Solid South, a bloc of states that for almost a century could be counted on to vote exclusively for Democratic Party candidates for national office. This political juggernaut led, eventually, to the defeat of Reconstruction governments at the polls.

The last showdown between the North and South in the 19th century came in the 1876 presidential election, which featured the campaigns of Democrat Samuel J. Tilden and Republican Rutherford B. Hayes. The redeemers crusaded against the graft and greed of Ulysses S. Grant's administration and its carpetbag rule—and intimidated blacks in order to stifle their votes. This tactic swung the Solid South behind Tilden and won the popular vote. The Republicans, however, reversed the electoral tally of the three Southern states they still controlled under Reconstruction laws and (there is no other term for it) stole the election. A deadlock resulted, followed by months of tense wrangling during which the nation had no clear president-elect and the threat of civil disunion loomed once again in the background. Hayes assumed office only because he agreed never again to tinker with the peculiar segregated social structures being established in the postwar South. Afterwards, even his closest associates sometimes in private called him Your Fraudulency.

The compromise left the South free to construct its separate and unequal world, a segregated society that unabashedly oppressed its racial minorities—and to a lesser extent its ethnic and religious minorities—until the civil rights upheavals of the 1960s. The Fourteenth and Fifteenth Amendments played no small role in the 20th-century movements for social equality, providing an activist Supreme Court under Chief Justice Earl Warren with the constitutional leverage it needed to at last protect the civil rights and expand the individual freedoms of all Americans, including the descendants of the slaves freed by the Civil War.

Part Nine

THE NEW IMPERIALISM

INTRODUCTION

The Americans, relying on British men-of-war to enforce a MONROE DOCTRINE it had declared but could not impose, called it the Era of Good Feelings—the Pax Britannica established by the indisputable supremacy of the British navy. With no country in a position to challenge Great Britain's dominance of the seas, the period between the Napoleonic Wars and the 1870s saw an evident falling off in conflicts between European powers. They did not disappear entirely, and there were wars against colonial peoples by the colonizing nations: Britain in India and Burma, in South Africa against the "Kaffirs" and in New Zealand against the Maoris; France in Algeria and Indochina; the Low Countries in Indonesia; the United States against its Native Americans. And there was some revolutionary turmoil on the Continent, especially in France leading to the rise of Napoleon III. As a whole, however, Europe was relatively calm compared to the constant fighting for colonial possessions in the 18th century or the rise again of intense rivalry between the Great Powers in the late 19th and early 20th centuries.

The very peace that Britain secured, during which the Empire became the world's champion of free trade and took the lead in such progressive matters as abolishing slavery, opened the Continent to greater industrial development and sparked the move toward national unification, especially in Italy and Prussia, that shattered the peace. It was during this period that there came on the scene one of the more remarkable diplomats in European history. The young Prussian premier Otto von Bismarck was inspired by the diplomatic and bellicose successes of Italy's able chief minister, Camillo di Cavour, in creating a new Italian state under his Piedmontese king. The Prussian minister was determined to copy those triumphs. Reforming Prussia's politics when necessary, engaging in aggressive warfare if need be, perfectly willing to aggrandize his country through negotiations when possible, Bismarck would in the end not only unite Germany under Prussia and defuse liberal and radical agitation almost completely within his new state, he would also launch a whole new era in international relations.

Bismarck's Europe

In 1866 ignoring the express objections of his king, Wilhelm I, Bismarck provoked a war within the aging German Confederation—the so-called Seven Weeks War—in order to destroy Austria's dominance of the league and thus unite the German states under Prussian hegemony. As a result, the old league was replaced by Bismarck's new North German Confederation. Bismarck then seduced the still-independent southern German states into joining the North German Confederation, playing off their hatred of Napoleon III, who would come to regret his role in giving birth to the confederacy.

In 1870, when Bismarck tried to place one of Kaiser Wilhelm's Hohenzollern relatives on the Spanish throne, Emperor Napoleon panicked. The last thing he wanted was Germans on both sides of him, giving rise to the potential for a Prussian-Spanish two-front war against France. The result was another short and brutal but even more momentous conflict, the Franco-Prussian War of 1870–71. The conflict brought about the fall of the Second French Empire, provided the impetus to the creation of the German Empire, and figured as the first modern European war, in which both combatant nations used railroads, the telegraph, modern rifles, and modern rifled, breechloading artillery. With the 1871 TREATY OF VERSAILLES came the birth of the Third Republic in France and Bismarck's New German Empire.

After 1871 Bismarck also made it clear that this new empire was a satisfied power as far as the continent of Europe itself was concerned. As the man who expelled Austria from Germany, humiliated France and toppled Napoleon III, and unified Germany and created the modern German Empire, he would loom over the European continent for three decades, from 1862 to 1890, and determine the course of its history. During his 19 years as Germany's imperial chancellor, Bismarck would employ a clear-eyed if sometimes ruthless diplomacy to install a network of interlocking alliances aimed at isolating Russia and keeping a defeated France weak and demoralized. By the 1878 Congress of Berlin, the "Iron Chancellor" had in effect moved the capital of continental Europe from Paris, or perhaps Vienna, to Berlin, where it was more comfortable for him to maintain single-handed Europe's balance of power.

Bismarck's "system" came to work so well, in fact, that world politics seemed, for a while, to enjoy something like an equilibrium reminiscent of the recent Pax Britannica, and Europe itself seemed to be entering an age of political and social progress. Germany and Italy were unified countries, instead of the old patchwork of central European principalities that had been engaged in internecine warfare since the heyday of the Holy Roman Empire. The venerable empires of Russia, Austria-Hungary, and Ottoman Turkey still prevailed, and the budding breakup of eastern and southeastern Europe into small, disputatious states had yet to threaten the general stability of these ancient regimes. The industrial age, with its demands for large-scale capital investment and economies of scale, had rendered many formerly powerful European states inconsequential, such as the Netherlands and Sweden, which were too small, and Spain, which was, in today's economic jargon, underdeveloped. Unless their own interests were directly involved, these lesser powers had little or no say in the affairs of the Great Powers, who were the sole arbiters of European politics.

Nothing like Europe's diplomatic system existed in the rest of the world. The United States, busy developing its own internal empire west of the Mississippi and having long settled its quarrels with Europe over the country's continental borders, was largely isolated from the "Great Game" of power politics and imperial adventure till the turn of the century. Backed by the British navy, the U.S. under the Monroe Doctrine ensured not only that it steered clear of Europe's multilateral balance-of-power system but also that Latin America remained free of such entanglement. For most of the 19th century, Africa (except North Africa, nominally under Ottoman rule, and a few European seaports) remained terra incognita. And, when Europe invaded what it called the Dark Continent in earnest late in the century, the alliance system itself seemed to facilitate the Great Powers' placement of their colonial

pieces in the jigsaw world they stitched together. The same could be said of the apparently sanguine collusion with which they "opened" Chinese seaports to Europe's "free" trade, while the rest of China, like Japan, remained xenophobic and isolationist. The fin de siècle cabinets of Europe's Great Powers seemed to have reached the zenith of their influence.

The alliance system, however, continued to flourish in large part because of the strength of the British Empire. As the home of the industrial revolution, Great Britain—with its factory system and its steam power as well as its triumphs at sea laying the foundation—had once already captained an era of calm and confidence in world affairs. Always a sea empire, Britain's worldwide naval supremacy following Admiral Nelson's defeat of Napoleon's armada at Trafalgar in 1805 had paved the way not only for the Pax Britannica but also for the new and aggressive colonial adventures of Queen Victoria's rule. During her reign, Britain completed its century long conquest of India and, late in the 19th century, oversaw the partitioning of Africa, ensuring its own dominance by taking control of Egypt and the Nile by 1898. More than any other nation, Britain was the center of the geopolitical world upon which the 20th century dawned.

By then, the widowed queen—as the paragon of the stuffy decorum and the figurehead for the ardent imperialism that together defined the Victorian Age—was popular, even beloved. But she was in fact more a ceremonial than a true monarch, and her real influence on the British government was slight. Actual power lay with her prime ministers: the liberal, deadly serious William Gladstone; the seductive and politic but lazy Benjamin Disraeli; the arch-Conservative Robert Cecil, third marquess of Salisbury. It was mostly Disraeli who, beginning at midcentury, cobbled together new pieces of colonial real estate in the name of the Crown, but after his death Lord Salisbury, Disraeli's foreign secretary, ably picked up the imperialists' mantle when he became prime minister, as well.

Few of Europe's politicians, even fewer of its soldiers, understood how the British Empire administered by Gladstone, Disraeli, Salisbury, and others actually worked. They were confused by the fact that one small island of constantly bickering people ruled over by a dowdy old matron with a ridiculously small army could control a quarter of the globe. It flabbergasted them that in India alone, 70,000 British troops somehow held onto a subcontinent of 300 million people. And it irritated them to no end that the obviously small and apparently fragile England should have so wide a range of action, even more so that the British just stood there, unchallenged and unflappable, aloof and patronizing, refusing to become embroiled in the petty passions and squabbles that consumed the political life of a Europe scarcely 20 miles away across the English Channel.

The British ministers knew well enough what they were doing, however. They realized, if their queen did not, that the technological change she so stoutly resisted, which included such basic modern inventions as the telegraph, the railroad, and the steam engine, was reshaping the face of European civilization and in many ways making her far-flung empire possible. Under their guidance, the British Isles—called with some exaggeration "the workshop of the world"—from 1846 led the globe in promoting free trade, which the other major European states soon fully embraced. It was no accident that the pound sterling became the internationally preferred reserve currency, nor that the Bank of England served as the hub of the world's finance. Britain's ministers eschewed all alliances, happy to cruise along in "splendid isolation," while their diplomacy aimed always to preserve the balance of power on the Continent and sought at all costs to protect the Empire's trade routes to India from Russian encroachment.

Otto von Bismarck understood this, and he took advantage of Britain's policy of aloofness. Placing his immense diplomatic talents at the service of peace and stability, Bismarck had all but built contemporary Europe. He feared no rivals military or economic, but he did worry about that two-front war and, thus, anti-German coalitions, especially those that might include France, which he knew would never reconcile herself to her reduced status and the loss of Alsace-Lorraine (imposed by the 1871 TREATY OF VERSAILLES, ending the Franco-Prussian War). Indeed, in 1873 he had formed the Three Emperors' League (Germany, Austria-Hungary, Russia) precisely to isolate France, but such a combination was always vulnerable to Austro-Russian dispute over the Balkans, the so-called Eastern Question of how to organize the peninsula's feuding nationalities as they freed themselves from an ailing Ottoman Empire. By century's end the Triple Alliance (Germany, Austria-Hungary, and the new nation of Italy) became the linchpin of German diplomatic strategy, which in addition to isolating France sought to check Russian ambition in the Balkans. Bismarck's maneuverings had created a dual alliance system: Germany and the Hapsburgs with their allies on one side, France and the Romanovs with theirs on the other.

Bismarck's system was premised on the very fact that Britain would not get embroiled, that she would continue to keep her distance from her historical enemies, Russia and France. It was not that Britain ignored Europe. Indeed, she meddled in the political affairs of other powers all the time all over the world. Instead, it was that she chose to stand outside the Bis-marckian system, depending on her naval supremacy and the industrial might of her seaborne empire instead of formal, even secret, alliances, to give her a free hand in international affairs. In fact, Lord Salisbury regarded such formal commitments as not only unnecessary but dangerous, believing that when the time came for a fight, a democratic electorate might well decide to bring down a government rather than go to war. As the Great Powers other than England—Germany, Austria-Hungary, France, and Russia—grouped into coalitions during the last decade of the 19th century, Salisbury stubbornly maintained England's splendid isolation, and one of the results was that by the beginning of the 20th century, Germany had became England's major competitor in world affairs.

The Pax Britannica rested on Britain's industrial dominance and its economic hegemony, and it would last only so long as they did. But both the dominance and the hegemony incited envy and longing in others, who sought to rival Britain by imitating her. Other nations also industrialized, built up their navies, and dreamed of owning and exploiting the riches of distant colonies—Germany chief among them, whose industrial might and huge economy were by 1900 second in Europe only to Britain and third in the world after England and the United States. This competitiveness was capitalism's "heart of darkness": its search for the markets its growing industries needed to stay healthy, the brutalities it exercised in the name of profits, the ever larger pools of capital it needed to develop full-blown industrial economies, and the gambler's ethic produced by the stock market financing it employed to raise funds. This heart lay beating just below the surface of the titular tranquility of the Pax Britannica and the clever calmness of the alliance systems. It promoted self-interest and prompted both an arms race and a scramble for colonies and increasingly justified both with a theory of racist superiority based on a survival of the fittest (i.e., the best bred and the best armed) called Social Darwinism.

On the other hand, since Bismarck's continental alliance system rested on British aloofness, if others grew to challenge the dominance and hegemony of the mighty British Empire, Britain might find herself unwilling, even unable, to maintain its splendid isolation. That's just what happened as new nations such as the United States and Japan launched themselves on colonizing courses and the crumbling of the more ancient empires on the Continent tempted others to new adventures at home. With the costs of empire escalating, with players new and old combining to challenge Britain's sway in the world, with hostile colonial peoples growing ever more quarrelsome, Britain could no longer afford to go it alone.

The New Imperialism

Although historians disagree sharply about the reasons—and the significance, if any—of the so-called new imperialism of the late 19th and early 20th centuries, they don't much dispute that some new departure from past policies did indeed occur. This new era was characterized by an acceleration in colonial acquisitions and the entry onto the field of a number of new players, all of which were undergoing the kind of rapid industrialization England, and to some extent France, had experienced much earlier.

UNITED STATES

One of these new colonial powers was the United States, except the United States was not so "new" a colonial power as she first appeared. When Europeans embarked on imperialistic adventures, they traditionally went to faraway places, to Africa, say, or to Asia, just as once they had gone to America, and in these remote corners of the earth they sought to impose their will on people of color and to master exotic environments. In America, the empire was built in. If an Englishman talked of his empire in those days as lying "somewhere east of Suez," an American could have responded with equal fervor that his could be found west of the wide Missouri. It was, the Americans said, their manifest destiny to advance the frontier between civilization and savagery into the land of the Sioux and the Nez Percé, the Navajo and the Apache, the Comanche and the Paiute.

Late in the century, however, the United States found its internal colonizing of the West at an end when the 1890 U.S. census announced that sometime after 1880 the "frontier line" in the West had disappeared. Not unrelated, 1890 was also the year of the massacre at Wounded Knee, when federal troops mowed down with a machine gun some three hundred Sioux in the last major U.S. confrontation with Native Americans. After Wounded Knee, the Indians would never again prove a military threat to the occupation of their former lands, which now "belonged" to the United States and in which the government could "count" its citizens. For the managers of the American economy and the financial markets behind it, the time had clearly come for new colonies, and they began to look beyond the American continent.

The Panic of 1893, which began when the Philadelphia and Reading Railroad went bankrupt, shook the New York Stock Exchange into the biggest selling spree on record. In the severe depression that followed, banks called their loans; credit dried up; the Erie, the Northern Pacific, the Union Pacific, and the Santa Fe all failed, one after another; and mills, factories, furnaces, and mines everywhere shut down. By the time it was over, five hundred banks and 15 hundred firms had fallen into bankruptcy, and a series of industrial strikes around the country had grown so violent that the country's municipalities began building local national guard armories to arm federalized strikebreakers. These events merely fired a fever already growing in the elite political and financial circles of American society. To the moneyed class it seemed that overseas markets for American goods might relieve the problem of underconsumption at home and that overseas sources of raw materials might weaken the position of an increasingly hostile labor force. In short, overseas colonies might prevent the kind of economic crisis that in the 1890s was bringing something approaching class war to America.

Young expansionists like Teddy Roosevelt could be fairly explicit in their private views that foreign adventures should divert farmers and laborers from their preoccupation with economic ills, though for public consumption they dressed those views in the racist and "manly" terminology that had been the heritage of the American West since John O'Sullivan coined the phrase "manifest destiny." But even William McKinley, one of the still numerous cautious, old "standpatters" in the Republican Party, had stated some years before he became president that "we want a foreign market for our surplus products."[1] In Congress, too, the consensus was growing. In 1897 Indiana's Senator Albert Beveridge declared that American factories were making more than the American people could use and American soil was producing more than they could consume. "Fate has written our policy for us," said Beveridge. "The trade of the world must and shall be ours."[2]

Economically, they were right. The United States outstripped all other imperialist nations with industrialized economies in its coddling of business, throwing open its doors to European immigrants who flooded its cities after the Civil War with unprecedented numbers even as it erected high protective-tariff walls around its new markets. An economy already expanding before the war exploded into massive growth in the decades following Appomattox, and what in 1860 had been a second-rate industrial country—lagging behind England, Germany, and even France—had by 1890 taken the lead. The United States had become the greatest free-trade market in the world: the value of its manufactured goods all but equaled the combined production of the three previous leaders. Farm products, especially tobacco, cotton, and wheat, had long depended on international markets for prosperity, and by then American trade in general exceeded that of every country in the world but England. In the two decades previous, new investments by American capitalists overseas had reached a billion dollars. Oil, too, had become a big export. By 1891 Rockefeller's Standard Oil Company produced 90 percent of America's kerosene export and controlled 70 percent of the world market, and oil had grown second only to cotton as the leading product shipped overseas.

Both industrialists and large commercial farmers—including some of Populist leaders—were demanding expansion into foreign markets for their huge agricultural surpluses. What they had in mind was not necessarily foreign conquest but an open-door trade policy, such as the United States was then helping to impose on China—in other words, what historian William Apple Williams called an "informal empire." But even informal empires sometimes fed real expansion, as the filibusters and merchant seamen who had drifted into the occupation of Texas and California back in the middle of the 19th century could attest. In Cuba, American policy makers and newspapers claimed they wanted to rescue freedom-fighting rebels intent on overthrowing an abusive Spanish rule. The Spanish-American War, fought on that pretext, in reality announced the United States' entry into the contest for world markets.

Not all Americans supported the war being whipped up by the circulation contest between Joseph Pulitzer's *New York World* and William Randolph Hearst's *New York Journal*. Anti-imperialists, led by William Jennings Bryan and Carl Shurz, rallied their forces in Congress against the warmongers, led by Roosevelt and Henry Cabot Lodge. Those arguing against intervention got Congress to pass the Teller Amendment, which prohibited annexation of Cuba as the result of any U.S. action.

Meanwhile, the business community had begun to rally. Newspapers and trade journals of the day were chock full of the bellicose sentiments of businessmen: Pittsburgh's iron industrialists claimed that the possibility of war had stimulated the iron trade; shipping merchants announced that an actual war would decidedly enlarge the business of transportation; banker Russell Sage told the press that there was no question where the rich men stood; while John Jacob Astor and William Rockefeller admitted they were feeling militant, and J. P. Morgan said he believed further talk with Spain would lead nowhere.

One Washington newspaper talked about a "belligerent spirit" inhabiting the Navy Department, which was being egged on toward war by arms manufacturers and supply contractors who had been camped in the department since the destruction of the *Maine*. That spirit was Teddy Roosevelt, McKinley's undersecretary of the navy. From deep within the administration, Roosevelt kept up steady pressure on the president for intervention in Cuba, turning the

famous frontier theories he had expounded in his multivolume history *The Winning of the West* now to the cause of Cuba. Basically, he argued that foreign adventure could renew the virility of the ruling Anglo-Saxon class just as the frontier once had done. He began forming a unit to fight under his command when the war came, consisting of the cowboys, hunters, sheriffs, Texas Rangers, a few outlaws, and a large number of former vigilantes he had met in his youthful travel about the American West. He called them the Rough Riders, which was the name of a segment of Buffalo Bill Cody's immensely popular Wild West Show, then touring the country.

The turning point came on March 21, 1898, when Boston Brahmin Henry Cabot Lodge informed McKinley that he had talked with bankers, brokers, businessmen, editors, clergymen, and other members of the city's elite, and that all of them, including the most conservative, wanted the Cuban question—which was, in short, what to do about the succession of rebellious spasms that were disrupting American commerce—solved. On March 25 an adviser in Cuba wired the White House a telegram informing McKinley that America's big corporations on the island believed a war was coming and what was more, welcomed it as a relief from the suspense and uncertainty of the current situation.

Two days later, McKinley presented Spain with an ultimatum demanding an armistice with the rebels. When Spain did not reply, McKinley asked Congress for a declaration of war on April 11, but he made no mention of recognition for Cuba or of its independence, which had initially been the reasons given for American intervention. After Congress by joint resolution gave McKinley the power to intervene nine days later, American forces, including Roosevelt's Rough Riders, invaded Cuba but ignored the rebel army. In fact, American major general William R. Shafter told rebel leaders to stay out of the Cuban city of Santiago, which he would put in the hands of a defeated Spain's civil authorities. Then Roosevelt staged a charge up San Juan Hill to little military benefit for the United States but to much political benefit for TR. It was all over in three months.

Given the strictures of the Teller Amendment, the United States did not annex Cuba, but it occupied the island. Fast on the heels of the army came American capital. Then came more railroads, more mines, more plantations. United Fruit moved into the Cuban sugar industry, the American Tobacco Company onto its tobacco lands. By 1901 an additional $30 million had been invested, and 80 percent of Cuba's mineral exports were in American hands, mostly those connected to the wrists of Bethlehem Steel. The army had to stay to protect such interests, and when the

Cubans went out on a series of strikes in 1899 and 1900, they were brutally suppressed. By the time the Cuban Constitutional Convention met in 1901, the United States simply informed the new government that the army would stay unless and until it included the Platt Amendment, passed by the U.S. Congress in February 1901, in its new constitution. The amendment gave the United States "the right to intervene for the preservation of Cuban independence" and "for the protection of life, property, and individual liberty," plus a few naval coaling stations on the island. In truth, there was no need to annex Cuba.

The Spanish-American War did lead to a series of annexations of countries not covered under the Teller prohibition operative in Cuba. These new colonies were Puerto Rico, Guam, and the Philippines, for which the United States paid Spain $20 million. The Hawaiian Islands had already been penetrated by American missionaries and pineapple plantation owners, who were now able to oust the only recently restored Queen Liliuokalani; they cost nothing since it was taken in time-honored Western tradition from the indigenous peoples themselves. Explaining his decision to annex the Philippines to a group of ministers visiting the White House, President McKinley said he had looked at all the options and decided "there was nothing left for us to do but take them all and to educate the Filipinos, and uplift and civilize and Christianize them, and by God's grace do the very best we could by them, as our fellow men for whom Christ also died. And then I went to bed and went to sleep and slept soundly."[3]

Teddy Roosevelt, now on McKinley's reelection ticket as vice presidential candidate, took up the issue of putting down the Philippine rebellion that followed annexation and used it as a cudgel against the perennial Democratic candidate, pacifist and Populist hero William Jennings Bryan. Soon made president himself when the newly reelected McKinley was assassinated, Roosevelt took to the new imperialism in America with gusto. He enthusiastically supported such initiatives as the construction of the Panama Canal, for which he not only had to practice a subtle diplomacy with Britain and France but also had to engineer the creation of the new Republic of Panama, expressly to provide the United States a canal zone. American muckrakers would call America's imperial policies "dollar diplomacy," and American businesses like United Fruit would prove every bit as effective as the British in taking control of foreign countries, especially in Central America, which the yellow press soon labeled "banana republics." Before the century was out, Roosevelt, whose navy was growing, as was Japan's and Germany's, into a threat for the British, would relish his role as "policeman" to the world, notably following the Russo-Japanese War. Tellingly, it was a role Great Britain had once reserved for itself.

RUSSIA

The other new imperial nations—Germany and Japan, for instance—also experienced something similar to America's post–Civil War industrial expansion, and a more intensely industrializing Russia also became decidedly expansionist in the second half of the 19th century. If not precisely new to the imperial game, Moscow was at least headed in new directions. As Bismarck's machinations began to check Russian ambitions in the West, the czars turned toward Asia, where a number of European nations were spreading their influence. Russia was, however, the only nation to approach Asia overland instead of by sea, and in this the nation rather resembled the United States before the 1890s, forcibly extending her continental frontiers.

The turning point for Russia had been the Crimean War, when Prussia, Britain, and the Hapsburg Austria, with Ottoman permission, marched into Moldavia and Wallachia to check Russian expansion into eastern Europe under the pretext of protecting Orthodox Christians against the outrages of infidel Turks. The war produced one of the age's great imperial works of literature, Alfred, Lord Tennyson's famous poem "The Charge of the Light Brigade," and frustrated for the time being the thoroughly trounced Russians in their ambitions in the Balkans and Middle East.

After Crimea, Russia turned with renewed vigor toward its eastern frontiers. The emancipation of the serfs in 1861 only served to feed the movement, as landless Russian and Ukrainian peasants now migrated in large waves into Siberia and central Asia, again somewhat resembling the trans-Mississippi West. As in the United States, a surge of industrialization, foreign trade, and railroad building not only stitched a vast country together but led to the colonization of an internal empire. And Russia was no more limited in its expansion eastward by the opposition of native peoples than had been the United States westward, though, as in the Wild West, sometimes fierce opposition proved a momentary stumbling block. The real trouble came as Russia ran up against competitive colonizers in the Far East, one of them, Great Britain, already familiar; the other, Japan, a truly new imperial nation.

JAPAN

Commodore Oliver Perry's 1854 expedition managed to open the door to Japan under the EMPIRE OF JAPAN TREATY, and for a few years the old pattern of colonial exploitation threatened Japanese sovereignty. After an intense internal power struggle, brought on by the usual causes—the danger of foreign military intervention, the rise of socially unsettling commerce, the growth of a disaffected peasantry—led to civil war between the rigid ruling Toguawa family and the supporters of Emperor Mutsuhito, long isolated from political affairs, the Meiji restoration brought not only peace but a thoroughgoing modernization that left Japan strong economically and militarily. Soon Japan had followed the West not only on the path of industrialization but also along the road to modern colonial empire. Japan swallowed up the Ryukyu Islands, the Kuril Islands, the Bonin Islands, and Hokkaido before moving on to Korea, which sparked a war with China. From the Chinese, Japan won Taiwan, P'eng-hu (the Pescadores), and southern Manchuria. By this time Russia, France, Britain, and Germany were already seeking ways to frustrate Japan's new imperial ambitions.

EUROPE

It was in Africa that Germany, its industrial might and its need for markets expanding together just as they were in other nations, made its first major bid to join the Great Powers' colonial club. In Africa, too, the smaller nations of Italy and Belgium entered the hallowed ranks. Even Portugal and Spain, their ancient imperial bones creaking, once again entered the fray. South-West Africa, Togoland, Cameroon, Zanzibar, the Congo—names Europeans would hardly have recognized a few years earlier—were suddenly destinations on a map filling up with colonial possessions and protectorates. The growing number of players sped up the race for conquest, and with so many people stirring so many pots, there was bound, sooner or later, to be trouble from the colonized and the colonizers alike.

BACKLASH

The ultimate result of these new imperial adventures was a destabilization, first in the colonial empires, then in the Europe of the Great Powers. Nowhere had so many rivals been vying for position in the same spot for so long as in Manchu China, to which English smugglers had opened the door in the Opium Wars a generation back under the onerous TREATY OF NANKING. At the turn of the 20th century, China was convulsed by an antiforeign uprising known as the Boxer Rebellion (see BOXER PROTOCOL), which as much as any event captured the destructive nature of the new imperialism for those nations outside the Great Power system of Bismarck's Europe.

By the late 19th century colonial empires were beginning in many ways to drain the resources and the emotions of the home countries, which had to garrison them against native insurgency and defend them against encroachment by others. For example, Britain's colonial wars with the Boers of South Africa—which were fought against the original Dutch settler population, now under British rule, and which, for that reason and the extreme harshness of the conflict, proved unpopular—signaled an exhaustion among the British public with Victoria's empire that presaged its precipitous decline in the 20th century. Finally, and perhaps inevitably, the expansionist powers themselves went to war with each other over their new imperial possessions.

Ultimately, the most damaging to the future stability of Europe's international relations was the Russo-Japanese War of 1904. The Japanese, realizing early that with Russia heading east toward Japan's Chinese and other Asian possessions, and Japan heading west, eventually the two would collide. So in 1903, the Japanese government proposed to the czar's ministers that each country should recognize the other's special interests and economic privileges in those colonies where conflict seemed most likely, Manchuria and Korea. Meanwhile, Japan had been building up its army and navy on the sly, and the Russians, unaware of the firepower the Japanese commanded, negotiated in lackadaisical fashion, angering the Japanese ambassador, who abruptly broke off the talks on February 6, 1904, and headed for home.

Three days later, the Japanese sank two Russian warships at Inchon in Korea and torpedoed the main Russian force at Lüshan, or Port Arthur, on China's Liaodong Peninsula. With the rest of the Russian fleet still icebound at Vladivostok, Japan quickly achieved superiority at sea, freeing her up to send thousands of troops inland into both Korea and Manchuria. The Japanese overran the former almost instantly, and by May 1 they were deep into the interior of the latter. They drove the Russians north to Mukden (now Shenyang) by September, and then they surrounded Port Arthur. After suffering through a grueling siege, the Russians surrendered on January 25, 1905.

The world was stunned by the victory, the first in modern times of an Asian nation over a Great Power. Europe associated such countries with weak, ancient governments, ripe for the picking, so the Japanese triumph was magnified even beyond its impressive speed and thoroughness. As a result, the czar's government came close to falling to revolution, and Russian prestige in Europe plummeted. Not only did the war announce the arrival of Japan as a great power, but it afforded U.S. president Theodore Roosevelt an opportunity to strut American muscle, as well, when his offer to mediate the peace was accepted and resulted in the TREATY OF PORTSMOUTH.

More important still, English observers aboard Japanese warships came away persuaded to launch an aggressive naval construction program for the huge Dreadnought class, which fueled a budding arms race with Germany and helped destabilize the European system of alliances that Bismarck had so carefully constructed and that Queen Victoria had once so effectively policed.

1. Howard Zinn, *A People's History of the United States* (New York: HarperCollins, 1980), 292.
2. Ibid.
3. Ibid., 305–306.

TREATIES

Mutual Defense Treaties, Military Alliances, and Nonaggression Pacts

TREATY OF CONSTANTINOPLE (UNKIAR SKELESSI)

TREATY AT A GLANCE

Completed (Ratified)
July 8, 1833, at Unkiar Skelessi, near Constantinople
(present-day Istanbul, Turkey)

Signatories
Russia and Ottoman Empire (Turkey)

Overview
The treaty reflects Czar Nicholas I's new approach to Turkey. Fearful of the tide of revolution sweeping Europe, the conservative czar attempted an alliance to bolster the faltering empire of Russia's traditional enemy. As a result, the Ottoman Empire became a virtual protectorate of Russia.

Historical Background

It is a measure of the remarkable degree to which Czar Nicholas I feared the onslaught of revolution that he concluded a treaty of alliance with an empire against which Russia had fought no fewer than 10 major wars and countless minor disputes since the 16th century. The most recent Russo-Turkish war, which accompanied the rebellion of the Ottomans' Greek subjects, had ended just three years earlier with the signing of yet another peace treaty that would not hold, the 1829 TREATY OF ADRIANOPLE.

The timing was right, though. Sultan Mahmud II was ready to accept the alliance with Nicholas because he was facing almost certain defeat by the insurgent Muhammad 'Ali Pasha of Egypt. He had already requested military assistance from Austria, Great Britain, and France, and been rejected by all three, when he accepted aid from the Russians in early 1833. In return, he signed a treaty at Unkiar Skelessi, a small village near Istanbul.

Terms and Consequences

An eight-year defensive alliance that proclaimed peace and friendship between the two nations, the Treaty of Constantinople obligated Russia to assist the Ottomans against not only external enemies but internal—that is, revolutionary, forces—as well.

The treaty is brief enough to quote in its entirety.

In the Name of Almighty God.

HIS Imperial Majesty the Most High and Most Puissant Emperor and Autocrat of all the Russias, and his Highness the Most High and Most Puissant Emperor of the Ottomans, equally animated by a sincere desire to maintain the system of peace and good harmony happily established between the two Empires, have resolved to extend and to strengthen the perfect amity and confidence which reign between them by the conclusion of a Treaty of defensive Alliance.

In consequence, their Majesties have chosen and nominated as their Plenipotentiaries, that is to say, his Majesty the Emperor of all the Russias, the most excellent and the most honourable Alexis Count Orloff, his Ambassador Extraordinary at the Sublime Ottoman Porte, etc. etc.

And Mr. Appolinaire Bouténeff, his Extraordinary Envoy and Minister Plenipotentiary at the Sublime Ottoman Porte, etc. etc.

And his Highness the Sultan of the Ottomans, the most illustrious and most excellent, the oldest of his Viziers, Hosrew-Mehmet Pacha, Seraskier Commander-in-chief of the regular

Troops of the Line, and Governor-general of Constantinople, etc. etc.; the most excellent and the most honourable Ferzi-Achmet Pacha, Mouchir and Commander of his Highness's Guard, etc. etc.; and Hadji-Mehmet-Akif Effendi, actual Reis Effendi, etc. etc.

Who, after having exchanged their full powers, which have been found in good and regular form, have agreed upon the following Articles.

ARTICLE I

There shall be for ever Peace, Amity, and Alliance between H. M. the Emperor of all the Russias, and H. M. the Emperor of the Ottomans, their Empires and their Subjects, as well by land as by sea. This Alliance having solely for its object the common defence of their States against all attack, their Majesties promise to have a mutual and unreserved understanding as to all objects which concern their tranquillity and safety respectively, and to lend to each other for this purpose *matériel* succours and the most efficacious assistance.

ARTICLE II

The Treaty of Peace concluded at Adrianople on the 2d of September, 1829, as well as all the other Treaties comprised in it, as well as the Convention signed at St. Petersburgh on the 14th of April, 1830, and the arrangement concluded at Constantinople on the 9th (21st) of July, 1832, relative to Greece, are confirmed throughout all their tenour by the present Treaty of defensive Alliance, as if the said Transactions had been inserted in it word for word.

ARTICLE III

In consequence of the principle of conservation and of mutual defence which serves as the basis for the present Treaty of Alliance, and by reason of the most sincere desire to assure the duration, the maintenance, and the entire independence of the Sublime Porte, H. M. the Emperor of all the Russias, in case that circumstances which might again determine the Sublime Porte to claim naval and military aid from Russia should occur, although the case be not now foreseen, if it please God, promises to furnish by land and sea as many troops and forces as the contracting parties shall deem necessary. It is accordingly agreed that in this case the forces by land and sea whose assistance the Sublime Porte shall demand, shall be held at its disposal.

ARTICLE IV

According to what has been said above, in case one of the two Powers shall have demanded assistance from the other, the expenses only of provisions for the forces by land and sea which shall have been furnished shall fall to the charge of the Power which shall have demanded the succour.

ARTICLE V

Although the two High Contracting Powers be sincerely disposed to maintain this engagement to the most remote period, inasmuch however as it is possible that hereafter circumstances may require some alterations in this Treaty, it has been agreed that its duration should be fixed at eight years, to run from the date of the exchange of the Imperial Ratifications. The two Parties, before the expiration of that term, shall agree, according to the state in which things shall be at that epoch, upon the renewal of the Treaty.

ARTICLE VI

The present Treaty of defensive Alliance shall be ratified by the two High Contracting Parties, and the ratifications shall be exchanged at Constantinople, within the period of two months, or sooner if possible.

The present Instrument, containing six Articles, and to which the last hand shall be put by the exchange of the respective ratifications, having been drawn up between us, we have signed and sealed it with our Seals, in virtue of our full powers, and delivered, in exchange for another of the like tenour, into the hands of the Plenipotentiaries of the Sublime Ottoman Porte.

Done at Constantinople, the 26th of June (8th of July), in the year one thousand eight hundred and thirty-three (the 20th of the moon of Safer, in the year 1249 of the Hegira).

[Signed]
[L.S.] COUNT ALEXIS ORLOFF.
[Signed]
[L.S.] A. BOUTÉNEFF.

The most significant aspect of the treaty, however, was a secret article. On the one hand, it limited Ottoman aid to Russia to the closing of the Strait of the Dardanelles to "any foreign vessels of war" except those of Russia. On the other, Mahmud did so at the request of the czar, which was much indeed. The secret clause gave Russia special international leverage since it could cut off a key avenue of passage for foreign warships.

SEPARATE ARTICLE OF THE TREATY OF ALLIANCE CONCLUDED BETWEEN RUSSIA AND TURKEY, ON THE 8TH OF JULY, 1833

In virtue of one of the clauses of the First Article of the Patent Treaty of defensive Alliance concluded between the Sublime Porte and the Imperial Court of Russia, the two High Contracting Parties have engaged to lend mutually *matériel* succours and the most efficacious assistance for the safety of their respective states. Nevertheless, as H. M. the Emperor of all the Russias, wishing to save the Sublime Ottoman Porte the expense and the inconveniences which might result to it from lending such *matériel* succour, will not demand this succour should circumstances place the Sublime Porte under the obligations to furnish it; *the Sublime Porte, in lieu of the succour which it is bound to lend in case of need according to the principle of reciprocity of the Patent Treaty, should limit its action in favour of the Imperial Court of Russia to shutting the Strait of the Dardanelles, that is to say, not to permit any foreign vessel of war to enter it under any pretext whatsoever.*

The present separate and secret Article shall have the same force and validity as if it were inserted word for word in the Treaty of defensive Alliance of this day.

Done at Constantinople the 26th of June (8th of July), in the year one thousand eight hundred and thirty-three (the 20th of the moon of Safer, in the year 1249 of the Hegira).

[Signed]
[L.S.] COUNT ALEXIS ORLOFF.
[Signed]
[L.S.] A. BOUTENEFF.

Consequences

The treaty aroused the suspicion of Russia's traditional imperial competitor, Great Britain, and the czar abandoned the Dardanelles privileges to sign the London Straits Convention in 1841. Meanwhile, Russian pressure continued to destabilize the Ottoman Empire in the Balkans. Using the guise of protecting Christian minorities under the ailing rule of the Turks, Russia attempted to grab Ottoman-controlled Moldavia and Wallachia in 1853, sparking the Crimean War. Defeated by a combined force of Turkish, British, French, and Sardinian troops, Russia turned its imperial ambitions east toward Asia for nearly a generation.

The decadent Ottoman Empire, called the Sick Man of Europe, became almost an obsession with European diplomats in their search for a balance of power on the Continent. Another Russo-Turkish war broke out in 1877, when Russia came unsuccessfully to the aid of Serbian rebels. Eventually, the festering situation between Russia and Turkey in the Balkans would play a significant role in the imbroglio that led to World War I.

Peace Treaties and Truces

TREATY OF ADRIANOPLE

TREATY AT A GLANCE

Completed
September 14 (September 2 old style), 1829, at Adrianople
(present-day Edirne, Turkey)

Signatories
Russia and Ottoman Empire (Turkey)

Overview
The treaty ended the Russo-Turkish War of 1828–29, which broke
out when Russia came to the assistance of Greece in its war of
independence. The war dealt the Ottoman Empire a heavy blow.

Historical Background

Russia declared war on the Ottomans on April 26, 1828, ostensibly with the purpose of aiding the Greeks in their struggle for independence. In fact, the war was an excuse for territorial expansion.

From obscure origins in the Islamic jihads (holy wars) of the 13th century, the Ottoman Turks had by the middle of the 1500s conquered most of eastern Europe, western Asia, and North Africa and ruled the Mediterranean and Black Seas. Over these lands, they established a strongly centralized but rigidly compartmentalized state, headed by a sultan whose Muslim subjects were legally barred from a significant role in government. At first flexible and tolerant, the Ottomans grew increasingly arrogant and corrupt, so that by the 19th century Ottoman rule had become a synonym in Europe for bureaucratic decadence. Their conquests had come to a halt, and their strength had begun to slowly weaken, in the 17th century, when they failed to break through the opposition of the Hapsburgs in Europe, of Russia in the Ukraine, and of the Safavid dynasty in Iran.

From 1700 on, the Ottomans tried to Westernize under the constant menace of increasing Russian power. Constant warfare with Russia led in 1774 to the Treaty of Kutschuk-Kaïnardji, which recognized the czar's control of the northern coast of the Black Sea and acknowledged his protectorate over the Christian subjects of the sultan. In 1783 Catherine the Great annexed the Khanate of the Crimea, the first major loss of primarily Muslim territory. By the beginning of the 19th century, the multiethnic nature of the Ottoman Empire, once a source of strength, was beginning to wear on the Turkish rulers, as Russia continuously hammered away at its edges. Separatist tendencies first manifested themselves in the Serbian uprisings of 1804 and 1815. The Greek war of independence was an ominous sign that the alienation of the empire's minority groups was not limited to the Serbs.

The Russian armies took Braila in Wallachia, then crossed the Danube and captured important Turkish fortresses. The city of Varna yielded after a three-month siege, and in the Caucasus, the Russians took Kars and Akhaltsikhe. Silistra likewise fell to the Russians, who were victorious as well in battles at Tcherkovna (June 11, 1829) and at Sliven (August 12). The Russians' more formidable enemy was the plague, which ravaged its armies and prompted Russian general Hans Diebitsch-Zabalkansky to conclude a treaty.

Terms

Principal terms of the Treaty of Adrianople included semiautonomy for the Danubian Principalities (Moldavia and Wallachia), Russian control of the mouth of the Danube, and free navigation through the Turkish straits. The treaty also granted Greece its independence. As to the Ottoman Empire, it was compelled to pay heavy war reparations and conceded religious freedom to the Orthodox who lived within its territories.

Article 7 of the Adrianople treaty was less ambiguous and more forceful than the Treaty of Kutschuk-Kaïnardji in asserting Russia's rights to control the fate of its nationals within the Ottoman Empire, particularly with regard to commerce:

The Russian nationals shall enjoy within the whole Ottoman Empire, both on land and sea, full freedom of commerce assured to them by the Treaties, previously concluded between the two Contracting Powers. This liberty of commerce shall by no means whatsoever be restricted and under no circumstances or pretexts interfered with, either by prohibition or restriction whatsoever, nor by any regulation or measure be it administrative or by central legislation. Russian subjects, vessels and merchandise shall be protected from any violence or chicanery: the former shall remain under the jurisdiction and police of the Russian Minister and Consuls only, the Russian vessels shall never be submitted to any visit whatsoever on board by the Ottoman authorities, neither on the open sea, nor at any of the ports or roadsteads under the domination of the Sublime Porte and all merchandise or commodity belonging to a Russian subject, after paying off duty according to tariffs, could be freely sold, deposited on land in the warehouses of the owner or consignee, or else shipped on another vessel carrying the flag of any nation whatever, without the necessity for the Russian subject to give notice thereof to the local authorities or ask at all their permission. It is explicitly agreed that the wheat coming from Russia shall enjoy the same privileges, and that its free transit shall never and under no pretext suffer the slightest difficulty or hindrance. The Sublime Porte undertakes moreover to watch closely that the commerce and navigation on the Black Sea in particular should not experience any obstacle of whatever nature. To this effect it recognizes and declares the passage of the Canal of Constantinople and of the Dardanelles Isthmus entirely free and open to Russian vessels carrying merchant flags, with or without cargo, whether coming from the Black Sea to enter the Mediterranean, or coming from the Mediterranean to enter the Black Sea. These vessels, provided they are merchant ones of whatever size or capacity, shall not be exposed to any impediment or vexation whatsoever, as provided above. The two Courts will agree upon the proper measures to be taken to avert any delay in the delivery of the necessary shipments. By virtue of the same principle the passage of the Canal of Constantinople and the Dardanelles Isthmus is declared free and open to all merchant vessels of the powers that are on a status of peace with the Supreme Porte, be it that they sail to the Russian ports of the Black Sea or that they come with or without cargo, under the same conditions as stipulated for vessels under the Russian flag.

Finally, the Sublime Porte recognizes to the Imperial Court of Russia the right to secure for itself the guarantees of this full freedom of commerce and navigation on the Black Sea and solemnly declares it shall never and under no circumstances or pretext place the slightest obstacle on its part. Above all, the Sublime Porte promises it shall never henceforth take the liberty of stopping vessels with or without cargo, either Russian or belonging to nations with which the Ottoman Empire is not at declared war, whilst passing through the canal of Constantinople and the Dardanelles Isthmus to sail from the Black Sea to the Mediterranean, or from the Mediterranean to the Russian ports of the Black Sea. And if, Heaven forbid, any of the stipulations contained in the present article should be violated, disregarding the claims made by the Minister of Russia to this effect—claims that should obtain prompt and full satisfaction—then the Sublime Porte recognizes in advance to the Imperial Court of Russia the right to consider such a violation as an act of hostility and to take immediate reprisals towards the Ottoman Empire.

Consequences

Russia had succeeded in its traditional policy of expanding at Turkey's expense using the rubric of protecting the Christians under Ottoman rule. The recognition of Greek autonomy by the Turks may have been merely the result of a knee-jerk Russian diplomacy whose historical goal was imperial expansion, but—along with the reduction in Turkish power imposed by the treaty—it led to full independence for Greece, accepted reluctantly, it is true, by the Porte (the Ottoman government), in 1832.

TREATY OF NANKING

TREATY AT A GLANCE

Completed
August 29, 1842, at Nanjing (Nanking), China

Signatories
Great Britain and China

Overview
This treaty ended the Opium War of 1839–42, and China ceded Hong Kong to Great Britain, opened several ports to unrestricted trade, and promised to conduct foreign relations on the basis of equality. The Chinese also agreed to the principle of extraterritoriality, whereby Westerners in China were exclusively subject to the jurisdiction of their own countries' consular courts.

Historical Background

The First and Second Opium Wars (1839–42 and 1856–60) were the first major military confrontations between China and the West. They not only ended Chinese isolation from other civilizations but began for China a century of mistreatment and humiliation at the hands of foreign powers, leading to the decay of the Qing (Ch'ing) dynasty and, ultimately, revolution, civil war, and the ascendancy of communist rule.

The First Opium War began when British merchants ignored a Chinese prohibition against the importation of opium. On March 30, 1839, a Chinese imperial commissioner seized the opium in British warehouses in Guangzhou (Canton). Britain responded by dispatching warships and troops. In rapid succession, the coastal cities of Hangzhou (Hangchow), Hong Kong, and Guangzhou fell under attack, and Guangzhou was captured in May 1841. Xiamen (Amoy) and Ningbo fell next. After a lull in the fighting due to disease among the British forces, renewed efforts resulted in the taking of Shanghai and Zhenjiang (Chinkiang). Outmatched by British troops and equipment, the Chinese capitulated and agreed to the harsh terms of the Nanjing Treaty.

Terms

In addition to agreeing to pay a $20 million indemnity, the Chinese opened the ports of Guangzhou, Xiamen, Fuzhou (Foochow), Ningbo, and Shanghai to British trade and residence. China also granted Britain the right of extraterritoriality, whereby British residents in China were subject not to Chinese legal jurisdiction but that of special consular courts. The greatest prize ceded to the Crown was Hong Kong, which was transferred to Britain in perpetuity.

Treaty of Nanking
Nanking, August 29, 1842
*Peace Treaty between the Queen of Great Britain and
the Emperor of China*

HER MAJESTY the Queen of the United Kingdom of Great Britain and Ireland, and His Majesty the Emperor of China, being desirous of putting an end to the misunderstandings and consequent hostilities which have arisen between the two countries, have resolved to conclude a Treaty for that purpose, and have therefore named as their Plenipotentiaries, that is to say:

Her Majesty the Queen of Great Britain and Ireland, Sir Henry Pottinger, Bart., a Major-General in the service of the East India Company, &c.;

And His Imperial Majesty the Emperor of China, the High Commissioners Keying, a member of the Imperial House, a Guardian of the Crown Prince, and General of the garrison of Canton; and Elepoo, of the Imperial Kindred, graciously permitted to wear the insignia of the first rank, and the distinction of a peacock's feather, lately Minister and Governor-General, &c., and now Lieutenant General commanding at Chapoo;

Who, after having communicated to each other their respective Eull Powers, and found them to be in good and due form, have agreed upon and concluded the following Articles:

I

There shall henceforward be peace and friendship between Her Majesty the Queen of the United Kingdom of Great Britain and Ireland and His Majesty the Emperor of China, and between their respective subjects, who shall enjoy full security and protection for their persons and property within the dominions of the other.

II

His Majesty the Emperor of China agrees, that British subjects, with their families and establishments, shall be allowed to reside, for the purposes of carrying on their mercantile pursuits, without molestation or restraint, at the cities and towns of Canton, Amoy, Foochowfoo, Ningpo, and Shanghai; and Her Majesty the Queen of Great Britain, &c., will appoint Superintendents, or Consular officers, to reside at each of the above-named cities or towns, to be the medium of communication between the Chinese authorities and the said merchants, and to see that the just duties and other dues of the Chinese Government, as hereafter provided for, are duly discharged by Her Britannic Majesty's subjects.

III

It being obviously necessary and desirable that British subjects should have some port whereat they may careen and refit their ships when required, and keep stores for that purpose, His Majesty the Emperor of China cedes to Her Majesty the Queen of Great Britain, &c., the Island of Hong-Kong, to be possessed in perpetuity by Her Britannic Majesty, her heirs and successors, and to be governed by such laws and regulations as Her Majesty the Queen of Great Britain, &c., shall see fit to direct.

IV

The Emperor of China agrees to pay the sum of 6,000,000 of dollars, as the value of the opium which was delivered up at Canton in the month of March, 1839, as a ransom for the lives of Her Britannic Majesty's Superintendent and subjects, who had been imprisoned and threatened with death by the Chinese High Officers.

V

The Government of China having compelled the British merchants trading at Canton to deal exclusively with certain Chinese merchants, called Hong merchants (or Co-Hong), who had been licensed by the Chinese Government for that purpose, the Emperor of China agrees to abolish that practice in future at all ports where British merchants may reside, and to permit them to carry on their mercantile transactions with whatever persons they please; and His Imperial Majesty further agrees to pay to the British Government the sum of 3,000,000 of dollars, on account of debts due to British subjects by some of the said Hong merchants (or Co-Hong), who have become insolvent, and who owe very large sums of money to subjects of Her Britannic Majesty.

VI

The Government of Her Britannic Majesty having been obliged to send out an expedition to demand and obtain redress for the violent and unjust proceedings of the Chinese High Authorities towards Her Britannic Majesty's officer and subjects, the Emperor of China agrees to pay the sum of 12,000,000 of dollars, on account of the expences incurred; and Her Britannic Majesty's Plenipotentiary voluntarily agrees, on behalf of Her Majesty, to deduct from the said amount of 12,000,000 of dollars, any sums which may have been received by Her Majesty's combined forces, as ransom for cities and towns in China, subsequent to the 1st day of August, 1841.

VII

It is agreed, that the total amount of 21,000,000 of dollars, described in the 3 preceding Articles, shall be paid as follows:

6,000,000 immediately.

6,000,000 in 1843; that is, 3,000,000 on or before the 30th of the month of June, and 3,000,000 on or before the 31st of December.

5,000,000 in 1844; that is, 2,500,000 on or before the 30th of June, and 2,500,000 on or before the 31st of December.

4,000,000 in 1845; that is, 2,000,000 on or before the 30th of June, and 2,000,000 on or before the 31st of December.

And it is further stipulated, that interest, at the rate of 5 per cent. per annum, shall be paid by the Government of China on any portion of the above sums that are not punctually discharged at the periods fixed.

VIII

The Emperor of China agrees to release, unconditionally, all subjects of Her Britannic Majesty (whether natives of Europe or India), who may be in confinement at this moment in any part of the Chinese empire.

IX

The Emperor of China agrees to publish and promulgate, under his Imperial sign manual and seal, a full and entire amnesty and act of indemnity to all subjects of China, on account of their having resided under, or having had dealings and intercourse with, or having entered the service of Her Britannic Majesty, or of Her Majesty's officers; and His Imperial Majesty further engages to release all Chinese subjects who may be at this moment in confinement for similar reasons.

X

His Majesty the Emperor of China agrees to establish at all the ports which are, by the IInd Article of this Treaty, to be thrown open for the resort of British merchants, a fair and regular tariff of export and import customs and other dues, which tariff shall be publicly notified and promulgated for general information; and the Emperor further engages, that when British merchandize shall have once paid at any of the said ports the regulated customs and dues, agreeable to the tariff to be hereafter fixed, such merchandize may be conveyed by Chinese merchants to any province or city in the interior of the Empire of China, on paying a further amount as transit duties, which shall not exceed * per cent. on the tariff value of such goods.

XI

It is agreed that Her Britannic Majesty's Chief High Officer in China shall correspond with the Chinese High Officers, both at the capital and in the provinces, under the term "communication"; the subordinate British Officers and Chinese High Officers in the provinces, under the terms "statement" on the part of the former, and on the part of the latter, "declaration"; and the subordinates of both countries on a footing of perfect equality: merchants and others not holding official situations, and therefore not included in the above, on both sides, to use the term "representation" in all papers addressed to, or intended for the notice of, the respective Governments.

XII

On the assent of the Emperor of China to this Treaty being received, and the discharge of the first instalment of money, Her Britannic Majesty's forces will retire from Nanking and the Grand Canal, and will no longer molest or stop the trade of China. The military post at Chinhai will also be withdrawn; but the Islands of Koolangsoo, and that of Chusan, will continue to be held by Her Majesty's forces until the money payments, and the arrangements for opening the ports to British merchants, be completed.

XIII

The ratification of this Treaty by Her Majesty the Queen of Great Britain, &c., and His Majesty the Emperor of China, shall be exchanged as soon as the great distance which separates England from China will admit; but in the meantime, counterpart copies of it, signed and sealed by the Plenipotentiaries on behalf of their respective Sovereigns, shall be mutually delivered, and all its provisions and arrangements shall take effect.

Done at Nanking, and signed and sealed by the Plenipotentiaries on board Her Britannic Majesty's ship *Cornwallis*, this 29th day of August, 1842; corresponding with the Chinese date, 24th day of the 7th month, in the 22nd year of Taoukwang.

[L.S.] HENRY POTTINGER.
[SIGNATURES OF THE THREE CHINESE
PLENIPOTENTIARIES]

Declaration Respecting Transit Duties

Whereas by the Xth Article of the Treaty between Her Majesty the Queen of the United Kingdom of Great Britain and Ireland, and His Majesty the Emperor of China, concluded and signed on board Her Britannic Majesty's ship *Cornwallis*, at Nanking, on the 29th day of August, 1842, corresponding with the Chinese date 24th day of the 7th month, in the 22nd year of Taoukwang, it is stipulated and agreed, that His Majesty the Emperor of China shall establish at all the ports which; by the IInd Article of the said Treaty, are to be thrown open for the resort of British merchants, a fair and regular tariff of export and import customs and other dues, which tariff shall be publicly notified and promulgated for general information; and further, that when British merchandize shall have once paid, at any of the said ports, the regulated customs and dues, agreeable to the tariff to be hereafter fixed, such merchandize may be conveyed by Chinese merchants to any province or city in the interior of the Empire of China, on paying a further amount of duty as transit duty;

And whereas the rate of transit duty to be so levied was not fixed by the said Treaty;

Now, therefore, the undersigned Plenipotentiaries of Her Britannic Majesty, and of His Majesty the Emperor of China, do hereby, on proceeding to the exchange of the Ratifications of the said Treaty, agree and declare, that the further amount of duty to be so levied on British merchandize, as transit duty, shall not exceed the present rates, which are upon a moderate scale; and the Ratifications of the said Treaty are exchanged subject to the express declaration and stipulation herein contained.

In witness whereof the respective Plenipotentiaries have signed the present declaration, and have affixed thereto their respective seals.

Done at Hong-Kong, the 26th day of June, 1843, corresponding with the Chinese date, Taoukwang 23rd year, 5th month, and 29th day.

[L.S.] HENRY POTTINGER.
[SEAL AND SIGNATURE OF THE CHINESE
PLENIPOTENTIARY]

Consequences

The trade and legal concessions made to the British under the treaty were soon extended to other Western powers, and China's long isolation came to an end. A Second Opium War erupted in 1856 and was concluded by the TREATY OF TIENTSIN. In 1860, following China's defeat in the Second Opium War, the Kowloon peninsula on the Chinese mainland was added to the Hong Kong colony, and in 1898 a large area beyond Kowloon, together with the surrounding islands (the "New Territories"), was leased to Great Britain for 99 years. With the expiration of the lease on July 1, 1997, all of Hong Kong was returned to Chinese sovereignty.

TREATY OF PARIS (1856)

TREATY AT A GLANCE

Completed
March 30, 1856, at Paris

Signatories
Great Britain, France, Sardinia, the Ottoman Empire, and Russia

Overview
The treaty ended the Crimean War, imposing stiff penalties on Russia, including the demilitarization and neutralization of the Black Sea (which ensured continued British maritime dominance in the eastern Mediterranean); the loss of the Russian protectorship over Balkan Christians, the Danubian principalities, and Serbia; and the return of southern Bessarabia to Moldavia (thereby cutting off Russian access to the Danube River).

Historical Background

The Crimean War (1853–56) may be seen as one in the long series of Russo-Turkish wars, which began in the 16th century. However, the 1853–56 conflict also brought in the British and the French, who saw the war as crucial to the resolution of the so-called Eastern Question: the fate of the Ottoman Empire, which, weak and corrupt, seemed ready to fall into whatever hands, Western or Eastern, were present to take it.

Russia relentlessly sought expansion of influence in the Balkans at the expense of the failing Ottoman Empire. Britain, however, wanted to preserve the Ottoman Empire in order to protect its interests in the eastern Mediterranean and Asia and prevent Russia from gaining strategic and economic control of Constantinople and the straits. For its part, France, under Napoleon III, wanted to protect Roman Catholic interests in the Holy Places of Turkish-controlled Palestine, which Eastern Orthodox Russia viewed as a threat to its national religion.

Tensions escalated during 1853 as Russia sought to reassert its protectorship over the Orthodox subjects of the Ottoman Empire. Lengthy negotiations broke down, and early in July 1853, Russia moved to occupy the Danubian principalities of Moldavia and Walachia, then under Turkish jurisdiction. Turkey protested, and Britain and France dispatched fleets to Besika Bay at the entrance of the Dardanelles. Despite continued negotiations, sporadic fighting broke out between Russian and Turkish forces after Russia declined to respond to a Turkish ultimatum (October 4, 1853) to withdraw from the Danubian principalities.

The crisis came to a head on November 3 with the so-called Sinope Massacre, in which the Russians annihilated the Turkish fleet at Sinope. Moved by public opinion, Britain and France jointly declared war on Russia on March 28, 1854. At this time, Austria, seeking to divert war from its frontiers, ordered Russian evacuation of the principalities. The czar agreed, having no desire to confront another enemy. A combined Anglo-French-Turkish expedition was launched against the Russian fortress at Sevastopol, on the tip of the Crimean peninsula, and a grindingly frustrating war, characterized by blundering (as at the Battle of Balaklava, commemorated in Lord Tennyson's "Charge of the Light Brigade") and plagued by disease (despite the ministrations of Florence Nightingale) culminated in the fall of Sevastopol in September 1855. This, combined with the death of Czar Nicholas I in battle (March 2, 1855) and an Austrian threat of intervention, convinced Russia to accede to the humiliating conditions imposed by the Treaty of Paris.

Terms

Russia agreed to restore to the Ottoman Empire all of the Ottoman territory its troops occupied, and all of the signatories agreed to respect the territorial integrity of the Ottoman Empire:

ARTICLE VII

Her Majesty the Queen of the United Kingdom of Great Britain and Ireland, His Majesty the Emperor of Austria, His Majesty the Emperor of the French, His Majesty the King of Prussia, His Majesty the Emperor of All the Russias, and His Majesty the King of Sardinia, declare the Sublime Porte admitted to participate in the advantages of the Public Law and System (*Concert*) of Europe Their Majesties engage, each on his part, to respect the Independence and the Territorial Integrity of the Ottoman Empire; Guarantee in common the strict observance of that engagement; and will, in consequence, consider any act tending to its violation as a question of general interest.

ARTICLE VIII

If there should arise between the Sublime Porte and one or more of the other Signing Powers, any misunderstanding which might endanger the maintenance of their relations, the Sublime Porte, and each of such Powers, before having recourse to the use of force, shall afford the other Contracting Parties the opportunity of preventing such an extremity by means of their Mediation.

For his part, the Ottoman sultan pledged his intention to treat his Christian subjects well:

ARTICLE IX

His Imperial Majesty the Sultan having, in his constant solicitude for the welfare of his subjects, issued a Firman, which, while ameliorating their condition without distinction of Religion or of Race, records his generous intentions towards the Christian population of his Empire, and wishing to give a further proof of his sentiments in that respect, has resolved to communicate to the Contracting Parties the said Firman, emanating spontaneously from his Sovereign will.

The Contracting Powers recognize the high value of this communication. It is clearly understood that it cannot, in any case, give to the said Powers the right to interfere, either collectively or separately in the relations of His Majesty the Sultan with his subjects, nor in the Internal Administration of his Empire.

Russia was compelled to accept demilitarization and neutralization of the Black Sea:

ARTICLE XI

The Black Sea is Neutralised; its Waters and its Ports, thrown open to the Mercantile Marine of every Nation, are formally and perpetuity interdicted to the Flag of War, either of the Powers possessing its Coasts, or of any other Power, with the exceptions mentioned in Articles XIV and XIX of the present Treaty.

ARTICLE XII

Free from any impediment, the Commerce in the Ports and Waters of the Black Sea shall be subject only to Regulations of Health, Customs, and Police, framed in a spirit favorable to the development of Commercial transactions.

In order to afford to the Commercial and Maritime interests of every Nation the security which is desired, Russia and the Sublime Porte will admit Consuls into their Ports situated upon the Coast of the Black Sea, in conformity with the principles of International Law.

ARTICLE XIII

The Black Sea being Neutralized according to the terms of Article XI, the maintenance or establishment upon its Coast of Military-Maritime Arsenals becomes alike unnecessary and purposeless; in consequence, His Majesty the Emperor of All the Russias, and His Imperial Majesty the Sultan, engage not to establish or to maintain upon that Coast any Military-Maritime Arsenal.

This had the effect of ensuring that Great Britain would continue to dominate the eastern Mediterranean.

By Article 20, Russia agreed to "rectification of [the] Frontier in Bessarabia":

The new Frontier shall begin from the Black Sea, one kilometer to the east of the Lake Bourna Sola, shall run perpendicularly to the Ackerman Road, shall follow that road to the Val de Trajan, pass to the south of Bolgrad, ascend the course of the River Yalpuck to the Height of Saratsika, and terminate at Katamori on the Pruth. Above that point the old Frontier between the Two Empires shall not undergo any modification.

Delegates of the Contracting Powers shall fix, in its details, the Line of the new Frontier.

ARTICLE XXI

The Territory ceded by Russia shall be Annexed to the Principality of Moldavia, under the Suzerainty of the Sublime Porte.

The Inhabitants of that Territory shall enjoy the Rights and Privileges secured to the Principalities; and during the space of 3 years, they shall be permitted to transfer their domicile elsewhere, disposing freely of their Property.

This cut off Russia's access to the important Danube River. Moreover, Russia renounced its claims to the exclusive protectorship over Balkan Christians and over the Danubian principalities and Serbia.

A convention subjoined to the treaty prohibited foreign warships in the Straits of the Dardanelles.

Convention between Great Britain, Austria, France, Prussia, Russia, and Sardinia, on the One Part, and the Sultan, on the Other Part, Respecting the Straits of the Dardanelles and of the Bosphorus.

Signed at Paris, 30th March, 1856

ARTICLE I

His Majesty the Sultan, on the one part, declares that he is firmly resolved to maintain for the future the principle invariably established as the ancient rule of his Empire, and in virtue of which it has, at all times, been prohibited for the Ships of War of Foreign Powers to enter the Straits of the Dardanelles and of the Bosphorus; and that, so long as the Porte is at Peace, His Majesty will admit no Foreign Ship of War into the said Straits.

And Their Majesties the Queen of the United Kingdom of Great Britain and Ireland, the Emperor of Austria, the Emperor of the French, the King of Prussia, the Emperor of All the Russias, and the King of Sardinia, on the other part, engage to respect this determination of the Sultan, and to conform themselves to the principle above.

ARTICLE II

The Sultan reserves to himself, as in past times, to deliver Firmans of Passage for Light Vessels under Flag of War, which shall be employed, as is usual in the service of the Missions of Foreign Powers.

ARTICLE III

The same exception applies to the Light Vessels under Flag of War, which each of the Contracting Powers is authorized to station at the Mouths of the Danube in order to secure the execution of the Regulations relative to the liberty of that River, and the number of which is not to exceed two for each Power.

Consequences

The Crimean War was a turning point in both Russian and European history. After the war, stymied in its traditional attempts to expand westward, Russia turned with renewed vigor toward its eastern frontiers. The emancipation of the serfs in 1861 only served to feed the movement, as landless Russian and Ukrainian peasants now migrated in large waves into Siberia and central Asia, somewhat resembling American settler migration into the trans-Mississippi West. As in the United States, a surge of industrialization, foreign trade, and railroad building not only stitched a vast country together but led to the colonization of an internal empire. Russia's eastward expansion led to opposition from native peoples. More severe troubles came as Russia vied with competitive colonizers in the Far East: Great Britain and Japan.

TREATY OF TIENTSIN

TREATY AT A GLANCE

Completed
June 26, 1858, at Tianjin (Tientsin), China

Signatories
Great Britain and China

Overview
The result of the Second Opium War, the treaty opened up more ports to the West, allowed foreign envoys to reside in Beijing, admitted missionaries to China, permitted foreigners to travel in the Chinese interior, and legalized the importation of opium.

Historical Background

The TREATY OF NANKING ended the First Opium War and resulted in the opening of several Chinese ports as well as the cession of Hong Kong to Great Britain. By 1856 the British (and the French) were restless for further trade concessions. In that year, Chinese officials seized the *Arrow*, a Chinese-owned ship flying the British flag and engaged in illegal opium trading. In response to the seizure, a combined English and French force attacked, occupying Guangzhou (Canton) by late 1857. Next the force took forts near Tianjin (Tientsin), and treaties were concluded between China and Britain as well as similar treaties between China and France, Russia, and the United States.

Terms

Articles 2–7 established full diplomatic relations between Britain and China:

II

For the better preservation of harmony in future, Her Majesty the Queen of Great Britain and His Majesty the Emperor of China mutually agree that, in accordance with the universal practice of great and friendly nations, Her Majesty the Queen, may, if she see fit, appoint ambassadors, ministers, or other diplomatic agents to the Court of Peking; and His Majesty the Emperor of China may, in like manner, if he see fit, appoint ambassadors, ministers, or other diplomatic agents to the Court of St. James.

III

His Majesty the Emperor of China hereby agrees that the ambassador, minister, or other diplomatic agent, so appointed by Her Majesty the Queen of Great Britain, may reside, with his family and establishment, permanently at the capital, or may visit it occasionally, at the option of the British Government. He shall not be called upon to perform any ceremony derogatory to him as representing the Sovereign of an independent nation on a footing of equality with that of China. On the other hand, he shall use the same forms of ceremony and respect to His Majesty the Emperor as are employed by the ambassadors, ministers, or diplomatic agents of Her Majesty towards the Sovereigns of independent and equal European nations.

It is further agreed, that Her Majesty's Government may acquire at Peking a site for building, or may hire houses for the accommodation of Her Majesty's Mission, and that the Chinese Government will assist it in so doing.

Her Majesty's Representative shall be at liberty to choose his own servants and attendants, who shall not be subjected to any kind of molestation whatever.

Any person guilty of disrespect or violence to Her Majesty's Representative, or to any member of his family or establishment, in deed or word, shall be severely punished.

IV

It is further agreed, that no obstacle or difficulty shall be made to the free movements of Her Majesty's Representative, and that he, and the persons of his suite, may come and go, and travel at their pleasure. He shall, moreover, have full liberty to send and receive his correspondence, to and from any point on the sea-coast that he may select; and his letters and effects shall be held sacred and inviolable. He may employ, for their transmission, special couriers, who shall meet with the same protection and facilities for travelling as the persons employed in carrying despatches for the

Imperial Government; and, generally, he shall enjoy the same privileges as are accorded to officers of the same rank by the usage and consent of Western nations.

All expenses attending the Diplomatic Mission of Great Britain in China shall be borne by the British Government.

V

His Majesty the Emperor of China agrees to nominate one of the Secretaries of State, or a President of one of the Boards, as the high officer with whom the ambassador, minister, or other diplomatic agent of Her Majesty the Queen shall transact business, either personally or in writing, on a footing of perfect equality.

VI

Her Majesty the Queen of Great Britain agrees that the privilege hereby secured shall be enjoyed in her dominions by the ambassadors, ministers, or diplomatic agents of the Emperor of China accredited to the Court of Her Majesty.

VII

Her Majesty the Queen may appoint one or more Consuls in the dominions of the Emperor of China; and such Consul or Consuls shall be at liberty to reside in any of the open ports or cities of China, as Her Majesty the Queen may consider most expedient for the interests of British commerce. They shall be treated with due respect by the Chinese authorities, and enjoy the same privileges and immunities as the Consular officers of the most favoured nation.

Consuls and Vice-Consuls in charge shall rank with Intendents of Circuits; Vice-Consuls, Acting Vice-Consuls, and Interpreters, with Prefects. They shall have access to the official residences of these officers, and communicate with them, either personally or in writing, on a footing of equality, as the interests of the public service may require.

Article 8 provided for the admission of Christian missionaries into China:

VIII

The Christian religion, as professed by Protestants or Roman Catholics, inculcates the practice of virtue, and teaches man to do as he would be done by. Persons teaching or professing it, therefore, shall alike be entitled to the protection of the Chinese authorities, nor shall any such, peaceably pursuing their calling, and not offending against the law, be persecuted or interfered with.

Article 9 broke down Chinese restrictions on travel in the interior:

IX

British subjects are hereby authorized to travel, for their pleasure or for purposes of trade, to all parts of the interior, under passports which will be issued by their Consuls, and countersigned by the local author-

ities. These passports, if demanded, must be produced for examination in the localities passed through. If the passport be not irregular, the bearer will be allowed to proceed, and no opposition shall be offered to his hiring persons or hiring vessels for the carriage of his baggage or merchandize. If he be without a passport, or if he commit any offence against the law, he shall be handed over to the nearest Consul for punishment; but he must not be subjected to any ill-usage in excess of necessary restraint. No passport need be applied for by persons going on excursions from the ports open to trade to a distance not exceeding 100 li and for a period not exceeding 5 days.

The provisions of this Article do not apply to crews of ships, for the due restraint of whom regulations will be drawn up by the Consul and the local authorities.

To Nanking, and other cities disturbed by persons in arms against the Government, no pass shall be given, until they shall have been recaptured.

The articles opening Chinese ports to Western trade also opened those cities to Western settlement:

XI

In addition to the cities and towns of Canton, Amoy, Fuchow, Ningpo, and Shanghai, opened by the Treaty of Nanking, it is agreed that British subjects may frequent the cities and ports of New-Chwang, Tang-Chow, Tai-Wan (Formosa), Chau-Chow (Swatow), and Kiung-Chow (Hainan).

They are permitted to carry on trade with whomsoever they please, and to proceed to and fro at pleasure with their vessels and merchandize.

They shall enjoy the same privileges, advantages, and immunities, at the said towns and ports, as they enjoy at the ports already opened to trade, including the right of residence, of buying or renting houses, of leasing land therein, and of building churches, hospitals, and cemeteries.

XII

British subjects, whether at the ports or at other places, desiring to build or open houses, warehouses, churches, hospitals, or burialgrounds, shall make their agreement for the land or buildings they require, as the rates prevailing among the people, equitably, and without exactions on either side.

XIII

The Chinese Government will place no restrictions whatever upon the employment, by British subjects, of Chinese subjects in any lawful capacity.

Yet, while the cities were thus forced open to British occupation, British residents were to be subject not to Chinese legal jurisdiction but to the jurisdiction of the British consulate:

XV

All questions in regard to rights, whether of property or person, arising between British subjects, shall be subject to the jurisdiction of the British authorities.

XVI

Chinese subjects who may be guilty of any criminal act toward British subjects shall be arrested and punished by the Chinese authorities, according to the laws of China.

British subjects who may commit any crime in China shall be tried and punished by the Consul, or other public functionary authorized thereto, according to the laws of Great Britain.

Justice shall be equitably and impartially administered on both sides.

The balance of the treaty established tariffs and other conditions of trade.

Consequences

The new treaties with the Western powers caused widespread outrage in China and failed to receive ratification. Foreign diplomats were refused entrance to Beijing, and a British force was slaughtered outside of Tianjing in 1859. A renewed Anglo-French assault captured Tianjing and defeated a Chinese army outside of Beijing. The Chinese emperor fled, and his commissioners concluded new treaties embodying the provisions of the Tientsin agreement and adding four more ports to the list of those now open to foreign trade.

TREATY OF VERSAILLES (1871)

TREATY AT A GLANCE

Completed
February 26, 1871, at Versailles, France

Signatories
Germany and France

Overview
The Treaty of Versailles was the preliminary peace treaty ending the Franco-Prussian War and marking the creation of a unified German empire, which had been proclaimed on January 18, 1871, in the very place at which the present treaty was signed, the Hall of Mirrors of the Palace of Versailles.

Historical Background

The Franco-Prussian War of 1870–71 was momentous for European civilization, bringing about the fall of the Second French Empire, providing the impetus to the creation of the German Empire, and figuring as the first modern European war, in which both combatant nations used railroads, the telegraph, modern rifles, and modern rifled, breech-loading artillery.

The nominal cause of the war was neither more nor less trivial than the causes of most European wars—in this case, the candidacy of a Hohenzollern prince for the Spanish throne. The deeper issue, however, was Prussia's growing power in Germany, which Emperor Napoleon III correctly saw as a threat to French security. For his part, Prussia's extraordinarily astute prime minister, Otto von Bismarck, deliberately exploited the issue of the Spanish succession to goad France into an act of war designed to frighten the south German states into joining the North German Confederation, organized in 1867 with Prussia the dominant member. On July 13, 1870, the Prussian king, who would become Kaiser Wilhelm I, sent a message to Napoleon III reporting a quite innocuous meeting with the French ambassador. Bismarck, edited this, the so-called Ems Telegram, to imply that the meeting had been an exchange of insults. In receipt of the telegram, the French course seemed either to accept a diplomatic defeat or to go to war.

With his government's prestige faltering at home, Napoleon III judged that he could ill afford to suffer an insult at the hands of Prussia, and he declared war on July 19, 1870. Unfortunately, Napoleon III had failed to consider that a military defeat was far worse than a diplomatic one. His armies were badly outnumbered and, even worse, outgeneraled. They quickly withdrew from the frontier—one army to Metz, where it was held under siege, and the other to Sedan, where it was quickly crushed. Napoleon III surrendered the army of Sedan as well as himself to Bismarck on September 2, 1870.

The humiliation of Sedan reached Paris two days later, and the Third Republic was proclaimed. In its name, the Government of National Defense carried on the war, or attempted to. From September 23 to January 28, Paris was besieged and then bombarded by German artillery. On January 28 the new government sued for peace, concluding an armistice that allowed France three weeks in which to elect a national assembly with authority to negotiate a peace in the name of France.

When the elections created an assembly overwhelmingly in favor of peace, the Treaty of Versailles was concluded.

Terms

The Versailles document was characterized by the legendary Prussia passion for efficiency. Without preamble, it began:

> ARTICLE I
> France renounces in favor of the German Empire all her Rights and Titles over the Territories situated on the East of the Frontier hereafter described.
>
> The Line of Demarcation begins at the Northwest Frontier of the Canton of Cattenom, towards the Grand Duchy of Luxembourg, follows on the South

the Western Frontiers of the Cantons of Cattenom and Thionville, passes by the Canton of Briey, along the Western Frontiers of the Communes of Montjois-la-Montagne and Roncourt, as well as the Eastern Frontiers of the Communes of Marie-aux-Chênes, St. Ail, Habonville, reaches the Frontier of the Canton de Gooze (which it crosses along the Communal Frontiers of Vionville, Bouxières, and Onville), follows the Southwest Frontier, south of the District of Metz, the Western Frontier of the District of Château-Salins, as far as the Commune of Pettoncourt, taking in the Western and Southern Frontiers thereof to follow the Crest of the Mountains between Seille and Moncel, as far as the Frontier of the District of Sarreburg, to the South of Garde. The demarcation afterwards coincides with the Frontier of that District as far as the Commune of Tanconville, reaching the Frontier to the North thereof, from thence it follows the Crest of the Mountains between the Sources of the White Sarre and Vezouze, as far as the Frontier of the Canton of Schirmeck, skirts the Western Frontier of that Canton, includes the Communes of Saales, Bourg-Bruche, Colroy-la-Rochet Plaine, Ranruptt-Saulxures, and St. Blaise-la-Roche of the Canton of Saales, and coincides with the Western Frontier of the Departments of the Lower Rhine and the Upper Rhine as far as the Canton of Belfort. The Southern Frontier of which it leaves not far from Vourvenans, to cross the Canton of Delle at the Southern Limits of the Communes of Bourogne and Froide Fontaine, and to reach the Swiss Frontier skirting the Eastern Frontiers of the Communes of Jonchery and Delle.

The German Empire shall possess these Territories in perpetuity in all Sovereignty and Property. An International Commission, composed of an equal number of Representatives of the two High Contracting Parties, shall be appointed immediately after the exchange of the Ratifications of the present Treaty, to trace on the spot the new Frontier, in conformity with the preceding stipulations.

This Commission shall preside over the Division of the Lands and Funds, which have hitherto belonged to Districts or Communes divided by the new Frontiers; in case of disagreement in the tracing and the measures of execution, the Members of the Commission shall refer to their respective Governments.

The Frontier, such as it has just been described, is marked in green on two identical copies of the Map of the Territory forming the Government of Alsace, published at Berlin in September 1870, by the Geographical and Statistical Division of the Staff, and a copy of which shall be annexed to both copies of the present Treaty.

Nevertheless, the alteration of the above tracing has been agreed to by the two Contracting Parties. In the former Department of the Moselle, the Villages of Marie-aux-Chenes near St. Privat-la-Montagne, and Vionville to the west of Rezonville, shall be ceded to Germany. In exchange thereof, France shall retain the Town and Fortifications of Belfort, with a Radius which shall be hereafter determined upon.

In addition to ceding Alsace and much of Lorraine to Germany, France agreed to pay an indemnity of unprecedented proportions: 5 billion francs (Article 2). Article 7 provided for negotiations toward a "Definitive Treaty of Peace," which resulted in the TREATY OF FRANKFURT:

ARTICLE VII

The opening of negotiations for the Definitive Treaty of Peace to be concluded on the Basis of the present Preliminaries shall take place at Brussels, immediately after the Ratification of the latter by the National Assembly and by His Majesty the Emperor of Germany.

Consequences

The treaty marked the coming to prominence of one of the greatest diplomats in European history, Otto von Bismarck, who would go on over the course of the next 20 years virtually to create modern Europe. More immediately, having succeeded by the war in persuading all the German rulers to join together in forming a new German Empire under Kaiser Wilhelm I, Bismarck declared the new empire from the Hall of Mirrors in the Palace of Versailles on January 18, 1871. The empire would thrive and expand until Germany's defeat in World War I.

TREATY OF FRANKFURT

TREATY AT A GLANCE

Completed
May 10, 1871, at Frankfurt, Germany

Signatories
Germany and France

Overview
This, the definitive treaty of peace ending the Franco-Prussian War—based on the preliminary treaty, the TREATY OF VERSAILLES (1871)—gave birth to the French Third Republic and a unified Germany, Otto von Bismarck's new German Empire.

Historical Background

In 1866 Prussian premier Otto von Bismarck ignored the objections of his king, Wilhelm I, and provoked a war within the aging German Confederation in order to overcome Austria's dominance of the league and unite the German states under Prussian hegemony. By occupying the duchy of Holstein, then administered by Austria, Bismarck sparked the so-called Seven Weeks' War, which pitted Austria and its allies—Württemberg, Saxony, Hanover, Baden, and a host of smaller German states—against the military-minded Prussians and their ally, Italy. Bismarck won, and in a peace mediated by France's Napoleon III, Austria was excluded from German affairs, Prussia took hold of Schleswig-Holstein, Hanover, Hesse, Nassau, and Frankfurt, and the old confederation was replaced by the new North German Confederation.

Bismarck immediately began to work on bringing the still independent southern German states into the North German Confederation, which, despite Napoleon III's midwifery, was virulently anti-French. When the Prussians tried to put a Hohenzollern prince related to the Prussian kaiser on the Spanish throne in 1870, the Emperor Napoleon felt the pressure of a possible Prussian-Spanish two-front war looming in his future, and he called a summit with Kaiser Wilhelm to discuss the matter, which Bismarck torpedoed with his infamous Ems Telegram. French-German relations ruptured, and Napoleon—having been assured the French army was invincible and believing a sure victory would destroy his declining prestige at home—declared the war Bismarck wanted on July 19, 1870.

It was another of the brief, brutal wars Bismarck liked to fight, although not so short as the 1866 conflict. Personally humiliated by defeat at Sedan on September 2, where he led the last vain charge before surrendering, Napoleon was deposed by a French provisional government set up in a Paris besieged by Bismarck's army. In January 1871 Paris fell, though fighting continued between the two armies in the French provinces until an armistice was declared in March. The peace, delayed by the outbreak of civil war in France, was not concluded till May, although an interim Treaty of Versailles was concluded.

Bismarck had what he wanted, as the North German Confederation was declared the German—read "Prussian"—Empire.

Terms

Under the Treaty of Frankfurt, France lost Alsace and much of Lorraine, incurred a massive indemnity of 5,000,000,000 francs, and saw the birth of the Third Republic from the ruins of Napoleon III's Second Empire, while Prussia became the center of a new, unified Germany.

As with the Treaty of Versailles (1871), the Frankfurt document began without preamble, plunging instead directly into the matter of redefining the Franco-German frontier:

ARTICLE I
The distance between the Town of Belfort and the Line of Frontier, such as it had been proposed during the negotiations of Versailles, and such as it is marked on the Map annexed to the Ratifications of the

Preliminaries of the 26th February, is considered as describing the Radius which, by virtue of the Clause relating thereto in Article I of the Preliminaries, is to remain to France with the Town and Fortifications of Belfort.

The German Government is disposed to extend that Radius so as to include the Cantons of Belfort, Delle, and Giromagny, as well as the western part of the Canton of Fontaine, to the West of a line to be traced from the spot where the Canal from the Rhone to the Rhine leaves the Canton of Delle to the South of Montreux-Château, to the Northern Limits of the Canton between Bourg and Félon where that Line would join the Eastern Limit of the Canton of Giromagny.

The German Government will, nevertheless, not cede the above Territories unless the French Republic agrees, on its part, to a rectification of Frontier along the Western Limits of the Cantons of Cattenom and Thionville which will give to Germany the Territory to the East of a Line starting from the Frontier of Luxembourg between Hussigny and Redingen, leaving to France the Villages of Thil and Villerupt, extending between Erronville and Aumetz, between Beuvillers and Boulange, between Triux and Lomringen, and joining the ancient Line of Frontier between Avril and Moyeuvre.

The International Commission, mentioned in Article I of the Preliminaries, shall proceed to the spot immediately after the Ratifications of the present Treaty to execute the Works entrusted to them and to trace the new Frontier, in accordance with the preceding dispositions.

Careful provision was made for French residents of the ceded territories, allowing any who wished, to move to France proper, without sacrificing their real property and without being accused of evading Prussian conscription laws:

ARTICLE II

French Subjects, Natives of the ceded Territories, actually domiciled on that Territory, who shall preserve their Nationality, shall up to the 1st October, 1872, and on their making a previous Declaration to that effect to the Competent Authority, be allowed to change their domicile into France and to remain there, that right in nowise infringing on the Laws on Military Service, in which case the title of French Citizen shall be maintained.

They shall be at liberty to preserve their Immovables situated in the Territory united to Germany.

No Inhabitant of the ceded Territory shall be prosecuted, annoyed, or sought for, either in his person or his property, on account of his Political or Military Acts previous to the War.

Article 7 spelled out the humiliating terms by which the French agreed to pay the unprecedented indemnity. Payment was tied to the process of evacuating the occupying German troops:

ARTICLE VII

The payment of 500,000,000 (1/2 milliard) shall be made within 30 days after the re-establishment of the Authority of the French Government in the City of Paris. 1,000,000,000 (1 milliard) shall be paid in the course of the year, and 500,000,000 (1/2 milliard) on the 1st May, 1872. The last 3,000,000,000 (3 milliards) shall remain payable on the 2nd March, 1874, as stipulated in the Preliminary Treaty. From the 2nd March of the present year the Interest on those 3,000,000,000 francs (3 milliards) shall be paid each year on the 3rd March, at the rate of 5 per cent. per annum.

All sums paid in advance on the last 3,000,000,000 shall cease to bear Interest from the day on which the payment is made.

The payment can only be made in the principal German Commercial Towns, and shall be made in metal, Gold or Silver, in Notes of the Bank of England, in Prussian Bank Notes, in Netherlands Bank Notes, in Notes of the National Bank of Belgium, in first class Negotiable Bills to Order or Letters of Exchange, payable at sight.

The German Government having fixed in France the value of a Prussian Thaler at 3 francs 75 centimes, the French Government accepts the conversion of the Moneys of both Countries at the rate above stated.

The French Government will inform the German Government, 3 months in advance, of all payments which it intends to make into the Treasury of the German Empire.

After the payment of the first 500,000,000 (1/2 milliard) and the Ratification of the Definitive Treaty of Peace, the Departments of the Somme, Seine Inférieure, and Eure shall be evacuated in so far as they shall be found to be still occupied by German Troops. The Evacuation of the Departments of the Oise, Seine-et-Oise, Seine-et-Marne, and Seine, as well as the Forts of Paris, shall take place so soon as the German Government shall consider the reestablishment of Order, both in France and Paris, sufficient to ensure the execution of the Engagements contracted by France.

Under all circumstances, the Evacuation shall take place after the payment of the third 500,000,000 (1/2 milliard).

The German Troops, for their own security, shall have at their disposal the Neutral Zone between the German line of Demarcation and the Paris enclosure on the Right Bank of the Seine.

The stipulations of the Treaty of 26th February relative to the occupation of French Territories after the payment of the 2,000,000,000 (2 milliards), shall remain in force. None of the deductions which the French Government might have a right to make shall be made on the payment of the first 500,000,000 (1/2 milliard).

The treaty went on to establish certain commercial as well as spiritual rights. For example, as specified in Article 12:

ARTICLE XII

All expelled Germans shall preserve the full and entire enjoyment of all Property which they may have acquired in France.

Such Germans who had obtained the authority required by French Laws to establish their Domicile in France shall be reinstated in all their Rights, and may consequently again establish their Domicile in French Territory.

The delay stipulated by French Laws to obtain Naturalization shall be considered as not having been interrupted by the state of War for persons who shall take advantage of the above-mentioned facility of returning to France within 6 months after the exchange of the Ratifications of this Treaty, and the time which has elapsed between their expulsion and their return to the French Territory shall be taken into account, as if they had never ceased to reside in France.

The above conditions shall be applicable in perfect reciprocity to the French Subjects residing, or wishing to reside, in Germany.

By Article 16, the two governments pledged to "respect and preserve the Tombs of Soldiers buried in their respective Territories." In Article 2 of "Additional Articles" appended to the treaty, the German government offered 2 million francs "for the rights and properties possessed by the Company of the eastern Railways on that portion of its system situated on Swiss territory from the frontier at Bâle, provided that the French Government signifies its consent within a period of one month."

Consequences

With the Treaty of Frankfurt, Bismarck declared the new German Empire a satisfied power, and he placed his not inconsiderable diplomatic talents at the service of European stability. Here, too, he would prove successful, and peace among the major powers of Europe, with a France free of Napoleon no longer dominant, would last until the outbreak of the Great War in 1914. So, too, would the empire.

TREATY OF SAN STEFANO

TREATY AT A GLANCE

Completed
March 3 (February 19 old style), 1878, at San Stefano
(present-day Yesilkoy, Turkey)

Signatories
Russia and Ottoman Empire (Turkey)

Overview
After suffering a setback in its control over the Ottoman Empire's Balkan possessions as a result of the Crimean War, Russia fought a new war with Turkey in 1877-78, forcing a peace that created a large Bulgarian state dominated by Russia.

Historical Background

In the Serbo-Turkish War of 1876–77, Russia aided the Serbian rebels, who nevertheless failed to cast off the Ottoman yoke, which included suppression of Orthodox Christians. Russia declared war on the Ottoman Empire on April 24, 1877, and was joined by Romania (a union of the former principalities Moldavia and Walachia). The Russians suffered initial reverses but captured the Shipka Pass and Plevna in the Balkans in 1877 and the Turkish fortress of Kars, in the Caucasus, on November 18, 1877, then laid siege to Erzurum. By the beginning of 1878, a Russian army was just outside the Ottoman capital, Constantinople (Istanbul). This brought the Turks to the negotiating table, which eventuated in the San Stefano treaty.

Terms

The most critical articles of the treaty were those relating to Bulgaria:

ARTICLE VI

Bulgaria is constituted an autonomous tributary Principality, with a Christian Government and a national militia.

The definitive frontiers of the Bulgarian Principality will be traced by a special Russo-Turkish Commission before the evacuation of Roumelia by the Imperial Russian army.

This Commission will, in working out the modifications to be made on the spot in the general tracing, take into account the principle of the nationality of the majority of the inhabitants of the border districts, conformably to the Bases of Peace, and also the topographical necessities and practical interests of the intercommunication of the local population.

The extent on the Bulgarian Principality is laid down in general terms on the accompanying map, which will serve as a basis for the definitive fixing of the limits. Leaving the new frontier of the Servian [Serbian] Principality, the line will follow the western limit of the Caza of Wrania as far as the chain of the Kara-dagh. Turning towards the west, the line will follow the western limits of the Cazas of Koumanovo, Kotchani, Kalkandelen, to Mount Korab; thence by the River Welestchitza as far as its junction with the black Drina. Turning towards the south by the Drina, and afterwards by the western limit of the Caza of Orchride towards Mount Linas, the frontier will follow the western limits of the Cazas of Gortcha and Starovo as far as Mount Grammos. Then by the Lake of Kastoria, the frontier line will rejoin the River Moglenitza, and after having followed its course, and passed to the south of Yanitza (Warder Venidje), will go by the mouth of the Warder and by the Galliko towards the villages of Parga and of Sarai-keui; thence through the middle of Lake Bechik-Guel to the mouth of the Rivers Strouma and Karassou, and by the sea-coast as far as Buru-Guel; thence striking northwest towards Mount Tchaltepe by the chain of Rhodope as far as Mount Krouschowo, by the Black Balkans (Kara-Balkan), by the mountains Eschekkoulatchi, Tchepelion, Karakolas, and Tschiklar, as far as the River Arda.

Thence the line will be traced in the direction of the town of Tchirmen, and leaving the town of Adrianople to the south, by the villages of Sugutlion, Kara-Hamza, Aronaut-keui, Akardji, and Enidje as far as the River Tekederessi. Following the Rivers Tekederessi and Tchorlouderessi as far as Loule-Bourgaz, and thence, by the River Soudjakdere as far as the village of Serguen, the frontier line will go by the heights straight towards Hakimtabissai, where it will strike the Black Sea. It will leave the sea-coast near Mangalia, following the southern boundaries of the Sandjak of Toultcha, and will come out on the Danube above Rassova.

ARTICLE VII

The Prince of Bulgaria shall be freely elected by the population and confirmed by the Sublime Porte, with the assent of the Powers. No member of the reigning dynasties of the great European Powers shall be capable of being elected Prince of Bulgaria.

In the event of the dignity of Prince of Bulgaria being vacant, the election of the new Prince shall be made subject to the same conditions and forms.

Before the election of the Prince, an Assembly of Bulgarian Notables, to be convoked at Philippopolis (Plowdiw) or Tyrnowo, shall draw up, under the superintendence of an Imperial Russian Commissioner, and in the presence of an Ottoman Commissioner, the organization of the future administration, in conformity with the precedents established in 1830 after the Peace of Adrianople, in the Danubian Principalities.

In the localities where Bulgarians are mixed with Turks, Greeks, Wallachians (Koutzo-Vlachs), or others, proper account is to be taken of the rights and interests of these populations in the elections and in the preparation of the Organic Laws.

The introduction of the new system into Bulgaria, and the superintendence of its working, will be intrusted for two years to an Imperial Russian Commissioner. At the expiration of the first year after the introduction of the new system, and if an understanding on this subject has been established between Russia, the Sublime Porte, and the Cabinets of Europe, they can, if it is deemed necessary, associate Special Delegates with the Imperial Russian Commissioner.

ARTICLE VIII

The Ottoman army will no longer remain in Bulgaria, and all the ancient fortresses will be razed at the expense of the local Government. The Sublime Porte will have the right to dispose, as it sees fit, of the war material and of the other property belonging to the Ottoman Government which may have been left in the Danubian fortresses already evacuated in accordance with the terms of the Armistice of the 19th [old style] 31st [new style] January, as well as of that in the strongholds of Schoumla and Varna.

Until the complete formation of a native militia sufficient to preserve order, security, and tranquillity, and the strength of which will be fixed later on by an understanding between the Ottoman Government and the Imperial Russian Cabinet, Russian troops will occupy the country, and will give armed assistance to the Commissioner in case of need. This occupation will also be limited to a term approximating to two years.

The strength of the Russian army of occupation to be composed of six divisions of infantry and two of cavalry, which will remain in Bulgaria after the evacuation of Turkey by the Imperial army, shall not exceed 50,000 men. It will be maintained at the expense of the country occupied. The Russian troops of occupation in Bulgaria will maintain their communications with Russia, not only through Roumania, but also by the ports of the Black Sea, Varna, and Bourgas, where they may organize, for the term of the occupation, the necessary depots.

ARTICLE IX

The amount of the annual tribute which Bulgaria is to pay the Suzerain Court, by transmitting it to a bank to be hereafter named by the Sublime Porte, will be determined by an agreement between Russia, the Ottoman Government, and the other Cabinets, at the end of the first year during which the new organization shall be in operation. This tribute will be calculated on the average revenue of all the territory which is to form part of the Principality.

Bulgaria will take upon itself the obligations of the Imperial Ottoman Government towards the Rustchuk and Varna Railway Company, after an agreement has been come to between the Sublime Porte, the Government of the Principality, and the Directors of this Company. The regulations as to the other railways (*voies ferrées*) which cross the Principality are also reserved for an agreement between the Sublime Porte, the Government established in Bulgaria, and the Directors of the Companies concerned.

ARTICLE X

The Sublime Porte shall have the right to make use of Bulgaria for the transport by fixed routes of its troops, munitions, and provisions to the provinces beyond the Principality, and *vice versa*. In order to avoid difficulties and misunderstandings in the application of this right, while guaranteeing the military necessities of the Sublime Porte, a special regulation will lay down the conditions of it within three months after the ratification of the present Act by an understanding between the Sublime Porte and the Bulgarian Government.

It is fully understood that this right is limited to the regular Ottoman troops, and that the irregulars, the Bashi-Bazouks, and the Circassians will be absolutely excluded from it.

The Sublime Porte also reserves to itself the right of sending its postal service through the Principality, and of maintaining telegraphic communication. These two points shall also be determined in the manner and within the period of time indicated above.

ARTICLE XI

The Mussulman proprietors or others who fix their personal residence outside the Principality may retain their estates by having them farmed or administered by others. Turco-Bulgarian Commissions shall sit in the principal centres of population, under the superintendence of Russian Commissioners to decide absolutely in the course of two years all questions relative to the verification of real property, in which either Mussulmans or others may be interested. Similar commissions will be charged with the duty of regulating within two years all questions relative to the mode of alienation, working, or use for the benefit of the Sublime Porte of the property of the State, and of the religious endowments (*Vacouf*).

At the expiration of the two years mentioned above, all properties which shall not have been claimed shall be sold by public auction, and the proceeds thereof shall be devoted to the support of the widows and orphans, Mussulman as well as Christian, victims of the recent events.

Consequences

An enlarged Bulgaria became a semiautonomous state under Russian authority, while Romania and Serbia, their own territories also enlarged by the treaty, gained independence. The rest of Europe moved quickly to block Russia's growing influence in the Balkans, and most of its "gains" in the current negotiations were soon greatly abridged by the TREATY OF BERLIN, concluded later in the year. The Balkans were quickly becoming that hotbed of international intrigue and Great Power competition that would ultimately erupt into world war.

TREATY OF SHIMONOSEKI

<table>
<tr><td>

TREATY AT A GLANCE

Completed
April 17, 1895, at Shimonoseki, Japan

Signatories
China and Japan

Overview
The treaty ended the Sino-Japanese War of 1894–95, victory in which brought Japan Taiwan, P'eng-hu (the Pescadores), and the Liaodong Peninsula of southern Manchuria, in addition to a large monetary indemnity.

</td></tr>
</table>

Historical Background

The Sino-Japanese War was the military culmination of Japan's emergence as a world power during the Meiji period. The origin of the war was rivalry for control of Korea. Earlier, in 1876, Japan compelled Korea to assert independence from Chinese suzerainty by opening itself to foreign trade. China responded with measures intended to check growing Japanese influence in Korea. Tensions mounted, and in 1894 Korea rebelled against its Chinese overlords. Both China and Japan sent troops into Korea. The war, which commenced on August 1, 1894, was brief, as the small but efficiently Westernized Japanese army made short work of the numerically superior Chinese forces.

China capitulated and signed the Treaty of Shimonoseki.

Terms

The treaty recognized Korean independence and ceded Taiwan, P'eng-hu (the Pescadores), and the Liaodong Peninsula of Manchuria to Japan. China's major concessions were addressed in the first four articles:

ARTICLE I

China recognizes definitively the full and complete independence and autonomy of Korea, and in consequence, the payment of tribute and the performance of ceremonies and formalities by Korea to China in derogation of such independence and autonomy, shall wholly cease for the future.

ARTICLE II

China cedes to Japan in perpetuity and full sovereignty the following territories together with all fortifications, arsenals and public property thereon:

(1) The southern portion of the Province of Fêng-Tien within the following boundaries:

The line of demarcation begins at the mouth of the River Yalu and ascends that stream to the mouth of the River An-ping; from thence the line runs to Fêng-Huang; from thence to Hai-Cheng, from thence to Ying-Kow, forming a line which describes the southern portion of the territory. The places above named are included in the ceded territory. When the line reaches the River Liao at Ying-Kow it follows the course of that stream to its mouth where it terminates. The mid-channel of the River Liao shall be taken as the line of demarcation.

This cession also includes all Islands appertaining or belonging to the Province of Fêng-Tien situated in the eastern portion of the Bay of Liao-Tung and in the northern part of the Yellow Sea.

(2) The Island of Formosa together with all Islands appertaining or belonging to the said Island of Formosa.

(3) The Pescadores Group, that is to say, all Islands lying between the 119th and 120th degrees of longitude east of Greenwich and the 23rd and 24th degrees of north latitude.

ARTICLE III

The alignments of the frontiers described in the preceding Article and shown on the annexed Map shall be subject to verification and demarcation on the spot, by a Joint Commission of Delimitation, consisting of two or more Japanese and two or more Chinese Delegates to be appointed immediately after the exchange of the ratifications of this Act. In case the boundaries laid down in this Act are found to be defective at any point, either on account of topography or in consideration of good administration, it shall also be the duty of the Delimitation Commission to rectify the same.

The Delimitation Commission will enter upon its duties as soon as possible and will bring its labors to a conclusion within the period of one year after appointment.

The alignments laid down in this Act shall, however, be maintained until the rectifications of the Delimitation Commission, if any are made, shall have received the approval of the Governments of Japan and China.

ARTICLE IV

China agrees to pay to Japan as a war indemnity the sum of 200,000,000 Kuping Taels. The said sum to be paid in eight instalments. The first instalment of 50,000,000 taels to be paid within six months, and the second instalment of 50,000,000 taels to be paid within twelve months, after the exchange of the ratifications of this Act. The remaining sum to be paid in six equal annual instalments as follows: The first of such equal annual instalments to be paid within two years; the second within three years; the third within four years; the fourth within five years; the fifth within six years, and the sixth within seven years, after the exchange of the ratifications of this Act. Interest at the rate of 5 per centum per annum shall begin to run on all unpaid portions of the said indemnity from the date the first instalment falls due.

China shall, however, have the right to pay by anticipation at any time any or all of said instalments. In case the whole amount of the said indemnity is paid within three years after the exchange of the ratifications of the present Act, all interest shall be waived and the interest for two years and a half or for any less period, if then already paid, shall be included as a part of the principal amount of the indemnity.

Consequences

The Japanese presence in Manchuria put Japan at odds with Russia, which enlisted the support of France and Germany in pressuring Japan to return Liaodong to China. After Japan restored possession of the peninsula, it leased it from China, together with other rights in Manchuria, and thereby maintained a Japanese presence there. Still, Japan was never reconciled to having given up Liaodong and would fight the Russo-Japanese War of 1904–05 in part to regain it.

TREATY OF ADDIS ABABA

TREATY AT A GLANCE

Completed
October 26, 1896, at Addis Ababa, Ethiopia

Signatories
Italy and Ethiopia

Overview
Italy lost its bid for imperialist control over Ethiopia when it suffered defeat in the Italo-Ethiopian War of 1895-96. This treaty restricted Italian activity in Ethiopia to the coastal trading areas only.

Historical Background

Italy established a presence on Ethiopia's Red Sea coastline at Massawa (Mitsiwa) in Eritrea in 1885 and also at the Eritrean port of Aseb. However, Italy wished to penetrate inland and began to do so with the aid and encouragement of the British. Ethiopian emperor Yohannes IV marched against the Italians, killing 500 at the Battle of Dogali on January 26, 1887. In response, Italy dispatched a large force of 20,000 men in a war that technically lasted from 1887 to 1889 but which saw little fighting, though much suffering from dysentery and fever. When Yohannes was killed by Muslim extremists (Mahdists) at the Battle of Metemma (Gallabat) on March 12, 1889, the Italians backed the ascension of tribal chieftain Menelik II to the throne and negotiated the Treaty of Uccialli with him on May 2, 1889.

As the Italians understood this treaty, Italy was given a protectorate over Ethiopia. In 1891, however, Menelik rejected this as a misinterpretation of the text. Great Britain, desirous of an Italian presence in the volatile region, recognized the protectorate. Tensions mounted, finally resulting in the Italo-Ethiopian War of 1895–96 when in 1895 the Italians occupied the district of Tigre. Menelik attacked a force of 2,400 Italians at Mekele, compelling their surrender. Italy then dispatched 20,000 men against approximately 80,000 Ethiopians at the Battle of Aduwa on March 1, 1896, and suffered a defeat so disastrous that they immediately sued for peace.

Terms

By the Treaty of Addis Ababa, Italy formally recognized Ethiopia's independence but was permitted to retain a small coastal colony in Eritrea. The Addis Ababa treaty was brief.

In the name of the Sainted Trinity

His Majesty Humbert [Umberto] I, King of Italy, and His Majesty Menilek II, Emperor of Ethiopia, wishing to end the war and resume their old friendship have agreed on the following Treaty.

To conclude this Treaty, His Majesty, the King of Italy delegated as his Plenipotentiary, Major Cesare Nerazzini, *Chevalier des Saints Maurice et Lazare, Officier de la Couronne d'Italie.* Major Nerazzini's authority having been duly authorized, His Excellency Major Nerazzini, in the name of His Majesty the King of Italy, and His Majesty, Menilek II, Emperor of Ethiopia and of the Galla countries in his own name, agreed on and concluded the following acts:

ARTICLE I

The state of war between Italy and Ethiopia has definitely been ended. Consequently perpetual peace and friendship shall be maintained between His Majesty, the King of Italy and His Majesty, the King of Ethiopia as it shall by their successors and subjects.

ARTICLE II

The Treaty concluded at Outchale, the 25th of *Miazia*, 1881 [corresponding to the 2nd of May, 1889] is and remains permanently annulled, as are its clauses.

ARTICLE III

Italy recognizes without reserve the absolute independence of the Ethiopian Empire as a sovereign and independent state.

ARTICLE IV

Since the two negotiating powers have not been able to agree on the question of frontiers, and since they wish to call a truce and establish peace without delay, thus assuring their respective countries the benefits of peace, it has been decided that within a year's delay, beginning as of this day, trusted delegates of both His Majesty, the King of Italy and His Majesty, the Emperor of Ethiopia, shall establish definite frontiers in the spirit of friendly talks. Until these frontiers are definitely fixed and agreed upon, the two Contracting Parties agree to observe the *status quo ante*. Each Party shall strictly refrain from crossing the provisory frontier which shall be determined by the flow of the Mareb, Belessa and Mouna Rivers.

ARTICLE V

Until the Italian and Ethiopian governments have established in common accord their definite boundaries, the Italian government pledges not to cede any or part thereof of the territory in question to any other Powers. Should the Italian government wish to abandon of its own free will any part of the territory it now holds, it would give said territory to Ethiopia.

ARTICLE VI

Pursuant to a goal favoring commercial and industrial relations between Italy and Ethiopia, subsequent agreements can be negotiated between the two governments.

ARTICLE VII

The present Treaty shall be made known to all other Powers and this task entrusted to the care of the two contracting Powers.

ARTICLE VIII

The present Treaty shall be ratified by the Italian government within three months, starting as of this day.

ARTICLE IX

The present Peace Treaty, concluded on this day shall be written in *Amharigna* and in French, both texts being identical in language and content, submitted in duplicate and signed by both Parties. One document shall remain in the possession of His Majesty, the King of Italy, and the other in the hands of His Majesty, the Emperor of Ethiopia.

Being in complete accord on the terms of this Treaty, His Majesty Menilek II, Emperor of Ethiopia, in his own name and His Excellency, Major Nerazzini, Emissary for His Majesty, the King of Italy, have approved and signed it.

Done in Addis Ababa, the 17th *Tekemt*, 1889 (corresponding to the 26th of October 1896).

[L.S.] MAJOR CESARE NERAZZINI
Plenipotentiary Emissary of His Majesty, the King of Italy

(signed by His Majesty, the Emperor Menelik II)

Ratified by His Majesty—Rome, 6th of January, 1897.
Sent to Parliament—24th of May, 1897.

AGREEMENT BETWEEN ITALY AND ETHIOPIA
FOR THE EXCHANGE OF PRISONERS,
SIGNED AT ADDIS ABABA, OCTOBER 26, 1896.

In the name of the Sainted Trinity.

The present agreement was drawn up and agreed upon between His Majesty Menilek II, Emperor of Ethiopia and the Galla countries and His Excellency, Plenipotentiary Envoy of His Majesty Humbert I, King of Italy, Major Cesare Nerazzini:

ARTICLE I

As a result of the Peace Treaty signed on this day between the Kingdom of Italy and the Ethiopian Empire, the Italian prisoners of war held in Ethiopia are thereby set free. His Majesty, the Emperor of Ethiopia pledges to bring them together without delay and transfer them to Harar where they shall be entrusted to the care of the Italian government Plenipotentiary Envoy as soon as the Peace Treaty is ratified.

ARTICLE II

In order to facilitate the repatriation of these war prisoners, and assure them all the necessary comforts, His Majesty, the Emperor of Ethiopia shall authorize a detachment from the Italian Red Cross to come to Gueldessa to meet with the prisoners.

ARTICLE III

His Majesty, the King of Italy's Plenipotentiary Envoy recognizing that these prisoners were receiving the greatest care and attention resulting from His Majesty, the Emperor of Ethiopia's solicitude in the matter of their repatriation, and that these proceedings were costly to the Ethiopian government, reworded the facts and let it be known that the Italian government would undertake to reimburse the Ethiopian government for all monies expended in this connection.

His Majesty, the Emperor of Ethiopia shall rely on the fairness of the Italian government in dealing with the question of compensation for their sacrifices and inconveniences.

Thus in good faith, His Majesty, the Emperor of Ethiopia, in his own name, and His Excellency, Major Cesare Nerazzini, for His Majesty the King of Italy, have approved, signed and sealed this present agreement.

Consequences

In 1900 Italy ceded most of the rest of its Eritrean colony and was left with a mere 80 square miles of Ethiopian territory. This humiliation would fester into the 1930s, when Benito Mussolini exacted a terrible vengeance against the African nation in the Italo-Ethiopian War of 1935–36, one of several preludes to World War II.

TREATY OF PARIS (1898)

TREATY AT A GLANCE

Completed
December 10, 1898, at Paris

Signatories
United States and Spain

Overview
The treaty ended the Spanish-American War, resulting in Spain's granting Cuba its independence and ceding to the United States Puerto Rico, Guam, and the Philippine Islands. The treaty marked the emergence of the United States as an imperialist power.

Historical Background

Although by no means unanimous, the prevailing sentiment in the United States during the closing decade of the 19th century was expansionist, and with the Native American population now subjugated on the continent, the only avenues to expansion lay offshore. When Cuban nationalists began a revolt against the repressive Spanish colonial government after 1895, and the island's military governor, General Valeriano Weyler, herded thousands of civilians into concentration camps (where many died of disease), U.S. expansionism found an urgent and noble reason to intervene on the island. The powerful publisher of the *New York Journal*, William Randolph Hearst, and others called for the annexation of Cuba by the United States, and Hearst obtained and published a private letter from the Spanish minister to the United States insultingly critical of President McKinley.

With the powder keg duly packed, all that was wanting was a match. That came on February 15, 1898, when the American battleship *Maine* exploded in Havana harbor, killing 266 sailors. A rapidly convened naval court of inquiry concluded that the ship had hit a Spanish mine (modern analysts believe that it was the ship's powder magazine that caused the disaster), and a public outcry of "Remember the Maine!" arose.

Spain, which was not eager for war, accelerated efforts to withdraw from Cuba without compromising its honor. However, on April 11, 1898, President McKinley yielded to public pressure and effectively requested a declaration of war, which Congress passed on April 25. The ensuing war was brief—10 weeks—and decisive, the Spanish proving far less for-

midable an enemy than the yellow fever endemic to the island of Cuba.

Commodore George Dewey steamed his Pacific Squadron to the Philippines, where on May 1 he handily demolished the obsolescent Spanish fleet as it lay at anchor. Reinforced by U.S. land forces, Dewey next besieged the Spanish garrison in Manila, capturing the city on August 13. In the meantime, the navy seized Spanish Guam as well as previously unclaimed Wake Island, and Congress acted to annex Hawaii.

In the Caribbean, Spanish warships slipped into the safety of the harbor of Santiago de Cuba, where, however, they were blockaded by the U.S. Navy in May. American troops landed in Cuba late in June (including such volunteer regiments as Theodore Roosevelt's Rough Riders) and won victories at the battles of El Caney and San Juan Hill (July 1). The Spanish admiral Pasqual Cervera attempted on July 3 to break out of the blockade holding his ships. Within four hours, most of his outnumbered and outgunned fleet was sunk. On July 17, the city of Santiago and Cuba's 24,000 Spanish troops surrendered, and Spain sued for peace nine days later. A protocol embodying the terms for peace was concluded on August 12, 1898, and the Treaty of Paris was signed on December 10.

Terms

Moral objections to outright expansionism had produced the Teller Amendment to the declaration of war, forbidding the annexation of Cuba. Therefore, the United States did not seek in the negotiations to annex Cuba, which Spain relinquished by Article 1:

ARTICLE I

Spain relinquishes all claim of sovereignty over and title to Cuba. And as the island is, upon its evacuation by Spain, to be occupied by the United States, the United States will, so long as such occupation shall last, assume and discharge the obligations that may under international law result from the fact of its occupation, for the protection of life and property.

However, at the insistence of President McKinley, United States negotiators secured Spanish cession of Puerto Rico, Guam, and the Philippine Islands:

ARTICLE II

Spain cedes to the United States the island of Porto Rico and other islands now under Spanish sovereignty in the West Indies, and the island of Guam in the Marianas or Ladrones.

ARTICLE III

Spain cedes to the United States the archipelago known as the Philippine Islands, and comprehending the islands lying within the following lines:

A line running from west to east along or near the twentieth parallel of north latitude, and through the middle of the navigable channel of Bachi, from the one hundred and eighteenth (118th) to the one hundred and twenty seventh (127th) degree meridian of longitude east of Greenwich, thence along the one hundred and twenty seventh (127th) degree meridian of longitude east of Greenwich to the parallel of four degrees and forty five minutes (4° 45') north latitude, thence along the parallel of four degrees and forty five minutes (4° 45') north latitude to its intersection with the meridian of longitude one hundred and nineteen degrees and thirty five minutes (119° 35') east of Greenwich, thence along the meridian of longitude one hundred and nineteen degrees and thirty five minutes (119° 35') east of Greenwich to the parallel of latitude seven degrees and forty minutes (7° 40') north, thence along the parallel of latitude of seven degrees and forty minutes (7° 40') north to its intersection with the one hundred and sixteenth (116th) degree meridian of longitude east of Greenwich, thence by a direct line to the intersection of the tenth (10th) degree parallel of north latitude with the one hundred

and eighteenth (118th) degree meridian of longitude east of Greenwich, and thence along the one hundred and eighteenth (118th) degree meridian of longitude east of Greenwich to the point of beginning.

The United States will pay to Spain the sum of twenty million dollars ($20,000,000) within three months after the exchange of the ratifications of the present treaty.

Even in the nations and territories that were not annexed, the Treaty of Paris provided for the basic "American" right of freedom of worship:

ARTICLE X

The inhabitants of the territories over which Spain relinquishes or cedes her sovereignty shall be secured in the free exercise of their religion.

Consequences

Imperialism so blatant did not sit well with many in the United States, and the Senate fight over ratification of the treaty was intense. Apologists for U.S. imperialism argued that the United States had an international duty to function as an agent of civilization; moreover, these Pacific holdings would give the nation a crucial threshold for trade with China. The treaty was ratified by a margin of 57 to 27, just two votes more than the number required.

Dubbed by U.S. secretary of state John Hay a "splendid little war," the Spanish-American War established the United States as a major power in the Far East and the dominant power in the Caribbean. It also initiated a four-year guerrilla insurrection against American dominion in the Philippines, which was granted virtual independence in the 1930s and full independence following World War II. Puerto Rico became an American territory, and Cuba, nominally independent, became a U.S. satellite, which included territory explicitly ceded to the United States for the Guantanamo Naval Base. Puerto Rico and Cuba also figured importantly as strategic points from which the Panama Canal could be defended.

TREATY OF VEREENIGING

TREATY AT A GLANCE

Completed
May 31, 1902, at Pretoria, South Africa

Signatories
Orange Free State and the South African Republic and Great Britain

Overview
The treaty ended the Second ("Great") Boer War, also known as the South African War, as a result of which the Boers, or Afrikaners, were compelled to submit to British rule, but British imperialism nevertheless suffered a blow that signaled its inevitable decline.

Historical Background

The Second "Great" Boer War of 1899–1902 was fought between Great Britain and the two Afrikaner governments of South Africa: the South African Republic (also called the Transvaal) and the Orange Free State.

The Afrikaners, also called Boers (the Dutch word for "farmers") were immigrants of Dutch descent primarily. In 1852 the Afrikaners established the South African Republic in the Transvaal region, and two years later, the Orange Free State was also established. The Transvaal lost its independence from Britain in 1877, but the First Boer War of 1881 restored it. Nevertheless, both the South African Republic and the Orange Free State remained under British suzerainty.

This situation was tolerable until 1886, when the discovery of gold in the Transvaal brought an influx of British Uitlanders ("foreigners") and resulted in deteriorating relations between the British and the Boers. Following an armed raid instigated in 1895 by British administrator Sir Leander Starr Jameson against the Transvaal, the Republic of South Africa forged an alliance with the Orange Free State and made protest against British reinforcement of their garrison in South Africa.

This soon led to the Second ("Great") Boer War. The Boers proved victorious during the early part of the war, greatly embarrassing the British, who dispatched fresh troops under Kitchener and Frederick Sleigh, Lord Roberts, who ultimately defeated the principal Boer forces. However, in the war's late phase, the Boers resorted to skillful guerrilla tactics, which prompted the British to respond with oppressive measures against Boer civilians, including confinement in concentration camps. Finally brought to heel militarily, the Boers remained almost defiant in the diplomacy following the truce.

Terms

By the brief Treaty of Vereeniging, both Boer republics became British colonies but exacted from Britain substantial monetary compensation and secured culturally representative institutions.

GENERAL LORD KITCHENER of Khartoum, Commander-in-Chief, and His Excellency Lord Milner, High Commissioner, on behalf of the British Government, and Messrs. S. W. Burger, F. W. Reitz, Louis Botha, J. H. De la Rey, L. J. Meyer, and J. C. Krogh, acting as the Government of the South African Republic, and Messrs. C. R. De Wet, W. J. C. Brebner, J. B. M. Hertzog, and C. H. Olivier, acting as the Government of the Orange Free State, on behalf of their respective burghers, desirous to terminate the present hostilities, agree on the following articles:

I

The burgher forces in the field will forthwith lay down their arms, handing over all guns, rifles, and munitions of war in their possession or under their control, and desist from any further resistance to the authority of His Majesty King Edward VII, whom they recognize as their lawful Sovereign.

The manner and details of this surrender will be arranged between Lord Kitchener and Commandant-General Botha, Assistant-Commandant-General De la Rey, and Chief-Commandant De Wet.

II

Burghers in the field outside the limits of the Transvaal and Orange River Colony, and all prisoners of war at present outside South Africa who are burghers, will, on duly declaring their acceptance of the position of subjects of His Majesty King Edward VII, be gradually brought back to their homes as soon as transport can be provided and their means of subsistence ensured.

III

The burghers so surrendering or so returning will not be deprived of their personal liberty or their property.

IV

No proceedings, civil or criminal, will be taken against any of the burghers so surrendering or so returning for any acts in connection with the prosecution of the war. The benefit of this clause will not extend to certain acts contrary to the usage of war which have been notified by the Commander-in-Chief to the Boer generals, and which shall be tried by court-martial immediately after the close of hostilities.

V

The Dutch language will be taught in public schools in the Transvaal and the Orange River Colony where the parents of the children desire it, and will be allowed in courts of law when necessary for the better and more effectual administration of justice.

VI

The possession of rifles will be allowed in the Transvaal and Orange River Colony to persons requiring them for their protection, taking out a licence according to law.

VII

Military administration in the Transvaal and Orange River Colony will at the earliest possible date be succeeded by civil government, and, as soon as circumstances permit, representative institutions leading up to self-government, will be introduced.

VIII

The question of granting the franchise to natives will not be decided until after the introduction of self-government.

IX

No special tax will be imposed on landed property in the Transvaal and Orange River Colony to defray the expenses of the war.

X

As soon as conditions permit, a commission on which the local inhabitants will be represented will be appointed in each district of the Transvaal and Orange River Colony, under the presidency of a magistrate or other official, for the purpose of assisting the restoration of the people to their homes and supplying those who, owing to war losses, are unable to provide themselves with food, shelter, and the necessary amount of seed, stock, implements, etc., indispensable to the resumption of their normal occupations.

His Majesty's Government will place at the disposal of these commissioners a sum of three million pounds sterling for the above purposes, and will allow all notes, issued under Law No. I of 1900, of the Government of the South African Republic, and all receipts given by officers in the field of the late Republics or under their orders, to be presented to a judicial commission which will be appointed by the Government, and if such notes and receipts are found by this commission to have been duly issued in return for valuable consideration, they will be received by the first-named commissions as evidences of war losses suffered by the persons to whom they were originally given. In addition to the above-named free grant of three million pounds, His Majesty's Government will be prepared to make advances as loans for the same purpose, free of interest for two years, and afterwards repayable over a period of years with three per cent. interest. No foreigner or rebel will be entitled to the benefit of this clause.

Signed at Pretoria this thirty-first day of May, in the year of our Lord one thousand nine hundred and two.

Consequences

British prestige, military as well as moral, was greatly eroded by the war. In Britain itself, anti-imperialist sentiment rose sharply, signifying the beginning of the end of the great British world empire. In South Africa the war proved not the death but the rekindling of Afrikaner nationalism. By 1910 the sometimes opposed Afrikaner interests had united as the Union of South Africa, which ultimately gained political supremacy.

Trade Agreements and Commercial Treaties

UNITED STATES–SANDWICH ISLANDS AGREEMENT

TREATY AT A GLANCE

Completed (Ratified)
December 23, 1826, at Honolulu, Waohoo, Sandwich Islands
(present-day Oahu, Hawaii)

Signatories
United States and the Sandwich Islands

Overview
In the wake of the tide of American missionaries flooding into the Sandwich Islands, the United States concluded its first diplomatic arrangement with Hawaii, launching them on a path that eventually led to U.S. annexation and ultimately Hawaiian statehood.

Historical Background

The Hawaiians most likely made their first contact with people from a different culture on January 18, 1778. That was the day British naval captain and explorer James Cook, having run across the islands by accident during a voyage from Tahiti to the Pacific Northwest, sailed into view. Cook's arrival corresponded with certain priestly predictions and Hawaiian stories, and the Hawaiians not only welcomed Cook warmly but hailed him as a god.

A year later, when Cook returned to the islands, the situation had changed. According to historian Gavan Daws, Cook probably walked into the middle of a power struggle among various chiefs and the priesthood; after a tense facedown between Europeans and Hawaiians on February 19, 1779, Cook was killed in the ensuing brawl. Cook's discovery, however, sparked four decades of growing European and American influence over the Hawaiians, as explorers, adventurers, trappers, and whalers stopped over for fresh supplies at what Cook had called the Sandwich Islands.

In 1796 King Kamehameha I, with European backing, unified the Hawaiian islands by conquest. Meanwhile, the virtually disease-free Hawaiians had already begun to experience the effects that diseases from both West and East would have because of their lack of natural immunity. Cook's sailors had introduced venereal disease to the islands, and as Europeans brought items

Hawaiians came particularly to value, such as livestock (horses, cattle, goats) and trees and fruits (eucalyptus and guava, for example), they also brought cholera, smallpox, measles, bubonic plague, and leprosy. By 1819 a population estimated at 300,000 before Cook's arrival had fallen to around 135,000.

Then came the missionaries. Protestants arrived from the United States in 1820, the first of some 15 New England missionary companies. Soon they dominated the island. Enthused by the new secular, or reform, Calvinism, men like the Reverend Hiram Bishop and missionary and physician Gerrit P. Judd preached the gospel, founded schools, and promoted agriculture. They also brought trade, which led to the first diplomatic agreement between the United States and Hawaii in 1826.

Terms

The treaty, drawn by a United States just then forcibly removing American Indians from North America east of the Mississippi, was a more subtle document than its treaties with the Indian nations had been. Seeking to enter fully the expanding market economy of the imperial European powers, the U.S. conducted its diplomacy in Hawaii in an atmosphere of growing competition in international trade in the Pacific.

Articles of Arrangement Made and Concluded at Oahu between Thomas ap Catesby Jones Appointed by the United States, of the One Part, and Kauikeaouli, King of the Sandwich Islands, and his Guardians, on the Other Part

ARTICLE 1ST

The peace and friendship subsisting between the United States, and their Majesties, the Queen Regent, and Kauikeaouli, King of the Sandwich Islands, and their subjects and people, are hereby confirmed, and declared to be perpetual.

ARTICLE 2ND

The ships and vessels of the United States (as well as their Consuls and all other citizens within the territorial jurisdiction of the Sandwich Islands, together with all their property), shall be inviolably protected against all Enemies of the United States in time of war.

ARTICLE 3RD

The contracting parties being desirous to avail themselves of the bounties of Divine Providence, by promoting the commercial intercourse and friendship subsisting between the respective Nations, for the better security of these desirable objects, Their Majesties bind themselves to receive into their Ports and Harbours all ships and vessels of the United States; and to protect, to the utmost of their capacity, all such ships and vessels, their cargoes officers and crews, so long as they shall behave themselves peacefully, and not infringe the established laws of the land, the citizens of the United States being permitted to trade freely with the people of the Sandwich Islands.

ARTICLE 4TH

Their Majesties do further agree to extend the fullest protection, within their control, to all ships and vessels of the United States which may be wrecked on their shores; and to render every assistance in their power to save the wreck and her apparel and cargo; and as a reward for the assistance and protection which the people of the Sandwich Islands shall afford to all such distressed vessels of the United States, they shall be entitled to a salvage, or a portion of the property so saved; but such salvage shall, in no case, exceed one third of the value saved; which valuation is to be fixed by a commission of disinterested persons who shall be chosen equally by the Parties.

ARTICLE 5TH

Citizens of the United States, whether resident or transient, engaged in commerce, or trading to the Sandwich Islands, shall be inviolably protected in their lawful pursuits; and shall be allowed to sue for, and recover by judgment, all claims against the subjects of His Majesty The King, according to strict principles of equity, and the acknowledged practice of civilized nations.

ARTICLE 6TH

Their Majesties do further agree and bind themselves to discountenance and use all practicable means to prevent desertion from all American ships which visit the Sandwich Islands; and to that end it shall be made the duty of all Governors, Magistrates, Chiefs of Districts, and all others in authority, to apprehend all deserters; and to deliver them over to the master of the vessel from which they have deserted; and for the apprehension of every such deserter, who shall be delivered over as aforesaid, the master, owner, or agent, shall pay to the person or persons apprehending such deserter, the sum of six Dollars, if taken on the side of the Island near which the vessel is anchored; but if taken on the opposite side of the Island, the sum shall be twelve Dollars; and if taken on any other Island, the reward shall be twenty four Dollars, and shall be a just charge against the wages of every such deserter.

ARTICLE 7TH

No tonnage dues or impost shall be exacted of any Citizen of the United States which is not paid by the Citizens or subjects of the nation most favoured in commerce with the Sandwich Island; and the citizens of subjects of the Sandwich Islands shall be allowed to trade with the United States, and her territories, upon principles of equal advantage with the most favoured nation.

Done in council at Honolulu, Island of Waohoo, this 23rd day of December in the year of our Lord 1826.

THOS. AP CATESBY JONES.
ELISABETA KAAHUMANU.
KARAIMOKU.
POKI.
HOWAPILI.
LIDIA NAMAHANA.

Consequences

The American missionaries and colonizers who came to the Sandwich Islands with their trade and their treaties touched off a stage in Hawaiian history that, despite the absence of major native Hawaiian Anglo-American armed conflicts, resembled the stages in the U.S. settlement of its trans-Mississippi West. Here again the settlement included the incidental devastation of an indigenous population by exotic diseases, concerted attempts to Christianize and Americanize the Hawaiians, the introduction of homesteading legislation as an enticement away from the feudal-like system of land ownership practiced by indigenous peoples, even the establishment of a reservation system for "pure-bloodied" Hawaiians, the confiscation of native land, and the annexation of the island to the new American empire.

On the other hand, and more immediately, the competition and political maneuverings of the Western imperial nations bent on trading in Pacific exotics—the United States, France, and Great Britain—presaged the kind of diplomatic contortions practiced with and against the Chinese a few decades later.

LORD RUSSELL'S TREATY
(ANGLO-HAWAIIAN TREATY)

TREATY AT A GLANCE

Completed
November 13, 1836, at Honolulu, Oahu, Sandwich Islands
(present-day Oahu, Hawaii)

Signatories
Great Britain and the Sandwich Islands

Overview
The growing competition in the Pacific among the European imperial nations led Britain to sign a diplomatic treaty with the Sandwich Islands to protect its trade and its nationals during a time of political unrest on the islands fostered by the growing power of American missionaries and the machinations of the U.S., British, and French councils and naval forces.

Historical Background

Britain's great 18th-century explorer Captain James Cook had not only discovered the Sandwich Islands in 1778 but was murdered there during a brawl with Hawaiians. With the coming of American missionaries in the 1820s and the arrival of such men as the Reverend Hiram Bishop and Dr. Gerrit Judd, the United States began to assert what in time would become an American hegemony over the islands. The missionaries produced a spiritual revolution, as members of the royal family, their basic beliefs in the Hawaiian religion undermined, tossed out the once powerful priests and abolished the kapu system in a series of deviant acts that shook the stability of the Hawaiian people and accelerated their decline. Their loss of faith in the old gods, their intense curiosity about the ways of Americans and Europeans, their lust for learning to read and write, and something like a need to identify spiritually with those coming to control the islands led the Hawaiians to adopt the new religion quickly.

Alarmed by the growing uncertainty of the Hawaiians' tribal rule and American influence, the consuls and navy officials of the United States, Britain, and France attempted to manipulate the local governments and peoples to their advantage, and in 1836 Britain signed a diplomatic treaty giving it basically the same rights the Americans had claimed by a similar agreement in 1826 (see UNITED STATES–SANDWICH ISLANDS AGREEMENT).

Terms

The treaty was brief enough.

English Treaty of
Lord Edward Russell, Nov. 16th, 1836

ARTICLES made and agreed on at Honolulu, Island of Oahu, the 16th of November, 1836.

ARTICLE I
English subjects shall be permitted to come with their vessels, and property of whatever kind, to the Sandwich Islands; they shall also be permitted to reside therein, as long as they conform to the laws of these Islands, and to build houses, and warehouses for their merchandize, with the consent of the King, and good friendship shall continue between the subjects of both countries, Great Britain and the Sandwich Islands.

ARTICLE II
English subjects, resident at the Sandwich Islands, are at liberty to go to their own country, or elsewhere either in their own or any other vessel; they may dispose of their effects, enclosures, houses, &c., with the previous knowledge of the King, and take the value with them, without any impediment whatever. The land on which houses are built is the property of the King, but the King shall have no authority to destroy the houses, or in any way injure the property of any British subject.

ARTICLE III

When an English subject dies on the Sandwich Islands, his effects shall not be searched or touched by any of the Governors or Chiefs, but shall be delivered into the hands of his executors or heirs, if present but if no heir or executor appear, the Consul or his agent shall be executor for the same; if any debts were owing to the deceased, the Governor of the place shall assist and do all in his power to compel the debtors to pay their debts to the heir or executor, or the Consul, in case no heir or executor appears, and the Consul is to inform the King or the death of every British subject leaving property upon the Sandwich Islands.

KAMEHAMEHA III,
EDWARD RUSSELL,
Captain of H.B.M.'s ship *Actcon*.

Consequences

Three years later, King Kamehameha III, under pressure from the missionaries, instituted a social revolution and laid the foundations for constitutional rule with a Declaration of Rights on June 7, 1839, an Edict of Toleration on June 17, 1839, and a written constitution on October 8, 1840. By then Bishop was dictator of Hawaii in all but name, and the islands were largely a Christian kingdom. That year Bishop returned to America, and two years later Judd succeeded him as prime minister.

Kamehameha's "progressive" actions were followed by formal avowals of Hawaiian independence from the United States, Great Britain, and France, but the ambitions of these nations continued unabated, and a succession of overt and covert diplomatic moves culminated in Hawaii's signing of the TREATY OF RECIPROCITY with the United States in 1876 and, ultimately, in the annexation of the islands by the United States.

TREATY BETWEEN THE HAWAIIAN ISLANDS AND THE UNITED STATES

TREATY AT A GLANCE

Completed
December 20, 1849, at Washington, D.C.

Signatories
United States and the Hawaiian Islands

Overview
Alarmed that France seemed prepared to seize the Hawaiian Islands, the United States signed a treaty reaffirming their mutual relationship, yet one more step toward U.S. annexation late in the century.

Historical Background

Even before the United States acquired Oregon and California following the war with Mexico in 1848, Americans had long been interested in Hawaii. In the late 18th and early 19th centuries, U.S. merchantmen engaged in trade with the Far East, and American whaling ships had stopped off for supplies at the Sandwich Islands, discovered by English explorer and captain James Cook. American missionaries began arriving in the 1820s, and men like the Reverend Hiram Bishop and Dr. Gerrit Judd began to exercise a vast influence over Hawaiian society and affairs.

Caught up in the international trading competition with other Western imperial powers, the United States signed a diplomatic agreement with the Sandwich Islands as early as 1826 (see UNITED STATES–SANDWICH ISLANDS AGREEMENT). The American missionaries and the imperial machinations of other nations such as France and Great Britain (see LORD RUSSELL'S TREATY) caused immense disruption in Hawaiian society and led to a precipitous decline in the native population. In the late 1830s and early 1840s, with the various foreign consuls and navy officers stirring up matters, the missionaries pushed the tribal king Kamehameha III into establishing a constitutional government that made Bishop a virtual dictator of the islands, before he left for the United States in 1840 and Judd replaced him as prime minister.

In these early years there was as yet little talk of annexation, especially since the influential Americans were coming to see Hawaii as their private economic fiefdom, but the imperial powers continued their diplomatic shenanigans, and in 1849, when France seemed on the verge of seizing the islands for herself, U.S. secretary of state John Clayton developed a desire to establish American sovereignty in Hawaii, signed a new treaty with the islands, and warned that the United States "could never with indifference allow [the islands] to pass under the domination or exclusive control of any other power."

Terms

The treaty was much more detailed and more inclusive than the 1826 agreement, since it had now not to do merely with native populations and an exotic trade but with the white immigrant population and a colonial export economy.

Treaty with the Hawaiian Islands

WHEREAS a treaty of friendship, commerce, and navigation. between the United States of America and his Majesty the King of the Hawaiian Islands, was concluded and signed at Washington, on the twentieth day of December, in the year of our Lord one thousand eight hundred and forty-nine, the original of which treaty is, word for word, as follows:

The United States of America and his Majesty the King of the Hawaiian Islands, equally animated with the desire of maintaining the relations of good understanding which have hitherto so happily subsisted between their respective states, and consolidating the commercial intercourse between then, have agreed to enter into negotiations for the conclusion of a treaty of friendship, commerce, and navigation, for which purpose they have appointed plenipotentiaries, that is to say The President of the United States of America, John M. Clayton, Secretary of State of the United States; and his Majesty the King of the Hawaiian Islands, James Jackson Jarves, accredited as his special commissioner to the government of the United States; who, after having exchanged their full powers, found in good and due form, have concluded and signed the following articles:

ARTICLE I

There shall he perpetual peace and amity between the United States and the King of the Hawaiian Islands, his heirs and his successors.

ARTICLE II

There shalt he reciprocal liberty of commerce and navigation between the United States of America and the Hawaiian Islands. No a duty of customs, or other impost, shall be charged upon any goods, the produce or manufacture of, one country, upon importation from such country into the other, other or higher than the duty or impost charged upon goods of the same kind, the produce or manufacture of, or tin-ported from, any other country; and the United States of America and his Majesty the King of the Hawaiian Islands do hereby engage, that the subjects or citizens of any other state shall not enjoy any favor, privilege, or immunity, whatever, in, matters of commerce and navigation, which shalt not also, at the same time, be extended to the subjects or citizens of the other contracting party, gratuitously, if the concession in favor of that other state shall have been gratuitous, and in return for a compensation, as nearly as possible of proportionate value and effect, to he adjusted by mutual agreement, if the concession shall have been conditional.

ARTICLE III

All articles, the produce or manufacture of either country, which can legally be imported into either country from the other, in ships of that other country, and thence coming, shall, when so imported, be subject to the same duties, and enjoy the same privileges. whether imported in ships of the one country, or in ships of the other; and in like manner, all goods which can legally be extorted or re-exported from either country to the other, in ships of that other country, shall, when so exported or re-exported, be subject to the same duties, and he entitled to the same privileges, drawbacks, bounties, and allowances, whether exported in ships of the one country, or in ships of the other; and all goods and articles, of whatever description, not being of the produce or manufacture of the United States, which can be legally imported into the Sandwich Islands, shall, when so imported in vessels of the United States, pay no other or higher duties, imposts, or charges, than shall be payable upon the like goods and articles, when imported in the vessels of the most favored foreign nations, other than the nation of which the said goods and articles are the produce or manufacture.

ARTICLE IV

No duties of tonnage, harbor, lighthouses, pilotage, quarantine, or other similar duties, of whatever nature, or under whatever denomination, shall he imposed in either country upon the vessels of the other, in respect of voyages between the United States of America and the Hawaiian Islands, if laden, or in respect of any voyage, if in ballast, which shalt not be equally imposed in the like cases on national vessels.

ARTICLE V

It is hereby declared, that the stipulations of the present treaty are not to be understood as applying to the navigation and carrying trade between one port and another, situated in the states of either contracting party, such navigation and trade being reserved exclusively to national vessels.

ARTICLE VI

Steam vessels of the United States which may be employed by the government of the said States, in the carrying of their public mails across the Pacific Ocean, or from one port in that ocean to another, shall have free access to the ports of the Sandwich Islands, with the privilege of stopping therein to refit, to refresh, to land passengers and their baggage, and for the transaction of any business pertaining to the public mail service of the United States, and shall be subject in such ports to no duties of tonnage, harbor, lighthouses, quarantine, or other similar duties of whatever nature or under whatever denomination.

ARTICLE VII

The whale ships of the United States, shall have access to the ports of Hilo, Kealakekua, and Hanalei, in the Sandwich Islands, for the purposes of refitment and refreshment, as well as to the ports of Honolulu and Lahaina, which only are ports of entry for all merchant vessels; and in all the above-named ports, they shall be permitted to trade or barter their supplies or goods, excepting spirituous liquors, to the amount of two hundred dollars ad valorem for each vessel, without paying any charge for tonnage or harbor dues of any description, or any duties or imposts whatever upon the goods or articles so traded or bartered. They shall also be permitted, with the like exemption from all charges for tonnage and harbor dues, further to trade or barter, with the same exception as to spirituous liquors, to the additional amount of one thousand dollars ad valorem, for each vessel, paying upon the additional goods and articles so traded and bartered, no other or higher duties than are payable on like goods and articles, when imported is the vessels and by the citizens or subjects of the most favored foreign nation. They shall also be permitted to pass from port to port of the Sandwich Islands, for the purpose of procuring refreshments, but they shall not discharge their seamen or land their passengers in the said Islands, except at Lahaina and Honolulu; and in all the ports named in this article, the whales ships of the United States shalt enjoy, in all respects whatsoever, all the rights, privileges, and immunities, which are enjoyed by, or shall be granted to, the whale ships of the most favored foreign nation. The like privilege of frequenting the three ports of the Sandwich Islands, above named in this article, not being ports of entry for merchant vessels, is also guaranteed to all the public armed vessels of the United States. But nothing in this article shalt be construed as authorizing any vessel of the United States, having on board any disease usually regarded as requiring quarantine, to enter, during the continuance of such disease on board, any port of the Sandwich Islands, other than Lahaina or Honolulu.

ARTICLE VIII

The contracting parties engage, in regard to the personal privileges that the citizens of the United States of America shell enjoy in the dominions of his Majesty the King of the Hawaiian

Islands, and the subjects of his said Majesty in the United States of America, that they shall have free and undoubted right to travel and to reside in the states of the two high contracting parties, subject to the same precautions of police which are practiced towards the subjects or citizens of the most favored nations. They shall be entitled to occupy dwellings and warehouses, and to dispose of their personal property of every kind and description, by sale, gift, exchange, will, or in any other say whatever, without the smallest hindrance or obstacle; and their heirs or representatives, being subjects or citizens of the other contracting party, shall succeed to their personal goods, whether by testament or ab intestato; and may take possession thereof, either by themselves or by others acting for them, and dispose of the same at will, paying to the profit of the respective governments, such dues only as the inhabitants of the country wherein the said goods are, shall be subject to pay in like cases. And in case of the absence of the heir and representative, such care shall be taken of the said goods as would be taken of the goods a native of the same country in like case, until the lawful owner way take measures for receiving them. And if a question should arise among several claimants as to which of them said goods belong, the same shall be decided finally by the laws and judges of the land wherein the said goods are. Where, on the decease of any person holding real estate within the territories of one party, such real estate would, by the law. of the land, descend on a citizen or subject of the other, were he not disqualified by alienage, such citizen or subject shalt be allowed a reasonable time to sell the same, and to withdraw the proceeds without molestation,. and exempt from all duties of detraction on the part of the government of the respective states. The citizens or subjects of the contracting parties shall not be obliged to pay, under any presence whatever, any taxes or impositions other or greater than those which are paid, or may hereafter be paid, by the subjects or citizens or the most favored nations, in the respective states of the high contracting parties. They shall be exempt from all military service, whether by land or by sea; from forced loans; and from every extraordinary contribution not general and by law established. Their dwelling, warehouses, and all premises appertaining thereto, destined for the purposes of commerce or residence, shalt be respected. No arbitrary search of, or visit to, their houses, and no arbitrary examination or inspection whatever of the books, papers, or accounts of their trade, shall be made; but such measures shall he executed only in conformity with the legal sentence of a competent tribunal; and each of the two contracting parties engages that the citizens or subjects of the other the residing in their respective states shall enjoy their property and personal security; in as full and ample manner as their own citizens or subjects, or the subjects or citizens of the most favored nation, but subject always to the laws and statutes of the two countries respectively.

ARTICLE IX

The citizens and subjects of each of the two contracting parties shall be free in the states of the other to manage their own affairs themselves, or to commit those affairs to the management of any persons whom they may appoint as their broker, factor, or agent; nor shall the citizens and subjects or the two contracting parties be restrained in their choice of persons to act in such capacities; nor shall they be called upon to pay any salary or remuneration in any person whom they shall not choose to employ.

Absolute freedom shall he given in all cases to the buyer and seller to bargain together, and to fix the price of any goods or merchandise imported into, or to be exported from the states and dominions of the two contracting parties, save and except generally such cases wherein the laws and usages of the country may require the intervention of any special agents in the states and dominions of the contracting parties. But nothing contained in this or any other article of the present treaty shall be construed to authorize the sale of spirituous liquors to the natives of the Sandwich Island, farther then such may be allowed by the Hawaiian laws.

ARTICLE X

Each of the two contracting parties may have, in the ports of the other, consuls,. vice-consuls, and commercial agents, of their own appointment, who shall enjoy the same privileges and powers with those of the most favored nations; but if any such consuls shall exercise commerce, they shall be subject to the same laws and usages to which the private individuals of their nation are subject in the same place. The said consuls, vice-consuls, and commercial agents, are authorized to require the assistance of the local authorities for the search. arrest, detention and imprisonment of the deserters from the ships of war and merchant vessels of their country. For this purpose they shall apply to the competent tribunals, judges and officers, and shall, in writing, demand the said deserters, proving, by the exhibition of the registers of the vessels, the rolls of the crews, or by other official documents, that such individuals formed part of the crews; and this reclamation being thus substantiated, the surrender, shall not be refused. Such deserters, when arrested, shall be placed at the disposal, of the -and consuls, vice-consuls, or commercial agents, and may be confined in the public prisons, at the request and cost of those who shall claim them, in order to be detained until the time when they shall be restored to the vessel to which they belonged, or sent back to their own country by a vessel of the same nation, or any other vessel whatsoever. The agents, owners, or masters of vessels on account of whom the deserters have been apprehended, upon requisition of the local authorities, shall be required take or send away such deserters from the states and dominion of the contracting parties, or give such security or their good conduct as the law way require. But if not sent back nor reclaimed within six months from the day of their arrest, or if all the expenses of such imprisonment are not defrayed by the party causing such arrest and imprisonment, they shalt be set at liberty, and shall not be again arrested fur the same cause. However, if the deserters should be found to have committed any crime or offence, their surrender may be delayed until the tribunal before which their case shall be depending shall have pronounced its sentence, and such sentence shall have been carried into effect.

ARTICLE XI

It is agreed that perfect and entire liberty of conscience shall be enjoyed by the citizens and subjects of both the contracting parties, in the countries of the one and the other, without their being liable to be disturbed or molested on account of their religious belief. But nothing contained in this article shall be construed to interfere with the exclusive right of the Hawaiian government to regulate for itself the schools which it may establish or support within its jurisdiction.

ARTICLE XII

If any ships of war or other vessels be wrecked on the coasts of the states or territories of either of the contracting parties, such ships or vessels, or any parts thereof, and all furniture and appurtenances belonging thereunto, and all goods and merchandise which shall be saved therefrom, or the produce thereof, if sold, shall be faithfully restored with the least possible delay to the proprietors, upon being claimed by them, or by their duly authorized factors; and if there are no such proprietors or factors on the spot, then the said goods and merchandise, or the proceeds thereof, as well as all the papers found on board such wrecked ships or vessels, shill be delivered to the American or Hawaiian consuls, or vice-consul, in whom district the wreck may have taken place; and such consul, vice-consul, proprietors, or factors, shall pay only the expenses incurred in the preservation of the property, together with the rate of salvage and expenses of quarantine which would have been payable in the like case of a wreak of a national vessel; and the goods and merchandise saved from the wreck shall not be subject to duties unless entered for consumption, it being understand that in case of any legal claim upon such wreck, goods, or merchandise, the same shall he referred for decision to the competent tribunals of the country.

ARTICLE XIII

The vessels of either of the two contracting parties which may be forced by stress of weather or other cause into one of the ports of the other, shall be exempt from all duties of port or navigation paid for the benefit of the state, if the motives which led to their seeking refuge be real and evident, and if no cargo be discharged or taken on board, save such tat may relate to the subsistence of the crew, or be necessary for the repair of the vessels, and if they do not stay in port beyond the time necessary, keeping in view the cause which led to their seeking refuge.

ARTICLE XIV

The contracting parties mutually agree to surrender, upon official requisition, to the authorities of each, all persons who, being charged with the crimes of murder, piracy, arson, robbery, forgery, or the utterance of forged paper, committed within the jurisdiction of either, shall he found within the territories of the other, provided that this shall only be done upon such evidence of criminality as, according to the laws of the place where the person so charged shall be found, would justify his apprehension and commitment for trial, if the crime had there been committed; and the respective judges and other magistrates of the two governments, shall have authority, upon complaint made under oath, to issue a warrant for the apprehension of the person so charged, that he may be brought before such judges or other magistrates respectively, to the end that the evidence of criminality may be heard and considered; and if, on such hearing, the evidence be deemed sufficient to sustain the charge, it shall he tile duty of the examining judge or magistrate to certify the same to the proper executive authority, that a warrant may issue for the surrender of such fugitive. The expense of such apprehension and delivery shall be borne and defrayed by the party who makes the requisition and receives the fugitive.

ARTICLE XV

So soon as steam or other mail pickets under the flag of either of the contracting parties shall have commenced running between their respective ports of entry, the contracting parties agree to receive at the post-offices of those ports all mailable matter, and to forward it as directed, the destination being to same regular post-office of either country, charging thereupon the regular postal rates an established by law in the territories of either party receiving said mailable matter, in addition to the original postage of the office whence the mail was sent. Mails for the United States shall be made up at regular intervals at the Hawaiian post-office, and dispatched to ports of the United States; the postmasters at which ports shall open the same, and forward the enclosed matter as directed, crediting the Hawaiian government with their postages as established by law, and stamped upon each manuscript or printed sheet.

All mailable matter destined for the Hawaiian Islands shall be received at the several post-offices in the United States, and forwarded to San Francisco, or other ports on the Pacific coast of tie United States, whence the postmasters shall dispatch it by the regular mail packets to Honolulu, the Hawaiian government agreeing on their part to receive and collect for and credit the post-office department of the United States with the United States rates charged thereupon. It shall be optional to prepay the postage on letters in either country, but postage on printed sheets and, newspapers shalt in all cases be prepaid. The respective post-office departments of the contracting parties shall in their accounts, which are to be adjusted annually, be credited with all dead letters returned.

ARTICLE XVI

The present treaty shall be in force from the date of the exchange of the ratifications, for the term of ten years, and further, until the end of twelve months after either of the contracting parties shall have given notice to the other of its intention to terminate the same, each of the said contracting parties reserving to itself the right of giving such notice at the end of the said term of ten years, or at nay subsequent term.

Any citizen or subject of either party infringing the articles of this treaty shall be held responsible for the same, and the harmony and good correspondence between the two governments shall not be interrupted thereby, each party engaging in no way to protect the offender, or sanction such violation.

ARTICLE XVII

The present treaty shall be ratified by the President of the United States of America, by and with the advice and consent of the Senate or the said States, and by his Majesty the King of the Hawaiian Islands, by and with the advice of his Privy Council of State, and the ratification shall he exchanged at Honolulu within, eighteen months from the date, of its signature, or sooner if possible.

In witness whereof, the respective plenipotentiaries have signed the same in triplicate, and have thereto affixed their seals,

Done at Washington, in the English language, the twentieth day of December, in the year one thousand eight hundred and forty-nine.

JOHN M. CLAYTON, [SEAL.]
JAMES JACKSON JARVES. [SEAL.]

Consequences

As the native population declined, settlers seized the best Hawaiian lands for large-scale commercial farming. For a decade, Judd had defended Hawaii from the imperialist designs of the British and the French and protected the whaling and ranching industries that were then Hawaii's main sources of wealth. By the 1850s, young Hawaiians, locally called Kanakas, who had shipped out on whaling crews, began to show up in San Francisco and San Diego. In 1853, the last year Judd was in office, the Hawaiian native population had dwindled to 70,036 (from an estimated high of about 300,000 prior to first contact in 1778). The next year, the new U.S. administration of Franklin Pierce pursued an even more aggressive policy toward Hawaii as Secretary of State William L. Marcy negotiated a treaty of annexation with the Hawaiian government. British protests and opposition in the U.S. Senate led Pierce to drop the matter.

After 1854 missionary influence over Hawaii dissipated as the islands' economy shifted toward plantation sugar and pineapple production; foreigners, first from China, then Japan, were shipped in to harvest the crops in the face of Hawaiian resistance and decline; and King Kamehameha III's successors lost sympathy for the preachers. Under the growing power of big plantation owners, Hawaiian politics quickly grew corrupt, especially during Kalakaua's reign from 1874 to 1891. This, the last Hawaiian king, could not even begin to match the power of the big planters, who in 1876 wrangled the TREATY OF RECIPROCITY, which protected their profits in sugar, which quickly became Hawaii's major source of income. Yet until the 1880s, the United States seemed content to eschew annexation for the moment and simply but jealously keep Hawaii free from foreign control.

EMPIRE OF JAPAN TREATY
(KANAGAWA TREATY, PERRY CONVENTION)

TREATY AT A GLANCE

Completed
March 31, 1854, at Kanagawa, Japan

Signatories
United States and the Empire of Japan

Overview
Japan barred all intercourse with the West until President Millard Fillmore commissioned Matthew Calbraith Perry to negotiate a treaty that established trade and other relations between Japan and the United States.

Historical Background

In order to open trade and diplomatic relations with the Empire of Japan, which barred all intercourse with the West, President Millard Fillmore commissioned Matthew Calbraith Perry, a distinguished naval officer and the brother of War of 1812 hero Oliver Hazard Perry, to negotiate a treaty. While Perry was doubtless a personally effective emissary, the fact that he anchored the full augmented Eastern Squadron in Yedo (Tokyo) Bay was in itself sufficiently impressive—or intimidating—to persuade Japanese officials to transmit President Fillmore's proposals to higher authorities.

Terms

The treaty was brief and included the following provisions.

Empire of Japan Treaty

Kanagawa, March 31, 1854
*Treaty between the United States of America and
the Empire of Japan*

THE UNITED STATES of America and the Empire of Japan, desiring to establish firm, lasting, and sincere friendship between the two nations, have resolved to fix, in a manner clear and positive, by means of a treaty or general convention of peace and amity, the rules which shall in future be mutually observed in the intercourse of their respective countries; for which most desirable object the President of the United States has conferred full powers on his Commissioner, Matthew Calbraith Perry, Spe-

cial Ambassador of the United States to Japan, and the August Sovereign of Japan has given similar full powers to his Commissioners, Hayashi, Daigaku-no-kami; Ido, Prince of Tsus-Sima; Izawa, Prince of Mima-saki; and Udono, Member of the Board of Revenue. And the said Commissioners, after having exchanged their said full powers, and duly considered the premises, have agreed to the following articles:

ARTICLE I

There shall be a perfect, permanent, and universal peace, and a sincere and cordial amity between the United States of America on the one part, and the Empire of Japan on the other part, and between their people respectively, without exception of persons or places.

ARTICLE II

The port of Simoda, in the principality of Idzu, and the port of Hakodade, in the principality of Matsmai, are granted by the Japanese as ports for the reception of American ships, where they can be supplied with wood, water, provisions, and coal, and other articles their necessities may require, as far as the Japanese have them. The time for opening the first-named port is immediately on signing this treaty; the last-named port is to be opened immediately after the same day in the ensuing Japanese year.

NOTE.—A tariff of prices shall be given by the Japanese officers of the things which they can furnish, payment for which shall be made in gold and silver coin.

ARTICLE III

Whenever ships of the United States are thrown or wrecked on the coast of Japan, the Japanese vessels will assist them, and carry their crews to Simoda, or Hakodade, and hand them over to their countrymen, appointed to receive them; whatever articles the shipwrecked men may have preserved shall likewise be restored, and the expenses incurred in the rescue and support of Americans and Japanese who may thus be thrown upon the shores of either nation are not to be refunded.

ARTICLE IV

Those shipwrecked persons and other citizens of the United States shall be free as in other countries, and not subjected to confinement, but shall be amenable to just laws.

ARTICLE V

Shipwrecked men and other citizens of the United States, temporarily living at Simoda and Hakodade, shall not be subject to such restrictions and confinement as the Dutch and Chinese are at Nagasaki, but shall be free at Simoda to go where they please within the limits of seven Japanese miles (or ri) from a small island in the harbor of Simoda marked on the accompanying chart hereto appended; and in shall like manner be free to go where they please at Hakodade, within limits to be defined after the visit of the United States squadron to that place.

ARTICLE VI

If there be any other sort of goods wanted, or any business which shall require to be arranged, there shall be careful deliberation between the parties in order to settle such matters.

ARTICLE VII

It is agreed that ships of the United States resorting to the ports open to them shall be permitted to exchange gold and silver coin and articles of goods for other articles of goods, under such regulations as shall be temporarily established by the Japanese Government for that purpose. It is stipulated, however, that the ships of the United States shall be permitted to carry away whatever articles they are unwilling to exchange.

ARTICLE VIII

Wood, water, provisions, coal, and goods required, shall only be procured through the agency of Japanese officers appointed for that purpose, and in no other manner.

ARTICLE IX

It is agreed that if at any future day the Government of Japan shall grant to any other nation or nations privileges and advantages which are not herein granted to the United States and the citizens thereof, that these same privileges and advantages shall be granted likewise to the United States and to the citizens thereof, without any consultation or delay.

ARTICLE X

Ships of the United States shall be permitted to resort to no other ports in Japan but Simoda and Hakodade, unless in distress or forced by stress of weather.

ARTICLE XI

There shall be appointed, by the Government of the United States, Consuls or Agents to reside in Simoda, at any time after the expiration of eighteen months from the date of the signing of this treaty; provided that either of the two Governments deem such arrangement necessary.

ARTICLE XII

The present convention having been concluded and duly signed, shall be obligatory and faithfully observed by the United States of America and Japan, and by the citizens and subjects of each respective Power; and it is to be ratified and approved by the President of the United States, by and with the advice and consent of the Senate thereof, and by the August Sovereign of Japan, and the ratification shall be exchanged within eighteen months from the date of the signature thereof, or sooner if practicable.

In faith whereof we, the respective Plenipotentiaries of the United States of America and the Empire of Japan aforesaid, have signed and sealed these presents.

Done at Kanagawa, this thirty-first day of March, in the year of our Lord Jesus Christ one thousand eight hundred and fifty-four, and of Kayei the seventh year, third month, and third day.

M. C. PERRY.

HERE FOLLOW THE SIGNATURES
OF THE JAPANESE PLENIPOTENTIARIES

Consequences

Despite the arrivals of European and American navies at mid-century that tried to "open the door," Japan would be the only Asian country not to fall victim to Western imperialism, mainly because it in many ways bested Europe at its own game. True, Commodore Oliver Perry's 1854 expedition managed to come away with a full commercial treaty, and for a few years the old pattern held: more ports opened, resident foreigners demanded extraterritorial rights, import and export duties were imposed, Japan lost control of its own trade, and its feudal society was shaken up. But as luck would have it, the Western powers had much else on their minds. The Indian Mutiny, the Taiping Rebellion in China, the Crimean War, French entanglements with Mexico, and the U.S. Civil War all combined to ensure that when the internal crisis came, the Japanese were freer than they might otherwise have been to work out matters for themselves. Seeing what havoc the Opium Wars were causing in China, the Japanese shrugged off their peculiar kind of trade-spawned subjection.

After an intense internal power struggle brought on by such causes as the danger of foreign military intervention, the rise of an urban merchant class, and the growth of a disaffected peasantry led to civil war between the ruling and rigid Togukawa family and the supporters of the politically impotent imperial family, the Meiji Restoration brought not only peace but a thoroughgoing modernization that left Japan strong economically and militarily. Soon Japan had not only followed the West on the path of industrialization but also along the road to imperialist expansion. Japan swallowed up the Ryukyu Islands, the Kuril Islands, the Bonin Islands, and Hokkaido before moving on to Korea, which sparked a war with China. From the Chinese, Japan won Formosa, the Pescadores, and southern Manchuria. There, by the time the Japanese ran into the equally expansion-minded Russians, France, Britain, and Germany were already seeking ways to frustrate Japan's new imperial ambitions.

TREATY OF RECIPROCITY

TREATY AT A GLANCE

Completed
September 9, 1876, at Washington, D.C.

Signatories
United States and the Kingdom of Hawaii

Overview
As big plantation owners replaced missionaries as the driving force in Hawaiian society and politics, the United States negotiated a treaty of reciprocity with their client King Kalakaua, which helped make sugar the islands' main cash crop and ensured the hegemony of the sugar kings, who in turn would be instrumental in the annexation of the islands by the United States decades later.

Historical Background

From the time the English sea captain and explorer James Cook first ran across what he called the Sandwich Islands in the mid-Pacific, Hawaii had been a crossroads of European imperial ambitions. Colonized by American missionaries beginning in the 1820s, the islands seethed with native unrest as the United States, Great Britain, and France vied for trading privileges and influence among the Polynesian tribal groups and signed various "exclusive" trade agreements, among them the UNITED STATES–SANDWICH ISLANDS AGREEMENT, LORD RUSSELL'S TREATY, and the TREATY BETWEEN HAWAII AND THE UNITED STATES.

By 1840 men such as the Reverend Hiram Bishop and Dr. Gerrit Judd, both Protestant missionaries, had pushed Hawaiian overlord Kamehameha III into Westernizing the island government and introduced a written constitution that brought them to power in what was basically now a Christian kingdom. By mid-century Hawaii boasted frame houses, horse-drawn buggies, Western-style schools, churches, taverns, retail shops galore, a written language, a sharply declining culture, and a rapidly dying population. About that time, too, the United States—skittish about French intentions to seize the islands for themselves—began negotiating for Hawaii's annexation, which brought howls of protest from British diplomats and American legislators alike, killing the idea for the present.

After 1854 the missionaries' influence over Hawaii began to slack off as the islands turned toward a plantation economy producing sugar and pineapples. American plantation owners shipped in foreigners—first from China, then Japan—to harvest their crops in the face of Hawaiian resistance and decline. King Kamehameha III's successors lost sympathy for the preachers, whom they blamed for many of the natives' woes. The big planters, grown rich and powerful, quickly corrupted Hawaiian politics, especially during Kalakaua's reign from 1874 to 1891. A year after the new king assumed his throne, the planters wrangled the suffocating Treaty of Reciprocity with an America hungry for Hawaiian sugar.

Terms

Lasting for seven years, the Treaty of Reciprocity with the United States protected profits in sugar and secured the planters' hold on the islands.

The United States of America and his Majesty the King of the Hawaiian Islands, equally animated by the desire to strengthen and perpetuate the friendly relations which have heretofore uniformly existed between them, and to consolidate their commercial intercourse, have resolved to enter into a Convention for Commercial Reciprocity. For this purpose, the President of the United States has conferred full powers on Hamilton Fish, Secretary of State, and His Majesty the King of the Hawaiian Islands has conferred like powers on Honorable Elisha H. Allen, Chief Justice of the Supreme Court, Chancellor of the Kingdom, member of the Privy Council of State, His Majesty's Envoy Extraordinary and Minister Plenipotentiary to the United States of America, and Honorable Henry A. P. Carter, member of the Privy Council of State, His Majesty's special Commissioner to the United States of America.

And the said Plenipotentiaries, after having exchanged their full powers, which were found to be in due form, have agreed to the following articles:

ARTICLE I

For and in consideration of the right and privileges granted by His Majesty the King of the Hawaiian Islands in the next succeeding article of this Convention, and as an equivalent therefor, the United States of America hereby agree to admit all the articles named in the following schedule, the same being the growth and manufacture or produce of the Hawaiian Islands, into all the ports of the United States free of duty.

Schedule
Arrow-root, castor oil, bananas, nuts, vegetables, dried and undried, preserved and unpreserved; hides and skins, undressed; rice; pulu; seeds; plants, shrubs, or tree; muscovado, brown, and all other unrefined sugar, meaning hereby the grade of sugar heretofore commonly imported from the Hawaiian Islands, and now known in the markets of San Francisco and Portland a "Sandwich Island Sugar"; syrups of sugar-cane, melado, and molasses; tallow.

ARTICLE II

For and in consideration of the right and privilege granted by the United States of America in the preceding article of this Convention, and as an equivalent therefor, His Majesty the King of the Hawaiian Islands hereby agrees to admit all the articles named in the following schedule, the same being the growth, manufacture, or produce of the United States of America, into all the ports of the Hawaiian Islands free of duty.

Schedule
Agricultural implements; animals; beef, bacon, pork, ham, and all fresh, smoked, or preserved meat; boots and shoes; grain, flour, meal, and bran. Bread and breadstuff, of all kinds; bricks, lime, and cement; butter, cheese, lard, tallow; bullion; coal; cordage, naval stores, including tar, pitch, resin, turpentine raw and rectified; copper and composition sheating; nails and bolts; cotton and manufactures of cotton, bleached and unbleached, and whether or not colored, stained, painted, or printed; eggs; fish and oysters, and all other creatures living in the water, and the produce thereof; fruits, nuts, and vegetables, green, dried, or undried, preserved or unpreserved; hardware; hides, furs, skins and pelts, dressed or undressed; hoop iron and rivets, nails, spikes and bolts, sacks, brads, or sprigs; ice; iron and steel and manufactures thereof; leather; lumber and timber of all kinds, round, hewed, sawed and unmanufactured, in hole or in part; doors, sashes, and blinds; machinery of all kinds, engines and parts thereof; oats and hay; paper, stationary, and books, and all manufactures of paper or paper and wood; petroleum and all oils for lubricating or illuminating purposes; plants shrubs, trees, and seeds; rice; sugar, refined or unrefined; salt; soap; shooks, staves, and headings; wool and manufactures of wool, other than read-made clothing; wagons and carts for the purposes of agriculture or of dryage; wood and manufacture of wood, or of wood and metal, except furniture either upholstered or carved, and carriages; textile manufactures made of a combination of wool, cotton, silk, or linen, or of any two or more of them other than when ready-made clothing; harness and all manufactures of leather; starch; and tobacco, whether in leaf or manufactured.

ARTICLE III

The evidence that articles proposed to be admitted into the ports of the United States of America, or the ports of the Hawaiian Islands, free of duty, under the first and second articles of this Convention, are the growth, manufacture, or produce of the United States of America or of the Hawaiian Islands, respectively, shall be established under such rules and regulations and conditions for the protection of the revenue as the two Governments may from time to time respectively prescribe.

ARTICLE IV

No export duty or charges shall be imposed in the Hawaiian Islands, or in the United States, upon any of the articles proposed to be admitted into the ports of the United States or the ports of the Hawaiian Islands free of duty under the first and second articles of this Convention. It is agreed, on the part of His Hawaiian Majesty, that, so long as this Treaty shall remain in force, he will not lease or otherwise dispose of or create any lien upon any port, harbor, or other territory in his dominions, or grant so special privilege or right of use therein, to any other power, state, or government, nor make any treaty by which any other nation shall obtain the same privileges, relative to the admission of any articles free of duty hereby secured to the United States.

ARTICLE V

The present Convention shall take effect as soon as it shall have been approved and proclaimed by His Majesty the King of the Hawaiian Islands, and shall have been ratified and duly proclaimed on the part of the government of the United States, but not until a law to carry it into operation shall have been passed by the Congress of the United States of America. Such assent having been given and the ratifications of the Convention having been exchanged provided in Article I., this Convention shall remain in force for seven years from the date at which it may come. into operation; and further, until the expiration of twelve months after either of the contracting parties shall give notice to the other of its wish to terminate the same; each of the high contracting parties being at liberty to give such notice to the other at the end of the said term of seven years, or at an time thereafter.

ARTICLE VI

The present Convention shall be duly ratified and the ratification exchanged at Washington City, within eighteen months from the date hereof, or earlier if possible.

In faith whereof the respective Plenipotentiaries of the high contracting parties have signed this present Convention, and have affixed thereto their respective seal.

Done in duplicate, at Washington, the thirteenth day of January, in the year of our Lord one thousand eight hundred and seventy-five.

HAMILTON FISH
ELISHA H. ALLEN
HENRY A. P. CARTER

Later, King Kalakaua, in his speech before the opening session of the 1887 Hawaiian Legislature, under pressure from the sugar kings who had foisted on him a new constitution removing most of his power and given them control of the legislature, extended the agreement for yet another seven years and added a clause, as he said, "granting to national vessels of the United States the exclusive privilege of entering Pearl River Harbor and establishing there a coaling and repair station."

Consequences

With passage of the Treaty of Reciprocity, sugar quickly became Hawaii's major source of income, and the sugar planters became powerful forces in American, as well as Hawaiian, society, especially in California. Meanwhile, Hawaii's native population continued to die off at an alarming rate, dropping to around 40,000 by 1890 (a 90 percent decline in a century's time), and the sugar kings imported ever more foreign labor, now from Portugal and Spain, as well as Japan.

When Kalakaua died, his sister, the willful and conservative Liliuokalani, became queen and ruled from 1891 to 1893. Like her brother, she could never match the power of the big planters. In 1893 the American-backed planters overthrew the autocratic Liliuokalani and formed, in 1894, the Republic of Hawaii under a new kind of autocrat, controversial judge and now president Stanford Ballard Dole. Four years of sporadic and maddingly complicated negotiations led to annexation by the United States in 1898 in the spasm of national expansion that produced, among other things, the Spanish-American War. Hawaii became an American territory on June 14, 1900.

Beset by a mixture of racial and ethnic groups, saddled with an unstable government, and in the throes of a rapidly expanding plantation economy, the Hawaiian Territory had its problems. Like all territories, it was afforded only limited self-government, and with an economy already essentially exploitative, Hawaii—like much of the trans-Mississippi West after the Civil War—had clearly been relegated to colonial status. Not unlike the copper kings in the Southwest or the railroad barons in California, Hawaii's sugar kings took advantage of the disenfranchised mixture of ethnic groups to monopolize the economy.

In 1903 President Dole's cousin, James Drummond Dole, launched a pineapple plantation. Thirty years later exported canned pineapples would be Hawaii's second most valuable cash crop. Meanwhile, five firms—American Factors, Brewer & Company, Alexander & Baldwin, Castle & Cooke, and the Davis & Co., Ltd.—had come to control Hawaii's plantations, and with them Hawaii itself.

KINGDOM OF CHOSON TREATY

TREATY AT A GLANCE

Completed
May 22, 1882, at Yin Chuen, Choson (present-day Korea)

Signatories
United States and the Kingdom of Choson

Overview
Korea was the last of the three major Asian empires, after China and Japan, with which the United States established commercial relations, which led in short measure to modernization, civil unrest, and rebellion within Korea.

Historical Background

Westerners had first arrived in East Asia in the mid-17th century, when the crew of a Dutch merchant ship had been jailed in Seoul after the vessel ran aground at Cheju Island in 1656. It had been Korean envoys to China the century before who brought the first contact with Christianity to the Kingdom of Choson along with a world atlas, a few books of literature and religion, and some scientific instruments made by priests. Still, only a few scholars had converted to Catholicism before Catholic missionaries began arriving in the late 18th century. Most Koreans adhered to Confucianism, and by the dawn of the 19th century, the Korean government had begun to persecute Catholics, whose numbers were growing slowly but steadily, spreading from aristocratic circles in Seoul into the provinces and the peasantry.

Even with these conversions, however, the influence of the West had hardly made much of an impact on Korea when in 1864 a new king ascended to the Korean throne. Kojong was too young to rule, so his father, Taewon-gun, became regent. Determined to restore all the ancient powers of the monarchy, Taewon-gun pursued a policy of national isolation—from China and Japan as well as from the West—while launching a series of bold reforms to shore up that power, such as expanding the civil service and abolishing most of the Confucian academies, private institutions exercising much influence over Korean politics.

It was during his regency that more secular Europeans began to take an interest in Choson. Hardly had he taken up the reins of government before European men-of-war and merchant ships appeared off the coast. Claiming they came seeking trade and friendship, these vessels of the new imperialism were as often in search of plunder or smuggling outlets for opium. Not only did the new regent turn them away, but Korean soldiers and citizens seeking vengeance for the looting of Pyongyang by Yankee sailors burned and sank a U.S. merchantman, the *General Sherman*. In 1866 French warships attacked Korea, and in 1871 an American flotilla appeared bent on retaliation for the *General Sherman*, but Taewon-gun beat back both assaults, more resolved than ever to keep his land's doors closed to such foreign "commerce."

As hard as the West tried to establish a diplomatic and commercial beachhead in Korea, Japan tried even harder. When Nippon's efforts proved futile, as well, the Japanese military began to demand a war of conquest against the standoffish Choson. At home, Taewon-gun was also under attack for the high cost of his policies and reforms. A decade after he had assumed the regency, he stepped down in response to the popular unrest. He was replaced by relatives of Queen Min, opposed to his policies in every particular. Japan, which had been keeping close watch on Korean politics, quickly dispatched a fleet to pressure the new government into a treaty of friendship and, of course, trade. Pusan, Wonsan, and Inchon opened their ports to Japanese traders.

China's Qing (Ch'ing) rulers were not happy with the turn of events, and they sought some way to check Japan's growing presence in the kingdom. When conservative soldiers tried to restore Taewon-gun to the regency, the Chinese jumped into the revolt as an excuse to station troops in the kingdom, which launched an era of Qing meddling in Korea's domestic affairs. The Qing forced a trade treaty favorable to

China on the Choson rulers and served as middlemen in the signing of a trade and friendship agreement with the United States.

Terms

Despite its origins, scholars regard the treaty as one of the more enlightened documents of 19th-century East-West relations. The first article of the treaty suggested a degree of cultural sensitivity on the part of the United States's negotiators. The treaty was framed, not as a relationship between two governments, but between two heads of state: "There shall be perpetual peace and friendship between the President of the United States and the King of Chosen [Choson]," then, secondarily, between "the citizens and subjects of their respective Governments."

In addition to the customary articles establishing trade and diplomatic relations between the countries, there were articles specifically prohibiting the opium trade and controlling trade in foodstuffs (at critical times) and arms and munitions:

VII

The Governments of the United States and of Chosen mutually agree and undertake that subjects of Chosen shall not be permitted to import opium into any of the ports of the United States, and citizens of the United States shall not be permitted to import opium into any of the open ports of Chosen, to transport it from one open port to another open port, or to traffic in it in Chosen. This absolute prohibition, which extends to vessels owned by the citizens or subjects of either Power, to foreign vessels employed by them, and to vessels owned by the citizens or subjects of either Power, and employed by other persons for the transportation of opium, shall be enforced by appropriate legislation on the part of the United States and of Chosen, and offenders against it shall be severely punished.

VIII

Whenever the Government of Chosen shall have reason to apprehend a scarcity of food within the limits of the kingdom, His Majesty may by Decree temporarily prohibit the export of all breadstuffs, and such Decree shall be binding on all citizens of the United States in Chosen upon due notice having been given them by the authorities of Chosen through the proper officers of the United States; but it is to be understood that the exportation of rice and breadstuffs of every description is prohibited from the open port of Yin-Chuen.

Chosen having of old prohibited the exportation of red ginseng, if citizens of the United States clandestinely purchase it for export, it shall be confiscated and the offenders punished.

IX

Purchase of cannon, small arms, swords, gunpowder, shot, and all munitions of war is permitted only to officials of the Government of Chosen, and they may be imported by citizens of the United States only under a written permit from the authorities of Chosen. If these articles are clandestinely imported, they shall be confiscated, and the offending party shall be punished.

A provision was also included that specifically encouraged cultural exchange:

XI

Students of either nationality, who may proceed to the country of the other, in order to study the language, literature, law, or arts, shall be given all possible protection and assistance in evidence of cordial goodwill.

Consequences

Similar treaties quickly followed with the other Great Powers who exercised influence in China—Great Britain, Germany, Russia, and France—and all these set up resident foreign missions in Seoul. Almost immediately, Korea felt the impact of Western modernization. Western-style schools and newspapers were founded, and students and officials were sent off to Japan and China. No matter how hard Korea's new "friends" pushed the government to bring itself in line with the modern world, however, it ran up against long-term obstacles: the king, even of age, turned out to be feebleminded, and the ruling classes split between radicals seeking change and moderates hoping to hold onto something of the old, Chinese-influenced culture.

In 1884, two years after the signing of the first treaty with a western power, the radicals—touting their bold blueprint for modern reform—seized power in a coup, and China moved in to stop things before they went too far. Three days later, the Qing overthrew the radicals and forced on Korea the Li-Ito Convention, designed to guarantee a Sino-Japanese balance of power on the Korean Peninsula and check the impact of the Western powers there.

Multinational Conventions and Agreements

GENEVA CONVENTION OF 1864 (RED CROSS CONVENTION)

TREATY AT A GLANCE

Completed (Ratified)
August 22, 1864, at Geneva, Switzerland

Signatories
Switzerland, Baden, Belgium, Denmark, Spain, France, Hesse, Italy, Netherlands, Portugal, Prussia, and Württemberg

Overview
The first of a series of international treaties concluded in Geneva, Switzerland, this established the terms and conditions for the operation of the International Red Cross.

Historical Background

The term "Geneva Convention" covers any of a series of international treaties concluded in Geneva, Switzerland, between 1864 and 1949, aimed at providing soldiers and civilians some relief from the ever-escalating effects of war. The history of the conventions established in Geneva, Switzerland, beginning in 1864, is closely tied to that of the Red Cross. It was Red Cross founder Henri Dunant who initiated the negotiations establishing that year the Convention for the Amelioration of the Wounded in Time of War.

Terms

The first Geneva Convention exempted all establishments, and the people who worked for them, that sought to treat wounded or sick soldiers from destruction or capture, called for the impartial treatment of all combatants, offered protection to civilians trying to aid the wounded, and established the Red Cross symbol as a means to identify those covered by the agreement.

Convention for the Amelioration of the Condition of the Wounded in Armies in the Field

ARTICLE 1
Ambulances and military hospitals shall be acknowledged to be neutral, and, as such, shall be protected and respected by belligerents so long as any sick or wounded may be therein.

Such neutrality shall cease if the ambulances or hospitals should be held by a military force.

ARTICLE 2
Persons employed in hospitals and ambulances, comprising the staff for superintendence, medical service, administration, transport of wounded, as well as chaplains, shall participate in the benefit of neutrality, whilst so employed, and so long as there remain any wounded to bring in or to succor.

ARTICLE 3
The persons designated in the preceding article may, even after occupation by the enemy, continue to fulfil their duties in the hospital or ambulance which they serve, or may withdraw in order to rejoin the corps to which they belong.

Under such circumstances, when these persons shall cease from their functions, they shall be delivered by the occupying army to the outposts of the enemy.

ARTICLE 4
As the equipment of military hospitals remains subject to the laws of war, persons attached to such hospitals cannot, in with-

drawing, carry away any articles but such as are their private property.

Under the same circumstances an ambulance shall, on the contrary, retain its equipment.

ARTICLE 5

Inhabitants of the country who may bring help to the wounded shall be respected, and shall remain free. The generals of the belligerent Powers shall make it their care to inform the inhabitants of the appeal addressed to their humanity, and of the neutrality which will be the consequence of it.

Any wounded man entertained and taken care of in a house shall be considered as a protection thereto. Any inhabitant who shall have entertained wounded men in his house shall be exempted from the quartering of troops, as well as from a part of the contributions of war which may be imposed.

ARTICLE 6

Wounded or sick soldiers shall be entertained and taken care of, to whatever nation they may belong.

Commanders-in-chief shall have the power to deliver immediately to the outposts of the enemy soldiers who have been wounded in an engagement, when circumstances permit this to be done, and with the consent of both parties.

Those who are recognized, after their wounds are healed, as incapable of serving, shall be sent back to their country.

The others may also be sent back, on condition of not again bearing arms during the continuance of the war.

Evacuations, together with the persons under whose directions they take place, shall be protected by an absolute neutrality.

ARTICLE 7

A distinctive and uniform flag shall be adopted for hospitals, ambulances and evacuations. It must, on every occasion, be accompanied by the national flag. An arm-badge (brassard) shall also be allowed for individuals neutralized, but the delivery thereof shall be left to military authority.

The flag and the arm-badge shall bear a red cross on a white ground.

ARTICLE 8

The details of execution of the present convention shall be regulated by the commanders-in-chief of belligerent armies, according to the instructions of their respective governments, and in conformity with the general principles laid down in this convention.

ARTICLE 9

The high contracting Powers have agreed to communicate the present convention to those Governments which have not found it convenient to send plenipotentiaries to the International Conference at Geneva, with an invitation to accede thereto; the protocol is for that purpose left open.

ARTICLE 10

The present convention shall be ratified, and the ratifications shall be exchanged at Berne, in four months, or sooner, if possible.

In faith whereof the respective Plenipotentiaries have signed it and have affixed their seals thereto.

Done at Geneva, the twenty-second day of the month of August of the year one thousand eight hundred and Sixty-four.

[For the Swiss Confederation:]
GENL. G. H. DUFOUR
G. MOYNIER
DR. LEHMANN

[For Baden:]
DR. ROBERT VOLZ STEINER

[For Belgium:]
VISSCHERS

[For Denmark:]
FENGER

[For Spain:]
J. HERIBERTO GARCIA DE QUEVEDO

[For France:]
CH. JAGERSCHMIDT
S. DE PREVAL
BOUDIER

[For Hesse:]
BRODRUCK

[For Italy:]
CAPELLO
F. BAROFFIO

[For the Netherlands:]
WESTENBERG

[For Portugal:]
M. JOSE ANTONIO MARQUES

[For Prussia:]
DE KAMPTZ
LOEFFLER
RITTER

[For Württemberg:]
DR. HAUN

Consequences

Most of the Great Powers in Europe ratified the Red Cross Convention within three years or so, and so had many of the lesser states, but the isolationist United States, intensely suspicious of any international entanglements until the late 19th century, when its own budding imperialism abroad began to require them, would not officially sign on until 1882. The convention was amended and extended by the second Geneva Convention in 1906 and also by the Hague Conventions of 1899 and 1907.

TREATY OF BERLIN

TREATY AT A GLANCE

Completed
July 13, 1878, at Berlin

Signatories
Great Britain, Austria-Hungary, France, Germany, Italy, Russia, and Ottoman Empire (Turkey)

Overview
The treaty was the result of the Congress of Berlin, convened on June 13, 1878, under the presidency of German chancellor Otto von Bismarck, to restore the balance of power following the Russo-Turkish War of 1877–78 and the one-sided Treaty of San Stefano.

Historical Background

Germany's "Iron Chancellor," Otto von Bismarck, had all but built contemporary Europe. He was the man who expelled Austria from Germany, humiliated France and toppled Napoleon III, unified Germany and created the modern German Empire, the man who for three decades, from 1862 to 1890, loomed over the European continent and determined the course of its history. During his 19 years as Germany's imperial chancellor, Bismarck employed a ruthless diplomacy—in lieu of the short brutal wars he had previously waged against Denmark, Austria, and France—to install a network of interlocking alliances aimed at isolating Russia and keeping a defeated France weak and demoralized. The TREATY OF SAN STEFANO, concluded on March 3, 1878, which greatly increased Russian influence in the Balkans, threatened Bismarck's work and prompted him to call the other European powers to a congress in Berlin, under his leadership, to readjust the balance of power. But the great diplomat used the Congress of Berlin not only to shore up his alliance system but, in effect, to move the capital of continental Europe from Paris, or perhaps Vienna, to Berlin, where it was more comfortable for him to maintain single-handedly Europe's balance of power.

Terms

The Treaty of Berlin, which resulted from the congress, reduced Bulgaria, created by the San Stefano treaty as a Russian puppet state, to a smaller entity under the suzerainty of the Ottoman sultan. As compensation, Russia received southern Bessarabia from Romania, and Kars, Ardahan, and Batum from Turkey. Serbia, Montenegro, and Romania were given additional territory, along with full independence from the Ottoman Empire. As to Bosnia and Herzegovina, Austria reserved the right to "occupy and administer" it but could not annex it from Turkey—an ambiguous state of affairs that was destined to create explosive tensions. As to Turkey, the provisions of the Treaty of Berlin virtually excluded it from Europe.

The very complexity of the Treaty of Berlin was telling, and nowhere was the complexity greater than in the actual delineation of borders. Article 2 redefines Bulgaria:

ARTICLE II

The Principality of Bulgaria will include the following territories:—

The frontier follows on the north the right bank of the Danube from the former frontier of Servia [Serbia] up to a point to be determined by a European Commission to the east of Silistria, and thence runs to the Black Sea to the south of Mangalia, which is included in Roumanian territory. The Black Sea forms the eastern boundary of Bulgaria.

On the south the frontier follows upwards from its mouth the midchannel of the brook near which are situated the villages of Hodžakiöj, Selam-Kiöj, Aivadsik, Kulibe, Sudžuluk; crosses obliquely the valley of the Deli-Kamčik, passes south of Belibe and Kemhalik and north of Hadžimahale after having crossed the Deli-Kamčik at 2 1/2 kilom. above Čengei; reaches the crest at a point situated between Tekenlik and Aidos-Bredza, and follows it by Karnabad Balkan, Prisevica

Balkan, Kazan Balkan to the north of Kotel as far as Demir Kapu. It proceeds by the principal chain of the Great Balkan, the whole length of which it follows up to the summit of Kosica.

There it leaves the crest of the Balkan, descends southwards between the villages of Pirtop and Dužanci, the one being left to Bulgaria and the other to Eastern Roumelia, as far as the brook of Tuzlu Dere, follows that stream to its junction with the Topolnica, then the latter river until it meets the Smovskio Dere near the village of Petricevo, leaving to Eastern Roumelia a zone with a radius of 2 kilom. above that junction, ascends between the brooks of Smovskio Dere and the Kamenica, following the line of the water-shed so as to turn to the south-west at the level of Voinjak and reach directly the point 875 of the Austrian Staff map.

The frontier line cuts at right angles the upper basin of the brook of Ichtiman Dere, passes between Bogdina and Karaúla, so as to rejoin the line of the watershed separating the basins of the Isker and the Marica, between Camurli and Hadzilar, follows that line by the summits of Velina Mogila, the "col" 531, Zmailica Vrh, Sumnatica, and rejoins the administrative boundary of the Sandjak of Sofia between Sivri Taš and Čadir Tepe.

From Čadir Tepe, the frontier, taking a south-westerly direction, follows the watershed between the basins of the Mesta Karasu on the one side, and the Struma Karasu on the other, runs along the crests of the mountains of Rhodope called Demir Kapu, Iskoftepe, Kadimesar Balkan, and Aiji Gedük up to Kapetnik Balkan, and thus joins the former administrative frontier of the Sandjak of Sofia.

From Kapetnik Balkan the frontier is indicated by the watershed between the valleys of the Rilska reka and of the Bistrica reka, and follows the ridge called Vodenica Planina, descending into the valley of the Struma at the junction of this river with the Rilska reka, leaving the village of Barakli to Turkey. It ascends then south of the village of Jelenica, and reaches by the shortest line the chain of Golema Planina at the summit of Gitka, and rejoins there the former administrative frontier of the Sandjak of Sofia, leaving, however, to Turkey the whole of the basin of the Suha reka.

From Mount Gitka the western frontier goes towards Mount Crni Vrh by the mountains of Karvena Jabuka, following the former administrative limit of the Sandjak of Sofia in the upper part of the basins of Egrisu and of the Lepnica, ascends with it the crests of Babina Polana, and reaches Mount Crni Vrh.

From Mount Crni Vrh the frontier follows the watershed between the Struma and the Morava by the summits of the Strešer, Vilogolo, and Mešid Planina, rejoins by the Gačina, Crna Trava, Darkovska, and Drainica Plan, then the Deščani Kladanec, the watershed of the High Sukowa and of the Morava, goes straight to the Stol, and descends from it so as to cut the road from Sofia to Pirot, 1,000 metres north-west of the village of Seguša. It ascends in a straight line the Vidlic Planina and thence Mount Radočina in the chain of the Kodža Balkan, leaving to Servia the village of Doikinci, and to Bulgaria that of Senakos.

From the summit of Mount Radočina the frontier follows towards the west the crest of the Balkans by Ciprovec Balkan and Stara Planina up to the former eastern frontier (l'ancienne frontière orientale) of the Principality of Servia, near to the Kula Smiljova Čuka, which it rejoins at Rakovitza.

This delimitation shall be fixed on the spot by the European Commission, on which the Signatory Powers shall be represented. It is understood—

(1) That this Commission will take into consideration the necessity for His Imperial Majesty the Sultan to be able to defend the Balkan frontiers of Eastern Roumelia.

(2) That no fortifications may be erected within a radius of 10 kilom. from Samakow.

On February 8 (January 27 old style), Russia and the Ottoman Empire concluded another Treaty of Constantinople, in which they agreed to abide by the terms of the Treaty of Berlin and those provisions of the Treaty of San Stefano that had not been annulled by the Berlin document.

Consequences

The interlocking alliance system created by Bismarck at Berlin not only helped to bring a half century of relative peace to Europe, it also laid the groundwork on the Continent for a new round of imperial ventures. In the long run, however, the attempts to maintain a balance of power within such a network of alliances resulted in a sort of diplomatic house of cards. The complex compromises of the Treaty of Berlin did indeed serve to postpone the open warfare between the rival Austro-Hungarian and Russian Empires, but they also created the factious Balkan states, where the suppressed conflict incubated, only to break out eventually in the early 20th century in a war more terrible than any humankind had ever fought before: the "Great War"—World War I of 1914–18.

GENERAL ACT OF THE BERLIN CONFERENCE

TREATY AT A GLANCE

Completed
February 26, 1885, at Berlin

Signatories
Great Britain, Austria-Hungary, Belgium, Denmark, France, Germany, Italy, the Netherlands, Portugal, Russia, Spain, Sweden and Norway, Turkey, and the United States (United States failed to ratify)

Overview
Ostensibly convened to "civilize" central Africa and suppress the slave trade, the Berlin Congress actually developed an agreement for the European commercial exploitation of the Congo.

Historical Background

From his youth, King Leopold II of Belgium had been fascinated by Africa and the potential it offered for economic and colonial expansion. It was Leopold who sponsored Sir Henry Stanley's 1879–84 expedition to the Congo, and in 1882 at Leopold's instigation, the International Congo Association was formed. An association of international bankers, it was personally dominated by Leopold, acting as a private individual rather than as king of Belgium. Indeed, Leopold ran the Congo as a private fiefdom, and the overseers of his various enterprises (primarily rubber plantations) inflicted great brutality against the Congolese. This, combined with border disputes involving Portugal, England, and France, led to the Berlin Conference, which was convened under the leadership of Otto von Bismarck on November 15, 1884, and was conducted through February 26, 1885.

Terms

While the assembled powers, including Leopold, agreed to certain principles of humanity in dealing with the peoples of Africa, the preamble to the Congress's February 26 General Act was clear on its priorities. The preamble gave a roll call of participants and a summary of the extent of the understandings reached:

> *In the Name of Almighty God.*
> Her Majesty the Queen of the United Kingdom of Great Britain and Ireland, Empress of India; His Majesty the German Emperor, King of Prussia; His Majesty the Emperor of Austria, King of Bohemia, &c., and Apostolic King of Hungary; His Majesty the King of the Belgians; His Majesty the King of Denmark; His Majesty the King of Spain; the President of the United States of America; the President of the French Republic; His Majesty the King of Italy; His Majesty the King of the Netherlands, Grand Duke of Luxembourg, &c.; His Majesty the King of Portugal and the Algarves, &c.; His Majesty the Emperor of All the Russias; His Majesty the King of Sweden and Norway, &c.; and His Majesty the Emperor of the Ottomans, wishing, in a spirit of good and mutual accord, to regulate the conditions most favorable to the development of trade and civilization in certain regions of Africa, and to assure to all nations the advantages of free navigation on the two chief rivers of Africa flowing into the Atlantic Ocean; being desirous on the other hand, to obviate the misunderstanding and disputes which might in future arise from new acts of occupation (*prises de possession*) on the coast of Africa; and concerned, at the same time, as to the means of furthering the moral and material well-being of the native populations; have resolved, on the invitation addressed to them by the Imperial Government of Germany, in agreement with the Government of the French Republic, to meet for those purposes in Conference at Berlin, and have appointed as their Plenipotentiaries to wit:—
>
> Her Majesty the Queen of the United Kingdom of Great Britain and Ireland, Empress of India
> Sir Edward Baldwin Malet, Her Ambassador Extraordinary and Plenipotentiary at the Court of His Majesty the German Emperor, King of Prussia;
> His Majesty the German Emperor, King of Prussia
> Otto, Prince von Bismarck, his President of the Prussian Council of Ministers, Chancellor of the Empire;

344

Paul, Count von Hatzfeldt, his Minister of State and Secretary of State for Foreign Affairs; Auguste Busch, his Acting Privy Councillor of Legation and Under-Secretary of State for Foreign Affairs; and Henri von Kusserow, Privy Councillor of Legation in the Department for Foreign Affairs;

His Majesty the Emperor of Austria, King of Bohemia, &c., and Apostolic King of Hungary
Emeric, Count Szechenyi de Sarvari Felso-Videk, Chamberlain and Acting Privy Councillor, his Ambassador Extraordinary and Plenipotentiary at the Court of His Majesty the German Emperor, King of Prussia;

His Majesty the King of the Belgians
Gabriel Auguste Count van der Straten-Ponthoz, Envoy Extraordinary and Minister Plenipotentiary at the Court of His Majesty the German Emperor, King of Prussia; and Auguste, Baron Lambermont, Minister of State, Envoy Extraordinary and Minister Plenipotentiary;

His Majesty the King of Denmark
Emile de Vind, Chamberlain, his Envoy Extraordinary and Minister Plenipotentiary at the Court of His Majesty the German Emperor, King of Prussia;

His Majesty the King of Spain
Don Francisco Merry y Colom, Count Benomar, his Envoy Extraordinary and Minister Plenipotentiary at the Court of His Majesty the German Emperor, King of Prussia;

The President of the United States of America
John A. Kasson, Envoy Extraordinary and Minister Plenipotentiary of the United States of America at the Court of His Majesty the German Emperor, King of Prussia, and Henry S. Sanford, ex-Minister;

The President of the French Republic
Alphonse, Baron de Courcel, Ambassador Extraordinary and Plenipotentiary of France at the Court of His Majesty the German Emperor, King of Prussia;

His Majesty the King of Italy
Edward, Count de Launay, his Ambassador Extraordinary and Plenipotentiary at the Court of His Majesty the German Emperor, King of Prussia;

His Majesty the King of the Netherlands
Grand Duke of Luxembourg, Frederick Philippe, Jonkheer van der Hoeven, his Envoy Extraordinary and Minister Plenipotentiary at the Court of His Majesty the German Emperor, King of Prussia;

His Majesty the King of Portugal and the Algarves, &c.
Da Serra Gomes, Marquis de Penafiel, Peer of the Realm, his Envoy Extraordinary and Minister Plenipotentiary at the Court of his Majesty the German Emperor, King of Prussia, and Antoine de Serpa Pimentel, Councillor of State and Peer of the Realm;

His Majesty the Emperor of All the Russias
Pierre, Count Kapnist, Privy Councillor, his Envoy Extraordinary and Minister Plenipotentiary at the Court of His Majesty the King of the Netherlands;

His Majesty the King of Sweden and Norway, &c.
Gillis, Baron Bildt, Lieutenant-General, his Envoy Extraordinary and Minister Plenipotentiary at the

Court of His Majesty the German Emperor, King of Prussia;

His Majesty the Emperor of the Ottomans
Mehemed Said Pasha, Vizir and High Dignitary, his Envoy Extraordinary and Plenipotentiary at the Court of His Majesty the German Emperor, King of Prussia;

Who, being provided with full powers, which have been found in good and due form, have successively discussed and adopted:-

(1) A Declaration relative to freedom of trade in the basin of the Congo, its embouchures and circumjacent regions, with other provisions connected therewith.

(2) A Declaration relative to the Slave Trade, and the operations by sea or land which furnish slaves to that trade.

(3) A Declaration relative to the neutrality of the territories comprised in the Conventional basin of the Congo.

(4) An Act of Navigation for the Congo, which, while having regard to local circumstances,. extends to this river, its affluents, and the waters in its system ("eaux qui leur sont assimilees"), the general principles enunciated in Articles CVIII and CXVI of the Final Act of the Congress of Vienna, and intended to regulate, as between the Signatory Powers of that Act, the free navigation of the waterways separating or traversing several States-these said principles having since then been applied by agreement to certain rivers of Europe and America, but especially to the Danube, with the modifications stipulated by the Treaties of Paris (1856), of Berlin (1878), and of London (1871 and 1883).

(5) An Act of Navigation for the Niger, which, while likewise having regard to local circumstances, extends to this river and its affluents the same principles as set forth in Articles CVIII and CXVI of the Final Act of the Congress of Vienna.

(6) A Declaration introducing into international relations certain uniform rules with reference to future occupations on the coast of the African Continent.

And deeming it expedient that all these several documents should be combined in one single instrument, they (the Signatory Powers) have collected them into one General Act, composed of the following Articles:—

By virtue of the Berlin Congress, the International Congo Association became the Congo Free State. Politically, it was anything but free; the congress recognized Leopold II as personal sovereign of the Congo Free State. Economically, however, the Congo Free State was free in that it was open to businessmen of all nations:

II

All flags, without distinction of nationality, shall have free access to the whole of the coast-line of the territories above enumerated, to the rivers there running into the sea, to all the waters of the Congo and its affluents, including the lakes, and to all the ports situated on the banks of these waters, as well as to all canals which may in future be constructed with intent to unite the watercourses or lakes within the entire area of the territories described in Article I. Those trading under such flags may engage in all sorts of transport, and carry on the coasting trade by sea and river, as well as boat traffic, on the same footing as if they were subjects.

III

Wares, of whatever origin, imported into these regions, under whatsoever flag, by sea or river, or overland, shall be subject to no other taxes than such as may be levied as fair compensation for expenditure in the interests of trade, and which for this reason must be equally borne by the subjects themselves and by foreigners of all nationalities. All differential dues on vessels, as well as on merchandize, are forbidden.

IV

Merchandize imported into these regions shall remain free from import and transit dues.

The Powers reserve to themselves to determine after the lapse of twenty years whether this freedom of import shall be retained or not.

V

No Power which exercises or shall exercise sovereign rights in the above-mentioned regions shall be allowed to grant therein a monopoly or favor of any kind in matters of trade.

Foreigners, without distinction, shall enjoy protection of their persons and property, as well as the right of acquiring and transferring movable and immovable possessions; and national rights and treatment in the exercise of their professions.

The powers whose citizens were now free to exploit the region pledged themselves to (as the British writer Rudyard Kipling put it in a related context) "take up the white man's burden" and look after the welfare of the African people (however these powers might define "welfare"):

VI

All the Powers exercising sovereign rights or influence in the aforesaid territories bind themselves to watch over the preservation of the native tribes, and to care for the improvement of the conditions of their moral and material well-being and to help in suppressing slavery, and especially the Slave Trade. They shall, without distinction of creed or nation, protect and favor all religious, scientific, or charitable institutions and undertakings created and organized for the above ends, or which aim at instructing the natives and bringing home to them the blessings of civilization.

Christian missionaries, scientists, and explorers, with their followers, property, and collections, shall likewise be the objects of especial protection.

Freedom of conscience and religious toleration are expressly guaranteed to the natives, no less than to subjects and to foreigners. The free and public exercise of all forms of Divine worship, and the right to build edifices for religious purposes, and to organize religious Missions belonging to all creeds, shall not be limited or fettered in any way whatsoever.

The slave trade was explicitly outlawed—

Chapter II
Declaration Relative to the Slave Trade

IX

Seeing that trading in slaves is forbidden in conformity with the principles of international law as recognized by the Signatory Powers, and seeing also that the operations, which, by sea or land, furnish slaves to trade, ought likewise to be regarded as forbidden, the Powers which do or shall exercise sovereign rights or influence in the territories forming the Conversitional basin of the Congo declare that these territories may not serve as a market or means of transit for the trade in slaves, of whatever race they may be. Each of the Powers binds itself to employ all the means at its disposal for putting an end to this trade and for punishing those who engage in it.

—and the region's neutrality guaranteed:

Chapter III

Declaration Relative to the Neutrality of the Territories Comprised in the Conventional Basin of the Congo

X

In order to give a new guarantee of security to trade and industry, and to encourage, by the maintenance of peace, the development of civilization in the countries mentioned in Article I, and placed under the free trade system, the High Signatory Parties to the present Act, and those who shall hereafter adopt it, bind themselves to respect the neutrality of the territories, or portions of territories, belonging to the said countries, comprising therein the territorial waters, so long as the Powers which exercise or shall exercise the rights of sovereignty or Protectorate over those territories, using their option of proclaiming themselves neutral, shall fulfil the duties which neutrality requires.

XI

In case a Power exercising rights of sovereignty or Protectorate in the countries mentioned in Article I, and placed under the free trade system, shall be involved in a war, then the High Signatory Parties to the present Act, and those who shall hereafter adopt it, bind themselves to lend their good offices in order that the territories belonging to this Power and comprised in the Conventional free trade zone shall, by the common consent of this Power and of the other belligerent or belligerents, be placed during the war under the rule of neutrality, and considered as belonging to a non-belligerent State, the belligerents thenceforth abstaining from extending hostilities to the territories thus neutralized, and from using them as a base for warlike operations.

XII

In case a serious disagreement originating on the subject of, or in the limits of, the territories mentioned in Article I, and placed under the free trade system, shall arise between any Signatory Powers of the present Act, or the Powers which may become parties to it, these Powers bind themselves, before appealing to arms, to have recourse to the mediation of one or more of the friendly Powers.

In a similar case the same Powers reserve to themselves the option of having recourse to arbitration.

Consequences

The Berlin Congress was an important step in Europe's involvement in Africa. Despite its provisions relative to the welfare of native populations, reports of horrible exploitation and abuse continued to flow out of Leopold's Congo. By the end of the 19th century, an international protest movement, with genuinely humane motives, was steadily mounting. Finally, in 1908 the Belgian parliament compelled the king to step down as personal sovereign of the Congo Free State and cede it as a colony of Belgium. It was granted independence on June 30, 1960. After a decade as being known as the Congo (Léopoldville)—the capital name tagged on to distinguish it from the formerly French-controlled Congo (Brazzaville) to its west—the Afro-conscious nation changed its name to Zaire in 1971, its capital's name to Kinshasa, and the next year ordered all Zairians with Christian names to change them to African names.

HAGUE CONVENTION OF 1899

TREATY AT A GLANCE

Completed
July 29, 1899, at The Hague, the Netherlands

Signatories
Austria-Hungary, Belgium, Bulgaria, China, Denmark, France, Germany, Great Britain, Greece, Italy, Japan, Luxembourg, Mexico, Montenegro, Netherlands, Persia, Portugal, Romania, Russia, Serbia, Siam, Spain, Switzerland, Turkey, United Kingdoms of Sweden and Norway, and the United States

Overview
The Hague Convention of 1899 was the product of an international conference called by Czar Nicholas II of Russia. Its official purpose was to promote general disarmament. No agreement was reached on this head; however, the conference formulated rules for mediation and international arbitration of disputes as an alternative to war.

Historical Background

The term "Hague Convention" stands for any of a series of international treaties issued by two multinational conferences at The Hague in the Netherlands, one in 1899, the other in 1907, aimed at arms limitations and setting a framework for settling international disputes at a time when much of Europe was fearful that the naval arms race, especially between Great Britain and Germany, had the potential for sparking a general war. It was Count Mikhail Nikolayevich Muravyov, minister of foreign affairs for Russia's czar Nicholas II, who extended the invitation for the first meeting. In a circular dated January 11, 1899, Count Muravyov proposed several topics for discussion, including limiting the expansion of armed forces and reducing the deployment of new armaments and applying the principles of the 1864 GENEVA CONVENTION to naval warfare. Most of the 27 nations attending the conference from May 18 to July 29 were European, who after all were those most interested in the dangers of a continental diplomatic system based on a balance of power and stitched together by a series of interlocking alliances, though China—a flashpoint of European (and American) imperialism—was there and two American states, the United States and Mexico, participated.

The Hague Convention, however, was not a meeting of Great Powers seeking to shore up the dangerous system they had created, but instead the result of a broader and worldwide liberal peace movement that sprang up at the turn of the century in response to the growing militarism of the imperial powers. With a mostly middle-class constituency, the movement flourished, producing by 1900 nearly five hundred peace organizations of various kinds, fully half of them in Scandinavia and most of the others in Germany, Britain, and the United States. Even at the time, the Hague conferences—doomed to fail in their larger goal of preventing war—were considered the greatest achievements to result from the agitation of the peace organizations.

Terms

Subtitled a "Convention for the Pacific Settlement of International Disputes," the Hague Convention of 1899 was subscribed to by most of the great powers present, which were listed in the preamble to the document:

> HIS MAJESTY the Emperor of Germany, King of Prussia; His Majesty the Emperor of Austria, King of Bohemia etc. and Apostolic King of Hungary; His Majesty the King of the Belgians; His Majesty the Emperor of China; His Majesty the King of Denmark; His Majesty the King of Spain and in His Name Her

Majesty the Queen Regent of the Kingdom; the President of the United States of America; the President of the United Mexican States; the President of the French Republic; Her Majesty the Queen of the United Kingdom of Great Britain and Ireland, Empress of India; His Majesty the King of the Hellenes; His Majesty the King of Italy; His Majesty the Emperor of Japan; His Royal Highness the Grand Duke of Luxembourg, Duke of Nassau; His Highness the Prince of Montenegro; Her Majesty the Queen of the Netherlands; His Imperial Majesty the Shah of Persia; His Majesty the King of Portugal and of the Algarves etc.; His Majesty the King of Romania; His Majesty the Emperor of all the Russias; His Majesty the King of Serbia; His Majesty the King of Siam; His Majesty the King of Sweden and Norway; the Swiss Federal Council; His Majesty the Emperor of the Ottomans and His Royal Highness the Prince of Bulgaria

Animated by a strong desire to concert for the maintenance of the general peace;

Resolved to second by their best efforts the friendly settlement of international disputes;

Recognizing the solidarity which unites the members of the society of civilized nations;

Desirous of extending the empire of law, and of strengthening the appreciation of international justice;

Convinced that the permanent institution of a Court of Arbitration, accessible to all, in the midst of the independent Powers, will contribute effectively to this result;

Having regard to the advantages attending the general and regular organization of arbitral procedure;

Sharing the opinion of the august Initiator of the International Peace Conference that it is expedient to record in an international Agreement the principles of equity and right on which are based the security of States and the welfare of peoples;

Being desirous of concluding a Convention to this effect, have appointed as their Plenipotentiaries, to-wit:-

HIS MAJESTY THE EMPEROR OF GERMANY, KING OF PRUSSIA:

His Excellency COUNT DE MÜNSTER, Prince of Derneburg, His Ambassador at Paris.

HIS MAJESTY THE EMPEROR OF AUSTRIA, KING OF BOHEMIA ETC., AND APOSTOLIC KING OF HUNGARY:

His Excellency COUNT R. DE WELSERSHEIMB, His Ambassador Extraordinary and Plenipotentiary.

Mr. ALEXANDER OKOLICSANYI D'OKOLICSNA, His Envoy Extraordinary and Minister Plenipotentiary at The Hague.

HIS MAJESTY THE KING OF THE BELGIANS:

His Excellency Mr. AUGUSTE BEERNAERT, His Minister of State, President of the Chamber of Representatives.

COUNT DE GRELLE ROGIER, His Envoy Extraordinary and Minister Plenipotentiary at The Hague.

The CHEVALIER DESCAMPS, Senator.

HIS MAJESTY THE EMPEROR OF CHINA:

My. YANG YU, His Envoy Extraordinary and Minister Plenipotentiary at St. Petersburg.

HIS MAJESTY THE KING OF DENMARK:

His Chamberlain Fr. E. DE BILLE, His Envoy Extraordinary and Minister Plenipotentiary at London.

HIS MAJESTY THE KING OF SPAIN AND IN HIS NAME, HER MAJESTY THE QUEEN REGENT OF THE KINGDOM:

His Excellency the DUKE OF TETUAN, formerly Minister of Foreign Affairs.

Mr. W. RAMIREZ DE VILLA URRUTIA, His Envoy Extraordinary and Minister Plenipotentiary at Brussels.

MR. ARTHUR DE BAGUER, His Envoy Extraordinary and Minister Plenipotentiary at The Hague.

THE PRESIDENT OF THE UNITED STATES OF AMERICA:

His Excellency Mr. ANDREW D. WHITE, Ambassador of the United States at Berlin.

Mr. SETH LOW, President of Columbia University, New York.

Mr. STANFORD NEWEL, Envoy Extraordinary and Minister Plenipotentiary at The Hague.

Captain ALFRED T. MAHAN.

Captain WILLIAM CROZIER.

THE PRESIDENT OF THE UNITED MEXICAN STATES:

Mr. DE MIER, Envoy Extraordinary and Minister Plenipotentiary at Paris.

Mr. ZENIL, Minister Resident at Brussels.

THE PRESIDENT OF THE FRENCH REPUBLIC:

Mr. LEON BOURGEOIS, formerly President of the Council, formerly Minister of Foreign Affairs, Member of the Chamber of Deputies.

Mr. GEORGES BIHOURD, Envoy Extraordinary and Minister Plenipotentiary at The Hague.

The BARON D'ESTOURNELLES DE CONSTANT, Minister Plenipotentiary, Member of the Chamber of Deputies.

HER MAJESTY THE QUEEN OF THE UNITED KINGDOM OF GREAT BRITAIN AND IRELAND, EMPRESS OF INDIA:

His Excellency the Right Honorable BARON PAUNCEFOTE OF PRESTON, Member of Her Majesty's Privy Council, Her Ambassador Extraordinary and Plenipotentiary at Washington.

Sir HENRY HOWARD, Her Envoy Extraordinary and Minister Plenipotentiary at The Hague.

HIS MAJESTY THE KING OF THE HELLENES:

Mr. N. DELYANNI, formerly President of the Council, formerly Minister of Foreign Affairs, His Envoy Extraordinary and Minister Plenipotentiary at Paris.

HIS MAJESTY THE KING OF ITALY:

His Excellency COUNT NIGRA, His Ambassador at Vienna, Senator of the Kingdom.

COUNT A. ZANNINI, His Envoy Extraordinary and Minister Plenipotentiary at The Hague.

Commander GUIDO POMPILJ , Deputy in the Italian Parliament.

HIS MAJESTY THE EMPEROR OF JAPAN:

Mr. I. MOTONO, His Envoy Extraordinary and Plenipotentiary at Brussels.

HIS ROYAL HIGHNESS THE GRAND DUKE OF LUXEMBOURG, DUKE OF NASSAU.

His Excellency Mr. EYSCHEN, His minister of State, President of the Grand Ducal Government.

HIS HIGHNESS THE PRINCE OF MONTE-NEGRO:

His Excellency the present Privy Councillor DE STAAL, Ambassador of Russia at London.

HER MAJESTY THE QUEEN OF THE NETHER-LANDS:

JONKHEER A. P. C. VAN KARNEBEEK, formerly Minister of Foreign Affairs, Member of the Second Chamber of the States-General.

General J. C. C. DEN BEER POORTUGAEL, formerly Minister of War, Member of the Council of State.

Mr. T. M. C. ASSER, Member of the Council of State.

MR. E. N. RAHUSEN, Member of the First Chamber of the States-General.

HIS IMPERIAL MAJESTY THE SHAH OF PERSIA:

His Aide-de-Camp General MIRZA RIZA KHAN, Arfa-ud-Dovleh, His Envoy Extraordinary and Minister Plenipotentiary at St. Petersburg and at Stockholm.

HIS MAJESTY THE KING OF PORTUGAL AND OF THE ALGARVES, ETC.:

COUNT DE MACEDO, Peer of the Kingdom, formerly Minister of the Navy and of the Colonies, His Envoy Extraordinary and Minister Plenipotentiary at Madrid.

Mr. D'ORNELLAS ET VASCONCELLOS, Peer of the Kingdom, His Envoy Extraordinary and Minister Plenipotentiary at St. Petersburg.

COUNT DE SELIR, His Envoy Extraordinary and Minister Plenipotentiary at The Hague.

HIS MAJESTY THE KING OF ROMANIA:

Mr. ALEXANDER BELDIMAN, His Envoy Extraordinary and Minister Plenipotentiary at Berlin.

Mr. JEAN N. PAPINIU, His Envoy Extraordinary and Minister Plenipotentiary at The Hague.

HIS MAJESTY THE EMPEROR OF ALL THE RUSSIAS:

His Excellency the present Privy Councillor DE STAAL, His Ambassador at London.

Mr. DE MARTENS, Permanent Member of the Council of the Imperial Ministry of Foreign Affairs, His Privy Councillor.

His present Councillor of State DE BASILY, Chamberlain, Director of the First Department of the Imperial Ministry of Foreign Affairs.

HIS MAJESTY THE KING OF SERBIA:

Mr. MIYATOVITCH, His Envoy Extraordinary and Minister Plenipotentiary at London and at The Hague.

HIS MAJESTY THE KING OF SIAM:

PHYA SURIYA NUVATR, His Envoy Extraordinary and Minister Plenipotentiary at St. Petersburg and at Paris.

PHYA VISUDDHA SURIYASAKTI, His Envoy Extraordinary and Minister Plenipotentiary at The Hague and at London.

HIS MAJESTY THE KING OF SWEDEN AND NORWAY:

BARON DE BILDT, His Envoy Extraordinary and Minister Plenipotentiary at Rome.

THE SWISS FEDERAL COUNCIL:

Dr. ARNOLD ROTH, Envoy Extraordinary and Minister Plenipotentiary at Berlin.

HIS MAJESTY THE EMPEROR OF THE OTTOMANS:

His Excellency TURKHAN PACHA, formerly Minister of Foreign Affairs, Member of His Council of State.

NOURY BEY, Secretary-General at the Ministry of Foreign Affairs.

HIS ROYAL HIGHNESS THE PRINCE OF BULGARIA:

Dr. DIMITRI STANCIOFF, Diplomatic Agent at St. Petersburg.

Major CHRISTO HESSAPTCHIEFF, Military Attache at Belgrade.

Who, after communication of their full powers, found in good and due form have agreed on the following provisions:

While the primary aim of the Hague Convention was disarmament, the nations present were unable to agree even on guidelines for arms control or arms reduction. However, the signatories did subscribe to a principle of peace:

TITLE I—On the Maintenance of the General Peace

ARTICLE I

With a view to obviating, as far as possible, recourse to force in the relations between States, the Signatory Powers agree to use their best efforts to insure the pacific settlement of international differences.

Title 2 of the convention provided for informal mediation of disputes through the "good offices" of "one or more friendly Powers":

TITLE II—On Good Offices and Mediation

ARTICLE II

In case of serious disagreement or conflict, before an appeal to arms, the Signatory Powers agree to have recourse, as far as circumstances allow, to the good offices or mediation of one or more friendly Powers.

ARTICLE III

Independently of this recourse, the Signatory Powers recommend that one or more Powers, strangers to the dispute, should, on their own initiative, and as far as circumstances may allow, offer their good offices or mediation to the States at variance.

Powers, strangers to the dispute, have the right to offer good offices or mediation, even during the course of hostilities.

The exercise of this right can never be regarded by one or the other of the parties in conflict as an unfriendly act.

ARTICLE IV

The part of the mediator consists in reconciling the opposing claims and appeasing the feelings of resentment which may have arisen between the States at variance.

ARTICLE V

The functions of the mediator are at an end when once it is declared, either by one of the parties to the dispute, or by the mediator himself, that the means of reconciliation proposed by him are not accepted.

ARTICLE VI

Good offices and mediation, either at the request of the parties at variance, or on the initiative of Powers strangers to the dispute, have exclusively the character of advice and never having binding force.

ARTICLE VII

The acceptance of mediation can not, unless there be an agreement to the contrary, have the effect of interrupting, delaying, or hindering mobilization or other measures of preparation for war.

If mediation occurs after the commencement of hostilities it causes no interruption to the military operations in progress, unless there be an agreement to the contrary.

ARTICLE VIII

The Signatory Powers are agreed in recommending the application, when circumstances allow, of special mediation in the following form:—

In case of a serious difference endangering the peace, the States at variance choose respectively a Power, to whom they intrust the mission of entering into direct communication with the Power chosen on the other side, with the object of preventing the rupture of pacific relations.

For the period of this mandate, the term of which, unless otherwise stipulated, cannot exceed thirty days, the States in conflict cease from all direct communication on the subject of the dispute, which is regarded as referred exclusively to the mediating Powers, who must use their best efforts to settle it.

In case of a definite rupture of pacific relations, these Powers are charged with the joint task of taking advantage of any opportunity to restore peace.

Title 3 took the principle of arbitration a step further by defining international commissions of inquiry—bodies to be constituted on an ad hoc basis as required:

TITLE III—On International Commissions of Inquiry

ARTICLE IX

In differences of an international nature involving neither honor nor vital interests, and arising from a dif-

ference of opinion on points of fact, the Signatory Powers recommend that the parties, who have not been able to come to an agreement by means of diplomacy, should as far as circumstances allow, institute an International Commission of Inquiry, to facilitate a solution of these differences by elucidating the facts by means of an impartial and conscientious investigation.

ARTICLE X

The International Commissions of Inquiry are constituted by special agreement between the parties in conflict.

The Convention for an inquiry defines the facts to be examined and the extent of the Commissioners' powers.

It settles the procedure.

On the inquiry both sides must be heard.

The form and the periods to be observed, if not stated in the inquiry Convention, are decided by the Commission itself.

ARTICLE XI

The International Commissions of Inquiry are formed, unless otherwise stipulated, in the manner fixed by Article XXXII of the present convention.

ARTICLE XII

The powers in dispute engage to supply the International Commission of Inquiry, as fully as they may think possible, with all means and facilities necessary to enable it to be completely acquainted with and to accurately understand the facts in question.

ARTICLE XIII

The International Commission of Inquiry communicates its Report to the conflicting Powers, signed by all the members of the Commission.

ARTICLE XIV

The report of the International Commission of Inquiry is limited to a statement of facts, and has in no way the character of an Arbitral Award. It leaves the conflicting Powers entire freedom as to the effect to be given to this statement.

Finally, Title 4 introduced and established the Permanent Court of Arbitration (popularly called the Hague Tribunal), the modern world's first permanent international body designed to resolve—peacefully—conflicts among nations:

TITLE IV—On International Arbitration

CHAPTER I On the System of Arbitration

ARTICLE XV

International arbitration has for its object the settlement of differences between States by judges of their own choice, and on the basis of respect for law.

ARTICLE XVI

In questions of a legal nature, and especially in the interpretation or application of International Conventions, arbitration is recognized by the Signatory Powers as the most effective, and at the same time the most equitable, means of settling disputes which diplomacy has failed to settle.

ARTICLE XVII

The Arbitration Convention is concluded for questions already existing or for questions which may arise eventually.

It may embrace any dispute or only disputes of a certain category.

ARTICLE XVIII

The Arbitration Convention implies the engagement to submit loyally to the Award.

ARTICLE XIX

Independently of general or private Treaties expressly stipulating recourse to arbitration as obligatory on the Signatory Powers, these Powers reserve to themselves the right of concluding, either before the ratification of the present Act or later, new Agreements, general or private, with a view to extending obligatory arbitration to all cases which they may consider it possible to submit it.

CHAPTER II On the Permanent Court of Arbitration

With the object of facilitating an immediate recourse to arbitration for international differences, which it has not been possible to settle by diplomacy, the Signatory Powers undertake to organize a permanent Court of Arbitration, accessible at all times and operating, unless otherwise stipulated by the parties, in accordance with the Rules of Procedure inserted in the present Convention.

ARTICLE XXI

The Permanent Court shall be competent for all arbitration cases, unless the parties agree to institute a special Tribunal.

ARTICLE XXII

An International Bureau, established at The Hague, serves as record office for the Court.

This Bureau is the channel for communications relative to the meetings of the Court

It has the custody of the archives and conducts all the administrative business.

The Signatory Powers undertake to communicate to the International Bureau at The Hague a duly certified copy of any conditions of arbitration arrived at between them, and of any award concerning them delivered by special Tribunals.

They undertake also to communicate to the Bureau the Laws, Regulations, and documents eventually showing the execution of the awards given by the Court.

ARTICLE XXIII

Within the three months following its ratification of the present Act, each Signatory Power shall select four persons at the most, of known competency in questions of international law, of the highest moral reputation, and disposed to accept the duties of Arbitrators.

The persons thus selected shall be inscribed as members of the Court, in a list which shall be notified by the Bureau to all the Signatory Powers.

Any alteration in the list of Arbitrators is brought by the Bureau to the knowledge of the Signatory Powers.

Two or more Powers may agree on the selection in common of one or more Members.

The same person can be selected by different Powers.

The Members of the Court are appointed for a term of six years. Their appointments can be renewed.

In case of the death or retirement of a member of the Court, his place shall be filled in accordance with the method of his appointment.

ARTICLE XXIV

When the Signatory Powers desire to have recourse to the Permanent Court for the settlement of a difference that has arisen between them, the Arbitrators called upon to form the competent Tribunal to decide this difference, must be chosen from the general list of members of the Court.

Failing the direct agreement of the parties on the composition of the Arbitration Tribunal, the following course shall be pursued:—

Each party appoints two Arbitrators, and these together choose an Umpire.

If the votes are equal, the choice of the Umpire is intrusted to a third Power, selected by the parties by common accord.

If an agreement is not arrived at on this subject, each party selects a different Power, and the choice of the Umpire is made in concert by the Powers thus selected.

The Tribunal being thus composed, the parties notify to the Bureau their determination to have recourse to the Court and the names of the Arbitrators.

The Tribunal of Arbitration assembles on the date fixed by the parties.

The Members of the Court, in the discharge of their duties and out of their own country, enjoy diplomatic privileges and immunities.

ARTICLE XXV

The Tribunal of Arbitration has its ordinary seat at The Hague.

Except in cases of necessity, the place of session can only be altered by the Tribunal with the assent of the parties.

ARTICLE XXVI

The International Bureau at The Hague is authorized to place its premises and its staff at the disposal of the Signatory Powers for the operations of any special Board of Arbitration.

The jurisdiction of the Permanent Court, may, within the conditions laid down in the Regulations, be extended to disputes between non-Signatory Powers, or between Signatory Powers and non-Signatory Powers, if the parties are agreed on recourse to this Tribunal.

ARTICLE XXVII

The Signatory Powers consider it their duty, if a serious dispute threatens to break out between two or more of them, to remind these latter that the Permanent Court is open to them.

Consequently, they declare that the fact of reminding the conflicting parties of the provisions of the present Convention, and the advice given to them, in the highest interests of peace, to have recourse to the Permanent Court, can only be regarded as friendly actions.

ARTICLE XXVIII

A Permanent Administrative Council, composed of the Diplomatic Representatives of the Signatory Powers accredited to The Hague and of the Netherlands Minister for Foreign Affairs, who will act as President, shall be instituted in this town as soon as possible after the ratification of the present Act by at least nine Powers.

This Council will be charged with the establishment and organization of the International Bureau, which will be under its direction and control.

It will notify to the Powers the constitution of the Court and will provide for its installation.

It will settle its Rules of Procedure and all other necessary Regulations.

It will decide all questions of administration which may arise with regard to the operations of the Court.

It will have entire control over the appointment, suspension or dismissal of the officials and employees of the Bureau.

It will fix the payments and salaries, and control the general expenditure.

At meetings duly summoned the presence of five members is sufficient to render valid the discussions of the Council. The decisions are taken by a majority of votes.

The Council communicates to the Signatory Powers without delay the Regulations adopted by it. It furnishes them with an annual Report on the labors of the Court, the working of the administration, and the expenses.

ARTICLE XXIX

The expenses of the Bureau shall be borne by the Signatory Powers in the proportion fixed for the International Bureau of the Universal Postal Union.

CHAPTER III On Arbitral Procedure

ARTICLE XXX

With a view to encourage the development of arbitration, the Signatory Powers have agreed on the following Rules which shall be applicable to arbitral procedure, unless other rules have been agreed on by the parties.

ARTICLE XXXI

The Powers who have recourse to arbitration sign a special Act ("Compromis"), in which the subject of the difference is clearly defined, as well as the extent of the Arbitrators' powers. This Act implies the undertaking of the parties to submit loyally to the award.

ARTICLE XXXII

The duties of Arbitrator may be conferred on one Arbitrator alone or on several Arbitrators selected by the parties as they please, or chosen by them from the members of the Permanent Court of Arbitration established by the present Act.

Failing the constitution of the Tribunal by direct agreement between the parties, the following course shall be pursued:

Each party appoints two arbitrators, and these latter together choose an Umpire.

In case of equal voting, the choice of the Umpire is intrusted to a third Power, selected by the parties by common accord.

If no agreement is arrived at on this subject, each party selects a different Power, and the choice of the Umpire is made in concert by the Powers thus selected.

ARTICLE XXXIII

When a Sovereign or the Chief of a State is chosen as Arbitrator, the arbitral procedure is settled by him.

ARTICLE XXXIV.

The Umpire is by right President of the Tribunal.

When the Tribunal does not include an Umpire, it appoints its own President.

ARTICLE XXXV

In case of the death, retirement, or disability from any cause of one of the Arbitrators, his place shall be filled in accordance with the method of his appointment.

ARTICLE XXXVI

The Tribunal's place of session is selected by the parties. Failing this selection the Tribunal sits at The Hague.

The place thus fixed cannot, except in case of necessity, be changed by the Tribunal without the assent of the parties.

ARTICLE XXXVII

The parties have the right to appoint delegates or special agents to attend the Tribunal, for the purpose of serving as intermediaries between them and the Tribunal.

They are further authorized to retain, for the defense of their rights and interests before the Tribunal, counsel or advocates appointed by them for this purpose.

ARTICLE XXXVIII

The Tribunal decides on the choice of languages to be used by itself and to be authorized for use before it.

ARTICLE XXXIX

As a general rule the arbitral procedure comprises two distinct phases; preliminary examination and discussion.

Preliminary examination consists in the communication by the respective agents to the members of the

Tribunal and to the opposite party of all printed or written Acts and of all documents containing the arguments invoked in the case. This communication shall be made in the form and within the periods fixed by the Tribunal in accordance with Article XLIX.

Discussion consists in the oral development before the Tribunal of the arguments of the parties.

ARTICLE XL

Every document produced by one party must be communicated to the other party.

ARTICLE XLI

The discussions are under the direction of the President.

They are only public if it be so decided by the Tribunal, with the assent of the parties.

They are recorded in the *procès-verbaux* drawn up by the Secretaries appointed by the President. These *procès-verbaux* alone have an authentic character.

ARTICLE XLII

When the preliminary examination is concluded, the Tribunal has the right to refuse discussion of all fresh Acts or documents which one party may desire to submit to it without the consent of the other party.

ARTICLE XLII

The Tribunal is free to take into consideration fresh Acts or documents to which its attention may be drawn by the agents or counsel of the parties.

In this case, the Tribunal has the right to require the production of these Acts or documents, but is obliged to make them known to the opposite party.

ARTICLE XLIV

The Tribunal can, besides, require from the agents of the parties the production of all Acts, and can demand all necessary explanations. In case of refusal, the Tribunal takes note of it.

ARTICLE XLV

The agents and counsel of the parties are authorized to present orally to the Tribunal all the arguments they may think expedient in defence of their case.

ARTICLE XLVI

They have the right to raise objections and points. The decisions of the Tribunal on those points are final, and cannot form the subject of any subsequent discussion.

ARTICLE XLVII

The members of the Tribunal have the right to put questions to the agents and counsel of the parties, and to demand explanations from them on doubtful points.

Neither the questions put nor the remarks made by members of the Tribunal during the discussions can be regarded as an expression of opinion by the Tribunal in general, or by its members in particular.

ARTICLE XLVIII

The Tribunal is authorized to declare its competence in interpreting the "Compromis" as well as the other Treaties which may be invoked in the case, and in applying the principles of international

ARTICLE XLIX

The Tribunal has the right to issue Rules of Procedure for the conduct of the case, to decide the forms and periods within which each party must conclude its arguments, and to arrange all the formalities required for dealing with the evidence.

ARTICLE L

When the agents and counsel of the parties have submitted all explanations and evidence in support of their case, the President pronounces the discussion closed.

ARTICLE LI

The deliberations of the Tribunal take place in private. Every decision is taken by a majority of members of the Tribunal.

The refusal of a member to vote must be recorded in the *procès-verbal*.

ARTICLE LII

The award, given by a majority of votes, is accompanied by a statement of reasons. It is drawn up in writing and signed by each member of the Tribunal.

Those members who are in the minority may record their dissent when signing.

ARTICLE LIII

The award is read out at a public meeting of the Tribunal, the agents and counsel of the parties being present, or duly summoned to attend.

ARTICLE LIV

The award, duly pronounced and notified to the agents of the parties at variance, puts an end to the dispute definitely and without appeal.

ARTICLE LV

The parties can reserve in the "Compromis" the right to demand the revision of the award.

In this case, and unless there be an agreement to the contrary, the demand must be addressed to the Tribunal which pronounced the award. It can only be made on the ground of the discovery of some new fact calculated to exercise a decisive influence on the award, and which, at the time the discussion was closed, was unknown to the Tribunal and to the party demanding the revision.

Proceedings for revision can only be instituted by a decision of the Tribunal expressly recording the existence of the new fact, recognizing in it the character described in the foregoing paragraph, and declaring the demand admissible on this ground.

The "Compromis" fixes the period within which the demand for revision must be made.

ARTICLE LVI

The award is only binding on the parties who concluded the "Compromis."

When there is a question of interpreting a Convention to which Powers other than those concerned in the dispute are parties, the latter notify to the former the "Compromis" they have concluded. Each of these Powers has the right to intervene in the case. If one or more of them avail themselves of this right, the interpretation contained in the award is equally binding on them.

ARTICLE LVII

Each party pays its own expenses and an equal share of those of the Tribunal.

ARTICLE LVIII

The present Convention shall be ratified as speedily as possible.

The ratifications shall be deposited at The Hague.

A *procès-verbal* shall be drawn up recording the receipt of each ratification, and a copy duly certified shall be sent, through the diplomatic channel, to all the Powers who were represented at the International Peace Conference at The Hague.

ARTICLE LIX

The non-Signatory Powers who were represented at the International Peace Conference can adhere to the present Convention. For this purpose they must make known their adhesion to the Contracting Powers by a written notification addressed to the Netherlands Government, and communicated by it to all the other Contracting Powers.

ARTICLE LX

The conditions on which the Powers who were not represented at the International Peace Conference can adhere to the present Convention shall form the subject of a subsequent Agreement among the Contracting Powers.

A final article provided for individual signatories' "denouncing" the convention and provided a one-year period from the announcement of the denunciation to its effective date:

ARTICLE LXI

In the event of one of the High Contracting Parties denouncing the present Convention, this denunciation would not take effect until a year after its notification made in writing to the Netherlands Government, and by it communicated at once to all the other Contracting Powers.

This denunciation shall only affect the notifying Power.

In faith of which the Plenipotentiaries have signed the present Convention and affixed their seals to it.

Done at The Hague, the 29th July, 1899, in a single copy, which shall remain in the archives of the Netherlands Government, and copies of it, duly certified, be sent through the diplomatic channel to the Contracting Powers.

Consequences

While the 1899 conference failed to achieve its primary goal of limiting arms production—and eventually general disarmament—it did accept three declarations banning certain "inhumane" weapons: one prohibited the use of asphyxiating gases, another the use of expanding bullets (dumdums), and a third the discharge of projectiles or explosives from balloons. Even more important were those conventions, discussed above, that it adopted defining the conditions of a state of belligerency and other customs relating to war on land and sea. Perhaps the Convention for the Pacific Settlement of International Disputes, which created the Permanent Court of Arbitration, would prove the most significant of all. For it was in these latter matters, rather than in the banning of certain weapons (which nations at war in 1914–18 would come simply to ignore), that the Hague Convention laid the groundwork for future international world peace organizations.

Meanwhile, however, the fin de siècle liberal peace movement foundered on its internal contradictions. While liberals might consider themselves good Europeans or even world citizens beyond the narrow call of national militarism, they wanted to outlaw war without endorsing the international status quo. So, when the Italians and Germans fought wars of unification or tiny Balkan states rebelled against the Ottoman Empire, the European middle classes tolerated them because they were fought for "progressive" ends—and liberals, even Social Democrats, were always ready to excuse a war claiming progressive ends. This meant, in the long run, they had no place to stand, except beside the tiny Bolshevik Party, despised by liberal and socialist alike, when the "Great War" they all feared came along in 1914.

BOXER PROTOCOL

TREATY AT A GLANCE

Completed
September 7, 1901, at Beijing (Peking)

Signatories
The "Great Powers" (Germany, Austria-Hungary, Belgium, Spain, United States, France, Great Britain, Italy, Japan, Netherlands, Russia) and China

Overview
After putting down an antiforeign uprising in China known as the Boxer Rebellion, the United States, the European powers, and Japan imposed an indemnity on China, effectively forcing it to yield to Western and Japanese imperialism. The Boxer Protocol spelled out the punitive provisions of this new relationship.

Historical Background

The so-called open-door policy between China and the rest of the world was first suggested by a British customs official, Alfred E. Hippisley, but it was U.S. secretary of state John Hay who formally proposed a policy whereby all nations would have equal trading and development rights in China. In 1899 Hay communicated the essence of the policy to France, Germany, Great Britain, Italy, Japan, and Russia. The Japanese resisted it, but the European powers replied that they would comply, provided the others did. Hay took this hedge as a positive endorsement, unilaterally announcing in March 1900 that the open-door policy had been agreed to and approved.

The trouble was that none of the nations involved intended to adhere unconditionally to the policy, and the interests of China itself were neglected entirely. The result of the foreign powers' high-handedness was an uprising during the spring of 1900 spearheaded by militia units in the north called Yihe Quang (I-ho Ch'uan)—the "righteous harmony fists," a name that produced the label "Boxers" in the foreign press. The virulently antiforeign empress dowager Cixi (Tz'u-hsi)—in default of China's ineffectual emperor the single most powerful person in China—encouraged the Boxers to attack and kill foreigners as well as Christian Chinese and Chinese with ties to foreigners. In Beijing (Peking), foreign legations were held under siege, and a number of officials slain. In response, an international force of British, French, German, Japanese, Russian, and American troops invaded the capital in August 1900.

Even before the expedition got under way, Secretary Hay was fearful that the foreign powers would use the Boxer Uprising to abrogate the open-door policy and simply dismember China. Accordingly, Hay issued a "circular letter" on July 3, stating it as the policy of the United States "to seek a solution which may bring about permanent safety and peace to China, preserve Chinese territorial and administrative integrity, protect all rights guaranteed to friendly powers by treaty and international law, and safeguard for the world the principle of equal and impartial trade with all parts of the Chinese Empire."

Despite the apparently noble intentions of Hay's circular letter, after the Chinese imperial court fled Xi'an (Sian) before the onslaught of the expedition sent to subdue the Boxers, and after the uprising was contained, the Great Powers forced upon the emperor (and the empress dowager) a harsh "protocol," which China accepted in September 1901.

Terms

The protocol called for China to pay an exorbitant punitive indemnity equivalent to $333 million, of which $24,500,000 was to go to the United States. China also agreed to the stationing of foreign troops at the legations in Beijing and along the routes to the sea. The punitive nature of the Boxer Protocol is made startlingly clear by its opening articles, which called for the erection of a monument to the German minister to China, killed by the Boxers (Article 1), detailed the "punishments on the principal authors of the attempts and of the crimes committed against the foreign Governments and their nationals" (Article 2), acknowledged an abject imperial Chinese apology to Japan for the assassination of the chancellor of the Japanese legation (Article 3), and ordered the erection of "expiatory monuments in each of the foreign or international cemeteries which were desecrated" during the Boxer Uprising (Article 4).

The protocol also forbade China to import arms, ammunition, and the materials for manufacturing arms and ammunition for at least two years, with extensions of the ban to be imposed "in case of necessity recognized by the Powers" (Article 5). And Article 6 of the protocol detailed the amount of indemnities to be paid and the terms of payment:

> By an Imperial Edict dated the 29th May, 1901, His Majesty the Emperor of China agreed to pay the Powers an indemnity of 450,000,000 of Haikwan taels.
>
> This sum represents the total amount of the indemnities for States, Companies, or Societies, private individuals and Chinese, referred to in Article 6 of the note of the 22nd December, 1900.
>
> 1) These 450,000,000 constitute a gold debt calculated at the rate of the Haikwan tael to the gold currency of each country, as indicated below:—

Marks	3.055
Austro-Hungary crown	3.595
Haikwan tael = Gold dollar	0.743
Francs	3.740
Lb. sterling	3s
Yen	1.407
Netherlands florin	1.796
Gold rouble (17.434 dolias fine)	1,412

> This sum in gold shall bear interest at 4 per cent. per annum, and the capital shall be reimbursed by China in thirty-nine years in the manner indicated in the annexed plan of amortization. Capital and interest shall be payable in gold or at the rates of exchange corresponding to the dates at which the different payments fall due.
>
> The amortization shall commence the 1st January, 1902, and shall finish at the end of the year 1940. The amortizations are payable annually, the first payment being fixed on the 1st January, 1903.
>
> Interest shall run from the 1st July, 1901, but the Chinese Government shall have the right to pay off within a term of three years, beginning January 1902, the arrears of the first six months ending the 31st December, 1901, on condition, however, that it pays compound interest at the rate of 4 per cent. a year on the sums the payment of which shall have been thus deferred.
>
> Interest shall be payable semi-annually, the first payment being fixed on the 1st July, 1902.

> 2) The service of the debt shall take place in Shanghai in the following manner:—
>
> Each Power shall be represented by a Delegate on a Commission of bankers authorized to receive the amount of interest and amortization which shall be paid to it by the Chinese authorities designated for that purpose, to divide it among the interested parties, and to give a receipt for the same.
>
> 3) The Chinese Government shall deliver to the Doyen of the Diplomatic Corps at Peking a bond for the lump sum, which shall subsequently be converted into fractional bonds bearing the signature of the Delegates of the Chinese Government designated for that purpose. This operation and all those relating to issuing of the bonds shall be performed by the abovementioned Commission, in accordance with the instructions which the Powers shall send their Delegates.
>
> 4) The proceeds of the revenues assigned to the payment of the bonds shall be paid monthly to the Commission.
>
> 5) The revenues assigned as security for the bonds are the following:—
>
> a) The balance of the revenues of the Imperial Maritime Customs, after payment of the interest and amortization of preceding loans secured on these revenues, plus the proceeds of the raising to 5 per cent. effective of the present tariff of maritime imports, including articles until now on the free list, but exempting rice, foreign cereals, and flour, gold and silver bullion and coin.
>
> b) The revenues of the native Customs, administered in the open ports by the Imperial Maritime Customs.
>
> c) The total revenues of the salt gabelle, exclusive of the fraction previously set aside for other foreign loans.
>
> 6) The raising of the present tariff on imports to 5 per cent. effective is agreed to on the conditions mentioned below. It shall be put in force two months after the signing of the present Protocol, and no exceptions shall be made except for merchandize in transit not more than ten days after the said signing.
>
> a) All duties levied on imports *ad valorem* shall be converted as far as possible and as soon as may be into specific duties.
>
> This conversion shall be made in the following manner:—
>
> The average value of merchandize at the time of their landing during the three years 1897, 1898, and 1899, that is to say, the market price less the amount of import duties and incidental expenses, shall be taken as the basis for the valuation of merchandize.
>
> Pending the result of the work of conversion, duties shall be levied *ad valorem*.
>
> b) The beds of the Rivers Whangpoo and Peiho shall be improved with the financial participation of China.

Subsequent protocol articles set aside the area of Beijing occupied by the foreign legations as "specially reserved" and under the "exclusive control" of the Great Powers. Chinese residents were excluded from this area, which was fortified and defended by foreign troops permanently quartered there. Strategic points between the capital and the sea were also to be manned by foreign troops, and the Chinese government was ordered expressly to outlaw—"for ever under pain of death"—membership in any antiforeign society. The penultimate article, 11, stipulated a program for the improvement of internal watercourses in order to make them accessible to foreign commerce. The expenses for this program were to be shared by China and the Great Powers.

Consequences

The United States was never very comfortable with its portion of the Boxer Protocol and subsequently reduced its indemnity to $12 million, forgiving the unpaid balance on the reduced amount in 1924. Despite the good faith shown by these concessions, the United States repeatedly acquiesced to violations of the open-door policy. The Taft-Katsura Memorandum of 1905, between the United States and Japan, established a foundation for a Japanese protectorate in Korea. America also acknowledged Japan's "special interests" in China by means of the Lansing-Ishii Agreement of 1917, setting the stage for the 1932 Japanese invasion of Manchuria, first of the preludes to World War II.

The most momentous and immediate effect of the Boxer affair and the punitive protocol that followed it was the final undermining of the Qing (Ch'ing), or Manchu, dynasty, which had ruled since 1644 and had barely survived a series of destructive civil wars in the mid-19th century. In 1911 the Qing were overthrown in a revolution that established a corrupt and chaotic republic torn by the jarring demands of a host of warlords. The nation was thus made ripe for further revolution and, eventually, for communist domination.

Annexations and Territorial Agreements

CLAYTON-BULWER TREATY

> ### TREATY AT A GLANCE
>
> *Completed (Ratified)*
> April 19, 1850, at Washington, D.C.
>
> *Signatories*
> United States and Great Britain
>
> *Overview*
> When diplomatic relations between Great Britain and the United States became strained over control of a potential canal through the Isthmus of Panama, they negotiated a treaty that was unpopular with America's expansionist lobby because, while neutralizing the canal issue, it also seemed to negate the MONROE DOCTRINE.

Historical Background

For centuries Europeans had dreamed of joining the Atlantic and Pacific Oceans by cutting a canal through the Isthmus of Panama, but the United States did not begin to take the idea seriously until after the Mexican War of 1846–48. That year the United States, seeking faster communication between its east coast and the Far West (and quick transport to the gold fields just discovered in California), signed a treaty with New Granada (today's Colombia) that gave Americans transit rights through Panama in exchange for a guarantee of New Granada's sovereignty over the isthmus province.

Meanwhile, American diplomats, influenced by speculators and adventurers, had become mired in the affairs of the tiny and politically volatile Republic of Nicaragua, which many of them saw as being every bit as promising a site as Panama for an interocean canal. However, they had come up against Great Britain, whose world trade, transoceanic navy, and numerous colonies ensured that she was keenly interested in such a canal. In fact, most people, recognizing the enormous cost involved in building a canal, assumed it would be British capitalists, bloated by imperial profits, who would finance and control it.

London had been keeping close watch on U.S. ambitions in Central America, and the British had established a beachhead at the mouth of the San Juan River, which was the most likely terminus for a Nicaraguan canal. Claiming a protectorate of the Mosquito Indians on Nicaragua's east coast, the British set off alarms within the American foreign policy community. The two countries exchanged diplomatic notes warning they would not permit the other exclusive control over a canal through the isthmus. In 1850 the British minister to the United States, Sir William Henry Lytton Bulwer, and Zachary Taylor's secretary of state, John Clayton, got together and agreed to terms in a treaty settling the dispute.

Terms

The Clayton-Bulwer Treaty provided that any canal built through either Panama or Nicaragua would be unfortified, neutral during war, and open to shipping from any country on equal terms, and that neither the United States nor the United Kingdom was to colonize or try to establish dominion over any part of Central America.

THE United States of America and her Britannic Majesty, being desirous of consolidating the relations of amity which so happily subsist between them, by setting forth and fixing in a convention their views and intentions with reference to any means of communication by ship canal, which may be constructed between the Atlantic and Pacific Oceans, by the way of the River San Juan de Nicaragua, and either or both of the lakes of

Nicaragua or Managua, to any port or place on the Pacific Ocean: the President of the United States has conferred full powers on John M. Clayton, Secretary of State of the United States; and her Britannic Majesty on the Right Honorable Sir Henry Lytton Bulwer, a member of her Majesty's Most Honorable Privy Council, Knight Commander of the Most Honorable Order of the Bath, and Envoy Extraordinary and Minister Plenipotentiary of her Britannic Majesty to the United States, for the aforesaid purpose; and the said plenipotentiaries, having exchanged their full powers, which were found to be in proper form, have agreed to the following articles:

ARTICLE I

The governments of the United States and Great Britain hereby declare, that neither the one nor the other will ever obtain or maintain for itself any exclusive control over the said ship canal; agreeing that neither will ever erect or maintain any fortifications commanding the same or in the vicinity thereof, or occupy, or fortify, or colonize, or assume or exercise any dominion over Nicaragua, Costa Rica, the Mosquito coast, or any part of Central America; nor will either make use of any protection which either affords or may afford, or any alliance which either teas or may have, to or with any State or people, for the purpose of erecting or maintaining any such fortifications, or of occupying, fortifying, or colonizing Nicaragua, Costa Rica, the Mosquito coast, or any part of Central America, or of assuming or exercising dominion over the same; nor will the United States or Great Britain take advantage of any intimacy, or use any alliance, connection, or influence that either may possess, with any State or government through whose territory the said canal may pass, for the purpose of acquiring or holding, directly or indirectly, for the citizens or subjects of the one, any rights or advantages in regard to commerce or navigation through the said canal which shall not be offered on the same terms to the citizens or subjects of the other.

ARTICLE II

Vessels of the United States or Great Britain traversing the said canal shall, in case of war between the contracting parties, be exempted from blockade, detention, or capture by either of the belligerents; and this provision shall extend to such a distance from the two ends of the said canal as may hereafter be found expedient to establish.

ARTICLE III

In order to secure the construction of the said canal, the contracting parties engage, that, if any such canal shall be undertaken upon fair and equitable terms, by any parties having the authority of the local government or governments through whose territory the same may pass, then the persons employed in making the said canal, and their property used or to be used for that object, shall be protected, from the commencement of the said canal to its completion, by the governments of the United States and Great Britain, from unjust detention, confiscation seizure, or any violence whatsoever.

ARTICLE IV

The contracting parties will use whatever influence they respectively exercise with any State, states, or governments, possessing, or claiming to possess, any jurisdiction or right over the territory which the said canal shall traverse, or which shall be near the waters applicable thereto, in order to induce such states or governments to facilitate the construction of the said canal by every means in their power; and furthermore, the United States and Great Britain agree to use their good offices, wherever or however it may be most expedient, in order to procure the establishment of two free ports, one at each end of the said canal.

ARTICLE V

The contracting parties further engage that, when the said canal shall have been completed, they will protect it from interruption, seizure, or Unjust confiscation, and that they will guarantee the neutrality thereof, so that the said canal may forever be open and free, and the capital invested therein secure. Nevertheless, the governments of the United States and Great Britain, in according their protection to the construction of the said canal, and guaranteeing its neutrality and security when completed, always understand that this protection and guarantee are granted conditionally, and may be withdrawn by both governments, or either government, if both governments, or either government should deem that the persons or company undertaking or managing the same adopt or establish such regulations concerning the traffic thereupon as are contrary to the spirit and intention of this convention, either by making unfair discriminations in favor of the commerce of one of the contracting parties over the commerce of the other, or by imposing oppressive exactions or unreasonable tolls upon passengers, vessels, goods, wares, merchandise, or other articles. Neither party, however, shall withdraw the aforesaid protection and guarantee, without first giving six months notice to the other.

ARTICLE VI

The contracting parties in this convention engage to invite every State with which both or either have friendly intercourse, to enter into stipulations with them similar to those which they have entered into with each other, to the end that all other States may share in the honor and advantage of having contributed to a work of such general interest and importance as the canal herein contemplated. And the contracting parties likewise agree that each shall enter into treaty stipulations with such of the Central American States as they may deem advisable, for the purpose of more effectually carrying out the great design of this convention, namely, that of constructing and maintaining the said canal as a ship communication between the two oceans, for the benefit of mankind, on equal terms to all, and of protecting the same; and they also agree, that the good offices of either shall be employed, when requested by the other, in aiding and assisting the negotiation of such treaty stipulations; and should any differences arise as to right or prop. arty over the territory through which the said canal shall pass,—between the States or governments of Central America,—and such differences should, in any way, impede or obstruct the execution of the said canal, the governments of the United States and Great Britain will use their good offices to settle such differences in the manner best suited to promote the interests of the said canal, and to strengthen the bonds of friendship and alliance which exist between the contracting parties.

ARTICLE VII

It being desirable that no time should be unnecessarily lost in commencing and constructing the said canal, the governments of the United States and Great Britain determine to give their support and encouragement to such persons or company as may first offer to commence the same, with the necessary capital, the consent of the local authorities, and on such principles as accord with the spirit and intention of this convention; and if any persons or company should already have, with any State through which the proposed ship canal may pass, a contract for the construction of such a canal as that specified in this convention, to the stipulations of which contract neither of the contracting parties in this convention have any just cause to object, and the said persons or company shall, moreover, have made preparations, and expended time, money, and trouble, on the faith of such contract, it is hereby agreed that such persons or company shall have a priority of claim, over every other person, persons, or company, to the protection of the governments of the United States and Great Britain, and be allowed a year from the date of the exchange of the ratifications of this convention for concluding their arrangements, and presenting evidence of sufficient capital subscribed to accomplish the contemplated undertaking; it being understood that if, at the expiration of the aforesaid period, such persons or company be not able to commence and carry out the proposed enterprise, then the governments of the United States and Great Britain shall be free to afford their protection to any other persons or company that shall be prepared to commence and proceed with the construction of the canal in question.

ARTICLE VIII

The governments of the United States and Great Britain having not only desired, in entering into this convention, to accomplish a particular object, but also to establish a general principle, they hereby agree to extend their protection, by treaty stipulations, to any other practicable communications, whether by canal or railway, across the isthmus which connects North and South America, and especially to the inter oceanic communications, should the same prove to be practicable, whether by canal or railway, which are now proposed to be established by the way of Tehuantepec or Panama. In granting, however, their joint protection to any such canals or railways as are by this article specified, it is always understood by the United States and Great Britain that the parties constructing or owning the same shall impose no other charges or conditions of traffic thereupon than the aforesaid govern. meets shall approve of as just and equitable; and that the same canals or railways, being open to the citizens and subjects of the United States and Great Britain on equal terms, shall also be open on like terms to the citizens and subjects of every other State which is willing to grant thereto such protection as the United States and Great Britain engage to afford.

The ratifications of this convention shall be exchanged at Washington within six months from this day, or sooner if possible.

In faith whereof, we, the respective plenipotentiaries, have sinned this convention, and have hereunto affixed our seals. Done at Washington, the nineteenth day of April, anno Domini one thousand eight hundred and fifty.

JOHN M. CLAYTON, [L.S.]
HENRY LYTTON BULWER. [L.S.]

Consequences

The treaty was ratified by the U.S. Senate and remained in force for half a century, but it was never very popular. American expansionists hated it because it disallowed the United States from acquiring territory in Central America, which they said was tantamount to applying the Monroe Doctrine against the country that proclaimed it in the first place. Along the same lines, they argued, the treaty implied that the British had equal interests (and a right to those interests) in the region. Many thought Bulwer had outwitted Clayton, and wags suggested he be given a peerage for his work on the document.

Great Britain only made matters worse when she, in typically haughty fashion, maintained that the treaty was not retroactive, meaning she still got to keep her protectorate over the Mosquito Coast. The Americans responded in a fashion just as typical: Tennessee filibuster William Walker led an expedition to Nicaragua in 1855 and took over the country. He was soon driven out, but not by the British. Instead, Cornelius Vanderbilt, who had first given Walker some more or less clandestine support but who now needed him out of the way in order to get on with the business of building a railroad across the isthmus, was the driving force behind his removal.

Ultimately, of course, it would be the United States, fueled by the needs of such men, who alone would build and control the canal.

ALASKA PURCHASE TREATY

TREATY AT A GLANCE

Completed
June 20, 1867 (concluded March 30, ratified May 28,
exchanged and proclaimed June 20), at Washington, D.C.

Signatories
United States and Russia

Overview
At the conclusion of a long period of external expansion, the
United States purchased from Russia its last holdings on the
American continent before turning to the populating and
economic development of its "internal" colony,
the trans-Mississippi region in the aftermath of the Civil War.

Historical Background

From the beginning the new American nation of the United States, born as a result of European colonial expansion, was itself expansion minded, as the LOUISIANA PURCHASE in 1803, the acquisition by treaty of Florida in 1819, the annexation of Texas and the taking by conquest of New Mexico, California, and Oregon in the Mexican War, and the GADSDEN PURCHASE following that war amply illustrate. So headlong was its expansion across the continent, in fact, that it created tensions that in large measure led the country to a civil war over issues once considered settled by a balance of power between internal regions. After the Civil War, with a capitalist economy in full boom, the country tended to expand still, but over those continental lands already acquired, treating the trans-Mississippi region much the way any European power treated its colonies. Since the expansion was economic and internal, some historians have argued that U.S. diplomatic isolationism was a product of this period, a withdrawal, as it were, from the world.

The United States had been isolationist in its diplomacy all along, though, even when it was wholeheartedly expanding its territory, much as the British Empire—which unarguably was expansionist—practiced a foreign policy of "splendid isolation" when it came to the internecine workings of continental Europe. The United States is better viewed as always operating with a tension between the desire to expand its territory and its wish to remain aloof from the broils of imperial Europe.

Thus, Secretary of State John Seward's treaty with Russia to purchase Alaska in 1867—just after the Civil War, when the country was in the throes of reconstructing the American South and a major impeachment battle was looming for Seward's president, Andrew Johnson—is yet another in a continuum of territorial expansions that began with the Louisiana Purchase and continued up to the Spanish-American War. These were deals simply too good for a growing nation to turn its back on, even had it wanted to. Significantly, the year after the U.S. Senate almost unanimously approved the purchase of Alaska, Seward also signed a Treaty of Friendship and Commerce with China and negotiated another treaty to buy the Virgin Islands from Denmark for slightly more than it paid the Russians. And throughout the "isolationist" period of the middle to late 19th century, America was carefully seeing to its interest in Hawaii with diplomatic and trade treaties that laid the groundwork for the islands' annexation at the turn of the century.

Russia, facing internal difficulties in ruling its vast lands, was eager to sell, but Seward was just as eager to buy, the vast lands of Alaska.

Terms

Like the Louisiana Purchase, the Alaska Purchase was a bargain, costing a mere $7.2 million.

By the President of the Unites States

A PROCLAMATION

Whereas a treaty between the United States of America and his Majesty the Emperor of all the Russias was concluded and signed by their respective plenipotentiaries at the city of Washington, on the thirtieth day of March, last, which treaty, being in English and French languages, is, word for word as follows:

The United States of America and His Majesty the Emperor of all the Russias, being desirous of strengthening, if possible, the good understanding which exists between them, have, for that purpose, appointed as their Plenipotentiaries: the President of the United States, William H. Seward, Secretary of State; and His Majesty the Emperor of all the Russias, the Privy Councillor Edward de Stoeckl, his Envoy Extraordinary and Minister Plenipotentiary to the United States.

And the said Plenipotentiaries, having exchanged their full powers, which were found to be in due form, have agreed upon and signed the following articles:

ARTICLE I

His Majesty the Emperor of all the Russias agrees to cede to the United States, by this convention, immediately upon the exchange of the ratifications thereof, all the territory and dominion now possessed by his said Majesty on the continent of America and in the adjacent islands, the same being contained within the geographical limits herein set forth, to wit: The eastern limit is the line of demarcation between the Russian and the British possessions in North America, as established by the convention between Russia and Great Britain, of February 28–16, 1825, and described in Articles III and IV of said convention, in the following terms:

"Commencing from the southernmost point of the island called Prince of Wales Island, which point lies in the parallel of 54 degrees 40 minutes north latitude, and between the 131st and the 133d degree of west longitude, (meridian of Greenwich,) the said line shall ascend to the north along the channel called Portland channel, as far as the point of the continent where it strikes the 56th degree of north latitude; from this last-mentioned point, the line of demarcation shall follow the summit of the mountains situated parallel to the coast as far as the point of intersection of the 141st degree of west longitude, (of the same meridian;) and finally, from the said point of intersection, the said meridian line of the 141st degree, in its prolongation as far as the Frozen ocean. "IV. With reference to the line of demarcation laid down in the preceding article, it is understood—

"1st. That the island called Prince of Wales Island shall belong wholly to Russia, (now, by this cession, to the United States.)

"2d. That whenever the summit of the mountains which extend in a direction parallel to the coast from the 56th degree of north latitude to the point of intersection of the 141st degree of west longitude shall prove to be at the distance of more than ten marine leagues from the ocean, the limit between the British possessions and the line of coast which is to belong to Russia as above mentioned (that is to say, the limit to the possessions ceded by this convention) shall be formed by a line parallel to the winding of the coast, and which shall never exceed the distance of ten marine leagues therefrom."

The western limit within which the territories and dominion conveyed, are contained, passes through a point in Behring's straits on the parallel of sixty-five degrees thirty minutes north latitude, at its intersection by the meridian which passes midway between the islands of Krusenstern, or Ignalook, and the island of Ratmanoff, or Noonarbook, and proceeds due north, without limitation, into the same Frozen ocean. The same western limit, beginning at the same initial point, proceeds thence in a course nearly southwest through Behring's straits and Behring's sea, so as to pass midway between the northwest point of the island of St. Lawrence and the southeast point of Cape Choukotski, to the meridian of one hundred and seventy-two west longitude; thence, from the intersection of that meridian, in a south-westerly direction, so as to pass midway between the island of Attou and the Copper island of the Kormandorski couplet or group in the North Pacific ocean, to the meridian of one hundred and ninety- three degrees west longitude, so as to include in the territory conveyed the whole of the Aleutian islands east of that meridian.

ARTICLE II

In the cession of territory and dominion made by the preceding article are included the right of property in all public lots and squares, vacant lands, and all public buildings, fortifications, barracks, and other edifices which are not private individual property. It is, however, understood and agreed, that the churches which have been built in the ceded territory by the Russian government, shall remain the property of such members of the Greek Oriental Church resident in the territory, as may choose to worship therein. Any government archives, papers, and documents relative to the territory and dominion aforesaid, which may be now existing there, will be left in the possession of the agent of the United States; but an authenticated copy of such of them as may be required, will be, at all times, given by the United States to the Russian government, or to such Russian officers or subjects as they may apply for.

ARTICLE III

The inhabitants of the ceded territory, according to their choice, reserving their natural allegiance, may return to Russia within three years; but if they should prefer to remain in the ceded territory, they, with the exception of uncivilized native tribes, shall be admitted to the enjoyment of all the rights, advantages, and immunities of citizens of the United States, and shall be maintained and protected in the free enjoyment of their liberty, property, and religion. The uncivilized tribes will be subject to such laws and regulations as the United States may, from time to time, adopt in regard to aboriginal tribes of that country.

ARTICLE IV

His Majesty the Emperor of all the Russias shall appoint, with convenient despatch, an agent or agents for the purpose of formally delivering to a similar agent or agents appointed on behalf of the United States, the territory, dominion, property, dependencies and appurtenances which are ceded as above, and for doing any other act which may be necessary in regard thereto. But the cession, with the right of immediate possession, is nevertheless to be deemed complete and absolute on the exchange of ratifications, without waiting for such formal delivery.

ARTICLE V

Immediately after the exchange of the ratifications of this convention, any fortifications or military posts which may be in the ceded territory shall be delivered to the agent of the United States, and any Russian troops which may be in the territory shall be withdrawn as soon as may be reasonably and conveniently practicable.

ARTICLE VI

In consideration of the cession aforesaid, the United States agree to pay at the treasury in Washington, within ten months after the exchange of the ratifications of this convention, to the diplomatic representative or other agent of his Majesty the Emperor of all the Russias, duly authorized to receive the same, seven million two hundred thousand dollars in gold. The cession of territory and dominion herein made is hereby declared to be free and unencumbered by any reservations, privileges, franchises, grants, or possessions, by any associated companies, whether corporate or incorporate, Russian or any other, or by any parties, except merely private individual property holders; and the cession hereby made, conveys all the rights, franchises, and privileges now belonging to Russia in the said territory or dominion, and appurtenances thereto.

ARTICLE VII

When this convention shall have been duly ratified by the President of the United States, by and with the advice and consent of the Senate, on the one part, and on the other by his Majesty the Emperor of all the Russias, the ratifications shall be exchanged at Washington within three months from the date hereof, or sooner if possible.

In faith whereof, the respective plenipotentiaries have signed this convention, and thereto affixed the seals of their arms.

Done at Washington, the thirtieth day of March, in the year of our Lord one thousand eight hundred and sixty-seven.

[L.S.] WILLIAM H. SEWARD.
[L.S.] EDOUARD DE STOECKL.

And whereas the said Treaty has been duly ratified on both parts, and the respective ratifications of the same were exchanged at Washington on this twentieth day of June, by William H. Seward, Secretary of State of the United States, and the Privy Counsellor Edward de Stoeckl, the Envoy Extraordinary of His Majesty the Emperor of all the Russias, on the part of their respective governments, Now, therefore, be it known that I, Andrew Johnson, President of the United States of America, have caused the said Treaty to be made public, to the end that the same and every clause and article thereof may be observed and fulfilled with good faith by the United States and the citizens thereof.

In witness whereof, I have hereunto set my hand, and caused the seal of the United States to be affixed.

Done at the city of Washington, this twentieth day of June in the year of our Lord one thousand eight hundred and sixty-seven, and of the Independence of the United States the ninety-first.

[L.S.] ANDREW JOHNSON
By the President:
WILLIAM H. SEWARD, Secretary of State

Consequences

Every American schoolchild knows that Seward was derided for the deal he had made, that Alaska was called "Seward's folly" or "Seward's icebox" by an unappreciative electorate that would wait nearly a century to enjoy the riches it held. But the same had been true for Louisiana: New England in particular had scoffed at the area as a vast wasteland, uninhabitable and ungovernable, and the country had basically let the purchased land sit idle for half a century while it filled up and developed the lands of the Old Northwest in the Ohio Valley and along the Great Lakes. Alaska, in time, as had Louisiana, was to demonstrate its important strategic position and immense economic value.

TREATY OF ANNEXATION OF HAWAII

TREATY AT A GLANCE

Completed
June 16, 1897 (Ratified by the U.S. Senate July 1898),
at Honolulu, Hawaii, and Washington, D.C.

Signatories
United States and the Republic of Hawaii

Overview
Passage of the McKinley Tariff by the U.S. Congress destabilized
Hawaiian sugar production, creating a political crisis that led to the
downfall of the islands' last Polynesian ruler, Queen Liliuokalani,
and the rise of the sugar kings, who cooperated with expansion-
minded American diplomats to engineer at last the annexation of
Hawaii by the United States.

Historical Background

American interest in Hawaii dated back to the late 18th century, when the islands were discovered for the Western world by the English sea captain James Cook and dubbed the Sandwich Islands. American missionaries followed seafaring traders and began arriving in the 1820s, converting the native Polynesians to Christianity in the second quarter of the 19th century. They were followed in turn by American sugar growers at mid-century. During the presidency of Franklin Pierce an aborted effort was made to annex the island, and Secretary of State William Seward (engineer of the ALASKA PURCHASE TREATY) later raised the issue again, only to be met with failure, as well.

Both Americans and Europeans had long-standing trading treaties with the islands—the UNITED STATES–SANDWICH ISLANDS AGREEMENT, LORD RUSSELL'S TREATY, and the TREATY BETWEEN HAWAII AND THE UNITED STATES—but the most significant by far was the 1875 TREATY OF RECIPROCITY, which opened a free market in the United States to Hawaiian sugar growers. In response to that market, Hawaiian sugar production increased tenfold over the next 20 years. So dependent did the islands' sugar kings become on the American market that when House Ways and Means Committee chairman William McKinley pushed through the 1890 tariff that bears his name, admitting other foreign sugar sales on the same terms and subsidizing domestic planters, the act precipitated an economic crisis in the island kingdom and contributed to the political unrest already growing there.

King Kalakaua, the penultimate ruler of the long-reigning royal family, had been forced by the sugar kings and the white business community in general to accept a new constitution in 1887 that curbed his power, made his ministers responsible to the legislature, and placed the legislature firmly in the hands of the plantation owners. Dissolute and corrupt, the old king died in 1891, to be succeeded by his autocratic sister Liliuokalani, who made it clear that she intended to throw out the new constitution, shake off the control of the sugar kings, and restore the royal house to its past power and glory.

Alarmed by her threats and shaken by the economic slump attendant on the McKinley Tariff, the distressed planters and businessmen quickly reached the conclusion that only annexation by the United States could save them. Encouraged by enthusiastic expansionists in the U.S. Congress and President Benjamin Harrison's administration, they concocted a plot to overthrow "Queen Lil." A committee of businessmen turned revolutionaries responded to the queen's announcement in January 1893 that she was going to proclaim a new constitution as a signal to begin their revolt. They demanded that she abdicate, and U.S. minister in Hawaii John L. Stevens promptly ordered the marines ashore. Stevens, a staunch expansionist, who had been handpicked for the job by Secretary of State James G. Blaine, watched with pleasure as the marines piled out of the cruiser U.S.S. *Boston* and hoisted the American flag over Hawaii. The queen, bemoaning realistically enough "the superior force of the United States of America," capitulated.

Scarcely a month later, on February 15, Harrison sent the U.S. Senate a treaty annexing the Hawaiian Islands. The treaty might have been ratified immediately if president-elect Grover Cleveland, whose second administration began a few days later, had not made it clear he wanted the matter held over until after his inauguration. Once president again, Cleveland dispatched a special commission to investigate the highly suspicious revolt in the islands that had led to the treaty. The commission's report convinced Cleveland he was dealing with a coup by the sugar king clique, which of course he was. Believing that the great majority of the Hawaiian peoples supported the queen, sure that the revolution would have fizzled without the aid of the minister and the marines, Cleveland withheld annexation and insisted that it was America's duty to restore Queen Lil to her throne. Hawaii's revolutionary provisional government refused to step down. They continued to rule the islands, biding their time, waiting for a friendly imperialist to come to power in Washington.

In 1896 annexation became a party issue in the presidential elections. The Republican platform contained a pro-annexation plank, and McKinley, initially cool to the idea, warmed considerably after he became president. The commissioners in Hawaii, comparing the new president to the Democrat Cleveland, observed that it was "the difference between daylight and darkness." The new secretary of state, John Sherman, signed a new treaty of annexation on June 16, 1897, and McKinley sent it to the Senate.

Terms

As ratified by the Hawaiian Senate, the treaty read as follows.

RESOLUTION
of the Senate of Hawaii Ratifying the Treaty of Annexation

BE IT RESOLVED, by the Senate of the Republic of Hawaii:

That the Senate hereby ratifies and advises and consents to the ratification by the President of the treaty between the Republic of Hawaii and the United States of America on the subject of the annexation of the Hawaiian Islands to the United States of America concluded at Washington on the 16th day of June, A.D. 1897, which treaty is word for word as follows:

The Republic of Hawaii and the United States of America, in view of the natural dependence of the Hawaiian Islands upon the United States of their geographical proximity thereto, of the preponderant share acquired by the United States and its citizens in the industries and trade of said Islands, and of the expressed desire of the government of the Republic of Hawaii that those Islands should be incorporated into the United States

as an integral part thereof, and under its sovereignty, have determined to accomplish by treaty an object so important to their mutual and permanent welfare.

To this end the high contracting parties have conferred full powers and authority upon their respectively appointed plenipotentiaries, to wit:

The President of the Republic of Hawaii: FRANCIS MARCH HATCH, LORRIN A. THURSTON, and WILLIAM A. KINNEY.

The President of the United States: JOHN SHERMAN, secretary of State of the United States.

ARTICLE I

The Republic of Hawaii hereby cedes absolutely and without reserve to the United States of America all rights of sovereignty of whatsoever kind in and over the Hawaiian Islands and their dependencies: and it is agreed that all the territory of and appertaining to the agreed that all the territory of and appertaining to the Republic of Hawaii is hereby annexed to the United States of America under the name of the Territory of Hawaii.

ARTICLE II

The Republic of Hawaii also cedes and hereby transfers to the United States the absolute fee and ownership of all public, government or crown lands, public buildings or edifices, ports, harbors, military equipment, and all other public property of every kind and description belonging to the government of the Hawaiian Islands, together with every right and appurtenance thereunto appertaining.

The existing laws of the United States relative to public lands shall not apply to such lands in the Hawaiian Islands: but the Congress of the United States shall enact special laws for their management and disposition. Provided: that laws for their management and disposition. Provided: that all revenue from or proceeds of the same, except as regards such part thereof as may be used or occupied for the civil, military or naval purposes of the United States, or may be assigned for the use of the local government, shall be used solely for the benefit of the inhabitants of the Hawaiian islands for educational and other public purposes.

ARTICLE III

Until Congress shall provide for the government of such Islands, all the civil, judicial and military powers exercised by the officers of the existing government in said Islands, shall be vested in such person or person, and shall be exercised in such manner as the President of the United States shall direct: and the President shall have power to remove said officers and fill the vacancies so occasioned.

The existing treaties of the Hawaiian Islands with foreign nations shall forthwith cease and determine, being replaced by such treaties as may exist, or as may be hereafter concluded between the United States and such foreign nations. The municipal legislation of the Hawaiian Islands, not enacted for the fulfill fulfillment of the treaty so extinguished, and not inconsistent with this treaty, not contrary to the Constitution of the United States, nor to any existing treaty of the United States, shall remain in force until the Congress of the United States shall otherwise determine.

Until legislation shall be enacted extending the United States Customs laws and regulations to the Hawaiian Islands, the existing Customs relations of the Hawaiian islands with the United States and other countries shall remain unchanged.

ARTICLE IV

The public debt of the Republic of Hawaii, lawfully existing at the date of the exchange of the ratification of this Treaty, including the amounts due to depositors in the Hawaiian Postal savings Bank, is hereby assumed by the Government of the United States: but the liability of the United States in the regard shall in not case exceed $4,000.000. So long, however, as the existing government and the present commercial relations of the Hawaiian Islands are continued, as herein before provided, said Government shall continue to pay the interest on said debt.

ARTICLE V

There shall be no further immigration of Chinese into the Hawaiian Islands, except upon such conditions as are now or may hereafter be allowed by the laws of the United States, and no Chinese by reason of anything herein contained shall be allowed to enter the United States from the Hawaiian Islands.

ARTICLE VI

The President shall appoint Once Commissioners, at least two of whom shall be residents of the Hawaiian Islands, who shall, as soon as reasonably practical recommend to Congress such legislation concerning the Territory of Hawaii as they shall deem necessary or proper.

ARTICLE VII

This treaty shall be ratified by the President of the Republic of Hawaii, by and with the advice and consent of the Senate, in accordance with the Constitution of the said Republic, on the one part: and by the President of the United States, by and with the advice and consent of the Senate, on the other: and the ratifications hereof shall be exchanged at Washington as soon as possible.

In witness whereof, the respective plenipotentiaries have signed the above article, and have hereunto affixed their seals.

Done in duplicate at the City of Washington, this sixteenth day of June, one thousand eight hundred and ninety-seven.

(Sig.)
FRANCIS MARCH HATCH, (SEAL)
LORRIN A. THURSTON, (SEAL)

WILLIAM A. KINNEY, (SEAL)
JOHN SHERMAN, (SEAL)

I hereby certify that the foregoing Resolution was unanimously adopted at the Special Session of the Senate of the Republic of Hawaii on the 9th day of September, A.D. 1897.

WILLIAM C. WILDER,
President
Attest:
J. F. CLAY,
Clerk of Senate

Consequences

Even with reciprocity, annexation still lingered tantalizingly just out of reach. Congress was enamored of Hawaii and alarmed by the interest Japan had begun to show in the islands, but domestic opinion against overseas expansion, often dubbed isolationist, was still too strong, and the treaty languished. In fact, Populists—who had mounted a strong showing in the election as a third party, which probably cost Cleveland his job—were opposed to the war lobby itching for a fight with Spain over Cuba and the Philippines. They instead wanted the government to concentrate on the plight of farmers and a destitute working class, and they saw foreign adventurism as an attempt to distract attention from what was virtually a class war in the interior of the country and its cities.

But the battleship *Maine* suddenly exploded in Havana Bay, the United States went to war with Spain, and the "splendid little war" opened the floodgates to American expansion (see UNITED STATES–CUBA MILITARY LEASE AGREEMENT of 1903). In July 1898 the Senate ratified the Hawaiian treaty, and Hawaii was annexed.

UNITED STATES–CUBA MILITARY LEASE AGREEMENT (MAY 1903)

TREATY AT A GLANCE

Completed
May 22, 1903, at Havana, Cuba

Signatories
United States and Cuba

Overview
By this treaty, marking a new imperialism in the United States, the recently independent republic of Cuba granted the United States the right to intervene in Cuban affairs in order to preserve Cuba's independence. In effect, the treaty made Cuba a U.S. protectorate.

Historical Background

Ever since George Washington had warned against "foreign entanglements" in the first Presidential Farewell Address of 1797, many Americans had cherished their isolation, particularly from the ever fractious nations of Europe. It was also true, though, that as the United States itself grew increasingly expansionist, taking over land on the North American continent that had formerly been claimed by the European imperialists, it could hardly avoid such entanglements.

As early as 1823 the United States was staking a claim of hegemony over the Western Hemisphere, warning European powers to stay out of its side of the world in the famous, if at the time fatuous, MONROE DOCTRINE. By midcentury American policy makers were claiming a "manifest destiny" to control all of the North American subcontinent below the 49th parallel, which it asserted by taking away the new Republic of Mexico's vast North American holdings in what John Hay would call a "splendid little war," the U.S.–Mexican War of 1846–48. The American Civil War interrupted America's "manifest destiny," and after the conflict was over, the United States concentrated on industrializing and developing the internal colony it called the American West.

Late in the 19th century, however, the spectacular post-Civil War economic growth resulted in a boom-and-bust economy that was creating great civil unrest and a fairly open, if not quite all-out, class warfare, which would not truly abate until the 1920s. In the face of growing economic hardship and a series of increasingly violent labor disputes at home, many policy makers in the United States began to look toward imperial adventures abroad to distract Americans from domestic strife and rescue big business from its doldrums.

On the threshold of the 20th century—when Americans were generally isolationists, while the elite of its businessmen and opinion makers were expansionists—General Valeriano Weyler arrived in Havana as Spain's new colonial governor of Cuba, an island no more than 90 miles off the coast of Florida. Weyler's mission was to put down the Cuban rebels who had been fighting against Spanish dominion for more than a year. Weyler began by rounding up Cuban citizens and putting them in "reconcentration" camps in order to keep them from covertly supplying the rebels. This act of tyranny only bolstered the rebels' resolve—and it gave U.S. imperialists the wedge they needed to turn American public opinion against Spain and permit national leaders to embark on the road to world power.

President Grover Cleveland, whatever his personal sympathies may have been, did not want his country to become involved in a conflict between Spain and its Cuban colony, and William McKinley, who succeeded him in 1896, publicly expressed the same sentiments. Yet, as the months of tyranny continued, many in the United States agitated for intervention. Not only were the Spanish atrocities considered intolerable by American opinion makers, but American business interests and citizens, both plentiful on the island, were at hazard. Into the growing national debate jumped two rival newspaper giants, Joseph Pulitzer and William Randolph Hearst, whose *New York World* and *New York Journal* were engaged in a bitter war of their own—a circulation war—and coverage of the situation in Cuba was a highly desirable spoil of that war. The papers outdid each other in publishing sensational stories of valiant rebels fighting cruel Spanish overlords.

At last, in January 1898, with fighting and rioting general in Cuba, President McKinley dispatched the battleship *Maine* to Havana Harbor in order to protect U.S. citizens. When the *Maine* blew up on February 15, killing 266 crewmen, most Americans blamed Spanish sabotage and called for immediate retaliation. The findings of a naval court of inquiry supported popular opinion, concluding that the ship had hit a submarine mine. (Modern scholars believe the ship actually exploded accidentally, when one of its powder magazines ignited.) Cries of "Remember the *Maine*!"—an echo of "Remember the Alamo!" (the battle slogan that had stirred the nation to action during the Texas Rebellion and the Mexican War more than 50 years earlier)—were heard throughout the country.

President McKinley still hoped to steer a neutral course, but when he realized that Congress was siding with overwhelming public opinion, he did not want war to be declared without him. In April, McKinley asked Congress for authority to send forces into Cuba. Congress also passed a resolution recognizing Cuba's independence, whereupon Spain, on April 24, declared war on the United States.

The first battle did not take place in Cuba but in the Spanish-occupied Philippine Islands. Immediately upon the declaration of war, U.S. admiral George Dewey took his Asiatic Squadron from Hong Kong to Manila Bay. There on May 1 he fired on the Spanish fleet, destroying all 10 ships anchored in the bay without suffering any losses himself. Eleven thousand U.S. ground troops were dispatched to the Philippines, where they collaborated with Filipino irregulars commanded by Emilio Aguinaldo to defeat Spanish forces in Manila on August 13.

The fighting war in Cuba was similarly swift and decisive. On May 29 the U.S. fleet blockaded the Spanish fleet at Santiago Harbor, and the next month 17 thousand troops invaded Cuba at Daiquiri, then advanced on Santiago. The fiercely fought battle for the city was at San Juan Hill, which American forces, including Lt. Col. Theodore Roosevelt's Rough Riders, took on July 1. In the meantime, Spanish admiral Pascual Cervera, under fire from U.S. ground forces and blockaded by the U.S. Navy, resolved to run the blockade. The result was a four-hour battle in which the American fleet completely annihilated the Spanish fleet while suffering the loss of only one sailor.

On August 12 Spain agreed not only to withdraw from Cuba but to cede Puerto Rico and Guam to the United States. Formal peace talks in Paris also resulted in Spain's selling the Philippines to the United States for $20 million. Conflict between the American military government President McKinley established in Cuba and Cuban rebel leaders came almost immediately. There was much talk of U.S. annexation of the island, but this scheme was abandoned in 1902, with negotiations under way for what became the first treaty between the North American giant and the recently liberated little island.

Terms

While the U.S. military continued to occupy Cuba, the newly independent nation drew up a constitution in 1900 but neglected to incorporate into the document provisions for the continuation of Cuban–U.S. relations. The United States made such provisions a necessary condition for U.S. withdrawal from the island. Secretary of State Elihu Root drew up the provisions and attached them to the Army Appropriations Bill of 1901. This so-called Platt Amendment, sponsored by U.S. senator Orville H. Platt, made Cuba in effect a U.S. protectorate by limiting the new nation's treaty making capacity, curtailing its right to contract public debt, and securing for the United States Cuban land for naval bases. Most important, it reserved to the United States the right to intervene in Cuban affairs in order to preserve Cuba's independence and maintain order.

The Platt Amendment provisions were incorporated into the Cuban constitution in 1901, and the United States withdrew its forces the next year. Relations as defined in the Platt Amendment and the Cuban constitution were further formalized in the 1903 treaty:

ARTICLE I

The government of Cuba shall never enter into any treaty or other compact with any foreign power or powers which will impair or tend to impair the independence of Cuba, nor in any manner authorize or permit any foreign power or powers to obtain by colonization or for military or naval purposes, or otherwise, lodgment in or control over any portion of said island.

ARTICLE II

The government of Cuba shall not assume or contract any public debt to pay the Interest upon which, and to make reasonable sinking fund provision for the ultimate discharge of which, the ordinary revenues of the island of Cuba, after defraying the current expenses of the government, shall be inadequate.

ARTICLE III

The government of Cuba consents that the United States may exercise the right to Intervene for the preservation of Cuban independence, the maintenance of a government adequate for the protection of life, property, and individual liberty, and for discharging the obligations with respect to Cuba imposed by the Treaty of Paris on the United States, now to be assumed and undertaken by the government of Cuba.

ARTICLE IV

All acts of the United States in Cuba during its military occupancy thereof are ratified and validated, and all lawful rights acquired thereunder shall be maintained and protected.

ARTICLE V

The government of Cuba will execute and, as far as necessary, extend the plans already devised, or other plans to be mutually agreed upon, for the sanitation of the cities of the island, to the end that a recurrence of epidemic and infectious diseases may be prevented, thereby assuring protection to the people and commerce of Cuba, as well as to the commerce of the Southern ports of the United States and the people residing therein.

ARTICLE VI

The island of Pines shall be omitted from the boundaries of Cuba specified in the constitution, the title thereto being left to future adjustment by treaty.

ARTICLE VII

To enable the United States to maintain the independence of Cuba, and to protect the people thereof, as well as for its own defense, the government of Cuba will sell or lease to the United States lands necessary for coaling or naval stations, at certain specified points to be agreed upon with the President of the United States.

ARTICLE VIII

The present convention shall be ratified by each party in conformity with the respective constitutions of the two countries and the ratifications shall be exchanged in the city of Washington within eight months from this date. . . .

Thus had the United States agreed to Cuban independence: by retaining the right to establish military bases on the island (see UNITED STATES–CUBA MILITARY LEASE AGREEMENT [February 1903]) and to intervene in Cuban affairs whenever necessary to "preserve" order and maintain Cuban independence.

Consequences

What Secretary of State John Hay dubbed a "splendid little war" gave the United States instant prestige in the eyes of the world, setting it on a course to become a true world power in the dawning century. Therein lay the splendor of that splendid little war, and therein also lay its burden, which was apparent from the start. Puerto Rico submitted to the establishment of a U.S. territorial government with some difficulty. The Philippines also proved troublesome, as nationalist guerrillas under Aguinaldo fought the American occupiers. Peace was restored by 1902, but Philippine independence from the United States remained a thorny issue until after the end of World War II, when the islands were granted independence in 1946.

President McKinley did not long savor the victory in Cuba. On September 6, 1901, he was shot by an anarchist, Leon Czolgosz, while attending the Pan-American Exposition in Buffalo, New York, and he died eight days later. His new vice president, Theodore Roosevelt, assumed office and was elected in his own right in 1904, whereupon, based upon the experience in Cuba, he established a policy toward the Caribbean islands and Latin America that came to be known as the Roosevelt Corollary to the Monroe Doctrine. It effectively made the United States an international police force for the region, a role that was destined to expand, for better or worse, throughout the century.

PANAMA CANAL TREATY
(HAY–BUNAU-VARILLA TREATY)

TREATY AT A GLANCE

Completed
February 26, 1904 (concluded November 18, 1903; ratified by
the Senate February 23, 1904; ratifications exchanged February 26,
1904; proclaimed February 26, 1904), at Washington, D.C.

Signatories
United States and the Republic of Panama

Overview
After a half century of foreign policy machinations, aborted
treaties, false starts, and a U.S.–backed revolution, the Hay–Bunau-
Varilla Treaty cleared the way diplomatically, if barely legally, for
the construction of a canal across the Isthmus of Panama, built and
controlled by the United States and connecting the world's two
greatest oceans, the Atlantic and Pacific.

Historical Background

The origin of the Panama Canal can be found in the
1840s, when would-be settlers of the American West
were looking for alternatives to the arduous overland
routes from the east. The United States negotiated an
agreement with New Granada (a nation consisting of
present-day Panama and Colombia) for rights of transit across the Isthmus of Panama, which separates the
Caribbean Sea from the Pacific. For many, crossing the
dense and disease-ridden isthmus jungle was preferable either to trekking across the North American continent or to making the long sea journey all the way
down one side of the South American continent and up
the other. The 1849 California gold rush, which sent
tens of thousands of Easterners west, prompted the
United States to fund the Panama Railroad across the
isthmus, but the ultimate goal—of the United States as
well as Great Britain—was to build a canal across the
isthmus. The two nations concluded the CLAYTON-
BULWER TREATY (1850), agreeing that neither would
assert exclusive control over the canal.

Whatever that treaty said, however, was not of
much importance, of course, until someone actually
built the canal. In 1881 a French firm under the direction of the brilliant Ferdinand-Marie de Lesseps began
construction of a canal but went bankrupt in short
order. Twenty years later, in the flush of imperialist fer-

vor brought by victory in the Spanish-American War
(1898) and encouraged after 1900 by the expansionist
president Theodore Roosevelt, who had played a
prominent role in that war, the United States persuaded Great Britain to relinquish its claims to share
control of a Central American canal. A treaty had been
negotiated in 1899 and 1901 by the American secretary
of state John Hay and Lord Pauncefote of Preston,
British ambassador to the United States, was amended
by the Senate in 1900 and was rejected by the British.
The second version of the Hay-Pauncefote treaty,
which the British government accepted and which the
Senate ratified in December 1901, superseded the
Clayton-Bulwer treaty and gave the United States the
right to construct and fully control an isthmian canal
in Central America. It retained, at least nominally, the
principle of neutrality under the sole guarantee of the
United States and provided that the canal would be
open to ships of all nations on equal terms, but it omitted the clause contained in the first draft that, following Clayton-Bulwer, had forbidden fortifications.

Then, in 1901 an American commission of experts
authorized by Congress had come to prefer a lock
canal through Panama, which would provide the
cheapest and shortest route between the two U.S.
coasts. (The original plan had been to build the canal
in Nicaragua, whose Mosquito Coast—and British protection of that coast—had been behind the brouhaha

that led to Clayton-Bulwer in the first place.) Accordingly, in June 1902 Congress directed the president to negotiate with Colombia the acquisition of a strip of land in Panama after the New Panama Canal Company, successors to de Lesseps's defunct firm, agreed to a reasonable timetable and reasonable terms for selling the United States its titles and equities in the area. Rather than the original asking price of $109 million for this right-of-way, the French company took the $40 million at which the American commission had valued their holdings.

With that out of the way, Roosevelt pressed Colombia, which had jurisdiction over New Granada, to surrender control over the 10-mile-strip of land in return for a $10 million cash payment and annual rent of $250,000, the terms presented by the diplomats to both the U.S. and the Colombian senates under the Hay-Herren Treaty. Early in 1902 the Congress authorized construction and the next year ratified Hay-Herren.

When the Colombian senate held out for a higher price and greater sovereignty in the Canal Zone, an outraged Roosevelt called the request—reasonable enough from the Colombians' point of view—"blackmail" and let it be known privately to those interests backing the canal that he would smile upon an insurrection in Panama. To the surprise of few, an insurrection did indeed occur in 1903, but if one had not, President Roosevelt would have been fully prepared to ask Congress for the authority to seize the zone from Colombia. The United States backed the uprising, using a warship to prevent Colombian forces from landing an attack on the revolutionaries, and immediately recognized the newly independent Republic of Panama, which just as promptly accepted Roosevelt's plans for the Canal Zone. A fresh treaty was concluded with the new government on the same terms that had been offered to New Granada. It was ratified in 1904.

Terms

The Hay–Bunau-Varilla Treaty of November 18, 1903, read as follows.

Convention for the Construction of a Ship Canal

The United States of America and the Republic of Panama being desirous to insure the construction of a ship canal across the Isthmus of Panama to connect the Atlantic and Pacific oceans, and the Congress of the United States of America having passed an act approved June 28, 1902, in furtherance of that object, by which the President of the United States is authorized to acquire within a reasonable time the control of the necessary territory of the Republic of Colombia, and the sovereignty of such territory being actually vested in the Republic of Panama, the high contracting parties have resolved for that purpose to conclude a convention and have accordingly appointed as their plenipotentiaries,—

The President of the United States of America, John Hay, Secretary of State, and The Government of the Republic of Panama, Philippe Bunau-Varilla, Envoy Extraordinary and Minister Plenipotentiary of the Republic of Panama, thereunto specially empowered by said government, who after communicating with each other their respective full powers, found to be in good and due form, have agreed upon and concluded the following articles:

ARTICLE I

The United States guarantees and will maintain the independence of the Republic of Panama.

ARTICLE II

The Republic of Panama grants to the United States in perpetuity the use, occupation and control of a zone of land and land under water for the construction maintenance, operation, sanitation and protection of said Canal of the width of ten miles extending to the distance of five miles on each side of the center line of the route of the Canal to be constructed; the said zone beginning in the Caribbean Sea three marine miles from mean low water mark and extending to and across the Isthmus of Panama into the Pacific ocean to a distance of three marine miles from mean low water mark with the proviso that the cities of Panama and Colon and the harbors adjacent to said cities, which are included within the boundaries of the zone above described, shall not be included within this grant. The Republic of Panama further grants to the United States in perpetuity the use, occupation and control of any other lands and waters outside of the zone above described which may be necessary and convenient for the construction, maintenance, operation, sanitation and protection of the said Canal or of any auxiliary canals or other works necessary and convenient for the construction, maintenance, operation, sanitation and protection of the said enterprise.

The Republic of Panama further grants in like manner to the United States in perpetuity all islands within the limits of the zone above described and in addition thereto the group of small islands in the Bay of Panama, named, Perico, Naos, Culebra and Flamenco.

ARTICLE III

The Republic of Panama grants to the United States all the rights, power and authority within the zone mentioned and described in Article II of this agreement and within the limits of all auxiliary lands and waters mentioned and described in said Article II which the United States would possess and exercise if it were the sovereign of the territory within which said lands and waters are located to the entire exclusion of the exercise by the Republic of Panama of any such sovereign rights, power or authority.

ARTICLE IV

As rights subsidiary to the above grants the Republic of Panama grants in perpetuity to the United States the right to use the rivers, streams, lakes and other bodies of water within its limits for navigation, the supply of water or water-power or other purposes, so far as the use of said rivers, streams, lakes and bodies of water and the waters thereof may be necessary and convenient for the construction, maintenance, operation, sanitation and protection of the said Canal.

ARTICLE V

The Republic of Panama grants to the United States in perpetuity a monopoly for the construction, maintenance and operation of any system of communication by means of canal or railroad across its territory between the Caribbean Sea and the Pacific ocean.

ARTICLE VI

The grants herein contained shall in no manner invalidate the titles or rights of private land holders or owners of private property in the said zone or in or to any of the lands or waters granted to the United States by the provisions of any Article of this treaty, nor shall they interfere with the rights of way over the public roads passing through the said zone or over any of the said lands or waters unless said rights of way or private rights shall conflict with rights herein granted to the United States in which case. the rights of the United States shall be superior. All damages caused to the owners of private lands or private property of any kind by reason of the grants contained in this treaty or by reason of the operations of the United States, its agents or employees, or by reason of the construction, maintenance, operation, sanitation and protection of the said Canal or of the works of sanitation and protection herein provided for, shall be appraised and settled by a joint Commission appointed by the Governments of the United States and the Republic of Panama, whose decisions as to such damages shall be final and whose awards as to such damages shall be paid solely by the United States. No part of the work on said Canal or the Panama railroad or on any auxiliary works relating thereto and authorized by the terms of this treaty shall be prevented, delayed or impeded by or pending such proceedings to ascertain such damages. The appraisal of said private lands and private property and the assessment of damages to them shall be based upon their value before the date of this convention.

ARTICLE VII

The Republic of Panama grants to the United States within the limits of the cities of Panama and Colon and their adjacent harbors and within the territory adjacent thereto the right to acquire by purchase or by the exercise of the right of eminent domain, any lands, buildings, water rights or other properties necessary and convenient for the construction, maintenance, operation and protection of the Canal and of any works of sanitation, such as the collection and disposition of sewage and the distribution of water in the said cities of Panama and Colon, which in the discretion of the United States may be necessary and convenient for the construction, maintenance, operation, sanitation and protection of the said Canal and railroad. All such works of sanitation, collection and disposition of sewage and distribution of water in the cities of Panama and Colon shall be made at the expense of the United States, and the Government of the United States, its agents or nominees shall be authorized to impose and collect water rates and sewerage rates which shall be sufficient to provide for the payment of interest and the amortization of the principal of the cost of said works within a period of fifty years and upon the expiration of said

term of fifty years the system of sewers and water works shall revert to and become the properties of the cities of Panama and Colon respectively, and the use of the water shall be free to the inhabitants of Panama and Colon, except to the extent that water rates may be necessary for the operation and maintenance of said system of sewers and water.

The Republic of Panama agrees that the cities of Panama and Colon shall comply in perpetuity with the sanitary ordinances whether of a preventive or curative character prescribed by the United States and in case the Government of Panama is unable or fails in its duty to enforce this compliance by the cities of Panama and Colon with the sanitary ordinances of the United States the Republic of Panama grants to the United States the right and authority to enforce the same.

The same right and authority are granted to the United States for the maintenance of public order in the cities of Panama and Colon and the territories and harbors adjacent thereto in case the Republic of Panama should not be, in the judgment of the United States, able to maintain such order.

ARTICLE VIII

The Republic of Panama grants to the United States all rights which it now has or hereafter may acquire to bee property of the New Panama Canal Company and the Panama Railroad Company as a result of the transfer of sovereignty from the Republic of Colombia to the Republic of Panama over the Isthmus of Panama and authorizes the New Panama Canal Company to sell and transfer to the United States its rights, privileges, properties and concessions as well as the Panama Railroad and all the shares or part of the shares of that company; lot the public lands situated outside of the zone described in Article II of this treaty now included in the concessions to both said enterprises and not required in the construction or operation of the Canal shall revert to the Republic of Panama except any property now owned by or in the possession of said companies within Panama or Colon or the ports or terminals thereof.

ARTICLE IX

The United States agrees that the ports at either entrance of the Canal and the waters thereof, and the Republic of Panama agrees that the towns of Panama and Colon shall be free for all time so that there shall not be imposed or collected custom house tolls, tonnage, anchorage, lighthouse, wharf, pilot, or quarantine dues or any other charges or taxes of any kind upon any vessel using or passing through the Canal or belonging to or employed by the United States, directly or indirectly, in connection with the construction, maintenance, operation, sanitation and protection of the main Canal, or auxiliary works, or upon the cargo, officers, crew, or passengers of any such vessels, except such tolls and charges as may be imposed by the United States for the use of the Canal and other works, and except tolls and charges imposed by the Republic of Panama upon merchandise destined to be introduced for the consumption of the rest of the Republic of Panama, and upon vessels touching at the ports of Colon and Panama and which do not cross the Canal.

The Government of the Republic of Panama shall have the right to establish in such ports and in the towns of Panama and Colon such houses and guards as it may deem necessary to collect duties on importations destined to other portions of Panama and to prevent contraband trade. The United States Shall have the right to make use of the towns and harbors of

Panama and Colon as places of anchorage, and for making repairs, for loading, unloading, depositing, or transshipping cargoes either in transit or destined for the service of the Canal and for other works pertaining to the Canal.

ARTICLE X

The Republic of Panama agrees that there shall not be imposed any taxes, national, municipal, departmental, or of any other class, upon the Canal, the railways and auxiliary works, tugs and other vessels employed in bye service of the Canal, store houses, work shops, offices, quarters for laborers, factories of all kinds, warehouses, wharves, machinery and other works, property, and effects appertaining to the Canal or railroad and auxiliary works, or their officers or employees, situated within the cities of Panama and Colon, and that there shall not be imposed contributions or charges of a personal character of any kind upon officers, employees, laborers, and other individuals in the service of the Canal and railroad and auxiliary works.

ARTICLE XI

The United States agrees that the official dispatches of the Government of the Republic of Panama shall be transmitted over any telegraph and telephone lines established for canal purposes and used for public and private business at rates not higher than those required from officials in the service of the United States.

ARTICLE XII

The Government of the Republic of Panama shall permit the immigration and free access to the lands and workshops of the Canal and its auxiliary works of all employees and workmen of Whatever nationality under contract to work upon or seeking employment upon or in any wise connected with the said Canal and its auxiliary works, with their respective families, and all such persons shall be free and exempt from the military service of the Republic of Panama.

ARTICLE XIII

The United States may import at any time into the said zone and auxiliary lands, free of custom duties, imposts, taxes, or other charges, and without any restrictions, any and all vessels, dredges, engines, cars, machinery, tools, explosives, materials, supplies, and other articles necessary and convenient in the construction, maintenance, operation, sanitation and protection of the Canal and auxiliary works, and all provisions, medicines, clothing, supplies and other things necessary and convenient for the officers, employees, workmen and laborers in the service and employ of the United States and for their families. If any such articles are disposed of for use outside of the zone and auxiliary lands granted to the United States and within the territory of the Republic, they shall be subject to the same import or other duties as like articles imported under the laws of the Republic of Panama.

ARTICLE XIV

As the price or compensation for the rights, powers and privileges granted in this convention by the Republic of Panama to the United States, the Government of the United States agrees to pay to the Republic of Panama the sum of ten million dollars ($10,000,000) in gold coin of the United States on the exchange of the ratification of this convention and also an annual payment during the life of this convention of two hundred and fifty thousand dollars ($250,000) in like gold coin, beginning nine years after the date aforesaid.

The provisions of this Article shall be in addition to all other benefits assured to the Republic of Panama under this convention.

But no delay or difference opinion under this Article or any other provisions of this treaty shall affect or interrupt the full operation and effect of this convention in all other respects.

ARTICLE XV

The joint commission referred to in Article VI shall be established as follows:

The President of the United States shall nominate two persons and the President of the Republic of Panama shall nominate two persons and they shall proceed to a decision; but in case of disagreement of the Commission (by reason of their being equally divided in conclusion) an umpire shall be appointed by tire two Governments who shall render the decision. In the event of the death, absence, or incapacity of a Commissioner or Umpire, or of his omitting, declining or ceasing to act, his place shall be filled by the appointment of another person in the manner above indicated. All decisions by a majority of the Commission or by the Umpire shall be final.

ARTICLE XVI

The two Governments shall make adequate provision by future agreement for the pursuit, capture, imprisonment, detention and delivery within said zone and auxiliary lands to the authorities of the Republic of Panama of persons charged with the commitment of crimes, felonies or misdemeanors without said zone and for the pursuit, capture, imprisonment, detention and delivery without said zone to the authorities of the United States of persons charged with the commitment of crimes, felonies and misdemeanors within said zone and auxiliary lands.

ARTICLE XVII

The Republic of Panama grants to the United States the use of all the ports of the Republic open to commerce as places of refuge for any vessels employed in the Canal enterprise, and for all vessels passing or bound to pass through the Canal which may be in distress and be driven to seek refuge in said ports. Such vessels shall be exempt from anchorage and tonnage dues on the part of the Republic of Panama.

ARTICLE XVIII

The Canal, when constructed, and the entrances thereto shall be neutral in perpetuity, and shall be opened upon the terms provided for by Section I of Article three of, and in conformity with all the stipulations of, the treaty entered into by the Governments of the United States and Great Britain on November 18, 1901.

ARTICLE XIX

The Government of the Republic of Panama shall have the right to transport over the Canal its vessels and its troops and munitions of war in such vessels at all times without paying charges of any kind. The exemption is to be extended to the auxiliary railway for the transportation of persons in the service of the Republic of Panama, or of the police force charged with the preservation of public order outside of said zone, as well as to their baggage, munitions of war and supplies.

ARTICLE XX

If by virtue of any existing treaty in relation to the territory of the Isthmus of Panama, whereof the obligations shall descend or be assumed by the Republic of Panama, there may be any privilege or concession in favor the Government or the citizens and subjects of a third power relative to an interoceanic means of communication which in any of its terms may be incompatible with the terms of the present convention, the Republic of Panama agrees to cancel or modify such treaty in due form, for which purpose it shall give to the said third power the requisite notification within the term of four months from the date of the present convention, and in case the existing treaty contains no clause permitting its modification or annulment, the Republic of Panama agrees to procure its modification or annulment in such form that there shall not exist any conflict with the stipulations of the present convention.

ARTICLE XXI

The rights and privileges granted by the Republic of Panama to the United States in the preceding Articles are understood to be free of all anterior debts, liens, trusts, or liabilities, or concessions or privileges to other Governments, corporations, syndicates or individuals, and consequently, if there should arise any claims on account of the present concessions and privileges or otherwise, the claimants shall resort to the Government of the Republic of Panama and not to the United States for any indemnity or compromise which may be required.

ARTICLE XXII

The Republic of Panama renounces and grants to the United States the participation to which it might be entitled in the future earnings of the Canal under Article XV of the concessionary contract with Lucien N. B. Wyse now owned by the New Panama Canal Company and any and all other rights or claims of a pecuniary nature arising under or relating to said concession, or arising under or relating to the concessions to the Panama Railroad Company or any extension or modification thereof; and it likewise renounces, confirms and grants to the United States, now and hereafter, all the rights and property reserved in the said concessions which otherwise would belong to Panama at or before the expiration of the terms of ninety-nine years of the concessions granted to or held by the above mentioned party and companies, and all right, title and interest which it now has or many hereafter have, in and to the lands, canal, works, property and rights held by the said companies under said concessions or otherwise, and acquired or to be acquired by the United States from or through the New Panama Canal Company, including any property and rights which might or may in the future either by lapse of time, forfeiture or otherwise, revert to the Republic of Panama, under any contracts or concessions, with said Wyse, the Universal Panama Canal Company, the Panama Railroad Company and the New Panama Canal Company.

The aforesaid rights and property shall be and are free and released from any present or reversionary interest in or claims of Panama and the title of the United States thereto upon consummation of the contemplated purchase by the United States from the New Panama Canal (company, shall be absolute, so far as concerns the Republic of Panama, excepting always the rights of the Republic specifically secured under this treaty.

ARTICLE XXIII

If it should become necessary at any time to employ armed forces for the safety or protection of the Canal, or of the ships that make use of the same, or the railways and auxiliary works, the United States shall have the right, at all times and in its discretion, to use its police and its land and naval forces or to establish fortifications for these purposes.

ARTICLE XXIV

No change either in the Government or in the laws and treaties of the Republic of Panama shall, without the consent of the United States, affect any right of the United States under the present convention, or under any treaty stipulation between the two countries that now exists or may hereafter exist touching the subject matter of this convention.

If the Republic of Panama shall hereafter enter as a constituent into any other Government or into any union or confederation of states, so as to merge her sovereignty or independence in such Government, union or confederation, the rights of the United States under this convention shall not be in any respect lessened or impaired.

ARTICLE XXV

For the better performance of the engagements of this convention and to the end of the efficient protection of the Canal and the preservation of its neutrality, the Government of the Republic of Panama will sell or lease to the United States lands adequate and necessary for naval or coaling stations on the Pacific coast and on the western Caribbean coast of the Republic at certain points to be agreed upon with the President of the United States.

ARTICLE XXVI

This convention when signed by the Plenipotentiaries of the Contracting Parties shall be ratified by the respective Governments and the ratifications shall be exchanged at Washington at the earliest date possible.

In faith whereof the respective Plenipotentiaries have signed the present convention in duplicate and have hereunto affixed their respective seals.

Done at the City of Washington the 18th day of November in the year of our Lord nineteen hundred and three.

JOHN HAY [SEAL]
P. BUNAU-VARILLA [SEAL]

Consequences

Teddy Roosevelt boasted that he "took Panama," and most Americans, certainly the American elite, at the time not merely condoned but applauded his behavior. Nevertheless, in the eyes of much of Europe, some Americans at the time, all Colombians, many in the rest of Latin America, and any number of historians since, the episode was a national disgrace. Some hinted at scandal, and the agents of the French Panama Canal Company, anxious to dump their worthless stock, had indeed influenced the State Department and a number of members of Congress to adopt their favorable view of the Panama route. When the time came, those agents also helped stir up the Panamanian revolution. Roosevelt personally had no stake in their game, and he probably could not have cared less about the ethics of their actions in pursuit of profit, but he was no less ruthless than they in pushing what he perceived as America's national interest. He was certainly much better than they at persuading primarily himself but also many others of the righteousness of his cause: stamping out lawlessness in Colombia and disorder in Panama. Thus did "stability" become a rationalization for American imperialism, and one on which the country would long rely, especially in Latin America.

As it turned out, construction of the canal through the Panamanian jungle was a logistical nightmare. Climate and terrain presented tremendous difficulties, but it was disease, chiefly yellow fever and malaria, that threatened to wreck the project even before it was fairly begun. U.S. Army colonel William Gorgas waged an all-out war against mosquito-breeding swamps, and he improved sanitation practices. By 1906 his efforts had largely eradicated the two jungle plagues

It was now up to Colonel George Washington Goethals, of the U.S. Army Corps of Engineers, actually to build the 40-mile-long channel, which was replete with a complex system of locks. Though opened for commercial use in 1914, the Panama Canal was not formally dedicated until July 12, 1920, by which time the United States, flexing its imperial muscles and showing off its know-how with the planning and construction of the canal, had succeeded in changing the political and the physical geography of the planet. After spending a decade and $300 million moving 240 million cubic yards of earth to overcome enormous obstacles of terrain and climate, the United States opened to shipping the Panama Canal, a symbol of the new world power's technological and financial might. It would remain so for nearly a hundred years, before negotiations on a new PANAMA CANAL TREATY, completed in the 1970s, would at last put the canal itself in Panamanian hands at century's end.

DIPLOMATIC TREATIES

UNITED STATES-CUBA MILITARY LEASE AGREEMENT (FEBRUARY 1903)

TREATY AT A GLANCE

Completed
February 23, 1903, at Havana, Cuba

Signatories
United States and Cuba

Overview
When Cuban independence was proclaimed following the Spanish-American War, the United States moved quickly to establish treaty relations with the island, making it a protectorate. These treaties included an agreement for leasing military bases and naval coaling stations, which the United States maintains even today in the long aftermath of a second independence movement, fueled by Soviet-style ideology, against the United States itself and its client dictators.

Historical Background

After losing what U.S. secretary of state John Hay dubbed "a splendid little war" on August 12, Spain agreed not only to withdraw from Cuba but to cede Puerto Rico and Guam to the United States. Formal peace talks in Paris also resulted in Spain's selling the Philippines to the United States for $20 million. The Spanish-American War gave the United States instant prestige in the eyes of the world and launched it on a course toward world power, but it did little for the Cubans in whose name it had mostly been fought. There was much talk among American policy mavens and businessmen of annexing the island, and conflict developed immediately with Cuban rebel leaders. It was a lopsided contest, as the Cubans realized, and by 1902 treaty negotiations were under way (see TREATY WITH CUBA).

Terms

As part of those negotiations, the United States retained in Article 7 of the treaty the right to establish military bases and coaling stations on the island, the details of which were worked out in this separate agreement.

Agreement Between the United States of America and the Republic of Cuba for the Lease (Subject to Terms to Be Agreed Upon by the Two Governments) to the United States of Lands in Cuba for Coaling and Naval Stations

The United States of America and the Republic of Cuba, being desirous to execute fully the provisions of Article VII of the Act of Congress approved March second, 1901, and of Article VII of the Appendix to the Constitution of the Republic of Cuba promulgated on the 20th of May, 1902, which provide:

> "ARTICLE VII. To enable the United States to maintain the independence of Cuba, and to protect the people thereof, as well as for its own defense, the Cuban Government will sell or lease to the United States the lands necessary for coaling or naval stations, at certain specified points, to be agreed upon with the President of the United States."

have reached an agreement to that end, as follows:

ARTICLE I

The Republic of Cuba hereby leases to the United States, for the time required for the purposes of coaling and naval stations, the following described areas of land and water situated in the Island of Cuba:

1st. In Guantanamo (see Hydrographic Office Chart 1857). From a point on the south coast, 4.37 nautical miles to the eastward of Windward Point Light House, a line running north (true) a distance of 4.25 nautical miles;

From the northern extremity of this line, a line running west (true), a distance of 5.87 nautical miles;

From the western extremity of this last line, a line running southwest (true) 3.31 nautical miles;

From the southwestern extremity of this last line, a line running south (true) to the seacoast.

This lease shall be subject to all the conditions named in Article II of this agreement.

2nd. In Northwestern Cuba (see Hydrographic Office Chart 2036).

In Bahia Honda (see Hydrographic Office Chart 520b).

All that land included in the peninsula containing Cerro del Morrillo and Punta del Carenero situated to the westward of a line running south (true) from the north coast at a distance of thirteen hundred yards east (true) from the crest of Cerro del Morrillo, and all the adjacent waters touching upon the coast line of the above described peninsula and including the estuary south of Punta del Carenero with the control of the headwaters as necessary for sanitary and other purposes.

And in addition all that piece of land and its adjacent waters on the western side of the entrance to Bahia Honda including between the shore line and a line running north and south (true) to low water marks through a point which is west (true) distant one nautical mile from Pta. del Cayman.

ARTICLE II

The grant of the foregoing Article shall include the right to use and occupy the waters adjacent to said areas of land and water, and to improve and deepen the entrances thereto and the anchorages therein, and generally to do any and all things necessary to fit the premises for use as coaling or naval stations only, and for no other purpose.

Vessels engaged in the Cuban trade shall have free passage through the waters included within this grant.

ARTICLE III

While on the one hand the United States recognizes the continuance of the ultimate sovereignty of the Republic of Cuba over the above described areas of land and water, on the other hand the Republic of Cuba consents that during the period of the occupation by the United States of said areas under the terms of this agreement the United States shall exercise complete jurisdiction and control over and within said areas with the right to acquire (under conditions to be hereafter agreed upon by the two Governments) for the public purposes of the United States any land or other property therein by purchase or by exercise of eminent domain with full compensation to the owners thereof.

Done in duplicate at Habana, and signed by the President of the Republic of Cuba this sixteenth day of February, 1903.

[SEAL]
T. ESTRADA PALMA
Signed by the President of the United States the twenty-third of February, 1903.
[SEAL] THEODORE ROOSEVELT

Consequences

The United States used the bases as stations not so much "to protect the independence of Cuba" as to ensure its dependency on the United States nor so much "to protect the people thereof" as to expose them to the sweatshops and plantations of a burgeoning American capitalism. By the 20th century so deep was the sense created by these treaties and leases that Cuba, in a real sense, "belonged" to the United States, that even today American diplomats cannot bring themselves to normalize relationships. Even after a half-century has passed since dictator Fidel Castro pulled the island out of the American orbit and aligned Cuba with a cold war foe, even after that foe has ceased to exist, even after the end of Cold War itself, U.S. diplomats continue to treat Castro's Cuba as a pariah nation.

ENTENTE CORDIALE

TREATY AT A GLANCE

Completed
April 8, 1904, at London

Signatories
Great Britain and France

Overview
This agreement ended antagonisms whose roots stretched back for centuries between Britain and France and paved the way for their diplomatic cooperation against growing pressures from Germany in the decade before World War I.

Historical Background

The French and British dislike for one another's foreign policies had a long historical pedigree, stretching back to the formation of both nations and fueled by centuries of imperial competition in the New World and Africa. But in 1901 Queen Victoria died, and her passing marked not merely the end of the up-to-then longest reign in England's history but the close of the era named after her, when Great Britain's imperial adventures reached their high-water mark. Gone with the Victorian Age was also the ability of the empire, on which the sun never set, to maintain its "splendid isolation" from continental Europe.

Kaiser Wilhelm II, one of Victoria's many grandchildren in the ruling houses of Europe, had launched an aggressive buildup of the German navy, threatening the basis of the British seaborne empire. The stable diplomatic world that Victoria and German chancellor Otto von Bismarck had built was based on the Continent's Great Powers holding each other in check on land while Britain policed the seas. If Wilhelm's obsession with boats was to upset the balance of power, not only Great Britain but France, too, had cause for alarm. Thus, it was a happy circumstance, diplomatically speaking, that the man replacing Victoria on the throne was King Edward VII, who as the Prince of Wales had been a notorious francophile, loving Paris perhaps even more than London, and certainly open to warmer relations with his boon companions across the Channel.

Both Lord Lansdowne, replacing Lord Salisbury, who had resigned the foreign office the year Victoria died, and France's foreign minister, Théophile Declassé, were anxious to exploit the diplomatic opening offered by Edward's pro-French inclinations. Since coming to office in 1898, Declassé had believed that a Franco-British understanding would give his country some security against the elaborate system of alliances Bismarck had created for Germany in western Europe, and he now put the French ambassador in London, Paul Cambon, to work hammering out an agreement with British foreign secretary Lord Lansdowne. The result was the Entente Cordiale.

Terms

The entente was certainly not in any sense a military alliance, and it scrupulously avoided entangling Great Britain with any French commitment to Russia, long England's bête noire among the Great Powers. Perhaps most importantly, the agreement granted Britain freedom of action in Egypt, and France freedom of action in Morocco—so long, that is, as French intentions there included a reasonable allowance for Spain's interest in the area. Great Britain gave up the Los Islands off French Guinea to France, redefined the Nigerian frontier to favor Paris, and accepted French control in the upper Gambia River valley. The French renounced their claim of exclusive rights to fisheries off Newfoundland. The treaty outlined French and British zones of influence in Southeast Asia and sought to allay the friction between British and French colonists in the New Hebrides.

379

Declaration between the United Kingdom and France Respecting Egypt and Morocco, Together with the Secret Articles Signed at the Same Time

ARTICLE 1

His Britannic Majesty's Government declare that they have no intention of altering the political status of Egypt.

The Government of the French Republic, for their part, declare that they will not obstruct the action of Great Britain in that country. . .

It is agreed that the post of Director-General of Antiquities in Egypt shall continue, as in the past, to be entrusted to a French savant.

The French schools in Egypt shall continue to enjoy the same liberty as in the past.

ARTICLE 2

The Government of the French Republic declare that they have no intention of altering the political status of Morocco.

His Britannic Majesty's Government, for their part, recognize that it appertains to France, more particularly as a Power whose dominions are conterminous for a great distance with those of Morocco, to preserve order in that country, and to provide assistance for the purpose of all administrative, economic, financial , and military reforms which it may require.

They declare that they will not obstruct the action taken by France for this purpose, provided that such action shall leave intact the rights which Great Britain, in virtue of treaties, conventions, and usage, enjoys in Morocco, including the right of coasting trade between the ports of Morocco, enjoyed by British vessels since 1901.

ARTICLE 3

His Britannic Majesty's Government for their part, will respect the rights which France, in virtue of treaties, conventions, and usage, enjoys in Egypt, including the right of coasting trade between Egyptian ports accorded to French vessels.

ARTICLE 4

The two Governments, being equally attached to the principle of commercial liberty both in Egypt and Morocco, declare that they will not, in those countries, countenance any inequality either in the imposition of customs duties or other taxes, or of railway transport charges. The trade of both nations with Morocco and with Egypt shall enjoy the same treatment in transit through the French and British possessions in Africa. An agreement between the two Governments shall settle the conditions of such transit and shall determine the points of entry.

This mutual engagement shall be binding for a period of thirty years. Unless this stipulation is expressly denounced at least one year in advance, the period shall be extended for five years at a time.

Nevertheless the Government of the French Republic reserve to themselves in Morocco, and His Britannic Majesty's Government reserve to themselves in Egypt, the right to see that the concessions for roads, railways, ports, etc., are only granted on such conditions as will maintain intact the authority of the State over these great undertakings of public interest.

ARTICLE 5

His Britannic Majesty's Government declare that they will use their influence in order that the French officials now in the Egyptian service may not be placed under conditions less advantageous than those applying to the British officials in the service.

The Government of the French Republic, for their part, would make no objection to the application of analogous conditions to British officials now in the Moorish service.

ARTICLE 6

In order to ensure the free passage of the Suez Canal, His Britannic Majesty's Government declare that they adhere to the treaty of the 29th October, 1888, and that they agree to their being put in force. The free passage of the Canal being thus guaranteed, the execution of the last sentence of paragraph 1 as well as of paragraph 2 of Article of that treaty will remain in abeyance.

ARTICLE 7

In order to secure the free passage of the Straits of Gibraltar, the two Governments agree not to permit the erection of any fortifications or strategic works on that portion of the coast of Morocco comprised between, but not including, Melilla and the heights which command the right bank of the River Sebou.

This condition does not, however, apply to the places at present in the occupation of Spain on the Moorish coast of the Mediterranean.

ARTICLE 8

The two Governments, inspired by their feeling of sincere friendship for Spain, take into special consideration the interests which that country derives from her geographical position and from her territorial possessions on the Moorish coast of the Mediterranean. In regard to these interests the French Government will come to an understanding with the Spanish Government. The agreement which may be come to on the subject between France and Spain shall be communicated to His Britannic Majesty's Government.

ARTICLE 9

The two Governments agree to afford to one another their diplomatic support, in order to obtain the execution of the clauses of the present Declaration regarding Egypt and Morocco.

In witness whereof his Excellency the Ambassador of the French Republic at the Court of His Majesty the King of the United Kingdom of Great Britain and Ireland and of the British Dominions beyond the Seas, Emperor of India, and His Majesty's Principal Secretary of State for Foreign Affairs, duly authorised for that purpose, have signed the present Declaration and have affixed thereto their seals.

Done at London, in duplicate, the 8th day of April, 1904.

(L.S.) LANSDOWNE
(L.S.) PAUL CAMBON

Secret Articles

ARTICLE 1

In the event of either Government finding themselves constrained, by the force of circumstances, to modify their policy in respect to Egypt or Morocco, the engagements which they have undertaken towards each other by Articles 4, 6, and 7 of the Declaration of today's date would remain intact.

ARTICLE 2

His Britannic Majesty's Government have no present intention of proposing to the Powers any changes in the system of the Capitulations, or in the judicial organisation of Egypt.

In the event of their considering it desirable to introduce in Egypt reforms tending to assimilate the Egyptian legislative system to that in force in other civilised Countries, the Government of the French Republic will not refuse to entertain any such proposals, on the understanding that His Britannic Majesty's Government will agree to entertain the suggestions that the Government of the French Republic may have to make to them with a view of introducing similar reforms in Morocco.

ARTICLE 3

The two Governments agree that a certain extent of Moorish territory adjacent to Melilla, Ceuta, and other presides should, whenever the Sultan ceases to exercise authority over it, come within the sphere of influence of Spain, and that the administration of the coast from Melilla as far as, but not including, the heights on the right bank of the Sebou shall be entrusted to Spain.

Nevertheless, Spain would previously have to give her formal assent to the provisions of Articles 4 and 7 of the Declaration of today's date, and undertake to carry them out.

She would also have to undertake not to alienate the whole, or a part, of the territories placed under her authority or in her sphere of influence.

ARTICLE 4

If Spain, when invited to assent to the provisions of the preceding article, should think proper to decline, the arrangement between France and Great Britain, as embodied in the Declaration of today's date, would be none the less at once applicable.

ARTICLE 5

Should the consent of the other Powers to the draft Decree mentioned in Article I of the Declaration of today's date not be obtained, the Government of the French Republic will not oppose the repayment at par of the Guaranteed, Privileged, and Unified Debts after the 15th July, 1910.

Done at London, in duplicate, the 8th day of April, 1904.

(L.S.) LANSDOWNE
(L.S.) PAUL CAMBON

Consequences

The Entente Cordiale helped bring both powers out of the virtual isolation into which they had of late withdrawn, the French involuntarily and the British with typical complacency, as they eyed each other suspiciously in Africa. Great Britain's only ally was Japan, useless in a war in Europe. France had just Russia, which was soon to be utterly discredited in the Russo-Japanese War of 1904–05 (see the TREATY OF PORTSMOUTH).

Not surprisingly, the new arrangement upset Germany, which had relied before on the bitter rivalry between the two new allies. Consequently, Wilhelm tried to check the French and unhinge the entente in Morocco in 1905. Such maneuvers only forged new bonds between Great Britain and France, sparking discussion even of a military alliance between their general staffs, and both reaffirmed their new solidarity in the 1906 ALGECIRAS CONVENTION. Thus was the stage set for Germany, in attacking France in 1914, to bring the once aloof Great Britain into a general war in Europe.

Part Ten

EPOCH OF THE GREAT WAR

INTRODUCTION

On June 28, 1914, in the obscure Balkan capital of Sarajevo, Gavrilo Princip, a Serb nationalist, gunned down the Austro-Hungarian Empire's heir apparent. Because, by the second decade of the 20th century, the European powers were bound together and torn apart by a ragged web of alliances and counteralliances, the act of the suicidally desperate assassin, member of a Bosnian nationalist secret society, did far more than end the lives of the Archduke Francis Ferdinand and his wife, Sophie. It sparked a lumbering juggernaut of mobilization during which, one by one, the countries of Europe declared war on each other and committed their hapless populations to a course of mindless self-destruction unparalleled in the experience of the world.

While World War I's widespread destruction may have been mindless, the combinations and coalitions that led up to the war were not. In large measure the work of Count Otto von Bismarck, Germany's "Iron Chancellor," these diplomatic arrangements were meant precisely to enhance the security of their members and deter potential aggressors. They had been built painstakingly on the notion of a balance of power as the key to European stability, an idea established by the CONGRESS OF VIENNA in 1815. Indeed, for half a century, they had kept the Great Powers at peace, a remarkable feat in the latter half of the 19th century, the age of the New Imperialism, when Europe's jingoistic leaders once again became determined to carve up the rest of the world.

In the end, the irony was not so much that a single act of political terrorism provoked two great alliance schemes, the Triple Alliance (Germany, Austria-Hungary, and the relatively new nation Italy) and the Triple Entente (England, Russia, and France), into mortal combat, not, in other words, that a local crisis spread to engulf the Great Powers and, with them, most of the world. The irony was that the long-term causes of World War I could be traced back to the developments that impelled the formation of the alliances in the first place. For these very same developments continuously increased tensions among the Great Powers and made a number of European leaders so desperate that they not only sought to obtain their objectives by force (which countries had always done since time immemorial) but that they also were willing to do so even at the risk of a general war. These developments—the growth of militarism and mass mobilization; the economic and political instability, both domestic and international, accompanying rapid industrialization; global imperialism; popular nationalism; the rise of social Darwinism and racist ideology—were the baggage an alliance-ridden Europe toted into the dawn of the new century.

The Winds of Change

By the end of 1901, Queen Victoria was dead; the Iron Chancellor had been put out to pasture; two new monarchs—Wilhelm II and Edward VII—set on the thrones of Germany and England, respectively; the United States had abandoned its centuries-old isolationism, had acquired overseas colonies and broken Britain's monopoly in the China trade, and was building a two-ocean navy; the Japanese, under the crash program of industrialization and militarization launched by the Meiji Restoration, had attacked and defeated China to take a seat beside the Europeans as an imperial power; and the Boers in South Africa were busy taking the bloom off the New Imperialism.

The unravelling of the Victorian Age was under way.

Germany's young kaiser Wilhelm II embraced the winds of change. He fired Bismarck and, using Alfred Thayer Mahan's *The Influence of Sea Power on History* as his compass, set a new course for Germany. Clever but often semicrazed, the kaiser was especially self-conscious about his withered left arm, which may help to explain some of the bluster of his militarism, of his extreme fondness for warships, and of his often reckless approach to European diplomacy. Bismarck believed in security and was willing to temper international ambitions to achieve it; the kaiser wanted Germany's standing in world affairs to match its growing industrial strength, and so he favored a flamboyant policy of worldwide meddling that became known, infamously, as *Weltpolitik.*

At home Bismarck feared social revolution (another threat often accompanying rapid industrialization), so he outlawed the Social Democrats and created a state social security system to buy off the working classes. The kaiser could not have cared less. Figuring he could distract the proletariat with a few social programs, with a seemingly bottomless prosperity, but most important with the Reich's new national glory, he allowed the anti-socialist laws to lapse and taxed his people's pocketbooks and patience with his expensive military programs. Abroad, where Bismarck considered overseas colonies a dangerous luxury, given German geography, the kaiser found them indispensable to German prestige and declared them the key to its future. Bismarck dreaded above all else a two-front war, the avoidance of which is what his alliance system was all about; Wilhelm and his chancellors calculated they could capitalize on the colonial squabbling among France, Britain, and Russia with no thought that they might drive erstwhile enemies into each other's arms.

In a way, then, the roots of the coming war did, as historians earlier in this century often claimed, lie in Europe's competition for colonies, in its imperial rivalries. Colonies were the source, most believed, of British wealth and power, and they were seen at the time as essential both for their rich raw materials and cheap labor and the safety valves they provided nations with restless, industrially displaced populations. However, as subsequent historians have pointed out, late-19th-century colonies were often so costly to obtain, develop, and hold that the benefits of their exploitation hardly justified the trouble. Instead, trade more often followed than led the flag, and it was pride and a faith in the future that drove the engines of the new imperialism.

It is true that the ruling elites of the European powers, and many among their literate classes, shared Wilhelm's notion that a new world order based on colonial empire rather than a balance of power was dawning, and that to lag behind in acquiring bits of Africa or Asia was to become second rate, even perhaps to sink to the level of some obscurity in the Balkans. It was not, then, so much that colonies were transforming others into Great Britain's economic and industrial

equals that made the imperial rivalries a danger to European peace—although gains were being achieved for a number of reasons despite the capital drain of new colonies, and Britain herself certainly at the time feared those changes. It was more that the acquisition of overseas empires was immensely complicating Bismarck's continental alliance system. When the Great Powers turned their attention back to Europe, the alliances that had once guaranteed peace had metastasized, and they would prove deadly beyond reckoning.

Such an outcome was probably too subtle for Wilhelm, even if he had considered it possible or important. He did not. As far as he was concerned, Bismarck was gone, and he—the kaiser—wanted Germany to be a world power just like Great Britain. So he needed colonies just like Great Britain. To get them (so Mahan's book persuaded him), he must have a high seas fleet, and in the early 20th century, that meant building the huge—and hugely expensive—dreadnoughts. Little matter that the costs of a naval arms race with the British created a fiscal crisis that cracked German politics wide open.

Bismarck's replacement as chancellor, Prince Bernhard von Bülow, had been playing a balancing act of his own, trying to maintain a coalition of conservative peasants, aristocratic landowners (Junkers), and wealthy industrialists in the teeth of working-class hostility and a growing consumer revolt over high taxes and costs of living. Popular resentment had so fueled the socialist opposition that other parties could command a majority only by banding together in politically uncomfortable coalition governments, which raised protective tariffs in a domestic trade-off with the kaiser for supporting his shipbuilding.

Neither resistance to political reform nor a general retreat after the 1870s from free trade to protect home industry were unique to Germany. The growth of trade unions, the appearance of revolution-minded proletariats, and the general increase in social tensions that come with population growth and industrialization afflicted all the Great Powers and affected their foreign policies. But none were growing as rapidly as Germany, and only Russia and Austria-Hungary, both still overwhelmingly agricultural, had autocrats as tone deaf as the kaiser to the complaints of their shopkeepers or the demands of their workingmen. The social conflicts ultimately cost von Bülow his job and left his replacement, Theobald von Bethmann Hollweg, with the impossible choice (for a German chancellor) of slashing the navy (and tossing *Weltpolitik* overboard in the process) or making democratic concessions to the left.

Not only did Bethmann Hollweg do neither (he could hardly stand up to Wilhelm's beloved Admiral Alfred von Tirpitz), but Germany's Junker-controlled army, the domestic bedrock of the kaiser's rule, refused to support increases in naval funding unless the army also received sharp spending increases. If a growing German navy made England especially nervous, an expanding German army equally worried France and Russia, and the massive military spending fanned the flames of unrest at home. Inevitably, it seems, as the situation heated up, those high in the swollen ranks of Germany's armed forces began talk of a preventative war. By 1912 both Vienna (for reasons discussed below) and Berlin were coming to view a European war of some kind not as a potential threat but as a necessity of state. What else, after all, could Germany and Austria-Hungary do? The English had abandoned their "splendid isolation" to ally themselves with the French and the Russians, and for a decade Germany's enemies had been closing in on all sides.

The kaiser would never admit that his *Weltpolitik* might well have helped Great Britain come to terms with its historical antagonists on the Continent. Since the beginning of the century, the English had cast a cold eye on the growing fleets not just of Germany but also of France, Russia, Japan, and the United States, fretting that England alone no longer ruled the waves. German companies muscled in on numerous British markets even as the kaiser's navy cavorted about England's home waters. In the South China Sea, French, Russian, and the Japanese ships each outnumbered England's, while on the Mediterranean the French and Italians—and potentially the Russians—threatened her lifeline to India. And the Americans were now building a canal through Panama (a country Theodore Roosevelt more or less created for the purpose) to accommodate their two-ocean navy.

A certain amount of disenchantment was probably inevitable in England with the death of Victoria on January 22, 1901, because if nothing else, her 63-plus-years' reign was the longest in British history. But her death was accompanied by these new worries and by the embarrassing close to the show the British put on in South Africa against the Boers (see TREATY OF VEREENIGING). Coming to the throne was the former Prince of Wales, now Edward VII, and as with the removal of Bismarck, the death of Victoria marked not just the passing of the old but a new beginning: for Edward's fans, the stuffy old Victorian Age was over and the liberated 20th century had arrived. Edward, 59, portly, balding, his triangle of moustache and beard running to gray, was a thoroughly modern man, with a reputation for high living, numerous affairs, and a fondness for gambling.

As everyone at court knew, his mother had blamed him for his father's death—Prince Albert had died of the cholera, which he picked up on a trip to put the lid yet again on one of Edward's many scandalous affairs—and she kept her son from participating in official affairs until he was 50 years old. Now, with her considerable presence no longer looming over him, Edward could speak off the cuff, run his horses in the Derby, race his yachts, and arbitrate fashion—all as the king of England. Content with the basically ceremonial role his mother had come to play in the latter years of her reign, he determined at least to preside over the decline of the empire with a sense of style, finishing in the process the groundwork for the modern constitutional monarchy. Edwardian England would last a decade, and in retrospect it came to seem a golden age of prosperity and cultural awakening, in part because Edward, like his nephew Kaiser Wilhelm II, embraced change, although he was, like his mother, more led than leader when it came to foreign affairs.

At the turn of the century, even a ceremonial king of England still had an effect on the politics of a dangerous world. A man perhaps more at home in Paris than London, Edward quickly warmed up to the French, much to the chagrin of the kaiser, whom Edward found a boor and a martinet, and whom he believed, as the Foreign Office suggested, was determined to conquer at the very least all of Europe. By 1904 Edward had by his geniality and his lovely speeches during a state visit to Paris the year before paved the way with millions of French citizens of all ranks for an official Anglo-French ENTENTE CORDIALE, a strictly colonial arrangement but also one that marked a step away from isolation for both Britain and France, since in the long run the entente was meant to keep both from being dragged into the new war between Russia (France's ally) and Japan (now Britain's ally).

Lord Salisbury, old, weary, and sick, had given up the Foreign Office the year Victoria had died, and he had stayed on as prime minister long enough to oversee the abandonment of his long-standing principles of diplomacy—primary of which was Britain's splendid isolation—and watch his replacement in the Foreign Office conclude an alliance with Japan in January 1902. British foreign policy was being driven by the perceived threat to British dominance and the new need for friends that the foreign secretary, Henry Petty-Fitzmaurice, fifth marquess of Lansdowne, imagined such a threat implied. Queen Victoria was hardly buried before Lord Lansdowne, setting about resolutely to trim the long list of Britain's potential enemies, shored up friendly relations with the United States in the 1901 Hays-Pauncefote Treaty (see PANAMA CANAL TREATY or HAY–BUNAU-VARILLA TREATY).

But he shocked all of Europe—and, for that matter, the world—with the military arrangement he forged with Japan.

To Lansdowne the alliance was immensely sensible. In the wake of the Boer War, the British public had lost the stomach for colonial brush wars, and the foreign office had long wanted to avoid a naval arms race with Germany, so it needed an ally in the Far East with a navy sufficient to thwart Russian expansionism. Treating with Japan and the United States allowed the empire to secure its interests in East Asia on the cheap and to concentrate its regional forces on its major asset, India. The move backfired, however, when the tensions developing between Japan and Russia over Manchuria erupted into war in 1904. After Japan, emboldened by the new alliance, soundly defeated Russia in a war that set the czar's empire tottering on the edge of collapse (see TREATY OF PORTSMOUTH), the unthinkable happened: Bismarck's European system became seriously destabilized.

The Russo-Japanese War of 1904–5 was, indeed, the turning point. Determined not to be dragged into the struggle, the French (Russia's established ally) and the English (Japan's new friend) buried their pride along with a centuries-old colonial rivalry and concluded the Entente Cordiale, in which France abandoned its long-standing opposition to British rule in Egypt and Britain recognized France's right to Morocco. The kaiser, who had made the French occupation of Morocco an international incident to begin with, seized upon Russia's precarious position to renew Berlin's pressure on Paris to give up the North African prize.

The result was an international summit, and at the Algeciras Conference in 1906, the kaiser discovered that instead of shattering the Entente Cordiale as he had hoped, he had only managed to unite his enemies. The English began secret talks with the French military, France loaned Russia the money to rebuild its demoralized armed forces, and a desperate Russia and a fretful Britain put to rest their old rivalry in central Asia. Not just these three Great Powers (constituting what would soon be the Triple Entente) but also the United States and even Italy (later a member, along with Austria-Hungary, of the German-led Triple Alliance) sided against the kaiser. Only the Hapsburgs supported the German position, the ominous beginning of a new trend in Continental diplomacy.

The war had an impact on world diplomacy in other, more subtle ways. As the first modern defeat of a European power by an Asian nation, it emboldened the Chinese, Indians, and Arabs to dream of the day they too might expel exploitative foreigners from their homelands. Europe also realized the implications of an Asian victory for subject populations, which in turn encouraged an already nigh ubiquitous imperial saber rattling as well as the Great Powers' increasingly apocalyptic insecurity concerning their future. At the same time, the speed with which Japan had dispatched the Romanov forces fueled the spreading belief that firepower and finances would make the next great continental conflict short and brutal. No one in Europe could imagine the dragged-out stalemate of trench-based fighting that was coming (although the United States, at least, had seen a harbinger of modern total warfare in the American Civil War). Instead, Europe's leaders assumed the initial clash of arms on their frontiers would prove decisive, and thus they schemed to mobilize mass numbers and deploy them as fast as possible to their borderlands (or, as an American Civil War general was said to have described it, getting there "firstest with the mostest"). Of more immediate import was the fact that Japan's navy had carried the day, which deeply affected Europe's march to war, proving perhaps the decisive factor in pushing England, whose navy officers observed the conflict from aboard Japanese warships, into the reckless naval arms race with Germany it had hitherto been trying to avoid.

The most significant fallout from the war, however, came from czarist Russia itself. Threatened by revolution at home, its hopes for expansion in Asia dashed, Russia looked once again to the Balkans to slake its thirst for imperial adventure and distract its peoples from the severe social disturbances facing the Romanov dynasty. In doing so, the czar truly set the stage for World War I, since Nicholas II could only gain ground on the peninsula by undermining the rule of the Hapsburgs, whose Austro-Hungarian Empire had long been the weak link in the chain of alliances that tied Europe together into an uneasy but relatively peaceful whole.

Careening toward Calamity

The Hapsburg Empire was the multinational heir of the Holy Roman Empire's universal approach to European government. Not as technologically retrograde as Russia, Austria-Hungary, the "Dual Monarchy," nevertheless remained, like Russia, a vastly agricultural land. But the Austrian Germans and the Hungarian Magyars did not enjoy the kind of dominance over their ethnic minorities that the Great Russians exercised over the czar's subject peoples (with the important exception of the Russian Poles). The House of Hapsburg sat precariously at the head of some 5 million Czechs and Slovaks, 3 million Serbs and Croats, an almost equal number of Romanians, 2.5 million Poles, and a million or so Slovenes, all longing to be free.

Russia's problem was its backwardness, Austria-Hungary's its so-called nationality question. The czar's major dilemma was how to industrialize, which he needed to accomplish for Russia to remain a Great Power, without somehow calling into existence the urban proletariat that would undermine his dynasty; Emperor Francis Joseph's problem was how to accommodate an ardent ethnic nationalism without sparking the dissolution of the empire itself. And whereas the czar—at least until recently—could use imperial adventures in Asia as a screen for instituting some of the reforms necessary to modernize Russian farming, education, and technology without democratizing his government, the emperor could only expand at the expense of his ancient enemy Ottoman Turkey. And exactly there he was hemmed in by Europe's elaborate alliance system.

Established six centuries earlier, the Ottoman Empire had at its height controlled most of central and eastern Europe, western Asia, and North Africa. For the last three hundred years, the Ottomans had steadily been losing ground, a process rapidly accelerated in the past quarter century. All but bankrupted by constant warfare and corrupt rulers, the Turks had watched their provinces slip away "like pieces falling off an old house": Cyprus in 1878, Tunisia in 1881, Egypt in 1882. However decadent, the empire yet encompassed a vast territory—including Macedonia, Albania, Palestine, Libya, Syria, Mesopotamia, Crete, parts of Bulgaria, and other lands along the Red Sea and Persian Gulf—and still played an important political role in the European balance of power established by Bismarck's system of interlocking alliances.

The Turks were well aware that all three of the Great Powers of central and eastern Europe—Germany, Austria, and Russia—longed for various Ottoman holdings, especially in the Balkans, but since no one on the Continent could agree on how to carve them up, it became essential to European peace that no major player alone stake a claim. Thus, the nations of Europe, including England and France, made sure the ailing old giant did not fall completely to ruin, precisely in order to check the potential growth of their competitors. Indeed, since the Congress of Vienna, Austria-Hungary owed its continued status as a Great Power chiefly to its uncertain symbiosis with the Ottomans. For had not Bismarck himself—unwilling to see Russia enhance its already vast domain with Balkan real estate—declared Austria-Hungary "a European necessity" in light of the Ottoman decline?

At the Congress of Berlin, Bismarck did the best he could to dampen the dangers the Balkans represented to European peace. He trimmed off the map of Europe the spacious lands of the new nation of Bulgaria, which the Russians had carved out of Ottoman holdings under the TREATY OF SAN STEFANO. Bulgaria survived the congress as an independent country but on the smaller scale of a Serbia, a Montenegro, and a Romania, each of which received in Berlin a full, if virtually meaningless, independence from the Ottomans, an independence "guaranteed" by the Hapsburgs. Bosnia and Herzegovina came under Austro-Hungarian administration. Only Macedonia and today's Albania remained part of

Balkan Turkey. The truth was that none of the tiny Balkan nations had the technology, the personnel, or the raw wealth to be economically independent of one or the other of its giant neighbors, however much it might cherish its nominal political sovereignty. Thus, Bismarck considered Austria-Hungary the centerpiece of his arrangement, its economic and diplomatic sway the antidote to chaos in the south-central and southeastern corner of Europe.

The arrangement had its drawbacks. As the various Balkan peoples shucked the cultural and political yoke of Istanbul (or, as they called it, Constantinople), they and their ethnic brethren just over the line in Austria-Hungary clamored for true freedom from Vienna, as well, which kept this, the least of the Great Powers, in seemingly permanent crisis. If Germany considered the Dual Monarchy a bulwark against czarist ambition and the keystone to Europe's balance of power, the other players—England, France, and Russia—increasingly found the Hapsburgs hopelessly out of step with the times and thought their empire close to moribund. For a while, though, the other three were willing to go along with Bismarck. With England maintaining its haughty isolation and France still weakened by the Franco-Prussian War, even Russia eventually agreed (in 1897) to put its dispute with Austria-Hungary over the Balkans on hold for a decade while it pursued better prospects to the Far East. By the time the agreement ran out in 1907, the Hapsburgs ruled the most despised country in Europe after Turkey, and the Great Powers—now realigned—were no longer willing to carry Austria-Hungary the way they had the declining Ottoman Empire for most of a century.

Russia loomed once again over the Balkans, and the Turks still controlled Macedonia. The latter, however, was ringed by "independent" Greece, Montenegro, Serbia, and Bulgaria, all vulnerable to Russia's seductive support. Together they would become the Balkan League, hoping to benefit by rivalry between empires. Serbia posed the biggest threat to Vienna because it had ethnic ties to Serbs and Croats inside the Dual Monarchy. In years past, Francis Joseph had bribed Serbia's ruling dynasty to keep its people in line, but in 1903 a bloody coup d'état had brought to power a violently anti-Hapsburg clan, and now Russia was egging its members on to action. The Balkan League, which would soon attack the Ottomans, was formed originally to limit Austria's increasing power in the region at the expense of Turkey.

But the real difference in the Balkans these days lay with the attitudes of England and France, who were disinclined to discourage the czar, who even (if unofficially) sympathized with the nationalist ambitions of Austria-Hungary's ethnic minorities. Heedless of the undermining of the Hapsburg dynasty that such policies—official and unspoken—encouraged, the Triple Entente pushed the emperor and his ministers toward a mortal choice: die fighting or die by slow diplomatic dismemberment, as the Turks were. At the same time, Austria's only reliable ally, Germany, was also coming—for internal reasons, as well as due to the international machinations of England, France, and Russia—to accept the inevitability of war. The keystone of Europe's balance of power, which provided the precarious stability that allowed other powers to follow their imperial dreams, was being worked loose. Once Austria-Hungary was in effect yanked from the protections of the overall alliance system, the entire diplomatic edifice would collapse.

No one in Europe was unaware of what was happening. Even Bismarck had predicted years before that the next war would come because of "some damn fool thing in the Balkans." Indeed, all the powers had been building up mass armies, just in case. Military uniforms had become de rigueur for kaiser, emperor, czar, and king alike. Sensational novels and popular histories that depicted the next war (or the spying and intrigue supposedly leading to such a war) became bestsellers. Since the turn of the century, a middle class peace movement had been gaining ground, starting with a conference in the Hague in 1899 and culminating with a second HAGUE CONVENTION in 1907. Now the movement foundered on internal contradictions, for its liberal members applauded "just" wars fought for "progressive" ends. They had tolerated, for example, the wars for German and Italian independence in the previous century, and they would not dismiss the nationalist dreams of those they saw as freedom fighters against ancient regimes when war came to the Balkans. Indeed, it seemed as if the very triumphs of European progress—technology, nationalism, cultural modernism, modern science—were causing civilization to careen toward calamity.

Then, on July 3, 1908, the Ottoman Empire's 3rd Army Corps in Macedonia launched a revolt against the provincial authorities in Resna, which quickly led to rebellion throughout the empire and brought into positions of power and authority European-influenced revolutionaries intent on modernizing Turkey: the Young Turks. Although eventually they would succeed internally in reforming the government and fostering Turkish nationalism, their revolt shook the already seriously destabilized Balkans and led directly to World War I, during which their ham-handed handling of foreign affairs resulted in the final dissolution of the Ottoman state.

Late in the 19th century, the empire's current ruler, Sultan Abdülhamîd II, had revoked the constitution governing its polyglot of provinces and unleashed a vicious secret police force. The sultan's state terror horrified the empire's intelligentsia, but it was his massacre of tens of thousands of Armenians in the 1890s that made him an international pariah. Beset by a tide of rising nationalism among its subject peoples and Balkan neighbors, twisted hither and yon by the ambitions and demands of the Great Powers, Ottoman rule verged ever closer toward total collapse. The Young Turks staged their revolt in 1908 to save the ailing empire, not to destroy it. The rebels did not demand that the sultan step down—he was after all, however corrupt and tyrannical, the caliph (or spiritual leader) of many of the world's Muslims. What the rebels wanted was a restoration of the constitution and a recall of parliament. On July 23, amid the spreading revolt, Abdülhamîd II surprised everybody by giving the rebels all they asked, in theory reducing his status to that of a constitutional monarch. But the deep-seated ideological differences between the Young Turks resurfaced, preventing them from taking effective control of the government, and over the next two years, the sultan staged a destabilizing counterrevolution. Not until 1913, when new leaders took over Riza's faction—the triumvirate of Talat Pasha, Ahmed Cemal Pasha, and Enver Pasha—did the Young Turks set themselves up as the arbiters of Ottoman politics.

Meanwhile, the old empire had fallen apart in the Balkans. Turkish Bulgaria promptly took advantage of the chaos to declare its independence in 1908, and that same year Austria-Hungary quickly annexed Bosnia and Herzegovina. Turkish Crete proclaimed its union with Greece, though threats from Istanbul kept Greece from immediately acting on the declaration. In 1911, Italy invaded and overran Tripoli (today's Libya). The Italian conquest spurred the ambition of the Balkans' small Christian states—Serbia, Montenegro, Greece, and Bulgaria—and this Balkan League suddenly attacked European Turkey in October 1912. The Turkish army collapsed. By November 3 the Bulgarians had reached Istanbul, and five days later the Greeks entered Salonika (now Thessaloníki). The Serbs took Durazzo on the Adriatic, and thus Serbia provided itself with a seaport on November 28. On December 5 the Turkish government begged the Balkan belligerents for an armistice.

Europe was shocked by the Ottoman defeat. England immediately called for a Conference of the Great Powers, which opened a week later in London, on December 10, 1912. The Turks agreed to give up all they had lost to Serbia and Greece, but they drew the line at turning over to Bulgaria the city of Adrianople (today's Turkish Edirne), which their troops still occupied. The Bulgars increased the volume of their demands; the Turks grew adamantine; the armistice collapsed.

As the Great Powers continued to confer, the Balkans went back to war with the Ottomans in February 1913. Adrianople promptly fell to a combined army of Bulgars and Serbs, and the Turks again sued for peace. Back in London, Austria—faced with the growing power of its ethnic minorities—insisted that Durazzo had to be either given back to the Turks or made independent; the Serbs simply couldn't have it. Russia put pressure on Serbia to give up the seaport, and the Serbs did so with much ill will. On May 30, 1913, everybody signed the TREATY OF LONDON. Adrianople went to Bulgaria, Salonika to Greece, and an entirely new state—Albania—was carved out of Durazzo and the surrounding area.

Everything seemed fixed for about a month. Then, on June 29, Bulgaria attacked her former Balkan allies, Serbia and Greece, grabbing up Salonika for herself and pulverizing the surprised Serbian army. Now Romania, neutral in the First Balkan War, got into the act, attacking Bulgaria from the rear, crossing the Danube and marching up to the outskirts of the Bulgarian capital, Sofia. Seeing that Bulgaria was for the moment distracted, the Turks took back Adrianople. Germany's kaiser announced that he would support his cousin King Carol of Romania, but the Russian czar refused to help out the czar of Bulgaria, Ferdinand, whom Nicholas considered a maverick. So, in the TREATY OF BUCHAREST, signed on August 6, Bulgaria lost everything she had won in the previous conflict, the Greeks took back Salonika, and a shank of Bulgarian territory was sliced off and handed to Romania.

By this time, of course, nobody was fool enough to think matters in the Balkans had been settled. Already, the term "balkanized" had been coined for any collapse into petty factions, and everyone balked at anything that did not precisely meet their fancy. For the Great Powers, still meeting in London, it didn't matter so much who was stabbing whom in the back, or which little country got which piece of real estate. What mattered was that they keep talking until they worked this thing out, until they were sure that little wars would not spread naturally through the entangling alliances into general war. As Bismarck had warned, however, without the Ottomans to keep in line, the Hapsburgs seemed to have lost their purpose in the European scheme, and since the Great Powers no longer planned to organize the Balkans around the arthritic needs of the Dual Monarchy, nobody could agree on just what to do about the Turks' former holdings in Europe. The talks continued for some 10 months after the end of the Second Balkan War, before the London Conference dissolved without settling anything, even the details of the new Albania's boundaries.

The Balkan Wars and the long London Conference left Hapsburg hopes in tatters, too. What to do about the rise of ethnic nationalism, debated by Austrian statesmen for half a century, was a question they could hardly dodge any longer. Most of Europe's diplomats had come to the opinion that some form of federalism, which allowed for political autonomy, was best, but such measures, even when the Austrians suggested them, had always been vetoed by the Hungarians, who—since the reforms would carve up half their empire—stood to lose their equal standing in the Dual Monarchy. Conrad Franz, count von Hötzendorf, Austria's chief of the General Staff, joined the growing chorus in Germany that favored a preventive war. The heir apparent, Archduke Ferdinand, however, took the longer, more liberal view, saying that he would live and die a federalist, since federalism was the only thing that could save the monarchy.

An apparently sensible man in troubled times full of passionate intensities, Ferdinand was naturally disliked by all around him: the emperor's court disapproved of his marriage to a commoner; the Hungarians and the conservatives deplored his liberal views; and the empire's Slavic radicals despaired of his popularity. The last of these proved the more dangerous; many of them had joined the secret societies that sprang up to liberate Bosnia in the wake of the raw deal Serbia had been handed in London—societies such as Nabrodna Obrana (the National Defense), which had been formed in Serbia in 1908 to agitate and propagandize across the border, or the more militant Ujedinjenje ili Smrt (Union of Death), which preached terrorist action over intellectual agitprop and was actually run by the head of the Serbian secret service. Agitators and assassins alike, young romantics all, worried that Ferdinand, if he came to the throne, might well be the one man to pacify the empire's ethnic nationalities and scuttle their radical dreams of a Greater Serbia. Like the German and the Austrian militarists, the terrorists feared the peacemaker more than the sworn enemy, and a bevy of the Union's assassins flocked to Sarajevo for the archduke's upcoming state visit.

Not only did Ferdinand happen to arrive in the Bosnian capital on the Serbian national holiday, he and his morganatic wife toured the streets of the city in an open car. Someone threw a bomb at them, but it missed, and the archduke steadily completed his official duties. Bosnia's nervous governor then suggested they break off from the planned—and widely announced—official route and make their return along safer roads. Ferdinand agreed. Their driver, however, took a wrong turn and paused the cavalcade for a moment to get his bearings. In that instant, a 19-year-old fanatic undid a century's worth of diplomacy when he stepped up to the car and shot the royal couple dead.

War to End Wars

At first nothing happened. Few imagined the assassination, though clearly an outrage, was Bismarck's "damned fool thing in the Balkans." Austria's von Hötzendorf did actually want to use the event as a pretext for his preventive war against Serbia, but Emperor Francis Joseph took a wait-and-see attitude. First establish Serbia's complicity, he suggested, then decide what to do, if anything. The kaiser was less temperate. He urged firmness, giving his ally a "blank check" in a famous memo that promised German support for any action Austria wished to take against the Serbs. It was something of a hollow gesture, since the Germans were fully convinced that Russia—still reforming its military and reconstructing its social fabric in the wake of its loss to Japan and the 1905 revolution—would back down from any commitment to protect Serbia. Even if the Russians did not hold fire, so bragged the German high command, they would prove no match for the military forces under its command.

Chancellor Bethmann Hollweg was not so sure. Predicting an attack on Serbia would spark a world war, he nevertheless went along with the kaiser and hoped against hope that his leader was right, that decisive action would keep the conflict local. Urged on by the Germans, Austria stumbled ahead. Austria's foreign minister, Leopold, count von Berchtold, took his cue from the kaiser, calling for a firm policy toward Serbia to prevent further damage to Austria's prestige, which would only encourage the Balkans to unite behind the czar. Count Tisza, Hungary's prime minister, demurred, demanding that diplomacy come before a clash of arms. First submit a list of demands for redress, he said. If Serbia accepted them, the Dual Monarchy would have pulled off a "brilliant" diplomatic coup; if the Serbs rejected them, then Austria-Hungary could go to war with a moral righteousness the rest of Europe, even Russia, might recognize, especially if Austria declared it had no intentions of annexing Serbian territory.

Russia's response was critical, and the kaiser was right at least about her continuing troubles at home. In fact, in July 1914, just as Raymond Poincaré and René Viviani—president and prime minister, respectively, of France—were paying the czar a state visit in St. Petersburg, the city's working class had gone out on strike. While strikers threw up barricades, President Poincaré assured Nicholas behind the scenes that France would stand by her alliance commitments. Massive demonstrations, clashes between strikers and police, large-scale arrests of socialist agitators—all these formed the backdrop as the czar and his ministers discussed what to do about this latest Balkan crisis. Perhaps it was understandable then that when news of Vienna's ulti-

matum to Belgrade reached Russia just after the French leaders left for home on July 23, the czar's foreign minister, Sergey Dmitriyevich Sazonov, erupted in anger at the terms: a shutting down of the secret societies, an end to anti-Austrian agitation, direct Austrian participation in the Serbian investigation of the Sarajevo crime, and an immediate response from Serbia within 48 hours. Russia's prestige was at stake, too, since the Balkans was the only place left in the world where St. Petersburg could demonstrate its vitality. Encouraged by the French ambassador, Sazonov announced that Russia would immediately begin mobilizing.

In retrospect, Russia had little choice. Its vastness and the sorry shape of its railways meant that Nicholas had to act in advance of continental developments. Sazonov knew this, of course, so he viewed mobilization as something in the nature of a political threat that could be called off well before it was completed. But in the more modern Europe, mobilization was a matter of complicated timetables and precise planning rather than the covering of long distances ever so slowly, and Germany and Austria felt impelled to begin their own mobilizations. Meanwhile, Serbia had responded to the ultimatum within the given time, accepting all but two of the conditions, both of which directly compromised its sovereignty. Within 48 hours, Berchtold had talked Francis Joseph into initiating a war. The kaiser, off on his yacht, suddenly got cold feet and tried to cool down Vienna, as well.

Austria declared war on July 28 and started shelling Belgrade. The czar, in response, approved the mobilization of his army against Austria. All of Europe finally realized a general war was imminent. Quickly, the British, the Germans, and the Italians each called for diplomatic negotiations. Austria could occupy Belgrade and make sure the Serbs complied with their demands, if that's what it took. St. Petersburg was reassured that Austria had no ambitions for Serb territory. But for the first time the grim logic of the alliance system—when coupled with modern mass mobilization—became clear, and no one seemed able to stop the clockworks. Russian generals were loath to call off mobilization, which would disrupt their contingency plans, and it made no sense to mobilize against Austria and not Germany, whose frontier with Russia lay naked and exposed. Nicholas II was no stronger a leader now than he had been against Japan in 1904, so he had bowed to the concerns of his military by authorizing the general mobilization on July 30.

In France patriotic crowds and worried generals met the returning president with calls for precautionary military action. In Berlin, too, there were demonstrations, anti-Russian ones, and a concerned high command demanding immediate action. The British put their fleet to sea. A frantic kaiser, issuing ultimatums to Russia to end its mobilization and to France demanding neutrality, managed merely to spur them on to action. One could hardly blame them, since as they well knew, the Germans had over the summer been secretly plotting with the Young Turks and with Bulgaria to smash Serbia.

The ultimatums expired. Germany put its war plan—the Schlieffen Plan—into action and come August 1, declared war on Russia; come August 3, on France. When Belgium refused the German army safe passage, the kaiser invaded the Netherlands. Europe's fate was sealed on August 4, when Great Britain—which did not care about Serbia but cared very much indeed about the invasion of Belgium and the prospect of the kaiser's fleet in the English Channel—joined its entente allies and declared war on Germany.

The horror was that, as in some nightmare world, the alliances held.

The war commenced with a sweeping German drive deep into France, which boded a German victory as devastating as that of the Franco-Prussian War of 1870–71. But some 30 miles outside of Paris, German forces, fearful of overextending their supply lines, wheeled about and dug in. It was as fateful a maneuver as any in any war. What followed for more than the next four years was the deadly stalemate of trench warfare, a brutal contest of mutual death and destruction without meaningful gains in territory.

If none of the combatant nations gained significant real estate, all concentrated their resources on developing and employing new instruments of murder. First the French, then the Germans, developed an arsenal of poisonous gases that dissolved the lungs and asphyxiated men on their own blood and tissue. The British fielded the tank, an armored, mechanized mobile artillery piece. The French and Germans invented successively more destructive fixed artillery. The Germans made extensive use of deadly submarines. And all sides turned out airplanes, capable of raining death from the very skies.

The European combatants hammered one another for almost three years before the United States, responding to German depredations on the high seas and an anti-American overture to the government of Mexico, entered the war on the side of the Allies. It was the American troops who would turn the tide against the Central Powers. Allied shipping losses were at an unprecedented high, major French land offensives had failed, leading to low morale and mass mutinies throughout the French army, and the British offensive in Flanders had been inconclusive and very costly. Worse, the Eastern Front was in collapse, as a vast but ill-equipped and poorly led Russian army suffered one terrible defeat after another, and the nation was propelled inevitably toward revolution and a humiliating

"separate peace" with Germany under the TREATY OF BREST-LITOVSK, which would have long-lasting effects on postwar diplomacy. However, the immediate result of Russia's withdrawal was that Germany could ship vast numbers of troops to the Western Front and drag out the war.

The United States, still rife with isolationists despite the imperial adventures it had launched beginning with the Spanish-American War, was poorly prepared for any major conflict, much less a world war. Although General John J. ("Black Jack") Pershing arrived in Paris on June 14, 1917, and his first troops followed at the end of the month, it was not until the spring and summer of 1918 that significant numbers of American forces were fielded. The Americans suffered heavy losses, but during July and August, they were instrumental in crushing the last major German offensives and turning the tide of the long war. From the end of September 1918, all available U.S. forces were concentrated along a sector between the Meuse River and the Argonne Forest. The campaign, aimed at cutting the Germans' principal line of supply, involved 1,200,000 American troops, who suffered a heavy 10 percent casualty rate. The success of this offensive brought Germany to its knees, though, and an armistice was declared on November 11, 1918.

The Aftermath

When it was over, the carnage seemed so vast and the costs so great that many wanted to believe it had meant something, so they were attracted by President Woodrow Wilson's justification for entering the conflict as a war to end wars. The Wilsonian vision, which came to play a central role in the TREATY OF VERSAILLES, was of war as an atavism connected to autocrats—to monarchs, and aristocrats, and imperialists. Such men represented the old diplomacy, with its secret alliances, military adventures, and balance-of-power politics. In the long run, such diplomacy solved nothing, because it bred distrust and suspicion, which inevitably led to conflict. The solutions Wilson proposed were democratic control of diplomacy, self-determination for all nations, open negotiations, disarmament, free trade, and—most important—a system of international law and collective security to replace the exercise of raw power, war, as the final arbiter among nations. Ultimately, Wilson reasoned, a League of Nations would correct the errors and iron out the injustices that might creep into some treaties in an imperfect world.

All of this might have been fine for a man like Wilson, who led his country into the war as an "associated power" and fought for a liberal and international agenda opposed to all imperialism, German and Allied alike, but that was not what the war had been about. Germany fought to win and dominate the Continent; the allies to frustrate Germany and to realize certain war aims, which grew more elaborate as the war continued. Having agreed to make no separate peace with the Central Powers, the allies shored up their collective will to fight with the promises of spoils. The SYKES-PICOT AGREEMENT, concluded during the war, divided much of the Ottoman Empire outside Europe into British and French spheres of influence, while the British promised the Jews a new national home in Palestine in the BALFOUR DECLARATION. The allies used the lure of new possessions—Trentino, Trieste, a third of Dalmatia, a piece of South Tirol—to entice Italy into the war on their side, and they kept the badly listing Russians involved by giving them Constantinople itself. Why, on the other hand, should the Allies respect the rights of the Balkan states, who joined the now-defeated Central Powers in hopes of carving up Serbia?

So it was that France came to the Paris Peace Conference as the avatar of the traditional, Bismarckian balance of power. In 1914 France alone had not chosen war but had it thrust upon her with Germany's summary attack. She served as the major battlefield. She suffered the most physical damage. She sacrificed a generation of manhood. She therefore had the most to reconstruct and the most to fear from German revenge in the future, since she—as Germany's closest neighbor among the allies—would be the one executing whatever terms were agreed to at the conference. Despite Germany's defeat, it still had more people than France, and its industry was yet more developed. Meanwhile, France's major European ally had vanished into the mists of socialist revolution. France was burdened with heavy war debts and faced with the need for more borrowing to rebuild her battered cities and her shattered industry.

Georges Clemenceau arrived at the conference determined not to betray France's sacrificial victory for some pie-in-the-sky vision. He wanted very concrete things: to weaken Germany permanently; to secure the influx of capital from abroad to restore French solvency; access to German coal and German markets, even perhaps a cartel to help France survive peacetime competition from Germany; to persuade the wealthy United States to forgive French war debts. France, for example, came to desire the Saar and Rhine regions of Germany for their coal and to dream of the long-awaited return of Alsace-Lorraine, with its rich iron deposits. As an added incentive, separating Germany from the Rhineland would increase France's security, a paramount concern given the devastation of the war.

Clemenceau cast a cynical eye on Wilson's idealism and his claims to be an "honest broker" of the peace, since much of what he proposed seemed somehow to enhance the power and prestige of the United States in world affairs. The crafty old Gallic diplomat was nothing if not a realist, and—recognizing that Wilson's liberal internationalism was setting the tone for the peace conference—he was perfectly willing to couch his demands in Wilsonian rhetoric, arguing his case on the grounds of justice rather than power.

As it turned out, it was Britain's Lloyd George who proved the broker, siding now with France, now with the United States. Although the Americans accused him of conspiring with Clemenceau in support of the old diplomacy of balance of power, but, more accurately, he followed the traditional British policy of shoring up the defeated power in a European war while seeking to constrain the ambitions of the victorious. Wilson's rigid principles proved mostly inappropriate in any case, some irrelevant, some inapplicable, all of them to European eyes insufficient to the day. In the end, the idealistic gloss Wilson's language put on the hard-nosed peace treaties undermined much of their legitimacy. The Germans, disappointed that their sudden postwar embrace of democracy failed to win the kind of mild peace Talleyrand engineered for the French at the Congress of Vienna in 1815, had little trouble dismissing the peace process as a sham and the Treaty of Versailles as an onerous Diktat.

The Paris Peace Conference ultimately produced five treaties, each named after the Paris suburb in which it was signed: the Treaty of Versailles with Germany, the TREATY OF ST. GERMAIN with Austria, the TREATY OF TRIANON with Hungary, the TREATY OF NEUILLY with Bulgaria, and the TREATY OF SEVRÈS with Ottoman Turkey. They satisfied nobody. France's Marshal Foch declared, "This is not a peace, but a truce for 20 years." British economist John Maynard Keynes quit the conference in disgust and returned to England to draft a scathing critique of Wilson and the treaties. Wilson's own government, recoiling at European cynicism into a final spasm of isolation, rejected both the treaties and the League of Nations charter, which grew out of them, forcing negotiations for separate treaties with each of the defeated belligerents. The Paris conference did not even begin to address the problems created by the Bolshevik Revolution for the peace and security of Europe in the future.

And right-wing German nationalists, who grew in strength amid the political chaos fostered in part by the more draconian measures of the Versailles document, called those who signed the armistice "November criminals" and those who signed the treaty "traitors." They fostered a myth that Germany did not actually lose the war but was instead "stabbed in the back" by socialists and defeatists. Hitler's rise to power owed much to this myth, and he would make of the Versailles Treaty itself a casus belli for World War II.

The conflict caused by the collapse of the old alliance system left the world economically, intellectually, and morally drained, determined never to fight another general war. Yet, as became tragically apparent, the Paris Peace Conference left it economically, intellectually, and morally incapable of averting just such a second, and even more destructive, worldwide conflagration.

TREATIES

Mutual Defense Treaties, Military Alliances, and Nonaggression Pacts

SECRET TREATY BETWEEN GERMANY AND THE OTTOMAN EMPIRE

TREATY AT A GLANCE

Completed (Ratified)
August 2, 1914

Signatories
Germany and the Ottoman Empire

Overview
A secret agreement concluded immediately before the outbreak of World War I, this treaty stipulated that Germany and Turkey would remain neutral in the conflict between Austria-Hungary and Serbia, but that if Russia intervened, Germany would enter the war on the side of Austria-Hungary, and a military alliance with Turkey would become active.

Historical Background

As legions of historians have observed, Europe was a powder keg, fully packed, in the years and months leading up to June 28, 1914, when the Austrian archduke Francis Ferdinand and his wife, Sophie, were assassinated in Sarajevo. The political murder set the match to the powder, and a series of interlocking alliances between the nations of Europe ensured that the entire continent—along with the nations' colonial interests—would be engulfed in war. The events of the summer of 1914 also triggered a series of additional treaties as nations further aligned themselves with one another.

On August 2, 1914, Germany concluded a hasty treaty with the Young Turks, who had taken control of what was left of the Ottoman Empire. The Young Turks were busy passing a whole slew of administrative reforms that would centralize their government, promote the industrialization of their economy, and secularize their legal system, and an alliance with Germany might give them just the shelter they needed to complete their program free of Russian interference. Especially if war broke out, the Russians were unlikely to resist the lure of Turkish holdings. In short, the Young Turks needed a powerful friend.

On the other side, snuggling up to the Young Turks fit well into Germany's grand scheme to stretch its influence "from Berlin to Baghdad" as part of its age-old competition with Russia. The agreement thus was aimed at seducing Turkey's new and untested rulers squarely into the German camp, regardless of the rapidly developing events in the Balkans, events that the revolt of the Young Turks had itself helped to set in motion.

Terms

Like most prewar treaties, the secret agreement was based on assumptions and contingencies. Germany and Turkey would remain neutral in the conflict the assassination had created between Austria-Hungary and Serbia unless Russia intervened on the side of Serbia. Once that contingency developed, Germany would intervene on the side of Austria, and a special military alliance would become active between Germany and Turkey: the German military mission to the Ottoman

Empire would exercise "effective influence" over the Turkish army, and it would also defend Ottoman territory as the need arose.

Secret Treaty of Alliance between Germany and the Ottoman Empire, 2 August 1914

ARTICLE 1
The two Contracting Powers undertake to observe strict neutrality in the present conflict between Austria-Hungary and Serbia.

ARTICLE 2
In the event that Russia should intervene with active military measures and thus should create for Germany a casus foederis with respect to Austria-Hungary, this *casus foederis* would also come into force for Turkey.

ARTICLE 3
In the event of war, Germany will leave its Military Mission at the disposal of Turkey.

The latter, for its part, assures the said Military Mission effective influence over the general conduct of the army, in conformity with what has been agreed upon directly by His Excellency the Minister of War and His Excellency the Chief of the Military Mission.

ARTICLE 4
Germany obligates itself, by force of arms if need be, to defend Ottoman territory in case it should be threatened.

ARTICLE 5
This Agreement, which has been concluded with a view to protecting the two Empires from the international complications which may result from the present conflict, enters into force at the time of its signing by the above-mentioned plenipotentiaries and shall remain valid, with any analogous mutual agreements, until 31 December 1918. . .

Article 8 held that the treaty was to be secret unless the signatories agreed otherwise.

Consequences

Of course, Russia did enter the war on the side of Serbia. Turkey refrained from entering the war immediately and directly, but it did give immediate shelter to two German warships stationed in Turkish waters, and it reflagged them as vessels of the Turkish navy. More importantly, on September 26 Turkey closed the straits, thereby cutting off the major supply route to Russia. By the end of October 1914, the Turkish army was mobilized and had entered the war on the side of Germany and Austria-Hungary, beginning operations against Russia. A new alliance was concluded between the Ottoman Empire and Germany in January 1915, to which Austria-Hungary also subscribed in March 1915.

In the longer view, the Young Turks made a fatal mistake in overestimating German might and hastily entering the Great War on the side of the Central Powers. Already dismembered by the Balkan Wars, the empire would be beheaded after the defeat in World War I.

TREATY OF LONDON (1915)

TREATY AT A GLANCE

Completed
April 26, 1915, at London

Signatories
France, Russia, Great Britain, and Italy

Overview
By promising Italy certain territories at the expense of the Austro-Hungarian Empire, the Allies enticed the Italians to join their cause and to declare war on Austria-Hungary on May 23, 1915.

Historical Background

As a member of the long-standing Triple Alliance with Germany and Austria-Hungary, Italy was pledged to remain "benevolently neutral" and make no alliances with the enemies of Germany and Austria-Hungary. During the second year of World War I, however, Italy accepted the Allies' offer to join the war on their side. This was accomplished by means of the secret Treaty of London. The agreement, which in effect "purchased" Italy's belligerency, fit into a general trend of the war that followed from the solemn promise of the Entente powers on September 5, 1914, to make no separate peace with any of the Central Powers. As a result, throughout the war, the Allies felt compelled to bolster each other's fighting spirit with the promise of spoils to come. The Allies' callous willingness to consign Istanbul (Constantinople) to Russia in March 1915 was perhaps the most shocking example of this tendency, but buying Italy's loyalty also certainly ranked high on the list.

Terms

The treaty promised that victory in the war would give Italy the Trentino, the South Tirol, Istria, and one-third of Dalmatia—all possessions of the Austro-Hungarian Empire. Italy would also enjoy sovereignty over the Dodecanese Islands, which it already occupied, and a "just share" of the Ottoman Empire, should that territory be partitioned as a result of the war. Finally, in the interests of maintaining a balance of power, France and Britain pledged to compensate Italy for any gains those two powers made at the expense of Germany's colonial holdings.

Agreement between France, Russia, Britain, and Italy (Treaty of London), 26 April 1915

ARTICLE 1

A military convention shall be immediately concluded between the General Staffs of France, Great Britain, Italy and Russia. This convention shall settle the minimum number of military forces to be employed by Russia against Austria-Hungary in order to prevent that Power from concentrating all its strength against Italy, in the event of Russia deciding to direct her principal effort against Germany.

This military convention shall settle question of armistices, which necessarily comes within the scope of the Commanders-in-chief of the Armies.

ARTICLE 2

On her part, Italy undertakes to use her entire resources for the purpose of waging war jointly with France, Great Britain and Russia against all their enemies.

ARTICLE 3

The French and British fleets shall render active and permanent assistance to Italy until such time as the Austro-Hungarian fleet shall have been destroyed or until peace shall have been concluded.

A naval convention shall be immediately concluded to this effect between France, Great Britain and Italy.

ARTICLE 4

Under the Treaty of Peace, Italy shall obtain the Trentino, Cisalpine Tyrol with its geographical and natural frontier (the Brenner frontier), as well as Trieste, the counties of Gorizia and Gradisca, all Istria as far as the Quarnero and including Volosca and the Istrian islands of Cherso and Lussin, as well as the small islands of Plavnik, Unie, Canidole, Palazzuoli, San Pietro di Nembi, Asinello, Gruica, and the neighboring islets. . . [frontier details]

ARTICLE 5

Italy shall also be given the province of Dalmatia within its present administrative boundaries, including to the north . . . [frontier details]

NOTE: The following Adriatic territory shall be assigned by the four Allied Powers to Croatia, Serbia and Montenegro:

In the Upper Adriatic, the whole coast from the bay of Volosca on the borders of Istria as far as the northern frontier of Dalmatia, including the coast which is at present Hungarian and all the coast of Croatia, with the port of Fiume and the small ports of Novi and Carlopago, as well as the islands of Veglia, Pervichio, Gregorio, Goli and Arbe. And, in the Lower Adriatic (in the region interesting Serbia and Montenegro) the whole coast from Cape Planka as far as the River Drin, with the important harbors of Spalato, Ragusa, Cattaro, Antivari, Dulcigno and St Jean de Medua and the islands of Greater and Lesser Zirona, Bua, Solta, Brazza, Jaclian and Calamotta. The port of Durazzo to be assigned to the independent Moslem State of Albania.

ARTICLE 6

Italy shall receive full sovereignty over Valona, the island of Saseno and surrounding territory of sufficient extent to assure defence of these points . . . [frontier details]

ARTICLE 7

Should Italy obtain the Trentino and Istria in accordance with the provisions of Article 4, together with Dalmatia and the Adriatic islands within the limits specified in Article 5, and the Bay of Valona (Article 6), and if the central portion of Albania is reserved for the establishment of a small autonomous neutralized State, Italy shall not oppose the division of Northern and Southern Albania between Montenegro, Serbia and Greece, should France, Great Britain and Russia so desire. The coast from the southern boundary of the Italian territory of Valona (see Article 6) up to Cape Stylos shall be neutralized.

Italy shall be charged with the representation of the State of Albania in its relations with foreign Powers.

Italy agrees, moreover, to leave sufficient territory in any event to the east of Albania to ensure the existence of a frontier line between Greece and Serbia to the west of Lake Ochrida.

ARTICLE 8

Italy shall receive entire sovereignty over the Dodecanese Islands which she is at present occupying.

ARTICLE 9

Generally speaking, France, Great Britain and Russia recognize that Italy is interested in the maintenance of the balance of power in the Mediterranean and that, in the event of the total or partial partition of Turkey in Asia, she ought to obtain a just share of the Mediterranean region adjacent to the province of Adalia, where Italy has already acquired rights and interests which formed the subject of an Italo-British convention. The zone which shall eventually be allotted to Italy shall be delimited, at the proper time, due account being taken of the existing interests of France and Great Britain.

The interests of Italy shall also be taken into consideration in the event of the territorial integrity of the Turkish Empire being maintained and of alterations being made in the zones of interest of the Powers.

If France, Great Britain and Russia occupy any territories in Turkey in Asia during the course of the war, the Mediterranean region bordering on the Province of Adalia within the limits indicated above shall be reserved to Italy, who shall be entitled to occupy it.

ARTICLE 10

All rights and privileges in Libya at present belonging to the Sultan by virtue of the Treaty of Lausanne are transferred to Italy.

ARTICLE 11

Italy shall receive a share of any eventual war indemnity corresponding to her efforts and her sacrifices.

ARTICLE 12

Italy declares that she associates herself in the declaration made by France, Great Britain and Russia to the effect that Arabia and the Moslem Holy Places in Arabia shall be left under the authority of an independent Moslem Power.

ARTICLE 13

In the event of France and Great Britain increasing their colonial territories in Africa at the expense of Germany, those two Powers agree in principle that Italy may claim some equitable compensation, particularly as regards the settlement in her favor of the questions relative to the frontiers of the Italian colonies of Eritrea, Somaliland and Libya and the neighboring colonies belonging to France and Great Britain.

ARTICLE 14

Great Britain undertakes to facilitate the immediate conclusion, under equitable conditions, of a loan of at least £50,000,000, to be issued on the London market.

ARTICLE 15

France, Great Britain and Russia shall support such opposition as Italy may make to any proposal in the direction of introducing a representative of the Holy See in any peace negotiations or negotiations for the settlement of questions raised by the present war.

ARTICLE 16

The present arrangement shall be held secret. The adherence of Italy to the Declaration of the 5th September 1914 shall alone be made public, immediately upon declaration of war by or against Italy.

After having taken act of the foregoing memorandum the representatives of France, Great Britain and Russia, duly authorized to that effect, have concluded the following agreement with the representative of Italy, also duly authorized by his Government:

France, Great Britain and Russia give their full assent to the memorandum presented by the Italian Government.

With reference to Articles 1, 2, and 3 of the memorandum which provide for military and naval cooperation between the four Powers, Italy declares that she will take the field at the earliest possible date and within a period not exceeding one month from the signature of these present . . .

In a declaration appended to the treaty, all four powers agreed, three of them for a second time, not to make a separate peace with the Central Powers.

Consequences

Italy declared war on Austria-Hungary on May 23, 1915, shortly after concluding the treaty. Russia, after it was transformed by the Bolshevik Revolution, broke from its agreements and specifically abrogated the 1914 declaration in the TREATY OF BREST-LITOVSK, by which the Soviet government made a separate peace with Germany.

TREATY OF GUARANTEE

TREATY AT A GLANCE

Completed
June 28, 1919, at Versailles, France

Signatories
Great Britain and France

Overview
As part of the complex of treaties ending World War I, Britain (and in a separate document the United States) guaranteed to come to the aid of France in the event of a German attack against it.

Historical Background

In the complicated negotiations at Versailles after World War I, France made it perfectly clear from the beginning that one of her goals was to protect herself from German aggression in the future. The Treaty of Guarantee was one such measure, by which, added to the draconian provisions of the other documents created and signed during the peace negotiations, France hoped to entangle its wartime allies, the United States and Britain, in any future war with Germany. Both the U.S. and British Treaties of Guarantee were signed on June 28, 1919, along with the TREATY OF VERSAILLES.

Terms

The terms of the treaty give some idea of the suspicion of the European allies toward even a defeated Germany and capture well the atmosphere at Versailles.

ARTICLE 1

In case the following stipulations relating to the Left Bank of the Rhine contained in the Treaty of Peace with Germany signed at Versailles the 28th day of June, 1919, by the British Empire, the French Republic, and the United States of America among other Powers:

ARTICLE 42. Germany is forbidden to maintain or construct any fortifications either on the left bank of the Rhine or on the right bank to the west of a line drawn 50 kilometres to the east of the Rhine.

ARTICLE 43. In the area defined above the maintenance and assembly of armed forces, either permanently, or temporarily, and military manoeuvres of any kind, as well as the upkeep of all permanent works for mobilization, are in the same way forbidden.

ARTICLE 44. In case Germany violates in any manner whatsoever the provisions of Articles 42 and 43, she shall be regarded as committing a hostile act against the Powers signatory of the present Treaty and as calculated to disturb the peace of the world.

may not at first provide adequate security and protection to France, Great Britain agrees to come immediately to her assistance in the event of any unprovoked movement of aggression against her being made by Germany.

The United States treaty, however, depended on the ratification of the U.S. Senate, and the British treaty was contingent upon passage of the U.S. treaty:

ARTICLE 2

The present Treaty, in similar terms with the Treaty of even date for the same purpose concluded between the French Republic and the United States of America, a copy of which Treaty is annexed hereto, will only come into force when the latter is ratified.

ARTICLE 3

The present Treaty must be submitted to the Council of the League of Nations and must be recognized by the Council, acting if need be by a majority, as an engagement which is consistent with the Covenant of the League; it will continue in force until on the application of one of the Parties to it the Council, acting if need be by a majority, agree that the League itself affords sufficient protection.

ARTICLE 4

The present Treaty shall before ratification by His Majesty be submitted to Parliament for approval.

It shall before ratification by the President of the

French Republic be submitted to the French Chambers for approval.

ARTICLE 5

The present Treaty shall impose no obligation upon any of the Dominions of the British Empire unless and until it is approved by the Parliament of the Dominion concerned.

The present Treaty shall be ratified, and shall, subject to Articles 2 and 4, come into force at the same time as the Treaty of Peace with Germany of even date comes into force for the British Empire and the French Republic.

Consequences

In the long run, when the American Senate refused to ratify the U.S. treaty and, therefore, the British treaty lapsed, the Treaty of Guarantee, like so much else at Versailles, proved a chimera, neither providing security to France nor helping secure peace in Europe.

Peace Treaties and Truces

TREATY OF PORTSMOUTH

TREATY AT A GLANCE

Completed
September 5, 1905, at Portsmouth, New Hampshire

Signatories
Japan and Russia

Overview
Brokered by U.S. president Theodore Roosevelt, the Treaty of Portsmouth ended the Russo-Japanese War, which much to Europe's surprise and chagrin marked the defeat of a world power by a new Asian aggressor. The humiliated Russian czar, his ambitions checked in Asia, his rule at home seriously destabilized, turned an imperialist eye toward the Balkans. There—where a century's worth of entangling alliances sought to prop up the ailing Austro-Hungarian Empire and hold the line on the crumbling domain of the Ottoman Turks—Russia's face-saving meddling would help to light the fuse for World War I.

Historical Background

On February 8, 1904, the Japanese fleet laid siege to a Russian naval squadron anchored at Russian-controlled Port Arthur (Lüshun) on the coast of the Liaodong Peninsula in southern Manchuria. Japan's surprise attack on Russia launched one of the largest armed conflicts the world had ever witnessed, a war that saw the first large-scale use of automatic weapons and one in which for the first time in modern history an Asian country defeated a European power.

For half a century Japan had watched with apprehension the Russian Empire expand into eastern Asia, threatening Japan's own imperial designs. Russia claimed historical ties with Manchuria that stretched back to Peter the Great, and certainly since beginning the construction of the Trans-Siberian Railroad in 1891, the czar had looked longingly toward China's huge province. After the decadent Qing (Ch'ing), or Manchu, dynasty lost a war with Japan in 1894, China had entered into an anti-Japanese alliance with Russia, granting the czar rights to extend the railroad across Manchuria to Vladivostok, in the process giving Russia control over an important strip of Chinese territory.

In 1898 Russia pressured the Chinese into leasing the strategically important Port Arthur after the czar's troops had occupied Manchuria during the Boxer Rebellion. In 1903 the czar reneged on his agreement to withdraw those troops, making the military occupation of the Liaodong Peninsula permanent. With Russia's imperial navy stationed at Port Arthur and its imperial army ensconced on the peninsula, it seemed to the Japanese only a matter of time before the czar would stake a claim to Korea, which lay just to the east of Manchuria like a dagger pointed at the heart of Japan.

Since defeating China, Japan had been building up its army, and by the turn of the century, it enjoyed a marked superiority over Russia in the number of ground troops in the Far East. All that held the Japanese in check locally was Great Britain, which ruled the sea with its all-powerful navy. Then, in 1902, Britain abandoned her policy of "splendid isolation"—i.e., its refusal to enter into official alliances with any national power—and signed a treaty with Japan in order to stop the headlong expansionism of Czar Nicholas II. Confident of England's neutrality, Japanese military leaders began planning for the war that world leaders, not unaware of the constantly escalating hostility between Russia and Japan, had long expected.

When the attack came, Japan was a small country little known in the West, and Russia was one of Europe's five Great Powers. Most of the world expected Russia to make short work of the island kingdom. No country, certainly not Japan's newfound ally England, much less Russia herself, imagined the Japanese could so easily debilitate the czar's Pacific fleet; to replace it, Nicholas promptly dispatched his Baltic fleet, which suffered equally disastrous treatment from the Japanese navy. Yet more shocking was the speed with which Japan's army overran Korea and crossed the Yalu River into Manchuria. In general, because the Russians were unable to transport sufficient troops and supplies to the battle zone, they suffered a series of stunning defeats, losing Port Arthur (January 1905) and incurring heavy losses at the Battle of Mukden (February–March 1905). The worst disaster befell the Russians in May 1905, when its Baltic fleet was destroyed in the Battle of Tsushima.

The war also spotlighted the severe problems of the Romanov dynasty. Nicholas, his czarina and imperial court under the dolorous influence of the half-crazed monk Rasputin, was slow to react to Japanese advances; yet, overmatched and outgunned, he refused to back down, vaguely trusting in God rather than sound military action to defend the honor and glory of Russia. "A soft haze of mysticism refracts everything he beholds and magnifies his own functions and person," a Russian minister complained to a colleague puzzled by the czar's lassitude.

Meanwhile, in less than a year, Japan had brought the mighty Russian Empire to its knees.

Terms

The consequences of Japan's great victory were swift to come and far-reaching. Theodore Roosevelt, a U.S. president with his own scarcely concealed imperial ambitions, mediated the peace conference held at Portsmouth, New Hampshire, between August 9 and September 5, 1905.

By the treaty, Russia recognized Japan's conquest of Korea:

II

The Imperial Russian Government, acknowledging that Japan possesses in Korea paramount political, military, and economical interests, engage neither to obstruct nor interfere with the measures of guidance, protection, and control which the Imperial Government of Japan may find it necessary to take in Korea.

It is understood that Russian subjects in Korea shall be treated exactly in the same manner as the subjects or citizens of other foreign Powers—that is to say,

they shall be placed on the same footing as the subjects or citizens of the most-favored nation.

It is also agreed that, in order to avoid all causes of misunderstanding, the two High Contracting Parties will abstain, on the Russo-Korean frontier, from taking any military measures which may menace the security of Russian or Korean territory.

And Russia transferred to Japan its lease of Port Arthur and the Liaodong Peninsula, in addition to ceding the southern half of Sakhalin:

V

The Imperial Russian Government transfer and assign to the Imperial Government of Japan, with the consent of the Government of China, the lease of Port Arthur, Ta-lien, and adjacent territory and territorial waters and all rights, privileges, and concessions connected with or forming part of such lease, and they also transfer and assign to the Imperial Government of Japan all public works and properties in the territory affected by the above-mentioned lease.

The two High Contracting Parties mutually engage to obtain the consent of the Chinese Government mentioned in the foregoing stipulation. The Imperial Government of Japan on their part undertake that the proprietary rights of Russian subjects in the territory above referred to shall be perfectly respected.

VI

The Imperial Russian Government engage to transfer and assign to the Imperial Government of Japan, without compensation and with the consent of the Chinese Government, the railway between Chang-chun (Kwang-cheng-tsze) and Port Arthur and all its branches, together with all rights, privileges, and properties appertaining thereto in that region, as well as all coal-mines in the said region, belonging to or worked for the benefit of the railway.

The two High Contracting Parties mutually engage to obtain the consent of the Government of China mentioned in the foregoing stipulation. . . .

IX

The Imperial Russian Government cede to the Imperial Government of Japan in perpetuity and full sovereignty the southern portion of the Island of Sakhalin and all islands adjacent thereto and public works and properties thereon.

The fiftieth degree of north latitude is adopted as the northern boundary of the ceded territory. The exact alignment of such territory shall be determined in accordance with the provisions of additional Art. II annexed to this treaty.

Japan and Russia mutually agree not to construct in their respective possessions on the Island of Sakhalin or the adjacent islands any fortifications or other similar military works. They also respectively engage not to take any military measures which may impede the free navigation of the straits of La Perouse and Tartary.

Two articles laid the foundation for regulating the two nations' commerce in Manchuria, specifically restricting the use of rail lines built by Japan and Russia to commerce rather than warfare:

VII

Japan and Russia engage to exploit their respective railways in Manchuria exclusively for commercial and industrial purposes, and in nowise for strategic purposes.

It is understood that this restriction does not apply to the railway in the territory affected by the lease of the Liao-tung Peninsula.

VIII

The Imperial Governments of Japan and Russia, with a view to promote and facilitate intercourse and traffic will, as soon as possible, conclude a separate convention for the regulation of their connecting railway services in Manchuria.

While the treaty brought a swift end to the Russo-Japanese War, it underscored the humiliation Russia had suffered, greatly undercutting the tottering government of the czar. Not only had Japan gained control of Korea, the Liaodong Peninsula, and Port Arthur (and the South Manchurian Railroad that led to Port Arthur), but a chastened Russia meekly agreed to evacuate southern Manchuria.

Consequences

Within two months of signing the treaty, Nicholas II was faced with a social revolution. Ragged Russian workers, starving serfs, and dispirited soldiers rose up en masse to plead for succor from their "Little Father," only to have pleas drowned and their bodies broken under the hooves of Cossack horses. Though Nicholas, one of the more inept autocrats in European history, had crushed the 1905 revolution, he did so only after buying off middle- and upper-class reformers by issuing the October Manifesto, the equivalent of a constitutional charter. Thus began the final march in Russia toward the Bolshevik Revolution.

Meanwhile, needing time, perhaps years, to recover from the war and the 1905 revolution, Russia could no longer hold its own in the tricky system of alliances aimed at maintaining peace, however fragile, in Europe through a precarious balance of power. Determined to hold its own in the Balkans, Russia was forced to turn to its age-old enemy England in a diplomatic alliance against Germany and Austria-Hungary, who also had sights set on certain Balkan holdings of the crumbling Ottoman Empire. Thus was England further seduced down a diplomatic slippery slope, as a new generation of policy makers destroyed the assumptions upon which Queen Victoria's ministers and Germany's Otto von Bismarck had perched a world. Although the Triple Entente that ensued between Britain, France, and Russia was not originally conceived as a check on German power, it had that effect, especially after British military leaders—bedazzled by what they had seen as observers aboard Japanese ships attacking Port Arthur—persuaded their government to begin building even bigger battleships. These dreadnoughts kicked off a dangerous new naval arms race between Great Britain and Germany.

Theodore Roosevelt, for his successful efforts, was awarded the Nobel Peace Prize, even as the whiff of gunpowder swept from the harbors and battlefields of Manchuria across Europe, intoxicating leaders already slouching toward a general conflagration.

TREATY OF LAUSANNE (1912)
(TREATY OF OUCHY)

TREATY AT A GLANCE

Completed
October 18, 1912, at Lausanne, Switzerland

Signatories
Italy and the Ottoman Empire (Turkey)

Overview
The treaty ended the Italo-Turkish War of 1911–12, triggered by Italy's attempt to annex the Turkish North African provinces of Cyrenaica and Tripolitania (together constituting modern Libya). The war further destabilized an already unstable Europe and was therefore a contributing factor to the outbreak of World War I.

Historical Background

The turn of the century found Italy, like the rest of Europe, in an expansionist and imperialist mood, as the government of Premier Giovanni Giolitti looked for colonial outlets to accommodate the nation's surplus population. Italy, Germany's erstwhile partner in the Triple Alliance, had sided with France in the ALGECIRAS CONVENTION, which settled the dispute between France and Germany over Morocco. In return, the French secretly pledged to support Italy in Libya should the Italians wish to take advantage of the turmoil created among the Ottomans by the revolt of the Young Turks.

On September 29, 1911, Italy concocted an excuse for grabbing this piece of the ever-weakening Ottoman Empire, and the final pre–World War I assault on Turkish rule had begun. Claiming that Italians were being mistreated in Cyrenaica and Tripolitania, Italy declared war on the Turks. At the same time, Russian ministers in the Balkans secured an alliance between the bitter rivals Serbia and Bulgaria in preparation for its own strike against Ottoman-controlled Europe, and the Balkans also erupted in rebellion against Turkey.

Italy invaded what is now Libya, sending a naval squadron as far as the Dardanelles and seizing Tripoli and other towns along the coast. The Turks found support from the Libyan Arabs, but Italy escalated the war to Rhodes and the other Dodecanese Islands directly off the coast of Turkey. By November, Italy had annexed the region. The Ottomans, plagued by rebellion in their Balkan possessions and by trouble at home, sued for peace.

Terms

Under the Treaty of Lausanne, Libya became an Italian protectorate, albeit the Turks retained a degree of religious authority in the region, and the Turks also ceded Rhodes and the Dodecanese Islands.

The substance of the treaty was contained in 10 articles.

I

The two governments pledge themselves to take steps necessary for the cessation of hostilities, immediately following the signature of the present Treaty. Special Commissioners shall be sent on the spot to assure prompt execution of such steps.

II

The two Governments pledge themselves to give orders recalling their officers, their troops and their civil servants, immediately following the signature of the present Treaty. Recall shall be effective respectively for the Ottoman Government in Tripolitania and Cyrenaica and for the Italian Government in the Islands of the Aegean Sea.

The evacuation of the Islands, above-mentioned, by the Italian officers, troops and civil servants, shall take place immediately following the evacuation of the Ottoman officers, troops and civil servants from Tripolitania and Cyrenaica.

III

War prisoners and hostages shall be exchanged without undue delay.

IV

The two Governments pledge to grant full amnesty; the Royal Government to the inhabitants of Tripolitania and Cyrenaica and the Imperial Government to the inhabitants of the Islands of the Aegean Sea, under Ottoman sovereignty who took part in the hostilities or compromised themselves to safeguard their safety, excluding those who committed civil crimes. Consequently, no individual, regardless of class or rank, shall be pursued or disturbed in his person or possessions. His political or military acts or his opinion, voiced during the hostilities shall also be exonerated. Persons detained or deported for such behavior shall immediately be given their liberty.

V

All Treaties, Conventions and Agreements of all types and qualifications, concluded or in force before the declaration of war, shall be reestablished between the two Contracting Parties and put back in working force. The two Governments shall return to their pre-war status as shall their respective subjects and each shall resume their relations to one another as they stood before the hostilities.

VI

Italy pledges itself to conclude with Turkey, at the time it shall review its Treaties of Commerce with other Powers, a Treaty of Commerce, based on European public rights, that is to say that she consents to give Turkey complete economic independence and the right to act in matters of commerce and custom duties, as do the European Powers, without being bound by conventions or agreements of bygone days. It is understood that said Treaty of Commerce shall not be put in effect until other Treaties of Commerce have been effectuated, under similar conditions, by the Sublime Porte, with other Powers. Moreover, Italy agrees to upgrade custom duties from eleven per cent to fifteen per cent *ad valorem* in Turkey, and also to the establishment of new monopolies and deduction of surtaxes on duties on the following five items: petrol, cigarette paper, matches, alcohol and playing cards. All this provided the same conditions prevail simultaneously and without distinction to imports of other Powers.

Insofar as imports of articles classified as monopolies are concerned, the agencies controlling the imports of these monopolies shall be expected to furnish articles of Italian origin, following established percentages based on annual importations of said articles, providing delivery prices of the articles conform to current market prices at the time of purchase, taking into consideration the quality of the merchandise in question and the current prices of said articles; these prices should be compared to prices quoted in the three years preceding the war and conforming to comparable quality standards. It is understood, nevertheless, that if Turkey instead of establishing new monopolies on the five above-mentioned articles decides to impose a surtax on sales, these surtaxes would be imposed under the same conditions and standards as those set up by Turkey and all other nations.

VII

The Italian Government pledges to discontinue Italian postal services operating in the Ottoman Empire, doing this at the same time as other states also having postal services in Turkey shall also discontinue their services.

VIII

The Sublime Porte proposes to investigate negotiations with European, and other interested Big Powers, in order to terminate capitulary regimes in Turkey and replace them by regimes adhering to international rights. Thus Italy, recognizing the well founded intentions of the Sublime Porte, declares that, as of this day, it shall extend her full and sincere support.

IX

The Ottoman Government desiring to prove its good feeling in regard to the loyal and faithful services rendered by Italian subjects employed in the government administration but who were dismissed at the time the hostilities started, are prepared to reinstate them in their pre-war position. Retroactive salaries shall be paid to all who were dismissed at the time, and this interruption of service shall in no way be held against those who were ready to retire on pension.

Moreover, the Ottoman Government pledges itself to use its good offices with organizations with whom it is in contact (The Finance Department, the Societies on Railroads, Banks, etc.), so that the same arrangements are made by these organizations, as those above-mentioned, with regard to Italian subjects in their employ where the same conditions prevail.

X

The Italian Government pledges to pay annually to the Ottoman Government the debt owed the Imperial Government corresponding to a sum total to the average of each of the three preceding years prior to the declaration of the war; said payments to be rendered to the Finance Department from receipts received from the two Provinces. The total on the aforementioned annual payments shall be determined by mutual agreement by two Commissioners named by the Royal Government and the Imperial Government. Should discord arise over these nominations, the decision shall be put in the hands of arbitrators, mutually named by the two Parties. Should this move still not be effective, each Party shall designate a different Power to represent it and the choice of final arbitrators shall be decided by the designated Powers.

The Royal Government and the Ottoman Finance Department shall have through the intercession of the Imperial Government the power to demand substitution of the aforesaid annuity by paying a corresponding sum, computed at four per cent interest.

Referring to the preceding paragraph, the Royal Government declares as of today that the annuity cannot be less than two million Italian lire, and it is ready to remit to the Finance administration the capitalized corresponding sum, as soon as a request is voiced.

Consequences

By further destabilizing the Ottomans and thus further upsetting the extremely fragile balance of power in Europe, the provisions of the treaty were a contributing factor in the outbreak of World War I just two years later.

TREATY OF LONDON (1913)

TREATY AT A GLANCE

Completed
May 30 (May 17 old style), 1913, at London

Signatories
Balkan League (Greece, Bulgaria, Serbia, and Montenegro)
and the Ottoman Empire (Turkey)

Overview
The treaty ended the First Balkan War (1912–13), by which the Balkan League (Greece, Bulgaria, Serbia, and Montenegro), with the help of Europe's Great Powers, forced the cession of almost all of Turkey's remaining European territory. The treaty left unresolved questions over the division of Macedonia and other spoils, and as a result the Second Balkan War erupted in June 1913.

Historical Background

Italy had exposed Turkey's weakness following the revolt of the Young Turks—and their insecure hold on power—by wrenching away Tripoli. The conflict with Italy still raged, when the small Christian states of the Balkans—Serbia, Montenegro, Greece, and Bulgaria— formed the Balkan League, ostensibly to check Austro-Hungarian ambitions on the peninsula. Now, their ambitions stirred by the Italian's successes, they suddenly attacked European Turkey, with Montenegro first declaring war on Turkey on October 8, 1912, only to be quickly followed by the others. The Young Turks almost immediately came to terms with Italy, but it did not help. The Turkish army, much to everybody's surprise, virtually collapsed in the face of the invasion. By November 3, 1912, Balkan troops stood before the walls of Constantinople. Five days later the Greeks entered Salonika (now Thessaloníki). By the end of the month, the Serbs had taken the port of Durazzo on the Adriatic, giving landlocked Serbia a link to the sea. On December 3 the Young Turks sued for peace.

The Balkan victory shocked and dismayed the three Great Powers of Central Europe. Germany had been husbanding new relations with the Young Turks while it constructed its Berlin-to-Baghdad railway. Austria, expecting the Turks to make short work of the Serbs, instead were treated to the sight of the Serbs triumphant on the Adriatic. The day Serbian troops marched into Durazzo, the emperor mobilized nearly a million men and demanded the Balkan state withdraw from the seaport. But Russia, which had taken to meddling again in the Balkans after its shocking defeat by Japan, now endorsed the Balkan League and promised to defend its Turkish conquests. The message was clear: if Austria moved against Serbia, Russia would respond, and a European war would surely follow. At the same time, Russia was not exactly thrilled by Bulgaria's success, since the czar had always intended that Russian troops should occupy Constantinople, not the Bulgarian army.

Recognizing that the actions of the Balkan League had the potential to badly destabilize an already potentially explosive Europe, England's foreign secretary, Sir Edward Grey, sought to contain the conflict by proposing a conference of the Great Powers, who agreed to meet in London beginning December 10, 1912. Even while Grey set about his mission, the armistice between the Turks and the Balkan upstarts broke down, and fighting resumed. But this time, Adrianople fell to a combined Bulgarian-Serbian army, and the Turks returned in haste to the peace table, ready now for the Great Powers to impose a settlement. On May 30, 1913, the Treaty of London was signed, bringing the First Balkan War to a close.

Terms

Under the treaty, the Ottoman Empire ceded to the Balkan states all of its remaining European territory, except for the region immediately adjacent to Constantinople. The Treaty of London consisted of seven brief articles.

I

Upon the exchange of ratifications of the present treaty there shall be peace and friendship between His Majesty and Emperor of the Ottomans, on the one part, and their Majesties, the Allied Sovereigns, on the other part, as well as between their heirs and successors, their respective States and subjects in perpetuity.

II

His Majesty the Emperor of the Ottomans cedes to their Majesties the Allied Sovereigns all the territories of his Empire on the continent of Europe to the west of a line drawn from Enos on the Aegean Sea to Midia on the Black Sea, with the exception of Albania.

The exact line of the frontier from Enos to Midia shall be determined by an international commission.

III

His Majesty the Emperor of the Ottomans and their Majesties the Allied Sovereigns declare that they remit to His Majesty the Emperor of Germany; His Majesty the Emperor of Austria, King of Hungary; the President of the French Republic; His Majesty the King of Great Britain and Ireland, Emperor of India; His Majesty the King of Italy; and His Majesty the Emperor of All the Russias the matter of arranging the delimitation of the frontiers of Albania and all other questions concerning Albania.

IV

His Majesty the Emperor of the Ottomans declares that he cedes to their Majesties the Allied Sovereigns the island of Crete and that he renounces in their favour all rights of Sovereignty and all other rights which he possessed in that island

V

His Majesty the Emperor of the Ottomans and their Majesties the Allied Sovereigns declare that they entrust to His Majesty the Emperor of Germany; His Majesty the Emperor of Austria, King of Hungary; the President of the French Republic; His Majesty the King of Great Britain and Ireland, Emperor of India; His Majesty the King of Italy; His Majesty the Emperor of All the Russias the task of determining the title to all the Ottoman islands in the Aegean Sea (except the island of Crete) and to the peninsula of Mount Athos.

VI

His Majesty the Emperor of the Ottomans and their Majesties the Allied Sovereigns declare that they refer the matter of settling questions of a financial nature resulting from the war which is ended and from the above-mentioned cessions of territory to the International Commission convened at Paris, to which they have deputed their representatives.

VII

Questions concerning prisoners of war, questions of jurisdiction, of nationality, and of commerce shall be settled by special conventions.

Consequences

The short treaty failed to specify just how the territorial gains would be distributed between the Balkan allies, but as the Great Powers worked it out in London, Macedonia was partitioned between the Balkan states, Crete went to Greece, and Albania of course was granted independence. Landlocked Serbia, however, continued to bid for additional territory in Macedonia, hoping, even in the face of Russian opposition, to hang onto a seaport. Bulgaria, traditionally a bitter rival of the Serbs in any case, responded by attacking both Serbia and Greece, thus beginning the Second Balkan War.

These conflicts undermined the House of Hapsburg by stripping Turkey of its European real estate. While the wars themselves disturbed the uneasy symbiosis between the Austro-Hungarian and Ottoman Empires, the treaties—dictated by other Great Powers, often over Austrian objections—further damaged the already severely tarnished prestige of the Dual Monarchy. In this way, the Balkan Wars were a prelude to the great conflagration of World War I.

TREATY OF BUCHAREST

TREATY AT A GLANCE

Completed
August 10 (July 28 old style), 1913, at Bucharest, Romania

Signatories
Romania, Greece, Serbia, and Montenegro and Bulgaria

Overview
The treaty ended the Second Balkan War (1913), which cost Bulgaria most of the gains of her wars against Turkey. The cause of Serbian nationalism in particular had been advanced, and the enmity between Balkan states still flourished. Secret societies and terrorist organizations abounded, and the region was highly unstable, a condition that led ineluctably to World War I.

Historical Background

The TREATY OF LONDON (1913), which concluded the First Balkan War earlier in the year and by which the Balkan League acquired Turkey's Balkan possessions, left questions of just to which victor should go the spoils. While the conference of Great Powers continued to meet in London to hammer out the remaining problems, Bulgaria precipitously challenged Greek and Serbian claims to Macedonia. On June 29, 1913, scarcely a month after signing the treaty, Bulgaria—swollen with hubris over her earlier conquests from Turkey—attacked her former allies, Serbia and Greece, seized Salonika, and crushed the ill-prepared Serbian army.

Bulgaria's hasty action backfired, however, when Romania, neutral in the last conflict, fell on the Bulgars' unprotected rear. Romania's army crossed the Danube and threatened Sofia. Meanwhile, Turkey allied herself with Greece and Serbia against Bulgaria, swiftly recapturing Adrianople. When the kaiser backed King Carol of Romania and the Russian czar refused to come to the aid of Bulgaria, its own maverick Czar Ferdinand quickly sued for an armistice. The Great Powers once again intervened with a blend of threats, coercions, and compensatory bribes to impose peace in the Treaty of Bucharest.

Terms

The treaty compelled Bulgaria to cede Salonika (present-day Thessaloníki) to Greece, the northern Dobruja to Romania, and much of Macedonia to Serbia. In a separate treaty (the 1913 TREATY OF CONSTANTINOPLE), Bulgaria returned most of Thrace to Turkey.

The Treaty of Bucharest was brief and read, in its entirety, as follows.

I

From the day on which the ratifications of the present treaty are exchanged there shall be peace and amity between His Majesty the King of Roumania, His Majesty the King of the Bulgarians, His Majesty the King of the Hellenes, His Majesty the King of Montenegro, and His Majesty the King of Serbia, as well as between their heirs and successors, their respective States and subjects.

II

The former frontier between the Kingdom of Bulgaria and the Kingdom of Roumania, from the Danube to the Black Sea, is, in conformity with the *procès-verbal* drawn up by the respective military delegates and annexed to Protocol No. 5 of July 22 (August 4), 1913, of the Conference of Bucharest, rectified in the following manner:

The new frontier shall begin at the Danube above Turtukaia and terminate at the Black Sea to the south of Ekrene.

Between these two extreme points the frontier line shall follow the line indicated on the 1/100,000 and 1/200,000 maps of the Roumanian General Staff, and according to the description annexed to the present article.

It is formally understood that within a maximum delay of two years Bulgaria shall dismantle the existing fortifications and shall not construct others at Rustchuk, at Shumla, in the intervening country, and in a zone of twenty kilometres around Baltchik.

A mixed commission, composed of an equal number of representatives of each of the two High Contracting Parties, shall be charged, within fifteen days from the signing of the present treaty, with delimiting the new frontier in conformity with the preceding stipulations. This commission shall supervise the division of the lands and funds which up to the present time may have belonged in common to districts, communes, or communities separated by the new frontier. In case of disagreement as to the line or as to the method of marking it, the two High Contracting Parties agree to request a friendly Government to appoint an arbitrator, whose decision upon the points at issue shall be considered final.

III

The frontier between the Kingdom of Bulgaria and the Kingdom of Serbia shall follow, conformably to the *procés-verbal* drawn up by the respective military delegates, which is annexed to Protocol No. 9 of July 25 (August 7), 1913, of the Conference of Bucharest, the following line:

The frontier line shall begin at the old frontier, from the summit of Patarica, follow the old Turco-Bulgarian frontier and the dividing line of the waters between the Vardar and the Struma, with the exception of the upper valley of the Strumitza, which shall remain Serbian territory; the line shall terminate at the Belasica Mountain, where it will bend back to the Greco-Bulgarian frontier. A detailed description of this frontier and the 1/200,000 map of the Austrian General Staff, on which it is indicated, are annexed to the present article.

A mixed commission, composed of an equal number of representatives of each of the two High Contracting Powers, shall be charged, within fifteen days from the signing of the present treaty, with delimiting the new frontier, in conformity with the preceding stipulations.

This commission shall supervise the division of the lands and funds, which up to the present time may have belonged in common to the districts, communes, or communities separated by the new frontier. In case of disagreement as to the line or as to the method of marking it, the two High Contracting Parties agree to request a friendly Government to appoint an arbitrator, whose decision upon the points at issue shall be considered final.

IV

Questions relating to the old Serbo-Bulgarian frontier shall be settled according to the understanding reached by the two High Contracting Parties, as stated in the protocol annexed to the present article.

V

The frontier between the Kingdom of Greece and the Kingdom of Bulgaria shall follow, conformably to the *procés-verbal* drawn up by the respective military delegates and annexed to Protocol No. 9 of July 25 (August 7), 1913, of the Conference of Bucharest, the following line: The frontier line shall start from the new Serbo-Bulgarian frontier on the summit of Belasica Planina and terminate at the mouth of the Mesta on the Aegean Sea.

Between these two extreme points the frontier line shall follow the line indicated on the 1/200,000 map of the Austrian General Staff, in accordance with the description annexed to the present article.

A mixed commission, composed of an equal number of representatives of each of the two High Contracting Parties, shall be charged, within fifteen days from the signing of the present treaty, with delimiting the frontier in conformity with the preceding stipulations.

This commission shall supervise the division of the lands and funds, which up to the present time may have belonged in common to the districts, communes, or communities separated by the new frontier. In case of disagreement as to the line or as to the method of marking it, the two High Contracting Parties engage to request a friendly Government to appoint an arbitrator, whose decision upon the points at issue shall be considered final.

It is formally understood that Bulgaria renounces from henceforth all claim to the island of Crete.

VI

The headquarters of the respective armies shall be immediately informed of the signing of the present treaty. The Bulgarian Government engages to begin to reduce its army to a peace footing on the day after such notification. It shall order its troops to their garrisons, whence, with the least possible delay, the various reserves shall be returned to their homes.

If the garrison of any troops is situated in the zone occupied by the army of one of the High Contracting Parties, such troops shall be ordered to some other point in the old Bulgarian territory and may not return to their regular garrisons until after the evacuation of the above-mentioned occupied zone.

VII

The evacuation of Bulgarian territory, both old and new, shall begin immediately after the demobilization of the Bulgarian army and shall be completed within a period of not more than fifteen days.

During this period the zone of demarcation for the Roumanian army of operations shall be determined by a line running as follows: Sistov—Lovcea—Turski—Isvor—Glozene—Zlatitza—Mirkov—Araba—Konak—Orchania—Mezdra—Vratza—Berkovitza—Lom—Danube.

VIII

During the occupation of the Bulgarian territories the various armies shall retain the right of requisition in consideration of cash payment.

Such armies shall have free use of the railways for the transportation of troops and of provisions of all kinds, without compensation to the local authority.

The sick and wounded shall be under the protection of the said armies.

IX

As soon as possible after the exchange of ratifications of the present treaty all prisoners of war shall be mutually restored.

The Governments of the High Contracting Parties shall each appoint special commissioners to receive the prisoners.

All prisoners in the hands of any of the Governments shall be delivered to the commissioner of the Government to which they belong, or to his duly authorized representative, at the place which shall be determined upon by the interested parties.

The Governments of the High Contracting Parties shall present to each other, respectively, as soon as possible after all the prisoners have been returned, a statement of the direct expenses incurred through the care and maintenance of the prisoners from the date of their capture or surrender to the date of their death or return. The sums due by Bulgaria to each one of the other High Contracting Parties shall be set off against the sums due by each of the other High Contracting Parties to Bulgaria, and the difference shall be paid to the creditor Government in each case as soon as possible after the exchange of the above-mentioned statements of expense.

X

The present treaty shall be ratified, and the ratifications thereof shall be exchanged at Bucharest within fifteen days, or sooner if it be possible.

In witness whereof the respective plenipotentiaries have hereunto affixed their names and seals.

Consequences

The Great Powers in London congratulated themselves on maintaining peace in a volatile region during precarious times and 10 days after the signing of the treaty disbanded their conference. But "peace" was hardly the word for what they had wrought. Although all of the Balkan allies, including Bulgaria, had gained territory at the expense of the Ottomans, Bulgaria refused to become reconciled to its defeat, and the other Balkan states remained restless for yet more land too.

As Croats and Slovenes, who had long been under Austrian Hapsburg rule, eyed the growth of Serbia, they dreamed of joining the Serbs in a union of south Slavs ("Yugoslavia"). Secret societies, many of them workshops for terror, formed in Serbia and began agitation and assassination across the border. The instability of the Balkans in general was especially dangerous because of the complex alliances with Russia and the powers of central and western Europe. Within a year, a Serb national would kill the moderate Austrian heir apparent, and the world would erupt into war.

TREATY OF CONSTANTINOPLE (1913)

TREATY AT A GLANCE

Completed
September 29 (September 16 old style) 1913, at Constantinople
(present-day Istanbul, Turkey)

Signatories
Ottoman Empire (Turkey) and Bulgaria

Overview
The treaty concluded a separate peace between the Ottoman Turks
and Bulgaria following the Second Balkan War (1913). During this
conflict the Ottoman Empire had allied with its recent adversaries
Romania, Greece, and Serbia to oppose Bulgaria's greedy claims to
territories ceded to the Balkan allies by the Ottomans and carved
up according to the dictates of the Great Powers.

Historical Background

The First Balkan War (1912–13) had been fought by
the Balkan League (which included Bulgaria) against
the Ottoman Empire in order to obtain control of
Ottoman-held European territory. When Bulgaria
attempted to seize too much of the Ottoman-ceded
land, the other Balkan states united to checkmate their
former ally. Turkey joined the fight against Bulgaria, as
well. Attacked from all sides, Bulgaria concluded a
hasty peace with the other Balkan states (TREATY OF
BUCHAREST) and a separate peace with the Ottoman
Empire.

Terms

For the most part, the Treaty of Constantinople (1913)
was a conventional document delineating frontiers and
establishing diplomatic and trade relations. Of special
interest, however, was the annex governing the protection of Islam within Bulgaria.

Annex II

ARTICLE I
A head mufti [expounder of Islamic law] shall reside
in Sofia and shall act as intermediary between the
muftis of Bulgaria in their relations with the Sheik-ul-
Islamat for religious and civil matters of the Sheri, and
with the Bulgarian Ministry of Public Worship.

He shall be elected by the muftis of Bulgaria and
from amongst them, assembled especially for that purpose. The mufti-vekilis shall take part in this assembly,
but only as electors.

The Bulgarian Minister of Public Worship shall
notify, through the Imperial Legation in Sofia, the election of the head mufti to the Sheik-ul-Islamat, which
shall send him a menshur and the murassele authorizing him to exercise his functions, and to grant in turn,
the same power to the other muftis of Bulgaria.

The head mufti shall have the right, within the limits prescribed by the Sheri, of supervision and control
over the muftis of Bulgaria, over the Moslem religious
and charitable institutions, as also over their staffs and
their mutevellis.

ARTICLE II
The muftis are elected by the Moslem electors of Bulgaria.

The head mufti verifies whether the mufti elected
possesses all the qualities required by the Sheri, and in
the affirmative case, he informs the Sheik-ul-Islamat of
the necessity of giving him the necessary authorization to issue fetvas (menshur). Together with the menshur thus obtained he shall deliver to the new mufti
the murassele necessary for conferring upon him the
right of religious jurisdiction over Moslems.

The muftis may, on condition of having their
choice ratified by the head mufti, propose the nomination, within the limits of their districts and in localities where the necessity has arisen, of muftivekilis,
who shall have to fulfil the duties determined by the
present arrangement, under the direct supervision of
the local muftis.

ARTICLE III

The remuneration of the head mufti, the muftis, and the mufti-vekilis, as well as of the personnel of their offices, shall be assumed by the Royal Bulgarian Government, and shall be fixed in consideration of the dignity and importance of their positions.

The organization of the bash-muftilik shall be fixed by a regulation elaborated by the head mufti and duly published.

The head mufti, muftis, and mufti-vekilis and their personnel shall enjoy all the rights which the laws assure to Bulgarian officials.

ARTICLE IV

The removal of muftis and their vekilis shall take place according to the law on public officials.

The head mufti, or his deputy, shall be called upon to sit in the disciplinary council whenever the latter shall have to pronounce upon the removal of a mufti or mufti-vekili. However, the opinion of the head mufti or his deputy shall serve the said council as the basis for its consideration of charges of a purely religious nature.

The order of removal of a mufti or mufti-vekili shall fix the day for the election of his successor.

ARTICLE V

The heudjets and judgments rendered by the muftis, shall be examined by the head mufti, who shall confirm them if he finds them conforming to the precepts of the Sheri, and transmit them to the proper department in order to be carried into effect.

The heudjets and judgments which are not confirmed by reason of non-conformity with the Sheri shall be returned to the muftis who rendered them, and the matters of which they treat shall be examined and settled again according to the provisions of the said law. The heudjets and judgments not found to conform to the prescriptions of the Sheri, or the examination of which by the Sheik-ulIslamat has been requested by the interested parties, shall be sent by the head mufti to His Highness and Sheik-ul-Islamat.

The heudjets and judgments confirmed by the chief mufti, or approved by the Sheik-ul-Islamat, shall be carried into effect by the proper Bulgarian authorities. In that case, they shall be accompanied by a Bulgarian translation.

ARTICLE VI

The head mufti shall, whenever the occasion arises, make to the other muftis the necessary recommendations and communications in matters of marriage, divorce, testaments, successions and guardianships, alimony (nafaka) and other matters of the Sheri, as also in regard to the administration of the property of orphans. Moreover, he shall examine complaints and claims relative to the above-mentioned matters, and make known to the proper department what is to be done according to the Sheri law.

The muftis being also charged with the supervision and administration of the vakoufs, the head mufti shall have among his principal functions that of requiring the rendering of their accounts and of ordering the preparation of statements of accounts relating thereto.

The books relative to the accounts of the vakoufs may be kept in the Turkish language.

ARTICLE VII

The head mufti and the muftis shall inspect, if necessary, the councils of public instruction and the Moslem schools, as well as the medresses of Bulgaria, and shall adopt measures for the creation of educational institutions in localities where their need may be felt.

The head mufti shall, if occasion arises, communicate with the proper department in matters concerning Moslem public instruction.

The Royal Government shall establish at its own expense primary and secondary Moslem schools in the proportion provided by the Bulgarian law on public instruction. Instruction shall take place in the Turkish language and in conformity with the official program, with obligatory instruction in the Bulgarian language.

All laws relating to obligatory instruction and to the number and rights of teachers shall continue to be applied to the teaching body in Moslem communities.

The salaries of the teaching and other personnel of these institutions shall be regulated by the Bulgarian treasury on the same conditions as for those who teach in Bulgarian schools.

A special institution shall also be created for the training of naibs.

ARTICLE VIII

In every centre or city having a numerous Moslem population a Moslem community charged with vakouf matters and secondary public instruction shall be elected. The corporate personality of these communities shall be recognized in all circumstances and by all authorities.

As the vakoufs of each district must be administered, according to the laws and provisions of the Sheri, by the respective Moslem community, it is the corporate personality of the latter which shall be considered as owner of these vakoufs.

The public Moslem cemeteries and those situated near mosques are included in the domain of vakouf properties belonging to the Moslem communities, who shall dispose of them at their convenience and in conformity with the laws of hygiene.

No vakouf property can in any case be expropriated unless its value is paid to the respective community.

The good preservation of vakouf real property situated in Bulgaria shall be safeguarded. No building devoted to religion or charity shall be torn down except in case of unavoidable necessity and in accordance with the laws and regulations in force.

In case a vakouf building shall be expropriated for imperative reasons, this can only be done after the designation of another lot of ground of the same value in respect to location, and after the payment of the value of the building.

The sums paid as the price of *vakouf* real property which shall be expropriated for imperative reasons shall be handed over to the Moslem communities to be entirely devoted to the maintenance of vakouf buildings.

ARTICLE IX

Within six months after the signing of the present arrangement a special commission, of which the head mufti shall by right be a member, shall be appointed by the Bulgarian Government and shall have as its object the examination and verification, within three years from the date of its constitution, of the claims formulated by the mutevellis or their agents.

Those of the parties interested who are not satisfied with the decisions of the commission may have recourse to the proper tribunals of the country.

Consequences

The 1913 Treaty of Constantinople was especially significant in that it established an affinity between Bulgaria and Turkey, so recently enemies, and led both to align themselves with Germany, thereby heightening tensions between Germany (and its allies) and Russia (and its allies). Ultimately, of course, these tensions would explode into World War I.

The treaty marked the last time the Ottoman Turks would have a diplomatic say in European politics, a privilege Turkey had enjoyed for several centuries and one it would seek to regain in less than a year. When World War I broke out, the Young Turks, now more firmly in command at home, quickly allied themselves with the Central Powers, hoping to make up lost ground at the war's victorious conclusion. Instead, having already lost control of Turkish Europe, the move ensured that the Ottomans would lose sovereignty over most of their vast holdings in Asia Minor and the Mideast, as well.

TREATY OF BREST-LITOVSK

TREATY AT A GLANCE

Completed
March 3, 1918, at Brest-Litovsk, Russia (present-day Brest, Belarus)

Signatories
Germany, Austria-Hungary, Bulgaria, and Turkey and
the Russian Federal Soviet Republic

Overview
The Treaty of Brest-Litovsk, concluded between the Central Powers and the new Soviet government of Russia, ended Russian participation in World War I, with the Soviets agreeing to huge territorial losses. The treaty freed Germany from its two-front war, allowing the transfer of troops to the Western Front and a prolongation of the conflict, while presenting the Allies with the difficult question of how to handle Soviet Russia in peacetime, a question that was the haunt most of the 20th century.

Historical Background

World War I had begun in August 1914 with a spectacular German push to the west, toward Paris. When the German armies failed to reach the French capital, however, the war settled into a long, grinding stasis, as trench-bound forces killed one another without achieving any major strategic objectives. With the approach of 1917, all of the belligerents were nearing exhaustion.

England, France, Germany, Austria-Hungary, and Turkey, however, would survive their 1917 crises; Romanov Russia would not. From the beginning, the war had gone very badly for Russia. Its army was enormous: Russia had mobilized roughly 10 percent of its population, putting in excess of 15 million citizens under arms. But they were poorly equipped and even more poorly led. By 1917 the Russian army had been "turned over" three times, its losses estimated at nearly 8 million men, half those mobilized. Morale was so bad that officers refused to lead their troops into battle for fear of being shot in the back. Desertions assumed overwhelming proportions, and whole regiments—often on orders from their officers—surrendered en masse to the Germans.

The man in charge of the disaster, Nicholas II, announced he was leaving his government in the hands of his wife, the emotionally distraught Empress Alexandra, to go to the front and direct the fighting himself. Alexandra turned the reins of power over to

the "debauched monk" Rasputin, who wrecked what little chance the czarist regime had of surviving, much less winning, the war, before he was assassinated by Grand Duke Dmitry, Nicholas's nephew, and Prince Yusupov, the husband of the czar's niece. Meanwhile, industrial mobilization had thrown the economy completely out of whack; farmers could not export their produce and refused to sell food on the open market; the ruble was nearly worthless, and there was precious little room for barter; the railway system had collapsed, and what few supplies existed could get through neither to the front nor to the towns; and Russia's industrial cities, including Petrograd (the Russian name the czar decreed in 1914 to replace the Germanic "St. Petersburg"), were threatened by famine.

It was no accident, as the marxists would say, that 1917 became the year the great Russian Empire heaved one final huge sigh—and vanished. But during the so-called February Revolution, when workers poured spontaneously onto the boulevards from every factory in Petrograd and Moscow, no one seemed to understand what was going on—not the czar at the front, not the liberal and aristocratic Cadets who had been agitating for reform, not the revolutionary leaders exiled in Siberia. Only Vladimir Ilyich Ulyanov—a.k.a. "Lenin," the acerbic leader of a splinter from the marxist revolutionary Union of Russian Socialist Democrats Abroad, called the Bolshevik Party, who was cooling his heels in Switzerland—seemed to notice that power lay in the frozen streets of Petrograd that winter, just waiting for somebody to pick it up. And he said so, doing everything in his power to book passage for Petrograd's Finland Station.

On February 22, 1917, there were mass demonstrations in Petrograd. Two days later, the leaderless workers of the city went out on general strike, fighting bloody battles in the street with the czar's police. By February 27 the army had gone over to the proletariat, and the powerful Petrograd Soviet of Workers' and Soldiers' Deputies was formed. A day later Moscow created its own soviet. Even Nicholas II realized the matter was hopeless. He abdicated—officially—on March 3.

The Russian parliament, or Duma, formed a provisional government. Prince Gyorgy Lvov was appointed prime minister, but the two leading figures in the government were Aleksandr Kerensky and Pavel Milyukov. As political liberals they valued Russia's ties to Britain and France, and—Russia having been promised Constantinople by the Allies as an enticement to continue fighting—they looked forward to capturing the Turkish capital as a means of legitimizing their regime. Kerensky reassured the entente powers in mid-March that his government would fight "unswervingly and indefatigably" till victory was achieved. The words bitterly disappointed German foreign service officers, who had long dabbled in various revolutionary intrigues, hoping to shatter Russia from within and thus force it out of the conflict. Now, so it appeared, the czar's regime had indeed been shattered, but Russia remained a belligerent.

Germany did not give up. Since 1914 the foreign office had both collaborated with nationalist agitators among Russia's Baltic, Finnish, Georgian, Polish, and Ukrainian peoples and supported the conspiracies of Russian social revolutionaries. One of these was Lenin. Living in Kraków when the war erupted, he was immediately arrested. Then an Austrian Social Democrat named Victor Adler persuaded Austria's minister of the interior that Lenin, as leader of the most militant of the Russian marxists, could be an asset in the fight against the Romanov Empire. The minister saw to Lenin's release and deportation to Switzerland, where he continued his insurrectionary correspondence with the Bolshevik underground back home. Meanwhile, in Constantinople another Russian émigré socialist, Alexander Helphand, had caught the eye of Germany's ambassador to Turkey. Impressed with Helphand's revolutionary credentials and connections, the ambassador had him shipped off to Berlin to brief the foreign office.

In March 1915 the foreign office set aside 2 million marks to spend on subversion in Russia. By 1917 the amount had swelled to 41 million marks, much of it going to Helphand's seditious organization, which sowed revolutionary and pacifist ideas among Russian soldiers, workers, and peasants. Then came the fall of the czar's government and Kerensky's declaration of support for the Allied war effort, and the German foreign office figured it needed more radical help than Helphand could offer. Germany decided to facilitate Lenin's return to Russia. On April 9, 1917, the Germans placed Lenin and his comrades, Leon Trotsky among them, on a sealed train in Zurich and cleared the tracks for a night run across Germany. A boat waited in Sweden to whisk the group to the Finland Station at Petrograd.

Once landed, Lenin lost no time. He began pushing the Bolsheviks steadily toward a takeover from his very first speech, which called for all power to the soviets and for social revolution. The Germans loathed Lenin's ultimate goal—he wanted to transform the European war of nations into an international class war—but they loved his current program for a revolutionary Russia: an immediate armistice, an end to secret diplomacy, and the negotiation of a peace involving, so his slogan said, "no annexations, no indemnities." Such brilliant sloganeering—"Peace, Bread and Land" was another Bolshevik cry—caught the imagination of the masses, of the common soldiers, urban workers, and poor peasants to whom the Bolsheviks pitched their message. Scarcely a month after Lenin's arrival, Prince Lvov was forced to accept as official Russian foreign policy the revolutionary no-annexation-no-indemnities formula. On May 15 Milyukov, in disgust, resigned as foreign minister; in short order, Prince Lvov's government collapsed.

The Petrograd soviet called for the abolition of the officer corps, and the new provisional government abolished courts-martial and issued a Declaration of Soldier's Rights. Nevertheless, this government too failed. Indeed, throughout the spring and summer and on into autumn, no fewer than four more governments—all with Kerensky's backing—would form and fall, at the rate of nearly one a month. The hungry and toiling masses moved further and further left, further left than Lenin, who warned them against anarchy. They demanded food and freedom from want, a living wage, and an eight-hour workday, but most often and most loudly they called for an end to the senseless slaughter of World War I. And because it was the one demand Kerensky would not accept, everything seemed up for grabs that summer. As Bolshevik propaganda penetrated deep into the ranks of the ordinary soldiers, the Russian high command came to consider its own army a huge, weary, shabby, and ill-fed mob of angry men.

Suddenly Russian politics swung to the right after the Bolsheviks failed to take charge of the country during violent antigovernment demonstrations on July 3 and 4. In reaction, a coalition government was formed that banned the party, sent Lenin into hiding under threat of arrest, threw Trotsky in jail, and appointed right-wing general Lavr Kornilov commander-in-chief of the Russian army. Kornilov had been urging a number of reforms to restore the army to fighting trim. Kerensky was sympathetic, but the old general was surrounded by conspirators who wanted to make him military dictator. Reactionary skulduggery abounded, and Kerensky, aware of the danger of a coup, outlawed troop movements in the capital. When Kornilov attempted to lead an army into town to institute his reforms, the troops simply walked off the job behind his ramrod-straight back. Kerensky had Kornilov arrested, and the counterrevolution, if that's what it was, fizzled. In any case, yet another government had collapsed, and the Duma seemed bereft of both will and authority. On September 24 Kerensky formed one last coalition. Figuring he could beat the Bolsheviks at the ballot box, he hoped to hold out until the elections for a Constituent Assembly scheduled in December.

Exactly a month later, Lenin took control of Russia in a bloodless coup d'état. The Bolsheviks themselves doubted they would last long. On October 25 prominent party member Zinoviev, admittedly a notorious pessimist, gave the new regime two weeks because of the Bolsheviks' incompetence and the strength of their enemies. On October 28 Lenin declared a state of siege in Petrograd. Antirevolutionary (or, at least, anti-Bolshevik) "Whites" had taken the Kremlin, and civil war was under way. Come November, nothing much was settled: power and peace yet lay in the balance, the Bolshevik Party was deeply divided, civil servants engaged in systematic sabotage, bankers kept their doors locked to the new government, municipal services ground to a halt, and the White Army was on its way from the countryside.

Clearly, Lenin needed to be free of the European war in order to consolidate Bolshevik power. On December 15 the regime signed an armistice with the Central Powers. That same month, Lenin created the All-Russian Extraordinary Commission for the Struggle against Sabotage and Counterrevolution. Arrests began immediately, even as Trotsky headed off to the peace conference convening on December 22 at Brest-Litovsk. But it took several months for the terror to get into full swing and for the commission's acronym, CHEKA, to send chills down the spine of anyone with a bank account, not coincidentally about the same amount of time it took Trotsky to give away half of European Russia to the Germans.

Terms

Immediately, the German imperialists and the Russian totalitarians-in-the-making began to bicker about the definition of "national self-determination," an understandably touchy point since Lenin, Trotsky, and Karl Radek had in the first days of Bolshevik power organized the apparatus to spread revolution abroad. Although the expected uprisings had nowhere occurred when Trotsky sat down across the table from the Germans, Lenin continued to fear that the Bolshevik Revolution would not survive without them, and Trotsky believed in the necessity of international revolution until his dying day. Recognizing how far apart the two sides were, Trotsky promptly asked for an adjournment in hopes that the tide of revolution might yet sweep throughout central Europe. A mutiny did flare up in the Austrian fleet, and a general strike erupted in Berlin, but both outbreaks were quickly suppressed, and the Russians returned to the talks on January 7, 1918.

As Trotsky saw it, the Bolsheviks faced three choices, all bad. They could continue to defy the Germans, risking the almost certain conquest of Russian lands and the overthrow of their government; they could relent and cede to the Germans virtually all of Russia's western territories; or they could pursue what Trotsky called "neither war nor peace" while awaiting the revolution in Germany. The Germans suspected Trotsky of using the peace talks themselves to do just that, although he was more likely dragging out the proceeding to avoid any question that he was working in collusion with the German military. Such caution was wise, given the means by which he and Lenin had arrived back in Russian from their foreign exile. The Bolsheviks were always a suspicious lot, shrewd and ruthless, none more so than the head of the CHEKA, Feliks Dzerzhinsky, perhaps at the time the most ruthless of them all. It was folly to give such a man, searching for subversives and seeing sedition everywhere, the slightest cause for doubt.

Meanwhile, as Trotsky bode his time, the Germans and Austrians concluded the *Brotfrieden*, or "bread peace," with representatives of the Ukraine, a hotbed of White Army activity. When the Red Army fought its way into the region, the German high command, weary in any case of Trotsky's long-winded rhetoric, broke off the conference and resumed hostilities against Russia on February 18, 1918. The French ambassador immediately offered the Bolsheviks all the aid they could use if they would fight the Germans.

But Lenin—his country's economy in tatters, his party menaced by factionalism, his people engaged in civil war—ordered an immediate capitulation. The Germans now pressed even harsher terms on the Bolsheviks, but Lenin's government yielded to the new demands et alia. On March 3 the Bolsheviks signed. The Romanians, always under Russian domination, made peace on the 5th. The newly independent Finland signed a separate treaty with Germany on the 7th.

By the Treaty of Brest-Litovsk, Russia delivered Poland, Lithuania, the Baltic Provinces, Finland, and the Ukraine to Germany, either to occupation or into the hands of puppet governments. The Bolsheviks signed away 34 percent of Russia's population, 32 percent of Russia's farmland, 54 percent of Russia's industrial plant, 89 percent of Russia's coal mines, and virtually all of Russia's cotton and oil. Article 1 of the treaty established the cessation of the "state of war," and Article 2, without naming names, quickly sought to neutralize the spread of revolution:

ARTICLE II

The contracting parties will refrain from any agitation or propaganda against the Government or the public and military institutions of the other party. In so far as this obligation devolves upon Russia, it holds good also for the territories occupied by the Powers of the Quadruple Alliance.

Article 3 summarily proclaimed the redrawn map of eastern Europe:

ARTICLE III

The territories lying to the west of the line agreed upon by the contracting parties which formerly belonged to Russia, will no longer be subject to Russian sovereignty; the line agreed upon is traced on the map submitted as an essential part of this treaty of peace (Annex I). The exact fixation of the line will be established by a Russo-German commission.

No obligations whatever toward Russia shall devolve upon the territories referred to, arising from the fact that they formerly belonged to Russia.

Russia refrains from all interference in the internal relations of these territories. Germany and Austria-Hungary propose to determine the future status of these territories in agreement with their population.

Appendix 1 to the treaty spelled out the new geography in detail:

APPENDIX I, PROVIDED FOR IN ARTICLE III OF THE TREATY OF PEACE BETWEEN RUSSIA AND THE CENTRAL POWERS, OF 3 MARCH, 1918

The line prescribed in Article III of the peace treaty with Russia, which in the west runs along Russian sovereignty, passes through the islands of Dago and Worms, between Mohn and the mainland, *between the islands Runo and Kuno,* and in segmental curve passing through the bay of Riga, reaches the mainland slightly to the northwest, [northeast] of the mouth of the Livonian Aa, then in continuation of the curve it passes around Riga and to the east of Uxkull (Oger Galle), crosses the Duna (Dvina). Then it follows the course of the Duna to the east of Dwinsk (Dunaberg) to the place where ended the former Courland frontier, almost to Druja, and from this place it extends in

a straight line *southwest crossing Strusty Lake* to the southern part of Lake Driswjaty, leaving the locality Driswjaty itself to the east of the line.

From here the line bends in a south-southwest direction close to *Mjelengjany on the German side.* The localities Widsy and Tweretsch remain east of the line. It crosses the railway line from Swenziany to Lyntupy upon midway. The line then passes along a stream by the localities Michalischki and Gerwjany, both of which are left to the west of the line, *along the rivers Oschmjanka and Loscha.* The line itself in manifold windings reaches the railway from Wilna to Smorgon, which it crosses somewhat west of Slobodka. Here the *line bends, running straight to Klewisa on the German side,* by Oschmjany and Dsewenischki on the east, and Geranony on the west, *along the rivers Opita and Gawja to the Niemen.*

The line now follows the downward course of the Niemen to a point above Mosty, and here it bends directly to the south into the river course of the Selwianka, which it follows to Roshany, which remains to the east of the line. From here it passes in a southwest direction (*along the Temra*) to the Ukrainian border where Prushany is reached. *From here it passes between Borowiri and Szolzhentiza, between Koski and Dobruschin, and west of the road from Prushany to Vidom, passes in straight line the bends of the river Liesna, leaving Vidoml on the Russian side. The line ends on the river Liesna north of Brest-Litovsk, Szmolienitza and Bobruschin remain to the east of the line, Riga, Jacobstadt, Dwinsk, Svenzjany, Vilna, Lida, Wolkowysk, and Konstantinow on the German side*

An absolutely exact determination of the line will be established through a Russo-German Commission.

Mutual evacuation of one another's territories was established in Article 4, and Article 5 mandated immediate Russian demobilization:

ARTICLE V

Russia will, without delay, carry out the full demobilization of her army inclusive of those units recently organized by the present Government.

Furthermore, Russia will either bring her warships into Russian ports and there detain them until the day of the conclusion of a general peace, or disarm them forthwith. Warships of the States which continue in the state of war with the Powers of the Quadruple Alliance, in so far as they are within Russian sovereignty, will be treated as Russian warships.

The barred zone in the Arctic Ocean continues as such until the conclusion of a general peace. In the Baltic Sea, and, as far as Russian power extends within the Black Sea, removal of the mines will be proceeded with at once. Merchant navigation within these maritime regions is free and will be resumed at once. Mixed commissions will be organized to formulate the more detailed regulations, especially to inform merchant ships with regard to restricted lanes. The navigation lanes are always to be kept free from floating mines.

Brest-Litovsk also obligated Russia to conclude peace with the Ukrainian People's Republic (with which Austria and Germany had concluded a treaty in February), and by Article 9, all signatories renounced "compensation for their war expenses." A complex series of appendixes and subappendixes defined virtually all aspects of relations between Germany and Russia, ranging from commerce to "quarantine regulations against epidemic diseases" (a pressing concern in 1918, when the great influenza pandemic was just beginning to sweep Europe). The two nations had little time in which to exercise their new relations, however, before the armistice that ended World War I specifically nullified the Treaty of Brest-Litovsk.

Consequences

With Russia out of the war, the Central Powers were no longer fighting on two fronts, and Germany was free to concentrate all of its forces in the west. Both the economic gains in the east realized by the treaty and the new maneuverability it afforded cheered the Germans to believe they might achieve victory before the Americans arrived on the Continent in force. But in the event, the Germans did not take full advantage of Brest-Litovsk. They left roughly a million men, some 60 divisions, in the east in order to intimidate the Ukrainians into relinquishing foodstuffs, to pursue the German political agenda in the Baltic, and to make sure the Bolsheviks complied with the agreement.

Still, Brest-Litovsk almost certainly would have changed the outcome of the war, had the United States not become an "associated" power of the Allies and spent so freely of its money, material, and men. Even as it was, the treaty enabled Germany to unleash a massive offensive during 1918, which put American forces in the thick of some of the most savage fighting of the war.

If the Germans did not trust the Bolsheviks, neither did Russia's former allies. Not a few on the left in London, Paris, and Washington sympathized with the Bolshevik cause or believed Lenin would bring some efficiency to his troubled country, at least compared to the czar. There was talk among the French and the English of supporting various of the factions forming within the party. Then the German advance into Russia in February (after it had called off the conference with Trotsky in midsentence) caused the Allied diplomatic missions to panic and flee Petrograd for remote Vologada.

There they waited to see which direction Lenin and Trotsky would take, and Brest-Litovsk gave them their answer. News of Brest-Litovsk was received as an unparalleled disaster by the beleaguered Allies, who felt they now had to consider intervention in Russia. If they could hook up with the White nationalists, they

reasoned, they might be able to reopen the eastern front and thus save their own disgruntled troops the full wrath of the German army in the west. Then there was all the Allied matériel stacked up in Russian ports—nearly 20 tons of supplies in Archangel alone—just waiting for seizure by the Germans or the Bolsheviks. The Allied plans were to take those supplies and distribute them to any Russians they could find still willing to fight Germans.

In short, when Bolshevik Russia signed a separate peace with Germany at Brest-Litovsk, the Allies sent troops to invade Russia from the east in support of the Whites. In March, the month the treaty was signed, an Anglo-French expedition docked at Murmansk. In April the Japanese, seeking an imperial foothold on the Asian mainland, used the treaty as an excuse to seize and occupy Vladivostok. In June an American cruiser and 150 marines joined the English and French forces at Murmansk. In August another Anglo-French expeditionary force occupied Archangel, this one also to be joined by the Americans, five thousand of them under British command arriving in September.

Hitherto, Comrade Lenin had gone out of his way to check—and even punish—Dzerzhinsky-inspired excesses. That did not mean there was no CHEKA brutality, no summary executions, but as of Brest-Litovsk the Bolshevik tribunals had yet to deliver a death sentence. That changed with the Allied invasions. On June 18, 1918, the Bolsheviks handed down their first death sentence. A month later to the day, the local soviet in Ekaterinburg took the czar, his empress, and his heirs down into a dingy basement and shot them dead. That same month, August, the CHEKA arrested two hundred British and French residents of Moscow, stormed their consulates, and murdered the British naval attaché.

In Paris and in London, the Bolsheviks were now considered thugs or bandits or German agents, but in the Balkans their revolution had become an inspiration. Even moderates were won over to the cause of independence from the Great Powers. As men like the Czechs' Tomáš Masaryk, the Slovaks' Edvard Beneš, the Poles' Józef Piłsudski set up rump national governments, they joined for the time being the side offering them the best deal, but they had their eyes on the future. As soon as Hapsburg authority collapsed or the war ended, these de facto governments would be ready to assume control of successor states, which would greatly increase the headaches at the Paris Peace Conference. When the armistice came, Germany played the other side of the Bolshevik card in order to gain better peace terms, raising the specter of international revolution—"Bolshevism"—against which it might serve as a bulwark. The Germans won only minor concessions, but the Armistice, signed on November 11, 1918, did renounce the Treaty of Brest-Litovsk and the TREATY OF BUCHAREST.

Nullifying Brest-Litovsk was not the same as negating the Bolshevik Revolution, however, nor did it solve the problem the Bolsheviks represented for the entente Great Powers at Versailles. For them, Wilson's views on national determination constituted a truly revolutionary idea with global, if unpredictable, implications. Lenin's ideas, embraced as an alternative to Wilsonianism by some of the lesser participants, were simply off the map. France's paranoia at the conference about a future German threat sprang in no small measure from the erasing of Romanov Russia as a player in the European balance of power. After Brest-Litovsk, Anglo-French policy had turned vehemently anti-Bolshevik, and now Georges Clemenceau negotiated for a cordon sanitaire in eastern Europe intended to check the potential of both German and Bolshevik expansion. Lenin, still in need of nothing so much as time to consolidate Bolshevik power, delayed his summons to European Socialists to form a Third International (the Comintern) in hopes of opening negotiations with the West in Paris and relieving Allied pressure on the Russian civil war. Thus, at the conference, dealing with the Russian question became at least as important as punishing Germany.

Just as the peace conference participants decided amongst themselves to make some initiative toward Russia, Lenin—disheartened by the snarled diplomacy that was clearly widening the gap between the two sides—finally issued his call on January 15, 1919, for an international meeting of communists. To the Allies the move made Lenin seem intent on remaining an international outlaw, calling for the utter destruction of those very powers with which he claimed he wanted to normalize relations. The Bolshevik reputation for deviousness was only made worse by the Comintern itself, founded on March 2, 1919. Imposing rigorous communist discipline and subordinating local parties to the will of Moscow, it created a schism between European socialists, with the majority rejecting Bolshevik tactics and Lenin's dictatorship.

The peace conference's inability to frame a common policy toward Lenin's regime meant that the civil war continued and that Russia's future was a military, and not a diplomatic, matter. The civil conflict was a grand, protean struggle stretching over five major theaters. When the Reds defeated General Feliks Kolchak's White Army in the summer of 1919, the Allies gave up the battle in north Russia and evacuated Archangel and Murmansk—after several clashes with Bolshevik forces—on September 30 and October 12, 1919, respectively. In October 1920 Lenin came to terms with the Poles, fixing the Russian-Polish border west of Minsk (which was far east of the Curzon Line proposed at the Paris peace talks) and freeing the Red Army to turn south and eliminate the last pockets of White resistance.

On October 25, 1922, the Japanese, under pressure from the United States, withdrew from Vladivostok, bringing all foreign intervention in Russia to a close. For Russia, five years after signing its separate peace with Germany, World War I was finally over. In the final count, Russia had lost Poland, Finland, the Baltic states, and Bessarabia, but the Bolsheviks had survived to inherit the remaining, and still vast, Russian Empire.

On December 30, 1922, they created the Union of Soviet Socialist Republics.

TREATY OF VERSAILLES (1919)

TREATY AT A GLANCE

Completed
June 28, 1919, at Versailles, France

Signatories
United States, British Empire, France, Italy, and Japan ("Principal Allied and Associated Powers"); Belgium, Bolivia, Brazil, China, Cuba, Ecuador, Greece, Guatemala, Haiti, the Hejaz (part of present-day Saudi Arabia), Honduras, Liberia, Nicaragua, Panama, Peru, Poland, Portugal, Romania, Serb-Croat-Slovene State, Siam, Czechoslovakia, and Uruguay ("the Allied and Associated Powers"); and Germany

Overview
The Treaty of Versailles ended World War I. The product of acrimonious debate among the Allies and excluding Germany and the other Central Powers, it was harshly punitive. A defeated Germany was further humiliated and compelled to admit war guilt, to give up territory, to disarm, to agree to Allied occupation of the Saar and Rhineland, and to pay heavy reparations. Failing to address any number of serious diplomatic issues raised by the war and undercut by the gap between the high tones of its idealistic justification and the low-down realism of its draconian measures, the treaty helped establish the poisoned postwar atmosphere that lead to the rise of Nazi Germany and World War II.

Historical Background

The guns of the "Great War" fell silent with the armistice of November 11, 1918. On November 17, under the terms of the armistice, Allied troops began to reoccupy those portions of France and Belgium that had been held by the Germans since their first big push during the opening weeks of the war, in 1914. Allied and U.S. troops followed the withdrawing Germans into Germany itself, and on December 9 the Allied armies crossed the Rhine, taking up positions at the bridgeheads agreed to in the armistice.

On January 18, 1919, a peace conference was convened at Paris. That it was bitter and tumultuous is, perhaps, no surprise. Yet the acrimony developed not against representatives of Germany and the other Central Powers, who were excluded from the conference, but between the 27 Allied nations, who disagreed on the terms of the peace. From the beginning it was understood that the four major Allied powers, Britain, France, Italy, and the United States (the last technically an "associated power"), would dominate the Paris Peace Conference. But in its politically charged atmosphere, delegations from the other nations harassed the Great Powers with their various—most often conflicting—complaints and demands. In addition, the Great Powers themselves sent five delegates each, and these were supported by sprawling staffs that included a bewildering myriad of geographers, historians, and economists, as well as lawyers, politicians, and junior diplomats. This global assembly of folks from professions that, whatever else they instilled in their members, provided them with the gift of gab and a love of argumentation that was clearly unwieldy, a congregation in which peace could not be made.

The five major victors—the four great Western powers plus Japan—consequently created a Council of Ten, consisting of the heads of government and their foreign ministers, but this also proved too many. Since Italy and Japan in any case tended to narrow their focus to matters of mostly local interest, the major decisions in Paris were hammered out in private by an informal group the press took to calling the Big Three: Woodrow Wilson, president of the United States;

David Lloyd George, prime minister of Great Britain; and Georges Clemenceau, premier of France.

The French tried at the outset to impose an agenda for the conference, but Wilson brushed this schedule of priorities aside and insisted on tackling his proposed League of Nations first, so as to prevent the others from rejecting the League later because they were tired and drained and wanted to go home or from using it as a bargaining chip in later disputes throughout the talks. (Although included as Part I of the Versailles document, the COVENANT OF THE LEAGUE OF NATIONS is so important in the history of the 20th century that it warrants treatment in a separate entry.)

In general, Wilson advocated a conciliatory settlement based on his Fourteen Points, which he had enumerated before a joint session of Congress on January 8, 1918, as the basis for a just peace. These were 1) "open covenants, openly arrived at"; 2) freedom of the seas; 3) removing economic barriers to international trade; 4) radical reduction of armament to the lowest point consistent with domestic security; 5) a modification of all colonial claims on the basis of the self-determination of peoples, that is, making sure colonial arrangements respected the will of the peoples involved; 6) national self-determination for the peoples of Russia (assuming, of course, as Wilson did, that the Bolsheviks were usurping thugs); 7) restoration of Belgium; 8) return of all the German invaded and occupied territory of France, plus Alsace-Lorraine, which France had lost to Germany back in the Franco-Prussian War; 9) Italian recovery of her irredenta; 10) autonomy for the ethnic nationalities of Austria-Hungary; 11) restoration of the Balkan states and access to the Adriatic for Serbia; 12) autonomy for the subject peoples of the Ottoman Empire and free navigation through the Dardanelles; 13) an independent Poland with access to the sea; 14) a "general association of nations" offering "mutual guarantees of political independence and territorial integrity."

In two other speeches that year—the "Four Principles" talk on February 11 and the "Five Particulars" address on September 27—Wilson further explicated his views on national self-determination. If not quite as revolutionary as Lenin's call for a worldwide class war, they were nevertheless quite radical enough for countries whose notions of foreign policy remained tied to the new imperialism of the Victorian Age and Bismarck's fixation on a European balance of power. Introduced as a standard in world diplomacy through the Paris Peace Conference, they would cause no little trouble throughout the rest of the 20th century, not just in a Europe (and Asia) headed for another world war but in the United States's own imperial backyard: Latin America, the Pacific Islands, and Southeast Asia.

In opposition to Wilson at the conference, Clemenceau, whose nation had suffered the worst destruction in the war, not only wanted to secure France against future German attack but, having lived through the humiliation of the Franco-Prussian War and now having seen the flower of French youth and young manhood crushed, favored a vengeful, punitive, and restrictive treaty. Britain's Lloyd George had his own agendas. Although moderate in his personal views, Lloyd George had been elected on the promise that Germany would be punished. Moreover, he had little taste for President Wilson's idealism and was concerned that the Fourteen Points would interfere with British colonial policy.

Terms

Ultimately, France conceded its principal demand, that the left bank of the Rhine be detached from Germany and put under French military control, in exchange for British and American promises of future alliance and support. Nevertheless, the Treaty of Versailles—not negotiated with Germany but simply presented to it as an accomplished fact—was harsh, punitive, and humiliating. Not only was Germany forced to admit its guilt in having instigated the war, but it had to relinquish large tracts of territory, disarm, yield to Allied occupation of the Saar and Rhineland, and agree to pay economically devastating reparations. Moreover, the treaty by no means conformed to Wilson's Fourteen Points. Nevertheless, Wilson was gratified by the realization of his 14th point, the creation of the League of Nations.

The Treaty of Versailles is a book-length document, comprising almost 300 printed pages and covering

- The creation of the League of Nations
- The boundaries of Germany
- "Political Clauses for Europe"
- "German Rights and Interests Outside Germany"
- The disarmament of Germany
- The repatriation of prisoners of war and the maintenance of soldiers' graves
- Penalties ("The Allied and Associated Powers publicly arraign William II of Hohenzollern, formerly German emperor, for a supreme offence against international morality and the sanctity of treaties")
- Reparations
- "Financial Clauses," pursuant to reparations
- "Economic Clauses," governing commercial and trade relations, debts, and property rights
- "Aerial Navigation" (an important recognition of the new technology, framed on the model of rights governing navigation of the sea)
- Provisions governing ports, waterways, and railways

- International regulations governing "humane conditions of labor" in order to establish a lasting peace based on "social justice."

The only major point on which the Allies unanimously agreed was the return of Alsace-Lorraine (lost to Germany in the Franco-Prussian War) to France:

Section V
Alsace Lorraine

The HIGH CONTRACTING PARTIES, recognizing the moral obligation to redress the wrong done by Germany in 1871 both to the rights of France and to the wishes of the population of Alsace and Lorraine, which were separated from their country in spite of the solemn protest of their representatives at the Assembly of Bordeaux,

Agree upon the following Articles:

ARTICLE 51

The territories which were ceded to Germany in accordance with the Preliminaries of Peace signed at Versailles on February 26, 1871, and the Treaty of Frankfort of May 10, 1871, are restored to French sovereignty as from the date of the Armistice of November 11, 1918.

The provisions of the Treaties establishing the delimitation of the frontiers before 1871 shall be restored.

ARTICLE 52

The German Government shall hand over without delay to the French Government all archives, registers, plans, titles and documents of every kind concerning the civil, military, financial, judicial or other administrations of the territories restored to French sovereignty. If any of these documents, archives, registers, titles or plans have been misplaced, they will be restored by the German Government on the demand of the French Government.

ARTICLE 53

Separate agreements shall be made between France and Germany dealing with the interests of the inhabitants of the territories referred to in Article 51, particularly as regards their civil rights, their business and the exercise of their professions, it being understood that Germany undertakes as from the present date to recognize and accept the regulations laid down in the Annex hereto regarding the nationality of the inhabitants or natives of the said territories, not to claim at any time or in any place whatsoever as German nationals those who shall have been declared on any ground to be French, to receive all others in her territory, and to conform, as regards the property of German nationals in the territories indicated in Article 51, with the provisions of Article 297 and the Annex to Section IV of Part X (Economic Clauses) of the present Treaty.

Those German nationals who without acquiring French nationality shall receive permission from the French Government to reside in the said territories shall not be subjected to the provisions of the said Article.

ARTICLE 54

Those persons who have regained French nationality in virtue of paragraph 1 of the Annex hereto will be held to be Alsace-Lorrainers for the purposes of the present Section.

The persons referred to in paragraph 2 of the said Annex will from the day on which they have claimed French nationality be held to be Alsace-Lorrainers with retroactive effect as from November 11, 1918. For those whose application is rejected, the privilege will terminate at the date of the refusal.

Such juridical persons will also have the status of Alsace-Lorrainers as shall have been recognized as possessing this quality whether by the French administrative authorities or by a judicial decision.

ARTICLE 55

The territories referred to in Article 51 shall return to France free and quit of all public debts under the conditions laid down in Article 255 of Part IX (Financial Clauses) of the present Treaty.

ARTICLE 56

In conformity with the provisions of Article 256 of Part IX (Financial Clauses) of the present Treaty, France shall enter into possession of all property and estate, within the territories referred to in Article 51, which belong to the German Empire or German States, without any payment or credit on this account to any of the States ceding the territories.

This provision applies to all movable or immovable property of public or private domain together with all rights whatsoever belonging to the German Empire or German States or to their administrative areas.

Crown property and the property of the former Emperor or other German sovereigns shall be assimilated to property of the public domain.

ARTICLE 57

Germany shall not take any action, either by means of stamping or by any other legal or administrative measures not applying equally to the rest of her territory, which may be to the detriment of the legal value or redeemability of Germany monetary instruments or monies which, at the date of the signature of the present Treaty, are legally current, and at that date are in the possession of the French Government.

ARTICLE 58

A special Convention will determine the conditions for repayment in marks of the exceptional war expenditure advanced during the course of the war by Alsace-Lorraine or by the public bodies in Alsace-Lorraine on account of the Empire in accordance with German law, such as payment to the families of persons mobilized, requisitions, billeting of troops, and assistance to persons who have been evacuated.

In fixing the amount of these sums Germany shall be credited with that portion which Alsace-Lorraine would have contributed to the Empire to meet the expenses resulting from these payments, this contribution being calculated according to the proportion of the Imperial revenues derived from Alsace-Lorraine in 1913.

ARTICLE 59

The French Government will collect for its own account the Imperial taxes, duties and dues of every kind leviable in the territories referred to in Article 51 and not collected at the time of the Armistice of November 11, 1918.

ARTICLE 60

The German Government shall without delay restore to Alsace-Lorrainers (individuals, juridical persons and public institutions) all property, rights and interests belonging to them on November 11, 1918, in so far as these are situated in German territory.

ARTICLE 61

The German Government undertakes to continue and complete without delay the execution of the financial clauses regarding Alsace-Lorraine contained in the Armistice Conventions.

ARTICLE 62

The German Government undertakes to bear the expense of all civil and military pensions which had been earned in Alsace-Lorraine on date of November 11, 1918, and the maintenance of which was a charge on the budget of the German Empire.

The German Government shall furnish each year the funds necessary for the payment in francs, at the average rate of exchange for that year, of the sums in marks to which persons resident in Alsace-Lorraine would have been entitled if Alsace-Lorraine had remained under German jurisdiction.

ARTICLE 63

For the purposes of the obligation assumed by Germany in Part VIII (Reparation) of the present Treaty to give compensation for damages caused to the civil populations of the Allied and Associated countries in the form of fines, the inhabitants of the territories referred to in Article 51 shall be assimilated to the above-mentioned populations.

ARTICLE 64

The regulations concerning the control of the Rhine and of the Moselle are laid down in Part XII (Ports, Waterways and Railways) of the present Treaty.

ARTICLE 65

Within a period of three weeks after the coming into force of the present Treaty, the port of Strasburg and the port of Kehl shall be constituted, for a period of seven years, a single unit from the point of view of exploitation.

The administration of this single unit will be carried on by a manager named by the Central Rhine Commission, which shall also have power to remove him.

This manager shall be of French nationality.

He will reside in Strasburg and will be subject to the supervision of the Central Rhine Commission.

There will be established in the two ports free zones in conformity with Part XII (Ports, Waterways and Railways) of the present Treaty.

A special Convention between France and Germany which shall be submitted to the approval of the Central Rhine Commission, will fix the details of this organization, particularly as regards finance.

It is understood that for the purpose of the present Article the port of Kehl includes the whole of the area necessary for the movement of the port and the trains which serve it, including the harbor, quays and railroads, platforms, cranes, sheds and warehouses, silos, elevators and hydro-electric plants, which make up the equipment of the port.

The German Government undertakes to carry out all measures which shall be required of it in order to assure that all the making-up and switching of trains arriving at or departing from Kehl, whether for the right bank or the left bank of the Rhine, shall be carried on in the best conditions possible.

All property rights shall be safeguarded. In particular the administration of the ports shall not prejudice any property rights of the French or Baden railroads.

Equality of treatment as respects traffic shall be assured in both ports to the nationals, vessels and goods of every country.

In case at the end of the sixth year France shall consider that the progress made in the improvement of the port of Strasburg still requires a prolongation of this temporary régime, she may ask for such prolongation from the Central Rhine Commission, which may grant an extension for a period not exceeding three years.

Throughout the whole period of any such extension the free zones above provided for shall be maintained.

Pending appointment of the first manager by the Central Rhine Commission a provisional manager who shall be of French nationality may be appointed by the Principal Allied and Associated Powers subject to the foregoing provisions.

For all purposes of the present Article the Central Rhine Commission will decide by a majority of votes.

ARTICLE 66

The railway and other bridges across the Rhine now existing within the limits of Alsace-Lorraine shall, as to all their parts and their whole length, be the property of the French State, which shall ensure their upkeep.

ARTICLE 67

The French Government is substituted in all the rights of the German Empire over all the railways which were administered by the Imperial railway administration and which are actually working or under construction.

The same shall apply to the rights of the Empire with regard to railway and tramway concessions within the territories referred to in Article 51.

This substitution shall not entail any payment on the part of the French State.

The frontier railway stations shall be established by a subsequent agreement, it being stipulated in advance that on the Rhine frontier they shall be situated on the right bank.

ARTICLE 68

In accordance with the provisions of Article 268 of Chapter 1 of Section 1 of Part X (Economic Clauses) of the present Treaty, for a period of five years from the coming into force of the present Treaty, natural or manufactured products originating in and coming from the territories referred to in Article 51 shall, on importation into German customs territory, be exempt from all customs duty.

The French Government may fix each year, by decree communicated to the German Government, the nature and amount of the products which shall enjoy this exemption.

The amount of each product which may be thus sent annually into Germany shall not exceed the average of the amounts sent annually in the years 1911–1913.

Further, during the period of five years above mentioned, the German Government shall allow the free export from Germany and the free reimportation into Germany, exempt from all customs, duties and other charges (including internal charges), of yarns, tissues, and other textile materials or textile products of any kind and in any condition, sent from Germany into the territories referred to in Article 51, to be subjected there to any finishing process, such as bleaching, dyeing, printing, mercerization, gassing, twisting or dressing.

ARTICLE 69

During a period of ten years from the coming into force of the present Treaty, central electric supply works situated in German territory and formerly furnishing electric power to the territories referred to in Article 51 or to any establishment the working of which passes permanently or temporarily from Germany to France, shall be required to continue such supply up to the amount of consumption corresponding to the undertakings and contracts current on November 11, 1918.

Such supply shall be furnished according to the contracts in force and at a rate which shall not be higher than that paid to the said works by German nationals.

ARTICLE 70

It is understood that the French Government preserves its right to prohibit in the future in the territories referred to in Article 51 all new German participation:

(1) In the management or exploitation of the public domain and of public services, such as railways, navigable waterways, water works, gas works, electric power, etc.;

(2) In the ownership of mines and quarries of every kind and in enterprises connected therewith;

(3) In metallurgical establishments, even though their working may not be connected with that of any mine.

ARTICLE 71

As regards the territories referred to in Article 51, Germany renounces on behalf of herself and her nationals as from November 11, 1918, all rights under the law of May 25, 1910, regarding the trade in potash salts, and generally under any stipulations for the intervention of German organizations in the working of the potash mines. Similarly, she renounces on behalf of herself and her nationals all rights under any agreements, stipulations or laws which may exist to her benefit with regard to other products of the aforesaid territories.

ARTICLE 72

The settlement of the questions relating to debts contracted before November 11, 1918, between the German Empire and the German States or their nationals residing in Germany on the one part and Alsace-Lorrainers residing in Alsace-Lorraine on the other part shall be effected in accordance with the provisions of Section III of Part X (Economic Clauses) of the present Treaty, the expression "before the war" therein being replaced by the expression "before November 1, 1918." The rate of exchange applicable in the case of such settlement shall be the average rate quoted on the Geneva Exchange during the month preceding November 11, 1918.

There may be established in the territories referred to in Article 51, for the settlement of the aforesaid debts under the conditions laid down in Section III of Part X (Economic Clauses) of the present Treaty, a special clearing office, it being understood that this office shall be regarded as a "central office" under the provisions of paragraph I of the Annex to the said Section.

ARTICLE 73

The private property, rights and interests of Alsace-Lorrainers in Germany will be regulated by the stipulations of Section IV of Part X (Economic Clauses) of the present Treaty.

ARTICLE 74

The French government reserves the right to retain and liquidate all the property, rights and interests which German nationals or societies controlled by Germany possessed in the territories referred to in Article 51 on November 11, 1918, subject to the conditions laid down in the last paragraph of Article 53 above.

Germany will directly compensate her nationals who may have been dispossessed by the aforesaid liquidations.

The product of these liquidations shall be applied in accordance with the stipulations of Sections III and IV of Part X (Economic Clauses) of the present Treaty.

ARTICLE 75

Notwithstanding the stipulations of Section V of Part X (Economic Clauses) of the present Treaty, all contracts made before the date of the promulgation in Alsace-Lorraine of the French decree of November 30, 1918, between Alsace-Lorrainers (whether individuals or juridical persons) or others resident in Alsace-Lorraine on the one part and the German Empire or German States and their nationals resident in Germany on the other part, the execution of which has been suspended by the Armistice or by subsequent French legislation, shall be maintained.

Nevertheless, any contract of which the French Government shall notify the cancellation to Germany in the general interest within a period of six months from the date of the coming into force of the present Treaty, shall be annulled except in respect of any debt or other pecuniary obligation arising out of any act done or money paid thereunder before November 11, 1918. If this dissolution would cause one of the parties substantial prejudice, equitable compensation, calculated solely on the capital employed without taking account of loss of profits, shall be accorded to the prejudiced party.

With regard to prescriptions, limitations and forfeitures in Alsace-Lorraine, the provisions of Articles 300 and 301 of Section V of Part X (Economic Clauses) shall be applied with the substitution for the expression "outbreak of war" of the expression "November 11, 1918," and for the expression "duration of the war" of the expression "period from November 11, 1918, to the date of the coming into force of the present Treaty."

ARTICLE 76

Questions concerning rights in industrial, literary or artistic property of Alsace-Lorrainers shall be regulated in accordance with the general stipulations of Section VII of Part X (Economic Clauses) of the present Treaty, it being understood that Alsace-Lorrainers holding rights of this nature under German legislation will preserve full and entire enjoyment of those rights on German territory.

ARTICLE 77

The German Government undertakes to pay over to the French Government such proportion of all reserves accumulated by the Empire or by public or private bodies dependent upon it, for the purposes of disability and old age insurance, as would fall to the disability and old age insurance fund at Strasburg.

The same shall apply in respect of the capital and reserves accumulated in Germany falling legitimately to other social insurance funds, to miners' superannuation funds, to the fund of the railways of Alsace-Lorraine, to other superannuation organizations established for the benefit of the personnel of public administrations and institutions operating in Alsace-Lorraine, and also in respect of the capital and reserves due by the insurance fund of private employees at Berlin, by reason of engagements entered into for the benefit of insured persons of that category resident in Alsace-Lorraine.

A special Convention shall determine the conditions and procedure of these transfers.

ARTICLE 78

With regard to the execution of judgments, appeals and prosecutions, the following rules shall be applied:

(1) All civil and commercial judgments which shall have been given since August 3, 1914, by the Courts of Alsace-Lorraine between Alsace-Lorrainers, or between Alsace-Lorrainers and foreigners, or between foreigners, and which shall not have been appealed from before November 11, 1918, shall be regarded as final and susceptible of immediate execution without further formality.

When the judgment has been given between Alsace-Lorrainers and Germans or between Alsace-Lorrainers and subjects of the allies of Germany, it shall only be capable of execution after the issue of an *exequatur* by the corresponding new tribunal in the restored territory referred to in Article 51.

(2) All judgments given by German Courts since August 3, 1914, against Alsace-Lorrainers for political crimes or misdemeanors shall be regarded as null and void.

(3) All sentences passed since November 11, 1918, by the Court of the Empire at Leipzig on appeals against the decisions of the Courts of Alsace-Lorraine shall be regarded as null and void and shall be so pronounced. The papers in regard to the cases in which such sentences have been given shall be returned to the Courts of Alsace-Lorraine concerned.

All appeals to the Court of the Empire against decisions of the Courts of Alsace-Lorraine shall be suspended. The papers shall be returned under the aforesaid conditions for transfer without delay to the French Cour de Cassation, which shall be competent to decide them.

(4) All prosecutions in Alsace-Lorraine for offenses committed during the period between November 11, 1918, and the coming into force of the present Treaty will be conducted under German law except in so far as this has been modified by decrees duly published on the spot by the French authorities.

(5) All other questions as to competence, procedure or administration of justice shall be determined by a special Convention between France and Germany.

ARTICLE 79

The stipulations as to nationality contained in the Annex hereto shall be considered as of equal force with the provisions of the present Section.

All other questions concerning Alsace-Lorraine which are not regulated by the present Section and the Annex thereto or by the general provisions of the present Treaty will form the subject of further conventions between France and Germany.

Annex

1

As from November 11, 1918, the following persons are *ipso facto* reinstated in French nationality:

(1) Persons who lost French nationality by the application of the Franco-German Treaty of May 10, 1871, and who have not since that date acquired any nationality other than German;

(2) The legitimate or natural descendants of the persons referred to in the immediately preceding paragraph, with the exception of those whose ascendants in the paternal line include a German who migrated into Alsace-Lorraine after July 15, 1870;

(3) All persons born in Alsace-Lorraine of unknown parents, or whose nationality is unknown.

2

Within the period of one year from the coming into force of the present Treaty, persons included in any of the following categories may claim French nationality:

(1) All persons not restored to French nationality under paragraph 1 above, whose ascendants include a Frenchman or Frenchwoman who lost French nationality under the conditions referred to in the said paragraph;

(2) All foreigners, not nationals of a German State, who acquired the status of a citizen of Alsace-Lorraine before August 3, 1914;

(3) All Germans domiciled in Alsace-Lorraine, if they have been so domiciled since a date previous to July 15, 1870, or if one of their ascendants was at that date domiciled in Alsace-Lorraine;

(4) All Germans born or domiciled in Alsace-Lorraine who have served in the Allied or Associated armies during the present war, and their descendants;

(5) All persons born in Alsace-Lorraine before May 10, 1871, of foreign parents, and the descendants of such persons;

(6) The husband or wife of any person whose French nationality may have been restored under paragraph I, or who may have claimed and obtained French nationality in accordance with the preceding provisions.

The legal representative of a minor may exercise, on behalf of that minor, the right to claim French nationality; and if that right has not been exercised, the minor may claim French nationality within the year following his majority.

Except in the cases provided for in No. (6) of the present paragraph, the French authorities reserve to themselves the right, in individual cases, to reject the claim to French nationality.

3

Subject to the provisions of paragraph 2, Germans born or domiciled in Alsace-Lorraine shall not acquire French nationality by reason of the restoration of Alsace-Lorraine to France, even though they may have the status of citizens of Alsace-Lorraine.

They may acquire French nationality only by naturalization, on condition of having been domiciled in Alsace-Lorraine from a date previous to August 3, 1914, and of submitting proof of unbroken residence within the restored territory for a period of three years from November 11, 1918.

France will be solely responsible for their diplomatic and consular protection from the date of their application for French naturalization.

The French Government shall determine the procedure by which reinstatement in French nationality as of right shall be effected, and the conditions under which decisions shall be given upon claims to such nationality and applications for naturalization, as provided by the present Annex.

While the clauses governing the disposition of Alsace-Lorraine were typical of the other "Political Clauses for Europe," every other major treaty provision regarding German territory were compromises:

PART II
BOUNDARIES OF GERMANY

ARTICLE 27

The boundaries of Germany will be determined as follows:

1. *With Belgium*:

From the point common to the three frontiers of Belgium, Holland, and Germany and in a southerly direction:

the north-eastern boundary of the former territory of *neutral* Moresnet, then the eastern boundary of the *Kreis* of Eupen, then the frontier between Belgium and the *Kreis* of Montjoie, then the northeastern and eastern boundary of the *Kreis* of *Malmédy* to its junction with the frontier of Luxembourg.

2. *With Luxembourg*:

The frontier of August 3, 1914, to its junction with the frontier of France of the 18th July, 1870.

3. *With France*:

The frontier of July 18, 1870, from Luxembourg to Switzerland with the reservations made in Article 48 of Section IV (Saar Basin) of Part III.

4. *With Switzerland*:

The present frontier.

5. *With Austria*:

The frontier of August 3, 1914, from Switzerland to *Czecho-Slovakia* as hereinafter defined.

6. *With Czecho-Slovakia*:

The frontier of August 3, 1914, between Germany and Austria from its junction with the old administrative boundary separating Bohemia and the province of Upper Austria to the point north of the salient of the old province of Austrian Silesia situated at about 8 kilometers east of Neustadt.

7. *With Poland*:

From the point defined above to a point to be fixed on the ground about 2 kilometers east of Lorzendorf:

the frontier as it will be fixed in accordance with Article 88 of the present Treaty;

thence in a northerly direction to the point where the administrative boundary of Posnania crosses the river Bartsch:

a line to be fixed on the ground leaving the following places in Poland: Skorischau, Reichthal, Trembatschau, Kunzendorf, Schleise, Gross Kosel, Schreibersdorf, Rippin, Fürstlich-Niefken, Pawelau, Tscheschen, Konradau, Johannisdorf, Modzenowe, Bogdaj, and in Germany: Lorzendorf, Kaulwitz, Glausche, Dalbersdorf, Reesewitz, Stradam, Gross Wartenberg, Kraschen, Neu Mittelwalde, Domaslawitz, Wedelsdorf, Tscheschen Hammer;

thence the administrative boundary of Posnania northwestwards to the point where it cuts the Rawitsch-Herrnstadt railway;

thence to the point where the administrative boundary of Posnania cuts the Reisen-Tschirnau road:

a line to be fixed on the ground passing west of Triebusch and Gabel and east of Saborwitz;

thence the administrative boundary of Posnania to its junction with the eastern administrative boundary of the *Kreis* of Fraustadt;

thence in a north-westerly direction to a point to be chosen on the road between the villages of Unruhstadt and Kopnitz:

a line to be fixed on the ground passing west of Geyersdorf, Brenno, Fehlen, Altkloster, Klebel, and east of Ulbersdorf, Buchwald, Ilgen, Weine, Lupitze, Schwenten:

thence in a northerly direction to the northernmost point of Lake Chlop:

a line to be fixed on the ground following the median line of the lakes; the town and the station of Bentschen however (including the junction of the lines Schwiebus-Bentschen and Zullichau-Bentschen) remaining in Polish territory;

thence in a north-easterly direction to the point of junction of the boundaries of the *Kreise* of Schwerin, Birnbaum, and Meseritz:

a line to be fixed on the ground passing east of Betsche;

thence in a northerly direction the boundary separating the *Kreise* of Schwerin and Birnbaum, then in an easterly direction the northern boundary of Posnania to the point where it cuts the river Netze;

thence upstream to its confluence with the Küddow:

the course of the Netze;

thence upstream to a point to be chosen about 6 kilometers southeast of Schneidemühl:

the course of the Küddow;

thence north-eastwards to the most southern point of the reentrant of the northern boundary of Posnania about 5 kilometers west of Stahren:

a line to be fixed on the ground leaving the Schneidemühl-Konitz railway in this area entirely in German territory;

thence the boundary of Posnania north-eastwards to the point of the salient it makes about 15 kilometers east of Flatow;

thence north-eastwards to the point where the river Kamionka meets the southern boundary of the *Kreis* of Konitz about 3 kilometers north-east of Grunau:

a line to be fixed on the ground leaving the following places to Poland: Jasdrowo, Gr. Lutau, Kl. Lutau, Wittkau, and to Germany: Gr. Butzig, Cziskowo, Battrow, Bock, Grunau;

thence in a northerly direction the boundary between the *Kreise* of Konitz and Schlochau to the point where this boundary cuts the river Brahe;

thence to a point on the boundary of Pomerania 15 kilometers east of Rummelsburg:

a line to be fixed on the ground leaving the following places in Poland: Konarzin, Kelpin, Adl. Briesen, and in Germany: Sampohl, Neuguth, Steinfort, Gr. Peterkau;

then the boundary of Pomerania in an easterly direction to its junction with the boundary between the Kreise of Konitz and Schlochau;

thence northwards the boundary between Pomerania and West Prussia to the point on the river Rheda about 3 kilometers northwest of Gohra where that river is joined by a tributary from the north-west;

thence to a point to be selected in the bend of the Piasnitz river about 1 1/2 kilometers north-west of Warschkau:

a line to be fixed on the ground;

thence this river downstream, then the median line of Lake Zarnowitz, then the old boundary of West Prussia to the Baltic Sea.

8. *With Denmark*:

The frontier as it will be fixed in accordance with Articles 109 to 111 of Part III, Section XII (Schleswig).

ARTICLE 28

The boundaries of East Prussia, with the reservations made in Section IX (East Prussia) of Part III, will be determined as follows:

from a point on the coast of the Baltic Sea about 1 1/2 kilometers north of Probbernau church in a direction of about 159° East from true North:

a line to be fixed on the ground for about 2 kilometers;

thence in a straight line to the light at the bend of the Elbing Channel in approximately latitude 54° 19 1/2' North, longitude 19° 26' East of Greenwich;

thence to the easternmost mouth of the Nogat River at a bearing of approximately 209° East from true North;

thence up the course of the Nogat River to the point where the latter leaves the Vistula (Weichsel);

thence up the principal channel of navigation of the Vistula, then the southern boundary of the Kreis of Marienwerder, then that of the *Kreis* of Rosenberg eastwards to the point where it meets the old boundary of East Prussia;

thence the old boundary between East and West Prussia, then the boundary between the *Kreise* of Osterode and Neidenburg, then the course of the river Skottau downstream, then the course of the Neide upstream to a point situated about 5 kilometers west of Bialutten being the nearest point to the old frontier of Russia;

thence in an easterly direction to a point immediately south of the intersection of the road Neidenburg-Mlava with the old frontier of Russia:

a line to be fixed on the ground passing north of Bialutten;

thence the old frontier of Russia to a point east of Schmalleningken, then the principal channel of navigation of the Niemen (Memel) downstream, then the Skierwieth arm of the delta to the Kurisches Haff;

thence a straight line to the point where the eastern shore the Kurische Nehrung meets the administrative boundary about 4 kilometers south-west of Nidden;

thence this administrative boundary to the western shore of the Kurische Nehrung.

ARTICLE 29

The boundaries as described above are drawn in red on a one-in-a-million map which is annexed to the present Treaty.

In the case of any discrepancies between the text of the Treaty and this map or any other map which may be annexed, the text will be final.

ARTICLE 30

In the case of boundaries which are defined by a waterway, the terms "course" and "channel" used in the present Treaty signify: in the case of non-navigable rivers, the median line of the waterway or of its principal arm, and, in the case of navigable rivers, the median line of the principal channel of navigation. It will rest with the Boundary Commissions provided by the present Treaty to specify in each case whether the frontier line shall follow any changes of the course or channel which may take place or whether it shall be definitely fixed by the position of the course or channel at the time when the present Treaty comes into force.

In addition to these basic boundary provisions, Allied occupation of the Rhineland was slated to continue for at least 15 years, and possibly longer. Moreover, the region was to remain perpetually demilitarized, as was a belt 30 miles wide along the right bank of the Rhine. With parts of the German provinces of Posen and West Prussia given to a newly reconstituted Poland (in order to provide it with access to the Baltic), and with the Baltic seaport of Gdansk (German Danzig) declared a free state, East Prussia was entirely cut off from the rest of Germany. This so-called Polish Corridor was destined to become a desperately troublesome political issue and contributed to the restless nationalism that provided fertile ground for the growth of Naziism.

If Germany's territories were greatly reduced in Europe, its colonial possessions were entirely thrown open to Allied occupation and were organized as "mandates," subject to the supervision and control of the League of Nations. Britain and France divided most of Germany's African colonies, while Japan took over its island possessions in the South Pacific:

PART IV
GERMAN RIGHTS AND INTERESTS OUTSIDE GERMANY

ARTICLE 118

In territory outside her European frontiers as fixed by the present Treaty, Germany renounces all rights, titles and privileges whatever in or over territory which belonged to her or to her allies, and all rights, titles and privileges whatever their origin which she held as against the Allied and Associated Powers.

Germany hereby undertakes to recognize and to conform to the measures which may be taken now or in the future by the Principal Allied and Associated Powers, in agreement where necessary with third Powers, in order to carry the above stipulation into effect.

In particular Germany declares her acceptance of the following Articles relating to certain special subjects.

Section I
German Colonies

ARTICLE 119

Germany renounces in favor of the Principal Allied and Associated Powers all her rights and titles over her overseas possessions.

ARTICLE 120

All movable and immovable property in such territories belonging to the German Empire or to any German State shall pass to the Government exercising authority over such territories, on the terms laid down in Article 257 of Part IX (Financial Clauses) of the present Treaty. The decision of the local courts in any dispute as to the nature of such property shall be final.

ARTICLE 121

The provisions of Sections I and IV of Part X (Economic Clauses) of the present Treaty shall apply in the case of these territories whatever be the form of Government adopted for them.

ARTICLE 122

The Government exercising authority over such territories may make such provisions as it thinks fit with reference to the repatriation from them of German nationals and to the conditions upon which German subjects of European origin shall, or shall not, be allowed to reside, hold property, trade or exercise a profession in them.

ARTICLE 123

The provisions of Article 260 of Part IX (Financial Clauses) of the present Treaty shall apply in the case of all agreements concluded with German nationals for the construction or exploitation of public works in the German overseas possessions, as well as any subconcessions or contracts resulting therefrom which may have been made to or with such nationals.

ARTICLE 124

Germany hereby undertakes to pay, in accordance with the estimate to be presented by the French

Government and approved by the Reparation Commission, reparation for damage suffered by French nationals in the Cameroons or the frontier zone by reason of the acts of the German civil and military authorities and of German private individuals during the period from January 1, 1900, to August 1, 1914.

ARTICLE 125

Germany renounce s all rights under the Conventions and Agreements with France of November 4, 1911, and September 28, 1912, relating to Equatorial Africa. She undertakes to pay to the French Government, in accordance with the estimate to be presented by that Government and approved by the Reparation Commission, all the deposits, credits, advances, etc., effected by virtue of these instruments in favor of Germany.

ARTICLE 126

Germany undertakes to accept and observe the agreements made or to be made by the Allied and Associated Powers or some of them with any other Power with regard to the trade in arms and spirits, and to the matters dealt with in the General Act of Berlin of February 26, 1885, the General Act of Brussels of July 2, 1890, and the conventions completing or modifying the same.

ARTICLE 127

The native inhabitants of the former German overseas possessions shall be entitled to the diplomatic protection of the Governments exercising authority over those territories.

Section II
China

ARTICLE 128

Germany renounces in favor of China all benefits and privileges resulting from the provisions of the final Protocol signed at Peking on September 7, 1901, and from all annexes, notes and documents supplementary thereto. She likewise renounces in favor of China any claim to indemnities accruing thereunder subsequent to March 14, 1917.

ARTICLE 129

From the coming into force of the present Treaty the High Contracting Parties shall apply, in so far as concerns them respectively:

(1) The Arrangement of August 29, 1902, regarding the new Chinese customs tariff;

(2) The Arrangement of September 27, 1905, regarding Whang-Poo, and the provisional supplementary Arrangement of April 4, 1912.

China, however, will no longer be bound to grant to Germany the advantages or privileges which she allowed Germany under these Arrangements.

ARTICLE 130

Subject to the provisions of Section VIII of this Part, Germany cedes to China all the buildings, wharves and pontoons, barracks, forts, arms and munitions of war, vessels of all kinds, wireless telegraphy installations and other public property belonging to the German Government, which are situated or may be in the German Concessions at Tientsin and Hankow or elsewhere in Chinese territory.

It is understood, however, that premises used as diplomatic or consular residences or offices are not included in the above cession, and, furthermore, that no steps shall be taken by the Chinese Government to dispose of the German public and private property situated within the so-called Legation Quarter at Peking without the consent of the Diplomatic Representatives of the Powers which, on the coming into force of the present Treaty, remain Parties to the Final Protocol of September 7, 1901.

ARTICLE 131

Germany undertakes to restore to China within twelve months from the coming into force of the present Treaty all the astronomical instruments which her troops in 1900-1901 carried away from China, and to defray all expenses which may be incurred in effecting such restoration, including the expenses of dismounting, packing, transporting, insurance and installation in Peking.

ARTICLE 132

Germany agrees to the abrogation of the leases from the Chinese Government under which the German Concessions at Hankow and Tientsin are now held.

China, restored to the full exercise of her sovereign rights in the above areas, declares her intention of opening them to international residence and trade. She further declares that the abrogation of the leases under which these concessions are now held shall not affect the property rights of nationals of Allied and Associated Powers who are holders of lots in these concessions.

ARTICLE 133

Germany waives all claims against the Chinese Government or against any Allied or Associated Government arising out of the internment of German nationals in China and their repatriation. She equally renounces all claims arising out of the capture and condemnation of German ships in China, or the liquidation, sequestration or control of German properties, rights and interests in that country since August 14, 1917. This provision, however, shall not affect the rights of the parties interested in the proceeds of any such liquidation, which shall be governed by the provisions of Part: X (Economic Clauses) of the present Treaty.

ARTICLE 134

Germany renounces in favor of the Government of His Britannic Majesty the German State property in the British Concession at Shameen at Canton. She renounces in favor of the French and Chinese Governments conjointly the property of the German school situated in the French Concession at Shanghai.

Section III
Siam

ARTICLE 135

Germany recognizes that all treaties, conventions and agreements between her and Siam, and all rights, title and privileges derived therefrom, including all rights of extraterritorial jurisdiction, terminated as from July 22, 1917.

ARTICLE 136

All goods and property in Siam belonging to the German Empire or to any German State, with the exception of premises used as diplomatic or consular residences or offices, pass *ipso facto* and without compensation to the Siamese Government.

The goods, property and private rights of German nationals in Siam shall be dealt with in accordance with the provisions of Part X (Economic Clauses) of the present Treaty.

ARTICLE 137

Germany waives all claims against the Siamese Government on behalf of herself or her nationals arising out of the seizure or condemnation of German ships, the liquidation of German property, or the internment of German nationals in Siam. This provision shall not affect the rights of the parties interested in the proceeds of any such liquidation, which shall be governed by the provisions of Part X (Economic Clauses) of the present Treaty.

Section IV
Liberia

ARTICLE 138

Germany renounces all rights and privileges arising from the arrangements of 1911 and 1912 regarding Liberia, and particularly the right to nominate a German Receiver of Customs in Liberia.

She further renounces all claim to participate in any measures whatsoever which may be adopted for the rehabilitation of Liberia.

ARTICLE 139

Germany recognizes that all treaties and arrangements between her and Liberia terminated as from August 4, 1917.

ARTICLE 140

The property, rights and interests of Germans in Liberia shall be dealt with in accordance with Part X (Economic Clauses) of the present Treaty.

Section V
Morocco

ARTICLE 141

Germany renounces all rights, titles and privileges conferred on her by the General Act of Algeciras of April 7, 1906, and by the Franco-German Agreements of February 9, 1909, and November 4, 1911. All treaties, agreements, arrangements and contracts concluded by her with the Sherifian Empire are regarded as abrogated as from August 3, 1914.

In no case can Germany take advantage of these instruments and she undertakes not to intervene in any way in negotiations relating to Morocco which may take place between France and the other Powers.

ARTICLE 142

Germany having recognized the French Protectorate in Morocco, hereby accepts all the consequences of its establishment, and she renounces the regime of the capitulations therein.

This renunciation shall take effect as from August 3, 1914.

ARTICLE 143

The Sherifian Government shall have complete liberty of action in regulating the status of German nationals in Morocco and the conditions in which they may establish themselves there.

German protected persons, semsars and "associés agricoles" shall be considered as having ceased, as from August 3, 1914, to enjoy the privileges attached to their status and shall be subject to the ordinary law.

ARTICLE 144

All property and possessions in the Sherifian Empire of the German Empire and the German States pass to the Maghzen without payment.

For this purpose, the property and possessions of the German Empire and States shall be deemed to include all the property of the Crown, the Empire or the States, and the private property of the former German Emperor and other Royal personages.

All movable and immovable property in the Sherifian Empire belonging to German nationals shall be dealt with in accordance with Sections III and IV of Part X (Economic Clauses) of the present Treaty.

Mining rights which may be recognized as belonging to German nationals by the Court of Arbitration set up under the Moroccan Mining Regulations shall form the subject of a valuation, which the arbitrators shall be requested to make, and these rights shall then be treated in the same way as property in Morocco belonging to German nationals.

ARTICLE 145

The German Government shall ensure the transfer to a person nominated by the French Government of the shares representing Germany's portion of the capital of the State Bank of Morocco. The value of these shares, as assessed by the Reparation Commission, shall be paid to the Reparation Commission for the credit of Germany on account of the sums due for reparation. The German Government shall be responsible for indemnifying its nationals so dispossessed.

This transfer will take place without prejudice to the repayment of debts which German nationals may have contracted towards the State Bank of Morocco.

ARTICLE 146

Moroccan goods entering Germany shall enjoy the treatment accorded to French goods.

Section VI
Egypt

ARTICLE 147

Germany declares that she recognizes the Protectorate proclaimed over Egypt by Great Britain on December 18, 1914, and that she renounces the regime of the Capitulations in Egypt.

This renunciation shall take effect as from August 4, 1914.

ARTICLE 148

All treaties, agreements, arrangements and contracts concluded by Germany with Egypt are regarded as abrogated as from August 4, 1914.

In no case can Germany avail herself of these instruments and she undertakes not to intervene in any way in negotiations relating to Egypt which may take place between Great Britain and the other Powers.

ARTICLE 149

Until an Egyptian law of judicial organization establishing courts with universal jurisdiction comes into force, provision shall be made, by means of decrees issued by His Highness The Sultan, for the exercise of jurisdiction over German nationals and property by the British Consular Tribunals.

ARTICLE 150

The Egyptian Government shall have complete liberty of action in regulating the status of German nationals and the conditions under which they may establish themselves in Egypt.

ARTICLE 151

Germany consents to the abrogation of the decree issued by His Highness the Khedive on November 28, 1904, relating to the Commission of the Egyptian Public Debt, or to such changes as the Egyptian Government may think it desirable to make therein.

ARTICLE 152

Germany consents, in so far as she is concerned, to the transfer to His Britannic Majesty's Government of the powers conferred on His Imperial Majesty the Sultan by the Convention signed at Constantinople on October 29, 1888, relating to the free navigation of the Suez Canal.

She renounces all participation in the Sanitary, Maritime, and Quarantine Board of Egypt and consents, in so far as she is concerned, to the transfer to the Egyptian Authorities of the powers of that Board.

ARTICLE 153

All property and possessions in Egypt of the German Empire and the German States pass to the Egyptian Government without payment.

For this purpose, the property and possessions of the German Empire and States shall be deemed to include all the property of the Crown, the Empire or the States, and the private property of the former German Emperor and other Royal personages.

All movable and immovable property in Egypt belonging to German nationals shall be dealt with in accordance with Sections III and IV of Part X (Economic Clauses) of the present Treaty.

ARTICLE 154

Egyptian goods entering Germany shall enjoy the treatment accorded to British goods.

Section VII
Turkey and Bulgaria

ARTICLE 155

Germany undertakes to recognize and accept all arrangements which the Allied and Associated Powers may make with Turkey and Bulgaria with reference to any rights, interests and privileges whatever which might be claimed by Germany or her nationals in Turkey and Bulgaria and which are not dealt with in the provisions of the present Treaty.

Section VIII
Shantung

ARTICLE 156

Germany renounces, in favor of Japan, all her rights, title and privileges—particularly those concerning the territory of Kiaochow, railways, mines and submarine cables—which she acquired in virtue of the Treaty concluded by her with China on March 6, 1898, and of all other arrangements relative to the Province of Shantung.

All German rights in the Tsingtao-Tsinanfu Railway, including its branch lines together with its subsidiary property of all kinds, stations, shops, fixed and rolling stock, mines, plant and material for the exploitation of the mines, are and remain acquired by Japan, together with all rights and privileges attaching thereto.

The German State submarine cables from Tsingtao to Shanghai and from Tsingtao to Chefoo, with all the rights, privileges and properties attaching thereto, are similarly acquired by Japan, free and clear of all charges and encumbrances.

ARTICLE 157

The movable and immovable property owned by the German State in the territory of Kiaochow, as well as all the rights which Germany might claim in consequence of the works or improvements made or of the expenses incurred by her, directly or indirectly, in connection with this territory, are and remain acquired by Japan, free and clear of all charges and encumbrances.

ARTICLE 158

Germany shall hand over to Japan within three months from the coming into force of the present Treaty the archives, registers, plans, title-deeds and documents of every kind, wherever they may be, relating to the administration, whether civil, military, financial, judicial or other, of the territory of Kiaochow. Within the same period Germany shall give particulars to Japan of all treaties, arrangements or agreements relating to the rights, title or privileges referred to in the two preceding Articles.

To guard France and the rest of the world against future German aggression, the treaty imposed stringent terms of disarmament on Germany. Its army was limited to 100,000 men and could not possess any heavy artillery or military aircraft. The army's general staff was abolished, as was the practice of universal conscription. Germany's navy was greatly reduced.

ARTICLE 159

The German military forces shall be demolished and reduced as prescribed hereinafter.

ARTICLE 160

(1) By a date which must not be later than March 31, 1920, the German Army must not comprise more than seven divisions of infantry and three divisions of cavalry.

After that date the total number of effectives in the Army of the States constituting Germany must not exceed one hundred thousand men, including officers and establishments of depots. The Army shall be devoted exclusively to the maintenance of order within the territory and to the control of the frontiers.

The total effective strength of officers, including the personnel of staffs, whatever their composition, must not exceed four thousand

(2) Divisions and Army Corps headquarters staffs shall be organized in accordance with Table No. 1 annexed to this Section.

The number and strengths of the units of infantry, artillery, engineers, technical services and troops laid down in the aforesaid Table constitute maxima which must not be exceeded.

The following units may each have their own depot:

An Infantry regiment;
A Cavalry regiment;
A regiment of Field Artillery;
A battalion of Pioneers.

(3) The divisions must not be grouped under more than two army corps headquarters staffs.

The maintenance or formation of forces differently grouped or of other organizations for the command of troops or for preparation for war is forbidden.

The Great German General Staff and all similar organizations shall be dissolved and may not be reconstituted in any form.

The officers, or persons in the position of officers, in the Ministries of War in the different States in Germany and in the Administrations attached to them, must not exceed three hundred in number and are included in the maximum strength of four thousand laid down in the third sub-paragraph of paragraph (1) of this Article.

Rarely have treaties between nations assigned personal liability and culpability to sovereigns. By Part 7, the Versailles document did just that, accusing the kaiser of war crimes and guaranteeing him a fair trial. Others—unspecified—might also be brought before military tribunals:

PART VII
PENALTIES

ARTICLE 227

The Allied and Associated Powers publicly arraign William II of Hohenzollern, formerly German Emperor, for a supreme offence against international morality and the sanctity of treaties.

A special tribunal will be constituted to try the accused, thereby assuring him the guarantees essential to the right of defence. It will be composed of five judges, one appointed by each of the following Powers: namely, the United States of America, Great Britain, France, Italy and Japan.

In its decision the tribunal will be guided by the highest motives of international policy, with a view to vindicating the solemn obligations of international undertakings and the validity of international morality. It will be its duty to fix the punishment which it considers should be imposed.

The Allied and Associated Powers will address a request to the Government of the Netherlands for the surrender to them of the ex-Emperor in order that he may be put on trial.

ARTICLE 228

The German Government recognizes the right of the Allied and Associated Powers to bring before military tribunals persons accused of having committed acts in violation of the laws and customs of war. Such persons shall, if found guilty, be sentenced to punishments laid down by law. This provision will apply notwithstanding any proceedings or prosecution before a tribunal in Germany or in the territory of her allies.

The German Government shall hand over to the Allied and Associated Powers, or to such one of them as shall so request, all persons accused of having committed an act in violation of the laws and customs of war, who are specified either by name or by the rank, office or employment which they held under the German authorities.

ARTICLE 229

Persons guilty of criminal acts against the nationals of one of the Allied and Associated Powers will be brought before the military tribunals of that Power.

Persons guilty of criminal acts against the nationals of more than one of the Allied and Associated Powers will be brought before military tribunals composed of members of the military tribunals of the Powers concerned.

In every case the accused will be entitled to name his own counsel.

ARTICLE 230

The German Government undertakes to furnish all documents and information of every kind, the production of which may be considered necessary to ensure the full knowledge of the incriminating acts, the discovery of offenders and the just appreciation of responsibility.

In addition to personal penalties, the Allies imposed harsh indemnities on the German nation. The indemnities debate was particularly acrimonious, perhaps second only to the security debate, with which it overlapped. It was an emotional issue, affecting every taxpayer in every country, and it was made worse by some severely disappointed expectations.

It seemed morally clear to most everyone that Germany, not her victims, should pay the cost for reconstruction. It also seemed morally clear to the French that, since they took the harshest hammering, the wealthy British and Americans ought to forgive France's war debts. Most Americans saw it the opposite way: they leant the money in good faith; they saved France from utter destruction; France should not only pay back the money but do so gratefully. The U.S. Treasury dashed French hopes for Allied economic unity when it refused even to discuss abrogation of war debts and then went further to reject French and Italian proposals for a "financial League of Nations." Indeed, the Americans opposed economic favoritism of any ilk, all in accordance, they insisted in high tones, with the Fourteen Points. The British saw in the American truculence a chance to free themselves of previous agreements to forgive France her war debts, made in the heat of battle at the 1916 Allied Economic Conference. England reputed the resolutions of the conference, claiming they would have to collect the money from France so long as the United States insisted on payment from London.

The German indemnity clauses, however, were not merely punitive but also designed for security purposes, that is, to prevent Germany from being able to finance any rearmament, if it decided to evade the military limitations specified in the treaty. The scope of the extensive catalog of reparations can best be appreciated by reproducing Part 8 of the treaty in full.

PART VIII
REPARATION

Section I
General Provisions

ARTICLE 231

The Allied and Associated Governments affirm and Germany accepts the responsibility of Germany and her allies for causing all the loss and damage to which the Allied and Associated Governments and their nationals have been subjected as a consequence of the war imposed upon them by the aggression of Germany and her allies.

ARTICLE 232

The Allied and Associated Governments recognize that the resources of Germany are not adequate, after taking into account permanent diminutions of such resources which will result from other provisions of the present Treaty, to make complete reparation for all such loss and damage.

The Allied and Associated Governments, however, require, and Germany undertakes, that she will make compensation for all damage done to the civilian population of the Allied and Associated Powers and to their property during the period of the belligerency of each as an Allied or Associated Power against Germany by such aggression by land, by sea and from the air, and in general all damage as defined in Annex I hereto.

In accordance with Germany's pledges, already given, as to complete restoration for Belgium, Germany undertakes, in addition to the compensation for damage elsewhere in this Part provided for, as a consequence of the violation of the Treaty of 1839, to make reimbursement of all sums which Belgium has borrowed from the Allied and Associated Governments up to November 11, 1918, together with interest at the rate of five per cent. (5%) per annum on such sums. This amount shall be determined by the Reparation Commission, and the German Government undertakes thereupon forthwith to make a special issue of bearer bonds to an equivalent amount payable in marks gold, on May 1, 1926, or, at the option of the German Government, on the 1st of May in any year up to 1926. Subject to the foregoing, the form of such bonds shall be determined by the Reparation Commission. Such bonds shall be handed over to the Reparation Commission, which has authority to take and acknowledge receipt thereof on behalf of Belgium.

ARTICLE 233

The amount of the above damage for which compensation is to be made by Germany shall be determined by an Inter-Allied Commission, to be called the *Reparation Commission* and constituted in the form and with the powers set forth hereunder and in Annexes II to VII inclusive hereto.

This Commission shall consider the claims and give to the German Government a just opportunity to be heard.

The findings of the Commission as to the amount of damage defined as above shall be concluded and notified to the German Government on or before May 1, 1921, as representing the extent of that Governments obligations.

The Commission shall concurrently draw up a schedule of payments prescribing the time and manner for securing and discharging the entire obligation within a period of thirty years from May 1, 1921. If, however, within the period mentioned, Germany fails to discharge her obligations, any balance remaining unpaid may, within the discretion of the Commission, be postponed for settlement in subsequent years, or may be handled otherwise in such manner as the Allied and Associated Governments, acting in accordance with the procedure laid down in this Part of the present Treaty, shall determine.

ARTICLE 234

The Reparation Commission shall after May 1, 1921, from time to time, consider the resources and capacity of Germany, and, after giving her representatives a just opportunity to be heard, shall have discretion to extend the date, and to modify the form of payments, such as are to be provided for in accordance with Article 233; but not to cancel any part, except with the specific authority of the several Governments represented upon the Commission.

ARTICLE 235

In order to enable the Allied and Associated Powers to proceed at once to the restoration of their industrial and economic life, pending the full determination of their claims, Germany shall pay in such installments and in such manner (whether in gold, commodities, ships, securities or otherwise) as the Reparation Commission may fix, during 1919, 1920 and the first four months of 1921, the equivalent of 20,000,000,000 gold marks. Out of this sum the expenses of the armies of occupation subsequent to the Armistice of November 11, 1918, shall first be met, and such supplies of food and raw materials as may be judged by the Governments of the Principal Allied and Associated Powers to be essential to enable Germany to meet her obligations for reparation may also, with the approval of the said Governments, be paid for out of the above sum. The balance shall be reckoned towards liquidation of the amounts due for reparation. Germany shall further deposit bonds as prescribed in paragraph (c) of Annex II hereto.

ARTICLE 236

Germany further agrees to the direct application of her economic resources to reparation as specified in Annexes, III, IV, V, and VI, relating respectively to merchant shipping, to physical restoration, to coal and derivatives of coal, and to dye stuffs and other chemical products; provided always that the value of the property transferred and any services rendered by her under these Annexes, assessed in the manner therein prescribed, shall be credited to her towards liquidation of her obligations under the above Articles.

ARTICLE 237

The successive installments, including the above sum, paid over by Germany in satisfaction of the above claims will be divided by the Allied and Associated Governments in proportions which have been determined upon by them in advance on a basis of general equity and of the rights of each.

For the purposes of this division the value of property transferred and services rendered under Article 243, and under Annexes III, IV, V, VI, and VII, shall be reckoned in the same manner as cash payments effected in that year.

ARTICLE 238

In addition to the payments mentioned above Germany shall effect, in accordance with the procedure laid down by the Reparation Commission, restitution in cash of cash taken away, seized or sequestrated, and also restitution of animals, objects of every nature and securities taken away, seized or sequestrated, in the cases in which it proves possible to identify them in territory belonging to Germany or her allies.

Until this procedure is laid down, restitution will continue in accordance with the provisions of the Armistice of November 11, 1918, and its renewals and the Protocols thereto.

ARTICLE 239

The German Government undertakes to make forthwith the restitution contemplated by Article 238 and to make the payments and deliveries contemplated by Articles 233, 234, 235 and 236.

ARTICLE 240

The German Government recognizes the Commission provided for by Article 233 as the same may be constituted by the Allied and Associated Governments in accordance with Annex II, and agrees irrevocably to the possession and exercise by such Commission of the power and authority given to it under the present Treaty.

The German Government will supply to the Commission all the information which the Commission may require relative to the financial situation and operations and to the property, productive capacity, and stocks and current production of raw materials and manufactured articles of Germany and her nationals, and further any information relative to military operations which in the judgment of the Commission may be necessary for the assessment of Germany's liability for reparation as defined in Annex I.

The German Government will accord to the members of the Commission and its authorized agents the same rights and immunities as are enjoyed in Germany by duly accredited diplomatic agents of friendly Powers.

Germany further agrees to provide for the salaries and expenses of the Commission and of such staff as it may employ.

ARTICLE 241

Germany undertakes to pass, issue and maintain in force any legislation, orders and decrees that may be necessary to give complete effect to these provisions.

ARTICLE 242

The provisions of this Part of the present Treaty do not apply to the property, rights and interests referred to in Sections III and IV of Part X (Economic Clauses) of the present Treaty, nor to the product of their liquidation, except so far as concerns any final balance in favor of Germany under Article 243 (a).

ARTICLE 243

The following shall be reckoned as credits to Germany in respect of her reparation obligations:

(a) Any final balance in favor of Germany under Section V (Alsace-Lorraine) of Part III (Political Clauses for Europe) and Sections III and IV of Part X (Economic Clauses) of the present Treaty;

(b) Amounts due to Germany in respect of transfers under Section IV (Saar Basin) of Part III (Political Clauses for Europe), Part IX (Financial Clauses), and Part XII (Ports, Waterways and Railways);

(c) Amounts which in the judgment of the Reparation Commission should be credited to Germany on account of any other transfers under the present Treaty of property, rights, concessions or other interests.

In no case, however, shall credit be given for property restored in accordance with Article 238 of the present Part.

ARTICLE 244

The transfer of the German submarine cables which do not form the subject of particular provisions of the present Treaty is regulated by Annex VII hereto.

Annex I

Compensation may be claimed from Germany under Article 232 above in respect of the total damage under the following categories:

(1) Damage to injured persons and to surviving dependents by personal injury to or death of civilians caused by acts of war, including bombardments or other attacks on land, on sea, or from the air, and all the direct consequences thereof, and of all operations of war by the two groups of belligerents wherever arising.

(2) Damage caused by Germany or her allies to civilian victims of acts of cruelty, violence or maltreatment (including injuries to life or health as a consequence of imprisonment, deportation, internment or evacuation, of exposure at sea or of being forced to labor), wherever arising, and to the surviving dependents of such victims.

(3) Damage caused by Germany or her allies in their own territory or in occupied or invaded territory to civilian victims of all acts injurious to health or capacity to work, or to honor, as well as to the surviving dependents of such victims.

(4) Damage caused by any kind of maltreatment of prisoners of war.

(5) As damage caused to the peoples of the Allied and Associated Powers, all pensions and compensation in the nature of pensions to naval and military victims of war (including members of the air force), whether mutilated, wounded, sick; or invalided, and to the dependents of such victims, the amount due to the Allied and Associated Governments being calculated for each of them as being the capitalised cost of such pensions and compensation at the date of the coming into force of the present Treaty on the basis of the scales in force in France at such date.

(6) The cost of assistance by the Government of the Allied and Associated Powers to prisoners of war and to their families and dependents.

(7) Allowances by the Governments of the Allied and Associated Powers to the families and dependents of mobilized persons or persons serving with the forces, the amount due to them for each calendar year in which hostilities occurred being calculated for each Government on the basis of the average scale for such payments in force in France during that year.

(8) Damage caused to civilians by being forced by Germany or her allies to labor without just remuneration.

(9) Damage in respect of all property wherever situated belonging to any of the Allied or Associated States or their nationals, with the exception of naval and military works or materials, which has been carried off, seized, injured or destroyed by the acts of Germany or her allies on land, on sea or from the air, or damage directly in consequence of hostilities or of any operations of war.

(10) Damage in the form of levies, fines and other similar exactions imposed by Germany or her allies upon the civilian population.

Annex II

1

The Commission referred to in Article 233 shall be called "The Reparation Commission" and is hereinafter referred to as "the Commission."

2

Delegates to this Commission shall be nominated by the United States of America, Great Britain, France, Italy, Japan, Belgium and the Serb-Croat-Slovene State. Each of these Powers will appoint one Delegate and also one Assistant Delegate, who will take his place in case of illness or necessary absence, but at other times will only have the right to be present at proceedings without taking any part therein.

On no occasion shall the Delegates of more than five of the above Powers have the right to take part in the proceedings of the Commission and to record their votes. The Delegates of the United States, Great Britain, France and Italy shall have this right on all occasions. The Delegate of Belgium shall have this right on all occasions other than those referred to below. The Delegate of Japan shall have this right on occasions when questions relating to damage at sea, and questions arising under Article 260 of Part IX (Financial Clauses) in which Japanese interests are concerned, are under consideration. The Delegate of the Serb-Croat-Slovene State shall have this right when questions relating to Austria, Hungary or Bulgaria are under consideration.

Each Government represented on the Commission shall have the right to withdraw therefrom upon twelve months' notice filed with the Commission and confirmed in the course of the sixth month after the date of the original notice.

3

Such of the other Allied and Associated Powers as may be interested shall have the right to appoint a Delegate to be present and act as Assessor only while their respective claims and interests are under examination or discussion, but without the right to vote.

4

In case of the death, resignation or recall of any Delegate, Assistant Delegate or Assessor, a successor to him shall be nominated as soon as possible.

5

The Commission will have its principal permanent Bureau in Paris and will hold its first meeting in Paris as soon as practicable after the coming into force of the present Treaty, and thereafter will meet in such place or places and at such time as it may deem convenient and as may be necessary for the most expeditious discharge of its duties.

6

At its first meeting the Commission shall elect, from among the Delegates referred to above, a Chairman and a Vice-Chairman, who shall hold office for one year and shall be eligible for re-election. If a vacancy in the Chairmanship or Vice-Chairmanship should occur during the annual period, the Commission shall proceed to a new election for the remainder of the said period.

7

The Commission is authorized to appoint all necessary officers, agents and employees who may be required for the execution of its functions, and to fix their remuneration; to constitute committees, whose members need not necessarily be members of the Commission, and to take all executive steps necessary for the purpose of discharging its duties; and to delegate authority and discretion to officers, agents and committees.

8

All proceedings of the Commission shall be private, unless, on particular occasions, the Commission shall otherwise determine for special reasons.

9

The Commission shall be required, if the German Government so desire, to hear, within a period which it will fix from time to time, evidence and arguments on the part of Germany on any question connected with her capacity to pay.

10

The Commission shall consider the claims and give to the German Government a just opportunity to be heard, but not to take any part whatever in the decisions of the Commission. The Commission shall afford a similar opportunity to the allies of Germany, when it shall consider that their interests are in question.

11

The Commission shall not be bound by any particular code or rules of law or by any particular rule of evidence or of procedure, but shall be guided by justice, equity and good faith. Its decisions must follow the same principles and rules in all cases where they are applicable. It will establish rules relating to methods of proof of claims. It may act on any trustworthy modes of computation.

12

The Commission shall have all the powers conferred upon it, and shall exercise all the functions assigned to it, by the present Treaty.

The Commission shall in general have wide latitude as to its control and handling of the whole reparation problem as dealt with in this Part of the present Treaty and shall have authority to interpret its provisions. Subject to the provisions of the present Treaty, the Commission is constituted by the several Allied and Associated Governments referred to in paragraphs 2 and 3 above as the exclusive agency of the said Governments respectively for receiving, selling, holding, and distributing the reparation payments to be made by Germany under this Part of the present Treaty. The Commission must comply with the following conditions and provisions:

(a) Whatever part of the full amount of the proved claims is not paid in gold, or in ships, securities and commodities or otherwise, Germany shall be required, under such conditions as the Commission may determine, to cover by way of guarantee by an equivalent issue of bonds, obligations or otherwise, in order to constitute an acknowledgment of the said part of the debt.

(b) In periodically estimating Germany's capacity to pay, the Commission shall examine the German system of taxation, first, to the end that the sums for reparation which Germany is required to pay shall become a charge upon all her revenues prior to that for the service or discharge of any domestic loan, and secondly, so as to satisfy itself that, in general, the German scheme of taxation is fully as heavy proportionately as that of any of the Powers represented on the Commission.

(c) In order to facilitate and continue the immediate restoration of the economic life of the Allied and Associated countries, the Commission will as provided in Article 235 take from Germany by way of security for and acknowledgment of her debt a first installment of gold bearer bonds free of all taxes and charges of every description established or to be established by the Government of the German Empire or of the German States, or by any authority subject to them; these bonds will be delivered on account and in three portions, the marks gold

being payable in conformity with Article 262 of Part IX (Financial Clauses) of the present Treaty as follows:

(1) To be issued forthwith, 20,000,000,000 Marks gold bearer bonds, payable not later than May 1, 1921, without interest. There shall be specially applied towards the amortisation of these bonds the payments which Germany is pledged to make in conformity with Article 235, after deduction of the sums used for the reimbursement of expenses of the armies of occupation and for payment of foodstuffs and raw materials. Such bonds as have not been redeemed by May 1, 1921, shall then be exchanged for new bonds of the same type as those provided for below (paragraph 12, c, (2).

(2) To be issued forthwith, further 40,000,000,000 Marks gold bearer bonds, bearing interest at 2 1/2 per cent. per annum between 1921 and 1926, and thereafter at 5 per cent. per annum with an additional 1 per cent. for amortisation beginning in 1926 on the whole amount of the issue.

(3) To be delivered forthwith a covering undertaking in writing to issue when, but not until, the Commission is satisfied that Germany can meet such interest and sinking fund obligations, a further installment of 40,000,000,000 Marks gold 5 per cent. bearer bonds, the time and mode of payment of principal and interest to be determined by the Commission.

The dates for payment of interest, the manner of applying the amortisation fund, and all other questions relating to the issue, management and regulation of the bond issue shall be determined by the Commission from time to time.

Further issues by way of acknowledgment and security may be required as the Commission subsequently determines from time to time.

(d) In the event of bonds, obligations or other evidence of indebtedness issued by Germany by way of security for or acknowledgment of her reparation debt being disposed of outright, not by way of pledge, to persons other than the several Governments in whose favor Germany's original reparation indebtedness was created, an amount of such reparation indebtedness shall be deemed to be extinguished corresponding to the nominal value of the bonds, etc., so disposed of outright, and the obligation of Germany in respect of such bonds shall be confined to her liabilities to the holders of the bonds, as expressed upon their face.

(e) The damage for repairing, reconstructing and rebuilding property in the invaded and devastated districts, including reinstallation of furniture, machinery and other equipment, will be calculated according to the cost at the dates when the work is done.

(f) Decisions of the Commission relating to the total or partial cancellation of the capital or interest of any verified debt of Germany must be accompanied by a statement of its reasons.

13

As to voting, the Commission will observe the following rules:

When a decision of the Commission is taken, the votes of all the Delegates entitled to vote, or in the absence of any of them, of their Assistant delegates, shall be recorded. Abstention from voting is to be treated as a vote against the proposal under discussion. Assessors have no vote.

On the following questions unanimity is necessary:

(a) Questions involving the sovereignty of any of the Allied and Associated Powers, or the cancellation of the whole or any part of the debt or obligations of Germany;

(b) Questions of determining the amount and conditions of bonds or other obligations to be issued by the German Government and of fixing the time and manner for selling, negotiating or distributing such bonds;

(c) Any postponement, total or partial, beyond the end of 1930, of the payment of installments falling due between May 1, 1921, and the end of 1926 inclusive;

(d) Any postponement, total or partial, of any instalment falling due after 1926 for a period exceeding three years;

(e) Questions of applying in any particular case a method of measuring damages different from that which has been previously applied in a similar case;

(f) Questions of the interpretation of the provisions of this Part of the present Treaty.

All other questions shall be decided by the vote of a majority.

In case of any difference of opinion among the Delegates, which cannot be solved by reference to their Governments, upon the question whether a given case is one which requires a unanimous vote for its decision or not, such difference shall be referred to the immediate arbitration of some impartial person to be agreed upon by their Governments, whose award the Allied and Associated Governments agree to accept.

14

Decisions of the Commission, in accordance with the powers conferred upon it, shall forthwith become binding and may be put into immediate execution without further proceedings.

15

The Commission will issue to each of the interested Powers, in such form as the Commission shall fix:

(1) A certificate stating that it holds for the account of the said Power bonds of the issues mentioned above, the said certificate, on the demand of the Power concerned, being divisible in a number of parts not exceeding five;

(2) From time to time certificates stating the goods delivered by Germany on account of her reparation debt which it holds for the account of the said Power.

The said certificates shall be registered, and upon notice to the Commission, may be transferred by endorsement.

When bonds are issued for sale or negotiation, and when goods are delivered by the Commission, certificates to an equivalent value must be withdrawn.

16

Interest shall be debited to Germany as from May 1, 1921, in respect of her debt as determined by the Commission, after allowing for sums already covered by cash payments or their equivalent, or by bonds issued to the Commission, or under Article 243. The rate of interest shall be 5 per cent. unless the Commission shall determine at some future time that circumstances justify a variation of the rate.

The Commission, in fixing on May 1, 1921, the total amount of the debt of Germany, may take account of interest due on sums arising out of the reparation of material damage as from November 11, 1918, up to May 1, 1921.

17

In case of default by Germany in the performance of any obligation under this Part of the present Treaty, the Commission will forthwith give notice of such default to each of the interested Powers and may make such recommendations as to the action to be taken in consequence of such default as it may think necessary.

18

The measures which the Allied and Associated Powers shall have the right to take, in case of voluntary default by Germany, and which Germany agrees not to regard as acts of war, may include economic and financial prohibitions and reprisals and in general such other measures as the respective Governments may determine to be necessary in the circumstances.

19

Payments required to be made in gold or its equivalent on account of the proved claims of the Allied and Associated Powers may at any time be accepted by the Commission in the form of chattels, properties, commodities, businesses, rights, concessions, within or without German territory, ships, bonds, shares or securities of any kind, or currencies of Germany or other States, the value of such substitutes for good being fixed at a fair and just amount by the Commission itself.

20

The Commission, in fixing or accepting payment in specified properties or rights, shall have due regard for any legal or equitable interests of the Allied and Associated Powers or of neutral Powers or of their nationals therein.

21

No member of the Commission shall be responsible, except to the Government appointing him, for any action or omission as such member. No one of the Allied or Associated Governments assumes any responsibility in respect of any other Government.

22

Subject to the provisions of the present Treaty this Annex may be amended by the unanimous decision of the Governments represented from time to time upon the Commission.

23

When all the amounts due from Germany and her allies under the present Treaty or the decisions of the Commission have been discharged and all sums received, or their equivalents, shall have been distributed to the Powers interested, the Commission shall be dissolved.

Annex III

1

Germany recognizes the right of the Allied and Associated Powers to the replacement, ton for ton (gross tonnage) and class for class, of all merchant ships and fishing boats lost or damaged owing to the war.

Nevertheless, and in spite of the fact that the tonnage of German shipping at present in existence is much less than that lost by the Allied and Associated Powers in consequence of the German aggression, the right thus recognized will be enforced on German ships and boats under the following conditions:

The German Government, on behalf of themselves and so as to bind all other persons interested, cede to the Allied and Associated Governments the property in all the German merchant ships which are of 1,600 tons gross and upwards; in one-half, reckoned in tonnage, of the ships which are between 1,000 tons and 1,600 tons gross; in one-quarter, reckoned in tonnage, of the steam trawlers; and in one-quarter, reckoned in tonnage, of the other fishing boats.

2

The German Government will, within two months of the coming into force of the present Treaty, deliver to the Reparation Commission all the ships and boats mentioned in paragraph 1.

3

The ships and boats mentioned in paragraph 1 include all ships and boats which (a) fly, or may be entitled to fly, the German merchant flag; or (b) are owned by any German national, company or corporation or by any company or corporation belonging to a country other than an Allied or Associated country and under the control or direction of German nationals; or (c) are now under construction (1) in Germany, (2) in other than Allied or Associated countries for the account of any German national, company or corporation.

4

For the purpose of providing documents of title for the ships and boats to be handed over as above mentioned, the German Government will:

(a) Deliver to the Reparation Commission in respect of each vessel a bill of sale or other document of title evidencing the transfer to the Commission of the entire property in the vessel, free from all encumbrances, charges and liens of all kinds, as the Commission may require;

(b) Take all measures that may be indicated by the Reparation Commission for ensuring that the ships themselves shall be placed at its disposal.

5

As an additional part of reparation, Germany agrees to cause merchant ships to be built in German yards for the account of the Allied and Associated Governments as follows:

(a) Within three months of the coming into force of the present Treaty, the Reparation Commission will notify to the German Government the amount of tonnage to be laid down in German ship-yards in each of the two years next succeeding the three months mentioned above.

(b) Within two years of the coming into force of the present Treaty, the Reparation Commission will notify to the German Government the amount of tonnage to be laid down in each of the three years following the two years mentioned above.

(c) The amount of tonnage to be laid down in each year shall not exceed 200,000 tons, gross tonnage.

(d) The specifications of the ships to be built, the conditions under which they are to be built and delivered, the price per ton at which they are to be accounted for by the Reparation Commission, and all other questions relating to the accounting, ordering, building and delivery of the ships, shall be determined by the Commission.

6

Germany undertakes to restore in kind and in normal condition of upkeep to the Allied and Associated Powers, within two months of the coming into force of the present Treaty, in accordance with procedure to be laid down by the Reparation Commission, any boats and other movable appliances belonging to inland navigation which since August 1, 1914, have by any means whatever come into her possession or into the possession of her nationals, and which can be identified.

With a view to make good the loss in inland navigation tonnage, from whatever cause arising, which has been incurred during the war by the Allied and Associated Powers, and which cannot be made good by means of the restitution prescribed above, Germany agrees to cede to the Reparation Commission a portion of the German river fleet up to the amount of the loss mentioned above, provided that such cession shall not exceed 20 per cent. of the river fleet as it existed on November 11, 1918.

The conditions of this cession shall be settled by the arbitrators referred to in Article 339 of Part XII (Ports, Waterways and Railways) of the present Treaty, who are charged with the settlement of difficulties relating to the apportionment of river tonnage resulting from the new international regime applicable to certain river systems or from the territorial changes affecting those systems.

7

Germany agrees to take any measures that may be indicated to her by the Reparation Commission for obtaining the full title to the property in all ships which have during the war been transferred, or are in process of transfer, to neutral flags, without the consent of the Allied and Associated Governments.

8

Germany waives all claims of any description against the Allied and Associated Governments and their nationals in respect of the detention, employment, loss or damage of any German ships or boats, exception being made of payments due in respect of the employment of ships in conformity with the Armistice Agreement of January 13, 1919, and subsequent Agreements.

The handing over of the ships of the German mercantile marine must be continued without interruption in accordance with the said Agreement.

9

Germany waives all claims to vessels or cargoes sunk by or in consequence of naval action and subsequently salved, in which any of the Allied or Associated Governments or their nationals may have any interest either as owners, charterers, insurers or otherwise, notwithstanding any decree of condemnation which may have been made by a Prize Court of Germany or of her allies.

Annex IV

1

The Allied and Associated Powers require, and Germany undertakes, that in part satisfaction of her obligations expressed in the present Part she will, as hereinafter provided, devote her economic resources directly to the physical restoration of the invaded areas of the Allied and Associated Powers, to the extent that these Powers may determine.

2

The Allied and Associated Governments may file with the Reparation Commission lists showing:

(a) Animals, machinery, equipment, tools and like articles of a commercial character, which have been seized, consumed or destroyed by Germany or destroyed in direct consequence of military operations, and which such Governments, for the purpose of meeting immediate and urgent needs, desire to have replaced by animals and articles of the same nature which are in being in German territory at the date of the coming into force of the present Treaty;

(b) Reconstruction materials (stones, bricks, refractory bricks, tiles, wood, window-glass, steel, lime, cement, etc.), machinery, heating apparatus, furniture and like articles of a commercial character which the said Governments desire to have produced and manufactured in Germany and delivered to them to permit of the restoration of the invaded areas.

3

The lists relating to the articles mentioned in 2 (a) above shall be filed within sixty days after the date of the coming into force of the present Treaty.

The lists relating to the articles in 2 (b) above shall be filed on or before December 31, 1919.

The lists shall contain all such details as are customary in commercial contracts dealing with the subject matter, including specifications, dates of delivery (but not extending over more than four years), and places of delivery, but not price or value, which shall be fixed as hereinafter provided by the Commission.

4

Immediately upon the filing of such lists with the Commission, the Commission shall consider the amount and number of the materials and animals mentioned in the lists provided for above which are to be required of Germany. In reaching a decision on this matter the Commission shall take into account such domestic requirements of Germany as it deems essential for the maintenance of Germany's social and economic life, the prices and dates at which similar articles can be obtained in the Allied and Associated countries as compared with those to be fixed for German articles, and the general interest of the Allied and Associated Governments that the industrial life of Germany be not so disorganized as to affect adversely the ability of Germany to perform the other acts of reparation stipulated for.

Machinery, equipment, tools and like articles of a commercial character in actual industrial use are not, however, to be demanded of Germany unless there is no free stock of such articles respectively which is not in use and is available, and then not in excess of thirty per cent. of the quantity of such articles in use in any one establishment or undertaking.

The Commission shall give representatives of the German Government an opportunity and a time to be heard as to their capacity to furnish the said materials, articles and animals.

The decision of the Commission shall thereupon and at the earliest possible moment be communicated to the German Government and to the several interested Allied and Associated Governments.

The German Government undertakes to deliver the materials, articles and animals as specified in the said communication, and the interested Allied and Associated Governments severally agree to accept the same, provided they conform to the specification given, or are not, in the judgment of the Commission, unfit to be utilized in the work of reparation.

5

The Commission shall determine the value to be attributed to the materials, articles and animals to be delivered in accordance with the foregoing, and the Allied or Associated Power receiving the same agrees to be charged with such value, and the amount thereof shall be treated as a payment by Germany to be divided in accordance with Article 237 of this Part of the present Treaty.

In cases where the right to require physical restoration as above provided is exercised, the Commission shall ensure that the amount to be credited against the reparation obligation of Germany shall be the fair value of work done or materials supplied by Germany, and that the claim made by the interested Power in respect of the damage so repaired by physical restoration shall be discharged to the extent of the proportion which the damage thus repaired bears to the whole of the damage thus claimed for.

6

As an immediate advance on account of the animals referred to in paragraph 2 (a) above, Germany undertakes to deliver in equal monthly installments in the three months following the coming into force of the present Treaty the following quantities of live stock:

(1) *To the French Government.*

500 stallions (3 to 7 years);

30,000 fillies and mares (18 months to 7 years), type: Ardennais, Boulonnais or Belgian;

2,000 bulls (18 months to 3 years);

90,000 milch cows (2 to 6 years); 1,000 rams;

100,000 sheep;

10,000 goats.

(2) *To the Belgian Government.*

200 stallions (3 to 7 years), large Belgian type;

5,000 mares (3 to 7 years), large Belgian type;

5,000 fillies (18 months to 3 years), large Belgian type;

2,000 bulls (18 months to 3 years);

50,000 milch cows (2 to 6 years);

40,000 heifers;

200 rams;

20,000 sheep;

15,000 sows.

The animals delivered shall be of average health and condition.

To the extent that animals so delivered cannot be identified as animals taken away or seized, the value of such animals shall be credited against the reparation obligations of Germany in accordance with paragraph 5 of this Annex.

7

Without waiting for the decisions of the Commission referred to in paragraph 4 of this Annex to be taken, Germany must continue the delivery to France of the agricultural material referred to in Article III of the renewal dated January 16, 1919, of the Armistice.

Annex V

1

Germany accords the following options for the delivery of coal and derivatives of coal to the undermentioned signatories of the present Treaty.

2

Germany undertakes to deliver to France seven million tons of coal per year for ten years. In addition, Germany undertakes to deliver to France annually for a period not exceeding ten years an amount of coal equal to the difference between the annual production before the war of the coal mines of the Nord and Pas de Calais, destroyed as a result of the war, and the production of the mines of the same area during the years in question: such delivery not to exceed twenty million tons in any one year of the first five years, and eight million tons in any one year of the succeeding five years.

It is understood that due diligence will be exercised in the restoration of the destroyed mines in the Nord and the Pas de Calais.

3

Germany undertakes to deliver to Belgium eight million tons of coal annually for ten years.

4

Germany undertakes to deliver to Italy up to the following quantities of coal:

July 1919 to June 1920	4 1/2 million tons
July 1920 to June 1921	6 million tons
July 1921 to June 1922	7 million tons
July 1922 to June 1923	8 million tons
July 1923 to June 1924	8 1/2 million tons
and each of the following five years	8 1/2 million tons

At least two-thirds of the actual deliveries to be land-borne.

5

Germany further undertakes to deliver annually to Luxembourg, if directed by the Reparation Commission, a quantity of coal equal to the pre-war annual consumption of German coal in Luxembourg.

6

The prices to be paid for coal delivered under these options shall be as follows:

(c) For overland delivery, including delivery by barge, the German pithead price to German nationals, plus the freight the French, Belgian, Italian or Luxembourg frontiers, provided that the pithead price does not exceed the pithead price of British coal for export. In the case of Belgian bunker coal, the price shall not exceed the Dutch bunker price.

Railroad and barge tariffs shall not be higher than the lowest similar rates paid in Germany.

(b) For sea delivery, the German export price f. o. b. German ports, or the British export price f. o. b. British ports, whichever may be lower.

7

The Allied and Associated Governments interested may demand the delivery, in place of coal, of metallurgical coke in the proportion of 3 tons of coke to 4 tons of coal.

8

Germany undertakes to deliver to France, and to transport to the French frontier by rail or by water, the following products, during each of the three years following the coming into force of this Treaty:

Benzol	35,000 tons.
Coal tar	50,000 tons.
Sulphate of ammonia	30,000 tons.

All or part of the coal tar may, at the option of the French Government, be replaced by corresponding quantities of products of distillation, such as light oils, heavy oils, anthracene, naphthalene or pitch.

9

The price paid for coke and for the articles referred to in the preceding paragraph shall be the same as the price paid by German nationals under the same conditions of shipment to the French frontier or to the German ports, and shall be subject to any advantages which may be accorded similar products furnished to German nationals.

10

The foregoing options shall be exercised through the intervention of the Reparation Commission, which, subject to the specific provisions hereof, shall have power to determine all questions relative to procedure and the qualities and quantities of products, the quantity of coke which may be substituted for coal, and the times and modes of delivery and payment. In giving notice to the German Government of the foregoing options the Commission shall give at least 120 days' notice of deliveries to be made after January 1, 1920, and at least 30 days' notice of deliveries to be made between the coming into force of this Treaty and January 1, 1920. Until Germany has received the demands referred to in this paragraph, the provisions of the Protocol of December 25, 1918, (Execution of Article VI of the Armistice of November 11, 1918) remain in force. The notice to be given to the German Government of the exercise of the right of substitution accorded by paragraphs 7 and 8 shall be such as the Reparation Commission may consider sufficient. If the Commission shall determine that the full exercise of the foregoing options would interfere unduly with the industrial requirements of Germany, the Commission is authorized to postpone or to cancel deliveries, and in so doing to settle all questions of priority; but the coal to replace coal from destroyed mines shall receive priority over other deliveries.

Annex VI

1

Germany accords to the Reparation Commission an option to require as part of reparation the delivery by Germany of such quantities and kinds of dyestuffs and chemical drugs as the Commission may designate, not exceeding 50 per cent. of the total stock of each and every kind of dyestuff and chemical drug in Germany or under German control at the date of the coming into force of the present Treaty.

This option shall be exercised within sixty days of the receipt by the Commission of such particulars as to stocks as may be considered necessary by the Commission.

2

Germany further accords to the Reparation Commission an option to require delivery during the period from the date of the coming into force of the present Treaty until January 1, 1920, and during each period of six months thereafter until January 1, 1925, of any specified kind of dyestuff and chemical drug up to an amount not exceeding 25 per cent. of the German production of such dyestuffs and chemical drugs during the previous six months period. If in any case the production during such previous six months was, in the opinion of the Commission, less than normal, the amount required may be 25 per cent. of the normal production.

Such option shall be exercised within four weeks after the receipt of such particulars as to production and in such form as may be considered necessary by the Commission; these particulars shall be furnished by the German Government immediately after the expiration of each six months period.

3

For dyestuffs and chemical drugs delivered under paragraph 1, the price shall be fixed by the Commission having regard to prewar net export prices and to subsequent increases of cost.

For dyestuffs and chemical drugs delivered under paragraph 2, the price shall be fixed by the Commission having regard to pre-war net export prices and subsequent variations of cost, or the lowest net selling price of similar dyestuffs and chemical drugs to any other purchaser.

4

All details, including mode and times of exercising the options, and making delivery, and all other questions arising under this arrangement shall be determined by the Reparation Commission; the German Government will furnish to the Commission all necessary information and other assistance which it may require.

5

The above expression "dyestuffs and chemical drugs" includes all synthetic dyes and drugs and intermediate or other products used in connection with dyeing, so far as they are manufactured for sale. The present arrangement shall also apply to cinchona bark and salts of quinine.

Annex VII

Germany renounces on her own behalf and on behalf of her nationals in favor of the Principal Allied and Associated Powers all rights, titles or privileges of whatever nature in the submarine cables set out below, or in any portions thereof:

Emden-Vigo: from the Straits of Dover off Vigo;

Emden-Brest: from off Cherbourg to Brest;

Emden-Teneriffe: from off Dunkirk to off Teneriffe;

Emden-Azores (1): from the Straits of Dover to Fayal;

Emden-Azores (2): from the Straits of Dover to Fayal;

Azores–New York (1): from Fayal to New York;

Azores–New York (2): from Fayal to the longitude of Halifax;

Teneriffe-Monrovia: from off Teneriffe to off Monrovia;

Monrovia-Lome: from about lat.: 2 degrees 30 inches N; long.: 7 degrees 40 inches W. of Greenwich:

to about lat.: 2 degrees 20 inches N.; long.: 5 degrees 30 inches W. of Greenwich;

and from about lat.: 3 degrees 48 inches N.; long.: 0 degrees 00 inches, to Lome

Lome-Duala: from Lome to Duala

Monrovia-Pernambuco: from off Monrovia to off Pernambuco;

Constantinople-Constanza: from Constantinople to Constanza;

Yap-Shanghai, Yap-Guam, and Yap-Menado (Celebes): from Yap Island to Shanghai, from Yap Island to Guam Island,

and from Yap Island to Menado.

The value of the above mentioned cables or portions thereof in so far as they are privately owned, calculated on the basis of the original cost less a suitable allowance for depreciation, shall be credited to Germany in the reparation account.

Section II
Special Provisions

ARTICLE 245

Within six months after the coming into force of the present Treaty the German Government must restore to the French Government the trophies, archives, historical souvenirs or works of art carried away from France by the German authorities in the course of the war of 1870–1871 and during this last war, in accordance with a list which will be communicated to it by the French Government; particularly the French flags taken in the course of the war of 1870–1871 and all the political papers taken by the German authorities on October 10, 1870, at the chateau of Cerçay, near Brunoy (Seine-et-Oise) belonging at the time to Mr. Rouher, formerly Minister of State.

ARTICLE 246

Within six months from the coming into force of the present Treaty, Germany will restore to His Majesty the King of the Hedjaz the original Koran of the Caliph Othman, which was removed from Medina by the Turkish authorities and is stated to have been presented to the ex-Emperor William II.

Within the same period Germany will hand over to His Britannic Majesty's Government the skull of the Sultan Mkwawa which was removed from the Protectorate of German East Africa and taken to Germany.

The delivery of the articles above referred to will be effected in such place and in such conditions as may be laid down by the Governments to which they are to be restored.

ARTICLE 247

Germany undertakes to furnish to the University of Louvain, within three months after a request made by it and transmitted through the intervention of the Reparation Commission, manuscripts, incunabula, printed books, maps and objects of collection corresponding in number and value to those destroyed in the burning by Germany of the Library of Louvain. All details regarding such replacement will be determined by the Reparation Commission.

Germany undertakes to deliver to Belgium, through the Reparation Commission, within six months of the coming into force of the present Treaty, in order to enable Belgium to reconstitute two great artistic works:

(1) The leaves of the triptych of the Mystic Lamb painted by the Van Eyck brothers, formerly in the Church of St. Bavon at Ghent, now in the Berlin Museum;

(2) The leaves of the triptych of the Last Supper, painted by Dierick Bouts, formerly in the Church of St. Peter at Louvain, two of which are now in the Berlin Museum and two in the Old Pinakothek at Munich.

Nor was this staggering list of reparations the only economic penalty Germany incurred. Parts 9 and 10, "Financial Clauses" and "Economic Clauses," made further stipulations regarding debt and setting forth international commercial arrangements that were highly advantageous to the Allies at the expense of Germany.

Consequences

It is not surprising that on May 7, 1919, when a German delegation headed by German foreign minister Graf Ulrich von Brockdorff-Rantzau was presented with the treaty terms, they denounced it. Brockdorff-Rantzau protested that the treaty abrogated the Fourteen Points, which had provided the basis for the armistice. He also insisted, quite rightly, that the economic provisions of the treaty were impossible to fulfill. Germany's chancellor, Philipp Scheidemann, likewise denounced the treaty when it was presented to him. However, the Allies maintained a stringent naval blockade of Germany. In protest, both Scheidemann and Brockdorff-Rantzau resigned on June 21. That same day, at Scapa Flow, where the German High Seas Fleet lay at anchor, German sailors scuttled all 50 of their warships, thereby depriving the Allies of this great prize. The new German chancellor, Gustav Bauer, sent another delegation to Versailles and, on June 28, signed the document only after informing the Allies that he accepted the treaty in order to alleviate the hardships caused by the "inhuman" blockade.

Much of the treaty was simply ignored. For example, neither the kaiser nor anyone else was tried for war crimes following World War I. Wilhelm fled to Holland after the war, and the Dutch government declined to extradite him to the jurisdiction of the Allies. He remained in Dutch exile until his death during the next world war, on June 8, 1941. In practice, Germany also increasingly ignored the provisions aimed at destroying its "militarism" as it rearmed under Adolf Hitler during the 1930s. Ironically, the abolition of conscription meant that the core of the post–World War I German army was an all-volunteer force—in effect, an elite body of professional soldiers around whom Hitler and his commanders built a highly effective and efficient army.

In another irony, one of history's bitterest, the United States ultimately failed to accept the Treaty of Versailles. Many in the U.S. Senate objected to joining the League of Nations, which, through President Wilson's efforts, was part and parcel of the Versailles treaty. Wilson campaigned vigorously for acceptance of the treaty, traveling across the nation to garner popular support for it. In the process, he destroyed his health, suffering a collapse in Pueblo, Colorado, and, subsequently, a debilitating stroke. Ultimately, the United States arranged separate treaties with Germany, Austria, and Hungary.

While some of the Allies were gratified by having punished Germany, the terrible fact was that the Treaty of Versailles created the political, economic, and emotional climate that promoted the rise of Adolf Hitler and Nazism. The product of the so-called War to End All Wars, the Versailles treaty sowed the seeds of what seemed inconceivable in 1919: an even more horrendous, costly, and destructive war.

TREATY OF ST. GERMAIN

TREATY AT A GLANCE

Completed
September 10, 1919, at St. Germain-en-Laye, France

Signatories
United States, British Empire, France, Italy, and Japan
("Principal Allied and Associated Powers"); Belgium, China,
Cuba, Ecuador, Greece, Nicaragua, Panama, Poland, Portugal,
Romania, Serb-Croat-Slovene State, Siam, and Czechoslovakia
("The Allied and Associated Powers"); and Austria

Overview
Besides the TREATY OF BREST-LITOVSK and the TREATY OF VERSAILLES
(1919), this was the most important treaty relating to World War I.
In concert with the Versailles document, it dissolved the Austro-
Hungarian Empire, raised the hackles of the Italians concerning
Italy's boundary with Austria and the newly created Yugoslavia,
caused the Italian government to fall, and created a bitterness that
fostered the rise of Mussolini's Fascists.

Historical Background

The end of World War I was accompanied by a series of treaties, of which the Treaty of Versailles was the central document. The Treaty of St. Germain (named for the Paris suburb in which the treaty was concluded), signed on September 10, 1919, made official the disintegration of the vast Austro-Hungarian, or Hapsburg, Empire, which had in actuality taken place during October and November 1918. By the treaty, Austria, now a small republic, recognized the political dispositions made by the Treaty of Versailles: the independence of Czechoslovakia, Poland, and Yugoslavia; and the award of Galicia to Poland and of the Trentino, south Tirol, Trieste, and Istria to Italy. The once major Austrian army was now cut to a maximum of 30,000 men, and Austria agreed to reparations. Most significantly, Austria was forbidden to unite with Germany—a dream cherished by many Germans as well as Austrians.

Czechoslavakia's foreign minister, Tomáš Masaryk, and Czechoslavakia's president, Edvard Beneš, avid fans of Woodrow Wilson and his self-determination policy for ethnic nationalities, exploited their personal friendship with the U.S. president to win two major concessions that violated the very principle of national self-determination they so admired. In order to give Czechoslavkia a riverine outlet, the Paris Peace Conference granted the two men control of territory stretching south to Bratislavia, which created within the newly established borders a minority of a million Magyars. Even more troublesome was the action taken to provide the vulnerable young country military protection from Germany: the diplomats placed the Sudety Mountains between the two nations. Thus did Czechoslovakia retain the entire historical province of Bohemia, bringing 3.5 million Sudeten Germans under the rule of Prague, a turn of events that would haunt the peacemakers when Adolf Hitler came to power.

Then, largely because of the Italians' traditional truculence and Wilson's typical sanctimoniousness, the negotiations to set Italy's boundaries between Austria and Yugoslavia became one of the more inflammatory issues of the entire peace talks. Italy's premier, Vittorio Orlando, clung to the Allied promises that had enticed Italy into the war in the first place under the 1915 TREATY OF LONDON.

The morally touchy Wilson, offended by the secret war-aims treaty, vented his frustrations with the peace process—disguised as righteous indignation—on the Italians. When he took to the streets of Paris to make his case publicly, not only did he commit a serious breach of diplomatic etiquette, but he provoked the easily aggravated Italians into bolting the conference.

They returned to promises of a sort of compromise spoils: Wilson would let them have Trieste, parts of Istria and Dalmatia, and the Upper Adige up to the Brenner Pass (with its 200,000 Austrians), but that was as far as he would go. No way would Italy get Fiume, a province with a Yugoslavian hinterland but an Italian port. On June 19 Orlando's government fell over the issue. A month later, a band of crypto-fascist freebooters under the command of the flamboyant Italian nationalist poet Gabriele D'Annunzio seized the port city and declared Fiume a free state.

Terms

As with the Treaty of Versailles, the COVENANT OF THE LEAGUE OF NATIONS was integral to the treaty as its Part 1. Part 2 of the treaty defined the new frontiers of Austria:

PART II
FRONTIERS OF AUSTRIA

ARTICLE 27

The frontiers of Austria shall be fixed as follows:

1. *With Switzerland and Liechtenstein:*

The present frontier.

2. *With Italy:*

From the point 2645 (Gruben J.) eastwards to point 2915 (Klopaier Spitz), a line to be fixed on the ground passing through point 1483 on the Reschen-Nauders road;

thence eastwards to the summit of Dreiherrn Spitz (point 3505), the watershed between the basins of the Inn to the north and the Adige to the south;

thence generally south-south-eastwards to point 2545 (Marchkinkele), the watershed between the basins of the Drave to the east and the Adige to the west;

thence south-eastwards to point 2483 (Helm Spitz),

a line to be fixed on the ground crossing the Drave between Winnbach and Arnbach;

thence east-south-eastwards to point 2050 (Osternig) about 9 kilometers northwest of Tarvis,

the watershed between the basins of the Drave on the north and successively the basins of the Sextenbach, the Piave and the Tagliamento on the south;

thence east-south-eastwards to point 1492 (about 2 kilometers west of Thörl),

the watershed between the Gail and the Gailitz;

thence eastwards to point 1509 (Pec),

a line to be fixed on the ground cutting the Gailitz south of the town and station of Thárl and passing through point 1270 (Cabin Berg).

3. *On the South, and then with the Klagenfurt area,* subject to the provisions of Section II of Part III (Political Clauses for Europe):

From point 1509 (Pec) eastwards to point 1817 (Malestiger),

the crest of the Karavanken;

from point 1817 (Malestiger) and in a north-easterly direction as far as the Drave at a point situated about 1 kilometer southeast of the railway bridge on the eastern branch of the bend made by that river about 6 kilometers east of Villach,

a line to be fixed on the ground cutting the railway between Mallestig and Faak and passing through point 666 (Polana);

thence in a south-easterly direction to a point about 2 kilometers above St. Martin,

the course of the Drave;

thence in a northerly direction as far as point 18711 about 10 kilometers to the east-north-east of Villach,

a line running approximately from south to north to be fixed on the ground;

thence east-north-eastwards to a point to be chosen near point 725 about 10 kilometers north-west of Klagenfurt on the administrative boundary between the districts of St. Veit and Klagenfurt,

a line to be fixed on the ground passing through points 1069 (Taubenbühel), 1045 (Gallinberg) and 815 (Freudenberg);

thence eastwards to a point to be chosen on the ground west of point 1075 (Steinbruch Kogel),

the administrative boundary between the districts of St. Veit and Klagenfurt;

thence north-eastwards to the point on the Gurk where the administrative boundary of the district of Völkermarkt leaves that river,

a line to be fixed on the ground passing through point 1076;

thence north-eastwards to point 1899 (Speikkogl),

the administrative boundary between the districts of St. Veit and Völkermarkt;

thence south-eastwards to point 842 (1 kilometer west of Kasparstein),

the north-eastern boundary of the district of Volkermarkt;

thence eastwards to point 1522 (Huhner Kogel),

a line to be fixed on the ground passing north of Lavamund.

4. *With the Serb-Croat-Slovene State*, subject to the provisions of Section II of Part III (Political Clauses for Europe):

From point 1522 (Hühner Kogel) eastwards to point 917 (St. Lorenzen),

a line to be fixed on the ground passing through point 1330;

thence eastwards to the point where it meets the administrative boundary between the districts of Marburg and Leibnitz,

the watershed between the basins of the Drave to the south and the Saggau to the north;

thence north-eastwards to the point where this administrative boundary meets the Mur,

the above-mentioned administrative boundary;

thence to the point where it meets the old frontier of 1867 between Austria and Hungary about 5 kilometers south-east of Radkersburg, the principal course of the Mur downstream;

thence northwards to a point to be fixed east of point 400 about 16 kilometers north of Radkersburg,

the old frontier of 1867 between Austria and Hungary;

thence north-eastwards to a point to be fixed on the watershed between the basins of the Raab and the Mur about 2 kilometers east of Toka, being the point common to the three frontiers of Austria, Hungary, and the Serb-Croat-Slovene State,

a line to be fixed on the ground, passing between the villages of Bonisfalva and Gedoudvar.

5. *With Hungary:*

From the point above defined north-eastwards to point 353 about 6 kilometers north-north-east of Szentgotthard,

a line to be fixed on the ground passing through point 353 (Janke B.), then west of the Radkersburg-Szentgotthard road and east of the villages of Nagyfalva, Nemetlak and Rabakresztur;

thence in a general north-easterly direction to point 234 about 7 kilometers north-north-east of Pinkamindszent,

a line to be fixed on the ground passing through point 322 (Hochkogel), then south of the villages of Zsamand, Nemetbukkos and Karacsfa, and between Nagysaroslak and Pinkamindszent;

thence northwards to point 883 (Trött Kö) about 9 kilometers south-west of Köszeg,

a line to be fixed on the ground passing through points 241, 260 and 273, then east of Nagynarda and Rohonez and west of Dozmat and Butsching;

thence north-eastwards to point 265 (Kamenje) about 2 kilometers south-east of Nikitsch,

a line to be fixed on the ground, passing south-east of Liebing,

Ohnod and Locsmand, and north-west of Köszeg and the road from Köszeg to Salamonfa;

thence northwards to a point to be selected on the southern shore of Neusiedler See between Holling and Hidegseg,

a line to be fixed on the ground, passing east of Nikitsch and Zinkendorf and west of Kovesd and Nemet-Pereszteg;

thence eastwards to point 115 situated about 8 kilometers south-west of St. Johann,

a line to be fixed on the ground, crossing the Neusiedler See, passing south of the island containing point 117, leaving in Hungary the branch railway running north-westwards from the station of Mexiko as well as the entire Einser canal, and passing south of Pamhagen;

thence northwards to a point to be selected about 1 kilometer west of Antonienhof (east of Kittsee), this point being the point common to the three frontiers of Austria, Hungary and the Czecho-Slovak State,

a line to be fixed on the ground, leaving entirely in Hungarian territory the Csorna-Karlburg railway and passing west of WüstSommerein and Kr. Jahrndorf,

and east of Andau, Nikelsdorf, D. Jahrndorf and Kittsee.

6. *With the Czecho-Slovak State:*

From the point above-defined north-westwards to the bend of the old frontier of 1867 between Austria and Hungary about 23 kilometers north-east of Berg,

a line to be fixed on the ground, cutting the Kittsee-Pressburg road about 2 kilometers north of Kittsee;

thence northwards to a point to be selected on the principal channel of navigation of the Danube about 4 1/2 kilometers upstream from the Pressburg bridge,

a line to be fixed on the ground following as much as possible the old frontier of 1867 between Austria and Hungary;

thence westwards to the confluence of the Morava (March) with the Danube, the principal channel of navigation of the Danube;

thence the course of the Morava upstream, then the course of the Thaya upstream to a point to be selected about 2 kilometers south-east of the intersection of the Rabensburg-Themenau road with the Rabensburg-Lundenburg railway;

thence west-north-westwards to a point on the old administrative boundary between Lower Austria and Moravia situated about 400 meters south of the point where this boundary cuts the Nikolsburg-Feldsberg railway,

a line to be fixed on the ground passing through points 187 (Dlouhyvrch), 221 (Rosenbergen), 223 (Wolfsberg), 291 (Raistenberg), 249 and 279 (Kallerhaide);

thence west-north-westwards the above-mentioned administrative boundary;

thence westwards to a point to be selected about 3 kilometers east of the village of Franzensthal,

the old administrative boundary between Lower Austria and Bohemia;

thence southwards to point 498 (Gelsenberg) about 5 kilometers north-northwest of Gmünd,

a line to be fixed on the ground passing east of the Rottenschachen-Zuggers road and through points 537 and 522 (G. Nagel B.);

thence southwards and then west-north-westwards to a point on the old administrative boundary between Lower Austria and Bohemia situated about 200 meters north of the point where it cuts the Gratzen-Weitra road,

a line to be fixed on the ground passing between Zuggers and Breitensee, then through the most southeasterly point of the railway bridge over the Lainsitz leaving to Austria the town of Gmünd and to the Czecho-Slovak State the station and railway works of Gmünd (Wolfshof) and the junction of the Gmünd-Budweis and Gmünd-Wittingau railways, then passing through points 524 (Grundbühel), 577 (north of Hohenberg) and 681 (Lagerberg);

thence south-westwards the above-mentioned administrative boundary, then north-westwards the old administrative boundary between Upper Austria and Bohemia to its point of junction with the frontier of Germany.

7. *With Germany:*

The frontier of August 3, 1914.

ARTICLE 28

The frontiers described by the present Treaty are traced, for such parts as are defined, on the one-in-a-million map attached to the present Treaty. In case of differences between the text and the maps, the text will prevail.

ARTICLE 29

Boundary Commissions, whose composition is fixed by the present Treaty, or will be fixed by a Treaty between the Principal Allied and Associated Powers and the, or any, interested States, will have to trace these frontiers on the ground.

They shall have the power, not only of fixing those portions which are defined as "a line to be fixed on the ground," but also, where a request to that effect is made by one of the States concerned, and the Commission is satisfied that it is desirable to do so, of revising portions defined by administrative boundaries; this shall not, however, apply in the case of international boundaries existing in August, 1914, where the task of the Commission will confine itself to the re-establishment of sign posts and boundary marks.

They shall endeavor in both cases to follow as nearly as possible the descriptions given in the Treaties, taking into account as far as possible administrative boundaries and local economic interests.

The decisions of the Commissions will be taken by a majority, and shall be binding on the parties concerned.

The expenses of the Boundary Commissions will be borne in equal shares by the two States concerned.

ARTICLE 30

In so far as frontiers defined by a waterway are concerned, the phrases "course" or "channel" used in the descriptions of the present Treaty signify, as regards non-navigable rivers, the median line of the waterway or of its principal branch, and, as regards navigable rivers, the median line of the principal channel of navigation. It will, however, rest with the Boundary Commissions provided for by the present Treaty to specify whether the frontier line shall follow any changes of the course or channel which frontier line shall follow any changes of the course or channel which may take place, or whether it shall be definitely fixed by the position of the course or channel at the time when the present Treaty comes into force.

ARTICLE 31

The various States interested undertake to furnish to the Commissions all documents necessary for their tasks, especially authentic copies of agreements fixing existing or old frontiers, all large scale maps in existence, geodetic data, surveys completed but unpublished, and information concerning the changes of frontier watercourses.

They also undertake to instruct the local authorities to communicate to the Commissions all documents, especially plans, cadastral and land books, and to furnish on demand all details regarding property, local economic relations, and other necessary information.

ARTICLE 32

The various States interested undertake to give assistance to the Boundary Commissions, whether directly or through local authorities, in everything that concerns transport, accommodation, labor, material (signposts, boundary pillars) necessary for the accomplishment of their mission.

ARTICLE 33

The various States interested undertake to safeguard the trigonometrical points, signals, posts or frontier marks erected by the Commission.

ARTICLE 34

The pillars will be placed so as to be intervisible; they will be numbered, and their position and their number will be noted on a cartographic document.

ARTICLE 35

The protocols defining the boundary, and the maps and documents attached thereto will be made out in triplicate, of which two copies will be forwarded to the Governments of the limitrophe States and the third to the Government of the French Republic, which will deliver authentic copies to the Powers signatories of the present Treaty.

Part 3 contained "Political Clauses for Europe," by which Austria acknowledged the relevant and applicable cessions and awards made in the Treaty of Versailles. By Section 5 of Part 3, Austria promised to protect minorities:

Section V
Protection of Minorities

ARTICLE 62

Austria undertakes that the stipulations contained in this Section shall be recognized as fundamental laws, and that no law, regulation or official action shall conflict or interfere with these stipulations, nor shall any law, regulation, or official action prevail over them.

ARTICLE 63

Austria undertakes to assure full and complete protection of life and liberty to all inhabitants of Austria without distinction of birth, nationality, language, race or religion.

All inhabitants of Austria shall be entitled to the free exercise, whether public or private, of any creed, religion or belief, whose practices are not inconsistent with public order or public morals.

ARTICLE 64

Austria admits and declares to be Austrian nationals *ipso facto* and without the requirement of any formality all persons possessing at the date of the coming into force of the present Treaty rights of citizenship (*pertinenza*) within Austrian territory who are not nationals of any other State.

ARTICLE 65

All persons born in Austrian territory who are not born nationals of another State shall *ipso facto* become Austrian nationals.

ARTICLE 66

All Austrian nationals shall be equal before the law and shall enjoy the same civil and political rights without distinction as to race, language, or religion.

Differences of religion, creed, or confession shall not prejudice any Austrian national in matters relating to the enjoyment of civil or political rights, as for instance admission to public employments, functions and honors, or the exercise of professions and industries.

No restriction shall be imposed on the free use by any Austrian national of any language in private intercourse, in commerce, in religion, in the press or in publications of any kind, or at public meetings.

Notwithstanding any establishment by the Austrian Government of an official language, adequate facilities shall be given to Austrian nationals of non-German speech for the use of their language, either orally or in writing, before the courts.

ARTICLE 67

Austrian nationals who belong to racial, religious or linguistic minorities shall enjoy the same treatment and security in law and in fact as the other Austrian nationals. In particular they shall have an equal right to establish, manage and control at their own expense charitable, religious and social institutions, schools and other educational establishments, with the right to use their own language and to exercise their religion freely therein.

ARTICLE 68

Austria will provide in the public educational system in towns and districts in which a considerable proportion of Austrian nationals of other than German speech are residents adequate facilities for ensuring that in the primary schools the instruction shall be given to the children of such Austrian nationals through the medium of their own language. This provision shall not prevent the Austrian Government from making the teaching of the German language obligatory in the said schools.

In towns and districts where there is a considerable proportion of Austrian nationals belonging to racial, religious or linguistic minorities, these minorities shall be assured an equitable share in the enjoyment and application of the sums which may be provided out of public funds under the State, municipal or other budgets for educational, religious or charitable purposes.

ARTICLE 69

Austria agrees that the stipulations in the foregoing Articles of this Section, so far as they affect persons belonging to racial, religious or linguistic minorities, constitute obligations of international concern and

shall be placed under the guarantee of the League of Nations. They shall not be modified without the assent of a majority of the Council of the League of Nations. The Allied and Associated Powers represented on the Council severally agree not to withhold their assent from any modification in these Articles which is in due form assented to by a majority of the Council of the League of Nations.

Austria agrees that any Member of the Council of the League of Nations shall have the right to bring to the attention of the Council any infraction, or any danger of infraction, of any of these obligations, and that the Council may thereupon take such action and give such direction as it may deem proper and effective in the circumstances.

Austria further agrees that any difference of opinion as to questions of law or fact arising out of these Articles between the Austrian Government and any one of the Principal Allied and Associated Powers or any other Power, a Member of the Council of the League of Nations, shall be held to be a dispute of an international character under Article 14 of the Covenant of the League of Nations. The Austrian Government hereby consents that any such dispute shall, if the other party thereto demands, be referred to the Permanent Court of International Justice. The decision of the Permanent Court shall be final and shall have the same force and effect as an award under Article 13 of the Covenant.

This was a provision consistent with President Wilson's Fourteen Points. (It was, of course, entirely abrogated by Austria's Nazi regime prior to and during World War II.)

By Part 4 of the treaty, Austria renounced all of its colonial possessions and other interests outside of Europe:

PART IV
AUSTRIAN INTERESTS OUTSIDE EUROPE

ARTICLE 95

In territory outside her frontiers as fixed by the present Treaty Austria renounces so far as she is concerned all rights, titles and privileges whatever in or over territory outside Europe which belonged to the former Austro-Hungarian Monarchy or to its allies, and all rights, titles and privileges whatever their origin which it held as against the Allied and Associated Powers.

Austria undertakes immediately to recognize and to conform to the measures which may be taken now or in the future by the Principal Allied and Associated Powers, in agreement where necessary with third Powers, in order to carry the above stipulation into effect.

Section I
Morocco

ARTICLE 96

Austria renounces, so far as she is concerned, all rights, titles and privileges conferred on her by the

General Act of Algeciras of April 7, 1906, and by the Franco-German Agreements of February 9, 1909 and November 4, 1911. All treaties, agreements, arrangements and contracts concluded by the former Austro-Hungarian Monarchy with the Sherifian Empire are regarded as abrogated as from August 12, 1914.

In no case can Austria avail herself of these acts and she undertakes not to intervene in any way in negotiations relating to Morocco which may take place between France and the other Powers.

ARTICLE 97

Austria hereby accepts all the consequences of the establishment of the French Protectorate in Morocco, which had been recognized by the Government of the former Austro-Hungarian Monarchy, and she renounces so far as she is concerned the regime of the capitulations in Morocco.

This renunciation shall take effect as from August 12, 1914.

ARTICLE 98

The Sherifian Government shall have complete liberty of action in regulating the status of Austrian nationals in Morocco and the conditions in which they can establish themselves there.

Austrian protected persons, semsars and "associes agricoles" shall be considered to have ceased, as from August 12, 1914, to enjoy the privileges attached to their status and shall be subject to the ordinary law.

ARTICLE 99

All movable and immovable property in the Sherifian Empire belonging to the former Austro-Hungarian Monarchy passes *ipso facto* to the Maghzen without compensation.

For this purpose, the property and possessions of the former Austro-Hungarian Monarchy shall be deemed to include all the property of the Crown, and the private property of members of the former Royal Family of Austria-Hungary.

All movable and immovable property in the Sherifian Empire belonging to Austrian nationals shall be dealt with in accordance with Sections III and IV of Part X (Economic Clauses) of the present Treaty.

Mining rights which may be recognized as belonging to Austrian nationals by the Court of Arbitration set up under the Moroccan Mining Regulations shall be treated in the same way as property in Morocco belonging to Austrian nationals.

ARTICLE 100

The Austrian Government shall ensure the transfer to the person nominated by the French Government of the shares representing Austria's portion of the capital of the State Bank of Morocco This person will repay to the persons entitled thereto the value of these shares, which shall be indicated by the State Bank.

This transfer will take place without prejudice to the repayment of debts which Austrian nationals may have contracted towards the State Bank of Morocco.

ARTICLE 101

Moroccan goods entering Austria shall enjoy the treatment accorded to French goods.

Section II
Egypt

ARTICLE 102

Austria declares that she recognizes the Protectorate proclaimed over Egypt by Great Britain on December 18, 1914, and that she renounces so far as she is concerned the regime of the capitulations in Egypt.

This renunciation shall take effect as from August 12, 1914.

ARTICLE 103

All treaties, agreements, arrangements and contracts concluded by the Government of the former Austro-Hungarian Monarchy with Egypt are regarded as abrogated as from August 12, 1914.

In no case can Austria avail herself of these instruments, and she undertakes not to intervene in any way in negotiations relating to Egypt which may take place between Great Britain and the other Powers.

ARTICLE 104

Until an Egyptian law of judicial organization establishing courts with universal jurisdiction comes into force, provision shall be made, by means of decrees issued by His Highness the Sultan, for the exercise of jurisdiction over Austrian nationals and property by the British Consular Tribunals.

ARTICLE 105

The Egyptian Government shall have complete liberty of action in regulating the status of Austrian nationals, and the conditions under which they may establish themselves in Egypt.

ARTICLE 106

Austria consents, so far as she is concerned, to the abrogation of the decree issued by His Highness the Khedive on November 28, 1904, relating to the Commission of the Egyptian Public Debt, or to such changes as the Egyptian Government may think it desirable to make therein.

ARTICLE 107

Austria consents, so far as she is concerned, to the transfer to His Britannic Majesty's Government of the powers conferred on His Imperial Majesty the Sultan by the Convention signed at Constantinople on October 29, 1888, relating to the free navigation of the Suez Canal.

She renounces all participation in the Sanitary, Maritime, and Quarantine Board of Egypt and consents, so far as she is concerned, to the transfer to the Egyptian Authorities of the powers of that Board.

ARTICLE 108

All property and possessions in Egypt of the former Austro-Hungarian Monarchy pass to the Egyptian Government without payment.

For this purpose, the property and possessions of the former Austro-Hungarian Monarchy shall be deemed to include all the property of the Crown, and the private property of members of the former Royal Family of Austria-Hungary.

All movable and immovable property in Egypt belonging to Austrian nationals shall be dealt with in accordance with Sections III and IV of Part X (Economic Clauses) of the present Treaty.

ARTICLE 109

Egyptian goods entering Austria shall enjoy the treatment accorded to British goods.

Section III
Siam

ARTICLE 110

Austria recognizes, so far as she is concerned, that all treaties, conventions and agreements between the former Austro-Hungarian Monarchy and Siam, and all rights, title, and privileges derived therefrom, including all rights of extra-territorial jurisdiction, terminated as from July 22, 1917.

ARTICLE 111

Austria, so far as she is concerned, cedes to Siam all her rights over the goods and property in Siam which belonged to the former Austro-Hungarian Monarchy, with the exception of premises used as diplomatic or consular residences or offices as well as the effects and furniture which they contain. These goods and property pass *ipso facto* and without compensation to the Siamese Government.

The goods, property and private rights of Austrian nationals in Siam shall be dealt with in accordance with the provisions of Part X (Economic Clauses) of the present Treaty.

ARTICLE 112

Austria waives all claims against the Siamese Government on behalf of herself or her nationals arising out of the liquidation of Austrian property or the internment of Austrian nationals in Siam. This provision shall not affect the rights of the parties interested in the proceeds of any such liquidation, which shall be governed by the provisions of Part X (Economic Clauses) of the present Treaty.

Section IV
China

ARTICLE 113

Austria renounces, so far as she is concerned, in favor of China all benefits and privileges resulting from the provisions of the final Protocol signed at Peking on September 7, 1901, and from all annexes, notes and documents supplementary thereto. She likewise renounces in favor of China any claim to indemnities accruing thereunder subsequent to August 14, 1917.

ARTICLE 114

From the coming into force of the present Treaty the High Contracting Parties shall apply, in so far as concerns them respectively:

(I) The Arrangement of August 29, 1902, regarding the new Chinese customs tariff;

(2) The Arrangement of September 27, 1905, regarding Whang-Poo, and the provisional supplementary Arrangement of April 4, 1912.

China, however, will not be bound to grant to Austria the advantages or privileges which she allowed to the former Austro-Hungarian Monarchy under these Arrangements.

ARTICLE 115

Austria, so far as she is concerned, cedes to China all her rights over the buildings, wharves and pontoons, barracks, forts, arms and munitions of war, vessels of all kinds, wireless telegraphy installations and other public property which belonged to the former Austro-Hungarian Monarchy, and which are situated or may be in the Austro-Hungarian Concession at Tientsin or elsewhere in Chinese territory.

It is understood, however, that premises used as diplomatic or consular residences or offices, as well as the effects and furniture contained therein, are not included in the above cession, and, furthermore, that no steps shall be taken by the Chinese Government to dispose of the public and private property belonging to the former Austro-Hungarian Monarchy situated within the so-called Legation Quarter at Peking without the consent of the Diplomatic Representatives of the Powers which, on the coming into force of the present Treaty, remain parties to the Final Protocol of September 7, 1901.

ARTICLE 116

Austria agrees, so far as she is concerned, to the abrogation of the leases from the Chinese Government under which the Austro-Hungarian Concession at Tientsin is now held.

China, restored to the full exercise of her sovereign rights in the above area, declares her intention of opening it to international residence and trade. She further declares that the abrogation of the leases under which the said concession is now held shall not affect the property rights of nationals of Allied and Associated Powers who are holders of lots in this concession.

ARTICLE 117

Austria waives all claims against the Chinese Government or against any Allied or Associated Government arising out of the internment of Austrian nationals in China and their repatriation. She equally renounces, so far as she is concerned, all claims arising out of the capture and condemnation of Austro-Hungarian ships in China, or the liquidation, sequestration or control of Austrian properties, rights and interests in that country since August 14, 1917. This provision, however, shall not affect the rights of the parties interested in the proceeds of any such liquidation, which shall be governed by the provisions of Part X (Economic Clauses) of the present Treaty.

In addition to the restrictions on the size of the Austrian army (30,000), the treaty set forth stringent recruiting requirements designed to prevent the government from training personnel and then nominally discharging them in order to circumvent the restrictions on the size of the army:

ARTICLE 125

All officers must be regulars (officers de carrière). Officers now serving who are retained in the army must undertake the obligation to serve in it up to the age of 40 years at least. Officers now serving who do not join the new army will be released from all military obligations; they must not take part in any military exercises, whether theoretical or practical.

Officers newly appointed must undertake to serve on the active list for 20 consecutive years at least.

The number of officers discharged for any reason before the expiration of their term of service must not exceed in any year one-twentieth of the total of officers provided for in Article 120. If this proportion is unavoidably exceeded the resulting shortage must not be made good by fresh appointments.

ARTICLE 126

The period of enlistment for non-commissioned officers and privates must be for a total period of not less than 12 consecutive years, including at least 6 years with the colors.

The proportion of men discharged before the expiration of the period of their enlistment for reasons of health or as a result of disciplinary measures or for any other reasons must not in any year exceed one-twentieth of the total strength fixed by Article 120. If this proportion is unavoidably exceeded, the resulting shortage must not be made good by fresh enlistments.

Heavy limitations were imposed on artillery, many naval vessels were disarmed and converted to merchant ships, and Austria was forbidden to maintain an air force.

Many of the reparations issues were deferred in this treaty until a Reparations Commission made its determinations. The treaty set forth the constitution and mandate of the commission:

Annex II

1

The Commission referred to in Article 179 shall be called the "Reparation Commission" and is hereafter referred to as the "Commission."

2

The Delegates to this Commission shall be appointed by the United States of America, Great Britain, France, Italy, Japan Belgium, Greece, Poland, Romania, the Serb-Croat-Slovene State and Czecho-Slovakia. The United States of America, Great Britain, France, Italy, Japan and Belgium shall each appoint a Delegate. The other five Powers shall appoint a Delegate to represent them all under the conditions indicated in the third sub-paragraph of paragraph 3 hereafter. At the time when each Delegate is appointed there shall also be appointed an Assistant Delegate, who will take his place in case of illness or necessary absence, but at other times will only have the right to be present at the proceedings without taking any part therein.

On no occasion shall Delegates of more than five of the above Powers have the right to take part in the proceedings of the Commission and to record their votes. The Delegates of the United States, Great Britain, France and Italy shall have this right on all occasions. The Delegate of Belgium shall have this right on all occasions other than those referred to below. The Delegate of Japan will have this right when questions relating to damage at sea are under consideration. The Delegate representing the five remaining Powers mentioned above shall have this right when questions relating to Austria, Hungary or Bulgaria are under consideration.

Each of the Governments represented on the Commission shall have the right to withdraw after giving twelve months' notice to the Commission and confirming it six months after the date of the original notification.

3

Such of the Allied and Associated Powers as may be interested shall have the right to name a Delegate to be present and act as assessor only while their respective claims and interests are under examination or discussion, but without the right to vote.

The Section to be established by the Commission under Article 179 shall include representatives of the following Powers: the United States of America, Great Britain, France, Italy, Greece, Poland, Romania, the Serb-Croat-Slovene State and Czecho-Slovakia. This composition of the Section shall in no way prejudge the admissibility of any claims. In voting, the representatives of the United States of America, Great Britain, France and Italy shall each have two votes.

The representatives of the five remaining Powers mentioned above shall appoint a Delegate to represent them all, who shall sit upon the Reparation Commission in the circumstances described in paragraph 2 of the present Annex. This delegate, who shall be appointed for one year, shall be chosen successively from the nationals of each of the said five Powers. . . .

12

The Commission shall have all the powers conferred upon it and shall exercise all the functions assigned to it by the present Treaty.

The Commission shall, in general, have wide latitude as to its control and handling of the whole reparation problem as dealt with in this Part, and shall have authority to interpret its provisions. Subject to the provisions of the present Treaty, the Commission is constituted by the several Allied and Associated Governments referred to in paragraphs 2 and 3 above as the exclusive agency of the said Governments respectively for receiving, selling, holding and distributing the reparation payments to be made by Austria under this Part of the present Treaty. The Commission must comply with the following conditions and provisions:

(a) Whatever part of the full amount of the proved claims is not paid in gold or in ships, securities, commodities or otherwise, Austria shall be required, under such conditions as the Commission may determine, to cover by way of guarantee, by an equivalent issue of bonds, obligations or otherwise, in order to constitute an acknowledgement of the said part of the debt.

(b) In periodically estimating Austria's capacity to pay the Commission shall examine the Austrian system of taxation first, to the end that the sums for reparation which Austria is required to pay shall become a charge upon all her revenues prior to that for the service or discharge of any domestic loan, and, secondly, so as to satisfy itself that in general the Austrian scheme of taxation is fully as heavy proportionately as that of any of the Powers represented on the Commission.

The Reparation Commission shall receive instructions to take account of:

(1) The actual economic and financial position of Austrian territory as delimited by the present Treaty; and

(2) The diminution of its resources and of its capacity for payment resulting from the clauses of the present Treaty.

As long as the position of Austria is not modified the Commission shall take account of these considerations in fixing the final amount of the obligations to be imposed on Austria, the payments by which these are to be discharged, and any postponement of payment of interest which may be asked for by Austria.

(c) The Commission shall, as provided in Article 181, take from Austria, by way of security for and acknowledgment of her debt, gold bearer bonds free of all taxes or charges of every description established or to be established by the Austrian Government or by any authorities subject to it. These bonds will be delivered at any time that may be judged expedient by the Commission, and in three portions, of which the respective amounts will be also fixed by the Commission, the crowns gold being payable in conformity with Article 214 of Part IX (Financial Clauses) of the present Treaty:

(1) A first issue in bearer bonds payable not later than May 1, 1921, without interest. There shall be specially applied to the amortisation of these bonds the payments which Austria is pledged to make in conformity with Article 181, after deduction of the sums used for the reimbursement of the expenses of the armies of occupation and other payments for foodstuffs and raw materials. Such bonds as may not have been redeemed by May 1, 1921, shall then be exchanged for new bonds of the same type as those provided for below (paragraph 12,(c) 2).

(2) A second issue in bearer bonds bearing interest at 2 1/2 per cent. between 1921 and 1926, and thereafter at 5 per cent. with an additional 1 per cent. for amortisation beginning in 1926 on the whole amount of the issue.

(3) An undertaking in writing to issue, when, but not until, the Commission is satisfied that Austria can meet the interest and sinking fund obligations, a further instalment of bearer bonds bearing interest at 5 per cent., the time and mode of payment of principal and interest to be determined by the Commission.

The dates for the payment of interest, the manner of employing the amortisation fund and all other questions relating to the issue, management and regulation of the bond issue shall be determined by the Commission from time to time.

Further issues by way of acknowledgment and security may be required as the Commission subsequently determines from time to time.

In case the Reparation Commission should proceed to fix definitely and no longer provisionally the sum of the common charges to be borne by Austria as a result of the claims of the Allied and Associated Powers, the Commission shall immediately annul all bonds which may have been issued in excess of this sum.

(d) In the event of bonds, obligations or other evidence of indebtedness issued by Austria by way of security for or acknowledgment of her reparation debt being disposed of outright, not by way of pledge, to persons other than the several Governments in whose favor Austria's original reparation indebtedness was created, an amount of such reparation indebtedness shall be deemed to be extinguished corresponding to the nominal value of the bonds, etc., so disposed of outright, and the obligation of Austria in respect of such bonds shall be confined to her liabilities to the holders of the bonds, as expressed upon their face.

(c) The damage for repairing, reconstructing and rebuilding property situated in the invaded and devastated districts, including re-installation of furniture, machinery and other equipment, will be calculated according to the cost at the date when the work is done.

(f) Decisions of the Commission relating to the total or partial cancellation of the capital or interest of any of the verified debt of Austria must be accompanied by a statement of its reasons.

The balance of the treaty covered economic and commercial relations and was, in this, consistent with the Treaty of Versailles.

Consequences

When the Italians began talk of their "mutilated victory" in the Great War, they were referring to the Treaty of St. Germain, and the passions this treaty evoked in Italy helped pave the way for the triumph of Mussolini's Fascists in 1922. Similarly, Adolf Hitler used the treaty in the late 1930s to justify his dismemberment of Czechoslovakia (to protect, he said, Sudeten Germans) and the establishment of the Anschluss (Nazi Germany's annexation of Austria).

TREATY OF NEUILLY

TREATY AT A GLANCE

Completed
November 27, 1919, at Neuilly-sur-Seine, France

Signatories
"Principal Allied Powers" (United States, British Empire [U.K.], France, Italy, and Japan); and the "Associated Powers" (Belgium, China, Cuba, Greece, the Hejaz [part of present-day Saudi Arabia], Poland, Portugal, Romania, the Serb-Croat-Slovene State, Siam, and Czechoslovakia); and Bulgaria

Overview
One of the complex of lengthy treaties concluding World War I, Neuilly officially ended hostilities with Bulgaria, which was compelled to cede territory to Serbia (the Serb-Croat-Slovene State) and Greece

Historical Background

Like the TREATY OF ST. GERMAIN and a series of others, the Treaty of Neuilly (named, as were the others, after the Parisian suburb in which it was signed) accompanied the TREATY OF VERSAILLES (1919), which was the central document in the peace concluding World War I. Like the St. Germain treaty, the Treaty of Neuilly also helped in its way to make official the disintegration of the vast Austro-Hungarian, or Hapsburg, Empire, which had in actuality taken place during October and November 1918.

Having contributed much to the tearing apart of central Europe that led to the war, Bulgaria was about to pay the price of allying itself with Germany during the hostilities. The victors outlined the costs of losing in more than 90 printed pages of provisions attached to the Versailles peace treaty, all applying specifically to Bulgaria.

Terms

Articles 27–35 redrew Bulgaria's borders, giving substantial territory to Serbia (the Serb-Croat-Slovene State) and to Greece. Articles 36–41 compelled Bulgarian recognition of the Serb-Croat-Slovene State and gave residents of territories ceded to the Serb-Croat-Slovene State the option of declaring Bulgarian or Serbian nationality:

ARTICLE 40

Within a period of two years from the coming into force of the present Treaty, Bulgarian nationals over 18 years of age and habitually resident in the territories which are assigned to the Serb-Croat-Slovene State in accordance with the present Treaty will be entitled to opt for their former nationality. Serb-Croat-Slovenes over 18 years of age who are Bulgarian nationals and habitually resident in Bulgaria will have a similar right to opt for Serb-Croat-Slovene nationality.

Option by a husband will cover his wife and option by parents will cover their children under 18 years of age.

Persons who have exercised the above right to opt must within the succeeding twelve months transfer their place of residence to the State for which they have opted.

They will be entitled to retain their immovable property in the territory of the other State where they had their place of residence before exercising their right to opt. They may carry with them their movable property of every description. No export or import duties may be imposed upon them in connection with the removal of such property.

Within the same period Serb-Croat-Slovenes who are Bulgarian nationals and are in a foreign country will be entitled, in the absence of any provisions to the contrary in the foreign law, and if they have not acquired the foreign nationality, to obtain Serb-Croat-Slovene nationality and lose their Bulgarian nationality by complying with the requirements laid down by the Serb-Croat-Slovene State.

Similar articles (42–47) applied to territory ceded to Greece.

Articles 49–57 bound Bulgaria to protect the rights of minorities. Bulgaria further assented to the authority of the League of Nations in matters relating to what nowadays would be called human rights:

Section IV
Protection of Minorities

ARTICLE 49

Bulgaria undertakes that the stipulations contained in this Section shall be recognized as fundamental laws, and that no law, regulation or official action shall conflict or interfere with these stipulations, nor shall any law, regulation or official action prevail over them.

ARTICLE 50

Bulgaria undertakes to assure full and complete protection of life and liberty to all inhabitants of Bulgaria without distinction of birth, nationality, language, race or religion.

All inhabitants of Bulgaria shall be entitled to the free exercise, whether public or private of any creed, religion or belief, whose practices are not inconsistent with public order or public morals.

ARTICLE 51

Bulgaria admits and declares to be Bulgarian nationals *ipso facto* and without the requirement of any formality all persons who are habitually resident within Bulgarian territory at the date of the coming into force of the present Treaty and who are not nationals of any other State.

ARTICLE 52

All persons born in Bulgarian territory who are not born nationals of another State shall *ipso facto* become Bulgarian nationals.

ARTICLE 53

All Bulgarian nationals shall be equal before the law and shall enjoy the same civil and political rights without distinction as to race, language or religion.

Difference of religion, creed or profession shall not prejudice any Bulgarian national in matters relating to the enjoyment of civil or political rights, as for instance admission to public employments, functions and honours, or the exercise of professions and industries.

No restriction shall be imposed on the free use by any Bulgarian national of any language in private intercourse, in commerce, in religion, in the press or in publications of any kind, or at public meetings.

Notwithstanding any establishment by the Bulgarian Government of an official language, adequate facilities shall be given to Bulgarian nationals of non-Bulgarian speech for the use of their language, either orally or in Writing, before the Courts.

ARTICLE 54

Bulgarian nationals who belong to racial, religious or linguistic minorities shall enjoy the same treatment and security in law and in fact as the other Bulgarian nationals. In particular they shall have an equal right to establish, manage and control at their own expense charitable, religious and social institutions, schools and other educational establishments, with the right to use their own language and to exercise their religion freely therein.

ARTICLE 55

Bulgaria will provide in the public educational system in towns and districts in which a considerable proportion of Bulgarian nationals of other than Bulgarian speech are resident adequate facilities for ensuring that in the primary schools the instruction shall be given to the children of such Bulgarian nationals through the medium of their own language. This provision shall not prevent the Bulgarian Government from making the teaching of the Bulgarian language obligatory in the said schools.

In towns and districts where there is a considerable proportion of Bulgarian nationals belonging to racial, religious or linguistic minorities, these minorities shall be assured an equitable share in the enjoyment and application of sums which may be provided out of public funds under the State, municipal or other budgets, for educational, religious or charitable purposes.

ARTICLE 56

Bulgaria undertakes to place no obstacles in the way of the exercise of the right which persons may have under the present Treaty, or under the treaties concluded by the Allied and Associated Powers with Germany, Austria, Hungary, Russia or Turkey, or with any of the Allied and Associated Powers themselves, to choose whether or not they will recover Bulgarian nationality.

Bulgaria undertakes to recognise such provisions as the Principal Allied and Associated Powers may consider opportune with respect to the reciprocal and voluntary emigration of persons belonging to racial minorities.

ARTICLE 57

Bulgaria agrees that the stipulations in the foregoing Articles of this Section, so far as they affect persons belonging to racial, religious or linguistic minorities, constitute obligations of international concern and shall be placed under the guarantee of the League of Nations. They shall not be modified without the assent of a majority of the Council of the League of Nations. The Allied and Associated Powers represented on the Council severally agree not to withhold their assent from any modification in these Articles which is in due form assented to by a majority of the Council of the League of Nations.

Bulgaria agrees that any Member of the Council of the League of Nations shall have the right to bring to the attention of the Council any infraction, or any danger of infraction, of any of these obligations, and that the Council may thereupon take such action and give such direction as it may deem proper and effective in the circumstances.

Bulgaria further agrees that any difference of opinion as to questions of law or fact arising out of these Articles between the Bulgarian Government and any one of the Principal Allied and Associated Powers, or any other Power, a Member of the Council of the League of Nations, shall be held to be a dispute of an international character under Article 14 of the Covenant of the League of Nations. The Bulgarian Government hereby consents that any such dispute shall, if the other party thereto demands, be referred to the Permanent Court of International Justice. The decision of the Permanent Court shall be final and shall have the same force and effect as an award under Article 13 of the Covenant.

Articles 64–104 regulate the Bulgarian military, severely restricting it.

Consequences

In keeping with the Allies' intentions to limit the future war making potential of all the German-allied Central Powers, the Treaty of Neuilly, like its parent Treaty of Versailles, only ensured that Bulgaria in its turn would embrace its local version of Nazism and once more tie itself to the German juggernaut in the next war.

TREATY OF TRIANON

TREATY AT A GLANCE

Completed
June 4, 1920, at Trianon, Versailles, France

Signatories
"Principal Allied Powers" (British Empire [U.K.], France, Italy, and Japan); the "Associated Powers" (United States, Belgium, China, Cuba, Greece, Nicaragua, Panama, Poland, Portugal, Romania, the Serb-Croat-Slovene State, Siam, and Czechoslovakia); and Hungary

Overview
The treaty was one of several that ended World War I. It reduced the area of Hungary from 109,000 square miles to less than 36,000 square miles, severely limited the strength of the Hungarian army, and called for unspecified reparations.

Historical Background

World War I spelled the end of the Austro-Hungarian Empire. The TREATY OF ST. GERMAIN broke up the dual empire, and the Treaty of Trianon—delayed until 1920 by the Communist coup in Hungary—took what was left of Hungary and subtracted three-fourths of it. As with the other peace treaties that followed those concluded at Versailles, the Treaty of Trianon began with the COVENANT OF THE LEAGUE OF NATIONS. The treaty then continued to establish the greatly contracted frontiers of Hungary. To Italy, Hungary renounced "all rights and title which she could claim over the territories of the former Austro-Hungarian Monarchy recognized as forming part of Italy in accordance with [the Treaty of St. Germain]." Similar cessions were made to the Serb-Croat-Slovene State, to Romania, and to Czechoslovakia.

The largely Italian Adriatic port city of Fiume (present-day Rijeka, Croatia), formerly a part of Austria-Hungary, was also renounced, but its disposition was left undecided. It had become a source of dispute between Yugoslavia and Italy, which had received it by the terms of the secret TREATY OF LONDON in 1915. In September 1919 the poet and political activist Gabriele D'Annunzio, leading a band of a thousand legionnaires, "liberated" Fiume and was governing it as self-proclaimed dictator at the time of the Treaty of Trianon. D'Annunzio was displaced in January 1921, when a coalition of political factions assumed control over Fiume.

Terms

In articles similar to those of the Allies' treaty with Bulgaria (TREATY OF NEUILLY), Hungary was bound to protect civil and human rights. The breakup of the Austro-Hungarian Empire and the reduction of Hungary created thorny problems of nationality, which were addressed in Articles 61–66 of the treaty:

Section VII
Clauses Relating to Nationality

ARTICLE 61

Every person possessing rights of citizenship (*pertinenza*) in territory which formed part of the territories of the former Austro-Hungarian Monarchy shall obtain *ipso facto* to the exclusion of Hungarian nationality the nationality of the State exercising sovereignty over such territory.

ARTICLE 62

Notwithstanding the provisions of Article 61, persons who acquired rights of citizenship after January 1, 1910, in territory transferred under the present Treaty to the Serb-Croat-Slovene State, or to the Czecho-Slovak State, will not acquire Serb-Croat-Slovene or Czecho-Slovak nationality without a permit from the Serb-Croat-Slovene State or the Czecho-Slovak State respectively.

If the permit referred to in the preceding paragraph is not applied for, or is refused, the persons concerned will obtain *ipso facto* the nationality of the State exercising sovereignty over the territory in which they previously possessed rights of citizenship.

ARTICLE 63

Persons over 18 years of age losing their Hungarian nationality and obtaining *ipso facto* a new nationality under Article 61 shall be entitled within a period of one year from the coming into force of the present Treaty to opt for the nationality of the State in which they possessed rights of citizenship before acquiring such rights in the territory transferred.

Option by a husband will cover his wife and option by parents will cover their children under 18 years of age.

Persons who have exercised the above right to opt must within the succeeding twelve months transfer their place of residence to the State for which they have opted.

They will be entitled to retain their immovable property in the territory of the other State where they had their place of residence before exercising their right to opt.

They may carry with them their movable property of every description. No export or import duties may be imposed upon them in connection with the removal of such property.

ARTICLE 64

Persons possessing rights of citizenship in territory forming part of the former Austro-Hungarian Monarchy, and differing in race and language from the majority of the population of such territory shall within six months from the coming into force of the present Treaty severally be entitled to opt for Austria, Hungary, Italy, Poland, Roumania, the Serb-Croat-Slovene State, or the Czecho-Slovak State, if the majority of the population of the State selected is of the same race and language as the person exercising the right to opt. The provisions of Article 63 as to the exercise of the right of option shall apply to the right of option given by this Article.

ARTICLE 65

The High Contracting Parties undertake to put no hindrance in the way of the exercise of the right which the persons concerned have under the present Treaty, or under treaties concluded by the Allied and Associated Powers with Germany, Austria or Russia, or between any of the Allied and Associated Powers themselves, to choose any other nationality which may be open to them.

ARTICLE 66

For the purposes of the provisions of this Section, the status of a married woman will be governed by that of her husband, and the status of children under 18 years

of age by that of their parents.

Articles 102–160 specified the reduced strength of the Hungarian armed forces and set a ceiling of 35,000 men on the army.

The amount of war reparations to be assessed was deferred to a later time:

ARTICLE 161

The Allied and Associated Governments affirm and Hungary accepts the responsibility of Hungary and her allies for causing the loss and damage to which the Allied and Associated Governments and their nationals have been subjected as a consequence of the war imposed upon them by the aggression of Austria-Hungary and her allies.

ARTICLE 162

The Allied and Associated Governments recognise that the resources of Hungary are not adequate, after taking into account the permanent diminutions of such resources which will result from other provisions of the present Treaty, to make complete reparation for such loss and damage.

The Allied and Associated Governments, however, require, and Hungary undertakes, that she will make compensation as hereinafter determined for damage done to the civilian population of the Allied and Associated Powers and to their property during the period of the belligerency of each as an Allied and Associated Power against Hungary by the said aggression by land, by sea and from the air, and in general all damage as defined in Annex I hereto.

ARTICLE 163

The amount of such damage for which compensation is to be made by Hungary shall be determined by an Inter-Allied Commission to be called the Reparation Commission . . .

Consequences

In keeping with the Wilsonian principles proclaimed at Versailles, the breakup of Austria-Hungary was supposed to lead to the establishment of national successor states, which the American president had designated as the essence of a "free" world. Instead, the peace created weak countries that made easy prey for the totalitarian governments of the 1930s while sowing the seeds of further ethnic discord in the future of eastern Europe.

TREATY OF SÈVRES

TREATY AT A GLANCE

Completed
August 10, 1920, at Sèvres, France

Signatories
"Principal Allied Powers" (United States, British Empire [U.K.], France, Italy, and Japan) and the "Associated Powers" (Armenia, Belgium, Greece, the Hejaz [part of present-day Saudi Arabia], Poland, Portugal, Romania, the Serb-Croat-Slovene State, and Czechoslovakia) and Turkey

Overview
The treaty was one of several that ended World War I, and, like the others, which treated the Central Powers (Germany and its allies) severely, it was harsh. The Ottoman Empire was formally dissolved, and the Allies largely divided it between themselves. However, the government that agreed to the treaty was almost immediately deposed by Mustafa Kemal, better known as Atatürk.

Historical Background

The Ottoman Empire was one of the first neutrals to join the fray in World War I, and the Young Turks' alliance with the Central Powers was a serious blow to the Entente. It effectively isolated Russia from its Western allies and weakened their hand in the Balkans' capitals. Having lost the Balkans to Europe in 1914, the Turks—under Young Turk leader Enver Pasha—concluded that an Allied victory would likewise lead to a partitioning of their Arab lands even if they remained neutral (Allied negotiations to this effect were already then under way). At least joining the Germans, whose military efficiency they admired, gave them a fighting chance to hang onto what was left of the Ottoman Empire, even perhaps to win some spoils from Russia. Enver also declared a jihad, a holy war, and incited Muslims to rise up against British and Russian rule in India, Persia, and Central Asia. The British paid him back in kind when the Allies began taking Ottoman land during the war by giving a chunk of it away in Palestine to the Jews, not even waiting till war's end before proclaiming their intentions in the BALFOUR DECLARATION.

The Young Turks were wrong about the Russian spoils, of course; those went to others—on the Allied side. But they were right about the partitioning. They had sided with the Germans during World War I and, like the Germans, were severely punished by the treaties ending the war. Here, too, as elsewhere, the Paris peace talks were based on secret war-aims treaties that reflected Allied ambitions in the Middle East, some predating the outbreak of hostilities. But Woodrow Wilson was less willing to challenge these ambitions than he had those of the Italians in the TREATY OF ST. GERMAIN, mostly because he believed the Arabs were not ready for self-rule.

To avoid the taint of imperialism, the victors took control of the spoils under "mandates" from the League of Nations, a prime example of the gap yawning between the high idealism of the peacemakers' rhetoric and the base reality of their actions. The result was the same in either case: the long-tottering and thoroughly corrupt Ottoman Empire was formally dissolved, and the Allies divided much of it between themselves. The straits into the Black Sea were neutralized, and a Greek army of occupation landed at Smyrna (now Izmir). Iraq, Transjordan, and Palestine went to the British, and Syria and Lebanon to the French, as Class A mandates, reserved for lands that were to be "prepared" for independence.

Terms

In most respects the Treaty of Sèvres is similar to the other treaties that followed the TREATY OF VERSAILLES. It begins with the COVENANT OF THE LEAGUE OF NATIONS,

462

and it provides for a restructuring of boundaries, protection of minorities, resolution of nationality, and reduction of military strength. Unlike the other treaties with the Central Powers, it does not assess war reparations. Of greatest particular interest is the neutralization of the commercially and militarily strategic Black Sea straits:

Section II
Straits

ARTICLE 37

The navigation of the Straits, including the Dardanelles, the Sea of Marmora and the Bosphorus, shall in future be open, both in peace and war, to every vessel of commerce or of war and to military and commercial aircraft, without distinction of flag.

These waters shall not be subject to blockade, nor shall any belligerent right be exercised nor any act of hostility be committed within them, unless in pursuance of a decision of the Council of the League of Nations.

ARTICLE 38

The Turkish Government recognises that it is necessary to take further measures to ensure the freedom of navigation provided for in Article 37, and accordingly delegates, so far as it is concerned, to a Commission to be called the "Commission of the Straits," and hereinafter referred to as "the Commission," the control of the waters specified in Article 39.

The Greek Government, so far as it is concerned, delegates to the Commission the same powers and undertakes to give it in all respects the same facilities.

Such control shall be exercised in the name of the Turkish and Greek Governments respectively, and in the manner provided in this Section.

ARTICLE 39

The authority of the Commission will extend to all the waters between the Mediterranean mouth of the Dardanelles and the Black Sea mouth of the Bosphorus, and to the waters within three miles of each of these mouths.

This authority may be exercised on shore to such extent as may be necessary for the execution of the provisions of this Section.

ARTICLE 40

The Commission shall be composed of representatives appointed respectively by the United States of America (if and when that Government is willing to participate), the British Empire, France, Italy, Japan, Russia (if and when Russia becomes a member of the League of Nations), Greece, Roumania, and Bulgaria and Turkey (if and when the two latter States become members of the League of Nations). Each Power shall appoint one representative. The representatives of the United States of America, the British Empire, France, Italy, Japan and Russia shall each have two votes. The representatives of Greece, Roumania, and Bulgaria and Turkey shall each have one vote. Each Commissioner shall be removable only by the Government which appointed him.

ARTICLE 41

The Commissioners shall enjoy, within the limits specified in Article 39, diplomatic privileges and immunities.

ARTICLE 42

The Commission will exercise the powers conferred on it by the present Treaty in complete independence of the local authority. It will have its own flag, its own budget and its separate organisation.

ARTICLE 43

Within the limits of its jurisdiction as laid down in Article 39 the Commission will be charged With the following duties:

(a) the execution of any Works considered necessary for the improvement of the channels or the approaches to harbours;

(b) the lighting and buoying of the channels;

(c) the control of pilotage and towage;

(d) the control of anchorages;

(e) the control necessary to assure the application in the ports of Constantinople and Haidar Pasha of the regime prescribed in Articles 335 to 344, Part XI (Ports, Waterways and Railways) of the present Treaty;

(f) the control of all matters relating to wrecks and salvage;

(g) the control of lighterage;

ARTICLE 44

In the event of the Commission finding that the liberty of passage is being interfered with, it will inform the representatives at Constantinople of the Allied Powers providing the occupying forces provided for in Article 178. These representatives will thereupon concert with the naval and military commanders of the said forces such measures as may be deemed necessary to preserve the freedom of the Straits. Similar action shall be taken by the said representatives in the event of any external action threatening the liberty of passage of the Straits.

ARTICLE 45

For the purpose of the acquisition of any property or the execution of any permanent works which may be required, the Commission shall be entitled to raise such loans as it may consider necessary. These loans will be secured, so far as possible, on the dues to be levied on the shipping using the Straits, as provided in Article 53.

ARTICLE 46

The functions previously exercised by the Constantinople Superior Council of Health and the Turkish Sanitary Administration which was directed by the said Council, and the functions exercised by the National Life-boat Service of the Bosphorus, will within the limits specified in Article 39 be discharged under the control of the Commission and in such manner as it may direct.

The Commission will co-operate in the execution of any common policy adopted by the League of Nations for preventing and combating disease.

ARTICLE 47

Subject to the general powers of control conferred upon the Commission, the rights of any persons or companies now holding concessions relating to lighthouses, docks, quays or similar matters shall be maintained; but the Commission shall be entitled if it thinks it necessary in the general interest to buy out or modify such rights upon the conditions laid down in Article 311, Part IX (Economic Clauses) of the present Treaty, or itself to take up a new concession.

ARTICLE 48

In order to facilitate the execution of the duties with which it is entrusted by this Section, the Commission shall have power to organise such a force of special police as may be necessary. This force shall be drawn so far as possible from the native population of the zone of the Straits and islands referred to in Article 178, Part V (Military, Naval and Air Clauses), excluding the islands of Lemnos, Imbros, Samothrace, Tenedos and Mitylene. The said force shall be commanded by foreign police officers appointed by the Commission.

ARTICLE 49

In the portion of the zone of the Straits, including the islands of the Sea of Marmora, which remains Turkish, and pending the coming into force of the reform of the Turkish judicial system provided for in Article 136, all infringements of the regulations and by-laws made by the Commission, committed by nationals of capitulatory Powers, shall be dealt with by the Consular Courts of the said Powers. The Allied Powers agree to make such infringements justiciable before their Consular Courts or authorities. Infringements committed by Turkish nationals or nationals of non-capitulatory Powers shall be dealt with by the competent Turkish judicial authorities.

In the portion of the said zone placed under Greek sovereignty such infringements will be dealt with by the competent Greek judicial authorities.

ARTICLE 50

The officers or members of the crew of any merchant vessel within the limits of the jurisdiction of the Commission who may be arrested on shore for any offence committed either ashore or afloat within the limits of the said jurisdiction shall be brought before the competent judicial authority by the Commission's police. If the accused was arrested otherwise than by the Commission's police he shall immediately be handed over to them.

ARTICLE 51

The Commission shall appoint such subordinate officers or officials as may be found indispensable to assist it in carrying out the duties with which it is charged.

ARTICLE 52

In all matters relating to the navigation of the waters within the limits of the jurisdiction of the Commission all the ships referred to in Article 37 shall be treated upon a footing of absolute equality.

ARTICLE 53

Subject to the provisions of Article 47 the existing rights under which dues and charges can be levied for various purposes, whether direct by the Turkish Government or by international bodies or private companies, on ships or cargoes within the limits of the jurisdiction of the Commission shall be transferred to the Commission. The Commission shall fix these dues and charges at such amounts only as may be reasonably necessary to cover the cost of the works executed and the services rendered to shipping, including the general costs and expenses of the administration of the Commission, and the salaries and pay provided for in paragraph 3 of the Annex to this Section.

For these purposes only and with the prior consent of the Council of the League of Nations the Commission may also establish dues and charges other than those now existing and fix their amounts.

ARTICLE 54

All dues and charges imposed by the Commission shall be levied without any discrimination and on a footing of absolute equality between all vessels, whatever their port of origin, destination or departure, their flag or ownership, or the nationality or ownership of their cargoes.

This disposition does not affect the right of the Commission to fix in accordance with tonnage the dues provided for by this Section.

ARTICLE 55

The Turkish and Greek Governments respectively undertake to facilitate the acquisition by the Commission of such land and buildings as the Commission shall consider it necessary to acquire in order to carry out effectively the duties with which it is entrusted.

ARTICLE 56

Ships of war in transit through the waters specified in Article 39 shall conform in all respects to the regulations issued by the Commission for the observance of the ordinary rules of navigation and of sanitary requirements.

ARTICLE 57

(1) Belligerent warships shall not revictual nor take in stores, except so far as may be strictly necessary to enable them to complete the passage of the Straits and to reach the nearest port where they can call, nor shall they replenish or increase their supplies of war material or their armament or complete their crews, within the waters under the control of the Commission. Only such repairs as are absolutely necessary to render them seaworthy shall be carried out, and they shall not add in any manner whatever to their fighting force. The Commission shall decide what repairs are necessary, and these must be carried out with the least possible delay.

(2) The passage of belligerent warships through the waters under the control of the Commission shall be effected with the least possible delay, and without any other interruption than that resulting from the necessities of the service.

(3) The stay of such warships at ports within the jurisdiction of the Commission shall not exceed twenty-four hours except in case of distress. In such case they shall be bound to leave as soon as possible. An interval of at least twenty-four hours shall always elapse between the sailing of a belligerent ship from the waters under the control of the Commission and the departure of a ship belonging to an opposing belligerent.

(4) Any further regulations affecting in time of war the waters under the control of the Commission, and relating in particular to the passage of war material and contraband destined for the enemies of Turkey, or revictualling, taking in stores or carrying out repairs in the said waters, will be laid down by the League of Nations.

ARTICLE 58

Prizes shall in all respects be subjected to the same conditions as belligerent vessels of war.

ARTICLE 59

No belligerent shall embark or disembark troops, munitions of war or warlike materials in the waters under the control of the Commission, except in case of accidental hindrance of the passage, and in such cases the passage shall be resumed with all possible despatch.

ARTICLE 60

Nothing in Articles 57, 58 or 59 shall be deemed to limit the powers of a belligerent or belligerents acting in pursuance of a decision by the Council of the League of Nations.

ARTICLE 61

Any differences which may arise between the Powers as to the interpretation or execution of the provisions of this Section, and as regards Constantinople and Haidar Pasha of the provisions of Articles 335 to 344, Part XI (Ports, Waterways, and Railways) shall be referred to the Commission. In the event of the decision of the Commission not being accepted by any Power, the question shall, on the demand of any Power concerned, be settled as provided by the League of Nations, pending whose decision the ruling of the Commission will be carried out.

Consequences

Within two years of the treaty's signing, Atatürk had reconquered Turkish Armenia, which the treaty had declared independent, and had ejected the Greek occupation forces. Atatürk also reoccupied Thrace (European Turkey), which the treaty had given to Greece. This accomplished, Atatürk agreed to abide by most of the other provisions of the Sèvres treaty, and the Allies acquiesced. The Turkish leader İsmet İnönü subsequently concluded the 1923 TREATY OF LAUSANNE, by which the Republic of Turkey was recognized.

TREATY OF RIGA

TREATY AT A GLANCE

Completed
March 18, 1921, at Riga, Poland (present-day Latvia)

Signatories
Poland and Russia and the Ukraine

Overview
The treaty ended the Russo-Polish War of 1919–20—but one theater in the vast Russian civil war—by resolving the Russian-Polish frontier, thus freeing the Red Army to isolate and destroy the remaining pockets of resistance to Bolshevik rule within the borders left Russia by the draconian TREATY OF BREST-LITOVSK.

Historical Background

After German troops withdrew from Poland in accordance with the provisions of the armistice that ended World War I in 1918, Bolshevik (Soviet) troops overran Polish-held territory as far as the Bug River trying to regain lands lost to the Germans under the humiliating Treaty of Brest-Litovsk. In response, by February 1919 General Józef Pilsudski led Polish forces against the Bolshevik "invaders," pushing them back to the Berezina River and into the Ukraine. In the meantime, the Supreme Council of the Allies approved a temporary eastern Polish border within Russia. Bolshevik leaders sought to establish one farther west, along the actual front of the war. For his part, Pilsudski wanted to restore Poland's 18th-century border, which encompassed the Ukraine.

Pilsudski forged an alliance with anti-Bolshevik Ukrainians under Simon Petlyura and captured Kiev during April 25 to May 7, 1920, only to be driven back by a strong Bolshevik counterattack. The Bolsheviks pushed on and reached the outskirts of Warsaw, where they were badly defeated. Once again, Polish armies took the offensive and dealt a severe blow to the Bolsheviks, defeating them on the Vistula River. The Russians agreed to an armistice on October 12, 1920. A preliminary treaty concluded at Riga was made definitive on March 18, 1921.

Terms

By the treaty, the Russians accepted Poland's territorial claims in the east. In addition to Poland's territorial gains, the treaty also exacted Russia's pledge to desist from attempting to extend the revolution:

V

Each of the Contracting Parties mutually undertakes to respect in every way the political sovereignty of the other Party, to abstain from interference in its internal affairs, and particularly to refrain from all agitation, propaganda or interference of any kind, and not to encourage any such movement.

Each of the Contracting Parties undertakes not to create or protect organizations which are formed with the object of encouraging armed conflict against the other Contracting Party or of undermining its territorial integrity, or of subverting by force its political or social institutions, nor yet such organizations as claim to be the Government of the other Party or of a part of the territories of the other Party. The Contracting Parties therefore, undertake to prevent such organizations, their official representatives and other persons connected therewith, from establishing themselves on their territory, and to prohibit military recruiting and the entry into their territory and transport across it of armed forces, arms, munitions, and war material of any kind destined for such organizations.

Consequences

Poland's victories and the Riga agreement effectively halted the spread of the Bolshevik revolution into Central Europe until Stalin's renewed Russian expansion during World War II and its aftermath.

UNITED STATES AND AUSTRIA TREATY OF PEACE

TREATY AT A GLANCE

Completed
August 24, 1921, at Vienna

Signatories
United States and Austria

Overview
While the armistice of November 11, 1918, ended hostilities between the United States and Austria, the U.S. Senate failed to ratify the subsequent major treaties of peace with the Central Powers (because these treaties required membership in the League of Nations, which the United States rejected) and therefore made a separate peace with Austria and the other Central Powers.

Historical Background

The treaty with Austria, officially ending the U.S. hostilities of World War I, was framed in large part as a joint resolution of the U.S. Congress, since the Senate had refused to ratify the settlements reached at the peace conference under the leadership of President Woodrow Wilson.

Terms

The treaty asserts the U.S. right to the benefits of the TREATY OF ST. GERMAIN, which the other Allies concluded with Austria, despite the United States Senate failure to ratify it. The brief document read in full as follows:

Considering that the United States, acting in conjunction with its co-belligerents, entered into an Armistice with Austria-Hungary on November 3, 1918, in order that a Treaty of Peace might be concluded;

Considering that the former Austro-Hungarian Monarchy ceased to exist and was replaced in Austria by a republican Government;

Considering that the Treaty of St. Germain-en-Laye [St. Germain] to which Austria is a party was signed on September 10, 1919, and came into force according to the terms of its Article 381, but has not been ratified by the United States;

Considering that the Congress of the United States passed a Joint Resolution approved by the President July 2, 1921, which reads in part as follows:

"*Resolved by the Senate and House of Representatives of the United States of America in Congress assembled,*

"That the state of war declared to exist between the Imperial and Royal Austro-Hungarian Government and the United States of America by the joint resolution of Congress approved December 7, 1917, is hereby declared at an end.

"SEC. 4. That in making this declaration, and as a part of it, there are expressly reserved to the United States of America and its nationals any and all rights, privileges, indemnities, reparations or advantages, together with the right to enforce the same, to which it or they have become entitled under the terms of the armistice signed November 3, 1918, or any extension or modifications thereof; or which were acquired by or are in the possession of the United States of America by reason of its participation in the war or to which its nationals have thereby become rightfully entitled; or which, under the Treaty of St. Germain-en-Laye or the Treaty of Trianon, have been stipulated for its or their benefit; or to which it is entitled as one of the principal Allied and Associated Powers; or to which it is entitled by virtue of any Act or Acts of Congress; or otherwise.

"SEC. 5. All property of the Imperial German Government, or its successor or successors, and of all German nationals which was on April 6, 1917, in or has since that date come into the possession or under control of, or has been the subject of a demand by the United States of America or of any of its officers, agents, or employees, from any source or by any agency whatsoever, and all property, of the Imperial and Royal Austro-Hungarian Government, or its successor or successors, and of all Austro-Hungarian nationals which was on December 7, 1917, in or has since that date come into the possession or under control of, or has been the subject of a demand by the United States of America or any of its officers, agents, or employees from any source or by any agency whatsoever, shall be retained by the United States of America and no disposition thereof made, except as shall have been heretofore or specifically hereafter shall be provided by law until such time as the Imperial German Government and the Imperial and Royal Austro-Hungarian Government, or their successor or successors, shall have respectively made suitable provision for the satisfaction of all claims against said Governments respectively, of all persons, wheresoever domiciled, who owe permanent allegiance to the United States of America and who have suffered, through the acts of the Imperial German Government or its agents, or the Imperial and Royal Austro-Hungarian Government or its agents since July 31, 1914, loss, damage, or injury to their persons or property, directly or indirectly, whether through the ownership of shares of stock in German, Austro-Hungarian, American, or other corporations, or in consequence of hostilities or of any operations of war, or otherwise and also shall have granted to persons owing permanent allegiance to the United States of America most-favored-nation treatment, whether the same be national or otherwise, in all matters affecting residence, business, profession, trade, navigation, commerce, and industrial property rights and until the Imperial German Government and the Imperial and Royal Austro-Hungarian Government or its successor or successors shall have respectively confirmed to the United States of America all fines, forfeitures, penalties, and seizures imposed or made by the United States of America during the war, whether in respect to the property of the Imperial German Government or German nationals or the Imperial and Royal Austro-Hungarian Government or Austro-Hungarian nationals, and shall have waived any and all pecuniary claims against the United States of America."

Being desirous of establishing securely friendly relations between the two nations;

Have for that purpose appointed their plenipotentiaries:

The President of the United States of America, ARTHUR HUGH FRAZIER, and the Federal President of the Republic of Austria, JOHANN SCHOBER;

Who, having communicated their full powers, found to be in good and due form, have agreed as follows:

ARTICLE I

Austria undertakes to accord to the United States and the United States shall have and enjoy all the rights, privileges, indemnities, reparations or advantages specified in the aforesaid Joint Resolution of the Congress of the United States of July 2, 1921, including all the rights and advantages stipulated for the benefit of the United States in the Treaty of St. Germain-en-Laye which the United States shall fully enjoy notwithstanding the fact that such Treaty has not been ratified by the United States. The United States in availing itself of the rights and advantages stipulated in the provisions of that Treaty, will do so in a manner consistent with the rights accorded to Austria under such provisions.

ARTICLE II

With a view to defining more particularly the obligations of Austria under the foregoing Article with respect to certain provisions in the Treaty of St. Germain-en-Laye, it is understood and agreed between the High Contracting Parties:

(1) That the rights and advantages stipulated in that Treaty for the benefit of the United States which it is intended the United States shall have and enjoy, are those defined in Parts V, VI, VIII, IX, X, XI, XII and XIV.

(2) That the United States shall not be bound by the provisions of Part I of that Treaty nor by any provisions of that Treaty including those mentioned in paragraph (1) of this Article which relate to the Covenant of the League of Nations, nor shall the United States be bound by any action taken by the League of Nations or by the Council or by the Assembly thereof, unless the United States shall expressly give its assent to such action.

(3) That the United States assumes no obligations under or with respect to the provisions of Part II, Part III, Part IV and Part XIII of that Treaty.

(4) That, while the United States is privileged to participate in the Reparation Commission, according to the terms of Part VIII of that Treaty and in any other commission established under the Treaty or under any agreement supplemental thereto, the United States is not bound to participate in any such commission unless it shall elect to do so.

(5) That the periods of time to which reference is made in Article 381 of the Treaty of St. Germain-en-Laye shall run, with respect to any act or election on the part of the United States, from the date of the coming into force of the present Treaty.

ARTICLE III

The present Treaty shall be ratified in accordance with the constitutional forms of the High Contracting Parties and shall take effect immediately on the exchange of ratifications which shall take place as soon as possible at Vienna.

In witness whereof, the respective plenipotentiaries have signed this Treaty and have hereunto affixed their seals.

Done in duplicate in Vienna, this twenty-fourth day of August, 1921.

[SEAL.] ARTHUR HUGH FRAZIER
[SEAL.] SCHOBER

Consequences

The rather hollow victory that the Republicans and isolationist Democrats achieved over Woodrow Wilson was made clear in these haphazardly produced separate peace documents, in which the Congress tried to have it both ways: asserting that the parts of the Paris Peace Conference settlements they agreed with were valid; those they did not like, invalid. In the long run, such actions served little purpose but to undermine an already shaky peace and help ensure the ineffectiveness of the League of Nations (see COVENANT OF THE LEAGUE OF NATIONS) in settling international disputes. Wilson lost the fight for ratification, which cost him his health and perhaps his life, but the opposition victory only helped the coming of a second worldwide 20th-century conflagration, in which their country once again would inevitably become embroiled.

UNITED STATES AND GERMANY TREATY OF PEACE

TREATY AT A GLANCE

Completed
August 25, 1921, at Berlin

Signatories
United States and Germany

Overview
While the armistice of November 11, 1918, ended hostilities between the United States and Germany, the U.S. Senate failed to ratify the subsequent major treaties of peace with the Central Powers (because these treaties required membership in the League of Nations, which the United States rejected) and therefore made a separate peace with Germany and the other Central Powers.

Historical Background

The brief treaty ending war between the United States and Germany was almost identical to that ending war between the United States and Austria (see UNITED STATES AND AUSTRIA TREATY OF PEACE).

Terms

Of greatest significance was the United States's claim to all rights accorded the other Allies by the TREATY OF VERSAILLES (1919), notwithstanding America's failure to ratify that treaty. And, because the United States did not ratify the Versailles document, the present treaty disclaimed many U.S. obligations under the Versailles treaty, even while claiming the rights it granted.

Considering that the United States, acting in conjunction with its co-belligerents, entered into an Armistice With Germany on November 11, 1918, in order that a Treaty of Peace might be concluded;

Considering that the Treaty of Versailles was signed on June 28, 1919, and came into force according to the terms of its Article 440, but has not been ratified by the United States;

Considering that the Congress of the United States passed a Joint Resolution, approved by the President July 2, 1921, which reads in part as follows:

"*Resolved by the Senate and House of Representatives of the United States of America in Congress assembled,*

"That the state of war declared to exist between the Imperial German Government and the United States of America by the joint resolution of Congress approved April 6, 1917, is hereby declared at an end.

"Sec. 2. That in making this declaration, and as a part of it, there are expressly reserved to the United States of America and its nationals any and all rights, privileges, indemnities, reparations, or advantages, together with the right to enforce the same, to which it or they have become entitled under the terms of the armistice signed November 11, 1918, or any extensions or modifications thereof; or which were acquired by or are in the possession of the United States of America by reason of its participation in the war or to which its nationals have thereby become rightfully entitled; or which, under the Treaty of Versailles, have been stipulated for its or their benefit; or to which it is entitled as one of the principal Allied and Associated powers; or to which it is entitled by virtue of any Act or Acts of Congress; or otherwise.

"Sec. 5. All property of the Imperial German Government, or its successor or successors, and of all German nationals, which was, on April 6, 1917, in or has since that date come into the possession or under control of, or has been the subject of a demand by the United States of America or of any of its officers, agents, or employees, from any source or by any agency whatsoever, and all property of the Imperial and Royal Austro-Hungarian Government, or its successor or successors, and of all Austro-Hungarian nationals which was on December 7, 1917, in or has since that date come into the possession or under control of, or has been the subject of a demand by the United States of America or any of its officers, agents, or employees, from any source or by any agency whatsoever, shall be retained by the United States of America and no disposition thereof made, except as shall have been heretofore or specifically hereafter shall have been provided by law until such time as the Imperial German Government and the Imperial and Royal Austro-Hungarian Government, or their successor or successors, shall have respectively made suitable provision for the satisfaction of all claims against said Governments respectively, of all persons, wheresoever domiciled, who owe permanent allegiance to the United States of America and who have suffered, through the acts of the Imperial German Government, or its agents, or the Imperial and Royal Austro-Hungarian Government, or its agents, since July 31, 1914, loss, damage, or injury to their persons or property, directly or indirectly, whether through the ownership of shares of stock in German, Austro-Hungarian, American, or other corporations, or in consequence of hostilities or of any operations of war, or otherwise, and also shall have granted to persons owing permanent allegiance to the United States of America most-favored-nation treatment, whether the same be national or otherwise, in all matters affecting residence, business, profession, trade, navigation, commerce and industrial property rights, and until the Imperial German Government and the Imperial and Royal Austro-Hungarian Government, or their successor or successors, shall have respectively confirmed to the United States of America all fines, forfeitures, penalties, and seizures imposed or made by the United States of America during the war, whether in respect to the property of the Imperial German Government or German nationals or the Imperial and Royal Austro-Hungarian Government or Austro-Hungarian nationals, and shall have waived any and all pecuniary claims against the United States of America."

Being desirous of restoring the friendly relations existing between the two nations prior to the outbreak of war;

Have for that purpose appointed their plenipotentiaries:

The President of the German Empire, Dr. FRIEDRICH ROSEN, Minister for Foreign Affairs, and the President of the United States of America; ELLIS LORING DRESEL, Commissioner of the United States of America to Germany;

Who, having communicated their full powers, found to be in good and due form, have agreed as follows:

ARTICLE I

Germany undertakes to accord to the United States, and the United States shall have and enjoy, all the rights, privileges, indemnities, reparations or advantages specified in the aforesaid Joint Resolution of the Congress of the United States of July 2, 1921, including all the rights and advantages stipulated for the benefit of the United States in the Treaty of Versailles which the United States shall fully enjoy notwithstanding the fact that such Treaty has not been ratified by the United States.

ARTICLE II

With a view to defining more particularly the obligations of Germany under the foregoing Article with respect to certain provisions in the Treaty of Versailles, it is understood and agreed between the High Contracting Parties

(1) That the rights and advantages stipulated in that Treaty for the benefit of the United States, which it is intended the United States shall have and enjoy, are those defined in Section I, of Part IV, and Parts V, VI, VIII, IX, X, XI, XII, XIV and IXV. The United States in availing itself of the rights and advantages stipulated in the provisions of that Treaty mentioned in this paragraph will do so in a manner consistent with the rights accorded to Germany under such provisions.

(2) That the United States shall not be bound by the provisions of Part I of that Treaty, nor by any provisions of that Treaty including those mentioned in paragraph (i) of this Article, which relate to the Covenant of the League of Nations, nor shall the United States be bound by any action taken by the League of Nations, or by the Council or by the Assembly thereof, unless the United States shall expressly give its assent to such action.

(3) That the United States assumes no obligations under or with respect to the provisions of Part II, Part III, Sections 2 to 8 inclusive of Part IV, and Part XIII of that Treaty.

(4) That, while the United States is privileged to participate in the Reparation Commission, according to the terms of Part VIII of that Treaty, and in any other Commission established under the Treaty or under any agreement supplemental thereto, the United States is not bound to participate in any such commission unless it shall elect to do so.

(5) That the periods of time to which reference is made in Article 440 of the Treaty of Versailles shall run, with respect to any act or election on the part of the United States, from the date of the coming into force of the present Treaty.

ARTICLE III

The present Treaty shall be ratified in accordance with the constitutional forms of the High Contracting Parties and shall take effect immediately on the exchange of ratifications which shall take place as soon as possible at Berlin.

IN WITNESS WHEREOF, the respective plenipotentiaries have signed this Treaty and have hereunto affixed their seals.

Done in duplicate in Berlin this twenty-fifth day of August, 1921.

[SEAL.] ROSEN.
[SEAL.] ELLIS LORING DRESEL.

Consequences

By a proclamation of the president signed November 14, 1921, war between the United States and Germany was declared to have terminated July 2, 1921. Whether American support of the Versailles accords would have made any difference to Germany's fate in the interwar years is more doubtful than for other countries, since those accords—even with Woodrow Wilson's palliative presence—remained fixed on punishing the Germans. Perhaps U.S. participation in the League of Nations would have somewhat offset French harshness, as Wilson's did in Paris, but it is hard to see how it would have changed Germany's pariah status or even prevented the rise of a figure like Hitler. What it might well have done, however, would have been to create a diplomatic order much more united than proved to be the case against the kind of international outlawry Hitler began to practice once he came to power.

UNITED STATES AND HUNGARY TREATY OF PEACE

> ## TREATY AT A GLANCE
>
> ### Completed
> August 29, 1921, at Budapest
>
> ### Signatories
> United States and Hungary
>
> ### Overview
> While the armistice of November 11, 1918, ended hostilities between the United States and Austria-Hungary, the U.S. Senate failed to ratify the subsequent major treaties of peace with the Central Powers (because these treaties required membership in the League of Nations, which the United States rejected) and therefore made a separate peace with Hungary (after it had been separated from Austria following the dissolution of the Austro-Hungarian Empire) and the other Central Powers.

Historical Background

Concluded within days following the U.S. treaties with Austria (UNITED STATES AND AUSTRIA TREATY OF PEACE) and Germany (UNITED STATES AND GERMANY TREATY OF PEACE), the Hungarian treaty was identical in principle to those.

Terms

It read as follows:

Considering that the United States, acting in conjunction with its co-belligerents, entered into an Armistice with Austria-Hungary on November 3, 1918, in order that a Treaty of Peace might be concluded;

Considering that the former Austro-Hungarian Monarchy ceased to exist and was replaced in Hungary by a national Hungarian Government;

Considering that the Treaty of Trianon to which Hungary is a party was signed on June 4, 1920, and came into force according to the terms of its Article 364, but has not been ratified by the United States;

Considering that the Congress of the United States passed a Joint Resolution, approved by the President July 2, 1921, which reads in part as follows:

"*Resolved by the Senate and House of Representatives of the United States of America in Congress assembled,*

"That the state of war declared to exist between the Imperial and Royal Austro-Hungarian Government and the United States of America by the joint resolution of Congress approved December 7, 1917, is hereby declared at an end.

"SEC. 4. That in making this declaration, and as a part of it, there are expressly reserved so the United States of America and its nationals any and all rights, privileges, indemnities, reparations, or advantages, together with the right to enforce the same, to which it or they have become entitled under the terms of the armistice signed November 3, 1918, or any extensions or modifications thereof; or which were acquired by or are in the possession of the United States of America by reason of its participation in the war or to which its nationals have thereby become rightfully entitled; or which, under the Treaty of Saint Germain-en-Laye or the Treaty of Trianon, have been stipulated for its or their benefit; or to which it is entitled as one of the principal Allied and Associated powers; or to which it is entitled by virtue of any Act or Acts or Congress; or otherwise.

"SEC. 5. All property of the Imperial German Government, or its successor or successors, and of all German nationals which was, on April 6, 1917, in or has since that date come into the possession or under control of, or has been the subject of a demand by the United States of America or any of its officers, agents, or employees, from any source or by any agency whatsoever, and all property of the Imperial and Royal Austro-Hungarian Government, or its successor or successors, and of all Austro-Hungarian nationals which was on December 7, 1917, in or has since that date come into the possession or under control of, or has been the subject of a demand by the United States of America or any of its officers, agents, or employees, from any source or by any agency whatsoever, shall be retained by the United States of America and no disposition thereof made, except as shall have been heretofore or specifically hereafter shall be provided by law until such time as the Imperial German Government and the Imperial and Royal Austro-Hungarian

Government, or their successor or successors, shall have respectively made suitable provision for the satisfaction of all claims against said Governments respectively, of all persons, wheresoever domiciled, who owe permanent allegiance to the United States of America and who have suffered, through the acts of the Imperial German Government, or its agents, or the Imperial and Royal Austro-Hungarian Government, or its agents, since July 31, 1914, loss, damage, or injury to their persons or property, directly or indirectly, whether through the ownership of shares of stock in German, Austro-Hungarian, American, or other Corporations, or in consequence of hostilities or of any operations of war, or otherwise, and also shall have granted to persons owing permanent allegiance to the United States of America most-favored-nation treatment, whether the same be national or otherwise, in all matters affecting residence, business, profession, trade, navigation, commerce and industrial property rights, and until the Imperial German Government and the Imperial and Royal Austro-Hungarian Government, or their successor or successors, shall have respectively confirmed to the United States of America all fines, forfeitures, penalties, and seizures imposed or made by the United States of America during the war, whether in respect to the property of the Imperial German Government or German nationals or the Imperial Austro-Hungarian Government or Austro-Hungarian nationals, and shall have waived any and all pecuniary claims against the United States of America."

Being desirous of establishing securely friendly relations between the two nations;

Have for that purpose appointed their plenipotentiaries:

The President of the United States of America, U. GRANT SMITH, Commissioner of the United States to Hungary; and Hungary, COUNT NICHOLAS BANFFY, Royal Hungarian Minister for Foreign Affairs;

Who, having communicated their full powers, found to be in good and due form, have agreed as follows:

ARTICLE I

Hungary undertakes to accord to the United States, and the United States shall have and enjoy, all the rights, privileges, indemnities, reparations or advantages specified in the aforesaid Joint Resolution of the Congress of the United States of July 2, 1921, including all the rights and advantages stipulated for the benefit of the United States in the Treaty of Trianon which the United States shall fully enjoy notwithstanding the fact that such Treaty has not been ratified by the United States. The United States, in availing itself of the rights and advantages stipulated in the provisions of that Treaty, will do so in a manner consistent with the rights accorded to Hungary under such provisions.

ARTICLE II

With a view to defining more particularly the obligations of Hungary under the foregoing Article with respect to certain provisions in the Treaty of Trianon, it is understood and agreed between the High Contracting Parties:

(1) That the rights and advantages stipulated in that Treaty for the benefit of the United States, which it is intended the United States shall have and enjoy, are those defined in Parts V, VI, VIII, IX, X, XI, XII and XIV

(2) That the United States shall not be bound by the provisions of Part I of that Treaty, nor by any provisions of that Treaty including those mentioned in paragraph (I) of this Article, which relate to the Covenant of the League of Nations, nor shall the United States be bound by any action taken by the League of Nations, or by the Council or by the Assembly thereof,

(3) That the United States assumes no obligations under or with respect to the provisions of Part II, Part III, Part IV and Part XIII of that Treaty.

(4) That, while the United States is privileged to participate in the Reparation Commission, according to the terms of Part VIII of that Treaty, and in any other commission established under the Treaty or under any agreement supplemental thereto, the United States is not bound to participate in any such commission unless it shall elect to do so.

(5) That the periods of time to which reference is made in Article 364 of the Treaty of Trianon shall run, with respect to any act or election on the part of the United States, from the date of the coming into force of the present Treaty.

ARTICLE III

The present Treaty shall be ratified in accordance with the constitutional forms of the High Contracting Parties and shall take effect immediately on the exchange of ratifications which shall take place as soon as possible at Budapest.

IN WITNESS THEREOF, the respective plenipotentiaries have signed this Treaty and have hereunto affixed their seals.

Done in duplicate in Budapest, this twenty-ninth day of August, 1921.

[SEAL.] U. GRANT-SMITH,
Commissioner of the United States to Hungary
[SEAL.] COUNT NICHOLAS BANFFY,
Royal Hungarian Minister for Foreign Affairs

Consequences

Thus did the United States conclude its involvement in World War I and turn its back on the already tottering peace arrangements. Henceforth, American involvement in Europe during the period between the wars would consist of its efforts to collect on war debts. When the Continent found itself yet again marching toward general war, once more those in Congress who had resisted ratifying the peace believed they could avoid fighting in the coming conflict. Once again, they were wrong.

Multinational Conventions and Agreements

ALGECIRAS CONVENTION

TREATY AT A GLANCE

Completed
April 7, 1906, at Algeciras, Spain

Signatories
Germany, Austria-Hungary, Belgium, Spain, the United States, France, Great Britain, Italy, Morocco, the Netherlands, Portugal, Russia, and Sweden

Overview
The convention was the result of a conference of European diplomats called to settle Germany's challenge to the impending partition of Morocco by France and Spain. Germany's chief motive was to dissolve the Anglo-French Entente of 1904 (see ENTENTE CORDIALE); in fact, as a result of the Algeciras Conference and Convention, the entente became stronger.

Historical Background

Northern Africa became the focus of much European power politics at the beginning of the 20th century. The French had tried and failed to gain control in the Egyptian Sudan in 1898 and so sought to strengthen their hold on Saharan Africa. In 1904 France reached a secret understanding with Spain over the partitioning of the Sultanate of Morocco, while at the same time reaching agreement under the Entente Cordiale with Britain not to oppose her ambitions in Egypt in exchange for a free hand in Morocco. France immediately moved on Morocco, presenting the sultan with a new economic program and a series of so-called political reforms, which basically established French hegemony.

All of this irritated Germany, whose rise to Great Power status had been premised on Britain's "splendid isolation" from the European balance of power. Britain's new rapport with France troubled a number of European countries, but it seemed to unhinge Germany's Kaiser Wilhem II, who arrived in Morocco from Tangiers and, in a dramatic show of imperial power, declared from his yacht on May 31, 1905, that the traditional open-door policy was still in effect concerning Morocco and that he backed her independence and integrity. Perhaps Wilhelm's temper was an indication of the vola-tility surrounding the budding naval arms race

between Britain and Germany, perhaps merely an example of his near-crazed competitive spirit when it came to his English cousin, Britain's King Edward VII. In any case, his actions resulted in an international panic that came to be known as the First Moroccan Crisis.

If the kaiser's hope was that his demonstration of personal pique would prompt England to back down from its recently concluded Entente Cordiale with France, he was to be sorely disappointed. Instead, Wilhelm's action served to draw England and France, traditional rivals, even closer together. The sultan of Morocco requested an international conference at Algeciras from January 16 to April 7, 1906, to resolve what was developing into a crisis that could result in war. The tension was relieved when the German emperor, evidently realizing he had overplayed his hand, prevailed upon U.S. president Theodore Roosevelt to help bring about the conference and to serve as mediator, much as he had the year before when he brought the Russo-Japanese War to an end with the TREATY OF PORTSMOUTH.

Terms

The Algeciras Convention included detailed "chapters" concerning the establishment of a paramilitary police force; the creation of a largely French-controlled state bank; reform of tax laws, customs, anti-smuggling controls, and public works and services administration. The chapter establishing a police force for Morocco is an apt demonstration of how imperialism gains a foothold in an ostensibly sovereign power.

Chapter I
Declaration Relative to the Organization of the Police

I

The conference summoned by His Majesty the Sultan to pronounce on the measures necessary to organize the police declares that the following provisions should be made:

II

The police shall be under the sovereign authority of His Majesty the Sultan. It shall be recruited by the Maghzen from Moorish Mohammedans, commanded by Moorish Kaids, and distributed in the eight ports open to commerce.

III

In order to aid the Sultan in the organization of this police, Spanish officers and noncommissioned officers as instructors, and French officers and noncommissioned officers as instructors, shall be placed at His disposal by their respective Governments, which shall submit their designation to the approval of His Shereefian Majesty. A contract drawn between the Maghzen and these instructors, in conformity to the regulation provided by article IV, shall determine the conditions of their engagement and fix their pay, which must not be less than double of the pay corresponding to the rank of each officer or noncommissioned officer. In addition they will be allowed living expenses, varying according to their residences. Proper lodgings will be placed at their disposal by the Maghzen, which will likewise supply them with their horses and the necessary fodder.

The Governments having jurisdiction over the instructors reserve the right to recall them and replace them by others, accepted and engaged under the same conditions.

IV

These officers and noncommissioned officers for a period of five years, to date from the ratification of the act of the conference, shall give their service to the organization of a body of Shereefian police. They shall assure instruction and discipline in conformity with the regulations to be drawn up in respect thereto. They shall also see that the men enlisted are fit for military service. In a general way they shall supervise the administration of the soldiers and superintend the payment of their salary, which shall be effected by the "Amin," assisted by the accounting officer instructor. They shall extend to the Moorish authorities invested with the command of these bodies their technical aid in the exercise of the said command.

The regulations to assure the recruital, discipline, instruction, and administration of the bodies of police shall be established by mutual agreement between the Shereefian Minister of War or his delegate, the inspector provided by article VII, and the highest ranking French and Spanish instructors.

The regulations shall be submitted to the Diplomatic Body at Tangier, which will formulate its opinion within a month's time. After that period the regulations shall be enforced.

V

The total strength of the police shall not be more than 2,500 men, nor less than 2,000. It shall be distributed, according to the importance of the ports, in groups varying between 150 and 600 men. The number of Spanish and French officers shall be between sixteen and twenty; of Spanish and French noncommissioned officers, between thirty and forty.

VI

The funds necessary to maintain and pay soldiers and officers and noncommissioned officer instructors shall be advanced by the State Bank to the Shereefian Treasury within the limits of the annual budget assigned to the police, which shall not exceed two million and a half pesetas for an effective strength of two thousand five hundred men.

VII

During the same period of five years a general inspection shall be made into the working of the police. Such inspection shall be intrusted by His Shereefian Majesty to a superior officer of the Swiss army, who will be submitted to His approval by the Swiss Federal Government. This officer will be styled Inspector-General and reside at Tangier.

He shall inspect at least once a year the different bodies of the police, and after such inspection he shall draw up a report which he will address to the Maghzen.

In addition to such regular reports, he will, if he regards it as necessary, draw up special reports with reference to the working of the police.

Without directly intervening either in the command or the instruction, the Inspector-General will ascertain the results obtained by the Shereefian police, as regards the maintenance of order and security in the places where this police shall have been established.

VIII

A copy of the reports and communications made to the Maghzen by the Inspector-General, with reference to his mission, shall at the same time be transmitted to the Dean of the Diplomatic Body at Tangier, in order that the Diplomatic Body be enabled to satisfy itself that the Shereefian police acts in conformity to the decisions taken by the conference, and to see whether it guarantees effectively, and in conformity with the treaties, the security of person and property of foreign citizens, subjects, and protégés, as well as that of commercial transactions.

IX

In the case of complaints filed with the Diplomatic Body by the legation concerned, the Diplomatic Body may, upon notice given to the representative of the Sultan, direct the Inspector-General to investigate and report for all available purposes in the matter of such complaints.

X

The Inspector-General shall receive an annual salary of 25,000 francs. In addition, he will be allowed 6,000 francs for the expenses of his tours. The Maghzen will place at his disposal a suitable residence and will look after the maintenance of his horses.

XI

The material conditions of his engagement and of his establishment, as provided by article X, shall be the subject of a contract drawn up between him and the Maghzen. A copy of this contract shall be communicated to the Diplomatic Body.

XII

The staff of instructors of the Shereefian police (officers and noncommissioned officers) shall be Spanish at Tetuan, mixed at Tangier, Spanish at Larache, French at Rabat, mixed at Casablanca, and French in the other three ports.

The United States assented to the convention but, characteristically, excluded itself from what George Washington would have called a "foreign entanglement." The convention concluded:

> The Government of the United States of America, having no political interest in Morocco and no desire or purpose having animated it to take part in this conference other than to secure for all peoples the widest equality of trade and privilege with Morocco and to facilitate the institution of reforms in that country tending to insure complete cordiality of intercourse without and stability of administration within for the common good, declares that, in acquiescing in the regulations and declarations of the conference, in becoming a signatory to the General Act of Algeciras and to the Additional Protocol, subject to ratification according to constitutional procedure, and in accepting the application of those regulations and declarations to American citizens and interests in Morocco, it does so without assuming obligations or responsibility for the enforcement thereof.

In Executive Session, Senate of the United States.

Resolved (two-thirds of the Senators present concurring therein), That the Senate advise and consent to the ratification of the general act and an additional protocol, signed on April 7, 1906, by the delegates of the powers represented at the conference which met at Algeciras, Spain, to consider Moroccan affairs.

Resolved further, That the Senate, as a part of this act of ratification, understands that the participation of the United States in the Algeciras conference and in the formation and adoption of the general act and protocol which resulted therefrom, was with the sole purpose of preserving and increasing its commerce in Morocco, the protection as to life, liberty, and property of its citizens residing or traveling therein, and of aiding by its friendly offices and efforts, in removing friction and controversy which seemed to menace the peace between powers signatory with the United States to the treaty of 1880, all of which are on terms of amity with this Government; and without purpose to depart from the traditional American foreign policy which forbids participation by the United States in the settlement of political questions which are entirely European in their scope.

Consequences

Since the conference included an affirmation of the independence of Morocco, Germany was, on the surface, placated; but France was accorded much control of this "independent" country, including regulation of the Moroccan police and finances, just as she had planned all along. Contrary to German expectations, only Austria-Hungary had backed the German position at the conference, while Italy, Russia, and, more importantly, Britain and the United States had lined up behind France.

For the true significance of the conference lay precisely here, in this substantial diplomatic support for France from the two English-speaking powers. Algeciras foreshadowed their actions in World War I, for which the Moroccon Crisis was a prelude. Wilhelm intervened again in the region in 1911, by sending a gunboat to Agadir after French forces punitively occupied the Moroccan capital of Fez. Faced with the same alliance, Germany backed down completely during this second crisis, and recognized French rights in Morocco. In 1912 most of the area became a French protectorate. Soon after, of course, the two countries were fighting the world war over the Balkans that they had avoided fighting over Morocco.

HAGUE CONVENTION (1907)

TREATY AT A GLANCE

Completed
October 18, 1907, at the Hague, Netherlands

Signatories
Argentina*, Austria-Hungary, Belgium, Bolivia*, Brazil*, Bulgaria, Chile*, China, Colombia*, Cuba*, Denmark, Dominican Republic*, Ecuador*, France, Germany, Great Britain, Greece, Guatemala,* Haiti,* Holland***, Italy, Japan, Luxembourg, Mexico, Montenegro, Nicaragua*, Norway**, Panama*, Paraguay*, Persia, Peru*, Portugal, Romania, Russia, El Salvador*, Serbia, Siam, Spain, Sweden**, Switzerland, Turkey, United States, Uruguay*, and Venezuela*

Overview
Like the Hague Conference of 1899, the Hague Conference of 1907 was called by Czar Nicholas II of Russia. The convention produced by the second conference amplified and extended the provisions for international arbitration of disputes as set forth in the HAGUE CONVENTION (1899).

Historical Background

Before the turn of the 20th century, a liberal peace movement with a middle-class constituency had sprung up worldwide, perhaps in response to the tensions of the naval arms race primarily between Great Britain and Germany, but also involving such newcomers as Japan and the United States, which was destabilizing the balance of power in Europe and, increasingly, fueling the threat of general war. By 1900, historians have estimated, somewhere in the realm of 500 world peace organizations existed, half of them in Scandinavia, but many in such Great Power strongholds as Germany, Great Britain, and the United States. The movement's crowning achievements were the Hague Conferences, the first in 1899 (see the Hague Convention 1899), the second in 1907.

While the 1899 conference succeeded in outlawing some inhumane weapons and establishing important conventions of warfare, it made no progress toward general disarmament. By 1907, with the dangers of the arms race growing each year in such crises as the Russo-Japanese War of 1904 (see the TREATY OF

*Did not sign the Hague Convention 1899
**Norway and Sweden signed the Hague Convention 1899 as United Kingdoms of Sweden and Norway
***Holland signed the Hague Convention 1899 as the Netherlands

PORTSMOUTH) and the First Moroccan Crisis of 1905 (see the ALGECIRAS CONVENTION), the parties were ready to try again.

Terms

Part 2 of the convention, addressing "Good Office and Mediation," was virtually identical to Title 2 of the 1899 document, except that the signatories were now referred to as "Contracting Powers" rather than "Signatory Powers," suggesting a desire to foster a greater spirit of comity among the signatories. The constitution and operation of international commissions of inquiry were specified in greater detail than in the earlier document.

PART III
INTERNATIONAL COMMISSIONS OF INQUIRY

ARTICLE IX

In disputes of an international nature involving neither honor nor vital interests, and arising from a difference of opinion on points of fact, the Contracting Powers deem it expedient and desirable that the parties who have not been able to come to an agreement by means of diplomacy, should, as far as circumstances allow, institute an International Commission of Inquiry, to facilitate a solution of these disputes by elucidating the facts by means of an impartial and conscientious investigation.

ARTICLE X

International Commissions of Inquiry are constituted by special agreement between the parties in dispute.

The Inquiry Convention defines the facts to be examined; it determines the mode and time in which the Commission is to be formed and the extent of the powers of the Commissioners.

It also determines, if there is need, where the Commission is to sit, and whether it may remove to another place, the language the Commission shall use and the languages the use of which shall be authorized before it, as well as the date on which each party must deposit its statement of facts, and, generally speaking, all the conditions upon which the parties have agreed.

If the parties consider it necessary to appoint Assessors, the Convention of Inquiry shall determine the mode of their selection and the extent of their powers.

ARTICLE XI

If the Inquiry Convention has not determined where the Commission is to sit, it will sit at The Hague.

The place of meeting, once fixed, cannot be altered by the Commission except with the assent of the parties.

If the Inquiry Convention has not determined what languages are to be employed, the question shall be decided by the Commission.

ARTICLE XII

Unless an undertaking is made to the contrary, Commissions of Inquiry shall be formed in the manner determined by Articles XLV and LVII of the present Convention.

ARTICLE XIII

Should one of the Commissioners or one of the Assessors, should there be any, either die, or resign, or be unable for any reason whatever to discharge his functions, the same procedure is followed for filling the vacancy as was followed for appointing him.

ARTICLE XIV

The parties are entitled to appoint special agents to attend the Commission of Inquiry, whose duty it is to represent them and to act as intermediaries between them and the Commission.

They are further authorized to engage counsel or advocates, appointed by themselves, to state their case and uphold their interests before the Commission.

ARTICLE XV

The International Bureau of the Permanent Court of Arbitration acts as registry for the Commissions which sit at The Hague, and shall place its offices and staff at the disposal of the Contracting Powers for the use of the Commission of Inquiry.

ARTICLE XVI

If the Commission meets elsewhere than at The Hague, it appoints a Secretary-General, whose office serves as registry.

It is the function of the registry, under the control of the President, to make the necessary arrangements for the sittings of the Commission, the preparation of the Minutes, and, while the inquiry lasts, for the charge of the archives, which shall subsequently be transferred to the International Bureau at The Hague.

ARTICLE XVII

In order to facilitate the constitution and working of Commissions of Inquiry, the Contracting Powers recommend the following rules, which shall be applicable to the inquiry procedure in so far as the parties do not adopt other rules.

ARTICLE XVIII

The Commission shall settle the details of the procedure not covered by the special Inquiry Convention or the present Convention, and shall arrange all the formalities required for dealing with the evidence.

ARTICLE XIX

On the inquiry both sides must be heard.

At the dates fixed, each party communicates to the Commission and to the other party the statements of facts, if any, and, in all cases, the instruments, papers, and documents which it considers useful for ascertaining the truth, as well as the list of witnesses and experts whose evidence it wishes to be heard.

ARTICLE XX

The Commission is entitled, with the assent of the Powers, to move temporarily to any place where it considers it may be useful to have recourse to this means of inquiry or to send one or more of its members. Permission must be obtained from the State on whose territory it is proposed to hold the inquiry.

ARTICLE XXI

Every investigation, and every examination of a locality, must be made in the presence of the agents and counsel of the parties or after they have been duly summoned.

ARTICLE XXII

The Commission is entitled to ask from either party for such explanations and information as it considers necessary.

ARTICLE XXIII

The parties undertake to supply the Commission of Inquiry, as fully as they may think possible, with all means and facilities necessary to enable it to become completely acquainted with, and to accurately understand, the facts in question.

They undertake to make use of the means at their disposal, under their municipal law, to insure the appearance of the witnesses or experts who are in their territory and have been summoned before the Commission.

If the witnesses or experts are unable to appear before the Commission, the parties will arrange for their evidence to be taken before the qualified officials of their own country.

ARTICLE XXIV

For all notices to be served by the Commission in the territory of a third Contracting Power, the Commission shall apply direct to the Government of the said power. The same rule applies in the case of steps being taken on the spot to procure evidence.

The requests for this purpose are to be executed so far as the means at the disposal of the Power applied to under its municipal law allow. They cannot be rejected unless the Power in question considers they are calculated to impair its sovereign rights or its safety.

The Commission will equally be always entitled to act through the Power on whose territory it sits.

ARTICLE XXV

The witnesses and experts are summoned on the request of the parties or by the Commission of its own motion, and, in every case, through the Government of the State in whose territory they are.

The witnesses are heard in succession and separately, in the presence of the agents and counsel, and in the order fixed by the Commission.

ARTICLE XXVI

The examination of witnesses is conducted by the President.

The members of the Commission may however put to each witness questions which they consider likely to throw light on and complete his evidence, or get information on any point concerning the witness within the limits of what is necessary in order to get at the truth.

The agents and counsel of the parties may not interrupt the witness when he is making his statement, nor put any direct question to him, but they may ask the President to put such additional questions to the witness as they think expedient.

ARTICLE XXVII

The witness must give his evidence without being allowed to read any written draft. He may, however, be permitted by the President to consult notes or documents if the nature of the facts referred to necessitates their employment.

ARTICLE XXVIII

A Minute of the evidence of the witness is drawn up forthwith and read to the witness. The latter may make such alterations and additions as he thinks necessary, which will be recorded at the end of his statement.

When the whole of his statement has been read to the witness, he is asked to sign it.

ARTICLE XXIX

The agents are authorized, in the course of or at the close of the inquiry, to present in writing to the Commission and to the other party such statements, requisitions, or summaries of the facts as they consider useful for ascertaining the truth.

ARTICLE XXX

The Commission considers its decisions in private and the proceedings are secret.

All questions are decided by a majority of the members of the Commission.

If a member declines to vote, the fact must be recorded in the Minutes.

ARTICLE XXXI

The sittings of the Commission are not public, nor the Minutes and documents connected with the inquiry published except in virtue of a decision of the Commission taken with the consent of the parties.

ARTICLE XXXII

After the parties have presented all the explanations and evidence, and the witnesses have all been heard, the President declares the inquiry terminated, and the Commission adjourns to deliberate and to draw up its Report.

ARTICLE XXXIII

The Report is signed by all the members of the Commission.

If one of the members refuses to sign, the fact is mentioned; but the validity of the Report is not affected.

ARTICLE XXXIV

The Report of the Commission is read at a public sitting, the agents and counsel of the parties being present or duly summoned.

A copy of the Report is given to each party.

ARTICLE XXXV

The Report of the Commission is limited to a statement of facts, and has in no way the character of an Award. It leaves to the parties entire freedom as to the effect to be given to the statement.

ARTICLE XXXVI

Each party pays its own expenses and an equal share of the expenses incurred by the Commission.

Likewise, the constitution and procedures of the Permanent Court of Arbitration are more fully spelled out, and, most significantly, a special procedure for summary arbitration is established.

ARTICLE XLI

With the object of facilitating an immediate recourse to arbitration for international differences, which it has not been possible to settle by diplomacy, the Contracting Powers undertake to maintain the Permanent Court of Arbitration, as established by the First Peace Conference, accessible at all times, and operating, unless otherwise stipulated by the parties, in accordance with the rules of procedure inserted in the present Convention.

ARTICLE XLII

The Permanent Court is competent for all arbitration cases, unless the parties agree to institute a special Tribunal.

ARTICLE XLIII

The Permanent Court sits at The Hague.

An International Bureau serves as registry for the Court. It is the channel for communications relative to the meetings of the Court; it has charge of the archives and conducts all the administrative business.

The Contracting Powers undertake to communicate to the Bureau, as soon as possible, a certified copy of any conditions of arbitration arrived at between them and of any Award concerning them delivered by a special Tribunal.

They likewise undertake to communicate to the Bureau the laws, regulations, and documents eventually showing the execution of the Awards given by the Court.

ARTICLE XLIV

Each Contracting Power selects four persons at the most, of known competency in question of international law, of the highest moral reputation, and disposed to accept the duties of Arbitrator.

The persons thus selected are inscribed, as members of the Court, in a list which shall be notified to all the Contracting Powers by the Bureau.

Any alteration in the list of Arbitrators is brought by the Bureau to the knowledge of the Contracting Powers.

Two or more Powers may agree on the selection in common of one or more members.

The same person can be selected by different Powers. The members of the Court are appointed for a term of six years. These appointments are renewable.

Should a member of the Court die or resign, the same procedure is followed for filling the vacancy as was followed for appointing him. In this case the appointment is made for a fresh period of six years.

ARTICLE XLV

When the Contracting Powers wish to have recourse to the Permanent Court for the settlement of a difference which has arisen between them, the Arbitrators called upon to form the Tribunal with jurisdiction to decide this difference must be chosen from the general list of members of the Court.

Failing the direct agreement of the parties on the composition of the Arbitration Tribunal, the following course shall be pursued:—

Each party appoints two Arbitrators, of whom one only can be its national or chosen from among the persons selected by it as members of the Permanent Court. These Arbitrators together choose an Umpire.

If the votes are equally divided, the choice of the Umpire is intrusted to a third Power, selected by the parties by common accord.

If an agreement is not arrived at on this subject each party selects a different Power, and the choice of the Umpire is made in concert by the Powers thus selected.

If, within two months' time, these two Powers cannot come to an agreement, each of them presents two candidates taken from the list of members of the Permanent Court, exclusive of the members selected by the parties and not being nationals of either of them. Drawing lots determines which of the candidates thus presented shall be Umpire.

ARTICLE XLVI

The Tribunal being thus composed, the parties notify to the Bureau their determination to have recourse to the Court, the text of their "Compromise," and the names of the Arbitrators.

The Bureau communicates without delay to each Arbitrator the "Compromise," and the names of the other members of the Tribunal.

The Tribunal assembles at the date fixed by the parties. The Bureau makes the necessary arrangements for the meeting.

The members of the Tribunal, in the exercise of their duties and out of their own country, enjoy diplomatic privileges and immunities.

ARTICLE XLVII

The Bureau is authorized to place its offices and staff at the disposal of the Contracting Powers for the use of any special Board of Arbitration.

The jurisdiction of the Permanent Court may, within the conditions laid down in the regulations, be extended to disputes between non-Contracting Powers or between Contracting Powers and non-Contracting Powers, if the parties are agreed on recourse to this Tribunal.

ARTICLE XLVIII

The Contracting Powers consider it their duty, if a serious dispute threatens to break out between two or more of them, to remind these latter that the Permanent Court is open to them.

Consequently, they declare that the fact of reminding the parties at variance of the provisions of the present Convention, and the advice given to them, in the highest interests of peace, to have recourse to the Permanent Court, can only be regarded as friendly actions.

In case of dispute between two Powers, one of them can always address to the International Bureau a note containing a declaration that it would be ready to submit the dispute to arbitration.

The Bureau must at once inform the other Power of the declaration.

ARTICLE XLIX

The Permanent Administrative Council, composed of the Diplomatic Representatives of the Contracting Powers accredited to The Hague and of the Netherlands Minister for Foreign Affairs, who will act as President, is charged with the direction and control of the International Bureau.

The Council settles its rules of procedure and all other necessary regulations.

It decides all questions of administration which may arise with regard to the operations of the Court.

It has entire control over the appointment, suspension, or dismissal of the officials and employees of the Bureau.

It fixes the payments and salaries, and controls the general expenditure.

At meetings duly summoned, the presence of nine members is sufficient to render valid the discussions of the Council. The decisions are taken by a majority of votes.

The Council communicates to the Contracting Powers without delay the regulations adopted by it. It furnishes them with an annual Report on the labors of the Court, the working of the administration, and the expenditure. The Report likewise contains a resume of what is important in the documents communicated to the Bureau by the Powers in virtue of Article XLIII, paragraphs 3 and 4.

ARTICLE L

The expenses of the Bureau shall be borne by the Contracting Powers in the proportion fixed for the International Bureau of the Universal Postal Union.

The expenses to be charged to the adhering Powers shall be reckoned from the date on which their adhesion comes into force.

CHAPTER III Arbitration Procedure

ARTICLE LI

With a view to encouraging the development of arbitration, the Contracting Powers have agreed on the following rules, which are applicable to arbitration procedure, unless other rules have been agreed on by the parties.

ARTICLE LII

The Powers which have recourse to arbitration sign a "Compromise," in which the subject of the dispute is clearly defined, the time allowed for appointing Arbitrators, the form, order, and time in which the communication referred to in Article LXIII must be made, and the amount of the sum which each party must deposit in advance to defray the expenses.

The "Compromise" likewise defines, if there is occasion, the manner of appointing Arbitrators, any special powers which may eventually belong to the Tribunal, where it shall meet, the language it shall use, and the languages the employment of which shall be authorized before it, and, generally speaking, all the conditions on which the parties are agreed.

ARTICLE LIII

The Permanent Court is competent to settle the "Compromise," if the parties are agreed to have recourse to it for the purpose.

It is similarly competent, even if the request is only made by one of the parties, when all attempts to reach an understanding through the diplomatic channel have failed, in the case of:—

1. A dispute covered by a general Treaty of Arbitration concluded or renewed after the present Convention has come into force, and providing for a "Compromise" in all disputes and not either explicitly or implicitly excluding the settlement of the "Compromise" from the competence of the Court. Recourse cannot, however, be had to the Court if the other party declares that in its opinion the dispute does not belong to the category of disputes which can be submitted to compulsory arbitration, unless the Treaty of Arbitration confers upon the Arbitration Tribunal the power of deciding this preliminary question.

2. A dispute arising from contract debts claimed from one Power by another Power as due to its nationals, and for the settlement of which the offer of arbitration has been accepted. This arrangement is not applicable if acceptance is subject to the condition that the "Compromise" should be settled in some other way.

ARTICLE LIV

In the cases contemplated in the preceding Article, the "Compromise" shall be settled by a Commission consisting of five members selected in the manner arranged for in Article XLV, paragraphs 3 to 6.

The fifth member is President of the Commission *ex officio*.

ARTICLE LV

The duties of Arbitrator may be conferred on one Arbitrator alone or on several Arbitrators selected by the parties as they please, or chosen by them from the members of the Permanent Court of Arbitration established by the present Convention.

Failing the constitution of the Tribunal by direct agreement between the parties, the course referred to in Article XLV, paragraphs 3 to 6, is followed.

ARTICLE LVI

When a Sovereign or the Chief of a State is chosen as Arbitrator, the arbitration procedure is settled by him.

ARTICLE LVII

The Umpire is President of the Tribunal *ex officio*.

When the Tribunal does not include an Umpire, it appoints its own President.

ARTICLE LVIII

When the "Compromise" is settled by a Commission, as contemplated in Article LIV, and in the absence of an agreement to the contrary, the Commission itself shall form the Arbitration Tribunal.

ARTICLE LIX

Should one of the Arbitrators either die, retire, or be unable for any reason whatever to discharge his functions, the same procedure is followed for filling the vacancy as was followed for appointing him.

ARTICLE LX

The Tribunal sits at The Hague, unless some other place is selected by the parties.

The Tribunal can only sit in the territory of a third Power with the latter's consent.

The place of meeting once fixed cannot be altered by the Tribunal, except with the consent of the parties.

ARTICLE LXI

If the question as to what languages are to be used has not been settled by the "Compromise," it shall be decided by the Tribunal.

ARTICLE LXII

The parties are entitled to appoint special agents to attend the Tribunal to act as intermediaries between themselves and the Tribunal.

They are further authorized to retain for the defence of their rights and interests before the Tribunal counsel or advocates appointed by themselves for this purpose.

The members of the Permanent Court may not act as agents, counsel, or advocates except on behalf of the Power which appointed them members of the Court.

ARTICLE LXIII

As a general rule, arbitration procedure comprises two distinct phases: pleadings and oral discussions.

The pleadings consist in the communication by the respective agents to the members of the Tribunal and the opposite party of cases, counter-cases, and, if necessary, of replies; the parties annex thereto all papers and documents called for in the case. This communication shall be made either directly or through the intermediary of the International Bureau, in the order and within the time fixed by the "Compromise."

The time fixed by the "Compromise" may be extended by mutual agreement by the parties, or by the Tribunal when the latter considers it necessary for the purpose of reaching a just decision.

The discussions consist in the oral development before the Tribunal of the arguments of the parties.

ARTICLE LXIV

A certified copy of every document produced by one party must be communicated to the other party.

ARTICLE LXV

Unless special circumstances arise, the Tribunal does not meet until the pleadings are closed.

ARTICLE LXVI

The discussions are under the control of the President.

They are only public if it be so decided by the Tribunal, with the assent of the parties.

They are recorded in minutes drawn up by the Secretaries appointed by the President. These minutes are signed by the President and by one of the Secretaries and alone have an authentic character.

ARTICLE LXVII

After the close of the pleadings, the Tribunal is entitled to refuse discussion of all new papers or documents which one of the parties may wish to submit to it without the consent of the other party.

ARTICLE LXVIII

The Tribunal is free to take into consideration new papers or documents to which its attention may be drawn by the agents or counsel of the parties.

In this case, the Tribunal has the right to require the production of these papers or documents but is obliged to make them known to the opposite party.

ARTICLE LXIX

The Tribunal can, besides, require from the agents of the parties the production of all papers, and can demand all necessary explanations. In case of refusal the Tribunal takes note of it.

ARTICLE LXX

The agents and the counsel of the parties are authorized to present orally to the Tribunal all the arguments they may consider expedient in defence of their case.

ARTICLE LXXI

They are entitled to raise objections and points. The decisions of the Tribunal on these points are final and cannot form the subject of any subsequent discussion.

ARTICLE LXXII

The members of the Tribunal are entitled to put questions to the agents and counsel of the parties and to ask them for explanations on doubtful points.

Neither the questions put, nor the remarks made by members of the Tribunal in the course of the discussions, can be regarded as an expression of opinion by the Tribunal in general or by its members in particular.

ARTICLE LXXIII

The Tribunal is authorized to declare its competence in interpreting the "Compromise," as well as the other Treaties which may be invoked, and in applying the principles of law.

ARTICLE LXXIV

The Tribunal is entitled to issue rules of procedure for the conduct of the case, to decide the forms, order, and time in which each party must conclude its arguments, and to arrange all the formalities required for dealing with the evidence.

ARTICLE LXXV

The parties undertake to supply the Tribunal, as fully as they consider possible, with all the information required for deciding the case.

ARTICLE LXXVI

For all notices which the Tribunal has to serve in the territory of a third Contracting Power, the Tribunal shall apply direct to the Government of that Power. The same rule applies in the case of steps being taken to procure evidence on the spot.

The requests for this purpose are to be executed as far as the means at the disposal of the Power applied to under its municipal law allow. They cannot be rejected unless the Power in question considers them calculated to impair its own sovereign rights or its safety.

The Court will equally be always entitled to act through the Power on whose territory it sits.

ARTICLE LXXVII

When the agents and counsel of the parties have submitted all the explanations and evidence in support of their case the President shall declare the discussion closed.

ARTICLE LXXVIII

The Tribunal considers its decisions in private and the proceedings remain secret.

All questions are decided by a majority of the members of the Tribunal.

ARTICLE LXXIX

The Award must give the reasons on which it is based. It contains the names of the Arbitrators; it is signed by the President and Registrar or by the Secretary acting as Registrar.

ARTICLE LXXX

The Award is read out in public sitting, the agents and counsel of the parties being present or duly summoned to attend.

ARTICLE LXXXI

The Award, duly pronounced and notified to the agents of the parties, settles the dispute definitively and without appeal.

ARTICLE LXXXII

Any dispute arising between the parties as to the interpretation and execution of the Award shall, in the absence of an Agreement to the contrary, be submitted to the Tribunal which pronounced it.

ARTICLE LXXXIII

The parties can reserve in the "Compromise" the right to demand the revision of the Award.

In this case and unless there be an Agreement to the contrary, the demand must be addressed to the Tribunal which pronounced the Award. It can only be made on the ground of the discovery of some new fact calculated to exercise a decisive influence upon the Award and which was unknown to the Tribunal and to the party which demanded the revision at the time the discussion was closed.

Proceedings for revision can only be instituted by a decision of the Tribunal expressly recording the existence of the new fact, recognizing in it the character described in the preceding paragraph, and declaring the demand admissible on this ground.

The "Compromise" fixes the period within which the demand for revision must be made.

ARTICLE LXXXIV

The Award is not binding except on the parties in dispute.

When it concerns the interpretation of a Convention to which Powers other than those in dispute are parties, they shall inform all the Signatory Powers in good time. Each of these Powers is entitled to intervene in the case. If one or more avail themselves of this right, the interpretation contained in the Award is equally binding on them.

ARTICLE LXXXV

Each party pays its own expenses and an equal share of the expenses of the Tribunal.

CHAPTER IV Arbitration by Summary Procedure

ARTICLE LXXXVI

With a view to facilitating the working of the system of arbitration in disputes admitting of a summary procedure, the Contracting Powers adopt the following rules, which shall be observed in the absence of other arrangements and subject to the reservation that the provisions of Chapter III apply so far as may be.

ARTICLE LXXXVII

Each of the parties in dispute appoints an Arbitrator. The two Arbitrators thus selected choose an Umpire. If they do not agree on this point, each of them proposes two candidates taken from the general list of the members of the Permanent Court exclusive of the members appointed by either of the parties and not being nationals of either of them; which of the candidates thus proposed shall be the Umpire is determined by lot.

The Umpire presides over the Tribunal, which gives its decisions by a majority of votes.

ARTICLE LXXXVIII

In the absence of any previous agreement the Tribunal, as soon as it is formed, settles the time within which the two parties must submit their respective cases to it.

ARTICLE LXXXIX

Each party is represented before the Tribunal by an agent, who serves as intermediary between the Tribunal and the Government who appointed him.

ARTICLE XC

The proceedings are conducted exclusively in writing. Each party, however, is entitled to ask that witnesses and experts should be called. The Tribunal has, for its part, the right to demand oral explanations from the agents of the two parties, as well as from the experts and witnesses whose appearance in Court it may consider useful.

Consequences

Like the earlier conference, the second Hague meeting failed to arrive at any workable scheme of disarmament or arms reduction. In substance, the principles and procedures for peacefully arbitrating international disputes were the same as those enumerated in the earlier convention. Although 17 additional nations—all South and Central American, except for Haiti—subscribed to the 1907 convention, the grim logic of the arms race was outrunning the idealistic logic of disarmament, as the predicament of Sir Edward Grey illustrated.

Britain's Liberal foreign secretary, Grey was the one European statesman most sympathetic to the peace movements. Swayed by the Hague Conferences, Grey made several overtures to Germany in hopes of ending the naval arms race, citing the waste, international tension, and social discord it caused. But these arguments failed to find sympathetic ears in Kaiser Wilhelm's Germany, and Grey concluded that Britain had little choice but to escalate the race. Even more radical liberals like David Lloyd George felt compelled to admit that, however much they deplored the arms race in theory, all that was liberal and decent in the world rested on Britain's security, and that rested on her control of the seas. Many at the Hague Conferences would have concurred.

In effect, by outlawing war, the middle class wished to endorse the status quo in Europe and thus the world. But when wars aimed at promoting progressive ends, such as the conflicts in the Balkans for national liberation from the decadent and corrupt Ottoman Empire, began erupting in the first two decades of the century, members of the peace movement stood less ready to condemn them. By 1912 the peace movement had begun to founder on such contradictions.

Beyond these immediate, and dire, circumstances in which Europe found itself and the end of the new century's first decade, the increasingly ignored Hague Conferences would have a lasting legacy. The Permanent Court of Arbitration was the progenitor of the League of Nations and of the United Nations. It was largely superseded in 1921 by the Permanent Court of International Justice, established under the COVENANT OF THE LEAGUE OF NATIONS, which was in turn replaced in 1945 by the International Court of Justice under the UNITED NATIONS CHARTER.

COVENANT OF THE LEAGUE OF NATIONS

TREATY AT A GLANCE

Completed
June 28, 1919, at Versailles, France (with amendments
adopted through December 1924)

Signatories
United States (signed, but failed to ratify), British Empire,
France, Italy, and Japan ("Principal Allied and Associated
Powers"); Belgium, Bolivia, Brazil, China, Cuba, Ecuador,
Greece, Guatemala, Haiti, the Hejaz, Honduras, Liberia,
Nicaragua, Panama, Peru, Poland, Portugal, Romania,
the Serb-Croat-Slovene State, Siam, Czechoslovakia, and
Uruguay ("the Allied and Associated Powers"); and Germany

Overview
Largely at the insistence of U.S. president Woodrow Wilson, the
Covenant of the League of Nations was made an integral part of the
TREATY OF VERSAILLES (1919) and other treaties relevant to the conclusion of World War I (including the TREATY OF ST. GERMAIN). The
covenant established the League as a permanent organization to
promote international peace, to resolve international disputes
without resorting to war, and to protect the rights, sovereignty, and
self-determination of all nations.

Historical Background

Since the two Hague conferences of 1899 and 1907
(see HAGUE CONVENTION OF 1899 and HAGUE CONVEN-
TION [1907]), convened at the instigation of Czar
Nicholas II of Russia, many of the world's nations
began seriously looking for alternatives to war as a
means of settling international disputes. The outbreak
of World War I in 1914 accelerated thought in this
area, and as the war ground on, schemes for world
organizations were proposed and garnered popular
support. Key leaders—among them Woodrow Wilson,
Jan Smuts of South Africa, and Lord Robert Cecil, a
member of the British cabinet—advocated an international league to prevent future wars. This concept
became the last of President Wilson's celebrated Fourteen Points, proposed toward the end of the war as the
basis for a just peace. In large part through Wilson's
insistence, the creation of a League of Nations became
a cornerstone issue and dominated the Paris Peace
Conference, which followed the armistice ending
World War I.

Terms

Unlike the later UNITED NATIONS CHARTER, which would
be a political document emphasizing diplomacy, the
League convenant was more a legalistic contract concentrating on judicial procedures to prevent war. The
covenant, consisting of 26 articles, outlined three
approaches to preventing war: arbitration in settling
disputes, disarmament, and collective security. All 63
member states were represented in an assembly, which
held sessions at least annually. Each member had a single vote, but unanimity was required for all decisions.

While the assembly regulated the budget and
membership of the league, also serving as a forum for
airing international opinion, the main political work of
the league, especially the settlement of international
disputes, fell to a more select body, the council. Permanent seats on the council were reserved for Britain,
France, Japan, Italy, and later Germany and the Soviet
Union. Had the United States Senate ratified the Treaty
of Versailles and thereby consented to join the League,
it too would have had a place on the council. Other
countries were elected to temporary representation on

the council to make a total of eight, later raised to 10, and then 14 members.

The activities of the League were administered by a third body, the secretariat. Finally, the League was also associated with the Permanent International Court of Justice, or World Court, which met at the Hague and had evolved from the Permanent Court of Arbitration (popularly called the Hague Tribunal), established by the Hague Convention of 1899, and also with the International Labor Organization. The League of Nations proper was headquartered in Geneva, Switzerland.

The Covenant of the League of Nations

THE HIGH CONTRACTING PARTIES,

In order to promote international cooperation and to achieve international peace and security

by the acceptance of obligations not to resort to war,

by the prescription of open, just and honorable relations between nations,

by the firm establishment of the understandings of international law as the actual rule of conduct among Governments, and

by the maintenance of justice and a scrupulous respect for all treaty obligations in the dealings of organized peoples with one another,

Agree to this Covenant of the League of Nations.

ARTICLE 1

The original Members of the League of Nations shall be those of the Signatories which are named in the Annex to this Covenant and also such of those other States named in the Annex as shall accede without reservation to this Covenant. Such accession shall be effected by a Declaration deposited with the Secretariat within two months of the coming into force of the Covenant. Notice thereof shall be sent to all other Members of the League.

Any fully self-governing State, Dominion or Colony not named in the Annex may become a Member of the League if its admission is agreed to by two-thirds of the Assembly, provided that it shall give effective guarantees of its sincere intention to observe its international obligations, and shall accept such regulations as may be prescribed by the League in regard to its military, naval and air forces and armaments.

Any Member of the League may, after two years' notice of its intention so to do, withdraw from the League, provided that all its international obligations and all its obligations under this Covenant shall have been fulfilled at the time of its withdrawal.

ARTICLE 2

The action of the League under this Covenant shall be effected through the instrumentality of an Assembly and of a Council, with a permanent Secretariat.

ARTICLE 3

The Assembly shall consist of Representatives of the Members of the League.

The Assembly shall meet at stated intervals and from time to time as occasion may require at the Seat of the League or at such other place as may be decided upon.

The Assembly may deal at its meetings with any matter within the sphere of action of the League or affecting the peace of the world.

At meetings of the Assembly each Member of the League shall have one vote, and may have not more than three Representatives.

ARTICLE 4

The Council shall consist of Representatives of the Principal Allied and Associated Powers, together with Representatives of four other Members of the League. These four Members of the League shall be selected by the Assembly from time to time in its discretion. Until the appointment of the Representatives of the four Members of the League first selected by the Assembly, Representatives of Belgium, Brazil, Spain and Greece shall be members of the Council.

With the approval of the majority of the Assembly, the Council may name additional Members of the League whose Representatives shall always be members of the Council; the Council, with like approval may increase the number of Members of the League to be selected by the Assembly for representation on the Council.

The Council shall meet from time to time as occasion may require, and at least once a year, at the Seat of the League, or at such other place as may be decided upon.

The Council may deal at its meetings with any matter within the sphere of action of the League or affecting the peace of the world.

Any Member of the League not represented on the Council shall be invited to send a Representative to sit as a member at any meeting of the Council during the consideration of matters specially affecting the interests of that Member of the League.

At meetings of the Council, each Member of the League represented on the Council shall have one vote, and may have not more than one Representative.

ARTICLE 5

Except where otherwise expressly provided in this Covenant or by the terms of the present Treaty, decisions at any meeting of the Assembly or of the Council shall require the agreement of all the Members of the League represented at the meeting.

All matters of procedure at meetings of the Assembly or of the Council, including the appointment of Committees to investigate particular matters, shall be regulated by the Assembly or by the Council and may be decided by a majority of the Members of the League represented at the meeting.

The first meeting of the Assembly and the first meeting of the Council shall be summoned by the President of the United States of America.

ARTICLE 6

The permanent Secretariat shall be established at the Seat of the League. The Secretariat shall comprise a Secretary General and such secretaries and staff as may be required.

The first Secretary General shall be the person named in the Annex; thereafter the Secretary General shall be appointed by the Council with the approval of the majority of the Assembly.

The secretaries and staff of the Secretariat shall be appointed by the Secretary General with the approval of the Council.

The Secretary General shall act in that capacity at all meetings of the Assembly and of the Council.

The expenses of the League shall be borne by the Members of the League in the proportion decided by the Assembly.

ARTICLE 7

The Seat of the League is established at Geneva.

The Council may at any time decide that the Seat of the League shall be established elsewhere.

All positions under or in connection with the League, including the Secretariat, shall be open equally to men and women.

Representatives of the Members of the League and officials of the League when engaged on the business of the League shall enjoy diplomatic privileges and immunities.

The buildings and other property occupied by the League or its officials or by Representatives attending its meetings shall be inviolable.

ARTICLE 8

The Members of the League recognize that the maintenance of peace requires the reduction of national armaments to the lowest point consistent with national safety and the enforcement by common action of international obligations.

The Council, taking account of the geographical situation and circumstances of each State, shall formulate plans for such reduction for the consideration and action of the several Governments. Such plans shall be subject to reconsideration and revision at least every ten years.

After these plans shall have been adopted by the several Governments, the limits of armaments therein fixed shall not be exceeded without the concurrence of the Council.

The Members of the League agree that the manufacture by private enterprise of munitions and implements of war is open to grave objections. The Council shall advise how the evil effects attendant upon such manufacture can be prevented, due regard being had to the necessities of those Members of the League which are not able to manufacture the munitions and implements of war necessary for their safety.

The Members of the League undertake to interchange full and frank information as to the scale of their armaments, their military, naval and air programs and the condition of such of their industries as are adaptable to warlike purposes.

ARTICLE 9

A permanent Commission shall be constituted to advise the Council on the execution of the provisions of Articles 1 and 8 and on military, naval and air questions generally.

ARTICLE 10

The Members of the League undertake to respect and preserve as against external aggression the territorial integrity and existing political independence of all Members of the League. In case of any such aggression or in case of any threat or danger of such aggression the Council shall advise upon the means by which this obligation shall be fulfilled.

ARTICLE 11

Any war or threat of war, whether immediately affecting any of the Members of the League or not, is hereby declared a matter of concern to the whole League, and the League shall take any action that may be deemed wise and effectual to safeguard the peace of nations. In case any such emergency should arise the

Secretary General shall on the request of any Member of the League forthwith summon a meeting of the Council.

It is also declared to be the friendly right of each Member of the League to bring to the attention of the Assembly or of the Council any circumstance whatever affecting international relations which threatens to disturb international peace or the good understanding between nations upon which peace depends.

ARTICLE 12

The Members of the League agree that, if there should arise between them any dispute likely to lead to a rupture they will submit the matter either to arbitration or judicial settlement or to enquiry by the Council, and they agree in no case to resort to war until three months after the award by the arbitrators or the judicial decision, or the report by the Council. In any case under this Article the award of the arbitrators or the judicial decision shall be made within a reasonable time, and the report of the Council shall be made within six months after the submission of the dispute.

ARTICLE 13

The Members of the League agree that whenever any dispute shall arise between them which they recognize to be suitable for submission to arbitration or judicial settlement and which cannot be satisfactorily settled by diplomacy, they will submit the whole subject-matter to arbitration or judicial settlement.

Disputes as to the interpretation of a treaty, as to any question of international law, as to the existence of any fact which if established would constitute a breach of any international obligation, or as to the extent and nature of the reparation to be made for any such breach, are declared to be among those which are generally suitable for submission to arbitration or judicial settlement.

For the consideration of any such dispute, the court to which the case is referred shall be the Permanent Court of International Justice, established in accordance with Article 14, or any tribunal agreed on by the parties to the dispute or stipulated in any convention existing between them.

The Members of the League agree that they will carry out in full good faith any award or decision that may be rendered, and that they will not resort to war against a Member of the League which complies therewith. In the event of any failure to carry out such an award or decision, the Council shall propose what steps should be taken to give effect thereto.

ARTICLE 14

The Council shall formulate and submit to the Members of the League for adoption plans for the establishment of a Permanent Court of International Justice. The Court shall be competent to hear and determine any dispute of an international character which the parties thereto submit to it. The Court may also give an advisory opinion upon any dispute or question referred to it by the Council or by the Assembly.

ARTICLE 15

If there should arise between Members of the League any dispute likely to lead to a rupture, which is not submitted to arbitration or judicial settlement in accordance with Article 13, the Members of the League agree that they will submit the matter to the Council. Any party to the dispute may effect such submission by giving notice of the existence of the dispute to the Secretary General, who will make all necessary arrangements for a full investigation and consideration thereof.

For this purpose the parties to the dispute will communicate to the Secretary General, as promptly as possible, statements of their case with all the relevant facts and papers, and the Council may forthwith direct the publication thereof.

The Council shall endeavor to effect a settlement of the dispute, and if such efforts are successful, a statement shall be made public giving such facts and explanations regarding the dispute and the terms of settlement thereof as the Council may deem appropriate.

If the dispute is not thus settled, the Council either unanimously or by a majority vote shall make and publish a report containing a statement of the facts of the dispute and the recommendations which are deemed just and proper in regard thereto.

Any Member of the League represented on the Council may make public a statement of the facts of the dispute and of its conclusions regarding the same.

If a report by the Council is unanimously agreed to by the members thereof other than the Representatives of one or more of the parties to the dispute, the Members of the League agree that they will not go to war with any party to the dispute which complies with the recommendations of the report.

If the Council fails to reach a report which is unanimously agreed to by the members thereof, other than the Representatives of one or more of the parties to the dispute, the Members of the League reserve to themselves the right to take such action as they shall consider necessary for the maintenance of right and justice.

If the dispute between the parties is claimed by one of them, and is found by the Council, to arise out of a matter which by international law is solely within the domestic jurisdiction of that party, the Council shall so report, and shall make no recommendation as to its settlement.

The Council may in any case under this Article refer the dispute to the Assembly. The dispute shall be so referred at the request of either party to the dispute, provided that such request be made within fourteen days after the submission of the dispute to the Council.

In any case referred to the Assembly, all the provisions of this Article and of Article 12 relating to the action and powers of the Council shall apply to the action and powers of the Assembly, provided that a report made by the Assembly, if concurred in by the Representatives of those Members of the League represented on the Council and of a majority of the other Members of the League, exclusive in each case of the Representatives of the parties to the dispute, shall have the same force as a report by the Council concurred in by all the members thereof other than the Representatives of one or more of the parties to the dispute.

ARTICLE 16

Should any Member of the League resort to war in disregard of its covenants under Articles 12, 13 or 15, it shall *ipso facto* be deemed to have committed an act of war against all other Members of the League, which hereby undertake immediately to subject it to the severance of all trade or financial relations, the prohibition of all intercourse between their nationals and the nationals of the covenant-breaking State, and the prevention of all financial, commercial or personal intercourse between the nationals of the covenant-breaking State and the nationals of any other State, whether a Member of the League or not.

It shall be the duty of the Council in such case to recommend to the several Governments concerned what effective military, naval or air force the Members of the League shall severally contribute to the armed forces to be used to protect the covenants of the League.

The Members of the League agree, further, that they will mutually support one another in the financial and economic measures which are taken under this Article, in order to minimize the loss and inconvenience resulting from the above measures, and that they will mutually support one another in resisting any special measures aimed at one of their number by the covenant-breaking State, and that they will take the necessary steps to afford passage through their territory to the forces of any of the Members of the League which are cooperating to protect the covenants of the League.

Any Member of the League which has violated any covenant of the League may be declared to be no longer a Member of the League by a vote of the Council concurred in by the Representatives of all the other Members of the League represented thereon.

ARTICLE 17

In the event of a dispute between a Member of the League and a State which is not a Member of the League, or between States not Members of the League, the State or States not Members of the League shall be invited to accept the obligations of membership in the League for the purposes of such dispute, upon such conditions as the Council may deem just. If such invitation is accepted, the provisions of Articles 12 to 16 inclusive shall be applied with such modifications as may be deemed necessary by the Council.

Upon such invitation being given the Council shall immediately institute an inquiry into the circumstances of the dispute and recommend such action as may seem best and most effectual in the circumstances.

If a State so invited shall refuse to accept the obligations of membership in the League for the purposes of such dispute, and shall resort to war against a Member of the League, the provisions of Article 16 shall be applicable as against the State taking such action.

If both parties to the dispute when so invited refuse to accept the obligations of membership in the League for the purposes of such dispute, the Council may take such measures and make such recommendations as will prevent hostilities and will result in the settlement of the dispute.

ARTICLE 18

Every treaty or international engagement entered into hereafter by any Member of the League shall be forthwith registered with the Secretariat and shall as soon as possible be published by it. No such treaty or international engagement shall be binding until so registered.

ARTICLE 19

The Assembly may from time to time advise the reconsideration by Members of the League of treaties which have become inapplicable and the consideration of international conditions whose continuance might endanger the peace of the world.

ARTICLE 20

The Members of the League severally agree that this Covenant is accepted as abrogating all obligations or understandings *inter* se which are inconsistent with the terms thereof, and solemnly undertake that they will not hereafter enter into any engagements inconsistent with the terms thereof.

In case any Member of the League shall, before becoming a Member of the League, have undertaken any obligations inconsistent with the terms of this Covenant, it shall be the duty of such Member to take immediate steps to procure its release from such obligations.

ARTICLE 21

Nothing in this Covenant shall be deemed to affect the validity of international engagements, such as treaties of arbitration or regional understandings like the Monroe doctrine, for securing the maintenance of peace.

ARTICLE 22

To those colonies and territories which as a consequence of the late war have ceased to be under the sovereignty of the States which formerly governed them and which are inhabited by peoples not yet able to stand by themselves under the strenuous conditions of the modern world, there should be applied the principle that the well-being and development of such peoples form a sacred trust of civilization and that securities for the performance of this trust should be embodied in this Covenant.

The best method of giving practical effect to this principle is that the tutelage of such peoples should be entrusted to advanced nations who by reason of their resources, their experience or their geographical position can best undertake this responsibility, and who are willing to accept it, and that this tutelage should be exercised by them as Mandatories on behalf of the League.

The character of the mandate must differ according to the stage of the development of the people, the geographical situation of the territory, its economic conditions and other similar circumstances.

Certain communities formerly belonging to the Turkish Empire have reached a stage of development where their existence as independent nations can be provisionally recognized subject to the rendering of administrative advice and assistance by a Mandatory until such time as they are able to stand alone. The wishes of these communities must be a principal consideration in the selection of the Mandatory.

Other peoples, especially those of Central Africa, are at such a stage that the Mandatory must be responsible for the administration of the territory under conditions which will guarantee freedom of conscience and religion, subject only to the maintenance of public order and morals, the prohibition of abuses such as the slave trade, the arms traffic and the liquor traffic, and the prevention of the establishment of fortifications or military and naval bases and of military training of the natives for other than police purposes and the defence of territory, and will also secure equal opportunities for the trade and commerce of other Members of the League.

There are territories, such as South-West Africa and certain of the South Pacific Islands, which, owing to the sparseness of their population, or their small size, or their remoteness from the centers of civilization, or their geographical contiguity to the territory of the Mandatory, and other circumstances, can be best administered under the laws of the Mandatory as integral portions of its territory, subject to the safeguards above mentioned in the interests of the indigenous population.

In every case of mandate, the Mandatory shall render to the Council an annual report in reference to the territory committed to its charge.

The degree of authority, control, or administration to be exercised by the Mandatory shall, if not previously agreed upon by the Members of the League, be explicitly defined in each case by the Council.

A permanent Commission shall be constituted to receive and examine the annual reports of the Mandatories and to advise the Council on all matters relating to the observance of the mandates.

ARTICLE 23

Subject to and in accordance with the provisions of international conventions existing or hereafter to be agreed upon, the Members of the League:

(a) will endeavor to secure and maintain fair and humane conditions of labor for men, women, and children, both in their own countries and in all countries to which their commercial and industrial relations extend, and for that purpose will establish and maintain the necessary international organizations;

(b) undertake to secure just treatment of the native inhabitants of territories under their control;

(c) will entrust the League with the general supervision over the execution of agreements with regard to the traffic in women and children, and the traffic in opium and other dangerous drugs;

(d) will entrust the League with the general supervision of the trade in arms and ammunition with the countries in which the control of this traffic is necessary in the common interest;

(e) will make provision to secure and maintain freedom of communications and of transit and equitable treatment for the commerce of all Members of the League. In this connection, the special necessities of the regions devastated during the war of 1914–1918 shall be borne in mind;

(f) will endeavor to take steps in matters of international concern for the prevention and control of disease.

ARTICLE 24

There shall be placed under the direction of the League all international bureaux already established by general treaties if the parties to such treaties consent. All such international bureaux and all commissions for the regulation of matters of international interest hereafter constituted shall be placed under the direction of the League.

In all matters of international interest which are regulated by general convention but which are not placed under the control of international bureaux or commissions, the Secretariat of the League shall, subject to the consent of the Council and if desired by the parties, collect and distribute all relevant information and shall render any other assistance which may be necessary or desirable.

The Council may include as part of the expenses of the Secretariat the expenses of any bureau or commission which is placed under the direction of the League.

ARTICLE 25

The Members of the League agree to encourage and promote the establishment and cooperation of duly authorized voluntary national Red Cross organizations having as purposes the improvement of health, the prevention of disease and the mitigation of suffering throughout the world.

ARTICLE 26

Amendments to this Covenant will take effect when ratified by the Members of the League whose Representatives compose the Council and by a majority of the Members of the League whose Representatives compose the Assembly.

No such amendments shall bind any Member of the League which signifies its dissent therefrom, but in that case it shall cease to be a Member of the League.

Consequences

The framers of the League had unwavering faith in a parliamentary system, through which, they believed, a consensus on most issues could be achieved. In practice, unanimity was rare, and the requirement of unanimity often paralyzed the institution.

Despite widespread public enthusiasm for the League, it proved a disappointment from its very establishment on January 10, 1920. To begin with, the inclusion of its covenant in the Treaty of Versailles made the League seem as if it were a tool of the victorious Allies rather than a genuinely representative and impartial body meant to serve all nations. Worse, the failure of the United States to join the League greatly crippled it from the outset. And, of course, achieving the required unanimity in the assembly more often than not proved impossible.

Nevertheless, the League was effective in resolving a number of relatively minor disputes, including that between Sweden and Finland over the Aland Islands in 1920 and between Greece and Bulgaria in 1925. Steps that might have stopped aggression by major powers, however, were repeatedly checked. The Geneva Protocol of 1924, which defined aggressive war as an ipso facto international crime, was opposed by Great Britain and failed. The apparatus the League set up for collective security was never tested: no international peacekeeping forces were ever assembled. Disarmament remained a topic of discussion, but languished in practice as no nation believed the League could actually guarantee its security.

On less politically sensitive fronts, the League did make progress, combating the traffic in illicit drugs, contributing to international child welfare, improving health conditions around the world, and promoting international trade. (The United Nations, too, would capitalize on these areas—nonpolitical work in economic development and social welfare—in which the League did enjoy some success.)

The first major challenge to the League came with the Japanese invasion of Manchuria in September 1931. The League dispatched a commission of inquiry to the scene in 1932, Japan withdrew from the League, and nothing was done to force that nation to return the territory it had seized. In 1933 Adolf Hitler withdrew Germany from the Geneva disarmament conference and soon after left the League itself. Nor did the League act as Germany rearmed in defiance of the Treaty of Versailles. In 1935 the League of Nations did impose economic sanctions against Italy in response to its aggression against Ethiopia, but the timorous reservations of Britain and France mitigated the sanctions, and Italy completed its brutal conquest. Two years later, Italy withdrew from the League and joined Germany in its intervention in the Spanish Civil War.

Hopelessly crippled, the League continued to meet but was wholly ineffective in stemming the tide that brought World War II. Nevertheless, the League must be regarded as a noble pioneering experiment paving the way to the postwar creation of the United Nations, which officially supplanted the League in 1946.

TREATY BETWEEN THE ALLIED AND ASSOCIATED POWERS AND POLAND ON THE PROTECTION OF MINORITIES

TREATY AT A GLANCE

Completed
June 28, 1919, at Versailles, France

Signatories
"Principal Allied Powers" (the United States, British Empire, France, Italy, and Japan) and "Associated Powers" (Belgium, Bolivia, Brazil, China, Cuba, Ecuador, Greece, Guatemala, Haiti, the Hejaz, Honduras, Liberia, Nicaragua, Panama, Peru, Poland, Portugal, Romania, the Serb-Croat-Slovene State, Siam, Czechoslovakia, and Uruguay) and Poland

Overview
The rights of Poland's German minority, as well as the rights of other minorities, were not guaranteed in the TREATY OF VERSAILLES (1919) but in this separate document adopted the same day.

Historical Background

With great idealism, driven in large measure by U.S. president Woodrow Wilson, the framers of the peace at Versailles following World War I were concerned to protect the rights of minorities in the former belligerent nations, because the fall of the Ottoman Empire and the reshaping of European boundaries placed many ethnic enclaves at risk in newly independent nations where majority populations were often xenophobic, given the rawness of their authority. This minorities treaty with Poland served as the model for similar documents concluded with Czechoslovakia, Yugoslavia, Romania, and Greece.

Terms

The treaty read in part as follows.

ARTICLE 2
Poland undertakes to assure full and complete protection of life and liberty to all inhabitants of Poland without distinction of birth, nationality, language, race or religion. All inhabitants of Poland shall be entitled to the free exercise, whether public or private, of any creed, religion or belief, whose practices are not inconsistent with public order or public morals.

ARTICLE 3
Poland admits and declares to be Polish nationals *ipso facto* and without the requirement of any formality German, Austrian, Hungarian or Russian nationals habitually resident at the date of the coming into force of the present Treaty in territory which is or may be recognized as forming part of Poland, but subject to any provisions in the Treaties of Peace with Germany or Austria respectively relating to persons who became resident in such territory after a specified date.

Nevertheless, the persons referred to above, who are over eighteen years of age will be entitled under the conditions contained in the said Treaties to opt for any other nationality which may be open to them. Option by a husband will cover his wife and option by parents will cover their children under eighteen years of age. . . .

ARTICLE 7
All Polish nationals shall be equal before the law and shall enjoy the same civil and political rights without distinction as to race, language or religion.

Differences of religion, creed or confession shall not prejudice any Polish national in matters relating to the enjoyment of civil or political rights, as for instance admission to public employments, functions and honours, or exercise of professions and industries.

No restriction shall be imposed on the free use by any Polish national of any language in private intercourse, in commerce, in religion, in the press or in publications of any kind, or at public meeting. . . .

ARTICLE 8
Polish nationals who belong to racial, religious or linguistic minorities shall enjoy the same treatment and security in law and in fact as the other Polish

nationals. In particular they shall have an equal right to establish, manage and control at their own expense charitable, religious and social institutions, schools and other educational establishments, with the right to use their own language and to exercise their religion freely therein.

ARTICLE 9

Poland will provide in the public educational system in towns and districts in which a considerable proportion of Polish nationals of other than Polish speech are residents adequate facilities for ensuring that in the primary schools the instruction shall be given to the children of such Polish nationals through the medium of their own language. This provision shall not prevent the Polish Government from making the teaching of the Polish language obligatory in the said schools. . . .

ARTICLE 11

Jews shall not be compelled to perform any act which constitutes a violation of their Sabbath, nor shall they be placed under any disability by reason of their refusal to attend courts of law or to perform any legal business on their Sabbath. This provision however shall not exempt Jews from such obligations as shall be imposed upon all other Polish citizens for the necessary purposes of military service, national defence or the preservation of public order. . . .

Consequences

As with so much else associated with the Treaty of Versailles, the guarantees of minority rights ultimately meant little. With the multiethnic empires of Austria-Hungary and Ottoman Turkey gone, the patchwork of ethnic populations and national borders throughout Europe virtually ensured volatile relations between minorities longing to be separate and majorities determined to dominate their nations. None of this lessened the traditional prejudices toward Europe's Jews and such international ethnic groups as the gypsies. For the most part, the nations of Europe simply ignored the injunctions against the persecution of minorities after Versailles and abused their minorities, sometimes for political reasons, more often for historical ones, in ways both overt (legal restrictions to employment or participation in government, for example) and covert (unpunished individual violence against minority group members and unofficial pogroms, for example).

Centuries of virulent anti-Semitism culminated in the Holocaust of World War II, during which six million Jews were exterminated by Nazi Germany. Some pause was then given to this European tradition, but with the collapse of the post–World War II multiethnic governments or governmental blocs, most of them communist, such as Yugoslavia or the Soviet satellites, ethnic hatred again took center stage. Not that persecution failed to occur in such governments, as it had under the Ottoman and Austro-Hungarian Empires, but that the fall of such governments, fueled by ideology rather than ethnic unity, removed any checks they provided on persecution, again as was the case with the pre–World War I empires. This treaty, used here emblematically, once again underscores the failure of Versailles to come to terms with its inner contradictions—the promotion of nationhood based on the strivings of individual "peoples" and the injunctions against intolerance, for example—by clothing them in an idealism in which only a few actually believed.

Annexations and Territorial Agreements
SYKES-PICOT AGREEMENT

TREATY AT A GLANCE

Completed (Ratified)
May 9, 1916, at London

Signatories
Britain, France, and Imperial Russia

Overview
A secret tripartite agreement defining the goals of the Allied powers of Britain, France, and Russia for the partition of the Ottoman Empire at victorious close of the Great War, the Sykes-Picot Agreement did not remain secret for long. News of the secret deal excited the territorial ambitions of the Italians and created what would become a long-term resentment among the Arabs, then in revolt and seeking postwar autonomy and nationhood.

Historical Background

Most, if not all, the belligerents entered World War I claiming that they did so defensively, either to protect territory that had been invaded or was threatening to be invaded by a foreign power, or to maintain their national honor by coming to the aid of an ally under such attack. As the war got under way and the body count and the costs began to mount, each side—Allies and Central Powers—began to define their war aims more broadly and to justify their involvement with dreams of adding new territory or colonies. Thus, under the guise of making the enemy pay for his perfidy, did the old imperial lusts resurface.

By 1916 the Allies pretty much understood that should they win, they would be dividing up spoils between themselves, and there was no greater spoil than the ailing Ottoman Empire, whose instability had contributed so much to the start of the war. It was in the spring of that year that two diplomats, Mark Sykes of Britain and Georges Picot of France, got together and hammered out the secret convention between Great Britain and France, with the assent of soon-to-be moribund Imperial Russia, for the dismemberment of the Turkish lands in the Middle East. The Sykes-Picot Agreement, as it came to be called, would lead to the division of Turkish-held Syria, Iraq, Lebanon, and Palestine into various areas administered by either the British or the French, despite the fact that some of those lands—sometimes even the same lands—were in effect promised to the leaders of the Arab Revolt on the one hand and, through the BALFOUR DECLARATION, to the Jews on the other.

Terms

The agreement promised that Russia should acquire parts of Armenia and some Kurdish territory to the southeast; that France would get Lebanon and Syria; and that to Britain would fall Mesopotamia, including Baghdad, and the Mediterranean ports of Haifa and Acre. Between the French and British holdings, Sykes and Picot agreed, there would fall either a confederation of Arab states or a single Arab state, which, however, would be divided into French and British spheres of influence. Egyptian Alexandria would be a free port, and Palestine, because it was a holy center for several religions, would be placed under "international" supervision. The agreement took form in an exchange of notes between April 26 and October 23, 1916, such as these two from British foreign secretary Edward Grey: one to French ambassador Cambon, one to Russian ambassador Benckendorff, both residing in London.

Grey to Cambon, 16 May 1916

I have the honour to acknowledge the receipt of your Excellency's note of the 9th instant, stating that the French Government accept the limits of a future Arab State, or Confederation of States, and of those parts of Syria where French interests predominate, together with certain conditions attached thereto, such as they result from recent discussions in London and Petrograd on the subject.

I have the honour to inform your Excellency in reply that the acceptance of the whole project, as it now stands, will involve the abdication of considerable British interests, but, since His Majesty's Government recognize the advantage to the general cause of the Allies entailed in producing a more favourable internal situation in Turkey, they are ready to accept the arrangement now arrived at, provided that the cooperation of the Arabs is secured, and that the Arabs fulfil the conditions and obtain the towns of Homs, Hama, Damascus, and Aleppo.

It is accordingly understood between the French and British Governments:

1. That France and Great Britain are prepared to recognize and protect [this was changed in August 1916 to read "uphold"] an independent Arab State or a Confederation of Arab States in the areas (A) and (B) marked on the annexed map, under the suzerainty of an Arab chief. That in area (A) France, and in area (B) Great Britain, shall have priority of right of enterprise and local loans. That in area (A) France, and in area (B) Great Britain, shall alone supply advisers or foreign functionaries at the request of the Arab State or Confederation of Arab States.

2. That in the blue area France, and in the red area Great Britain, shall be allowed to establish such direct or indirect administration or control as they desire and as they may think fit to arrange with the Arab State or Confederation of Arab States.

3. That in the brown area there shall be established an international administration, the form of which is to be decided upon after consultation with Russia, and subsequently in consultation with the other Allies, and the representatives of the Shereef of Mecca.

4. That Great Britain be accorded (1) the ports of Haifa and Acre, (2) guarantee of a given supply of water from the Tigris and Euphrates in area (A) for area (B). His Majesty's Government, on their part, undertake that they will at no time enter into negotiations for the cession of Cyprus to any third Power without the previous consent of the French Government.

5. That Alexandretta shall be a free port as regards the trade of the British Empire, and that there shall be no discrimination in port charges of facilities as regards British shipping and British goods; that there shall be freedom of transit for British goods through Alexandretta and by railway through the blue area, whether those goods are intended for or originate in the red area, or (B) area, or area (A); and there shall be no discrimination, direct or indirect, against British goods or any railway or against British goods or ships at any port serving the areas mentioned.

That Haifa shall be a free port as regards the trade of France, her dominions and protectorates, and there shall be no discrimination in port charges or facilities as regards French shipping and French goods. There shall be freedom of transit for French goods through Haifa and by the British railway through the brown area, whether those goods are intended for or originate in the blue area, area (A), or area (B), and there shall be no discrimination, direct or indirect, against French goods on any railway, or against French goods or ships at any port serving the areas mentioned.

6. That in area (A) the Baghdad Railway shall not be extended southwards beyond Mosul, and in area (B) northwards beyond Samarra, until a railway connecting Baghdad with Aleppo via the Euphrates Valley has been completed, and then only with the concurrence of the two Governments.

7. That Great Britain has the right to build, administer, and be the sole owner of a railway connecting Haifa with area (B), and shall have a perpetual right to transport troops along such a line at all times.

It is to be understood by both Governments that this railway is to facilitate the connection of Baghdad with Haifa by rail, and it is further understood that, if the engineering difficulties and expense entailed by keeping this connecting line in the brown area only make the project unfeasible, the French Government shall be prepared to consider that the line in question may also traverse the polygon Banias-Keis Marib-Salkhad Tell Otsda-Mesmie before reaching area (B).

8. For a period of twenty years the existing Turkish customs tariff shall remain in force throughout the whole of the blue and red areas, as well as in areas (A) and (B), and no increase in the rates of conversion from ad valorem to specific rates shall be made except by agreement between the two powers.

There shall be no interior custom barriers between any of the above-mentioned areas. The customs duties leviable on goods destined for the interior shall be collected at the port of entry and handed over to the administration of the area of destination.

9. It shall be agreed that the French Government will at not time enter into any negotiations for the cession of their rights and will not cede such rights in the blue area to any third Power, except the Arab State or Confederation of Arab States, without the previous agreement of His Majesty's Government, who, on their part, will give similar undertaking to the French Government regarding the red area.

10. The British and French Governments, as the protectors of the Arab State [the phrase "protectors of the Arab State" was deleted in August 1916], shall agree that they will not themselves acquire and will not consent to a third Power acquiring territorial possessions in the Arabian peninsula, or consent to a third Power installing a naval base either on the east coast, or on the islands, of the Red Sea. This, however, shall not prevent such adjustment of the Aden frontier as may be necessary in consequence of recent Turkish aggression.

11. The negotiations with the Arabs as to the boundaries of the Arab State or Confederation of Arab States shall be continued through the same channel as heretofore on behalf of the two Powers.

12. It is agreed that measures to control the importation of arms into the Arab territories will be considered by the two Governments.

I have further the honour to state that, in order to make the agreement complete, His Majesty's Government are proposing to the Russian Government to exchange note analogous to those exchanged by the latter and your Excellency's Government on the 26th April last. Copies of these notes will be communicated to your Excellency as soon as exchanged.

I would also venture to remind your Excellency that the conclusion of the present agreement raises, for practical consideration, the question of the claims of Italy to a share in any partition or rearrangement of Turkey in Asia, as formulated in Article 9 of the Agreement of 26th April 1915, between Italy and the Allies.

His Majesty's Government further consider that the Japanese Government should be informed of the arrangements now concluded.

Grey to Benckendorff, 23 May 1916

I have received from the French Ambassador in London copies of the notes exchanged between the Russian and French Governments on the 26th ultimo, by which your Excellency's Government recognize, subject to certain conditions, the arrangement made between Great Britain and France, relative to the constitution of an Arab State or a Confederation of Arab States, and to the partition of the territories of Syria, Cilicia, and Mesopotamia, provided that the cooperation of the Arabs is secured.

His Majesty's Government take act with satisfaction that your Excellency's Government concur in the limits set forth in that arrangement, and I have now the honour to inform your Excellency that His Majesty's Government, on their part, in order to make the arrangement complete, are also prepared to recognize the conditions formulated by the Russian Government and accepted by the French Government in the notes exchanged at Petrograd on the 26th ultimo.

In so far, then, as these arrangements directly affect the relations of Russia and Great Britain, I have the honour to invite the acquiescence of your Excellency's Government in an agreement to the following terms:

1. That Russia shall annex the regions of Erzeroum, Trebizond, Van, and Bitlis, up to a point subsequently to be determined on the littoral of the Black Sea to the west of Tebizond.

2. That the region of Kurdistan to the south of Van and of Bitlis between Mush, Sert, the course of the Tigris, Jezireh-ben-Omar, the crest-line of the mountains which dominate Amadia, and the region of Merga Var, shall be ceded to Russia; and that starting from the region of Merga Var, the frontier of the Arab State shall follow the crest-line of the mountains which at present divide the Ottoman and Persian Dominions. These boundaries are indicated in a general manner and are subject to modification of detail to be proposed later by the Delimitation Commission which shall meet on the spot.

3. That the Russian Government undertake that, in all parts of the Ottoman territories thus ceded to Russia, any concessions accorded to British subjects by the Ottoman Government shall be maintained. If the Russian Government express the desire that such concessions should later be modified in order to bring them into harmony with the laws of the Russian Empire, this modification shall only take place in agreement with the British Government.

4. That in all parts of the Ottoman territories thus ceded to Russia, existing British rights of navigation and development, and the rights and privileges of any British religious, scholastic, or medical institutions shall be maintained. His Majesty's Government, on their part, undertake that similar Russian rights and privileges shall be maintained in those regions which, under the conditions of this agreement, become entirely British, or in which British interests are recognized as predominant.

5. The two Governments admit in principle that every State which annexes any part of the Ottoman Empire is called upon to participate in the service of the Ottoman Debt.

Consequences

The secret arrangement was in direct conflict with British pledges already made to Hussein ibn Ali, sharif of Mecca, the Hashimite king, who—with, most famously, the help of the British agent T.H. Lawrence ("Lawrence of Arabia")—was about to launch the Arab Revolt against the Turks, with the understanding that the Arabs would get a much larger and more important share of the fruits of victory. The good news was that the Arabs did not yet know about the agreement, and would not know about it until late in 1917, when the new Soviet government published Sykes-Picot along with several other secret treaties entered into by the czar's government.

Meanwhile, the Italians, who as nominal allies did indeed know about the agreement, began to clamor for spoils of their own. The Allies promptly promised them southwestern Anatolia in another secret agreement. Russia lost her piece of the pie when the Russian Revolution took her out of the conflict prematurely, and Italy never got the lands she wanted because of the Young Turks' nationalist victories following the military collapse of the old empire during the war.

When the Arabs finally heard about the agreement, they were scandalized, and Britain only added salt to the diplomatic wounds it had inflicted on them by promising the Jews a homeland in Palestine. Arab resentment persisted beyond the concessions made to them in the Allies' conference at San Remo in April 1920. In some measure, it persisted through the rest of the century, long after the breaking up of the Middle East after the war into newly constructed, sometimes arbitrary kingdoms, in which Sykes-Picot played its role, which had become a fixed and problematic reality that haunts modern diplomacy.

Declaration

BALFOUR DECLARATION

TREATY AT A GLANCE

Completed (Ratified)
November 2, 1917, at London

Signatories
Great Britain and the Zionist Federation (these were the concerned parties; the Balfour Declaration was not a formal treaty, so there were no formal signatories)

Overview
This statement of British policy concerning Zionism endorsed the establishment of "a national home" for the Jewish people in Palestine. Its substance was written into the League of Nations mandate for Palestine (1922).

Historical Background

Zionism, the dominant Jewish nationalist movement, is closely identified with Theodor Herzl and other individuals and groups active in the late 19th century. However, its roots are as old as the commencement of the Jewish Diaspora, the Babylonian Exile of the sixth century B.C.E., during which the Jews longed for Zion (Jerusalem). But it was not until the emancipation of the Jews in 1791 during the French Revolution that organized Zionist movements began to appear. Then, during the 19th century, largely in response to rising nationalist sentiment throughout Europe coupled with persecution of European Jews, especially in Russia, Jewish political activists, including Moses Hess, David Luzatto, Leo Pinsker, Zvi Kalischer, and Yehudah Alkalai, worked to raise the national consciousness of ghetto Jewry. Financiers such as Moses Montefiore, Edmond de Rothschild, and Maurice de Hirsch backed several plans for the return of Jews to the Middle East. In 1897 Herzl's World Zionist Congress, held at Basel, Switzerland, created a worldwide political movement.

Terms

After some 20 years of struggle, the Zionist Congress secured the so-called Balfour Declaration, contained in a November 2, 1917, letter from Balfour to Lord Rothschild.

The Balfour Declaration
(Letter from Balfour to Lord Rothschild),
2 November 1917

I have much pleasure in conveying to you, on behalf of His Majesty's Government, the following declaration of sympathy with Jewish Zionist aspirations which has been submitted to, and approved by, the Cabinet:

His Majesty's Government view with favor the establishment in Palestine of a national home for the Jewish people, and will use their best endeavors to facilitate the achievement of this object, it being clearly understood that nothing shall be done which may prejudice the civil and religious rights of existing non-Jewish communities in Palestine, or the rights and political status enjoyed by Jews in any other country.

I should be grateful if you would bring this declaration to the knowledge of the Zionist Federation.

Consequences

Shortly after the Balfour Declaration, British general Sir Edmund Allenby invaded Palestine, capturing Jerusalem in December. In 1922 the League of Nations approved a British "mandate" over Palestine and neighboring Transjordan, and the provisions of the Balfour Declaration were written into the mandate.

The mandate was intended to encourage the development of self-government, and indeed Transjordan (modern Jordan) became autonomous in 1923 and was recognized as independent in 1928. However, in Palestine, independence was withheld because of apparently hopeless conflict between Arab and Jewish claims. Throughout the 1920s and 1930s, Arab-Jewish violence was often intense, especially as more and more Jewish immigrants fled to Palestine from Nazi-dominated Europe. From 1936 to 1939 Palestine erupted into civil war. Finally, in 1939 the London Round Table Conference produced a White Paper promising the creation of an independent Palestine within a decade and limiting Jewish immigration to 1,500 individuals per month until 1944, when Jews would no longer be admitted to Palestine.

Zionists turned from Britain to the United States for support, demanding, in the May 1942 Biltmore Conference in New York, the formation of an independent Jewish state—a demand that attracted much U.S. support. Following World War II, large numbers of Holocaust survivors sought homes in Palestine. By 1947 a war-weary Britain turned the entire problem over to the United Nations, which voted to partition Palestine into Arab and Jewish states. On May 14, 1948, the eve of Britain's evacuation, Palestine's Jews proclaimed the state of Israel.